WITHDRAWN

REDWOOD LIBRARY

THE LINE
UPON A WIND

Also by Noel Mostert

Supership

THE LINE UPON A WIND

The Great War at Sea, 1793–1815

Noel Mostert

W. W. Norton & Company
New York   London

Copyright © 2007 by Noel Mostert
First American Edition 2008

All rights reserved
Printed in the United States of America

For information about permission to reproduce selections from this book,
write to Permissions, W. W. Norton & Company, Inc.,
500 Fifth Avenue, New York, NY 10110

For information about special discounts for bulk purchases, please contact
W. W. Norton Special Sales at specialsales@wwnorton.com or 800-233-4830

Manufacturing by RR Donnelley, Harrisonburg

Library of Congress Cataloging-in-Publication Data

Mostert, Noël.
The line upon a wind : the great war at sea, 1793–1815 / Noel Mostert. — 1st american ed.
p. cm.
Includes bibliographical references and index.
ISBN 978-0-393-06653-1 (hardcover)
1. Anglo-French War, 1793–1802—Naval operations. 2. Napoleonic Wars,
1800–1815—Naval operations. 3. Seafaring life—History—18th century.
4. Seafaring life—History—19th century. 5. Europe—History, Naval—18th century.
6. Europe—History, Naval—19th century. I. Title.
DC226.4.M68 2008
940.2'745—dc22
2007039313

W. W. Norton & Company, Inc.
500 Fifth Avenue, New York, N.Y. 10110
www.wwnorton.com

W. W. Norton & Company Ltd.
Castle House, 75/76 Wells Street, London W1T 3QT

1 2 3 4 5 6 7 8 9 0

DC
226.4
.M68
2008

JUL 07 2008

166023

To Ghailan Boujerrar,
for his loyalty, friendship and support
over the past forty years

CONTENTS

PART THREE: The Conclusive Struggle, 1805–1816

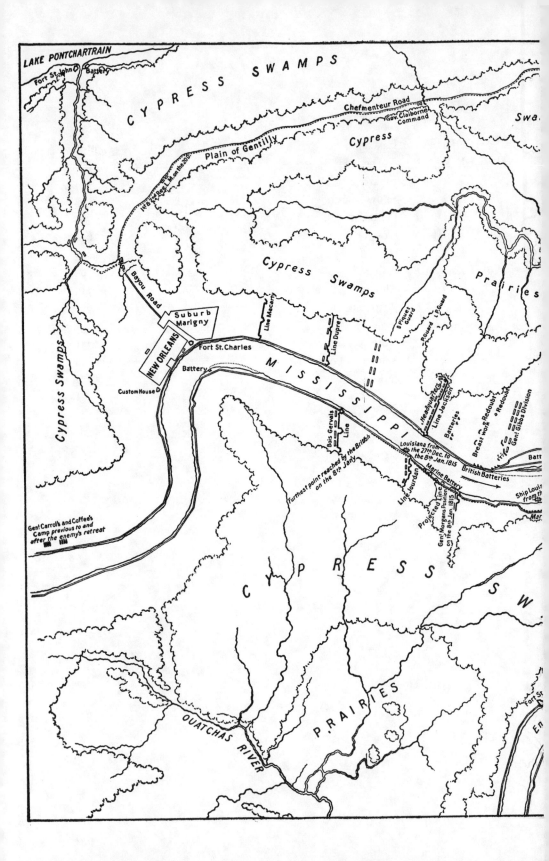

PRAIRIES

mps

Prairies

Fishermen Village

Track of the British Barges

LAKE

Strongwork
commenced by
the British to con-
tain 1000 men

BAYOU BIENVENU

Breast
work

BAYOU des PÊCHEURS

BORGNE

Fort Villere

Prairies

Breastwork where was
placed the advanced pi-
quet guard of the British after
their retreat

MAP

SHOWING THE LANDING OF THE

BRITISH ARMY

Strong Redoubt enclosing huts
for Deposit and Commanding
the entrance of the 3 Canals

BAYOU MAZANT

PRAIRIES

its several Encampments and Fortifications on the Mississippi and the
Works they erected on their Retreat;
also the different Posts, Encampments
and Fortifications made by the several
Corps of the American Army during the
whole Campaign

by Major A. LACARRIERE LATOUR
Late Principal Engineer 7th Military District U.S. Army 1815

CYPRESS

SWAMPS

SCALE OF MILES
½   0   1   2

Genl Keanes
Division

Genl Lambert
Villeres
Division

Villeres Canal
Road made and used by the British
of Quarters

British
Hospital

Battery

Battery

siana
ng 23rd to 27th morning
Carolina Blown up on the
27th Dec

ch of the B. Troops on the 8th Jan

RIVER

Redoubt

CYPRESS   SWAMPS

MPS

Leon

glish   Turn

TERRE   AUX   BŒUFS   SETTLEMENTS

Cypress Swamps

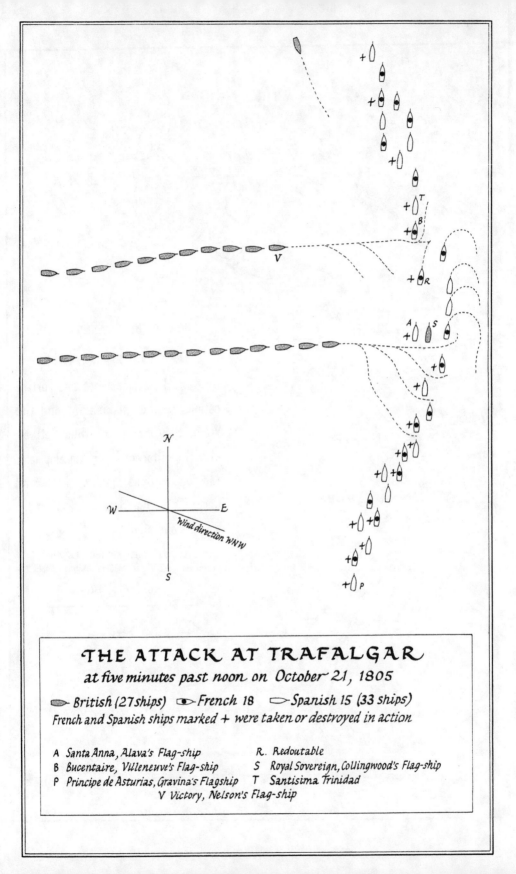

N

W   E

Wind direction WNW

S

THE ATTACK AT TRAFALGAR
at five minutes past noon on October 21, 1805

British (27 ships)   French 18   Spanish 15 (33 ships)
French and Spanish ships marked + were taken or destroyed in action

A   *Santa Anna, Alava's Flag-ship*   R.   *Redoutable*
B   *Bucentaire, Villeneuve's Flag-ship*   S   *Royal Sovereign, Collingwood's Flag-ship*
P   *Principe de Asturias, Gravina's Flagship*   T   *Santisima Trinidad*
            V   *Victory, Nelson's Flag-ship*

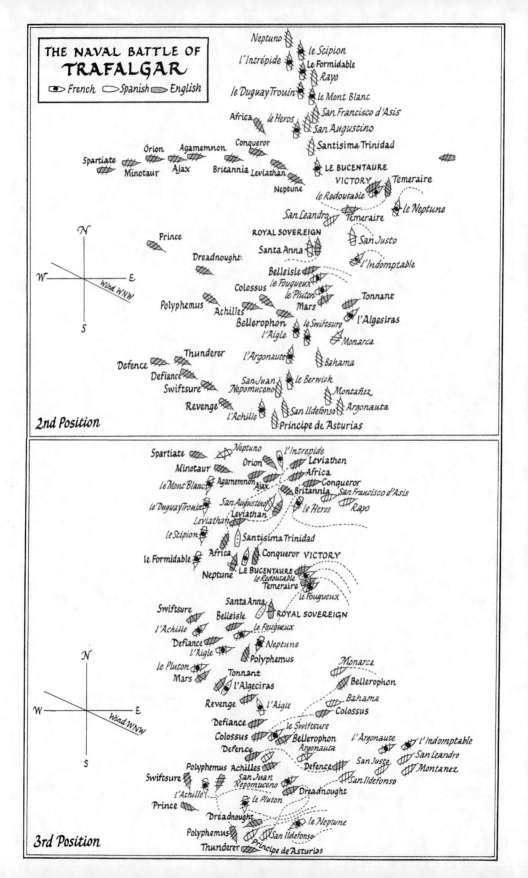

THE NAVAL BATTLE OF
TRAFALGAR

French   Spanish   English

2nd Position

Neptuno
le Scipion
l'Intrépide
Le Formidable
Rayo
le Duguay Trouin
le Mont Blanc
San Francisco d'Asis
Africa
le Heros
San Augustino
Santisima Trinidad
Conqueror
Spartiate   Orion   Agamemnon
Minotaur   Ajax   Britannia   Leviathan   LE BUCENTAURE
Neptune   VICTORY   Temeraire
le Redoutable   le Neptune
San Leandro   Temeraire
Prince   ROYAL SOVEREIGN   San Justo
Santa Anna
Dreadnought   l'Indomptable
Belleisle
le Fougueux
Colossus   le Pluton
Polyphemus   Mars   Tonnant
Achilles   Bellerophon   le Swiftsure   l'Algesiras
l'Aigle   Monarca
Thunderer   l'Argonaute   Bahama
Defence
Defiance   San Juan   le Berwick
Swiftsure   Nepomuceno   Montañez
Revenge   San Ildefonso   Argonauta
l'Achille   Principe de Asturias

N
W   E
Wind WNW
S

3rd Position

Spartiate   Neptuno   l'Intrepide
Orion   Leviathen
Minotaur   Africa
le Mont Blanc   Agamemnon   Conqueror
Ajax   Britannia   San Francisco d'Asis
le Duguay Trouin   San Augustino   le Heros   Rayo
Leviathan   Leviathan
le Scipion   Santisima Trinidad
Africa   Conqueror   VICTORY
le Formidable   LE BUCENTAURE
Neptune   le Redoutable
Temeraire
le Fougueux
Santa Anna
Swiftsure   Belleisle   ROYAL SOVEREIGN
l'Achille   le Fougueux
Defiance   Neptune
l'Aigle   Polyphemus
le Pluton   Monarca
Mars   Tonnant   Bellerophon
l'Algeciras   Bahama
Revenge   l'Aigle   Colossus
Defiance   le Swiftsure
Colossus   Bellerophon   l'Argonaute   l'Indomptable
Defence   Argonauca   San Juste   San Leandro
Defence   Montanez
Polyphemus   Achilles
Swiftsure   San Juan   San Ildefonso
Nepomuceno   Dreadnought
l'Achille   le Pluton
Prince
Dreadnought   le Neptune
Polyphemus   San Ildefonso
Thunderer   Principe de Asturias

N
W   E
Wind WNW
S

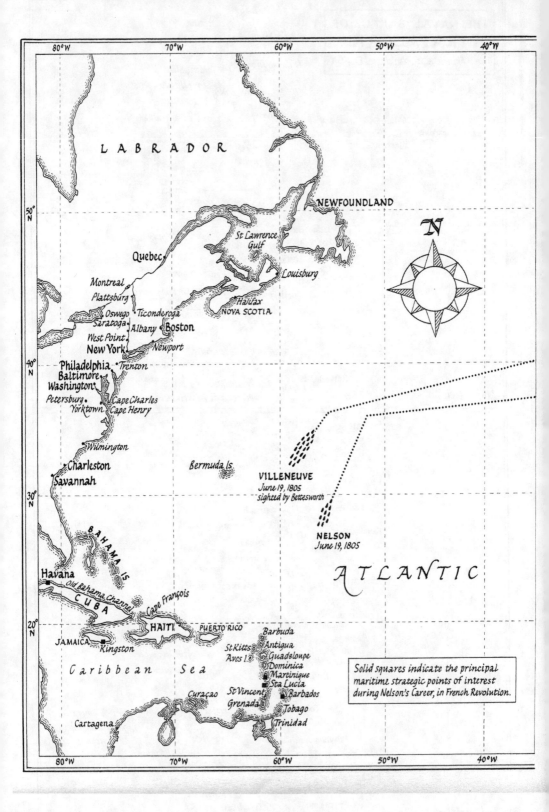

80°W 70°W 60°W 50°W 40°W

L A B R A D O R

NEWFOUNDLAND

50°N

St Lawrence Gulf

Quebec

Louisburg

Montreal
Plattsburg
Oswego · Ticonderoga
Saratoga
West Point · Albany · Boston
New York · Newport

Halifax
NOVA SCOTIA

N

40°N

Philadelphia · Trenton
Baltimore
Washington
Petersburg · Cape Charles
Yorktown · Cape Henry

Wilmington

Charleston
Savannah

Bermuda Is.

VILLENEUVE
June 19, 1805
sighted by Bettesworth

30°N

B A H A M A · I S

Havana
Old Bahama Channel
C U B A
Cape François

NELSON
June 19, 1805

A T L A N T I C

20°N

HAITI
JAMAICA
Kingston

PUERTO RICO
Barbuda
St Kitts Antigua
Aves Is. Guadeloupe
Dominica
Martinique
Sta Lucia
St Vincent Barbados
Grenada Tobago
Trinidad

C a r i b b e a n   S e a

Curaçao

Cartagena

Solid squares indicate the principal
maritime strategic points of interest
during Nelson's Career, in French Revolution.

80°W 70°W 60°W 50°W 40°W

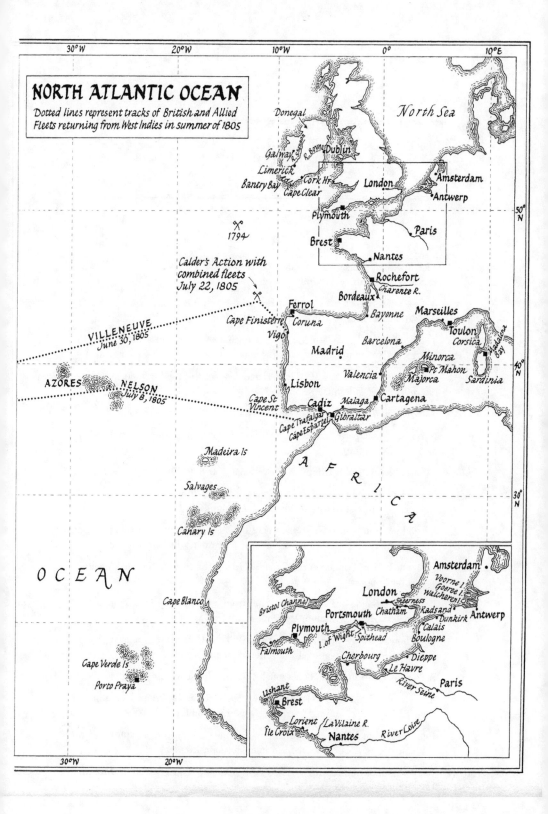

NORTH ATLANTIC OCEAN

Dotted lines represent tracks of British and Allied
Fleets returning from West Indies in summer of 1805

North Sea

Donegal
Galway
Limerick
Bantry Bay
Cape Clear
Cork Hr.
Dublin
R. Boyne
London
Amsterdam
Antwerp
Plymouth
50° N
Brest
Paris
Nantes
Rochefort
Charente R.
Bordeaux
Bayonne
Marseilles
1794
Calder's Action with
combined fleets
July 22, 1805
Ferrol
Cape Finistère
Coruna
Vigo
Toulon
Corsica
VILLENEUVE
June 30, 1805
Madrid
Barcelona
Minorca
Pt Mahon
Sardinia
Majorca
40° N
AZORES
NELSON
July 8, 1805
Lisbon
Valencia
Cape St
Vincent
Cadiz
Malaga
Cartagena
Cape Trafalgar
Cape Espartel
Gibraltar
Madeira Is
A F R I C A
Salvages
30° N
Canary Is
O C E A N
Cape Blanco
Amsterdam
Voorne I.
Goeree I.
Walcheren I.
London
Sheerness
Kadsand
Dunkirk
Antwerp
Bristol Channel
Portsmouth
Chatham
Calais
Boulogne
Plymouth
I. of Wight
Spithead
Cape Verde Is
Falmouth
Cherbourg
Dieppe
Le Havre
Paris
Porto Praya
River Seine
Ushant
Brest
Lorient
La Vilaine R.
Île Croix
Nantes
River Loire
30° W
20° W

LIST OF ILLUSTRATIONS

Every effort has been made to trace and contact copyright holders. The publishers will be pleased to correct any mistakes or omissions in future editions.

ACKNOWLEDGEMENTS

MY preparation for this book has taken me through many different libraries. As ever, with any historical reading and research, I am deeply grateful to the staff at the British Library and the Public Record Office. I am most especially thankful as well to the Garrison Library of Gibraltar and its inestimable librarian, Lorna Swift, a grandly impressive lady who has saved and revived what appeared to be a precious and little known Mediterranean treasure. After standing closed and inaccessible for many years the library's nominal owner, the British Army, sent one of its most experienced librarians to reopen this splendid institution. Founded by a military governor of Gibraltar in the late eighteenth century, the Garrison Library offers in its grand halls a magnificent assembly of volumes and records covering the political and military world through from the eighteenth century to the mid-twentieth.

I wish to offer as well my grateful thanks and appreciation to editor in chief Starling Lawrence at W. W. Norton and editorial assistant Molly May. I am grateful as well to my London agent, David Godwin, and Will Sulkin at Jonathan Cape for helping to bring this book to its close. And, personally, in Canada, most especially, my gratitude to Dusty and Samuel Solomon of Montreal for moral support; as ever it has been during sixty years of valued friendship. And, equaling for the same, to Boyce and Shirley Richardson at Ottawa.

START

THREE-thirty of a fine imminent dawn on 18 June 1793, out into the south-western stretch of the Channel, off Start Point on the Devonshire coast, and Captain Edward Pellew, commanding the 36-gun frigate *Nymphe*, received report of a sail bearing north-east, some twenty miles ahead.

Nymphe had sailed from Falmouth two days before to hunt its counterpart French frigates now active across the Channel. There was acute hunger for action in a war already five months old and yet lacking any serious naval encounter, for which the British public had grown impatient. The big ships of the line, the main battle fleet of Britain, those of the home waters, were either still at berth in Plymouth and Portsmouth, or lying off Spithead. Only two battle squadrons had sailed out for oceanic combat, one for the West Indies, the other for the Mediterranean.

Nymphe had already had a brush that came close to action. A week before, *Nymphe*, accompanied by another frigate, had encountered the 36-gun French frigate *Cléopâtre*, which, faced by a stronger force, had fled into Cherbourg. Pellew since then had been scouting for *Cléopâtre* which, with other frigates, had been falling with savage success upon British merchantmen.

At four a.m. Pellew, with *Nymphe* under all sail, closed towards his quarry sure that she was indeed *Cléopâtre*. They were together running with a light wind. Pellew feared that *Cléopâtre*, also under a press of canvas, was again seeking to escape. But, at five a.m., the French ship hauled up her foresail and lowered her topgallant sails to cut her speed, indicating that she awaited the fight.

For the next hour a great silence lay upon that sun-lit, slow-rolling and diminishing space of sea between the two ships as they drew steadily closer.

At six a.m. they were within hailing distance. *Cléopâtre*'s commander, Captain Jean Mullon, was the first to hail. Pellew answered, 'Hoa, hoa!', which was followed by three cheers from *Nymphe*'s sailors, waiting at their stations. Mullon, waving his hat, cried, '*Vive la Nation!*', and his own men responded with their own cheers.

With *Cléopâtre*'s acceptance of the challenge and the ships lying so close, and drawing closer, Pellew recognized the close nature of the combat about to start and ordered his men aloft from some of their stations into the shrouds. Observing that, Mullon made the same move. On each ship, therefore, men were manning the yards, preparing to fight and board from there. And then, at six fifteen, with *Nymphe*'s foremost guns bearing on the starboard quarter of *Cléopâtre*, Pellew, hat still in hand from raising it to hail his opponent, put it back on his head, his signal for starting action.

In this manner of ceremonious grace and courtesy began the first serious naval action of a war that had appeared curiously reluctant to get underway at sea, as if yet seeking to hold back from what was already bloodily swerving across the Continent. Or so it could seem in Britain through the months after 1 February 1793, when Revolutionary France had declared war on Britain and Holland.

As Captain Pellew replaced his hat the two frigates, running before the wind, opened their artillery upon one another. Within half an hour *Cléopâtre* had her mizzen mast and her wheel shot away in succession. This disaster made her ungovernable and brought her lying heavily against *Nymphe*, with her jib boom passing between *Nymphe*'s fore- and mainmasts. *Nymphe*'s mainmast had been badly damaged. It had become heavily entangled with the other ship's rigging. The strain of that threatened to bring down the mainmast. Pellew called out ten guineas to any man who would go up and cut the rigging. But, invisible in the smoke of battle, his maintopman had already run up the shrouds and cut the ropes, allowing the ships to draw apart.

The hottest part of the battle was by then being fought aloft. As the ships became entangled the seamen who on both vessels had been sent up to the yardarms began fiercely contesting each other's yards. *Nymphe*'s sailors were the first to cross and fought for possession of *Cléopâtre*'s yards. Other British sailors jumped on to *Cléopâtre*'s quarterdeck and shortly after seven a.m. hauled down the French colours.

Cléopâtre's Captain Mullon lay severely wounded. A round shot had torn open his back and crushed his left hip. His last action was as heroic as his stance had been throughout. In spite of his agony, he sought to destroy a list of the coast signals of the French navy by stuffing it into his mouth and chewing it to pieces. The action was, alas, in vain, for he had instead drawn from his pocket his own commission as an officer. He died with his teeth fixed on it. Five days later Pellew accompanied Mullon to his grave, along with full military honours. 'The enemy fought us like brave men,' Pellew said in his tribute, 'neither ship firing a shot until we had hailed.'

Given the scope of the tremendous maritime struggle that was to come, it was appropriate that the next action followed just a month later, on the other side of the Atlantic.

The 32-gun British frigate *Boston*, Captain George Courtenay, was cruising off New York, waiting for the 36-gun French frigate *Embuscade*, Captain Jean-Baptiste Bompart, to emerge from that port. *Embuscade* had captured or destroyed sixty British merchantmen before going to anchor off New York.

From his anchorage Bompart mistook *Boston* for a frigate, *Concorde*, that was due to put in to receive orders from him. In the belief that *Boston* was indeed *Concorde* Bompart sent over his first lieutenant, an American by birth, with twelve men to give his instructions to *Concorde*. Courtenay had deceived the pilot boat cruising off Sandy Hook by putting all French-speaking members of his crew on deck, talking loudly. On his way out *Embuscade*'s American lieutenant became suspicious of the frigate and rested on his oars. But the pilot boat in passing assured him that *Boston* was indeed French.

The American lieutenant went on board and he and his men were captured. When Courtenay told him that he wished to challenge *Embuscade* the American declared that Bompart was sure to accept and suggested that he himself write a letter to Bompart relaying the challenge. The letter went ashore with the Sandy Hook pilot. Bompart had a council of his officers. They agreed at once to accept Courtenay's challenge.

Boston and *Embuscade* met at dawn on 31 July 1793, off the New Jersey shore. Between five and six a.m. *Boston* lost command of her sails. Too much of her rigging had been shot away. Her jib and foremast staysail were gone. Shortly after six her main topmast and the yard with it fell. Then Courtenay and a lieutenant of the marines were killed by the same cannon-ball on the quarterdeck. The mizzen, mizzen topmast and mizzen staysail were shot away. The mizzen mast was expected to go at any moment. The only officers alive, two lieutenants, John Edwards and Alexander Kerr, were below, seriously wounded. Kerr had lost his sight, Edwards was wounded in the head. Without officers there was confusion on deck. Edwards, suffering severely, went on deck to take command. Unable to manoeuvre with her sails, *Boston* was exposed to raking fire from *Embuscade*, which was nearly as damaged as the British ship.

In that distressed state they drifted apart at eight a.m. and vanished from sight of one another.

These two distinctive frigate actions marked the start of the twenty-two years of sea warfare of the linked Revolutionary and Napoleonic Wars, which became the greatest war under sail and the first real world war. It was many things besides.

Nothing comparable preceded it in history. It became the longest, hardest and cruellest war ever fought on the waters, sea war on such a scale and of such a diversity that the only comparable sequence of naval operations lies with World War Two. The similarity between the maritime aspects of the two conflicts is indeed remarkable, for the naval side of the war of 1793–1815 saw deployment across all the oceans and upon most seas, with seaborne assaults and landings of the same sort upon which so much would similarly depend between 1939 and 1945. It was a war that saw the first ocean battle distant from shore. Only in the Pacific in World War Two would deep-sea naval battle be witnessed again. And, as in World War Two, the duress of conflict at the turn of the eighteenth century had demanded inventiveness. It was a war where the words rocket, torpedo, submarine and flight sprang alive through innovative experiment, helping to affirm that significant transition to the modern world that the war came to mark, further underlined by the fact that the two decades of its duration saw the passage of the eighteenth into the nineteenth century.

The tragically splendid formal duel between *Boston* and *Embuscade* off Sandy Hook had its own value as a pronouncement of the war's Atlantic reach, for the war's impact upon North America was to be profound, for both the United States and Canada.

It established the United States as a power before the world in a manner that the War of Independence never had or could have done, in a way that the Americans in 1793 never expected, and which initially they certainly did not relish. They would be fighting three distinct wars of their own within the Great War, in the Mediterranean with Barbary, with France in the Caribbean and with Britain all over the oceans as well as again on their own soil. By the end, however, the gift of it all would be an asserted sense of nationhood and global stature arrived to match the great beckoning of the West.

Much the same could be said for the Canadians who, in fighting an attempt by the American Westerners during the war to incorporate them into the United States, would possessively declare their own identity, a whole people, distinct from the mere colonial.

The Great War it was justly called at the time, and the name remained firmly attached to it until the twentieth century transferred that title to the first of its two world wars. But Great War is how this mighty and epochal struggle between Land and Sea will be referred to throughout this book.

Britain's Royal Navy was the most conservative, the most rigidly composed and severely governed naval force. Against this emblematic model of power afloat, Land duly presented the newest, most finely disciplined and marshalled military force the world had yet seen, the sudden product of the greatest soldier the world would know. And Sea for its part faced that soldier, Napoleon Buonaparte, with its own special example of drive, spirit and character as symbolized by Horatio Nelson: thus these two were called by that most special confrontation to stand forth far beyond all others, in the manner of the select of all ages, those who suddenly and mysteriously manifest the special qualities and instincts that intend them as if destined only for a particular moment and a special function at a particular time.

The Great War provided the climactic conclusion to the three centuries of oceanic conquest and naval rivalry that gradually had accompanied the emergence of the modern world. Nevertheless, navy and naval warfare in the character distinctive of the Great War had a realistic background of little more than a century and a half at the time that the boy Horatio Nelson stepped aboard his first ship. A Europe perpetually gripped by dynastic warfare and territorial dispute certainly never doubted the need for land armies, whether national or mercenary. But navy as a national necessity with established permanence had an uneven struggle into becoming the fierce instrument for obtaining or disputing command of the seas during the age of sail. In his classically innovative work of 1890, *The Influence of Sea Power upon History*, the great American naval historian Captain (subsequently Admiral) A. T. Mahan saw the year 1660 as being the point at which navies and naval power finally arrived in the form recognisable to later epochs. The new age that came in with the eighteenth century made ever-increasing strategic and tactical demands upon sail, which by then already was practically at the limit of its ability to respond any further. It was to be that period between the middle of the seventeenth century and the last decade of the eighteenth that had to furnish the navies and shape the talents and dispositions of the sailors of the war of 1793–1815. For this reason, to understand completely and properly the Great War one therefore has to cast back to what preceded it, for it is the tortuous evolution of the tactical means of ensuring the ultimate triumph of Sea over Land that first needs to be grasped.

PART ONE

THE TACTICAL EVOLUTION

I

OCEAN

NAVAL warfare in the broadly familiar historic sense that we understand it was the creation of the Western world.

It sprang from the heart of the Mediterranean to find its finished product at Europe's Atlantic shores. Little of that was neatly sequential. Time spaced it widely and unevenly.

To understand the ocean, to learn how to survive on it, to know how to move on it propulsively, and eventually to penetrate the long blue horizons that demarcated two-thirds of the face of the globe had to be fundamental to the rise and progress of humankind. But it had a different emergence in the different hemispheres.

On the other side of the world another seaborne history of ancient existence on the Indian Ocean and the eastern seas had long preceded that of the West. The character of it was demonstratively pacific in contrast to the incipiently aggressive nature of Western sea venture that showed itself from the start.

Upon that incompatibility of two wholly distinct forms of nautical impulse much of the oceanic future of the world eventually would turn. Modern global maritime history began with the seaborne fusion of the two hemispheres in the fifteenth century as the East reluctantly confronted the oceanic arrival of the West. Half a millennium of fiercely active collision followed, driven by the quickening demands of commercial rivalry in the West. But why should humankind's initial foraging courses upon the seas have emerged in such extreme contrast between the hemispheres?

If you look east, some sense of the answer comes from ocean there, for sailing the deep was an early skill upon the Indian Ocean. That familiarity with the deep seemed to lay a wider, less intimidated outlook upon Eastern seagoing. Ocean obviously was not the only factor shaping the Eastern maritime character. Nevertheless it was a considerable one. Western man's early seagoing lacked that sense of confident movement within the boundless that the Indian Ocean allowed. Instead it was coastal, headland to headland. Venture beyond sight of shore was practical only where it was of short span and familiar. Coastal and insular settlement brought warfare through proximity and raiding. Fighting afloat was a natural development. Trade, as it developed, incited piracy, an early school of maritime warfare which, for millennia, nevertheles remained simply an extension of land fighting.

The fundamentals of early European maritime experience, in commerce and warfare, were acquired in the confined basins and short passages of the eastern Mediterranean, where the steady evolution of sea experience leaped forward with huge impact upon legend and history, and gave to the world its first and longest enduring fighting ship, the galley. This slender, oar-driven vehicle provided the dynamic from which Western man's martial sailoring evolved.

The simple oar, which at some remote point replaced paddles on the Nile, must be the single greatest invention yielded by man's search for fully controlled movement upon water. It became the most enduring instrument of naval warfare. In its many different forms, the galley had an existence of 2,500 years, probably more, but certainly from early in the first millennium BC. Its last fighting appearance was to be against Nelson at Copenhagen in 1801.

The galley arrived to meet the specific need of warfare in the eastern Mediterranean, particularly the Aegean. The great commerce that spread across the Mediterranean was mainly transported in broad, sturdy merchantmen that allowed as much space as possible for cargo. They carried oars for calm weather or perhaps to help evade pirates, but otherwise depended principally on their large square sail, possibly complemented with a foresail.

The basic form of the galley had to be entirely different – long and narrow for speed and manoeuvrability. Sail was carried but the galley fought only under oar. Sail was used for setting course, or for getting away in face of defeat.

The main tactical weapon of the galley became the ram, a strong underwater projection at the prow. Apart from its destructive power, it aided speed, in the same way as a similar bulbous projection below the bows of a modern supertankers does. The ram was for attacking the enemy head-on, splintering the oars and fatally damaging the hull of the other vessel; it remained the principal basis of naval tactics for two thousand years, until a forward-firing gun was mounted by it, allowing damage to be inflicted on the foe before contact.

The galley's speed and sustainable performance were of course tied up with the endurance and strength of the oarsmen. The most celebrated model of the ancient world, the trireme, the standard fighting ship of the Greek navy, was carried forward through successive designs from around the late sixth century BC until it reached its ultimate, a three-decked vessel carrying 170 oars of three different types. A study by two American academics, Vernard Foley and Werner Soedel, published in *Scientific American* in 1981, put the trireme's top speed at a good deal more than earlier estimates of 11.5 knots, with the oarsmen able to reach their top speed in thirty seconds from a standing start. Foley and Soedel calculated that the moving oars had to be kept parallel within about twelve inches.

In 483 BC we have the first detailed account of a critical naval battle, that of Salamis, fought in September 480 BC. Beyond Salamis, naval warfare continued across the centuries throughout the Mediterranean. The Romans were military-minded more than sea-minded and gave nothing new and innovative to sea warfare. But their vast empire demanded naval power, seamanship and naviga-tion, the cumulative knowledge and experience of which made them the greatest naval force of antiquity. They gave commercial unity to the Mediterranean. Then, as the Roman world disintegrated under the weight of the Barbarian invasions, and as it entered deeper into the Christian era, the empire moved its capital from Rome to Byzantium on the Bosporus, the city that would eventu-ally be renamed Constantinople after the emperor Constantine. Here was born the Western global impulse, for it was the expansive flow of goods from the East that gave the Bosporus its supreme niche in history.

It was this hemispheric trade of peppers and spices, silks and brocades, that was ultimately to act as the spur to Western oceanic venture and the opening of the world. For here at Constantinople began the rise of that commerce whose enticement, with its promise of huge wealth, perpetual profit and empire, would launch commercial competition and consequent naval rivalry among the European powers. As the old Western empire of the Romans disappeared, there came the shock of the rise of Islam as the warrior followers of the Prophet Mohamed were seized by a spiritual drive that gave them a command from the Indian Ocean to the Atlantic. Their onslaught westwards from Arabia was achieved in the span between the death of Mohamed in 632 and the successful landing at Gibel Tarik, Gibraltar, in 711. They went in a mere eighty years from Arabia to Spain, absorbing in their rush, one after the other, the Persian Empire, Syria, Egypt, all of North Africa to Morocco, and from there across the Straits into Spain.

The unity of the Western world, once centred upon the Mediterranean, was broken for centuries to come.

On the other side of the world, an immense sweep of trade brought unifying communication between four civilisations, the Irano-Arabic,

Hindu, Indonesian and Chinese. It created, according to K. N. Chaudhuri, historian of that trade, 'an invisible sense of unity' among them all, a concept of co-existence that in the West died with the Roman Empire.[1]

Early maritime development in eastern waters placed steadfast emphasis upon peaceful oceanic commerce, which was of a venturesome magnitude that would take the West many centuries to achieve in like scale, though never with similar lack of belligerence.

The Indian Ocean was naturally encouraging to early maritime ranging across huge spans of deep open ocean because nowhere else were the prevailing winds so predictably favourable. Sailors of the Chinese Han Empire appear to have traversed the Indian Ocean as early as AD 2. During the late seventh and eighth centuries Arabs and Persians were already sailing to Canton. Around the ninth and tenth centuries the Arabs were sailing regularly to Africa and founding settlements all along the eastern coast of the continent as far south as Sofala opposite Madagascar on the Mozambique Channel. Before and after 1000 AD it was a network that linked half the world, from Nagasaki to Cairo.

Across all the seas between the Persian Gulf and Canton other trade routes of every sort crisscrossed. It was a vast self-sustaining oceanic commerce whose cohesion had achieved remarkable balance during the millennium that preceded Europe's intrusion.

The Indian Ocean was the pumping heart of this system, its navigation fostered by the regularity of the monsoon winds.

A pivotal point of Chaudhuri's landmark examination of the Indian Ocean trading network is his demonstration of the fundamental lack of belligerence or attempt at aggressive domination within it. Piracy was a permanent menace, as of course it was in the Mediterranean. But, as Chaudhuri says, before the arrival of Europe on the Indian Ocean 'there had been no organized attempt by any political power to control the sea-lanes and the long-distance trade of Asia . . . The Indian Ocean as a whole and its different seas were not dominated by any particular nations or empires.'[2]

The outstanding fact of this vigorous enterprise was that the Arabs were sailing the deep ocean, confidently far beyond shore, many centuries before the Europeans dared to venture far out into the Atlantic.

By the time Charles Martel stopped the Arab advance into the European heartland at Poitiers in 732 the great thriving pattern and connection of the Roman world was all but gone. The economy of north-western Europe had fallen back on agriculture instead of commerce. In its retreat into agricultural self-sufficiency society became feudal, producing only for its own needs, or for the armies it fostered. Existence was rural or military. There was nothing else, except the Church.

By the end of the eighth century Europe had a few points of embryonic sea trade on the Narrow Seas between the Continent and Britain. It was trade developed by the Frisians of Friesland, that region at the lower reaches of the Rhine that would be embraced by the future Holland. The Frisians in their broad-hulled, river-type craft sailed to England and France but, more importantly, perhaps also to the Baltic, laying the basis for the future mercantile power of the Dutch.

The focal points of revival were to be Venice and Kiev, which became the commercial pivot for trade moving up from Constantinople to the Baltic. By the end of the eleventh century Christian navigation had reasserted itself across the Mediterranean. The fighting ship of Venice and the other Italian maritime republics was the galley, revived through a succession of forms, larger, with greater oar power, more varied sail, otherwise still long, lean and fast, still ferociously dependent upon the ram, and recognizably the vessel of antiquity. Between the Baltic and the North Sea a rich and expansive trading pattern developed. New ship types evolved, better suited to carriage of the expanding trade in the region. They were versions of 'round ship', broad, barrel-like vessels working under sail, the best known of which was the 'cog'.

The cog was flat-bottomed, with straight stem and stern, a large stern rudder and a keel, a single mast and broad sail. It could be between seventy and eighty feet long, with a width of about twenty-four feet. A particular distinction, because of its cargo-carrying capacity, was that it sat high out of the water.

The armed cog was in a sense Europe's first real warship, adapted to naval purposes by Denmark and the Dutch of Friesland and Zeeland in particular. It became the essential dual-purpose vessel. The Dutch remained the principals of this intensive north European sea trading, masters of the carrying trade in those seas, a success that was to take them far beyond as well, bearing them to greater riches and eventually to possession of the first true naval command of Europe in defence of their commerce. For the moment, however, the deep ocean was yet a barrier to them.

The Portuguese in the fourteenth century had become active seafarers around the European coasts. They had sailed to the Azores, Madeira and the Canaries taking advantage of familiar wind patterns which ensured their return. By the end of the fifteenth century Portugal, with its established Atlantic experience, led the way to wider oceanic horizons. Their ships began a steady descent of the north-western African coast and then found that they could safely go no further.

The problem was Cape Bojador, roughly 100 miles south of the Canary Islands. To beat back home against the headwinds required a vessel that would sail closer to the wind than anything Europe then possessed.

Commonly at the start of the fifteenth century European ships were square-rigged, with a single large square sail on one, two or three masts. The giant sail of square rig had not yet been divided into the variety of sail that would give such distinction to the ships of later centuries. Topsails had appeared but were yet to become general. The large square sails were fine for running before the wind but not for sailing into it. This was not a ship for venturing out on the deep, open ocean beyond sight of land and all visible markers.

The deep-sea ship that evolved to defeat the barrier of Cape Bojador was the caravel. To the square rig of the northern ships was added the lateen sail. This characteristic sail of the Indian Ocean had the great advantage of allowing a ship to beat to windward close-hauled. It was a square sail that crossed the width of the boat. The lateen is said to have passed into the Mediterranean by the fourth century AD. It seems surprising, therefore, that it took so long for its Atlantic possibilities to be realized. A possible reason was supplied by Alan Villiers after a voyage on an Arab dhow in the late 1930s. Villiers found that the lateen sail of the dhow was the big problem when tacking. Lateen sail is a triangular sail working from a very long boom, or yard. 'So we always wore her round,' Villiers says, 'running off with the wind behind the sail, and swinging the huge yard when she was dead before the wind . . . it was a complicated and difficult process. The whole sail was thrown over, the sheet and the tack changing from end for end, and the manoeuvre had to be done carefully when there was anything of a wind lest the sail take charge.'[3]

Clearly something less arduous was required for the more violent and unpredictable waters of the Atlantic. From the time of its first appearance around 1430 the caravel was adapted until it took new form as the carrack, first developed by Biscay shipbuilders. This ship had square sails, topsail and course on the foremast and lateen rig on the main and mizzen. The lateen itself had undergone transformation. It had shortened yards and was fitted more snugly to the mast, always on the same side of it, enabling the ship to go about without the necessity of taking the yard over the top of the mast.

Bartolomeu Dias, who sailed for the South Atlantic in 1487, was the first to round the Cape of Good Hope into the Indian Ocean. By that time Columbus had made two voyages to the Caribbean and John Cabot had persuaded the Tudor King Henry VII to back him in seeking a northern route to the Indies. In a mere three months Cabot crossed the North Atlantic, found his own 'new found land', and returned. He had not found the Indies he sought but he had shown the way to the Grand Banks of Newfoundland, having reported the seas alive with fish.

The rigid command and monopoly that the Portuguese in 1500 sought to lay upon the Indian Ocean, their private preserve, like that of the Spanish soon to follow in the Americas, launched the concept of global naval warfare. The sense of that was immediate. The sudden arrival of active commercial and ideological belligerence was difficult to understand among those who for nearly two millennia had sailed without any serious menace, other than that of piracy and privateering. As K. N. Chaudhuri concluded, 'The phenomenon that is in need of explaining is not the system of peaceful but that of armed trading.'

The harsh explanation was, of course, that the inspirational value of the early oceanic search for the world had been framed by the Portuguese as Holy Crusade, drawn from the stark spiritual polarities of the late Middle Ages and its fervent commitment to the ultimate defeat of Islam.

During the century after Columbus the ocean and its mastery, the quest beyond the horizon, the seaborne union of the hemispheres, the drive for possession and command of all that discovery might deliver, formed the dominating secular obsession of Europe. Naval rivalry swiftly became integral to that expanding global vision projected from the shores of the western Atlantic in the sixteenth century.

In this manner the oceanic future of the world arrived with startling suddenness.

Where the whole of the fifteenth was the century of search, the sixteenth right from the outset was the century of the realized world, for after Columbus and da Gama came Magellan and Juan Sebastián Elcano, who completed Europe's first circumnavigation of the world. The sixteenth century opened the world to those who had the seacraft and power to lay possession to wherever they set their flag and their beacons. What now swiftly unfolded became fundamental to the story of the modern world, the subsequent missions of conquest, the rush for colonial acquisition, the rise of ruthlessly competitive mercantilism, the vision of global imperial greatness, the dream of universal sway, and withal the necessarily aggressive need for naval power that outbalanced that of one's rivals. This quest, grown upon the North Atlantic's western shores, would henceforth be fervently nourished and driven forward, accumulating its momentum over the next three centuries. Unlike the Indian Ocean's tradition of commercial harmony and tolerance, the motivating factor on the Atlantic would finally be fight for command of profit upon the seas and with it enforcement of the victor's rights.

From that struggle inevitably evolved a fully focused consciousness of the need for purpose-built standing navies requiring experienced admirals and trained sailors. It would require another century for the mature emergence of the concept, but all the circumstances that would mould its emergence would soon be obvious.

At the start of the sixteenth century neither France nor England was able to challenge the Iberian monopoly of the oceans and Portugal and Spain's proclaimed exclusion of all others. Only the Netherlands, masters of the North Sea carrying trade, could boast a truly extensive continuity of armed mercantile seagoing experience.

While the ship of the Narrow Seas was in a state of slow evolution naval combat essentially remained what it had always been – land fighting afloat. That is, galley fighting. The galley itself was still firmly in use with the French and English, the former especially. In the Mediterranean the continual naval warfare between the Italian states and between the Christian powers and the Turkish Ottomans had developed galleys and galley warfare to a high point of artistry and skill.

In basic principle galley warfare remained scarcely different from that of Salamis, with the ships advancing line abreast, prow to prow, towards one another. But galley battle came to resemble a board game in its tactical manoeuvring. The British naval historian Julian Corbett described it thus: 'A great school of Italian admirals had grown up whose services were sought by all the Mediterranean powers . . . their influence was strong enough, supported as it was, by classical tradition, to outweigh the oceanic experience of Spanish and Portuguese seamen. In the scientific spirit of the age the art of commanding a fleet had become akin to a branch of mathematics, and an admiral of the Italian school would manoeuvre a squadron with almost as much pedantic intricacy as a *maestro di campo* could handle his *tertia* of infantry.'[4] Sail had no real place in this Mediterranean galley warfare. That became a problem as the galley established itself firmly in the naval forces on the Narrow Seas and in the Baltic. Its disadvantages in those rougher seas compelled the development of its necessary equivalent under sail along the Atlantic seaboard.

Corbett saw the matter of reconciling sea endurance with free movement as being the main problem at the heart of naval history. Sea endurance meant the degree of bad weather that a vessel could support. The essence of naval strategy therefore meant the degree of a fleet's capability of keeping the sea: 'The galley was a vessel of low sea endurance but of highly free movement. The great-ship, or ship-of-the-line, was of large sea endurance but entirely subservient to the wind for its power of movement . . . In the first period, the period of oars, when the focus of empire lay within the confined waters of the Mediterranean, we see mobility taking precedence of sea endurance; in the second, the period of sails, when the arena of history widens into the ocean, sea endurance becomes of first importance . . .'

It was from Italy and out of the galley itself, however, that the prime model for the future ship of sea endurance came, the *galleazza*, or galleon as it eventually came to be known. The *galleazza* succeeded where the round ship had failed. The latter's 'tumble home' sides curved inboard at the top of the hull, giving them their characteristic dumpy appearance. They were ponderously slow, short in proportion to beam and with high freeboard. The *galleazza*, or galleass as it was first to be called in England, had a length three times its beam against a round ship's length of twice its beam. It had lower freeboard than a round ship. It was rigged with three masts, the foremast carrying square sails, the main and mizzen lateens. Its more graceful proportions gave it speed and sea endurance that allowed it the assurance to pass from the Mediterranean into the Atlantic, and thereby made it the ship for the Venetian carrying trade between the Mediterranean and Antwerp. Once arrived on the Atlantic seaboard it was swiftly adopted by all the maritime powers there, the French, Portuguese, Spanish and the English.

What this necessary ship of sea endurance still lacked, however, was its proper use in naval warfare. The arrangement of the galleon's firepower and its tactical deployment in naval war were questions that arose even as it supplanted the galley. On those matters it was swiftly obvious that all the centuries of galley fighting had nothing to offer.

In England the concept of an established navy came rapidly alive with Henry VIII. The greatest change he helped to bring lay with ordnance. The French, though heavily reliant upon galleys, were said to have been the first, in 1501, to have put heavy guns between decks and cut ports in the sides of their big ships through which the guns would fire. Henry was credited with the invention. Whoever was first with it, the idea was an astounding change. It was nevertheless inevitable because, as the weight of gun metal increased, the top deck guns, each of some three tons, would make the ship top heavy. Taking them closer to the waterline gave balance and stability.

This change meant that guns were now arranged along the sides of the ship. But the fundamental form of galley fighting persisted, of ships advancing upon a foe in a line with all abeam of one another. That was obviously impractical with galleons. Sailing in line abeam of one another they could only have firepower right forward in the bows, otherwise they would be firing across at one another.

One of the most decisive lessons in naval warfare came on 15 August 1545, when an attempted French invasion of England failed off Shoreham. Both sides fought with galleys but Henry had also lined up his galleasses, which made use of the destructive unity of the firepower extended along the length of their decks. That came to be called 'broadside'. Henry's galleasses 'did so handle the galleys, as well with their sides as their prows, that your great-ships in a manner had little to do'. With that observed and learned, the battle term broadside was established: it meant the simultaneous unleashing of shot from the length of a vessel at an adversary, and became the fundamental tactic of firepower for the naval warfare that henceforth would be played out between the great naval powers of the Western world. With that the oar began to recede into history, for the ship of the line had arrived. So, too, it seemed, had arrived an enhanced awareness of Britain's status as an island, and realization of both the strength and the vulnerability of that. Or, as Julian Corbett proposed in his classic on naval strategy in 1911,[5] . . . limited war is only permanently possible to island Powers or between Powers that are separated by sea, and then only when the Power desiring limited war is able to command the sea . . . to render impossible the invasion of his home territory. Here, then, we reach the true meaning and highest military value of what we call the command of the sea, and here we touch the secret of England's success against Powers so greatly superior to herself in military strength.'

The balance of power in Europe became a critical matter of national policy, integral to the need of a navy, even before the demands of oceanic commerce compounded that need. Europe's quarrels were being resolved militarily at levels of strength and ferocity on land that now lay far beyond any English participant capability, whether in men or money. From the sixteenth century, therefore, British maritime strategy stands fully emergent, the necessary resistance to forces across the Channel. For the dynastic complexity of emergent Europe was increasingly accountable for its military turbulence. A bewildering pattern of royal marriages during the fifteenth century and the unpredictable inheritances that arose in consequence of them was the origin for much of the antagonism that was released within the Continent. And accompanying that was the ideological turmoil of the Reformation and subsequent Counter Reformation that would continue to tear at Europe until the middle of the seventeenth century.

That turmoil initiated the eventual ruin of Spain and loss of her naval dominance. Through Philip II's marriage to Mary Tudor he sought, as king of England, to have possession of England's resources, not least its seafaring instincts and abilities. But his rigorous refusal to allow English 'trespass' within the Spanish Empire and denial of any portion of its New World oceanic trade raised up a buccaneering generation of English privateers who went out to help themselves. They had the broadside to help them do it. Here at the outset Philip II created the beginnings of an altogether different English naval spirit, one of obduracy, tenacity and abhorrence of the Continental powers that sought to master the island.

In the Netherlands the Hapsburgs similarly set in motion an equally powerful situation that eventually would act against them. The Netherlands was the richest and most prosperous part of Europe. It provided Spain with a permanent source of revenue through the taxes laid upon its bankers and merchants. There was pride and independence in a compact region that had become the banking, manufacturing and trading centre of the Western world. It was that very pride and independence that reacted against an occupying Spanish army and the Inquisition.

The Dutch revolt against Spanish dominance broke open in 1567. It was to be an eighty-year struggle, but well before the end of it the formidable future naval power of the Dutch and their new republic had been well established. As with the English, Dutch naval ascendancy began with ruthless privateering, the so-called 'Sea Beggars', *gueux de mer*, who attacked Spanish transports, captured the Spanish silver fleet and at one point scattered and sank the Spanish navy in the North Sea, taking its admiral prisoner.

The English were everywhere in the Mediterranean, trading to the Moslem as well as the Christian ports. English agents used the Levant to pass through Syria and Persia to the Indian Ocean and on to the Indies. The East India Company was founded in 1600. The Dutch too swarmed into the Mediterranean, in Fernand Braudel's expressive phrase 'like so many heavy insects crashing against the window panes'. Simultaneously they ignored Portuguese claims of exclusive right to the East, circumnavigated the Cape, occupied Java, captured Mauritius and visited Siam and China. Their own East India company was founded in 1602.

What, meanwhile, of the French? Their promising and exciting oceanic ventures into Canada at the early part of the century had been halted by wars with the Hapsburgs and violent internal religious wars. The French throne had passed to the House of Bourbon, with Henry IV as king. Henry revived oceanic ambition. Port Royal (Nova Scotia) was founded in 1604, Quebec in 1608. The outline of the great mercantile and naval contest of the future was being drawn. The three principal contestants, England, Holland and France, were coming to their allotted places. It was the essential competitive pattern that would continue to hold and to be built upon through all the ups and downs of the dynastic, religious and national convulsions yet to come.

II

NAVY

THE seventeenth was the century of the rise of navies.

At the start of the century the commercial exclusivity upon the great waters attempted by Portugal and Spain was already gone. The determining race for power and mastery upon the seas had begun, with the Iberians already seen as the weakening participants in the race against the swiftly rising powers of England, Holland and France. Navy had not yet resolved into any firm concept of permanent standing navies. War at sea depended upon any existing warships being hastily supported by armed merchantmen.

Sea fighting itself remained in its brawling infancy still heavily influenced by galley fighting. Nowhere had there yet arrived any firmly defined tactical rules for sea battle manoeuvre, or set rules governing use of sail and wind in battle. Much less were there sustained ideas embracing grand oceanic strategy. Ocean was still too large a vision for comfortably adjusted existence in most Western minds, which were yet too obsessed with the religious convulsions of Europe to be seriously distracted by a goal still too abstract. Terrestrial conflict was the principal menace. Military power, land fighting and armies, therefore naturally remained the predominant concern, diminishing the role of navies and their professional evolution. But since the struggles on land were seldom far removed from the Atlantic coasts or the Narrow Seas of north-western Europe, the Channel and the North Sea, it was in those confined waters that Western naval development had to find its evolution.

All of Europe was convulsed by the last great surge of religious and dynastic upheaval at the heart of which burned the bitter enmity between Bourbon France on the one hand and the alliance of the Hapsburgs of Austria and Spain on the other. Europe was plunged into crisis, and from crisis into prolonged war. The conflict that raged from 1618 to 1648 became known as the Thirty Years War, more cruel and savage than anything so far.

Out of that bloody upheaval would emerge a new Europe, and with it new and different concepts of naval strategy. The Thirty Years War might well be regarded as the signal period that delivered naval strategy to the Western mind, bringing with it the concept that the deployment of naval power could seriously hamper or affect the battle fortunes of the land, and with it the fate of nations and the destiny of empires. And it restored the Mediterranean to a central role in Western maritime history.

It was with France, however, under Louis XIII's chief minister, Cardinal Richelieu, that the strongest effort to restructure naval power was begun. He laid down a programme for a fleet of some forty major warships, half of them 34- to 40-gun ships. But Richelieu's greatest contribution may have been his innovating establishment of the principle of a navy on two seas, with an Atlantic fleet at Brest and a Mediterranean force at the new naval base he established at Toulon. France's own Mediterranean naval strategy was thereby set in motion, with dramatic impact when France finally entered the Thirty Years War in 1635.

Richelieu had seen his new base at Toulon as a key to defeat of the powerful Austro-Spanish armies that were fighting the Dutch in the Lowlands and the Germans east of the Rhine and would be fighting the French along their own German frontiers once France became fully involved. Richelieu's surprising and original strategy centred upon Toulon as a means of cutting Spanish supply and reinforcement of its armies inside Europe. For Spain the shortest route for maintaining her armies inside the Continent was from Corunna up through the Narrow Seas to the Spanish enclave of Dunkirk and on to the Spanish Netherlands (modern Belgium). But that had become impracticable. The Dutch with their experienced and belligerent navy controlled the Narrow Seas.

Denied the direct supply route through the Narrow Seas Spain's alternative route of reinforcement and supply had to lie through Genoa. From there they passed to Milan and thence through various Alpine passes to the valley of the Rhine. Toulon became Richelieu's base for cutting communication between Spain and Genoa, thereby undermining the whole Spanish-Austrian campaign inside the Continent. That shift of the Brest fleet to Toulon initiated the great strategic deployment that would prevail in French naval policy in the future as it shifted fleets to match requirement: if not Brest to Toulon, then Toulon to Brest. Toulon became a name, a strategic determinant, to be coupled eventually with that of Gibraltar. The two were to become the opposing points of critical strategic command in the western basin of the Mediterranean. From the Straits to the Italian peninsula they would create a maritime reach of 'transcendent importance' where, in Mahan's memorable words, preponderant naval power determined gigantic issues, swaying the course of history again and again in successive wars of that century and thereafter when 'it was not chiefly in the clash of arms, but in the noiseless pressure by the navies, and largely in the Mediterranean, that the issues were decided'.

In the Thirty Years War the western Mediterranean thus assumed a new significance in the power struggles of Europe that it was never to lose.

In reply to the French example Charles I set out to match Richelieu's naval construction programme, the controversial expense of which was to contribute to the circumstances that cost him his crown and his life. The British navy's real future was moulded by his usurpers. For revolution, civil war and regicide in England were to deliver a wholly new concept of navy and naval administration. New ideas and new commitment were infused by the rigorous military minds that had come to control England's reconstituted Commonwealth destiny.

For the British, Oliver Cromwell and his soldier-generals fathered the modern navy. Cromwell delivered to the quarterdecks of a new fleet of ships military commanders, colonels who were called generals-at-sea, some of whom were to establish themselves in the front rank of Britain's greatest sailors. It was these soldiers who set the English navy on its evolutionary course towards its greatness in the century ahead, and who by deciding that universal supremacy at sea was the navy's rightful goal helped to mould the particular prowess that went towards ensuring its achievement.

The unique distinction of Cromwell's sailoring soldiers was that they were to combine pride of seamanship with drilled military efficiency and crisp tactical command, without imposing any distinction of land commanding sea, which remained the inclination of the French and the Spanish. With Cromwell there finally arrived the full commitment to a standing navy. The established tradition of composing a navy in an emergency by hurriedly arming merchantmen was abandoned. A standing navy meant ships built by the state and maintained by it only for naval purposes, the principal of which became defence of commerce. For Julian Corbett no change in English naval history was greater or more far-reaching than that. 'It was no mere change of organisation; it was a revolution in the fundamental conception of naval defence. For the first time protection of the mercantile marine came to be regarded almost as the chief end for which the regular navy existed, and the whole of naval strategy underwent a profound modification in English thought . . . the main lines of commerce became also the main lines of naval strategy . . . what they were really aiming at was the command of the sea by the domination of the great trade routes and the acquisition of focal points as naval stations.'[1]

The Dutch, with their command of Europe's carrying trade and their expanding colonial empire across the world, had shown the way, notably with their seizure of the Cape of Good Hope. Their squadrons were protectively posted wherever their trade moved. And it moved everywhere, nourishing the wealth of their tiny state. The example was too powerful to be ignored.

A new class of warship had emerged, the frigate, small, fast-sailing, flush-decked ships that originated from the dockyards at Dunkirk where design was affected by the demands for the privateering vessels built and stationed there. Frigates were among the first ships ordered for the Commonwealth navy, whose reconstruction had passed from the hands of politicians to professionals. Aboard the new wooden walls pay and conditions for sailors were improved.

After the turmoil of the Thirty Years War the Dutch republic, the now wholly independent United Provinces, might have seemed to be the natural ally of the English military republic. But the mercantile strength and naval power of the Dutch had aroused both the ire and the envy of Cromwell's Commonwealth.

Released from the burden of war, Holland was left free to concentrate upon the accumulation of wealth and power from its vast mercantile resources. Its merchant fleet totalled ten thousand vessels employing 168,000 seamen. England scarcely possessed a thousand merchantmen. The carrying trade of most of Europe, from the Baltic to the Levant, and including much of England's, was with the Dutch. They now had the monopoly of the eastern trade, having seized many of Portugal's Asian possessions. They held the monopoly of trade with Japan. Their colonial possessions in the East extended from India to include Ceylon and the whole of the Indonesian archipelago. They had colonies in West Africa, South America and, notably, held New Amsterdam in North America. In 1652 they seized the pivotal point of east–west trade, the Cape of Good Hope. Backing them was a strong navy led by experienced seamen.

All of this Cromwell was driven to challenge, despite a desire for a compact between the Protestant states as a caution against the rising power of France.

By 1653 England was at war with the Dutch, the first of three wars that would follow in quick succession before the end of the century. With Spanish sea power now in permanent decline, the English–Dutch wars represented the beginning of the final process of elimination between the three surviving naval powers, Holland, England and France, for command of the sea.

These Anglo-Dutch wars were radically different from any that preceded them, the real beginning of modern naval warfare. They changed the tactical and strategic character of naval war and rivalry, being sea war between equals, between sailors of the highest professional proficiency and commitment, and fought within a confined sea space that demanded exceptional tactical skill.

With these wars mercantilism had arrived in full, determining manifestation. It would be the motor of a new age of oceanic commercial
rivalry dedicated to ruthless elimination of opponents. Mercantilism was
the conviction that oceanic commerce compelled narrow self-interest, the
need to overtake or drive out rivals in trade and colonial possession, and
to deny access wherever profits were greatest, particularly in the East and
the Caribbean. Mercantilism was the fever that had developed naturally
and ever more rapaciously through the seventeenth century as sea power
diversified and the Dutch, the English and the French as well as others
began intruding upon Spain and Portugal's attempts at global exclusivity.
Elizabethan piracy and privateering had been mercantilism's first offspring.
Established naval power became the next.

This first of the Dutch wars was an uneven affair. It saw the rise of the
foremost of the Dutch admirals, Tromp, de Ruyter and de Wit. They were
opposed by the British commander in chief Robert Blake and a new general
seconded to the navy, General George Monck. It was a war in which the
English and the Dutch were evenly matched in strength and seamanship.
But by concentrating on control of the vital approaches to the Dutch coast
the English cut off Dutch trade and brought Holland near to ruin. It was left
to Cromwell in 1654 to allow a generous peace, for fear of wholly ruining
a potential Protestant ally against France.

The Western world had come to yet another point of pivotal change.
Cromwell died in 1658. In 1660 Charles II was restored to the English throne.
A wholly different Europe had arisen from the destruction of the Thirty
Years War. The chaotic age of religious tumult and its savage wars was over.
Spain, the source of so much of it, was in rapid and permanent decline. The
power of the Austrian Empire too was crippled. Hapsburg Austria, humbled
by the defeat of its overambitious lunge for Continental power, now found
itself facing an ambitiously ascendant France to the west and to the east
continuing assaults against its empire from the Ottoman Turks.

In France Louis XIV's finance minister, Jean-Baptiste Colbert, set out
to transform France's naval power and character as profoundly as Cromwell
had changed that of England. When Colbert took office in 1661 he visualized
a huge navy of ships ranging from twenty-four to 120 guns. In 1664, as
Colbert's vast naval programme was being laid out, the Dutch and English
were again at war. The English peremptorily seized New Amsterdam,
or New York as we now know it. There was no quibbling about motive.
General Monck laid it out bluntly: 'What matters this or that reason? What
we want is more of the trade which the Dutch now have.'[2] This short war
stands as one of the most significant in naval history.

The circumstances were different from the last. The Commonwealth
Navy was now Charles II's 'Royal Navy', with his brother, the Duke of

York, the future James II, as Lord High Admiral of England. Restoration had brought demoralizing factional tensions within the navy. But Monck, who had helped organize the king's return from exile, was still afloat, commanding the larger division of the battle fleet, with Prince Rupert, the Duke of York's cousin, the other division.

The war was fought in the Narrow Seas and essentially settled through three battles, which together defined basic naval tactics for the next hundred years. For it was this war that made visible, clearly and distinctly for the first time, that grand vision of two battle fleets passing parallel in strict line of battle while firing broadsides at one another: the Line. Naval warfare had so far lacked any clear directional control. In action the impulse was towards melee with the ships of the various squadrons breaking off into individual engagement. Clear, firm instructions covering the movements of a fleet in action were yet to emerge. But Cromwell's soldier-admirals, with their rigorous military minds, had made the first serious effort to approach naval battle formation and tactical strategy as a matter of ordered, scientific procedure that required strict compliance. Their instructions were issued in 1653 during the first Dutch war. One of these was that 'all the ships of every squadron shall endeavour to keep in line with the chief, unless the chief be . . . disabled . . . Then every ship of said squadron shall endeavour to keep in line with the admiral, or he that commands in chief next unto him . . .' That battle code was amplified in 1666 by the Duke of York, who strengthened the instructions for keeping the line. But it was only towards the end of this second war that the line made its first full appearance before a surprised maritime world. It did so with one of the greatest battles in naval history: the Four Days Battle in the first week of June 1666.

Mahan described the battle as 'the most remarkable, in some of its aspects, that has ever been fought upon the ocean'.[3] Certainly nothing was ever to match it for horror and endurance: four days of near ceaseless fighting, seven thousand dead, nineteen ships lost. Only at Jutland in 1914 would Britain suffer as severely.

The fleets were huge, the English with some eighty ships, the Dutch with around one hundred. Fought in the Narrow Seas, in the waters bounded by Dover and North Foreland and Calais and Dunkirk, the action veered indecisively from one coast to the other over four days until it exhausted itself, with the Dutch admiral de Ruyter having the better of the English in the final action. The loss of the English over the four days was the greater of the two, with five thousand killed and three thousand taken prisoner. They lost seventeen ships. The Dutch lost two thousand men and two ships. The English had had the worst of it but it was de Ruyter who preferred to withdraw before carrying it into a fifth day.

The courage of the English was the more remarkable for the fact that the Royal Navy under Charles was in a poor state. There was no money. The sailors were hungry, rations were short. Pay was years in arrears. Maintenance aboard ship and on shore had been low. Those conditions had induced some three thousand English and Scottish sailors to sell their services to the Dutch. Shamelessly and derisively they had shouted their dollar price to their brothers from the decks of the Dutch ships.

What the battle would always stand for above everything else was its vivid display of the new tactic of line. General Monck had at the start signalled for 'line of battalia'. The close-hauled 'line' thereafter was performed with a skill and perfection that hardly suggested its novelty. One French observer, the Comte de Guiche, marvelled at the admirable order of the English. Nothing equalled their order and discipline, 'leading from the front like an army of the land'.

Line represented the final rejection of the lingering influences of galley fighting. Right into the Four Days Battle the Dutch, like all others, still preferred that for battle their ships should continue sailing in line abreast, as galleys did, with consequent melee. But with the English the primacy of the big gun had become established and they had come to put emphasis upon their broadsides, which for maximum effect meant that gunfire should be positioned directly opposite the enemy, a beam of it, that is, parallel to it, unloading shot at its rigging and into its sides.

Why would the seemingly obvious have taken so long to evolve? The idea of line was, nevertheless, old. The first suggestion of it had shown in fighting instructions prepared by Sir Edward Cecil, one of Sir Walter Raleigh's commanders in the fleet Raleigh took to Guiana in 1617. Cecil suggested that in action the whole fleet should follow the leading ship 'every ship in order, so that the headmost may be ready to renew the fight against such time as the sternmost hath made an end, by that means keeping the weather of the enemy, and in continual fight until they be sunk . . .' But the concept received little favour. Fighting instructions for a fleet remained vague or absent. By 1618, however, it was plainly recognized that sea fighting had changed from all times before. A Commission of Reform had described the demise of galley traditions by reporting that 'sea fights in these days come seldom to boarding, or to great execution of bows, arrows, small shot and the sword, but are chiefly performed by the great artillery breaking down masts, yards, tearing, raking, and bilging the ships, wherein the great advantage of His Majesty's navy must carefully be maintained by appointing such a proportion of ordnance to each ship as the vessel will bear'.

There were sound reasons for line of battle by the time of the Dutch wars. The sizes of navies and of ships were both at a stage of rapid growth. Greater size of fleets brought forward the problem of battle confusion.

The smoke and melee arising from a denser concentration of ships locked in battle than in former times made signals and instruction more difficult during action. Huge opposing fleets produced intensive close action on a scale never before experienced. This demanded order upon confusion.

The second Dutch war expired with a peace in which Britain acknowledged the supremacy of Holland in the East Indies but retained New York and New Jersey, thereby joining all her colonies along the eastern seaboard of North America. It was an outstanding prize for a war in which Britain could by no means claim to have been entirely victorious. The greatest gift of the war, however, was line, shared by all.

Although the rest of the seventeenth century was convulsed by the dynastic and military upheaval that accompanied the domineering ascent of Louis XIV, it offered nothing to naval development. France had now been raised to the height of the new power assembled for her by Colbert. Louis XIV wanted sea power, colonial empire and dominance of oceanic trade. France looked set for an eventual challenge to English ambition in all of that. But by focusing on the Continental domination Louis forfeited what Colbert was striving for on his behalf.

The final quarter of the sixteenth century saw Europe convulsed by its greatest sequence of dynastic wars, the last of which, the War of the Spanish Succession, changed the map of Europe and colonial possession.

The sickly Spanish king, Charles II, a Hapsburg, had died and in his will declared Louis XIV's seventeen-year-old grandson Philip, the Duke of Anjou, to be his heir, possessing an undivided Spanish empire. Louis XIV began to rule Spain from Versailles on behalf of the adolescent Philip of Anjou, now Philip V of Spain. For England and Holland France's command over all Spanish possessions became intolerable provocation. On 15 May 1702, England, Holland and Austria declared war on France. This war, like its immediate predecessor, was also to be a war of land battles, marked by an absence of notable naval action, except for a single battle at the very end.

The Duke of Marlborough, in charge of the combined English and Dutch forces, demanded a strong Mediterranean squadron to go out to seize Toulon. The response by Sir George Rooke, the admiral appointed to command the Mediterranean squadron, was obstructive. When early in 1704 Rooke unavoidably found himself in the Mediterranean his performance initially was dismal. He made no show at Toulon. The French fleet there under Admiral Comte de Toulouse had been reinforced by the fleet from Brest. Rooke felt that the combined fleet was too powerful for his squadron and retreated towards the Straits of Gibraltar where, peremptorily, as if to compensate for the lack of anything to show before he returned home, he seized Gibraltar, on 23 July 1704. That brought Toulouse with his Toulon fleet down in an effort to recapture the Rock. He met Rooke off Malaga. This, the only naval battle of the war, was hard but indecisive. The combatants drifted apart and made no further contact, which was just as well since Rooke had used up all his ammunition.

The Treaty of Utrecht concluded the War of the Spanish Succession in 1713 and, in addition, gave England the island of Minorca where Port Mahon provided a key base from which to operate against Toulon. England's Mediterranean situation gained further advantage under Utrecht as Spain lost Sicily and Naples to Austria, with Sardinia going to another ally, Savoy. This meant further strategic limitation upon France and its navy within the Mediterranean. Austria acquired the Spanish Netherlands, which for England removed the fear of France on the Scheldt and the North Sea coast. As icing upon the cake of prizes England had Nova Scotia, Newfoundland and Hudson's Bay ceded to her by France. The war had been as costly to Britain as to the others, yet she had emerged from it wealthier than before, her trade flourishing and her credit unsurpassed.

With France, however, the situation was bleak. Regardless of her immense domestic resources, she was in a state of ruinous depression. Reconstruction of the country's naval and economic fortunes required a long peace. Holland was the worst off. Her naval strength and commerce had suffered badly from the war, the cost of which had drained her wealth. She would never recover the commercial supremacy of the past two centuries.

England had now become Great Britain: the union of England and Scotland in 1707 had made it so. Usage of 'England' would now begin to fall away in official though less so in common use. A new dynasty occupied the English throne. Queen Anne died in 1714 and was succeeded by the Hanoverian George I.

Britain could with much satisfaction review the evolution of her own maritime accomplishments after such a tumultuous century. A standing, professional navy was solidly established.

For all, a powerful new stream of history had begun to flow, and mingled with it a different sense of the underlying power and significance of naval strength.

III

CENTURY

THE eighteenth century came in bearing the world, the hemispheres, the oceans, in a frame different from any preceding it. The wars of the second half of the seventeenth century had helped to obscure the larger, more dynamic and steadily altering picture within the frame. The world looked accessible in a way it never had before. Intensified commerce across the seas carried sailors in a steadily denser throng across a wider hemispheric range and their vividly communicated experience passed into the public view. and perception. The intimidation of global distance was gone.

As the century advanced the sailor, merchant and naval, became even more distinctly a man apart from the rest. Marcus Rediker describes the former in his fine study of the merchant seaman at mid-century: 'In an age when most men and women in England and America lived in small, clustered local communities, the early eighteenth-century sailor inhabited a world huge, boundless, and international. The seaman sailed the seven seas; he explored the edges of the earth. He toiled among a diverse and globally experienced body of workingmen, whose labours linked the continents and cultures of Europe, Africa, Asia, and North and South America ... The seaman was central to the changing history and political economy of the North Atlantic world.'[1] The merchant seaman would as likely as not be a naval sailor at some point of his life, voluntarily or through impressment. The range of the latter's experience differed only in the rigidity of naval life against the informality of the other. And, as Captain Basil Hall, a contemporary memorialist, recorded of the naval sailor's life: 'His range of duties includes the whole world; he may be lost in the wilderness of a three-decker, or be wedged into a cock-boat of a cutter; he may be half fried in Jamaica, or wholly frozen in Spitzbergen; he may be cruising during six days of the week in the midst of a hundred sail, and flounder in solitude on the seventh; he may be peaceably riding at anchor in the morning, and be in hot action before sunset.'[2]

The outstanding fact of naval existence through most of the first half of the new century was the absence of war between Britain and France. But new forces were stirring across Western Europe.

Russia had become a Baltic power with the ability to influence this principal source of essential naval supplies for Britain as well as the other naval powers. From the Baltic came wood, tar, hemp and other commodities required for the construction and furnishing of the modern warship. Conflict in the region between the Ottoman Empire and Russia during this period added a new threat to the balance of power. The conflict with the Turks centred upon Peter the Great's desire for the Sea of Azov and the Crimea, which thereafter became a Russian obsession. Russia's domination of the Black Sea potentially meant increased Russian influence into the Mediterranean. The Ottoman Turks thus entered into an entirely new role and significance in the eastern Mediterranean. It was a factor that would affect all Mediterranean strategies in the century ahead.

What balances would emerge in the eastern Mediterranean if the Ottomans were decisively defeated there by the Russians? Not since the fall of Constantinople had so many questions descended upon that ancient basin. Similar concerns now existed in northern Europe as the Hohenzollern dynasty began its ascent to power with the coronation of the reigning Elector as Frederick II, King of Prussia. Prussia was spread in scattered segments, with Berlin at its heart. Prussian enlargement and consolidation therefore became an active Hohenzollern preoccupation. For Britain, the new century brought in Prussia as a particular and peculiar problem because of the Hanoverian dynasty newly established on the British throne. Hohenzollern Brandenburg, the Prussian seat, adjoined Hanover, the protection and sustaining of which was a foremost concern for the Hanovers of Britain. This was an involvement that threatened to take Britain deep into whatever boiled up through dynastic disturbance on the Continent in the decades ahead. But the prospect of that was in abeyance as three decades of comparative peace settled upon Europe and with it a broadly comfortable diplomatic rapport between Britain and France.

France, meanwhile, was rapidly gaining commercial advantage. Her maritime prosperity bounced back and the French colonies in the Caribbean became the most successful and profitable there. Wealth flowed in with French coffee, sugar and other tropical produce everywhere outpricing British equivalents, which were as much as 30 per cent higher and consequently driven out of Continental markets. French textiles similarly displaced British in markets of the Mediterranean and the Ottoman Empire. The intensity of French exploitation of the Grand Banks off Newfoundland gave France a commanding lead in exports of salt fish to Europe. More than five hundred ships manned by 25,000 seamen worked the banks, providing France with a huge reserve of manpower for her navy in any future conflict.

Louisbourg, built during the 1720s on Cape Breton Island at Cabot Strait, the southern entrance to the Gulf of St Lawrence, was the base for France's huge fishing operations on the Grand Banks as well as its thrust into the continent. New France – a narrow, extended thrust into the continent from the Gulf of St Lawrence – was the base from which France aimed to link the settlements of the St Lawrence with Louisiana and the Gulf of Mexico. Fortified posts were already being constructed along the Mississippi and the intention appeared to be nothing less than encirclement and containment of the thirteen British colonies. But it was a waterborne penetration that, ultimately, was dependent upon the fortress of Louisbourg.

The French Empire in India was also expanding. Both the British and French East India companies had established themselves on the Coromandel – southern – Coast of India in the seventeenth century. France had gained great strategic advantage on the Indian Ocean by occupying the two main islands of Mauritius, which she called Ile de France and Ile de Bourbon, and establishing a naval base that lay halfway along the passage between the Cape and India, ideally placed for interception and patrol on the Indian Ocean.

Reflective of this new rise of France was the increase of its mercantile fleet. After Utrecht the French merchant marine had consisted of a mere three hundred vessels. By 1735 it numbered 1,800, sixty of which belonged to the East India Company. This astonishing revival of French commercial fortunes spurred British resentment. Britain, meanwhile, was close to war with Spain over mercantile confrontations in the Caribbean; they went to war in October 1739. The Anglo-French truce ended as France moved to support Spain, thus bringing to a close the comfortable relationship that had existed with Britain since 1713. Finally, in 1744, France and England were formally at war.

Forty years of naval inactivity between Britain and France dominated the sudden prospect of war. Their navies had aged into decrepitude. The French navy had only forty-five ships of the line and sixty-seven frigates against the Royal Navy's ninety ships of the line and eighty-four frigates. For both, naval action was a distant memory. Absence of serious naval engagement had frozen the Royal Navy's outlook and imagination into rigid dependence upon the last experience of it – the Battle of Malaga in 1704. Though Malaga had been an undistinguished action, Rooke's direction of the battle, through lack of further example, had become established as the essential lesson for all. And Malaga thus became for subsequent generations in the British navy the rigidly entrenched format for naval engagement.

At Malaga Rooke's ships had fought in line, as had the French. It was a hard, uninspired, indecisive battle with both fleets passing abeam and flinging

tons of shot at one another. Rooke's instructions required his ships to stand
to battle in carefully spaced line proceeding parallel to the enemy line van
to van, centre to centre, rear to rear, with each ship required to contest its
opposite number. Brilliant though the concept was at its historic inception
in 1666, there had been no serious revision of the tactic since then.

As an Admiralty Standing Instruction at the approach of mid-century,
line was set with an inflexibility that denied any impulsive action. Its iron
rigidity barred any captain from breaking away from line for whatever reason,
whether to take prize of a ship that had lowered its colours or to finish off
a severely crippled opponent. There was licence for nothing other than to
fight one's slot while following in the allotted place behind the ship ahead.
Change and adaptation were severely proscribed, despite the fact that some
of the deficiencies of line as a tactic practised in the Rooke manner had been
recognized even before Malaga. The matter had been publicly argued just
two years before Malaga. 'What is your opinion of fighting in line?' a veteran
seaman is asked by a younger, in an exchange set down in a tract published
in 1702. 'I don't approve of it at all . . . I'll give you my reasons against your
line. When the fleets engage in a line, supposing the admiral's post to be in
the centre and the fight be begun by the windward squadron, the ship first
begun can only be supported by its second; for the admiral, by reason of the
smoke, cannot see how to send her convenient succour, for signals are useless
soon after the commencement of the action. Now when we fought without
a line, every one made the best of his way to engage the enemy. We looked
for no signals, but when we saw how one of our ships was overcharged by
the enemy, we immediately bore down to her assistance . . .'

What was lost was recourse to individual action, to melee. Line, up to
that time the greatest tactical evolution under sail, was thereby neutralized
to ineffectiveness, for nothing more was allowed to evolve from it. For yet
another four decades Admiralty Instructions were to deprive the Royal
Navy of inventive impulse, individual risk and originality. By scrubbing out
any possibility of individual action, Admiralty Instructions allowed nothing
for intuition, deductive reasoning or swift sea instinct. They padlocked the
naval mind. Without that, without the melee that invited it, there was no
decisive victory in naval battle. A frustrating paralysis thereafter sat upon
all naval engagement.

Malaga was the crippling legacy that lay upon the British commanders
when preparing for battle off Toulon, where in 1744 the British and French
resumed their naval confrontation. This was to be the only formal naval
battle of the war that had now begun.

A Spanish fleet had sought shelter at Toulon and been trapped there by
a British fleet cruising vigilantly off. On 19 February 1744 a combined

Spanish–French fleet put out from Toulon towards the waiting British fleet. Against this combination the British admiral, Thomas Mathews, signalled his ships to form line. Then, fearing that the enemy would escape, Mathews followed his signal to form line with a second signal, to engage. He himself broke from the line to engage the ship bearing the flag of the Spanish admiral. The admiral commanding the British rear, Richard Lestock, made no move to break from line, Some captains followed Mathews in breaking from the line, while others lay back with Lestock. What ensued as Mathews and some of the captains broke line to fight was the melee of individual engagement, violation of the Admiralty's Standing Instruction to hold to line.

When at court martial Lestock was asked why he held back he declared that he did so because the signal for line of battle was flying at the same time as the signal to engage. As he saw it, he could not obey the latter without disobeying the former. But from the start Lestock had never taken up his proper station. Nevertheless, given the signal confusion, he had the Fighting Instructions on his side.

Both Mathews and Lestock were difficult and unpopular characters. Mathews was sixty-eight and had returned to sea only two years before after an absence of sixteen years. Lestock was older and bitterly resentful that the Mediterranean command had fallen to Mathews rather than himself. As some saw it he set out to frustrate his commander. One historian of the time believed that he should have been shot, describing him as 'an artful, vindictive disciplinarian'. Rodney, in a later verdict, said that Lestock 'plainly showed that he meant to betray his country, even to his Admiral'.

In the event it was Lestock who got off free and Mathews who was broken by court martial, though the king, believing that the admiral had behaved bravely, refused to confirm the sentence. Eleven captains were put on trial. Only two were acquitted. The majority of the accused were men whose gallantry and service had never before been questioned.

It was specifically for his breaking of the line that Admiral Mathews was cashiered. That he believed he had no other option and that he fought with outstanding courage finally counted for nothing against the fact that he had broken the foremost standing instruction of Admiralty, to hold the line. To question that instruction therefore became a challenge to the entire naval order, mutinous disloyalty even. That could be the only conclusion after Toulon. It was a brutal lesson that went deep, as it was intended to. The absurdity of it was magnified by the fact that licence for melee actually existed under a different set of rules, those of 'chase', which allowed freedom of individual and close action. Chase was the option if an enemy force appeared to be escaping, or, as with convoys, the escorting men-of-war were on widely distributed stations.

The Treaty of Aix-la-Chapelle that closed the war in 1748 brought the curious formality of peace declared for a war that continued beyond Europe. The lack of any clear outcome in North America and India was where the struggle between Britain and France was maintained, regardless of Aix-la-Chapelle. That meant on the oceans as well. Only thus could the question of maritime supremacy and commercial dominance finally be settled, something already well understood by the adversaries.

That phenomenon of waging war without there being a formal war while maintaining the pretence of peace in Europe would now persist in India and North America. From the end of one war in 1748 to the start of the next in 1756, the strife in those opposite corners of the world mounted steadily.

From the Coromandel Coast to Bengal and from Louisbourg through to the Ohio and the Mississippi armed conflict slid into open war. Now, in the forests and inland waters of North America, on the hot plains and mangrove estuaries of Asia, the critical contests for the main prizes of colonial mastery had begun.

The American colonials far outnumbered the French. They were tough, pugnacious and made restless by the temptations of the vast continent that lay beyond their narrow eastern seaboard settlements. But the French sought to hem them in between the Allegheny Mountains and the sea. The French dream was possession along a line from Montreal through Lakes Ontario and Erie along the Ohio into the Mississippi basin and on down to New Orleans. In 1753 the French began an attempt to establish their control by building new forts and posts from the lakes down towards the Ohio basin. Virginia colonists retaliated by building a fort at the forks of the Ohio. The French seized it and named it Fort Duquesne, site of the future Pittsburgh. George Washington led the retaliatory Virginian forces against the French but was compelled to surrender.

The British government, fearing further French entrenchment west of the Alleghenies, decided on an Atlantic response, intense activity having been observed at Brest and other Channel ports. The quarrel over a small fort in an obscure corner deep inside North America thus shifted to the seas. For France, without naval strength to match British naval dominance, the dream of aggressively boxing in the thirteen colonies by extending Canada to Louisiana had never been realizable.

William Pitt, Earl of Chatham, had laid out that Britain, when faced by the combination of Continental and Atlantic issue, should set absolute priority upon the latter. By unequivocally declaring the primacy of Britain's maritime destiny over the demands of the Hanoverian connection, Pitt became the dominating figure who at mid-century defined the course that he saw as obligatory upon British power for the future of the nation. He was driven to destroy the commerce and power of France as Britain's only rival and he saw French expulsion from Canada as the initial key to that. It was, as Julian Corbett said, 'a question of life and death between two empires, and the continued existence of France as a maritime power'. Pitt's ideas on Canada had been rejected by the Duke of Newcastle, in whose government he served as Paymaster of the Forces. His opportunity awaited him, however, in the real war with France that both sides for their various reasons still avoided formally declaring, even while furiously pitted against one another in America, in the East and on the seas.

It was to be nearly a year before war would actually be declared. During that time the French appeared to be preparing a large-scale invasion from Brest and Rochefort, but they had other plans. They struck where the British least expected it.

In April 1756 a French fleet convoyed 150 transports carrying fifteen thousand troops and invaded Minorca. The British garrison there was besieged in Port Mahon when French warships blockaded the harbour. When news of the invasion reached London England declared war on France, on 17 May. Thus began the Seven Years War.

A British fleet commanded by Admiral John Byng was at that time already en route to help the defence of Minorca. He arrived at the island on 20 May to find it held by the French, though the British military were still besieged in the fortress of Port Mahon.

The battle that followed was the first of what was at last formal war. It was a success for the French and a fateful tragedy for the British, since the demand for obedience to Admiralty Instructions on line was again involved, highlighted this time by tragedy.

The prevailing wind had created a difficult situation. The fleets were not parallel when Byng gave the signal to engage. Instead they approached at an angle of between thirty and forty degrees. That made it difficult for each ship to engage its opposite, as was required by line. The whole line was prevented from coming into action near enough at the same time. Byng sought rigorously to cling to line in spite of near-impossible circumstances. He stuck to it because the fate of Mathews at Toulon was heavily on his mind. 'You see that the signal for line is out,' he told his flag captain. 'You would not have me as admiral of the fleet, run down as if I were to engage a single ship. It was Mr Mathews's misfortune to be prejudiced by not carrying down his force together, which I shall endeavour to avoid.' Thus the rigid instructions on maintaining line stifled choice and initiative. Had he in fact followed Mathews's example and borne down upon the French it might have been different. The outcome was indecisive, as it invariably was with line, and Byng consequently withdrew his ships to Gibraltar. He was sent home to face court martial for failing to defeat the French, but mainly for failing to relieve the besieged Mahon garrison and consequently

NAVAL TACTICS

I. THE DESCRIPTION OF ADMIRAL BYNG'S ENGAGE-
MENT WITH THE FRENCH FLEET OFF MINORCA, MAY
20. 1756.[*]

38. B. (Plate VI. Fig. 1.) The British fleet, about one o'clock afternoon, upon the starboard tack, and after they had weathered *the French fleet, F,* then upon the larboard tack.

39. B. (Plate VI. Fig. 2.) The British fleet edging or lasking down to attack the enemy, F, lying to, to receive them. (Vide No. 18. 28. and 29.)

40. A. The van of the British obeying the signal, by bearing away two points from the wind, but each ship steering upon her opposite in the enemy's line.

41. A. (Fig. 3.) The five headmost ships of the British line *brought to*, and engaged in a smart cannonade, but not till after having greatly suffered in their rigging by three broadsides received from the enemy, during a course of some miles, while, at the same time, they had it not in their power to make retaliation. (No. 17.)

[Fig. 4 shows the British incapable of pursuing the French, Fig. 5 indicating the French victorious.]

---

[*] British, 13 ships, 4 frigates, 1 sloop. French, 12 ships, 5 frigates.

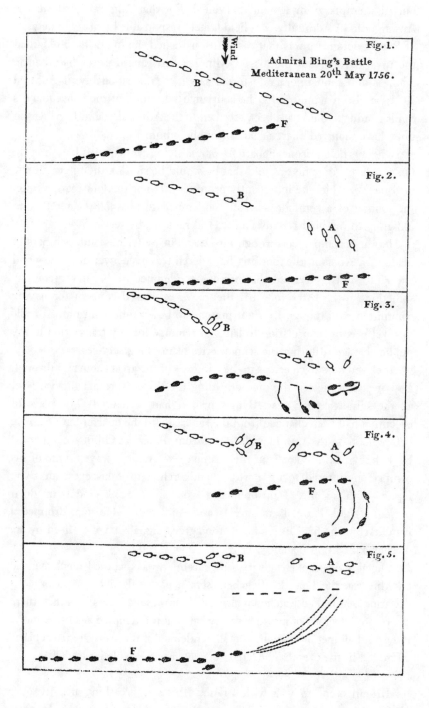

Fig. 1.

Admiral Bing's Battle
Mediteranean 20th May 1756.

Wind

B

F

Fig. 2.

B

A

F

Fig. 3.

B

A

Fig. 4.

B

A

F

Fig. 5.

B

A

F

for the loss of Minorca. He was acquitted of cowardice but nevertheless sentenced to death by firing squad. The court recommended him to mercy but all attempts to implement that failed. For that Admiral Lord George Anson, head of Admiralty, was held largely responsible by many. The view of Byng's defenders was that, had Anson wished, he might have obtained the royal pardon, but the loss of Minorca had caused great disturbance. And, as one contemporary historian saw it, 'Unquestionably, if Admiral Byng had been acquitted by the court martial, much of the consequences of his conduct would have been ascribed to the Admiralty, and Lord Anson must have incurred a large share of public odium.'[3]

Byng was held prisoner aboard *Monarque*, lying at anchor off Portsmouth. On 13 March 1757 he was told that he would be shot on the forecastle the next day, to which he indignantly protested, 'Is not this putting me upon the footing of a common seaman condemned to be shot? Is not this an indignity to my birth, to my family, and rank in the service?'

He was accompanied through his last night by friends and members of his family. At six in the morning he ordered tea, his conversation easy and cheerful: 'I have observed that persons condemned to die, have generally something to be sorry for, that they have expressed concern for having committed; and though I do not pretend to be exempt from human frailties, yet it is my consolation to have no remorse for any transaction in my public character, during the whole series of my long services.'[4]

At eleven he walked across to the windows of the great cabin and through a spying glass viewed the men crowding the decks, shrouds and yards of all the ships that lay near. Byng's protest had registered. The place of execution had been changed from the forecastle to the quarterdeck. Shortly before noon on the 14th he walked out from the Great Cabin accompanied by a clergyman. He knelt on the cushion set for him, prayed. One of his companions offered to tie a white handkerchief over his eyes but Byng replied with a smile, 'I am obliged to you, sir; I thank God I can do it myself; I think I can; I am sure I can.' And tied it. He then dropped a handkerchief he held in his hand, the agreed signal. A volley fired by six marines killed him instantly.

A notable aspect of Byng's trial and execution was that the French marshal on Minorca, the Duc de Richelieu, sent a personal appeal to George II, declaring that he had watched it all, that Byng was blameless, and that 'there can be no higher act of injustice than what is now attempted against Admiral Byng, and all men of honour, and all gentlemen of the army are particularly interested in the event'. The letter was entrusted to Voltaire to deliver.

As Britain went to war with France, Prussia, breathing heavily over Hanover, had become hostile. George II demanded a defence of Hanover, in spite of inadequate military resources. For Pitt, who now had command of the war, that amounted to the subordination of Britain's oceanic interests to preservation of the House of Hanover on the Continent.

Britain turned to Russia. An alliance was concluded in which Russia undertook to prevent the conquest of Hanover. The effect on Frederick was dramatic. He immediately guaranteed the neutrality of the Electorate of Hanover. England and Prussia signed an alliance in January 1756, just a few weeks after the Russian agreement. With George II pacified Pitt had gained the priority he wanted for Britain's colonial and maritime interests. That fell neatly into place in September when Frederick marched into Saxony, precipitating war across the Continent. And, once more, against the logic of her American and oceanic ambitions, France was drawn into European war, just when her maritime forces and national energies were required to be fully committed against those of Britain.

In July 1757 Pitt became Principal Secretary of State, with the absolute control of the war. He began planning his American campaign. In February 1758, with Admiral Edward Boscawen in command, the first large fleet convoying troops and supplies sailed for Halifax, Britain's new naval base on the Nova Scotian coast. Twelve thousand soldiers and as many seamen formed a combined assault against Louisbourg that summer and the base capitulated in July. The collapse continued point by point thereafter within Canada. In India, meanwhile, French possessions began to fall to a remarkable English East India Company employee named Robert Clive.

Faced by these calamities as well as by devastating raids on the Channel ports and the destruction of their commerce and their navy, the French recognized the disastrous error of attempting to fight an oceanic war as well as a continental one. As ever, invasion appeared as a quick solution. It was projected as an invasion far beyond anything ever contemplated before. Fifty thousand men were to go into England, twelve thousand into Scotland. Two fleets were to be assembled, one at Toulon and the other at Brest. The Toulon fleet was to make it through the Straits of Gibraltar to augment the one at Brest. But the Toulon fleet was broken by Boscawen off the Portuguese coast. The Brest fleet of twenty ships of the line sailed for the Clyde under Maréchal de Conflans. Its first destination, however, was the Loire, where the transports were waiting. There, in Quiberon Bay on 20 November 1759, Admiral Hawke broke the French fleet, through destruction, capture and putting the remnants to flight. It was the end of the invasion.

Pitt was out of the government before the war ended, forced out by his resistance to an early peace demanded by those bemoaning the rising cost of the war. It was time for peace. The Treaty of Paris of 1763 brought extensive changes to the map of global power. Britain got from France the whole of Canada, Nova Scotia and Cape Breton Island, Minorca, Senegal, Grenada, St Vincent, Dominica and Tobago. Restored to France were her fishing rights on the Grand Banks, the Atlantic islands of St Pierre and Miquelon, Guadeloupe, Martinique and St Lucia, and Goree in West Africa. In India she got back Pondicherry and Chandernagore, though on an unfortified basis. Britain now held the whole of North America, except for Louisiana. France had got back the richest of her Caribbean islands and a foothold in India. Could she restore her naval power? The answer was already there.

France now appeared finally to have learned that neglect of her navy during military involvement on the Continent was far too costly. An unprecedented national cry for restoration of the navy had arisen across France even during the war, with Louis XV's minister the Duc de Choiseul as its advocate and visionary. New, better and faster ships were built. Dockyards and naval arsenals were raised to a high point of efficiency. Stores of all kinds, including ship timber, were built up. Training of both officers and seamen was improved. Ten thousand gunners were drilled every week. A system of reserve training for seamen was established.

Britain could no longer make easy assumptions over the defeat of France, in spite of the vast national rejoicing that her victories had brought. A powerful new French navy partnered by the ever-mighty military power of France meant that Britain remained as vulnerable from invasion across the Narrow Seas. But Choiseul scaled down the imperial vision to the practicable. There was no plan for recovery of Canada. The emphasis fell upon the Caribbean, from where France had drawn so much wealth before the war and which she now wished to revive. The diversity of her coasts was one of her finest assets. So French policy focused now, as in the past, upon the Mediterranean, where new forces were at work and where France saw opportunity.

Tsar Peter III had died in July 1763, five months after the peace. His wife Catherine, a powerfully minded German princess, had declared herself her husband's successor as Catherine II. Her ambitions for the expansion of Russia were focused upon Sweden, Poland and Turkey: Sweden as her Baltic rival, Poland for territorial enlargement, Turkey as historic menace in eastern Europe and the obstacle to Mediterranean access and the Levant. Of the three, Turkey became the greatest obsession, as it had been with her predecessors. This time there was a difference, for it was swiftly coupled with Catherine's plans for a greater navy, the strategic outlook of which would reach beyond mere challenge to Sweden for command of the Baltic.

Russia began to recruit British seamen. This infusion became a particular naval phenomenon that would have no subsequent parallel elsewhere. More than half the entire list of officers in the Russian navy were soon to be British. As one historian of the subject put it, 'The Russian navy may almost be said to be the creation of British seamen.'[5] A British admiral, Samuel Greig, in fact a Scot, was to become known as the Father of the Russian navy. There was no apparent discouragement from Britain where, as usual at the end of a war, the navy was being demobilized, its manpower paid off.

Russia simultaneously began its attempt to dominate Poland. War began there in 1768. French forces went to the assistance of the Poles as French diplomacy began working intensively at Constantinople against Russia. Turkey declared war against Russia in the autumn of 1768, striking from the Crimean peninsula on the Black Sea. The Russians sent an army into the Balkans and occupied Bucharest. But the big shock to France was the descent of a Russian fleet under its British admiral from the Baltic to the eastern Mediterranean. Britain gave conspicuous assistance to the expedition. The fleet of twenty ships of the line used Spithead to refit. Russian soldiers landed and were drilled by British marine sergeants.

The fleet passed through the Straits of Gibraltar and was refitted and stocked again at the British dockyard of Port Mahon. The Russian and Turkish fleets met off Chios in July 1770. Under Admiral Greig and his commanders the Turkish fleet was destroyed. Peace in 1774 gave Russia the fortress of Kerch on the Sea of Azov. From there she had passage through the straits connecting the Sea of Azov with the Black Sea. In effect, Russia, with the aid of British seamanship, had obtained her access to the Mediterranean. And with it she had become recognized as a naval power.

The French had observed all of this in anger and frustration. There was nothing they could do about it, but they had their compensation elsewhere. As this chapter closed another was opening on the other side of the world.

France, ruing the loss of Canada, found herself watching with satisfaction as Britain sought to cope with rebellion in the thirteen colonies of the American seaboard.

France had never been more ready for naval encounter, should it arise. Choiseul had been dismissed from office in 1770 but his naval enterprise was continued by his successors. Here, then, was grand opportunity for France to balance the North American account. Aid and assistance passed to the colonial rebels, followed by recognition of the independence of the United States, notification of which London received on 13 March 1778. War with France was inevitable.

France now had eighty ships of the line and 67,000 sailors on the conscription books. Ten thousand gunners were drilled every week. Her potential ally, Spain, had sixty ships of the line. Both had large numbers of ships of other classes. It was the start of a desultory war at sea, hardly

comparable to the dramatic events on land. Nevertheless it was the sea where
the war was decided. As war between Britain and the Bourbon kingdoms
of France and Spain it was, uniquely, a purely maritime war. For this time
neither France nor Spain had distracting and debilitating military involvement on the Continent. Their navies being powerful and technically in
better shape than Britain's meant that Britain was on the defensive, France
firmly on the offensive.

For France it appeared to be the great opportunity against Britain too
long delayed, too often missed.

In March 1780, Rear Admiral Sir George Rodney arrived as commander
in chief in the Caribbean. Rodney was an unusual character: sixty-four years
old, irascible, suffering severely from gout, the usual eighteenth-century
penalty for extravagant living. He was a gambler who had found himself
exiled by his debts. He was in France at the start of the war and was only
able to return to Britain when his French host, Maréchal de Biron, in typical
chivalrous response of the *ancien régime*, undertook to pay his debts after
Rodney had boasted of his ability to deal with the French fleet, if he were
able to get back to Britain.[6] Against this life of play stood the steadfast naval
character of the day, the quarterdeck martinet. In his gouty state Rodney
might not have appeared to be in top form for the West Indies command,
but his irritation with his own physical state of being, the ill-tempered
impatience it engendered, might have been what came to serve him well.
For it was possibly that personal irritation and aggravation that acted upon a
deeper irritation and impatience with the rigid tactical codes of the navy he
returned to. Rodney was about to become the embodiment of the greatest
revolution in naval tactics in more than a century.

At a time when challenge to everything on every level of human society
was either nascent or imminent it could hardly be surprising that the Royal
Navy should find, finally, that fighting in line was suddenly in question.

Naval actions ruled by line had proved indecisive, with enemy ships
neither captured nor sunk. Clear-cut victory had become evasive. Worse, the
French, in practising line, had adapted it to their own advantage, something
which the British appeared to facilitate.

Line of battle was fought either from the windward or the leeward
position. Windward was to have what was called the weather-gauge, the
advantage of the wind, allowing a fleet to steer down upon the enemy.
The fleet to windward was less affected by gun smoke, better situated for
observing signals. It was the aggressive tactic for attack, the one fixedly
preferred by the British. The French preference was leeward, downwind,
which offered several options for advantageous manoeuvre. Damaged ships
could fall back, giving place to others not yet in action. It was the more

defensive position, allowing easier retreat from battle, a principal reason why line battle remained indecisive.

The British practice was to range each ship upon its opposite in the enemy line. They therefore sought to place their line the length of the enemy line, van to van, centre to centre, rear to rear for attack upon the enemy's van. To the French this was illogical, if not actually mad. In their determined progression towards the enemy van the British line exposed itself to the full fire of the French, with the British leading ships, or van, taking the heaviest punishment. British ships were thus severely disabled, particularly since the French tactic was to fire at masts and rigging, destroying British motive power. The familiar experience was 'the British admiral, having his ships crippled in the first onset, never after was able to close with, follow up, or even detain one single ship of them for one moment'.

For the British what was so obviously missing from this now static form of battle was the possibility of any form of close combat, the melee of old, which could only come through ships breaking away from line to get near or alongside an opponent. More important was lack of tactic that could defeat French evasiveness by engaging them before they could fall away and make off. The answer to all that was the painfully simple one of bearing down upon the enemy line, breaking through it, and coming up on its lee to attack from that other side. Why had the British, in the seventy-five years since Malaga, demonstrated such a stubborn lack of insight to counter the brilliant evasiveness of the established French battle plan? How long could logic be defied? The response was to come from land as much as from the sea.

The matter was put to the public in the middle of the War of the Independence of the American colonies, expressed thus by the man who caustically asked for the answers and then proffered them: '. . . it may be asked, have the French ever effected anything decisive against us? Have they ever, in any of these reencounters, taken any of our ships? Have they ever, presuming upon their superior skill, dared to make the attack? No. But confident in their superior knowledge in naval tactics, and relying on our want of penetration, they have constantly offered us battle to leeward, trusting that our headlong courage would hurry us on to make the customary attack, though at a disadvantage almost beyond the power of calculation; the consequences of which have always been, and always will be, the same, as long as prejudices prevent us from discerning either the improvements made by the enemy, or our own blunders.

'To be completely victorious cannot always be in our power; but, to be constantly baffled, and repeatedly denied the satisfaction of retaliation, almost on every occasion, is not only shameful, but, in truth, has been the cause of all our late misfortunes.'[7]

That comment was contained in the first detailed assessment and analysis of British naval tactics ever offered to the broad public, *An Inquiry into Naval Tactics* by John Clerk, another Scot. It made its first informal manuscript appearance about 1780, to be revised and printed in 1782. It was an astonishing work, for Clerk of Eldin had never been to sea.

Clerk offered detailed diagrammatic plates and observations on every notable battle of the century since those of Mathews and Byng, but particularly of those in the prevailing American War:

From these examples, it appears, that the attack, in every one of them, without variation, has been made by a long extended line, generally from the windward quarter, by steering or directing every individual ship of that line upon her opposite of the enemy, but more particularly the ships in the van, in preference to an attack upon the rear. That the consequences of this mode of attack have proved fatal in every attempt, given the enemy an opportunity of disabling our ships, and preventing us from coming close alongside of them. Our ships have been so disabled, and so ill supported, that the enemy have been permitted not only to make sail and leave us, but, to complete the disgrace, have, in passing, been permitted to pour in the fire of their whole line upon our van, without a possibility of retaliation on our part. The cause, then, of these miscarriages, can never be said to have proceeded from a fault in our shipping, and far less from a want of spirit in our seamen.

For the naval establishment of the day the shock of Clerk's work was in his proposal that instead of holding rigidly to line in battle there should be licence to make for the enemy's line and break it for close action, to ensure destruction, capture or flight. The value of line naturally remained. It marshalled a fleet. But what Clerk was asking for was a flexibility that allowed the option of close combat, melee, so long denied to the navy. Melee could only be achieved by breaking line in order to break through the enemy's line, thereby sanctioning the individual impulse of any captain who saw opportunity.

Clerk was fifty when the war began. His fascination with ships and the sea had begun as a boy. The natural inclination to go to sea had been quashed by his family because of heavy losses of other members at sea and with the army. He spent much of his boyhood studying ships at Leith, acquired and made models of ships which he sailed on waters in the grounds of his father's estate, drew knowledge from those of his family still at sea, and 'courted connexion with other professional seamen and shipbuilders, of all ranks and capacities, wherever they were to be met with'. As he matured, Clerk cross-examined all those he could on the battles and actions of the period and studied the offical despatches and courts martial. He had also begun composing diagrams of fleet and ship movements. Small models of ships were constantly in his pockets, 'every table furnishing sea-room sufficient on which to extend and manoeuvre the opponent fleets at pleasure; and where every naval question, both with respect to situation and movement, even of every individual ship, as well as the fleets themselves, could be animadverted on – in this way not only fixing and establishing my own ideas . . .'

Clerk was rash in claiming to be the originator of 'breaking the line', for what had struck him had already also struck some of the most capable naval officers, notably Rodney. It was at Maréchal de Biron's table, Rodney subsequently said, that the idea of breaking the line first occurred to him. The extended ease of after-dinner speculative exchange apparently produced another similar occasion, in London, where Rodney was said to have once outlined the manoeuvre with an 'arrangement of two hostile squadrons of cherry stones'.[8]

Clerk's lack of sea experience had made him hesitant about publishing his work, although his ideas had already begun to find a wider private and influential audience. In 1780 he claimed to have got a copy of his manuscript delivered to Admiral Sir George Rodney before Rodney sailed to take up his West Indies command. Clerk maintained that the manuscript accompanied Rodney to the Indies. As with all aspects of what became one of the most partisan controversies in naval history, certainly of its day, there was to be some strong witness against those claims, although Rodney himself provided notes to a later edition of Clerk's *Inquiry*.

Rodney's first attempt to implement breaking the line was in his encounter with Admiral de Guichen off Dominica on 17 April 1780.

It was a hard, confused and indeterminate fight, brilliantly conducted on both sides as each fleet sought advantage on a light wind and Rodney and de Guichen intelligently read the other's battle intentions. Rodney subsequently said that de Guichen was the opponent he most admired.

The French fleet fought in an extremely extended line, the British in closer drawn formation. Rodney intended to use this difference to his advantage. He wanted to throw his whole force against the enemy's rear and centre. His tactic was to change the character of his line by reducing the distances between his ships in contrast to the greater distances between the French ships. That would help to concentrate his attack on the French rear. By falling upon first one portion of the French fleet he could cut it off. As Rodney saw it, the French centre and the rear would have been savaged before the French van could have come about again to help.[9]

Once he had his fleet sailing compactly in line ahead positioned abreast of the enemy's rear Rodney signalled that every ship should break off and steer for the ship directly opposite in the enemy's line. But his captains instead adhered to the principles of line as they understood it. Rodney's lead ship, instead of attacking the rear of the French line as Rodney wished, put on canvas and made towards the French van. Others followed her example. Rodney's plan disintegrated into disorder and confusion.

As if in violent demonstration of his rage against the disobedience of his captains Rodney threw himself into battle with remarkable ferocity, putting three French ships out of the line. His own ship lost its foremast and had some seventy men killed or wounded. By contrast, some of his captains never fired a shot during the engagement.

Rodney blamed his captains, they blamed him. A prime fault was a lack of the proper signals for his differing instructions, and lack of any standing model for his radical ideas. There were no court martials. There were too many conflicting accounts, the situation itself too controversial. Cutting the enemy's line or massing the greater part of the force of a fleet against only the rear squadron of the enemy line, both of which appear to have been in Rodney's mind that day, were certainly not part of the Standing Instructions his captains possessed.

A bitter Rodney nevertheless regarded his subordinates thereafter with an avenging eye and, describing his attitude to them after the de Guichen battle, remarked that 'after their late gross behaviour, they had nothing to expect at my hands but instant punishment to those who neglected their duty . . . admirals as well as captains, if out of their station . . .' But subsequent naval historians would see in the episode the lingering intimidating shadow of Mathews and Byng in the minds of the officers and, on top of that, corruption at an Admiralty where 'every one feared that blame would be shifted on him, as it had been on to Byng . . . The navy was honeycombed with distrust, falling little short of panic. In this state of apprehension and doubt, the tradition of line of battle, resting upon men who . . . had seen officers censured, cashiered, and shot, for errors of judgment . . .'[10]

The end of that enduring constriction upon the naval mind and imagination was imminent. The hold that line possessed upon the navy nevertheless produced one more disastrous consequence to lay against line's morbid history since 1704.

In North America the British invasion of the southern states had seen forces under General Cornwallis driven steadily back northwards until Cornwallis decided to make his stand at Yorktown on the southern cape of the Chesapeake. There he found himself invested by land and sea. The only hope for reinforcements was by sea. But the French admiral Comte de Grasse was determined to prevent this. He reached the Chesapeake with twenty-eight ships of the line at the end of August 1781. Another fleet under Comte Barras, meanwhile, sailed from Newport to reinforce de Grasse.

Admiral Thomas Graves sailed from the Hudson with more than twenty ships to help Cornwallis. Aware that de Grasse was at sea and that Barras hoped to join him, Graves sought to arrive before the two Frenchmen could combine their fleets. He arrived off the capes of the Chesapeake in the morning of 15 September 1781 and was unpleasantly surprised to find de Grasse's fleet at anchor at the entrance to the bay, lying between the middle ground and Cape Henry.

There followed an extraordinary set of tactical moves from Graves. Half the French sailors were ashore when Graves hove up. Instead of sailing to attack the anchored French ships and entering the Chesapeake to relieve Cornwallis, which he could have done without difficulty, he lay off. De Grasse, once his sailors were on board, sailed out to meet Graves. This alone provided Graves with rare opportunity since the French ships had to tack out slowly from a difficult situation. Their van was painfully vulnerable. Graves could have picked them off in turn as they came out and destroyed the van squadron before the rest were out. Instead he waited to engage the French formally, by line.

This meant that battle started only late that afternoon. After heavy mutual destruction the action broke off. For five days the two fleets drifted in sight of one another out at sea off the capes. In this stalemate they remained until de Grasse calculated that Barras had arrived in the Chesapeake, which he indeed had. De Grasse went in. Faced by the combined fleet of thirty-six ships Graves sailed away, leaving Cornwallis to his fate. On 19 October Cornwallis capitulated. De Grasse's squadron had ensured victory at Yorktown for the colonial rebels. One verdict on Graves's actions is representative of the general reaction to it that followed: 'Had Admiral Graves succeeded in capturing that squadron, it would have greatly paralyzed the besieging army (it had the siege train on board), if it would not have prevented its operations altogether; it would have put the two fleets nearly on an equality in point numbers, would have arrested the progress of French arms for the ensuing year in the West Indies, and might possibly have created such a spirit of discord between the French and Americans as would have sunk the latter into the lowest depths of despair, from which they were only extricated by the arrival of the forces under De Grasse.'[11] Or, as the American naval historian Admiral Samuel Eliot Morison put it, 'without De Grasse's victory off the Virginia capes, it is not Cornwallis's capitulation but Washington's that history would have recorded at Yorktown'.

It was this exemplary example of the hold that line exercised upon the naval mind that finally persuaded Clerk of Eldin to go public with a printed edition of his *Inquiry into Naval Tactics*. Here finally for all to consider was a public plea for manoeuvres of 'greater ingenuity', for the navy to go to battle in a manner that would ensure decisive action. Off Dominica in 1780 Rodney had failed to implement the tactic of breaking the line but two years later, almost to the day, on 12 April 1782, he brought it into history. This was again in the West Indies, where the greater part of naval action of the American War of Independence was concentrated because of dependence by all upon their wealth there.

The force was as great as any that had yet been assembled for naval battle. The British fleet had thirty-six ships of the line, the French thirty-four. The French ships were larger, more powerful and faster. They met between Guadeloupe and Dominica, in the vicinity of a group of islands known as the Saints.

Line was formed at daybreak on 12 April, after a two-day chase. Half an hour before the action started Rodney, his flag captain Sir Charles Douglas, a post captain, Lord Cranstoun, and the surgeon Sir Gilbert Blane, were at breakfast aboard the flagship *Formidable*. Blane, in his account of the day's events, said that in discussing their position it became clear that, if they held to the tack on which they were sailing close-hauled, they would inevitably converge with the French line and necessarily pass through it. Rodney 'visibly caught the idea', Blane said, 'and no doubt decided in his own mind at that moment to attempt a manoeuvre at that time hitherto unpractised in naval tactics'.

For twelve hours the two fleets lay in their parallel lines pounding at one another, a brutal ceaseless fire that, with hardly any wind, practically obscured sight of all but the closest. As the wind freshened and the smoke cleared the French line was seen to be more disordered than the British. A gap existed at the centre of the French line. Instead of waiting for the French to re-form their line Rodney left his own line and steered his flagship for the gap. Others followed his example. The result was melee and, at the end, decisive victory.

Blane was on Rodney's quarterdeck throughout. Victory was decided, Blane said, the moment *Formidable* broke the French line. The signal for line was hauled down and 'every ship annoyed the enemy as their respective commanders judged best, and the French struck their colours in succession'. So there it was: after seventy-six years of obdurate insistence upon holding to what stood simply because it had become the rule, the Royal Navy had found the solution to its frustration with indecisive action, hitherto the only outcome of battle, however furious the spirit and courage expended. With his own relief, Blane expressed what now fell upon all: '. . . it has generally been the fashion of late . . . to ridicule as vulgar and groundless prejudice, the opinion of our being superior to our neighbours in naval skill and courage; and of this I was more than half persuaded myself . . .' It was a rare moment.

For once there were captured ships to display, including the flagship with de Grasse on board. De Grasse's fleet had been formed to carry an expedition against Jamaica. Part of the land force, its artillery and ammunition were aboard some of the captured ships. With that and with de Grasse sitting prisoner in Rodney's stern gallery, the victory was as complete as any could be.

Did the Battle of the Saints, as it came to be known, owe its success and fame to Admiral George Brydges Rodney's own touch of genius, or had he been influenced by Clerk of Eldin's ideas? The question was to inflame naval and public discussion of the Battle of the Saints across the next generation. When news of the victory at Saints and the method of it reached Britain four months later Clerk's immediate response was to claim to have been the inspiration for breaking the line. But Clerk's claim that when Admiral Rodney sailed for the West Indies in January 1780 he carried the Scot's manuscript with him was denied by close friends of Rodney's.

Off the Saints in 1782 there was no apparent forethought by Rodney that he intended using such a tactic. He gave no indication of anything like it to his officers, unless one accepts Blane's breakfast-table incident. Everything leading up to the historic breaking of the French line was preceded by absolute adherence to convention. The only signals were for battle and close battle. The British fleet stood in a line that Rodney's flag captain Sir Charles Douglas described as 'one of the best lines of battle I ever saw'. According to Douglas Rodney's action sprang wholly from the sudden surprise of a break in the French line and the opportunity it instantly suggested. Mahan, writing a century later, described Rodney as belonging 'rather to the wary, cautious school of the French tacticians than to the impetuous, unbounded eagerness of Nelson',[13] adding, however, that Rodney, 'meant mischief, not idle flourishes'. But the impetuosity of Rodney's drive through the French line might surely have sprung from that other side of his character, a gambler's impulse. All the cards were suddenly his, and he played them.

Rodney or Clerk? Ultimately there seems little point to any argument, for Rodney it was who first broke line, who was in a position to do so, did so, and who remains the hero of it. Clerk was a genius who brought an original, wide and necessary questioning of the established and seemingly unassailable (Nelson for one was to become a keen student of Clerk's theses). The two should therefore be seen together as the outstanding characters who loosened forever the restrictive inflexibility of what was known as Standing Instructions and thereby brought enlightenment for a new and different naval generation. The undismissible importance of Clerk was that his work was in print for all to read and debate.

The British were obviously not in a cheering mood at the end of the American War. Nevertheless, the war had given them a unique gift for the future. For the younger generation of commanders the fall of Standing Instructions was a new beginning that shone upon the future. Naval warfare had entered the Age of Reason. They had been delivered freedom of action, the concept of individual risk and intuitive judgement. For the moment, more could not be asked.

IV

DECADE

THE Treaty of Paris, signed in September 1783 at Versailles, gave the United States its independence and became one of the great markers in history for what it closed, but perhaps more so for what it opened. If one were required to define the particular period that marked the onset of the modern age it would be difficult to quarrel against the decade between the years 1783 and 1793, between the formal end of the American War of Independence and the start of the Great War.

The ten years between these dates offer the start of the turning of the Western world, with rapid and profound change affecting every aspect of life and outlook, politically, philosophically, morally, economically, productively, scientifically and aesthetically. Across every form of public cognizance and sensibility a new consciousness took hold, seemingly to displace all that had gone before. It was the unprecedented nature of the American War, a new Atlantic state and the shock of triumphant rebellion and its inflaming republican principles that gripped the Western nations as formal peace was concluded amid the mirrors of Versailles. But in 1793, at the end of the decade, Versailles was a hollow shell, emptied of its Bourbon grandeur, the proclamation of the earlier republic having been superseded by the precipitous arrival of another quite different republic, militant and hostile to all that challenged it.

The foundations of the apparently changeless and immovable had been shaken and began to shift. In those last days of the *ancien régime* the symbol of a virile new nation across the Atlantic, commercially active, productively self-sustaining, potentially powerful and morally triumphant, was a bright new political and social headland blazing democratic example. The singularity of that was immediately matched by political drama in the Old World as well. For the triumph of American idealism, having crossed the Atlantic with the returning battle fleets, had brought immediate incitement to an established and already active political radicalism in both Britain and France. The intensifying ferment took a different form in each.

In France the pace was to be faster and more politically violent, carrying the nation inexorably towards the fall of the Bastille on 14 July 1789 and with it the start of the French Revolution. Movement had come there earlier, though inexorably, as Alexis de Tocqueville described: 'Some thirty or forty years before the Revolution . . . a change came over the scene . . . every Frenchman was dissatisfied with his lot and quite decided to better it. And this rankling discontent made him at once impatient and fiercely hostile to the past; nothing would content him but a new world utterly different from the world around him.'[1]

Much the same could be said of Britain. In Britain it was all at different speed though equally irreversible momentum. Society and governance were being carried through sudden breaches of the established order towards a future that from 1783 began to impose itself ever more emphatically.

For Britain the end of the old and the beginning of the new came with the signing of the preliminary Anglo-American articles of peace on 30 November 1782. Between that formality and the conclusive one to follow at Versailles, Britain was compelled to absorb the impact of its losses.

There was little room for optimism in the land through 1783 as the protracted writing of the final treaty of peace continued. The shock of losing America at first appeared incalculable. The largest and most valuable part of the British colonial empire had been lost and gone with it, so it seemed, was the biggest and most important market for British manufactures.

The prevailing pessimism was expressed in a dismal summary of the state of the nation offered in February 1783, by young William Pitt, speaking as Chancellor of the Exchequer. The fabric of naval supremacy, he declared, 'was visionary and baseless'. The 'memorable era of England's glory' belonged to the past. The nation now lay 'under the awful and mortifying necessity of employing a language which corresponds with her true condition; the visions of her power and pre-eminence are passed away'.[2]

More such recriminative bitterness flooded parliament. As one voice cried out to the Commons in March 1783, 'It had been easy to foresee that American independence must tend to great convulsions in our commerce, the emigration of manufacturers, the loss of seamen, and all the evils incident to a declining country. The hour of calamity has now come.' The Americans, he continued, must 'in a course of years possess themselves of the carrying trade. Thus the kingdom must gradually lose its great nursery of seamen, and all the means of manning ships in times of emergency, and thus decline and languish during peace, and be helpless and dependent during war.'[3]

Whatever the manning loss to the Royal Navy, always so dependent upon the press gang, fear of the Americans as maritime trading rivals was sound.

The coastal-living Americans had already demonstrated a superior ability as a seagoing people. Their own expansive merchant fleet and privateering operations during the war had amply demonstrated that. So had the exploits of John Paul Jones, the American naval commander who had brought his personal war to the Narrow Seas.

Such dramatized anguish sounded against every basic premise implanted in every Briton concerning the nation's existence and survival. Never before had so little faith been expressed in, so little credit been given to, the naval and mercantile future of Britain. It was a memorably bizarre grief.

As if to underscore this sense of national tribulation, parliament had already been informed of 'an extraordinary event'. Lying in the Thames while this talk was going on was an American ship with 'the thirteen stripes flying on board'. It seemed to have arrived to press home all the fears being expressed. The ship had offered to enter at Custom-House but as peace was not yet formal 'the officers were at a loss how to behave'.[4]

In face of so much pessimism, confusion and bitterness parliament refused to allow Pitt to pass a bill that granted Americans unrestricted trade with Britain, in spite of strong argument that the practical common sense of such a measure was more realistic than the fears of the cost to British carrying trade. For no other nation, the House was assured, could supply on better terms the Manchester and Birmingham manufactures that the Americans required. Apart from that, the American states were in greater need of credit than any time before. That could be had only in Britain. The French, who had previously given the Americans credit, were bankrupt.[5]

The political state of Britain and its parliament in 1783 appeared as agonizing and uncertain as the economic situation. The political turbulence that had marked British political life during the American War had produced a growing tension between George III and those who had opposed the war and who subsequently converted that opposition into a campaign against personal government by the king. Since his accession George had sought to maintain royal authority over parliament. The challenge to that had become a dominant note of British political life, led by Charles James Fox. Fundamental to Fox's political stance was liberty of parliament, the nation and the individual. With parliament that meant that the leader favoured by the majority in the House of Commons governed the nation, not the king.

In 1783 the coalition government of Lord North and Fox ran foul of George III over a bill for a new form of governance of India. Commissioners for India would be appointed or dismissed by parliament, not by the crown. The king saw it as violation of his constitutional right. After the Commons passed the India Bill, George III allowed it to be known that any who then helped pass the bill in the House of Lords would be his 'enemy'. Within twelve hours of the bill's consequent defeat in the Lords on 17 December

1783, the king dismissed the government of Fox and North and offered the government to William Pitt. On 19 December 1783 William Pitt became the youngest Prime Minister in history. Pitt had to establish himself on a stronger footing than as head of an interim government called to office by the king. Early in 1784, he called a general election that would decide whether he or Fox would lead the land.

Pitt's victory was decisive and in May 1784 he began a prime minister-ship that would manage the fortunes and survival of the nation across one of the most compelling spans of historic change that the world has seen.

In his own manner Pitt was as dedicated to parliamentary reform as Charles James Fox. He just went about it in quieter style. Above all his would be a parliament dedicated to economic and administrative reform. Within three years of taking office the national revival guided by Pitt was effacing the gloom and losses of the American War, in counter to his own dismal predictions of February 1783.

Pitt had been the younger and favourite son of his masterful father, William the elder. Tall, lanky, withdrawn, he was described by one colleague as 'without elegance or grace . . . cold, stiff, and without suavity or amenity. He seemed never to invite approach, or to encourage acquaintance, though when addressed he could be polite, communicative, and occasionally gracious. Smiles were not natural to him . . .'[6]

Whatever else he was, William Pitt was certainly very much a child of the world and of the age in which he lived. In France and Britain the Enlightenment had hardened from philosophical prospect into the firmer practicalities of the Age of Reason. The gospel of Rousseau's *Social Contract*, 'man is born free and everywhere he is in chains', was superseded, in Britain particularly, by the greater realism and wider appeal of Thomas Paine's more precisely enunciated *Rights of Man* with its cry for universal suffrage and the abolition of monarchy. Pitt was hardly a disciple of Paine. But all those determining influences nevertheless were upon him, as they were on his whole generation, and as his impact upon the independence of parlia-ment would demonstrate. He became an ardent supporter of the crusade to abolish slavery, was a disciple of Adam Smith and a devoted reader of Gibbon's *Decline and Fall of the Roman Empire*, so propitious to that time with its classical account of the rise and fall of dynastic power. And it was Gibbon who, writing from Switzerland, hailed the 'revolution' of Pitt's election in phrases that seemed to leap from Gibbon's own masterwork: 'A youth of five-and-twenty, who raises himself to the government of an empire by the power of genius and the reputation of virtue, is a circum-stance unparalleled in history, and, in a general view, is not less glorious to the country than to himself.'[7]

The decade that Pitt and his coevals of the age would command was already offering vastly more than political change. Economic success was also being drawn from new sources that were increasingly visible all across the land. New inventions and machines affected agriculture and industry alike, with accompanying shifts of population. The year 1783 itself marked the first significant acquisition of steam engines by a small number of industries. In 1785 the steam engine began spinning cloth. Its use soon extended to flour and other mills. In 1784 a rolling process for large-scale coal-fuelled production of iron was invented thereby ensuring iron as the basic material of the industrial revolution.

Industry required finance and transport. After 1780 banks began rising rapidly in number, in the country especially. By 1784 there were more than one hundred country banks in England alone. To emerging industry they offered deposit facilities, credit, transfers of money, paper money, bills of exchange. But goods, like money, needed to move. The canal age had already begun. Through the 1780s a network of canals spread across Britain, allowing easy communication between production centres as well as from inland to the seaports. Roads were simultaneously improved.

In 1783 striking comparisons were drawn in the *Gentleman's Magazine* between that present and the recent past. It was an image of a faster, looser, more prosperous and more secular world.

In 1763, it said, one stagecoach set out once a month from Edinburgh for London, a journey that took fifteen days. By 1783 there were sixty stagecoaches monthly from Edinburgh to London, fifteen every week, and they reached the capital in four days.

In the year 1750 Hackney coaches were plain, awkward, clumsy things, hung by leathers. At present they are almost as handsome as those belonging to people of fashion. At that time country gentlemen and their families kept at home, or made a journey once a year with a Pair of dock-tailed horses; whereas now they spend all their fortunes in London, and drive hunters 100 guineas the pair. Fashions in the former period did not reach any place 50 miles from London, till they were nearly out: now they travel down in coaches and diligences in a few hours ... Formerly citizens wore round wigs, and worsted stockings: now nothing but queus and silk hose are worn by their apprentices and porters ... The number of merchants at that time was very small ... Now merchants are as numerous as clerks; and their families are emulous in dissipation.[8]

Edinburgh was marked as a city that particularly reflected the phenomenal changes that were affecting Britain in the second half of the century.

In 1763 it was fashionable to go to church ... Sunday was strictly observed by all ranks as a day of devotion, and it was disgraceful to be seen in the streets during

the time of public worship . . . In 1783 attendance on church is much neglected . . .
The streets are often crowded in the time of worship, and, in the evenings, they
are shamefully loose and riotous. Family worship is almost totally abolished . . . It
may now be said that the generality of young men are bold in vice, and that too
many of the young women assume the meretricious airs and flippancy of courtezans
. . . In 1763 a young man was termed a fine fellow who, to a well-informed and
accomplished mind added elegance of manners, and a conduct guided by principle . . . In 1783 a fine fellow is one who can drink three bottles . . . who swears
immoderately, and before ladies, and talks of his word of honour; who ridicules
religion and morality, as folly and hypocrisy . . . who is very jolly at the table of
his friend, and will lose no opportunity of seducing his wife.

Duelling, understandably, was common.

In such a free climate crime was rampant, in the country and on the
highways as much as in the city. Retribution was harsh. Hanging, drawing
and quartering was still on the books for the military. Burning on the stake
lingered, for counterfeiters. 'Nine malefactors were executed before the
debtors door at Newgate . . . They behaved in a decent manner . . . The
woman for coining was brought out after the rest were turned off, and
fixed to a stake and burnt, being first strangled by the stool being taken
from under her.' There was no lessening of severity for the young. 'Were
executed before Newgate . . . Joseph Wood, aged fourteen, and Thomas
Underwood, aged fifteen, for robbing William Beedle, a lad of twelve years
old, of a jacket, shirt, waistcoat and five pence in half pence . . .'

The *Gentleman's Magazine* in this unique review added of 1783 that
'convicts under sentence of death in Newgate, and the gaols throughout the
kingdom, increase so fast that . . . England would soon be marked among
the nations as the *Bloody Country*'.

There were wondrous new spectacles, however, more compelling than
the mass turnout for executions.

Man was in the air. Flight was everywhere, first in France and then in
Britain and America. On 7 January 1785 a Frenchman, J. P. Blanchard,
and an American, Dr John Jeffries, made the first flight across sea. They
took off from Dover for Calais in a gas-filled balloon.

The serenity and composure visible on the countenances of these two extraordinary
characters, the display of two beautiful flags, the Red Ensign of England and the
Royal Standard of France, the elegance of the little wherry that sustained the passengers . . . the stupendous magnificence of the balloon itself, with the sun-beams full
upon them, was a sight which leaves all description at a distance . . . The salutations
from the Castle, the Beach, the Forts and the Town were general, and gracefully
returned by the two Aeronauts, moving their hats and waving their flags . . . At

the distance of about half seas over they descended so rapidly, that the spectators were exceedingly alarmed . . . but in a few minutes they were relieved from their apprehension by their ascending higher than before . . . the sky was so clear that the French land and town of Calais were plainly discernible, and the eye scarcely lost sight of the Voyagers for near an hour and a half, and with good glasses they were seen till safe within the opposite coast . . . Philosophy may hereafter improve this science, and accommodate Balloons to some useful purpose, and less astonish the world; but all future ages must applaud the abilities, and admire the cool, intrepid, determined conduct of these two men, who first crossed the Ocean suspended in ethereal regions by the power only of inflammable air.[9]

Aeroflation, the French called it.

The future was being opened on and below the water as well. In 1783 the Marquis de Joffroy d'Abbans ran a steam-powered craft for fifteen minutes on the River Saône. In 1787 James Rumsey of Maryland propelled a boat with steam pressure on the Potomac. Other experiments with steam-propelled craft followed hard on one another. Already in the American War a rough form of 'submarine navigation' had been attempted by an American, David Bushnell, with a craft called *American Turtle* that nearly succeeded in damaging a British warship in New York. Throughout the 1780s, another American, Robert Fulton, was working on an advanced form of Bushnell's submerged naval vessel.

The ordinary man was empowered by being better informed. Bigger and better newspapers served the public. From 1783 journalists were allowed to take notes in parliament. New magazines published debates in full. They carried as well reviews of new books, long reports on scientific, medical and mechanical 'transactions'. Their pages were open to a full range of comment and discussion. The world was reported on from Europe, America, the East, and all points in between as the British traveller roamed in unprecedented manner.

A new morality had long been offering itself. Britain had been prepared for it by John Wesley who, since his evangelical conversion in 1783, had travelled a quarter of a million miles on horseback all over the country preaching in 'straightforward and pointed address', usually outdoors, to 'plain people of low education and vulgar taste . . . strangers to the refinements of learning and politeness'. Wesley's evangelical movement gradually took fire. For the next forty years it brought new meaning and perspective to the old crisis word of Christian belief, Dissent.

Wesley was preaching to the masses that had remained excluded from the established church. To those bound by the rigid codes of social deference he offered equality of all men before God. Itinerant preachers, 'illiterate enthusiasts', mobilized the religious revival of British society. They drew huge crowds to their open-air meetings to hear exhortations to repent sin and claim salvation. A 'violent and impetuous power' took hold at these meetings through wild scenes of passionate conversion. From this 'new birth' the evangelical revival took firm hold upon the land, gradually advancing even into the upper classes where dissent, in the form of 'Methodism' especially, was first regarded with scorn and punitive disapproval.

By coupling virtue, piety, the work ethic and human progress with salvation and associating idleness and drink with sin and damnation, the Evangelical faith became the necessary religion for the oncoming industrial revolution. Indeed, as the French historian Elie Halévy expressed it, the 'moral cement' of British society in the nineteenth century 'which invested the British aristocracy with almost stoic dignity, restrained the plutocrats who had newly risen from the masses from vulgar ostentation and debauchery, and placed over the proletariat a select body of workmen enamoured of virtue and capable of self-restraint . . .'

Like everything else, the British navy was in a state of suspension between the old and the new. It had become a time for vital reassessment.

The thirteen American colonies had been lost through the biggest maritime war yet fought. The Royal Navy's performance had, except at the very last, been at best an inconclusive draw with the French and Spanish navies. Rodney's victory off the Saints barely redeemed that. Looking to the future, it could appear that the mercantile dominance that the navy was required to maintain might be seriously doubtful if the French and Spanish maintained their superior skills and again offered themselves in such powerful naval union. Their ships had been superior, the seamanship outstanding. Earl Howe, after his appointment as First Lord of the Admiralty in January 1783, attributed a great deal of final British success to chance. The British navy had been inferior in strength, its ships in poor condition. His plea was that peace should bring determined effort to prepare the navy for any future hostility.

For the Royal Navy an immediate question at the close of the American War had to be whether, as ships were laid up, the navy would suffer the slow decline that usually followed a war.

Custom was that mass discharges immediately reduced the swollen manpower of the navy. Ships consequently deteriorated for lack of maintenance, except those kept on an active basis. Cost was the short-term view of it all. The Royal Navy thus invariably found itself seeking to re-establish and man itself in a rush whenever a new crisis developed. But in 1783 a newly appointed Comptroller of the Navy, Charles Middleton, eventually to be Lord Barham, committed himself to care and preservation of the navy after the close of the war. Middleton, a strong evangelical, applied himself with all the fervour of such. Dockyards and naval administration were still accursed by corruption, incompetence and negligence. The greatest obstacle, however, came from the Pitt government's insistence on economy which, in spite of Middleton's furious resistance, continued to affect maintenance of ships and the whole naval establishment.

Naval command belonged to the ageing. Rodney had seen his last sea service. Others, such as Earl Howe and Lord Samuel Hood, were approaching sixty and far from fit. Howe was ever taking the waters at Bath for gout and other ailments. But, though reluctant, he had been thrust into being First Lord of the Admiralty and, at the end of the decade, was destined to take active command of the navy. Hood, who had seen hard service in the American War, was to have the Portsmouth command from 1786 through into the early 1790s. Those moving up close behind them included John Jervis, forty-eight in 1783. Jervis had been at the capture of Quebec in 1759, had commanded the 80-gun *Foudroyant* in the American War and had captured the French 74-gun *Pégase* without losing a man on his own ship. But of particular interest now had to be the generation composed of the young captains and the midshipmen of the American War. These now had a special light shining upon them, for they were come of age to be the beneficiaries of Rodney's breaking-the-line example and Clerk's tactics. The new was theirs to exploit.

Distinctive among these was Captain Horatio Nelson, who had already marked himself distinctively as a young man of unusual character, bravado, leadership, enthusiastic sea sense and forceful dedication. He had gone to sea at twelve and served an apprenticeship markedly different from many in that part of his initiation had been as able seaman in the merchant service, from which he had emerged with sympathy for the freer association that existed there among officers and men. He was twenty when the American War began and had just obtained captain's rank. By that time he had seen a remarkable amount of the world, from the Arctic to the Indian Ocean, and most of the waters of Europe and the Americas. During the war he had demonstrated his courage and audacity in an assault upon Nicaragua. The end of the war found him sharing command in the Leeward Islands, with Antigua as his base.

Commanding a 64-gun ship in the West Indies at this time was Cuthbert Collingwood, ten years older than Nelson. Between the two of them a remarkable and historic friendship arose. Collingwood, aged thirty-five in 1783, had earned his lieutenancy for intrepidly supplying the soldiers fighting at Bunker Hill. In 1786 Nelson, off Martinique, would write, 'This station has not been over pleasant: had it not been for Collingwood, it would have been the most disagreeable I ever saw.' That bond would continue strongly.

Of quite different character was young William Sidney Smith who, at age thirteen, joined the navy in 1777. Five years later, now eighteen, the youth was appointed a post-captain by George Rodney, under whom he had served with conspicuous courage in several battles. In a navy where able men could wait half a lifetime for promotion, Smith's teenaged captaincy was an extraordinary thing. Smith would eventually stand as one of the Great War's small group of particularly distinctive adventurists, wilful men who set themselves up in whatever roles they wished to play, and which were never to be minor or of small consequence. 'There was an evident eccentricity about him which perhaps stood in the way of his being employed in the ordinary routine of service,' one acquaintance wrote. Smith was never to demonstrate anything different.

At the end of the American War Smith travelled widely on the Continent, embodying the *beau idéal* eighteenth-century cosmopolite, described as 'perhaps the best English-Frenchman that ever lived'. In 1786 he was in naval service to King Gustavus of Sweden in that monarch's war with Russia.

Of these three individuals, Nelson was to make the peace a difficult period for himself, by creating his own extension of the American War.

In the Caribbean Americans and islanders had acted together to continue free trade between the islands and the United States. For Nelson this amounted to giving Americans the special privilege which they had lost by rebellion and which Westminster had denied them by refusing Pitt's bill. Nelson sought energetically to suppress that trade, arousing the resentment and ire of Americans and island colonials alike. 'I hate them all,' he wrote. Nelson found himself ostracized socially on his station, and threatened by lawsuit within British jurisprudence by Americans for seizure of their ships. On the West Indies station he met a young widow, Fanny Nisbet, whom he married in 1787. He also formed a close friendship with Prince William Henry, the future King William IV, who had arrived in the Caribbean during the American War as a seventeen-year-old midshipman, and who returned to the Caribbean as a post-captain. The prince escorted the bride at Nelson's marriage to Fanny Nisbet.

At the end of 1787 Nelson found himself back in Britain and, after his ship had been paid off, sat waiting in vain for a new command. He was further harassed by the litigation over his seizures of American ships which had pursued him to Britain. In making his plea for a new command Nelson got nowhere. A barrier had been set against him. His campaign against the American trade with the islands had brought repercussion in London, where the islanders had exercised their influence.

Instead of the command he wanted Nelson found himself farming his father's land as the last decade of the century began. The new age of full reportage of the world and its crises brought solace. His principal relief came from taking the weekly *Norfolk Chronicle* to a secluded spot on the farm, there to immerse himself in the events from which he felt excluded. The wider world that he surveyed from rural Norfolk during this period of frustration and lengthening inactivity was one that had menacingly emerged since the American War and during his years in the Caribbean.

Even as 1783 folded into 1784, mere months after the Treaty of Paris had been blotted and put away, there were already abundant indications that the call upon the navy to defend British interest might be soon.

The American War had helped to distract attention from new crises reaching across the face of the Old World, generated particularly by the rise of Russia and the ambitions of its sovereign, Catherine II, to reach for the Levant. Alongside this lay the rivalry between Prussia and Austria for the allegiance and command over the German peoples. Russia and Prussia sought increased possession and control in Poland. In the Baltic hostility between Russia and Sweden was fast building. Between Sweden and Denmark hostility was entrenched.

A curtain was suddenly rising on aggressive situations that had emerged across practically the whole face of Europe during the American War. Heavy clouds were gathered over the Continent even as the peace treaties were concluded. Exhausted though the big powers were, they saw themselves immediately drawn into a spread of critical events that suggested that they were stepping without pause from one war on to the threshold of the next.

So it was to remain.

Across the decade from 1783 to 1793 Britain and the continental powers henceforth were to confront a continually shifting prospect of threat of war, immediate imminence of war or war itself in one part or another of the map of the Western world. It became a brooding panorama of menace and violence, of aggressive militarism, dynastic ambition and manipulative diplomacy that set into motion a linked sense of crisis from the Narrow Seas across to Prussia and Russia, from Paris to all points, from the Ottoman Porte to St Petersburg and Vienna, from St Petersburg across the Baltic to Stockholm, and between Stockholm and Copenhagen. All were inextricably involved whether through direct hostility or through binding alliances in situations of accelerating intensity that either mastered crisis or continued steadily and unswervingly onward towards more fateful resolution.

A particular focus for the naval powers was that Catherine II's dream of a Greater Russia reaching more directly to the Mediterranean had gathered new force. The lush peninsula of the Crimea had become particularly attractive to the man who dominated Catherine's life, Prince Grigori

Potemkin, a Lithuanian. Potemkin had become Catherine's lover as well as the strongman of Russia. In 1782 Catherine and Potemkin decided on the annexation of the Crimea. A year later Russia seized the Crimean peninsula, with only slight resistance from the Turks. Potemkin immediately began to build Russia's Black Sea naval base. Practically the whole of it was organized and supervised by Britons. The naval ports and facilities became the work of Admiral Samuel Greig's son, Alexis.

Through Thomas Jefferson the empress had engaged the American naval hero of the War of Independence, John Paul Jones, to take one of the senior commands in the Russian navy. But the British officers already serving in the Russian navy promptly resigned, or threatened to resign. In deference to the hostility of her British sailors Catherine, instead of using Jones on the Baltic as she first intended, sent him to the Black Sea as vice admiral in the operations there.

This assertive strategy and naval emergence arising at the eastern Mediterranean was highly disturbing to all the principal onlookers. France, traditional supporter of Turkey, had never liked the prospect of Russia looming over the eastern Mediterranean, gateway to the East. For Britain, Russia now represented a maritime force of great significance on the Baltic and of potentially serious threat in the eastern Mediterranean and to the Indian Ocean beyond.

The Ottoman Porte, exasperated by Russia's continuing encroachments, itself finally put an end to the crisis by declaring war on Russia on 24 August 1787. On 10 February 1788 the emperor of Austria joined Russia and declared war against Turkey. On 21 June Sweden invaded Russian Finland and nine days later Russia declared war against her.

Events moved swiftly on the Black Sea. The Russians wanted the Turkish fortress of Ozchakov. It sat at the point where the Dnieper and the Bug joined the Black Sea, whose waters Ozchakov had effectively controlled before the new Russian establishments arose close by.

As Potemkin laid siege to Ozchakov, an inglorious naval action in the waters below it saw the Turkish fleet of galleys and light shallow-draught ships mostly destroyed after an engagement with a similar Russian force commanded by John Paul Jones. Ozchakov was taken by the Russians on 17 December 1788. But the entry of Sweden into the war against Russia meant that the naval contest transferred from the Black Sea to the Baltic, where a different aspect of eighteenth-century naval warfare had become established.

Sea warfare on the Baltic, like that of the Black Sea, was different from that practised elsewhere by the major naval powers. Peter the Great had recognized the necessity of galleys during the Great Northern War at the beginning of the eighteenth century. The nature of much of the Baltic coastline had compelled it. Offshore runs of rocks and small islands often prevented sailing ships from approaching the mainland, except at projecting headlands. Sheltered channels inside the rocky shore were ideal for oared craft, which could move armies where sail could not. These 'galleys' were mainly flat-bottomed, some with two decks mounting guns as heavy as thirty-two pounds. Some had topsides that could be lowered to a horizontal position for landing cavalry, artillery and ammunition, and with that presaging the landing craft of twentieth-century seaborne invasions.

The Russian Baltic fleet was under Admiral Samuel Greig, still in command after nearly two decades of building Russia's naval power. While Greig was commanding the Russians the Swedes had their own British naval adviser in Captain Sidney Smith, who had become a close confidant of the Swedish king, and whose triumphant achievement in this Baltic war came in 1789 when he extracted the Swedish fleet from the Finnish port of Viborg, into which it had fled and lay blocked by the Russians. Forty of the Russian galleys were captured. The Turkish prisoners driving them were released by Sidney Smith who, in a deft gesture of switched fate, then got them to continue at the oars in pursuit of the fleeing Russian galleys. For that he was knighted by Gustavus with the Grand Cross of the Swedish Order of the Sword, an honour acknowledged by George III with a British knighthood. After Sweden, Sidney Smith took himself to Constantinople.

In France finally exploded into life the greatest event of that decade, and of the century. There the future truly had arrived. That fateful summer of 1789, Europe saw the Bourbon dynasty in France struck down to a state of humiliating compliance with the public demands set upon it.

Britain simultaneously found itself distracted by prospect of war, with Spain. It was to be the first of two major events, 'Armaments': crises that threatened war.

American oceanic commerce had begun to expand resourcefully since the end of the war. American merchant ships were crossing the Atlantic in increasing numbers, to Britain, north-west Europe and the Mediterranean. They had virtually taken over the Caribbean and South America trade and were building their China trade as well, with fifteen-month voyages between Philadelphia and Canton. American zeal had also taken them into the Pacific, where they were exploiting an entirely new form of China trade, the supply to the Chinese market of furs and ginseng from north-west America.

The base the Americans established was on Nootka Sound on Vancouver Island. Captain Cook had surveyed this coast and sailed into this sound but no Europeans had yet formed settlement so far north, although the Spanish professed prior claim to the entire coastline from Mexico to sixty degrees north.

This new line of American commerce immediately attracted the attention of the East India Company which backed a venture to Nootka in 1786 under two British officers, Lieutenant Mears and Captain Douglas of the Royal Navy. Land was purchased from a local chief at Nootka, a house built and the British flag raised above it. But in May 1789, after wintering at Nootka with two American ships, Douglas was surprised by the sudden appearance of two Spanish warships under Don Estevan Martínez, commander of the Mexican base of San Blas.

Martínez arrested Douglas and his crew and the captains and crew of three other British ships as they came into harbour. The British flag was hauled down and the prisoners compelled to assist in building fortifications, after which they went sent as prisoners to San Blas. The American ships by contrast were left alone. Martínez appeared more cautious about molesting them.[10]

British protest brought the unsatisfactory response that the British seamen had trespassed on the dominion of Spain. For Britain no such Spanish dominion existed on the north-west coast of America. Simultaneously, intelligence was received of Spanish fleets being prepared for war at Cadiz and Ferrol. On 4 May 1790 an order for the general impressment of seamen was announced. The following day a message from the king, announcing the prospect of war, was presented to both houses of parliament. Lord Howe was called to command a squadron in the Channel. He hoisted his flag aboard the 100-gun *Queen Charlotte*.

Plans were made for reprisal attacks on Spanish possessions in the Caribbean and South America. By 17 August the fleet had been fully assembled and was ready for sea 'in the readiest and most perfect state that has been known in the annals of Great Britain'. This was to be known as 'The Spanish Armament'. It had the desired effect. In October Spain agreed to restore all it had taken from the traders at Nootka, to pay an indemnity and not to interfere again in commerce or settlement on America's north-west coast.

The Spanish navy, with fine but poorly manned ships, was certainly ill-suited to confront Howe's fleet. A British captain, Jahleel Brenton, and an English pilot accompanied the Spanish line ship that carried the Nootka indemnity money to Britain. Brenton found that in rough weather all the officers except the captain were unable to dine in the wardroom, all being seasick. Nearing England the ship was caught in a severe squall. Brenton was roused by the English pilot crying that the ship had become unmanageable. Going on deck Brenton found total confusion, with the ship 'running away'. It took some hours 'to get things to rights'.

Nelson, still farming in Norfolk, had been mortified not to be called to a command during the Nootka crisis, crying to the Admiralty that it was an affront he did not deserve. 'I am more hurt than surprised,' he wrote to

Prince William, to whom he had again appealed. He was so far disturbed that he thought of exiling himself to France, or joining the Russian navy, as so many before him had done.

Nootka had considerable significance in that it had brought the British navy swiftly up to mark.

The second 'Armament' now followed. As if emboldened by Nootka, and certainly encouraged by Britain's improved diplomatic, political and economic situation, Pitt became drawn into a policy to curb Russia's expansion in south-east Europe. A particular concern was the threat of Russian power to Britain's Baltic trade, especially for the naval supplies the Royal Navy required. Pitt's diplomatic plan was for Britain and Prussia to compel Russia to make peace with Turkey and for Russia then to return Ozchakov to the Ottomans. Demand to that effect was sent to Catherine at the end of 1790. Her absolute refusal of British and Prussian involvement in her war with the Turks came back in February 1791.

Pitt found himself trapped into prospect of war. As with Nootka, he turned to the navy as the simplest form of intimidation. Admiral Hood was ordered to hoist his flag in *Victory* to lead a fleet to the Baltic. The fleet, assembled at Spithead, consisted of thirty-six ships of the line and twenty-nine smaller vessels. Impressment was ordered on 31 March. This was known was the 'Russian Armament'. But it all fell apart.

The idea of Baltic war over an unknown fortress in the Black Sea was hugely unpopular in parliament as well as with the public. The cost of such a war in waters unfamiliar to the navy horrified Pitt's critics. Charles James Fox led the assault in the House. Was it really so vital to British interests whether Russia did or did not retain Ozchakov? Was it really worth incurring all the costs and calamities of war for a desolate tract of marshes, and for a fortress already half in ruins?

Pitt was compelled to retreat. It was a major setback for him, at home and abroad. For Fox it was a conspicuous return to centre stage. In admiration of his efforts on her behalf Catherine obtained a bust of Fox from England and placed it in a gallery in her palace between those of Demosthenes and Cicero.

Austria and the Ottomans signed their peace on 4 August 1791, Russia and the Porte a week later. Russia kept her hold on Ozchakov.

Whatever the political cost, the Ozchakov crisis, like that of Nootka, had been of huge benefit to the navy. Both crises had brought the British navy to a high state of readiness as Britain and Europe regarded the plight of the Bourbon monarchy in France. American challenge to the divine right of kings had been an ocean away. This nearer manifestation compelled the emperor of Austria and the king of Prussia to declare that the situation of the king of France was a matter of common concern to other kings. They got immediate support from Catherine of Russia and Gustavus of Sweden. A sweeping war across Europe looked imminent.

Against that sombre outlook, Pitt, on 17 February 1792, offered an astonishing view of Britain's own expectations. His remarks were a review of the decade since the dark days following the end of the American War in 1783. He now projected peace practically everlasting. 'We must not count with certainty on a continuance of our present prosperity . . . but unquestionably there never was a time in the history of this country, when, from the situation of Europe, we might more reasonably expect fifteen years of peace, than we may at the present moment.' It was a dizzily wishful utterance from a British premier standing in sight of a world already on the boil for France declared war against Austria and Prussia just a month later, on 20 April 1792. In August 1792, Louis XVI and his family were imprisoned in the Temple, followed by the butchery of the September Massacres.

The pace thereafter was headlong. On 21 September France was declared a republic. That same month the French army turned back the Austrian and Prussian invaders. And they then began launching themselves against their enemies. By the middle of November they had entered Brussels and were masters of Belgium. The British navy was again put on alert. Pitt, while believing that British involvement might be inevitable, continued to put his faith in diplomacy. The drive to mobilize the navy nevertheless accelerated.

With the navy on alert and the crisis building, Captain Nelson received apologies for the long delay in giving him a ship and was told that he would have his command as soon as a suitable vessel had been brought from lay up in ordinary.

Britain continued its diplomatic efforts but the execution of Louis XVI on 21 January 1793 changed everything. When the news of the regicide reached London the French ambassador, Chauvelin, was told to leave Britain. On 1 February France declared war on Britain and Holland.

The news reached London a week later. The day before it arrived Captain Horatio Nelson boarded his new command, the 64-gun *Agamemnon*, lying at Chatham. He was thirty-four.

On 11 February George III announced to the nation through his message to parliament that the country was at war with France. Only a year earlier Pitt had made his declaration of reasonably expecting fifteen years of peace for Britain.

PART TWO

THE GREAT WAR, FIRST PHASE, 1793–1805

V

WOOD

Eighteenth-century navies were floating memorials to the lost grandeur of Western Europe's hardwood forests of antiquity. These were fast vanishing, where they had not already disappeared. Of nowhere was this truer than Great Britain, whose great oak forests, once of unique splendour, appeared to be dwindling to extinction.

A century of expanding global commerce, of greater navies and of recurring, extended naval warfare had entirely changed an earlier relaxed view of the abundance and accessibility of forests, and of the availability of the wood for the ships upon which national existence had become dependent. Recognition of the severity of a potential crisis had developed steadily during the past quarter-century.

Ships were of wood. With the ship, that plain self-evident fact was not quite as simple as it might seem. Most trees were unsuitable for ship construction. Every ship required different varieties of wood for its different parts. To complicate the matter, the life of wood was variable. Wood rotted. The sea and ship life had its own effects upon that, whatever the natural character of the timber. By the later stages of its life any ship, though it might appear the same, had been so made over piece by piece that often it was scarcely the original. Apart from worm, decay and the violence of the seas, battle played its own havoc. To keep a ship afloat and in service repair and replacement were constant. One way or another, a ship of the late eighteenth century was in permanent reconstruction, insatiable in its requirement of the appropriate timbers.

There was, in Britain, a sense of intensifying alarm over retention of naval mobility and deployment. In its way that was comparable to any major seagoing power of the early twentieth century facing limitation of its sources of coal to drive its steamships or, in our own time, of being cut off from oil. Wind, the source of power, was always there. But the ship it drove required that there always be at that vessel's disposal the particular and traditional selections of wood that ensured its continued serviceability and existence.

Already by the end of the eighteenth century a British ship-of-war, because of its many different wooden structural parts, embodied a certain far-ranging compositional character as few other things yet did. Apart from English oak, a British warship might also have oak from Ukraine, masts of fir from Lithuania and Russia. Thus, as Robert Albion summarized it in his *Forests and Sea Power*, 'Probably not more than a man in a thousand who looked at a ship of the line reflected that her great mainmast had been cut in the forests of Maine, that the topmast had grown in the Ukraine, or that the little spars came from some Norwegian mountainside . . . that part of the planking of those yellow sides had floated down the Vistula to Dantzig, while the curved frame timbers which gave shape to the bulging hull had come from tough, crooked hedgerow oaks in Sussex.'[1]

The naval and commercial oceanic future viewed in terms of existing fleets and their maintenance and expansion was thus a frightening one for any informed figure pondering the rapidly accelerating depletion of resources at the end of the eighteenth century.

Take the example of the 74-gun ship, the building of which, according to one estimate, required about two thousand oak trees. Altogether a 74 consumed three thousand loads of timber, representing the produce of fifty-seven acres of land. A load represented fifty cubic feet. An average oak contained about a load of timber. The Royal Navy's annual consumption of timber for building and repairs was estimated to be sixty thousand loads, or forty thousand full-grown trees. The building of merchant ships of all types consumed 72,500 loads a year. How could it last? This was nature, requiring a century for oak to reach maturity.

The Spanish and Russian 'Armament' crises had twice taken Britain to the brink of war within the first two years of the 1790s, even as the situation on the Continent worsened. All of that together had sharply focused attention upon the timber crisis. Already in 1772 concern over timber had brought a demand that the East India Company and other merchant owners reduce their construction of new ships to leave more timber for the navy. Ten years later, in 1792, a report demanded by parliament from the Commissioners of Woods and Forests declared that 'such is the present state of the growing timber, and the prospect of future supply, that this country will in all probability experience a *fatal* want of great oak timber and become dependent on other powers for the means of supporting her navy . . .'.

Allied to this mounting problem of the availability and accessibility of wood was the growing recognition of the limitations of wood and therefore of the ship itself, for there was little difference between the ship of the late eighteenth century and those of a century and a half before.

Already, by the start of the Great War, the limitations of naval architecture sat heavily upon the insightful. It could hardly be otherwise as the

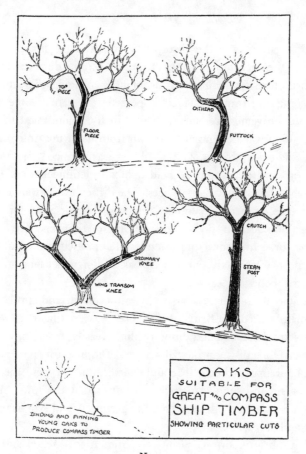

OAKS
SUITABLE FOR
GREAT and COMPASS
SHIP TIMBER
SHOWING PARTICULAR CUTS

BINDING AND PINNING
YOUNG OAKS TO
PRODUCE COMPASS TIMBER

No. 1

A MIDSHIP SECTION OF A 74 GUN SHIP WITH A
DEEP WAIST AND TUMBLE HOME SIDES, AS
BUILT IN HIS MAJESTY'S DOCK YARDS

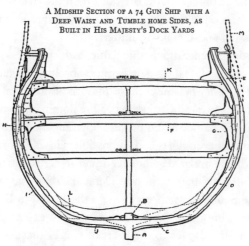

CROSS-SECTION
OF A
SEVENTY-FOUR
SHOWING TIMBERS
USED IN CONSTRUCTION

FROM 11 CLR; H.C.J., 1792,
PLATE 1.

A KEEL (ELM)   G KNEE
B KEELSON (ELM) H THICKSTUFF
C FLOOR PIECE   I PLANK (BALTIC OAK)
D FUTTOCK   J GARBOARD STRAKES (ELM, BEECH)
E TOP PIECE   K DECK DEALS (BALTIC OAK OR FIR)
F BEAM (FIR)   L CEILING

M SNODGRASS PLAN FOR STRAIGHT SIDES TO SAVE
COMPASS TIMBER. ENGLISH OAK USED IN ALL PARTS
EXCEPT WHERE SUBSTITUTES NOTED

rising industrial age and the absorption with new technologies gathered pace beyond the dockyards. As the war progressed the demands upon naval architecture intensified. But the continuously changing character of what would become a hard-fought, widely dispersed war meant that the influences upon ship improvement remained small. Finally, it all came back to wood and what new advantage might be drawn from it for the time being.

One of the big problems of shipbuilding was the need for timber. The construction of a ship could be held up for indefinite periods as forests were searched for the necessary pieces. The difficult ones were curved and crooked pieces, known as 'compass' timbers. The demand for these was mainly in the gracefully flowing main frame of the ship. The stem with its demand for tightly curved pieces presented particular difficulty. So did the stern post, which required a single oak log forty feet long and perhaps twenty eight inches thick.

At the start of the Great War oak, elm, beech, fir and spruce were the timbers mainly used for British ships. Oak was dominant. It was tough, water-resistant, bent well and did not splinter easily in action, when flying splinters were one of the principal sources of injury. Fir, pine and spruce were used for masts. The Baltic and North America were the principal sources for fir and pine. American pine provided the lower masts and bowsprits of ships of the line, Riga fir larger masts and Norwegian spruce topmasts and yards.

British timber imports came mainly from Riga, Memel and Dantzig. With all three it was timber that floated down on the rivers Duna, Niemen and Vistula from many different parts of eastern Europe, including from deep in the Russian and Ukrainian hinterlands.

For Britain dependence upon the Baltic had been heavy through the century, but with the Great War it became absolute. Britain's vanishing oak and the range of her dependence for the rest of her naval timbers upon foreign sources thus prescribed the first of the dominating strategies of the Great War: that the Baltic should be kept open for the unimpeded flow of naval stores and timber imports and, if possible, closed to France, Holland and Spain who had similar dependence upon it. This was asking a great deal, especially of a frequently hostile Denmark that controlled access to the Baltic at the Sound. Any threat to close the Sound to British trade, or even any threat within the Baltic to stop the flow of exports, clearly would be the equivalent of a dagger to the heart of naval existence.

The navy that had to be replenished and maintained in face of this rising timber crisis numbered just short of five hundred ships of all types at the start of the Great War. The whole fleet was organized into six classifications, with the ships rated from first- to sixth-rate. The main force of the fleet was formed by the ships of the line: the big ships that would form line of battle, broadly distinguished by the number of decks and guns. First-rates were the largest ships afloat in their day. They were three-deckers and carried from 100 to 120 guns. The second-rates were also three-deckers, with 90 to 98 guns. Third-rates were two-deckers, with 60, 74 or 80 guns. Fourth-rate ships carried 50 to 60 guns. Fifth- and sixth-rates were mainly frigates, which ranged from 28, 30 to 44 guns. All were three-masted and square-rigged.

Below these six rates lay a large assembly of unrated vessels, the flotilla, consisting of sloops, brigs, gunboats, cutters, bomb ships, transport-hospital ships.

As a picture of the whole this composition was relatively new and reflected the surge in naval thought and innovation that had gathered momentum from the mid-eighteenth century, notably in consequence of the Seven Years War. As Julian Corbett points out, the classification of British ships up to then had become purely arbitrary, in that it lacked precise definition of function for various types of vessel within a fleet, But that long hard-fought war, unique in that it so single-mindedly divorced itself from the Continental struggle to concentrate upon colonial seaborne commerce, had delivered 'a new and more scientific conception of naval warfare'.[2]

Before that mid-century struggle there had been no logical distinction between the large and the small type of battleship and none between the lesser battleship and the frigate or between the frigates and the flotilla. The 100-gun and 90-gun three-deckers headed a fleet of 80-, 70-, 60- and 50-gun vessels, with the latter all regarded as battleships and classed as ships of the line. The very nature of the war suggested the need for an intermediate vessel 'to combine battle and commerce-protection properties in one type'. And, Corbett adds, 'We can see growing up a clearer analysis of the various services required; a germ of their classification into battle, scouting, and inshore work; and side by side an attempt to organize the fleet upon a corresponding threefold basis of battleships, cruisers, and flotilla.'

Two ships of distinctive role and purpose came to the fore from this 'silent pressure . . . forcing the fleet into the shape it demanded'. These were the 74-gun ship of the line and the frigate. The origin of both ships was largely French.

To the frigate fell the broadened concept of 'cruiser', the all-purpose ship, fast sailing, capable of heroic single-ship actions as it went cruising to encounter the enemy frigates, but with an operational flexibility that could assign it as patrol ship, fleet scout, fleet support, convoy escort, messenger, privateer and for close inshore work.

France, through the ceaselessly inventive capacity of its maritime genius, had developed the original seventeenth-century model of the frigate from the racy lines of the Mediterranean galley. For the French, frigates were the ideal *guerre de course* ship. The privateer port of Dunkirk became their natural base. An early English model was the 32-gun *Southampton* of 1757. She carried her guns on a single whole deck, with a slight quarterdeck and a forecastle. Though the basic form remained steady, frigate armament continued to vary, from twenty guns to as high as forty-four. The frigate continued to change under the influence of new models, especially those emerging from France and, eventually, America. What the Royal Navy still urgently needed was a better intermediate ship of the line.

When Britain captured the two-decked *Invincible* from the French in 1757 the navy recognized that it had found the model to serve that mid-eighteenth-century quest for a new hybrid, multi-purpose ship of the line. *Invincible*, built in 1744, was wrecked shortly after capture, but she had already served as the model for the British-built 74s that followed. The 74 was to be the most valuable ship of the fleet of the Great War. Its versatility made it indispensable. With it, the fighting power of a ship of the line was matched to the ranging flexibility of the frigate. Excellent sailing qualities and powerful metal allied to intermediate size made the 74 a formidable ship of the line. Half the line of battle would eventually consist of 74s. Apart from service in the line, the 74s commanded squadrons in various operational areas, as well as being ideal for solitary special missions.

The American War of Independence had left a bitter, smarting recollection of how defenceless the commerce in the Narrow Seas had been in face of devastating *guerre de course*. That, together with the perpetual threat of invasion, had raised the importance of flotilla and had called for new designations or remodelling of vessels such as sloop, brig, gunboat, bomb vessel and cutter. These would serve against privateers, for coastal watch and protection and for night raids on the opposite shores.

For most, however, then and ever since, the great symbol of the eighteenth-century navy simply and unarguably was the ship of the line in its fullest emergence, the three-decked 90-, 100- and 110-gun colossus in decorated wood that stood for naval power and achievement.

The pictorial image of such a ship with full sail upon its towering masts, with the alternate yellow-painted lines along the sides each offering its regular sequence of gun ports, the windowed and brightly shining galleries at the stern, and the whole of it gracefully and solidly embedded in the sea, remains steadfastly beguiling. It was the fighting machine that changed the course of history, and it looked the part.

For all its beauty, the ship of the line was a hard place to be, especially for months or even years on end. Such service would be particularly true of a 74, whose deployment could range far beyond the Western Squadron and its guardianship of the Narrow Seas.

Most of the 74 guns of the 74 were on two decks that ran the length of the ship. Other guns were on the poop, quarterdeck and the forecastle. The length of the lower gun deck of a 74 would be 170–175 feet, with a beam of forty-five feet or just over. The ship had a tonnage of around 1,700 and carried between six and seven hundred men.

Between the forecastle and the quarterdeck lay the waist, an open space above the upper gun deck, along the bulwarks of which were nettings of rope into which, on being roused, the men ran to stow their hammocks. Similar nettings were on the quarterdeck and forecastle. On the forecastle stood the ship's bell, with its lanyard for striking the time. Right in the bows by the bowsprit were the 'heads', the open and uncomfortably exposed latrine. The ship's kitchen was in the forecastle, its chimney projecting near the bell.

The quarterdeck was the guiding heart of the ship. The after part of it ascended to the poop, a slightly raised, small expanse of open deck from whose flagstaff a giant ensign flew. Beside it was the large stern light. Here, too, were two lifebuoys which were cut loose and flung into the sea upon a cry of 'man overboard'. Midships on the quarterdeck stood the giant steering wheel and the binnacle with the compass.

The captain's quarters, extending under the poop, were entered from the quarterdeck, the most spacious corner of the ship which opened on to the stern walk. Immediately below the quarterdeck was the upper gun deck. Right aft along it, just below the captain's quarters, was the officers' wardroom with small private compartments for the lieutenants along one side, each just large enough to hold a swinging cot and a desk.

Below this deck, occupying practically the length of the ship, was the lower gun deck, where the men slept and ate in their messing space between the guns. The midshipmen's quarters were in the gun room right aft on this deck. In bad weather, with the ports closed, the place was dark, damp and foul- smelling. Even darker and more noisome was the deck below, the orlop (overlap) deck. This was the hidden life of the ship. Here were many of the stores, the sailmaker's, the carpenter's, the boatswain's for the fitting and repairing of the rigging, and the surgeon's place of business. The surgery, called the cockpit, was a large space right aft that the surgeon shared with senior midshipmen, junior lieutenants, the purser and master's mates. They all had small cabins. The mess table in the middle of the large room around which they lived served as an operating table during action. Suitably, as elsewhere in the ship, the sides were painted blood-red to minimize the splash and running of blood in action. Here the sick were kept and treated.

The ship's holds were below the orlop deck. They contained the powder magazines as well as the main stores, the salted fish and meat, the biscuit, the wine and rum, and the water, and also the ballast. There could be some five months of stores. The entrances to the magazines were covered by copper lids and padlocked, guarded by a marine with loaded musket. The magazines were well below the water line, to prevent shot during action hitting there. In this permanent darkness they required illumination, without the entry of candles or lanterns. Light was therefore provided by small rooms with double-glass windows peering into the magazines. Lanterns in those rooms provided the required light beyond the glass.

The magazine walls and floors were thickly covered with felt or other material. No one was allowed to enter except in thick felt slippers and with any form of metal emptied from his pockets. Magazines were fitted with water pipes in case of fire.

The common big guns of the 74 were 32-pounders, weighing fifty-five hundredweight, the 24-pounder, of similar weight, and the 18-pounder, of slightly less. The 32-pounders were on the lower gundeck with 24-pounders on the deck above.

Guns were mounted on four-wheeled red-painted carriages placed at the gun port, whose hinged lid was secured above the gun. Of themselves, guns represented great danger to the men who handled them. They had to be secured with great care, in rough weather and in action, and especially in both. The guns were secured by ropes, breechings, which were passed through a ring on the pomelion of the gun and were attached to ring bolts on the ship's side, at each side of the gun port. The breeching held the gun from rolling backwards across the deck, and checked its recoil when fired. The motion of a ship could make the recoil unpredictable, allowing the gun's leap back to severely wound or even kill a man. Many suffered in this manner. Even more dangerous was a gun that broke loose and ran wildly across the deck, gathering sufficient motion on a steep roll to crash through the ship's sides.

To fire the gun, a powder-filled cartridge was rammed down the bore followed by the ball and then by a wad by which ball and cartridge were rammed tight together. Flame from a lighted match or a flintlock spark was applied through a vent. Before reloading the bore had to be cleaned of any hot detritus that remained. First it was scraped then a sponge was thrust down the bore. These tasks were dangerous for the sailor doing them because he had to at least partly lean out of the port to get his instruments down the bore. He thus made himself a target for French sharpshooters. Swift, deft skill was necessary.

Shot was not explosive but the damage and carnage it could wreak was nevertheless huge. For the men one of the nastiest aspects of shot was splinters. More men were said to be killed by splinters than by shot itself. Surprisingly, the effect in close action was said to be less than from afar. In close action the velocity of the cannonball was so great that in penetrating the ship's side few or no splinters were torn off. A spent ball from distance produced innumerable splinters, all flying like so many daggers. Instead of neatly holing the ship's side it shattered the wood and tore it apart widely and extensively, creating more splinters. The proportion of wounded to killed was estimated to be four to one in distant action against three to one in close action.

Two small chained balls and bar shot, like doubled-headed barbells, were used to damage masts and rigging. Grapeshot was also fired to kill crew. The injury and havoc that all of these could inflict was horrifying. In its path across a crowded deck a ball could in sequence decapitate one man, cut another body in half, remove limbs from others before smashing into the ship itself.

The American War had seen a new form of armament delivered to the Royal Navy. This was a gun invented in Scotland in 1779 and called the carronade or, popularly, the 'smasher'. It was a short, light carriage gun designed to take a large ball, equivalent to long-gun shot. It had been designed as a weapon for merchant ships, but the navy seized upon it. The large ball propelled by a small charge of powder had short range, making it essentially a weapon for close contact, in which its effect was powerfully destructive. As breaking the line had renewed the possibility of close contact, the carronade would seem to have arrived as a perfect match for this newly licensed tactic. The forecastle and poop or quarterdeck became its natural lodging places.

The carronade was one British technical contribution to naval warfare of the late eighteenth century, but the Royal Navy still lagged behind its rivals in naval architecture and proficiency of design. French naval architecture had been ahead since the days of Colbert's navy. Already before the end of the seventeenth century Jesuit scientists had been investigating the resistance of bodies moving through water of different forces. In 1681 conferences were called in Paris to promote naval architecture on a scientific basis. Subsequently Paul Hoste, professor of mathematics at Toulon, began investigating a range of vital questions. These included speed and resistance, the lines of the hull, stability and stowage and other such studies. By 1750 the French Société Royale des Sciences was offering prizes on an international level for contributions to marine science and design. The French government involved itself closely with the whole field of inquiry, out of which came new insight into speed and water resistance along different lines of hull formation, particularly at bow and stern.

Such scientific pursuit had never been as common to Britain as with the French. Ships had been built according to tradition, or by the few who made themselves masters of the art. Stability, the flow of water upon bows and stern, the complexities of size and weight, the mysteries of proportionate length and beam, were not questions of zealous pursuit. They were mysteries left to the genius of those who rose as undisputed masters of the craft. In Britain, as late as 1711, a noted shipwright of the Portsmouth and Deptford Yards could write 'our art can only be allowed notional, and the safest way of building and equipping will be to go to precedent, if there be any to be found. But . . . tis very customary, that let a ship be fitted never so well by one hand, it will not suit the temper of another. Besides, the proper business of a shipwright is counted a very vulgar imploy, and which a man of indifferent qualifications may be master of.'

Shortly before the American War the British began doing what the French had long done, copper-sheathing their ships against worm and decay. Efforts were simultaneously made to improve ventilation, reinforce structure and improve sail patterns.

A particular defect of many British ships was the low placement of their lowest gun deck. The 100-gun *Victory* had its midship guns just four feet six inches above the water. The midship sills of 80-gun French ships could be nearly eight feet above the water, even when loaded with stores for five months and near 400 tons of water. Low gun ports meant that in high seas they shipped the seas on a roll and had to be closed.

The French and the Spanish also built bigger. Size brought architectural advantages. Gun ports were wider, adding length to the ships and proportionate beam. The balance achieved greater buoyancy, and faster sailing. The Spanish had traditionally been first with size. They continued to set the example. They built higher out of the water, and broader. The proportions of their newer ships, in breadth especially, provided superior buoyancy. When British officers first boarded a French 120-gun they were astonished at the thickness of the sides which seemed impenetrable to shot.

The French, throughout the eighteenth century, continued to forge ahead in experiment and design. The British, ironically, were to become perhaps the principal beneficiary of that. 'The navy of Britain, like that of Rome, has been improved by copying from their enemies,' said the contemporary naval historian Edward Brenton in his work on the Great War. For, he said, the French and Spanish ships were 'generally superior to those of England, both in size, weight of metal, and number of men, out sailing them in fleets, and often in single ships, carrying their guns higher out of the water . . .'

Against recognition of some advance in ship design, a *Naval Chronicle* writer nevertheless saw a dead end: 'The size of ships seems now to have reached nearly its ultimatum.'[3] The French had built what they regarded as the largest ship but she had been pronounced unfit for service. The Spanish were said to have built one even larger but, with so little faith in her as she set out, two ships were sent out to tow her back in again. It seemed nature herself had fixed the limits of such big ships for 'It is *man* who is to navigate and manage them; and unless our bodily strength could be increased likewise, every manoeuvre on board them must be conducted with difficulty and delay ... The cordage, when made larger, will be rendered difficult to pass through the pulleys, and so large, at last, as not to pass at all. Timber, the growth of nature, as much as man, cannot be made to grow larger ... And let it be remembered, as a certain axiom in mechanics, that what we gain in *power* we must be contented to lose in *time*. Every operation on board will therefore become laborious, dilatory, and even uncertain.'

This reaction to the idea of maritime progress having reached its tidal mark reads strangely for a time of accelerating technology and visible industrial change on land. It was, however, a common view and one that was evident in much of the nautical writing of the time. Nevertheless, British concern with the science of naval architecture took life rapidly with the start of the Great War. The dilemmas that lay upon maritime improvement had become suddenly too great to avoid deep and systematic consideration. The ocean could hardly remain entirely severed from the spirit of the age.

Fast voyages were not unfamiliar. During the Great War the remarkable passage of the frigate *Arethusa* was recorded. She covered the 2,400-mile passage from Vera Cruz to England in nine days. The perplexed comment was 'It would be a fit subject of investigation, in what degree this remarkable velocity is attributable to physical or to mechanical causes.' Another remarkable passage was that of the merchantman *Pacific*, which crossed from New York to Liverpool in twelve days. But such fast voyages were usually the result of a constant rate of speed under varying conditions of wind and weather rather than bursts of very high speed in favourable conditions.

A new body, the Society for the Improvement of Naval Architecture, began experiments 'to ascertain the laws respecting bodies moving through the water with different velocities'. The inventor and zealously reform-minded Earl Stanhope, an early experimenter with steam navigation (and husband to Pitt's eccentric sister, Hester), was a driving force behind the society which between 1793 and 1798 undertook some ten thousand experiments in ship form, at bow, midships and stern, 'of all kinds of navigable vessels'. In its first report the definitions of water pressures, friction and resistance were written by Stanhope.

The emphasis was upon speed, and thereby form and stability. The French had already published notable papers on form and resistance. The British, through men like Stanhope, began to follow. But for both sides it would continue to prove an essentially frustrating exercise, demonstrating that with speed they could go only so far and discernibly not much further under sail. The French ships were stronger and they were faster, but they, like all the others, were still held in the slow, restraining grip that affected form and speed under sail. The slender, sharp-ended, sea-breaching power of the clipper ship bearing grain and passengers in commercial race through the Roaring Forties was still more than half a century away.

As Howard Chapelle declared in his exhaustive inquiry *The Search for Speed under Sail*, what anyone looking back from the modern age had to understand was the far greater complexity of wind propulsion set against mechanical propulsion. Sail power could not be expressed in terms of mechanical power because the velocity of wind was never constant for long. Wind could increase and decrease almost constantly over a wide area of sea and under certain conditions and points of sailing the individual sails could be distorted by wind pressure or produce interference with each other by cutting off wind from another sail or creating eddies: 'Aerodynamic forces, for the calculation of which there are no real constants, make the sailing rig of a vessel impossible to estimate in terms of comparative horsepower or in any other reasonably precise quantitative measurement.'[4]

The relatively small driving power of sail meant that the hull design had to be that which drove most easily with the least wind. But the multiple varieties of wind strength meant that there simply did not exist one ideal hull form to suit all. It was gradually understood that the length of the hull influenced the speed of a vessel. That, in turn, required elements such as the bows and stern and deadrise in the midsection, all of which involved hydrodynamics, to be allied to design.

As with all modern wars, of which the Great War was truly the first, invention flourished where it was immediately required.

Chapelle sums it up: 'Designers and builders now had economic reasons for improved design, construction, and fitting. A new era of great shipbuilding and design activity began; perhaps one of the most productive in American maritime history.' Here was where the great epoch of the clipper ship had its inception, where eighteenth-century sail began to fold into that of the nineteenth century.

American shipbuilding began to boom along the shores of the Chesapeake after the Great War began, with an emphasis upon fast schooners. Once they got going, the British were constantly experimenting with ideas – some sound, some erratic and some simply ahead of their time. New forms of sail were tested, underwater bow-fitted shields were suggested for breaking the power of waves thereby enabling a ship to travel faster, hollow iron masts were proposed accompanied by the idea that 'even the whole hull may be made of wrought iron', and whole new experimental vessels were attempted.

Whatever all sides might come up with on new hull and sail patterns, for Britain and the other belligerents it all still came back to the crisis more pressing than any other – the availability of wood. For Britain the problem was growing every day. Before even thinking of new construction, however, there sat the question of maintaining the existing fleet, and at the heart of that was decay. Of all the problems that wood entailed the worst for those at sea was the slow disintegration of their ships. It was a problem as old as seagoing. But in this war the demand laid upon the Royal Navy was for extended sea time to a greater degree than ever before, and it became steadily more extended as the war progressed. Ships stayed out for long periods without overhaul. Existing decay advanced more rapidly under those circumstances. There were many additional causes, however, for the increasingly swift deterioration of British naval vessels.

Shipboard decay was affected by the natural quality of the wood with which they were built, the condition of the material when used, the care taken in building the ships and, not least, the treatment of the vessels in service.

Dry rot, a fungus infestation that reduced timber to powder, had always been a curse of wood. There were particular shipboard reasons for its exist-ence and active life. Those were many, some of which were impossible to prevent. Foreign wood was usually found to be more susceptible to dry rot than domestic. Wood from both the Baltic and North America was floated down long rivers from the interior on rafts. That months-long saturation in water could change the state of the wood, which was further affected by long exposure to frost or snow after being landed. The effects of this were enlarged when ships were built without shelter and their frames and fittings exposed to ever-changing weather.

Venice had long set example by building its ships under cover, inside sheds, where they were also kept when laid up. The Swedes and the French also built under cover. Such ships often existed many years without mark of decay. Saturation with water on river journeys and extended exposure in dockyards meant that wood fibres lost their natural texture and became porous. Early stages of dry rot could set in. The pores never closed again, allowing the wood to absorb the damp and stagnant air of the ship's interior. Apart from the risk of dry rot being present in new wood used in building a ship, a frequent and fatal habit was to repair or build ships with wood taken out of old, laid-up vessels. Dry rot in such wood could infect the entire ship.

The near-futile battle against decay that the British navy struggled with during the Great War was described by a Plymouth shipbuilder, Isaac Blackburn, in his *A Treatise on the Science of Ship-Building; with observations on the British Navy; the extraordinary Decay of the Men of War.* Published at the end of the Great War, it offered a particularly grim portrait of the atmosphere that had to be taken for granted by those who had to live for long periods within wooden walls: 'The exhalations from bilgewater, when ships are not pumped out frequently, are extremely noxious: pure water let in often has a very salubrious tendency, both with respect to the ship and the health of the crews; hence why leaky ships are found to be so sweet and healthy. The foetid air from the warm breaths of a numerous crew, and from the filth and dirt below, the closeness of the different storerooms and cabins, and the want of a circulation of pure air, operates most destructively on our ships; and the wet pent up in the timbers in foul stagnant air changes its nature, and fills the pores of the timbers with putrifying and corrupt matter, and brings on that most fatal of all causes of the decay of our ships – the dry-rot.'[5]

Dry rot had particular affinity for the part of the ship just above the water line, where exposure constantly alternated between air and water, where strain was greatest and where, within the ship, the air remained heavily stagnant. This was where leaks most frequently originated. And with that, in turn, lay the source of countless mysterious tragedies of the sea in the global era of sail.

Frequently during that great span, when sail was distributed across all the oceans, vessels would be met at sea with no living soul on board. On those occasions when survivors were found their usual story was that the ship had sprung a leak and that, in spite of all their efforts to pump, the water had risen too fast and they had taken to the boats. Why a ship remained afloat after all was sometimes explained by empty casks in her hold or some other factor of unforeseen buoyancy, such as a cargo like sugar dissolving. But the number of drifting, empty vessels was probably small against the uncountable number of vessels that foundered because their timbers leaked and the leak became a rush of water that took the ship down, never to be heard of again.

VI

SHIPBOARD

THE late-eighteenth-century man-of-war of the Royal Navy contained a shipboard society that stands as the most distinctive of its kind in naval history, if only because of the tremendous burden that the Great War of 1793–1815 laid upon its ships.

Two decades of continuous service, frequently endured with scarcely any relief by the ships and the men who sailed them, was the relentless hardship laid upon most of Britain's warships, whether in home waters, the Mediterranean or elsewhere. Instead of comparable sea time, the ships of the French and Spanish navies were too frequently blockaded for long periods in their home ports.

For the British sailors the Great War's sea time in all its various phases became an endurance of mind and body, of will and patience, and a required faith in mission and self, beyond anything that any other form of dutiful service demanded. The burden of it was a great deal more than merely prolonged time. The confinement of their sea days was for too many an ordeal of hardship and torment which, for long after, remained as a dark stain upon the naval record.

While much of that was broadly true, it was nevertheless a sweeping condemnation of the worst without offering any of what could and did sometimes alleviate it.

Those in any position of authority had before them a ready and obediently mute human assembly upon which they could wilfully project all their inner dissatisfaction with themselves or the world. Life aboard ship intensified the particular conflict of changing outlook that marked the time. As the principal instrument of the island nation's survival the Royal Navy evolved into the most rigorous form of military discipline in the world, the severity of which increased rather than diminished as the war progressed. The hard codes of duty and obedience were naturally accepted by all who served in the navy. Its commanders, even those of the most equable manner and disposition, saw them as the necessary instrument of discipline. Their minds were trained to it. But the new radicalism of late-eighteenth-century society infiltrated everywhere, even within those wooden walls so resolutely defiant of any assault upon custom and tradition.

The social structure of a ship of the Great War began with the fundamental division of quarterdeck and lower deck, meaning officers and the others, though with many shadings within the two groups and between them.

On top were the admirals, the principal of whom would be in wartime the commander in chief of any large fleet such as the Western Squadron in home waters, a Mediterranean fleet or a West Indies one. Aboard the flagship of a principal fleet the admiral would have beside him a captain of the fleet, a position distinct from that of captain of the ship. The captain of the fleet was the one upon whom the commander in chief principally depended for agreement or advice on tactical manoeuvre or decisions during action. Aboard a flagship the ship's own captain was therefore in a subservient position. The tactical control of the ship was out of his hands. But in all other circumstances a captain was as absolute in his command of the ship and the tight community within it as any feudal baron in his moated castle. He could be a monster without equal to those who served below him, or a hero for whom they were willing to die. The rest fell somewhere in between. But most captains probably stood more or less at the middle, capable of harsh discipline but ruled overall by their need to maintain a steady, responsibly functioning ship under harshly changing circumstances, and to do so best by avoiding a mood of insubordination and, with that, a reputation for incompetence among those who mattered.

A captain bore the weight of many different roles he might be called to fulfil, atop of mere command of his ship. Apart from their function in line battle, captains could also be called upon to undertake critical land actions, small boat actions, night coastal assaults, and, in sudden switch, ambassadorial missions. Such captains might peremptorily be named commodore and elevated to rear admiral status for command of squadrons detached from the fleet, or sent on special mission, such as would often fall to Nelson. With mission accomplished such a commodore would revert to captain's rank.

A harsh social profile of the quarterdeck by a naval officer was to appear near the close of the Great War. It is an account strongly affected by evangelical moralizing but it nevertheless helps to convey the ever-present tensions and social composition that was so distinctive to the Royal Navy:

The lieutenant and midshipman, who are subject to the vilest abuse from their superiors, suffer a mental degradation that in time unfits them for their situation; the spirited and gentlemanly officer seldom dares to bring his superior to a court-martial, or call him to private account, the first stops his promotion, the latter ensures him a disgraceful end . . . The power invested in the different captains, of appointing their midshipmen, has probably been the most abused. Numbers of improper men, sometimes from the worst classes of foremast men, have been thrust into the society of gentlemen; this has contributed more than any other cause, to the vulgarity of manners and ideas but too common; undoubtedly many respectable officers have been before the mast; but . . . a favourite quarter master, coxswain, or cabinet maker are generally selected; these men, athletic, powerful, and overbearing, soon acquire an influence highly injurious with their weaker and more youthful companions; the oaths, vulgarities and abusive language of the forecastle, the pugilistic contests of blackguards . . . owe their introduction to this class . . . it is from this cause we so frequently find the descendants of noble families vying with the vulgar in the meanest debauchery, and the still more ruinous vice of drunkenness. Few captains are anxious for the improvement of young men committed to their care . . . many abandon them to the caprice of their lieutenants, often still more unfit, and frequently jealous of the talents or interest of the younger officer.[1]

In an age where society was rigidly classified by class the quarterdeck of a man-of-war was principally drawn from the upper levels, though not entirely so. In France and Spain officers had almost exclusively meant the aristocracy. In Britain it meant gentry more than aristocracy. And gentry itself was a wide swathe that fetched up in many diverse corners of gentle-born society. Nelson's background, although possessing high social connections, was nevertheless that of remote and modest country parsonage. Officers naturally included many from the aristocracy, including the royal family, as well as from all the professional classes; from business and commerce and, of course, from navy itself, from those bearing a family tradition of generations of naval service. They also came in from the merchant marine, whose social standing was certainly lower than that of the navy. But the quarterdeck also occasionally drew officers from its lower deck, from the 'working class'. That was testament to an outlook that saw naval requirement as the priority above all else. It became particularly true under the demands of the Great War. A seaman of outstanding character and ability could be elevated, if he got the attention of a sympathetic captain.

'Tarpaulin' was the word for such an officer. A memorable description of one of them was offered by one of the Great War's most renowned seamen, Thomas Cochrane, who, on joining his first ship, found the first lieutenant on deck 'dressed in the garb of a seaman, with marlin-spike slung round his neck and a lump of grease in his hand, and was busily engaged in setting up the rigging'.

That could not have happened in either the French or the Spanish navies. Furthermore, the principle of it, of being able if necessary to do the seaman's job, was regarded as important. Nelson's first lieutenant aboard *Victory* at Trafalgar, John Quilliam, had risen from the lower deck. So had his signal lieutenant, John Pasco, who would later hoist the historic signal, 'England expects . . .'

For most, the journey on to the quarterdeck started at a very young age – anything from seven years onwards. One captain took his son on board at the age of three; Nelson was twelve when he went in. Routes of entry varied. Nelson, for example, joined the navy through 'interest', which meant having some close connection in the navy, usually a senior serving officer, or managing it through influence in high quarters. Either way, at the end of the route stood the captain, upon whom the hopeful depended for his place. Admiralty appointed a ship's commissioned and warrant officers but the captain could additionally take into his ship anyone he wanted. Those he picked were the boys who, under his initial guidance, would help form the officer corps of the future. They were moulded into midshipmen who, after at least six years of sea service and examination on essential matters, might be commissioned as lieutenant. Those who for some reason or another failed to pass on could find themselves at middle age still in the midshipmen's mess.

A midshipman already at sea and expecting to move upward received careful admonition on what not to lose sight of:

You are by this time fully acquainted, not only with the names, but the use and direction of every rope in the ship; and have long since, to use the seaman's term, 'paid your footing' in each top; for it is in the tops, and on the mast heads, that you must qualify yourself thoroughly to understand the duties of a working seaman; a knowledge absolutely necessary to make yourself respectable as an officer in their eyes . . . unless the seaman thinks that you are equally acquainted with his minor duties, that in case of emergency you could take his place on the yard, or assist him in knotting a shroud, or splicing a cable, he would be apt to think lightly of your other qualifications, valuable as they really are, because he finds you deficient in those which more immediately come within the sphere of his own comprehension.[2]

A ship of the line carried from three to eight lieutenants, ranked according to the dates of their commissions. The first lieutenant was, effectively, the commander of the ship. Day and night, he was responsible for the proper running of it, the discipline, order, maintenance, navigation, the whole general state of it. His duties were ceaseless, his vigilance all-embracing. With such a load lying upon him, the first lieutenant was understandably often the harshest shipboard tyrant of them all.

After the lieutenants came the warrant officers. They were the master, surgeon, purser and chaplain. Ships sometimes also carried a schoolmaster to continue the education of the boys. They had no official rank. The warrant officers were all quarterdeck and dined in the wardroom. The principal of them was the master. He was the real navigating officer of the ship. Upon him lay full responsibility for the ship's course. He ordered the sail that was carried and in battle directed the manoeuvring of the vessel. He took the ship's daily position and in unfamiliar waters guided her using such charts as he possessed.

The master's control of the sailing of the ship meant that his position was special. He had an independence on board that no one else under the captain possessed. The lieutenants had no control over him. He could challenge a captain's orders if he felt he saw error. This could be so particularly in action if he judged the ship to be moving into dangerous exposure to the enemy, or to a position of hampered manoeuvrability. The master was also in charge of the ship's water, its ballast and the loading and supervision of its stores. He was assisted by master's mates.

The purser was one to whom history has never been kind. As the man in charge of the ship's accounts, which meant the provisioning of the ship, he accounted for the essential domestic wellbeing of the vessel. That provided practically limitless scope for fraud, fully exercised by the worst villains. Pursers got rich by buying the lowest quality stores, cutting supplies of firewood and tallow, and adulterating wine and grog. He had a percentage on tobacco sales and on 'slops', the clothing and bedding that a sailor might require if in need of replacement. The purser kept the ship's muster book, which carried the name of every person on board. This book was referred to whenever the crew was mustered, usually every ten days and always after action. The muster book allowed free play with the wages of those transferred from the ship without receiving their wages, those who deserted and those who were killed. By keeping names in the book the purser could collect wages due to the person.

Another category of warrant officers was those who were not of wardroom or quarterdeck standing, including the master-at-arms, carpenter, sailmaker and the cook. The principal of these, however, were the gunner and the boatswain.

The gunner was the man in charge of the guns, the ordnance and ammunition and gunnery instruction. The boatswain had the broadest range of duties on board. Together with his boatswain's mates he effectively ran the daily functioning of the ship. He was responsible for the boats, the sails, the rigging, the anchors and chains, all of which he had to maintain in good order. He was the principal overseer of the seamen, the day-long embodiment of discipline. The boatswain and his mates were often the most detested of all figures of discipline aboard ship. With them rested the practice of 'starting', which in a hard ship was relentlessly constant. With their rattans and rope's ends the boatswain and the boatswain's mates beat the seamen into doubling their pace even as they rushed to fulfil their tasks. Those who were the last to clamber into the shrouds got the worst of it. They could expect the same again when they came down. Where it was habitual, starting could accompany practically every activity, hoisting sail, hoisting boats in and out, hoisting in supplies. The prolonged torment of starting on such occasions was described in one account: '. . . when they were not done with smartness, the captain stationed the boatswain's mates at different parts of the deck, each with a rope's end, with orders to beat every man as he passed them . . . Thus, whether good or bad, whether old or young, whether exerting himself or not, nearly every man in the ship got a beating. Sometimes these evolutions were frequently repeated, for the sake of exercise and order; and I have seen them last so long, that when done, the whole ship's company were lying about the decks like so many hard-hunted greyhounds.' And for the beaten it was 'forbid even to *look* displeased, as that is "Contempt" or "Disrespect"'.

To those who fell foul of an ill-tempered captain, fear had to be their guide. That stood for his officers as well as the men. He could make or break the officers. The men he could literally break, with flogging by the 'cat'. A dozen lashes was supposedly the minimum that a captain might inflict but, while there were those captains who sought to avoid all flogging where possible, there were the others who decided lashes in number that suited their disposition of the moment, with three to four dozen lashes by no means unusual.

For the ordinary sailor, punishment could be arbitrary. Some of it is described in a notably severe criticism of naval discipline published in 1813 by an officer, Lieutenant Thomas Hodgskin, who wrote, 'At a very early age I went to sea, with my head full of stories of the valour, generosity, and chivalric spirit of sailors . . . much was I disappointed at finding one universal system of terror – no obedience but what was forced – no respect but what was constrained.'[3]

Hodgskin was particularly agitated by abuse of the twenty-seventh Article of War, which threatened the severest punishment for any duty negligently performed:

I have seen it acted upon, that no such thing as an accident could happen; consequently, any misfortune must have arisen in some person's neglect, and some person must be punished to prevent its recurrence . . . Some of the iron allotted to a man to polish does not shine well; his hammock has not been clean scrubbed; his clues have not been blacked; his clothes have wanted mending; his shirt has been dirty;

or perhaps he may have neglected the captain's stock, or the wardroom dinner: these, and a thousand similar trifles, are what seamen are flogged for, as neglect of duty. The captain's orders have made doing these things their duty; and custom sanctions his inflicting flogging for their neglect. No person who reads over these items for which sailors are flogged, whether sailor or not, must know greater part of them have no real value in themselves; they have a beginning in the captain's will, and when he is pleased their utility ends.[4]

Occasionally, though not often, retribution caught up with particularly tyrannical commanders. One case of the sort of wilful, fastidious punishment that Hodgskin complained about resulted in the dismissal of the captain, Sir Edward Hamilton. Before going ashore Hamilton had ordered the gunner to clean the quarterdeck guns and carronades but when he returned he swore that his orders had not been complied with, damned the gunner as a rascal and ordered him and four of his men to be tied up in the shrouds in 'cold frosty weather'. The first lieutenant told Hamilton's court martial that the guns appeared to him to have been remarkably well cleaned. The gunners had remained tied up until the surgeon intervened on their behalf. It is reasonable to suppose that the action of the surgeon and the unhesitant corroboration of the first lieutenant indicated a broader state of tyranny than that single incident. Hamilton had been at sea since the age of seven.[5]

One custom especially abhorrent to Hodgskin was that of flogging all of the men involved in a particular task aloft: '. . . such as the main topsail-yard men, etc., if they were last at executing a part of their duty, or if, in the captain's opinion, they stood conspicuous for neglect . . . This custom . . . yet has, the evil effect of begetting hatred to the service . . . not many years have passed since I saw all the men stationed on the main-topsail-yard severely flogged for their dilatoriness.'[6]

Flogging was a dreadful, methodical business, designed properly to impress its awfulness upon all. The condemned was stripped to his waist and tied to a raised grating. The lashes were inflicted alternately by the boatswain and his mates, each apportioned a certain number of lashes to ensure that the force of the punishment was not mitigated by one man's arm grown weary. The cat's tails were an inch thick and two feet long.

If the offence was considered to deserve more severe punishment the man was held for court martial ashore, where the view of misdemeanour was, if anything, even harsher.

The most horrendous form of punishment was for those landed for trial at the naval stations and then sentenced to be flogged around the fleet. The sufferer was tied to a grating or some such support erected in a boat and borne from ship to ship, with drums beating the Rogue's March. The crews of all the ships were massed on deck to observe. The sentence could be anything from two hundred to five hundred lashes. It was inflicted in portions beside every ship, with a boatswain's mate from each vessel descending to perform the allotted share there. Against these ordeals hanging was merciful, for no one could survive whole in mind and body such a prolonged annihilation of spirit and self. If they did not subsequently die from shock and torment, they would be maimed for life. As examples of these, a sentence of two hundred lashes round the fleet was given for 'skylarking', during which the sentenced man's companion was accidentally killed, and the same for a shipboard crime of having robbed a fellow seaman of a blue jacket and trousers, sold them, 'and gotten drunk'. These were by no means unusual.

One of the sharpest accounts of life aboard a late-eighteenth-century ship-of-war is that of a youth, Samuel Leech, who went to sea expecting to become a midshipman and instead found himself as merely a boy on the lower deck. He gives a disturbing description of a flogging:

The boatswain's mate is ready, with coat off and whip in hand. The captain gives the word. Carefully spreading the cords with the fingers of his left hand, the executioner throws the cat over his right shoulder; it is brought down upon the now uncovered Herculean shoulders of the man. His flesh creeps – it reddens as if blushing at the indignity; the sufferer groans; lash follows lash, until the first mate, wearied with the cruel employment, gives place to a second. Now two dozen of these dreadful lashes have been inflicted: the lacerated back looks inhuman; it resembles roasted meat burnt nearly black before scorching fire; yet still the lashes fall; the captain continues merciless. Vain are the cries and prayers of the wretched man . . . Four dozen strokes have cut up his flesh and robbed him of all self-respect; there he hangs, a pitied, self-despised, groaning, bleeding wretch; and now the captain cries, forbear! . . . and the hands sullenly return to their duties.[7]

Leech's account, written later in life, had this to say on the consequences of flogging: 'One of two results always follows. The victim either lives on, a lone, dark-minded, broken-spirited man, despising himself and hating everyone, because he thinks every one hates him; or he lives with one fearful, unyielding purpose . . . REVENGE. I have heard them swear – and the wild flashing eye, the darkly frowning brow, told how firm was the intent – that if ever they should be in battle, they would shoot their officers. I have seen them rejoice over the misfortunes of their persecutors, but more especially at their death.'

As might have been expected, under Nelson's command flogging was a rarity. He similarly went to any length to avoid hanging a man. Of equal standing in model behaviour towards his seamen was Captain Cuthbert Collingwood, later Admiral Lord Collingwood. This was Nelson's close friend from his earliest days at sea and his second in command at Trafalgar. He survived Nelson by five years.

Collingwood, like Nelson, provided a model example of how a ship of the line could be run with fullest discipline but without resort to brutality and abuse. A year could pass aboard his ship without a flogging and when he did order a flogging it was for serious reason, and the lashes were few.

Collingwood substituted a variety of punishments for the lash, such as watering the offender's grog or extra duty. He never used coarse language with his men and forbade it from his officers. 'If you do not know a man's name,' he told them, 'call him sailor, and not you-sir, and such other appellations; they are offensive and improper.' When the men were sick he visited them daily and nourished them from his own table. The same consideration was extended to his officers. It was little wonder that free-flowing tears accompanied his departure when he changed ship, as was the case with Nelson, and the many others who behaved similarly: they were not simply a few, but certainly they were not the majority.

Tyranny aboard a late-eighteenth-century man-of-war could be widely distributed through the vessel, and not merely from the quarterdeck. Where a captain might be lenient, punishment could come on the demand of his lieutenants. Often the frequency was due to bad temper. 'These severities filled our crew with discouragement,' Leech said. 'A sailor dreads the dishonour of the lash. Some, urged by a nice sense of honour, have preferred death to its endurance. I have heard of one man who actually overloaded himself with shot and deliberately walked overboard. Among our ship's company the effects of these severe measures showed themselves in frequent desertions . . . some ran off when ashore with the boats, others dropped overboard in the night, and either swam on shore or were drowned.'

The malice of an ill-tempered officer, once attracted, could manifest itself endlessly in all sorts of ways that broke the spirit or simply humiliated. Midshipmen, too, could be vicious tyrants. Mere boys, they frequently liked, as small masters, to exercise the authority that rank allowed them. Seamen hated them for that. 'Those little minions of power drove me round like a dog' was how Leech described them. The midshipmen of *Ramillies* were described as 'being of a most cruel and vindictive disposition'. But midshipmen themselves could be victims of severe punishment. 'I have seen,' wrote a master's mate, 'young men of the highest respectability . . . unmercifully flogged, on the bare back, at the publick gangway; brought there but too often, not from their own impropriety, but from the malice of a superior, who, fiend like, poisons the mind of his captain, and then works their disgrace.' The common punishment for midshipmen was mast-heading. Here the offender was sent to the topmast or the topgallant cross-trees, to remain there for hours, even twenty-four hours, in all weathers, themselves dependent there upon the topmen sailors for food and drink.

The cost of unrelenting shipboard tyranny and the other harsh circumstances that accompanied resulted in massive desertion throughout the war. Men deserted wherever opportunity presented itself, in foreign ports, even those of Barbary, and to all other naval flags. As in the Dutch wars, they even went to the enemy, to the French (a few British sailors were fighting aboard the French flagship at Trafalgar). But the most popular choice was the United States, and the Americans made every effort to lure British seamen when they could to help man their own growing navy. The astounding scale of desertion was revealed in figures for one period between May 1803 and June 1805, when more than thirteen thousand seamen walked away, the majority of them among the finest, being both able seamen and ordinary seamen.

Wise instinct nevertheless decreed that there had to be at least a small break to the hardness of the shipboard regime. This came on Sunday which, as Leech affirmed, was a day of revelry rather than worship. And, once a year, the whole rigid structure broke down entirely and dramatically: '. . . at Christmas our ship presented a scene such as I had never imagined. The men were permitted to have their "full swing". Drunkenness ruled the ship. Nearly every man, with most of the officers, were in a state of beastly intoxication at night. Here, some were fighting, but were so insensibly drunk, they hardly knew whether they struck the guns or their opponents; yonder, a party were singing libidinous or bacchanalian songs, while all were laughing, cursing, swearing or hallooing; confusion reigned in glorious triumph; it was the very chaos of humanity.'

Were sailors such outright ruffians and laggards that they deserved the consistently vile treatment that so many suffered?

The sailor was admired for his bravery but not for his morals. But contemporary pronouncements on matelot vice were heavily influenced by the rising evangelical fervour of the time. For the evangelicals the ship-of-war was simply an extension of the brawling, gin-sodden and prostitute-enlivened scene in every naval dockyard. On board the ship lucky to be moored at Plymouth or Portsmouth a riotously bawdy scene prevailed. As Leech, a youth pronouncedly evangelical in outlook, indignantly described it, 'Bad as things are at sea, they are worse in port. There, boat-loads of defiled and defiling women are permitted to come alongside; the men, looking over the side, select whoever best pleases his lustful fancy, and by paying her fare, he is allowed to take her and keep her on board as his paramour, until the ship is once more ordered to sea.'

As with practically everything else, there could be no easy generalization on the social character of the eighteenth-century seaman. For, like the social origins of the quarterdeck, the lower-deck sailors, too, came from a variety of backgrounds. Well into the war their usual shipboard composition could be described as 'a proportion of seamen and the rest landsmen of all denominations'.

Although the late-eighteenth-century sailor had no prescribed uniform he was easily identifiable, for there was certain uniformity in the manner of dress when going ashore. The sailor then usually wore a short blue jacket with brass buttons down the right side and on the cuffs. His shirt was popularly one of blue and white horizontal stripes, like that of a modern Russian sailor. The shirt collar was wide, with a black silk handkerchief loose around the throat. Gaudy yellow or scarlet waistcoats were worn under the jacket, decorated with collared ribbons. Trousers were white, and floppily loose. White stockings and tight black shoes completed the picture. Unlike the nineteenth-century sailors who followed him, the sailor of the Great War was clean-shaven. But perhaps his most distinctive feature was his queue, or pigtail, with the hair heavily greased and tightly bound with a black ribbon.

Apart from the boys who went into the navy as prospective midshipmen and officers, other boys were brought in from an institution known as the Marine Society, which took in waifs and orphans. These boys went into the navy either as 'apprentices' or as 'servants'. Apprentices could be trained up to be gunners, carpenters or other such ratings. The servants became real servants to the officers. Other boys and young men entered the navy as volunteers because it was the life they fancied.

Arrival on board for newcomers was an intimidating experience. That this was a world of iron discipline of a special character was immediately apparent as the confinement of those wooden walls closed in. On those crowded decks every man was seen to be moving at the double, driven by the boatswain and his mates. Every man had his task, his place, from which there was no deviation. Samuel Leech gave a description that sprang directly from the new industrial age burgeoning around him: 'A vessel of war contains a little community . . . governed by laws peculiar to itself . . . when its members first come together, each one is assigned his respective station and duty . . . each task has its man, and each man his place. A ship contains a set of *human* machinery, in which every man is a wheel, a band, or a crank, all moving with wonderful regularity and precision to the *will* of its machinist – the all-powerful captain.'

The strength of intimacy, of loyalty, affection and mutual support within those many small individual groups of messmates aboard a man-of-war was, as many recounted, the bond that helped carry them through much that was unbearable. It was the family solace, the inviolable trust, the necessary dependence in a hostile and punitive world.

Eight seamen usually formed a mess, a berth between two guns. A mess table was lowered from its place secured to the beams above. This was the sailor's living space on board, when not on duty. Here at night he slung his hammock. He had two, one in use and a clean one in reserve. The allotted space for a hammock was supposed to be fourteen inches in width. An eighteenth-century scale drawing of the gun deck of a man-of-war shows the impossibility of this if fully exercised for the entire crew. The system was made possible by the fact of alternating watches.

When the boatswain's whistle piped them up in the morning, 'Up all hammocks ahoy', the sailors leaped from their hammocks, dressed themselves in seconds, lashed the hammock into a tight roll and then ran on deck to stow it in its allotted place with the others in the hammock nettings that ran round the upper decks. And hastened in all these efforts by the rope's end of the boatswain's mates. Then all to their duties. At noon dinner was piped and, at half-past, the sound of the fifer sounding a popular tune, immediately picked up by all, who went to draw their grog. This was the best moment of the day. Half an hour of merriment and back to work. At four p.m. supper and a second tot of rum or wine was served. Half an hour later all mustered at their stations, which were then meticulously inspected. When that was over the men ran down to collect their hammocks. At eight o'clock the first night-watch turned in, until called at midnight.

During the night the officer of the watch maintained strict lookout with one on each side of the bow, port bow and starboard bow, one on each gangway, and one on each quarter, those being the after parts of the ship close to the stern. The mate of the watch passed round every half-hour to see that the lookout men were awake and attentive to their duty. A midshipman went down every half-hour between decks to see that no improper light was burning and that all was quiet.

The ship was pumped out at four every morning. The rule was that there should never be more than eighteen inches of water in her, hard to sustain aboard a ship at sea for months on end through all types of weather. At four the decks were to be holystoned and washed. At daylight a man was sent to the main and fore topgallant mastheads to look out. The officer of the morning watch had to ensure that the sails were properly set, the sheets close home, the sails taut up and the yards well trimmed, with everything clear for making sail on other course at daylight if necessary. The captain of the forecastle, the gunner's mate and captain of the afterguard examined the rigging of the lower masts and yards, the captains of the tops everything above the tops, and a carpenter's mate the masts and yards as soon as the deck was washed. All these activities were reported to the officer of the watch, after which the rest of the ship was roused and the hammocks piped up and stowed, and a new full day began.

The eighteenth-century man-of-war was a natural vehicle for sickness and disease. It living spaces were badly ventilated. In fine weather canvas ventilators were rigged to pass fresh air below. But the uncertainties of weather and operations meant that this was sporadic. In some operational areas such as the Narrow Seas, ships were permanently battened down. The atmosphere of permanent damp became steadily more rancid from the spray and rain that entered, from leaking timbers and, not least, from condensation of the mass of men inside. Portable fires were burned in attempt to dry the interior, but the stench of this polluted air could not be dislodged. Below the main deck it lay heavily throughout, rising up from the bilges. The usual form of disinfectant was to wash decks and walls with vinegar. In that atmosphere disease nevertheless spread rapidly.

By the late eighteenth century it had become commonly realized that for the navy cleanliness was vital. Sailors were required to keep themselves as well as their clothes and sheets and blankets clean. The lower decks were cleaned every day, washed on Saturdays, but hygiene was a constant problem. Seasickness and other sickness could foul below. A large intake of impressed men meant that the seasick were vomiting wherever they found themselves. Dysentery created its own havoc, with men loosening their bowels before they could reach the heads to relieve themselves. There was harsh punishment for those who unobtrusively tried to do their 'dirt' in some corner of the lower decks. Regulations stipulated that the men 'are never to make water on the decks, or throw dirt of any kind on the gunwale, nor any out of the ports, as the head is the place for such purposes'.

When a lower deck had become drenched, stoves were lit and moved from place to place and no one allowed below until the deck was dry. Twice a week the men had to wash their clothes.

Much more now depended upon the surgeon than before. He was a man whose profession and standing had risen sharply by the time of the outbreak of the Great War. His craft had altered gradually through the eighteenth century from a rough business of sawing and sewing and trusting to luck for recovery to sawing and sewing accompanied by increasing enlightenment on some common diseases and on medical care. Even at its best, however, what was known was scarcely anything at all in modern terms.

The shocking fact remained that sickness and disease devastated the navy more than battle action ever could. In the American War of Independence 1,243 were killed against 18,541 who died of disease. In the Seven Years War it had been even worse, with 1,512 killed against 133,708 men lost to disease or desertion.[8] But during the Great War, the rate of such medical loss, though still appalling, diminished slowly but steadily.

Scurvy was a traditional affliction. From 1753, the single greatest benefit for seamen was the knowledge that scurvy had a cure, but it was only in

1795 that Admiralty ordered lemon juice to be issued to the whole crew
of a ship. That came at the insistence of Gilbert Blane, one of the small
number of physicians who left their notable mark upon naval health and
hygiene, and thereby saved innumerable lives. But daily intake of lemon
juice in the rum was by no means yet the end of scurvy; the risk remained
for long voyages.

The greatest killers of the eighteenth-century sailor were the tropical
fevers such as yellow fever and malaria that fell like an onslaught upon
ships arriving in the West Indies and other tropical operational areas. At
a time when it was believed that 'only bare conjectures' could be made on
the causes of fever, the most insightful proposition came from a celebrated
medical scientist, Dr James Lind, whose investigations into tropical diseases
persuaded him that to save men ships should lie as far as possible off
tropical coasts.

The acute manning problem that the navy continually faced made
the manpower loss through these diseases one of the most critical issues
confronting Admiralty. The pursuit of cure or remedy by medical men afloat
and ashore was ceaseless. Much of what was administered would be alarming
to our eyes, but for fever and malaria some were close to the mark.

A notable medication for fever was a tincture of cinchona, called Peruvian
tree bark, which would eventually become the source for quinine and other
anti-malarial alkaloids. Cinchona was used for medical purposes by Andean
Indians, and Jesuit missionaries passed it to Europe in the seventeenth
century. The bark was reduced to a powdered state. An early experiment
with Peruvian bark was undertaken by Leonard Gillespie, surgeon aboard
the sloop *Weasel* on a voyage to West Africa and the West Indies in 1787.[9]
Gillespie, in common with others at the time, believed that tropical downpour was dangerous to European constitutions. In the tropics Gillespie made
seamen coming on watch strip to the waist when it rained to enable them to
put on dry clothes when they came off watch. They also drank a dose of bark
in wine. Coming off watch they had to bathe in seawater before putting on
the dry clothes. They then took another dose of bark in wine. It was in its
way a strangely tentative combination of wildly speculative supposition with
ingestion of the unfamiliar. But that sort of experimentation was common.
Gillespie simultaneously insisted on total cleanliness and fresh air. The
ship was well ventilated throughout and below decks washed with vinegar.
Humidity was controlled with fires. A sick berth was established under the
forecastle and the sick were kept separated from those in health.

The system worked. *Weasel* arrived at Antigua after her eight-month
voyage from England without a sick man on board. Few had taken ill during
the voyage itself. Only one man had died since sailing from England.

Gillespie had morbid affirmation of his success through the performance of *Weasel*'s companion ship out of England, the 32-gun frigate *Minerva*, which had sailed a few days before *Weasel* to follow the same course. *Minerva*'s allocation of bark had been left behind to sail with *Weasel*. But since the ships never came together in West Africa *Minerva* never got her bark. In West African waters her crew, as was usual, came down heavily with fever. Her captain was among the victims.

It required another West African trial, in 1792 by the physician to the Royal Hospital at Greenwich, Dr Robertson, before Admiralty accepted that two daily doses of cinchona and wine should be issued to sailors who were sent ashore in West Africa. Cinchona bark thereafter became the medication common to the surgeon's shipboard dispensary in tropical seas.

To the modern mind few images can seem more appalling than that of a shipboard sick bay during an action, with the wounded coming down one after another with their torn and bleeding bodies. They were treated strictly in succession. Many therefore lay bleeding to death before the surgeon got to them. When he did, the crush of work around him meant that there was little time for decision on whether a limb might be saved. Amputation was the quickest solution. The patient was given a quick slug of rum and a thick leather gag put between his teeth. An assistant held the man as the surgeon amputated. Skill meant that the operation was mercifully swift. A primitive form of antiseptic was to draw the skin over the wound. That also helped stem the flow of blood, but blood was nevertheless everywhere, flowing in stream across the deck already soaked with it, lying thick on the clothes and arms of the surgeon and his assistants and splashed on everything in sight. All of this took place in circumstances as unhygienic as anything could be, with no sterilization of instruments or of the place where the patient lay. Gangrene and transmission of infections were a frequent consequence.

The courage and fortitude of the patients were remarkable. So was their recovery in these circumstances. They put body and duty together again with a promptness that is testament to their mental and physical powers of endurance. Mercifully, they usually got the best that the circumstances of their ship could offer. They were treated with consideration and got the best of the provisions on board.

The Royal Navy's disease-mortality death rate was three times that of ordinary Britons of comparable age: navy being 1 in 30.25 against the national mortality rate of 1 in 80. Set against that astonishing disparity was the fact that the Great War presented situations that aggravated the problem of maintaining shipboard health. There was, of course, the global range of the war and the long voyages it demanded. Unaccustomed land operations in unhealthy climates took their toll.

Feeding the deep-sea sailor had been an intractable problem since oceanic venture began, and continued to be through the eighteenth century. The basic diet was repellent and nutritionally barren. To the newcomer it was likely to be distasteful at first sight, whatever the circumstances of the man before he came to sea. The longer a ship stayed at sea without fresh provisioning the worse it got. It could hardly be otherwise with salted meat that might be years old, certainly many months, and stone-hard biscuit. Salt was the only means of preserving meat. It was barrelled and stored in the victualling warehouses until required. A ship taken out of service returned its meat to the warehouse, where it remained until reissued to another vessel. Darkened and hardened by age, these lumps bore little resemblance to meat. It required long soaking before the cook could do anything with it, by which time its resemblance to anything nutritious was nonexistent.

Biscuit presented a similarly sorry tale. It was baked in dockyard ovens from a mixture of wheat and pea flour. As it aged it bred weevils and, growing still older, the weevils metamorphosed into maggots. It was noted that the French, ever resourceful, had installed ovens to bake fresh bread daily. But there was no move to follow their example. Equally repugnant was the breakfast mess called 'burgoo', oatmeal boiled in the foul-tasting ship's water. An alternative breakfast was 'Scotch Coffee', burnt biscuit boiled in water to the consistency of paste. Midday dinner consisted of the salted meat and pea soup.

Small wonder, then, that the greatest moments of the day came with the issue of grog and wine or beer. Small wonder, too, that drunkenness and the obliteration that it brought of all that daily assaulted the sailor became the most zealously sought release. 'One of the greatest enemies to order and happiness in ships of war is drunkenness,' Samuel Leech wrote. 'To be drunk is considered by almost every sailor as the *acme* of sensual bliss . . . Hence it almost universally prevails. In our ship the men would get drunk, in defiance of every restriction.'

The drunkenness of sailors was indeed legendary. The quantity of liquor issued daily was considerable, albeit diluted with water. The sailor got either a gallon of beer, a pint of wine or half a pint of rum or brandy twice a day. Beer taken on board before the ship sailed was issued until it ran out. There was no issue of rum or brandy while beer lasted. Wine was usual in the Mediterranean. But rum or brandy, easily kept, were the common issue, and certainly the preferred. It was never difficult for a sailor to get drunk on any day he wished. He could do so by saving his noon ration to augment the supper one and by purchasing the rations of those willing to bargain.

In that light it becomes easier to understand how it was that two judgements of the day, on the character of the British sailor, arose from his supposedly questionable morals on the one hand and his unquestioned courage on the other.

Hodgskin offered an unusual perspective on seamen's courage and how it enabled them to endure the worst of their circumstances. He saw a certain defiant vanity: 'On the whole, the character of the seamen may be summed up, by saying, that they are courageous, because they are our countrymen, and because they ardently love fame.' Their heroic status, their fame, had been so liberally bestowed upon seamen that it had made them 'peculiarly sensible of praise . . . It is this love of praise, and the general success of the navy, that makes desertion so much less frequent than it otherwise would be; or, indeed, that makes seamen serve at all.'

'Two of the brightest points in the character of a seaman seem to be, intrepidity, and presence of mind,' wrote J. P. Andrews, a compiler of social images of 1789, in touching on the secular self-sufficiency of the British sailor. 'In the hour of extreme danger he does not, like the Portuguese, the Italian, or the Russ, either ask assistance from, or denounce vengeance against, his patron-saint. No, he trusts to his own agility and resolution for safety; and if he imprecates curses on *any* head, it is on his own, or on that of some *lubber*, who is not as active as himself in the general work of preservation.'[10]

Beyond the tone of evangelical urgency of a Hodgskin, the portrait of the late-eighteenth-century British sailor that emerges is a fine one of an individual bound by his own distinctive values. Those, formed by the worst and the best in his seagoing life, raised him to his own special niche. One can see him, as a hardy, easy-going type, simple in manner and outlook, equipped with a buoyant spirit that determined his survival. All of that is true enough. Being mostly illiterate, he left few individual accounts of what drove him and his fellows, but there is plenty available from the sources that surrounded him. From all of it we can see that the worst of what he endured yielded much of the best in him. It invested him with consistent qualities of loyalty, stoicism, generosity and the humane that set him quite apart. The wilful nature of survival in his world, from battle and the elements or the fevers that beset him, gave him a secular wit and humour that was wholly his own.

Kindness is a quality that always recurs in portraits of the eighteenth-century sailor: '. . . that fraternal regard which reigns among them all, let the outsides of some be ever so rugged,' as J. P. Andrews put it. 'No tie of free masonry, no oath, no bond of society, can unite any denomination of mankind together as sailors are united.' Hodgskin concurred: '. . . from the vices connected with avarice, they are eminently and conspicuously free . . . none want while the others possess. At sea, every man is engaged in prosecuting the same end, and the interests of all is the same: this begets a similarity of feeling and opinion; and possessing these is the surest bond of union . . .'

Leech described the joy of the sailors when a popular member of the lower deck escaped a flogging. 'So joyous were we all at his escape from punishment that we insisted on his giving a concert, which went off well. Seated on a gun surrounded by scores of the men, he sung a variety of favourite songs amid the plaudits and encores of his rough auditors. By such means as these, sailors contrive to keep up their spirits amidst constant causes of depression and misery . . . these things are often resorted to, because they feel miserable, just to drive away dull care. They do it on the same principle as the slave population in the South, to drown in sensual gratification the voice of misery that groans in the inner man . . .'

Finally, even when all of the bad of shipboard has been accounted for, there arose those occasions when all ranks and all ratings were bound together as one, each for the other. One such occasion arose when the 18-gun brig *Penguin* fell in with three French ships, each with more metal than she had. After two hours *Penguin* was ungovernable. As her topmast crashed down, Captain Mansel took hold of the hand of the next man to him 'and the whole crew followed his example; there was a moment of awful silence; not a word was spoken, but we all knew what it meant, to stand by each other to the last, and never to strike – three cheers to our brave captain followed'.[11]

BALLAD

Spanking Jack was so comely, so pleasant, so jolly,
Though winds blew great guns, still he'd whistle and sing;
Jack loved his friends, and was true to his Molly;
And if honour gives greatness, was as great as a king:
One night as we drove, with two reefs in the main-sail,
And the scud came on low'ring upon a lee shore,
Jack went up aloft, for to hand the top-gallant-sail,
A spray wash'd him off, and we ne'er saw him more!

But grieving's a folly,
Come let us be jolly,
If we've troubles at sea boys, we've pleasures ashore.

Whistling Tom still of mischief or fun in the middle,
Through life in all weathers at random would jog,
He'd dance, and he'd sing, and he'd play on the fiddle,
And swig with an air his allowance of grog:

Long side of a Don, in the Terrible frigate,
As yard-arm and yard-arm, we lay off the shore,
In and out whistling Tom did so caper and jig it,
That his head was shot off, and we ne'er saw him more.

But grieving's a folly, etc.

Bonny Ben was to each jolly messmate a brother,
He was manly and honest, good-natur'd and free;
If ever one Tar was more true than another,
To his friends and his duty, that sailor was he:
One day with the davie to heave the cadge anchor,
Ben went in a boat on a bold craggy shore,
He overboard tipt, when a shark and a spanker,
Soon snipt him in two, and we ne'er saw him more.

But grieving's a folly, etc.

But what of it all, lads! Shall we be down-hearted
Because that mayhap we now take our last sup;
Life's cable must one day or other be parted,
And death in safe moorings will bring us all up;
But 'tis always the way on't, one scarce finds a brother,
Fond as pitch, honest, hearty, and true to the core,
But by battle, or storm, or some damn'd thing or other,
He's popped off the hooks, and we ne'er see him more.

But grieving's a folly, etc.[12]

VII

TOULON

NEVER had Britain been launched upon a war that, once started, remained so lacking on all sides in certainty of aim and direction, and of any semblance of cohesive vision and intent.

In February 1793 no one in Britain had any idea of where this war was going, other than that momentum was still provided only by the flare or lapse of the passions from which it all initially arose on the Continent.

Across the Continent deposition of the French monarchy followed by regicide had shattered seemingly safe thousand-year-old dynastic assumptions of God-given right and privilege. Monarchies falling upon one another in their perpetual dynastic play with balance of power in Europe was one thing, but the prospect of universal challenge to the entire concept of dynastic rule and legitimacy arising from the hitherto obediently inert masses below their thrones was something else. Nevertheless, resistance to France and its declared universal republican mission was a crisis that they appeared incapable of coping with through any manifest concerted drive and generalship, even after the French armies were driven back from most of their initial conquests.

On the Continent the core alliance against France was an uneasy collaboration between traditional enemies Prussia and Austria. Apart from their natural suspicions of one another, both had other preoccupations as well.

Austria had concluded its war with Turkey but stood alert in the partition of Poland, where Prussia and Russia had in the past year seized what suited their greed for territorial gain and defensive interests. Prussia remained heavily watchful of any further Russian moves to gain more for itself in Poland. Through the spring and early summer of 1793 Austria and Prussia maintained their advance against the French, encouraged by the continuing disarray and low morale of the republican armies.

The belief seemed to be that it would not last long. In spite of the horror over regicide and terror there was, on many sides, an underlying though reluctant recognition that a republican France was a fact that eventually might have to be accepted.

In his address to the House on the declaration of war Pitt had spoken forcefully of checking the progress of a system 'the principles of which, if not opposed, threaten the most fatal consequences to the tranquillity of this country, the security of its allies, the good order of every European government, and the happiness of the whole human race'. Even so, there was nowhere any sense of the mighty conflict about to fall upon the world. Nor would there be any intimation of such for at least a year or so. Pitt, with no enthusiasm for any deep involvement on the Continent, was to continue to hold in mind the idea of negotiated settlement. Most expected the war to be over sooner rather than later. But the strategic situation everywhere gave no comfort, for all that.

The Baltic had grown into a menacing problem during the peace. The continuing rise of Russia under Catherine the Great and Potemkin had established Russia not only on the Baltic but in the eastern Mediterranean as well. Russia therefore presented a large and worrisome conundrum at the start of this war. But she herself helped to resolve it in the short term by offering to send a naval squadron to work with the British Channel fleet. The value of the offer lay not so much in any effective contribution from the ships but in having Russia on side as guarantee of the free flow of Baltic trade.

As ever, to protect trade, the western Mediterranean was for Britain the European theatre of greatest consequence and concern after the Narrow Seas. For the moment, however, Britain's situation in the Mediterranean looked reasonably comfortable because of the Revolution's recklessly indulged impulse to go to war with so many of France's neighbouring Mediterranean states and territories. France and Spain were at war just a month after Britain. Britain and Spain were therefore nominal allies. But Spain was a resentful partner, for the Nootka affair still rankled. Nevertheless, her powerful navy was on side. Alliance with Spain also gave use of Spanish harbours. Cadiz offered facilities that Gibraltar lacked. The Spanish Mediterranean ports could help serve any action against Toulon and its fleet.

Britain's other principal Mediterranean ally was the Bourbon Kingdom of Naples, which embraced southern Italy and Sicily itself. Naples was its capital. The kingdom's queen, Maria Carolina, was a sister of Marie Antoinette. She was as powerful in her influence in her realm as her sister had been in hers. Naples, Palermo and Syracuse offered good operational bases, if necessary. The Neapolitan fleet had four 74-gun line ships and an army of six thousand at Britain's disposal if she needed them. The island of Sardinia belonged to the kingdom on the mainland of the same name, with its capital at Turin, and offered good anchorage at different points. In this war Britain thus began with a surfeit of Mediterranean alternatives, if she required them.

Beyond European waters, the West Indies was an immediate concern. The great wealth that the Caribbean gave to both Britain and France established the early priority the islands had with each. A French fleet sailed just over a week after the declaration of war. A British fleet under Admiral Gardner sailed nearly a month later, on 24 March.

In St Domingue (Haiti) the former black slaves and mulattos had seized the island, which was now under the rule of Toussaint L'Ouverture. He was to declare St Domingue neutral but his disposition towards Britain was sympathetic. Gardner returned to England, leaving part of his squadron behind.

In India, Britain had made little effort to bolster its naval forces, which consisted of only one 64-gun ship at Madras and a few frigates and sloops at Calcutta. News of the war reached the British posts before the French heard it. Swift action allowed the British to seize the French ports of Chandernagore, Karica, Yanam and Mahe and finally Pondicherry. After that, defence of the Indian coast was left to a single warship and armed Indiamen. But with the powerfully fortified French base at Mauritius, the Ile de France as it was known, the ports of the Indian Ocean remained widely vulnerable.

The Indian Ocean now had significantly greater value than before. Apart from the huge importance of India itself to Britain, the Indian Ocean had become an access to the new settlements of Australia and the Pacific. In the new geographical consciousness that enthralled the western nations at the end of the eighteenth century, the Indian Ocean had become the critical half of the navigable circumference of the earth. But its strongest new aspect in 1793 was the rising value of the China trade, especially given the American intrusion there. For all those reasons Britain now had its first embassy to China embarked on its long mission to Pekin via the Cape, Batavia and Chusan.

With invasion as the immediate fear, it was upon home waters, however, that the naval focus was necessarily and urgently directed at the start of any war. Defence of the island rested primarily with the navy and its guardianship of the Narrow Seas. But mobilization of the line ships was painfully slow.

Earl Howe was admiral and commander in chief of the British fleet, as he had been through the Spanish and Russian armaments. His subordinate flag officers were Vice Admirals Thomas Graves and Sir Alexander Hood, brother of Lord Hood. This was the top rank of the American War again in command (Rodney had died in 1792). But it was not until three months later, on 27 May, that Howe was ordered to proceed to Portsmouth to take command of his flagship, the 100-gun *Queen Charlotte*, and only on 1 July that he received more specific instructions, which were to protect Britain's trade, intercept that of the enemy and 'molest' the enemy's ships.

By contrast the serviceability of the French fleet was pronouncedly evident. That was first demonstrated little more than a week after the declaration of war by the fleet that had sailed for the West Indies from Brest. It was a squadron of three 74s together with frigates and corvettes commanded by Rear Admiral Guillaume Sercey. About the same time ships began sailing from Brest, Lorient and Rochefort to assemble in Quiberon Bay. By midsummer twenty-one line ships and four frigates either lay in Quiberon Bay or were at sea off that coast. They were there as a defence against any British move to give support to a royalist insurrection in La Vendée, the hinterland beyond the Brittany coast.

While the British line ship force remained largely immobile at Spithead the French ships of the line moved freely. But the French took no direct aggressive advantage. Instead, they practised a damaging irregular role by moving about the Bay of Biscay and taking merchant prizes or supporting privateers engaged in the same activity. The French Channel ports were reported to be filled with captured English ships.

Ironically, never had the Royal Navy been in a better state for immediate action. The armaments of Nootka and Ozchakov had left the navy primed. Of the 113 line ships in the navy, between eighty and ninety were in good condition. Nevertheless, this was a fleet of old ships. The age, quality and slowness of the ships was to become a source of frequent, angry remonstration among British officers in this war, with bitter contrast drawn between the British ships and the speed and newness of the French. Then there was the fact of manning. In spite of the unusual state of their preparedness at the start of this war, the Royal Navy lacked the crews to man its ships.

This was the perennial problem of the British navy. The country simply did not possess the manpower that France had at its disposal for both army and navy. Impressment was the traditional means of coping with that. The manning problem meant that even ships fully ready for sea had to wait until they had their necessary complement. Even at the end of 1793, more than a quarter of the total number of line ships still lacked men.

On shore, the press gangs went out across the country to bring in those who did not manage to elude them. Offshore, inbound merchantmen were intercepted and stripped of part of their crews. For those returning from a long voyage, life's rawest cruelty was to be seized within sight of the land upon which they had expected to be stepping ashore perhaps that day or the next. They knew that for perhaps years they would be trapped aboard the ships to which they were delivered. Often they would never see the pay they had expected to draw for their labour aboard the merchantmen.

Nelson provided a rare exception in the manning of his ship *Agamemnon*. Like everyone else he needed the press. 'I have only got a few men, and very hard indeed they are to be got, and without a press I have no idea our fleet can be manned,' he wrote to his father on 10 February, three days after joining *Agamemnon* at Chatham.[1] He nevertheless started by sending out a naval team to call for volunteers in Norfolk seaports and made his own appeal among the farms and villages around his home. The result was a ship that had the family spirit of men from the same or nearby communities. His midshipmen, too, were drawn from the gentry of his area. They included his thirteen-year-old stepson, Josiah, and twelve-year-old William Hoste, son of a neighbouring clergyman. Like all the boys answering the call to sea at the start of this war, these young gentlemen, if they survived, were to form the mature generation that concluded it.

France had entered the war with one of the most powerful navies it had ever possessed, the creation and pride of Louis XVI. It had 250 vessels, eighty-two of which were of the line. Three-quarters of them were ready for sea or in a serviceable state. After the start of the war a massive addition of seventy-one new ships was ordered, including twenty-five of the line. Five of the latter were to mount 100 guns. One 130-gun ship was ordered. For the rest there were 80s and 74s.

For all that, the French navy was nevertheless a vastly different creature from what it might otherwise have been. The Revolutionary troubles of the past two years had taken their toll within a service whose officers were exclusively from the nobility or from those close to it in the social hierarchy. Mutinous outbreaks occurred in all the major seaports. Officers were insulted, threatened with death and gaoled when they sought to restore order. All of this occurred in the early years of the Revolution, even while Louis XVI was still recognized as king. Like many of the nobility, naval officers began to leave the service, and fled the country itself.

The purge of officers continued. Many of the most distinguished went to the guillotine. 'And,' said the French naval historian Jurien de la Gravière, 'that navy so glorious, so devoted, so redoubtable to the enemies of France, seemed to disappear entirely in a single year of terror.'[2] But, for all its difficulties, that was far from being entirely so. There were those who remained, loyal to their service and to the country. One such was Lieutenant Villaret-Joyeuse, who of necessity was soon to be elevated to admiral. And while all of this helped explain the lack of any aggressive drive in the French navy at the start of the war in spite of its strength, and though it continued to labour under great difficulties, it was nevertheless a huge and intimidating force whose courage was fierce.

Initially, however, the French preoccupation with Quiberon together with the immobility of the larger part of the British line fleet created an interlude of suspended main event on the seas, lasting from February to midsummer. That was not to say that this was a war that lacked action. There had already been a great deal of it, right from the start. While the big ships lay quiet, the smaller ones were not, as demonstrated by the actions of *Nymphe* and *Cléopâtre* and *Boston* and *Ambuscade*.

For all the great resounding battles that would mark it so indelibly upon history, this war from start to finish would be one of unceasing action by under-line ships, the frigates, sloops, brigs and lesser craft. For twenty-two years theirs was to be a show of sustained action. Upon these ships and their boat operations would fall the burden of a continuous fighting war. It was frequently solitary, lone-vessel war, with one-on-one vessel engagement, as well as dangerous inshore work in unfamiliar waters, mounting landing incursions of seamen and marines into hostile territory, open-boat boarding parties with ferocious close combat in the galley manner. The under-line efforts were unceasing. With the big line ships lay the ultimate responsibility of decisive engagement that would settle the grand issues of mastery at the points wherever it was vitally necessary. Theirs was the task of finding and drawing into battle the enemy's equivalent force and then destroying that force's ability to shield an invasion or maintain operations that could drastically affect the course of the war. Formal battle was what the line ships sought, and only rarely got. Line ship strength was collective, as a fleet in being. Such stationing was limited to where the enemy's like concentration lay. And, since the French were largely to avoid full-scale line battle by holding their line ships in harbour, blockade of those ports where they lay, Brest and Toulon especially, would become the frustrating main preoccupation of the British line ships. Upon the under-line ships therefore was to fall much of the responsibility for the vast pattern of operational involvement that lay outside the confining mission of the line ship battle fleets. The under-line war on both sides did not lose a day from the start of the war, when these ships were immediately active. They remained active to the very end. When not in pursuit of privateers or prizes the under-line ships sought one another. Whatever the mission or the encounter, the under-line ships represented the unceasing battle at sea. Raw courage, intrepid daring and brutal endurance aboard the small ships produced a sustained heroism on both sides that has become one of the lost memories of the Great War, and those under-line sailors its forgotten heroes.

It was two months after Admiral Gardner sailed for the West Indies with his squadron that a second battleship fleet sailed, under the command of Lord Hood, who had been named commander in chief of the Mediterranean forces. Nelson's *Agamemnon* was part of the force. As with Howe's Channel fleet, Hood's ships were slow in preparation.

On 22 May Hood finally sailed from Spithead, with his flag in the 100-gun *Victory*. The force was united at Gibraltar and sailed from there on 27 June, fifteen ships of the line and nine frigates, whose task was to blockade Toulon and Marseilles and, if possible, to bring out the French fleet at Toulon to fight. They were off Toulon on 16 July. There they were to be joined by a Spanish fleet of twenty-four ships of the line under Admiral Juan de Langara. Seventeen French line ships, including two 100-gun vessels, lay in the Great Road of Toulon. With such a mighty force arrayed against them it was highly unlikely that they would come out to confront it.

For the next month, until 25 August, Hood's ships were engaged in their vigilance of Toulon and Marseilles and the adjacent waters. The uneventful monotony got to Nelson. 'I can hardly think the war can last,' he wrote to his wife, 'for what are we at war about?' And to his brother, 'Time must discover what we are going after.'[3]

At the other end, Earl Howe finally put to sea on 14 July, five months after the start of the war, with twenty-three sail of the line.

The sailing might of Britain's home fleet was at sea at last. Off Belle Ile on 31 July cries from the masthead reported enemy topsails just above the horizon. The French fleet consisted of fifteen line ships and two frigates. The ships sighted were the Quiberon fleet under Admiral Morard-des-Galles bringing in the merchant convoy from the West Indies. For two days the British ships tried to catch up. But on 2 August none of the French were in sight. The first line battle of the war had failed to offer itself.

While the Royal Navy was thus seeking to come to action new Revolutionary tumult was tearing France apart. This was to be of great significance to the fleet lying off Toulon.

The counter-revolutionary insurrection that had broken out among the peasants of La Vendée in March had begun to have effect across the country, even as the French army was being driven back from its early gains. La Vendée provided an example that was followed by the cities of Marseilles, Lyons, Bordeaux, Toulon and other regions, all of which rose against the capital. Then, as the Austrian commander, the Prince of Coburg, marched on Paris, from this extreme situation arose revolution within the revolution itself. On 2 June 1793, the governing party, the Girondins, were overthrown by the other republican party, the more extremist Jacobins, the men of the 'Mountain' as they were known. This was the climax of the Revolution, the launch of the real Terror, the instrument by which new, ruthless organization was laid upon the country to control from Paris every aspect of the national life. Patriotic fervour was aroused across the nation to help confront the invading forces and to suppress the counter-revolutionaries. It was a renewed passion that was to save France as she faced invasion north and south, east and west.

The Committee of Public Safety, the machine of Jacobin power, decreed a *levée en masse* to defend France. A military engineer, Lazarre Carnot, became the 'organizer of victory'. A new army was conscripted from all the *départements*, all the food and materials that would sustain it were requisitioned. Those who were resistant or who were suspected of a lack of patriotism got summary justice, but the zeal that infused the new army gave it an entirely different character. Its soldiers became seized by a strengthened revolutionary élan that carried them forward with a rage that was soon to have decisive impact upon the fractious efforts of their invading opponents. Coburg's march to Paris faltered. An attempt by the Duke of York to seize Dunkirk failed.

In the western Mediterranean the prospect looked better for the counter-revolutionaries. Toulon and Marseilles were divided by royalist insurrection. Delegates from Marseilles in July persuaded sections of the civil and military establishments at Toulon to raise the Bourbon flag. Toulon nevertheless remained a base holding powerful Jacobin loyalists. A significant part of the naval force and strategic points retained Jacobin support. The fall of Toulon to the royalists could not be assumed, even with the Bourbon flag flying.

The flagship of the Toulon fleet, the 100-gun *Commerce de Marseille*, was typical. Her commander in chief, Rear Admiral Trogoffe, was a man of the old navy. While he and his captain supported the royalists, other officers and crew were republican. The other 100-gun ship in the port, *Commerce de Bordeaux*, was commanded by Toulon's second in command, Rear Admiral St Julien who, together with his officers and the rest of the ship's company, was an ardent republican.

On 23 August Hood had a dramatic surprise. Commissioners from all the *départements* around the mouth of the Rhône, including those of Marseilles, boarded *Victory* and declared they had full authority to negotiate peace. They had expected to find delegates from Toulon on board but these had not turned up. The absence of the Toulon delegates prompted Hood to send ashore one of his French-speaking officers, Lieutenant Edward Cooke, to try to contact the Toulon delegates. He was given full authority either to bring the delegates back with him or to negotiate terms.[4]

Cooke was picked because he had been ashore when the fleet first arrived, to treat for an exchange of prisoners. Accompanied by a midshipman he waited until ten that night to row into the harbour. It was dark and windy, which helped them slip past ships that Cooke knew to be republican in sympathy. But they ran into a boom and a gunboat emerged. Fortunately Cooke, on his first mission the month before, had become acquainted with the man who commanded the craft. No alarm was sounded and word was sent to the royalist Commissioners to come to the harbour. Delegates promptly came down and Cooke gave them Hood's terms on submission of the port.

Cooke and the midshipman were told to remain in their boat and not to land. In the morning they were taken to the French navy's quarantine station where they received a letter fixing a meeting with the Commissioners. Cooke sent off the midshipman in *Victory*'s boat to deliver a written report to Hood. At dusk a guide arrived with a horse and Cooke was taken on a long ride from the outer harbour to inside the fortified walls of Toulon. Meanwhile, the midshipman in *Victory*'s boat had been seized and taken aboard Admiral St Julien's ship. He was interrogated on how he and Cooke had got to the city and where Cooke was. Cooke's letter to Hood was read and its contents relayed to the other ships, accompanied by St Julien's threat that if Cooke were caught he would be hanged.

On arrival in Toulon, Cooke was taken to a chamber where the Committee General was sitting. Hood's proposals were unanimously accepted. The British would be put in full possession of all the outlying forts, together with the city and its fortifications. The French ships would all move into the inner harbour. All officers civil and military would be at Hood's disposal. But grain shipments should immediately be allowed.

Cooke listened to it all in astonishment and joy. He was negotiating the surrender of the greatest base on the Mediterranean. Nothing like it could have been imagined when the fleet had arrived offshore. He promised that the British would protect them, whatever Revolutionary force might be sent against Toulon. Cooke's guide took him to a coastal village, from where a boat got him to *Victory*. Cooke arrived on board at midday, just forty-eight hours after his departure.

Hood was pleased but remained doubtful, unwilling to trust anything until the French ships lying in the outer harbour had been moved into the inner one. The difficulty of achieving that was the likely resistance of the republican officers and crews aboard some of the ships. Cooke immediately offered to return to Toulon to have the Commissioners canvas the response of the fleet. He left at daylight.

To get ashore he had to pass a French frigate. On his approach the frigate manned and sent off her longboat to intercept him. They began firing when it became evident that he was trying to escape them. The shots passed over his head and he got ashore. He remained under heavy fire along the path he had to follow round the bay, compelled to pause among the rocks to catch his breath and regain his strength. The firing persisted as he reached trees above the rocky shore. Hiding there until the frigate appeared to have given up, Cooke continued his breathless run to the town, where he was greeted 'amidst the acclamations of the greatest multitude I ever beheld'. But the news was bad.

Republican sailors had sent word ashore that they would do their utmost to preserve Toulon for the republic. That froze the negotiations of the town's people. Admiral St Julien had deposed Admiral Trogoffe as commander of the fleet and had also taken command of forts on the left of the harbour.

Cooke set off back to the fleet mid-afternoon, accompanied by a guide and a deputy. All journeys circuitous of that huge bay were long and difficult. The three had to cover thirty-five miles to a point where they were likely to get a boat. They got there at daylight and some hours later seized a Genoese fishing boat. At four o'clock that afternoon Cooke was back aboard *Victory*.

Hood summoned all his admirals and senior officers to a council aboard *Victory*. A naval landing was decided upon. It would be the first of countless such, large and small, that the Royal Navy would be called upon to launch in this war with sailors and the marines, and on this occasion also with the two regiments that had sailed out with Hood. Together sailors and military formed a small force of fifteen hundred men. Their objective was a huge and powerful fortress, Fort La Malgue, that dominated the Great Road beyond the outer harbour. It mounted forty-eight pieces of cannon.

Cooke was delegated to lead the sailors. One of Hood's captains, Keith Elphinstone, commanded the troops. At nine in the morning of 28 August the ships covering the landing stood towards Fort La Mague, which was effortlessly captured. At noon Captain Elphinstone entered the fort at the head of the troops. Even as all of this was taking place the Spanish fleet commanded by Admiral Juan de Langara hove up over the horizon. By the time they came to anchor near the British fleet Toulon and all its fortifications had fallen.

Elphinstone sent a flag of truce to Admiral St Julien with the warning that ships failing to proceed to the inner harbour and put their powder on shore would be treated as enemies. But St Julien had fled during the night together with the greater part of the crews of the seven line ships that had been attached to him. The ships were brought into the inner harbour. The next day Hood's fleet anchored in Toulon outer road, followed by the Spanish. One thousand Spanish soldiers were landed to reinforce the British.

Here at Toulon it seemed that the future had begun, for Britain, her allies and France. As Pitt saw it, the fall of Toulon was a blow that had to be 'in every view the most important which could be struck towards the final success of the war'.

Over five days, with great daring, Edward Cooke had helped to secure what looked like becoming one of the greatest strategic victories in all the history of Britain's wars with France, the more remarkable for being practically bloodless in its initial accomplishment.

Nelson, meanwhile, was speeding towards a special encounter, on an urgent mission intended to obtain more soldiers for the future defence

of Toulon. Nelson was to sail first to the small Genoese port of Oneglia
to leave despatches for transmission to the British minister at Turin,
Mr Trevor, asking him to do all he could to get Sardinian troops. From
Oneglia he was to proceed to Naples to press upon the British minister
there, Sir William Hamilton, that he in turn should similarly press the
Bourbon king of Naples to send as many Neapolitan soldiers as possible
to Toulon.

Nelson had strongly regretted having to leave. 'I should have liked to
have stayed one day longer with the fleet, when they entered the harbour,'
he wrote to his wife, 'but service could not be neglected for any private
gratification . . . What an event this has been for Lord Hood; such an one
as History cannot produce its equal; that the strongest place in Europe and
twenty-two sail of the Line, should be given up without firing a shot. It is
not to be credited.' But the wonder of it was already looking threatened.

Marseilles, meanwhile, had submitted to the French general leading the
assault against the insurgent south of France, Generel Carteaux, whose
attention was immediately directed at Toulon. The French army thereafter
began establishing itself more firmly on the heights above Toulon. An
advance force from Carteaux's army with ten cannon arrived at the village
of Ollioules above Toulon. On 30 August Captain Elphinstone led a force
of six hundred British and Spanish troops and sailors and deployed them so
skilfully in an encircling movement to gain the high ground that the French
were chased from the village and their cannon captured. Elphinstone's
force continued to maintain the defence of the outlying districts of Toulon
and to hold command of the heights, even as Carteaux's army grew in
strength there, with reinforcements continually arriving. By the middle of
September, however, Toulon was under constant alarm.

The large Spanish contribution in ships and men compelled Hood to
appoint one of the Spanish admirals, Gravina, commandant of Toulon
in overall land command. The weight upon Hood increased daily. Lord
Mulgrave, a soldier-diplomat sent by Pitt to obtain a picture of the situation in the region arrived at Toulon on 6 September. Hood gave him
command of the British land forces, working with Admiral Gravina.
Their problem was numbers. Eight hundred Sardinian troops arrived.
The British fighting force, sailors and soldiers, was around two thousand.
The Spanish had landed one thousand soldiers and 1,500 of the French
in Toulon had volunteered. But already some fifteen thousand French
were on the heights above Toulon.

A continuous struggle was now underway for the posts on the heights that
offered the most advantageous command over Toulon. The French were
constantly firing upon the fleet and gunboats below. Although the French
posts were repeatedly destroyed others quickly replaced them.

*   *   *

On the night of 11 September the *Agamemnon* lay anchored in the Bay of Naples, with all on deck admiring 'the throws of fire from Mount Vesuvius'. The Neapolitan flagship lay anchored nearby. King Ferdinand IV was on board and the following morning summoned *Agamemnon*'s captain to his ship. A treaty of friendship and common purpose had been signed between Britain and the Kingdom of Naples (the largest in Italy) earlier that year.

Nelson went straight from this royal interview to deliver Hood's letters to Sir William Hamilton. Mutual admiration was quickly established. Hamilton was so taken with Nelson that he offered to put him up in his own house, something he had never before done with any other officer. Nelson for his part was said to have declared to Hamilton, 'You are a man after my own heart; you do business in my own way.' Together they went to see Ferdinand's principal adviser, an Englishman, Sir John Acton, who immediately promised that two thousand Neapolitan troops would be sent. Ferdinand subsequently doubled the number.

Nelson was now to meet Sir William Hamilton's wife, Emma, of whom he said in a letter to his own wife, 'Lady Hamilton has been wonderfully kind and good to Josiah. She is a young woman of amiable manners, and who does honour to the station to which she is raised.'

The king twice more sent for Nelson to talk, and also invited him to dine, placing Nelson on his right. Ferdinand invited him to watch the drilling of troops destined for Toulon. There were entertainments at the Hamilton *palazzo* and at Acton's, and aboard *Agamemnon*. All of it was a cheerful, easily intimate fusion.

Agamemnon's brief stay at Naples was a warm interlude that brought together in their initial contact a small group of oddly assorted individuals whose reunion and involvement at a later time would be under far more dramatic and straining circumstances. They were figures who composed their own particular tableau image of those aspects of late-eighteenth-century society that effortlessly and amiably set an outlook free of moralizing constraint within the formal structures of mannered living.

Emma Hamilton was a beauty who had made an effortless ascent from the bottom to the top. The daughter of a blacksmith, she had progressed through early episodes either of brothel existence or something similar to life at the highest end of the scale as mistress to two succeeding members of the aristocracy, the last of whom, Charles Greville, second son of the Earl of Warwick, had become a love match. But Greville, with debts and lacking private fortune, required to marry an heiress. In an extraordinary negotiation he had passed Emma on to his widowed uncle, Sir William Hamilton, who at first received her reluctantly but then in his turn fell in love with her.

Hamilton, grandson of the third Duke of Hamilton, was a passionate art collector, a man of quiet grace and high intelligence. Tall, lean, sunburned by twenty years of southern Italian sunshine, he was at sixty-two of striking distinction to those who met him. He and Emma had a close and comfortable relationship with Ferdinand and his queen, whom Nelson could not meet on this occasion because she was pregnant with her eighteenth child. Ferdinand, physically unattractive, bearing the distinctive large Bourbon nose, pursued women and wild boar with equal intensity. He had a peasant coarseness that he enhanced by another of his hobbies, dressing as a fisherman, spending the night with his nets, and then selling the fish in the market, where he weighed them and took the money himself. It was a character that gave no pleasure to the aesthetic Hamilton, but a necessary intimacy had to be maintained with a monarch whose kingdom was of such indispensable strategic importance to the British navy. It was an intimacy anyway unavoidable through Emma Hamilton's close relationship with Queen Maria Carolina, who was the effective ruler of the kingdom and brought to it the total preoccupation with methodical and absolute rule derived from her Hapsburg lineage. She governed her husband as effectively as she did the kingdom. Working in close liaison with the queen was John Acton, the 'prime minister' of Naples. Acton came from an old Shropshire family. His father, a physician, had married a Frenchwoman. He had grown up on the Continent, served in the Tuscan navy, been drawn from there into the Neapolitan navy and within that service gradually built his position and influence in the Kingdom of Naples.

Into this wayward group Captain Horatio Nelson was now warmly accepted. But he had to sail away in haste, without embarking the troops, on receiving a report that a French warship and the merchantmen it was convoying were anchored in a Sardinian bay. It would be five years and in quite different circumstances before there was a reunion with his Neapolitan friends. It is impossible to know what he carried away with him concerning the plump, vivacious Emma Hamilton, other than gratitude for a brief, generously hospitable interlude.

VIII

BUONAPARTE

On the heights above Toulon a young artillery captain had joined the French forces. He had hoped to be elsewhere.

In July, Captain Napoleon Buonaparte had been ordered to join the army of General Carteaux while it was attempting to put down the anti-Jacobin insurrection in and between Lyons and Marseilles. Buonaparte was in Avignon as rebel resistance began to collapse across Provence. Anxious to get himself elsewhere, he had applied for a transfer to the Army of the Rhine.

Buonaparte was twenty-four and in a poor state of mind and body. Born of one of the leading families of Ajaccio, Corsica, his line was traceable to a noble Florentine family that went back to the eleventh century. Influence had got him into a school for the sons of French nobility at Brienne. He had gone on to the Ecole Militaire in Paris and from there graduated into the artillery regiment, Régiment de La Fère. Part of his subsequent training had been at the artillery school at Auxonne, where he continued to excel. The young Buonaparte was at Auxonne when the Revolution began. He saw it as an opportunity for the independence of Corsica and arranged a transfer from the regular army to a Corsican battalion. But Pasquale Paoli, the political leader for Corsican independence, broke with the French government and sought British help. Buonaparte and his family fled to Provence condemned by the Paolists to 'perpetual execration and infamy'.

Buonaparte had obtained his reinstatement in the French army before his family's flight from Corsica. The shortage of officers as a result of the emigration of the *noblesse* meant that he was promoted from lieutenant to captain. His salary was all that his family now had to survive on. Little was left for himself. Thin, emaciated, bitter and disillusioned, he embraced Jacobinism in a fierce pamphlet, urging France to unite under the Jacobins to save the country from its invaders and the vengeance of the emigrant nobles. With a formerly bright career now lying inconclusively upon him, he sought to make his own contribution where the greater action was.

But instead of getting a transfer to the Army of the Rhine Buonaparte was ordered to join General Carteaux's army above Toulon as chief of a battalion of artillery.

On 16 September 1793 Buonaparte arrived at Carteaux's camp near the village of Ollioules. He found disorder. The French were well placed but lacked cannon and munitions. Carteaux was ignorant of the range of his few cannon and Dommartin, the artillery commander, had been disabled by a wound. The continuous arrival of more troops added to the confusion. Trying to bring order to the situation was Salicetti, a Corsican friend of the Buonaparte family who, like Napoleon, had left the island after Paoli's successful seizure. Salicetti was one of the Commissioners of the Convention who had been sent to this critical scene to try and impose order and to inject patriotic drive. For France loss of this celebrated arsenal and Mediterranean command base was impossible to suffer. To Salicetti the arrival of this entirely professional artillery captain in whom he knew he could put his trust and dependence was miraculously opportune.

Salicetti appointed Captain Napoleon Buonaparte commander of the artillery above Toulon. Buonaparte was astonished to discover that he had pathetically little to work with. The accurate return fire of the allied forces from Toulon harbour had left only a few field pieces and fewer heavy guns. There were hardly any munitions and no tools. There was no discipline. Buonaparte imposed it. 'You mind your business,' he told infantrymen who objected, 'it is artillery that takes fortresses: infantry gives its help.' He then set about organizing supplies. From his knowledge of the forces, resources and dispositions of the army at its positions in Provence he began collecting cannon, mortars, munitions and stores from various points.

The view from Paris was that an extended siege would be required to dispossess the British from Toulon. The Committee of Public Safety sent plans and instructions on how the siege should be managed. A band of fortifications experts was sent down and a council was called above Toulon, presided over by one of the Deputies, Gasparin. The confusion was such that Barras, another Deputy, went so far as to recommend that the whole of Provence should be abandoned. From the outset Napoleon had believed a siege to be unnecessary if a headland – l'Eguillette – that commanded both the inner and the outer harbour could be taken. That was the plan that he himself put forward and the one that was eventually put into effect, for which in his memoirs he thanked Gasparin, the man he therefore regarded as truly opening his career.[1]

Unfortunately, l'Eguillette was commanded by Fort La Malgue, which the British had captured and renamed Fort Mulgrave. It was to be three months to the day after Napoleon's arrival before those critical positions were overwhelmed. Buonaparte needed that time to create batteries ever closer to Fort Mulgrave, which the French called 'Little Gibraltar'. Meanwhile, the bombardment upon the British from the heights continued, with heavy fighting as each side sought to capture the other's batteries. In this fierce combat the Spanish admiral Gravina was wounded.

Nelson was back at Toulon on 5 October. The change in the situation there since his departure was immediately apparent to him, and pithily summarized. 'Shots and shells are throwing about us every hour. The enemy have many strong posts on the hills which are daily augmented with men.' *Agamemnon* was welcomed back for the contribution she could make to reinforcement of the allied forces. Nelson immediately had a large portion of his men taken from him.

On the heights the fighting now ranged to and fro. It became an indecisive struggle for the same strategic points as across the south the republicans were restoring their power. After the capture of Marseilles Carteaux's army had begun to take the other insurgent *départements* of the south of France. Lyons, the critical point for domination of the south of France, fell on 9 October. The full concentration would now be on Toulon.

The fall of Lyons meant more weaponry for Napoleon up at Ollioules, where he had established an arsenal with eighty workers. He had sent an officer to Lyons, Briançon and Grenoble to procure all that could be useful. Cannon were being brought from Antibes and Monaco, and requests for horses went to everywhere between Nice and Montpellier. Carteaux had been succeeded by General Doppet, who reported that Napoleon was ceaselessly busy. When he needed rest, Doppet said, Buonaparte merely lay down on the ground and wrapped himself in his cloak.

Down below Nelson stood on *Agamemnon*'s deck watching the action on the heights and envying his own seamen and those naval officers who were called upon to participate. In this war he was yet to see action. His frustration at Toulon had already been expressed several times. Inaction in the presence of action was unbearable to anyone whose every instinct in such a situation raised a total involvement of mind, spirit and demanding energy. But for the onlooker gazing back across two centuries what taunts the imagination is that first circumstantial bonding between the two junior officers, the two captains, in that place and at that moment, the one on the heights and the other on the water below.

It is strange to reflect on how alike these two were at that moment. They were types as unprepossessing as any within their respective milieux. Both were poor physical specimens, almost fragile in their thin, unimpressive frames, hardly the movers and shakers of land and sea. Yet it was all already powerfully there. In Nelson, a mere junior post-captain, the thrust to impose himself upon the war and its direction wherever he found himself was ever determined, irrepressible. So, too, with Napoleon. These two whose war it swiftly would become, upon whose genius and actions so much of fate and future would be decided, were here at the start the closest that they would ever be to one another. As he moved between his posts to place cannon and to engineer fortifications, Napoleon's attention would continually be drawn to the harbour below and the ships that were seeking the range of his battlements. And from his quarterdeck Nelson would perpetually be scanning through his glasses the heights where the other was, clearly seeing the small figures bent on destruction of his own ship and the other vessels around him. Did each in his sweeping view of the scene on some occasion have fleeting, unwitting sight of the other? Here the metaphysical, never far from the historical imagination, intervenes. For it is impossible not to be drawn to the strange quirk of destiny that should have brought them here, so close together at the very start: two minor players placed on stage as the curtain rises on the first major act of the long drama that will steadily enlarge their roles and characters until they are finally delivered to a climactic duel.

Agamemnon lay just two weeks at Toulon before sailing on another assignment for Hood, whose dependence upon Nelson grew. Nelson was increasingly picked for assignments that required the particular combination of zeal, perception, daring and intelligence that Hood, as chief of Mediterranean operations, required. This preference of Nelson for particular tasks owed much to Nelson's own determination to put himself forward at every opportunity that allowed him the action he perpetually sought, as well as the public recognition he craved.

The new assignment was to accompany a diplomatic mission to the Bey of Tunis. For Nelson the main significance of this diversion was to be that he did not return to Toulon while the British were still there.

At Toulon the situation through October deteriorated rapidly for the allies. Hood's problems were on all fronts, with his allies as well as with the enemy on the hills above.

On 18 October the Spanish admiral Langara told Hood that a Spanish officer, General Valdes, had arrived to command the Spanish troops, replacing Admiral Gravina who was still recovering from the wound suffered in the battle of 1 October. Then, five days later, on 23 October, Hood was informed by letter from Admiral Langara that on account of the valour of Admiral Gravina the Spanish king had promoted him to the military rank of lieutenant-general and consequently had appointed Gravina commander in chief of the combined forces at Toulon.

An astounded Hood declared vehemently that Toulon and its dependent forts been surrendered to the British alone and that, moreover, before the Spanish fleet had arrived. The Sardinian and Neapolitan troops who were there had been put at Britain's disposal under Hood's command where they and the British forces had to remain.

Adding to this crisis was the fact that two senior British officers had just arrived, Lieutenant General O'Hara and Lieutenant General David Dundas. Their arrival further compounded Hood's problems because Lord Mulgrave, Pitt's emissary, had been working closely and satisfactorily with Gravina, and was not prepared to take second place to the new British officers. He returned to London. For Hood a further blow had been that O'Hara and Dundas had brought only half the one-thousand-man reinforcement of soldiers he had requested from the governor of Gibraltar. Hood's ships had become seriously weakened by the substantial number of sailors that had been drafted ashore to man the outlying forts for, as it had been from the start, much of the hard drive in the land fighting remained naval.

The Spanish then made a move with their ships that the British read as intentionally menacing. Hood had only ten sail of the line in Toulon against Spain's twenty. Many of his gunners were ashore. On the excuse of moving his ships to more convenient anchorages Langara brought his three-deckers to what the British officers saw as clearly threatening positions near the British ships. Langara's own ship was brought broadside alongside *Victory*. Two other line ships were anchored on her bow and quarter.

A man of Langara's caste and diplomatic sophistication well knew that the British were the least likely to consider themselves intimidated by such a move. He would also have known the power of provocation in a man like Hood. The shift was certainly Langara's stern reminder that the greater part of the shipboard metal there was under his command to move or dispose with as he saw fit, distinct warning that the relationship between Britain and Spain could change.

The Spanish had good reason to be aggrieved. They were in every sense the largest party there. Apart from having the largest fleet, and with it the strongest artillery, the six thousand troops they had landed represented by far the largest contribution, three times the size of the British force. For their own reasons they were nevertheless pleased to have that force there. The suspicion had arisen in the Court at Madrid that the long-range intention of the British was to retain Toulon, despite Hood's assurance in the terms of the surrender that Britain would simply hold Toulon on behalf of the Dauphin, Louis XVII. If this war were to be as short as many still believed it might be, the idea of Britain retaining two of the greatest strategic points in the western Mediterranean, Toulon as well as Gibraltar, was insufferable.

Langara renewed his demand for more power in the naval, military and civil government of Toulon. He got nowhere. With Hood, he was unlikely to. The British admiral remained coldly brusque with the Spanish, in manner and correspondence.

Mulgrave had worked closely with the Spanish. General O'Hara followed his example and shared command, but Hood dealt with any Spanish approach with a resolute bluntness and lack of diplomacy. Both Langara and Gravina were described as having the exemplary manners of men of rank. Gravina especially was said to be 'a very pleasing and gentlemanlike man'. To such men Hood's manner created great continuing offence.

Hood was nearly seventy. Like Howe and the other senior commanders, he had been called from what in effect had been a well-earned retirement after the American War. He embodied as much as any man could that conviction of the indomitable that was so particularly a naval trait. It sat upon his sharp, angular features and the look of disciplinary authority that his portraits convey. But the situation in which he now found himself was wholly different from anything in his experience. What had looked like unique triumph was fast gathering the appearance of being a trap closing upon him, flight from which would be a defeat as distinctive as the triumph first had seemed to be. The humiliation of retreat now daily confronted him. By mid-November it was already evident that he was powerless to avoid it, without a miraculous infusion of new forces. That prospect had become remote.

Britain had asked Austria for a contribution and was promised five thousand soldiers. But when Hood sent a ship to Vado Bay to collect them none were there. The Austrians apparently had no intention of fulfilling their part of the bargain. In spite of railing against Austria for failing to meet a commitment at this hour of greatest need at Toulon, Britain itself was preparing to send a force of seven thousand soldiers to the West Indies. They sailed on 26 November, escorted by a squadron under Sir John Jervis. Simultaneously a force to assist the failing Vendée rebellion was being considered. Toulon appeared to have the least priority of all, perhaps because of a lingering belief in London that France would collapse during the winter. For Toulon Britain laughably promised only a small detachment of cavalry. It would be easy to surmise from all of this that British intention to hold on to Toulon was hardly a full and serious commitment. Yet neither was there any demonstrable suggestion of any ready willingness to evacuate, least of all with Hood, who was to spurn suggestions from General Dundas that they should.

The Spanish by now were more realistic about any possibility of holding on to Toulon. As early as 3 October the Spanish Foreign Minister, Duque d'Alcuida, had suggested to the British ambassador at Madrid that contingency plans should be made to sink or set on fire French warships to avoid the French navy making use of them, if eventually Toulon were to be abandoned.

By mid-November the French had some forty thousand men above

Toulon. Defending Toulon the allies had sixteen thousand, many of whom were sick or wounded. Between them the defenders had to cover a circumference around town and harbour of fifteen miles and twenty main posts beyond, as well as minor ones.

The idea of British retention began to vanish steadily as the French hold tightened. By November, Napoleon had ringed Fort Mulgrave and the headland of l'Eguillette with batteries. The fate of Toulon had come to depend upon possession of these. Once Fort Mulgrave, 'Little Gibraltar', fell, the General-in-Chief, Dugommier, would have Fort l'Eguillette, which commanded all – the outer harbour, the inner harbour and Toulon itself – which meant that in French hands l'Eguillette would suggest immediate withdrawal of the allied fleets or their destruction from the fort. The imminence of that fate grew as the French increased their assaults against 'Little Gibraltar'. In an allied retaliation on 10 November, O'Hara was wounded and taken prisoner. General Dundas, now in command, was already advising Hood to abandon Toulon. But Hood clung on. The end came on 17 December.

At two that morning, in the middle of a wild storm, the French attacked Fort Mulgrave. Napoleon's horse was shot dead under him in the first rush. The Spanish gave way. The British were unable to hold. All retreated. At dawn on 17 December Toulon was lost.

Dugommier advanced from Mulgrave to l'Eguillette, where the British and Spanish fleets lay before him. Hood was fortunate. Napoleon had hoped to cannonade the combined fleets before noon but poor construction of the batteries at l'Eguillette meant that this had to be postponed until the guns could be planted in new positions. That could not be until the next day. Had it not been so, Buonaparte would have had his own Trafalgar right there, a naval triumph to match his first military triumph.

A council of war of all the commanders, British, Spanish and the others, was urgently called aboard *Victory* before midday on the 17th. Evacuation was to be immediate. The troops were called in from the posts. They were assembled at Fort La Malgue to be taken off in the boats of the fleet. The sick and wounded were embarked immediately. So were some fifteen thousand loyalist men, women and children from Toulon. Within twenty-four hours most of this had been accomplished.

Spain's recommendation on 3 October of the need of a contingency plan for evacuation had never been acted upon – it had been dismissed out of hand. Too little preparation meant that many of the finest French ships, including the grand *Commerce de Bordeaux* lay in the inner harbour. These had to be destroyed, together with the arsenal, the general magazine and all the storehouses, packed with valuable pitch, tar, tallow, oil and hemp. And to the fore stepped Sir Sidney Smith, last heard of fighting the Russians while serving in the Swedish navy. He had arrived at Toulon two weeks before from Constantinople.

Smith was a naval captain without immediate employment and therefore on half-pay. He immediately volunteered himself to Hood as the one to destroy all that should not be left behind. His offer accepted by Hood, Sidney Smith collected a party of other officers and took a small fleet composed of a tender, three English and three Spanish gunboats into the inner harbour. The dockyard people had already replaced the white Bourbon cockade with the Revolutionary one. Triumphant shouting and republican songs could be heard from the French soldiers rampaging into Toulon town. The immediate menace was a surprising one. Prisoners, whom the French often assigned to galleys, had freed themselves from their chains on board the galleys and attacked the party. Sidney Smith kept the guns of the tender aimed at the galleys as the other craft went about sinking the French ships.

Instead of sinking a frigate, as they had been ordered to do, the Spanish on one of the gunboats set her alight. She had been packed with one thousand or more barrels of gunpowder and the explosion nearly destroyed the entire party. One gunboat was blown to pieces, others badly damaged. One of Sidney Smith's officers and three sailors were killed in the blast or from the rain of flaming debris, but they gathered themselves and continued sinking and burning ships. Then another powder ship blew up. The conflagration and roar and ceaseless firing imposed itself indelibly upon the minds of those present. Napoleon on St Helena recalled his own awe of it: 'The whirlwind of flames and smoke from the arsenal resembled the eruption of a volcano, and the thirteen vessels blazing in the roads were like so many displays of fireworks: the masts and forms of the vessels were distinctly traced out by the flames, which lasted many hours and formed an unparalleled spectacle.'

As the inner harbour exploded on 18 December, the British fleet withdrew from the outer harbour and road of Toulon to lie between Hyères Bay and the Iles d'Hyères, there to consider the immediate tactical future.

As an anticlimax, on that very day a message went from London to Hood advising that two thousand men would be sent from Ireland.

There was now a great deal to mull over, both aboard *Victory* off Hyères and in London. To the last Hood made no practical gesture towards possible evacuation. When the decision was finally forced there was no time for any systematic destruction of the port and the formidable French fleet that lay there. A huge fleet was lost to the British. Although twenty-five French warships were set alight, including thirteen ships of the line, half of them were recovered and restored to action by the French. Three French line ships, including the 120-gun *Commerce de Marseille*, together with three frigates and seven corvettes, sailed out with the British, this their modest prize from the great fleet that might have been theirs. Rear Admiral Trogofte, commanding the flagship *Commerce De Marseille*, had allied himself to the British from the start.

Across Britain loss of Toulon was coupled with dismay over the lack of action on the Atlantic. Howe had either been at sea with his fleet vainly searching for the French, or briefly at Torbay for supplies. For the people at large all of this seeming inaction was as poor a showing as Toulon. Scorn from the public prints focused on the fact that the French fleet was several times sighted by Howe's Western Squadron yet there had been no captures, no battle fought. Howe was widely blamed. The uncomfortable fact to be faced was that a full decade of peace had brought a generation of inexperienced men to sea.

As Howe's young signal lieutenant Edward Codrington later said, 'When our fleet, composed of inferior men and of inferior ships, and commanded by officers, some of whom in the commonest evolutions betrayed a want of seamanship and of knowledge of their profession, got a distant view of the French fleet, superior in numbers, on our first putting to sea in July, 1793, Lord Howe did his utmost to get them in order to bring them to battle.' But for his failure with them Howe paid dearly in public perception for, as Howe's biographer John Barrow commented, '. . . if they hear not of a battle and a victory, are apt to become dissatisfied, and to conclude that, as nothing of the kind has taken place, blame must rest somewhere, and where can it be more appropriately fixed than on the shoulders of the commander-in-chief? . . . Such was the clamour that prevailed in the year 1793 among all ranks and descriptions of men . . . The public prints of the day . . . were exceedingly and offensively scurrilous against the British admiral, sometimes gravely or ridiculously critical, at other times sarcastic.'

Howe and his ships and their crews were in desperate need of their break when, finally in the middle of December, this grand fleet of eighteen sail of the line and five frigates was brought into port and laid up, half at Portsmouth and the other half at Plymouth. There they were to remain until May 1794.

A small, brilliant feat followed as postscript to Toulon. Hood's nephew, Captain Samuel Hood, commanding the 32-gun frigate *Juno*, brought his ship into Toulon harbour some two weeks after the evacuation, ignorant of what had taken place. Unable to see the British fleet he guessed them to have moved into the inner harbour. He took his ship in. Passing a brig at anchor Captain Hood hailed her to ask where the British admiral lay. He made no sense of the answers.

As *Juno* anchored a boat full of French officers and officials boarded her. Hood assumed them to be French working with the British. But a midshipman observed that they all wore republican cockades. A lieutenant said, 'I believe, sir, we shall be able to fetch out, if we can get her under sail.'

Hood instantly ordered the French below. Marines with pikes forced them down. In less than three minutes every sail was set and braced for casting. As soon as the cable was taut it was cut. The head sails filled and *Juno* moved out. The brig and the forts began firing on her, but she made the open water, firing at the shore as she found her way out.[2]

IX

CORSICA

As the first year of the war drew to a close Britain and her allies confronted general uncertainty, with a stalemate on land and a lack of any result upon sea. The broad situation that the British parliament surveyed as it met at the end of January 1794 offered little of immediate prospect to build upon, with scant gain so far against the turbulent power that commanded France.

France's rush against Holland and Belgium had been held. But strong doubts were arising concerning the staying power and involvement of Prussia, which remained preoccupied with Poland and territories it wanted there. Austrian mistrust of Prussia was deep and growing. The coalition and its military thrust appeared stalled. So it would remain, deep into 1794, accompanied by increasing anxiety about the rising strength, cohesion and success of the French army under the organizing vitality of Carnot.

The spirited new French army was everywhere demonstrating its recovery. Across the south the anti-Jacobin revolt had been fully suppressed. But for the British it was the failure at Toulon and the lack of any line ship action in the western approaches during 1793 that had provoked real dismay.

The overall strategy for the Continent visualized by Pitt was destruction of the Jacobin government. This was seen as the most likely means of terminating the war. The Austrians preferred it as the quickest solution and it was agreed that Paris should therefore be the target of a new campaign. But who would bear the fullest burden of the cost of it all, particularly the huge Austrian and Prussian armies?

The formula taking shape was the traditional one in which a Britain weak in land forces and chary of committing those she possessed to Continental warfare instead contributed to the costs of others or paid for mercenaries who fought on her behalf. But the picture that was forming even in late 1793 already hinted that the position against France might not hold even on that familiar basis. Weighing it up, Britain at the start of 1794 could, with perspicacity, recognize the other side of that situation, something equally familiar, which was that somewhere along she might find herself on her own. And that brought her back where her own certainties dwelled, what she felt sure of: the sea and her navy. But in January 1794 anxious questions touched that as well.

Earl Howe's failure to bring the French grand fleet to battle sat badly upon the nation as a whole. The British public wanted battle from its navy. They wanted it in their home waters, where their real security lay. They wanted the assurance of it in a war the direction and balance of which no one yet could properly fathom. It was from the navy, so closely tied to British emotion and sentiment and conviction of destiny, that some positive assurance was required. Some affirmation of British naval mastery was needed to alleviate the ingrained fear of invasion.

Whatever the outcome on the Continent there had to be assurance that the navy retained its full capability of defending Britain's shores, her primal defence, while maintaining its dominance upon the broad oceanic strategic picture, the source of Britain's power and wealth.

The man committed to the latter was Secretary of State for War Dundas, a hard, ruthless, greedy Scot who later, as Lord Melville, head of the Admiralty, was to face a difficult trial in parliament on charges of corruption. He effectively dominated colonial policy under Pitt. Unlike Pitt, he upheld slavery and the slave trade, attracting the implacable hostility of the Evangelical Abolitionists. It was symptomatic of Pitt's broadly balanced position in the fractured society of late-eighteenth-century Britain that as Prime Minister he was equally comfortable in his working relationships with such different characters and viewpoints.

Dundas had already declared that in this war he never wanted to have to choose between colonial defence and that of the Continent. Here was the revived voice of Chatham, Pitt the Elder. For Henry Dundas, too, if forced to choose, his priority would ever be oceanic, attached to colonial possession and trade rather than Continental Europe. In early 1794 his colonial focus was anxiously fixed upon the West Indies.

After Britain's loss of the American colonies and France's loss of Canada, the West Indies had become the focal point of colonial interests. The West Indies stood as the immediate indispensable source of colonial wealth. Troops that would have made a big difference at Toulon were mustered for the West Indies instead. Departure of the Indies force was delayed until the end of November, after deployment to the French coast in the futile attempt to give assistance to the rebellion in La Vendée. Finally, on 27 November 1793, a powerful squadron commanded by Vice Admiral Sir John Jervis, bearing seven thousand troops under Lieutenant General Sir Charles Grey, sailed from St Helens for a winter crossing of the Atlantic.

The loss of Toulon signified something greater than the loss of the base itself. After sweeping away rebellion in the south, the French now had what they called the Army of Italy, a new threat to all the British allies along the coasts of the Ligurian Sea. Sardinia, Genoa, Leghorn (Livorno) and, though much more distantly, Naples and Sicily, all suddenly looked more vulnerable.

This was what Hood contemplated in January 1794, as his fleet lay anchored in its retreat at Hyères Bay, just a few miles from Toulon. Hood had lost the place that Marlborough in his war had considered being the key to Mediterranean and trans-Alpine military action. French success in the south of France and French pressure on the Austro-Sardinian forces around and beyond the Alps meant that Marlborough's Mediterranean strategy had become as relevant to this war as it had been to his.

Unhappily for Hood the French fleet at Toulon and the extensive naval facilities there, the command base of French power on the western Mediterranean, would soon be restored.

Hood required a new base to cope with that. It had to be somewhere accessible to supplies, where storage depots could be maintained and ships repaired and refitted. And from where Austrian and Sardinian military operations could be supported. Hood looked at his maps and with Corsica lying large before him it was the obvious choice. It offered good harbours, easy provisioning and, best of all, plenty of timber for ship repair.

Corsica, formerly the possession of Genoa, had been ceded to France in 1768. It was the Genoese connection that had given Napoleon Buonaparte his Italian antecedents. The nationalist leader, Pasquale Paoli, was fighting the French and had already asked George III to take the island under British protection. In 1793 his partisans had established positions of strength across much of this wild, mountainous island, but the French commanded its principal strategic bases.

The objective for Hood would be the large bay of San Fiorenzo at the northern end of Corsica. Fiorenzo was the natural shelter for a fleet with defensive outposts at the fortresses of Bastia and Calvi. With these three points taken from the French, the British navy would cover the most vitally strategic stretch of coast in the entire Mediterranean, the Ligurian coast.

Fiorenzo lay a mere two hundred or so kilometres directly south of Genoa across the Ligurian Sea. Within easy reach stretched the entire coastline from Toulon to Elba. Apart from Toulon itself, this reach embraced such diverse points as Nice, Genoa, Spezia and Leghorn. A tight blockade of Toulon would be maintained with French trade and supply through Genoa and Leghorn to Corsica equally tightly controlled, if not curtailed.

To Captain Nelson, Hood promptly delegated the task of preparation for this critical offensive through which British command of the Mediterranean might become absolute. The zeal with which Nelson committed himself to his new task indicated his own conviction of that. From the last days of the old year into the first weeks of the new he had been blockading the Corsican coastline to lock in the French ships at their Corsican anchorages and to deny the French army its supplies. Two French frigates were destroyed at their anchorage. Garrison stores on land were destroyed by *Agamemnon*'s guns from the sea. Supply ships were captured. Nelson in short time made himself master of the coast around Bastia. *Agamemnon*'s sailors began to regard themselves as 'invincible, almost invulnerable', he wrote to his wife. 'They really mind shot no more than peas.'

The first assault on Fiorenzo nevertheless failed. Hood suspected treachery from islanders who, though fighting the French, were ever hostile to any invaders of their shores. On 12 January Hood sent a delegation from the fleet to Corsica for new discussions with Paoli at his base. The party consisted of two army officers and Sir Gilbert Elliot, who was to represent Britain on the island. The group reported favourably and Hood immediately sailed for Fiorenzo from Hyères Bay.

As the siege of Fiorenzo began sailors undertook the task of reducing one of the outlying fortifications, Forneilli, whose guns covered Fiorenzo. Forneilli was a formidably fortified redoubt that appeared to defy any form of assault. Its natural defence, height and steep access, was the common one of a place as ruggedly mountainous as Corsica. It was dominated, however, by a rock-like projection, several hundred feet above sea level, which the French had failed to fortify, in an apparent belief that it was inaccessible. The ascent to the top appeared close to perpendicular in places, seldom much wider than what allowed one person to stand. But up that path the sailors dragged the heavy guns brought ashore to form a battery, from which they poured shot upon Forneilli, forcing the French to retreat into Fiorenzo. Getting the guns to the top was an astonishing feat of strength, endurance and determination, a tough accomplishment of a kind not at that time associated with naval sailors. But the precedent had been set at Toulon, where a naval officer had led the invading force ashore and where artillery had similarly been hauled to the heights and manned there by sailors.

Nelson initiated on Corsica the sort of sailor landings and land operations that would become a frequent and indispensable form of naval assault throughout this war. On Corsica those provided the fuller action and excitement that Nelson had been craving. Toulon had denied him action, although many of his own sailors had been taken ashore to fight. Corsica at once promised something different, and delivered it. This sudden licence for what Nelson relished most, independent action, enlivened him. He wrote to his wife, 'I have not been one hour at anchor for pleasure in eight months; but I can assure you I never was better in health.'

Hood's dependence upon Nelson mounted steadily. Certainly he would have found no one else with the same zest for what was allocated to him. All of it resounds from Nelson's correspondence at the time. Hood, he said, trusted his 'zeal and activity'. On the business of contacting and conferring with Paoli, 'This business going through my hands is a proof of Lord Hood's confidence in me, and that I shall pledge myself for nothing but what will be acceptable to him.'

On 19 February the French abandoned Fiorenzo and retreated to Bastia. That same day Nelson had gone ashore with sixty troops and marched to within three miles of Bastia. He was surveying Bastia's defences at the time of the Fiorenzo assault and delivered an exhaustive report on the fortifications, their vulnerabilities and on how the place might be taken. That task became the fire in his mind.

Hood's faith in Nelson had reached the point where he took care to avoid placing a senior captain over him on these Corsican operations, the next phase of which, Bastia, was thus entirely entrusted to Nelson, who now had six frigates under his command.

Closing off Bastia was vital. From Bastia across to Leghorn offered the shortest direct passage between Corsica and the mainland. It was therefore the main supply point for the French. Bastia was a walled town of ten thousand inhabitants with a citadel at its centre. The main fortifications were along the sea front, with others in the hills above guarding the approaches from Fiorenzo. The high batteries would also intimidate any force that might manage to seize the town. But Nelson was all for rushing and taking the place at once. He had examined landing places near Bastia and believed that troops and cannon could be landed with great ease on level country south of the town. His reports went over almost daily from *Agamemnon* to Hood aboard *Victory* lying off Fiorenzo. He reported that the French were ceaselessly strengthening the defences of Bastia. Nevertheless, 'Bastia, I am sure, in its present state, would soon fall,' he wrote to Hood.

On 23 February Nelson decided on close reconnoitre and bombardment of Bastia from the sea. It was to be a studiedly slow-paced challenge to Bastia's firepower from his frigates, led by *Agamemnon*. 'I backed our main top-sail and passed slowly along the town.' Twenty-seven identifiable guns and four mortars firing from the shore, the heights and the town itself commenced pouring shot and shells upon the small fleet of frigates. The cannonading between ships and shore lasted nearly two hours. Although every ship was struck not a man was killed or wounded aboard any of them.

During the action British troops appeared on the heights above Bastia. They were under Lieutenant General Sir David Dundas, who had commanded the military at Toulon. He was a close relative of Minister Henry Dundas, to whom he sent 'whining' letters that the ever-optimistic Dundas contemptuously rejected. The troops had come over on the twelve-mile land route from Fiorenzo. They made no move down to attack from the heights.

The appearance of the military raised impatient reflection with Nelson. In a letter to his wife detailing the events of that day he said, 'If I had carried with me five hundred troops, to a certainty I should have stormed the Town, and I believe it might have been carried. Armies go so slow, that Seamen think they never mean to get forward; but I dare say they act on a surer principle, although we seldom fail. You cannot think how pleased Lord Hood has been with my attack . . .' In a letter to his brother on the same event he gave the army less allowance: 'Our troops are not yet got to work. I can't think what they are after.'

What he himself was after, now even more determinedly so, was to do what he felt the army was failing to do. Hood, in remarkable concurrence with such precipitate possibility of conflict between the two services, was swiftly of the same mind. But when Dundas brought his troops back down to Fiorenzo, Hood sought to persuade him to return and attempt to take Bastia. Dundas refused. He believed that starvation by blockade would in due course bring submission, without the loss of life that would result from direct assault. And, he forcefully asserted, Hood indubitably would be of the same opinion were the whole responsibility of such an attack to rest upon *his* shoulders.[1]

'Nothing would be more gratifying to my feelings, than to have the whole responsibility upon me,' Hood coldly corrected.

'What the general could have seen to have made a retreat necessary, I cannot conceive,' Nelson wrote in his journal. 'I wish not to be thought arrogant, or presumptuously sure of my own judgment, but it is my firm opinion that the Agamemnon with only the frigates now here, lying against the town for a few hours with 500 troops ready to land . . . would to a certainty carry the place. I presumed to propose it to Lord Hood and his Lordship agreed with me.'

Hood agreed that Nelson might take the town with five hundred troops backed by three ships of the line from Hood's squadron but doubted that Nelson could take the heights as well. Hood therefore went back on shore from *Victory* two days after his first meeting with Dundas to press the matter with him again. But he got no further: Dundas refused even more vehemently than before, declaring that an attack on Bastia was impracticable without the reinforcement of two thousand troops requested from Gibraltar, adding 'I consider the siege of Bastia, with our present means and force, to be a most visionary and rash attempt, such as no Officer could be justified in undertaking.' Dundas's force consisted of sixteen hundred regulars and 180 artillery men. Nelson's estimate of the strength of the French in Bastia had been one thousand regulars and fifteen hundred 'irregulars', the latter Corsicans.

Hood's written reply to Dundas was sharply edged: 'I must take the liberty to observe, that however visionary and rash an attempt to reduce Bastia may be in your opinion, to me it appears very much the reverse, and to be perfectly a right measure . . . and I am now ready and willing to undertake the reduction of Bastia at my own risk, with the force and means at present here, being strongly impressed with the necessity of it.'[2]

Faced by that intractable declaration of intent Dundas resigned his command. Unfortunately for Hood the successor to the command, General d'Aubant, shared Dundas's views. And he unrelentingly stuck by them. He not only refused soldiers for an assault on and siege of Bastia but also withheld from Hood mortars, field guns and ammunition from the stores he controlled at Fiorenzo. Hood was compelled to send to Naples for the materiel he lacked. But he exercised his own powers by recalling on board his ship's soldiers from four regiments who had previously been allocated to him to do temporary service as marines and whom he had loaned to Dundas for the capture of Fiorenzo. Since these soldiers were now registered as part of the complements of the ships aboard which they were quartered d'Aubant was unable to refuse to release them.

The siege of this remote Corsican fortress of Bastia became bitter infighting between the Royal Navy and the army. With the soldiers under d'Aubant's command confined to their garrison in Fiorenzo, this was the navy's war or, so to speak, Hood's and Nelson's personal campaign. For Nelson, Bastia had to fall, and soon. To him the attitude of the army in refusing to join with Hood in the assault was incomprehensible. 'Not attacking it I could not but consider as a national disgrace. If the Army will not take it, we must, by some way or the other.'

Through March Nelson maintained the blockade of Bastia, with *Agamemnon* riding out near-continuous gales and thick weather. From his storm-lashed quarterdeck Nelson angrily watched the town daily strengthening its defences: '. . . how that has hurt me'. Some of the hardship he was imposing upon Bastia was being experienced aboard *Agamemnon* as well. On 16 March he reported to Hood, 'We are really without firing, wine, beef, pork, flour and almost without water: not a rope, canvas, twine or nail in the ship . . . We are certainly in a bad plight at present, not a man has slept dry for many months.' As postscript to that same note in his journal he added, 'But we cheerfully submit to it all, if it but turns out for the advantage and credit of our country.' Holding on was critical for Nelson personally, his fear being that if *Agamemnon* were compelled to go to Leghorn for stores he would lose his own role in the attack on Bastia. He was in something like near panic over missing out on another land operation, one so closely involving his own efforts and persuasion. He put it to Hood, 'My wish is to be present at the attack of Bastia; and if your Lordship intends me to command the Seamen who may be landed, I assure you I shall have the greatest pleasure in doing it, or any other service where you may think I can do most good: even if my ship goes into port to refit, I am ready to remain.' Hood responded and *Agamemnon*'s deficiencies were supplied from the squadron and other sources.[3]

Nelson, together with an army artillery officer and an army engineer, then made steady reconnaissance ashore to decide landing beaches and sites for batteries northward of Bastia. He pitched a tent on a beach with the union flag hoisted above it, and was thereafter in continual movement between tent and *Agamemnon*. His presence on land was constant because his sailors, with others from the squadron, were building batteries, clearing roads and hauling guns and ammunition to the batteries. Like the earlier effort, it was a phenomenal task dragging guns up those rocky and precipitous heights, requiring physical strength and stamina that astonished all who witnessed it. 'It is very hard service for my poor seamen, dragging guns up such heights as are scarcely credible,' Nelson wrote. And, after his sailors had dragged guns to a pinnacle just seven hundred yards from the town, he described it as a feat 'which never, in my opinion, would have been accomplished by any other than British seamen'.

Hood took full command on 4 April, though preparation for the siege remained with Nelson. By 11 April three batteries equipped with sixteen heavy guns and mortars were ready to open fire on Bastia. Hood sent in a flag of truce demanding surrender. The answer he got from La Combe St Michel, Corsica's commissioner, was defiant: 'I have hot shot for your ships and bayonets for your troops. When two-thirds of our troops are killed, I will then trust to the generosity of the English.'

The battle for Bastia began at once. Navy and Bastia began pouring shot and mortars upon one another. The cannonade was immense. From commanding positions over the town, the citadel and the outworks five British 24-pounders, four mortars and two heavey carronades poured their fire while the ships opened up from the sea. Thus it was to remain through April and on into the third week of May. Bastia continued to hold out defiantly, in spite of the destruction raining upon it and the starvation afflicting its garrison and populace.

Bizarrely, throughout the campaign General d'Aubant and his officers had simply stood by as interested observers.

On 19 May the French asked for negotiation. A boat went from *Victory* to the town. 'The enemy met us without arms, and our officers advancing, they shook hands, and were good friends: they said it was all over, and that Bastia was ours,' Nelson recorded in his journal. General d'Aubant and the soldiers from Fiorenzo simultaneously appeared on the hills above the town. They were there because reinforcement had just arrived from Gibraltar. They then proceeded to occupy Bastia and all its outposts.

The garrison was far stronger than Hood believed and had held out longer than expected. Nelson, however, *had* known. He knew it two months before the siege began. Here, then, was the near-fearful recklessness that ever pulsed in this extraordinary man. He had got the information from a packet boat intercepted by *Agamemnon*. The mailbag on board contained a letter from Corsica's commissioner, General La Combe St Michel, declaring that he needed subsistence for eight thousand French and Corsican soldiers. This was four times as many as estimated by Nelson and Hood, but Nelson kept that critical information to himself. He rightly believed that disclosure would set Hood against any assault against Bastia. It would embarrassingly confirm Dundas's verdict that such an attack would be 'visionary and rash'. Failure to attack had been insufferable to Nelson. It went wholly against his disdain for holding off and failing to try. There was as well the conviction that his sailors could master any situation given the proper leadership and motivation.

Had he persuaded Hood into the sort of landing that he had cried out for at the start it could have finished them both, for they likely would have suffered heavy loss in the attack. This provided illustration of the length to which Nelson was prepared to go, whatever the risk and circumstances, to ensure action for himself. It worked at sea, and much of his future glory would be based upon it. But he never learned the point that Napoleon, in his memoirs, made on the difference at battle scene between land and sea: 'A marine general has nothing to guess; he knows where his enemy is, and knows his strength. A land general never knows anything with certainty, never sees his enemy plainly . . . When the armies are facing each other, the slightest accident of the ground, the least wood, may hide a party of the hostile army. The most experienced eye cannot be certain whether it sees the whole of the enemy's army, or only three fourths of it . . . The marine general requires nothing but an experienced eye; nothing relating to the enemy's strength is concealed from him.'[4] A year after Bastia had fallen Nelson was to confess, 'I never yet told Lord Hood that . . . I had information given me of the enormous number of troops we had to oppose us; but my own honour, Lord Hood's honour, and the honour of our country must have all been sacrificed, had I mentioned what I knew.'[5] He had been prepared for that risk, and would be again. And in his correspondence on this matter he described as well as he ever would the settled principles that drove him: 'I feel for the honour of my country, and had rather be beat than not make the attack. If we do not try we can never be successful . . . My reputation depends on the opinion I have given; but I feel an honest consciousness that I have done right. We must, we will have it, or some of our heads will be laid low. I glory in the attempt,' he told his wife in one of his many assertive letters at the time. Or, on another occasion, 'My disposition cannot bear tame and slow measures.' Also, '. . . our country will, I believe, sooner forgive an officer for attacking his enemy than for letting it down'. And, in response to his wife's continual fears over his safety, 'Only recollect that a brave man dies but once, a coward all his life long.'

At all events, Bastia had been won. He and his sailors had done it. 'The more we see of this place, the more we are astonished at their giving it up,' Nelson said. Starvation was probably the greatest factor in compelling early surrender. On that point at least General Dundas has been insightfully correct.

The surrender and occupation of Bastia and its fortifications were complete by 22 May. The army had taken over, under Lieutenant Colonel Villettes, and for Nelson what had been his operation no longer was. An attack was about to be launched against the other fortress, Calvi, and he saw his own role diminished and uncertain. Although Hood had allowed Nelson a free hand while the army held off, he had never in any way defined Nelson's command. In the new circumstances Nelson saw himself at a disadvantage with the army. He was, he said in a letter home, 'everything, yet nothing ostensible'.

Nelson then put his unease to Hood: 'Your Lordship knows exactly the situation I am in here. With Colonel Villettes I have no reason but to suppose I am respected in the highest degree . . . but yet I am considered as not commanding the seamen landed. My wishes may be, and are, complied with; my orders would possibly be disregarded. Therefore, if we move from hence, I would wish your Lordship to settle that point.'

Hood gave sympathetic acknowledgement without, however, issuing any decisive clarification of the sort Nelson wanted. Hood had already had too many difficulties with the army without inviting more. The idea of conceding clearly defined authority to Nelson as his man there may have raised fear in Hood of Nelson's impatience and impetuosity provoking trouble with the army.

For Hood defeat at Toulon had been followed, after much uncertainty, by triumph at Fiorenzo and Bastia. Towards Calvi all now directed their attention. There was no basis for doubting another imminent triumph there as well. Hood was in poor health and expected soon to be going home. He would wish to return expecting the sort of salutation and honours that these successes would ensure. He now possibly believed that Nelson's energetic and impulsive bravado needed to be subdued. Hood was by this time certainly aware of the possible loss that might have been suffered had he yielded to Nelson's early impetuous conviction that Bastia might be won by merely five hundred seamen. Nevertheless, he had benefited in the end from that impetuosity. What Hood's reputation had gained here he owed to Nelson. Difficult therefore to understand what Hood now officially delivered concerning Nelson's part at Bastia.

Aboard *Victory* lying off Bastia, on 22 May Hood wrote his first report, his general order of thanks directly to the participants in the action. It was brief, direct. 'The commander in chief returns his best thanks to Captain Nelson . . . as well as to every officer and seaman employed in the reduction of Bastia . . .' But when Hood sat down and composed his official report to the Admiralty his tributes were framed differently.

Hood's report to Admiralty began with particularly fulsome praise for 'the unremitting zeal, exertion and judicious conduct' of Colonel Villettes. As for the other army officers, 'their persevering ardour, and desire to distinguish themselves, cannot be too highly spoken of; and which it will be my pride to remember to the latest period of my life'. Then, 'Captain Nelson, of His Majesty's ship Agamemnon, who had the command and direction of the seamen, in landing the guns, mortars and stores; and Captain Hunt, who commanded at the batteries . . . have an ample claim to my gratitude; as the seamen . . .' This praise for Hunt particularly riled Nelson, for Hunt was a protégé of Hood who had made minimal contribution to their success.

Apart from the spareness of the praise in comparison with that which extolled the army officers, for Hood to have so limited Nelson's part in all of it to that of a mere supervisor of the landing of guns and stores coldly denigrated the whole of Nelson's extraordinary achievement there, ignored Hood's own faith in and dependence upon him, dismissed the boldness and endurance that had helped to establish their very presence on the Corsican coast.

Like the others, Nelson saw Hood's initial congratulatory General Order at once. But it would be several weeks before copies of the Admiralty report reached him. When it did it was to be a jolting shock. Regardless of that brutal insensitivity and lack of consideration, it was nevertheless Hood's gift of responsibility on Corsica that finally meant everything. For here on Corsica in the first half of 1794 began the remarkable ascendancy in this war of this unique character, Horatio Nelson. So much of what was to mould his greater role in such a determining war was cast here. In Corsica Nelson drew upon himself the sort of command he sought in which to exercise his independence and express the individuality so vital to him. The conquest of Corsica was Nelson's achievement. Land battle thus arrived before sea battle for Nelson in this war. He had had his first action at sea, a small encounter on the way to Tunis, but what he ardently longed for was to be part of the confrontation between the French and the British navies on that large and decisive scale that might settle the issue on this sea and on the ocean beyond. That was yet distant.

*   *   *

On the other side of the world the considerable naval force commanded by Sir John Jervis and accompanied by a military force of seven thousand troops under General Sir Charles Grey had commenced operations in the West Indies.

They had arrived at Barbados at the beginning of January and within three months the French had lost every one of their West Indian possessions. But the British operation quickly suffered a reverse. A small French force turned up unexpectedly and overcame the small British force at Guadeloupe's strongest post, Fleur d'Epée. For the next six months the British were engaged in ceaseless, ineffectual and debilitating struggle to regain the island and secure St Dominigue (Haiti).

The West Indies campaign became a deep morass into which the British continued to sink. It was to be one of the worst experiences in all British military history. Yellow fever ravaged the forces, on land as well as aboard the ships. On shore, the soldiers in their thick, tight uniforms that made no allowance to climate had to fight in the steamy, torridly heavy climate of the islands against blacks and Creoles for whom those conditions were a natural environment.

The constant drastic depletion of the military forces in the West Indies and lack of reinforcement from Britain meant that the navy had to be constantly called upon. An outstanding feature of these West Indian operations in 1794 therefore became a unique dependence upon seamen. Never before in war had the navy been inducted so swiftly and comprehensively into military land activity. On Martinique and Guadeloupe the naval contribution was as distinctive as that of Corsica. Sailors dragged cannon and mortars up heights that appeared impossible to others but they also had to pull them for many miles along rough roads. Some roads they cut themselves, through thick wood. In one especially remarkable achievement they astonished the army when, in three days, they cut a road nearly a mile long through thick forest, made a passage across a river by filling the crossing point with huge slabs of rock and stone, got a 24-pounder cannon to the base of a mountain whose summit was a mile distant, and on the following day dragged the gun and two additional 24-pounders up an ascent so steep that a loaded mule could not walk up it in a direct manner. They manned the batteries they built. They assaulted forts with scaling ladders they made from thick bamboo.

On the Atlantic, meanwhile, there had arrived what all had so desperately longed for. After a year and a half of a war that had lacked naval action of the consoling and decisive sort upon which British morale depended, Earl Howe had finally brought the French Grand Fleet to battle.

X

BATTLE

THE winter lay-up of the Royal Navy's battle fleet between the end of 1793 and the spring of 1794 was an astonishing six months.

Lay-up was common to all Atlantic fleets. Although the late-eighteenth-century wooden ship was capable of toughing out hurricane in the West and East Indies and riding the Atlantic at its worst, formal winter battle was never sought. Until late into the eighteenth century it was considered unwise for line ships to dare the Bay of Biscay after October. The price of winter operations was considered too high even in the Narrow Seas. The wear upon ships was far too costly. Storms prevented or thwarted tactical manoeuvre. So, too, with gunnery. Firing from decks that were alternately swinging skywards or down to near beam ends with unpredictable velocity was hardly practicable. And then there was the problem of the gun ports. The risk of them open in rough weather was huge: the ship could instantly be flooded. This was especially dangerous for the British, whose gun ports were usually closer to the water than those of France and Spain. As the heaviest guns were on the lower deck, rough weather limited their use. The late summer and autumnal gales of 1793 had demonstrated how difficult maintaining large wooden ships in the Channel for protracted periods could be even in what should be fair season. Howe had come in with badly strained ships and crews in low morale. So much repair was required that it extended far into the spring.

The navy's lack of action in 1793 weighed heavy on the public mind. The public knew that the French fleet had beén constantly on the move through the year but Earl Howe's squadron, guardian of the home waters, had been ineffectual even in catching up with it. With Howe's squadron already laid up for winter, two ships of the line, both 74-gun, accompanied by two frigates and a brig, sailed from Brest on 26 December under Rear Admiral Van Stabel escorting a merchant fleet of 130 ships. The convoy was destined for the West Indies and America, to bring back American grain and West Indian produce. The reputation of Howe and his fleet would therefore depend upon the interception of that convoy on its return in the spring of 1794. It would be a contest with the Grand Fleet that would indubitably go out to help to bring the convoy into Brest and Rochefort.

France's dire need to protect her inbound trade meant that the mandatory reach and focus of the French navy was now out into the Atlantic, bringing in the convoys. The convoying meant that the main operational area of the French fleet now included the whole of the Biscay coast south of Ushant and the westward reach beyond out into the Atlantic. The main area of operational deployment that thus arose might roughly be said to have formed a block of ocean covering about five hundred square miles, if you took a line drawn from the westernmost point of Ireland down to the latitude of Cape Finisterre, with the sweep of it pivoted upon Ushant.

Although no great sea battle had yet been fought deep into the ocean, the probability had now arrived. The dependence of both countries upon trade had determined this, with Britain no less than France. While wishing to intercept the French convoys to deprive the French of what they needed, the British navy had to protect its own merchant shipping, whose inbound and outbound passage necessarily crossed the main arena of French naval deployment. And that meant any early encounter between the two grand fleets now was destined to be out on the open Atlantic within or just without Biscay, an expanse of ocean that could be as violent in its temper as practically any other on the face of the earth.

For an experience so radically new fortunately the British navy was equipped with the new. It had a code of signals that Earl Howe had devised during the long peace. Together with this clearer signalling system the navy had unprecedented freedom of manoeuvre, thanks to Rodney and Clerk of Eldin. The latter's role provoked sharp controversy. The notion of a man without naval experience writing the navy's first textbook of tactics based on drawings was anathema to much of the naval mind, further incensed by the introduction to a new edition of Clerk's *Inquiry*: 'It was Clerk, then, who gave our naval commanders the first idea of the proper mode for attacking and bringing on decisive action. The Navy must admit that they did learn this from Clerk.'

The *Naval Chronicle*, the publication that was to become an intimate record of the war, was prepared to concur: '. . . experience has proved that we were defective in tactics. As our mode of attacking was then to range along the line of the enemy, until the van of our fleet came opposite the rear of his; thus our ships ran the gauntlet of the enemy's whole fleet, giving them an opportunity to cripple each ship as it passed, of which the French never failed to take advantage . . . The leading principle of Mr Clerk's system is, to force an enemy's fleet to close engagement, whatever efforts he may make to avoid it, and the breaking through his line of battle, and cutting off one division of his fleet from another, so as to prevent the enemy from being able to extricate himself, is recommended as a certain means of capturing the division you have cut off, or of bringing on a general engagement. The uniform success of this manoeuvre, now so well known, leaves no room to doubt the infallibility of Mr Clerk's system.'

There were those, however, who were still not prepared to give Clerk any credit. One was Edward Brenton, a historian of the war who served in the navy throughout. Of Clerk's work he wrote in 1823, '. . . a landsman has now the credit of having instructed our Admirals, and of being the founder of a system by which we have acquired the empire of the seas. To this proposition I can never subscribe.'

Nevertheless, all of this meant that the whole idea of tactical fluency was alive throughout the navy. If that had been wanting before, it was not now. The tactic was very much in Howe's mind at this time. So far he had been allowed no opportunity to emulate Rodney at the Saints. The urgent question with him aboard his 100-gun flagship *Queen Charlotte* in the spring of 1794 had to be whether that chance might now present itself.

Howe had behind him a career as distinguished as the Royal Navy in its combative history of that century could offer. In the American War, as commander in chief of the fleet on the American station, the conquests of New York, Rhode Island and Philadelphia were all attributed to his deployment of the fleet.

Howe's immediate objective would be to encounter on its return the big French convoy that had sailed out of Brest in December, and to engage the Grand Fleet that sailed out from Brest to escort it safely into port. It was known that the convoy had loaded heavily in the West Indies and then passed to Chesapeake Bay to load American grain. The pattern for such convoys was familiar. For fullest protection of its valuable freight it would avoid the worst of the winter but seek to get away as early as possible with the change of season. It would be expected to sail from the other side of the Atlantic in April with an early summer arrival at its eastern destination. The convoy and its escort had in fact sailed from Norfolk, Virginia, on 11 April 1794, bound for Brest, though this intelligence was not available to Howe before he sailed.

Howe's squadron, meanwhile, was handed its own convoying obligations. Its sailing instructions were to deliver out of the Biscay danger zone a convoy of ninety-nine merchantmen bound for three different destinations, the East Indies, West Indies and Newfoundland. The merchantmen were to be escorted by thirty-four ships of the line and fifteen other warships. This mighty assembly sailed from Spithead on 2 May. Two days later, off the Lizard, the merchantmen broke into their separate convoys. A squadron of six line ships and two frigates under Rear Admiral James Montagu detached from the main force to see the East Indies ships as far as the latitude of Cape Finisterre. Montagu's squadron was then to cover the southern area of the Bay of Biscay in case the French convoy out of Norfolk made its approach there. The main fleet under Howe put about and sailed for Ushant, off which they arrived on 5 May.

Howe's own task now was to cover the northern stretches of the bay to intercept the inbound French convoy and its escort. Three frigates ran in to reconnoitre Brest Roads. They returned to report that the main force of the French fleet was still lying in the anchorage. Howe then took his force of twenty-six line ships and seven frigates out deep into Biscay and began sailing to and fro across the likely approach of the Norfolk convoy. He remained on this station from 5 to 18 May.

On 6 May an initial escort of five ships of the line, accompanied by frigates and corvettes under Rear Admiral Nielly, sailed from Rochefort with orders to meet and help bring in Van Stabel's convoy out of Norfolk. That was followed on 16 May by the Grand Fleet of France, twenty-five line ships and a large accompanying force of frigates and corvettes, under Rear Admiral Villaret-Joyeuse. Bringing the grain safely to harbour was the French admiral's first task and responsibility. Battle was not. Robespierre himself had told Villaret-Joyeuse that failure to bring in the grain meant the guillotine. From the start, battle with the British navy was something to be avoided. Villaret-Joyeuse nevertheless bravely decided that, in the event of an encounter with the British fleet, his tactic had to be to draw the British fleet away from the approach of the American convoy.

Villaret-Joyeuse had all the polish and bearing of an officer of the old school. Like Howe, he was a veteran of the American War and was regarded as one of the best officers under Suffren, the greatest French admiral of the century (renowned for his near-mastery of the British navy in the Indian Ocean).

For Villaret-Joyeuse and Howe their moment in history might have arrived the day after the former sailed from Brest. Thick fog lay on the water on 17 May. The French fleet passed so close to the British that the latter's fog signals of beating drums and ringing bells were distinctly heard. But when the fog cleared on the 18th they had no sight of one another.

Five fleets – two British and three French – and four convoys – three British and one large French – were now moving within and about that defined space of five hundred square miles of ocean, each unit conscious that any moment of those lengthening spring days could bring a masthead cry declaring one or the other in sight.

By all calculation the French convoy out of Norfolk should now have been at the approaches to that area of the Atlantic, if not already inside it.

The *Redoutable* faces *Victory* and *Téméraire*, 5 October 1805

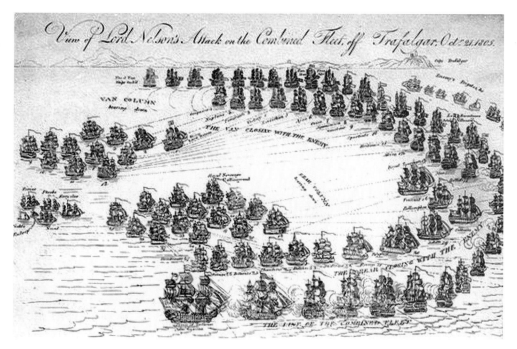

Nelson's attack on the Combined Fleet, Trafalgar, October 1805

The Impressment
of an American Seaman

A Scene on the Main Deck

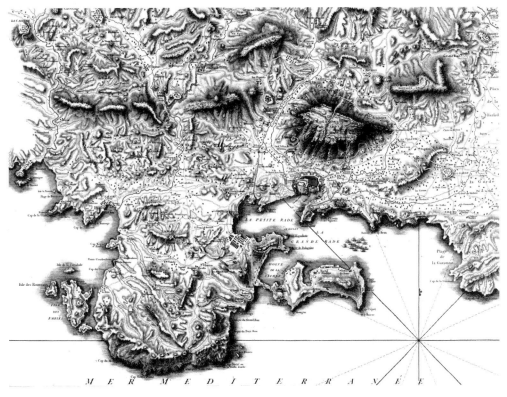

The Siege of Toulon, 18 September–18 December 1793

Napoleon Buonaparte,
Emperor of the French People, 1812

Rear Admiral Horatio Nelson

Alexander Hood, Lord Bridport

Sir Sidney Smith, imprisoned in
Temple Prison, Paris, 1796–1798

Sir Hyde Parker,
Captain of the *Phoenix*

Admiral Lord Keith

Rear Admiral Sir Thomas Troubridge

A view of Porto Ferrago, the capital of Elba and residence of Napoleon Buonaparte
May 1814–February 1815

Vice Admiral
Sir Thomas M. Hardy

John, Earl of St Vincent,
Admiral of the Fleet

Emma, Lady Hamilton

Horatia Nelson with a rocking horse

Sir Sidney Smith Defending the
Breach of Acre, May 1799

The attack on Copenhagen,
2 April 1801

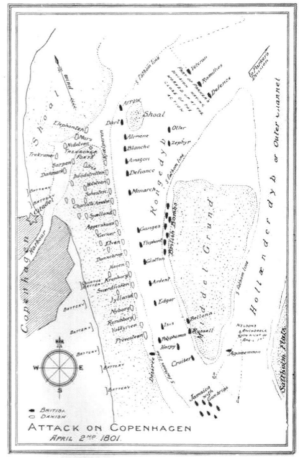

Captain Ellison's Action off Guernsey, 8 June 1794

The view of the British Fleet under the command of Admiral Duncan, breaking through the
Dutch line off Camperdown, near the Texel, 11 October 1797

Six weeks would be the assumption for a reasonably good passage, eight for slower. If the former, its arrival could now be any day. Howe, unaware of how close he had been to the Grand Fleet, remained ignorant that it had actually sailed from Brest. But on 19 May he sent two frigates to look into the harbour. They reported it empty. For the British the urgent search was now on for the missing fleet.

An unusual drama of catch now played itself out. Early success went to the French. The squadron that had sailed out of Rochefort under Admiral Nielly had encountered a British convoy inbound from Newfoundland and captured most of its ships as well as an escort, the 32-gun frigate *Castor*. On the same day Villaret-Joyeuse's Grand Fleet encountered another inbound convoy of fifty-three ships, mostly Dutch, and took half of them before the rest escaped with their escort.

Some of the French success was immediately reversed. Nielly had assigned a 20-gun corvette to escort ten of the captured Newfoundland ships to Rochefort. On 15 May the ships were recaptured together with their escort by Admiral Montagu's squadron. Montagu had delivered the East India convoy in his charge to south of Finisterre. He had then begun his own assigned patrol area between Cape Ortugal and the latitude of Belle Ile and almost immediately made his capture. What he obtained, together with his prizes, was first-rate intelligence.

Those who had briefly been prisoners of the French had accurate information on the strength of Nielly's squadron and on the composition and imminence of the Norfolk convoy. Howe received the news at four in the morning on the 20th. He then directed his fleet towards the position.

The next day, at two in the morning, the lookout cried a large fleet in sight. It proved to be the merchant fleet captured by Villaret-Joyeuse and under escort to Brest. Ten ships were recaptured. The others, with their escort, escaped. Howe, afraid of weakening his own crews by sending the ten ships into port as prizes, burnt them all after taking off their crews. The logbooks of the captured merchant ships now gave him his first positive position of Villaret-Joyeuse's fleet, two days since. From seamen brought aboard he also had the course steered by Villaret-Joyeuse's fleet when it parted from them.

All of this was electrifying to a fleet desperate for action. The excitement was the greater when French prisoners told them that Villaret-Joyeuse and his officers were determined, in the event of battle, to engage the British at close quarters. On 23 May three ships captured by the French fleet were encountered and retaken. From these logbooks Howe knew that he was closing. On 25 May other merchant prizes taken by Villaret-Joyeuse were also retaken. Howe knew that he was now running into Villaret-Joyeuse's cruising area.

What was crucial here for Howe was a notable example of what Julian Corbett regarded as the old and basic British naval creed. As Corbett saw it that creed was: 'Whatever the nature of the war in which we are engaged, whether it be limited or unlimited, permanent and general command of the sea is the condition of ultimate success. The only way of securing such a command by naval means is to obtain a decision by battle against the enemy's fleet. Sooner or later it must be done, and the sooner the better . . .'

Never was it to be so eagerly sought, however, as then. Howe and his sailors needed decisive battle as a vindication as much as necessity. But, as Corbett also pointed out:

In naval warfare we have a far-reaching fact which is entirely unknown on land. It is simply this – that it is possible for your enemy to remove his fleet from the board altogether . . . In land warfare we can determine with some precision the limits and direction of our enemy's possible movements. We know that they must be determined mainly by roads and obstacles. But afloat neither roads nor obstacles exist. There is nothing of the kind on the face of the sea to assist us in locating him and determining his movements . . . Consequently in seeking to strike our enemy the liability to miss him is much greater at sea than on land, and the chances of being eluded by the enemy whom we are seeking to bring to battle become so serious a check upon our offensive action as to compel us to handle the maxim of 'Seeking out the enemy's fleet' with caution.

The ocean nevertheless did possess its own signposts. There was now example of how on the wide and empty ocean the hunter could find his quarry. Passing merchantmen of all nationalities were usually stopped for news. Their logbooks, better than any mile post, would give time, day and position. That was what Howe now had from recaptured ships. And by the end of the eighteenth century intensified seagoing meant that commercial and naval passage had brought substantial familiarity that allowed reasonable basic calculations. That had allowed fairly accurate calculation on an approximate arrival of the Chesapeake convoy as well as some estimate of where Villaret-Joyeuse would be meeting it.

At six-thirty on the morning of 28 May, a rough sea running, the lookout frigates of the British fleet sighted sail, then a fleet, directly to windward ahead. One sighting was by Howe's young signal lieutenant, Edward Codrington, who at daylight was scouring the horizon from the masthead.

They were in the deep ocean, some four hundred miles west of Ushant.

By nine the approaching fleet was seen bearing down towards the British. Howe gave the signal to prepare for battle. The lookout frigates were recalled. At ten the French fleet, twenty-six ships of the line and five frigates, had approached to within nine or ten miles, then lay to. A three-decker was seen passing along the line, as if to speak to each ship. The French then formed their line.

At ten thirty-five the British fleet wore round on to the same tack as the French and advanced to windward in two columns. Shortly after that Howe signalled that there was yet time for the ships' companies to dine. Thereafter the British stood ready for action. But the French suddenly appeared to have a change of mind. At one p.m. the French ships made sail and began tacking. Howe signalled his lead ships, three 74s, *Russell*, *Marlborough* and *Thunderer*, to harass the enemy's rear ships. Then, when it appeared that the French were making off, he signalled for a general chase and for each ship to engage the enemy it caught up with.

The first shots were fired at two thirty by the *Russell* at the enemy's stern-most ships. The French returned the fire but the two fleets, with a squally wind and heavy sea, continued to tack for position, with the French twelve to fifteen miles to windward. At five, one of the largest of the French ships, the 110-gun *Révolutionnaire*, made a curious and, according to subsequent official reports, apparently unauthorized move. She removed herself from the van and passed to the rear of the enemy line, where she was engaged by several of the van ships of the British line. It was possible that her commander on his own initiative had taken her superior gun power from the van to the rear to offer protection to the weaker ships there. But the move was fatal. *Révolutionnaire* bore the fire of five different British ships and, as night settled, remained in furious engagement with one of them, *Audacious*. The fight was so close, so fierce, that the two effectively disabled one another as their fleets passed on into the night. But both *Audacious* and *Révolutionnaire* subsequently made it to their respective home ports.

A heavily dark night gave the inexperienced in the fleet their first awesome sight of the flash of guns blazing at the near-invisible forms on the water. A hard gale was blowing and the mounting seas prevented ships from getting up to the enemy and maintaining action, which ceased at half-past nine. The men nevertheless continued at their quarters all night.

Through the night, showing lights, the two fleets were on parallel courses, constantly manoeuvring as Howe sought to get to windward to facilitate attack.

At seven in the morning of the 29th, when Howe sent his first signal to his fleet to form their line, the weather was still rough. The French were still to windward, the position traditionally preferred by the British. Howe's intention was to cut through the French line and to engage. He had approached the battle zone with that strategy borne whole in mind: to bear down on the French line from windward, pass through it and then to engage at close quarters from leeward.

Here, then, was the first intentional return exercise of Rodney's tactic. But this was different. Rodney's action at the Saints in 1783 leaped from impulse presented by a different situation before him, notably a sudden change of wind that offered unexpected opportunity. He had sprung forward towards the French line and passed through it, leading others to do the same, thereby setting the historic example. But when Howe on 29 May signalled that he would cut through the enemy's line and engage to leeward he had that tactic firmly in mind as his *deliberate intention*. Howe thereby claimed his own special place in history, for on 29 May 1794, he was the first who, with premeditated intent, instructed his ships to bear down upon the French line, pass through, and create melee beyond.

Regrettably, 29 May was to offer Howe little success with the tactic. The sea was still building. Heavy pitching was soon to bring down the fore topmast of one of the French ships. Howe had his line assembled at seven a.m. The French were still to windward, where Howe wished to be. At seven thirty, to gain that position Howe signalled to pass through the enemy line and to come to windward. But little was achieved other than heavy broadsides and damage between the lead ships of both fleets. Howe's van ship, *Caesar*, by keeping her topsails reefed, failed to raise sufficient sail and appeared to ignore demands that she make more in order to lead the attack, in spite of being the best sailing ship in the fleet. As a result those astern of her also had to shorten sail, including *Queen Charlotte*. Damaging broadsides were exchanged between ships of both fleets without any advance of the situation being achieved.

The signal to pass through the enemy line was again raised at eleven thirty. *Caesar* again should have begun the manoeuvre but made no reply. The order was repeated. *Caesar* signalled an inability to tack and went about. It appeared to be laying off instead of bearing towards the enemy. Except for one ship, *Queen*, Rear Admiral Gardner, all the other lead ships in position ahead of *Queen Charlotte* also went about.

Queen, 98 guns, second in the line, continued towards the French line and, unable to pass through, continued along the line, firing and taking fire. She suffered so much damage that she eventually had to signal disability.

Invincible had accompanied *Queen* in cutting through the line. Joined by the *Royal George* the two brought to action the two rearmost ships in the French line, *Tyrannicide* and *Indomptable*.

Caesar's failure or unwillingness to set example meant that the French fleet was now drawing so far ahead that Howe feared his manoeuvre was about to fall away entirely. Watching *Queen* and *Invincible* take heavy punishment as they passed leeward along the French line Howe told Bowen, the master, 'Tack the Queen Charlotte, sir, and let us show them the example.'

The signal to cut through the French line and to engage was raised. At one thirty p.m. *Queen Charlotte* tacked and, like an expression of Howe's own contempt for his miscreant vessel, *Queen Charlotte* passed around the *Caesar* and under a press of sail made for the French line. She was followed by two other ships, those just ahead and just astern of her. These were *Bellerophon* and *Leviathan*. All three cut through the French line.

Howe's signal lieutenant, Edward Codrington, had his battle quarters on the lower deck. This was young Codrington's first action. His quarters were the foremost guns, larboard (port) and starboard, right up in the bows. The gun ports were all lowered to prevent the heavy seas washing in. Codrington was impatiently at his post as they came up to the French line. He had had no instruction to fire but, hauling up one of the weather-side ports, he saw that they were at that moment passing through the French line. He had all seven ports within his quarters instantly hauled up and fired his seven guns. He then hastened to the lee side and fired those as well.

While the guns were loading again Codrington was standing by the second gun from the bow when it suddenly went off. The recoil knocked Codrington senseless. The deck was by now filled with water from the open ports. Codrington was washed across the ship into the lee scuppers. The cold water probably brought him to his senses. He had no recollection of how he got where he was. He could just raise his head out of the water by leaning on his left arm. In his first action, instead of enemy shot, a drowning in Atlantic water washing about inside his ship was what nearly claimed him.

Queen Charlotte followed by *Bellerophon* and *Leviathan* were through the French line. Howe signalled for a general chase. The battle continued unevenly, confused by weather, tactical disorder and the succouring of disabled ships.

A distinctive incident came when Admiral Villaret-Joyeuse put his whole line about in order to rescue two heavily disabled ships, *Tyrannicide* and *Indomptable*, that were in imminent danger of capture by the British. It was a bold challenge to which Howe was unable to respond. Unsupported, Howe had near him only *Bellerophon* and *Leviathan*, both badly damaged. At four he called the other ships about him and sought to give cover to two, *Queen* and *Royal George*, that were crippled and struggling and towards which Villaret appeared to be making. The vans of the two fleets thereby ran within shot of one another again. The exchange was brief. The action finally died at five that afternoon.

The British had lost a total of sixty-seven killed and 128 wounded. Howe had lost only one man killed aboard *Queen Charlotte*, one of his lieutenants.

Here in this indecisive encounter was fully demonstrated the difficulty and risk of engagement in heavy weather on the open sea. Howe's own ship, *Queen Charlotte*, had taken in a great deal of water through her ports, as Edward Codrington discovered. The pumps had been working through the day, and were to be kept busy all that night.

Queen had taken the heaviest beating. She had lost her master and twenty-one seamen. Her captain had lost his leg. The sixth lieutenant and twenty-five seamen were wounded. Her hull had taken many shots but none so low that it brought in the sea. She had lost her mizzen topmast and foreyard. Her mainmast, bowsprit and fore topmast were badly shattered by shot. But by nightfall a main topsail yard had been got up for a foreyard, a fore topgallant mast for a mizzen topmast, and a fore topgallant yard for a mizzen topsail yard. New sails were bent fore and aft. *Queen* was then reported ready for service.

These astonishing efforts by battle-weary men who had hardly slept or eaten for two days can seem scarcely credible when one tries to imagine that struggle to restore motoring life to shattered masts and yards on a breaking sea.

At last sight of one another at sunset on 29 May the two fleets were about ten miles apart. At dawn on the 30th the French were still in sight to the north-west but on a different tack. Howe demanded a report from all ships on their readiness to renew action. All except *Caesar* reported themselves ready. Howe then signalled to form line in two columns and the fleet bore steadily towards the enemy, but fog descended so heavily that no ship could see the vessel ahead or astern. Fog thus gradually scattered the fleet. It did the same to the French. The morning of 31 May found the weather clearer. Through the day the fleets drew slowly closer. At five p.m. they were about five miles apart. Movement in the French line suggested that Villaret-Joyeuse was preparing for battle. Howe had similarly signalled engagement of the van, centre and rear of the French line. A full general action appeared imminent, to carry them through the night. At seven that evening Howe hauled up his fleet having decided to avoid night action, to avoid the sort of misunderstanding of his signals already experienced, especially with *Caesar*.

Maintaining line and a full press of sail, the two fleets stood on parallel course westward through the night towards the dawn of 1 June. Villaret-Joyeuse was now buoyantly confident, the more so since his fleet had been augmented by new arrivals from Admiral Nielly's squadron. By this time, too, Howe should have had support from Montagu's squadron but a failed rendezvous had left the two ignorant of each other's position and situation.

As hoped for, the next day came better than the previous two. The weather had moderated. The sea was smoother. At seven the two fleets were about four miles apart. They were in perfect parallel.

Both fleets had taken heavy punishment from three days of action or near-action. With the French, the 110-gun *Révolutionnaire* had already been towed away to France. The 80-gun *Indomptable* and 74-gun *Tyrannicide* were so badly damaged that they were under tow, though still with the fleet and ready to deliver fire power. The British, too, had sent home one ship, *Audacious*. Most of the others had suffered loss and damage. But as day dawned Howe had what the British always wanted, the weather-gauge. He had zealously been manoeuvring during the past three days to obtain it. He could now attack from windward. The wind was south by west. The French line ran east to west. Breaking from a parallel course for their descent to cut the French line put the British on a heading of north-west. That meant a slanting angle of approach to the French line. On that approach the British ships could expect heavy exposure to French fire.

Between seven and seven thirty Howe sent out two signals that declared his plan of attack. He would cut through the enemy's line and engage to leeward, though it was hoped that this time the plan would be more determinedly exercised by Howe's captains than it had been on the 29th.

The French hove to, to await the attack. Howe arranged his line. *Caesar* was still to be the van ship. Frigates and small craft were positioned behind the line. Three frigates chosen as Repeaters of Signals would move with the line. The British then hove to as well and the fleet was ordered to breakfast.

Shortly after eight the fleets moved to engage. On his quarterdeck Howe observed one of his midshipmen, a mere child, standing in what he deemed to be a dangerous position. 'You had better go below, you are too young to be of service here,' he told the boy.

'My lord,' replied the blushing boy, 'what would my father say, if I was not to remain upon deck during action?'

Howe's plan was for the British ships to steer for their opposite number in the French line, to attack as they approached and then to pass between the enemy ships, administering a raking fire as they did so, and then, once beyond, on the lee side of the French line, to continue the attack from there. Raking shot, contrary to broadside, passed lengthwise end to end of the ship. The random havoc it could create included the officers on the quarterdeck, the rudder and the wheel.

Howe's signal unfortunately offered discretionary power. Those captains unable to effect his intention were at liberty to 'act as circumstances may require'.

As he brought the signals down and surveyed a battle line that appeared to be holding as accurately as he ever could hope for, Howe remarked to *Queen Charlotte*'s master, Bowen, 'I now shut up my signal book, and I trust I shall have no occasion to re-open it today.' Unfortunately he had to open it almost immediately, after the French van opened fire, just before nine thirty. The line then no longer held its form. The problem again lay with *Caesar*, which should have begun the manoeuvre.

Instead of bearing down to run through the line and engage the French van ship to leeward of it, *Caesar* had its main topsails aback. *Caesar* was firing, although it lay still short of its proper firing range. This was the same performance that had been witnessed on the 29th. In holding back, *Caesar* affected the entire van. Four other ships had backed fore and main topsails, thus arresting their advance. An inevitable conclusion was that *Caesar* was exercising the option that Howe had allowed his captains of acting as they themselves judged necessary in their circumstances.

For a year now Howe had been severely critical of *Caesar*'s captain, Anthony James Molloy. Events of the previous two days had done nothing to make him think better of the man. He had had misgivings over retaining Molloy and his ship as the van of the fleet, a position of distinction as well as responsibility. But the captain of the fleet, Sir Roger Curtis, whose station was aboard *Queen Charlotte* with Howe, had pleaded for Molloy to be kept. Now, with *Caesar* once more at fault, out of line, Howe tapped Curtis on the shoulder and said, 'Look, Curtis, there goes your friend. Who is mistaken now?'

That preoccupation had to be quickly passed over, for Howe was more immediately concerned with making his own cut of the French line. James Gambier, captain of the 74-gun *Defence*, had been the first one through. Howe was slower because Villaret-Joyeuse's flagship, *Montagne*, was his target. He intended to cut through the line immediately astern of the 120-gun *Montagne*, regarded as possibly the finest ship in the world at that time. To reach *Montagne*, however, meant that *Queen Charlotte*, on closing with the French line, found herself running almost parallel to it. This in turn meant running the gauntlet of two other ships in the French line, *Vengeur* and *Achille*, both of which directed fire on her as she ran in past them at nine thirty. *Queen Charlotte* set topgallant sails to carry her past them more swiftly.

Howe wanted Bowen, the master, to bring *Queen Charlotte* as close as possible to *Montagne* as they passed astern of her. As *Queen Charlotte* cut through the French line and passed between *Montagne* and the next ship in the French line, the 80-gun *Jacobin*, Bowen took her so close that the French ensign aloft was brushing *Queen Charlotte*'s mizzen rigging.

This immediate need of skill and daring was in marvellous concentration across the ship as she entered these final critical moments of the approach. The fore topmast stays had been cut in the fire as *Queen Charlotte* ran down the French line. The captain of the foretop saw that in rounding to as she came to leeward of *Montagne* the fore topmast was likely to go over. He went aloft with a light hawser to secure it. Exactly as he foresaw, the topmast went as *Queen Charlotte* hauled up and came to the wind. The seaman fell on the starboard gangway with the whole wreck of the mast but miraculously was not hurt. The same thing was to happen to the captain of the main top when the main topmast stay was shot away. He went up to attempt to secure it. When the topmast went he too went down with it, into the water. He also managed to survive by clambering back on board. Another captain of the top remained in the top with his leg shot off. Other men were badly hurt when loose rigging flayed or wound round them.

Queen Charlotte let loose a broadside as she came to leeward and slid past *Montagne*'s starboard quarter. As all the action so far had been to larboard, which was the weather side of the French line, the French flagship was unprepared for this shift of fire as *Queen Charlotte* cut through the line and came up to her leeward side. *Montagne*'s gun ports there were all closed: the French never expected assault from leeward. *Montagne* was unable to retaliate immediately and swiftly as *Queen Charlotte* poured fire upon her. Villaret later reported that three hundred of his men were killed or wounded from that fire.

The *Jacobin*, meanwhile, in coming up behind *Montagne*, slid between *Queen Charlotte* and the French flagship, the position where Howe himself had wished to be. As the three ships sought to manoeuvre in their tight cluster Bowen cried out, 'Then let's rake them both.' But *Montagne* dropped away, still without having fired a shot from her leeward guns. *Queen Charlotte* was left lying between *Jacobin* and *Juste*, the latter ahead of *Montagne* in the line. *Jacobin* brought down *Queen Charlotte*'s fore topmast and then, like *Montagne*, dropped away.

The 80-gun *Juste* was already engaged with the 74-gun *Invincible*. *Juste* now became simultaneously engaged with *Queen Charlotte*. She sent two broadsides into *Queen Charlotte*. As the action continued *Juste* lost her foremast, then her main- and mizzen masts. She was out of it and struck her colours. In this exchange *Queen Charlotte* lost her main topmast. With one topmast already gone and rigging and yards badly damaged Howe's flagship had become practically unmanageable. The state of the *Queen Charlotte* impelled Captain Thomas Pakenham of the *Invincible* to send one of his lieutenants to Howe to say that, although badly damaged, his ship was sufficiently manageable should Howe wish to transfer his flag to it. Howe was not prepared to leave his ship. He sent the lieutenant to take possession of *Juste*.

Montagne was in a similarly distressed state from *Queen Charlotte*'s raking broadsides. Masts, rigging and sails stood, but her rudder was hanging from a shattered stern post. The binnacle and wheel were destroyed, as well as all her boats. Many guns were dismounted and more than 250 shot had struck her along the starboard water line, particularly near the stern. She was leaking badly, and swiftly. She had lost many of her officers, including the flag captain, two or three lieutenants and several midshipmen. Villaret narrowly escaped when the seat on which he stood was shot from under him.

One of the ships in that first rush to cut the line, *Gibraltar*, did not go through the line but instead remained to windward firing on the French ships. As *Montagne* drew ahead *Gibraltar*'s fire hit *Queen Charlotte*. The captain, Sir Andrew Douglas, was wounded in the head. He went below and returned with the wound tightly bound.

Quarterdeck injuries, fatal or otherwise, were common that day, as would have been expected among men who, in their distinctive and decorative uniforms, were prime targets for the sharpshooters the French posted aloft. The raised quarterdeck anyway was more exposed than practically any other place on a line ship. All the officers not at quarters elsewhere on the ship would be there. Certainly none of those present could presume upon survival at the end of it all. Cuthbert Collingwood was captain of *Barfleur* under Rear Admiral George Bowyer. As they stood together on the quarterdeck some time before ten on 1 June, just before the action began, Collingwood reminded the admiral of it being Sunday. 'I observed to the admiral that about that time our wives were going to church, but that I thought the peal we should ring about the Frenchmen's ears would outdo their parish bells.' The admiral dropped ten minutes after the action began. 'I caught him in my arms before he fell,' Collingwood said. Admiral Bowyer, shot in the leg, was to lose it when carried to the surgeon. The first lieutenant was also wounded.

Across that exploding, missile-charged and smoke-darkening patch of ocean, a battle like no other yet in that century was building in its uncommon fury as the most active of Howe's ships renewed the forgotten experience of close individual combat, melee, lost to the Royal Navy for more than a century and here regained. For their part, the French, whose own traditional tactic was to avoid where possible the destruction of full and extended battle, came to this day determined instead to commit themselves with all their spirit and valour to making their own mark upon it. And so it was to be.

Within that blazing smoke cloud diverse encounters of unique character were being played out.

Captain James Gambier's 74-gun *Defence* had been the first to cut the French line, having got ahead of her own line when all responded to the signal to engage. She paid a heavy price for her alacrity by receiving the full weight of the initial French fire. She cut the French line between two 74-gun ships, *Mucius* and *Tourville*, which together engaged her heavily. Their fire brought down *Defence*'s main- and mizzen masts. Seeing their opponent so seriously disabled, *Mucius* and *Tourville* gave themselves to the intensifying action around them.

In a navy whose religious beliefs were for the most part still lightly carried, still affected by eighteenth-century secularist token observance, Gambier was fervently evangelical. As *Defence* drifted away from *Mucius* the 110-gun *Républicain* appeared out of the battle smoke. The man who first saw her, a lieutenant whose quarters were on the main deck, ran up to the quarterdeck and cried to Gambier, 'Damn my eyes, sir, but here is a whole mountain coming upon us. What shall we do?'

Instead of direct response Gambier said, 'How dare you, sir, at this awful moment, come to me with an oath in your mouth? Go down, sir, and encourage your men to stand to their guns, like brave British seamen.'

Républicain shot away *Defence*'s remaining mast, the foremast, and moved off. *Defence* signalled for assistance and one of the frigates came to take her in tow. This was a common task of frigates on both sides.

The 74-gun *Marlborough*, captained by Cranfield Berkeley, was another of the swift and heavily engaged assailants of the French line. Her properly selected opponent was the 74-gun *Impétueux*. *Marlborough* cut through the line by passing under *Impétueux*'s stern, but in coming up to leeward she ranged so close that the two ships became entangled at the mizzen shrouds and at *Impétueux*'s bowsprit. In this fatal embrace they turned their fire upon one another at close range. *Marlborough*'s raking fire drove the French sailors from their upper decks. Some of the British sailors boarded the French ship but were called back. All *Impétueux*'s masts went over.

After breaking from its action with *Defence*, *Mucius* moved to assist *Impétueux*. In the French line *Mucius* had been the ship astern of *Impétueux*. As she moved up to the two tangled ships *Mucius* sought to rake *Marlborough* and in the process moved against the latter's bows, from where an attempt to board was made. It was repelled by carronades and marine musketry. The three ships lay in this now-triple embrace of fire. *Mucius* lost all its masts. As *Marlborough* sought to back away from the entanglement the *Montagne*, itself then disengaging from *Queen Charlotte*, fired upon her. All *Marlborough*'s masts were carried away and Captain Berkeley was wounded. His first lieutenant, Monckton, took the command. They were still trying to move away from *Impétueux*, which was on fire and, since she had ceased to fire, Monckton allowed the French sailors to extinguish the flames without firing on them. With remarkable skill and command Monckton then proceeded to save his own severely damaged ship.

Monckton began clearing away wreckage. Then, seeing the rear of the enemy's fleet coming up and determined to avoid surrender, he ordered the men to lie down at their quarters to receive the fire. With her masts gone, *Marlborough* was rolling too deep to allow the lower deck gun ports to be opened. The French ships fired as they passed but the only men killed were those still standing at their quarters. It was a gauntlet that a helpless *Marlborough* continued to run through the hours that remained of the battle, until finally she was taken in tow by a frigate.

The 98-gun *Queen* was another that suffered heavily from gunfire on the approach to the French line. She was already in a bad way in her sails and rigging when she engaged the new 74-gun *Jemmappes*. The two-hour contest between them saw so much flaming metal fall upon each ship that at the end both were useless. *Jemmappes*'s mizzen mast was the first to go; *Queen*'s mainmast followed. Then *Jemmappes*'s mainmast and foremast. From her broken decks her crew waved submission with their hats. But *Queen* was too disabled to take possession. Her mizzen topmast had been shot away, her foremast and bowsprit were shattered in places, her mizzen mast was expected to fall at any moment, and her rigging and sails were cut or shredded. Thus she floated through the smoke, fearing her end from a reassembled French line standing towards her.

Of all these individual actions that exploded upon the ocean after Howe had signalled to run down on the French line one stands out as the epic of the whole war. As Mahan says, it should be commemorated as long as naval history shall be written. It was the action between the 74-gun *Brunswick* captained by John Harvey and an equal, the 74-gun *Vengeur*, commanded by a masterful seaman, Captain Renaudin, who had his twelve-year-old son on board as an ensign.

Brunswick was second to *Queen Charlotte* in the line. The instant the signal was raised for every ship to bear down *Brunswick*'s helm was put up simultaneously with *Queen Charlotte*'s. The two ran down together towards the centre of the French line. The slanting (lasking, it was called) manner of the approach exposed the ships to heavy fire as they ran in. But *Brunswick*, being slightly ahead, served as a shield for *Queen Charlotte* and took much of the fire directed at the flagship. Her fore topgallant mast was shot away. Many of her crew were killed or wounded before *Brunswick* had even fired a shot. But greater difficulty followed.

Harvey had intended to cut through the French line astern of *Jacobin*, his designated opponent, that ship being second to *Montagne*. But *Jacobin* had moved to the defence of *Montagne* and the French ships following behind her had bunched up. The only opening was a narrow one between the third ship, *Patriote*, and the fourth, *Vengeur*. The gap drew even tighter as *Brunswick* sought to pass through. As a result her three starboard anchors hooked into the fore chains of *Vengeur*.

Brunswick's master asked Harvey whether they should cut clear. 'No!' Harvey cried. 'We have got her, and we will keep her!' In this manner, locked together, drawn broadside alongside one another, the two ships drifted away about a mile to leeward of the others to resolve this tight action of their own.

Brunswick lay with her starboard side against *Vengeur*'s larboard side. As the closeness of the two ships prevented the opening of the lower starboard gun ports the British simply blew off their own lids. They maintained lower deck fire in a way that the French could not. To ram their shot and sponge their guns the French used long wooden staves that compelled them to reach outside the gun ports, which was impossible with the sides of the two ships touching. The British used flexible ropes that enabled them to work entirely inside. The French could use only a few of their forward and after guns. But, as the British blasted into *Vengeur*'s larboard side the French had a mastery on the upper deck.

Vengeur's carronades and the musketry of her sailors played havoc across *Brunswick*'s open decks. The carronades fired the vicious shot called langridge (old nails and pieces of iron). Several of the officers and a marine captain were among the dead. Captain Harvey was already hit twice. A musket ball took off part of his right hand. He wrapped the wound in his handkerchief. Then a splinter struck him on the loins and threw him to the deck. He was helped to his feet but still refused to go below to the cockpit for treatment.

The action had been underway just over an hour when through the smoke another French ship was seen to larboard bearing down hard upon *Brunswick*. Her decks and rigging were crowded with men ready for boarding. This was later to be identified as the 74-gun *Achille*. As the *Achille* approached within musket reach Harvey ordered the larboard guns, which from the way *Brunswick* and *Vengeur* lay together were unable to be used against *Vengeur*, to be directed upon the new enemy. The guns were loaded with a particularly brutal shot. Atop a single 32-pound shot each gun was additionally given a double-headed shot. Between five and six rounds were directed against *Achille*, even as the struggle with *Vengeur* continued. All of *Achille*'s masts were brought down and lay over her starboard side. Her firing ceased and the French colours came down. But *Brunswick* was in no position to take possession of her. In a while *Achille* rehoisted her colours and, setting a spritsail (a square sail set beneath the bowsprit), she sought to labour away.

The slaughter on *Brunswick*'s upper deck had so enfeebled the British there that *Vengeur*'s captain, Renaudin, was on the point of preparing to carry the day by boarding her. But he was frustrated in this by a British ship coming up to support *Brunswick*. That ship was the 74-gun *Ramillies*, commanded by Harvey's brother, Henry Harvey.

As *Ramillies* stood closer to *Brunswick* figures on the former's deck were waving signs that *Brunswick* should endeavour to cut *Vengeur* adrift, to diminish risk to itself from *Ramillies*'s broadsides. That still appeared difficult, but it suddenly happened of its own accord. Brunswick then swung clear of *Vengeur*, tearing away three anchors from the latter's bows.

Ramillies waited for *Brunswick* to drift quite clear of her opponent, then poured two tremendous broadsides into *Vengeur*. *Brunswick*, having drifted well clear, then administered the fatal shots. All *Vengeur*'s masts except the mizzen came down. The mizzen followed soon after. *Vengeur*'s rudder and stern post were shattered and she had a huge hole in her counter. Water poured in. Guns were thrown overboard. The pumps were unable to cope. The action had lasted some three hours without pause.

As she began sinking *Vengeur* displayed the British flag in submission and appealed for help. But all *Brunswick*'s boats had been destroyed. There was nothing she could do to help her stricken opponent. Her mizzen mast, damaged earlier, suddenly went overboard. The other masts and much of her rigging were badly damaged. The mainmast and foremast were wholly crippled. All the running and much of the standing rigging had been shot away. Yards were in a shattered state. The ship had been on fire three times.

The close fighting meant that the wounded were in a particularly bad way. The langridge shot of iron pieces and nails had lacerated flesh; flame pots thrown through the ports had inflicted frightful burns on faces and arms.

Harvey had been wounded for the third time, this time more seriously, in the fighting before the ships parted and when the threat of a boarding looked imminent. A shot struck his right arm near the elbow and shattered the arm to pieces. Faint from loss of blood he refused assistance to help him below, saying, 'I will not have a single man leave his quarters on my account! My legs still remain to bear me down to the cockpit.' And, as he went, had cried out, 'The colours of Brunswick shall never be struck!' What was left of his arm was amputated but the loss of blood left him fighting for his life.

Whatever insult and menace preceded battle foe to foe, compassion ruled the end. Such determined valour on both sides as *Brunswick* and *Vengeur* demonstrated produced a respect that left no rancour when it was all over. The agony at the end was shared. The cries for help from the sinking *Vengeur* only produced pity and a futile desire to be able to do something, which a lack of resources on *Brunswick* prevented.

Aboard *Brunswick* the exhausted crew set about securing what they could. The sails were all useless, shot to shreds. Wherever it was yet possible to carry sail they would have to bend (affix to the yards) completely new sails. One of her lower studding sails was set forward to enable her to steer. In this manner she drifted away from what remained of battle, which was very little.

Vengeur, in a sinking state that worsened as, on the roll, her shattered gun ports scooped in more water, nevertheless rehoisted her colours and set a small sail on the stump of her foremast. In this manner, pumps working, bailing, she struggled to survive another two hours as a continuing unit of the French navy.

The rehoisting of colours after having lowered them in submission was a particularly distinctive feature of this battle. That, as much as anything, reflected the difference that close combat brought to the battle, endowing so much of its novel character. Two ships in tight mutual onslaught inflicted so much punishment upon one another that even when one of them submitted the other was too disabled to take possession. As a result, after an interval, pride was regained and up went the colours again, defiantly fluttering wherever there was a modest elevation to which they could be attached. The ship could then be rescued and towed away by frigates, avoiding the fate of being a prize. That became one of the most controversial aspects of the Battle of June the First, as it would be known to history. It had got fully underway between nine thirty and ten. *Queen Charlotte*'s own firing had started eight minutes before ten. Ten minutes after ten *Montagne* was already so severely damaged from *Queen Charlotte*'s raking fire that she began to draw away. Between half-past ten and eleven the action had abated, though was not yet over.

One of the hardest actions of the morning, between *Queen* and *Jemmappes*, was then drawing to its conclusion. At eleven *Queen*'s mainmast went over the lee side, carrying away the mizzen yard and parts of the poop and quarterdeck. At eleven fifteen the mainmast of *Jemmappes* came down, followed by the foremast. The French crew emerged waving submission, which *Queen* in her own wrecked state could do nothing about.

Howe was looking out anxiously from the taffrail to make some assessment as the smoke showed signs of clearing. At the same time, Villaret-Joyeuse was himself making an assessment of the state of his fleet from *Montagne*. Of the twelve ships ahead of him in his line when the battle began seven had given ground and five of those now lay to leeward, the other two were astern and lay to windward. Of the balance, one ship had lost main- and mizzen masts and the remaining four were totally dismasted. Of the thirteen ships astern of *Montagne* in the line six had lost all their masts, one had only the foremast standing, the remaining six had their spars and rigging in serviceable condition. All lay to leeward.

Villaret-Joyeuse signalled the serviceable ships to gather round him. He formed a new column of twelve and moved to a leeward position where he could receive the disabled ships that lay to windward as well as those brought to him by frigates. These manoeuvres set his line of twelve bearing down to where *Queen* was struggling to make her way.

Howe, like Villaret-Joyeuse, sought to reform his line. He had already signalled all ships to close round *Queen Charlotte* and to form line ahead or astern of her. Then, with a clearer view of the ocean before him, he had seen the French line advancing towards *Queen*. He hurried to the forepart of the poop and called down to the captain of the fleet, Sir Roger Curtis, below on the quarterdeck, 'Go down to the Queen, sir. Go down to the Queen.'

Curtis cried back, 'My lord, we can't. We're a mere wreck! The ship won't steer. What can we do when the ship herself won't steer?'

Bowen, the master, who was by the helmsman, burst out, 'She *will* steer, my lord.'

'Try her, sir,' Howe commanded Bowen who, taking over, got her slowly before the wind with her head towards the French line, getting the spritsail well filled to assist her round.

All sail that could be set was spread and *Queen Charlotte*, accompanied by more than five of the line ships, stood towards *Queen* and the newly assembled French line. But Villaret-Joyeuse had never been intent on *Queen*. His purpose was to collect together and save four disabled French ships that were being towed towards him. The 110-gun *Terrible* that he now had with him was the first that he had picked up. The ships that he now gathered in were the 110-gun *Républicain*, the 80-gun *Scipion* and two 74s, *Jemmappes* and *Mucius*. He had salvaged a formidable force. Or, more pertinently as many would see it, deprived the British of their best prizes.

General firing stopped shortly after one p.m. A signal had been sent by Howe for ships to stand by prizes. There were six of them, one 80-gun and five 74s. Howe sought as well to round up his own disabled ships. Eleven of his fleet, including *Queen Charlotte*, had been dismasted, apart from other serious damage. Villaret-Joyeuse, meanwhile, was completing his recovery of his broken ships, two of which had struck their colours and subsequently raised them again when their opponents were unable to take possession of them. That object accomplished, the French fleet of nineteen line ships and attendant smaller vessels stood away northward. By six fifteen that afternoon it had vanished from sight, with only a frigate left behind to watch the British movement.

The real conclusion to the battle was the final end to the tragedy of *Vengeur*. At about the time that the French fleet was disappearing across the horizon the fight to keep her afloat with pumps and bailing was at an end. Three British ships came up at about six fifteen and sent their boats across to take off the French sailors. They were just in time. More than four hundred were rescued in the very last minutes left to *Vengeur*. Most were wounded. Understandably there were some who, expecting that the ship's end would be their own, had gone to the brandy kegs. As *Vengeur* took her plunge, some were heard crying, '*Vive la Nation!*', '*Vive la République!*' She went down so quickly that it was feared she took most of her seriously wounded with her.

From aboard *Orion* Midshipman William Parker wrote a moving account of *Vengeur*'s end to his father. 'You could plainly perceive the poor wretches climbing over to windward and crying most dreadfully. She then righted a little, and then her head went down gradually, and she sunk. She after that rose again a little and then sunk, so that no more was seen of her. Oh, my dear Father! when you consider of five or six hundred souls destroyed in that shocking manner, it will make your very heart relent. Our own men even were a great many of them in tears and groaning, they said God bless them.' But there was one happy episode to finish it all. Captain Renaudin, who had fought his ship as bravely as any man that day, was reunited with his twelve-year-old son at Portsmouth. The two had been taken off by different boats. Each had thought that the other had gone down with the ship.

Aboard *Queen Charlotte* the personal cost of the battle to Howe was evident. He had not been to bed the whole time of the three-day chase. To the strain of constant tactical calculation had been added the shortcomings of many of his captains in the manoeuvres he sought. On top of it all was this new experience of battle in storm on the open ocean. The lifting of it all from him with the flight of the French fleet seemed to bring on a state of deferred collapse. He was so weak that suddenly he was unable while on his feet to balance against the roll of the ship. Edward Codrington caught him as he staggered. 'Why, you hold me as if I were a child,' Howe said, with good humour.

'I beg your pardon, my lord, but I thought you would have fallen.'

The state of the fleet was itself little better. It took two more days for his ships and their prizes to repair damage sufficient for the collective return to Britain. It was only at five a.m. on 3 June that Howe's fleet made sail from the area of the battle. Nine of his ships were ordered to Plymouth. The rest, together with the prizes, made for Spithead, where they anchored on the morning of the 13th.

Huge crowds gathered on shore when the fleet was seen standing in from the horizon. As *Queen Charlotte* came to anchor salutes boomed from the batteries on shore. Howe landed an hour later as a band played 'See the Conquering Hero Comes'. People cheered and wept with joy. It was, as one report had it, a scene that baffled description in its excitement and celebration. Thus it continued, ever more splendidly. The royal family arrived at Portsmouth on the 26th and proceeded to *Queen Charlotte* in barges. On the quarterdeck George III presented Howe with a sword set with diamonds and a gold chain to which would be attached a medal. Medals and honours descended upon many of the others in the fleet.

What of that part of Howe's fleet under Rear Admiral Sir James Montagu that had sailed with Howe at the very outset? Montagu's orders had been to rejoin Howe on 20 May. He had delayed four to five days in proceeding to the proposed rendezvous off Ushant. Then, learning that Howe was far to the westward into the ocean, Montagu returned to Plymouth, where he arrived on 30 May. He had made no further effort to find and reinforce Howe. *Audacious*, disabled in the first actions on 28 May, arrived at Plymouth on 3 June, bringing the first news of the battle. Montagu was sent out the next day with his squadron of eight line ships.

At seven a.m. on 9 June, off the Bay of Bertheaume, Montagu sighted Villaret-Joyeuse's battle-worn Grand Fleet standing in with five of his ships in tow. Lying inside the bay at this time was another French fleet of eight line ships. Montagu's position was between Bertheaume and the approaching fleet. Villaret-Joyeuse immediately formed a compact line and at noon gave chase to the British squadron. Montagu, with several excessively slow ships in his squadron and apparently afraid of being caught between two forces, headed away. At five p.m. Villaret-Joyeuse abandoned the chase, fearful of being drawn too far from the shelter his suffering fleet sought. On 11 June Villaret-Joyeuse anchored in Bertheaume. Montagu continued for Plymouth, where he arrived on the 12th. Two days later the Chesapeake convoy entered Brest.

There was a victory for the British, but for the French as well. They, by common agreement among their foes, had fought more ferociously and bravely than ever before, with determined staying power. Howe had set out with two objectives – to engage the enemy and to intercept the Chesapeake convoy. He had succeeded only with the first. French success lay with the safe arrival of the grain convoy. That, after all, was the objective that Robespierre himself had laid down for the Grand Fleet. Battle was something that Villaret-Joyeuse had been specifically told to avoid. He therefore had masterfully evaded action for as long as he could, intent on drawing Howe as far away as possible from the convoy route. Once in action, however, he made no attempt to evade it. He was indifferent to the loss of the ships that Howe took home as prizes. 'While your admiral amused himself refitting them, I saved my convoy, and I saved my head,' he told the historian Brenton on a voyage they made together from the West Indies later in the war.

After sixteen months of war Howe had delivered the naval battle that Britain had wanted for assurance of its naval capability and continuing naval supremacy. And he had delivered it brilliantly, the more so for the deficiencies of many of his captains, notably Molloy of *Caesar*. After being severely censured by Howe, Molloy asked for a court martial, where he was charged with not having brought his ship into action or exerted himself to the utmost of his power. Molloy was dismissed from command of his ship.

Molloy was not the only one. Howe's instructions to make for the French line and pass through were never complied with by the majority of his captains. Howe himself had to share the blame for that, for allowing it as an option fitted to circumstances judged by individual captains. He had set the example, however, for all to follow by making for the French flagship and producing melee, the element absent from battle all that century and through which alone could line battle produce decisive result. Only five of his captains followed his example by passing through the French line. These and other factors meant that, for all the cheering that greeted Howe as he stepped ashore, a background murmur of criticism soon attached to the Battle of June the First. It ran throughout the fleet.

Howe was criticized on two grounds. These were for not pursuing Villaret-Joyeuse and continuing the battle and, failing that, for allowing the escape of the five dismasted French ships, which got away from the battle area either under tow or mere spritsail. Allowing the five potential prizes to get away appeared to rankle deeper with many than the failure to chase Villaret-Joyeuse. It was as though Howe had allowed the symbol and significance of victory to be towed away, for Villaret-Joyeuse then to present his fleet at Brest as denial of complete defeat and of any British claim to full success.

Edward Brenton, one of the two contemporary historians of the naval Great War, was a severe critic of June the First. Brenton had some advantage in that he had been a midshipman aboard one of Montagu's ships. He declared that by failing either to capture the five dismasted French ships or to pursue Villaret-Joyeuse, Howe had 'turned a victory into a defeat, while the expert French admiral obtained from his own defeat all the advantages of a victory'. The other historian, William James, disagreed with Brenton's criticisms of Howe and Montagu. James, like Clerk of Eldin, was a landsman obsessed with naval matters. Like Clerk he, too, was a meticulous student of his subject, and produced what is certainly the superior work, painstakingly accurate, immensely detailed, yet occasionally prone to his own insistent convictions.

Whatever the balance in the criticisms of it, the Battle of June the First 1794 stands in its own supreme niche for being the first naval battle on the open ocean as much as for the dominant tactical aspect of it: the deliberate aforethought cutting of the line, thereby bringing on close engagement, melee. It provided the essential lesson for Nelson and the others who followed. For that Howe holds his own uniquely distinctive place in naval history.

XI

UNCERTAINTY

AFTER June the First, as the cheering and celebrations for Howe's victory faded, there followed a hollow sense of return to the inconclusive level of naval achievement in home waters before the battle, and through the previous year. What rankled was that the French fleet remained scarcely less powerful.

Lying at Brest were thirty-five ships of the line, thirteen frigates, as well as corvettes and brigs. They were still a threat in the Narrow Seas, and to the West Indies. Quite as dangerous was the potential of Brest to detach a squadron to reinforce the fleet at Toulon. The French Grand Fleet had a new sense of pride. Neither within the Grand Fleet nor in Paris and across France was June the First regarded as a French defeat or a British victory. The fierce courage of the French sailors had been as triumphantly saluted in France as the return of Howe's fleet had been in Britain. But with the French fleet recovering in Brest there was no immediate expectation in midsummer 1794 of major action upon the near seas.

For the British, trade protection, meanwhile, was as vital as the need permanently to cripple or destroy the Grand Fleet. Squadrons of French frigates continued their havoc upon British trade in the Channel and around the British coasts. British frigate squadrons were constantly out in pursuit of their French counterparts. Valiant resistance came from the merchantmen themselves. Some of their tales of courage became small legends of that particular side of the war.

In July the ship *Betsey*, inbound for London from Jamaica, was captured off the Lizard by a squadron of French frigates. The master and crew were taken off, leaving only the mate, cook, carpenter, a ship's boy and a passenger, Mrs Williams. A French lieutenant and thirteen sailors took charge of the prize. Three days later, in sight of Guernsey, the mate formed a plot to retake the ship. When outlining the part proposed for her in it Mrs Williams fainted, having been told that if they failed all could expect to be killed. On recovering, she declared that she would play her part.

At eleven that night, when the French lieutenant was asleep in his berth and the other French in the fore part of the ship, the signal was given. Mrs Williams went to the lieutenant's cabin and locked the door. She stood with her back against it to prevent it being forced. On deck the mate, cook, carpenter and the ship's boy surprised the French sailors and forced them down the hatchway, threatening death if they tried to come up again. The small band sailed on for another two days, until they reached Cowes Road. When a boat party came aboard from the shore they found Mrs Williams still in the same positon at the lieutenant's door, pistol in hand.

June the First and the fall of Bastia had for the British reassuringly, though briefly, smoothed over a façade of wartime coalition that was cracking and splintering, with no way yet of judging for how long all would continue to hold together.

A new campaign in the Austrian Netherlands had begun in April, financed by Britain and Holland. By May it had already begun to fade. The outcome became steadily more unpredictable, compounded by events in France. In July, six weeks after Howe's victory, Robespierre went to the guillotine. The Terror was over. Did that lend itself to the possibility of peace? No one could tell. The hope had to be that it might, for the course of the allied Continental campaign continued to falter ominously.

The Austrians were fast retreating from Flanders. They, in fact, appeared near indifferent to its fate. Like the Prussians their attention was fixed on Poland, where patriotic insurgency had a new leader, Kosciuszko, who was moving from one triumph to another after the seizure of Warsaw. The attention of Prussia and Austria had deflected eastwards. They were concerned about those territories that they already had partitioned off from Poland. Austria also saw the Kosciuszko insurgency as likely excuse for further Prussian aggrandizement. Against that background Prussian and Austrian zeal and commitment for the western campaign against France had diminished.

Austria's distraction eastwards hastened the crisis for Pitt's ministry as Brussels was abandoned on 11 July, and Antwerp two weeks later. For Britain, hostile power in possession of the coast of the Scheldt was historically a matter of morbid apprehension, arising from fear of the Scheldt becoming a prime marshalling point for invasion. The French now had all of that. And French possession of Holland as well looked imminent.

Collapse in Holland was inevitable if the Austrian Netherlands fell. That spelled disaster of special dimensions for Britain. The Dutch had been Britain's partner in doling out subsidies to the Prussians and Austrians and Amsterdam's banking was the financial buttress of London, in support of those on the Continent wishing to raise their own loan funds. The Dutch had a large naval fleet that would be at the disposal of the French. Holland commanded much of the trade on the Indian Ocean, and possessed the strategic point of access between the hemispheres, the Cape of Good Hope. Was all of that to fall to France? Britain's anxiety was understandable.

Britain sought to buy her way out of the crisis by throwing more money at the Prussians and Austrians. But it was money that brought little significant gain on the battlefields. Relations between the coalition partners soured steadily.

The French on the other hand were holding up well, with a poor, ragged army whose revolutionary spirit remained intact, its ardour fed by significant gains in the Netherlands and the south. In Paris the National Convention saw the need for strong advances along the Riviera because of the British landings on Corsica. The Army of Italy was therefore becoming of much greater significance. This owed a lot to the strategic calculations fed to the National Convention by its commissioner on the Riviera, Augustin Robespierre, brother of Maximilien. His organizational skill had helped rebuild the Army of Italy after the recapture of Toulon, where a close friendship had developed with young Napoleon Buonaparte. In April 1794 Buonaparte had been appointed general in command of artillery with the Army of Italy. Augustin Robespierre then gave Napoleon another staff job as well. He was to plan the future operations of the Army of Italy. In June Augustin took Buonaparte's memorandum on future operations of the Army of Italy to Paris. Augustin died in the attack on the Committee of Public Safety in July, but with that assignment Augustin Robespierre had unwittingly provided Napoleon with the key to his future. However, it nearly became Napoleon's death warrant as well. The fall of the Jacobins the following month and the execution of Maximilien Robespierre meant that Napoleon's associations with the Robespierres put him in immediate danger. He was arrested in the south, interrogated and then released. He returned to his plans for the Army of Italy.

This had been topographical staff work, but it became inflamed by the expansive visions that sprang from it. What he planned for Italy he saw in relation to a larger objective. Alive in his mind was the basis of a campaign that expanded from the Riviera coast across northern Italy and Venice, and over the Alps into Austria, to link up with advances from the Rhine. Under General Maséna the Army of Italy had taken the passes of the Maritime Alps and Apennines. They had outflanked the Austro-Sardinian forces in the Maritime Alps and had driven the Sardinians back along the Riviera. The Army of Italy had crossed the Sardinian boundary on the Riviera, taken Nice, and passed on into the territory of independent Genoa as far as Vado Bay. The Army of Italy therefore already held much of the indispensable coastal route from Toulon to Vado, the arrow into the heart of northern Italy, as well as Alpine passes, which represented the potential access beyond into the Tyrol. For Napoleon, the eviction of the British from Corsica naturally became central to his designs for the Army of Italy.

Possession of Fiorenzo and Bastia already suggested secure British command over the western Mediterranean, and by extension of the entire Mediterranean. But, though nothing on this wild and rough island could yet be taken for granted, Hood moved on to the attack against Bastia's companion fortress of Calvi. 'We shall now join heart and hand against Calvi,' Nelson had written when the French colours were lowered on Bastia on 20 May. The operation against Calvi began on 16 June, when *Agamemnon* anchored in deep water off the fortress.

Calvi was a tougher proposition than Bastia. Like Bastia, the walled town enclosed a citadel. The place sat on a promontory on a bay. Calvi's own defences were supported by batteries on outworks surrounding it. These commanded approaches from the interior as well as the sea.

The assault was a repetition of the hardships of Bastia. The sailors once more were hauling guns to heights, cutting roads and building batteries. This time they, and Nelson, were subordinate to the army. But as Hood's intermediary with the army Nelson retained intimacy with the operation. A change in the army command initially made the relationship easier. Dundas and d'Aubant had been succeeded by a harder soldier, General Charles Stuart, whom Nelson respected. Land and sea were nevertheless once more in discord as intense mutual resentment arose between Stuart and Hood.

Nelson threw himself into the preparation for assault as fully as he had done at Bastia. Hood's dependence continued for, once again, it was upon Nelson's reports that he relied, whose observations he sought, and through whom a proper relationship with the army had to be maintained. But for Nelson a bitterness now attached to his relations with Hood for it was at this time that he learned of the scant recognition Hood had given him in the official report to the Admiralty on the Bastia operation.

To his uncle he wrote, 'The whole operations were carried on through Lord Hood's letters to me. I was the mover of it – I was the cause of its success. Sir Gilbert Elliot will be my evidence, if any is required.' Nelson's patriotism was his solace. To his wife he wrote, 'I am well aware my poor services will not be noticed: I have no interest; but however services may be received, it is not right in an officer to slacken his zeal for his country.'

The intense heat of the Corsican high summer brought mosquitoes and malaria. By the end of June the conditions for the army and navy around Calvi could hardly have seemed different from what was being endured in the West Indies. 'We have upwards of one thousand sick out of two thousand, and others not much better than so many phantoms. We have lost many men from the season, very few from the enemy,' Nelson wrote.

He was on his feet while others lay sick or dying from malaria, typhoid or dysentery. His own fever was different. To his wife he wrote, 'I am very busy, yet own I am in my glory; except with you, I would not be anywhere but where I am, for the world.' No one possessed that sustaining inner fire like Nelson. It is a patriotism real to the times, though more distinctive in his case for the near-mystical character of it. 'Life with disgrace is dreadful,' he once told his wife. 'A glorious death is to be envied; and if anything happens to me, recollect that death is a debt we all must pay, and whether now, or a few years hence, can be but of little consequence.' It becomes a repetitive litany in his correspondence, tightly enclosing the core of his commitment.

His passion for being at the forefront of the action naturally made him vulnerable. On 12 July Nelson was at a naval battery when, at daylight, heavy fire from Calvi showered surprise down upon it. Nelson was watching the bombardment from a rock that gave him a view of Calvi and the whole field of operation. A shot barely cleared his head but blasted sand and stones against his breast and into his face with such force that his right eye was blinded. He was bleeding profusely and in great pain.

His face was badly cut, the worst cut being in the right brow. It had penetrated the eyelid and eyeball. He kept the eye but the verdict was that he would never again have good sight from it. Nelson's own comment was that he could do little more than 'distinguish light from dark'. He was soon compelled to wear a dark eyeshade to diminish the intense Corsican light.

To Hood on the night of his injury he merely reported, 'I got a little hurt this morning.' To his wife he wrote, 'Amongst the wounded, in a slight manner, is myself, my head being a good deal wounded and my right eye cut down . . . It confined me, Thank God, only one day . . .' And later, 'No, nothing but the loss of a limb would have kept me from my duty, and I believe my exertions conduced to preserve me in this general mortality.'

Nelson had indeed stayed off-duty only the regular twenty-four hours allotted for what were considered lighter injuries. He then returned to an increasingly difficult liaison with the army, which was demanding five hundred more sailors for labour and manning the batteries. The army complained that those soldiers who were not sick were exhausted. Hood reluctantly gave the sailors. General Stuart believed that without more troops, more seamen and more ammunition the siege of Calvi might have to be abandoned. It was the height of summer and sickness was daily wasting more of the strength they had. Unless the siege were soon brought to an end sickness among the troops would do it anyhow.

The steady hammering of Calvi saved the situation. The houses in the citadel were either in ruins or flames. On 10 August the fortress capitulated.

Nelson was relieved to see the end of it. His wound was troubling him. Once again he was to be lashed by a lack of acknowledgement for his services. He got no mention in Stuart's list of commendations. Hood for his part was outraged that his own name had not appeared in the capitulation. Nelson's name did not even appear in the list of wounded. 'One hundred and ten days I have been actually engaged, at sea and on shore, against the enemy. I do not know that any one has done more,' he wrote. 'I have had the comfort to be always applauded by my commander-in-chief, but never to be rewarded: and what is more mortifying, for services in which I have been wounded, others have been praised, who, at the same time, were actually in bed, far from the scene of action. They have not done me justice. But, never mind . . .'

There were some broader reasons for that, for Calvi and Bastia marked a bitter moment between the two services. It left a deep mark. The classic historian of the British Army, J. W. Fortescue, blamed Hood. The army, Fortescue believed, suffered badly in reputation from Corsica because, in the general view, the navy was exalted as incomparable in the operations there and the army as useless. That, he declared, 'may be traced in great measure to the arrogant and contemptuous attitude which Hood assumed, and taught his officers to assume, towards the Army'.[1] At Calvi, Fortescue acknowledged, 'Nelson's zeal and industry were indefatigable; but the extremely able dispositions whereby Stuart mastered the town were the general's only, and Nelson did no more than carry out his instructions.'

For Nelson and his ship there was respite at last. *Agamemnon* sailed for Leghorn, where the crew was found to be quite unfit. Recovery for all was slow. The ship lay there a month under repair.

Hood had been recalled to Britain; he was never to be employed again. Admiral Hotham was temporarily commander in chief Mediterranean. Hood did at least now make a determined attempt before he left for home to reward Nelson for his extraordinary support. He wanted Nelson to accept command of a larger ship, the first 74 whose command became available in the Mediterranean, but it was a promotion that Nelson felt unable to accept since it meant saying goodbye to a ship's company with whom he had shared too much, suffered too much in common, to make leave-taking easy.

A spell at home was what Nelson had also hoped for, but the strength of the French fleet at Toulon remained too serious for *Agamemnon* to be detached. The fleet needed reinforcement, which Hood had long begged for. Hood nevertheless sailed home in *Victory*, an indispensable line ship, provoking the surly though perhaps justifiable comment from the army that it was 'singular' that he should take *Victory* home 'when he might be conveyed equally well in a frigate'.

The French were preparing for assault on Corsica. At Marseilles a fleet of large transports had been assembled and were said to be ready for the transport of a landing force. But by holding the principal defensive positions at the northern end of the island the British now had effective possession and control of Corsica.

Britain had never commanded such a position of dominance in the Mediterranean, the finest possible for surveillance and control over the strategically vital western basin of the sea. Any full assurance of holding it nevertheless depended upon bringing the Toulon fleet to battle and reducing its strength to the point where it was effectively powerless to muster an assault. One opportunity for that had already been lost when Vice Admiral Hotham failed to engage Admiral Martin's squadron when it set out to relieve Calvi. But British command and retention of Corsica would also depend upon the continued independence of the Ligurian and Tuscan coastline and their ports of Genoa and Leghorn, which together offered facilities of a sort that Corsica lacked.

The Army of Italy had already assaulted the independence of Genoa by taking Vado. It could not be supposed that they would halt there. Against the uncertainties of that a disturbing shadow had fallen upon the navy lying at Fiorenzo.

Mutiny had erupted aboard the 98-gun *Windsor Castle*, under the flag of Rear Admiral Robert Linzee. The mutineers refused to continue serving under the admiral, their captain, the first lieutenant and a boatswain. They declared their dislike of them all. Vice Admiral Hotham, who had now officially succeeded Hood as commander in chief in the Mediterranean, together with Rear Admiral Hyde Parker and the captains of other ships lying at Fiorenzo, all went aboard *Windsor Castle* to plead with the mutineers to return to duty. Notwithstanding such an intimidating force of persuasion, they still refused. *Windsor Castle*'s captain demanded a court martial to redeem his reputation. He got it and was exonerated. The subsequent outcome for the mutineers was astonishing for a navy where mutiny or any semblance of it was, as a rule, unfailingly punishable by hanging. But in this instance the mutineers were all pardoned. The captain, the lieutenant and the boatswain were all replaced.

The absence of punitive measure was reflective of how scant were the resources of this fleet. The siege of Calvi had demonstrated how critically short of manpower the British forces were in the Mediterranean. Death and continuing sickness had steadily worsened the situation. The first thing Hotham required was restoration of such a mighty ship to functional normality. The last thing wanted was fear of example, a possible contagion of sympathetic insurrection too difficult to cope with so far from home waters and disciplinary intervention. The mutineers' stubborn resistance to any form of plea had been alarming.

Just three weeks later similar drama burst upon the Western Squadron at Spithead.

On 3 December the greater part of the crew of the 74-gun ship *Culloden*, under Captain Thomas Troubridge, refused to take the ship to sea. Late that night the mutineers unshipped the ladders from the main deck and barricaded themselves below. They broke into the magazine and loaded two guns with shot. A trio of admirals came on board and tried to persuade the men to return to duty. Their pleas were rejected and the sailors, forming the greater part of the ship's crew, remained shut in below for a week, until 10 December, when a captain from another ship persuaded them to surrender. Ten of the suspected ringleaders were seized. Eight were sentenced to death, two acquitted. Five of the eight were hanged aboard *Culloden*, the other three pardoned.

The winter of 1794-5 was one of the severest on record in Britain and Europe. A savage cold fell with heavy demoralizing impact upon the faltering campaigns on the Continent. It all looked steadily worse for Britain and its coalition partners as the French entered Holland and drove the Austrians and Prussians back across the Rhine. They had also driven the Spanish back across the Pyrenees.

For Britain difficulty lay everywhere. Only in Corsica were there positive results. In the West Indies the battle for Guadeloupe was finally stumbling to its end, with final British withdrawal on 10 December. In Holland British soldiers were fast withdrawing from the Continent as the Duke of York, the commander there, retreated. The war situation thereafter began to deteriorate ever more rapidly. The first six months of 1795 were dramatic. Amsterdam fell in January, and William of Orange fled to England. Holland was all but lost. What now had to be confronted was the huge imbalance in strategy and resources that this represented: a new operational front on the North Sea, French acquisition of the Dutch navy and merchant fleet, and of the Dutch colonial empire. Up to now all of that had been apprehensively dreaded but hopefully wished away as possible fact. Unrealistically, hope of saving Holland still lingered, tied to subsidies dangled before Austria, Prussia and Russia.

Between them the staggering sum of five and a half million pounds was now on offer from Britain, four million six hundred thousand for Austria alone. The latter was to be the largest single loan proffered in that entire war.

Decisions had already been made concerning Dutch shipping and warships. If complete collapse of Holland looked imminent Dutch ships would be held in British ports. Warships could be taken when encountered. More immediately pressing, however, was the urgent issue of the Cape of Good Hope and the Dutch possessions on the Indian Ocean such as Ceylon. The flight of the Prince of Orange to Britain in January provided the key to that. He was pressed to give sanction to British occupation. He did so reluctantly. Had he not done so Britain would have occupied Dutch territories anyway, to forestall any French attempt. There was no colonial wealth at the Cape. All the value was in the place itself, for it dominated the passage to the East as imposingly as Gibraltar did the Straits between the Mediterranean and the Atlantic. As one naval officer, John Blankett, expressed it in a letter to War Secretary Dundas's under-secretary, 'What was a feather in the hands of the Dutch will become a sword in the hands of France.'

Preparations for seizing the Cape of Good Hope were hastily begun. A small squadron of four ships bearing the Prince of Orange's authority for relinquishing command of the Cape to Britain sailed under Commodore John Blankett on 27 February, the main squadron under Sir George Keith Elphinstone sailed from Spithead on 3 April, and the main body of troops on 15 May.

The greatest immediate anxiety, however, lay with the West Indies, as it had done from the outset. Neither of the two fleets that already had gone out had achieved conspicuous success. The forces in the islands had been so drastically reduced by disease that they were scarcely capable of holding their own. The French had reinforced Guadeloupe after the British had abandoned their operations there. The campaign in St Domingue was barely holding. A further complication arose as slave uprisings swept the islands and threatened even Jamaica. But the West Indian operations had to be maintained, to deny the French the financial advantages they got from their island trade, and to maintain Britain's own trade as Continental subsidies continued to drain the exchequer.

In the Mediterranean the fleet under its new commander, Admiral Hotham, was constantly at sea during a stormy winter: '. . . nothing but gales of wind, but in *Agamemnon* we mind them not; she is the finest ship I ever sailed in, and, were she a seventy-four, nothing should induce me to leave her whilst the war lasted; for not an hour of this war will I, if possible, be out of active service; much as I shall regret being so long parted from you,' Nelson wrote to his wife in January from Fiorenzo. 'I hope we have many happy years to live together.'

He was obsessed with the growing threat to Corsica from a Toulon fleet that had been restored to a strength of fifteen line ships. One hundred and twenty-four large troop transports were lying at Marseilles for the anticipated assault on Corsica. The British had thirteen line ships, most in a bad state of wear and all undermanned. This fleet was now almost constantly at sea, on watch for the expected attack.

On 25 February *Agamemnon* was lying at Leghorn with the fleet, in from 'a very bad cruise', when Tuscany concluded peace with France and declared its neutrality. The fall of this particular domino led Nelson to ask, with a note of unusual despair yet also a touch of foresight, '. . . as all the Powers give up the contest, for what has England to fight? I wish most heartily we had peace, or that all our troops were drawn from the Continent, and only a Naval war carried on, the war where England alone can make a figure.'[2] His despair mounted as he found that, in their deteriorating circumstances, the new commander, Hotham, appeared the least likely to make an impact.

A week later, on 6 March, still at Leghorn, Hotham got news that the Toulon fleet of fifteen line ships accompanied by three frigates was at sea. They escorted a convoy that had embarked between five and six thousand troops for Corsica. Apparently hopeful of achieving a lightning coup, the force had sailed on learning that the British were laid up at Leghorn. Hotham's inadequacy for his task was now to become disturbingly clear.

Hotham ordered his fleet to prepare to sail at once, which they did at daybreak the following morning. On 10 March they came in sight of the enemy. The British were practically becalmed. But at dawn on the 13th, with a change of wind, Hotham signalled a general chase. *Agamemnon*'s speed, the fastest in the fleet, soon put her far in advance of the rest. Nelson, for two hours alone, then fought a ship massively more powerful than his own until Hotham sent a signal of recall.[3]

The battle was to be resumed the next morning. An advanced French squadron moved forward to join the fight but then bore off. As the French fleet made off under all possible sail Nelson hastened aboard Hotham's flagship *Britannia*, lying just astern of *Agamemnon*. He pleaded with Hotham to pursue the French, but to Nelson's frustration Hotham said, 'We must be contented, we have done very well.' Nelson's subsequent comment on that placid retort was: 'My disposition cannot bear tame and slow measures. Sure I am, that had I commanded our fleet on the 14th, the whole French fleet would have graced my triumph, or I should have been in a confounded scrape.' With that compact pronouncement he declared the formula of his present and foreseeable existence.

Hotham believed that it was sufficient to have frustrated the French attempt to retake Corsica, but it was already evident that the situation in the Mediterranean was shifting dangerously. Leghorn, Tuscany's principal port, had been tantamount to being a British mainland base, for ship maintenance, supplies and hospice for weary sailors. As a neutral port the French now had access to it. What would be its future? Nelson already had his doubts about Corsica. On 25 March he wrote, 'I am not even now certain Corsica is safe, if they undertake the expedition with proper spirit.' As if to underline that apprehension ten days later, on 4 April, six line ships and two frigates from Brest arrived at Toulon, which threatened to change the naval balance on the Mediterranean. But on 14 June six sail of the line under Admiral Robert Man joined Hotham's force off Minorca. This was the reinforcement that Hood had promised to demand.

On 29 June word was received at Fiorenzo that the French fleet was at sea again, seventeen ships of the line. Hotham, rather than stirring to action, preferred to believe that the French were simply exercising their men. He began refitting and watering his ships at Fiorenzo. He posted no guard frigates.

While the others refitted Nelson was then given a special mission. On 13 June the Austrians and Sardinians had launched an offensive against the French along the Ligurian coast. By driving the French back along the Riviera the Austrians believed they would control supplies to the Army of Italy. The Austrians had counted on cooperation from the British navy, but Hotham had been unable to provide that until the arrival of Admiral Man's reinforcement.

Nelson's assignment was to collaborate with the Austrian General Devins.[4] On 4 July *Agamemnon*, accompanied by a frigate, a gun ship, sloop and cutter, sailed for the Ligurian coast, but Nelson's small force fell in with the French fleet and returned to Fiorenzo with the French in pursuit. Off Fiorenzo *Agamemnon* began firing signal guns to attract the attention of the fleet at anchor in Fiorenzo Bay. The French, on sight of the large British fleet lying in the bay, made off at once. In doing so they lost the chance to catch the British off guard. Occupied with the refit and watering, Hotham's ships were unable to unmoor for chase, which only got underway some twelve hours after the appearance and disappearance of the French.

At daybreak on the 13th, south of Hyères and with a heavy gale blowing, the French fleet was sighted about five miles off, to the lee of the British. At four a.m. Hotham signalled his ships to form line. At eight he signalled general chase. But as the ships closed the gale dropped and light, changeable winds set in.

The British van, eight ships including *Agamemnon* and *Victory*, found themselves well ahead of the rest of the fleet, including Hotham's flagship *Britannia*. At half-past noon the van ships caught up with the sternmost French ship, *Alcide*, and opened fire. In less than an hour *Alcide* was disabled and struck her colours. Meanwhile, the light wind had changed from north-west to east, making it difficult for the French to escape as easily and quickly as they wished. *Britannia* was some eight miles away and, from that distance, Hotham was unable to make out the action. Fearing that the ships were getting too close to shore and the batteries there, Hotham sent a signal to discontinue. To the surprise of the French, the action was called off.

The French had lost their opportunity off Fiorenzo, the British off Hyères, where a superior fleet of twenty-three British ships had failed to come to action with an inferior French fleet of seventeen. It was to prove a disastrous failure. For the naval historian Brenton the French fleet should have been attacked by a general chase as soon as it was sighted at daybreak, when the British were still sailing with the last strength of the overnight gale, before the calms and shifts that followed affected action. Hotham should not have lost time forming a line. He should have dashed for the enemy. Instead the French were allowed to increase their distance. When, after a lapse of four hours Hotham finally made chase, the wind had failed and the best opportunity was lost. Even so, as Brenton's fellow historian William James declared, if Hotham had persevered in the action a few hours longer than he did he would have benefited from a change of wind. There was also the great inferiority of the British sailing ability against that of the French. The eight miles that lay between Hotham aboard *Britannia* and the seven ships that saw action against the French provided as effective an illustration of that as anything could.

For the British the consequences of Hotham's failure were soon to become apparent.

There was nothing better on offer from the Channel fleet at the Western Approaches. On 22 June an unusually powerful Channel fleet, with seventeen line ships including two 100-gun ships and six 98-gun, was cruising under command of Lord Bridport, formerly Viscount Alexander Hood and brother of Lord Hood. Bridport commanded because Howe, once again, was ill.

For two days the fleet had been seeking to close with the French fleet of twelve line ships under Villaret-Joyeuse. At seven a.m. Bridport signalled chase. But calms and shifting winds prevented action that day. Battle finally began shortly after daybreak on the 23rd. Two-thirds of each fleet became engaged. Three of the French ships struck their colours. Shortly before nine, to the amazement of the contending officers on both sides, Bridport sent out signals to disengage. The French retreated to Lorient where, at a conference summoned by Villaret-Joyeuse, it was frankly admitted by one French officer that Bridport had lost the opportunity of capturing or destroying the entire French fleet.

Bridport's explanation echoed Hotham's off Hyères: he feared the proximity of the land and of the batteries there. But the action was three miles off. There was no wind that might have carried the fleet towards shore. The batteries had not fired a shot.

On three occasions now in this year large French and British fleets were brought to action, 'and in each of which French ships were taken, so as to clothe each action with the appearance of victory; nevertheless the

circumstances under which each engagement was terminated were such as
to damage rather than to enhance the reputation of the British Admirals,
and to cause shame rather than exultation . . .'

It would be three years before the line ships of the Royal Navy were
offered their next opportunity against the Grand Fleet.

Spring 1795 had delivered a deeply clouded outlook for Britain on the
Continent. On 5 April Prussia signed a treaty with the French, which
brought Prussia's neutrality. Tuscany, too, in the same month concluded
its treaty with France. Holland finally surrendered on 16 May. The Triple
Alliance that had so confidently gone to war with an apparently weak and
disorganized Revolutionary France belonged to history.

All the other partners were faltering as well. Sardinia was losing heart;
the neutrality of Venice and Naples was being undermined by the submission to neutrality of others; French advances into Catalonia had brought
strengthening inclination towards peace in Madrid.

Great Britain saw isolation advancing upon her. She nevertheless resolutely sought to stem it, even to reverse the situation. Her policy mid-1795
was on three fronts. The main one was continued support and subsidy of
Austria; the other was for tentative direct approaches on peace with France;
the third was, on the face of it, a wild gamble, being yet another attempt
to encourage insurrection on mainland France.

The summer of 1795 had been unrest in much of France. The popularly elected National Convention had governed France since October
1792. From 1793 France was ruled by the Convention's Committee of
Public Safety, the Jacobin dictatorship dominated by Robespierre until he
fell in July 1794. In that summer of 1795 anti-Jacobin feelings and desire
for revenge saw royalists inflicting their own terror in parts of the south
and the west. There were popular risings in Paris. The Revolutionary
constitution was revoked and replaced by a new governing cabal, the
Directory. But the old guard, fearful of an election driven by royalists
sweeping away the republic, held on to power. When Paris exploded
Paul Barras was appointed to command the army. He then turned to the
young officer whose artillery work he had admired at Toulon, Napoleon
Buonaparte.

Napoleon had come to Paris as an officer in the infantry instead of the
artillery, a change that had angered him. He was assigned to a command
against the royalist uprising in La Vendée but refused it. His name was
removed from the list of general officers. Three weeks later, as Paris rose,
he received that call from Barras. In a single day of brilliant deployment
of soldiers and cannon on the streets of Paris the mob was crushed. The
future was open to the rise of Napoleon Buonaparte.

* * *

On 11 June Blankett and Elphinstone arrived together off Simon's Town, in False Bay at the southern end of the peninsula that formed the Cape of Good Hope. The main body of force arrived on 7 July. There was resistance, quickly overcome. The Cape was surrendered on 16 September.

The passage to India was secure. The Mediterranean, however, was not.

On 22 July Spain had withdrawn from the war. The immediate concern was the fate of her considerable fleet of twenty-one line ships at Mahon. With such a force allied to the Toulon fleet the balance in the western basin would be massively against the British.

The other point of uncertainty was on the Ligurian coast. Nelson had gone back to his mission there to assist the Austrian commander, General Devins, whose efforts to drive the French from the Riviera all the way to Nice had stalled after limited success. It had become even more urgent to deny the French the stores and supplies their forces depended upon from Genoa, Leghorn and other Italian ports. Failing that, according to the British minister at Genoa, 'it is almost impossible for the Allied Army to hold their present situation, and much less possible for them to make any progress in driving the French out of the Riviera'.[5]

Immediate strategy centred upon Vado Bay, which had just been recaptured by the Austrians. Vado was the best anchorage on that coast. With the Maritime Alps and the Apennines descending so close to the coast, communication along their rough slopes was difficult for a manoeuvring army. Military movement along the poor coastal road was exposed to fire from the sea and supplies depended heavily upon small coasting vessels. Attack on both became Nelson's task.

Nelson was briefly spirited as he commanded the coast, surveying its features, devising strategy. The Corsican experience was resurgent in him. He was impressed by the Austrian soldiers and started off well with General Devins. He proposed landings to create new bridgeheads, which he could maintain from sea. He begged more ships to assist him and went to Leghorn to press his request personally on Hotham. Instead Hotham reduced his squadron and, on top of the tasks he was already charged with, ordered Nelson continually to reconnoitre Toulon. Once more, at a critical point in a critical operation, he was left in seething frustration in face of inaction tied to overload. Gradually at first and then ever more rapidly, he found himself watching a vital front needlessly disintegrating before him, powerless to do what he knew might hold it. Hotham certainly had the ships to spare. Apart from an occasional cruise off Toulon his fleet was either lying at Fiorenzo or at Leghorn. He seemed to need the show of numbers around him without putting any of it at risk. But, as Mahan points out, 'the employment of adequate force upon the Riviera, in active aggressive work under Nelson during the summer, when it was practicable to do so, would have compelled the French fleet to come out and fight, or the French army to fall back'.

General Devins practised his own form of negation. Like Hotham, he could not be pinned down to any of the strategic suggestions that Nelson proffered, and considered drastically urgent. The French were steadily strengthening their positions along the coast and in the mountains. By the autumn Nelson had lost faith in all whom he had been designated to serve. He was writing them all off. On 27 October he summed it up in a cynical letter to his uncle: 'The campaign of our Allies, the Austrians and Piedmontese, is, I suppose, almost over . . . My situation with this Army has convinced me . . . of the futility of Continental Alliances . . . the Admiral has given me directions to look after the French Fleet at Toulon (Whilst he lies quiet in Leghorn Roads) . . .' Nelson's scorn for Hotham here expressed was perhaps the sharpest he had so far allowed himself. He now wanted to see an early end to it all: 'Peace, I believe, will yet be with us before next January; at least I hope so, if it can be on honourable terms.'[6]

Hotham's Mediterranean term was over. On 1 November he struck his flag and left. Sir Hyde Parker had temporary command. The situation that Hotham left to him had grown still more serious.

Peace with Spain meant that the French troops fighting on the peninsula were beginning to arrive as reinforcements for the Army of Italy. The French were assembling flatboats, transports, gunboats and other vessels for close inshore action at different points on the Riviera. Supply depots were established and constantly being stocked. It was a situation that invited assault. This, after all, was the original operational purpose for which the Austrians had called for the British fleet.

The greatest assembly point for these transports, small craft and supplies was at Alassio Bay. The place was defended by formidable batteries erected by the French. Nelson believed that with three ships of the line he could destroy all that was there. Hyde Parker not only refused the request for line ships but reduced Nelson's force of frigates.

Nelson stood confronted by a great event building before him, one that was pulsing with its imminence, quite unpredictable in its immediate outcome, yet vulnerable to his or another's determining influence at the right place, at a certain moment. He was placed to read the circumstances and fated possibilities with a comprehension that seemed to elude others. Since he was in constant survey along that coast between Genoa and Toulon, Nelson had a better overall picture of the situation than anyone.

With Hyde Parker, like Hotham before him, sailing fruitlessly in and out of Leghorn, Nelson took the unusual step of sending an urgent report to Evan Nepean, under-secretary at the Admiralty, apologizing should it be taken as presumptuous, '. . . I hope their Lordships will think I have done right in giving them this information, without its coming through the Admiral, which is the proper channel'. He reported the position of the 28,000-strong French army along the mountains as impregnable, the Austrian position similarly so. But the winter had begun stormy and cold. Up in the mountains where the French and Austrian forces were entrenched the weather was savage. Men were dying from it. 'Thus both armies remain to see who can stand the cold longest.'[7] Meanwhile, down in Genoa the French were arrogantly insulting the authority of the republic by openly enlisting its citizens and inciting others to rise. Nelson was pleading for the action that winter stalemate briefly offered, the looming threat being loss of Genoa, the bank and supply point for both the French and the British. The strategic consequences of its loss would be considerable. Right then the French had a frigate lying in Genoa with a force that was intended to cut communications between the Austrian army and the city.

Agamemnon was lying at Vado. On learning of the frigate's intention Nelson sailed at once for Genoa and laid *Agamemnon* across the harbour mouth to prevent the French warship from leaving to land its troops along the coast. Here again, one prompt, bold, decisive and necessary move upon a huge and complex operational area springs from the remarkable individual that is Horatio Nelson, he the only one who, in a rapidly deteriorating scene of potentially grave consequences, holds clear image of need and specific action. On 20 November he declared the situation to Hyde Parker with unusually sharp tone: 'I have not, which you probably know, been on former occasions backward in presenting my thoughts to Admiral Hotham, that at one time or another, the French would make a push for this coast, as also my wishes for a reinforcement of two 74-gun ships, and that the Frigates should not be diminished; the latter, I am sorry to say, is done. The extraordinary events which have taken place here, and the Expedition which would now sail from this Port, were I to withdraw the Agamemnon, will always render it a measure of necessity to keep a superior force to the French at this place, with orders to attack the enemy, if they presume to sail.'[8] Unfortunately, Napoleon was already master of the situation.

Two days later, on 24 November, the Army of Italy struck.

The French overwhelmed the Austrians up in the mountains and drove down to the coast to the small port of Loano. In this astonishing assault, to be known as the Battle of Loano, the Austrians lost seven thousand soldiers killed. The rest fled in what was riot. Thousands remote from the enemy were said to have fled. The Ligurian Riviera was abandoned by the Austrians and their allies. The French now held the coast up to Voltri, nine miles from Genoa. All of it was accomplished by a ragtag army that looked as though it might have been scattered by a gust of wind. But it carried a spirit and drive that surprised all who encountered it.

Nelson had a lieutenant, two midshipmen and sixteen sailors captured on shore at Vado. They gave him a disturbing picture of those who had caught them: '. . . few of the French soldiers are more than twenty-three or twenty-four years old; a great many do not exceed fourteen years, all without clothes'. They were ill fed and unpaid.

As the Austrians were gone from the coast, General Devins with them, *Agamemnon*'s own purpose there was over. Nelson took her to Leghorn, there to reflect upon it all.

Recrimination poured from the Austrians on lack of support from the British. Nelson understood them. 'They say, and true, they were brought on the coast at the express desire of the English, to co-operate with the fleet, which fleet nor admiral they never saw.' But at least, as Francis Drake, British minister at Genoa, consoled him, the Austrians laid no blame to him personally: 'their complaints turn upon the insufficiency of the force under your command, and not upon the mode in which that force was employed . . .'[9]

Nelson's own reflections were forthright. 'Our admirals will have, I believe, much to answer for in not giving me that force which I repeatedly called for, and for at last leaving me with Agamemnon alone. Admiral Hotham kept my squadron too small for its duty; and the moment Sir Hyde took the command of the fleet he reduced it to nothing – only one frigate and a brig; whereas I demanded two seventy-four-gun ships and eight or ten frigates and sloops to insure safety to the army.'[10]

Nelson had long feared loss of Italy and all its allies, down to Naples. He now was to say, with his usual perspicacity, 'If the French mean to carry on the war, they must penetrate into Italy. Holland, Flanders, with their own country, they have entirely stripped: Italy is the gold mine, and if once entered, is without the means of resistance.' Or, as he had said on another occasion, 'If we are not completely victorious – I mean, able to remain at sea whilst the enemy must retire into port – if we only make a Lord Howe's victory, take a part, and retire into port, Italy is lost.'

That possibility was now the looming crisis for Britain in the Mediterranean.

Napoleon Buonaparte's defeat of the mob uprising in Paris had re-established him with the army. He was appointed second to Barras, who commanded the Army of the Interior. When Barras resigned Napoleon moved up to command.

Only twenty-seven, small, thin and sallow-cheeked, Napoleon was entirely unprepossessing until he began to speak on what obsessed him; at the end of 1795, that subject was still his plan for an Italian campaign.

The success against the Austrians on the Ligurian coast had reinforced his passion for it.

In January 1796 Napoleon took his plan to the Directors. They forwarded it to General Scherer, then in command of the Army of Italy. Scherer's response was dismissive. If that was what they wanted then the man who had drafted the plan ought to come out and put it into effect. A month later the Directors took Scherer at his word and in February they appointed Napoleon to command of the Army of Italy.

XII

CHANGE

A different war had fallen upon all.

The war thrust its varying character upon the combatant world from the very first days of 1796 through to the last ones of the year, by which time the magnitude of an altogether changed struggle was to be fully perceptible. It would now rapidly develop at heart into a war for the Mediterranean between a new and transformed British navy on the one hand, and a new and transformed French army on the other. Soon gone was the desultory and characterless war of the past three years for the direction was in new hands on both sides.

Napoleon's design for the Army of Italy called for domination of the Kingdom of Sardinia and the Austrian possessions south of the Alps, the Hapsburg-controlled duchies of Milan and Tuscany. To consolidate any such control he needed the great fortress of Mantua below Milan. From there the French could descend to the Papal States and Naples. The British requirement in face of such an assault against Italy was firm blockade of Toulon, sweeping command of the Riviera coasts, retained possession of Corsica and the continuing neutrality of the commercial ports of Genoa and Leghorn, from which they drew their principal supplies.

Loano had demonstrated how fully the Ligurian coast was already the seat of this struggle. But Napoleon's strategic vision was fixed above the coast, specifically at the juncture of the Maritime Alps and the Apennines above the coastal town of Savona. From the passes above Savona roads ran directly to Turin and Milan.

From that location would follow the final humiliation of Britain's remaining Continental allies, Sardinia and Austria, driving the conflict rapidly into a contest between Britain and France. There, upon that coastline, Britain's isolation began and the Great War became an epic struggle between the opposing concepts of hegemony that the two powers had come to symbolize. And there, too, in that western basin of the Mediterranean, the two individuals for whom this war became a decisive personal duel would be fully liberated upon their heroically distinctive courses.

Horatio Nelson was thirty-eight, Napoleon Buonaparte ten years younger. Physically, they might almost have been brothers. The same thin, emaciated physique, the same spectral pallor, and the same impression of a frailty unlikely to be able to sustain the huge repetitive weight of fatal decision-making that was already descended upon them. But with Nelson, too, as Madame Junot, wife of General Junot, said of Napoleon, there were the 'eyes sparkling with keenness and will power', before which questioners retreated. Never perhaps in all history have two combatants been so uniquely alike, at least in the deceptive masking, to the uninitiated, of the innate driving forces that would ultimately so drastically affect the run of the world. As they approached their respective destinies in the first months of 1796, Nelson and Napoleon both still bore that inner fire closer to themselves than wider visibility yet allowed. But that was about to change, with Napoleon especially, after receiving command of the Army of Italy in February, when he promptly set about planning the invasion of northern Italy.

With Nelson the determining factor was quite as opportune as that which fell to Napoleon. After Hotham's departure and the interim command of Sir Hyde Parker, the Mediterranean command went to Sir John Jervis, a man of a different naval character entirely from the other two: a character as stern as any but ameliorated by fairness, balance and, above all, deductive common sense. Jervis had arrived in Fiorenzo Bay aboard *Victory* on 30 November 1795.

With Jervis came a new navy. If not quite new in wood and canvas, new certainly in force of insight, discipline, overhaul of deficiencies and, not least, recognition of the dangers that had mounted in the Mediterranean, as well as the default that had allowed so much to pass unchallenged.

Admiral Hotham's much lamented failure to pursue the evasive French fleet under Admiral Martin in the Battle of Hyères the year before had left the Toulon fleet as a powerful instrument in aiding the defeat of the Austrians at Loano and advancing the French along the Ligurian coast. In his *Naval Strategy* Mahan declared that Hotham's refusal to chase and destroy the Toulon fleet had thus 'made possible Napoleon's Italian campaign of 1796, from which flowed his whole career and its effects upon history'.

Nelson could never have disagreed with that. He had been furiously alive to the consequences of Hotham's ineptitude, followed by that of Hyde Parker. It thereafter gnawed at him. 'You will now bear me out in my assertion,' he was to write to Lord Keith at the Admiralty in 1800, 'when I say that the British fleet could have prevented the invasion of Italy; and if our friend Hotham had kept his fleet on that coast, I assert, and you will agree with me, no army from France could have been furnished with stores or provisions; even men could not have marched.'¹ Nelson's loyal supporter, the viceroy of Corsica, Sir Gilbert Elliot, concurred: 'I have always thought that it is a great and important object in the contest between the French republic and the rest of Europe, that Italy, in whole or in part, should neither be annexed to France as dominion, nor affiliated in the shape of dependent republics; and I have considered a superior British fleet in the Mediterranean as an essential means for securing Italy and Europe from such a misfortune.'

Jervis had unfortunately arrived too late to affect the momentum of what was about to follow on from the Austrian catastrophe of Loano. But he had Nelson, and for Nelson in turn here was a commander who had the insight to comprehend to the full any situation laid before him. Their rapport was immediate when they first met at Fiorenzo on 19 January 1796. He was received, Nelson told his wife, 'not only with the greatest attention, but with much apparent friendship'. And, later, that Jervis 'seems at present to consider me more as an associate than a subordinate officer; for I am acting without any orders. This may have difficulties at a future day; but I make none, knowing the uprightness of my intentions.'

With Jervis this trust and familiarity so quickly extended to Nelson was greater tribute than anything received from Hood, for Jervis was a man with whom every disciplinary caution was necessary. Such licence to a junior officer did not come easily.

Jervis was rigidly severe, intolerant of any, even the slightest, breach of discipline. This embraced his officers as much as it did the men. His view was that the discipline of the fleet depended upon that of the wardroom. 'It is not the insubordination on the part of the men that I apprehend,' he told Nelson, 'but the imprudent talk of the officers, and their presumptuous disposition to discuss the orders they receive. That is the real danger, and the true cause of insubordination.' Or, on another occasion, 'When the forms of discipline are observed, the substance will soon follow.'

'The business of a captain should be no sinecure,' he said. 'With me the commander of a ship is responsible for everything that goes on board, and he must answer for the conduct of his officers and his crew.' True to that, he put under arrest the captain and all the wardroom officers of a ship against which he had cause of complaint. On another occasion, he charged the pay of a negligent officer of the watch for the repairs and damages to the flagship after another ship had run foul of her.

Smartness had to be observable in everything. Young lieutenants of the fleet were warned that their hats had to be taken off to their superior officers and not merely touched 'with an appearance of indifference'. No officer was allowed to board *Victory* in other than the prescribed uniform.

In broader respects, Jervis had done as much as anyone in that time to change the Royal Navy. His severity was leavened by active concern for the wellbeing of his men. Accompanying discipline was his demand for cleanliness to ensure good health. Jervis revolutionized medical care aboard his ships. He brought the sick up from the low orlop deck and created a sickbay in the forecastle, ventilated by two large ports. Hammocks and bedding had to be scrubbed once a week, when sailors were also allowed to mend their clothing. To reduce damp within the ship he stopped the washing of the lower decks. All these changes had to be entered by his captains in the logs of their ships. He was deeply sceptical of the medical qualifications of his surgeons and demanded that 'the surgeons of this squadron should never walk the decks or go on shore, whether for duty or pleasure, without having their case of instruments in their pockets'. He insisted that the sickbay be provided with flannel shirts for those who had a cough or common cold, and that the sailors should be obliged to put them on. He also insisted on doses of lemon juice as a defence against scurvy.

Another aspect of his discipline was his demand from his captains for complete order in station at sea, as well as frequent military drill on board. 'It is of first importance,' he declared to his captains, 'that our crews should be perfect in the use of their guns; I therefore wish that every day, whether in harbour or at sea, a general or partial exercise should take place on board every ship in the squadron.'

An interesting aspect of all this was the fact that, as a member of parliament, Jervis had voted Whig and, with Fox, had regarded this war as useless, impolitic and lamentable. But when war came he resigned his seat and, with the full force of his proven naval character, applied himself to this rigorous determination on success for his own contribution to the struggle. All of it was of a piece with the manner in which he had raised himself without patronage into the highest levels of naval command. His father was counsel and solicitor to the Admiralty in the early eighteenth century, then treasurer of Greenwich Hospital. Jervis was himself intended for law. He ran away from his Greenwich grammar school at twelve. A year later he entered the navy. He retained a strong consciousness of a naval ascent without privilege. At the time of the Nootka crisis, when he took command of the 98-gun *Prince*, his quarterdeck was packed with young gentlemen from great and wealthy families, but he gave lieutenant's commission to the son of an old naval officer without family or fortune. His grateful recognition of special merit in Nelson was likely accompanied by his awareness that there was much in Nelson's social background that was similar to his own.

Certainly if Jervis himself was not yet fully appraised of the full gravity of their situation Nelson now left him in no doubt of it.

Nelson believed more strongly than ever that a full invasion of Italy by the French was imminent. 'If they mean to carry on the war, they must penetrate into Italy,' he said, in further conviction that for the French Italy represented the next round of spoil. He believed that French possession of Vado Bay as a result of Loano meant that the troops for the invasion of Italy would sail from there to Tuscany, a quick transfer presumably protected by the Toulon fleet.

Jervis was impressed, and appreciative. This was in satisfying contrast to the frustration Nelson had endured under Hotham. Jervis, Nelson wrote, 'was so satisfied with my opinion of what is likely to happen, and the means of prevention to be taken, that he had no reserve with me respecting his information and ideas of what is likely to be done'.

This instant observable bond between them naturally raised resentment among those who got less attention. One of the other captains promptly told Nelson, 'You did just as you pleased in Lord Hood's time, the same in Admiral Hotham's and now again with Sir John Jervis; it makes no difference to you who is commander-in-chief.' Nelson told his wife that 'he returned a pretty strong answer to this speech'. The attack reflected envy and resentment that would accompany Nelson further along the way. It also reflected the lingering incapacity of some in that squadron who, after Loano, yet failed to recognize the particular service that he had already rendered, and continued to do in confronting the huge crisis rapidly mounting for them in that sea. For Nelson, and no one else so far, had been the principal agent in every naval exploit of importance in the Mediterranean.

Under Jervis, Nelson began the rapid progress towards the achievements that would fully establish him in the public mind. No time was wasted. He sailed off instantly, just forty-eight hours after his arrival at Fiorenzo and his first encounter with Jervis.

Jervis had a fleet of twenty-five ships of the line, twenty-four frigates, ten corvettes and a range of flotilla vessels. He immediately offered Nelson the *St George* of 98 guns or the *Zealous*, a 74, but Nelson retained his attachment to *Agamemnon*. Jervis allowed him the pendant of a commodore which, though not officially a rank, allowed a captain to command as an admiral. With that floating above him, Nelson aboard *Agamemnon*, accompanied by three frigates and two corvettes, sailed back to the Riviera coast.

Jervis himself also moved off at once to blockade Toulon. What he encountered there corroborated the large-scale intent that Nelson had conveyed to him. A large French force of thirteen ships of the line as well as frigates lay in the outer roads, bustling with activity and apparently ready for sea. Five new line ships had been built at Toulon since Hood's departure. These were now fitting out.

Jervis promptly imposed the most rigid and efficiently organized blockade yet laid upon a French port, one that was to become the model for future blockade of Brest and other French ports. He divided his fleet into an offshore and an inshore. The offshore fleet sailed in two disciplined lines, with Jervis aboard *Victory* as lead ship of the one line. An inshore squadron of four line ships was commanded by Captain Thomas Troubridge. This steady vigil would be kept up month after month, supplied from the mainland, without need to enter port.

When a transport with supplies arrived it was put under tow of the first ship to be served. Once the tow was secured, the boats of the ship being supplied were launched and began ferrying the supplies from the transport, which afterwards slipped back to the next recipient. If any ship required repairs signal was made for the skilled workmen of all the ships to be put aboard, under the supervision of the flagship's carpenter. A two-deck 44-gun ship accompanied the fleet solely as hospital ship. Anyone taking ill was immediately transferred to the hospital ship in a cot and returned only when cured. In this manner infection was prevented from spreading.

As fresh fruit, vegetables and meat were constantly delivered from shore the health of the sailors remained excellent. Jervis established a system of three watches for the sailors, one of which was for mending clothes or simply amusing themselves. It brought greater ease to the monotony of blockade. A steady harmony prevailed throughout that spring and summer of 1796. There were no courts martial.

All of it demonstrated the commanding style of Jervis who, though renowned for the severity of his discipline, nevertheless held the loyalty and respect of his sailors. They knew they would have the best he could manage, and that he expected the same of them.

Beyond the Mediterranean, the naval war had fallen slack again. Apart from actions between cruising frigates, a somnolent quiet lay upon naval activity. June the First had become a receding memory of great battle action, though the promise of another major confrontation appeared to be in preparation at Brest.

The main activity was with the frigates that freely roamed the Narrow Seas as they sought encounter with their French counterparts or hunted the privateers that steadily preyed on commerce. One such was the adventurer Sir Sidney Smith, captain now of the 38-gun frigate *Diamond*. By April 1796, Sidney Smith had already gained a reputation for daring inshore incursions along the French coast. On 17 April he went foraging into Le Havre. After anchoring in the outer road he saw lying in the inner road a notorious privateer whom he particularly wished to catch. The vessel in question was a fast-sailing lugger, *Vengeur*, whose commander was well known for his daring and seamanship.

After a short struggle *Vengeur* was boarded and seized without casualty, but her crew had cut the anchor cable and Sidney Smith found the ship being carried into Le Havre inner harbour on a fast inflowing tide. An armed lugger and small craft filled with troops surrounded *Vengeur* and, after a fierce fight with muskets, Sidney Smith was compelled to surrender. Four of his group had been killed.

The surviving British officers and men were marched from Le Havre to Rouen. But Sidney Smith and one of his midshipmen, John Wesley Wright, were separated from the others and taken under escort to Paris, where they were imprisoned in adjoining cells in the Temple, the prison where Louis XVI and his family had been incarcerated three years before. This imprisonment separate from the rest in such a special gaol was highly unusual. It spoke of the international reputation Sidney Smith already possessed.[2]

In the Mediterranean the lack of naval action simply increased the tensions over a wholly new course of the war building within Italy.

Nelson's own immediate task was to ascertain French strategy along the Riviera and to inflict whatever damage he could upon their progress or preparations. As he investigated that whole line of coast Nelson became steadily more despairing. His immediate proposal to the Austrians was that they should reoccupy Vado. Without a point of occupation on the coast it would be impossible to frustrate the French plans. On 15 March, in neutral Genoa, he found that Napoleon's close confidant, the army commissioner Salicetti, was also in the city, together with other French army commissioners. For Nelson this was confirmation of all his worst fears. They were there, he believed, 'for the express purpose of expediting the operations of the French Army towards the invasion of Italy'. Salicetti was in fact in Genoa to raise a loan for supplies the Army of Italy needed.[3]

To the British minister at Genoa, Francis Drake, Nelson again strongly urged the recapture of Vado, otherwise the French would freely pass along the Ligurian coast. They would be able to send light guns on mountain carriages as well as men along the coast road and the Toulon flotilla of small craft would ferry ammunition and stores from Nice to Savona. 'I moreover beg it may be understood, that if the French flotilla proceeds along the coast, our ships-of-war cannot molest them; not being able to approach the coast, from the shallowness of the water,' Nelson advised Drake.

The new commander of the Austro-Sardinian forces, seventy-one-year-old General Beaulieu, was reluctant, however, to advance to the coast from his position in the mountains above Savona. On 6 April Nelson sought persuasion through Drake at Genoa: '. . . assure General Beaulieu, that on whatever part of the coast he comes, I shall never quit him. If he is able, and willing, and expeditious, I am sure we shall do much . . .'[4]

On that same day Beaulieu had other, unexpected, means of persuasion.

The French vanguard on the coast under General Scherer had unexpectedly moved to Voltri, practically the gates of Genoa. Beaulieu hastily took a strong column down to capture Voltri, believing that the French thrust into Italy was now moving along the coast which, as he saw it, would therefore become the main theatre of operations.

Napoleon was in the process of moving his headquarters to Savona, where he arrived on 9 April. He had left Paris on 21 March, after being invested with the command of the Army of Italy over its then incumbent head, General Scherer. He was at Nice on 27 March. What he surveyed as he encountered his army was hardly encouraging.

His soldiers were young and desperate. Unpaid, hungry, shabbily and inadequately clothed, and badly equipped. For all their misery they nevertheless demonstrated the fierce motivating spirit that Nelson's officers had observed when they were captive of the young French soldiers at Vado. Those at Nice got a further infusion of that spirit from Napoleon. Sharing with them at least the kinship of youth, he cried out to them the exhortation that became legendary. 'Soldiers, you are half starved and half naked. The government owes you much, but can do nothing for you. Your patience and courage are honourable to you. But they procure you neither advantage nor glory. I am about to lead you into the most fertile valleys of the world: there you will find flourishing cities and teeming provinces: there you will reap honour, glory and riches. Soldiers of the Army of Italy, will you lack courage?'

That plea was supported by immediate efforts to feed and dress and pay them, partly from the funds that Salicetti had secured at Genoa and from loans from bankers at Nice.

The Army of Italy was a force of just under fifty thousand against fifty-two thousand of the Austro-Sardinians. The forward positions of the French were mainly near the coast from Savona to Loana. The Austro-Sardinians were in the heights above them, north of Savona, at the pass that separated the Apennines from the Maritime Alps. They were effectively in control of the position between two vital roads that went inland, one north-east towards Milan, the other north-west towards Turin, the Sardinian capital. But their situation was weakened by mountainous heights between the two roads. It was at that point of vulnerability between the Austrian and Sardinian forces that Napoleon planned to strike, to sever the allies, and to pass on beyond to Turin. Before his own intended move, however, the Army of Italy's van under Scherer moved towards Voltri and it was this move that brought General Beaulieu down to the coast, where Nelson had all along pleaded for him to be.

Napoleon, who established his headquarters at Savona on 9 April, had not sanctioned Scherer's advance to Voltri. It angered him because it had eliminated the element of surprise that he was counting on for springing upon the Austrians in the mountains above the coast. In the event it worked to his advantage for Beaulieu, in his belief that the centre of operations was to lie on the coast, had weakened his own situation in the mountains by rushing a large force down to the coast.

Just as he had promised, Nelson was present in full support on the night that he had been advised the Austrians would attack. *Agamemnon*, accompanied by another line ship and two frigates, lay abreast of the Austrian positions at eleven o'clock on the night of 10 April, in station for when the Austrians attacked. But Nelson found himself watching a bungled operation. Beaulieu had started the assault twelve hours before the time he had specified. When the Austrians attacked Voltri with ten thousand men some three hundred French were killed or wounded but four thousand retreated into the mountains. 'I beg you will endeavour to impress on those about the general the necessity of punctuality in a joint operation, for its success to be complete,' Nelson wrote to Francis Drake in Genoa. But that warning was already too late, as he explained in a letter to the Duke of Clarence eight days later: 'Our ships so entirely commanded the road, that had the general's concerted time and plan been attended to, I again assert, none of the enemy could have escaped.' This may have been wishful thinking, for Beaulieu's operation was fatal anyway for weakening the centre between the Austrian and Sardinian forces in the mountains and it was there, as he had intended from the first, that Buonaparte struck on 12 April. Beaulieu was compelled to rush up from the coast as hastily as he had descended to it.[5]

When Nelson wrote his letter to the Duke of Clarence on the 18th the Austrians and the Sardinians had already been separated. The Austrians had lost some ten thousand men killed or wounded or taken prisoner, the mountain posts of Montenotte and Dego had fallen, Beaulieu was already out of the mountains on the plain of Piedmont and the Sardinians were confronting the French at the pass of Ceva, from where the road to Turin was open.

In one week of brilliant deployment of his forces against the confused and extended line of the Austro-Sardinians Napoleon had completely outmatched them. Ceva fell and on 23 April the Sardinians asked for armistice. It was signed at Cherasco on 28 April. A fortnight later France and the king of Sardinia signed their peace agreement. The territories of Savoy and Nice were surrendered to France as well as the three principal fortresses of the Piedmont plain.

Napoleon now saw emergence of his original 1794 plan of campaign for the Army of Italy, with its ultimate thrust to the Rhine. After the signing at Cherasco he wrote to the Directory, 'Tomorrow I shall march against

Beaulieu, force him to cross the Po, cross myself immediately after and seize the whole of Lombardy: within a month I hope to be on the mountains of the Tyrol, in touch with the Army of the Rhine, and to carry the war in concert into Bavaria . . .'

The course to that connection proved to be slower than Napoleon anticipated but the sweep of his advance into Italy nevertheless continued triumphantly. On 10 May he threw his full force against the town of Lodi on the River Adda, south of Milan. Access to Lodi was across a long, narrow bridge, an obstacle that ensured close, fierce combat of the most bloody and heroic kind. Here Napoleon was in the heat of the fighting, placing guns. It was at Lodi that he rose to be a national hero, and it was there that his men first saluted him as *le petit caporal*. The storming of the bridge at Lodi became enshrined as the first of Napoleon's golden moments. He himself saw it in fuller terms. At St Helena he told his aide, General Montholon, that 'it was only on the evening after Lodi that I realized I was a superior being and conceived the ambition of performing great things, which hitherto had filled my thoughts only as a fantastic dream'. On 14 May Napoleon entered Milan.

Down on the Mediterranean Nelson had news of Lodi just six days after it fell. By now he had a sound appreciation of the force of the French drive. 'The story is very ill told, and I should doubt much had I not unfortunately been in the habit of believing accounts of French victories,' he wrote to Sir Gilbert Elliot from Leghorn. 'I very much believe that England, who commenced the war with all Europe for her allies, will finish it by having nearly all Europe for her enemies. Should all the powers in this country make peace . . . Corsica will be the only tie to keep our great fleet in the Mediterranean.' His pessimism and despair rise from the very words as he concludes, 'I beg pardon for the readiness of my pen, it has, I fear, gone further to your Excellency on this subject than it ought.'[6]

He knew, as they all did, that a defining moment had arrived, or was close.

Once more, as at Toulon, one is drawn to the fact that on that coast Nelson and Napoleon Buonaparte had been close to one another. Again, too, much the same scene – Nelson aboard *Agamemnon*, Napoleon on the heights immediately above. The symbolism of the arriving duel is stronger. The image is etched more sharply than before. For this time each is already well removed from obscurity. If Lodi lit Napoleon's aura, Nelson is fast moving into illumination of his own. Jervis assured that. Unlike his service with Hood, Nelson could now expect to receive whatever accolade would be his due for any achievement, and for Jervis's critical dependence upon him.

For the moment, however, the flow of events on the Mediterranean was temporarily stilled by uncertainty. Nelson concentrated his efforts upon

Riviera coastal traffic and the batteries that the French had laid all along the coast. But he did so with a mounting sense of futility. Were they really of any use there? he asked. 'If not, we may serve our country much more by being in other places.'

Napoleon's brilliant tactic of striking inland meant that the French coasting trade had less significance since it no longer represented the Army of Italy's main supply train. The Army of Italy now had Piedmont and Lombardy to feed it. In a letter to Jervis on 18 May Nelson more fully expressed his exasperation over the great change that was making their own efforts appear so futile: 'Money, provisions, and clothes the enemy have in abundance; and they command arsenals to supply their wants in arms and ammunition.' French surfeit was the cruel reality that all now had to come to terms with.

In England the deteriorating state of France through 1795, the royalist insurgence and general unrest together with food shortages and soaring inflation, had induced Pitt to believe that a hard peace might be drawn from France. Pitt had talked of 'a gulf of bankruptcy' so severe that he could 'almost calculate' when French resources would be consumed. Britain's own situation, though fundamentally different, for its own reasons often appeared scarcely better. Public unrest, widespread distress and shortages in Britain together with the growing unpopularity of the war created pressure for peace, in spite of strong objections from George III. The colossal cost of the war and the unprecedented size of the subsidies paid out to the Continental allies alone formed a strong argument for peace. Pitt already foresaw Britain's isolation, with Spain, Sweden and Denmark as potential enemies. All of that had given strength to Dundas's continued insistence that Britain could dictate peace only through success in the West Indies and depriving the French of their resources there. It was the view that George III fully backed. But, given the economic state of France, Pitt had steadily envisaged arrival at an early compromise of benefit to Britain and her allies. The French had hardened steadily, however, and on 26 March 1796, the day before Napoleon took direct command of the Army of Italy, the Marquis de Barthélemy, the French envoy with whom Britain was dealing at Berne, made impossible demands for peace. Pitt recognized 'no option between war and peace'. And then, just two months later, there for all to see was the Army of Italy drawing the financial succour of France from Turin, Milan, Parma and Modena and advising the Directory that 'you can now count on six to eight millions in gold or silver ingots or jewels, which are at your disposal in Genoa'. Napoleon was already giving his troops, who themselves had ransacked the country across which they stormed, half their pay in silver. By July Italy would have provided France with sixty millions of francs.

* * *

The collapse of the naval front on the Mediterranean became inevitable as one base after another disappeared from British grasp, and as Spanish belligerence rapidly increased to the point where war with the Iberian Peninsula looked imminent.

Change arrived for Nelson himself. The beloved *Agamemnon* was in a sorry state and in need of return to Britain for complete overhaul. On 11 June 1796 Nelson shifted his pennant to the 74-gun *Captain*. Most of his officers accompanied him to his new command as *Agamemnon* sailed for home. It was a momentous month in other respects. On 3 June Napoleon had established his headquarters at Verona. This fortress on the River Adige put him where he strategically wished to be, able eventually to reach northwards into the Tyrol while able to deploy southwards, whence he suddenly sent two diversionary forces to occupy Leghorn and to intimidate the Papal States and Naples, both nominal allies of Britain. On 5 June the Court of Naples signed an armistice and withdrew its troops and ships from support of the British. The Pope signed an armistice on 24 June. Nelson was at Genoa on 23 June when confused accounts of these events reached him. With his usual perspicacity he sailed at once for Leghorn, arriving there 27 June to find the British merchants of the place, the traditional suppliers of the British navy in the western Mediterranean, already on their way out of the port aboard ships laden with their personal property. The French arrived the following day, 28 June.

Nelson's immediate conviction was that an invasion of Corsica was planned. But Napoleon, after a brief visit to Leghorn, which was immediately sacked of its treasure, returned to Verona. Buonaparte did not need to mount an invasion of Corsica for he was fomenting uprisings on the island with Corsican refugees shipped over from Genoa under a French general. The British viceroy on Corsica, Sir Gilbert Elliot, shared Nelson's fears and directed him to occupy the island of Elba which, halfway between Corsica and the mainland, provided the perfect stepping stone for hostile forces. On 10 July Nelson reported that Elba's fortress of Porto Ferrajo had been occupied by a detachment of troops landed by his squadron. That accomplished, Nelson maintained tight blockade of Leghorn, while Jervis continued his of Toulon. Loss of fresh supplies from Leghorn meant that Jervis now feared scurvy in his fleet, a fear heightened when in August, under pressure from the French, Genoa was declared closed to the British fleet.

Nelson advocated seizure of Leghorn. Both Viceroy Elliot and Jervis approved of it. But the proposed assault on Leghorn fell away as word of continuous French victories on the mainland descended to them. And, in the middle of August, he was dismally prophetic to Jervis: 'Austria, I suppose, must make peace, and we shall, as usual, be left to fight it out: however, at worst, we only give up Corsica, an acquisition which I believe we cannot keep, and our fleet will draw down the Mediterranean.'[7]

Through the blazing heat of the height of a Mediterranean summer the British navy, with increasing discomfort and alternating surges of bravado, confidence and resignation, awaited the critical outcome on the Continent that would decide its immediate future. Mahan described the biding situation with a splendour of rhetoric and succinct summation. In his *Life of Nelson* he wrote:

The summer of 1796 was in truth the period of transition, when the victories of Bonaparte, by bringing near a cessation of warfare upon land, were sweeping from the scene the accessories that confused the view of the future, removing conditions and details which perplexed men's attention, and bringing into clear relief the one field upon which the contest was finally to be fought out, and the one foe, the British sea-power, upon whose strength and constancy would hinge the issues of the struggle. The British navy, in the slight person of its indomitable champion, was gradually rising to the appreciation of its own might, and gathering together its energies to endure single-handed the gigantic strife, with a spirit unequalled in its past history, glorious as that had often been. From 1796 began the rapid ascent to that short noontide of unparalleled brilliancy, in which Nelson's fame outshone all others, and which may be said to have begun with the Spanish declaration of war, succeeded though that was by the retreat in apparent discomfiture from the Mediterranean now at hand.

In that emergence of the Royal Navy that Mahan defined Jervis surely stood for the constancy as Nelson did for the spirit. It was a partnership as remarkable as any that the navy had known.

Constancy lay with the embedded resolution of Jervis's character. The spirit that drove Nelson was far from being anything so straightforwardly readable, being of its own unique complexity. It could be dangerous. Jervis recognized that. 'The commodore is the best fellow in the world to conduct the naval part; but his zeal does now and then (not often) outrun his discretion,' he told Gilbert Elliot. The reference was to Nelson's desire to seize Leghorn with troops and sailors. Before Leghorn, Nelson had sought to promote a similar landing on the Tuscany coast. These and other enthusiastic impulses for ventures of doubtful value or success could, had they been given completely free rein and then brought on disaster, have broken Nelson and this partnership as surely as the earlier faulted proposal for an assault on Bastia could resoundingly have broken Nelson and Hood. The visible tumult in Nelson mostly seems to have been less from despair over deterioration of the big picture than simply from the lack of action. Action was ever what he craved. There was in that his ache for glory, for the eventual 'Gazette' that would extol the individual, himself. But the seeming outrageous vanity of that was merely expression of the ardent longing for the concrete, for the adamantly elusive, for what stubbornly refused to manifest. And that had to be understandable for such a character who in any contemplation of action saw himself at the heart of it. That was to be his ongoing frustration throughout 1796, a year barren of any significant naval action.

On 19 August 1796 Spain entered into offensive alliance with France. This remained short of actual war, but that could now hardly be long delayed. Nine days later, on 28 August, Secretary of War Dundas advised the Admiralty to evacuate Corsica. This despatch reached Jervis on 25 September. He himself was told to retire to Gibraltar, but to remain in the Mediterranean as long as possible. On 5 October Spain finally declared war.

Neither Jervis nor Nelson was surprised: they had been expecting it for too long. What they feared was that they would again have a situation like that of the American War of Independence with the Spanish and French fleets in joint operation against them. The concern was numbers. They had no fear of the Spanish navy on its own but the fifty line ships of the Spanish fleet joined to the Toulon fleet represented a formidable challenge to Jervis's force of fewer than twenty line ships. This was something that Nelson, typically, looked forward to rather than dreaded. To the Duke of Clarence he wrote: 'I will venture my life Sir John Jervis defeats them; I do not mean by a regular battle, but by the skill of our Admiral, and the activity and spirit of our officers and seamen. This country is the most favourable possible for skill with an inferior fleet; for the winds are so variable, that some one time in twenty-four hours you must be able to attack a part of a large fleet, and the other will be becalmed, or have a contrary wind, therefore I hope Government will not be alarmed for our safety . . . there is nothing we are not able to accomplish under Sir John Jervis.'

Jervis at once sought to augment his fleet by lifting the blockade of Cadiz that had been imposed by Hotham just a year ago under Rear Admiral Robert Man, who had pursued a squadron that escaped from Toulon under Admiral Richery. The blockade was imposed in October 1795, when Richery took refuge in Cadiz. Since then Man had maintained the blockade with six line ships and a frigate. He was now ordered to bring these into the Mediterranean to reinforce Jervis.

Admiral Man immediately provided another example of the sort of individuals common enough to the navy of the time, those who lacked the comprehension of crisis, the wit and initiative to deal with it, of whom Hotham had so far been an outstanding example.

When Man arrived at his rendezvous with Jervis he had come so precipitately that he had failed to provision his ships at Gibraltar. With all the usual supply points now closed to the British fleet, Jervis sent Man back immediately to get supplies and, with those on board, to return at once.

But Man never came back. On his way to Gibraltar he met a Spanish fleet of nineteen line ships under Admiral Langara. Man and his seven ships escaped from Langara and went on to Gibraltar where he called a conference of his captains and, with their agreement, sailed into the Atlantic instead of the Mediterranean, cruised about for a while, and then sailed for Spithead, while Jervis waited anxiously and in bewilderment for him to return as instructed to reinforce and supply the fleet.[8]

After receiving his instruction to abandon Corsica, Jervis decided to make Elba's Porto Ferrajo the navy's temporary base. To Nelson now fell the galling task of dismantling Bastia to which he had given so much of his energies. It took him from 30 September to 19 October before he was ready to leave.

Corsica, in any event, had become untenable, without a large military force. The insurrection there had gathered momentum, with steady infiltration from the mainland. The tricoloured republican cockade was being openly worn by French partisans. Hostility against the British was so powerful that all naval stores had been brought from shore and embarked in ships. It had become impossible for the British to go into the interior from Bastia or San Fiorenzo. When Nelson wanted to consult with Jervis at Fiorenzo he was warned that he could not do it with safety by going overland. As viceroy, Sir Gilbert Elliot had lost all authority.

Nelson was the last one off, at dawn on 20 October. The French by then had already entered Bastia's citadel. Nelson's ships then joined the rest of the fleet at Fiorenzo, to which, after seven months off Toulon, Jervis had finally withdrawn to assist with the evacuation of Corsica. Watch frigates remained posted at Toulon but with the main blockade removed the doors were open to the French to join forces with the Spanish.

By this time the Spanish fleet under Langara had appeared offshore, daily sighted by Jervis's lookout frigates. This was when Admiral Man's absence began to look critical. With the Toulon fleet likely to join the Spanish Jervis decided that the odds were building against him and so waited impatiently for sight of Man, Fiorenzo Bay being the appointed rendezvous.

On 20 November Nelson sent a note across to his old companion, Captain Cuthbert Collingwood, who all along had been part of Jervis's fleet, commanding the 74-gun *Excellent*: 'We have reports that Man is gone through the Gut,' he told Collingwood, 'not to desert us, I hope, but I have my suspicions.' 'The Gut' was the term used for the Straits of Gibraltar.

Collingwood later gave his own account of the tensions of waiting for Man.

For a fortnight after the island was completely in possession of the French, we waited in St Fiorenzo Bay, with the utmost impatience, for Admiral Mann [*sic*], whose junction at one time seemed absolutely necessary to our safety. We were all eyes in looking westward, from the mountain tops: but we looked in vain. The Spanish fleet, nearly double our numbers, were cruising almost in view, and our reconnoitring frigates sometimes got almost among them, while we expected them hourly to be joined by the French fleet, who had already possession of the harbour in which we lay. But no Man appeared; and, as the enemy began to annoy us from the shore, we sailed on the 2d of November.[9]

Daily rations were down to a third of the usual as they waited for Man. There was nowhere to draw from in Fiorenzo. Nelson was ever-optimistic of a decisive action as they sat it out. He wrote, 'When Man arrives, we shall be twenty-two sail of such ships as England hardly ever produced, and commanded by an admiral who will not fail to look the enemy in the face, be their force what it may . . . There is not a seaman in the fleet who does not feel confident of success.' Sir Gilbert Elliot, present with the fleet, echoed that: 'The admiral is as firm as a rock. He has at present fourteen sail-of-the-line against thirty-six, or perhaps forty. If Man joins him, they will certainly attack, and they are *all* confident of victory.'

Abandonment of the Mediterranean and those posts that he himself had done so much to secure sat bitterly with Nelson. To his wife he wrote, 'We are all preparing to leave the Mediterranean, a measure which I cannot approve. They at home do not know what this fleet is capable of performing; anything, and everything. Much as I shall rejoice to see England, I lament our present orders in sackcloth and ashes, so dishonourable to the dignity of England.'

When they finally moved off from Fiorenzo the early winter voyage was rough and extended, with a passage of twenty-eight days down to Gibraltar, where they arrived on 1 December. Jervis had been instructed to base himself at Lisbon. Valuable though it was, Gibraltar could not service a fleet. The Rock was cut off from fresh supplies by Spain's entry into the war. Its own garrison was often on salt rations. There was no anchorage safe from the weather, from the levanter especially. This was forcibly driven home when, on 10 December, two of Jervis's line ships were driven from anchor to sea in an easterly gale. One was totally lost with most of her crew, driven on to the Moroccan shore opposite. The other was so disabled that she was sent back to Britain. A third ship had gone ashore at Gibraltar itself and had to remain at the Rock.

As though that were not enough, there was on the very same day the galling sight of five ships of the line of the Toulon fleet, under Admiral Villeneuve, sailing through the Straits, flying out with the very gale that was wrecking Jervis's own ships.

Jervis sailed for his new base at Lisbon on 16 December, to await reinforcement there. He lost a fourth ship 21 December on entering the Tagus inbound for Lisbon, leaving him with a mere eleven ships of the line. He had been instructed to evacuate Elba, a task that, inevitably, was assigned to Nelson.

Nelson shifted his broad pennant to a frigate, *Minerve*, and accompanied by another frigate, *Blanche*, left Gibraltar on 15 December for Porto Ferrajo to bring away the garrison, stores, and also to pick up the Corsican viceroy, Sir Gilbert Elliot. It was to be a swift, memorable excursion for Nelson finally got another taste of the action he had been craving.

Off Cartagena on 19 December, at around eleven p.m., Nelson encountered two Spanish frigates, *Sabina* and *Ceres*, and gave chase. In *Minerve* he came up with *Sabina* and engaged her fiercely for close to three hours. *Minerve* was fitted with four carronades, which made her the more powerful and damaging of the two, the 'fire of hell' the Spanish called it. But the Spanish captain several times refused Nelson's demands to surrender. He finally did, after all his officers had been killed. When the captain came aboard to surrender his sword he identified himself as Don Jacobo Stuart, a lineal descendant of James II and Arabella Churchill. Nelson, impressed by the lineage and the resistance, returned the sword: 'I felt this consonant to the dignity of my Country, and I always act as I feel right, without regard to custom.'

That action was scarcely over before Nelson was engaged by another Spanish ship. He beat her off but *Minerve* was so badly damaged that Nelson was unable to chase her. Then, while repairing damage, two Spanish line ships accompanied by two frigates appeared bearing down upon them, drawn by the gunfire heard from a distance. Nelson and his captain, George Cockburn, quickly got away from their likely destruction. *Sabina*, which was in tow, was abandoned, with two of Nelson's officers still aboard her. *Ceres*, which had been captured by *Blanche*, was also abandoned.

The necessary retreat before the superior Spanish force that advanced on *Minerve* and *Blanche* could not detract from the fierce satisfaction that this duel allowed. They were at least going out of the Mediterranean with something clear and distinct as final curtain.

Minerve and *Blanche* reached Porto Ferrajo on 26 December. Christmas entertainment was still underway. 'It was ball night, and being attended by the captains, I was received in due form by the General, and one particular tune was played: the second was "Rule Britannia".' An impatient Nelson was held at Elba for a month. General de Burgh, commander of the Elba garrison, had received no instructions to evacuate. Until he got them, he intended to remain. Nelson was blunt. He would withdraw all naval stores and belongings and 'should you decline quitting this post, I shall proceed down the Mediterranean with such ships of war as are not absolutely wanted for keeping open the communication of Elba with the Continent'. But he still had to wait for the arrival of Sir Gilbert Elliot, who was visiting Naples. Nelson finally sailed on 29 January 1797, leaving behind on that small, barren island Britain's only foothold garrison inside the Mediterranean, stubbornly and unimaginatively awaiting its last orders, or possible capture by the French.

In this manner, near enough to the date, closed three years of inconclusive war in the Mediterranean, with Britain evicted from any decisive control within that sea, and with no immediately visible prospect of return.

The British navy had arrived in the western Mediterranean without clear mandate except to protect trade and blockade the French navy. They had obtained possession of two of the principal controlling points, Toulon and Corsica, and lost both. Much of the blame for that lay with Jervis's predecessors who, as naval commanders in chief, were too inept to recognize the advantages they possessed and to seize advantage when it offered. It lay as well with serious mismanagement of the war by Pitt and Dundas, the latter especially, with his focus upon the West Indies, which had denied Mediterranean reinforcement of ships and men.

The decision to abandon Corsica and fall back out of the Mediterranean was nevertheless probably premature; the chagrin of both Jervis and Nelson had expressed that. On the Continent at this time the French had momentarily lost advantage. The Austrians under Archduke Charles had regained the initiative at the Rhine and Napoleon found his own extended campaign stalled by lack of reinforcement. The Austrians managed to strengthen the defence of Mantua, the fall of which Napoleon depended upon for his control of northern Italy. He had personally suffered a setback close to his headquarters at Verona. 'Perhaps we are on the eve of losing Italy,' Napoleon wrote on 13 November 1796. 'None of the expected help has arrived.'

Through all of that one comes back yet again to Rear Admiral Man's failure to keep his appointed rendezvous at Fiorenzo. For someone as bound to duty and obedience as Jervis, Man's actions were beyond all reason. Byng had been shot for less. Jervis was later to transmit his indignation to Admiralty: 'The conduct of Admiral Man is incomprehensible: he acknowledges to have received my orders and the duplicates, and that he opened the dispatches which directed my continuance in the Mediterranean. I had taken the liberty of cautioning him against consulting with the Captains under his orders, who all wanted to get to England; and yet, by a passage in his public letter, it appears that he acted with their concurrence.'[10]

Jervis subsequently believed, as did Nelson, that had Man joined with his reinforcement at Fiorenzo the decisive battle for the Mediterranean could have been fought and won in those last weeks of a year that was marked by an absence of naval event of any consequence in that sea or anywhere else. Instead, after three years, they were withdrawing in humiliation. Had Man turned up, Jervis, backed by Nelson, would undoubtedly have gone after the Combined Fleet, with a different turn of history in both the Mediterranean and the Atlantic. As Napoleon himself wrote, 'The expulsion of the English has a great effect upon the success of our military operations in Italy. We must exact more severe conditions of Naples. It has the greatest moral influence upon the minds of Italians, assures our communications and will make Naples tremble even in Sicily.'

For some reason Man evaded a court martial, even though he had left Jervis and his fleet in a dangerous situation. He was told to strike his flag and to come ashore. He was never employed again.

As viceroy of Corsica Sir Gilbert Elliot had repeatedly urged that Corsica become a base for offensive military operations. But the Mediterranean, unfortunately, had never seriously figured in any military plans. In September 1793 Pitt spoke of a force of nearly ten thousand troops for Toulon. That was never fulfilled. When the British were close to abandoning Toulon word was finally received of a risibly modest cavalry detachment available as reinforcement. Dundas's obsession with the West Indies had made that the main focus for military attention. The West Indies in consequence became the principal British military graveyard of the early years of the war. And still, through 1796, Dundas pressed for more to go out to the Indies, this at increasing cost to the navy, for the sweep of the press for both services steadily yielded fewer men as well as fewer of real worth.

Britain did at least sail from the Mediterranean with certain assets distinctly superior to those she had when she went in. These, of course, were the rise of Nelson and the steady development of his skills and outlook: that, and the new stature of command created by Jervis. During his time in the Mediterranean Nelson may not have got all the accolade he deserved, but with Hood, even with Hotham and then with Jervis he had obtained responsibility, opportunity and experience that he would not have got elsewhere during that period.

Leaving Porto Ferrajo, Nelson divided his force and the fleet of store-ships they were to convoy into two divisions, to proceed on different courses to avoid capture. He himself, with the viceroy and Elliot's entourage on board *Minerve*, was intent on a final scouting of the enemy's western Mediterranean naval bases. What they found was like a declaration of a great struggle gone elsewhere. Fiorenzo was empty, Toulon practically so. Cartagena was empty. It was Langara's base. He had apparently taken his fleet somewhere else. Together with Villeneuve's gale-assisted flight through the Straits, all of this appeared to be merely further indication that naval battle had shifted to the Atlantic.

Minerve anchored in Rosia Bay, Gibraltar, on 9 February. The Spanish fleet had passed through the Straits into the Atlantic four days before. Two of the line ships and a frigate had detached to deliver supplies to the Spanish base at Algeciras, opposite the Rock. They were still there when Nelson arrived. On board one of them, *Terrible*, were two of Nelson's lieutenants, Hardy and Culverhouse, who had been taken prisoner when *Sabina* had been recaptured. An exchange was negotiated. Nelson was happy to delay for that, less so waiting for Elliot's party to dine with the Gibraltar governor. Nelson had himself refused the invitation. His impatience rang from a note sent to Elliot's private secretary: 'I most heartily wish you all good appetite, and only beg you will be on board as early in the evening as possible – say eight o'clock – for I shall sail the first moment after; but I fear a *westerly* wind.' A westerly prevented, or at least severely hampered, passage to the Atlantic.

Minerve got away, but only the following morning, 11 February. The Spanish ships at Algeciras were held ready and promptly moved as *Minerve* left Rosia Bay.

Nelson had some advantage as he got away from the lee of the Rock since the Spanish ships, once they had raised anchor, had some distance from Algeciras island off the western shore of the bay to Cabrita Point from where they rounded into the Straits. But once in the Straits *Terrible* appeared to be gaining on *Minerve*. Nelson prepared the frigate for action. Colonel John Drinkwater Bethune, a member of Sir Gilbert Elliot's staff, asked Nelson whether action was probable. Nelson declared it very possible. Then, gesturing towards his broad pennant laying itself out in the wind above them, he declared: 'But before the Dons get hold of that bit of bunting, I will have a struggle with them, and sooner than give up the frigate, I'll run her ashore.' After this, the whole party descended for dinner.

Bethune was congratulating Lieutenant Hardy on no longer being a prisoner of war aboard *Terrible* when the cry 'Man overboard' rang down from above. The officers ran up on deck while the passengers crowded the stern windows to watch. *Minerve*'s jolly boat was lowered with Hardy and a party of sailors.

The sailor who had gone overboard had disappeared and was never seen again. He had been carried away by the fast eastwards-flowing current, which then was also carrying the jolly boat towards *Terrible*, with Lieutenant Hardy thus facing further imprisonment on board just a day after his release from her. Nelson was not having it. 'By God, I'll not lose Hardy,' he cried, 'Back the mizzen topsail!'

That action checked *Minerve*'s advance, allowing the current to carry her back towards the jolly boat and towards her pursuers. Close action appeared imminent. But, astounded by such an inexplicable manoeuvre, *Terrible* itself shortened sail, as if seeing it as challenge, and also prepared to drift on the current to allow her Spanish companions to catch up. *Minerve* came along-side the jolly boat and, as Hardy and the sailors clambered back on board, Nelson ordered to make sail again.

The Straits were wider where they now found themselves, between Tarifa and Cape Malabata. They had more advantage of the wind, and with that swiftly put distance between themselves and *Terrible*, which by nightfall had been lost sight of. But during the night *Minerve* suddenly found itself in the middle of a fleet. The night was hazy and the ships unidentifiable But Nelson believed it to be the Grand Fleet, outbound from Cartagena. Jervis had been told to cruise in the vicinity of Cape St Vincent and it was twenty-five miles off that promontory where he arrived at daybreak on 13 February. He was joined by Nelson before midday that same day.

Jervis could confirm that it was the Grand Fleet making towards them. His scouting frigate had already been shadowing them when *Minerve* had found itself in their midst. Nelson now removed his pennant back to *Captain*, and from there he and Jervis aboard their respective ships that night listened to the signal guns of the Grand Fleet, like a drumming to the action that both were so fervently longing for.

XIII

TRIUMPH

THIS was the day, St Valentine's Day 1797, that Jervis and Nelson had been praying and waiting for since their partnership was sealed at their first meeting at Fiorenzo the previous year.

'A victory is very essential to England at this moment,' Jervis was heard to say as he surveyed the force advancing towards him. His chances of having victory would, to most, have appeared gravely uncertain, given his own strength and that of the oncoming armada. Nevertheless, with Jervis those words were a firm declaration of intent and not mere wishful utterance. It was also his personal demand for redress against the humiliation of being forced out of the Mediterranean to fight where he now was.

With the reinforcement brought by Admiral Parker, Jervis commanded a fleet of fifteen line ships, two 100-guns, three 98s, one 90, eight 74s and one 64. The modern armada descending upon him represented a naval force as powerful as any that had ever existed, with close to double the gun power of the British.

The Spanish Grand Fleet was commanded by Admiral Don Josef de Cordova, who had taken over from Admiral Langara. He had sailed from Cartagena with twenty-seven line ships and twelve 34-gun frigates. Pride of place in the fleet belonged to the giant four-deck *Santissima Trinidad* of 130 guns, largest warship in the world. Accompanying her were six 112s, two 80s, and eighteen 74s. The fleet approaching the British off Cape St Vincent lacked some of the ships that had been diverted into Algeciras. It nevertheless still consisted of practically all of the main armament, its strength here being twenty-five line ships and eleven frigates.

Admiral Cordova approached the British fleet with a mind eased by assurance of his own superiority. An American ship that had passed through the British fleet before Jervis received the reinforcement of Admiral Parker's five ships had reported that Jervis had no more than nine ships. Even so, when sighted the enhanced British force of fifteen line ships was still greatly inferior to the Grand Fleet's twenty-five.

The east wind had dropped during the night but the usual humid haze of a heavy levanter remained as dawn broke. Jervis's scout frigate had informed him just before daybreak that the Grand Fleet was some nine to twelve miles off. First light revealed to the British a fleet straggling across the horizon, its big ships magnified by the mist. Shortly before eleven the officers on *Victory*'s quarterdeck began taking clearer stock. 'By my soul,' *Victory*'s signal lieutenant cried, 'they are thumpers. They look like Beachy Head in a fog.'

Standing beside Jervis was his captain of the fleet, Sir Robert Calder, who was counting the approaching ships. 'There are eight sail of the line, Sir John.'

'Very well, sir.'

'There are twenty sail of the line, Sir John.'

'Very well, sir.'

'There are twenty-five sail of the line . . . twenty-seven, Sir John.'

'Enough, sir. No more of that, sir,' Jervis peremptorily ordered him. 'The die is cast and if there are fifty sail I will go through them. England badly needs a victory at present.'

'That's right, Sir John, that's right,' another captain, a Canadian, cried out, and in his exuberance slapped Jervis on the back, a startling familiarity but apparently passable in that prevailing mood. 'And by God, we shall give them a damned good licking.'

Having been carried so far out into the Atlantic by the levanter the Grand Fleet was benefiting from the change of wind during the night. It was now running nearly before the wind, sailing east-south-east towards Cadiz. But they were approaching loosely in two groups, well spaced. The British were almost at right angles to them. Jervis ordered his ships to form a single column and signalled that he would cut through the disordered Spanish line.

Jervis's immediate decision had to be whether to go for the larger force of sixteen ships to his weather side, or against the leeward nine. The Spanish apparently expected the latter. Instead Jervis went for the main force. As Collingwood, commanding *Excellent*, described it, 'We flew to them as a hawk to his prey, passed through them in the disordered state in which they were, separated them into two distinct parts, and then tacked upon their largest division.' Cordova's main force and the British were then sailing nearly parallel, on opposite course. Heavy cannonade was exchanged. When Jervis signalled to tack it was to bring his line on the same course as the Spanish. That meant that as the line tacked and turned it would come up behind the Spanish rear.

Culloden, Captain Thomas Troubridge, was the lead ship of Jervis's van. Troubridge had anticipated that very signal. He already had it at the masthead and, as *Victory*'s instruction fluttered out, his acknowledgement promptly unfurled as he began to tack. Jervis, watching from *Victory* at the centre of the British line, cried out, 'Look at Troubridge! He handles his ship as if the eyes of all England were upon him, and would to God they were!'

Ship after ship of the British line tacked to follow *Culloden*. The run of British line through the gap between the two Spanish divisions meant that the line ships proceeded one by one to the point where *Culloden* had put about, and where each in succession tacked to join the pursuit of the main Spanish fleet. This was around one p.m. on the 14th, with the weather fine, the wind light. But such tacking of an entire line to come up with and proceed along the Spanish line was slow. As the rest of the British line followed in *Culloden*'s wake Cordova thought he saw opportunity to reunite his entire force by passing behind the last ships in the British rear to join the leeward division of nine. The last ships of the British rear at this time were still standing in line, each awaiting its turn to tack. But the slowness of the process meant that they themselves remained abeam of the Spanish van.

Nelson's *Captain* was third from the end of the British line. He had just come abreast of the rearmost of the Spanish line. On his own line he had five of the British ships ahead of him that still had to tack before he himself did. It was this methodical one after another that made the manoeuvre such a slow process. But, alert as ever, being at the end of the British line, Nelson saw that the van of the Spanish line was manoeuvring to cross behind *Captain* and the other last ships of the British column. Cordova's intention to double back towards the other Spanish group of ships to unite with them was immediately apparent to Nelson. The slowness of the British tacking manoeuvre had presented Cordova with his opportunity. In their full force of twenty-five ships the Spanish would represent a different field of action for the fifteen British.

Instead of proceeding to tack in his allotted position as he was meant to do, Nelson instantly on his own initiative broke from the line, wore his ship, put *Captain* about on to the reverse course, to pass alone towards and then among the leaders of the Spanish van to the flagship itself. His 74-gun *Captain* promptly engaged Cordova's 130-gun *Santissima Trinidad*, a challenge of David to Goliath. Never in the Royal Navy had any captain ever dared to take such single-minded action upon himself.

Such an astonishing and unprecedented individual action probably caused more surprise among the Spanish than the British. It brought confusion to the Spanish manoeuvre. They never recovered from it, for Nelson's action destroyed all semblance of formal battle. The Spanish ships had maintained no proper order. They had even less after this startling break in the British fleet's own strictly marshalled order. Some of their ships became clustered close together, hindering one another's fire but presenting better target to the British, some of whose ships quickly followed Nelson's example or went to his assistance. It became melee.

Apart from *Santissima Trinidad* Nelson had found himself engaged with the 112-gun *San Josef*, the 112-gun *San Salvador del Mundo* and the 80-gun *San Nicolas*. He needed help. He got it. *Culloden*, leader of the British line, was soon right in there in support of *Captain*. The two ships took heavy punishment. They were unsupported at first.

Aboard *Victory* Jervis's captain of the fleet, Robert Calder, said, 'Sir, the Captain and Culloden are separated from the fleet, and unsupported: shall we recall them?'

'I will not have them recalled. I put my faith in those ships: it is a disgrace that they are not supported and separated.'

Captain and *Culloden* were both crippled in what Nelson nevertheless defiantly called 'this apparently, but not really, unequal contest'. *Blenheim* then came up and gave them respite, allowing Nelson to bring up more shot from the hold, all having been exhausted by the rapid and continual fire.

Collingwood's *Excellent*, a 74, had been stationed last in the British line. He also made for *Captain* and the heart of the action. Collingwood had already taken prizes but abandoned them to go to Nelson's assistance. As Nelson put it, Collingwood 'most gallantly pushed up, with every sail set, to save his old friend and messmate, who was to appearance in a critical state'. *Excellent* had initially engaged the *San Salvador del Mundo*, won its surrender, and then passed to the *San Isidro*, 74, 'so close alongside, that a man might jump from one ship to the other. Our fire carried all before it; and in ten minutes she had hauled down her colours . . . Then making all sail, passing between our line and the enemy, we came up with the San Nicholas, of 80 guns, which happened at the time to be abreast of the San Joseph, of 112 guns; we did not touch sides, but you could not put a bodkin between us, so our shot passed through both ships and, in attempting to extricate themselves, they got on board each other.'

Captain by this time had paid severely for the unequal weight of metal that she had brought against herself. She was completely disabled, having lost her fore topmast, all sail and shroud and with her wheel shot away. She was lying by 80-gun *San Nicolas* and had been taking shot from five different hostile ships for an hour. *Blenheim*, in coming to support of *Captain*, came under the same fire. She took 105 shot in her sides alone. *Blenheim*'s masts and rigging were shattered. Her boatswain subsequently declared that it was impossible to find a whole rope in the ship.

In spite of the disabled state of his own ship, Nelson saw more fight in her, and for himself. The *San Nicolas* and *San Josef* had become locked together close beside *Captain*, which was too disabled to detach herself under sail but manoeuvrable for what Nelson now required. Nelson told his captain, American-born Ralph Miller, to put the helm a-starboard to bring *Captain* hard against *San Nicolas*, and simultaneously called for boarders.

Captain's bow was hard against the starboard quarter of *San Nicolas*, with her spritsail yard passing over the poop and hooking in the Spaniard's mizzen shrouds. *Captain* was carrying soldiers of the 69th Regiment. These, together with sailors, prepared to leap aboard *San Nicolas*. As Nelson's captain, Miller, rushed forward to lead them Nelson restrained him, 'No, Miller, *I* must have that honour.'

With the upper quarter gallery and its large ornamental windows hanging over them, a soldier broke a window and jumped in, followed by Nelson, with the others crowding in behind, while more were leaping aboard above them. The cabin doors were fastened and Spanish officers fired their pistols through them but the soldiers broke the doors open. The soldiers fired as they pushed towards the quarterdeck, killing the Spanish brigadier who sought to bar their way.

Lieutenant Edward Berry, who had been travelling as passenger with Nelson, had already taken the poop above the quarterdeck and was hauling down the Spanish colours there. Nelson passed on to the forecastle, where a group of Spanish officers who had been taken prisoner by his seamen handed over their swords. Pistol and musket fire then opened from the admiral's stern gallery of the *San Josef* alongside.

Rear Admiral Don Francisco Xavier Winthuysen had decided to resist seizure of *San Josef*. Nelson ordered more men to go over from *Captain* and himself crossed to *San Josef* by the main chains. A stiff resistance continued briefly. During it Winthuysen fell. A Spanish officer then told Nelson from the quarterdeck rail that the ship had surrendered. On the quarterdeck the captain, with bended knee, handed over his sword and said that Admiral Winthuysen was dying of his wounds below. The other officers then handed their swords one by one and, as they did so, Nelson passed them to one of his sailors who 'put them with greatest sangfroid under his arm'.

This part of the action concluded around four p.m. *Victory* passed soon after and saluted *Captain* with three cheers.

The *San Josef* and *San Nicolas* were the last Spanish ships to be taken prize, after *San Salvador del Mundo* and *San Isidro*. This was practically the end of what had been a five-hour battle of great intensity. But Cordova's flagship, *Santissima Trinidad*, after being engaged one after the other by all the main participants – Jervis, Nelson, Troubridge, Collingwood and Frederick – was now engaged again, this time with Sir James Saumarez, *Orion*, and *Blenheim*. Their action with her began at ten past four. In this bout *Santissima Trinidad*, already shattered, lost her fore- and mizzen masts and was totally disabled. She struck shortly before five, or at least was assumed to have done so for her ensign came down, was seen trailing in the water from the taffrail, and no attempt was made to rehoist it. But Saumarez and Frederick were unable to take possession of her because the nine ships that had formed the isolated part of the Spanish fleet, and which had taken little part in the general action, appeared intent on rescuing Cordova and his flagship. As several of their large ships bore down towards the action *Orion* and *Blenheim* opened fire and the Spanish hauled off, successful, however, in having collected *Santissima Trinidad*. She would live to fight another day, on an even greater occasion.

Jervis then decided to call off the action. *Captain*, which had borne the brunt of the battle, was a wreck in hull and masts. Her losses were the greatest of any ship. The British fleet had lost seventy-three killed, twenty-four of whom were aboard *Captain*. One-quarter of the 227 wounded were also hers. Nelson himself had been wounded, struck at the groin by a fragment of something that, without creating an open wound, caused severe contusion.

Jervis himself had a narrow escape that day. A marine who stood beside him on the poop had had his head blown off. His blood and brains and fragments of bone splattered across Jervis, who was first thought to be badly wounded. He was untouched and, calm, asked a midshipman to fetch an orange to freshen his dry mouth.

As *Captain* was now quite out of any further action, a boat was sent from *Minerve* to pick up Nelson and he was taken to *Irresistible*, a 74, for refreshment and rest, and where his pennant was raised. He did not stay long before heading for *Victory*. He had not changed. He had not even washed. His shirt and coat were badly torn. He had lost his hat and his face was still streaked with gunpowder. His urgency was to present himself to Jervis.

Nelson still had no idea what reaction he would get from Jervis for his unorthodox break from line and single-handed engagement of the main force of the Spanish battle fleet. He knew perfectly well that the day owed to him, and he could not have been too concerned after receiving three cheers from *Victory*. But Jervis, a man of absolute discipline, could never be predictable on such a matter. He had had his own distinct plan of action, which Nelson had violated by breaking from line to make his own engagement. Although line was no longer as sacrosanct as it had been, it nevertheless imposed a necessary order and control, as Jervis himself had strictly required for this very action. Such individual deviance from an order of battle signalled by a commander as rigorous as Jervis was something that would still commonly have been regarded as beyond contemplation. But, as Nelson recounted, 'At dusk, I went on board Victory, when the Admiral

received me on the quarterdeck, and having embraced me, said he could
not sufficiently thank me, and used every kind expression which could not
fail to make me happy.'

Jervis refused to accept the sword of the Spanish admiral who fell aboard
San Josef. 'Keep it,' he said, 'it belongs, by just right, to him who received
it from his prisoner.'

At six, as night descended, the British and Spanish fleets lay to on
different tacks, with the British ships busy all night in repairing damage,
to be ready to renew the action at daylight if required. Dawn on the 15th
saw the Spanish fleet to windward in line of battle, with a Spanish frigate
towing *Santissima Trinidad*. British sailors continued repairing and splicing
their rigging. But Jervis had decided against renewing the battle.

After Jervis's praise Nelson got the same from all around. His singular
achievement was indisputable with them all. Collingwood sent over a
letter first thing on the morning of the 15th. 'My dear good Friend, First
let me congratulate you on the success of yesterday, on the brilliancy it
attached to the British navy . . . The highest rewards are due to you and
Culloden; you formed the plan of attack – we were only accessories to
the Dons' ruin; for had they got on the other tack, they would have been
sooner joined, and the business would have been less complete.' Gilbert
Elliot and Bethune had watched the action from the decks of the frigate
that was to carry them to England immediately after the battle, carrying
Jervis's report of it. Elliot wrote, 'You will easily believe, I trust, the joy
with which I witnessed your glory yesterday. To have had any share in it
is honour enough for one man's life, but to have been foremost on such
a day could fall to your share alone. Nothing in the world was ever more
noble than the transaction of the Captain from beginning to end, and the
glorious group of your ship and her two prizes, fast in your grip, was never
surpassed, and I dare say never will.'

Perhaps the greatest praise, however, was a further tribute from Jervis
that night when he was reviewing the day with the captain of his fleet,
Captain Calder, a man whose cautions had already twice vexed him that
day. Calder, with some reserve, now broached the matter of Nelson's
spontaneous action and the fact that it had carried Nelson, Troubridge
and Collingwood into the brunt of the battle. Was it not an unauthorized
departure from the prescribed mode of attack?

Jervis promptly answered: 'It certainly was so, and if ever you commit
such a breach of your orders, I will forgive you also.'

Calder's question said as much as anything could how against the grain
Nelson's action could be for the older generation.

Like 'the First of June', as Howe's fight was always called, there was
again question of whether the Spanish fleet should have been pursued and

brought to further action, or whether *Santissima Trinidad* at the very least should have been retrieved as the outstanding prize it had been. The French historian of the naval side of the Great War, Jurien de la Gravière, expressed one view, that 'Jervis feared to compromise the important advantage he had gained by any partial engagements . . . To have dashed recklessly after the enemy's 21 ships, of which the majority had hardly been engaged, he should have been Nelson. Sir. J. Jervis was neither great enough nor rash enough for that; besides . . . at this period, it seemed too natural, too much in conformity with established usages, to tarnish the glory of this brilliant victory.'[1] But Mahan believed that '. . . [Nelson's] genius in no way detracts from the credit due to the commander-in-chief . . . To Jervis alone belongs the honour of attacking such heavy odds, as well as of the correct and sufficient combination by which he hoped to snatch victory from superior numbers . . . It has been thought that further pursuit of a fleet so disgracefully beaten would have increased the British triumph; but Jervis was not the man to risk a substantial success, securely held, for a doubtful further gain.'[2]

The shortcomings of the battle were nevertheless to weigh quietly upon the victors. As Nelson wrote shortly after, speaking of *Captain*, *Culloden* and *Excellent*, 'We are the only three ships who made great exertions on that glorious day: the others did their duty, and some not exactly to my satisfaction. We ought to have had the Santissima Trinidad and the Soberano, seventy-four. They belonged to us by conquest, and only wanted some good fellow to get alongside them, and they were ours. But it is well; and for that reason only we do not like to say much. Sir John Jervis is not quite contented, but says nothing publicly.'

Admiral Cordova and his senior officers had all fought bravely but they were woefully deficient in experienced sailors. They had been manned at Cartagena by peasants brought in from the fields or men taken from the prisons. On one ship several guns on the side on which the ship had been engaged had never been discharged.

Cordova was sent to Madrid under arrest after landing at Cadiz. He was expelled from the service. Other officers suffered similar humiliation.

Jervis remained conscious that the biggest prize of the battle, the four-decked 130-gun *Santissima Trinidad*, the biggest ship in the world, a trophy without equal to deliver to Britain, had eluded him. Three frigates were sent to look for her and after four days found her but again she managed to escape. Ten days later, on 1 March, a frigate again fell in with her but was held off by her powerful broadsides. Spanish line ships appeared and the great ship eventually made it to Cadiz.

In his official report Jervis gave special commendation to none, but in a separate, private report to the First Lord of the Admiralty, Earl Spencer, he was more forthcoming on the individual contributions. There was anyhow no way this time that Nelson's achievement could escape public notice. The mere fact of a victory ensured that. News of it swept the land, bringing relief, exultation and national gratitude. Jervis's pronouncement at the outset of the battle on Britain's need of a victory might have been regarded as an understatement in the country at large.

The cost of the war had brought Britain to a critical state. Before news of St Vincent reached Britain the Bank of England was compelled to suspend cash payments. Bankers and merchants agreed to accept banknotes. Unrest continued across the country. On the Continent things could not have been worse. The Austrians had been routed at Rivoli on 14 January. Mantua capitulated on 2 February. The Pope had come to terms with Napoleon, paid a heavy indemnity and ceded Bologna, Ferrara and the Romagna. Catherine the Great had died and her heir, the Tsar Paul, showed none of her disposition to lend any support on the Continent for the defeat of France. Continuing military disaster on the Continent and the fact that it could not be long before the Austrians began preliminaries for peace had made a combined French–Spanish assault on Britain more than likely. But this ignominious defeat suffered by the Spanish Grand Fleet meant that union of the French and Spanish fleets was not in prospect. The indifferent showing of the Royal Navy so far in the war had heightened apprehension over its ability to cope with a serious assault on British shores. Cape St Vincent restored pride and confidence. It was a necessary solace in face of uncomfortable odds. Britain now made the most of it.

What Nelson's father wrote to him was reflective of the response across the land: 'The name and services of Nelson have sounded throughout the city of Bath, from the common ballad singer to the public theatre. Joy sparkles in every eye, and desponding Britain draws back her sable veil and smiles.'

Nelson received a Knighthood of the Bath, with an accolade that broadly covered all of his services that had lacked previous acknowledgement. It was, the First Lord wrote, 'to cover the Royal approbation of your successful and gallant exertions on several occasions during the course of the present war in the Mediterranean, and more particularly of your very distinguished conduct in the glorious and brilliant victory obtained over the fleet of Spain'. With that came a pension of £1,000 a year and elevation to rear admiral. Jervis was made Earl of St Vincent, and given a pension of £3,000 a year. 'Though we can afford no more than a cottage – yet, with a contented mind, my chains, medals, and ribbons are all sufficient,' Nelson wrote to his wife.

Unfortunately, upon a Royal Navy restored to the nation's high esteem an unpleasant surprise was about to explode.

XIV

MUTINY

ACROSS the land the bells were still tolling for the victory, the hymns of thanksgiving still being sung, praise upon the Royal Navy still ringing out, when from the decks of the battle fleet in whose honour all had stood in celebration arose a crisis threatening the immediate fate of the nation. The Royal Navy had risen in open mutiny. It had finally become participant, it seemed, in the revolutionary turbulence of the last decade of the eighteenth century.

For Britain, but for England especially, the shock was barely credible. Upon the navy depended the whole nation's sense of existence and survival. Such a crisis had never before existed. As one Civil Lord of the Admiralty informed the First Lord, Earl Spencer, it 'forms the most awful crisis that these kingdoms ever saw'. Few, right then, could easily doubt it.

On the Continent the allied war against France was on the brink of final collapse. Buonaparte had demonstrated that this was now a war totally different from anything previously visualized, even mere weeks before when Pitt's last emissary sent to negotiate peace was brusquely told to leave Paris. A French armada for the invasion of Ireland was then underway out of Brest. Through the summer and autumn of 1796 the French had assembled their massive force for the invasion of Ireland, with fifteen thousand regular troops at Brest under command of General Lazare Hoche, of the Army of the Rhine. The British navy had failed to intercept them. Fortunately for Britain storm had wrecked the assault at the very point of the proposed landings, Bantry Bay. But the French intent on Ireland remained, affirmed by knowledge that yet another invasion attempt was being organized in Holland, assisted by Admiral de Winter of the Dutch navy.

The attempt to talk peace in Paris in December had failed when the British insisted on the return of Belgium to Austrian control. Here, as always, was the central British preoccupation: that enemy possession of the North Sea coast should be avoided. Thus, at one stroke, Britain appeared to stand deprived of the neutrality of the one Continental strategic disposition she regarded as indispensable to her security as well as the only defence she could rely upon against hostile possession of it, namely her navy. What other defence had Britain against assault from the Continent other than the navy?

The only surprise about rebellion in the British navy should have been surprise itself.

Since the start of the war seamen on several occasions had complained of vicious treatment by unnecessarily cruel officers. The men had dared to write to the Lords of the Admiralty begging either the removal of the offending captains or lieutenants, or if not then the transfer of the crew members themselves to other vessels. They rarely got such satisfaction.

Mutiny was a comparatively rare event. This war had already seen two major mutinies, both at the end of 1794: aboard the 98-gun *Windsor Castle* at Fiorenzo and *Culloden* at Spithead. What was particularly notable was the difference in the response to them. With *Windsor Castle* the mutineers were pardoned and certain officers they complained about removed. With *Culloden*, there were eight death sentences; five men were hanged on board.

Soon after, early in 1795, the Admiralty received from Admiral Philip Patton a warning that a general mutiny was possible throughout the navy because of discontent, which was already causing a rising rate of desertions. Men were running away wherever opportunity offered, going mostly to American ships but some even going over to the French and to the Barbary powers of North Africa. Nothing was made of Patton's warning even though through 1795 and on through 1796 letters arrived at Admiralty from sailors protesting of cruelty aboard particular ships. Those aboard *Shannon* wrote in June, 1796, that 'the ill-treatment which we have and do receve from the tiriant of captain . . . is more than the spirits and harts of true English Man can cleaverly bear, for we are born free but now we are slaves . . . which treatment and bad usages is anufe to make the sparites of Englishmen to rise and steer the ship into an enimies port'.[1] Then, at the end of 1796, petitions began arriving at the Admiralty from various ships complaining of their low pay and poor victuals. And in February 1797 anonymous letters continuing these demands were sent in from ships at Spithead and in Portsmouth harbour.

The British sailor had not seen a rise in pay since the reign of Charles II. Pay was measured by the lunar month. An able seaman of 1797 got twenty-four shillings, an ordinary seaman nineteen shillings. To talk in terms of monthly remuneration was derisive. It could be years before they got their pay, which was issued only when the ship paid off. The sailor was then paid through tickets which had to be cashed at the port where he was commissioned into the navy. When transferred to another ship he had to be sure to collect his tickets from the purser. If he failed to do that the purser was likely to pocket the sum for himself. By the time he was actually paid the seaman had in any event been mulcted of his monies in a variety of ways. From the purser he had to buy his clothing and bedding, at extortionate prices. The sailor would draw on his pay for any extras that might improve the bad food he daily got when fresh supplies were unavailable.

Of all the grievances of the late-eighteenth-century sailor the one that particularly raises disbelief in anyone familiar with accounts of the horrors of battle in that time is that sailors got no pay when in the sickbay, even when wounded.

The soaring inflation that accompanied wartime shortages and crop failure had made the sailor's pittance more miserably inadequate than it already had been. On board ship they were paying 30 per cent more for their 'slops', purchased from the purser.

In 1795 sailors had seen a rise of pay for marines aboard their ships. There had been no suggestion in the interim that they themselves would receive the like. Navy lieutenants had requested and received a rise in pay in 1796. Captains were making the same demand. One of them, Captain Thomas Pakenham, now took the liberty of advising the First Lord that something should be done for the seamen as well. Seeing the officers receive more money the lower deck would make its own demand, unless the 'underpaid condition of the thoroughbred seaman' was improved. Earl Spencer pleaded that the financial state of the nation meant the 'absolute impracticability' of raising seamen's pay. But the agitation was already far advanced.[2]

The iron disciplinary control of the navy had allowed much to be taken for granted. National conviction of the sailor's inherent patriotism allowed the broad impression of a navy resistant to radical influences. What was most taken for granted, therefore, was the supposition that the navy was somehow outside the social turmoil from which a new society already stood emergent. Every level of the Royal Navy's executive structure reflected that outlook. But the new rigorous forms of impressment of 1795 had drawn into the navy many who came directly from involvement in the upheavals on shore, landsmen who had benefited from the surge for education that accompanied evangelical influence and the early industrial revolution. The lower deck of the navy had thereby become more articulate and socially diverse than at any time in its history.

Demonstration of that accompanied the victory of St Vincent. While the fate of the Spanish Grand Fleet was being settled off that Cape a well-organized effort in framing a lower-deck petition to Admiralty was underway among the ships of the Channel fleet lying off Spithead. Everything about it was unprecedented. First of all there was the surprising fluency of communication between the ships and the tight secrecy between several thousand men that accompanied it. Drafts of the proposed petition were circulated between the ships, discussed in secret conclave aboard each, and comment forwarded to the originators, who appeared to belong to the crew aboard *Queen Charlotte*, Earl Howe's former flagship. The petition itself and the letters that circulated with it were articulate, emotionally balanced and logically argued. 'Messmates' was the introductory salutation in the correspondence. The plea was for 'reason, peace and good fellowship' in framing their petition.

There was some argument whether the petitions should be sent to Admiralty or to the House of Commons. It was eventually agreed the petition should be sent to Earl Howe, whom the mutineers designated a friend of the sailors. *Queen Charlotte*'s petition, dated 27 February, 'on behalf of themselves and their Brethren on Board of the Fleet at Spithead' begged that Howe would take the hardships they complained of into consideration and lay them before the Lords of the Admiralty 'not doubting in the least from your Lordship's interference in their behalf they will obtain a speedy redress'. Their plea focused entirely on their low wages, pointing out that the army and militia wages had been increased.

Howe saw it all as 'the fabrication of the same individual'. He declared that to Sir Peter Parker, the port admiral, and Lord Bridport. Both concurred. From Earl Spencer Howe got much the same response.

The fleet returned to Spithead on 30 March. It was quickly obvious to the sailors that their appeal to Howe had been to no effect. The round-the-fleet consultations were immediately restored. On 12 April Sir Peter Parker and Lord Bridport had got word that the seamen were to take command of the ships from the officers on 16 April. This intelligence was immediately sent to London. On the morning of the 15th, Easter Sunday, Bridport, who had just received and studied a petition from *Queen Charlotte*, wrote hastily to Admiralty about the 'disappointment and ill-humour which at present prevails in the ships under my orders' and asked that the fleet be not directed to put to sea 'before some answer is given to these petitions'. In the event, even as his letter went ashore instruction arrived by telegraph from London for the fleet to put to sea at once.

Bridport ordered the fleet to prepare for departure. That became the signal for mutiny to leap alive. The sailors of *Queen Charlotte* manned the fore shrouds and gave three cheers, swiftly taken up throughout the fleet. The leaders aboard *Queen Charlotte* then put off in a boat, followed by those aboard *Royal George*. The boats visited ship after ship, telling them to send two delegates to *Queen Charlotte* that evening. Boats from each ship joined the procession, winding through the fleet even as Easter Divine Service was being conducted. Only one ship, the 98-gun *London*, refused to allow the delegates to board. Its commander, Admiral Colpoys, ordered the marines to fire if they did. The delegates, encouraged by the sailors aboard *London*, were prepared to face this threat, but Bridport sent an officer to intervene and allow the delegates to board.

By nightfall the mutiny was firmly established across the Channel fleet. The thirty-two delegates met in the formal glitter of the state cabin aboard *Queen Charlotte*. Oath of loyalty to the cause was demanded from each delegate, with the same required of all the others aboard the ships. Any ship showing signs of disregard of what was agreed would be put in the centre of the fleet under the guns of all the rest. Rules were drawn up for maintaining strict order aboard the ships. Yard ropes were rove at the yardarm of each ship as warning of immediate execution for those who might betray them. Drunkenness would be punished by flogging. Officers were deprived of command, but sailors were told to pay them due respect. Those officers who were hated for their severity were ordered ashore. The guns were shotted and watch was kept on deck the same as at sea. A red flag of defiance was raised aboard *Royal George*. The sailors declared that they would not weigh anchor until their demands had been complied with, unless the enemy's fleet put to sea, in which case they would go out and fight, and then return expecting their complaints to be heeded.

Those complaints were amplified in the final petition signed by all the delegates aboard *Queen Charlotte* on 18 April. Apart from the demand for better wages, they wanted an increase in the weight and quality of their provisions, sufficient vegetables when in port 'which we grievously complain and lay under want of', better care for the sick, that a wounded man should receive his pay until cured or discharged, and that there should be opportunity 'to taste the sweets of liberty on shore, when in any harbour'. But the shock of the mutiny appeared too much a betrayal of the nation for even some of the most liberal- minded to sympathize with it. One of the latter was the former Comptroller of the Navy, Sir Charles Middleton, who had actually resigned his office because he could not carry out reforms which he believed would prevent the breaking out of a serious mutiny. Middleton, one of the most stalwart evangelicals in the navy, pleader for the abolition of slavery, was called in by Pitt and the First Sea Lord. Pitt said, 'Bad news from the fleet, Sir Charles. A ship has mutinied. What are we to do?'

Middleton answered, 'You know how ill I think these poor fellows have been used, but now that it has come to a mutiny, there is but one thing to be done. You must show them that you have the superiority. You must order a ninety-gun ship on each side of her, and sink her on the spot, if she does not submit.'

Pitt was staggered. 'That is a strong measure. What if they should refuse to obey?'

'Then indeed all would be over. But they will not refuse to obey if you give the order resolutely, and it is the only thing which can be done.'[3]

So much for evangelical humanity. Fortunately more merciful response would follow from the more secularly disposed commanders of the navy.

At eight the first morning the sailors mounted the rigging and gave three cheers. They did the same at sunset. The practice continued daily while the mutiny lasted. Thus did the prestige fleet of the Royal Navy become the subdued captive of its sailors.

For Britain the situation was desperate.

As the navy rose demanding more pay, Britain's credit was failing. The drain upon the Bank of England had been relentless through the export of bullion in subsidies and loans to Continental powers, the governance of unruly Ireland and the massive running costs of a global war. As the price of gold rose sharply and the situation worsened a nation-wide run on the banks began. Depositors drained the country banks, which in turn withdrew their deposits from the Bank of England, which stood threatened by insolvency.

On 26 February Pitt stopped cash payments from the Bank. One of the most revolutionary steps in British financial history was adopted with the decision to make bank notes instead of cash legal tender. Gold was withdrawn even from small coins, with notes issued for one and two pounds each.

Pitt went ahead to secure yet another huge subsidy for the emperor of Austria, no less than three and a half millions, in the continuing belief that Austria remained resolute. But ground for such hope had already expired. Parliament voted approval of this final Austrian subsidy on 4 May. The following day Pitt got the tidings that the war was now finally, single-handedly, Britain's to maintain, if she could.

On 19 February the Pope had, with the Treaty of Tolentino, ceded the greater part of the papal territories which Napoleon had already seized. On 6 March Austria's Archduke Charles was defeated at Tagliamento and Napoleon continued his march towards Vienna. The emperor recognized reality and sent envoys to talk peace. On April 18 Napoleon and the Austrians signed the preliminaries of peace at Leoben. The published terms of the preliminaries ceded Belguim to France and extended the French frontier to the Rhine. Leoben, then, was the news that reached Pitt on 5 May.

Britain was alone, with an inadequate army, a home navy in revolt and open to assault the full length of its south and east coasts, even as preparations continued in Holland for an attack by the Dutch navy.

In face of national shock and alarm, the Lords of the Admiralty had responded swiftly and submissively to the demands of the sailors by conceding increases of pay and provisions. On 21 April three admirals, Gardner, Colpoys and Pole, went on board *Queen Charlotte* to inform the delegates, but the admirals were told that until all their demands were met, confirmed by an act of parliament and accompanied by a royal pardon, no ship would lift an anchor.

The admirals returned to London where all the demands were promptly agreed to by government proclamation and George III's pardon was sent down from Windsor. Bridport delivered these to *Queen Charlotte* and, after some discussion, the delegates accepted and the fleet returned to duty. The fleet prepared to sail but parliamentary approval of the pay demand was still lacking. Parliamentary delay unsettled the mutineers again. They saw evasion from the promises made to them. On 7 May Bridport got news that the French fleet was preparing to sail. He made the signal for the fleet to weigh anchor and put to sea. The sailors refused to obey.

This time round it was to be rougher. The centre of the action was to be aboard *London*, whose commander, Vice Admiral Colpoys, had sought to resist delegates at the start of the mutiny. From the deck of his ship Colpoys saw boats pulling to and fro among the ships and decided that he would resist. He ordered his own seamen below and told the officers and marines to arm themselves. As the delegates arrived alongside and began clambering on board Colpoys ordered the officers to fire on them. One of *London*'s seamen began to unlash a main deck gun to point it aft towards the quarterdeck. He ignored the order to stop and was shot dead by First Lieutenant Peter Bover. The enraged crew turned upon the officers to disarm them. Two of the crew were shot. The foremost guns were trained on the quarterdeck as the sailors took command of the decks. They then seized Bover and took him to the forecastle to be hanged. The rope was around his neck when one of the delegates, who knew Bover from an earlier ship, pleaded on his behalf. Colpoys also stepped forward and said that he alone was to blame.

As the seamen stood deciding whether to hang the admiral instead of Bover a man was heard to call Colpoys 'a damned bloody rascal'. Colpoys had a harsh reputation. But in spite of the rage of the moment the habit of tradition and respect inverted the collective state of mind. The crowd turned upon the offender and threatened to throw him overboard. It was a strange illustration of the instinctive power of ingrained deference and the protocols of class. It saved Colpoys.

Colpoys and his officers were then confined to their cabins. On 11 May Colpoys was asked to go ashore, followed by the captains of other ships.

On the same day Earl Howe, accompanied by Lady Howe, was hastening down to Portsmouth from London. Pitt, in final desperation, had turned to the man whom the seamen themselves had first regarded as their best interlocutor. On 9 May Pitt had brought in the bill for increasing the pay and allowances for the seamen. In one day it passed through all its stages in the House at one sitting, and through the Lords with equal speed. Armed with this parliamentary act and again carrying a full pardon from the king, Howe spent two days at Spithead visiting one ship after another. On the 13th on board *Royal William* the mutiny was concluded. Part of the settlement was that Colpoys, four captains and one hundred other officers and petty officers were removed from their ships. Howe did not like it but saw it as necessary. For that he was damned for being in his dotage, too infirm and exhausted. And indeed it was to be his last great service to the navy. He never sailed again.

A bizarre conclusion wound it all up. The day after the settlement aboard *Royal William* the delegates landed from Spithead, were entertained to refreshment at Government House, Portsmouth, marched to the port where they embarked in barges, all the while accompanied by Lord and Lady Howe, officers of high rank and 'persons of distinction'. Having visited all the ships the party returned to Portsmouth. Howe, for his infirmity, was carried on the shoulders of the delegates to Government House, where they all dined, the delegates at table with Howe and Lady Howe. The fleet sailed the next day.

As with so much in that fast-moving age, there was an element of modernity that played a significant part throughout the mutiny. Crisis impelled communication faster than mail coach. It was done by telegraph. Already well developed in France, Britain had four telegraph lines, from the Admiralty to Portsmouth, Plymouth, Deal and Yarmouth. Signals were transmitted from towers through a vertical board with six large holes, each of which was controlled by shutters. Messages were read from the natural light of the openings or from red and blue lamps mounted in them. Later towers were fitted with arms for sempahoric signalling, from which subsequently evolved human semaphore ship to ship.

Hope that Howe's settlement meant the end of the crisis, however, was instantly dispelled. The example of the Spithead fleet was now followed by that of the Nore, the anchorage in the Thames estuary around Sheerness from where part of the North Sea fleet operated. The flagship and the main fleet were usually off Yarmouth, since the Texel, the sandbar behind which the Dutch fleet sheltered, was more accessible from there. The Nore fleet usually consisted largely of frigates because it fulfilled a variety of scouting and escort functions. It was therefore less of a uniform entity than the main fleet under Admiral Adam Duncan, who at Yarmouth had fifteen ships of the line, but none bigger than 74 guns, which was the strength of Duncan's flagship, *Venerable*. Nelson's old favourite, *Agamemnon*, was part of his fleet.

As early as 1 May sailors aboard *Venerable* lying off Yarmouth had surprised Duncan by giving three cheers in the style of those at Spithead. He went among them and pardoned the leaders. The disturbance died down. But at the Nore on 12 May mutiny became general among all the ships there, including three line ships and a depot ship. One of the Nore ships, *Director*, was commanded by William Bligh, of *Bounty* renown. For the second time in his unfortunate career Bligh found himself driven from his ship by mutiny, he as hated in this instance as he had been aboard *Bounty*.

The red flag was hoisted but the example of Spithead was strictly followed, no laxity allowed, routine as normal, any drunkenness flogged, and noose prepared for those who fell out of step. Unpopular officers and pursers were packed off ashore. Bligh was told that he had been succeeded by his first lieutenant and ordered to quit the ship. Delegates rowed about with bands in the boats playing 'Rule, Britannia!', 'God Save the King' or other tunes. But dilemma quashed frivolity when the delegates they had sent to Spithead and who were present at the concluding festivities presided over by Howe brought news of the settlement. Should the Nore immediately fall into accord with what had been accepted at Spithead? Or had they grounds of their own? Was there more to accomplish?

That they would not fall in line was immediately evident, and this rebellion became something greatly more serious than the Spithead mutiny. The Nore suddenly produced a leader of unusual ability, an intellect straight from the ferment of ideas ashore, with social scores of his own to settle. Here to the fore was what John Barrow called the contagion of liberty, equality and the rights of man.

That individual was a strange thirty-year-old character called Richard Parker. His background was the sort of curious mixture of class, mind and experience that became unique to the late eighteenth century, as bright individuals began to move more easily, and to their own confusion, between the various levels of society in that discordant time. Parker, tall and darkly handsome, was the son of a well-to-do baker who did sufficiently well to retire to an estate in Exeter. From initial schooling Parker entered the Royal Navy in 1782, at fifteen, and passed along much the same route as Horatio Nelson, going from able seaman aboard a ship on which a cousin was second lieutenant and then on to another as midshipman. After a period of recurrent illness he obtained his discharge from the navy and joined the merchant service, where he remained until the war, when he went back into the navy as master's mate, to do duty as a lieutenant, with prospect of being confirmed in the rank. But clear definition of rank did not come. What followed instead was a troubled period aboard different ships as supernumerary and finally as midshipman aboard *Assurance*, from which he was discharged after behaving in a 'contemptuous and disobedient manner' to the lieutenant. He was disrated and ordered to another ship. But another period of uncertain illness saw him finally discharged, in 1794, still as a supernumerary. He married, was briefly in gaol for debt, and in 1797 took £20 from the navy to re-enter on quota. His recurring illness was said to be mental, rather than the rheumatism that was on his illness tickets.

After enlisting on quota Parker was taken to the North Sea fleet's depot ship, *Sandwich*, at Sheerness, where he was once again entered as supernumerary able seaman and confined with more than one thousand other supernumeraries to wait for transfer to a ship. *Sandwich* was a moored vessel of indescribable filth and sickness, according to its surgeon. The impact of that upon the disturbed mind of Richard Parker undoubtedly helped to account for the swift emergence of the personality that followed.

Parker had no part in initiating the mutiny at the Nore. He was ignorant of any of it at Sheerness and was working below decks when the crew of *Sandwich* took over the ship. It was three days before he was asked to join the delegates, but swiftly thereafter he rose to leadership. He had immediately sympathized with the sailors and, being highly articulate and impassioned in his presentation, proved a natural spokesman. The many denials of advancement he had suffered in the past appeared to have affected him for, once his leadership had been acknowledged by the others, he promptly called himself 'President of the Committee of the Delegates of the Fleet'.

Their demands were stronger and by no means irrational. They again pressed the point of liberty to go ashore when a ship returned to harbour. Nothing had come of the similar request from the Spithead mutineers. Besides, they wanted all arrears of wages paid before a ship went to sea; impressed men who were not on the ship's pay records should be given two months' advance to cover the cost of immediate necessities; a more equal distribution of prize money should be made; and the harsher elements of the antiquated Articles of War that ruled life on board should be expunged. They wanted a delegation from Admiralty like the one that had gone to Spithead, and they wanted the king's pardon. But for the Admiralty the thing had been settled: the Nore should accept what Spithead had accepted and get back to duty.

In his relations with his men Adam Duncan was of the same humane outlook as Nelson and Collingwood. He had some time previously sent a paper to Admiralty urging that the number of lashes be reduced, that stoppage of rum for punishment should cease, leave should be regulated, tobacco, soap and lemon juice should be issued, and prize money more equally distributed. But on disobedience Duncan proved more strong-minded than most, with physical strength to match. He had already had disturbance when news of the Nore reached Yarmouth. On the 13th the situation became serious.

When sailors aboard the line ship *Adamant* refused to obey orders Duncan went across and addressed them all. 'My lads, I am not in the smallest degree apprehensive of any violent measures you may have in contemplation. And though I assure you I would much rather acquire your love than incur your fear, I will with my own hand put to death the first man who shall display the slightest sign of rebellious conduct.'

He then put it to them: Was there any man who wished to dispute his authority, or that of any officer? One of the six who had been marked as the ringleaders stepped forward and said, 'I do.'

'Do you, sir, want to take command of this ship out of my hands?'

'Yes, sir.' Upon which Duncan grabbed the man and held him over the side of the ship, crying out, 'My lads, look at this fellow, he who dares to deprive me of the command of the fleet.' One account had Duncan making motion to draw his sword to run the man through, but he was restrained by the chaplain. Duncan's bravado at any rate settled the issue for the moment.[4]

On 24 May the Admiralty, informed that the Dutch fleet was about to put out from the Texel, ordered Duncan to take his fleet across.

The signal to weigh was made on 29 May but one by one Duncan's ships deserted him. The historian Edward Brenton was at this time fourth lieutenant of *Agamemnon*, now part of that fleet. Soon after the ship sailed from Yarmouth the men laid a barricade of hammocks across the lower deck and pointed loaded 24-pounders at the quarterdeck. After speaking to the men Captain Fancourt surrendered to the situation and calmly led his off-duty officers down to dinner. The master-of-arms approached Brenton and, speaking before the others, said that the ship had been given away by the officers despite the fact that the best part of the men and all the marines were against the mutiny. Brenton went down and relayed this to Fancourt, who said, 'Mr Brenton, if we call out the marines some of the men will be shot, and I could not bear to see them lying in convulsions on the deck; no, no, a little patience, and we shall all hail unanimity again.' It was in extraordinary contrast with Duncan's resolution some days before, indicating the great difference of response that could so often occur in any circumstance in that navy. Brenton wrote, 'I quitted the cabin and walked the deck until my watch was out, too irritated to say a word more.'

Out of his fleet of eleven line ships at one p.m. on the 29th Duncan was left with but two, one of them being his own flagship, *Venerable*, the other *Adamant*. With them was the frigate *Circe*. The mastery of the man was now demonstrated even more remarkably. Instead of abandoning his mission, he continued with his three ships for the Texel to maintain watch over the fleet of fourteen line ships and eight frigates under the Dutch admiral de Winter, and to confront them if they came out.

What Duncan now proceeded to do would stand as one of the outstanding acts of resourceful composure of the war. *Venerable* and *Adamant* anchored at the outer buoy of the Texel in plain sight of de Winter's fleet which, with flotilla vessels, numbered fifty altogether. *Circe* stood off, far out, in the guise of signal station, making and receiving signals as if relaying messages between Duncan and the main fleet in the offing beyond *Circe*. It was an extraordinary act of bluff and, amazingly, it worked. Duncan could not suppose that it would for long. But it did.

When Duncan arrived the wind had been favourable for the Dutch fleet putting out to sea, but the Dutch made no effort to come out. The British successfully maintained their bluff for eight days, when two British line ships arrived, soon followed by other ships.

The arrival of the ships proved to be the welcome signal to Duncan that the mutiny was over. It had rapidly begun to disintegrate. On board *Sandwich* the sailors turned against Richard Parker, who was arrested by the ship's officers and taken ashore. Many mutineers got away, some to France, others to Holland. By 16 June all the ships had surrendered.

Parker went on trial on 22 June, was found guilty and hanged aboard *Sandwich* on the 30th. 'I hope my life will be the only sacrifice,' he pleaded. 'I trust it will be thought sufficient atonement. Pardon, I beseech you, the other men; they will return with alacrity to their duty.' At the execution he asked the captain of *Sandwich* to shake his hand in forgiveness. The request was granted. George III, on the other hand, made a personal plea for the body to be suspended in chains 'on the most conspicuous land in sight of ships at the Nore'. But Parker was taken to a graveyard on shore. Four hundred of the sailors were tried, fifty-nine condemned to death, twenty-nine of whom were actually executed. Others were severely flogged or sent to prison.

Far from dying, the infection began to spread abroad. After the Battle of Cape St Vincent, Jervis, now Earl St Vincent, had remained cruising off Cadiz in blockade of the port, with provisioning at Lisbon. His fleet was the next to be struck, at Lisbon and off Cadiz. St Vincent provided his own special note to retribution. Four men who mutinied aboard *St George* off Cadiz were tried by court martial on Saturday 8 July. St Vincent instructed that with a guilty verdict execution had to be immediate. The verdict came too late that Saturday for it to be carried out. The president of the court martial told the prisoners that, the next day being Sunday, they had until Monday to prepare themselves. But St Vincent promptly ordered execution for nine o'clock Sunday morning, drawing protest from chaplains and one of his vice admirals that they would be profaning the Sabbath. Ignoring them, he pronounced another unusual aspect of the execution.

Executions were usually attended by boat crews from the different ships. The hanging itself would be performed by men from across the fleet. Lots were drawn in each boat to decide which of them would go aboard the ship where execution would take place to man the yard ropes hoisting the condemned. This time St Vincent ordered that the crew of *St George* alone should be the executioners, and that as soon as the culprits were suspended every ship in the fleet should start divine service.[5]

These were unusual instructions. The officer charged with the execution went nervously to St Vincent's cabin early on Sunday to verify them. St Vincent was in his dressing gown and shaving. Turning his head sharply to see his visitor he cut himself severely. As blood poured from the wound the officer apologized. 'No apology is necessary, sir,' St Vincent said, 'the duty you are engaged in is too important to be trifled with, and I never should have forgiven you if you had made any mistake.'

At nine, as the gun was fired to run up the men, each ship immediately hoisted the pennant for divine service, which began even as the condemned struggled in their final convulsions, one of the uniquely dreadful images of the Royal Navy in the Great War.

Passing down the Atlantic the fever first touched the island of St Helena then the Cape of Good Hope. At St Helena the crew of the *Dortrecht* rose against their officers, but the captain, Charles Brisbane, seized one of the ringleaders, wound a cord around his neck, as if to drag him to immediate execution, but instead, face close to face, declared that if he again dared to open his mouth in disobedience he would hang. The shock of such imperative action subdued the rest. At the Cape a larger scene was enacted. The crew of *Tremendous* rose against their captain, George Stephens, accusing him of cruelty and misconduct, and threatened to bring him to court martial by their delegates. The outbreak spread to *Sceptre* and other ships in Table Bay. The governor of the newly acquired Cape Colony, Lord Macartney, ordered one hundred cannon on the ramparts of the battery to be prepared with shot heated red-hot in furnaces. The mutineers were given two hours to lower their red flag, after which the ships would be fired upon. Submission came ten minutes before the time expired. The ringleaders were tried and executed, others severely flogged.

For the Royal Navy, worse was yet to come, with the most notorious single-ship mutiny of that war.

The 32-gun frigate *Hermione* was undoubtedly one of the unhappiest ships that ever sailed, for reason that her commander, Captain Hugh Pigot, was one of the most ferociously ill-tempered and cruelly tyrannical masters afloat in his day. His officers appear to have been scarcely less offensive to the crew, whether for their own faults or merely as the detested instruments of the savage Pigot it is impossible to say. But on the fatal night they got no more mercy than he did.

Hermione was on West Indies station, always an enervating and soul-trying place to be, where rancorous disposition was liable to be daily incremental, where hope was a burned-out scar.

On the evening of 21 September 1797, *Hermione* was lying off Porto Rico after an impressive boat operation against a shore battery and three French privateers. When sailors were sent aloft to reef the mizzen topsail yard Pigot, to lend alacrity, shouted that he would flog the last man down. It was a warning that all took seriously, knowing that he meant it. In the general competitive rush to gain the topmast rigging and to avoid being Pigot's victim, two sailors missed their hold and fell on the quarterdeck and were killed. Their smouldering shipmates committed them to the deep and decided that, finally, the moment of vengeance had arrived. It came the following night.

The marine sentinel outside Pigot's cabin was knocked down. Pigot, hearing noise outside his cabin, ran out to find himself facing a group of armed seamen led by a maintop man, David Forrester, and a seaman named Crawley. Pigot, immediately slashed by bayonets, retreated into his cabin, where he sought to defend himself with his dirk. The seamen appeared momentarily appalled by sight of the wounded Pigot, but Crawley yelled his impatience with them: 'What four against one, and yet afraid? Here goes then!' And plunged his bayonet into Pigot, who cried out, 'Forrester are you against me too?' and got the answer, 'Yes, you bloody rascal!' whereupon Forrester plunged his own bayonet into Pigot two or three times and then helped throw him out of the stern window. Pigot, in spite of his wounds, was heard to cry out in final despair as he fell.

On the quarterdeck First Lieutenant Samuel Read begged for his life, saying he had a wife and three children totally dependent upon him for support. But he was thrown overboard alive. A cry was then heard through the ship that Second Lieutenant Archibald Douglas could not be found. Forrester, accompanied by others, went below with a lantern. Douglas was found hiding by the marine officer's cabin. He was drawn up the ladder by his hair. His servant, a fourteen-year old boy named James Allen, cried out, 'Let me have a cut at him!' and, presumably in resentment of treatment from his master, struck at him with a tomahawk, severely wounding him. But Douglas was still crying 'Mercy, mercy!' as they dragged him across the deck and threw him overboard. The lieutenant of marines was similarly dragged up to deck, with a dozen men chopping at him with cutlass or tomahawk as he went. There was no mercy even for the fifteen-year-old midshipman who, making an effort to escape, was chopped with tomahawk before being thrown overboard. Also killed were the purser, surgeon, the captain's clerk and the boatswain. Other warrant officers that were spared were cast adrift in a small boat.

Hermione was taken into the South American port of La Guiria and handed over to the Spanish who, delighted to have a British frigate, paid ten dollars to each of the mutineers, then manned and equipped her. For the next two years she would sail the Caribbean as a Spanish ship, continually hunted by the British as a most particular stigma on the honour of the Royal Navy. And that she certainly was, for there had never before been such a ferociously bloody uprising within the navy. She would keep that distinction.

Several of its principals, including Forrester and the boy Allen, were caught long after when they returned to Britain and were court-martialled and hanged. Forrester, perhaps foolishly, re-entered the navy and served five years aboard a sloop with a reputation for good behaviour, before being spotted in Portsmouth dockyard by one of *Hermione*'s former stewards.[6]

The eccentricity of the British navy lay in its obstinate refusal to recognize what many of its own commanders did or to respond in the manner of a Nelson and a Collingwood by acknowledging the plain normality of grievance and demand. But the concessions yielded to the mutineers at Spithead rankled with monarch, government and Admiralty. The pressure was for the punitive rather than for understanding.

The paradoxical nature of the British sailor's life was that his horizons were the widest that had ever been, but his shipboard confinement was the tightest there was. The demand upon him was allegiance to a servitude without equal among free men. What was imposed upon him and what he suffered were often compared even in those days, and indeed by himself, as being little different from that of the African slave. Under men like Pigot of the *Hermione* the comparison was valid enough.

That he fought as he did, with ferocity and heedless courage when required, can seem a matter of wonder to anyone going through the record of what, in ordinary circumstances, the British sailor was compelled to endure. It was this ability to rise instantly above his circumstances in response to the call upon him that stands out above everything.

The British sailor was the steadfast hero of his nation. All history had consigned him to that. He saw himself as bound to it. At the core of it was his island's dependence upon the sea as its first defence. Though Jack Tar embodied British trust and pride, what was laid upon him aboard ship represented the hardest example of national indifference. And it cannot be really surprising therefore that when he turned against it and broke his link with the loyalties within his shipboard environment the British sailor showed remarkable facility to turn traitorously against it all. It was almost a tradition of its own. British deserters in steady stream offered themselves to other flags. That was how, ultimately and often, the British sailor served the gall deep set within him.

XV

TENERIFE

AFTER the Battle of Cape St Vincent, Nelson's station remained with Jervis, now Earl St Vincent, in maintaining the blockade of Cadiz, where the defeated Spanish fleet were locked in. The Spanish made no move to come out, although the odds remained in their favour, with thirty Spanish sail of the line against a force of twenty or twenty-two British. 'The Spaniards threaten us they will come out, and take their revenge,' Nelson wrote, 'the sooner the better, but I will not believe it until I see it . . . but fear we shall have a peace before they are ready to come out. What a sad thing that will be!'

The British lay close in, in clear sight of the white city of Cadiz, looking at the traditional evening *paseo*, 'the ladies walking the walls and Mall of Cadiz', and at the ships cooped up behind the mole. Nelson's vigilance was from a new command, *Theseus*, once more a 74.

A certain courtesy commonly prevailed between British and Spanish. Madrid's harsh treatment of the admirals and officers who commanded at the Battle of Cape St Vincent dismayed those who had so successfully fought them. In keeping with that outlook Nelson, on 30 May, sent a note ashore to Admiral Don Josef de Mazarredo, declaring, 'I embrace the opportunity of assuring you of my high esteem of your character. The 4th of June being the birthday of my Royal master, Sir John Jervis intends firing a *feu de joie*, at eight o'clock in the evening; and has desired me to mention it to your Excellency, that the ladies at Cadiz may not be alarmed at the firing. Believe me your Excellency's most faithful servant, Horatio Nelson.' To which the admiral replied: 'My dear Sir, I correspond to the urbanity merited by the letter with which you honoured me. The ladies of Cadiz, accustomed to the noisy sounds of salutes of the vessels of war, will sit, and will hear what Sir John Jervis means to regale them with, for the evening of the 4th in honour of his Britannic Majesty's birthday; and the general wish of the Spanish nation cannot but interest itself in so august a motive. God preserve you many years. I kiss your hand.'

The other side of this protocol was called for on 3 July when St Vincent, to bring life to the monotony of blockade, but more in hope of inciting the Spanish navy to come out to battle, decided to bombard Cadiz.

Since the Spanish shore batteries were highly accurate in getting the range of the British fleet should they move in closer, the bombardment had to be left to St Vincent's bomb vessel escorted by the inshore squadron, which was commanded by Nelson.

'I wish to make it a warm night in Cadiz,' Nelson told St Vincent. The bomb vessel itself did little damage to Cadiz. The fight was between Nelson's armed launches and those of the Spanish fleet that swarmed out to engage them. Nelson's function as commander should have been to direct from the side, but he ran his own boat with its complement of thirteen, himself included, against that of the commander of the Spanish flotilla, Don Miguel Tyrason, who, with thirty men, tried to take Nelson's barge by boarding. The fighting was hand to hand, cutlass to cutlass. Nelson was twice saved by his coxswain, John Sykes, who interposed himself, on one occasion shoving his head forward to receive directly a sword cut aimed at his admiral. Tyrason surrendered only after eighteen of his men had been killed. Of Tyrason, Nelson was to say, 'his resistance was such as did honour to a brave man'.

Admiration of an opponent's courage was never grudging. In that duelling age, the satisfaction of a challenge resolutely met drew the same response in wartime combat as on the field, with an honourably courageous fight diminishing animosity. For Nelson this was particularly so. For him, the whole of it was a constant, intensely personal duel. It rings from his satisfaction in seeking close, intimate, almost private, engagement such as that with Don Miguel Tyrason, and earlier with Don Jacobo Stuart. It was an aspect of his vanity, of relishing his individual distinction above the rest, the private quest upon the field of honour. The narrow escape from near certain death enhanced it all. 'My late affair here will not, I believe, lower me in the opinion of the world. I have had flattery enough to make me vain, and success enough to make me confident.' While all of that flowed, nothing else mattered.

Lack of any prospect of drawing out the Spanish fleet threw Nelson and St Vincent back on to a project already long established between them, and which appears to have originated with Nelson. This was an assault on Tenerife, the westernmost of the Canary Islands.

With the British squadron in firm possession of the approaches to Cadiz the fear of the merchants and traders of this great entrepôt had been that the fleet bearing the treasure from South America and the Philippines, upon which Spanish finances depended, might show up and be snared. That they had not showed suggested they had sought temporary haven at the mole of Santa Cruz, the fortified town lying at the base of Tenerife's volcanic heights. Such became Nelson's firm conviction. His excitement enlarged it into extravagant vision 'of the great national advantages that would arise to our country, and of the ruin that our success would occasion to Spain'. The treasure fleet reportedly lying at Santa Cruz could, Nelson declared, represent a sudden ingestion of six to seven million of hard currency to a British economy that had just gone off the gold standard and resorted to paper notes: 'If this sum were thrown into circulation in England what might not be done. It would insure an honourable peace with innumerable other blessings. It has long occupied my thoughts.' He, naturally, was to command the expedition.

Nelson and St Vincent both recognized that a military force was required to supplement their own strength. Efforts to obtain soldiers from the governor of Gibraltar, General O'Hara, got nowhere. O'Hara regarded the scheme as impracticable. St Vincent nevertheless decided to go ahead.

The lack of military assistance did not apparently concern Nelson. He had, after all, got by without it at Corsica. When the squadron designated for Tenerife left the fleet on 15 July Nelson was therefore entirely dependent upon its own men for a landing upon what all knew to be an especially difficult shore.

Edward Brenton said he knew no other place 'more invulnerable to attack from a naval force, or more easily defended, than Teneriffe'. He put that down to inshore waters too deep to allow anchorage, rock-strewn beaches composed of slippery stones and pounded by perpetual surf, and an air prone either to calms or sudden violent squalls that could without warning take a ship's topmasts over the side. Nevertheless, Blake in the time of the Protectorate had indeed made a successful attack against Santa Cruz by laying his ships close in alongside the town. 'I do not reckon myself equal to Blake,' Nelson said, 'but if I recollect right, he was more obliged to the wind coming off the land, than to any exertions of his own: fortune favoured the gallant attempt, and may do so again.'

That was Nelson: luck and good fortune were tactical possibilities as calculably good as any others.

Nelson's force consisted of three 74s, his own *Theseus*, *Culloden* under Captain Troubridge, *Zealous* under Samuel Hood as well as the 50-gun *Leander*, three frigates, a cutter and a mortar boat.

On the way to Tenerife Nelson went over his plans for the assault in detail with his captains. The intention was to make a night landing of a thousand sailors and marines from the frigates. They were to take a twenty-six-gun fort on the heights commanding the town. A summons to surrender the treasure-laden galleon *El Principe de Asturias* as well as other cargoes in the port would then be sent to the governor of Santa Cruz. The line ships would move in at dawn to back up the summons by menacing the town fortifications with their broadsides.[1]

The squadron had the volcanic peak of Tenerife in sight at six in the afternoon on 21 July. The landing party under Troubridge assembled aboard the frigates, which were to carry them close inshore where they would debark into boats that would land them on the beach. But at midnight the frigates were no closer than three miles from the landing place, buffeted by a gale and fighting a powerful inshore current that threatened to put them aground. The boats never made it to the beach and Troubridge returned to *Theseus* to confer with Nelson. Together they decided to make another immediate attempt. By then Santa Cruz was in a state of high alert. Troubridge's next assault was at nine a.m. Those who landed from the boats struggled in the midsummer heat of that semi-tropical island to seize the heights above the town. But Troubridge and his men were driven back to the boats. The outlook was deeply unpromising. Nelson declared that the next assault would be commanded by himself.

For the next two days the squadron lay off Santa Cruz, adjusting sail in persistently strong gales as final plans were made for a new landing, which was set for the night of 24 July. The squadron found anchorage two miles off the town. Nelson was unusually conscious that he might not survive the night. He called for his stepson, Lieutenant Josiah Nisbet, to help destroy Fanny's letters. Nisbet, who had the watch on deck, appeared bearing arms required for going on shore. Nelson begged him to remain on board: 'Should we both fall, Josiah, what would become of your poor mother? The care of Theseus falls to you. Stay, therefore, and take charge of her.'

'Sir,' Nisbet replied, 'the ship must take care of herself. I will go with you tonight, if I never go again.' His stubborn determination was to put him in place to be the instrument of saving Nelson's life.[2]

Nisbet was one of two remaining youths who, as mere boys, had embarked with Nelson aboard *Agamemnon* five years earlier, as war loomed. The other was William Hoste who, like Nisbet, had remained steadily with Nelson ever since, transferring with him to successive ships. Nisbet had already advanced to lieutenant but Hoste was still midshipman. They were the only ones of *Agamemnon*'s original complement of officers still with Nelson.

At eleven the force of some seven hundred men embarked in the boats, which were fastened together to ensure that they all landed simultaneously. The night was so dark and the sea so rough that the Spanish watch was slow in discovering them. But when they did Santa Cruz's bells began ringing out and heavy cannonading and musket fire began to spray the water before the town. Nelson ordered the boats to cast loose and spread out. A gigantic surf was piling up along the shore. The proposed landing place on the mole was difficult to achieve. As Nelson, with drawn sword, tried to step from the boat his right arm was shattered above the elbow by grape shot. He sought to grasp his sword with the left hand but, bleeding profusely, growing faint, he cried, out, 'I am shot through the arm. I am a dead man!' Nisbet, close beside him, laid his stepfather in the bottom of the boat and, noticing the heavy rush of blood, with great presence of mind took the silk handkerchiefs from around his own neck and tied the arm tightly above the wound. One of the seamen in the boat hastily made a sling and, calling back five others, Nisbet struggled to get afloat again and away against the crashing surf. He himself took one of the oars and directed the others to row close under the shore batteries, to escape under the arch of their shot.

The cutter *Fox* heading inshore nearby them was struck below the water-line and went down, taking with her most of the 180 men aboard.

Nelson asked to be raised. As Nisbet lifted him *Fox* took its last plunge. Hearing the cries of her drowning seamen Nelson told Nisbet to try and pick up as many as he could. They then made for the frigate *Seahorse*, whose captain, Fremantle, had his wife on board. Nelson refused to go on board. Nisbet pleaded that from the state of his wound he was risking his life by delay in reaching *Theseus*. 'Then I will die,' Nelson cried, 'for I had rather suffer death than alarm Mrs Fremantle by her seeing me in this state, and when I can give her no tidings whatsoever of her husband.'

Aboard *Theseus* William Hoste despairingly watched the boat draw along-side bearing the man 'who I may say has been a second father to me'. In spite of his pain and weakness Nelson refused all assistance to climb aboard his ship: 'Let me alone, I have yet my legs left, and one arm.' With his left arm he then helped himself jump up the ship's side 'with a spirit that astonished everyone'. He then instructed, 'Tell the surgeon to make haste and get his instruments. I know I must lose my right arm, so the sooner it is off the better.'[3]

A surgical improvement of sorts arose from the operation, for what seemed to give Nelson more discomfort with the surgery than the actual cutting was the coldness of the knife 'making the first circular cut through the integu-ments and muscles'. Henceforth, he instructed, at the start of any naval action a hanging stove had to be ready with water warmed for the instru-ments. Surgeon Thomas Eshelby's entry in the medical journal of *Theseus* said: '1797. July 25. Admiral Nelson. Compound fracture of the right arm by a musket ball passing through a little above the elbow, an artery divided. The arm was immediately amputated and opium afterwards given.'

Meanwhile, those successfully led on shore by Troubridge were in a hopeless situation. Their landing had also been disastrous. Several of the boats had hit shore together. The surf filled them with water and stove them against the rocks. The men's pouches were soaked. All the ladders meant for scaling the citadel were smashed. The surf was so high that, seeing the fate of those before them, some of the boats put back.

Troubridge, with neither men nor equipment to attack the citadel, and ignorant of Nelson's fate, began rounding up the survivors of the landing. By daybreak he had collected eighty marines, eighty pikemen and 180 small-armed seamen. They were all that remained of those who had landed. Troubridge nevertheless sought resolutely to lead them against the citadel, but some eight thousand Spaniards as well as French advanced against them from all sides. Santa Cruz was far better garrisoned and defended than anyone had expected. There was no escape since all the boats had been stove in by the surf. There was no possibility of reinforcement, their ammunition was wet and they had no provisions.

From their cover in a convent Troubridge sent forward a flag of truce with an address to the governor of Santa Cruz, Don Antonio Gutierrez. He would burn the town if the Spanish continued to advance against him, Troubridge said. It would be done with regret as he had no wish to harm the inhabitants, but he and his men had to be allowed to leave quietly together with their arms in boats provided by the Spanish. It was an unrealistic show of bluff, even though he had compelled the priests under the threat of death to prepare torches and fireballs. As the only men with him with immediately usable weapons were the pikemen, Troubridge had little chance of making good his threat. In a second message after the rejection of the first Troubridge ludicrously even demanded surrender of whatever treasure was held in Santa Cruz. His final message to the governor was a bleak request that they simply be allowed to return to their ships without loss of military honour, with a promise that the British would withdraw without further attack on the Canary Islands. This was accepted and later that morning, accompanied by band music on either side of them, the British seamen and marines were marched down to board the boats the Spanish provided, after having been treated to wine, bread and fruit. The officers were invited to dine with the commandant of the Spanish forces.

Spanish generosity went beyond those gestures. The wounded were all taken to hospital, cared for, and later ferried to their ships. The squadron was allowed use of the markets before departure. Nelson sent as gift to Gutierrez a cask of English beer and cheese, the best that his limited resources allowed. Preparing to sail away on the 27th, he expressed his gratitude to Gutierrez: 'Sir, I cannot take my departure from this island without returning Your Excellency my sincerest thanks for your attention towards me, by the humanity in favour of our wounded men in your power and under your care, and for your generosity towards all our people who were disembarked ... hoping also, at a proper time, to assure your Excellency in person how truly I am, Sir, your most obedient, humble servant, Horatio Nelson.'

Tenerife had been a dismal miscalculation. The weight of that rested on Nelson, whose idea it principally was. There was about the whole venture strong reminder of his earlier miscalculation over the feasibility of an easy capture of Bastia on Corsica. As with Bastia, the strength of the Santa Cruz garrison and overall strength of likely resistance had been wholly under-estimated. Too little account had been taken of the operational difficulties on that shore which, as Brenton indicated, had been sufficiently well known since the time of Blake. The objective of the enterprise – capture of the treasure ship – was an empty one since the ship was not there at all. And the Spanish had simply laughed at the idea of emptying into British holds whatever might have been in their treasury. The price for the British had been 263 killed and wounded, not far short of the loss at Cape St Vincent. Nelson had paid with the severity of his own wound. But, at least in the immediate aftermath, he paid as well with some apparent sobering reflection upon it all. Two days after the operation, writing to St Vincent the first letter with his left hand, he said: 'My dear Sir, I am become a burthen to my friends, and useless to my country . . . When I leave your command, I become dead to the world; I go hence, and am no more seen . . . I hope you will be able to give me a frigate to convey the remains of my carcase to England.' The main object of the letter, encircled by the above despair, was to ask for promotion for Josiah Nisbet, who had saved him. A powerful source of that despair was his regret that he himself had not led the original assault: 'Had I been with the first party, I have reason to believe complete success would have crowned our efforts. My pride suffered.' The vanity remained irrepressible.[4]

Nelson sought what consolation he could from the prospect of home. Expressing that to Fanny, he said, 'I shall not be surprised to be neglected and forgot, as probably I shall no longer be considered as useful. However, I shall feel rich if I continue to enjoy your affection.'

In spite of his seeming physical fragility, the thinness, the paleness, Nelson possessed that extraordinary resistance so often witnessed when others were dying around him from climate and hardship, as in the West Indies and on Corsica. His physical courage and conviction of a special role carried him through innumerable ordeals, as they would this one. His endurance, as on the night he was wounded, was persistent testimony to a character remote from the ordinary. His recovery, as on the earlier occasion with his eye, appeared quickly mastered. The day after his operation the surgeon noted that he had 'rested pretty well and quite easy. Tea, soup and sago. Lemonade and Tamarind drink.' No fever. Four days later, the 'stump looked well. No bad symptom whatever occurred. The sore reduced to the size of a shilling. In perfect health. One of the ligatures not come away.'

The Tenerife squadron rejoined St Vincent's fleet off Cadiz on 16 August. St Vincent warmly welcomed him, dismissing the failure: 'Mortals cannot command success.' Nelson was sent home in the frigate *Seahorse*, which anchored off Spithead on 1 September. When he stepped ashore later that day he had been away from Britain for more than four years. Upon Fanny would fall the task of dressing his wound but he at least brought to her the news that Josiah Nisbet had been given command of the hospital ship *Dolphin*, although he was still short of the qualifying sea time necessary for such a command, modest though it was. 'Pretty quick promotion, I think,' Hoste ruefully commented in a letter to his father. Still a midshipman with months to go before his time as such expired, there was at least some compensation in having been brought up to the wardroom from the dark depths of the midshipman's quarters on the water-line orlop deck. 'I mess in the wardroom with a jovial set of officers. Pray don't you wish me joy of leaving the lower regions, after a spell of five years?' Upon such, spirit was required to thrive.

XVI

CAMPERDOWN

During the period of the preceding events France had begun to heave with political unrest as the Directory, the ruling executive, became divided in face of further resurgent royalist forces that sought to end republicanism.

There were five members of the Directory, one of whom was replaced each year. Supporting this executive was the Assembly composed of two legislative councils. National elections were held in May 1797 to replace one-third of the Deputies in each council. The results gave a majority to the moderates, amongst whom there was powerful feeling towards restoration of the monarchy. The Directory itself became divided, with two of its members in sympathy with the moderates. The political crisis in France escalated sharply as the three remaining Jacobinical Directors stood firm against anything that smacked of royalist restoration.

It was hardly surprising that the peace negotiations begun with Austria at Leoben on 18 April 1797 became affected by this political upheaval in France. Across Europe hope swiftly arose for a different prospect of peace, with a new order in France. Austria played for time and delayed for six months the final treaty which its emperor had so eagerly grasped for at Leoben when Napoleon was advancing on Vienna. The circumstances at Paris encouraged the Hapsburgs to hope that Leoben might quietly lapse to await a triumphal peace with a restored Bourbon dynasty.

For a financially strapped Britain, however, the desire for quick peace was immediate and overwhelming. 'I feel it my duty,' Pitt said, 'as an English minister and a Christian, to use every effort to stop so bloody and wasting a war.' Before him was a war going nowhere, stalled upon every scene, including all of naval activity. Sailors continued to be run up to the yardarms somewhere or the other in the brooding discontent that persisted. Across the nation poverty and hardship aggravated by inflation provoked discontent that brought unease to all.

The drive for peace worked so urgently upon William Pitt that he was even willing to recognize Belgium as a French possession and Holland as a

French dependency. The French Minister of Foreign Affairs, M. Delacroix, set Lille as the seat for negotiations, and on 3 July Lord Malmesbury, on his third peace mission for Pitt within the past year, once more landed at Calais. At Lille he broadened British concessions: Britain was willing to restore all the conquests she had made from France and the allies of France, except for Trinidad, taken from the Spanish, and the Cape of Good Hope, taken from the Dutch.

As these peace negotiations began on 8 July the political ferment in Paris was stirring. Republican Jacobinism was steadily losing ground. The Assembly had elected as its president Pichegru, who had conquered Holland for the Revolution but who was now said to be in the pay of the royalists. Another revolutionary hero, Carnot, was one of the two Directors who favoured the moderates. Fear of a 'white terror' in the hands of royalist supporters gripped republicans.

To all onlookers outside as well as inside the country it became evident that, given the condition of intrigue and conspiracy within the capital, the political future of France was likely to be decided one way or another by some form of *coup d'état*.

Ostensibly well removed from the Parisian political turmoil through that nervous summer was the conqueror of Italy. Napoleon Buonaparte was preoccupied with grander things. He was changing the historical face of much of southern Europe, and doing so cartographically, politically and constitutionally. He had installed himself regally in the palace of Montebello near Milan, and there it was that he rearranged the map and institutional composition of the Italianate states he had conquered or now intimidated.

His main creation was the Cisalpine Republic embracing Lombardy and its capital Milan, to which was added the former papal territories of Bologna, Ferrara, Modena and Romagna. The Cisalpine constitution was modelled on that of France. Among the guiding principles of this new democratic state were to be religious liberty and civic equality. Genoa, compelled to accept French protection, became the Ligurian Republic on the same principles. Venice was another casualty. As with Genoa, Napoleon imposed the French model of republicanism.

Napoleon's resolute preoccupation with the restructure of northern Italy seemingly kept him out of the Parisian turmoils. The three beleaguered Jacobin directors, Barras, Reubell and Revelliere, knew the army to be their only salvation. They first sought to appoint the strongly republican General Hoche of the Army of the Rhine as Minister of War but the Deputies resisted it. Napoleon had himself been regarding with alarm the prospect of a Bourbon restoration. He had the loyalty and affection of the army, which remained strongly republican in sentiment. And, faced by the prospect of a civil war in France, Napoleon therefore appeared to be the one upon whom the future of republicanism rested. On 14 July he accused the Directory of weakness in face of royalist conspiracy. The republican Directors called on him for support. On 27 July Napoleon accordingly advised the Directory that General Augereau, a dedicated republican, had requested leave to return to Paris on personal matters. But on arrival Augereau was made commandant of the army in Paris. On 4 September 1797 Augereau sent troops into the Tuileries, where the Deputies were sitting. Royalists and moderates favouring restoration were sent to the Temple and their leaders such as Pichegru and Carnot condemned to imprisonment in French Guiana, a sentence known as the 'dry guillotine'. Carnot managed to escape before he was arrested.

All the elections in which royalists had been victorious were declared void. Jacobin power was triumphant, republicanism affirmed. A new repressive order was established in Paris. Though he had remained at Montebello, the figure of Napoleon was now dominant upon all, in association with another remarkable individual whom he did not know, but with whom he now collaborated by messenger between Montebello and Paris.

That person was Charles Maurice de Talleyrand-Périgord, known to history simply as Talleyrand, the man who more than any other offered a certain late-eighteenth-century image. His fame rested upon a unique embodiment within aristocratic mannered grace of a whole set of notorious proclivities – profligate lover and gambler, avidly greedy seeker of personal fortune, master of wit and supreme faceless self-control, yet committed libertarian reformer of the established order, architect of a new house of Europe. Born of one of the grand ducal families of France, Talleyrand enjoyed a youthful libertine existence in Paris until persuaded into a bishopric, a gift from Louis XVI to Talleyrand's dying father. While continuing to indulge his social pleasures, Talleyrand's intellect nevertheless drove him to become part of the force for reform that had fallen upon the land. So that he came, eventually, to represent a unifying link between the *ancien régime* and the Revolution, between the libertarian reformers and revolutionaries, in that dawning. As a bishop of the old clergy he was defrocked as a priest for his service with the new secularist order: he had notoriously promoted the transfer of ecclesiastical property to the state. But as with so many of the early sympathizers with the Revolution he had been compelled to flee with the onslaught of the Terror. After exile in Britain and the United States, Talleyrand had returned to France in July 1796 and immediately been absorbed back into the intellectual ferment of post-Terror Paris. He was swiftly re-established as a figure at the centre of affairs. In July 1797 he was appointed Minister of Foreign Affairs and, just a few days after his appointment, he wrote a letter of flattery

and praise to Napoleon, whom he had never met. A strong correspondence developed through which each recognized the value of the other to
himself. It was discussion between them that helped settle on the choice
of General Augereau as the organizer of the coup that came to be known
as 18 *Fructidor*, the date for 4 September in the Revolutionary calendar.

The impact of *Fructidor* upon the war and upon Europe was immediate.

Pitt's peace negotiator at Lille, Lord Malmesbury, had reported at the
outset of their negotiations on 8 July that it was impossible 'for any men
to have conducted themselves with more cordiality, good humour, and
good faith than the whole of the French Legation have done'. But one
week after *Fructidor* the French plenipotentiaries were replaced and the
new instructed to tell Malmesbury that unless all French demands were
met he should leave Lille within twenty-four hours. Since the negotiations
had previously gone well, this peremptory demand meant that Britain was
required to surrender those points she sought to keep, the Cape, Ceylon and
Trinidad, and that Gibraltar should be returned to Spain and the Channel
Islands ceded to France.

Malmesbury's crude expulsion and the ruthless end of the talks were such
a severe shock to Pitt that he even considered a secret offer of settlement
through a bribe. He considered offering the French a two million pound
bribe for the Cape and Trinidad in hope that it might buy both retention of those bases as well as the peace that he so urgently wanted. The
celebrated venality of Talleyrand was said to be the origin of the proposed
payment, a substantial portion of which undoubtedly would have passed
into the Foreign Minister's own pockets. Even though Pitt succeeded in
winning over George III on it, the contempt of Foreign Secretary Grenville
helped kill any such thing. 'If this country could but be brought to think
so,' he wrote to Pitt, 'it would be ten thousand times safer (and cheaper
too) to face the storm than to shrink from it. And above all, I dread the
loss of consideration which must, I fear, infallibly result from any mode
of *purchasing* our safety; and such this is and will be felt to be, let us say
or do what we will.'[1]

After the Jacobin coup and suppression of royalist emergence in France
the Austrians hastened to conclude the peace treaty roughly outlined at
Leoben six months earlier. On 17 October the final treaty was formally
signed at the village of Campo Formio on the frontier between Venice and
Austria. It concluded Napoleon's Italian campaign with a shock decision
that resounded across Europe. The independence of Venice was traded to
Austria in return for Belgium. Austria recognized the Cisalpine Republic,
thereby conceding the loss of Lombardy. But it was the absorption of
Venice and the bulk of its territories that shook Europe. Thus ended more
than a thousand years of Venetian history: a unique republic traded to the

Hapsburg throne by the soldier who had just fervently supported a coup to ensure the survival of republicanism in France. But Napoleon kept for France a significant Venetian possession, the Ionian Islands, which for him became at once stepping stones into the global vision that had suddenly grown to possess him. His own involvement with the great romantic city that for a millennium had stood as the West's portal to the Levant could only have inflamed that vision, which was that of Choiseul: France in Egypt.

On 16 August he had written to the Directory: 'The time is not far distant when we shall feel that, in order truly to destroy England, we must occupy Egypt. The approaching death of the vast Ottoman Empire obliges us to think in good time of taking steps to preserve our trade in the Levant.' Talleyrand became an eager proponent of the venture. To him, on 13 September, Napoleon wrote: 'We could leave here with twenty-five thousand men, escorted by eight or ten ships of the line or Venetian frigates and take it. Why should we not occupy Malta? . . . We shall be masters of the Mediterranean.'

Napoleon had already made his first moves in anticipation. In June he had ordered Rear Admiral Brueys to sail from Toulon to Corfu with six sail of the line and a number of frigates. At Corfu Brueys seized six Venetian 64-gun ships and six frigates. Brueys was followed from Toulon by a fleet of French transports bearing troops and provisions with which all the Ionian Islands were occupied and garrisoned.

With that, the French looked to be indisputable masters of the Mediterranean, which Britain appeared to have abandoned without a backward reflection. Even the victory of Cape St Vincent had not drawn her back, except for Nelson's brief mission to evacuate the soldiers left on Elba after the abandonment of Corsica at the end of 1796. The British navy stayed at Cadiz, held fast by the interminable blockade there. Instead of some reassertive venture in the Mediterranean, lives and effort had been wasted on a wishful excursion to Tenerife. There were other reasons for the limit set to British operations beyond Cadiz. They could allow no deployment eastward through the Straits while serious threat of invasion existed, particularly from across the North Sea. French retention of Belgium and war with Holland, or the Batavian Republic as it now called itself, meant that it was from those coasts, specifically from the Texel, that the next assault was expected to come. Cadiz was a necessary aspect of the defence against it, to hole up or destroy the Spanish fleet to prevent any union between it and the fleets at Brest and the Texel.

Invasion was what the reconstituted Jacobinical Directory especially demanded. Napoleon was in apparently firm agreement. 'The present moment offers us a fine game. Let us concentrate all our activity upon the navy, and destroy England. That done, Europe is at our feet.'

After Campo Formio with its settlement between France and Austria to end the contest on land, the war against France's remaining adversary, Britain, fell back entirely on to the sea.

For this new phase of the maritime confrontation the Dutch fleet lying at the Texel had been assigned the main assault task, which once more was intended for Ireland. The failure of the first attempt in December had done nothing to deter French willingness to have another go at it. The Dutch had been induced to pay for it all, for fifteen thousand men and their arms to be carried to Ireland by their navy under Admiral de Winter. Quarrel between the Dutch and the French over the supreme command, which the French wanted for General Hoche, had delayed the expedition. So had Admiral Duncan's skilful bluff of fleet in the offing. Thereafter the Dutch ships were confined to port the entire summer because of adverse winds, allowing Duncan, who remained in persistent blockade, to be reinforced.

The Irish rebel leader Wolfe Tone, counting on this expedition to achieve what the first had been unable to do, had embarked aboard de Winter's flagship on 8 July, expecting to sail at once. Eleven days later his journal noted: 'Wind foul still. Horrible! Horrible! Admiral de Winter and I endeavour to pass away the time playing the flute, which he does very well; we have some good duets.'

With no let-up in the contrary winds, in mid-August de Winter finally advised Tone that reinforcement of Duncan's fleet outside the Texel and the reduction of provisions in his ships meant that the Irish expedition was, for the time being, impossible. General Hoche, not yet thirty, died unexpectedly soon after, apparently from consumption, and with his death the Irish expedition was momentarily dead anyway. In the interim de Winter was required by the Directory to effect a union with the Brest fleet at the first opportunity. He was instructed that, once, clear of the Texel, he had to avoid an action with the British before he got to Brest, to enable a joint naval force to be available for the next plan of invasion.[2]

De Winter's singular problem all along had been that he could not easily leave the Texel without suffering serious hurt in the process: the channel out of the Texel was so narrow that only one ship at a time could pass out. With a reinforced British fleet lying off, the destruction upon the emerging Dutch fleet had to be considerable before it managed to get into line of battle. But de Winter got his opportunity to clear the Texel safely when, in early October, Duncan was compelled, through lack of provisions and damage from the bad weather, to take his fleet back to Yarmouth for provisioning and repair. On 7 October de Winter sailed out from the Texel, chasing away the watch ships that Duncan had left on vigil. The cutter *Active*, one of the watch ships posted by Duncan, raced for Yarmouth. Her signal that the enemy was at sea was read as she came into Yarmouth Roads on 9 October. Duncan had his whole fleet under weigh even before *Active* came alongside. From *Active* and from ships that Duncan had sent back to the Texel he got accurate position of the enemy.

The British fleet caught up with de Winter at seven on the morning of 11 October, off the village of Camperdown on the Texel shore.

Duncan at Camperdown, as the ensuing battle came to be called, demonstrated as forcefully as Nelson at Cape St Vincent and Howe on 'the first of June' that the Royal Navy's new school of tactics was truly and widely dominant. This battle would provide further evidence of how deeply all of that had penetrated during the decade and a half since the Saints and publication of Clerk's *Inquiry*. With ship-of-the-line battle full scope now existed. For the willing, the options for individual action were open. So it was now with Duncan, for Camperdown proved to be a battle that could only be fought by breaking the enemy's line to create melee.

The British had fifteen line ships against fifteen Dutch. The principal line ships on both sides were 74s. Duncan's fleet consisted of seven 74s, seven 64s, one 50-gun ship and a flotilla of two frigates and smaller vessels. De Winter had four 74s, seven 64s, four 50s and a large flotilla of frigates and other craft.

Two powerful fleets under strong-minded commanders and manned by determined experienced sailors stood against one another in the dangerously variable conditions of the North Sea. It was a direct fallback to the matching of equals last experienced in the Anglo-Dutch wars of the previous century.

Duncan's situation was particularly dangerous as he approached de Winter, who at sight of the British began forming line of battle while moving steadily towards the Texel shore. There was great variation in the sailing qualities of Duncan's ships. As a result their approach to action was a straggling one. Duncan had little scope for manoeuvre, since de Winter appeared to be drawing him steadily inshore where, lacking familiarity with those waters, the disadvantages would be greater: 'The enemy at this time in a line of battle on the larboard tack, with their main-top-sail yards square, but keeping them shivering, and sometimes full, by which their line was gradually advancing toward their own shore, not seven miles distant.' The day was already approaching noon, the wind was onshore, the water perilously and unpredictably shoal. There was little time for tactical deliberation. Instead of any attempt to form line Duncan quickly decided to get his ships between de Winter's fleet and the Texel shore. Seven minutes before noon Duncan signalled his fleet to pass through the enemy line. That order now had its own life in the signal books, Signal 34, followed shortly after with the signal for close action, melee. The action began at twelve thirty and by one p.m. it was general.

Duncan took two reefs in his topsails and steered *Venerable* for the centre of the French line accompanied by the three ships nearest him. Others followed the example though, with hazy weather, the signal was at first not seen by all.

Admiral Onslow in *Monarch* found himself leading the van. As he bore down on the Dutch his captain drew his attention to the fact that the enemy's ships lay too close and that he would find no passage through them. 'Monarch will make a passage,' Onslow replied, and *Monarch* promptly did.

What followed was the first action entirely melee arising from breaking the line.

Camperdown was fought with the same unflinching ferocity and courage of the historic Four Days Battle of 1666. It was indeed the bloodiest naval action since the Four Days. The fighting was close, the ships ranging along-side one another, pouring shot into each other's hulls, raking the decks, which ran thickly with blood of the fallen. Two individuals stood out with unusual distinctness. Duncan and de Winter were both over six feet, robust physical figures, tall on their quarterdecks as their two ships pounded at one another. De Winter at the end was the only person on his quarterdeck not killed or wounded. With all swept away around him, he himself lowered his colours around three in the afternoon. His ship, *Vryheid*, had by then lost all her masts. Battle ended just in time. They were by now in nine fathoms of water and no more than five miles from land.

The British lost more than a thousand killed, the Dutch far more. Such unusually huge losses compared to actions with the Spanish and French were testimony to the severity of the battle. Dutch colours only came down when there was no fight left in a ship. As always in such actions of unstinting courage and bloody suffering on both sides, triumphalism in the victors was subdued by respect for the fighting qualities of the defeated. When de Winter was brought prisoner aboard *Venerable* and presented his sword to Duncan it was courteously returned to him.

The British took six prizes, including two 74s, before the rest of the Dutch fleet made off. Prizes they were in name, but all were so severely damaged that none was ever again considered seaworthy. One of the prizes, *Delft*, began sinking soon after being taken in tow. British ships sent their boats to bring off the crew. As the ship settled the officer commanding the prize crew, Lieutenant Bullen, invited the Dutch first lieutenant, Heilberg, to leave in one of the boats. 'How can I go and leave these poor men?' Heilberg said, pointing to the wounded. Bullen promptly grasped his hand and said that then he too would stay. They remained together beside the wounded as boats continued to take off as many as possible, until *Delft* suddenly plunged and went down. Bullen managed to swim to a ship but Heilberg was never seen again.

Aboard *Venerable*, Admirals de Winter and Duncan dined and then sat down to a game of whist together. Losing the rubber, de Winter remarked that it was a little hard to be beaten twice in one day by the same opponent. Thus it so often ended, in the stately quarters of the victorious admiral, a courteous, relieving hospitality, everything so quiet suddenly, those other violent hours abruptly gone, being now absorbed by familiar civil pleasantries, with just the rock of the sea, memory softened by the steadfast glow from the candles in their lantern cases. And soul soothed by the graces of mutual support for an impossible comprehension.[3]

Camperdown was a battle that, with posterity, somehow lost rank and significance against the greater and more romantically glorious events that followed. But it was at the time an event of huge effect, with far consequences.

This victory was clear-cut. The Dutch navy, a formidable force as it had just proved itself to be, was for any foreseeable calculation out of the picture, unlike the Spanish Grand Fleet that still kept Earl St Vincent and his ships tied to Cadiz. St Vincent, who had consciously restrained himself about too loudly expressing the doubts that he held over aspects of his own victory off Cape St Vincent, proved unpleasantly scornful of Duncan's achievement: 'He was a brave officer, little versed in the subtleties of naval tactics, and who would have been quickly embarrassed by them. When he saw the enemy, he rushed upon him without thinking of such and such an order of battle. To conquer, he calculated upon the brave example he set his captains, and the event justified his expectation.'

It was a strange comment from a man whose own victory was notably assisted by the brave example of one of his captains veering from the prescribed order of battle. But this criticism of Duncan 'of having gone confusedly and hurriedly to work' was answered by one of Duncan's younger captains, William Hotham, nephew of Admiral Sir Henry Hotham: '. . . the advanced season of the year, and the close proximity of the enemy's coast all made what, upon another occasion, might have appeared haste imperatively necessary, for it was the prompt decision of the Admiral that occasioned the result . . . I was interrogated confidentially upon this subject by one high in office and this was the spirit of the answer I gave.' And, as the logbook of Duncan's flagship *Venerable* further recorded, 'Had our time been lost in making a regular distribution of our ships, the Dutch fleet must have got so near their coast, it would have been impossible to follow them with any view of advantage.' In other words, waiting to form line would have been at the expense of battle and its victory.

The government and public relief over Camperdown was enormous.

In the wake of the Nore and, as reports continued to come in, of recurrent mutiny at various other points, Camperdown provided a necessary reassurance of the steadfast qualities of the British sailor. A despondent government and a deeply unsettled public were in need of substantial solace. Through Camperdown, the Brest fleet lost its closest as well as its most valuable and dependable partner for reinforcement. With the Treaty of Campo Formio France had acquired Belgium. Defeat of the Dutch navy brought respite from that concern. Successful invasion of Ireland would have raised insurmountable problems for the survival of Britain. For the moment, therefore, Camperdown offered a relief that neither 'the First of June' nor Cape St Vincent had given, which was victory off the home shores, in the very waters across which assault had looked imminent. But in the wider arena Camperdown was much more.

As Julian Holland Rose points out in his biography of Napoleon, before the victory of Duncan over the Dutch at Camperdown Britain seemed to have lost her naval supremacy. That was the way it looked to France and onlookers. The Directory certainly appeared convinced of it when, in November, Napoleon, who was still at Montebello, was appointed to the command of the Army of England. Pitt's financial crisis, the mutinies and Irish insurrection combined to suggest a final exhaustion and demoralization of Britain, and with that the likely success of assault across the Narrow Seas. But with Camperdown Duncan had met Grenville's ardent demand to Pitt for Britain 'to face the storm than to shrink from it'. And in doing so Duncan had re-established Britain's naval dominance more emphatically in Continental strategic calculations than any other Royal Naval action in the war so far. Though the Directory retained its obsession with invasion, Napoleon was shortly to pronounce himself against it. Camperdown had assured that. Napoleon consequently turned to the alternative challenge that he earnestly preferred, his proposed eastern adventure.

The dispiriting apathy and fear of no longer being required that had settled upon Nelson after the disaster at Santa Cruz was short-lived after his arrival at Spithead on 1 September. 'My pride suffered,' he had said after Santa Cruz. It was restored in London.

His welcome by his nation was all that he could have wished, he wrote to St Vincent. His physical state, however, had deteriorated. He was now suffering severe pain and discomfort from infection of the ligature on the stump of his severed arm. He needed opium to sleep. His wife dressed his arm. For her it was a period of attentive care and intimacy of a nature that she was never to experience again. Nelson's public attentions to Fanny were described as those of a lover. He himself was saying that her care alone was saving his life. 'I found my domestic happiness perfect,' he told St

Vincent. But the persistence of the infection suggested more professional attention, and he and Fanny moved from Bath to London, into lodgings on Bond Street.

That he still was wanted by his nation had been made clear to him by George III who, on the day that Nelson went to St James's Palace to receive his Order of the Bath, said to him, 'Your country has a claim for a bit more of you.'

Camperdown gave insight into his public standing. Public joy over victory there saw London all lit up, with candles in every window. Cheering mobs rampaged through the streets demanding that all houses join the celebratory illumination. Nelson had taken laudanum to allow him to sleep when they arrived. The mob hammered loudly and violently on the door demanding to know why the house was not lit up in celebration of Duncan's victory. A servant opened the door and told them that Sir Horatio Nelson who had been so badly wounded lodged there and could not be disturbed. 'You will hear no more from us tonight,' the leader said, and they withdrew.

The capital's surgeons had little in that day that could offer much relief, except laudanum and opium. 'Time and nature' was their recommendation. So it proved to be. On 4 December the silk ligatures that had tied the wound and become infectiously absorbed into it suddenly came away. Relief was instant. 'I am now perfectly recovered,' Nelson wrote immediately after, 'and on the eve of being employed.'

The man selected to be captain of whatever new command Nelson received was Edward Berry, who had led the boarding party to the *San Nicolas* at Cape St Vincent. On 17 December Nelson accompanied Berry to Chatham to inspect the ship that would receive his flag, *Vanguard*, a 74.

As so often was seen with Nelson and Napoleon Buonaparte, a special defining moment in their ascent was simultaneously come for both. This time it was for each of them the end of the critical first phase of their emergence from anonymity into legend. For each of them it was a public arrival from triumph.

Napoleon was by now twenty-eight, Nelson thirty-nine. Like Nelson, back from St Vincent, Napoleon at that moment was a hero who had returned to the metropolitan heart of affairs to receive personally, after long absence, the public accolades accumulative since the start of the Italian campaign.

The hero of Italy arrived in Paris on 5 December 1797, which for Nelson on the other side of the Channel was his first full day of relief from pain. For each, therefore, that day was one of freshness, of reinvigorated youth, renewal of mission and purpose as only their individual excess of zeal and animation and conviction of personal destiny could make it.

The acclamation was intense for the young soldier who had brought the Hapsburg Empire to its knees, humbled Sardinia and the Vatican, laid republicanism across northern Italy and in the process poured gold into the French Treasury and art treasures into the Louvre. Talleyrand was the one whom the hero was most anxious to meet. This meeting came the day after Napoleon's arrival. 'At first sight,' Talleyrand said, 'his face appeared to me charming. A score of victories go so well with youth, with fine eyes, with paleness, and with an appearance of exhaustion.' He might have been describing Nelson, so easily did it fit. Each drew, after all, from near the same form of illumination.

XVII

DUEL

EVEN with the shock of lower deck mutiny lying heavily upon it, the Royal Navy was hardly prepared for the equivalent on quarterdeck level, with one naval officer shot by another for refusing to obey an order.

It was an event without precedent. Or, as described at the time, 'an awful lesson on the duty of subordination, being the only case of summary punishment for an offence against that duty in the upper ranks that, we believe, has occurred in our navy'.

What exploded in English Harbour, Antigua, on the evening of 13 January 1798, was a shocking surprise even for a navy where acrimonious relations on quarterdeck between particular officers were a common experience, especially aboard ships long at sea.

The quarterdeck was seldom an easy place of temperate emotions. Quarrel could build or flare for many reasons other than the inevitable tensions that could arise from extended close confinement together of disparate individuals. But the licence of quarrel was naturally confined to those of equal rank. The full severity of naval regulations descended upon anyone who dared to face up to a senior. Among those of equal rank, resentment was strong when they saw a promotion they expected given to someone of lesser seniority, especially when 'interest' was involved. Seniority in any form, who might order whom, was therefore always a matter of extreme sensitivity. It had to be in a service where many could wait years for upward recognition while watching others inexplicably advancing through favour.

These were the factors that appeared principally involved at English Harbour when Lieutenant Camelford shot Lieutenant Peterson for what he regarded as mutinous behaviour.

Two small vessels lay as guard ships in that harbour. These were the sloop *Favorite*, commanded by twenty-three-year-old Lieutenant Lord Camelford and *Perdrix*, a captured French ship, under Lieutenant Charles Peterson. They were both comparatively new arrivals. Peterson had taken

over *Perdrix* when its captain went on leave. Camelford similarly arrived
to replace a commander who had fallen ill.

Little is known of Lieutenant Peterson but Lieutenant Lord Camelford
came with a full weight of aristocratic and establishment connections behind
him. He was born Thomas Pitt, second Baron Camelford, of a well-established
family in Boconnoc, Cornwall. The Prime Minister William Pitt was a
cousin. His sister was married to Foreign Secretary Lord Grenville. Another
cousin was Sir Sidney Smith, at that time languishing in prison in France,
but representing as much as anyone could the social as well as the adventurist
dilettantism of late-eighteenth-century upper-class society. Camelford was
of that breed, but strangely so. He was a disturbed man.

Brought up in Switzerland, he was educated at Charterhouse. His social
graces were those of class arrogance, that special definition of gentleman
that in certain characters accompanied disdainful contempt of most of those
around them but in particular of those below them. It was the manner that
attached quick sensitivity to insult, real or imagined; the inveterate duellist.
But Camelford was a man strange in many other respects. He had gone
into the navy at fourteen. He had accompanied Captain Vancouver in 1791
on his exploration of northwest America but was discharged by Vancouver
at Hawaii for insubordination. When he met Vancouver three years later
he challenged him and was prevented by bystanders from caning him in
the street. His life was said to be 'punctuated by disorderly adventures'.
Camelford had confessed to one intimate, Sir Anthony Carlisle, a renowned
surgeon at Westminster Hospital, that

he had no animal courage and laboured by any means to get the better of a weakness
of nerves in this respect, by attending cock-fightings, pugilism, etc. etc. That in
him Courage was a struggle of sentiment against Constitution. He was industrious
to acquire knowledge of many things. He was a good Chemist, a most excellent
geographer, a good seaman – could do business of a Turner and work in *fineering*
as a cabinet maker – he was very desirous of being reckoned much upon as a *Man*
independent of his title and wished his friends to lay that aside and to address him
familiarly – But he desired to be at the head notwithstanding – to have the best
horses – in points of dress, and in other things to be first. When in a passion it was
a kind of phrenzy it disordered him. But otherwise his mind was gentle and easy
. . . In political matters he was democratick. He hated all the Royal Family except
the Prince of Wales who he thought had good qualities. He disliked William Pitt,
his cousin and the whole family of the Grenvilles.

Carlisle was describing a man whose character left him tumbling in the
turbulence of the transition of the centuries. Camelford appeared to be overwhelmed by the contest between the aggressive physical assertion that was a

male requirement for that violent epoch and the starburst of the intellectu-
ally new that struggled for its own different illumination within an active
mind, which he appeared to have. It was a familiar demand of the times
that lay upon all of any distinctive capability and had to be met. When it
was met, it resounded. Where it failed, it could be fatal.

This was the tormenting personal conflict that the second Baron Camelford
brought to Antigua. All of it descended at once upon Lieutenant Peterson.
Peterson had been first lieutenant of *Favorite* when Camelford arrived to take
command. They were together for three months in that situation, Peterson
necessarily subordinate to Camelford. Peterson was said to have executed
Camelford's orders as he had done under former captains, but it was a fact
'most notorious', Camelford said, that Peterson was a man 'with whom on
service I never could agree, which rendered him by no means a desirable
second to a commander . . . I have often been heard to express myself vexed
and concerned that he could not be treated like a gentleman . . . his character
was so different from mine, that we were not formed to sail together; and as
I was loath to take away his commission, I desired him to leave the ship.'

Rancour between the two had obviously built up during that relationship. The situation eased when *Perdrix*'s captain took leave and Peterson
replaced him. Through all that time the senior officer of the port had been
the captain of the sloop *Babet*, Jemmet Mainwaring. The climax to the bad
blood between the two lieutenants came when *Babet* was ordered to Fort
Royal Bay, Martinique. Peterson was dead just a little over twenty-four
hours after *Babet* sailed.

Camelford and Peterson appeared to have put their previous differences
aside until Mainwaring's departure aboard *Babet* produced sudden fateful
confrontation on the evening of the 13th. 'We seemed totally to have forgot
each other,' Camelford said at his court martial, 'and probably would have
remained in that state of forgetfulness ever after if duty (the only point
on which it ever can be said we disagreed) had not interposed, on the
unfortunate occasion that places me where I now stand.'

Mainwaring's departure as the appointed senior officer of English Harbour
created an entirely new situation since neither Camelford nor Peterson had
been officially designated his successor in that specific command. Both were
'acting commanders' of their respective ships. The language used by the
admiral in appointing Camelford to *Favorite* certainly did not specifically
declare him to be in overall command of English Harbour. His responsibility
was 'strictly charging and commanding all the officers and company of the
said sloop . . . and you likewise to observe and execute . . . such orders and
directions as you shall, from time to time, receive from me . . .' But when
Mainwaring sailed each of the lieutenants assumed that command of the
port now was his.

Peterson saw one indisputable fact in his favour. On the navy's list of lieutenants through which advancement progressed Peterson stood ahead of Camelford. He told the master of *Perdrix*, Masser Crawford, that he regarded himself to be senior commander of English Harbour because the directions sent to Camelford aboard *Favorite* by the admiral for Leeward Islands were addressed to 'Lieutenant Lord Camelford' and that since he, Peterson, was a senior lieutenant on the list to Lord Camelford, the post fell naturally to him. The fact that 'lieutenant' preceded 'Lord' appeared to be Peterson's basis for seeing level ground for his own case. Had 'Lord' preceded 'lieutenant' perhaps Peterson would have deferred to it. Hard to know, but there is a strong sense in his argument of the ever-brooding resentment in the navy of 'interest' among those who lacked it. To Peterson, apparently, there here appeared to be another instance of leap-frogged advancement through 'interest'. He was not having it. Camelford's assertion of his right to seniority was never questioned at his court martial, although the jurors at the coroner's inquisition at Antigua found themselves compelled to conclude 'that a mutiny had taken place, but on which side such mutiny did exist, they cannot pretend to say'. The documents presented at the opening of Camelford's court martial included the Antigua jurors' statement but the proceedings failed to offer any clarification of their puzzlement. Only in the brief verdict of the court martial acquitting Camelford was there any official declaration of Camelford as 'the senior officer at English Harbour, at that time'. Camelford's claim very likely was based upon Captain Mainwaring having delegated him as commanding senior before *Babet* sailed. That would seem to be supported by the fact that Mainwaring was a member of the court martial, accounting for any lack of question among the judges.

Apart from that, Camelford, having at one point at English Harbour had Peterson as a subordinate, would have found it difficult thereafter to regard Peterson as anything other than that. It is nevertheless evident that, if Mainwaring had indeed delegated Camelford as senior officer, it had not been made officially or generally known there.

In Camelford's court martial witnesses were asked whether Camelford had at any time after *Babet* sailed worn 'commander's coat'. No one had seen him do so. Nor, said the *Perdrix* master Crawford, had Peterson received any message from Camelford indicating superiority before the fatal one sent on the evening of the 13th.

That Peterson was lieutenant senior to Camelford on the list was something that Crawford and others aboard *Perdrix* had by then come to accept. It attached their loyalty to him as the thing began to blow out of control.

What set it all off at sunset on the 13th was a signal sent down from the fort above the harbour that ships had been sighted standing in either for English Harbour or an adjacent port. Mainwaring had maintained a standing order that a rowing guard should be maintained at the entrance to the harbour. On receipt of the signal Camelford sent an instruction to Peterson amending that order. He instructed that a midshipman was to be put in charge of the boat instead of a warrant officer and the boat should be kept at a grapnel at the entrance of the harbour instead of maintaining a rowing guard there. He required Peterson's acknowledgement.

Camelford's message was headed, 'By Lieutenant Lord Camelford, commanding his Majesty's sloop Favorite, and senior officer of his Majesty's ships and vessels lying in English Harbour, Antigua'. It bore the instruction, 'Sir, You will be pleased to acknowledge the receipt of the enclosed letter on service. I am, etc. Camelford.'

It was that outright declaration of Camelford's seniority and the direct order that accompanied it that incensed Peterson.

Both Camelford and Peterson were messing ashore in lodgings at opposite sides of the small harbour. Peterson was in quarters ashore at the capstan house beside his ship. A short boat journey was usually taken from one place to the other. To and fro across that close space of water the crisis now built, drawing into its small frame its sequence of witnesses.

When Camelford had written and sealed his instruction he handed it to an acting lieutenant of *Favorite*, Clement Milward, who in turn passed it over to *Favorite*'s first lieutenant, Lieutenant Parsons, who passed it to William Granger, master's mate of *Favorite*. It was nearly eight o'clock when Granger arrived at the capstan house, guarded by a sentry with a cutlass. He was told that Peterson was in the mess room upstairs.

Peterson broke open Camelford's instruction, read it and, dismissing Granger, told him to return to Camelford and to tell him that Lieutenant Peterson considered him very presumptuous to write to him in that manner.

On hearing that, Camelford ordered Lieutenant Parsons to tell Granger to convey to the master of *Perdrix* that he should confine Lieutenant Peterson to his cabin and take upon himself temporary command of the ship. Fifteen minutes after his return Granger was on his way back to the capstan house.

When Granger arrived there he found Peterson with Samuel Piguenit, purser of *Perdrix*, and Crawford, who was expected to put Peterson under arrest. Crawford showed no response to the instruction he had received. Peterson told the purser to take down the message that Granger had brought, made Granger sign it, and then dismissed him. Throughout all of it Peterson had kept on repeating his astonishment at Camelford's presumption to send him such an instruction.

After Granger left, Peterson, in his conviction of seniority, wrote his own letter of instruction to Camelford. Addressed to 'Lieutenant Lord

Camelford of His Majesty's sloop Favorite' he headed it, 'By Lieutenant Charles Peterson, commander of his Majesty's ship Perdrix, and senior officer of his Majesty's ships, *for the time being*, in English Harbour'. It read, 'Whereas the island of Antigua is now under an alarm – You are hereby required and directed, to cause the crew of his Majesty's sloop Favorite, under your direction, to hold themselves in readiness to man the batteries round this harbour; also to cause a guard to be rowed round the entrance of this harbour, during this night, and report to me their proceedings in the morning.' Crawford was told to deliver it to Lieutenant Parsons, who took it in to Camelford.

In this near tragicomic manner the drama gathered momentum, with messages handed from rank to rank in strict order of etiquette for the brief passage to and fro across the harbour.

Peterson's own letter of instruction to Camelford, declaring himself as senior officer, was for that already seething man the limit of his endurance. 'This letter,' Camelford declared, 'appeared to me to be throughout so highly mutinous and refractory, inasmuch as it not only set me at defiance, and usurped my authority as senior officer of the port that I immediately and without hesitation gave directions to Lieutenant Parsons to despatch Lieutenant Milward at the head of a party of marines, to arrest the person of Lieutenant Peterson, and to bring him over to the easternmost capstan house either dead or alive.'

That brutal command of a summary execution as option was discarded by Parsons, who instead instructed Milward to make use of force of arms if necessary but always to avoid bloodshed. If he could not arrest Peterson without endangering his life, he said, Milward should return and report to Camelford. Parsons's verbal lessening of the harsh licence allowed to Milward was to enrage Camelford, who subsequently came close to court-martialling Parsons for disobedience because of it. At his court martial Camelford blamed Parsons for allowing Peterson time for preparation. It became a principal point in justifying his act, proffered to his jury with an accompanying image of Peterson and those loyal to him aboard *Perdrix* as forcefully prejudicial as he could make it. He knew, he said, that 'from the arrogant and seditious turn of mind which he displayed on all occasions he would never allow himself to be apprehended while the means were left him for defence, and whilst the evil-disposed persons surrounding him were ready at his side to pour their pernicious advice'.

From that and from the swift sequence of what immediately followed it seems clear that Camelford's enraged state made the final outcome inevitable. Too much had accumulated between Peterson and himself. All of it carried the emotional trappings of a duel, which in other circumstances would have allowed the release required by such an inherently disturbed mind. Need for that satisfaction had become an overwhelming demand.

Camelford was unlikely to remain patient for long.

Milward had taken a party of marines over the water and marched them to the mess room door of the capstan house. After receiving the first message from Camelford, Peterson had doubled the sentries at the capstan house door. They bore fixed bayonets when Milward arrived. They asked him what he wanted. 'To see Lieutenant Peterson on service,' he replied. He was told that he could not go upstairs to the mess room without Peterson's permission. Milward asked them to send a servant upstairs to ask Peterson to allow him in. The servant returned and told Milward to go up.

Milward went up, calling his marines to follow him. Peterson listened as Milward related the orders from Parsons.

'I will not go,' Peterson said and went to a table at the other end of the room from which he took up a sword. Milward advanced toward him saying that he was come to take him to the other capstan house under arrest. Peterson told Crawford, the master, to arm himself. He then advanced towards Milward pointing the sword at Milward's breast and ordering him with the marines down the stairs.

Peterson told Milward that if he did not go down he would run him through, and with that made a feint towards Milward with the sword. Milward deflected the sword with his own. Peterson went to a table and took up two brass pistols. Crawford took one, Peterson kept the other. Milward told the marines to seize Peterson.

Crawford pointed his pistol at the marine sergeant's breast and shoved him back, telling him to get out of the room. 'Don't shove me,' the sergeant said. 'I have my commanding officer here and I will cut your head off directly.'

Milward, remembering Parsons's injunction and afraid of endangering Peterson's life, told his marines to stop.

Peterson walked to the other side of the room and rapped on a partition with the sword, called down to the gunner and master-of-arms, 'Get the people under arms.' Leaning from the window, Peterson shouted, 'Perdrix's, Perdrix's, arm yourselves! Load with powder and ball.'

Camelford, meanwhile, had appeared in the yard below, drawn by the clamour. He arrived to find *Perdrix*'s ship's company hurriedly falling in under arms. He called out, 'Mr Milward!' When Milward answered Camelford cried, 'Desist, desist!'

Milward went down with his marines. Camelford was standing a short distance from the capstan house. *Pedrix*'s men were still turning out. Milward formed up his own marines facing them. Battle between the two ships' groups appeared imminent for Peterson, who had descended, asked his men if they were ready. They answered, 'No, sir.' Peterson then said, 'Load with ball cartridge, and fix bayonets.' And repeated, 'Are you ready?'

Camelford had hailed *Favorite* and called for the rest of the ship's company to be sent over. As he and Milward waited for the boat, the *Perdrix* men having loaded, Peterson called, 'Stand by!'

Camelford and Milward stood expecting to be fired on. Camelford, Milward said, was 'in a great rage'.

Camelford then asked Milward if he was armed. Milward said he was. Had he pistols? Milward said he had. Camelford asked for one. He was given one.

'Is it loaded?'

'Yes.'

Camelford walked towards *Perdrix*'s men and called out, 'Where is Mr Peterson?'

Somebody answered, 'He is here, sir.'

Camelford called again for Peterson, who emerged. Standing before Camelford, hands on his hips, he rose on his toes and lowered back on his heels as he answered, 'I am here, damme, sir!'

Camelford went up to him, cocked his pistol and put it to Peterson's breast, and asked, 'Do you still persist in refusing to obey my orders?'

'I do, sir.'

Camelford repeated the question. Peterson said, 'No, sir, I will not.'

The question was repeated a third time. The answer was 'I will not obey.' Camelford fired.

As Peterson fell Camelford jumped back, expecting the *Perdrix* men to shoot him and calling to his marines to support him. Milward handed Camelford another cartridge and told him to load as he expected them to be fired at. But shock appeared to have affected all. The *Perdrix* men, staring at their fallen commander, did nothing. Crawford, seeing that Peterson was dead, cried out, 'Mr Peterson is shot. Return your arms. Dismiss.'

Camelford told them, 'I have shot Lieutenant Peterson for mutiny.' He then asked Crawford whether he would obey his orders or not. He had to repeat the question three times before Crawford, who had been close to Peterson, answered 'Yes.' Camelford then said, 'Mr Crawford, your commanding officer is killed for downright mutiny; dismiss the people, return their arms, and conceive yourself commanding officer of the Perdrix.'

What emerged with absolute clarity at the court martial was that *Perdrix*'s men were ready to fire on the other if ordered to do so. They were forthright about it. 'I certainly would have fired at them, if I had received orders from Lieutenant Peterson,' one of *Perdrix*'s seamen said. 'I would not have obeyed

Lord Camelford. I conceived Lord Camelford as an inferior officer. I would not have fired without orders. If I had received orders from Lieutenant Peterson, I should have fired, thinking it my duty.'

The marine sergeant from *Favorite* who had accompanied Milward into the capstan house mess was asked, 'Did you not conceive that as soon as the Perdrix's company were ready to fire, they would begin?'

'Yes.'

The support Camelford called for from *Favorite* arrived after Peterson was shot and Crawford, as senior officer of *Perdrix*, had dismissed his men. From the testimony on both sides it was clear that what would have been one of the ugliest scenes in British naval history had narrowly been avoided, one where the ship's companies of the only two vessels in port would have fired upon one another on the orders of their respective commanders. If *Perdrix*'s men had fired, *Favorite*'s would have responded in self-defence. The attitude of Milward's sergeant of marines had already made the latter clear enough.

Through that chilling episode one nevertheless sees reflected, ironically in view of what provoked it, the absolute compliance with any instruction from an officer that the Royal Navy rigidly demanded of its lower ranks, without any question ever allowed on the right or wrong of it.

The first outsider on the scene was Captain Henry Mitford, whose ship *Matilda* arrived with a convoy of provisions for Antigua the very night of the 13th. He arrested Camelford, ordered Lieutenant Parsons of *Favorite* to take command of *Perdrix* and the master of *Favorite* to prepare that ship for sea. Mitford's immediate report to the commander in chief on what he found saw Camelford's motives as private pique and resentment. It was a view that appears to have gathered strength within the navy. But the court martial's verdict was that, since Peterson had committed 'acts of mutiny highly injurious to the discipline of His Majesty's service', Camelford was 'unanimously and honourably acquitted'.

Camelford was to lose his own life in a duel in 1804. In his diary the artist Joseph Farington noted, 'Westmacott called. He mentioned that Lord Camelford is little regretted. At Lord Darnley's he heard some gentlemen say "that it was dangerous to sit in company with such a man".'

XVIII

OFFENSIVE

ON 5 April 1798 William Pitt tentatively approached one of the greatest decisions he was to make during the war, certainly the most critical he was ever to make regarding the Royal Navy.

The Prime Minister pondered whether it was feasible to send a strong naval squadron into the Mediterranean, to initiate a new strategy there. At Downing Street on the 5th he sat down and composed a set of queries for Earl Spencer, First Lord of the Admiralty. The next day Spencer outlined his serious doubts and reservations to Foreign Secretary Grenville. But on the 7th, pursuing the matter with Grenville, Pitt was resolved. He would act.[1]

In two days he had taken Britain from the defensive to the offensive.

It was a remarkable about-turn from the Pitt who at Lille had seemed willing to defer to the French on practically everything, even bribe them, simply to have an end to a war that seemed to be crippling Britain financially. One might guess that Pitt had been stiffened by Grenville's rousing admonition to face the storm rather than shrink from it, but there were several sudden factors. Britain's commercial fortunes were changing. Camperdown had revived the flagging spirit of the land and with it, presumably, Pitt's own. The defiance that Duncan's victory had roused across the land was manifest in the Thanksgiving at St Paul's that on 19 December had celebrated together the victories of 'the First of June', St Vincent and Camperdown. The immediate influence, however, was that events on the Continent had changed the outlook there. Austria, in consequence, was making a firm plea to Britain to return to the Mediterranean with a fleet, after more than a year's absence during which the French had come to regard that sea as solely theirs for manoeuvre. Naples, too, had been pleading for it, to deter French threat against the existence of the Kingdom of the Two Sicilies. One nevertheless feels that Pitt could not so easily have opened himself so widely to those pleas without the dramatic infusion of the overall confidence that suddenly appeared to possess him.

On 17 March the Austrian Chancellor, Baron Franz Thugut, sought to know through his ambassador in London whether Britain would help Austria against a France 'irrevocably determined on the total subversion of Europe, and rapidly marching to that end'. The idea of the Mediterranean fleet would reassert British presence there and assist the fusion of a new resistance to France. Remarkably this was just six months after Austria had concluded her peace with France at Campo Formio, thereby finally burying the First Coalition against France. But, far from settling Continental nerves, Campo Formio had left the Continent in continuing uncertainty after the French sought to relieve their financial difficulties by marching on Rome and Switzerland.

French troops had entered Rome and declared the civil authority of the Pope at an end. Paintings and statues were looted. Miles-long convoys of wagons loaded with art treasures wound out of Rome bound for Paris. The French similarly raided Switzerland's cantonal treasuries and replaced the confederation of Swiss oligarchies with the Helvetic Republic.

In tentative prospect was a Second Coalition against France, with Russia and possibly even Prussia coming in on side. Tsar Paul was involving himself more directly in the Continental turmoil than his mother Catherine had been prepared to be at the end. The Directory gave him reason when, on 12 January 1798, it declared that the movement of any ships carrying Baltic goods to Britain through the Sound would be tantamount to declaration of war by their flags against France. He himself sent a fleet of twenty-two line ships and 250 galleys to the Sound 'to protect trade in general against the oppression of the Directory'. He also offered part of his Baltic fleet to England to help blockade the coast of Holland.

The emergence of any such new alliance was likely to be a straggling process, however, and the value of a Mediterranean distraction looked questionable to Spencer as he reviewed Pitt's proposal. He saw dangerous overextension of an undermanned fleet, in spite of the fact that at Toulon Buonaparte was assembling a naval and military armada that clearly, from all report and observation, was the mightiest yet put together by the French. Its intent was unknown but the common assumption was that it was meant for Ireland, to complement the preparations for invasion observable in all the Channel ports. The strategic situation looked as serious as it ever could be for Britain. The Directory had sworn its full commitment to Irish liberation and Ireland was in a state of fervent rebellion. For Britain a mighty combined assault on her own as well as the Irish coasts spelled more than her available resources appeared likely to be able to cope with.

Spencer informed Pitt that the fleet at his disposal was thirty-four ships for the Channel and the coast of Ireland and twenty-four for Lord St Vincent at Lisbon, the base for the Cadiz blockade. Additionally, three ships were fitting for sea while eight others were nearing completion. The biggest problem was with men, eight thousand more being needed. To Grenville he was more forthright. In laying out his fears in his letter to the Foreign Secretary on the 6th, Spencer appeared like a man staring at a board upon which his limited forces were deployed in a manner that left little or no room for manipulation.

Even if a Russian squadron appeared to assist them in the North Sea it was impossible for Britain to maintain a permanent squadron in the Mediterranean, he declared. For Pitt's proposed policy he required at least seventy ships of the line, instead of the fifty-eight immediately disposable. Those seventy would have to be evenly allocated, meaning thirty-five for the Channel and Ireland and thirty-five for St Vincent. Those for St Vincent would be barely enough to watch Cadiz as well as command the Mediterranean. Spencer, moreover, believed that Portugal would soon succumb to combined French and Spanish pressure and that the British would then be expelled from the Tagus. He accordingly saw the best plan as being to hang on as long as they were able to their command between Lisbon and Cadiz. When that base went then St Vincent, with the fleet he had, could 'take a sweep round the Mediterranean and do all the mischief he can to the French navy'. That, Spencer said, was the plan he advocated, if Austria could be satisfied with such an eventual sweep around the Mediterranean.[2]

For Pitt that evidently lacked immediacy. On the 7th he told Grenville that Austria had to be encouraged to play a decisive part in resisting French aggression. He was prepared to face the risks of invasion as preferable to a lingering and indecisive war. On 29 April the cabinet formulated its orders for St Vincent. He should do all he could to intercept and spoil or defeat the force that was being assembled at Toulon. If possible the blockade of Cadiz should be maintained. But it was left to St Vincent to decide whether to enter the Mediterranean at the head of his entire fleet, or to send a squadron of at least nine or ten ships of the line commanded by a flag officer of his choosing. In a private letter to St Vincent the First Lord summarized the risk as well as the urgency of the assignment:

The circumstances in which we now find ourselves oblige us to take a measure of a more decided and hazardous complexion than we should otherwise have thought ourselves justified in taking; but when you are apprized that the appearane of a British squadron in the Mediterranean is a condition on which the fate of Europe may at this moment be stated to depend, you will not be surprised that we are disposed to strain every nerve, and incur considerable hazard in effecting it ... how absolutely necessary it is at this time to run some risk, in order, if possible, to bring about a new system of affairs in Europe, which shall save us all from being overrun by the exorbitant power of France ... it is impossible not to perceive how much depends on the exertions of the great Continental powers ... no good will be obtained from them if some such measure as that now in contemplation is not immediately adopted ... if, by our appearance in the Mediterranean, we can encourage Austria to come forward again, it is ... probable that the other powers will seize the opportunity of acting at the same time ...

To that Spencer added a vital rider: 'If you determine to send a detachment into the Mediterranean (instead of going in person with the fleet), I think it almost unnecessary to suggest to you the propriety of putting it under the command of Sir. H. Nelson, whose acquaintance with that part of the world, as well as his activity and disposition, seem to qualify him in a peculiar manner for that service.'[3]

There it was, Pitt's suddenly sprung offensive: a Britain quite alone, threatened by seemingly imminent and massive assault on her coasts and Irish flank, yet prepared to deploy a significant part of her limited resources upon an uncertain mission of merely persuasive intent, hopefully to draw the Continental powers into a Second Coalition. Put differently, a Mediterranean gamble for a new alliance against France was specifically to be entrusted to the 'peculiar' talents of Horatio Nelson.

British fears of assault across the near waters were entirely real since invasion remained the obsessive demand of the Directory. Napoleon had gone along with that by unhesitatingly accepting command of the Army of England. His own obsession, however, remained with venture to Egypt, and its grip on him had grown powerfully: 'If the success of a descent upon England appear doubtful, as I suspect it will, the Army of England shall become the Army of the East, and I go to Egypt.'

In February 1798 he toured the Channel and North Sea coast. His report to the Directory effectively squashed any immediate further thought of invasion across the Narrow Seas. Camperdown had ensured that. 'Whatever efforts we make,' Napoleon reported, 'we shall not for some years gain the naval supremacy. To invade England without that supremacy is the most daring and difficult task ever undertaken.' If such naval ascendancy continued to seem impossible, they should nevertheless be satisfied with keeping up the pretence of it, 'to exhaust them by ruinous preparations against expected descents on their southern coasts, on Ireland, and even on Scotland'. The alternatives to invasion, therefore, were either to concentrate on the Rhine, to deprive England of Hanover and Hamburg, or 'undertake an eastern expedition which would menace her trade with the Indies'.[4]

The Directory's hopes for a direct assault on Britain nevertheless remained tied to an invasion of Ireland in coordination with Wolf Tone and the Irish rebel organizations. The Egyptian expedition was, however, what Napoleon wanted and was determined to have. It required extended persuasion of a reluctant Directory but, financed by the looting of the treasuries of Switzerland and Rome, agreement for the Egyptian expedition was finally reached on 12 April 1798.

By then the aims of the expedition had been broadened into something new in the chronicles of colonial and mercantilist adventure. Not even Britain had ever set out with such a rashly comprehensive plan for power and enrichment that, with missionary zeal, would unite the hemispheres and their cultures. In Napoleon's immediate vision the British were to be excluded from all their possessions in the East. To facilitate that, a canal was to be cut across the isthmus of Suez, to ensure free and exclusive use of the Red Sea. Idealistically, in accord with the principles of the Revolution, he was to improve the living conditions of the people of Egypt. Good relations were to be maintained with the Porte, the governance of the Ottoman Empire, within the long view that ultimately Constantinople was to be seized and the Ottoman Empire overthrown to enable France 'to take Europe in the rear'. An impressive contingent of French savants was to accompany the expedition to bring back the arts, literature and science of Egypt and Mesopotamia. Malta was to be seized en route to Alexandria.

The organization and furnishing of the expedition was astonishing, a tribute to the disciplined functioning of the French army that had brilliantly emerged from the motivated but disorganized rabble that first Carnot then Hoche, Kléber and Napoleon had sorted out and moulded into the finest fighting force in Europe. An army of fifty-five thousand men and an armada of some four hundred sail assembled at Toulon, Genoa, Ajaccio and Civita Vecchia. The main force was at Toulon, where 130 transports were to embark seventeen thousand troops, as many sailors and marines, as well as hundreds of vehicles, horses and a vast quantity of artillery and ammunition. They would sail out of Toulon escorted by thirteen ships of the line, forty-two frigates as well as brigs and other naval vessels. The naval force was dominated by the 120-gun, three-deck *L'Orient* commanded by Vice Admiral François Brueys with Rear Admiral Ganteaume as captain of the fleet, the 80-gun *Franklin* under Rear Admiral Blanquet Du Chayla, the 80-gun *Guillaume Tell* under Rear Admiral Villeneuve and the 80-gun *Tonnant* under Commodore Du Petit-Thouars.

At dawn on 19 May, with Napoleon watching from the deck of *L'Orient*, this colossal armada began moving out of Toulon, to be joined at sea by the convoys from the other ports. To all of them, conscious of the heavy and apprehensive British preoccupation on the other side of the Continent, the sparkling blue sea before them, whipped by an unseasonable mistral, appeared reasonable declaration of unhindered passage ahead.

*   *   *

Nelson had joined St Vincent at the Tagus on 30 April. St Vincent of his own accord, even before receiving Spencer's instruction, had meanwhile decided on a Mediterranean incursion. Alarmed by what he already had heard of the preparations at Toulon he ordered Nelson to go down to Gibraltar and to take the ships he found there on a scouting mission to ascertain if he could find out the intended destination of the expedition.

On 2 May Nelson left Cadiz for Gibraltar. On the night of 3 May Napoleon left Paris for Toulon. Again, this one was to be uncannily close. There seems to be something like an affiliation between the positive dates of their lives and the critical moments in their history when they found themselves unwittingly close within the same frame. So it was with these dates, and would be even more so off Toulon within the month.

Nelson, 'elated beyond description' to be back in the Mediterranean, sailed from Gibraltar on 8 May accompanied by two 74s, *Orion* under Captain Sir James Saumarez and *Alexander* under Captain Alexander Ball, as well as two 32-gun frigates. They were off Cape Sicie, a headland near Toulon, on 17 May and captured a French corvette. Nelson personally interviewed the entire crew individually but all professed ignorance of the expedition's destination. He was variously told that the force would sail from Toulon in a few days or a fortnight.

As Napoleon sailed out of Toulon on the 19th, Nelson was still off Cape Sicie, practically at Toulon, a short distance just west of it. But the expedition's course was in the opposite direction, eastward along the Ligurian coast to pass between the mainland and Corsica. The next day, the 20th, the very mistral that had carried Napoleon's huge convoy away from Toulon gathered sudden violent force and struck Nelson's small group. His own ship, *Vanguard*, got the worst of it. She was progressively dismasted. The main topmast went overboard followed by the mizzen topmast. The foremast crashed in two pieces upon the forecastle. In this state they tried to ride a worsening gale for the next forty-eight hours. *Vanguard* was eventually taken in tow by *Alexander*. But the ordeal was far from over for, in trying to make for the Sardinian island of San Pietro, heavy swell was driving them towards the shore. The situation looked so hopeless that at one point Nelson ordered *Alexander* to drop the tow and leave *Vanguard* to her fate rather than lose two ships. Captain Ball ignored the order and the ships eventually made the harbour of San Pietro. There they were told that, since Sardinia had a neutrality pact with France, they had to remove themselves as soon as possible.

With no help from the shore, *Vanguard* was refitted in four days. *Alexander* and *Orion* had ridden the storm without serious damage. All the ships fell to in fixing *Vanguard*. 'If the ship had been in England, months would have been taken to send her to sea,' Nelson wrote to his wife; 'here my operations will not be delayed four days . . . Vanguard is fitted tolerably for sea . . . We are all health and good humour.'

There was no possibility of masts of proper size. A main topmast had to serve as a foremast and a topgallant mast as topmast. As *Vanguard* sailed unusually well Nelson saw all of that as sufficient to allow his search to continue instead of falling back down to Gibraltar for more serious repairs.

It was another of those smaller episodes of memorable effort that marked the less publicized but no less dramatic side of Nelson's career. The resilience, skill, resourcefulness, spirit and determination of this event say a lot not only about Nelson and his captains and men, but of that whole navy in its day. All of it was the commonplace of survival, what sailors expected of one another aboard their easily broken vessels in situations where the worst looked imminent, where succour lacked credence, where there was only makeshift and themselves.[5]

Meanwhile, St Vincent at the Tagus had, on 19 May, received First Lord Spencer's instructions on despatching a Mediterranean fleet. He was told as well to expect a reinforcement for his own squadron to make up for the ships he would allocate to Nelson. He immediately put together the necessary squadron. It was a historic moment, this full return of Britain into the Mediterranean, and St Vincent was highly conscious of it. Nelson could not have done better than St Vincent then did on his behalf in picking the sort of men that Nelson would want on such a mission, several of them being his closest friends. St Vincent picked out ten sail of the line to form, with the three ships already with Nelson, a fleet of thirteen 74s. Also joining would be the 50-gun *Leander*, Captain Thomson. The brig *Mutine*, captained by Nelson's old friend Thomas Hardy, was sent off at once to carry the news to Nelson.

On 28 May, while still at San Pietro, Nelson learned that Napoleon had sailed from Toulon, though the destination and course of his fleet remained unknown. With repairs to *Vanguard* completed he sailed to a fixed rendezvous that had been agreed for reunion in the event of the division being scattered. There he expected to find his four frigates waiting. On 4 June Nelson was at the rendezvous. No frigates in sight. The next day, still waiting, perplexed at the absence of his ships, Nelson had a joyful surprise of *Mutine* arriving with St Vincent's instructions, and the news that the fleet he was to command would soon be with him. Hardy also brought news of Nelson's frigates. On his way up from the Straits he had run in with them and been told that they were returning to Gibraltar. The senior frigate captain, George Hope, had assumed that *Vanguard* was so badly wrecked that Nelson would take her to Gibraltar for lay-up and repair. 'I thought that Hope would have known me better,' Nelson said, a bitter dismissal. The frigates were never to rejoin him, a woeful disadvantage through the many weeks ahead.[6]

Hardy also brought 'Additional Instructions' that St Vincent had received from Admiralty. Nelson could never have supposed such a sweeping assignment, such licence to hunt, as he now possessed. This intelligence was received, said his captain, Edward Berry, 'with universal joy throughout our little squadron'. The Mediterranean was theirs to track as freely as necessitated from one end to the other and up all its adjacent parts, such as Adriatic, the Greek archipelago and even into the Black Sea should the destination of the French expedition 'be to any of those parts'. They were to remain on this commission as long as their supplies lasted or at any rate as long as they could obtain provisions from any of the ports in the Mediterranean. With regard to the latter, they should at least try and draw on the Tuscan ports, Naples, Sicily, Malta, Venice and the Ottoman ports. There was good reason to believe that they would be received with goodwill at all the principal ports of Barbary, Algiers, Tunis and Tripoli.

That was all very well but no one could yet surmise where the expedition was headed for. Every possibility was proposed, except the actual one. Was it for an attack on Naples and Sicily, the conveyance of the army to Spain for marching upon Portugal, or was it bound for the Straits, with Ireland as its ultimate destination? Egypt and the Levant appear to have occurred to no one, until Nelson would hit upon it. British intelligence had never been so poor. Something should have been picked up in Paris. But, with so little to go on, Nelson was the one person not to be fazed. To St Vincent he wrote, 'You may be assured I will fight them the moment I can reach, be they at anchor or under sail.'

Two days later, on 5 June, the new squadron showed up: Captains Troubridge of *Culloden*, Miller of *Theseus*, Hood of *Zealous*, Foley of *Goliath*, Darby of *Bellerophon*, Louis of *Minotaur*, Peyton of *Defence*, Gould of *Audacious*, Westcott of *Majestic* and Hallowell of *Swiftsure*.

The one good friend missing from among the new arrivals was the oldest friend of all, Cuthbert Collingwood, who remained with the blockade off Cadiz. 'Our good chief has found occupation for me,' he wrote in a bitter letter to Nelson; 'he has sent me to cruise off San Lucar, to stop the Spanish boats which carry cabbages to Cadiz. Oh humiliation! If I did not feel that I had not deserved such treatment, if I did not say to myself, that the caprices of power could never lower me in the eyes of honourable men, I think I should have died of indignation.'

After nearly two years Britain was back in the Mediterranean, with the most effective and assured fleet she had ever had there. Its purpose, the biggest naval chase yet witnessed on that sea, was therefore now on, starting this day, 5 June. But without his wide-ranging scouting destroyers Nelson was seriously hampered in the pace of his pursuit, dependent instead upon the slower *Mutine* to forage forward for intelligence along the Ligurian coast. Lack of the destroyers was a drawback that made the entire mission more difficult, frustrating and exhausting, with the fleet's course a matter of continual supposition and guesswork based upon scanty intelligence gleaned from ships encountered along the way. Here once more, in fullest example, was Julian Corbett's definition of the strategical character of war at sea, the far-reaching fact that, apart from the enemy's ability to remove his fleet from the board altogether, there was nothing on the face of the sea itself to assist in locating the enemy and determining his movements. Passing or captured vessels had to be the main form of intelligence, short of a sighting. His scouting frigates had been Nelson's principal means for both, for a ranging interrogation of commerce or an actual sighting.

The first positive report Nelson got of the French fleet was accompanied by an immediate example of the astonishing swiftness of the deductive ability he possessed.

On 14 June a Tunisian cruiser told him that the French fleet had been sighted off Trapani on 4 June at the north-west end of Sicily, steering to the eastward. 'If they pass Sicily,' Nelson reported in a letter to Spencer on 15 June, 'I shall believe they are going on their scheme of possessing Alexandria, and getting troops to India – a plan concerted with Tippoo Saib, by no means so difficult as might at first view be imagined.' Tippoo Sahib was the powerful Sultan of Mysore, hostile to the British presence in India. Nelson's was the first proper insight into where Napoleon might be heading. It was a conviction that grew on him.[7]

Nelson sent Troubridge to Naples to ask Sir William Hamilton, the British minister at the Neapolitan Court, to find out how much aid the fleet could expect. He especially wanted Neapolitan frigates if available, and pilots for Sicilian waters. On 17 June the squadron hove to ten miles off Naples. Troubridge boarded with news that the French were off Malta with the intention of attacking it and that the Neapolitan government was in dire fear of French retaliation if they assisted the English. Naples would reluctantly provide supplies *sub rosa* (secretly) but nothing else.

As *Vanguard* bore away for Malta Nelson expressed his indignation over the Neapolitan timidity to Hamilton: 'Here we are, and are ready, and will shed our blood in preventing the French from ill-treating them. On arrival of the king's fleet I find plenty of goodwill towards us, with every hatred towards the French; but no assistance for us . . . On the contrary the French minister is allowed to send off vessels to inform the fleet of my arrival, force, and destination, that instead of surprising them, they may be prepared for resistance.'

On the 20th, passing Messina, the British consul there boarded *Vanguard* and told Nelson that Malta had surrendered on the 15th. The squadron continued close inshore towards Syracuse in case the French might be there. At daylight on the 22nd, off Cape Passaro, the south-eastern point of the island, they sighted two French frigates. It was for Nelson the most aggravating moment he had yet suffered, soured anew by the absence of his own frigates. 'All my ill fortune, hitherto, has resulted from want of frigates,' he wrote to St Vincent in relating the incident. 'These would have fallen to me if I had had frigates.' He had been unwilling to break his squadron for a chase after the French frigates, thereby losing time when they were flying to Malta, expecting within twenty-four hours to be engaged with the main French fleet. But that same morning they spoke to a Genoese brig that had sailed from Malta the day before. The master confirmed that Malta had surrendered on the 15th and the French fleet had sailed the next day, leaving a garrison behind with the French flag flying.

The high elation of anticipation that had seemed to be carrying them forward as much as the very wind itself was instantly deflated. So where were the French now? How could such a huge enterprise covering many square miles of the sea prove so elusive? The best clue came from the prevailing wind, which was blowing steadily from the north-west. After leaving Malta the French fleet was seen running before the wind. Spain was thus instantly ruled out. With such a huge expedition it would have been difficult suddenly to put it about and head westwards. The management of such an operation with such a vast armada could only have brought chaos. What point anyway when they had already come halfway down the Mediterranean and were driving steadily eastwards? Sicily was also ruled out. Whatever the French objective, it therefore clearly had to be somewhere in the eastern Mediterranean. Egypt or Constantinople?

Nelson was now convinced that it was Egypt. Four captains in whom he placed particular confidence – Saumarez, Troubridge, Ball and Darby – were summoned to *Vanguard* to present their opinions. Saumarez reflected Nelson's own belief, '. . . under all circumstances I think it most conducive to the good of His Majesty's service to make the best of our way for Alexandria, as the only means of saving our possessions in India, should the French armament be destined for that country'.[8]

Returning to his ship, *Orion*, Saumarez set down the weight of the frustration and responsibility that lay upon them all, but upon Nelson especially:

I am just returned from on board the Admiral and we are crowding sail for Alexandria; but the contrast to what we experienced yesterday is great indeed, having made sure of attacking them this morning. At present it is very doubtful whether we shall fall in with them at all, as we are proceeding upon the merest conjecture only, and not on any positive information. Some days must now elapse before we can be relieved from our cruel suspense; and if, at the end of our journey, we find we are upon a wrong scent, our embarrassment will be great indeed. Fortunately, I only act here *en second*; but did the chief responsibility rest with me, I fear it would be more than my too irritable nerves would bear.[9]

Here was quieter testimony to Nelson's greatness, a subdued tribute to what could be expected of him above the others in bearing such a responsibility in such a bewildering maze, where weaker ones might flag or desist.

Nelson was the more conscious of what lay upon him for his appointment had raised extreme ire among some in the navy. In selecting him St Vincent had passed over two senior officers attached to the Cadiz fleet, Sir William Parker and Sir John Orde, both of whom took violent umbrage at being superseded by a junior for such an important command. Orde was second in command to St Vincent. His reaction, therefore, was particularly violent, seeing it as a breach of standing naval etiquette. He promptly challenged St Vincent to a duel whensoever the opportunity would present itself. It was the second duel provoked by this sharpened focus upon the navy. Pitt, too, had been challenged when, in May, as St Vincent's instructions sailed out to him, the Prime Minister brought in a bill for the more effectual manning of the navy. When a member of the opposition, George Tierney, declared it precipitate, Pitt accused him of a desire to obstruct the defence of the country. When Pitt refused to retract Tierney challenged him for the very next day. Pitt accepted and they met on Putney Heath. They twice fired without effect. The seconds then intervened. It was an extraordinary episode that provoked consternation with the public, George III among the most irate, all astonished that the Prime Minister should take such a risk at one of the most dangerous and critical moments of the war when everything depended upon him. Meanwhile, Nelson himself was being mocked by those who questioned his entitlement to the command, or who jealously envied his reputation. St Vincent wrote to him: 'Sir William Parker and Sir John Orde have written strong remonstrances against your commanding the detached squadron instead of them. I did all I could to prevent it, consistent with my situation, but there is a faction, fraught with all manner of ill-will to you, that, unfortunately for the two Baronets, domined over any argument or influence I could use: they will both be ordered home the moment their letters arrive.'[10] And, as another admiral supportive of Nelson wrote to him, '. . . how often have I been questioned: "What is your favourite hero about? The French fleet has passed under his nose," etc. etc.'[11] The latter type of derision was, of course, a familiar manifestation when any particular naval operation appeared to be inconclusive, prolonged without decisive resolution. It was a national impatience that can seem to have been blinded to the limitations of sail with its cruel vagaries of weather, the long calms and extended gales, as well as the spaced emptiness that Corbett, a century later, would recognize as the sea's strategic deficiency. For Nelson this special and favoured command given to him in preference to others therefore made the weight of their lack of success so much the heavier at that council aboard *Vanguard* on 22 June. And the fears and doubts could only intensify as they bore on for Alexandria.

The French fleet had sailed from Malta on the 19th, not the 16th as they had been told, which meant that they were close. So close that they in fact passed one another that very night of the 22nd in thick haze, with Brueys hearing the signal guns of the British squadron. Had Nelson had his scouting frigates they would probably have sighted the French then or the following day. But the British fleet itself, sailing in close order in hazy weather and on its steady bearing for Alexandria, had little possibility of chance encounter, particularly since Brueys was on a bearing for Crete, so that the gap between them widened to around one hundred miles. Nelson was on the shorter, direct passage.

On 26 June Nelson sent *Mutine* ahead, a single ship being able to move more quickly than a close-sailing squadron tied to the speed of its slowest vessel. Hardy carried a letter to George Baldwin, British consul at Alexandria, asking for news of any French preparation in Egypt 'to fix themselves at the head of the Red Sea, in order to get a formidable army into India; and, in concert with Tippoo Saib, to drive us, if possible from India'. *Mutine* sailed into Alexandria on the 27th. Unfortunately Baldwin was away. The Mameluke governor had heard of the French capture of Malta and the city was preparing its defences. Hardy was first assumed to be a Frenchman. Identifying himself as British made no difference: he was told to go away. British presence was as little wanted as French. Nelson arrived the next day, to survey a harbour occupied only by Turkish vessels and to suffer what right then looked like the crowning disillusionment of his career. The shock was brutal. The mark of it was to be forever with him, as he subsequently admitted.

The dilemma of where the French were was now even greater than on the 22nd. Where, then, had they gone after sailing from Malta? Nelson immediately feared again for Sicily. They sailed from Alexandria on the 29th and beat steadily westward against the northwesterly that had carried them so effortlessly eastward, this time with the squadron occasionally scattered when the wind turned to gale. Why did he not merely wait another day or so? His anguished desperation simply would not allow it.

On the day that Nelson arrived at Alexandria Napoleon's troops, in preparation for landing, listened to a proclamation read out to them, with injunctions on how to behave in the land where they were going. It was a declaration that retains resonance in the twenty-first century:

You are about to undertake a conquest whose effects on the world's civilization and trade are incalculable . . . We shall make some wearisome marches; we shall fight a few battles; we shall succeed in all our enterprises; destiny is for us . . . The Mameluke Beys, who exclusively favour English trade . . . and who are tyrannizing over the unhappy people of the Nile valley, will cease to exist a few days after our landing.

The people with whom we shall live are Mohammedans. Their chief creed is this: 'There is no God but God and Mohammed is his Prophet'.

Do not contradict them. Act towards them as in the past you have acted toward the Jews and the Italians. Respect their muftis and imams, as you have respected the rabbis and bishops. Show the same tolerance towards the ceremonies prescribed by the Koran and towards the mosques as you have shown toward the convents and synagogues, towards the religions of Moses and of Jesus Christ.[12]

Two days later, on 1 July, Napoleon's armada anchored off Alexandria and the people there 'when they looked at the horizon, could no longer see water, but only sky and ships: they were seized by an unimaginable terror'.[13]

Aware that a British fleet was hunting for him, to avoid risking his army on the water Napoleon swiftly put them ashore at Marabout near Alexandria, which he then seized on 2 July. With General Kléber left in command there, Napoleon left on the night of 4 July to march across the desert to Cairo, with General Menou assigned to capture Rosetta and descend to Cairo by a flotilla of boats on the Nile.

After a desert march of new and terrible hardships unlike anything the soldiers had been led to expect, thirst in particular since the Bedouin filled the wells with stones, Napoleon reached the Pyramids on 21 July and there fought the first great battle of this, the first secular western Crusade, before he entered Cairo.

The great French fleet had required a safe base after the troops and equipment were landed. On 3 July, as he prepared for his advance upon Cairo, Napoleon told Admiral Brueys to decide whether 'the squadron can enter the port of Alexandria, or whether in Aboukir Roads, bringing its broadside to bear, it can defend itself against the enemy's superior force; and in case both these plans should be impracticable, he must sail for Corfu . . .'.

Brueys had taken soundings at the narrow entrance of the Old Port and he and his captain, Casabianca, considered that the entrance was too shallow. Apart from the risk of stranding in the channel there was also the possibility of it being blocked by the enemy, trapping the fleet inside. Brueys, with an active desire to remain close to hand in the event of a need for the squadron, decided on Aboukir Bay, where he anchored his fleet on 7 July. He believed that he could create a defensible position at Aboukir, and be ready to fight at anchor if necessary. The option of proceeding to Corfu therefore fell away.

On 18 July Nelson's squadron was back off Cape Passaro and on the 19th anchored at Syracuse. He sat weighted by the empty sense of failure. 'Do not fret at anything,' he was later to say to Troubridge. 'I wish I never had, but my return to Syracuse in 1798, broke my heart, which on any extraordinary anxiety now shows itself, be that feeling pain or pleasure . . . More people, perhaps, die of broken hearts than we are aware of.'

On 20 July at Syracuse Nelson sat down to write one of the most plain-tive letters of his life on what had passed. To St Vincent he said, 'Yesterday I arrived here, where I can learn no more than vague conjecture that the French are gone eastward. Every moment I have to regret the frigates having left me, to which must be attributed my ignorance of the movements of the enemy . . . I feel that I have the zeal and activity to do credit to your appointment, and yet to be unsuccessful hurts me most sensibly. But if they are above water, I will find them out, and if possible bring them to battle. You have done your part in giving me so fine a fleet, and I hope to do mine in making use of them.' To Sir William Hamilton he wrote, 'All my ill fortune, hitherto, has proceeded from want of Frigates . . . You will, I am sure, and so will our Country, easily conceive what has passed in my anxious mind, but I have this comfort, that I have no fault to accuse myself of. This bears me up, and this only.' And to his wife, 'Glory is my object, and that alone.'

As ever, through all of it, his mind was on the welfare of his men, declaring to Hamilton that the provisions he was fighting to get from the Sicilians had to be of the best quality or he would not take them, 'for, as no fleet has more fag than this, nothing but the best food and greatest atten-tion can keep them healthy. At this moment, we have not one sick man in the fleet.' But the Hamiltons, Sir William and Emma, stretched all the influence they possessed to ensure that he got what he wanted.

On 25 July they were on their way again from Syracuse, towards the Greek archipelago. Three days later Troubridge was sent inshore in the Gulf of Messina and, off the small port of Koroni, captured a French brig laden with wine. But he brought back a bigger prize in the news that four weeks earlier Buonaparte's armada had been seen steering south-eastwards of Crete: for Egypt obviously. They got the same news later that day from a vessel they spoke to. And so, four days on, 1 August, they were back approaching Alexandria. Two of the ships, *Alexander* and *Swiftsure*, now served as scouts. They were the first off the port. They saw the transports, the tricolour everywhere. But no battlefleet. So the main squadron followed the coast eastwards with Hood's *Zealous* and Foley's *Goliath* in the van.

And, almost simultaneously aboard both ships, lookouts cried sight of the fleet lying at Aboukir. 'The utmost joy seemed to animate every breast at sight of the enemy,' Edward Berry said, and especially noted Nelson's vibrant relief. It was four in the afternoon of that hot summer's day. The sun would soon slant into its blazing descent, but for all who stood there looking at the French mastheads it might just as well have been the fresh start of day.

XIX

NILE

THE Bay of Aboukir was a great shallow indentation some eighteen miles across lying between Alexandria and the Rosetta mouth of the Nile. It was a placid expanse of water that offered some shelter from the prevailing north-west summer wind. At the western end of the open roadstead was Aboukir Point, which held a fort. Across from that was the small island of Aboukir. Wide though it appeared, Aboukir Bay was a dangerously deceiving inroad from the sea for, like everywhere else in that great estuary, it was mainly shoal water, highly dangerous for any unfamiliar with its shifting sandy depths.

The four-fathom line ran virtually across the middle of the roadstead, three miles from the beach, and it was just off that concave line that Admiral Brueys had anchored his ships at the western end of the bay. Only along the four-fathom line did the soundings guarantee safe anchorage. But the great distance to the beach across the inner shoal meant heavy, constant labour for the ships' boats ferrying water and supplies.

The van ships were close to the four-fathom line, in five fathoms of water, the centre and rear ships in deeper water. The five van ships, *Guerrier, Conquérant, Spartiate, Aquilon* and *Peuple Souverain* were all 74s. Between these and the rear lay the forbiddingly powerful centre composed of, in sequence of line, the 80-gun *Franklin*, 120-gun *L'Orient* and 80-gun *Tonnant*. The five ships of the rear were *L'Heureux, Mercure,* and *Timoleon,* 74s, the 80-gun *Guillaume Tell,* and *Généreux,* a 74.

The distance between Brueys's ships was considerable, about one hundred and sixty yards, making the whole line about a mile and three-quarters long across the bay. The principal weakness was that it left gaps too wide between the ships, thus allowing an enemy to pass between. They should have been lying nearer to the shoal to ensure that there was little room for a passage between their lee and the shoal, thereby preventing an enemy from getting on both sides of his ships. They also had no springs on their cables, the rope system that would have enabled them to turn broadside in the direction they wished if called upon to fight at anchor.

Apart from those obvious and serious defects, Brueys believed that he was in the best possible defensible position. His van ships were close to the outer shoal that encircled Aboukir Island at the western approach to the bay. Brueys regarded that seaward-extending outer shoal as sufficient deterrent to any attack on his van since oncoming ships could round Aboukir Island only with the greatest caution. He therefore expected any attack to be laid against his centre and rear. And since the van ships lay headed into the prevailing north-west wind it meant that they could easily fall back down the line to help the centre or rear if required.

Brueys had intended to correct the several serious faults in his line, particularly to have cable taken from ship to ship to prevent the enemy from passing between. Drawn closer they would have offered a formidable broadside of five hundred guns. But the ships' boats were necessary for the task. Their constant use to and from the shore had delayed it all. Neither that nor any other improvement had been effected by the close of that hot summer's day of 1 August 1798, as Nelson's squadron closed with Aboukir Bay. And there was little chance for last-minute effort when, at two o'clock that afternoon, one of the rear ships of the French line, *L'Heureux*, signalled that a fleet of ships of war was in sight from the masthead, standing west-north-west of Aboukir. Surprise was total since Brueys had failed to post any of his four frigates on lookout off the coast. His shortage of sailors for work parties was probably one reason for that.

Brueys had found himself in a difficult situation from the start because of a demand by Napoleon that the fleet unload all its own stores for use by the land army and instead victual itself from the shore. All the French ships therefore constantly had a large part of their crews on shore, digging wells and drawing water, with strong marine guard to protect them against Bedouin. Others were occupied transporting water and supplies in the ships' boats across the wide expanse of shoal water. On 1 August several hundred sailors had gone to Alexandria and Rosetta to buy rice and wheat. Altogether an estimated 20 to 30 per cent of the crews were ashore. Brueys's health, understandably, had begun to deteriorate under these insecurities, aggravated by dysentery.

As it bore down on Aboukir Bay Nelson's main force consisted of ten 74s, his flagship *Vanguard*, *Minotaur*, *Audacious*, *Defence*, *Zealous*, *Orion*, *Goliath*, *Majestic*, *Bellerophon* and *Theseus*. Two other 74s, *Alexander* and *Swiftsure*, had been sent to cruise as lookout ships while another, *Culloden*, had fallen behind because of towing a prize. Accompanying the 74s was the 50-gun ship *Leander*. First sight of the French fleet came from *Zealous* at four p.m. At five the main force, running strongly before the fresh north-west wind, hauled up to round Aboukir Island and the wide shoal that encircled it. The van of Brueys's line lay moored just a mile and a half off from the British as they came up to the island.

Nelson had no maps or charts of Aboukir other than a rough diagram obtained aboard a prize merchantman. But to the perceptive eye there would have been a great deal to suggest the dangers of those waters, a line of breakers between Aboukir Point and Aboukir Island declaring the presence of reef, and the three-mile expanse of water between the French line and the shore providing clear indication of the limits of navigable depth. The French line itself, with its obtuse curve beyond the centre towards the rear, seemed to trace the very edge of the shoal.

As he came up to it, however, Nelson approached Aboukir with that combination of foresight, tactical intuition and hard resolve unique to him.

One of the most celebrated features of Nelson's distinction as commander was his intensive instruction to his captains on what he had in mind for any action. Broad strategy and tactical manoeuvre were exhaustively projected upon whatever scene and circumstances could be in prospect. No aspect of a potential action was ignored or overlooked. It was a rigorous drill that left an insight into the genius of that marshalled mind that stayed with those exposed to it perhaps more forcefully than anything else about him. For it was the seed of whatever good fortune they shared with him. It became the masterful guide within their own careers. In battle itself it was the basis of their confidence and trust. In Nelson's scheme of things no man could ever feel alone. It was, therefore, the basis not merely of their admiration but also of their love. Upon that bond rested the very concept of Nelson and his 'band of brothers'. Aboukir would demonstrate all of that more powerfully, more necessarily, than any other of Nelson's great actions.

As Nelson's squadron ranged in chase to and fro across the Mediterranean, whenever weather and circumstances allowed he called every captain in his squadron to his flagship *Vanguard* where, as his captain, Edward Berry, described it, 'he would fully develop to them his own ideas of different and best modes of attack, and such plans as he proposed to execute upon falling in with the enemy, whatever their position or situation might be, by night or day'. There was no possible position or advantageous form of attack that Nelson had not digested and taken into his calculation, Berry said in his narrative account of the Battle of the Nile: 'With the masterly ideas of their admiral, therefore, on the subject of naval tactics, every one of the captains of his squadron was most thoroughly acquainted; and upon surveying the situation of the enemy, they could ascertain with precision what were the ideas and intentions of their commander, without the aid of any further instructions; by which means signals became almost unnecessary.'

The most remarkable aspect of that preparation was his calculation, two months before Aboukir, that among all the possibilities which might confront him at some point was that of fighting a battle at anchor, an unfamiliar occurrence in the then history of naval warfare. But the American War had provided example of action involving anchored squadrons. At the island of St Kitts in 1782 Hood had contemplated tactical attack on an anchored de Grasse squadron on the night of 25 January, but had lost his surprise. The very next day he found himself in the reverse situation, himself moored awaiting attack from de Grasse.

Nelson's mind carried a compendium of every tactic or strategy of significance in naval history from which he constantly drew for caution or instruction. He naturally sought illumination mainly from the past century and a half of developed naval activity, but looked especially to his own foundation experience, the American War.

From that episode at St Kitts in 1782 Nelson had drawn up his own plan for an attack at anchor, which he had minutely and precisely outlined to his captains two months before the arrival off Aboukir Bay, long before there could have been any remote idea of fighting there or in a place like it. His plan was distinct from the previous example at St Kitts. The principle of Nelson's own tactic was for his ships to anchor by the stern, broadside to broadside alongside the enemy's moored vessels. That, according to the naval historian Brenton, was to be the first time recorded in the naval history of Great Britain of preparing to fight anchored by the stern: 'His object in doing this was to deprive the enemy of the advantage of raking him, as he would have swung round and exposed the bow, or the stern of his vessels, had he brought up in the usual way.' To prepare for it, cables were passed out of the stern ports, carried along the side, and bent to the anchors, with a spring on the anchor cable and one topsail loose to be able to shift position in case of need.

The fierce sun was in its final glaring descent when, at five thirty, off Aboukir Island shoal, Nelson ordered his ships to form line of battle. The French line lay vividly presented to them against the setting sun as they came round the island in a wide loop. As the British approached the outer shoal the French sought to decoy them into its shallows by sending two brigs towards Aboukir Island. But the British lead ships *Zealous* and *Goliath* had been making soundings as they cautiously stood in and the ruse failed. So expertly was the British rounding of the shoal accomplished that the French were convinced Nelson had experienced pilots on board, '. . . as he did not pay any attention to the brig's track, but allowed her to go away: he handled well round all the dangers'.

'We hoped to have deceived the enemy but he was not to be misled,' Rear Admiral Villeneuve of the 80-gun *Guillaume Tell* later said, with the further observation that 'to see and to attack us was the affair of the moment'. Or, as Berry wrote, 'The Admiral viewed the obstacles with the eye of a seaman DETERMINED ON ATTACK.'

Nelson hailed Samuel Hood of *Zealous* to ask if they were already far enough eastward of the Aboukir Island shoal to clear it. Hood replied that *Zealous* was in eleven fathoms and would press ahead with soundings to provide a clear approach for the rest of the line. This *Zealous* and Captain Thomas Foley in *Goliath* proceeded to do, drawing the squadron into the five-fathom water where the French lay.

As they moved towards the French line all ships in the squadron prepared to go to action at anchor, with men aloft furling sails or at the stern preparing the anchor and springs there, ready for when each ship drew alongside its moored opponent. Nelson, making his observations, overheard two sailors talking at a gun near him. 'Damn them, look at them,' one said. 'There they are, Jack, if we don't beat them, they will beat us.'

Mahan, always succinct, provides a neat summation of that approach: 'The proceedings of the British fleet, under its leader, show an instructive combination of rapidity and caution, of quick comprehension of the situation, with an absence of all precipitation; no haste incompatible with perfect carefulness, no time lost, either by hesitation or by preparations postponed.'

On sight of the French fleet Nelson was driven by that powerful element of the reckless so deep set in his character, that overriding impulse that made the possibility of action impossible to resist, regardless of obvious risk. On the face of it Aboukir Bay represented a gigantic gamble. Rounding the Aboukir Island outer shoal was immediately the greatest danger, soon to be proven when *Culloden* ran hard aground. Taking it on that alone, it must be doubted that anyone else would ever have done what Nelson proceeded to do: go for such a powerful quarry at that hour, with the sun in fast descent and the shadows drawing in over perilously shallow waters. The risk of it he himself eventually came to admit, '. . . but I knew my captains'. In any event, after the bitter dead ends suffered in the chase any hesitation here, whatever the difficulties, was unlikely.

The dangers of rounding the Aboukir Island shoal to make attack was of course what Brueys had counted upon in laying out his line, with the strength of metal placed at the centre and the rear, where he expected attack. Brueys had seen his position as an absolutely sound one, with his van ships lying head to the prevailing wind, thus able to fall back to the assistance of the centre and rear ships if they required it. But it was with the same sense of facility on that very wind that Nelson's squadron was riding down so effortlessly and directly upon those van ships, now the most vulnerable.

There was deep unease, therefore, when the mast-head lookout on *L'Heureux* reported a fleet in sight early that afternoon, so many of the squadron's men being ashore with small hope of having them back on board in time. An immediate signal for their return was sent from the flagship but it had to be hours before they could all be back. In the event, only a fraction of them returned.

The absence of the boats meant that urgent attempts to draw the ships closer with cables between them and springs to enable them to manoeuvre their broadsides when required could not be fully accomplished. Nevertheless, the French considered that the superior force of their own fleet was more than capable of coping with what they saw bearing down upon them: ten 74s sighted against nine French 74s, the 120-gun flagship and three 80-gun three-deckers. Their deficiency was in the experience and discipline of the crews 'composed of men picked up at hazard, and almost at the moment of sailing'. The majority were said to be around eighteen or under. The situation had been plaintively outlined from the flagship by Rear Admiral Ganteaume to the Minister of Marine on 9 July: 'Our crews are very weak, both in numbers and the quality of the men: our ships are, in general, ill-armed; and I think it requires considerable courage to undertake command of ships so ill-fitted.'

An hour after the sighting of the distant fleet Brueys no longer had any doubt that it was the British. At three p.m. he ordered the hammocks to be stowed for action. But the urgent question at the council called aboard his flagship *L'Orient* was whether they should fight under sail. Rear Admiral Blanquet Du Chayla of the 80-gun *Franklin* was in favour, supported by Commodore Du Petit-Thouars of the 80-gun *Tonnant*. Their belief was that the superior strength of the French fleet held the sure advantage in meeting the British out at sea. But the rest were against it. With so many men ashore Brueys himself felt that he did not have enough men to engage under sail. The notion of perhaps getting the fleet to sea nevertheless lingered and at five p.m. Brueys actually directed that the topgallant yards be sent up and squared, a preliminary to getting a ship under weigh. In doing so Brueys was clinging to a new hope that, with the day fast fading, the British might defer their attack until morning. In that event Brueys saw a chance of getting to sea in darkness, thereby either meeting the enemy on the open water or avoiding battle. But the British were then seen to be forming line off Aboukir Island and Brueys recognized that they intended to attack at once. And at five-thirty p.m., as Nelson had already done, Brueys too signalled that he intended engaging the enemy at anchor.

Nelson's plan of battle had declared itself the moment he had full clear view of the French line, widely spaced on single anchor. 'By attacking the enemy's van and centre, the wind blowing directly along their line, I was enabled to throw what force I pleased on a few ships. This plan my friends readily conceived by the signals.'

His captains had firmly in mind at this moment an important injunction that Nelson had stressed to them, 'that where there was room for an enemy's ship to swing, there was room for one of ours to anchor'. Brueys, by failing to lay his line of ships closer along the edge of the shoal, had left them free to swing. Nelson and his captains were thus free to engage on both sides of the French line.

Of that benefit Foley in *Goliath* took immediate advantage.

At 6.20, as *Goliath* and *Zealous* approached the French line, the van ships *Guerrier* and *Conquérant* opened fire on them. *Goliath* and *Zealous* were some distance ahead of the rest of the squadron. Just ahead of *Zealous*, as *Goliath* advanced upon the French van ship *Guerrier*, Foley saw that there was depth for him to pass between the shore and the inside of the French line. He passed *Guerrier* on the inside, intending to anchor beside her. But when the anchor hung and failed to drop on time he passed on to the next ship in the line, *Conquérant*, and laid himself beside her. *Zealous*, close behind, anchored beside *Guerrier*. The next three ships in the British line, *Orion*, *Theseus* and *Audacious*, also followed on the inside of the French line to anchor and engage with *Spartiate*, *Aquilon* and *Peuple Souverain*.

Nelson in *Vanguard* had dropped to sixth place in his line, but instead of following his lead ships on the inside he took *Vanguard* down on the outside, the seaward side, and laid her close to the third French ship, *Spartiate*, which was already engaged with *Theseus*. Nelson was followed on the outside of the French line by *Minotaur* engaging *Aquilon* and *Defence* athwart *Peuple Souverain*. *Bellerophon* found itself in the toughest situation, abreast of the 120-gun *L'Orient*. *Majestic* engaged *Mercure*.

From the outset the British line had 'doubled' on the French line, engaging it on both sides. Foley had led the way to that. He had promptly exercised that full liberty that Nelson allowed his commanders of making their own tactical decision if they saw advantageous opportunity within an agreed plan of battle. The fact that four other ships unhesitatingly followed when he took *Goliath* down the inside of the French line was further demonstration of the latitude that all knew to be theirs, should they see the advantage of it.

For Brueys the fate of his fleet was practically sealed at the outset, for what he had assumed to be his strength became his weakness. His most powerful ships were lying from the centre to the rear. He had placed them there on the reasonable assumption that that was where the main thrust of any attack would come. But as the battle began it raged fiercely down from the van to the centre of the French line, with the rear five ships, including two of the 80-guns, outside the action.

The full force of action began at six thirty. Some of the British ships came broadside to broadside with their antagonists, others engaged with two ships simultaneously, lying on the quarter of one and the bow of another. In this cruel intimacy they poured shot and musket fire upon one another along the lee side of the French line while *Vanguard* and the others on the seaward side of the line similarly ranged alongside their opponents.

The night was closing in as these preliminary actions began. By seven it was dark, though in such an exploding scene dark was relative.

For such close combat Nelson had ordered his ships to hoist four lanterns horizontally arranged for easy recognition. Instead of his Admiral's Blue, which would be difficult to see in the dark, the White Ensign was hoisted.

Fifteen minutes after the action began *Guerrier* had lost all her masts from broadsides poured into her by *Zealous*, *Orion* and *Theseus*, but her furious resistance continued for another two hours. So it went with the rest of Brueys's van ships, *Conquérant*, *Spartiate*, *Peuple Souverain* and *Aquilon*, though *Conquérant* was compelled to strike after fifteen minutes. The others, like *Guerrier*, fought resolutely through those first two hours, seemingly blinded to the mounting destruction and carnage by the ferocity of their determination to hold out. The loss of life was severe, including two of the commanders. In these actions the British suffered much more lightly. Where *Guerrier* lost half her complement killed or wounded, her opponent *Zealous* had only seven men wounded.

Vanguard had suffered more than the five lead ships that had preceded her into action. She had been under simultaneous fire from *Spartiate* and *Aquilon*, with thirty killed and seventy-six wounded; among whom was Nelson himself.

Nelson was on the quarterdeck when a metal splinter struck him on the forehead. The skin fell over his good eye, which was blinded by the rush of blood. He cried out, 'I am killed. Remember me to my wife!' He was falling but Edward Berry caught him in his arms. When carried to the cockpit he refused to be attended to before the other injured had been seen to. In searing pain from what seemed a broken head, he remained convinced that his wound was mortal, but the surgeon examined him and assured that it was not. He was nevertheless totally incapacitated.

Nelson had launched his attack with his squadron short of three of its 74s. *Culloden*, commanded by Troubridge, had been held back by the prize it was towing. The scout ships *Swiftsure* and *Alexander* had been summoned from their station and were making for Aboukir. *Culloden* discarded its tow but unfortunately ran aground on the Aboukir Island shoal shortly after the action began, suffering the fate that all the others before her had evaded. The 50-gun *Leander* went to her assistance but could do nothing and *Culloden* remained stranded until the following morning. *Swiftsure* and *Alexander* were under a press of sail coming up hard behind *Culloden* as night fell but *Culloden*'s signals saved them from sharing its fate on the shoal. Together with *Leander* they cleared the island and made for the centre of the action. *Leander*, the only 50-gun ship in the squadron, earned special praise from Nelson for laying itself beside the 80-gun *Franklin*.

The British ships that understandably took the most punishment were those anchored beside or close to the big guns at the centre of the French line. The heaviest sufferer was *Bellerophon*, which had laid itself broadside alongside Brueys's flagship, the 120-gun *L'Orient*. *Bellerophon* was swiftly shattered, her mizzen and mainmasts soon went over, with carnage and destruction on deck and inside of her from *L'Orient*'s broadsides. The ship was on fire at several points. *Bellerophon* had already lost nearly two hundred killed and wounded, almost half her complement, when her commander, Captain Darby, cut her cable and, under spritsail, *Bellerophon* drifted away. Two of her lieutenants were killed. Darby himself was wounded. Her foremast came down as she moved off. Drifting down the French line *Bellerophon* took more punishment, including a broadside from the 80-gun *Tonnant*.

As the French van collapsed, the battle focused upon the French centre where, apart from *Bellerophon*, a tangled close action was being fought between the British *Orion*, *Defence* and *Majestic*, and the French *Peuple Souverain*, the two 80-guns, *Tonnant* and *Franklin*, and *L'Orient*. In one tightly focused exchange of fire between *Peuple Souverain* on the one hand and *Orion* and *Defence* in combination on the other, each side had badly disabled the other through the intensity of their fire, with masts shattered or gone and yards and rigging torn apart. *Majestic*, in close exchange with *Tonnant*, had lost her captain. As *Peuple Souverain* drifted out of the action the British fire concentrated upon *L'Orient*, and *Franklin* and *Tonnant*. Into the cannonading heart of this fury *Swiftsure*, *Alexander* and *Leander* now entered.

This for the British was akin to the arrival of fresh reserves. The French were dismayed by this hearty, impetuous reinforcement. Rear Admiral Du Chayla aboard *Franklin* had hoped for a better combination of fire with *L'Orient*. But each was now preoccupied with its own immediate adversaries. And here, in perhaps the tightest concentration of fire yet experienced in naval battle, the outcome was to be decided.

Swiftsure moved into the place beside *L'Orient* that *Bellerophon* had abandoned, arriving there at three minutes past eight. Aboard *Swiftsure* as she closed a superb small lesson in disciplined self-control was being enacted. Her captain, Hallowell, was conscious of the ill effects of breaking men off from the guns once they had begun to use them. In spite of coming under heavy fire from *L'Orient* and *Franklin* he allowed no shot to be fired from *Swiftsure* until all preparations for coming to anchor were complete. As *L'Orient*'s fire poured upon her, *Swiftsure*'s sailors were aloft furling sails or on deck preparing everything for placing the ship in the best situation at anchor, half-gunshot distance from the French flagship. Then they swiftly descended. Two minutes after anchoring abeam of *L'Orient* and *Franklin*, *Swiftsure* opened fire.

Alexander and *Leander* had passed through the open French line. *Leander* anchored off the line, abreast of *L'Orient* and *Franklin*, upon both of which she maintained steady fire. After passing through the French line *Alexander* anchored in a position that put her broadside to *L'Orient*'s larboard (land) side. As Admiral Du Chayla subsequently put it, 'The action in this part then became extremely warm.'

The next hour, between eight and nine, was the fiercest of the battle. Around nine, as this centre battle raged, firing among the van ships slackened and finally died away as they struck. When a shot cut *Peuple Souverain*'s cable it drifted out of the picture. The fight became tightly concentrated as the new arrivals, *Swiftsure*, *Alexander* and *Leander* joined *Defence* and *Orion* in pouring their fire on to *L'Orient* and the 80-gun *Franklin*, both of which already had taken heavy punishment. So had *Tonnant*, the other 80-gunner that was engaged, principally, with *Leander* and *Majestic*.

At three minutes past nine those aboard *Swiftsure* saw that fire had broken out in the grand cabin of *L'Orient*. Lying half a pistol shot from *L'Orient*, Captain Hallowell immediately ordered that as many of *Swiftsure*'s guns as could be spared from firing on *Franklin* should be directed instead upon the scene of the fire aboard *L'Orient*. *Alexander* from the other side did the same. In face of all of this Brueys, who lay dying on his quarterdeck, still refused to lower his colours. Already wounded in the head, a body shot in the belly then almost cut him in half. He refused to be carried below, wanting to be left to die on deck: 'A French admiral should die on his quarterdeck.' He lasted another agonizing fifteen minutes. His gunners on the lower deck continued firing, even as the conflagration appeared to be enveloping the entire ship.

Brueys's captain, Commodore de Casabianca, was also wounded and lay attended by his ten-year-old son, a midshipman, who refused to leave his side and died there, eventually inspiring that sentimental tribute to the valiant innocence of boy sailors that became one of the most enduring of the popular poetized memorials of that war:

> The boy stood on the burning deck,
> Whence all but he had fled
> . . .
> . . . beautiful and bright he stood
> . . .
> A proud though child-like form.
> . . .

> . . . the noblest thing which perished there
> Was that young faithful heart!

Felicia Hemans, 1793–1836

The fire extended along the upper decks. As the flames climbed the masts and enveloped the ship many of those on deck began jumping overboard. But still the sailors at the guns on the lower deck kept firing; in the words of Rev. Cooper Willyams, the chaplain observing from aboard *Swiftsure*, they were 'either insensible of the danger that surrounded them, or impelled by the last paroxysms of despair and vengeance'. At all events, this grandest flagship of the French navy followed the example of her commanding admiral and fought furiously even as her final moments lay upon her.

Nelson, in severe pain, had hastened on deck from the cockpit on being told of the fire. He immediately gave instructions for those fleeing from *L'Orient* to be picked up by any boats in his squadron that had not been shattered. By this time fear of imminent explosion of the ship began to affect all. The surrounding ships began giving distance to *L'Orient*. Battle lapsed as ships on both sides took precautions, wetting sails, closing ports and hatches, removing all explosive items from deck. Firemen with buckets were organized to fight any fires. *Tonnant* and two other French ships cut their cables to enable them to drift from close proximity.

The full force of the fire was already visible on the middle gun deck, fast approaching the area of the magazine. At thirty-seven minutes past nine, that being the time that *Swiftsure* recorded, the fire apparently reached the magazine and *L'Orient* blew up. The force and brilliance of it was greater than anyone could have supposed. All on that scene remained deafened by it for some time.

The explosion shook *Swiftsure* from top to the very bottom, as if shaken by a violent earthquake. It shook all ships to their keelsons and opened seams. The blazing debris of *L'Orient* was flung to such a vast height that it took some moments for the fragments to descend. Then it all came down like a hail of fire from the heavens. But in the immediate aftermath a great silence fell upon a battle that had become stilled in awe. 'An awful silence reigned for several minutes,' the *Swiftsure*'s chaplain recorded, 'as if the contending squadrons, struck with horror at the dreadful event, which in an instant had hurled so many brave men into the air, had forgotten their hostile rage in pity for the sufferers.'

A solemn aspect was that the moon had risen just before *L'Orient* blew up and it now cast down a different, stranger light on everything. The cannonading brilliance of gunfire that had torn at the dark and offered only fragmented images of the battle was suddenly gone. Instead the silent ships lay illuminated before one another with a softness that allowed the first broad picture of the battle scene. All saw the others in quiet, distinct detail, with only the fires lit by shot on some ships suggesting what had suddenly died. Then came the rain of fire as what was left of *L'Orient* fell from the skies.

Large pieces of the wreck dropped into the main and foretops of *Swiftsure* but fortunately the men had been brought down from there. One of the pieces was a big section of a mast, which Hallowell subsequently had made into a coffin that he would present as a gift to Nelson. Blazing wreckage also nearly set *Alexander* on fire.

Franklin also took a heavy descent of burning fragments. While *L'Orient* was burning *Franklin* suffered a blaze that looked as serious as that of the flagship. The arms chest filled with musket cartridges blew up and set fire to several places on the poop and quarterdeck but sailors managed to extinguish those. *Franklin* had already suffered a heavy raking fire from the 50-gun *Leander* that damaged her severely. Both *Franklin*'s commanders, Admiral Blanquet Du Chayla and his captain, Maurice Gillet, had been severely wounded. They had been carried off the deck, leaving command to the junior officers. But *Franklin*, having raised Brueys's flag, that of the commander in chief, fittingly was the first to reopen fire after the long, awed silence that had fallen upon Aboukir Bay. As Rev. Willyams expressed it, 'short was the pause of death: vengeance soon roused the drooping spirits of the enemy ... Franklin opened her fire with redoubled fury on the Defence and Swiftsure, the signal for renewed hostilities'.

Franklin's continued resistance was brief. All the guns on her main deck had been knocked out. She had only a few guns on her lower deck but with these she took on *Defence* and *Swiftsure* and in less than an hour after loss of *L'Orient* her main- and mizzen masts came down. She finally struck her colours. By then *Franklin* had lost more than half her complement killed and wounded and practically all her artillery, but she had fought on well past the point of futility.

The issue had been effectively decided, but the remnants of Brueys's great fleet stubbornly persisted in their resistance. And it would drag on desultorily for another day and a half. At midnight on 1 August *Tonnant* was the only ship fully engaged, in action with *Alexander* and *Majestic*, the latter badly disabled with her main- and mizzen masts gone. At about three a.m. *Tonnant* lost her three masts, shot away close to the deck. Her cable had also been cut, severing her from her last anchor. She was a wreck, but with her colours still up she continued firing while drifting in an unmanageable state. Her commander, Commodore Du Petit-Thouars, had first both his arms shot away, then one of his legs. His dying command was not to surrender the ship. Thus, with her colours still up, *Tonnant* drove ashore.

Firing stopped altogether for about an hour. It was as though exhaustion had laid sudden agreement for respite upon both parties. As Captain Miller of *Theseus* observed after having been told to move his ship to another position, 'My people were so extremely jaded that as soon as they had hove our sheet anchor up they dropped under the capstan bars, and were asleep in a moment in every sort of posture, having been then working at fullest exertion, or fighting, for near twelve hours.'

Firing resumed at dawn. And, for the first time in this battle, the ships that formed the rear of the French line became sporadically involved. These were the 80-gun *Guillaume Tell*, flagship of Rear Admiral Villeneuve, and two 74s, *Généreux* and *Timoleon*. Around midday, accompanied by two frigates, they got underway and stood out to sea but *Timoleon* ran aground, striking with such force that her foremast went overboard. Her colours were still flying, but she was too near in for any British ship to approach her. Two other ships, *L'Heureux* and *Mercure*, had also run ashore. Helpless, they too struck their colours.

To *Zealous*, originally the lead in Nelson's line when it first bore up to Aboukir Bay at five on the afternoon of 1 August, now also belonged the final act of the drama some twenty hours later, at something past midday on the 2nd. She went in pursuit of the four fleeing French ships but, after coming close and suffering heavy damage to her rigging and sails, was recalled by Nelson.

By daylight Aboukir Bay was a scene that recorded itself as powerfully as the explosive night had done. Upon a red sea floated hundreds of burned and broken bodies as well as many hundreds of body parts. They floated amidst the scorched remnants of *L'Orient* and what had been hurled from other ships. In that hot sun a suffocating stench rose from the dead. Attempts to sink the corpses failed. They only rose again, creating fears of pestilence among the living.

The visible destruction of the French fleet was hard to credit even for the victors. 'Victory is not a name strong enough for such a scene,' said Nelson. Of the seventeen French ships that had awaited him all but the four that had escaped were scorched hulks.

Only *Timoleon* and the irrepressible *Tonnant* remained active, both ashore, but both with colours still aloft, and thus they remained another twenty-four hours while the victorious British took stock of what their fleet had suffered and what they had achieved. On the morning of 3 August *Timoleon*'s captain and those of her crew who had not already fled ashore set her alight before they themselves fled and, colours still flying, she exploded. *Theseus* and *Leander* approached *Tonnant*. The situation was hopeless, and the last French colours finally came down in Aboukir Bay.

The British had not lost a single ship, though several were disabled or

badly damaged, Nelson's *Vanguard* among the latter. An accurate account
of the French dead and wounded was never possible. One calculation put it
at five thousand. Two thousand was the figure settled for by the historian
William James. The British had 218 dead and 678 wounded. The heaviest
loss, fifty dead and 143 wounded, was suffered by *Majestic*, from her heavy
engagement with *Tonnant*. *Zealous*, actively engaged from start to finish,
miraculously suffered only one dead and seven wounded.

After *L'Orient* exploded Nelson had been persuaded to return below to
his bed but, in spite of severe pain in the head, blinded and constantly sick,
he sought to maintain grip on the situation from there. In such a relentless
action this was close to impossible. Nevertheless, through the night he was
taking reports and sending messages, but in the end he depended upon his
captains to maintain the battle discipline and tactical lessons he had instilled
in them. He gave them full credit for that. Responding to Lord Howe's
congratulatory letter, Nelson said, 'I had the happiness to command a Band
of Brothers; therefore night was to my advantage. Each knew his duty; and
I was sure each would feel for a French ship.' But he smarted that four of
the French ships had got away. In that he saw fault through his absence,
adding that had he not 'been wounded and stone blind, there cannot be a
doubt but that every ship would have been in our possession. But here let
it not be supposed that any officer is to blame. No, on my honour, I am
satisfied each did his very best.'

Whatever the lurking regret over the escaped vessels, there nevertheless
had never been a naval battle more decisive, '. . . the most complete, probably,' Mahan said, 'in the annals of naval war'. Tactically alone it had been
a battle like no other. The brilliance of it was to tackle a greatly superior
force piecemeal: first attacking its weakest part, in this case the van, aware
of the rear's inability easily to come to its assistance, and progressively
thereafter to engage the rest. Then there was the method, the formula
for fighting at anchor, a plan fully prepared and kept on hand in readiness, though the likelihood of it proving essential in such circumstances
as Aboukir Bay could scarcely have been visualized as Nelson's squadron
scoured the Mediterranean.

Here, then, was closure of the great tactical revolution, the final blasting
away of any of the lingering old, for both the British and the French. Howe
at 'the First of June' had descended on the wind to break the French line
but, with less than full cooperation from his captains, was compromised in
his intentions by 'the inexperience of many of the captains and the rawness
of the crews'. At Cape St Vincent, Jervis (as Earl St Vincent then was) had
laid out the traditional line of battle, from which Nelson had flung himself
away in bold independent action. Duncan at Camperdown, unable to form
effective line, had strikingly settled for melee. Each of those had represented

some determined assertion of the new in naval warfare. But the Battle of
the Nile was comprehensively different from everything before. At Aboukir
Bay line of battle was simply a starting point from which the rest, all of it
new, took off.

Dominating all was the unprecedented freedom of Nelson's captains, the
Band of Brothers, a eulogium that declared the trust and dependence that
had been laid upon them and which they strikingly fulfilled before and,
more vitally, after their commander was brought down. This was what
Earl Howe instantly picked out in his verdict on the battle: 'I will only say,
on the splendid achievements of Nelson, that one of the most remarkable
features in the transaction consists in the eminently distinguished conduct
of *each* of the captains of the squadron. Perhaps it never before happened
that *every* captain had equal opportunity to distinguish himself in the same
manner, or took equal advantage of it.' It was one of the most meaningful
accolades that Nelson ever got. That his captains had such complete freedom
of action, that they were indeed entirely capable of being entrusted with
it, that they were so demonstrably able to exercise their own individuality
was totally new. That was the essence of Howe's tribute. For he recognized
that it derived entirely from Nelson's brilliance.

Here at Aboukir Bay Nelson's free-playing gift of the foreseen, the
assumed, the likely or the possible were attached to his confidence, conviction, self-reliance and the undeviating missionary assumption of destiny to
explode together with a force and brilliance that remained unrivalled, even
against his later achievements.

For the French a cruel circumstance of Aboukir was that, while the
British at mid-battle had brought in three ships from their outside stations,
Brueys's own potential powerful reinforcement lay inert at the end of his
line, hopeless spectators of the gradual destruction of the flagship and its
consorts. Of the controversies that arose from the Battle of the Nile, as
the action at Aboukir Bay came to be known, that perhaps was the most
bitterly unanswerable. As Jurien de la Gravière asked, 'In that fatal night
. . . what unaccountable fatality kept Villeneuve's ships in the rear, and
detained them as passive spectators of an unequal combat, unconcerned
masters of the only means that could have given us victory? These ships
were lying to leeward of those engaged, but under any circumstances, save
a dead calm, which did not exist, they could have easily stemmed the feeble
current which prevails on that coast, and gained, in a single tack, a more
honourable post for a brave man.'

Villeneuve's ships could have cut their cables during the battle as easily
as they did when they sought to effect their escape, Jurien de la Gravière
argued. Or they could have fought under sail right there. 'Villeneuve,
stationary and resigned, waited for orders, which Brueys, surrounded on all

sides, was no longer in a condition to give. He passed the night exchanging a few uncertain shots with the English ships, and – strange conduct from a man of such undoubted courage – left the battle with a ship almost unscathed amidst his mutilated consorts.' Those were the same accusations that greeted Villeneuve when he got back to France from Aboukir. He pleaded in a letter to Admiral Du Chayla: 'I neither could, nor should have weighed . . . there was no instruction as to bringing the rear to support of the Van, because the thing was impossible . . . the loss of the squadron was decided from the moment when the English ships doubled our line to attack us on both sides.'

It was, then, the greatest contest that had ever taken place between the two navies, the remarkable and unforeseen outcome of William Pitt's sudden and inspired decision for the offensive.

Aboukir Bay offered to both entirely new experience of the other. For the British, it was the courage and fight of the French. Respect for it became a particular memorial of the battle. Young and inexperienced Brueys's sailors may have been, but when it came to the test they more than made up for it with raw courage. They fought as the hungry, ill-equipped boy soldiers in the Italian campaign had fought.

For the French, it was their first experience of Nelson large. He had never before existed for them as absolute commander of any action, least of all as a figure one might recognize as a potential determinant of the whole course of war, which he now decidedly had become. That recognition went far beyond Napoleon and his staff. It reached all over Europe. For everyone Aboukir Bay stipulated to whom Napoleon now should look as his first true protagonist in this war. No one else that he so far had had to contend with, whether at land or sea, had possessed the stature and gift of being someone with the ability to decide the fate of Buonaparte's ambitions. But such Rear Admiral Horatio Nelson had become. As Nelson himself wrote, 'Bonaparte had never yet to contend with an English officer, and I shall endeavour to make him respect us.'

Apart from the blow to the morale and pride of the French navy, other factors arising from the disaster at Aboukir Bay were more immediately severe for France. The first of these was, of course, the establishment of British naval supremacy in the Mediterranean, never again to be lost. Scarcely less important for Britain in consequence of Aboukir Bay was the immediate block upon the French reach for India through conquest of the Middle East. With Napoleon's communications controlled by the British navy future reinforcement and supplies for his force in Egypt would be difficult if not impossible. Although Buonaparte's intended march from Egypt across Palestine, Syria and Asia Minor and on beyond was seriously affected, it was yet far from being entirely spoiled. He was in Egypt with a huge and capable army and in spite of Aboukir Bay nothing could be taken for granted. But on 2 September the French ambassador at Constantinople and all French consuls and merchants in the vicinity were arrested and on 9 September the Ottoman Empire delivered its formal declaration of war on France to the Spanish Embassy, for transmission to Paris. And, as the intercepted letter of one high French officer declared, '. . . the people of Egypt, whom we wished to consider as friends and allies, instantaneously became our enemies; and, entirely surrounded as we were by Turks, we found ourselves engaged in a most difficult defensive war, without a glimpse of the slightest future advantage to be derived from it'.

Nelson's first command on 2 August was for a Thanksgiving to be held aboard all the ships at two that afternoon. A touching image of the two faces of the opponents of that new age was offered at the Thanksgiving aboard *Vanguard*. The secular French prisoners watched in quiet astonishment as all activity stilled and, in place of triumphalism, the quiet, solemn service expressive of devout humility proceeded before them.

After the battle Nelson was in a bad way. He had survived, but only just, it must have seemed on the day after. Something of his cry that he was dead when the shot hit him probably still lingered. In intense pain of the head, he was a man wondering why he was still alive, and for how long that might be: 'I never expect, my dear Lord, to see your face again,' he wrote to St Vincent.

To his correspondents he repeatedly said his head was splitting and that he was constantly sick. The wound had healed but the scar remained vivid. The gratitude for victory was sobered by his nagging regret that some of the French ships should have got away. Other reflections were indicated in a short, sharp interlude with Saumarez, the one captain there who did not easily fit into the wide-embracing 'band of brothers'.

Something had always existed between Nelson and Saumarez. They had never got on, although Saumarez was admired as a seaman. He appeared to have offended Nelson before the battle during discussion of the possible modes of attack when we had argued against 'the evil consequences of doubling upon an enemy, especially in a night action'. Saumarez's argument was that 'it never required two English ships to capture one French, and that the damage which they must necessarily do each other might render them both unable to fight an enemy's ship which had not been engaged'. It was foresight of what exactly occurred.

On the second morning after the battle Saumarez went on board *Vanguard* to congratulate Nelson on his triumph. After the formal exchange on the quarterdeck Saumarez appeared on the point of bringing up the matter again. 'It was unfortunate,' he began, 'that we did not—' but he was cut off. He had meant to add, 'all anchor on the same side'. Nelson had guessed what was coming and cut in with 'Thank God, there was no order.' He left the quarterdeck and retired to his cabin.

It was hardly the proper moment for the intended criticism, if indeed such a moment was ever likely to be welcome in the wake of that resounding triumph, but Saumarez believed he had a valid point. He believed, too, that they might have done equal mischief to the enemy, with less risk to themselves, if they had been anchored on the bow and quarter of each Frenchman instead of on opposite sides. The French ships would then have fired only one broadside instead of two, and there would have been less risk of British seamen being killed by shot fired from their own ships on the other side. It was certainly believed that many British seamen were killed by shot fired from their own guns. Also, that by doubling the French line the British left the rear part of that line unengaged, free at the end to make sail away. Nelson's manner indicated that he did not need to be reminded of any of that, least of all to argue it out in the state that he was in. For him, always, victory was the sum that mattered. Dissatisfaction was tied to what was incomplete or indecisive. Whatever any faults that subsequent reflection might yield, the point right then was that which his captains had given him. And for Saumarez to come across with whys and wherefores at an hour yet so near to it all, with the whole scene around them still smoking and burning, could only have enraged him furiously, as it evidently did.

Six of the hastily repaired French prizes accompanied by seven of the British ships of the line sailed for Gibraltar on 14 September. The other prizes were destroyed. Several frigates arrived to assist in the blockade of Alexandria and to intercept the enemy's communications by sea. They brought Nelson urgent orders from St Vincent recalling him for an operation against Minorca. On 19 September Nelson sailed with his three most damaged ships, his own *Vanguard* accompanied by *Culloden* and *Alexander*. Their destination for repair was Naples, where encounter of a different order awaited Nelson.

XX

BARBARY

THE Great War involved the United States from the start, as it was bound to do in a conflict where commerce was ultimately a decisive element, within the ranging assertions of British sea power. For neutrals, and for the United States in particular, neutrality was something that would continually shift between benefit and loss.

Tom Paine had proposed immunity from the wars of Europe as one of the principal rewards that independence would bring. John Adams in 1776 had likewise declared that 'we ought to lay it down as a first principle and a maxim never to be forgotten, to maintain an entire neutrality in all future European wars'.

All of that was a fanciful vision of an unencumbered Atlantic future never to come. Emptiest of all within that would be the concept of neutrality, which, paradoxically, would eventually provide the core of America's fiercest antagonisms with both belligerents.

Within this all-enveloping conflict of the Great War the United States would fight its first foreign war, with the Islamic states of North Africa; a 'quasi-war' with France; and a full-scale war with Great Britain. Mars thus insistently intruded upon the easy self-preoccupied torpor that sought to settle upon an American people for whom the Old World seemingly had packed its bags and should have been gone for good.

There was no way, however, in which involvement in the far struggles could be avoided by a young nation of Atlantic coastal states the most prosperous of which still had their eyes steadfastly seaward, whose national credit depended upon commerce for its revenues, the principal source of which was the duty collected upon imports. Seaward indeed it looked since there could be little dependence yet on an interior fraught with undiminished echoes of the War of Independence, with the Canadian governor-general, Lord Dorchester, promoting incursions in the Great Lakes region. And with no serious advancement yet into and beyond an Indian-dominated Northwest Territory that held a scattered colonial population of merely some twenty-five thousand and whose westward limits were largely defined by a river, the Mississippi, the free use of which for a decade after independence was still challengeable by Spain.

As previously noted, the Americans were already well established as venturesome oceanic traders across the hemispheres. This could hardly be otherwise since the thirteen colonies had been strongly involved in the rapid development of North Atlantic commerce in the first half of the eighteenth century. Colonial shipyards had built ships more cheaply than the British and with these Americans had freely traded products to Britain, Europe, Africa and the West Indies, and brought imports back, British especially. After independence a resentful Britain was unwilling to concede the same freedom in its own ports or with the rest of the empire. American commerce through risk and ingenuity nevertheless prospered. But the broadening range of the American flag abroad brought unexpected shock when the United States found itself intimidated by an unforeseen opponent, one that had not properly been taken into consideration: Barbary.

This became the first belligerent overseas involvement laid upon the republic as it sought its independent course in the world.

Like all who traded into the Mediterranean, American ships had fallen victim to the privateering activities of Barbary, which meant the three militant North African city-states of Tripoli, Tunis and Algiers together with the less aggressively menacing Kingdom of Morocco. Since the early sixteenth century raiders from the three North African Mediterranean cities, and Sale on the Atlantic coast of Morocco, had practised their own distinctive form of maritime piratical marauding. It had established them not only as the scourge of the Mediterranean but took them ranging into the Atlantic, even to the coasts of Ireland and south-western England. The consequences for any flag that came through the Straits of Gibraltar without some form of established tribute or treaty were severe. The crews of all ships that were taken by the Barbary corsairs, as they were known, were enslaved until ransom was paid. If not paid, the captives remained slaves. Algiers had at the end of the eighteenth century become the most aggressively determined of them all.

In July 1785 the schooner *Maria*, of Boston, was seized by Algerines outside the Straits of Gibraltar. Her crew were enslaved. That same month another ship, *Dolphin*, of Philadelphia, suffered the same.

Before independence the thirteen colonies had come under British protection. Now, lacking any treaty of its own, the United States sought some promise of continued protection from Britain. That was refused. Britain was in fact urged, in a pamphlet on American trade by Lord Sheffield, that the Algerine and other corsairs served a useful purpose in keeping down the trade of the United States. America turned to its former allies, the French and the Dutch. Nothing was forthcoming from either of them. The republic therefore went ahead on its own and made a successful treaty with Morocco. Signed in 1786, it put trade between the two on reciprocal most-favoured basis and required no tribute. But when nothing was achieved with the other North Africans the United States, lacking any form of retaliation in the area, decided in 1792 to appoint John Paul Jones as consul at Algiers to negotiate the liberation of the enslaved. Jones died in Paris before the commission got to him. The situation got worse when, in 1793, Portugal suddenly withdrew from the Straits a force it had long maintained there against Algerine excursions into the Atlantic. The Algerine corsairs took immediate advantage. They sailed out of the Straits and in October 1793 four more American ships were seized by them. The crews were enslaved.

By this time the United States was approaching decision on its own remedial action. Creating naval power was seen as the only solution. After more than a dozen American ships had been seized on 27 March 1794 Congress authorized the construction of six large frigates, none to mount fewer than thirty-two guns. The models of Joshua Humphreys of Philadelphia were accepted.

What was now begun was a navy that in concept, structure and envisaged power was quite different from what had been hustled together during the War of Independence. It was a radical step that would leave its own distinctive mark upon the Great War, for what was to serve against Barbary was rapidly to find further purpose for standing up to the presumptions of the belligerent powers within and outside American waters.

Before the naval programme could be completed, however, the Dey of Algiers signed a treaty that required a tribute of nearly one million dollars in total value. Treaties of tribute, though of lesser value, were also concluded with Tripoli and Tunis. A relieved Congress immediately stopped work on three of the ships, allowing construction to proceed on two 44-gun frigates and one 38-gunner. But that falter of intent was not to last long for, as the European war got underway, work on the ships for the United States navy was resumed. Barbary's depredations had proved providential, for the existence of a United States navy swiftly became a necessary asset as Americans were increasingly drawn into that larger conflict. But it was that first foreign war of their independent nation, against the Islamic states of North Africa, that first bewildered and bemused Americans, and which had to be understood.

The three city-states of Tripoli, Tunis and Algiers had gradually established their distance from the executive reach of the Ottoman Turks whose empire along the southern Mediterranean coasts had followed in the wake of the eighth century's explosive westward expansion of Islam. Their belligerence upon the Mediterranean was thus as old as the contest between Christianity and Islam. That sea from the earliest had served as a source of privateering enrichment to them.

The Tunisians in the thirteenth century had made a business out of intercepting aid and assistance that sailed from France and Spain to the Christian armies in the Holy Land. In 1270 Louis IX sought to subdue them and, like most of his army, died a cruel death there, on the shores of the old Carthage. After expelling the Moors from Spain at the end of the fifteenth century the Spanish continued the pursuit by sending a large army to North Africa in 1504 and seized Oran, which they managed to hold until 1708, when the Algerines expelled them.

Algiers came to prominence in the early sixteenth century when two Greek brothers from the island of Lesbos began to establish their power there. As subjects of the Ottomans, they served that empire and its Mediterranean outposts. Aruj, the elder of the two, became known as Barbarossa because of his red beard. The name transferred as well to his younger brother, Kheyr-ed-din who, after building up the Turkish navy, began to create the Mediterranean's newest and most fearsome sea power at Algiers, which became the formidable base it remained. Algiers threw its dominance across much of the Mediterranean and beyond, eventually joined by Tunis and Tripoli. Charles V, the Holy Roman Emperor, saw it as a duty of his faith to mount a Crusade against Barbary in 1541. But, like all those that followed, the attack played itself out with scenes of horror and suffering that ultimately left the menace and existence of Barbary unaffected.

The aggressive power that the Barbarossa brothers helped establish on the North African coast at the beginning of the sixteenth century became for Europe in the centuries ahead a scourge seemingly impossible to deal with. Diplomatic appeal through the Turks at Constantinople had little effect as Barbary became self-assertive, and the Ottoman Empire weakened. Tripoli was the last to expel the Turks, which it did in 1714. With Venice in decline and the Spanish navy episodic in maintaining its deployable strength, the Barbary states remained the apparently unassailable predators of the Mediterranean, holding its commerce to ransom and ravaging its coasts. Their privateering power looked inviolable even in face of the new navies that arose with the seventeenth century. That was inevitable since British and European renegades who transferred themselves to Barbary for the enrichment, free-ranging adventure and sensual appeal of corsair life brought with them whatever was new in sailing prowess and shipcraft as well as gunnery. And the technical materials for all of that duly became part of the ransoms demanded of those in treaty tribute with the Barbary states. They invariably got it.

The early vessels of corsair privateering and warfare were galleys, which were gradually, though never entirely, replaced by the influence of the round ship. The vessel that emerged was the xebec, a fast-sailing, three-masted ship with a rig adaptable to the highly variable winds of the Mediterranean, allowing either square rig or lateen rig. The Barbary fleets were nevertheless a mix of many sorts of other vessels they had captured.

Enraged assaults against Barbary by the different maritime powers laid a pattern of determined, violent and ultimately futile episodes of retaliatory vengeance upon the history of the Mediterranean through the seventeenth century into the eighteenth. It was a heated fervour on both sides that never abated. In 1775 the Spanish sent a force of fifty thousand against Algiers and were routed as they tried to breach its fortifications. In 1784 Spanish ships sought to destroy Algiers by bombardment, inflicted heavy damage, and retired only after running out of powder and shot. They returned again to the attack the following year accompanied by ships from Portugal, Naples and Malta but, with likewise no resultant success, they settled by paying a hefty tribute for an end to depredations. And so it went. The scourge remained.

The ravages of North African privateering were matched by their surprise descents on the coastal towns of the Mediterranean, especially in southern Italy, Sicily, Sardinia, Corsica and also Spain and France. But such ventures took them to Ireland and the coasts of Devon and Cornwall as well. The seizure of slaves, women especially, was a prime objective. The fear they invoked was described in one account of an Algerine corsair xebec wrecked in a storm on the Cornish coast in September 1760: 'I shall never forget the terrors of that night. I was about eleven years of age, and was called up by my mother, amidst the ringing of the alarm bell, and the beating of drums.' But fear abated for the ship was a hopeless wreck. 'At break of day what a spectacle presented itself! A huge vessel of the most singular construction, at least to an English eye, wrecked and mutilated among the rocks! Men with long beards standing in groups, and having turbans on their heads . . . They had imagined our shore was the Spanish coast, and expected, of consequence, certain slavery; but when convinced they were on English ground, exclaimed with great joy, "Ingleterra! Ingleterra! Bona Ingleterra!".' Admiral Edward Boscawen went down to Tregothen and advised that the Algerines should be treated 'with the greatest kindness and civility as they were at that time very friendly to our nation'. He was assured that there was plenty of good provisions, including excellent pork but very little beef. 'Pork!' Boscawen cried, 'Damn you, and the Navy Board and Victualling Office together! Do not these blockheads know that the religion of Turks and Moors forbids them to eat Pork?'[1]

The Algerines were sent home to Algiers in a frigate. This courtesy and the hospitality they received reflected the various accommodations that were made and influences brought to bear as the eighteenth century advanced. They were necessary. There was no alternative. Both sides in their different ways recognized that.

The navies of Britain and Europe had become far more powerful and determined. They could inflict greater and more consistent damage to the Barbary ports, and blockade them. They could be more efficient in pursuing Barbary fleets. But they were severely limited in all of that. In peace their forces were kept to basic requirement because of cost. In war the situation was even more difficult. Britain, France and Spain were too fully preoccupied with one another. All three, besides, sought to play the individual Barbary states against each other, for whatever advantage might be gained in some situation. The French had the closest relations with Algiers, supplying them with naval stores from Marseilles. The British were required to maintain a close and obliging relationship with the Kingdom of Morocco. Gibraltar, evidently the ideal base for operations against Barbary, which on occasion it served to be, was nevertheless wholly dependent on Morocco for fresh provisions when Britain was at war with Spain. When difficulties arose with Morocco the five thousand-strong garrison of the Rock as well as the inhabitants were reduced to salted provisions as much as though that rearing hump of limestone were itself a vessel sailing the sea on short rations.

By the last quarter of the eighteenth century all these factors had enforced a system of self-interested acknowledgement between the opposing Christian and Islamic coasts of the Mediterranean. Britain and France were ever conscious of their Levant trade and its protection. They and others in regular trade across the Mediterranean arrived at their separate arrangements of tribute and treaty with the Barbary states. British ships carried a Mediterranean certificate that, according to the provisions of the treaties Britain had concluded with the various states, allowed her ships to pass safely across the Mediterranean as well as having free entry into the ports of the Barbary states. Consuls were established at Tripoli, Tunis and Algiers.

All of that was very well, but it left unaffected the fate of the tens of thousands of British and European slaves for whom ransom had never been paid or was unlikely to be paid and whose enslavement, except for unforeseen circumstances, would continue for the rest of their lives.

As a subject of public outrage white slavery had a fiercely active existence in British and European consciousness that black slavery was unable to summon until well into the nineteenth century. The horrors of the West African human traffic impinged but little until liberal evangelical conscience began to stir in the final decade of the century. The issue of release for the white slaves and emancipation for the black, though quite separate in the public mind, nevertheless gathered strength simultaneously at the end of the century. Few would have seen it as a single issue. Black slavery became a slow-developing moral cause whose momentum, in Britain notably, required the expansion of evangelical influence. Reaction to white slavery in Barbary was a matter of accumulative rage, already centuries old, that Britons and Europeans should be seized for enslavement or ransom on the high seas and off their coasts by enemies that had never yet been vanquished as they should have been. Moral conscience had less to do with it than the rage of apparent impotence. The Great War hastened resolution, with white slavery to be the final objective of the victors: the final Crusade.

This white slavery was the product of hostile proximity and lasting war. It was also a Mediterranean tradition. Enslavement of defeated foes and weaker neighbours was a settled part of all earlier Mediterranean history, a tradition as ancient as any there, as any Greek in Roman or Turkish service could verify. Barbary offered the final full historic manifestation of that. But with Barbary it was enhanced, of course, by the missionary zeal of an Islam that retained a potency in North Africa that no longer resounded with similar impact within a debilitated Ottoman Empire. Mutual despising of Faith was a vibrant factor between these slavers and those fearful of enslavement. Though hatred could obsess both, Barbary janissaries and Christians got on remarkably well when they sought it or when circumstances were conducive to it. By embracing Islam white slaves had options for freedom that did not exist for black slaves in the Atlantic world beyond.

One modern historian has estimated that more than one million Christians were enslaved by the Barbary states between 1500 and 1800 alone. Whatever the accuracy of that particular figure, the total of the enslaved covering three centuries had to be large, certainly in the hundreds of thousands. Visitors to the Barbary states during those centuries usually came up with estimates ranging from five to ten thousand slaves in one city or the other. But Algiers, Tunis and the Moroccan ports fronted well-developed hinterlands where construction of fortifications and other projects requiring European skill would have been in constant demand for slaves.

Many Westerners saw corsair life in Barbary as something more attractive than what England or Europe offered them and consequently took themselves there, 'taking the turban', as they called it. For many sailors, soldiers and others of humble origin, reared in the squalor of the darker side of Western life, tired of the heavy disciplinary codes that ruled them, the cities of Barbary could be a vision of the unattainable suddenly attainable. They happily embraced the bright, attractive streets of Algiers, with the absence there of any excluding social stratification, offering brothels and the somnolent cafés with their sweetly pungent aroma of smoked weed. With wealth earned from corsair life they could reasonably aspire to live in one of the 'handsome country houses on the neighbouring hills, which are covered with olive, lemon and banana trees'. Sailors, being worldly, and upon whom their own religion sat more lightly than with most in their societies, had perhaps the least difficulty in 'taking the turban'. British, French and American sailors were among those who decided for it.

Those unable to bring themselves to take that option had it hard. Slavery was slavery, whatever the whimsical character of the masters. When captives were landed their hands were examined for evidence of manual work or an easier life. For most of the former the future lay in building harbours and fortifications or labouring on the land. From Morocco to Tripoli huge defensive walls and harbour moles bear testimony today to the labour of the Christian slaves. The ones with indications of an upper-class life were marked for ransom and easier employment, as were those who had particular skills such as carpentry or baking. After being given local dress, captives were taken to the slave market and sold there, a higher price in demand for any skill.

Slaves, *beyliks*, were housed in *bagnios*, typical Moorish structures set around a courtyard. They had iron rings around their ankles with chains attached. They could be tied to other slaves, or they might simply walk unfettered. Conditions varied from place to place. One ameliorative custom all had in common: Islamic law required all work to stop three hours before sunset. During those three hours slaves were, as one of them later recalled, 'at free liberty to play, work for themselves, or steal'. For theft, if caught, they could expect to be bastinadoed: hung upside down and beaten on the soles of their feet with a hard stick.

Tales of the severity of the hardships suffered by the slaves in Barbary were sometimes balanced by accounts of a lesser severity. As one former resident of Algiers said of the harrowing account of enslavement there written by a priest: 'O fie, Father! Tho' it is part of your function to make a dismal story of slavery among the Infidels, yet you should, methinks, adhere only to the truth . . . thousands of Algerian captives live abundantly happier (want of freedom excepted) than ever they can even hope to do at home; and that very many are excused with a few bastinadoes for crime for which they would have suffered the wheel in most parts of Europe, or at least made their exit in a halter.'

Women were generally treated with respect and sold, depending on their attractiveness, into the harem of a high official or into domestic service.

Longing for freedom was hard to suppress, even for those who had the best of it. Such was the tale of William Okeley who was taken from the ship *Mary*, of London, in 1639. He had a kind master who loaned him enough money with which to open a shop, where he sold 'strong waters', tobacco and other goods, with a portion of the profits going weekly to his patron. In spite of these benefits he formed a plan of escape with John Anthony, a carpenter who had been a slave for fourteen years, William Adams, who during eleven years of slavery had learned brick making, and four others, a sailor and another carpenter, both of whom had been slaves for five years, and two whose work was to wash clothes at the seaside.

What they achieved was impressive. A boat was gradually built in Okeley's cellar. Its twelve-foot keel and all the other items, ribs and angled timbers, canvas, oars, tarpaulin, pitch, tallow and tar were brought to the cellar and the boat assembled. The finished work was eventually dismantled and carried away piece by piece in its various parts. The task of getting these out of town without detection was highly dangerous, but they got it all to the sea, where they found that the weight of seven was too much. Two of them therefore stepped away and returned to slavery. After more than a week of horrendous suffering, having brought too little food and water, compelled to drink their own urine, they washed up on Majorca, where the Spanish treated them kindly and got them on their way to London via Cadiz.

Others had a similar experience to Okeley's, of intimacy with the master. Emanuel d'Aranda, a Fleming, wrote of a patron he had in Algiers in 1671.

Though he was but a poor soldier, yet I lived well enough with him; for he would often say to me, 'Emanuel, be not melancholy, imagine that you were my patron and I your slave'. I did eat with him out of the same dish, sitting down with him cross-legged, after the Turkish way. He made me the best cheer he could, and often said to me, 'Emanuel, have I not reason to make much of myself, for I have neither wife nor children and when I die the Bashaw will be my heir?' I told him, 'You do prudently and have reason to live as much as may be at your ease.' I could say no less because I did eat and drink with him. But these words did not please a renegado boy who waited on him, kept his money and washed his linen; in a word the boy did the work of a woman in the family and was perpetually grumbling and saying 'You make away with all you have and there are so many days before the pay comes in; you should be ashamed to be drunk every day, this is not the life of a right Turk'. But my patron lived nevertheless at the same rate.

The domestic nagging of the renegade boy, who presumably took the turban after captivity, suggests a homosexual relationship. This was common in Barbary, then and into modern times. Handsome young captives were commonly persuaded into the relationship of concubine. It was a guarantee of being spoiled and, for many, preferable to the alternative hard labour.

Towards the end of the eighteenth century any ease of conditions appear to have deteriorated seriously at all the Barbary ports. This seems to have been particularly so during the period of the Great War. There was frequent witness from the consuls there and from the many emissaries sent to negotiate ransom or plead for release of captives. 'No sooner is anyone declared a slave,' said one account,

than he is instantly stripped of his clothes, and covered with a species of sackcloth; he is also generally left without shoes or stockings, and often obliged to work bareheaded in the scorching rays of an African sun ... Some of these wretched beings are destined to make ropes and sails for the squadron: these are constantly superintended by keepers, who carry whips ... Some like beasts of burthen, are employed in carrying wood and stones for any public buildings that may be going on: these are usually in chains, and justly considered as the worst among their oppressed brethren ... Two black cakes, thrown down as if intended for dogs, is their principal daily sustenance; and had it not been for the charity of a rich Moor, who left a legacy for that purpose, Friday, the only day they are exampted from work, would have seen them without any allowance whatsoever.

By the end of the eighteenth century it seemed to make little difference if British captives produced their certificates of protection. Even the supposedly immune consuls were treated with contempt. As one naval emissary reported,

You will judge, what an English officer's feelings must have been, when surrounded by these miserable men who, with tears, inquired if England knew their fate ... on arrival of these new slaves, our consul sent his interpreter to the bani, or bagnio, and hospital to find out if any of them had claims on the English protection. The infidels would not permit him to enter either place ... I plainly saw that he had used all his influence to effect their release, but to no purpose; his influence ... is greater than that of the consul of any other nation ... The Danish consul, a respectable and amiable man, was once actually taken to the bani, and irons put on him, until his nation paid some tributary debt! The Swedes are obliged to furnish artists for making gunpowder for them. The French government have sent them a builder for their navy ... The Spanish vice-consul of Bona, I myself saw in heavy irons, working with other slaves! Thus these infidels trample equally on all the rights of nations and of nature.[2]

Such was the implacably hostile legacy of medieval history that the young American nation had now entered, and had to be prepared to deal with on its own. It came in at a new crisis point, for Barbary's menace was developing into a robust sideshow of the Great War as the North Africans saw advantage for themselves in it all.

As the war progressed, particularly after the British withdrawal from the Mediterranean at the end of 1796, xebecs and galleys began swarming across that sea.

The United States had thus inescapably become partner to the last Crusade.

At ten a.m. on 20 January 1798, America sent off from Portsmouth, New Hampshire, a hefty instalment of the tribute it was paying to the Dey of Algiers in its humbled plea for the safe passage of its ships and their crews. Captain Newman, his chief officer and many of the sailors had all been prisoners at Algiers. So had Richard O'Brien, who had been ten years a prisoner there, and was sailing now to reside at Algiers as consul general to all the Barbary states. The frigate *Crescent*, 'one of the finest specimens of elegant naval architecture which was ever borne on the Piscataqua's waters', was itself part of that tribute. So were the twenty-six barrels of dollars stacked in her hold.

XXI

NEUTRALITY

ONE of the many axioms of Julian Corbett on naval strategy was that every step towards gaining command of the sea tended to turn neutral sea powers into enemies. Like all Corbett's pronouncements on the evolution of naval strategy that one stands as an incisive historical assessment of a particular aspect of what, when it suited, was ruthlessly employed in the rise of naval power: brush neutrality aside, seize their ships and confiscate their cargoes, impress their seamen, ignore their protests, if any of it in any way appears necessary to one's interests in the course of war.

Never was that proved truer than in the Great War. Yet, one of the most remarkable maritime aspects of the first half of the Great War was the way that maxim was turned upon its head. For in no other time of naval war were neutral flags allowed such licence as they began to obtain during the last five years of the eighteenth century. It created a situation unprecedented in oceanic trade. Britain was raised to the highest levels of maritime trade it had known. So, too, the United States. Furthermore, in rough inverse of Corbett's maxim, America saw this obverse of the usual neutrality situation foster its own naval ascent.

At a point when Great Britain appeared to stand on the edge of ruin – its darkest hour, February 1797, her navy out of the Mediterranean; the navy mutinous withal; the drain of bullion; financial credit threatened; the Bank suspended – that ascent towards a new wartime commercial situation on the Atlantic was already gathering momentum. For a Britain in peril, with a navy whose clear dominance was yet to be affirmed, dependence upon her oceanic commerce was absolute. Commerce would decide the war. Out of that came a new view of neutral shipping, which in turn became the manipulated instrument for British survival.

The war did not start in any way like that. The familiar conflict between belligerents and neutrals was immediately operative from the beginning.

Corbett's principle was enunciated in relation to the Seven Years War at mid-eighteenth century when Britain reasserted its doctrine that an enemy's goods were justifiable prize everywhere upon the high seas. Once activated it became an oppressive interference with the trade of those maritime powers nominally at peace with Britain.

For Britain command meant denial of essential war or revenue-earning goods to its enemies. It was an exercise fully matched by France who, when lacking the wider offensive scope of the British navy, sought to balance that with sweeping edicts for its cruising frigates and vessels of *guerre de course* that were ruthlessly and cynically applied wherever possible. Neutral flags were ever sailing dangerously. Definitions of what was regarded by one side or the other as contraband could be arbitrary. But, with the commerce of the preoccupied belligerents open to incursion, the war itself was a major stimulus to neutral flags to move in where exclusion once prevailed and to run through the vigilance of one side with goods it forbade the other. No one was out of the act. Neutrality, the moral cloak of non-belligerence, was for the most part simply a form of warfare within a war.

The principal neutral flags in the Great War were the United States and the Baltic powers of Sweden, Denmark and Russia. But for no country was this issue of neutrality to be more immediately contentious than for the young republic of the United States.

As with Barbary, America found itself dealing with something from which it had been sheltered by British protection in the past. That protector had now become assailant. For the new nation neutrality became a hard process by which to arrive at strategic maritime maturity: of seeking precise definitions, demanding recognition of rights and recompense for the unjustifiable, all of it continually conducted within unfamiliar diplomatic shuffle and connivance. The learning curve had to be swift, which sometimes it was, often not.

The Great War arrived with the United States on a better diplomatic footing with France in the event of European war than with Britain. Their 1778 treaty of friendship and respect defined the privileges to be enjoyed by the ships and commerce of both during a war in which the United States was neutral, France a belligerent. The treaty was broadly lenient for the United States. It sanctioned carriage of non-contraband freight to enemy ports. Contraband goods consisted almost exclusively of arms and ammunition. Outstandingly, France would have special privileges in American ports which would be denied to the opposing belligerent. French ships-of-war and privateers were free to bring their prizes into American ports and to stay or leave with them without interference. But this privilege had to be denied to whomsoever was France's enemy. Inevitably this meant Britain.

Congress completed similar treaties with the Netherlands, Sweden and Prussia. Britain held out, however, from any such treaty-making with America. It could hardly be otherwise, in face of such leniency allowed by the United States to the French in case of war. Besides, in its peace treaty with the United States at the end of the War of Independence Britain had avoided commercial arrangement of any sort, and refused to make any agreement on protection for neutral trade in the event of war. The effect of this when war came was quick. Britain set out ruthlessly to cut off France from the domestic sustenance the French people needed at the time, as well as from any source of colonial wealth.

On 8 June 1793 commanders of cruisers were ordered to detain all ships carrying flour or grain to France. On 6 November the order was amplified to cover 'all ships' carrying the produce of any French colony or supplies for any French colony. In support of those decrees at the outset Britain decided that neutrals trading with France or with French colonies would be considered as effectively part of the French merchant marine and therefore subject to seizure. All of this hit America hard. The West Indies trade was one of the most active areas of American shipping. Several hundred American ships were seized by British cruisers in the Caribbean and taken into port.

In spite of the 1778 treaty, on the outbreak of war in 1793 more than a hundred American ships were held at Bordeaux, their cargoes confiscated. The Great War thus began with neutrality sidelined by both the principal belligerents.

All of this made an unwelcome load upon a nation that just four years earlier had come into its own, with adoption of its Constitution and inauguration of its first administration. In April 1794 George Washington, now the first President, sent the Chief Justice of the Supreme Court, John Jay, to London to negotiate these issues and, effectively, thereby to attempt to keep the United States out of the war.

On 19 November 1794 in London Jay signed the first treaty between Britain and an independent United States. It helped to keep the peace by freeing the northern frontier of British garrison posts but it failed to secure disarmament on the Great Lakes. On other points the treaty earned scorn from many in a Congress where there was still much sympathy for France and strong feeling against the British. For some Jay's treaty looked too much like meek submission to British power, naval and military. The United States agreed that enemy goods as well as provisions bound for enemy ports might be taken from neutral ships and that naval stores should be regarded as contraband. But the treaty yielded to the British navy the privileges France held under her 1778 treaty. As with the French, British warships and privateers were now also to be admitted freely to American ports during war.[1]

There were no guarantees against impressment, but Britain put the United States on a most-favoured-nation basis of trade and allowed

American ships to trade directly with the British West Indies as well as the East Indies. With that the bitter British resentments of American commerce in the immediate aftermath of peace in 1783 were laid aside.

What was gained with the one, however, was swiftly lost with the other.

France was enraged by Jay's treaty: it saw it as an abrogation of its own treaty of 1778 with the United States as well as an act of ingratitude for the help France had given Americans in the War of Independence. While many in Congress could sympathize with that, for American mercantile forces a new dawn had arrived.

For Britain an easing of her old, restrictive mercantilist practices had become imperative. The trade that she required for the flow of revenue to uphold credit, afford the rising cost of the war and pay subsidies was under severe duress. It was slowly recognized that she was incapable of maintaining this vital commerce unaided.

Britain's naval power was badly stretched and forces available for mercantile protection were limited. The greatest risks to shipping were in the Channel through which passed nearly two-thirds of British commerce, most of it bound up the Thames for London. That made those seas the natural hunting ground for French privateers of every description. This assault against British commerce through *guerre de course* intensified in 1795 and steadily thereafter, harassing the regular flow of trade that Britain so urgently required.

Two factors brought Britain triumphantly through the critical mercantile setbacks of those early years of the war. One was the convoy system. Huge merchant fleets, numbering hundreds of vessels, even as many as one thousand, gathered at specified points. Once assembled, they sailed for their overseas destinations under naval escort. But in such an inevitably motley group sailing qualities were diverse. Owners of fast vessels therefore often preferred to sail without convoy. Continuing losses in 1798, however, brought the Convoy Act, which made taking convoy compulsory. But the principal factor that kept British trade moving was a steadily broadening extension of the privileges allowed to America under the Jay Treaty. Restrictions upon other neutrals were similarly eased, to help counter shipping losses. To bring in its colonial trade and to deliver its manufactured goods to the American, Continental and other markets meant that British commerce was of necessity thrown open to all neutrals to carry British goods.

Apart from losing ships at a rate of many hundreds a year, the merchant navy was also losing its men to the urgent demands of the Royal Navy. An early adjustment to British neutrality decrees was compelled as the Royal Navy drew heavily on the merchant service for its own sailors. A rule that required three-quarters of a merchant ship's crew to be British was set aside immediately after the outbreak of war. It was reversed, to allow three-quarters of a crew to be foreigners.

Such drastic review became necessary in the hard months after the Royal Navy abandoned the Mediterranean at the end of 1796. The British Levant trade that had been exclusive to British ships then had to be passed to neutral flags. Gradually, neutral shipping began to move in Atlantic trade as well without serious British restriction. The consequences of that for all concerned were to be dramatic, remarkably so for Britain, and equally so for the United States, which became by far the principal beneficiary among the neutrals.

During the first seven years of the war British trade underwent total transformation. In 1792, the last year of peace to 1800, British exports and imports doubled. The proportion of British goods moving in foreign ships had risen from 13 to nearly 43 per cent. As one observer noted, 'Our commerce has become more than double its greatest extent during the happiest years of peace.'[2]

Nothing like it could have been visualized even at the start of the war, certainly not the seemingly unhindered liberties allowed to American shipping, given the hostility that had existed at independence and, with certain British commercial forces, still did. Substantial areas of transatlantic trade fell almost exclusively to the Americans. Through the first and second terms of Washington's presidency United States commerce flourished hugely.

The American merchant marine became second only to Britain's. In 1790 American ships arriving in home ports from abroad totalled 355,000 tons while foreign vessels totalled 251,000 tons. In 1801 those totals stood at 799,304 for the American flag, against a mere 138,000 tons of foreign. The tonnage of American shipping in foreign trade rose from 363,100 in 1791 to 848,300 by 1807. Exports increased nearly fourfold, imports by 75 per cent, much of the latter simply on the basis of transhipment.[3]

For the first decade and a half of the Great War American shipping was in an extraordinary situation that could never have been anticipated in its own near waters, let alone in the European. Americans were handling a lion's share of the Caribbean trade into their own ports, and were carriers of it to the Continent as well as to Britain.

Britain was now in command of the greater part of the West Indian products so valued by Britain, France and the rest of Europe: the coffee, sugar, cocoa, molasses and cotton that all the Western world had got used to consuming as necessities more than mere luxuries. Although many of the main French, Spanish and Dutch possessions had either been seized by Britain or were blockaded by the British navy. The colonies and bases retained by France, Holland and Spain were thus powerless to move their products to Europe. American ships largely began to do it for them. One device was the 'broken voyage'. An American ship might, for example, load sugar at Martinique, discharge it at an American port, and then reload it as export. It could all be done within a week. The ship then sailed for France equipped with papers describing the cargo as export from the United States.

British merchants were free to import produce from French, Dutch and Spanish colonies in neutral flags, not for consumption in Britain but for re-export under the same flags after paying a toll. In January 1798 Britain formally exempted from capture Danes, Swedes and other neutrals when carrying coffee and sugar from the colonies of hostile powers to their own country, or to England.

For British and American merchants a fundamental of this extraordinary boom, companion to the trade in tropical produce, was the demand for British manufactures throughout the world, wherever trade routes ran, including in America. The significance of this trade to Britain was indicated when, in January 1798, the British government assigned a ship of the line and two frigates to convoy a fleet of American ships to their own coast. Other neutrals similarly sought British convoy. The demand for British goods was even greater on the Continent, where they were as insatiably required by France as much as by anyone else there. Under the pressures of war manufacturing had suffered severely on the Continent while in Britain it had expanded to meet the strengthening demands from all. All of that, naturally, had increased the demand for bottoms to cope with this unprecedented and soaring commerce.

The colonial produce and manufactured goods that poured into the Continent passed through the ports of northern Germany, Hamburg especially. Shipping cleared from British ports for Hamburg was practically non-existent in 1793. In 1795 it totalled 53,000 tons. By 1798 it had risen to 74,000 tons. Across the whole of northern Germany in 1798 imported tonnage stood at 303,000. Three-fifths of the foreign merchandise landed at German ports were exports from Britain.[4]

This commerce was paid for in specie, gold or silver coin, instead of paper, the value of which was dubious. France itself paid American traders in specie for what they delivered to her ports. This helped America pay for the manufactures it imported from Britain while the British for their part were earning back much of the subsidies they had been paying to their Continental allies.

Adam Smith thus briefly, one could say gloriously, triumphed on the oceans in the last decade of the eighteenth century and the first years of the nineteenth with resounding success for Britain and the United States. The commerce that moved across the oceans and seas was driven to converge upon Britain, which in that period established itself as the natural hub of seaborne trade, 'forcing neutrals to make England the storehouse and toll gate of the world's commerce'. It was a position of dominance that Britain continued to hold, and which eventually would establish her as the emporium of global trade.

By contrast in the last year of the century the Directory was compelled to admit the astonishing fact that France had not a single merchant ship sailing the seas.

What France was suffering on the seas was a bitter offset against Napoleon's victorious sweep across Italy and against Austria. The Chef du Bureau du Commerce, M. Arnould, described the commercial condition of France in 1797: 'The former sources of our prosperity are either lost or dried up. Our agriculture, manufacturing, and industrial power is almost extinct . . . The maritime war paralyzes our distant navigation and even diminishes considerably that on our coasts; so that a great number of French ships remain inactive, and perhaps decaying in our ports.'[5]

What Napoleon exacted in specie and treasure from those he conquered or intimidated on the Continent was hardly sufficient compensation for such a loss of the former enormous commercial power and economic stature of France. In face of such mounting humiliation there had to be a reaction from France. It came savagely in 1798.

A law forbidding the possession of British goods in France had been active since 1796. On 18 January 1798 the Directory decided to renew it more forcefully. On country roads wagons were searched rigorously for British products. It was further decreed that any ship of any flag bearing English goods would be considered lawful prize, since carrying for Britain made such vessels effectively enemies of France.

This retaliation by the Directory against neutrals had become particularly focused upon the United States, which had benefited so hugely from the British laxity.

Relations between America and France had deteriorated rapidly after the Jay Treaty was ratified by the two signatories in London in October 1795. When a newly appointed United States representative to France, C. C. Pinckney, arrived in Paris in 1796 the Directory refused to receive him. The French minister to the United States was recalled and the American government was informed that he would not be replaced.

American commerce thereafter began to suffer steadily and severely from the depredations of French cruisers and privateers. In November 1796 the French powers remaining in the West Indies added to the Directory's edicts by calling for the capture of American ships sailing to or from British ports. By the end of 1797 more than three hundred American ships had been seized in West Indies and European waters. Washington's successor, John Adams, elected in November 1796, sent a three-man commission to Paris to attempt to negotiate a diplomatic settlement and respect for American rights.

The three commissioners were waiting to be received by the Directory when intermediaries from Talleyrand suggested that they would be recognized by the Directory but the price was a major loan to France. Furthermore, the loan should be accompanied by a substantial personal present to Talleyrand. The commission packed its bags and carried its indignation back to Congress, to which it recommended that the nation arm itself for defence and possible war.

The response of Congress in April 1798 was immediate. The President was authorized to raise a 'provisional army' of ten thousand in addition to the established army. Washington was recalled to command the new army. But more urgent was the need of a Navy Department, which was created under Benjamin Stoddert as the first Secretary of the Navy. On 7 July 1798 the old treaty of alliance with France was abrogated. On 9 July United States naval ships and armed merchantmen were authorized to attack and capture armed French vessels wherever they might be found in the Atlantic and the Caribbean. On 11 July a new Marine Corps was established and a large naval force was ordered on July 16.

In his speech to Congress in December 1796 Adams had already recommended the increase of the navy. The three large frigates that had been authorized in 1794 to contend with the depredations of Barbary were by now afloat. The 44-gun *United States* had been the first, followed by the *Constellation*, 38, and *Constitution*, 44. Work suspended on companion ships ordered in 1794 was to resume. The new fleet sanctioned by Congress would consist of six 74s, twelve large frigates, twelve ships of 20 and 24 guns, six 18-gun sloops, as well as galleys and revenue cutters. All were to be built within a year. To service these, two dockyards would be established, one for the 'Eastern' and the other for the 'Middle' states. On that basis the United States set forth swiftly to defend itself along its coasts and upon the oceans.

Although already afloat, the fitting-out of *United States*, *Constellation* and *Constitution* was still in progress at this time. Various ships had, meanwhile, been bought to serve as temporary sloops and cruisers. One of these, an Indiaman named *Ganges*, was fitted with 24 guns and, under the command of Captain Richard Dale, sailed on 22 May 1798, with instructions to capture all French cruisers he encountered on the American coast. *Ganges* was therefore the first ship of the new United States Navy to proceed to sea. But the first capture was by another ship, the 20-gun *Delaware*, Captain Stephen Decatur, which in June brought in to the Delaware River the 14-gun French privateer *Croyable*. She was renamed *Retaliation* and, flying the Stars and Stripes, was soon back at sea hunting her former companions.[6]

By the end of the year twenty-three American naval ships were at sea, operating on the coast, in the West Indies or convoying between the islands and the United States.

Thus the new American navy came into service, and thus too began what was called the 'quasi-war' with France. It certainly was war, but the preference in Congress was that it should stay formally undeclared.

XXII

'QUASI-WAR'

THE American naval ascent was to surprise the British as much as the French, perhaps because the British, as they demonstrated with continuous impressment of Americans, gave little thought to America being a nation to whom they owed any form of deference.

In principle, although the British and the Americans were now allies against the French, British naval squadrons in the Caribbean nevertheless continued to stop and search American ships for sailors they regarded as British subjects. A particularly determined example of that soon greeted the operational emergence of the United States Navy.

On 16 November 1798, when the 20-gun sloop *Baltimore*, Captain Phillips, was escorting a convoy of merchantmen inbound to Havana from Charleston, a cruising British squadron was sighted. The Morro Castle was already in sight and Phillips, conscious of continuous British harassment of American merchantmen, signalled his ships to carry sail hard to make the port. As the squadron cut off three vessels in the convoy and captured them Phillips took *Baltimore* alongside the British flagship *Carnatick*, a 74, and was requested by Commodore Loring, the senior officer of the squadron, to come on board. Loring told Phillips that he intended to take from *Baltimore* all the men who were not carrying American Protection papers. Phillips declared that as an insult to his flag and said that he would simply surrender his ship if Loring carried through his intent.[1]

Returning to *Baltimore* Phillips found a British lieutenant already on board mustering the crew. Seizing the muster roll he ordered the lieutenant to stand aside and ordered his own people to their quarters. Phillips then confronted his situation. The power of the British squadron was overwhelming. *Carnatick* was accompanied by another 74, as well as a 98-gun and two 32-gun frigates. In these early days of American naval deployment *Baltimore* had sailed without the document now specified for such a commission, signed by the President of the United States, and which included the instruction 'I wish particularly to impress on your mind, that should you ever see an American vessel captured by the armed ship of any nation at war, with whom we are at peace, you cannot lawfully interfere to prevent the capture, for it is to be taken for granted, that such nation will compensate for such capture, if it should prove to have been illegally made.'

For Phillips in his dilemma that clause also seemed to justify his immediate decision to submit to the superior force, lower his flag, surrender his ship, and send fifty-five of his crew to *Carnatick*, and leave it to the American government to resolve the issue.

Loring kept five of the *Baltimore* men and sent fifty back. He then told Phillips that he had a number of impressed Americans in his squadron and would exchange them for an equal number of Englishmen that Phillips might have. The proposition was angrily refused. Loring sailed away with the five men and the three merchant ships, as well as the impressed Americans he had confessed to having.

The episode raised sensation in the United States. It served at least to change forthwith the future response of the United States Navy. On 29 December 1798 Navy Secretary Benjamin Stoddert issued to all American naval commanders the order that 'on no pretence whatever' was any ship of war in future to be detained or searched or any officers or men taken away by ships of a foreign nation 'so long as you are in a capacity to repel such outrage on the honour of the American flag'. It should be resisted to the utmost but if overpowered by superior force 'you are to strike your flag, and thus yield your vessel as well as your men, but never your men without your vessel'.[2]

In his account of the incident to Congress on 7 January 1799, President Adams retained something of the deferential mildness that characterized the instruction that had helped to influence Phillips in his actions: 'It is but justice to say, that this is the first instance of misbehaviour of any of the British officers towards our vessels of war that has come to my knowledge ... I have no doubt that this first instance of misconduct will be readily corrected.' It was not readily corrected, however, by the lack of release of the impressed Americans that Commodore Loring had confessed to having in his squadron.

On 10 January Captain Phillips was dismissed from the United States Navy, without court martial. The unfortunate man had served as the example that brought necessary results. Stoddert's firm injunction set the code that allowed no further deference in face of presumptuous intimidation.

On 9 February *Constellation* fought the first major action of this new navy.

The different squadrons operating in the Caribbean had already taken a considerable number of privateers and small cruisers of the French navy when, cruising off Nevis, *Constellation*, 38, Commodore Thomas Truxton, sighted the French frigate, *L'Insurgente*, 40, which first set American colours before hoisting the French ensign. *L'Insurgente* fired a gun to declare combat and eased her sails to await the American, who stood to windward. As *Constellation* drew abeam fierce fire was opened between the two. The French, as they usually did, concentrated on the masts and rigging and *Constellation* suffered heavy damage. But the weight of her fire proved to be the greater and, after an hour, *L'Insurgente* struck her colours. The French ship lost twenty-nine killed, forty-one wounded against only three wounded aboard the American.

One man died aboard *Constellation*, a small tragedy of the unaccustomed. At the start of combat, one sailor sought to flee from his gun. The third lieutenant, who was standing by, instantly killed him.[3]

This victory had to have resounding impact upon America. It declared a different form of independence for the United States, particularly after the *Baltimore* incident. The United States had demonstrated assertive presence offshore, and raised its challenge there. News of the action swept exuberantly through the homeland, raising enthusiasm for the navy and naval service, with the well-to-do seeking to enrol their sons on the navy lists.

The navy had besides also learned *ruse de guerre*, so frequently practised by the belligerents, the French especially. Later that year *Constellation* and *L'Insurgente* sought to bring out privateers from Guadeloupe by approaching each other offshore from opposite directions and then starting an apparently furious action, *Constellation* under American and *L'Insurgente* under French colours. An 18-gun privateer was rushed out to the assistance of *L'Insurgente* but, discovering the trap, struck without contest.

Before the end of the year the United States Navy took itself much further afield, on a mission that could only seriously disturb the British as a possible portent of the future, since American trade to the East was mounting. Two of the newest frigates, *Congress*, 38, and *Essex*, 32, were assigned to convoy merchantmen as far as Batavia, with the American pennant thereby for the first time carried round the Cape of Good Hope by an American warship.

The new century began with an American naval fleet of thirty-five ships. It also brought another action for *Constellation* and Commodore Truxton.

At half-past seven in the morning of 1 February 1800 *Constellation* was again off Guadeloupe when she encountered a 52-gun French frigate, *Vengeance*, to leeward and gave chase. But it was only at eight p.m. the following day before she hauled alongside. Truxton had hoisted his colours 'and had the candles in the battle lanthorns all lighted, and was in the lee gangway ready to speak to him, and to demand the surrender of his ship to the United States of America, when at that instant he commenced a fire from his stern and quarter guns, directed at our rigging and spars . . . and as sharp an action as ever was fought between two frigates commenced and continued until within a few minutes of one a.m. when the enemy's fire was completely silenced . . .' But Truxton was unable to secure his prize.

Constellation's mainmast was totally unsupported by rigging, every shroud having been shot away. Truxton ordered men aloft to attempt to secure the mast to catch up with the enemy again, 'but every effort was in vain, for it went over the side in a few minutes after, and carried with it the topmen, among whom was an amiable young gentleman, who commanded the main top, Mr James Jarvis, son of James Jarvis, Esq. of New York. This young gentleman, it seems, was apprized of his danger by an old seaman, but he had already so much the principle of an officer ingrafted on his mind, not to leave his quarters, that he replied, if the mast went, they must go with it, which was the case, and only one of them were saved.'

Constellation had fourteen killed, twenty-five wounded, *Vengeance* fifty killed and 110 wounded.[4]

The two actions of *Constellation* had demonstrated critical weaknesses in the ship already noticed in others. While the Americans had by now established themselves as superb builders of merchant vessels the demand for naval cruisers from their yards and architects had been suddenly sprung upon them. What initially resulted was something so different that, arguably, it immediately put the Americans alongside the French as the prime innovators in naval architecture in that century. The French had always gone for hull form and speed. The Americans in their experiment – for it appeared to be nothing less – went for a marriage of frigate and line ship, with the end product seeming closer to the latter than the other. Ships of the *Constellation* class were larger than any other frigates afloat, with the size and measurements and weight of metal that brought them close to a 74. In concept they were ahead of their time, to make them both damned and feared as well as reluctantly admired by the British for their innovation. But initially they proved to be difficult sea ships, troubled by their weight of metal and heavy rigging. They rolled heavily 'nearly gunwale to', and on different occasions in bad weather suffered the loss of masts, which were mostly 'single sticks' instead of being made. But they were remarkable ships for their day, fitting objects of pride for a newly founded navy. (It was an experiment that would be repeated successfully in the twentieth century when Germany, restrained from acquiring a battle fleet by the Treaty of Versailles, built 'pocket battleships' the size of cruisers but with greater speed and heavier armament than many battleships of the day.)

While America's western ocean war against French cruisers and privateers was fiercely pursued across the Caribbean, the humiliating truce with Barbary was of necessity being maintained. Some two hundred American merchantmen were every year engaged in Mediterranean trade. Their unmolested passage was what was being paid for.

In May 1800 the 24-gun *George Washington*, Captain William Bainbridge, sailed with tribute to the Dey of Algiers. On arrival at Algiers in September, Bainbridge anchored under the mole to unload the presents. He was then told by the American consul at Algiers that the Dey demanded the *George Washington* be placed at his disposal. Flying the Algerian flag, it was to be used to send tribute to the Ottoman Porte.

Bainbridge was outraged and demanded audience of the Dey, to whom he declared that he was unable to comply with any such request. The response was that Bainbridge and his ship were now in the power of the Dey, *his* to command. Bainbridge went into violent argument with the Dey until the American consul, who before his appointment had spent many years as a captive in Algiers, advised Bainbridge that unless he complied his ship would be seized. Bainbridge then said that he would carry the Dey's ambassador and the presents to Constantinople. He stipulated that this should be regarded not as an act of the Dey's right but as one of friendly concession by the United States and that on his return from Constantinople no further demands should be made.

Fresh argument arose, however, when *George Washington* was about to sail and the Dey insisted that the Algerian flag be at the main, the American ensign shown forward. Again Bainbridge protested, then yielded, but on clearing the mole he set his own ensign as usual. *George Washington* sailed on 19 October and anchored in the outer harbour of Constantinople on 9 November.

Bainbridge had brought this new world navy to the ancient frontier of the hemispheres which to all its old world predecessors had defined the division of the world and civilizations, the source and objective of the global commercial riches that should be sought. Passing through the Dardanelles and the point where two castles stood opposite one another, one on the European shore, the other on the Asiatic, he had without instruction fired respectful salute. At Constantinople the official who boarded demanded to know what the ship's flag was. Told that it was the ensign of the United States the official went away and returned to say that his government had never heard of such a nation as the United States of America. He wanted explanation. *George Washington* belonged to the New World, he was told. The answer was accepted.[5]

George Washington sailed from Constantinople on 30 December, reaching Algiers on 21 January 1801. This time Bainbridge kept the ship outside, beyond reach of the Algerine batteries. The Dey wanted a return to Constantinople. Bainbridge refused, ignoring the threat of war against the United States. But on his first visit he had borrowed ballast in the form of old guns. He began discharging the ballast into lighters, which the Dey promptly withdrew, again threatening war unless the ballast was returned, which meant coming into the mole. Bainbridge reluctantly took *George Washington* into the mole and offloaded the ballast. Another ferocious interview with the Dey followed, with Bainbridge again threatened with enslavement. But the Algerian ambassador he had carried to Constantinople had, on parting, given Bainbridge a Barbary Protection, which he now presented to the Dey who, on reading it, changed his manner entirely. Bainbridge was now offered friendship and promises of whatever service he required.

The advantage that Bainbridge took of that was nobly inspired. Algeria itself was at war with France. The French consul and the fifty to sixty Frenchmen in Algiers had all been imprisoned and enslaved. Bainbridge now asked for their freedom. It was granted and he took them all away aboard *George Washington*, which landed them at Alicante on the Spanish coast. Bainbridge had made that grace gesture while believing that the United States was still at war with France but a new treaty of peace had in fact been signed while *George Washington* lay at Algiers after its first arrival there.

For Bainbridge it had been a mission of perplexing and unforeseen responsibility. He was called upon to uphold the honour of his nation and his service, yet yield in humiliating fashion to the rage and threats of a despot who could at a word enslave him and his men, as that ruler perpetually did to others. Bainbridge was in a world of established deference beyond his understanding. The great naval powers of Europe were accustomed to performing the sort of demands that had been put upon him by the Dey. Bainbridge arrived there with a straightforward patriotism that made no allowance for such mortification of self and flag. The consul had swiftly convinced him, however, that on his own he risked provoking a war that, on top of the prevailing contest with France, was something the United States could ill afford at that moment. But the arbitrary humiliation of the United States Navy and its flag that had accompanied the payment of tribute rankled deeply when Bainbridge brought account of it home. Within a year the United States found itself at war with Barbary.

The quasi-war with France had been concluded after Talleyrand had developed a vision of acquiring Louisiana from Spain and rebuilding a French North American empire. He wanted a quick peace with the United States to enable him to advance his project. President Adams had declared that he would never send another minister to France unless he would be 'received, respected, and honoured as the representative of a great, free, powerful, and independent nation'. Talleyrand sent word that in such manner an American minister would indeed be received. Secretary of State

Timothy Pickering and other members of the cabinet wanted the undeclared war to continue but Adams named a three-man negotiating commission, which sailed for France.

The commission arrived to find that Talleyrand had already ordered an end to the capture of American ships and was about to release captured American sailors. A treaty was signed 30 September 1800. After it had been ratified the 18-gun *Herald* was despatched to the West Indies to recall the whole US naval force there.

In this manner ended the instructive early education of America's new-founded navy.

XXIII

IMPRESSED

HOWEVER satisfying the British concessions on trade, violation of neutrality nevertheless still rankled fiercely on the matter of impressment.

Faced by its continual shortage of men, experienced sailors especially, the British navy from early in the war had given itself licence to grab seamen on the high seas to fill the shortages aboard its own ships. None reacted more furiously than the Americans. No other issue in that war incensed them more, this violation as they saw it of the liberty and independence for which only the other day they had been fighting the British.

Impressment in all its aspect became much more sweeping, however, as the war progressed. American merchant seamen sought so far as possible always to be armed with a 'Protection' against the press gang, especially if going ashore either in Britain or in a British possession. Those, however, could be summarily brushed aside. The tales and experiences of the impressed for most part were to be of bitterly resented hardship. That, nevertheless, could be broken into something rare and strange, which was usually when opportunity for escape arose. Take the story of Joshua Penny of Southold in the county of Suffolk, Long Island, who offered a particularly striking account of the divergent experiences that impressment might deliver.

In 1794, at the age of twenty-one, Penny was serving aboard a British ship lying at Port Royal, Jamaica. He held a 'Protection', obtained when his ship lay at Liverpool. Soon after arrival at Port Royal, however, the whole of the ship's crew was impressed by the British. 'We were put into the *Alligator* frigate of 28 guns. Four of us were Americans, the others chiefly Danes and Swedes. A fever raged in this ship, and out of forty men, there were eleven corpses to be interred on the first morning. No sooner was the captain on deck in the morning than we were ready with our American protections. He said, "Men, I will not look at your protections – my ship is in distress, and I will have men to carry me to England."'

Alligator then moved to Montego Bay where she arrived the following

evening. Her boats promptly raided the merchantmen there. 'This business of kidnapping continued until daybreak, when they got underway in
season to prevent applications for relief. There were forty men impressed
that night, some of whom were American mates and supercargoes – some
had been taken out of their beds onshore, without liberty to dress themselves.'

Alligator was part of the escort of a convoy of 114 merchantmen. At
Spithead they were transferred to the 64-gun *Stately*, Captain Douglas.
Joshua Penny and companions found that they were part of the British
force, Blankett's and Elphinstone's, sent out to seize the Cape of Good
Hope. On arrival the fleet and transports rounded the Cape and anchored
off Simon's Town in False Bay on the Indian Ocean coast. The Dutch had
abandoned the fort there and retreated to Cape Town.

Penny was part of a force of sailors landed to reinforce the regular troops
for the attack on Cape Town. They were drilled by their own lieutenants.
'We were pronounced fit for action, but must be exercised in shooting
at a target. Accordingly a rock was fired at which was in the water. The
admiral had given out that whenever an American should fire, the rock
would smoke. About one of ten who fired drew smoke from the rock; and
on being asked by the general, "What countryman are you?" the answer
uniformly was, "I am an American".'

Opportunity to escape came when Penny and some of the other impressed
men were in a scouting party under a sergeant and saw a Dutch patrol
advancing upon them. The sergeant decided to evade the patrol and ordered
his men to follow, but Penny and the other impressed laid down their arms.
The Dutch took them to their camp – 'treated us with Constantia wine
and mutton tails of the best quality. In short they had nothing too good
for us. They knew we had deserted, for this was not the first party, and
asked us the cause of our desertion? We answered them truly, that we had
been impressed and wished to return home. They sent us to Cape Town
in a waggon without a guard; the inhabitants on the road where we halted
treated us very handsomely.'

At Cape Town they were presented to the governor, who ordered them
clothed and lodged at a boarding house. 'We had as much wine as we could
drink and ran about the streets as we pleased.' The day before Cape Town
was surrendered the governor called in the deserters, forty all told, and
advised them to go into the interior where they would be well received.
'Our knapsacks were loaded out of the company stores, with as much as
we could carry away. We retired to bushes on a hill about two miles from
town, and drank Dutch wine that night.'

They split into groups of three. Penny moved off with another American,
Jacob Cogswell of Boston, and a young Dutchman from Holland. They

were hospitably received everywhere as they continued into the interior for four days. They were put up at the house of a farmer named Sarel Overalsten and accompanied his sons to the coast, to a river mouth where they went fishing.

We had been two weeks at the river's mouth, living on fish and ostrich eggs, when this course of life became an old affair. The ostriches were always in sight, and in such numbers that at a distance they appeared like a drove of cattle. While fishing one day we discovered two men walking on the beach, which first alarmed us. They approached us, and being interrogated, stated that they had deserted from the whaling ship *John*, of London, which was then lying forty miles from us – that Captain Gardiner, formerly of Nantucket, commanded her – that he had killed one man and split the head of another with a broad axe – that they had left the ship at anchor and were very hungry. They lodged with us that night; for if they were English, they had also suffered under the tyranny exercised on board an English ship.

Cogswell and myself took it into our heads to visit this ship at anchor, whose crew was waging war on whales. We set off next morning with fish and a calibash of water, reached the ship in twenty-four hours. A whale-boat at the mouth of the Groot Vis Riviere, which belonged to the *John*, was watering. The crew confirmed the story which the two deserters related. They said it was a murdering ship, and they had calculated to leave her, but had heard of the surrender of the Cape to the English. With them we went on board, and satisfied the inquiries of the captain. He said he was much in want of men; for two of his damned rascals had deserted him. He said they had ten more days of whaling to be done before they sailed for St Helena. We shipped, and a few days after she was discovered to be so leaky, that it was doubtful whether she would reach St Helena.

The character of the captain was correctly given. One evening after killing two or three whales, I asked Cogswell whether he preferred to remain here or go among the Hottentots? He chose to stay.

Penny returned to the camp by the river and then back to the farm. There was more wandering in the interior, staying on farms, but he had grown weary of it, in spite of the hospitality he received from the Dutch inhabitants. He was often among the Hottentots (Khoikhoi, the original inhabitants of southern Africa). After more than a year of these varied adventures he met another American, John Johnston, of Rhode Island, and together they decided that they would return to the Cape in hope of finding a ship back to the United States. The Cape was by then completely under British control. Outside the Cape they met another of those who had deserted with them. He told them that the fleet that had brought them out was gone but the *Stately*, the ship from which Penny had escaped, was still there, along with a sloop, *Rattlesnake*. 'He further stated that seven men had recently been shot for desertion, and there had been a great naval mutiny in England.' Their new companion told them that the British mutiny had manifested itself at the Cape as well.

Penny and Johnston nevertheless decided to go into the town, 'dressed like the inhabitants of the country', and confident that as usual they would get sympathetic assistance from the Dutch. At the lodging house where they took rooms the landlord told them that there were merchant ships in port in need of men but it was impossible to avoid the English patrols that were searching every house for deserters. A patrol came that very night and demanded to know their nationality. 'We all answered that we were American. Johnston and myself were lodged in jail that night. The next morning we were told by the Fiscal that every such character in town who could not give a correct account of himself must be kept in jail until the trials of the sailors for the mutiny were terminated.'

Penny got a shock when, peering through the bars of the cell, he saw an officer from his old ship *Stately* appear. 'I lost my courage at the sight of the officer. But before he entered the prison door my fear forsook me. I was perfectly at ease. The officer, tapping me on the shoulder, asked if I was an American? Yes, I answered. "Is not your name Joshua Penny?" "My name is Jonas Inglesburg. I never deny my name nor country." He continued, "Can you deny that you know me?" No sir, I replied angrily, every officer who has been here these three weeks interviewing me has known me, and of course, you *must* know me.'

Penny was transferred to *Sceptre*, 64, aboard which he remained four to five months lying in Table Bay.

One of Penny's companions aboard *Sceptre* was another American, James Hall, who swam from *Sceptre* to an Indiaman and stowed himself on board. When Hall was reported missing *Sceptre*'s captain ordered all boats out to search the ships in the bay. Hall was found on the first ship they searched and brought back for punishment. Penny's account of the flogging provides a rare example of some humanity and even humour brought to the occasion.

All hands were called to see the culprit flogged, and stood as usual with their hats off. Hall was young, with a thin skin, and on receiving three strokes of the cat, cried out, 'Oh captain! For God's sakes forgive me!' The captain then suspending the punishment asked the unfortunate young man if he would now promise to attempt no more to run away. To which Hall answered, 'No, by God, captain, I will never give it up for one bad job.' As often as this solemnity occurs, the surgeon stands by the captain, to give notice of the man's fainting. After three strokes more were given the surgeon communicated the danger of the patient, upon which the cat was again arrested. Hall, scarcely able to articulate, addressing himself to the captain, said, 'Captain, we Americans can't bear flogging like you Englishmen, we are not used to it.' The captain turned, and walking off, with difficulty refrained from laughing aloud. But the whole ship's company smiled, though they dared not laugh. Hall was released because this captain did not happen to be a barbarian.

Penny concludes with his own observation on the episode: 'I have always noticed that when an American was whipped he fainted.'

From *Sceptre* Penny was transferred to the sloop *Rattlesnake*. On an Indian cruise *Rattlesnake* captured a Danish merchantman 'laden with silks and satins'. Penny was put aboard the prize, which sailed for the Cape. 'This pleased me, for I hoped to have another opportunity to get from the fangs of these harpies.' Instead he was drafted to the 20-gun *Sphinx*, assigned to cruise off the island of St Helena, where the right opportunity to get away finally appeared to present itself. James Hall and Penny were still together. Two other Americans messed with them aboard *Sphinx*. At St Helena they found an American whaling ship lying near *Sphinx* and decided to escape to the whaler. Hall and the others succeeded but Penny failed: 'not being a good swimmer I rested on our buoy and got with difficulty into the ship's head by climbing on the cable'.

When the three were reported missing Penny was called in to give his account of their escape. His lame retort was that he had believed the three were on ashore on watering duty. This captain's responses were not those of the *Sceptre*'s captain. The captain asked if he could swim. 'No, I answered. He then said, "You are a Yankee, sir, and have been seven years in the navy without ever being flogged, and now I'll flog you if you are God Almighty's first lieutenant."'

Penny fainted after the first three strokes. The surgeon informed the captain, who answered, 'He shall take his dozen, dead or alive!' This was done. 'I was cut down, and at the first recollection of myself, they were washing my face with a tub of water.'

Penny had some satisfaction when they got back to the Cape. On the way there *Sphinx* fell in with a French privateer which brought them to action. But the 20-gun *Sphinx* apparently considered itself at a disadvantage and made away. 'On our arrival at the Cape Captain Alexander was taken out of his ship and sent to England to be tried for cowardice. Cowards are always cruel. I shall forbear to dwell on this wretch's character, in order to shun the censure of being revengeful.'

Penny found himself back aboard *Sceptre*, lying in Table Bay, awaiting his next draft in this circuit from which escape had worked for others but eluded him. There was one bright moment.

Not long after this the 4th of June came, when the seamen are allowed to get drunk, because this is their king's birthday; and when the 4th of July came I applied to Lieutenant Pingally for liberty to get drunk. He said, 'go along forward, you Yankee rascal'. The captain then spoke to him, and when he, as I suppose, informed him of my request. He called me to him, and asked – 'What do you mean, sir, by asking permission to do what is contrary to the regulations of this ship?' 'I recollect, sir,' said I, 'that about a month ago you gave the English liberty to get drunk because it was their king's birthday; and now I want the liberty to rejoice on my nation's birthday.' The captain laughed heartily, ordered that two gallons of wine and one of brandy be procured from the shore for me and my yankee mess to rejoice. We all liked this captain.

Penny suffered an injury to his hand. He pretended continued inability to use it. The surgeon decided to send him ashore to hospital in Cape Town. 'The Yankee feigns his sickness so as to get at liberty, to run away from the hospital,' the captain said. But the doctor insisted. Filing through the town with his escort of two Penny pleaded thirst when they came to a wine house. The others were ready to comply. Penny ordered a bottle of wine. He drank a glass and went in to pay while the sailors drank theirs. 'I proposed going immediately, judging however that they would never budge while any wine remained. As soon as they became engaged I pretended an occasion of necessity to retire out of the back door, and helped myself by the chairs until fairly out, and it was safe to become as well as ever I was in my life.' He hid on the mountainside until night when he returned to the town 'and laid in my supply of goods – this was two loaves of bread, a calabash of brandy and a flint. This was as much I could take, although my money was not all spent, which had been saved out of my rations of grog for this purpose. My dress was composed of one shirt, one Guernsey frock, and one pair of duck trousers with a hospital cap.'

What followed was surely one of the most extraordinary escapades of desertion in the Great War. For the next fourteen months Penny lived the life of a wild creature on Table Mountain and within the long range that extended beyond it along the Cape Peninsula. 'I resolved to become a breakfast for a lion, sooner than be taken to another floating dungeon.

'It was unsafe to make a fire that night on a mountain fronting the ships, yet I was in danger from the wild beasts, who were often near me . . . The next morning I perceived that the ships lay far below, and could not discover me. I began to think of preparing subsistence . . .' His wanderings in the interior, especially among the Khoikhoi, had taught him a great deal about survival in the bushveld, the South African wild. These lessons were immediately applied.

. . . on searching, I soon found a hive of bees among the rocks. The Hottentots had taught me the process of obtaining this honey, and having a wooden pipe and introducing the stem of my pipe blew in the smoke . . . I could make a fire under the cover of a rock, and regale myself with brandy and honey. When I had ascended four days from the mountain's foot, I lost sight of the fleet and the bay . . . I saw innumerable herds of goats, hosts of antelopes, wolves and leopards. The baboons were numerous and large. At first, they would apparently take no notice of me; but soon after would be seen on a precipice, 100 feet above, throwing stones at me . . . I occupied a cavern which secured me from storms, near a spring of good water. My whole stock of provisions being nearly exhausted I sallied out with a stone in my hand, and had not advanced a great distance when I spied an antelope on the brow of a precipice. I threw the stone at the back of his head and tumbled him to the bottom where I found my game, whose skin I drew over his head, and cutting the meat into strings, hung it on sticks put into the crevices of my habitation. This meat when dried I broiled and eat with toad-sorrel for my sauce.

While among the Hottentots I had learned their method of making a very pleasant beverage resembling metheglin (mead). I was fortunate to find an old hollow tree, which I cut off with my knife and seized a green hide on one end for a bottom. Into this tub honey and water was put to stand twenty-four hours, then was added some pounded root to make it foment. My clothes, by creeping through the rocks and bushes, were so tattered that I had become almost naked. In this extremity I made a needle from the bone of a beast, the eye of which being made with my sharp-pointed knife, enabled me to sew with the sinews of my antelopes. With the skins I equipped myself from head to foot.

Thus I lived, unannoyed by wild beasts or press gangs. At each full moon I cut a notch in the root, which hung to a silken cord about my neck; and this was the only account I kept of time . . . I had become perfectly reconciled to my condition – had abundance of meat, sorrel, honey and water; and every night could sing my song with as much pleasure as at any period in my life. In fine, I never enjoyed life better than while I lived among the ferocious animals of Table Mountain . . . I now left my numerous habitations for the last time. The second day on my descent, the air being clear, I saw the bay, and one vessel only. I perceived that vessel to be a brig, and having no topgallant masts, took her for a merchantman.

I marched through the town unobserved by anyone except two or three servants, who continued to gaze obliquely at me as long as I could see them. The boat was coming to the shore as I approached it, with two men and the captain, as I supposed. I tried my power of speech to prepare myself. The captain landing advanced guard-edly towards me, I stepped up to meet him and asked if he wanted to ship a man? He was surprised to hear me speak, and asked, 'What in the name of God are you? Man or beast?' He at last stepped up to me and giving me his hand said, 'This is no place to talk – jump into the boat and go on board.' Into it I sprung and was soon snug on board. When the captain returned he sent for me and ordered me two suits of clothes. He then heard a short story of myself and said he had supposed me to be a deserter, but that I had nothing to fear if I would go with him.

The brig was under Danish colours, but the captain and property were English – and was bound to St Helena, and thence to London. On learning I had deserted the *Sceptre*, he informed me that she had been sunk fourteen months: he pointed to a monument on shore over the bodies of her crew, which had been driven on shore and there interred.

We were a few days making ready to sail to St Helena, which place we reached without accident. The governor detained us here until the India fleet arrived to take us under convoy. Lying there four months I found this captain to be a truly good, humane man. He let me have money to spend there, and although no agreement was made for any wages he had compassion on me. While we lay there the India ship *Indian Chief* of Philadelphia lay near us. I wished to return home in her, yet I could not without deserting – and who would be so ungrateful as to desert from such a captain. At sight of the American flag tears streamed from my eyes. I rushed on board and every American I saw seemed nearer of kin than my brother I left at home. Among other things I told them of the loss of my protection and asked if they had lost a hand? A young man answered 'Yes, we have lost my brother, John Porter, of your height and complexion'. Taking his protection I went to our brig and told the captain to put me down on the log book John Porter. He laughed and said it was very well thought of.

The India fleet arrived and I was taken into the *Admiral Hughes*, an India built ship of 2200 tons, which took our captain's brig in tow to England. When I was take out of the brig and alongside of the *Admiral Hughes* – who should I behold but Lieutenant Pingally, 1st of the *Sceptre*, which had foundered when he was on shore. He was the first person who spoke to me. He stood on the gangway, called me aside and said, 'Inglesberg, don't you know me?' 'Yes, your honour, perfectly.' The first opportunity that offered so as not to expose me, he asked where I had been, etc. I hope said he it was nothing that I had done which made you desert. He then told me what had happened after I had left *Sceptre*. He said that the surgeon's mate was unable to give a satisfactory account of the dead Inglesberg. You and I, he said, seem born for some fortunate end.

We arrived at the Downs. The regulating captain at the Downs made us all pass in review before him and answer his interrogatories. 'What countryman are you?' 'An American, sir.' 'Where is your protection?' Here it is, said I, showing him the one I obtained at St Helena. I told him I entered at St Helena. Lieutenant Pingally stood all this while looking at me, over the interrogating captain's shoulder, and laughed. He, however, after seeing me clear of these fellows clutches, called me aside and told me that he was appointed to command of a 20 gun ship and if I would go along with him, I should have as good an office as I could merit. I refused, and he said, 'Well, I wish you safe home: if I can never man my ship without impressment I never wish her manned. I knew you to be an American, or perhaps I should not have suffered you to get off as you have.' This was a good Englishman, and any one who was acquainted with him would gladly leave any other ship and run to him.

The captain of our brig, at Deptford, was glad to see us once more. He paid us all off, with two dollars extra to those who had fared so well in the *Admiral Hughes*, and then discharged us.

We went to London, with too much money not to lose a little. At length I sought a birth in an American vessel. Fortunately I found the ship *Dauphin*, of Boston, Captain Wallace, bound to Charleston, South Carolina. In her I had a pleasant passage to Charleston. When I beheld my country I was in an ecstasy of joy.

XXIV

NAPLES

News of Nelson's victory at the Nile took two months to reach London, arriving there only on 2 October 1798.

In Britain there had been acute concern. On 22 August Pitt wrote to his mother: 'The account of Bonaparte's arrival at Alexandria is, I am afraid, true; but it gives us no particulars, and leaves us in entire suspense as to Nelson.' Alarm at Westminster was high. Even at this point no one had expected the seizure of Malta and invasion of Egypt, much less any intent towards India. Pitt's worries at that date had yet long to go.

Nelson's captain, Edward Berry, was deputed to carry the despatches to St Vincent off Cadiz. Berry had sailed in the 50-gun *Leander* on 6 August but *Leander* was captured by *Généreux*, one of the ships that escaped from Aboukir Bay.

Fortunately duplicates were sent to Admiralty via Naples. They were put aboard *Mutine*, an armed brig commanded by Captain Thomas Capel, who was to take the despatches on from Naples to London via Vienna. At Naples Capel was to hand command of *Mutine* to eighteen-year-old William Hoste, the last of the old *Agamemnon* pupils waiting for promotion to his own ship. After Tenerife, Hoste had been posted to *Theseus*, which became part of Nelson's Mediterranean squadron. Hoste had been praised for his conduct aboard *Theseus* during the battle and was supervising refitting aboard the wrecked *Tonnant* when, to his astonishment, he was summoned and told that command of *Mutine* would fall to him when Capel left the ship at Naples. He had obtained his certificate while off Cadiz; this, then, was the long-awaited prize attendant upon that.

Naples was therefore to be the first point in Europe to receive the news of the victory at Aboukir Bay. Tumultuous though its reception would be elsewhere, nowhere would quite equal the hysterical scenes enacted within the royal palace when *Mutine* arrived on 3 September at three in the afternoon. Hoste and Capel went ashore to deliver the news to Sir William Hamilton. Overcome by the excitement, Emma Hamilton promptly fainted.

The performance of her friend, Queen Maria Carolina, was even more dramatic, according to Emma Hamilton: 'How shall I describe the transports of the Queen! 'tis not possible. She cried, kissed her husband, her children, walked frantic about the room, cried, kissed, and embraced every person near her; exclaiming, O brave Nelson! O God bless and protect our brave deliverer! O Nelson, Nelson! What do we not owe you! O Victor! Saviour of Italy! O that my swollen heart could not tell him personally what we owe to him?' All of that was in a letter from Emma Hamilton that Nelson received at sea before his arrival. Anticipating his own reception when he got to Naples, he dryly commented: 'I only hope I shall not have to be witness to a renewal of it.'

Until Nelson's arrival young Hoste served as Emma's trophy. 'Lady Hamilton made us get into her carriage and parade through the streets till dark; she had a bandeau round her forehead with the words "Nelson and Victory" . . . "Viva Nelson!" resounded through the streets . . . Bonfires and illuminations all over the town.'

Nelson's small squadron was, meanwhile, struggling towards Naples, beating against the wind. The three ships, *Vanguard*, *Culloden* and *Alexander*, were in need of urgent structural repair.

The painfully slow and heavily buffeted four-week passage from Aboukir Bay to Naples was a passage of another sort for Nelson. His condition was at the outset scarcely any better than that of his ship. He was still in that shattered state that had led him to tell St Vincent that he doubted he would ever see his face again. He suffered severely from concussion. In a fevered state, he sought an early return to England. 'My head is ready to split, and I am always so sick,' he wrote to St Vincent. And later, 'I know I ought to give up for a little while; my head is splitting at this moment.'

Underlying that was the shock that he said would always work on him, that of arriving off Alexandria high with expectation on the first part of his chase only to view a mole empty of the French armada he sought. The driving power that had sustained him had collapsed there. The impact of apparent failure achieved permanence, an inner turmoil 'which on any extraordinary anxiety now shows itself, be that feeling pain or pleasure'. That disturbance had therefore become the invisible wound which, along with that of the flesh, he carried from Aboukir Bay to Naples. He was a man listlessly in search of relief from both the scars upon him.

He had won the greatest victory yet in British naval history. The wider world was still unaware. He was for that short while alone with it. He understood the tremendous implications, but his enormous powers of resilience were being severely tested. He was in a state of extreme nervous irritation. Or, to see it differently, the man approaching Naples had become temperamentally vulnerable in a manner that left him open to the play of any new and different emotional circumstance.

Halfway through the passage, however, Nelson appeared restored to himself. He abandoned the idea of returning home. In a letter to Samuel Hood, who had been assigned the blockade of Alexandria, Nelson declared that he would not go home until the French army in Egypt had been destroyed and Malta and Corfu captured. He was now fully focused upon the changed strategic circumstances on the Mediterranean that he had made possible: the consolidation of British dominance from Sicily to the Levant. With that came strong resentment of the need to go to Naples, which was unavoidable, however, because of the need to repair his ships. 'I detest this voyage to Naples,' he wrote to St Vincent. 'Nothing but absolute necessity could force me to the measure. Syracuse in future, whilst my operations lie on the eastern side of Sicily, is my port, where every refreshment may be had for a fleet.' And to Sir William Hamilton at Naples he declared that he hoped not to be there more than four or five days.

By fixing upon Syracuse as his intended base Nelson, in the last days of this signal voyage from Aboukir to Naples, marshalled in his head and in his correspondence the necessary strategy he saw ahead for the Levant. He had aboard with him the senior French officers who had been captured, including Admiral Du Chayla, and they were minutely questioned on French intentions and strategy. And, having drawn from his prisoners their belief that Napoleon merely needed a communication opened by sea to vanquish Syria, that became Nelson's own conviction. Nothing else was in mind as *Vanguard* closed with Naples.

A week before her straggling arrival at Naples under tow *Vanguard* was met by *Mutine*, now commanded by William Hoste, who brought out all the letters and despatches that had arrived at Naples. Among the letters was an invitation from Sir William Hamilton declaring that an apartment awaited him in their *palazzo*.

It was more than five years since Nelson and the Hamiltons had met during the British occupation of Toulon. Although Nelson and Sir William had been in close communication to have *Vanguard* and the fleet supplied during the chase after Napoleon's armada. But Nelson had not gone ashore and seen them again.

A flotilla of small craft set out to meet *Vanguard* when she was sighted on 22 September. Long before she reached the anchorage King Ferdinand came out in his barge. The Hamiltons accompanied him in theirs. The court musicians played from another barge. Emma Hamilton was overcome as she came on board. Nelson described the scene to his wife: 'Up flew her ladyship, and exclaiming, "Oh God, is it possible?" She fell into my arm more dead than alive. Tears, however, soon set matters to rights.' And to

Fanny Nelson he offered her own share of the accolade: '. . . if it were so affecting to those who were only united to me by bonds of friendship, what must it be to my dearest wife, my friend, my everything which is most dear to me in this world?'

Nelson's victory was received with equal though less hysterical celebration by others on the Continent and around the Mediterranean. Gifts and accolades descended upon him from Tsar Paul, the Ottoman Sultan and the king of Sardinia. At Naples Ferdinand conferred on Nelson the dukedom of Bronte in Sicily, together with a supposed income of £3,000 a year. The East India Company, grateful that he had frustrated French ambitions in India, gave him £10,000. Only with London did it seem that he got less than many considered his due within carefully scaled titular merit. St Vincent had been raised from a barony to an earldom after St Vincent. Camperdown made Duncan a viscount. A viscountcy was what Pitt swiftly pronounced as Nelson's inevitable reward the day after the news reached London. Instead, Nelson got the lesser barony. The declared reason was another question of naval etiquette, namely that a new title higher than barony could not be sanctioned since, at Aboukir Bay, Nelson was not the Mediterranean commander in chief. His old commander at Toulon, Lord Hood, was among those who protested. In a letter to Nelson he said, 'In my humble judgment, a more flimsy reason was never given . . . I am not singular in the sentiments I have stated; they are in unison with the general voice of your grateful country.' Nelson's privately expressed view was that 'it is proof how much a battle fought near England is prized to one fought at a great distance'.

All of this was illustrative of the rigid social stratification that bound even the most splendid achievements, as Nelson's wife in different way also now discovered. 'Since . . . my husband has gained this victory, I have been honoured with the notice of the great in this neighbourhood – truly I don't thank them: they ought to have found their way to the cottage before.'

Any smallness of that was more than balanced, however, by the huge celebration that raced across Britain. A nation whose fears and uncertainties had been renewed after Camperdown by puzzlement over the objective of the Toulon armada now gave itself to Nelson with a fullness of trust and idolization that thereafter would build steadily.

The spare nature of the official British tribute can seem astonishing given that Nelson had changed the picture for all. He had accomplished precisely what Austria and Naples had required of Pitt. Indeed, more than anyone could have imagined, if only because no one had correctly read Napoleon's intentions with the armada. Suddenly, dramatically, totally unforeseen, instead of a massive assault on Britain or the Continent Napoleon was locked up in Egypt, descending the Nile instead of landing in Sicily, Portugal or Ireland.

Napoleon was out of the way and French sea power on the Mediterranean effectively removed but France still lay dominant across the Continent of Europe. She controlled the coasts from Bremen and Antwerp across to Genoa, ruled over most of Italy and the critical bastion of Switzerland, with her intimidating influence reaching into Spain and across to Portugal. Her revolutionary passion was easily incited, it was affecting many peoples aside from her own, for the idea of republicanism had begun to exercise strong appeal among the intelligentsia in many parts of Europe. For France's enemies the future nevertheless looked different.

A Second Coalition was in process. On 17 May, the very day that Napoleon sailed from Toulon for Egypt, Austria and Naples had signed a commitment detailing the forces each would provide on resumption of war with France. Russia and Britain were moving towards an alliance, finally to be concluded in the last days of the year. In a renewal of hostilities on the Continent Tsar Paul would, on payment of handsome subsidies by Britain, provide an army of forty-five thousand men. Prussia formed the other hoped-for partner in this coalition. So Foreign Secretary Thomas Grenville's brother went to Prussia to attempt to persuade Frederick William III against France. He got nowhere. But, remarkably, Paul I of Russia and the Ottoman Porte were committed to the alliance. The savage hatred that Catherine the Great had maintained against the Ottomans appeared to have been laid aside with Paul. The Ottoman Porte had already declared war on France as a result of Aboukir Bay. Powerful alliance against France thus seemed to be emerging, though not as hastily as Austrian Chancellor Thugut's initial plea for a Mediterranean naval demonstration by Britain might have suggested once news of Aboukir Bay had been received by all. Austria was not yet ready for a resumption of war.

In Britain, there were other reasons for optimism.

The surge of confidence released by Nelson's victory was now matched by the optimism of Pitt's national budget. In proposing a 10 per cent tax on income, Pitt did so on the basis of a complete assessment of the nation's resources, which demonstrated that after nearly six years of war British imports and exports exceeded those of any year of peace. The subsidies that the greedy potential allies would require were thus provided for.

There was as well relief that the Irish rebellion had been quashed. Tired of waiting for help from France, Wolfe Tone's United Irishmen had risen in rebellion in May. French assistance arrived too late. Tone was captured and committed suicide in prison.

Over as well for the moment was the costly struggle for St Domingue (Haiti) against the black rebel leader Toussaint L'Ouverture who had risen to power there. A junior British officer, Lieutenant Colonel Maitland, found himself responsible for the campaign there and Maitland had taken upon himself the decision of total evacuation of St Domingue, defying the powerful West Indian interests that objected to any example of independence under insurgent black rule. He negotiated a peace treaty with Toussaint in which Britain recognized the island as neutral territory. Toussaint for his part declared his ports open to free trade and prohibited the use of the ports by privateers. St Domingue was finally evacuated on 3 October.[1]

The West Indian morass was now easily cloaked by the triumph of the Nile. The British navy had made the single biggest contribution to the feasibility of another land campaign on the Continent. With Napoleon and his army stranded in Egypt and the Second Coalition to all intents and purposes established, France on the Continent looked vulnerable on all fronts, around the Mediterranean and its hinterland especially.

After three hard years off Cadiz St Vincent had moved to Gibraltar in October. He went ashore from *Victory* and established himself at Rosia House on Rosia Bay, from where the entire Straits lay before him, with the North African coast from Ceuta to Cape Spartel in view opposite, and the Spanish coast from Cabrita Point receding beyond the Rock. His arrival at Gibraltar was accompanied by a widely embracing set of Admiralty instructions for Nelson's squadron, dated 3 October 1798.

Nelson's responsibilities now were 'most particularly' to protect the coasts of Sicily, Naples and the Adriatic in 'active co-operation' with the Austrian and Neapolitan armies in the event of war being renewed in Italy. He had as well to blockade Malta, prevent communication between France and the French army in Egypt, and to cooperate with the Russian and Turkish squadrons that were to be sent into the Greek archipelago.

On his own initiative, however, Nelson, well before Admiralty's new strategic instructions arrived, became seized by desire to push Naples into war against France.

The hectic Neapolitan celebration of Aboukir had held Nelson entrapped in its frenzy day and night, with all of it capped a week after his arrival by a grand party the Hamiltons gave to celebrate his fortieth birthday on 29 September. A dinner for eighty at the Hamilton's *palazzo* was followed by a ball for seventeen hundred guests, with a supper laid for eight hundred. The next day Nelson appeared to have had enough of it all. His earlier disturbed condition was revived. He sat down on the 30th to write to St Vincent: 'I trust, my Lord, in a week we shall all be at sea. I am very unwell, and the miserable conduct of this Court is not likely to cool my irritable temper. It is a country of fiddlers and poets, whores and scoundrels.' To his wife he wrote, 'Our time here is actively employed; and between business, and what is called pleasure, I am not my own master for five minutes. The continued kind attention of Sir William and Lady Hamilton must ever make you and I love them . . . My pride is being your husband, the son of my dear father, and in having Sir William and Lady Hamilton for my friends.'

He might be seen here to be clutching at all that hitherto suggested stability in his life for, apart from the dizzy acclamations rapidly descending upon him, other unfamiliar forces now pressed upon him in that feverish environment.

The two women who dominated that scene had instant possession of him in their different ways. For Emma Hamilton it was, initially, the theatrical side of it, herself directing the whole show of the Hero's Return. With that, however, Nelson's private fascination with her had begun. At the end of a letter to St Vincent he gave his commander and the world its first glimpse of a new emotional disturbance arising within him: 'I am writing opposite Lady Hamilton, therefore you will not be surprised at the glorious jumble of this letter. Were your lordship in my place, I much doubt if you could write so well; our hearts and our hands must be all in a flutter: Naples is a dangerous place, we must keep clear of it.'

Aside from her blazing entertainments, Emma Hamilton had assumed another more serious role, as intermediary between Nelson and Queen Maria Carolina, who had promptly seen the victory at the Nile as the basis for an immediate further assault against the French and Nelson as party to it. If Emma Hamilton suddenly presented a new form of the feminine to him, the Neapolitan queen offered another. Nelson had never before experienced anything like either.

Marie Antoinette's sister was a driven woman who ruled her husband and the kingdom. Her hatred and fear of France sought release in vengeance upon it. Nelson's victory, as she constantly cried out, had delivered the Kingdom of the Two Sicilies from the French threat to its existence. What she wanted in consequence was to see the French driven right out of Italy. Right then, in compliance with the new treaty signed in May between Naples and Austria on the forces each would deliver if war came, an Austrian general, Baron Karl von Mack, was on his way to command the Neapolitan army. To Maria Carolina, with Nelson already in Naples and General Mack daily expected, the circumstances for a strike against the French in Italy looked propitious.

Nelson probably came to that conclusion on his own as he surveyed the strategic picture from Naples. He was swiftly seized by the concept of surprising the French. As he saw it, the French were so widely distributed in the Papal States that a surprise attack without formal declaration of war would prove triumphant, with instant welcome from the local population. For this he had full support from Sir William Hamilton and the Neapolitan prime minister, Sir John Acton. They were strongly opposed, however, by the Neapolitan Court. It was left to the eager queen to work upon the king, who found himself caught between Carolina and the Court.

Ferdinand and Carolina had reason to fear the French. The Kingdom of the Two Sicilies was the last in Italy to retain its independence from French intrusion. The French seizure of Italy had halted at the Papal States. Since Rome was but a short march from Naples the threat of the French seizure of Naples and Sicily was real enough. But French command of the Mediterranean and the lack of British presence in the Middle Sea had eased the threat, which was maintained only in the shape of stern warnings to Naples strictly to maintain its neutrality.

Just ten days after landing at Naples Nelson on his own was ready to go to war with France in Italy. Given the disturbed man that he already was, everything about him in that momentous week had helped to produce his own obsessive zeal. His head, as evident from his correspondence, was a strange dizzying mixture of all that had fallen upon him since he stepped ashore. The calm that the four weeks at sea had gradually and mercifully delivered to him had been severely affected by the hectic immersion in a fervid idolizing of himself of a sort he had never before experienced, which he saw as entirely his due, from which he could not, nor wished to, step aside, but aspects of which nevertheless raised his contempt and anger. The lavish entertainments ceaselessly raised in his honour, the cheers that accompanied him wherever he went, exposed to him the frivolous, corrupt and inept character of the Neapolitan Court. It helped raise the critical scorn he felt for what he saw as delinquent effort to muster their strength against a threat to the Kingdom of the Two Sicilies that he regarded as inevitable. Although Naples was then daily expecting the appearance of Austrian General Mack, Nelson was incensed that there was no evident military preparation in anticipation of his arrival.

He began urging an immediate attack by Naples upon Rome. On 4 October, Nelson wrote to St Vincent, 'This country by its system of procrastination will ruin itself; the Queen sees it, and thinks as we do . . . War at this moment can alone save these kingdoms . . . I have scolded; anger is necessary.'

Nelson overlooked several realities in the situation. This was in character when unrestrainable impulse for action took over and he found himself driven to act of his own accord, with something less than full consideration of the cost and possible consequences.

Such a tactical strike might have been realistic if combined with the eventual intended attack upon the French in northern Italy. But the Austrian emperor was reluctant to go to war against France yet, in spite of having gained from Britain the Mediterranean action that Chancellor Thugut had so earnestly pleaded for to Pitt earlier in the year. Emperor Francis II wanted to wait for the spring before any move against the French. He preferred that it be the French who started hostilities, which could be expected once they saw a Second Coalition that included Russia marshalled against them.

What Nelson also failed to comprehend was that, as elsewhere on the Continent, French republicanism held strong appeal for the Neapolitan intelligentsia as well as the liberal-minded of the aristocracy. Away from the Court, King Ferdinand's support lay with the Church, the peasants and the mob, the *lazzaroni*. Soon after his arrival the queen made her first plea to Nelson that Naples Bay should never thereafter be left without the protection of a British ship of the line, 'that in case of any mishap, that their Majesties think their persons much safer under the protection of the British flag than under any other'. Ferdinand and Maria Carolina clearly did not see themselves equally safe aboard one of the Neapolitan navy's own line ships.

It would be many weeks yet before the Admiralty's new instructions reached Nelson via St Vincent. Whatever the wisdom of urging Naples to war, the oncoming Admiralty directives did at least provide full protective cover from blame for Nelson, for they allowed that 'the protection of the coasts of Naples and Sicily, and an active co-operation with the Austrian and Neapolitan armies are the objects to which a principal part of the squadron should be most particularly directed'.

Notwithstanding his urgent demand for this independent Italian campaign, Nelson had to remain preoccupied with his established strategic objectives, which were necessarily focused upon the Levant.

His fleet was reduced. He had nine sail of the line, some frigates and sloops. These were equally divided between himself, Hood and Ball. Hood was off Alexandria with three line ships and two frigates. Ball was blockading Malta with a similar squadron. Nelson had the same strength but one of his three line ships was repairing at Naples. With most of this modest force held at Naples or occupied with blockade of Alexandria and Malta, its scope was severely limited.

A sense of the incomplete lay heavily upon Nelson as he contemplated the wide operational scene from which he had withdrawn. He had changed the strategic picture in the Levant only to find himself absent from it all, notably Egypt 'where my whole heart is, for I long to see the destruction of Buonaparte and his boasted Armament', as he declared to the British minister at Constantinople. But for the moment Hood's blockade was all that could be managed.

General Mack, meanwhile, had arrived at Naples to command the Neapolitan army, but a courier from Vienna brought word that the Austrian emperor wanted the French to be the aggressors. Austria was not yet prepared to start a war and could give no assurance of help if Naples did so on its own. The king and queen were in great distress over this, Nelson told St Vincent. But he had rallied them: 'I ventured to tell their Majesties directly that one of the following things must happen to the king, and he had his choice – Either to advance, trusting to God for his blessing on a just cause, to die with *l'épée à la main*, or remain quiet and be kicked out of your kingdoms.'

On 22 November an ultimatum was sent to the French to abandon the Papal States and Malta. The following day General Mack marched on Rome at the head of his Neapolitan army. On 6 December Nelson wrote to St Vincent, 'General Mack is marching against them with 20,000 men. I think the result of the battle doubtful, and on it depends the safety of Naples. If Mack is defeated this country is lost in fourteen days.' It required less than that.

Mack's army was routed, with the Neapolitans fleeing ignominiously before the French commander at Rome, General Championnet. As Championnet began advancing towards Naples the royal family prepared to flee to Sicily. Naples was in chaos with the intelligentsia and upper classes ready to welcome the French but the lower classes, the *lazzaroni*, swore loyalty to Ferdinand, begged him to stay, and prepared to fight the French at the gates. The king appeared on a balcony to assure them that he would stay, even as the royal household behind him packed for flight.

It was to be a dramatic three-day operation. The head of the Neapolitan navy, Admiral Francesco Caracciolo, was required to assist Nelson. That clearly sat ill with him. British sailors had been assigned to vessels of his own navy when the officers and seamen deserted their ships. Nelson had then removed all the Neapolitan naval vessels from the mole and sent them to anchorage. A British woman was struck by Caracciolo's manner at a dinner party, declaring that she 'never saw any man so utterly miserable. He scarcely uttered a word, ate nothing, and did not even unfold a napkin.'

Caracciolo's state was common to many of the upper classes observing the disintegration of their society and fearing for themselves as the *lazzaroni* roamed the streets swearing to lynch those they believed might be prepared to welcome the French. The royal family itself was in fear of the *lazzaroni* preventing their flight. A heavy, furtive secrecy descended upon all their activities as they sought to get their valuables and possessions away.

It was the night of 21 December before Nelson got everyone on board his own and the other ships that had arrived to assist. Once away the ships ran into a storm that Nelson described as 'harder than I have ever experienced since I have been at sea'.

Aboard *Vanguard* on that violent three-day voyage to Palermo, Emma Hamilton further demonstrated her devotion to the queen by steadfastly caring for her and the family. Her performance made a strong impression upon Nelson, who recounted to St Vincent, 'It is my duty to tell your Lordship the obligations which the whole Royal Family as well as myself are under on this trying occasion to her Ladyship . . . Lady Hamilton provided her own beds, linen, etc, and became *their slave* for . . . no person belonging to Royalty assisted the Royal Family, nor did her Ladyship enter a bed the whole time they were on board.' Emma Hamilton nursed the seasick, terrified children. On Christmas morning the youngest child, six-year-old Prince Alberto, had convulsions and died in Emma Hamilton's arms.

At two a.m. on the 26th *Vanguard* anchored off Palermo. The queen, grieving for her child, went quickly ashore before dawn to avoid the formality and trumpeting of a public landing, which the king made at nine that morning.

The impact of great change and loss lay upon all. The cost of the ill-considered lunge against the French made for a black approach of the new year of 1799.

Maria Carolina was mourning the loss of a child but beyond that, for her and her husband, lay loss of half of their kingdom and likelihood of losing the rest of it as well. Ferdinand was blaming his wife and her friend Lady Hamilton for leading him into the military disaster. While Emma Hamilton sat weeping with the queen, her husband was equally inconsolable. Sir William Hamilton was distraught over his own losses. At the evacuation he had put his treasures, the prized collection of a lifetime, aboard ships to carry them to England. He was to learn that one of the ships had been wrecked off the Scilly Isles with its cargo of some of his most valued Grecian vases. But he mourned as well for what had been abandoned in Naples: his 'three houses elegantly furnished, all our horses and six or seven carriages'. The distress was something more than material, however, being that of a man almost seventy who saw swept away the special richly sustaining Mediterranean existence that he had created for himself and loved.

For Nelson what had occurred was equally immeasurable. He sat with the consequences of his impulsive obsession to drive the Neapolitans to have their go at the French. It was impossible for a mind as astute as his to escape sense of his own culpability in the disaster. The depressed state that he had been in after the Nile came back upon him, together with headaches, irritability, nausea and the heart palpitations that he had specifically ascribed to the embedded shock and disillusion that had overwhelmed him when he had arrived at Alexandria expecting to see the French fleet and found only an empty mole.

What settled upon Nelson at Palermo was a temperamental state that in one form or another would stay with him to the end. Sir Harris Nicolas, who compiled and edited Nelson's letters and papers, said that it was from this time that an increasing irritability became apparent. The truth of that is continually evident in the subsequent correspondence and reports, which reflect frequent despair. For the past five years Nelson had consistently carried more direct active responsibility than any other individual in the British armed forces. No one else had had laid upon him such total trust and dependence in situations so closely associated with the nation's survival. He bore the scars of that on his head and on his body and, as was increasingly apparent, in his heart and mind as well.

Apart from the calamity of defeat and flight, after arrival at Palermo Nelson suffered an unpleasant personal shock on being advised by St Vincent that Sir William Sidney Smith had been given the naval command in the Levant. In effect, the most critical theatre of operations consequent on the triumph of the Nile had been detached from Nelson's control. The direct confrontation with Napoleon had been taken from him. For the man who in those very seas had just secured for Britain effective control of the entire Mediterranean it was a bitterly offensive jolt.[2]

Earl Spencer had never particularly distinguished himself as head of Admiralty. His handling of Smith's appointment was particularly insensitive. Sidney Smith's insouciantly presumptuous character was well known. He was admired for his boldness and daredevil courage. Few could match his romantic image of the warrior chivalrous and intrepid. But he was equally known for his insubordination and contempt of those in authority over him. He had escaped from captivity in Paris and had been assigned a fine, newly overhauled ship, the 80-gun *Tigre*, and then sent out to serve under St Vincent at Gibraltar. Spencer decreed that Sidney Smith should be regarded as the senior officer in the Levant except if a major fleet were sent there, then Sidney Smith would have to defer to those who were his seniors. Sidney Smith thus was allowed licence to consider himself in full command in that wide basin, responsible to no one beyond, although Nelson's command of the entire Mediterranean under St Vincent was clearly defined and understood. Sidney Smith's subservience within Nelson's overall command had not been defined.

True to form, Sidney Smith immediately rubbed that in. He wrote to Sir William Hamilton that Samuel Hood, whom Nelson had assigned to the blockade of Alexandria, naturally fell under his orders 'as being my junior'. By that he indicated that he now had complete charge of Hood's squadron.

For Nelson all of it was insufferable. On New Year's Eve he wrote to St Vincent, '*I do feel, for I am a man*, that it is impossible for me to serve in these seas . . . he has no orders from you to take my ships away from my command; but it is all of a piece. Is it to be borne? Pray grant me your permission to retire . . .'

St Vincent, in swift response, set things right. Sidney Smith was firmly advised that he was under Nelson's orders. To Nelson St Vincent said, 'For the sake of your Country, and the existence of its power in the Levant, moderate your feelings and continue your command . . . Employ Sir Sidney Smith in any manner you think proper: knowing your magnanimity, I am sure you will mortify him as little as possible . . .'[3]

Obedient to St Vincent's plea, Nelson stayed and applied himself to the evolving situation in Italy and the Levant. But it was obvious that, given his worn, nervous and debilitated state, he required deep relief in some form from all his pressures, those of command and his physical condition. He had already found a sustaining comfort in his dependence upon the friendship and hospitality of Sir William and Emma Hamilton. With Emma it had steadily become something far more, however, and this developed rapidly after the arrival at Palermo.

The observations left to posterity on Emma Hamilton's character, manners and behaviour obviously had to come principally from the literate upper classes, a full range of whom she necessarily met on equal terms after her marriage to Hamilton and as confidante of the queen of the Two Sicilies. In that elevated station that had come to her she naturally became a figure of constant comment in the diaries and letters of those of high social station who passed through Naples. Her background alone assured their interest. So did her flamboyance. The opinions sounded much the same note. Artful, vulgar, affected, were frequent terms. Or, as in one summation, '. . . bold, daring, vain even to folly, and stamped with her first situation much more strongly than one would suppose, after having represented Majesty, and lived in good company fifteen years'.

Emma Hamilton was always feeding her natural exuberance, putting herself at centre stage. In one of the most remarkable social advances of her epoch she had arrived at a setting that allowed her to exist in all the roles that Romney had cast her on canvas in her youth. Only Naples, with its vibrant southern conviviality, its cheerful spontaneity, its open sensuality, could so fully have allowed her that stage. The Neapolitan Court unavoidably reflected the tone, laxity and unstressed languor of the ancient society that surrounded it. In no other Court in Europe could Sir William Hamilton so effortlessly have introduced his wife and counted on her easy acceptance there.

Emma Hamilton's figure had become bountifully large, a classical Daphne or Venus. Hamilton called her his Grecian. Or, as one visitor to Naples put it, she was 'full in person, not fat, but *embonpoint*'. That suited her in the theatrical performance she liked to present, for she was an actress actual as well as in manner, always ready to perform an act she called 'Attitudes'. In that, people saw a different woman. Sir Gilbert Elliot described one occasion: 'We had the Attitudes a night or two ago by candle light. They come up to my expectations fully, which is saying everything. They set Lady Hamilton in a very different light from any I have seen her in before; nothing about her, neither her conversation, her manners, nor her figure, announce the very refined taste which she discovers in this performance, besides the extraordinary talent which is needed for the execution.' Another view was, 'It is a beautiful performance, amusing to the most ignorant, and highly interesting to the lovers of art. It is remarkable that although coarse and ungraceful in common life, she becomes highly graceful, and even beautiful, during this performance. It is also singular that, in spite of the accuracy of her imitation of the finest ancient draperies, her usual dress is tasteless, vulgar, loaded and unbecoming.'

Through that very conflict within the common view of her one glimpses more of what attracted Nelson. She offered what he could not have imagined he needed as he approached Naples, the voluptuous excess of Renaissance canvas that smothered him as he landed, the soothing softness that drew him away into an erotic befuddlement he had never experienced before. It came at the very moment in his life that he was most vulnerable to it. There was no suggestion, however, of sexual intimacy before the flight to Palermo. But her courageous and masterful role in the evacuation of the royal family took him beyond the seductive and the erotic in revealing something more of her to him. Her stalwart performance on the violent voyage to Palermo, herself as sleepless below as she tended her charges as he was on the quarterdeck seeing to their survival, solidly affirmed that other side of her character with him.

It was what they had in common in their lives and character that thereafter sounded with him: fortitude in crisis and endurance against obstacle. He had seen in her the same qualities he expected of his captains and seamen. She was brave, capable, efficient, dependable. She matched his own driving forces, the same defiance to the world and what stood against them: he, in the unceasing contest over his rightful due as he had even then over Sidney Smith, she in her triumph over the social odds ever against her. And she met him as well on his own level of excess, of vanity and self-glorification. The difference in class and upbringing together with the moral element attached to her earlier life that others could not ignore fell away entirely with him. Nelson wrote to St Vincent soon after arriving at Palermo, 'Our dear Lady Hamilton, whom to see is to admire, but, to know, are to be added honour and respect; her head and heart surpass her beauty, which cannot be equalled by anything I have seen.' It was already difficult for any outcome to their relationship other than that which now began to overwhelm them.

XXV

ACRE

THE start of the final year of the eighteenth century found the opposing forces of the Western world poised at the brink of a new future whose unpredictable course appeared set for resolution somehow or other between the deserts of the Middle East and Europe.

After two years of quiet on the Continent, war was about to erupt again, on the Rhine, in the Tyrol and northern Italy, even as Napoleon's bizarre dream of colonization in the Middle East sought its own momentum.

Buonaparte and his generals, Desaix and Kléber, had overrun Egypt. They were cut off, without communication to France. That nevertheless brought no disillusion. Napoleon had lost his Toulon fleet but with such a powerful army with him he could not regard himself as defeated. Far from it, his vision expanded. It remained limitless. Stretching before him he saw broad highways to world conquest. He would advance into Syria, on across the Levant eventually to take Constantinople as well as descending to India. He even dared to hope to reach the Indus by March 1800. The Ottoman Turks for their part were about to advance against him by land and sea. Formerly the closest ally of the French in the Levant, they had now declared war on France and were preparing to march down the Lebanese coast to free Egypt. They had, meanwhile, entered into dubious naval alliance against France with their old enemy Russia. Simultaneously with all of this a Russian army was marching across the Continent to join the Austrians for the war that the Austrian emperor wanted but avoided declaring.

In January 1799 understandably it was upon the Mediterranean, however, that the full focus lay. Pitt, St Vincent and Nelson together had restored British presence on that sea. But it was a limited presence, liable to be weakened should the Brest fleet get to Toulon and form a combination with the Spanish Grand Fleet. But the central preoccupation of the forces that St Vincent and Nelson commanded was that Napoleon and his army be kept locked in Egypt and denied all supplies and reinforcements. The burden of that task was intended to fall upon the Russian and Ottoman navies with whom Sir Sidney Smith was now to be the intermediary to convey Nelson's instructions.

It will be recalled that Sidney Smith, the wandering adventurer who had served the king of Sweden against the Russians in the Baltic, then the Ottoman Porte, and who had performed the final necessary sabotage at Toulon before the British evacuation from there in 1793, had subsequently been captured by the French on a reconnoitring expedition across the Channel. That was on 18 April 1796. After his capture he was at first threatened with being shot as a spy.

Many of the émigré royalists had returned to Paris after the fall of Robespierre. Sidney Smith had friends among them. These were enrolled to help him escape. After one failed attempt Sidney Smith, on instruction from the Directory, was placed under severe vigilance. A more elaborate scheme was prepared by Edmond de Philipeaux, a former artillery officer in Louis XVI's army. Philipeaux had been a fellow pupil at the Ecole Militaire in Paris with Buonaparte. He forged orders for Sidney Smith's removal to another prison. It was Sidney Smith's facility to pass for French that had put him in danger of being shot as a spy, but it was that as well that facilitated his relations in gaol, his escape, and moving comfortably about Rouen, where he spent several days before embarking for England. In May 1798 Sidney Smith was back in London, received with acclamation, including a private interview at Buckingham House with George III. In June he was given command of the 80-gun *Tigre* and in November sailed for the Mediterranean, and the assignment in the Levant that followed.

Nelson had strong suspicions of Russian intentions in the Mediterranean, in the Aegean especially. He wanted the Russian and Turkish fleets to take over the blockade of Alexandria and the watch on the Syrian coast. However, on entering the Mediterranean in October, the Russo-Turkish squadrons, instead of posting themselves off the Levant, had begun capturing the Ionian Islands. All the islands except Corfu had been captured from the French. The Russians were simultaneously laying claim to Malta, on grounds that the Knights of Malta had ceded it to the tsar after Napoleon turned them off the island.

Nelson believed that the Russians had their own sinister designs in the Mediterranean. His mistrust of them created desire for an independent liaison with the Turks. 'Those Russians seem to me to be thinking more of securing ports for themselves in the Mediterranean than destroying Bonaparte's army,' he wrote to Spencer Sidney Smith, the British minister at Constantinople, brother of Sidney Smith. 'How can the worthy Turk be blind to this danger?'

Nelson remained in the poor state that had settled upon him in the aftermath of the Neapolitan military debacle and the French thrust he had helped to release down to Naples, which General Championnet had occupied on 22 January. The Neapolitan half of the Kingdom of the Two Sicilies was now known as the Parthenopean Republic. Nelson therefore increasingly felt the weight of what he and the Sicilian monarchs had landed upon themselves. His fear was the imminent loss of Sicily. To St Vincent he wrote, 'As to myself, I see but gloomy prospects, look which way I will . . . In short, my dear Lord, everything makes me sick, to see things go to the Devil, and not to have the means of prevention.'

In that agitated state, Nelson was constantly railing against the Russians and Turks for not taking on the blockade of Alexandria. He wanted his own ships back from the Levant, to concentrate his forces around Italy as the situation on the Continent built to war. All of it can seem strange when set against the triumph that the achievement at the Nile should have ensured right then. But the great and bitter dismay that lay upon Nelson after the flight from Naples appeared to worsen rather than ease. One sees it in the rage that seethes through his correspondence, including that with Sidney Smith, with whom Nelson seems to find fault sometimes on merest pretext. Nelson is seen here as a man chronically unsettled and deeply ill at ease with himself. And by this time any guilt over pushing Naples to war would be compounded by guilt arising from his relationship with Emma Hamilton.

The venom that he directed against the Russians was even more powerfully expressed against the French. He now saw them in terms of purest hatred, which, notably, was also specifically directed for the first time against Napoleon Buonaparte. When he heard that the Bey of Tripoli had received emissaries from Napoleon, Nelson in a letter to the Bey described Napoleon as 'that man of blood, that despoiler of the weak, that enemy of all good Musselmen; for, like Satan, he only flatters that he may the more easily destroy . . . since the year 1789 all Frenchmen are of exactly the same disposition'. Of the French generally, he was to write, 'Down, down with the French! Is my constant prayer . . . my blood boils at the name of a Frenchman. I hate them all – Royalists and Republicans.'

By contrast, that object of Nelson's scorn was himself buoyant, for Napoleon was about to make the first advance down that visionary highway that he saw forking towards his twin ultimate goals of Constantinople and India.

Napoleon's immediate objective was to gain the ports on the Syrian coast, particularly Acre, through which communication with France could be re-established and upon which the British blockade of Alexandria depended for its supplies. But that operation had necessarily come to mean conquest of Syria and its ruler, Achmed Jezzar Pasha, who held as well the title of

Pasha of Egypt. Jezzar, whose name signified 'cut-throat', was the cruellest and most powerful pasha in the Middle East.

In a campaign against Jezzar and his Ottoman forces Napoleon expected to win the support of the Christians and Druzes on the Levant. Expectation of such an alliance was in conflict, however, with his own effort in the Arab world to suggest himself as Moslem in soul rather than being Christian. He had steadfastly sought to convey the idea that since he and his soldiers were secular the historical antipathy between Moslem and Christian did not exist with them. His government, he said, would be based on the principles of the Koran 'which alone are true and capable of bringing happiness to men'. But Christian, nevertheless, was how his conquered subjects saw him. And that, coupled with his determination to eradicate the Mameluke power that had ruled Egypt for half a millennium, had meant that prospects of a peaceful governorship were elusive from the start. His struggle with the Mamelukes took him, besides, into conflict with Jezzar Pasha.

The Mamelukes had their origin in a force of youths brought to Egypt from the Caucasus in the thirteenth century to form the elite corps of the Egyptian sultan's army. The Mamelukes eventually took power and held it even after the Turkish conquest in 1517. To the Turkish pashas who came as Ottoman governors the Mamelukes gave nominal obedience, but the real power remained with them. Through the centuries they continued to buy boys from the Caucasus to train as warriors. Mameluke power broke into factions, at the head of which stood the Bey. When Napoleon landed in Egypt power in the land was shared between two beys, Ibrahim Bey and Murad Bey. Napoleon set out to break them both. General Desaix was assigned to Murad Bey and pursued him all the way to the First Cataract of the Nile. But decisive defeat was elusive and, despite Desaix's efforts, Murad eventually found his way back to a position near the Pyramids. Napoleon himself took on Ibrahim Bey and defeated him. Ibrahim escaped across the Sinai Desert into Syria, where he allied himself with Jezzar.

After his defeat of Ibrahim Bey, Napoleon sent a letter by sea to Djezzar declaring that the French Republic sought to live at peace with him but demanded that Jezzar dismiss Ibrahim Bey and his Mamelukes and refuse them all aid. In response Jezzar put in irons all the French living at his capital, Acre, and began making military dispositions for resisting the French. It was against Jezzar and the Turkish forces along the Levant that Napoleon therefore found himself compelled to move without delay early in 1799 if he were to secure the two harbours he wanted, Acre and Jaffa. It was more than a month since Napoleon had learned that Turkey was at war with France. He had had no intelligence on Ottoman dispositions since receiving that news on 5 February. But the possibility of an Ottoman advance along the Levantine coast gave greater strategic meaning to possession of Acre.

Jezzar had earned that soubriquet (cut-throat) because few in the Ottoman Empire of his day could match his reputation for cruelty and casual slaughter. Napoleon's second in command, General Berthier, wrote that Jezzar was a monster who '. . . cuts off with his own hands the heads of his confidants, cuts off nose, ears, hands, and feet upon the most trivial suspicions, makes those who displease him rot alive to the very head'.

Jezzar was a native of Bosnia, from a prominent family from whom he fled at sixteen after attempting to rape his sister-in-law. At Constantinople he sold himself to slave merchants who in turn sold him to Ali Bey, the Mameluke ruler at Cairo. After a rough and violent career serving various Ottoman masters he eventually received from Constantinople the tributary sovereignty of all of Syria as well as the title Pasha of Egypt. He established himself at Acre, to amass wealth and a harem of white women.

Since Aboukir the British had drawn supplies at Acre for the Alexandria blockade. When *Swiftsure*, part of the blockading squadron, went in for fresh provisions of wine, rice and meat, her chaplain, the Rev. Cooper Willyams, visited Jezzar and added more to the legend:

The pacha is a venerable old man, with a beard as white as snow, yet he possessed great activity, both of mind and body, and seemed endowed with a much larger share of energy and spirit than characterised the generality of his countrymen . . . but he was cruel and oppressive in the extreme . . . from our consul we learnt that lately he had put to death the whole of his officers of his customs, whom he suspected of defrauding him . . . the unhappy objects of his suspicion, to the number of fifty-nine, were drawn up on the strand where the soldiers attacked them with their sabres . . . We were also told that lately, in a fit of jealousy, he had put to death all his wives: a Frenchman had penetrated his harem; fortunately for him he escaped.

The Syria that Jezzar ruled and into which Napoleon intended to march covered what today would be the states of Syria, Lebanon, Israel and Jordan. It consisted of five regional pashaliks, or governments, Aleppo, Damascus, Tripoli, Jerusalem and Akko (Acre). Jaffa, modern Jafo, Napoleon's first intended destination, is close to Tel Aviv. Acre, modern Akko, is on the Bay of Haifa. Napoleon's march and campaign beyond Egypt was thus practically entirely contained within what is modern Palestine and Israel.

Acre was originally a Phoenician city. Then and through its subsequent history it successively served as a strong fortress of the Ptolemies, the Romans and, during the Crusades, alternately the Saracens and the Christians, to whom it was St Jean d'Acre. Fortress ramparts and harbour, however, had long since gone into decay and ruin.

The town sat on a promontory at the north end of the Bay of Acre (Bay of Haifa), directly opposite Mount Carmel at the south end of the bay, at the foot of which lay the old castle of Khaiffa (Haifa). Mount Carmel, a 2,000-foot cone, had been home to the prophets Elias and Elisha. The River Kishon that flowed into the bay was where Elijah had slain the 450 prophets of Baal. To that scene so tightly compacted with so much of the ancient clash in human story now came yet another fatefully distinctive event.

As the loading of fresh supplies aboard *Swiftsure* demonstrated, Acre had been recognized on both sides as a point upon which Levantine strategy could succeed or fail. For Napoleon its acquisition was essential for control inland to Damascus as well as on the reach for Constantinople along the Levantine coast. He intended it as a base for the small naval force he retained in Alexandria whenever it might manage to break out through the blockade. Nelson had intercepted that intelligence. It had worried him even in the midst of preparing for the Neapolitan military attack on the French. On 17 December 1798 he had written to the commander of the Turkish squadron off Corfu, 'If any event drives us from the coast of Egypt, St Jean d'Acre will be attacked by sea. I have Bonaparte's letter before me.' And on the same day to the British minister at Constantinople he had declared his wish that four British frigates assemble at Acre, 'for I know that is the place where Buonaparte has ordered a part of his fleet to go to . . .'

Napoleon's move towards Acre was launched the first week of February with an army of just under thirteen thousand troops. They were the elite of his army. He would not have wanted anything less beside him. Jezzar had built up a force of Mamelukes and Turkish troops at the town of El Arish, on the coastal edge of the Sinai Desert. General Kléber arrived there with his troops on 11 February. Napoleon, who had left Cairo on the 6th, arrived at El Arish on 17 February. Jezzar's outpost fell soon after and the army pressed on towards Jaffa. But Napoleon's soldiers by then were already weary and disillusioned. Losses crossing the Sinai had been serious in men and horses. Heat and lack of water had worn them down. The troops had survived on biscuit alone. Some had shot themselves. Moving north from El Arish their difficulties increased. It was different weather, cold and wet, with the force now struggling through mud instead of dust. Gaza was taken on 24 February. Its stores provided supplies for the rest of the march to Jaffa, below whose walls Napoleon arrived on 3 March.

On that same day Commodore Sidney Smith arrived off Alexandria to start his own controversially assigned tour of operations off the Levant. As was usual when a post-captain was assigned to such a special task, Sidney Smith had been elevated to the rank of commodore for the duration of the assignment.

Whatever might be said about Captain Sir William Sidney Smith's disposition to infuriate through presumptuous self-regard and arrogance, no one ever questioned his courage. He was, as his admirers liked to affirm, too much of an adventurer to be easily confined by the stiff rules that bound others in naval service to tight obedience, though he had now been sternly instructed to heed and respect Nelson as his commander.

There had in fact been good reasons for sending Sidney Smith to the Levant. He had his brother, Spencer, as British minister at Constantinople. Off the Levant Sidney Smith was therefore back in familiar waters. He was well known to the Turkish navy, with which he was associated at the start of the war in 1793. The British government had wanted a naval officer capable of assuming full diplomatic power if necessary in working with the Turkish fleets and armies. Sidney Smith appeared ideal for the task, given his fluent French, the foreign language more commonly used than any other in the Levant. The operational demands of the Levant were anyway too great to be handled from as far off as Sicily. Nelson himself had foolishly underlined that when he had distracted himself with a war in Italy in defence of a corrupt society he despised.

Aboard his flagship, the 80-gun *Tigre*, Sidney Smith took over the Alexandria blockade from Troubridge on 7 March. And on that very day came an appeal to the squadron from Jezzar giving news of the fall of El Arish and of Napoleon's advance into Syria towards Jezzar's own capital, Acre.

Sidney Smith had with him aboard *Tigre* two men who had close association with his imprisonment in the Temple and who had become devoted friends. These were the fifth officer aboard *Tigre*, Lieutenant John Wesley Wright, who had been a fellow prisoner, and Edmond de Philipeaux, who had effected Sidney Smith's escaped from the Temple. At Constantinople Philipeaux had been assigned the rank of colonel in the Turkish forces. Sidney Smith immediately put Philipeaux and Wright aboard *Theseus*, commanded by Ralph Willett Miller, who had commanded *Captain* under Nelson at St Vincent. *Theseus* sailed for Acre the following day, to enable Philipeaux and Wright to inspect the fortifications in preparation to resist Napoleon.

After bombarding Alexandria and closely inspecting the coast beyond, *Tigre* followed *Theseus* to Acre.

Early in the afternoon of 4 March Napoleon began his assault on Jaffa. It was swiftly over, and then became one of the ugliest military episodes of his career.

Something fatal struck the French soldiers after they had successfully broken their way into the town. Perhaps the hardship, suffering and disillusion they had endured since the first day of their landing in Egypt and the torments of the very march to Jaffa went to their heads in a fury of hatred against their situation. They went berserk. Napoleon's own comment was, 'The soldiers' fury was at its height: everybody was put to the sword.' Or, as another said, 'anybody with a human face fell victim to their fury'. That included women, children, whether Christian, Jew or Moslem.

Some three thousand soldiers, Turks, Moroccans and Egyptians, had taken shelter in the Jaffa citadel where they were besieged. Napoleon sent two aides to negotiate with them. The soldiers called out that they would surrender if their lives were spared. The young aides gave their promise of that. They then led the prisoners out of the city to where Napoleon was camped. 'What do they want me to do with them?' he cried in consternation when he saw several thousand prisoners advancing towards him. The answer to that came on 10 March.

The Moroccans were taken to the beach where they were shot down. Many sought refuge in the sea but boats were sent after them. That afternoon the others were marched into the sand dunes near Jaffa. As one witness recorded, 'The Turks, marching without order, shed no tears, and uttered no cries, but resigned themselves to the fate of which they were already conscious.' They were halted beside a pool of water and then led off in groups to be shot, 'all the remaining Turks calmly performed their ablutions in the stagnant water, then taking each other's hand, and placing them according to the Moslem form of salutation, successively upon their heart and on their lips, they gave and received an eternal adieu . . . There at last remained those only by the water. Our soldiers had consumed their ammunition; it became necessary therefore to put to death the remainder with the bayonet and the naked sword. I could no longer bear this inhuman sight, but fled from it pale and fainting.' By the end of the day on 10 March the French had executed near three thousand surrendered soldiers who had been promised their safety.

In defence of Napoleon it was thereafter usually said that he had not enough soldiers for escort of the prisoners or food. Jaffa then delivered its own retribution. When they arrived there bubonic plague was said to be in every house in the town. Jaffa laid the plague upon the French, and it stayed with them thereafter, more dreaded and feared by them than anything else in that land. On 12 March Napoleon began the sixty-mile march to Acre, unaware that the British navy was now there and preparing for his arrival.

Tigre had anchored off Acre on the 15th. *Theseus* had arrived two days before and in that time Philipeaux had made extraordinary effort in shoring up the decayed defences he found. The few guns there were small and defective. Not a single heavy gun was mounted on the land side. But the walls were thick and Acre had the advantage that two-thirds of the fortress town faced the sea. The landward walls were flanked by towers. The gates were described as 'worse than good barn doors in England'. The moat was mostly filled in with the debris of years. But guns were landed and a remarkable refortification effected by Philipeaux. Equally vital, Sidney Smith had persuaded Jezzar to remain instead of taking flight with his army of Albanians.

Sidney Smith, having assessed Napoleon's movements, sent *Theseus* to reconnoitre down the coast while he, aboard *Tigre*'s boats, patrolled close inshore around the base of Mount Carmel for sight of the French approach he knew to be imminent. At ten o'clock on the night of the 17th a force was sighted, mounted on asses and dromedaries, passing along the seashore. Sidney Smith sent a lieutenant in a gunboat to circuit the Bay of Acre beside the marching men, so close to them in the dark that their talk was audible. Since the men were wearing turbans the lieutenant held his fire until he knew unmistakably that they were French and not Jezzar's men. Then he opened fire. The French disappeared up the slopes of Mount Carmel.

Napoleon had arrived that day at the roadstead of Khaiffa below Mount Carmel, six miles from Acre across the bay and with full view of the fortress. The sight of *Tigre* and *Theseus* as well as several gunboats on the water before Acre had been an alarming discovery, because of the unsuspected presence of the Royal Navy but more because a flotilla of small craft bearing his siege train, the artillery, cannon, ammunition, scaling ladders and battering equipment for any siege of Acre, was on its way to Khaiffa. Napoleon gave urgent orders that an effort should be made to intercept the flotilla and divert it into Jaffa. He was too late. The flotilla even then was approaching Acre, its assigned destination. It was sighted from *Tigre* as it rounded Mount Carmel. *Tigre* immediately slipped her anchors and went after them, capturing six of the transports just before dark.

Sidney Smith had the entire siege train. Had the French retained their siege equipment they would probably have carried the Acre fortress. The onslaught that now began was to be maintained with relentless ferocity against weaker forces in a barely defensible situation. Sidney Smith was to say, '. . . the town is not, nor ever has been, defensible according to the rules of art, but according to every other rule it must and shall be defended, not that it is in itself worth defending'.

On 19 March Napoleon established his army in camps around the town walls. The following day the digging of trenches began, first to form encircle-ments parallel to the town walls, and then from those trenches others were dug leading directly to and into the walls, to be mined with explosives to blow breaches for assault. The first wave of attackers would then attempt an entry through the breach, bearing ladders for scaling where the collapse was insufficient. Slaughter through these successive attempts was always heavy in any siege, as it was to be here, with the defenders on the ramparts pouring shot and explosives upon the heads and shoulders of those seeking to fight their way in below them. As the trenching continued, the sailors and marines and Jezzar's troops were simultaneously strength-ening the defences.

The full besieging assault began after eight days of digging. In spite of heavy fire upon them, a pattern of shallow trenches had been laid. It was enough for Napoleon to become impatient. He ordered attack for early on 28 March. It began at 4 a.m. Guns from the captured flotilla had been mounted on the walls and Philipeaux directed their destructive crossfire. A high breach had nevertheless been achieved by the French guns, in the walls twenty feet above the moat, and Napoleon ordered scaling ladders to be laid against it. But the punishment was too severe for the French. After this attack a mining operation was immediately begun under one of the towers. It was finished in three days in spite of the continuous fire laid upon those working on it. The British were immediately pressed to destroy the mine. For that they had to go out through the gates. At dawn on 7 April they made a rush from the fortress. They had counted on surprise but the French were alerted by the heedless noise of Jezzar's men. Sidney Smith's companion from the Temple, Lieutenant John Wesley Wright, wounded with two shots in his right arm, nevertheless entered the mine with pike-armed sailors, who pulled down the supports of the mine. A French account of the attack described it as 'headed by naval troops belonging to the English ships, their colours seen waving in conjunction with those of Jezzar'.

Thus began the siege of Acre. Jaffa had fallen so easily that a similar collapse was reasonably expected at Acre, but some French officers appeared to recognize at once that this was different. After the first French assault on the 28th and the heavy onslaught of the British naval guns, one of the officers recorded in his diary, 'Many of us were of the opinion from that moment on that we could never take the place.' Whatever their misgivings, they attacked with unflinching courage. They had to. They had shown no mercy in their wild rampage at Jaffa. They knew there was none here for them. Jezzar, acting on his own, had murdered prisoners he held. Their bodies washed up on the beach. When his men returned from fighting they always brought back French heads. Of his opponents, Sidney Smith wrote, 'Nothing but desperation can induce them to make the sort of attempts they do, to mount a breach practicable only by means of scaling ladders, under such fire as we pour in upon them; and it is impossible to see the lives even of our enemies thus sacrificed, and so much bravery applied without regret . . . The enemy repair in one night all the mischief we do them in the day, and continue within half pistol shot of the walls in spite of constant fire kept up from the ramparts . . .'

Jezzar had called upon the pashas of Aleppo and Damascus to come to his aid. Generals Junot, Murat and Kléber routed various forces. General Kléber, with two thousand men, at one point found himself surrounded by twenty-five thousand horsemen and ten thousand infantry. After ten hours of desperate fighting cannon signals were heard: Napoleon was leading a division to the rescue. The Ottomans fled.

By the end of April Napoleon had already made four determined attempts to storm the fortress. The fighting was continuous even between those assaults. 'We throw stones at each other when flints fail and ammunition runs short,' Sidney Smith wrote. The French were constantly attempting to mine the walls while the British sailors and marines and Jezzar's men made sorties to impede that tunnelling work. 'We have thus been in one continued battle ever since the beginning of the siege, interrupted only at short intervals by the excessive fatigue of every individual on both sides,' Sidney Smith reported. He saw his own situation as becoming desperate. One of the Turkish admirals, Hassan Bey, had been placed under his command. Sidney Smith had ordered him to come to his assistance with ships and a regiment, but a month after that instruction Hassan Bey had still not arrived. Napoleon had himself sent an appeal to Cairo for more guns. The squadron that was trapped at Alexandria, three frigates and two corvettes, escaped when the blockading ships went to Cyprus for water. They landed six guns at Jaffa on 15 April and then sailed to intercept Turkish communications between Cyprus and Rhodes. Napoleon received the first of the guns from Jaffa on 30 April.

For Sidney Smith the situation looked steadily more insecure. He believed that without Hassan Bey's reinforcement he would be unable to hold on at Acre. Edmond de Philipeaux died of the plague on 2 May, after only two days of illness. 'His superior genius has in a great measure saved the town,' John Keith, Sidney Smith's secretary, recorded. Philipeaux's death tolled the alternative fate hovering over them all. But it was death outside the walls that lay ever more suffocatingly upon them for the air was dense with the noxious stench of putrefaction from the bodies piled up around the fortress, Jezzar having refused truce to bury bodies.

With his new artillery Napoleon appeared to have decided that a point of finality had indeed come. Within the first six days of May 1799 he threw three desperate assaults against the fortress, in quick succession. On 7 May, the fifty-first day of the siege, Napoleon had his new guns in position and at 9 a.m. began the fiercest onslaught so far. It was guns manned by sailors from *Theseus* and *Tigre* upon whom fell the greatest responsibility for they were within grape shot of the head of the attacking column. They threw shells into the centre of this column and helped stall it but the French nevertheless gained ground. With this attack came the first real success for Napoleon. The upper part of one of the main towers had been entirely battered down by the siege artillery. The rubble fell into the moat and provided ascent for the French. But as the evening closed Hassan Bey's fleet of corvettes and troop transports appeared at last. It was an unpleasant surprise for Napoleon but at daybreak on the 8th he delivered his own surprise to Sidney Smith and Jezzar for he raised the French tricolour over the seized tower.

The critical point had been reached. The fate of Acre was on the brink. After the success of the previous day, on the morning of 8 May 1799 Napoleon had good reason to believe that the place would fall to him that day, provided he could do it before the Turks landed. The breach into the fortress was wide enough for a column of fifty men to pass through and possession of the tower had rendered much of the flanking fire from within the fortress ineffectual. Besides that, the French, with sandbags and the bodies of their dead, had effectively screened the approaches to the breach during the night.

Sidney Smith had the same recognition. Ammunition was short, the breach looked fatal and of Jezzar's original force of one thousand Albanians merely some two hundred were still alive. Napoleon began such vigorous assault and bombardment at daylight that there seemed small chance of holding Acre unless the Ottoman relief landed at once. Sidney Smith had left that responsibility to John Keith, who had to pass to Hassan Bey urgent instruction to come ashore without delay. In his official report Sidney Smith was to say, 'This was a most critical point of the contest; and an effort was necessary to preserve the place for a short time till their arrival.'

Instead of himself waiting to see Hassan Bey, Sidney Smith had left *Tigre* at daybreak with all the sailors he could muster from his different ships to bolster what remained of Jezzar's men. He landed his sailors, armed with pikes, at the mole and led them up to the breach, where they found Jezzar's men holding the French advance back by hurling large stones at the heads of the foremost men who, in falling, at least helped block the passage for the rest.

At that moment the thread upon which Acre's fate was dependent was slender indeed, for aboard *Tigre* John Keith stood in disbelief as he confronted the reaction of Hassan Bey and his accompanying generals when they boarded *Tigre* at six thirty and, on being told that Sidney Smith was on shore already, said they would call again in the afternoon. An apoplectic Keith repeated to Hassan Bey that he was transmitting orders for an instantaneous disembarkation of the Ottoman Chiftlik Regiment. 'He seemed averse to go into Acre; but on my repeating the order, he resigned with a heavy groan; and requesting me to go in his boat, we proceeded towards the town, as I supposed, when all of a sudden he ordered the boat to go to his frigate. I was completely angry with him at this time, and became still more so when, from his cabin, I discovered the middle division of the French army all drawn up before the camp, and making every exertion for attack.' Keith grew angrier still when, with 'a tone of mirth', coffee and pipes were ordered, 'which, with their bearers, I almost flung overboard'. He then got Hassan Bey ashore and they joined Sidney Smith, whom they found on the pinnacle of the ruined tower.

The savage fight atop the breastwork was well underway, 'the muzzles of their muskets and the spear-heads of their standards locked, with Jezzar sitting on the parapet, to reward such as should bring him the heads of the enemy and distributing musket cartridges with his own hands', until finally the Ottoman regiment arrived. Sidney Smith then persuaded Jezzar to open the town gates to allow a rush of the newly arrived Turks to take the French in the flank. The Turks streamed out but were driven back to the town with heavy loss. The sortie had prompted the French to expose themselves above the parapets on the tower and they had been practically annihilated there 'so that the small number remaining on the lodgment were killed or dispersed by our few remaining hand grenades thrown by Mr Savage, midshipman of the Theseus'. Every small gain by one side or the other seemed to be immediately balanced, however, by a loss. The French, with incessant fire, had begun a new breach near the other one, 'every shot knocking down whole sheets of wall much less solid than that of the tower'. This success apparently convinced Buonaparte that victory was at hand. As the day began to fade he was seen at the centre of a semicircle of his generals on a small hill named Richard Coeur-de-Lion just above the town. Through his spyglass Sidney Smith judged that Napoleon was giving directions for an attack and the despatching of an aide-de-camp indicated that reinforcement was being summoned from Kléber at Khaiffa. Just before sunset a massive column began advancing towards the new breach 'with solemn step'. Jezzar decided to allow some of the column to pass into the town. They came over the breach into the garden of Jezzar's seraglio 'where, in a very few minutes, the bravest and most advanced of them lay headless corpses; the sabre, with the addition of a dagger in the other hand, proving more than a match for the bayonet'. It was the bloodiest moment of that entire siege. For John Keith two images stood out: Jezzar sitting on a bag near the gate receiving from his Albanians the heads of Frenchmen, with already some seventy 'arranged by him like cabbages in a market', and his cashier paying fifty piastres for each; and, 'the balls were so thick that in passing through the garden the ground was in a manner of motion. Never was Sir. S. so merry, nor did he ever utter such *bon mots* as in the very thick of it.'

General Berthier, giving a French account of that episode, told of combustible materials pouring down on those passing through the breach and fire from houses, the streets and the palace of Jezzar. 'The action was then fought man to man . . . but the column no longer retained the same impulsion, notwithstanding the heroic efforts of General Lannes, who was

severely wounded . . . Night now came, and orders were given to retreat.'
Or, as Sidney Smith concluded, 'And thus the contest of twenty-five hours
ended, both parties being so fatigued as to be unable to move.'

The exhaustion was such that Sidney Smith, in his report written that
night, conceded the likelihood of his yet losing Acre. 'Be assured, my Lord,'
he wrote to St Vincent, 'the magnitude of our obligations does but increase
the energy of our efforts in the attempt to discharge our duty; and though
we may, and probably shall be overpowered, I can venture to say, that the
French army will be so much farther weakened before it prevails, as to be
little able to profit by its dear-born victory.'

Even such a Pyrrhic victory was, however, to be denied to Buonaparte,
who the following day made another full-scale attack upon the breach. It
was the last such. The loss was again frightful. The actions of the Ottoman
regiment this time proved decisive. Kléber's soldiers, fighting in the hideous
stench of their decaying comrades, were driven back before getting through
the breach.

After this attack on 10 May Napoleon decided upon his retreat. But he
allowed no indication of it to pass to Sidney Smith, who could not yet be
sure of anything, for Napoleon continued to bombard Acre for several days
after. He continued to attack, but nothing again on the previous scale. 'I am
but half dead,' Sidney Smith wrote on the 14th; 'Buonaparte brings fresh
troops to assault two or three times in the night, and we are thus obliged to
be always under arms . . . our ammunition is nearly expended . . . I am almost
blind, what with the dust from the shells, hot sun, and much writing . . .' He
had, besides, just suffered another grievous loss. An explosion aboard *Theseus*
had killed Captain Miller and disabled the ship, depriving the besieged of
her firepower. But their ordeal was in fact at its end: Napoleon began his
retreat after dark on 20 May. When the sentries on Acre's ramparts looked
out at dawn on the 21st the French camp was empty.

In his preliminary report on the retreat, Sidney Smith recognized the
decisive impact of the dreadful events of 10 May. 'After this failure, the
French Grenadiers absolutely refused to mount the breach any more over
the putrid bodies of their unburied comrades, sacrificed in former attacks
by Buonaparte's impatience and precipitation, which led him to commit
such palpable errors as even seamen could take advantage of.'

With those words the Royal Navy laid its first claim of victory against
the person of Napoleon. That of itself gave a special rarity to the siege of
Acre, for it would represent one of the Royal Navy's greatest achievements
in the Great War. As John Keith rightfully said, 'I hope government will
(and if it doth not, I hope our country will) observe that 2 ships of the
line, and a small ill-armed store-ship, have checked an hitherto invincible
army of above 12,000 men; which, had it not been for Sir Sidney's most

extraordinary genius, backed by every one of our little squadron, would by this time have been menacing the very capital of the Turkish empire.'

Napoleon, Sidney Smith said, '. . . seemed to have no principle of action but that of pressing forward, and appeared to stick at nothing to obtain the object of his ambition . . . He has lost the flower of his army in these desperate attempts to storm (as appears by the certificates of former services, which we find in their pockets) and eight generals.' Given his meagre resources, Sidney Smith's own tactical handling of the siege was skilfully considered and managed. He and the small band upon whom he depended, Philipeaux foremost, Miller of *Theseus*, Wesley Wright, and the marine commanders from *Tigre* and *Theseus*, had to cope with a military situation of the first order suddenly sprung upon them. Opposed by a force that at that moment was probably the most professional military unit on the face of the earth, facing a situation affecting the course of the entire conflict, they delivered another of the special instances of naval resolution in that war – capability and courage against the odds. One incident strikingly reflected Sidney Smith's own attitude. He had ordered *Tigre* to be taken in closer to the shoal water of the bay for better firepower and was himself preparing to go ashore to be at the breach. As he was going over the ship's side his first lieutenant presented him with a written protest declaring that his orders and his actions were placing *Tigre* in danger of being lost. Sidney Smith replied: 'Gentlemen, His Majesty's ships are built on purpose to be placed in danger of being lost, whenever His Majesty's service requires it, and of that, the commanding officer is the best judge.'

The task they had expected to fulfil originally had been simply blockade of Egypt and supervision of the Russian and Ottoman flotillas in those seas. Nelson, worried about the fate of Sicily should Championnet invade from Messina, had even been prepared, as late as 6 March, to recall Sidney Smith and the Levant squadron. And he continued to nag at St Vincent over Sidney Smith's loose form of address to him in defiance of navy protocol, declaring that he despised 'such frippery and nonsense as he is composed of'. But, as he came to recognize, perhaps reluctantly, Sidney Smith had achieved a block upon Napoleon's military course, wherever it had been due to run after Acre.

Of the elite French force that had left Cairo more than two thousand were dead, either killed in action or victims of the plague, and more than two thousand ill or badly wounded.

Napoleon probably rightly attributed his failure to the loss of his besieging equipment to Sidney Smith. 'Had it not been for that, I would have taken Acre,' he told his surgeon on St Helena, Barry O'Meara. But he expressed great admiration of Smith, whom he described as 'active, intelligent, intriguing, and indefatigable' but also half-crazy.

What Napoleon's actual course would have been had he taken Acre is impossible to say. He had sent a message to his command in Cairo on 19 April saying that he expected to take Acre by 5 or 6 May and, with that accomplished, would himself immediately return to Cairo. As master of the Levant that would have been a return for triumphant strategic reassessment, or something like it. To General Murat he had said, gesturing at Acre before the great sequence of assaults on the 7th and the 10th, 'The fate of the east is in that shanty. The fall of this place will be the end of my expedition. Damascus will be the fruit.'

The night before the Battle of Austerlitz in 1805 Napoleon said, 'If I had been able to take Acre, I would have put on a turban . . . I would have made myself emperor of the East, and I would have returned to Paris by way of Constantinople.' That was repeated aboard *Northumberland* on his way to St Helena. 'I would have been emperor of the East,' he was reported to have said in talk about Acre. So be it. History is rich with afterthought. But there is this at any rate, that the denial of his grandest vision of omnipotence was for him an extremely personal infliction at the hands of a British sailor.

XXVI

RETURN

On 17 April 1799 Admiral Lord Bridport resumed command of the Western Squadron, after the continuous vigilance over Brest and the Narrow Seas had been maintained by junior admirals through the winter. Under Bridport the winter cruising fleet of eight or nine ships was now at the fuller strength of sixteen sail of the line and several frigates. With these Bridport sailed from Spithead for Brest to start the more intensive watch of the summer months.

The blockade of Brest had been Bridport's responsibility for the past two years. The seventy-three-year-old admiral, formerly Viscount Alexander Hood, had been in command of the home fleet since taking over from Earl Howe in 1797. On 25 April he was off Brest where, instead of the usual somnolent inactivity, it presented Bridport's squadron with the immediate excitement and anticipation of something afoot, for the French ships were apparently getting ready to put to sea. But, as always with that station, wind enforced its own dictate. Coping with the wind freshening from north-east, Bridport fell back to a position twelve miles off Ushant. When he put back to Brest on the 27th the harbour was empty. The French had sailed out the night of the 25th, just a few hours after Bridport had been observing them.[1]

The watch upon Brest and the large naval force lying there was the principal preoccupation of the Western Squadron, the guardian of those home and encircling waters. Central to its task was the perpetual British fear of invasion when Brest showed signs of activity. If not invasion then some other significant strategy had to be assumed, invariably either an Irish operation or one in the Mediterranean.

Of all the insistent naval operations of the Great War the blockade of Brest was the most testing and unpopular of all, for its gruelling monotony and its demand for endurance through the inconstant winds and weathers of the area and, for the sailors, the pain of the sight and unreachable nearness of home, since leave was seldom granted even when they got back to port. Winter, with its restraint upon line ship activity, brought a reduced force on the blockade through those months. The watch nevertheless had to be rigorously maintained, though the elderly commanding admiral of the squadron usually went ashore for the winter.

The British navy was better situated than at any time so far in this war. At the beginning of 1799 it had 105 ships of the line at sea supported by 469 cruisers. Around half of the line ships were with the Channel fleet under Bridport, on guard against Admiral Bruix's Brest fleet of twenty-five line ships. Admiral Duncan covered the Baltic convoys and the blockaded Dutch fleet at the Texel with sixteen British line ships and ten Russian. Admiral Lord George Keith blockaded Cadiz with twenty-two line ships. The Mediterranean was the most modestly served of all, with just three squadrons of three line ships each assigned to three stations, with one squadron attached to Nelson at Palermo and the others blockading at Alexandria and Malta.

The Mediterranean represented a principal concern in the vigilance upon Brest because of the threat of a union of the Brest and Toulon fleets, whether Toulon to Brest or Brest to Toulon. Along with fear of this union was the companion fear of any link-up of such a force with the Spanish Grand Fleet. Brest and Toulon: Cardinal Richelieu's inestimable gift to the naval life of France of a permanently active existence on two seas! Until that very year of 1799 Britain had nothing comparable to that strategic balance that France possessed. Gibraltar had never provided any such balancing role since its seizure early that century. Its defects for provisioning, shelter and refit were too many. Napoleon on St Helena gave neat appraisal of the Rock's questionable value other than symbolic. Admiral George Cockburn had remarked that the British had always suspected him of planning an attack on Gibraltar. Napoleon answered: 'We knew better than that. It was in our interest to leave Gibraltar in your possession. It is of no advantage to you; it neither protects nor intercepts anything! It is only an object of national pride, which costs England very dear, and gives great umbrage to Spain. It would have been very injudicious in us to destroy such arrangements.' Gibraltar nevertheless had always served as a vital watch point of movement through the Straits. The Rock had finally become the British navy's operational command post for the Mediterranean and its Atlantic approaches only when St Vincent established himself ashore there at Rosia Bay early in 1799.

Nelson's destruction of the Toulon fleet at Aboukir Bay had left France disastrously incapable of relieving Napoleon's entrapment in Egypt or of coping with the other operations in the Mediterranean. The naval impotence that confronted France on the Mediterranean could therefore only be addressed by rapidly moving the Brest fleet down through the Straits and calling on Spain to join with its own fleet for a powerful muster against the modest force that was all that Britain was able to deploy east of Gibraltar. Such a powerful potential combination had to be an immediate speculation in pondering where Admiral Bruix was taking his squadron and for what purpose when Bridport saw Brest empty of its fleet on 27 April 1799.

What was now underway was a chase whose bewildering character and disputed management on both sides created a strategic crisis that, properly resolved by one or the other, might have written an entirely different naval history of the war.

This was the second time in Bridport's tenure as commander in chief of the Western Squadron that a great fleet had slipped out of Brest without him preventing it. The first occasion had nearly brought full disaster upon Britain. That was in the winter of 1796–7 when the mighty expedition for the invasion of Ireland sailed out, only to be wrecked in storm at Bantry Bay. This time Bridport, though at the scene, had positioned himself out of sight of Brest in spite of having observed a fleet preparing to sail. He had taken position off Ushant island at the north end of the Iroise Channel which formed the approach to Brest. Bruix sailed out at the southern end of the Channel past Pointe du Raz, a passage that took ships directly out into Biscay. This was at least forty miles from where Bridport lay. The wind was fresh from the north-east, helping Bruix to get away swiftly and smoothly.

A patrolling British frigate, *La Nymphe*, sighted the fleet as it was clearing Raz at nine on the morning of 26 April 1799, and raced forward to get the signal to Bridport who, after checking that Brest was indeed emptied of the French fleet, set course for Ireland. The assumption of another invasion attempt there was perhaps understandable given the previous experience. Messages had been sent by cutter, however, to Admiral Keith off Cadiz and St Vincent at Gibraltar. Bridport simultaneously sent messages to all the other Channel squadrons to join him off Cape Clear on the south coast of Ireland. That was precisely what the French had wanted. They got a cutter among his frigates with false despatches for Ireland, to maintain the suspicion of Bruix's intent. Bridport therefore remained stubbornly off Ireland even after he got word that the French had been sighted on a southerly course.

Bruix, who was Minister of Marine, commanded a formidably powerful fleet, the best that France had possessed. His twenty-five line ships included one 120-gun, three 110s, and two 80s, the rest being 74s. His instructions were to cooperate with the Spanish fleet to relieve Malta and Corfu and then carry supplies and reinforcements to Buonaparte in Egypt.[2]

As the Channel squadrons at early to mid-May made for or gathered off Cape Clear, Bruix was already deep into the Mediterranean, where St Vincent, Keith and Nelson found themselves confronting the unexpected strategic crisis thrust upon them.

Keith, off Cadiz, was the first affected. He had his shock on 3 May when a British frigate appeared with news that it was being chased by the French fleet, which showed up in all its strength and magnificence the next day. Keith and his fifteen ships were caught between Bruix and his twenty-five on the seaward horizon and the nineteen Spanish lying before him in Cadiz, 'between the devil and the deep sea', as Keith himself expressed it. Keith nevertheless formed line of battle, seeing that, with an onshore gale, the Spanish would have difficulty in easily bringing themselves out of Cadiz to support the French. Bruix in any event had no desire to engage at that point.[3]

The gale blowing off Cadiz was a strong northwesterly. For Bruix that meant quick, effortless passage through the Straits into the Mediterranean and on towards his assigned tasks. The decision had to be immediate, in the event of the westerly changing to a levanter that would hinder passage through the Straits. So he ran for the Straits. The next day, 5 May, St Vincent at Rosia Bay saw the gale carrying the French fleet past him and safely away towards their still-unknown assignment.

Consternation had reigned in Britain over what was described as 'the extraordinary escape of the French fleet'. Fear for Ireland was followed by fear for Portugal, invasion of which had long been dreaded. The Mediterranean did not seem to jump immediately to mind but when Bruix was known to be on that sea alarm was greater still. Nelson's victory at the Nile had allowed too much to be taken for granted in the Mediterranean, especially since the situation there faced a new situation on the Continent.

The Austrian emperor, Francis II, had wanted war with France without himself starting it, trusting on his alliance with Russia to provoke the French. The Directory was finally goaded to action as Russian troops under Marshal Suvorov moved into Europe to join the Austrians. French armies had finally crossed the Rhine on 1 March 1799. Francis II declared war on France on the 12th.

From the start the French campaign lacked the strategic overview of a Buonaparte. The Directory launched into three widely separated campaigns that made mutual support between the three armies difficult. General Masséna crossed into Switzerland but on 25 March was defeated near Lake Constance. General Scherer in Italy was defeated by the Austrians at Magnano on 5 April. The following day General Jourdan, who had crossed the Rhine, retreated back across it when faced by superior forces near Strasbourg. Command of the combined Austro-Russian forces in Italy was given to Suvorov. On 29 April they entered Milan. The French had already withdrawn from Naples and the War of the Second Coalition thus appeared to be rapidly erasing French control of central Europe and northern Italy. But such a mighty fleet entering the Mediterranean, presumably with an army on board, changed the whole strategic picture.

Bruix entered the Mediterranean as the final battles for Acre were fought and Napoleon was starting his retreat. None of this would be known in Britain or on the Continent for some time. Even when it was, however, it could hardly diminish the significance of this great fleet moving freely on a sea that had been considered safely dominated by the British navy which, because of its sparse and wide distribution, now appeared dangerously vulnerable.

The Middle Sea, Mittel Meer, *medius terra*, Between the Continents: Mediterranean. It was the name that operated with more literal significance within the conflicts of the Western world than that of any other stage. It was the operational scene more appropriately placed than any other, ever central. For whatever was raging across the Continent in wartime, the Mediterranean always seemed to be the real heart of it, the strategic middle, where the point of ultimate decision in all likelihood probably lay, where the course towards outcome was ever finely balanced. And, not least, where surprise was always forthcoming, as it now was.

Upon all who were concerned with the dispositions of the British navy great fright descended following this dramatic reappearance of the French in the Mediterranean in such force. The one bearing the full immediate weight of the crisis had to be St Vincent. Watching the French ships fly past Rosia Bay and vanish into the Mediterranean he immediately decided to call Keith and the Cadiz squadron to Gibraltar to form a chase. The Cadiz squadron was the only force available to him for pursuit of Bruix. Unable to get an immediate message to Keith by boat because of the tempestuous gale roaring through the Straits, St Vincent got his instructions to Keith overland through Spain. Concession was obtained from the governor of St Roche, adjacent to Gibraltar, to allow a British official a pass for travel to Lisbon. The official took a boat at Faro at the Portuguese end of the Gulf of Cadiz and got St Vincent's message to Keith, who arrived at Gibraltar on 10 May.

St Vincent, feeling his age, sick, worn out by the years of extended command on the Mediterranean and off Cadiz, was hardly in the best state to face a crisis of such overwhelming implications. The entire naval situation around the Straits and in the Mediterranean was drastically changed by it. Calling Keith to Gibraltar had removed the blockade of Cadiz. After seeing Bruix fly through the Straits, St Vincent had to watch the Spanish Admiral Mazarredo follow through, taking his fleet from Cadiz to Cartagena, for possible joint operation with Bruix. Thus two great fleets were now loose on the Mediterranean, to operate either singly or in combination.

St Vincent sent off messages to all his squadrons but it was obvious that, individually, they had little prospect of escaping destruction if Bruix showed up before any one of them. Their individual power to resist such a mighty fleet was minimal. Minorca had only four ships under Commodore Duckworth, Nelson had one ship at Palermo, Troubridge three in watch off Naples, Ball three in blockade of Malta. An urgent plea for reinforcement went to Bridport, at that time still off Ireland, but any such succouring assistance was weeks away. 'The Brest squadron had such a game to play at Malta and Sicily, that I trembled for the fate of our ships employed there, and for the latter island,' St Vincent wrote to Spencer at Admiralty.

The many possibilities of great strategic setback were obvious: Minorca taken, an army landed on Sicily, Malta relieved, Alexandria's blockade broken and Napoleon and his army brought back to help counter the advance of Suvorov and his Austro-Russian army.

Faced by those circumstances St Vincent, sick though he was, decided to go back aboard his flagship, *Ville de Paris*, and to lead in the hunt for Bruix. In his message to Nelson he had said that he believed the French to be intent on the relief of Malta and thence on to Egypt but that he himself intended to go to Minorca, where he arrived on the 20th to find it safe but to learn that there had been a sighting of the French fleet north of Minorca ostensibly bound for Toulon, which Bruix reached on 14 May.

Nelson, on receiving St Vincent's conviction that Bruix was bound for Malta and Alexandria, brought all his ships together and then took them to station off a small island west of Sicily, Maritimo, in the middle of the passage to the east. He had merely seven ships but intended to lie in wait there to intercept the French, heedless of any superiority in numbers, determined to cripple them sufficiently to make the force ineffectual, even if it meant destruction of his own force. And, as always, with the prospect of action his spirits were up, declaring to St Vincent: '... the squadron under my command shall never fall into the hands of the enemy; and before we are destroyed, the enemy will have their wings so completely clipped that they may be easily overtaken by you'.

None of that was to be, neither battle nor heroics. Not even sight of the enemy.

St Vincent with his fleet of twenty sail continued after Bruix towards Toulon. On 30 May he heard that the French had sailed from Toulon four days before, headed eastwards. But St Vincent had come to a point where he was incapable of further deductive effort. Three days later, 2 June, he said his health had finally failed him: 'such a rapid decline of health, as to bereave me of all power both of body and mind'. He handed command of the fleet to Keith and broke away to return to Minorca. Keith continued along the coast.

Bruix, meanwhile, had sailed from Toulon with supplies for the beleaguered French forces in northern Italy. He had anchored at Vado Bay on 4
June, sent supplies into Genoa, where General Masséna was besieged, and
sailed again on 6 June, sailing closely in along the Provençal coast, passed
Toulon without entering, and then made course down the Spanish coast
for Cartagena, where he joined the Spanish fleet on 22 June.

Keith knew of the French at Vado Bay the day after they had arrived
there. He then continued along the French coast towards Vado Bay, where
he expected to encounter Bruix, but he received instructions from St Vincent
to make for the Bay of Rosas, on the coast just south of the Golfe du Lion,
and to take position there to prevent Bruix joining the Spanish at Cartagena.
St Vincent still believed that for Bruix combining with the Spanish had to
be a prime objective for any serious operation. He believed Rosas to be the
best point for intercepting Bruix. But instead of making for Rosas, Keith
abandoned the chase off Monaco and descended directly to Port Mahon. As
he explained to Nelson, 'I had no doubt of overtaking them before they had
left the coast of Italy . . . but the defenceless state of Minorca, without a fleet
. . . will oblige me to relinquish the pursuit, and return to the protection of
that island . . . I am confident the French are not thirty leagues [ninety miles]
hence at this moment.'

It was Mahan's conviction that, had Keith obeyed and made for Rosas,
he unfailingly would have encountered Bruix. But he equally well could
have met Bruix off the Provençal coast if he had persisted there. Such was
Nelson's belief. With Bruix only thirty leagues distant it should well have
been possible. Poor though his physical and mental capabilities were, St
Vincent nevertheless had sought to exercise decision on distant deployment
from Port Mahon, where he lay aboard *Ville de Paris*. In such a strategic
situation blame could fly in any direction. One can only come back to
Corbett and the blindness of oceanic search.[4]

Keith arrived at Port Mahon on 12 June. St Vincent immediately transferred full command of the Mediterranean to him. Keith sailed for Toulon
on the 15th and spent the next three weeks in futile search for the French
across that whole western Mediterranean basin between Minorca and the
Ligurian coast.

With Nelson's station off the island of Maritimo being the critical one
for covering Sicily and the access to Malta and the Levant, Keith sent him
a reinforcement of two 74s, in the belief that Bruix might descend upon
Sicily and Naples, where, in spite of Championnet's withdrawal, the French
held the principal fortresses and the Neapolitan Republicans, or Jacobins
as Nelson called them, were still in power. Nelson had already received
four line ships for reinforcement, including the 80-gun *Foudroyant*, which
became his flagship. He had constant pleas from the Sicilian queen and

king to maintain their protection and, more urgently, retrieve Naples to
their sovereignty.

Meanwhile a Calabrian peasant army had successfully marched upon
Naples. The force behind this accomplishment had been a sixty-year-old
militarist priest, Cardinal Fabrizio Ruffo, a Calabrian, who on his own had
landed at Scilla and from there progressed up Calabria assembling as he
went an army of peasants and brigands and rabble that saw opportunity
for loot. By early June they were outside Naples, where the Neapolitan
populace, the *lazzaroni*, faithful to the king, eagerly awaited their arrival.
What Maria Carolina and Ferdinand IV now wanted was that Nelson should
immediately take his fleet in support of Cardinal Ruffo. Emma Hamilton
was, of course, the instrument for enforcing their pleas. On 12 June Nelson
had a particularly powerful letter from her: 'I have just passed an evening
with the Queen. The Queen beseeches you, my dear lord, supplicates and
implores you, if the thing be possible, to repair to Naples. For Heaven's
sake consider it, and do what the queen asks.'

On 20 June, Nelson got St Vincent's despatch informing him of two
events: that he had relinquished the entire Mediterranean command to
Keith, and that the arrival at Port Mahon of a reinforcement of twelve
line ships from the Channel was imminent. He said as well that Keith was
still searching for Bruix, whose whereabouts were still mystifying to all.
Simultaneously, another plea arrived from the Sicilian Court declaring that
the appearance of the British fleet at Naples would boost those fighting the
republicans, who now believed that Bruix was coming to their assistance.

The two letters had strange impact upon Nelson. He had for some
time again been declaring in his correspondence from his watch station
at Maritimo how ill and spiritless he was. The contents of the two letters
seemed to unbalance him completely. He promptly decided to abandon his
vital station off Maritimo and to go to the defence of Naples, justifying his
action with the belief that Naples had become the destination of the French
fleet. No one understood better than Nelson the seriousness of abandoning
such a key station without Keith's consent.

St Vincent's departure upset him deeply, as did Keith's elevation to the
Mediterranean command. His resentment against Keith was building with
the belief that Keith had given him inadequate strength for any battle with
Bruix. The news that Keith was receiving a reinforcement of sixteen ships
for his search was therefore another likely factor in Nelson so peremptorily abandoning his station off Maritimo. There was a sullen inference of
'You handle it all now' in his explanation to Keith of his departure from
station: 'As I had now no prospect of being in a situation to go in search
of the Enemy's fleet . . . I determined to offer myself for the service of
Naples, where I knew the French fleet intended going.' That sounded like

a contradiction in terms: unable to search for the enemy yet going to where he believed they would appear. On June 21 he was back at Palermo, where he remained only two hours before sailing for Naples, with the Hamiltons on board *Foudroyant*.[5]

What Nelson now embarked upon was the sorriest episode of his life, and character.

Late on the evening of 24 June *Foudroyant* anchored in the Bay of Naples where, to the surprise of all, subjection of the French garrison and the 'Jacobin' insurrection there appeared to have been accomplished. Flags of truce flew from the principal fortresses.

The governing body of the Parthenopean Republic had become an unusual combination of all who despised the sordidly corrupt, debauched and spineless Neapolitan Court. In common with much of Europe the philosophical ideals and republican commitment of the French Revolution had taken hold of the intelligentsia and middle classes of Naples. But detestation of the Court and the unlovely pair of Ferdinand IV and Maria Carolina had made republicans of the nobility as well. Among those who gave themselves to the service of the republic were nobles such as Prince Santa-Severina, Count Nuovo, the Duke of Andria and Schipani, the Duke of Rocca Romana and Prince Caracciolo, head of the small Neapolitan navy.

The French garrison and the Parthenopean republicans had rallied in the belief that Bruix's fleet was on its way to help them and had routed Ruffo's Calabrians on the outskirts of Naples. Nelson's only watch in the Bay of Naples at this time was Captain Edward Foote aboard his frigate *Seahorse*. Cardinal Ruffo, shaken by unexpected defeat and the prospect of the French arriving, had asked Captain Foote to arrange a truce. Foote complied and brought them all together. The defenders of the republic were operating from three fortresses. The French soldiers occupied the fort of St Elmo, the Neapolitan republicans were in two fortified castles, Nuovo and Uovo. The French and the Neapolitan republicans, after some hesitation, accepted terms of capitulation which stated that they would march out from their forts with colours flying to embark for Toulon with safe conduct. Those republicans who remained in Naples were to have their safety and property guaranteed. To all of that Foote had agreed.[6]

Nelson had sailed from Palermo with what he believed to be full powers to act for the king in the name of the king. The truce enraged him. For him, Captain Foote and Cardinal Ruffo had been dealing with rebels who had betrayed the king and were not entitled to any conditional terms of surrender. He called the truce 'infamous' and annulled it, declaring that he would not allow the French and the rebels to quit the forts to embark. The rebels had to surrender themselves 'to His Majesty's royal mercy'. His outlook at that moment was graphically expressed to a friend, to whom he wrote, 'I hope all those who are false to this king and country will be hanged, or otherwise disposed of, as their sovereign thought proper.'[7]

In the nervous state that he carried with him to Naples, Nelson was the more vulnerable to be inflamed by anything suggesting treason or disloyalty, for him always the ultimate descent in debased morality. There was no room for benign tolerance as *Foudroyant* anchored and he saw truce flag flying from a ship of his own squadron.

For Cardinal Ruffo and Captain Foote, however, the promises they had concluded with the French and the republicans were a matter of honour. Tense argument between Ruffo and Nelson took placed on *Foudroyant*'s quarterdeck on the 25th. On the 26th Nelson appeared to relent. He advised Ruffo that he had decided to do nothing that might break the armistice. The republicans were allowed to leave the two castles where they sheltered. They promptly did so that afternoon and went aboard the fleet of coasters, *polaccas*, that had been assembled to carry them to Toulon. They expected to sail at once, but Nelson promptly went back on his word. The following day, 27 June, he sent armed boats to bring the *polaccas* with the Neapolitan republicans on board and moored them alongside British warships, each *polacca* laid under a cannon. On the same day he sent Captain Troubridge with thirteen hundred sailors to besiege St Elmo castle where the French garrison remained.

The reason for this turnabout from one day to the next lay with letters that arrived, one from Acton saying that the king wanted nothing less than unconditional surrender of all, and another from the queen to Emma Hamilton that, in virulent terms, made the same point: 'I recommend Lord Nelson treat Naples as if it were an Irish town in a similar state of rebellion . . . They deserve to be branded that others may not be deceived by them. I recommend . . . the greatest firmness, vigour and severity.' And that was what all now got.

Foudroyant became the stage for early scenes in the tragedy that unfolded. The first of the great names of the nobility to suffer there was Admiral Prince Francesco Caracciolo, Duke of Brienza, commander of the Neapolitan fleet which had gone over to the republic. He was brought on board *Foudroyant* in irons, 'who with his hands bound behind him, and wretchedly attired, displayed a painful instance of the uncertainty of all worldly grandeur. When last on board, this prince had been received with all the respect and deference that were then due to his rank and character,' as one officer observed. Nelson immediately ordered a court martial before Neapolitan naval officers. Caracciolo was sentenced to be hanged in two hours. Nelson decreed that the execution should be aboard a Neapolitan frigate, that Caracciolo should hang until sunset and his body then be thrown into the sea, ignoring Caracciolo's plea that he be shot instead.

After Caracciolo the punitive process was relentless. It continued ferociously for weeks, still active even months later. It was another Jaffa in its
savagery, except that Jaffa was brief. What became offensive to the British
officers and other witnesses of the violence that fell upon Naples was
the sense of being participant in the vengeance of Ferdinand and Maria
Carolina. But Nelson's intimacy and repeatedly sworn duty of service
to this monarch, whom few others could bring themselves to respect,
compelled obedience to Nelson's orders. His officers therefore unhappily
saw themselves complicit in what they had to witness. Prisoners from Naples
incarcerated aboard *Foudroyant* were brought up on deck before being
imprisoned in the boats alongside. 'Many, very many, of Italy's beauteous
daughters, and those of high rank, have I seen prostrated on our deck,
imploring protection,' one midshipman recorded. 'Their graceful forms
bent with misery – their dark eyes and clasped hands raised to the Father
of all for mercy – their clear, olive complexion changing to a sickly hue
from anguish of mind. How could men, possessing human hearts, refrain
from flying to their relief?'[8] There was more of that when the prisoners
were brought up again from the boats to be taken ashore for their trials
and execution. The beheadings, hangings and other horrors were great
public spectacles in the main piazza of the city. Many of those begging
for help on *Foudroyant*'s deck were nobles and great ladies with whom the
Hamiltons had been close friends, in whose palaces they had been lavishly
entertained. Emma Hamilton, to whom many appealed directly, read their
beseeching letters but could do nothing. She herself had gone too far in
pushing the circumstances that helped launch the fate they confronted,
though her husband had become dismayed by the many distinguished
victims who had been his friends. None in this party went on shore from
Foudroyant, not even the king when he arrived and made the flagship his
home. They thus all spared themselves sight of the worst. The roar of the
mob at the executions in the central piazza nevertheless could be heard
on the ships. Aboard *Foudroyant*, as one midshipman recorded, there was
different music: 'The day of the king's arrival was passed in administering
justice (Italian fashion) to the wretches who fell into the grasp of Cardinal
Ruffo's lambs, enlivened by the bombardment of St Elmo. At noon dinner
was served to the royal party and their guests on the quarterdeck, Lady
Hamilton's graceful form bending over her harp and her heavenly music
gave a gusto to the dessert.'
    Nelson offered frequent justification of all that was occurring around
them. First of all, on breaking the truce arranged by Cardinal Ruffo and
Captain Foote, 'Let us suppose that the French fleet had entered Naples
Bay, would the French or the rebels have respected the truce for one
instant? No: the French admiral would have said, I do not come here to

play the part of spectator but to act.' Nelson persisted in his ever-more fatuous eulogizing of a man few others from outside that scene could see in similar terms. To Keith he wrote that 'it was impossible to witness without emotion the joy of the Neapolitans, to hear the shouts of enthusiasm with which they hailed their father, for the king was no longer designated by any other name'. A month later, on 20 August, Troubridge, who lay off Naples in *Culloden*, could still write, 'This day eleven of the leading Jacobins, princes, dukes, and representatives of the people, have been executed, and women have shared the same fate. I sincerely hope they will . . . proclaim a general amnesty, for death is nothing compared to their prisons.'

The best summation of the influences upon Nelson that helped form his outlook upon these events was to be offered by Sir Harris Nicolas, who compiled Nelson's despatches and letters. Writing of Nelson at Naples in the appendix of volume three of his collection Nicolas said: '. . . and if his judgment was in any degree perverted, there were ample causes for it in the character and events of the time, as well as in the peculiar feelings of his own mind. The French Revolution and its effects, especially in Italy, had inspired him with horror and disgust. Loyalty was his predominant passion. He detested those who entertained democratic opinions; a Rebel or a Traitor was, in his opinion, the impersonation of every crime that disgraces human nature; and "no terms with Rebels", was with him as sacred a principle as that he ought to destroy the enemies of his country . . . where men who had fought against their king were concerned, severity was an imperative duty.'[9]

Abhorrent as all of that might have been to its Royal Navy witnesses, yet two days later a sailor was sentenced to 250 lashes for theft from the quarters of a Neapolitan officer on shore. As Nelson's biographer Oliver Warner observed, no Neapolitan sadist over on the piazza could have exceeded the horror of the cat-o'-nine-tails laid in such excess upon a bare back.

Yet another bright scene offered illumination against the horrors being perpetrated beyond the moorings of the British fleet. The first anniversary of the Nile victory was celebrated, organized, of course, by Emma Hamilton. Nelson described the event to his wife in one of the rare letters he was writing to her at this time, always blaming his negligence on the many pressures upon him for the lack of them. A large vessel was fitted out like a Roman galley, 'on its oars were fixed lamps, and in the centre was erected a rostral column with my name; at the stern were elevated two angels supporting my pictures . . . An orchestra was fitted up and filled with the very best musicians and singers. The piece of music was in great measure to celebrate my praise, describing their previous distress "*but Nelson came, the invincible Nelson, and they were preserved and again made very happy*". This must make you think me vain; no, far, very far from it. I relate it more from gratitude than vanity . . .'

* * *

Through this period Admiral Keith was continuing his pursuit of the French navy. On 29 June the French fleet had sailed from Cartagena enforced with sixteen Spanish line ships. Keith had some intimation of this and was acutely concerned about the safety of Minorca against such a combination. On 27 June he sent an urgent request to Nelson 'to send such ships as you can possibly spare off the island of Minorca to wait my orders'. Keith declared a new situation but without clarifying what it was. Nelson received Keith's order on 13 July. Responding the same day he said that he needed all his ships 'for the safety of His Sicilian Majesty, and his speedy restoration to his kingdom'. Nelson better than anyone knew that refusing to send even a single ship to help Keith in whatever his new situation was could be seen as outright disobedience of a commander facing critical circumstances. For a man supposedly fearing descent of the French upon Naples he had weakened his squadron by taking 120 sailors from each ship to assist a military expedition against two inland fortresses. Explaining this to Spencer in justifying his refusal to send any ships to Keith, he said: 'I am prepared for any fate that may await my disobedience . . . I have done what I thought right; others may think differently; but it will be my consolation that I have gained a Kingdom, seated a faithful ally of his Majesty on his throne, and restored happiness to millions.'[10]

Keith wrote again with the same demand on 9 July and on the 14th, peremptorily demanding 'the whole or greater part' of Nelson's force for the protection of Minorca. Nelson received both on 22 July and then immediately sent four ships to Minorca. By that time, however, both Bruix and Keith were out in the Atlantic. Keith had finally picked up pursuit of Bruix, who was making for the Straits. On 7 July St Vincent, who had arrived at Gibraltar on his way home to England, saw the French fleet pass through the Straits.

He had seen them go in, and he saw them go out.

Bruix took the fleet into Cadiz. He sailed again from there on 21 July, shepherding his Spanish charges to Brest. Keith came through the Straits on the 30th and continued up the Atlantic after them. But Bruix brought his allied force safely into Brest on 13 August.

For Bruix it was an enormous triumph. Simultaneously it was an incomprehensible failure. He had undermined the settled conviction of unbreachable British command on the Mediterranean without a shot being fired. He had drawn the British navy about in a confused muddle of pursuit, but he had missed an opportunity that would never arise as advantageously again to inflict setback and defeat upon the British in that sea. He had allowed the British to concentrate their existing forces and to receive reinforcement. Before that, several options had been richly available to him. Pressing through to Alexandria was open. Attack on Sicily and the relief of Malta were possible. So was the recapture of Minorca. The British squadrons that stood in defence of all those initially offered no serious obstacle. 'Your lordship knows what Admiral Bruix might have done had he done his duty,' Nelson was to say to St Vincent some time after. But Bruix had allowed his opportunities to pass until, with a strong fleet mustered against him, he had preferred to evade any damaging action, collect the Spanish, and make it out. The last chance for any form of serious French naval assertion on the Mediterranean sailed out with him.

The British for their part were hardly in a position to celebrate. The tactical confusion between St Vincent and Keith had lost them the opportunity either to defeat or create serious havoc upon what remained of the French navy. Instead they found that they had in Brest a newly formidable force able to serve any invasion attempt. They were pinned to blockade there more unremittingly than ever.

Nelson had become a serious casualty of it all. An unfavourable view of his judgement and sense of responsibility was forming. His relationship with Emma Hamilton was becoming a matter of wide ribald discussion. Immediately more serious, however, was his disobedience of Keith's demands for ships to cover Minorca: a triple disobedience if measured by the number of demands Keith had felt compelled to make. The Admiralty secretary, Evan Nepean, in a sharp letter conveyed the Admiralty's disapproval of that as well as for drawing his best sailors from his ships to fight on land for the Neapolitans, '. . . their Lordships by no means approve of the seamen being landed to form a part of an army to be employed in operations at a distance from the coast, where, if they should have the misfortune to be defeated, they might be prevented from returning to the ships, and the squadron be thereby rendered so defective, as to be no longer capable of performing the services required of it . . .' For many, the laurels laid upon the victor of the Nile were beginning to look as though withering prematurely.

After Acre, glory now lay tenuously upon Nelson's rival as well. Napoleon saw urgent need to restore his position and for him that immediately lay in France. Soon after his return to Cairo he sent Rear Admiral Ganteaume to Alexandria to inspect two frigates lying in the port and to prepare them for his return to France. Before that could be, however, the Ottomans offered Napoleon a restorative encounter.

On 11 July an armada of 113 vessels appeared off Aboukir Bay. Thirteen 74s as well as frigates and gunboats had brought a convoy of transports reportedly carrying eighteen thousand troops who promptly disembarked. The fleet was commanded by Hassan Bey, with Sidney Smith aboard *Tigre* in attendance. Napoleon mustered ten thousand troops and, on 25 July 1799, destroyed the Ottoman force on the beach at Aboukir. But he himself lost more than two hundred killed and 750 wounded. Such continued loss was unsustainable. As Sidney Smith said to Nelson, 'a few more victories like this will annihilate the French army'.

When Napoleon sent two officers aboard *Tigre* to negotiate an exchange of prisoners Sidney Smith courteously gave them a pack of European and British newspapers he had on board. These gave Napoleon his first picture of what was happening in Europe. 'Italy is lost' he cried in pain on learning of the advance of the Austro-Russian forces. He returned briefly to Cairo and then went to Alexandria where, on 17 August, it was observed that Sidney Smith's blockading squadron had gone, presumably to Cyprus for water and provisions. Escape had to be immediate. At ten p.m. on the 22nd Napoleon embarked together with a small group of his generals, leaving General Kléber in command in Egypt. The frigates followed the African coast and then made it across to Corsica where, on 1 October, they anchored in the port of Ajaccio. On 9 October Napoleon and his suite disembarked at Fréjus on the Provençal coast.

XXVII

CONSUL

FRENCH domination of the Europe to which Napoleon Buonaparte returned had begun to look as shattered as his own dreams in the Middle East.

By the autumn of 1799 it seemed as if the Second Coalition was maintaining its initially successful way. Turin had followed Milan when, on 20 June, it capitulated to the Austro-Russian forces under Suvorov. Alessandria followed on 21 July and Mantua on the 30th. On 14 August the young French general Joubert was defeated at Novi. Suvorov moved on to the Papal States, from which the French withdrew on 27 September.

Britain, ever reluctant to see Holland continue in hostile possession, regarded the coalition's success on the Continent as opportunity to restore the authority of the House of Orange and its prince, the Stadtholder. The comfortable assumption was that the Dutch, in hatred of the French, would rise to support the invasion. An arrangement was arrived at with the tsar to land an expeditionary force in Holland. With Britain paying the cost, Russia sent a squadron of eleven ships and seventeen thousand soldiers. Together with thirty thousand British troops the force sailed on 13 August. The men were landed at Den Helder, commanded by Sir Ralph Abercromby, under the Duke of York.

An immediate achievement by Admiral Duncan and his second-in-command, Vice Admiral Mitchell, was capture of what remained of the Dutch navy, twenty-five ships. And with it another lesson in the lack of spontaneous enthusiasm for the restoration of monarchy. The official report declared, 'The Dutch officers have surrendered themselves prisoners of war to the British fleet, but refuse to acknowledge obedience to the Stadtholder. The whole fleet is however taken possession of in his Serene Highness's name, and the Orange flag now flies over every ship in the Texel.' Or, as another account depicted it, 'Certainly there was no appearance of any popular rising, and the Duke of York perceived that he must rely on his own forces alone.' The Duke of York's expedition capitulated two months after going ashore. It had lost ten thousand men.

Further setback followed. On 25 September General Masséna defeated the Russian general Korsakov at Zurich. That victory was blamed on the Austrians withdrawing their army under Archduke Charles thereby undermining Korsakov. The Russians and Austrians were forced from Switzerland. Suvorov pulled his troops out of action in October and went into winter quarters in Bavaria. He swore that he would never work with the Austrians again. The tsar backed him with the same pledge. In this manner the Second Coalition began its gradual disintegration. As the eighteenth century entered its final months this war of the Second Coalition stood wavering between apparent success and new uncertainty. That was the background against which Napoleon Buonaparte now made his startling reappearance.

Certainly no one, even in France, had expected him to turn up in such dramatic fashion. 'Your friend Buonaparte and his army are no more,' the Prince of Wales wrote to Nelson on 4 August 1799 expressing the conviction of the day. 'Sure France cannot withstand all these attacks and misfortunes and tranquillity must at length be restored to Europe.'[1]

Nelson himself blamed Admiralty for Napoleon's escape saying that it had removed to the Malta blockade the two ships whose stations should have ensured interception, 'therefore no blame lays at my door'. The only one who paid a price for it was the Turkish captain stationed off Alexandria. He was beheaded.

The map of the Continent that Napoleon was compelled to regard was the bitter pill he now had to swallow. The greater part of his conquests in Italy had by now been recovered by the Coalition. Austria, already holding Venice, was intent on spreading itself across northern Italy, absorbing Piedmont and displacing the king of Sardinia from there, and reaching down as far as the Papal States. With established Russian designs on the Ottoman Empire, the tsar wanted greater power on the Mediterranean in support of that. Apart from Malta he now also wanted Corsica. For emperor and tsar a weakened, defensive France suggested the way open to whatever territorial acquisition they had in mind. And at the time of Napoleon's arrival there was little to suppose that they were seriously wrong in their assumptions. The situation in France was desperate. Commerce was dead. Soaring national debt was accompanied by inflation. The budget deficit was in hundreds of millions. Royalist revolt was flaring again along the Atlantic coast. The rousing reception that Napoleon got when he landed at Fréjus told of popular relief to have a figure of strength back in a land that was tired of war and that on every level appeared to be in a chaotic state. He was cheered all the way to Paris.

Napoleon might almost be said to have chosen his moment. For he and for his friend Talleyrand his arrival in Paris on 16 October was fortuitous.

A new conspiracy was playing out against the Directory, with Talleyrand involved at the heart of it. Other military figures had been considered for leadership to the coup but here suddenly was the very one for whom the task seemed designed.

As the ruling entity at the summit of government the Directory had become deeply unpopular in 1799. Reform of the system had come to be seen as essential to redeem France. Napoleon was immediately absorbed into the conspiracy. A new post was required for him that suited the plot. Command of the armed forces in and near Paris was quickly arranged by the conspirators. They struck on 9 and 10 November. The outcome was a new form of government at the head of which were three Consuls. The First Consul was to be effective head of state. That position fell to Napoleon. The other two Consuls were primarily advisers. The Consuls presided over three legislative bodies of the popularly elected. The new constitution was promulgated on 15 December and early in 1800 was approved overwhelmingly by a public plebiscite. By that time Napoleon had already manipulated the powers of the First Consul into something different from what had first been intended. He controlled the army, the navy and diplomatic service as well as the general administration. At thirty-one the way to absolutism was spread before him.

The task he faced was intimidating, even for such as he. Napoleon himself summarized it in a legendary outburst to Barras, the most infamous of the Directors, on the first day of the coup: 'What have you done with that France which I left so bright in your hands? I had left you peace, I found war! I left you victories, I found defeats! I left you Italy's millions, I found nothing but predatory laws and poverty! What have you done with the hundred thousand Frenchmen whom I knew, who were my comrades in glory? They are dead.' To all of that he now applied himself.

Even as he took stock of the military situation, Napoleon saw the fall of two of the last fronts still fighting in Italy. Ancona surrendered in November and Coni on 4 December. He faced a gigantic task of reassessment and reconstruction, with the army first of all, to rebuild it and restore its spirit. The Army of Italy was in the same situation it had been in when he had taken command there in 1795, being locked into the very same narrow strip of the Ligurian coast around Genoa. The state of the army was the same. The Directory had gone to war against Austria, without money to pay for the army. The young soldiers, being without food or pay, in rags and shoeless, deserted in hundreds, or died from want and exposure.

Across France itself anarchy reigned on the roads with rampant highway robbery, many of the brigands being army deserters. The highways of France had to be brought under control, with armed soldiers on every regular diligence. Royalist insurrection in La Vendée had to be suppressed. And along with all of that stood the urgent demands of civil, administrative and financial reform. All of it to be managed before he could move to push the Austrians back across the Rhine and out of Italy. So, looking for time, on Christmas Day 1799, he sought to close the eighteenth century by establishing peace. He made his appeal directly to George III and Emperor Francis, relayed by Talleyrand, now once again handling Foreign Affairs.

Napoleon's peace proposal failed to appeal to the trio directly involved with the response, Pitt, Foreign Secretary Grenville and Secretary of War Henry Dundas. In parliament, however, Napoleon's gesture nevertheless brought resurgence of doubt among the opposition over the need for prolonging the war, given the state of France and the fact that the Revolution was already history. Pitt was asked to give sound reason why the war should be continued in face of Napoleon's offer. The Whig party's spokesman, Tierney, Pitt's former duelling opponent, declared that the government obviously would never be satisfied with any terms of peace short of the restoration of the Bourbons. Why else, he demanded, was the war continued? Tierney therefore wanted Pitt to state in one sentence what was now the object of the war and to define that 'without ifs and buts'. Pitt complied: '. . . it is security; security against a danger the greatest that ever threatened the world – a danger such as never existed in any past period of society'. And what could be expected that was different in a Napoleon, 'reared and nursed' in the bosom of the French Revolution 'and who was at once the child and the champion of all its atrocities'? As for the Bourbons, 'The restoration of the French monarchy I consider a most desirable object, because I think it would afford the best security to this country and to Europe.'[2] And that consequently became the basic principle for any British peace agreement with Napoleon. But, as Pitt's biographer J. Holland Rose suggested, Pitt could not have devised a better way to ensure a rush of popular support for Napoleon than proposing in such determined voice to all France the return of the Bourbons: 'This ranks among the greatest mistakes of the time. It made the name of the Bourbons odious and that of Bonaparte popular throughout France.' Apart from the Bourbons, Pitt had shown how determined he was to restore the House of Orange to the Netherlands throne. In these views he was completely in tune with his alliance partners, for the war of the Second Coalition was the final struggle of the Old World seeking to put the clock back. The dogged aim of the principals in the Continental alliance, Austria and Russia, was the restoration of the absolutism of monarchical sway. And with that went suppression of whatever spark of enlightenment and concept of social equality had settled fixedly among the literate classes everywhere. The acceptance of those values in the array of republics that Napoleon Buonaparte had laid down from the Batavian Netherlands to Helvetia Switzerland and on down the Italian peninsula was impressive, even in face of hostility against French overlordship. The struggle of the Neapolitan upper classes to hold on to the Parthenopean Republic was poignantly reflective of that. So was the refusal of the Dutch naval officers to raise the Orange standard. Of Pitt's stance on all of that Holland Rose said, 'There is no sign that Pitt set much store on winning over public opinion of Europe by siding with the oppressed against the oppressors . . .' Pitt and Foreign Secretary Grenville, he said, had no conception of the dynamics of nations: 'For they were essentially men of the eighteenth century; and herein lay the chief cause of their failure against Revolutionary France. They dealt with lands as blocks. She infused new energy into peoples.'

Eighteenth-century man Pitt certainly was in those respects but, as the century closed, he had already created nineteenth-century Britain. This sprang from Britain's altogether restructured economic energy. Far from throwing her into decline as many had expected, war had brought Britain to the top. There was that astonishing fact that, after six years of war, British exports and imports exceeded those of any year of peace. Illustrating that, during the summer trading season of 1799 the popular periodical the *Gentleman's Magazine* reported, 'A most pleasing view of the prosperity of the commerce and revenue of this country lately presented itself, on a part of the vacant ground belonging to the Crown upon Tower Hill, which was never before so usefully occupied. An extraordinary overflow of business of import and export, occurring this time at the legal quays, a seasonable indulgence was granted by the Governor of the Tower, whereby the principal officers of the Port of London . . . instructed to carry the cargoes to Tower Hill, and there to ascertain and secure the duties.'

While Britain's improved financial situation and expansive economic development created the principal basis of the new confidence and the exhaustion of France suggested little hope of early resurrection of her power, any appraisal of the war nevertheless allowed little of clear certainty.

On the Continent the Austrians had not been halted in spite of the Russian withdrawal from the Second Coalition. The Austrians were still advancing in Italy against a French army that appeared to be steadily folding before them. For all that, Britain remained painfully vulnerable as she faced the new century. The enmity of France, driven by naval and colonial rivalry, was unrelenting. The previous success of Masséna in Switzerland and Brune in Holland allowed nothing to be taken for granted. Furthermore, the Austrians, while devouring vast subsidies, had never allowed assurance of staying power. For Pitt and Foreign Secretary Grenville there was constant apprehension of huge financial investment in the military prowess of the Hapsburgs wasting away without durable achievement. Both partners in this round, a cautious Austrian emperor and a manic tsar, had already shown themselves notably unpredictable and unreliable.

This, then, was the situation as the eighteenth century passed away, that most remarkable century of emergence and transition, unequalled in history for the profundity of change it delivered. The *Gentleman's Magazine* paid due tribute to it:

... the world is (now) but as ONE FAMILY, and whatever is known is as freely communicated.

The scientific theorist and the practical labourer have shaken hands, and united into one common stock the result of their labours; and however men may differ in opinions or in rank, there exists an universal harmony as to their connexions and conduct as men, in search of useful truths, the result of which is an unexampled progress in all the arts of utility to the comfort and existence of man ... In looking at the changes that have taken place among individual nations, it is impossible not to be filled with a degree of astonishment, to find that one single century has made such changes, when so many had passed over before without leaving almost any trace of alteration.

With the door firmly shut against any immediate peace negotiation, war against this new manifestation of Napoleon Buonaparte was declared ongoing. The nature of Pitt's rejection of his peace offering was, in many senses, a new declaration of war, the first specifically directed against Napoleon himself, the individual who now personally embodied France in a manner that would remain distinctive. In that particular sense this stood as a different war, still obviously lacking any discernible vision of ultimate Napoleonic course and definition for those now viewing it, but already firmly attached to the person of the one who had come back from morass and who, from a new position of power, began to impose himself upon a world that briefly thought that it had closed the book on him. Or, as Corbett put it, 'Our great duel with him had begun.'[3]

Symbolically, and in reality, the Great War had evolved into war between Britain and France. As such Pitt ever saw it. It was now unlikely to be anything else until the end, whatever the Continental sideshows. Napoleon's return made that absolute. The new century's gift to him was his gathering sense of the invincibility of his position, and his projection from that of a vision of the greatness of a new France rising. With the old century went the wasted years of the Directory and its disorganized management of post-Jacobin France. The new structure would be Napoleon's, a civil reorganization of state through all its levels from education upwards. Around that had to be the encirclement of his and France's global power and influence. Something as bright in its magnitude and universal embrace as the drive that had taken him to Egypt: the fusion of military and savants upon which empire would rise. But that had to bring him back to the source of his likely frustration, to the impregnable island and to the waters. That was where the ultimate issue, the fundamental dream of triumph, still rested. For upon waters that were totally nursed by Britain was borne the wealth that he himself desired, the subsidies that undermined him on the land. This remained the prize that had to be pondered and sought even as Napoleon considered the strategic deployments that might retrieve his military position within the Continent. And he had at this time a goading reminder of naval inadequacy in a letter written to the Directory by General Kléber, whom Napoleon had left behind in command in Egypt. The letter, written after his departure and dated 8 October 1799, bitterly assessed the desperate position in which Napoleon had abandoned Kléber and the rest of the force. Napoleon only saw it after he became First Consul. 'I know all the importance of the possession of Egypt,' Kléber wrote. 'I used to say in Europe that this country was for France the fulcrum, by means of which she might move at will the commercial system of every quarter of the globe; but to do this effectually, a powerful lever is required, and that lever is a navy. Ours has ceased to exist. Since that period everything has changed; and peace with the Porte is, in my opinion, the only expedient that holds out to us a method of fairly getting rid of an enterprise no longer capable of attaining the object for which it was undertaken.'[4] It could only have been a vicious shaft through Napoleon's pride as he read it: the savage truth of France's abiding deficiency upon the waters, the cruellest of postscripts on the recent price of it in the Levant from the one man then indisputably the most qualified to deliver it.

William Pitt's own concerns were quite as much with Egypt, but more immediately with Brest, for the return of Bruix with the French fleet augmented by that of the Spanish had changed the situation in home waters.

Brest and its armada of line ships therefore continued as an enlarged threat of invasion or another mission to the Mediterranean and demanded stricter blockade and vigilance than ever. Bruix's venture had been too much of a fright. The possibility of another like it was so strongly feared that Nelson had lost most of his ships, which had been sent from Gibraltar under command of Admiral Duckworth to take station off Ferrol.

Nelson had been appointed temporary commander in chief in the Mediterranean pending the return of Keith. To Sidney Smith he wrote, 'All our Mediterranean operations are pretty nearly at a stand-still; for the enemy have no fleet at this moment to make us keep a good look-out . . . at this moment I have only two sail of the line and not more than two frigates in a condition to go to sea.'

The main activities in the Mediterranean were support of the Austrians along the Italian coast and the continuing blockade of Malta. It might have helped if there had been more compelling events to engage Nelson's mind and spirits, which at this time and through the months ahead were in steady descent. The picture of him that passed to the world was a sad one of a man who, in losing his heart, appeared also to have lost his way. The most disturbing image is of the hero of the Nile who, in spite of the laborious mound of correspondence daily demanded of his one arm and defective eye, nevertheless suppressed his weariness by nightly sitting up with Emma Hamilton at the casinos while she played faro, gambling away his and her husband's money. Fanciful rumours about the two abounded in Palermo, throughout the service and in London. All manner of stories reached his friends and disturbed them. His devoted friend Troubridge wrote, 'If you knew what your friends feel for you I am sure you would cut out all the nocturnal parties . . . I beseech your Lordship, leave off. Lady H's character will suffer . . . A gambling woman in the eyes of an Englishman is lost.' Reference to the poor state of his mind and health was constant in Nelson's correspondence at this time. None of it had been helped by his surprise and anger on finding that Keith had been officially appointed commander in chief in the Mediterranean succeeding St Vincent, an elevation he had had good reason to suppose might be his.

One unexpected occasion did restoratively illuminate this period for him, thanks to Keith who, on returning to the Mediterranean in his new capacity, called Nelson away from Palermo to confer with him. The meeting was chilly. They had little in common. Disobedience from Nelson was already a jarring experience for Keith, who besides was familiar with all the gossip about Nelson and the Hamiltons. Keith then decided that Nelson should accompany him to review the situation at Malta. Stopping at Palermo on the way, Keith found the scene there to be one 'of fulsome vanity and absurdity'.

It had continued to rankle with Nelson that two of the thirteen line ships at Aboukir had escaped, the *Généreux*, 74, and *Guillaume Tell*, 80. *Généreux* had made it back to Toulon but *Guillaume Tell* was locked in at Valletta by the blockade of Malta. Keith's squadron, with Keith aboard *Queen Charlotte*, Nelson with *Foudroyant*, arrived off Malta on 15 February. Once arrived they received report that a French squadron had been sighted on course for Malta, to throw in relief supplies. The squadron consisted of a 74, soon to be identified as *Généreux*, a transport and three corvettes. Nelson had seldom expressed himself so ecstatically on paper as he did on this occasion, recording the pursuit in a letter to Emma Hamilton: 'Here I am in a heavy sea and thick fog – Oh God! The wind subsided – but I trust to Providence I shall have them. 18th in the evening. I have got her – Le Genereux – thank God! 12 out of 13, only the Guillaume Tell remaining: I am after the others.'

Sir Edward Berry had replaced Thomas Hardy as captain aboard *Foudroyant*.

The brief action fell to *Foudroyant* and to Nelson's delight it was to her that *Généreux* lowered her colours. Berry went aboard and received the sword of her commander, Admiral Perrée, who was mortally wounded and died the following day. Uplifting though it was, even this unexpected gift of action did not, however, sustain Nelson for long. In leaving Nelson responsible for the continuing blockade of Malta, Keith directed him to discontinue using Palermo as his base and to substitute Syracuse instead. But Palermo was the only place where Nelson then wished to be, with Emma Hamilton. And, on receiving Keith's instructions, he answered him on 24 February, saying 'My state of health is such that it is impossible I can much longer remain here. Without some rest I am gone.' He wanted permission 'to go to my friends at Palermo for a few weeks'.

Nothing could have irked Keith more. The French ships in Valletta, including *Guillaume Tell*, were preparing to leave. Nelson's friends on the blockade, Troubridge and Ball, did their best to save Nelson from himself, Troubridge writing, 'I beseech you hear the entreaties of a sincere friend, and do not go to Sicily for the present.' But to Palermo he went, and there he remained. With that he denied himself the satisfaction of intercepting *Guillaume Tell* on its escape from Valletta, commanded by Admiral Decres. He missed what was probably the most memorable battle by a French ship in that war.

Guillaume Tell was pursued right after she got away, at eleven at night after the moon had gone down. She was recognized in the dark by the frigate *Penelope*, which immediately engaged her. At dawn the 64-gun *Lion* came up to within musket shot of *Guillaume Tell*, whose bowsprit became entangled in the shrouds of *Lion*. French sailors made two attempts to board *Lion* but failed as that ship, without a single sail left and her rigging cut to pieces, drifted off to repair damage. *Guillaume Tell* had already lost her main and mizzen topmasts when, at six in the morning, Edward Berry came up with *Foudroyant*, hailed the French ship and called to it to strike colours, simultaneously pouring in a broadside. The two ships were soon alongside each other, with *Penelope* close as well on *Guillaume Tell*'s quarter. 'The fire at that moment on both sides was terrible,' Decres said in his report. 'We continued as close to each other as it was possible without being able to board. In about thirty-six minutes the fore-mast of *Guillaume Tell* gave way, and at three quarters past six her main-mast shared the same fate.' At that time, *Foudroyant*'s log recorded, 'Saw a man nail the French ensign to the stump of the mizzen-mast.' This ferocious battle between the *Guillaume Tell* and her three adversaries, all of them badly shattered, continued for another two hours, until past eight. Rigging aboard the ships had several times caught fire. *Guillaume Tell*'s mainmast had twice been cut, with one fourteen-foot piece lying across the quarterdeck, obstructing movement. 'Notwithstanding this accident, and the appearance of blood, which overflowed all the decks, the resolution of the crew seemed to increase,' Decres wrote,

and not withstanding the fire of three ships the defence of Guillaume Tell, at half past eight, was still vigorous; at that moment her mizzen mast fell on the larboard side . . . Guillaume Tell received the fire of all three, without a mast standing, the ship ungovernable, and reeling from the violent motion of the waves, which she had no mast or sail to counteract, we were obliged to shut her lower ports to prevent her filling. In this situation it was too evident not only that it was impossible to save the ship, but that it was out of my power further to injure the enemy. I was sensible that the men I might lose by a longer resistance, would be the useless victims of a vain obstinacy; upon this conviction, and persuaded that the defence of Guillaume Tell had been in every respect truly honourable, I thought it my duty to submit to fortune, and at about thirty-five minutes past nine, after the ship was a wreck, the flag was struck.

Mahan declared that no ship had ever been more gallantly fought than *Guillaume Tell*.

Edward Berry reported the capture to Nelson. 'In great haste. My dear Lord, I had but one wish this morning – it was for you. After a most gallant defence Le Guillaume Tell surrendered . . . How we prayed for you, God knows . . .'

Responding, Nelson wrote, 'I am sensible in your kindness in wishing my presence at the finish of the Egyptian fleet, but . . . I would not for all the world rob you of one particle of your well-earned laurels . . . My task is done, my health is lost, and the orders of the great Earl St Vincent are completely fulfilled – thanks, ten thousand thanks, to my brave friends. Bronte Nelson of the Nile.'[5]

XXVIII

HOME

WITHIN the relative calm that broadly lay upon the Mediterranean there remained the disquiet over Egypt.

For Britain as much as Napoleon, Egypt was seriously unfinished business. Napoleon, without communication with General Kléber, could for the moment do nothing. Britain had had no immediate action in mind after Acre but Kléber's letter to the Directory had fallen into British hands.

Kléber's letter offered new intelligence. In suggesting peace with the Porte he had outlined the desperate state of the army in Egypt. It had, he said, been reduced to half its strength. Disease was endemic and the soldiers were in rags, their pay far in arrears. With Kléber's suggestion that French submission was imminent the terms of a surrender had sudden urgency in London. The need was to ensure that the twenty thousand troops estimated still to be there should lay down their arms and be declared prisoners of war, prevented from returning to Europe to assist the Army of Italy. Nelson had been vehement on that point, that no Frenchman should leave Egypt except as prisoner of war. 'I own myself wicked enough to wish them all to die in that country they chose to invade. We have scoundrels of French enough in Europe without them,' he wrote to the British minister at Constantinople on 21 December 1799. Admiralty on 17 December had already transmitted instructions to Admiral Keith for relay to Sidney Smith that the French soldiers in Egypt should not be allowed to return to reinforce the French army. Keith received Admiralty's instructions on 8 January 1800. He forwarded them to Sidney Smith that same day. In the Levant, however, it was already too late for any of that.

Sidney Smith, still aboard *Tigre* off the Levant, had come to a different arrangement before those instructions could reach him.

The Grand Vizier of the Ottoman Empire (a title that designated the effective ruler of the empire under its reigning sultan) was marching down the Levantine coast with an army of eighty thousand. Kléber had written to him suggesting negotiations. He then appealed to Sidney Smith to act as mediator. On 22 December Sidney Smith began discussing terms with the French negotiators aboard *Tigre*.

The Grand Vizier, meanwhile, had advanced to the fortress of El Arish, where an ugly incident occurred. When the Ottomans arrived the 250 men in the French garrison refused to resist. They mutinied, looted the wine store, pulled down the French flag and threw down ropes for the Turks to scale. Unhappily, once inside, the Turks began to massacre the French, of whom only one hundred were saved. It served as sad illustration of the depths to which French morale had sunk. The unpleasantness did not, however, stop the negotiations. The Grand Vizier's army was almost in as poor a state as Kléber's after the long march through Syria. Kléber would probably have defeated it as soundly as Napoleon had broken the earlier Turkish force at Aboukir Bay, but he wanted his army out of Egypt and the terms that he got from the Grand Vizier were generous. The French were to withdraw to Alexandria and other embarkation points where they would embark in Turkish transports sent to carry them and their arms back to France. The Grand Vizier had also agreed to pay for maintenance of the French army until their departure from Egypt. This Treaty of El Arish was signed on 28 January 1800.[1]

Keith's instruction to nullify any such treaty reached Sidney Smith early in March and got to Kléber on the 18th. Keith had included a letter for General Kléber in which, curtly and with little grace, he informed him that the only terms of capitulation Britain would allow were for the abandonment of arms and stores and the soldiers to be considered as prisoners of war.

The reaction with both Sidney Smith and Kléber was shock and outrage that their efforts to remove the French army so smoothly from Egypt should thus be undone. Kléber brandished Keith's letter before the army with the cry, 'Soldiers! We know how to reply to such insolence – prepare for battle!' To Keith, Sidney Smith wrote, 'I own, in my office of mediator in this business, it never entered into my ideas that *we* could put any obstacle in the way of an arrangement so very beneficial to us in a *general* view, and which evidently could not take place on any terms disgraceful to a veteran, unbeaten, and uninvested army.'

There can be no doubt that he did it all in good faith, with judgement based on the propitious circumstances apparent at El Arish, with both armies eager to see resolution, neither disposed to continue in the depleted state they were. He had mediated the treaty between the French and the Turks but had not actually signed it himself.

Kléber stopped the evacuation, advised the Grand Vizier that the truce was over, and two days later, on 20 March, attacked the Vizier's army and drove it from Egypt. The forces in Cairo erupted in resistance but, after savage violence within the city, on 22 April the Turks were marched out and put on the road to Syria. Thus, with the Ottomans defeated, the French occupation of Egypt continued unchallenged by the Turks. The war that El Arish had so agreeably sought to extinguish thus continued. But there was to be yet another act to this muddle and confusion.

The British government had, meanwhile, received the news of the El Arish agreement and, though disapproving of it and of Sidney Smith's sanction of it, decided that it would be best to ratify the treaty after all. And on 29 March the Admiralty, in the strained terminology of its embarrassment, told Keith that it had 'judged it proper that his Officers should abstain from any act inconsistent with the engagements to which Captain Sir Sidney Smith has erroneously given the sanction of His Majesty's name'.[2]

The delivery of that belated effort produced its own particular drama.

On 27 April Captain Courtenay Boyle of the frigate *Cormorant*, having received from Keith the packet of despatches containing the Admiralty's new instructions on El Arish, sailed from Leghorn for Alexandria. He was told to get to Alexandria 'without loss of time'. And fast his passage was. Carrying all possible sail in a fair wind *Cormorant* was just thirty-eight miles from Alexandria when, at ten p.m. on the night of 20 May, she struck. At daylight it was found that she had run deep into the shoal, grounded within a mile and a half of a low sandy shore 'without a tree or any object to give us the least idea of our situation on that coast – a heavy stern sea striking and setting her fast in shore . . . At noon, the haze clearing over the land, we discerned, with our glasses, a town bearing S.W. distance about eleven miles, which we supposed to be Alexandria, but were quite uncertain as no one on board had ever been on that coast.'

There followed in Boyle's account a classic description of the vicissitudes of naval diplomatic mission and Royal Naval management of shipwreck on an alien coast:

It now appeared to be the general opinion that the ship could not be saved; the rudder pintles had been broken from the ship's heavy striking, the rudder itself unhung and gone . . . The carpenter reported to me the pumps choked and the ship filling fast; and that he thought no exertion could save her. My first consideration then was, by what method I was likeliest to preserve the lives of my people in quitting the wreck. To keep them sober was absolutely necessary. Having ordered the spirit room to be opened, their allowance of grog was now served, and the hatches were then finally secured. The first lieutenant was directed to break the people off from their work, for ten minutes, in order that they might drink their grog, and collect a few cloaths together to take with them; a sail was then cut up, and, to each man, a piece of canvas was given, to put their cloaths into. On their return to work, the carpenter was ordered to turn-to directly, and make rafts for the landing of the people . . . and had now given orders to Lieutenant Blyth, for their quitting the ship with him. They were to have a sufficient number of arms, and ammunition headed up in casks thrown overboard to float on shore before him; and he himself was to go with part of this division on the first raft; and was on landing to distribute their arms to them, collecting and preserving whatever casks had beached . . . and when we should all be landed, the officers had my orders to form their respective divisions into a solid square, placing the boys in the centre, with pikes, to appear as formidable as possible in case of meeting with the Arabs . . . In this manner it was intended to march to the first French post; and there, delivering up our arms, claim the privileges attendant on a flag of truce . . . I opened the public despatches entrusted to my care, and which I had Lord Keith's directions to do, and act thereon myself, should Sir Sidney Smith be absent on my arrival off Alexandria . . . From these powers, I judged that, according to the law of nations, I might consider myself as, and claim the right of, negotiator; and under such an idea I ordered a flag of truce to be hoisted, continuing our signal guns of distress, which we had fired from our first striking . . . At half-past four, the officer bearing the French flag of truce arrived on the beach, with a party of cavalry; when I sent Mr John Blyth, first lieutenant, to him in the launch, to claim his protection and to acquaint him with my mission, at the same time ordering Mr Blyth to take on shore a coil of ? rope, with the hope of having a fixed raft rope to depend on. This order, from the heavy sea running and surf breaking on the beach, could not be complied with, and the launch was upset, drove up and stove in – the men, however, were landed safe. I then ordered the main-top-sail and mizen-stay-sail to be set on the ship to forge her as near the shore as possible, both to shorten the distance for the rafts getting on shore, and that we might have a better opportunity of saving the men's lives. In this attempt I was fortunate, for with a heavy stern sea she lifted in, to about a quarter of a mile from the beach; and made such a bed for herself, as to prevent the enemy ever getting her off, or her being of the least service to them. She was bulged, and her between decks full, and the sea making a fair breach over her . . . We were employed in making rafts all the evening, heaving the shot, arms, ammunition, etc., overboard, and destroying the signal flags and other stores. At six p.m. two rafts had left the ship and landed the men safe . . . these had carried ashore between 40 and 50 persons . . . Night was now fast approaching and dark . . . I in the next placed directed my attention to the remaining part of the ship's company, who had worked hard during a long and hot day, and had been up all the former night. The cold meat, together with some bread and cheese, which my servants had saved, was distributed amongst them; and by muster they were each served with a pint of port wine. They were then ordered to hang their hammocks up, under a raft lodged on the gunwales between the main and mizzen masts, covering it with the painted hammock cloths to keep the people dry as the sea was then making a fair breach over the ship . . . At 5 . . . a message from the officer commanding the French troops on the beach, aide-de-camp of General D'Estang, who commanded at Rosetta, the town in sight, to say it was the general's wish that I should come immediately on shore and acquaint him with the purport of my letter to General Kléber . . . and at 9 a.m. I took the surgeon and two men on shore with me leaving the 2nd lieutenant and the master with the necessary orders for the remaining people quitting the ship.

They were all taken to Cairo, after having seen practically all their possessions plundered from them by the French officers and soldiers at Rosetta. But at Cairo Boyle was hospitably received by Kléber and put up in Kléber's own house. Kléber pointed out the obvious, that the British ratification of El Arish had arrived too late and that, after securing Egypt in wake of Keith's earlier letter nullifying the treaty, he now had no intention of quitting Egypt. He promised to send Boyle to Sidney Smith at the first opportunity. Until then he and the ship's company would be cared for.

When Kléber left Cairo on an operation Boyle moved next door into a suite in General Damas's house. Kléber had housed *Cormorant*'s officers with other generals and put the men in a good camp at Gizeh. He had also instructed Damas to supply Boyle with any money he needed.

Kléber returned on 14 June. He went over to Damas's house to lunch with his officers. Strolling in the garden afterwards with an architect who was making alterations to his house a young Arab approached him, offered his hand and, as Kléber offered his, he was stabbed several times. Boyle had been on a visit to the Pyramids. He arrived back to find Cairo in turmoil. At Damas's house, in the sitting room of the suite he occupied, the assassin, Soliman Aleppy, was being interrogated by French officers while suffering the bastinado. In the midst of this hysterical scene of grief and vengeance Boyle heard one of the French officers cry out, 'There is the English captain who is the ally of this wretch.' Forthwith, as if it somehow helped ameliorate their distress, Boyle, the other officers and the men were imprisoned in the citadel, where they were lodged in the vilest part of that prison.

Kléber's funeral procession was halted where Soliman Aleppy was to be executed. As a preliminary Soliman's hand was roasted. After that he was impaled and the pole raised upright. It took him four hours to die. On 12 August Boyle and his surviving sailors were embarked at Alexandria aboard a British frigate bearing a flag of truce and taken to Cyprus to join Sidney Smith.[3]

For the French, 14 June 1800 was to have yet another great significance – the return of decisive military victory on the Continent.

Through the spring of 1800 Napoleon had built his prospective military campaign against the Austrians. The Austrian general, Melas, had attacked Masséna along the Apennines until Masséna found himself locked into Genoa. On 6 May Napoleon left Paris for Geneva. His planned to descend from Switzerland and, in one of the most distinctive manoeuvres of his military career, followed the example of Hannibal and took his force of some twenty thousand across the Alps, St Bernard Pass down to Piedmont. Milan was taken on 1 June and on 14 June he confronted Melas at the town of Marengo. Napoleon spread his troops too widely, allowing Melas at one point to believe he had won the day. But Desaix, who had just arrived from Egypt, followed up and put the Austrians to flight. Melas withdrew from Genoa and agreed to abandon Piedmont and Lombardy.

For Napoleon, it was the turning point. A mighty Austrian army was stopped and turned back, its victorious momentum shattered. France had regained Nice and most of northern Italy. Its army was back in step. General Moreau further affirmed this by crossing the Rhine and Danube, marching across Bavaria and entering Munich.

At mid-1800 Egypt had stood as the unheralded but decisive arbiter of destiny for the two figures who so conspicuously emerged as the near-symbolic protagonists representing the two principal parties to the Great War.

Egypt had given to the one triumph, the other defeat. But the fates that had guided play between the two had wickedly played another game. Triumph for the one had become dissipated by sensual inertia. Defeat and the threat of punitive oblivion with the other had, through the chance of fateful timing, become converted to a position of supremacy. And suddenly it all seemed to have changed in this play of fortune between these two men, the sailor and the soldier, in the apparent issue between them of whether Sea War in this epoch decided Land War, whether the sailor would master the soldier, or falter in the attempt.

As Napoleon returned in triumph to Paris, Nelson was about to start his own return: a long and controversial journey home that, to many, would suggest the decisive retreat from the field of triumph of a weary, fully dispirited hero, who was losing respect from even some of his most ardent admirers. That he already had lost much of it at Admiralty was made plain in the letters written to him by the First Sea Lord, Earl Spencer, and which reached Nelson at Leghorn on 14 June, a day already fatefully marked by Marengo and Kléber's assassination.

Spencer, like Keith, had become weary of the pleas of ill health from Nelson that accompanied his self-indulgent disobedience. That and the scandal of his passion at the corrupt Sicilian Court were reflected in the terse politeness of Spencer's phrases. In the first, official, letter Spencer said bluntly, '. . . all I shall say is, to express my extreme regret that your health should be such as to oblige you to quit your station off Malta, at a time when I should suppose there must be the finest prospect of its reduction . . . If the enemy should come into the Mediterranean, and whenever they do, it will be suddenly, I should be much concerned to hear that you learnt of their arrival in that sea, either on shore or in a transport at Palermo.' In the private letter that arrived with the official one Spencer made clear that this was the recall that Nelson had requested: 'It is by no means my wish or intention to call you away from service, but having observed that you have been under the necessity of quitting your station off Malta, on account of your health, which I am persuaded you could not have thought of doing without such necessity, it appeared to me much more advisable for you to come home at once . . . I believe I am joined in opinion by all your friends here, that you will be more likely to recover your health and strength in England than in an inactive situation at a Foreign Court, however pleasing the respect and gratitude shown to you for your services may be . . .'

Nelson's close friend on the Malta blockade, Troubridge, tried to persuade him to remain in the Mediterranean. So did Keith, indication of a greater sense of amity and forbearance than Nelson allowed him. 'I hope you will not be obliged to go,' Keith wrote, '. . . particularly as I am directed to send you, if you like it, to Egypt; but when a man's health is concerned, there is an end of all, and I will send you the first frigate I can lay hold of.' In spite of that, Keith was yet to experience more extreme irritation with Nelson.

Queen Maria Carolina had decided that she wanted to go from Palermo to Vienna to visit her Hapsburg relatives. To carry her and a large royal party and all their baggage from Palermo to mainland Italy, Nelson withdrew *Foudroyant* and another line ship, *Alexander*, from the blockade of Malta. Keith was enraged by this unwarranted reduction of the force on station. No sooner was she at Leghorn than the queen, afraid of French movement in Italy, wished to return to Palermo.

In the end the party crossed Italy to Vienna via Ancona and Trieste. Sir William Hamilton had received his own recall shortly before Nelson got permission to return. They therefore travelled back together. Emma Hamilton at this time was pregnant. Nelson and the Hamiltons went on from Vienna to Prague, where Nelson marked his forty-second birthday, thence on to Hamburg via Dresden. They landed at Yarmouth on 6 November.

It had been a strange, sad journey. William Hamilton was described as broken, distressed and harassed. With his wife carrying Nelson's child and with his former idyllic existence in Naples now irretrieveably far behind, he was a man who had lost all. An unpleasant distinction of the journey was the harsh scorn that Emma Hamilton provoked. Coarse, ill-mannered, vulgar were some of the familiar opinions of her. The same pursued her into London. The social consequences of their relationship were made plain to Nelson when he went to Court. George III merely asked the Hero of the Nile if he had recovered his health and without waiting for an answer turned to a general at his side and talked to him for half an hour without further attention to Nelson. Aside from this Nelson had to confront his relationship with his wife. They stayed together for just over a month in lodgings in London before parting for good.

Marengo re-established Napoleon's military stature, but Egypt remained the obsessive source of his oceanic fantasies, the inextinguishable dream hovering beside and beyond any vision of power in Europe. There was yet reality to it inasmuch as a large French army remained in Egypt. To strengthen and rebuild it had to remain a predominant goal, which was unachievable, however, without a naval strength to match Britain's. But, in the final half of the year 1800, that did not appear as unlikely as it might have seemed at the time of Buonaparte's return twelve months earlier. Triumph at Marengo and the armistice with the Austrians that followed had allowed Napoleon to pull together in mind the broad strategy through which he saw the maritime contest progressively winnable.

In the wake of the Austrian armistice discussions with France, the British ambassador at Vienna, Lord Minto, was instructed in August to take part in any negotiation for a broader, general peace. The First Consul's response to the British proposal was swift. From Napoleon came perhaps the most brazen diplomatic initiative ever attempted by him in the Great War. In a move of extraordinary gall he demanded a Naval Armistice previous to negotiating any form of peace treaty. Nothing like it had ever before been suggested, much less attempted. The specifics of this unique demand were scarcely credible to those who began studying them.

The negotiation had moved from Vienna to London, where Foreign Secretary Grenville dealt with M. Otto, the French agent established there as Commissioner for French prisoners. What Otto delivered from the First Consul was that, preceding any talk of a final peace, there should be immediate suspension of hostilities between the British and French fleets. Squadrons should withdraw to their own coasts from the blockades of Brest, Toulon, Cadiz, Flushing, Malta and Alexandria. Provisions should be allowed into Malta and Alexandria, and troops into Egypt. Six frigates should sail to Alexandria and return without being searched by the blockading British squadrons. In short, the Mediterranean should revert to a pre-Nile status quo.[4]

Reaction was not as peremptory as might have seemed likely. Pitt was concerned that absolute refusal would produce immediate renewal of hostilities between Austria and France with likely fresh military disasters and 'an immediate separate peace on the worst terms'. In this way the defensive yet had to meet the brash with diplomatic suavity instead of its own unmitigated astonishment. And Grenville formally responded declaring that such a Naval Armistice was unusual before a full peace treaty was completed, but that the king's desire for a general peace at length induced him to accede to it under certain conditions. Malta and the maritime ports of Egypt could be provisioned only for fourteen days at a time but nothing could be admitted by sea that would give additional means of defence. If British squadrons were withdrawn from Brest, Toulon and other ports no ships within those ports should be removed to any other station.

Otto in response 'threw out the most positive assertions' that without the Naval Armistice France would carry its victorious campaign in Italy down to the conquest of Naples and Sicily, to give it the stations it required for the relief of Malta and Alexandria. But his threat lost much of its force when the French garrison on Malta finally surrendered to the British on 4 September. That released the blockading British squadron to other purposes, notably for strengthened blockade of Egypt.

Public response to the proposed Naval Armistice was reflected in one London morning newspaper which considered it 'somewhat astonishing' that the government deigned to give an answer to the Naval Armistice proposal. 'Such an armistice,' it declared, 'would in fact, have established French power in Egypt; and would have rendered completely fruitless and ineffectual the glorious victory of the Nile, and the no less glorious defence of Acre . . . In short, to allow six frigates to go to Alexandria, loaded with the assassins and assassinating weapons of Bonaparte, would be to deliver Egypt into the hands of the French forever . . . paving their way to India, and laying the foundation of the ruin of England.'[5]

On 9 October the British government informed Otto that 'all farther discussions on the terms of a Naval Armistice would be superfluous'. Those talks had indeed become superfluous because just three days before, on 6 October, the British government had finally decided to mount a military expedition to remove the French. It was something that War Secretary Dundas had urgently pleaded for in a letter to Pitt on 19 September: 'The importance of expelling the French from Egypt is obvious; for it is clear that Bonaparte will subordinate every object to the retention of that colony . . . by our subsidies and naval help we have borne our fair share in the Coalition. Further efforts in that direction will be fruitless. We must now see to our own interests. By occupying all the posts of Egypt, we can coop up the French and force them to capitulate. Action must not be postponed for any consideration whatever.'[6]

Upon that urgent note preparation of the expedition now went ahead, though overshadowed by a closer, more immediately urgent and swiftly mounting crisis.

Any disappointment in Napoleon over failure to draw a Naval Armistice from Britain was swiftly balanced, however, by what was working out with Tsar Paul, through the hostility that had developed between the tsar and his coalition partners.

Paul now bore as much resentment against Britain as he did against Austria. The faults and failure of the Dutch expedition had embittered him, the more so since, after their withdrawal from Holland, the Russian troops had been quartered in the Channel Islands, where they had complained of poor treatment, which resulted, however, from their own misbehaviour. Napoleon, by contrast, had sent back to Russia the Russian prisoners of war France had taken in the campaigns with Austria. They went home well dressed and fully armed, unaccompanied by the usual demand for ransom. And, working on the fact that the tsar had been elected Grand Master of the Order of St John by the exiled knights, he offered to cede Malta to Paul if the French garrison there was finally compelled to evacuate the island. Out of this developed a Franco-Russian alliance as the tsar suddenly assembled his own hostile coalition against Britain.

As this account has already detailed, neutrality from the start had been a bitter issue in this war. The most irate victims initially were the Americans and the Scandinavians, both of whose commerce had boundlessly expanded with the war by British laxity of its neutrality strictures. The Danes and the Swedes had expanded so ubiquitously on all major trade routes that the British became increasingly more alert on what they might be delivering directly or indirectly to France and the nations it dominated. British boarding of Scandinavian ships had become so frequent that the Danes and Swedes jointly established their own system of convoys shepherded by frigates that carried instruction to resist British interference. Two such episodes involving Swedes and Danes provoked punitive response from the British and brought matters to a head that summer of 1800.

On 25 August an identical event followed off the Downs. The Danish frigate, *Frega*, convoying six ships, was told to await a boat. She answered that she would fire upon it, which she did. But the shot hit the British frigate, killing one man. The British ship fired a broadside. A spirited action followed, until the Dane lowered her colours. Then, in October, a British warship seized a Prussian merchantman carrying naval stores into Cuxhaven. The Prussians sent two thousand troops into Hamburg until the ship was restored. Through these events the Baltic nations had been brought to a state of rage against Britain.

The tsar seized upon that to propose revival of the Armed Neutrality of 1780 that had been formed by the Empress Catherine. And on 16 December 1800 Russia and Sweden signed, followed soon after by Denmark and Prussia.

Together they denied the British any right to stop their convoys, search their ships and confiscate what they deemed unlawful. They declared their intention to resist any such attempts with force. An embargo was placed on British vessels in Baltic ports. The tsar accordingly seized some three hundred British ships, imprisoned their crews and sealed British warehouses and other property. Prussian and Danish troops occupied Hanover, a direct slap at George III.[7]

All of this was the reward to Napoleon for his cultivation of Tsar Paul. It had yielded the required effect by finally producing full hostility in the unbalanced Paul against his former coalition partners and, so it seemed, locked the British out of the Baltic. Without formal declaration of war, the Baltic nations stood in what was tantamount to belligerent unity with France against Britain. On 14 January 1801 Britain laid its own embargo on all Russian, Swedish and Danish vessels in the ports of the United Kingdom.

Britain, without making threat of formal war, began to prepare its own ultimatum to the northern powers. It would be borne to the Baltic, to Copenhagen specifically, by as powerful a fleet as could be mustered in home waters. The Danes, whose capital was first in line of approach, would be required to withdraw their Baltic sanctions on British trade and the threat of combined force to resist British interrogation of their ships. After Copenhagen the British would move on against Russia and Sweden.

On the night of 3 February Pitt told the Commons, 'The question is, whether we are to permit the navy of our enemy to be supplied and recruited – whether we are to suffer neutral nations, by hoisting a flag upon a sloop or fishing boat, to convey the treasures of South America to the harbours of Spain, or the naval stores of the Baltic to Brest or Toulon?' It was his last speech after seven years of government. He resigned that very night on the question of Catholic emancipation, which George III refused to sanction. Henry Addington took over the premiership.[8]

Great Continental triumph for Napoleon accompanied these crises. On 28 November the war with Austria resumed. The Austrians were crushed in five days. On 3 December at Hohenlinden Moreau broke completely an Austrian army advancing in three columns that failed to make their proper connection because of heavy snow. Armistice was renewed on 25 December. In Italy the Austrians and Neapolitans were also defeated, with an armistice there on 16 January. On 9 February 1801, at Luneville, the First Consul's brother, Joseph Buonaparte, and the Austrians signed a peace treaty that, among other things, established the Rhine as the frontier of France, from Switzerland to Holland. Britain again stood alone.

The tsar, who had gone to war with anti-revolutionary zeal to restore the Bourbons to the French throne, now declared his intention to send an ambassador to Paris. Napoleon wrote to Joseph at Luneville, 'Peace with the emperor is nothing in comparison with the alliance with the czar, which will dominate England and preserve Egypt for us.' Russia he saw as his ally against the Ottoman Empire, to help ensure Egypt. To Talleyrand on 27 January he wrote, 'In the embarrassment about to come upon England, threatened in the Archipelago by the Russians and in the northern seas by the combined Powers, it will be impossible for her long to keep a strong squadron in the Mediterranean.' All of that, Mahan points out, showed how heavily sea power at this time weighed upon Napoleon's estimation. For Britain the Baltic crisis arrived to compound the weight that renewed isolation laid upon her.

XXIX

BALTIC

IT could be said that Nelson with his marvellous instincts and uncanny good fortune in his career got himself home just in time for the Baltic crisis. But the cloud that lay upon him was heavy, though everywhere he went the public clamoured to cheer him.

He asked for a new command immediately after arrival, declaring his health restored. He was assigned one under St Vincent, now in command of the Channel fleet. But when he reported to St Vincent on 16 January he was informed that a naval force had been decided upon for the Baltic and that he would sail as second to the commander in chief designate, Admiral Sir Hyde Parker.

On 17 January at Torbay Nelson hoisted his flag aboard the 110-gun *San Josef*, which he had captured at the Battle of St Vincent. When his flag was hoisted it was cheered by the whole fleet. On 1 February he was told of the birth to Emma Hamilton of their daughter Horatia. And on 12 February, mindful of the Baltic shallows, he transferred to a lighter ship, *St George*. Hardy remained with him as captain. *St George* moved from Torbay to Spithead and on the 23rd Nelson had three days' leave and went up to London to see Emma and his child. On his return the ship left Spithead for Yarmouth, where she arrived on 6 March. This was the departure point for the Baltic.

Any such critical expedition assembled in home waters might logically have expected some advance naval council with its commanders before setting out, but practically nothing was known of the strategy of this force before Nelson sailed from Spithead.

That they were going to the Baltic to deliver an ultimatum to Denmark and, by implication, to the other northern powers as well was generally known. Pitt had broadly briefed Nelson himself on the necessity of the mission, before the change of administration. It was that political change, presumably, that had affected plans and communication for the change of government carried with it changes at Admiralty. It was closer insight into the real character of their mission that Nelson therefore sought on arrival at Yarmouth.

Hyde Parker's flagship *London* was in the roads but the commander was living ashore. That Hyde Parker was ashore instead of on his ship preparing to sail was Nelson's first irritation, enlarged to fury on subsequently learning that Hyde Parker's young wife was planning a ball for a whole week hence, on the 13th.

Aboard *St George* and constantly at Nelson's side since coming aboard was Lieutenant Colonel William Stewart, second son of the Earl of Galloway, who commanded the troops on this expedition. From their first meeting Stewart had taken to Nelson and, in common with all those of lively mind who came close to Nelson, had become wholly fascinated by the strikingly original character that unfolded before him day after day. Stewart's account of the expedition was to be the fullest and most detailed. His fascination with Nelson the man made it an account enlivened by personal detail.

Nelson went to pay his respects to the commander the morning after *St George*'s arrival. 'I remember,' Stewart said, 'that Lord Nelson regretted Sir Hyde being on shore. We breakfasted that morning as usual, soon after six o'clock, for we were always up before daylight. We went on shore, so as to be at Sir Hyde's door at eight o'clock, Lord Nelson choosing amusingly exact to that hour, which he considered a very late one for business.' The amusement ended there, for Hyde Parker scarcely noticed him, which appeared to be a deliberate snub.

For a man whose whole being was entirely enlivened at the prospect of action such a stalled situation was unbearable. Even without clear intelligence on their mission he wanted a start to it instead of lying in a mixed state of preparation at Yarmouth. He was conscious that delay gave the Baltic powers time to strengthen their defences and prepare their navies. Nelson wanted those ships that were ready to sail to do so at once to deliver the intended ultimatum at the approaches to Copenhagen. The rest of the fleet was to follow when ready. By the time the fleet was fully assembled off the Sound response to the ultimatum would have been delivered and, with intelligence gathered on the defences by the advance force, action by the combined fleet could start if the Danes were unyielding. But he was allowed no opportunity to advance this proposal and discuss it either with Hyde Parker or in council. He remained in ignorance of whatever Hyde Parker himself thought. Thus it remained until they sailed.

Action at Copenhagen would be an operation bottled within a narrow strait where a severely restricted passage among shoals was defended by artillery batteries along the shore as well as a strong navy, the whole played upon by confused and variable winds. That much they all knew. Upon the necessary appreciation of that lay the wide difference in character and drive between Nelson and the commander in chief, Admiral Sir Hyde Parker, a wealthy, sixty-year-old socialite who had recently married a young woman of nineteen.

Hyde Parker was a man of long service but modest naval achievement. That he should have been selected as commander of such a vital mission with its critical bearing upon so many aspects of the war was difficult for many to understand then and after. It was equally difficult to understand why the talents of Nelson should have been confined as second. Nelson had in fact been Earl Spencer's choice to head the squadron but his recent erratic behaviour in the Mediterranean appeared to have worked against him at Admiralty. Hyde Parker nevertheless from every point of view appeared a baffling alternative. 'His health and strength were declining, and he was unequal to the charge,' was Edward Brenton's view of Hyde Parker. Collingwood described Hyde Parker as 'full of vanity, a great deal of pomp, and a pretty smattering of ignorance'.

Nelson himself carried his own firmly established doubt of Hyde Parker's ability as a commander. He had served under him in the Mediterranean in 1795 when Hyde Parker had succeeded Hotham in command there. Nelson had seen both Hotham and Hyde Parker as culpable in the eventual loss of the Mediterranean, for they had deprived him of the means to destroy or neutralize the Toulon fleet or to destroy coastal communications of the French as the campaign for Italy mounted. That damning view had certainly reached Hyde Parker in the past. All of it made for an uncomfortable beginning between the two.

The change of administration from Pitt to Addington had meant that St Vincent replaced Earl Spencer as First Lord of Admiralty. Thomas Troubridge joined him on the board. The changes did not become formally effective until a few days before the expedition sailed, but they at least brought the immediate advantage for Nelson in knowing that two of his closest friends and admirers were presiding over naval direction just as the expedition got underway.

For Nelson nothing was more inexcusable in preparation for such an expedition than delay. The value of time was repetitively expressed throughout his career. It produced a host of phrases from him, the basic theme being: 'Time – time is everything. Five minutes often makes the difference between victory and defeat.' 'Say what you will, it is on time that all depends in war.' To sit in idleness at Yarmouth for six days more waiting for Hyde Parker's wife to give a ball was to Nelson a mockery of all that they were about. 'I only now long to be gone,' he wrote from Yarmouth. 'Time is precious and every hour makes more resistance; strike quick, and home.' And to St

Vincent he had already written, 'Time, my dear Lord, is our best ally, and I hope we shall not give her up, as all our allies have given us up.' And, in guarded reference to Hyde Parker, 'Our friend here is a little nervous about dark nights and fields of ice, but we must brace up; these are not times for nervous systems.' That had been written before St Vincent and Troubridge took over at Admiralty. But once they were established there Nelson swiftly appealed to Troubridge, guardedly: 'I know, my dear Troubridge, how angry the Earl would be if he knew I, as second-in-command, was to venture to give an opinion, because I know his opinion of officers writing to Admiralty . . . Consider how nice it must be laying in bed with a young wife, compared to a damned cold raw wind. But, my dear Troubridge, pack us off. I am interested, as I want to return.'

The appeal was immediately effective. Troubridge apparently managed to pass its substance to St Vincent after all for he penned a hard command to Hyde Parker: 'I have heard by a side wind that you have intention of continuing at Yarmouth until Friday on account of some trifling circum-stance . . . I have . . . sent down a messenger purposely to convey to you my opinion, as a private friend, that any delay in your sailing would do you irreparable injury.'

That command arrived at Yarmouth on 11 March. 'The signal is made to prepare to unmoor at twelve o'clock,' Nelson triumphantly acknowledged to Troubridge that same day. 'Now we can have no desire for staying, for her ladyship is gone, and the *Ball* for Friday knocked up by yours and the Earl's unpoliteness, to send gentlemen to sea instead of dancing with white gloves. I will only say that as yet I know not that we are even going to the Baltic, except from newspapers.'

The whole fleet, fifty sail, sixteen of which were line ships, was at sea on the 12th. But Nelson's frustration remained. He still knew nothing of their official instructions.

For any second-in-command, but especially for a man of Nelson's feverishly focused strategic deductions before battle, absence of collabora-tive effort with the commander when approaching a target destination was intolerable. His mind was bereft of the activity it demanded in preparation, himself as if heading nowhere, except beating northwards in a heavy gale. He knew that what ultimately devolved upon him was the expectation that he would influence the commander on those tactical and strategic aspects that mattered most. It was the undeclared expectation that had sailed with them. Failure in the mission would fall back upon him regardless of whatever grounds Hyde Parker might offer for any lack of success.

Hyde Parker had made his snub too deliberate for it to be mistaken. He had some grounds, however, for not calling a council with Nelson and his officers. Although they all knew they were on course to deliver

an ultimatum to Denmark to withdraw from the threats levelled by the
Armed Neutrality they had sailed before Hyde Parker had received his full
instructions from Admiralty. These had caught up with the fleet after it had
cleared Yarmouth. The changeover at Admiralty was probably responsible
for the delay because it was only on 15 March that they were formally
drawn up and signed by St Vincent, Troubridge and another member of
the Admiralty board. In these the fundamental object of the expedition
was clearly defined as intent to break Russian naval power on the Baltic.
Once matters at Copenhagen had been settled, the fleet should proceed
first to Revel to destroy the Russian squadron there, and then to Cronstad
to finish off what lay there. The scope of it clearly demanded an intensity
of strategic consideration before reaching the Baltic. But for Nelson there
was still no communication concerning any of it. A copy of the instructions
should have been the least he received, before storm prevented contact by
boat between the flagship and *St George*.

The torment of the professional was accompanied by that of the personal.
Nelson was a wounded, suffering man. This was a moment of anguish,
rage and despair unequalled in his life, before or after. At the heart of it
all burned his passion for Emma Hamilton, accompanied by jealousy over
some possible liaison with the Prince of Wales, who had demonstrated his
interest in her and to which she had artfully responded in manner instinctive to her. The thought of it brought painful alternating hot and cold
seizures of the heart. Remembrance of their passion aroused him further:
'What must be my sensations at the idea of sleeping with you! It sets me
on fire, even the thoughts, much more would be the reality.' The arrival of
his child on the eve of their departure and the many questions concerning
her future that inevitably arose was a new form of turmoil. The questions
of his and Emma Hamilton's own future burned. If he survived, and as
usual he doubted that, he saw them quitting England at the end of this
campaign and retiring to Sicily. Withal, there had to be some conscience
over the fact that before sailing he had taken, coldly, his final departure from
Fanny Nelson. He had written her: 'Living, I have done all in my power
for you and, if dead, you will find I have done the same; therefore my only
wish is to be left to myself; and wishing you every happiness, believe me
that I am, your affectionate Nelson and Bronte.' With all of that seething
through his head and heart, the resentment, the fury, the frustration,
over the dismissive attitude of Hyde Parker was so much harder to bear,
an intolerable daily reminder of the guarded view of him that had settled
upon Admiralty, and the further reflection of all of that in the snub he had
received from George III at Court. 'They all hate me and treat me ill,' he
cried to Emma Hamilton, referring to Admiralty both past and present, to
the whole institution of navy. 'I cannot, my dear friend, recall to mind any

one real act of kindness, but all of unkindness.' And in that driven state, with that sense of all the world against him and his, and of the need to demonstrate with a final conclusive show of his worth his own contempt for them all, Nelson retrieved the force lost to him for the past year and a half. In his enraged state he was ready for the Baltic. As if in acquiescent response to that, change came at once.

Nelson was improbably rescued from his situation with Hyde Parker by an inspiration flown upon him halfway up the North Sea. What occurred to him was something that belonged entirely to the scathing wit and caustic view of society that continually lay exposed in his correspondence.

Nelson had received aboard *St George* a young lieutenant, William Layman, of striking personality. Layman was a nervous, gifted youth, part of whose strong appeal was an often self-sacrificing desire to be of service. On sailing from the Downs for Yarmouth one of Nelson's ships, *Warrior*, had gone aground. Nelson sent Layman to her assistance, which he success-fully accomplished. On his return to *St George* Nelson said, 'You deserve credit. I have written to the Admiralty in your favour.'

Layman modestly replied, 'I am much obliged to you, my lord, but I cannot think that what I did last night deserves it.'

In return Layman got a small, typical Nelsonian response. 'But *I* do,' Nelson replied, 'the loss of one line-of-battle ship might be the loss of a victory.'

The incident sealed a bond of respect and affection between the two. It allowed the sort of easy exchange that Nelson enjoyed with those with whom he felt close. Sailing up the North Sea Layman happened to remark that North Sea fish were superior to all caught on the western coast of England, the finest being turbot caught on the Dogger Bank. Nelson immediately began asking when *St George* would be on the Dogger Bank. When he was informed that they were already on the Bank he turned to Layman and asked, 'Do you think we could catch a turbot?'

'I don't know, my lord, but we can try.'

'To be sure, there is no doing anything without trying.' And overboard went the trawl. After some effort a small turbot was yielded. Delighted, Nelson cried out, 'Send it to Sir Hyde. I know the chief is fond of good living, and he shall have the turbot.' Some protest was made over a rising sea, lowering weather and swift-descending dark, but the turbot went over by boat. Back came a note expressing cordial gratitude. A small fish had established the necessary restorative, a gift without which, it was later commonly agreed, the Baltic might have had a different history. But heavy gales prevented Nelson from benefiting from the improved disposition of Hyde Parker to have a meeting with him until the squadron was at the approaches to the Baltic.

Passage to the Baltic took ships up the North Sea coast of Denmark to the tip of the Danish peninsula, a point known as the Skaw which, being rounded, took vessels on descent of the eastern coast, down the inland sea known as the Kattegat that separated the Denmark peninsula from the Swedish mainland. Actual entry into the Baltic was blocked at the end of the Kattegat by the great island of Zealand. Two passages flowing around the coasts of Zealand allowed entry into the Baltic. Zealand was separated from the Danish peninsula by a passage known as the Great Belt. The other passage, separating Zealand from Sweden, was the Sound, which contained Copenhagen.

The usual course for shipping entering the Baltic from the Kattegat was through the Sound, navigation of the Great Belt being more difficult. The Sound was where Denmark collected duties from ships using this key entry to the Baltic. That demand was facilitated by the fact that at its actual entrance the Sound was no more than three miles wide. Here on the Danish side were the fortress of Cronenburg Castle and close by to it the town of Elsinore. Hostile guns menaced the passage on both the Danish and Swedish sides.

. On 19 March, the fleet after its scattering by gale collected together off the Skaw. The Foreign Office emissary who accompanied the fleet, Nicholas Vansittart, was sent off in a frigate to deliver Britain's ultimatum to the Danes, who were given forty-eight hours to comply. The wind was fair for continuing down through the Kattegat to the Sound but Hyde Parker held off, to Nelson's annoyance, he believing that any ultimatum should have been delivered right off Copenhagen because 'a Danish minister would think twice before he would put his name to war with England, when the next moment he would probably see his Master's fleet in flames and his capital in ruins . . . The Dane should see our flag flying every time he lifted up his head.' Nelson saw every day's delay as still more time unnecessarily allowed to the Danes to strengthen their defences.

On 20 March at this anchorage he had his first meeting with Hyde Parker: 'I staid an hour, and ground out something, but there was not that degree of openness which I should have shown to my second in command.'

On 24 March the fleet moved up to just off Cronenburg Castle and Elsinore, where Nelson, on the morning of the 24th, was summoned to his first actual council aboard the flagship *London*. 'Now we are sure of fighting,' Nelson wrote to Emma. 'I am sent for. When it was a joke I was kept in the background.'

Layman accompanied Nelson to the flagship, to steer the gig. They found that Hyde Parker was attempting negotiations with the governor of Cronenburg Castle, to know whether he had orders to oppose entry of the British into the Sound. That clearly self-enfeebling inquiry offered its own assurance to their opponents, who were already defiant. The British envoy

Vansittart had boarded *London* at the same time as Nelson. He brought word that the Danes had rejected the British ultimatum. On top of that he reported that the Danes had greatly increased the defences of Copenhagen with batteries and block ships. He believed that if the fleet attacked it would be defeated. That, of course, corroborated what Nelson had maintained all along, that every day's delay was to the Danish advantage. And even then, at that very moment, with the wind strong and favourable to an immediate descent upon Copenhagen, he was in a fever to use that advantage. But for those who surrounded him such a bold risk was the very last option. On negotiation being mentioned, 'Lord Nelson curled up his lip and emphatically said, "Beat the enemy first, and negotiate afterwards."'

The realities now lay starkly before Hyde Parker, a moment of strategic decision that allowed no vacillation or avoidance of action of the sort that Nelson had laid against him in the Mediterranean in 1796. Yet, in the torpor of uncertainty, stalled initiative and anticipated defeat that lay upon all in the Great Cabin avoidance of action was the dominant preference. Captain Domett, Hyde Parker's captain of the fleet, himself saw that as being the only realistic option. The Danes were too strong for them to attack, he told Layman, who answered, 'We must have a better story to go back with than that.' All this despondency was actively encouraged by the pilots who had accompanied the fleet, merchant seamen terrified by the responsibility that rested upon them of taking battleships into channels which they had only experienced in small, light vessels. But the main source of the prevailing defeatism was the lack of spirit in the commander himself. As Nelson later recalled, 'The difficulty was to get our commander-in-chief either to go past Cronenburg or through the Belt because, what Sir Hyde thought best, and what I believe was settled before I came on board the London, was to stay in the Kattegat, and there wait the time when the whole naval force of the Baltic might choose to come out and fight – a measure, in my opinion, disgraceful to our country. I wanted to get at an enemy as soon as possible to strike a *home* stroke, and Czar Paul was the enemy most vulnerable, and of the greatest consequence for us to humble.'

It is strange how often during the course of the Great War one is led to wonder how the Royal Navy actually achieved the striking success that became its legacy. The disturbing question hovers from the very start with Earl Howe's 'the First of June' battle and the constraint on that occasion in the effort of many of his captains. But it is particularly manifest throughout the career of Nelson in that war as one often comes up against the obstructions laid in his way. The singular greatness of the man has always to be measured by that. What would the outcome have been without Nelson? That thought is assertively present with every major action involving him, but never more so than at the gate to the Baltic.

On 24 March in the Great Cabin of *London* undoubtedly came the critical moment when Hyde Parker, scanning his own irresolution, finally though slowly began to recognize where lay the solution to his own limitations. He got full affirmation of that the following morning for, on his return to *St George*, Nelson had sat down and with brutal frankness told Hyde Parker in the most powerful letter he had ever written to a senior what was required in this instance of the commander. Or, as Mahan described the letter, '. . . inspired by the spirit of the writer when in a state of more than usual exaltation, it possesses a unity of purpose and demonstration absent from most of his letters'. In that state Nelson addressed Hyde Parker, '. . . here you are, with almost the safety, certainly with the honour of England more intrusted to you, than ever yet fell to the lot of any British officer. On your decision depends, whether our country shall be degraded in the eyes of Europe, or whether she shall rear her head higher than ever: again I do repeat, never did our country depend so much on the success of any fleet as on this.' And with that proffered his own advice on what now should be done.

The Danish fleet had to be destroyed and Copenhagen 'made so hot that Denmark would listen to reason'. Simultaneously any junction between the Russians, Swedes and Danes had to be prevented, then Russian naval power destroyed. The sequence of those actions was adaptable, dependent on which of the two courses they took into the Baltic. Having absorbed that, Hyde Parker was advised on the merits of the two passages available to them, either straight down through the Sound from where they were, or skirting the coast of Zealand to pass down through the Great Belt. With such a favourable wind then blowing, Nelson's deepest wish was to push off at once into the Sound. The risks were damage from the guns of Cronenburg, as well as down at Copenhagen where ships would, of course, be crippled, one or two lost, and the wind that carried them in would not allow crippled ships to be brought out. For Nelson those dangers had to be accepted. He had less enthusiasm for rounding Zealand through the Great Belt, involving a passage of four or five days to come off Copenhagen whereas from where they were, some thirty miles from Copenhagen, the descent would be swift. Not a moment should be lost in attacking the enemy for 'they will every day and hour be stronger; we never shall be so good a match for them as at this moment'.

Irresolution persisted, however, for the next day the fleet still lay at anchor. The day after, the 26th, Hyde Parker at morning council decided against testing the guns of Cronenburg and the fleet set off along the northern Zealand coast towards the Great Belt passage. But they had gone scarcely any distance, perhaps no more than eighteen miles or so, before the fleet was brought to and Nelson sent for. The captain of *London*, Robert

Otway, was not a member of the council. His position as captain of the ship was distinct from that of the captain of the fleet, Captain Domett, with Otway responsible only for *London* the ship and not involved with tactical dispositions as Domett was. The Great Belt passage was apparently Domett's preference. But after the council broke up Otway, who had had some experience of the passage, advised Hyde Parker against it. Captain George Murray, whose ship *Edgar* was to lead the fleet, supported Otway, who was then sent to fetch Nelson to the flagship. Nelson's reaction when Otway boarded reflected the bewilderment and outrage that this new interruption to their course had provoked: 'I don't care a damn by which passage we go, just so that we fight them. Let it be by the Sound, by the Belt, or anyhow, only lose not an hour.' But the urgent summons to cross to *London* by boat in rough seas to affirm the new course was clear indication that the theatre was now his and at sunset, when the fleet returned to the anchorage six miles from Cronenburg that it had vacated that morning, Nelson was already a different man.

He was writing to Emma practically every day and back on board *St George* on this day he told her, 'Sir Hyde Parker has by this time found out the worth of your Nelson, and that he is a useful sort of man on a pinch; therefore, if he ever has thought unkindly of me, I freely forgive him. Nelson must stand among the first, or he must fall.'

His place established, Nelson nevertheless first had to confront yet more hesitation from Hyde Parker, and thereafter delay from the weather. Hyde Parker the following day again sent to the governor of Cronenburg to know whether he would fire on the English fleet if it passed into the Sound and got the inevitable answer that a fleet whose object was unknown to him would certainly be fired on. A three-day calm then settled upon the area. During that time Nelson shifted his flag from *St George* to a lighter ship, *Elephant*, a 74, captained by his old companion Thomas Foley, who had so distinctively led the line in the attack at Aboukir Bay. Finally, at daylight on 30 March, a breeze blew in from the north-west, the signal was made for line of battle and the fleet moved off to pass through the Sound. Once again Nelson's constant plea for risk was proven for there was no assault from the batteries on the Swedish side. The fleet had simply passed along the Swedish side of the Sound, evading the furious firing from Cronenburg. Not a ship suffered damage or any man injured from artillery that Hyde Parker had feared might cripple the fleet before it even got beyond Cronenburg.

At midday the fleet anchored about five miles from Copenhagen. That evening the surrounding waters and their defences were surveyed. Buoys removed by the Danes were replaced, Nelson himself supervising the work. The surgeon of *Elephant* recorded Nelson's activity in that: 'I could only silently admire when I saw the first man in the world spend the hours of the

day and night in boats, amidst floating ice, and in the severest weather; and
wonder when the light showed me a path marked by buoys, which had been
trackless the previous evening.' Colonel Stewart and other artillery officers
with the fleet meanwhile made their assessment of the Danish batteries.
'We soon perceived that our delay had been of important advantage to
the enemy,' Stewart wrote. The shoals had been lined with new batteries.
Existing batteries had been reinforced. A formidable flotilla lay before the
harbour, more ships inside it. The survey continued the next day, the 31st,
with Nelson and Stewart aboard the frigate *Amazon* commanded by Captain
Edward Riou, a man unfamiliar to Nelson but who in this activity raised
his admiration for the seamanship demonstrated in all their operations that
day. Finally a Council of War was summoned aboard *London* to discuss the
plan of attack for the impending battle.

For Nelson the council was an occasion of both satisfaction and needlessly
vexing irritation. 'During this Council of War, the energy of Lord Nelson's
character was remarked,' Colonel Stewart reported, '. . . Lord Nelson kept
pacing the cabin, mortified at everything which savoured either of alarm
or irresolution.' Even at this late stage, so irreversibly close to the hour of
action, plenty of both were demonstrated. Fears were expressed, difficulties
raised, should the Russians and Swedes intervene and how the British fleet
should meet such reinforcement force of numbers. 'The more numerous
the better,' Nelson cried, referring to the Swedes. As for the Russians, his
contempt was harshly flung out: 'So much the better, I wish they were
twice as many, the easier the victory, depend on it.'

With his disdain for the other partners of that Northern Alliance so
forcefully expressed Nelson declared his plan of attack. To mollify the
apprehensive, he proposed to launch the initial assault with only ten line
ships from the fleet of fifteen. By the end of the council he had so demonstrated his command of the entire operation that Hyde Parker appeared to
have submitted entirely to him, and strengthened Nelson's intended force
by adding two more ships to it.

Nelson's brilliant plan of action has to be understood within the geog-
raphy of the Sound. The exhaustive surveys he had undertaken over the
two days that they lay just above Copenhagen had demonstrated to him
that to overcome the formidable defences of the Danes required, as with
Aboukir Bay, attack from where they least expected it. There were in fact
many similarities with Aboukir Bay in that they were dealing with heavily
shoaled water and an enemy fleet anchored in line off the main shoal.

There were two approaches to Copenhagen within the Sound. The
city lay where the Sound broadened at its middle. The expanse of water
before the town encircled a large shoal called the Middle Ground. It was
this shoal that created two courses for approach. The main and obvious

approach was directly down from the north passing off the western side of the shoal. The other approach was to descend from the north and, passing down the eastern side of the shoal, to round the end of it and come up from the south.

The former approach, direct from the north, was down the King's Channel, which was the flow of deep water between the town and the western side of the Middle Ground. This, therefore, was the most strongly defended stretch of shore. Copenhagen was dominated by its great citadel before which stood its most formidable fortress battery known as the Tre Kronen, 'Three Crowns', constructed offshore on piles. Two old line-of-battle ships, *Mars* and *Elephanten*, were placed before Tre Kronen to augment its strength. Along with those two ships the face of the town was defended by a line of hulks and other old ships carrying 628 guns and manned by close to five thousand men. The whole line of defence from one extreme point to the other was estimated by Stewart to be nearly four miles. The Danish fleet was anchored in line before the town in the King's Channel.

Nelson's plan was to invert the apparent logic of direct attack from the north to an indirect one from the south. For the British to advance directly down from their northern anchorage required a northern wind. That meant that defeat of the Danes had to be ensured in the attack, for in face of setback return northwards would be difficult, if not impossible, without a south wind conveniently setting in. Crippled ships would not make it back. By descending down the Outer Channel, that which flowed on the eastern side of the Middle Ground, and then rounding the Middle Ground, the fleet would enter the King's Channel from the south, below Copenhagen. Such a course avoided much of the worst of the terrible onslaught that could be expected from Tre Kronen and the concentration of batteries there. The disadvantage was that a squadron carried down the Outer Channel on a north wind had to wait at the southern end of the Middle Ground for a southerly wind to carry them into the King's Channel to attack Copenhagen. They would be exposed to the batteries along that shore. But this was Nelson's preference. As Layman said, 'The penetrating eye of Lord Nelson had discovered sufficient to verify his ideas that although the crown and head of the Danish line of defence were truly formidable, yet the tail was more vulnerable . . . he therefore determined to visit the Danes *sans ceremonie*, by the back entrance.'

It was a bold plan, yet again reflective of his conviction that only with risk could there be achievement. The plan meant taking his twelve line ships, accompanied by a fleet of twenty-three other craft, frigates, bomb and gun vessels, down the Outer Channel for the main attack while Hyde Parker waited to the north with the remaining eight line ships to give support when and if possible.

On the morning of 1 April Nelson, aboard *Amazon*, made his final survey before returning to *Elephant* where at one p.m. he gave the signal to weigh. The shout that greeted the decision from all the ships of his squadron was heard for miles around. 'The effect produced on every person's countenance, and the enthusiastic joy expressed by every one in this squadron, when the signal was made to weigh, is indescribable,' Layman said. This was something most particularly British. The signal to action always seemed to knock away whatever misery or resentment might prevail in fleet or aboard individual ships, and with it as well any fear of imminent death or the terrible injuries that would soon be inflicted on many. In spite of it all, the Royal Navy always went into action with a visible joy and excitement that remains something to marvel at.

The wind was light, favourable, and *Amazon* led the way down the narrow channel. At nightfall they doubled the Middle Ground and anchored south of it, just two miles from the Danish line of warships, there to wait for a southerly breeze. 'I will fight them the moment I have a fair wind,' Nelson declared.

They had been fortunate in escaping attack on the descent, with the Danes believing that the British were bound up the Baltic to the Russians. At anchor they were within mortar range and the Danes might yet have inflicted heavy damage since the ships were all collected close together. Even then, however, the Danes, according to Stewart, 'were too much occupied during this night in manning their ships and strengthening their line, conceiving the channel impracticable to so large a fleet'.

As soon as the fleet anchored the signal to prepare for action the following day had been made. We now have from Colonel Stewart a fascinating picture of the activity in the main cabins aboard a flagship on the eve of battle. After anchoring Nelson called his closest companions to *Elephant* and they sat down 'in the highest spirits, and drank to a leading wind, and to the success of the ensuing day'. With him were Riou of the *Amazon*, Foley, Hardy, Stewart and others. The party broke up at nine, when Nelson, Foley and Riou retired to the after-cabin to arrange the order of battle and to prepare the orders for it. Thomas Hardy took himself off on his own special mission, bravely to sound the depth of the water right up to the nearest ship of the enemy line.

Nelson, his strength drained by the surveying and assessments of the past two days, dictated his orders until one in the morning. His appearance became so exhausted that the other officers as well as his faithful servant, Allen, insisted that he go to bed. Instead Allen brought his cot in and Nelson, lying down, dictated from there. The orders were meticulous. As one today reads his 'Orders for the Attack' one marvels yet at the astonishing detail of instruction for every one of those ships, directed on anchoring position, rake of fire, support of partners, cutting cables, boarding, change of station. No circumstance appears overlooked. The strength and position of even the small raft-like floating batteries was noted, and its British opponent located. At eleven Hardy returned. He had rowed round the nearest ship in the Danish line, sounding all the way round, using a pole for fear of being heard. It was a remarkable effort, for he was able to report the practicability of the channel and the depth of the water right up to the enemy's line. At one a.m. Nelson's orders were delivered to the half-dozen clerks in the foremost cabin who were to transcribe them for delivery to all the ships. Instead of sleeping undisturbed in his cot he was every half-hour calling to the clerks to hasten their work, for the wind was coming fair. This he learned from the constant reports he had demanded be brought to him through the night. The clerks finished their work at six. Nelson was already up, dressed and breakfasted. All the captains were summoned for a final meeting at seven. The instructions were delivered to each captain by eight o'clock. Captain Riou was given special licence to act as he thought circumstances required. The pilots were brought aboard between eight and nine o'clock but, as before, 'an unpleasant degree of hesitation prevailed amongst them all'. With the wind suitable and the signal made for action this was the last thing Nelson wanted. They had, he later said, 'no other thought than to keep the ship clear of danger and their own silly heads clear of shot'. The masters of the ships took over the pilotage. And at half-past nine the signal was given to weigh in succession and they moved off, with *Elephant*'s station at the centre of the line.

The British were to advance in column. The three lead ships would engage the rearmost ships in the Danish line, with the rest of the British line following in succession. As each ship arrived nearly opposite to her number in the Danish line, she let her anchor go by the stern and, the wind being favourable to it, presented her broadside to the enemy. The oncoming British ships would pass outside those who were engaged, each anchoring as it cleared the headmost ship already in action.

The action began just after ten on 2 April. Within half an hour half the fleet was engaged. Before eleven thirty the battle was general. As the action started Hyde Parker moved the eight line ships left to him nearer to the harbour but too far to take an active part in the fighting.

An immediate misfortune was that three of Nelson's line ships ran aground. Nelson's old ship *Agamemnon* was one, and was unable to participate in the battle but the other two, *Bellona* and *Russell*, were able to use their guns and did so. The grounding was blamed on the faulty advice of the pilots and poor judgement of the masters who had taken over the pilotage. They might not have suffered those accidents, Stewart declared, had they abided with the report that Hardy had brought during the night.

But worse might have been suffered had Nelson not promptly decided that Hardy was right, the others wrong, and given instruction to navigate according to Hardy's soundings. Hyde Parker promptly sent three of his ships to Nelson to replace those on shore.

Copenhagen would be remembered for the savagery of the slaughter between two peoples without deep historic antagonism and who saw one another in blood and shared values as closely alike. They held the same quality of resistance that accompanied a distinctive sense of an independence entirely unbonded to others. As seagoing peoples, they shared the endurance and hardihood of an oceanic background. In Copenhagen no press gangs were required to muster the defence of the hulks, batteries and gun platforms. The schools and universities emptied as students flocked to volunteer, along with the aged veterans of former campaigns.

Between ships and ships, ships and batteries, between the mixture of small craft employed on both sides, a ceaseless barrage was maintained from just after ten until one p.m. without any apparent favour to one side or the other. The unlikeliest match appeared to be when Riou in *Amazon* took on the Tre Kronen fortress, each unleashing steady fire upon the other.

His early wounding at the Nile had denied Nelson his full participation there, but here he was walking the starboard side of the quarterdeck during the whole action, 'sometimes much animated, and at others heroically fine in his observations'. Colonel Stewart was at his side throughout. When a shot through the mainmast knocked a shower of splinters upon them Nelson said to Stewart with a smile, 'It is warm work, and this day may be the last to any of us at a moment.' Then, halting his pacing at the gangway, he added with emotion, 'But mark you, I would not be elsewhere for thousands.' At this time *Elephant* was anchored on the bow of the Danish flagship *Dannebrog*, fighting her as well as some floating batteries adjacent to her. In that rain of burning metal the odds against survival were indeed heavy.

After three hours of such fire and destruction and with no clear result yet apparent Hyde Parker considered breaking off the action. There followed one of the most celebrated incidents of Nelson's career. Lieutenant Tom Southey, brother of Nelson's contemporary biographer Robert Southey, was aboard *London* and eventually gave his brother his own account of what occurred there. Hyde Parker is recorded as saying to his captain of the fleet, Domett, 'I will make the signal of recall for Nelson's sake. If he is in condition to continue the action successfully, he will disregard it; if he is not, it will be an excuse for his retreat, and no blame can be imputed to him.' Otway, captain of *London*, opposed the signal and got Hyde Parker's permission to row down to *Elephant* to obtain Nelson's own view. He shoved off at once but before he got to *Elephant* the signal to discontinue action, No. 39, was raised aboard *London*.

Colonel Stewart was with Nelson when No. 39 was raised. The signal lieutenant immediately reported it. Nelson continued his walk. The normal procedure was for No. 39 then to be raised aboard *Elephant* itself, indicating obedience to the order. When asked whether this should be done, Nelson replied, 'No, acknowledge it.' That meant simply raising a flag to indicate that the signal was seen and understood, without implying obedience. He then asked, 'Is No. 16 still hoisted?' The signal lieutenant affirmed that it was. 'Then keep it so,' Nelson said. No. 16 was 'For Close Action' and had been flying since the start of the battle.

The exchange over, Stewart asked Nelson what Signal No. 39 meant.

'Why, to leave off action.' Then repeated to himself, 'Leave off action!' And then added with a shrug, 'Now damn me if I do.' To his captain, Foley, he said, 'You know, Foley, I have only one eye – I have a right to be blind sometimes.' And then, as Stewart put it, 'with an archness peculiar to his character, putting the glass to his blind eye, he exclaimed, "I really do not see the signal."' Or, as biographer Southey put it, 'putting the glass to his blind eye, in that mood of mind which sports with bitterness, he exclaimed, "I really do not see the signal." Presently he exclaimed, "Damn the signal; keep mine for closer fighting flying: that's the way I answer such signals! Nail mine to the mast."'

Nelson's act was usually to be seen as one of admirably stubborn daring, disobedience in the interest of fighting on for the assured victory he already saw as achievable, part of the 'archness' that Stewart described. But the sense of mockery in the gesture that gave mirth to subsequent generations tended to dim one of the greatest moments in the career of Nelson. For, as he himself would later declare, 'everything would have been lost if these signals had been obeyed'. His refusal to obey the commander in chief's order saved his squadron from destruction, and the Royal Navy from probably total defeat. His recognition of that was instant. For victory at that point was by no means clearly apparent. Withdrawing from the action then would therefore have meant ordering his ships up the King's Channel, past its many still furiously active batteries, including the largely untouched Tre Kronen. Or, as Mahan put it, 'To retire, with crippled ships and mangled crews, through difficult channels, under the guns of a half-beaten foe, who would renew his strength when he saw the movement, would be to court destruction – to convert probable victory into certain, perhaps overwhelming, disaster.' It made Hyde Parker's signal, Mahan said, 'one of the most dangerous and ill-judged orders that ever was conveyed by flags'. And he thus further summed up Nelson's action: 'The pantomime of putting the glass to his blind eye was, however unintentionally, a profound allegory. There is a time to be blind as well as a time to see.'

The price that might have been paid by the rest of the squadron was illustrated by the experience of Riou's *Amazon*, which had so bravely engaged Tre Kronen. *Amazon* and the squadron of frigates obeyed Hyde Parker's signal and hauled off. With that manoeuvre *Amazon* showed her stern to Tre Kronen and took the fortress's raking firing along her length. As Stewart described it, 'Captain Riou was sitting on a gun, was encouraging his men, and had been wounded in the head by a splinter. He had expressed himself grieved at being thus obliged to retreat, and nobly observed, "What will Nelson think of us?" His clerk was killed by his side; and by another shot, several of the marines, while hauling on the main-brace, shared the same fate. Riou then exclaimed, "Come then, my boys, let us die all together!" The words were scarcely uttered, when the fatal shot severed him in two. Thus, in an instant, was the British service deprived of one of its greatest ornaments, and society of a character of singular worth, resembling the heroes of romance.'

The action continued vigorously until two-thirty p.m. when the resistance of the Danes at some points began to slacken. The Danish fire from ships and batteries astern of the British ships, those south of the Tre Kronen, had ceased, except for four ships. The ships ahead and Tre Kronen itself were still active. The Danish flagship *Dannebrog* was drifting in flames, shortly to blow up. But Nelson was infuriated when ships that had struck were reoccupied by volunteers who repulsed those sent by Nelson to possess them. Ships that the British considered silenced thus resumed vigorous action. He went below to the stern gallery and summoned the purser to take down a letter to be sent ashore under a flag of truce, addressed to the Crown Prince.

Standing at the casing of the rudder head Nelson wrote with his own hand, 'To the Brothers of Englishmen, the Danes. Lord Nelson has directions to spare Denmark, when no longer resisting; but if the firing is continued on the part of Denmark, Lord Nelson will be obliged to set on fire all the floating batteries he has taken, without having the power of saving the brave Danes who have defended them.' The purser, Thomas Wallis, simultaneously made his own copy then put the letter into an envelope which he was about to seal with a wafer. But Nelson insisted that the letter be sealed with wax. A sailor was sent to fetch wax and candle. On the way down his head was taken off by a cannonball. Nelson simply said, 'Send another messenger for the wax.' It was done and the letter was sealed with a large amount of wax stamped with his coat of arms. Stewart said to him, 'May I take the liberty of asking why, under so hot a fire, and after so lamentable an accident you have attached so much importance to a circumstance so trifling?' And was answered, 'Had I made use of the wafer it should still have been wet when presented to the Crown Prince; he would have inferred that the letter was sent off in a hurry, and that we had some very pressing reasons for being in a hurry. The wax told no tales.'

The inference of British victory already conveyed by the letter was a striking boldness, an assumption being that the Danes might be prepared to concur. In the event that they did not Nelson called together two of his most valued friends, his own captain, Foley, and Thomas Fremantle, who came over from *Ganges*. The pressing question he put to them was, What was the practicability of attempting a breakthrough with their least damaged ships past Tre Kronen and the other active batteries? Foley and Fremantle saw everything rationally against it given the destruction they would suffer, but agreed on the urgent need for removing the fleet from its vulnerability within an intricate channel while the wind favoured them and any armistice held.

The firing continued as Nelson waited for an answer, which was brought to him verbally by the Danish Adjutant-General, Lindholm. The Crown Prince's response was simple, direct, by no means yielding. What was Nelson's particular object in sending the flag of truce? Nelson replied in writing declaring his object to be humanity, further that he wanted to take his prisoners out of his prizes, land wounded Danes and burn or remove the prizes. He concluded that he would regard this the greatest victory he had ever gained if it could be the cause of a happy reconciliation and union between his own sovereign and the king of Denmark. The Crown Prince sent orders to the batteries to stop firing. Both sides hoisted flags of truce.

Nelson advised Lindholm to proceed to Hyde Parker, whose ships lay at anchor four miles off, to pursue formalities with him as commander in chief. Lindholm agreed. Nelson saw the long four-mile row to the flagship as his opportunity to get his own squadron away. The lead ships moved off at once but two, one of them *Elephant*, ran aground, just a mile from Tre Kronen, indicating the peril they all would have suffered had they remained and the truce failed. With *Elephant* held fast, Nelson returned to *St George* and British sailors laboured all night until they had freed the grounded ships.

The Danes were indeed defeated at Copenhagen, as the German historian Barthold Niebuhr, then living in the city, his place of birth, wrote at the time: 'We cannot deny it, we are quite beaten.' But as Nelson's swift retreat of his ships showed it had been a near thing for the British, whose ships had been cut to pieces, though not one was lost. Nevertheless, naval historians of the future saw it as perhaps Nelson's most distinctive achievement. Mahan saw the victory of Copenhagen as 'second in importance to none that Nelson ever gained; while in the severity of the resistance, and in the attendant difficulties to be overcome, the battle itself was the most critical of all in which he was engaged'. And in support of that he quoted the French naval historian Jurien de la Gravière that Nelson's Copenhagen 'will always be in the eyes of seamen his fairest title to glory. He alone was capable of displaying such boldness and perseverance; he alone could confront the immense difficulties of that enterprise and overcome them.'

Nelson's wish was to pass on directly to get at the Russian fleet and destroy it. But Hyde Parker passed negotiation of the truce to Nelson. It took a week, during which both sides continued preparing for any resumption of hostilities. Eventually, on 9 April, an armistice treaty was signed. Denmark withdrew from the Armed Neutrality.

Three ships were sent home with the wounded. Nelson again wished to go off to prevent a conjunction of the Russian and Swedish fleets, but Hyde Parker insisted on him remaining at Copenhagen and went off himself. On the evening of 19 April Nelson received a message from Hyde Parker informing him that a Swedish fleet was at sea, twenty-four miles from Copenhagen. Nelson, suffering severely from the fatigue and strain of the past three weeks, immediately left *St George* and went aboard a six-oared cutter to row the whole distance to join Hyde Parker. It took six hours of hard rowing in harsh cold, Nelson without a coat. An officer with him said, 'It was extremely cold, and I wished him to put on a great coat of mine which was in the boat. "No I am not cold; my anxiety for my country will keep me warm. Do you think the fleet has sailed?" "I should suppose not, my lord." "If they are, we shall follow them to Karlskrona in the boat, by God!"'

It was a futile hardship inflicted upon himself. He soon began paying for it severely with complications of his already exhausted condition arising from that exposure. Nor was there the reward of action, for the Swedes ran into Karlskrona on sight of the British. News was then received that Tsar Paul had been murdered and his successor, Alexander I, wished to come to terms with Britain. Hyde Parker withdrew to Copenhagen, where on 29 April he received his recall, with Nelson appointed commander in chief.

For Nelson this elevation was an understandable bitterness. He said, 'Had the command been given me in February many lives would have been saved, and we should have been in a very different situation; but the wiseheads at home know everything ... Sir Thomas Troubridge had the nonsense to say, now I was commander-in-chief I must be pleased. Does he take me for a greater fool than I am?' From an old friend with whom he associated a more insightful comprehension that was especially hard to take.

Nelson was suffering severely at this time from his exposure on the night of the 19th. For weeks at a time he was unable to leave his cabin. He wanted only to be home with Emma, 'to live a country life, and to have many (I hope) years of comfort, which God knows I never yet had – only moments of happiness'. As the new C-in-C he nevertheless immediately did what he had sought from the start of the entire operation – to get at the Russian fleet at Revel before the ice that locked it in had broken up.

He sailed for Revel on 7 May and arrived there on 12 May, to find that the Russian fleet had gone, the ice having disintegrated early. On that same day he expressed the sum of his frustration to Nicholas Vansittart, on how Hyde Parker's cautions had disgracefully held them back from the start: 'Paul was the enemy most vulnerable, and of the greatest consequence for us to humble. On the 2nd of April we could have been at Revel, and I know nothing at present which could have prevented our destroying the whole Russian force at that port.' For all of that, as with Hood after Bastia, Nelson held no personal animosity against Hyde Parker, whom he knew was going back to face possible court martial, to a cold reception at any rate. 'His friends in the fleet wish everything to be forgot,' he wrote in a later letter to Alexander Davison, 'for we all love and respect Sir Hyde; but the dearer his friends, the more uneasy they have been at his *idleness*, for that is the truth . . . I believe Sir H.P. to be as good a subject as His Majesty has.'

Tsar Alexander was anxious to mend with Britain. After some mild manoeuvring and resentment over a British fleet off a Russian port on 19 May the embargo placed on British ships by Tsar Paul and the Swedes was lifted. The Baltic crisis was settled. Nelson now only wanted to get home. Sanction of that finally arrived on 13 June. On the 19th he left the Baltic aboard a brig, arriving at Yarmouth on 1 July.

Nelson's new friend, Colonel Stewart, had returned to him after bearing to London the despatches on the battle and armistice at Copenhagen. As quiet returned to the Baltic and Nelson awaited his desperately wished-for recall, Stewart penned a postscript to battle with a small portrait of life with Nelson aboard *St George*:

The keeping of his fleet continually on the alert, and thus amply furnishing it with fresh water and provisions, were the objects of his lordship's unremitted care; and to this may in a great measure be ascribed the uniform good health and discipline which prevailed. Another point to which he gave nearly equal attention, was his economy of the resources of the fleet in regard to stores; their consumption was remarkable for its smallness in the Baltic, as it was in the fleet that was afterwards under his command in the Mediterranean. His hour of rising was four or five o'clock, and of going to rest about ten; breakfast was never later than six, and generally nearer to five o'clock. A midshipman or two were always of the party; and I have known him send during the middle watch to invite the little fellows to breakfast with him, when relieved. At table with them, he would enter into their boyish jokes, and be the most youthful of the party. At dinner he invariably had every officer of his ship in their turn, and was both a polite and hospitable host. The whole ordinary business of the fleet was invariably dispatched, as it had been by Earl St Vincent, before eight o'clock. The great command of time which Lord

Nelson thus gave himself, and the alertness which this example imparted throughout the fleet, can only be understood by those who witnessed it, or who know the value of early hours ... At Rostock ... the greatest veneration was shown to the name of Nelson; and some distant inland towns of Mecklenburg sent even deputations, with their public books of record, to have his name written in them by himself. Boats were constantly rowing round his flagship, the St George, with persons of respectability in them, anxious to catch a sight of this illustrious man. He did not again land whilst in the Baltic; his health was not good, and his mind was not at ease; with him, mind and health invariably sympathized.

XXX

STRAITS

THE Mediterranean at the time of the Baltic operation was intensely alive again, transformed from some six months earlier when Nelson had seen it as lacking activity, except on the monotonous blockades of Malta and Alexandria. For the Admiralty and the government, and Napoleon, it all still turned on Egypt.

Britain, once again solitary except for her weak Ottoman ally, was in a tough situation. The war was pressing on her at home. The cost of bread had soared, so had the National Debt. The inevitable dislocations involved with change of government from Pitt to Addington brought their own difficulties. France, in spite of her own mercantile losses, drew sustenance from her conquered lands. Her own soil and natural resources were more generous than those of Britain. A sense of national wellbeing had been restored. Among the British the national longing for peace had never been greater. The French were no less eager. The failure of the attempted Naval Armistice had not closed the efforts towards peace with Britain. After Hohenlinden the pressure for it increased on both sides. Talleyrand continued negotiating for a peace treaty with the British, but while he did so Napoleon was seeking to create the particular strategic balance he wanted for when signatures were quilled on documents.

Consolidation of the hold on Egypt was his first requirement before there was peace. Beyond that lay yet another grand imperial dream, for which Talleyrand on 30 September 1800 had already prepared by closing France's quasi-war with the United States. The driving impulse behind peace with America had been the prospect of building a new colonial empire on the banks of the Mississippi through acquisition of the Spanish colony of Louisiana. Cession of Louisiana to France was agreed in a secret treaty with Spain on 1 October 1800. In support of these ambitions all Talleyrand's efforts went into securing a peace that the change of government in Britain appeared to suggest might be more advantageous than one supervised by Pitt and Dundas.

For Napoleon, the effort to maintain and reinforce the French soldiers in Egypt was therefore assigned the greatest urgency, to be driven forward at all cost.

Napoleon's confidence in that was supreme, for the picture on the Continent was one that he could regard with satisfaction. He had redeemed the Continental losses incurred by the Directory during his Egyptian campaign. Italy, from the Alps to Messina, was under his control. So were the two republics upon which so much rested for him strategically: the Lowlands for the North Sea, Switzerland for its dominant military passage in the heart of Europe. Spain at his bidding had menaced Portugal with a short-lived invasion, as a result of which Lisbon was closed to British ships. Spain had also passed to the French navy six of the Spanish fleet's ships at Cadiz. Naples and Sicily similarly were jumping to command. The British navy and merchantmen were locked out of Naples and the Sicilian ports by the peace treaty that the Neapolitans had been compelled to accept after their defeat as Napoleon moved down Italy. Through that treaty Taranto and other Calabrian ports were now occupied by French soldiers destined for Egypt. These were to be the bases that facilitated communication between the Army of Egypt and France.

To set his ambitions in motion, at the end of October 1800 Napoleon had ordered Admiral Ganteaume to sail from Brest with seven ships of the line bearing four thousand troops and stores for the relief of the army in Egypt. Ganteaume was unable to get away until 8 January 1801, only to be spotted and compelled to return to Brest, where he remained until, on 23 January, a violent northerly gale scattered the blockading British ships and he finally got away.

For the Royal Navy another critical naval chase was now underway, until the destination of the French squadron could be verified. But the French squadron, beset by storm in the Atlantic and then the Mediterranean, suffered too severely to fulfil its mission.

Unfortunately for the First Consul the British expedition to Egypt demanded by Dundas before the change of government was then completing its own tortuous journey to make good the pathetic muddle that arose over the treaty drawn up by Sidney Smith at El Arish in January 1800.

Had El Arish been honoured, Napoleon would have been incapable of so soon reviving his Egyptian dream and all that accompanied it. This was perhaps the greatest strategic error by the British in the Mediterranean in that war. Had Kléber been allowed to take his whole army quietly away a year before without fuss over the need for them to go only as prisoners of war, there would have been no need for such a costly British military expedition and the naval deployments that accompanied it. And the first peace of the Great War, now under laborious negotiation, undoubtedly would have come sooner.

The army of some sixteen thousand under Sir Ralph Abercromby, carried in a fleet of between sixty and seventy sail under Admiral Keith, came to anchor off Aboukir Bay on 2 March. Some five thousand men formed the first disembarkation, moving in against four thousand French settled behind formidably prepared defences.

What was now well started was a hard fight for Egypt to last many months. For Sidney Smith, commanding the navy's involvement on shore, that must have been bitter reflection as he saw the soldiers and sailors fall around him. The British began their slow, arduous advance towards Cairo.

Napoleon, exasperated by Ganteaume's failure to land his troops in Egypt, ordered another attempt. Ganteaume's squadron of four ships of the line, including his 80-gun flagship *Indivisible*, and a frigate sailed from Toulon on 27 April. They were off the Egyptian coast, about to land their troops at Durasso on 7 June, when ships from Keith's fleet showed up. Ganteaume abandoned his forlorn effort and once more made sail for Toulon. Napoleon had lost his last chance at Egypt.

Ganteaume's failure to deliver some relief to General Menou in Egypt led Napoleon to refocus upon the western Mediterranean in order to cut supplies to the British at Malta and in Egypt. That required a force at the Straits that he lacked. Three ships that had withdrawn from Ganteaume's squadron to return to Toulon for repair of storm damage were ordered to join the Spanish ships taken over by the French at Cadiz.

The three line ships and a frigate, under Rear Admiral Linois, sailed from Toulon for the Straits on 13 June. Two of the line ships, *Formidable* and *Dessaix*, were 80-gun. The other, *Indomptable*, was a 74.

An interesting episode marked the passage south. Among those of the younger generation now thrusting forward into prominence in the Royal Navy was Thomas Cochrane, son of the Earl of Dundonald, who had first brought attention upon himself by delivering *Généreux* to Port Mahon after its capture by Nelson's squadron. With sick and invalided men as his crew Cochrane was hard put to save the ship when a violent gale hit them. Only by leading his weak men aloft himself, accompanied by his brother Archibald, was *Généreux* saved. Cochrane had gone on to build more of a reputation for himself when, given command of a brig, *Speedy*, he vigorously pursued Spanish coastal traffic in privateering style. While busy with that he ran into Linois's squadron. Cochrane gallantly resisted this superior force for many hours.

A broadside from *Dessaix* finally persuaded Cochrane to haul down his colours. On boarding *Dessaix* Cochrane presented his sword to her captain, Christie Pallière, who refused it, saying that he could not accept the sword of an officer who had for so long struggled against impossibility. Pallière also told him to continue wearing his sword as prisoner. 'After this reception,' Cochrane wrote, 'it is scarcely necessary to add that I was treated with great kindness by my captors.'

From Cochrane Linois learned that Admiralty had meanwhile sent a squadron of six line ships under Rear Admiral Sir James Saumarez to renew the blockade of Cadiz. The immediate question for Linois was whether he should pass through the Straits and risk the challenge he could expect from Saumarez. Or hold off. On 4 July Linois passed the Rock of Gibraltar and crossed the bay to anchor off Algeciras, the fortress four miles directly across the bay from Gibraltar town.

When Linois's squadron sailed into the bay the commander of the only British ship then anchored at Gibraltar, a sloop, immediately sent one of his ship's boats through the Straits to inform Saumarez off Cadiz. The east wind that had brought Linois into Gibraltar Bay meant that the same wind carried the advice boat fast through the Straits, enabling the news to get to Saumarez the following day. Saumarez had the further good fortune that, as he summoned his squadron, the wind changed to westerly, ensuring a relatively easy passage for him as well through the Straits, to Cabrita Point at the eastern end. Saumarez in his 80-gun flagship *Caesar* was accompanied by five 74s, *Venerable*, *Pompee*, *Audacious*, *Spencer* and *Hannibal*. The ships rounded Cabrita Point to approach Algeciras shortly before eight on the morning of 6 July. Saumarez had ordered them to anchor in line by the stern off Algeciras.

The Bay and Straits of Gibraltar taken as one was always seen as the least promising, even impossible, area for naval action. This twenty-two-mile-long Strait is often referred to in the plural in past documents, and even today in ordinary speech (and generally throughout this book). That is understandable given that, as the divide between two continents, it has two quite distinct identities, dependent upon which shore you stand.

The commonly prevailing winds, the east wind, levanter, and the westerly, poniente, could each in its own manner be either gift or curse for sail using the Straits. The difficulties they created were compounded by the fast and different currents within the Straits, whose narrow course funnelled both wind and current and thereby further powered them both. If making for the Atlantic from the Mediterranean, the levanter delivered the sailing ship swifly through. The levanter also helped ride the confused currents of the Straits, with its different flows on each side, one flowing in and the other flowing out. Riding in from the Atlantic to the Mediterranean on the poniente similarly took a ship comfortably through, strongly affecting the current in the middle of the Strait whose own flow could augment with westerlies to run a ship eastwards with a rapidity of seven miles an hour. For a ship seeking to pass from the Mediterranean to the Atlantic against a westerly was an obvious struggle, as it was for a vessel inbound from the Atlantic that had to fight a levanter. Tacking in both cases was onerous, slow and dangerous. Then there was the bay itself, between the Rock and Algeciras. The great Rock together with the high ground above Algeciras as well as the cliff-like Mons Abyla on the opposite North African shore, and the funnelling process of the Straits, all created shifts and eddies, calms and gusts, upon the bay, whatever the force of the wind.

The confinement of the bay and the difficulties it made for naval action were to be harshly imposed upon Rear Admiral Sir James Saumarez on 6 July 1801.

Aboard *Dessaix* Thomas Cochrane and his captor, Captain Pallière, were on deck when the topgallant masts and pendants of the British squadron were sighted rounding Cabrita Point. The French were surprised to see such a large force moving in. Pallière asked Cochrane if he thought an attack would be immediately made or whether the British squadron would proceed to anchor off Gibraltar. Cochrane replied that an attack certainly would be made and that before night both British and French ships would be lying below the Rock, when it would be Cochrane's pleasure to return to Pallière and his officers all the kindness he had experienced aboard *Dessaix*.

On that note Cochrane and Pallière went down to breakfast, with Pallière saying that arrival of the British would not spoil their meal. But before the meal was ended a round shot crashed through the stern windows of *Dessaix*, showering the room with broken glass and debris. They jumped up and went on the quarterdeck. When a shot from one of the British ships swept away a file of French marines close to Cochrane he decided that exposure of himself was pointless and went below to find a safer point of observation.

As his ships rounded Cabrita Point and passed along the shore, Saumarez was simultaneously engaged by the batteries on shore, by Linois's ships, the battery on Isla Verde and the gunboats lying there.

When the British ships were first sighted rounding Cabrita Point, Linois ordered boats lowered to start warping the ships inshore to be more completely under the protection of the land batteries. Many of the crew were then sent ashore to help man the batteries.

As they sought to position themselves the British ships were affected by wind that constantly changed in character. *Venerable*, Captain Samuel Hood, was the first into the bay and opened fire on the *Indomptable*, also 74. But *Venerable* became becalmed and was passed by *Pompee*, which began to take the fire of all the ships of the Linois squadron. She anchored close to Linois's flagship, the 80-gun *Formidable*, which began to draw away as the warps pulled her towards the shore. *Audacious* came up to join the other two British ships. The action was then between the whole of the Linois squadron and the three British ships. But *Caesar, Spencer* and *Hannibal* then also came up. *Caesar* became engaged with the 80-gun *Dessaix* and was soon joined by *Hannibal. Spencer*, becalmed, was unable to close with the action. Saumarez ordered *Hannibal* 'to go and rake the French admiral'. *Hannibal* cut her cables and sought to obey, making use of what little wind there was to tack closer inshore to intercept *Indomptable* but *Hannibal* ran aground. *Pompee*, disabled, was under tow by boats from ships that had them intact.

In the uncertain airs upon which they depended the British ships had severe difficulty of manoeuvre. Rarely had any naval action been more confused. Edward Brenton succinctly described the scene: 'The ships remained here for nearly two hours, under every disadvantage of calm, light, and baffling airs, with their heads all round the compass; the boats incessantly employed in towing them, so as to bring their broadsides to bear, until called away to assist Hannibal, now immoveably fixed on the shoal, whence no effort could extricate her.' *Hannibal* continued to fire from the shoal until, with many of her guns disabled, her masts wrecked and with dead and wounded strewn on her decks, Captain Ferris ordered firing to stop and then commanded his officers and men below to avoid further loss. It was a memorably distinctive act of compassion for those who served under him. *Hannibal*'s colours were then hauled down. The horror of the action even down in the cockpit was described by *Hannibal*'s surgeon in a letter to the father of a lieutenant of the marines who was badly wounded: 'Your son's right leg was entirely smashed to pieces, and the left very much shattered. I amputated his right leg, and dressed and took every possible care of him till the action was over, which lasted five hours, after which the ship caught fire in three different places in the cockpit; and I wish I could draw a veil over the dreadful catastrophe which then followed, as the French and Spanish soldiers and sailors, in extinguishing the fire, trod great numbers of the wounded to death. Your son, however, survived and I got him sent to the hospital at Algeziras, but from loss of blood he expired the next day.'

In the heat of the action there was a fine instance of an act of voluntary bravery by a British sailor. *Caesar* broke her sheer and could not get her guns to bear on the enemy. Sheering occurred when an anchored ship suddenly became difficult to hold in a required direction because of rolling and veering from wind or current. Captain Jahleel Brenton, brother of the historian Edward, ordered a cutter to be lowered from the stern to carry a warp to *Audacious*, but the cutter was found to be shattered by enemy shot. A young sailor named Collins, nineteen, belonging to *Caesar*'s mizzen top seized the end of a lead line saying, 'You shall soon have a warp', stripped, and leaped overboard from the quarterdeck. He swam to *Audacious* fifty yards off through water churning with shot and other red-hot metal. The line was taken aboard and a warp duly passed to *Caesar*.

At one thirty-five p.m. the action ceased and Saumarez withdrew his five surviving ships to Gibraltar. For the British, defeat in such a full naval action was difficult to absorb, especially after Copenhagen and the Nile. Linois had effectively repulsed the British attack, which made it his victory. Captain Pallière could have the satisfaction that night of reminding Cochrane that he was still Pallière's guest, not the other way round. Saumarez's ships had been severely mauled, his own ship *Caesar* in particular. Loss in killed and wounded was high on both sides, but the sting of their reverse created a fury of British effort to redeem it.

The flagship *Caesar* was so severely damaged that Saumarez considered transferring his flag to *Audacious*. The chances of swift repair to *Caesar* and *Pompee* appeared nil, the more so since many of the men working in Gibraltar dockyard had gone over to Algeciras in boats to help haul away the damaged *Hannibal* and had been captured. But *Caesar*'s captain, Jahleel Brenton, made a heartfelt appeal to his men to make the attempt to get *Caesar* seaworthy: 'All hands to work day and night until she is ready.' It was the sort of emotional, patriotic appeal that invariably had the electric effect upon British sailors. They responded with three cheers. They warped their ship into the mole and within two days had stripped the lower masts and got a new mainmast in. At Algeciras Linois was making similar effort to repair his ships and to get his prize, *Hannibal*, afloat. He had, meanwhile, sent an urgent appeal to the two admirals at Cadiz, the Spanish Mazarredo and French Dumanoir Le Pelley, for reinforcement. The assembled response was powerful: six ships of the line, including two Spanish of 112 guns, *Hermenegildo* and *Real Carlos*, as well as the 80-gun *San Fernando Arrogante*, two 74s, *San Augustin* and the French-manned *San Antonio*, and three frigates. At daylight on 9 July this tremendous fresh armament sailed from Cadiz. Sight of them moving out of the port led the three British ships still on guard off Cadiz to hasten to precede them through the Straits. These were the 74-gun *Superb*, the frigate *Thames* and a brig. Their warning, followed by sight of the Cadiz reinforcement rounding Cabrita Point, increased the efforts of the British sailors repairing their ships to demonic level and, on the morning of the 12th, when the ships at Algeciras were seen to loosen sails, they were ready.

A movement at Algeciras would have been expected anyway by those at Gibraltar for a fresh east wind had settled in. Without its allowance of swift passage through the Straits retirement to Cadiz could not have been

contemplated by the big force at Algeciras, for the British pursuit of such
a considerable enemy on an east wind within the confines of the twenty-
two-mile Strait offered practically no possibility of tactical manoeuvre.
With the wind driving Linois's ships straight on through, hard towards the
Atlantic, the tactic had to be to catch up with them and fight on the run, as
it were, bearing alongside where possible. The unsatisfactory alternative was
to hold in tight pursuit until the open sea, but the challenge of this action
within 'the Gut' was what Saumarez and his captains were determined on
at midday as the ships at Algeciras began to move.

The battle in Gibraltar/Algeciras Bay on the 6th had been watched by
thousands on both sides. Once more the entire population of Gibraltar, civil
and military, crowded to the waterfront as on that hot humid afternoon the
ships moved off, with *Caesar*'s band playing 'Heart of Oak' ('Come cheer up
my lads, 'tis to glory we steer') while the military band on shore answered
with 'Britons, Strike Home'. The prevailing emotion was so strong that
even the wounded men begged to be taken on board to share the honours
of the approaching action.

At three p.m. Saumarez, back on board *Caesar*, made the signal for the
squadron to prepare for battle, which first appeared likely off Cabrita Point,
where Linois and his Spanish counterpart, Admiral Moreno, appeared to be
forming their line, directed by Linois and Moreno from a frigate. Moving
off from mole or anchorage and forming line was a slow business in the lee
of the Rock and it was already seven before the British line was well away.
At seven forty-five p.m. both forces were at the eastern head of the Strait
in the comparatively wide stretch of water between Cabrita Point and Mons
Abyla. The British squadron consisted of five line ships, *Caesar*, *Venerable*,
Audacious, *Spencer* and *Superb* and the frigates *Thames* and *Carlotta*. The
Franco-Spanish force was nine line ships: Linois's original four and the
five that had come round as reinforcement from Cadiz.

As the long summer evening dimmed into night both fleets became
enclosed within the walled darkness of the Strait. Instead of manoeuvring
for battle the confrontation had become chase, with the Franco-Spanish
ships running with the freshening wind on through the Strait. The enemy
was taking advantage of the fact that the east wind gathers force from the
narrowing of the Strait, driving ships harder towards the open Atlantic
beyond Tarifa and Cape Spartel, on towards safer tactical battle there
or refuge at Cadiz. It would have been difficult then to know Linois's
intention. But at about eight forty, with the Franco-Spanish force already
invisible ahead, Saumarez hailed *Superb*, running just ahead of *Caesar*, and
directed her captain, Keats, to make sail ahead to attack the sternmost of
the enemy ships.

All sail was instantly set on *Superb*, the quickest ship in the squadron.

As *Caesar* and the other lead ship, *Venerable*, faded from sight behind her, *Superb* caught up with three enemy ships. These were the two 112 guns, *Real Carlos* and *Hermenegildo*, and the French-manned 74, *San Antonio*. *Superb* shortened sail and moved close in to *Real Carlos*, upon which she loosed three broadsides. The Spanish ship lost her fore topmast and was seen to be on fire. *Superb* passed on to *San Antonio* and in thirty minutes of close engagement as the two ships rode along together with the wind the colours of the French ship were lowered.

It was just after midnight and, as *Caesar*, *Venerable* and the frigate *Thames* came up, the British on these ships and *Superb* became witness to undoubtedly the most astonishing and appalling naval accident of the Great War, if not in all naval history, at all events unprecedented. In the thick darkness that lay upon the Straits the two 112-gun ships had mistaken one another as enemy and poured their fire upon each other; then, having fallen alongside, the fires aboard them combined and the two blew up. Of the two thousand aboard them only three hundred survived, picked up by *Superb* and other ships.

By dawn the east wind had carried all well clear of the Straits. *Venerable* and *Thames* were the only British ships in a position to continue the chase, close inshore below Cadiz. Their closest quarry was the 80-gun *Formidable*, which at five a.m. became engaged with *Venerable*. The east wind had dropped and in its final flurries the two ships were thrown close together. *Venerable* lost her mizzen topmast, then her mainmast and her foremast and finally grounded on shoal. With *Caesar* and the other British ships coming on, *Formidable* made for Cadiz, to join the others of her force already there. *Venerable* was hauled off the shoal and taken in tow for Gibraltar.

As if in strange anticipation, the final engagement of this battle was along the edge of the shoals just below Cape Trafalgar. Or, as Edward Brenton put it, 'Thus ended the first battle of Trafalgar.' It was a valid assessment of the large consequences of the action. Saumarez had drawn victory from defeat. He had done so brilliantly on waters that could easily be described as among the most difficult for naval action to be found anywhere in the world. Algeciras has generally been regarded as a single, linked battle. That helped diminish the sting of defeat in the first part of it, on the bay.

The defeat of the combined fleets in the Straits of Gibraltar meant that Napoleon had lost all possibility of further serious naval activity in the Mediterranean in support of his army in Egypt. For Napoleon maritime peace had meant triumph over the British navy in the Mediterranean, and through that holding on to Egypt. In July 1801 all of it finally fell apart.

Even as Linois entered Cadiz and Saumarez retired to Gibraltar the bulk of the French army was marching from Cairo for evacuation from Rosetta to Aboukir Bay. General Belliard had ignored an order from Menou

at Alexandria that his soldiers should defend Cairo to the death. He had
capitulated without firing a shot, before the investment of the city by the
surrounding British and Ottoman forces had properly begun. It took the
intending besiegers completely by surprise. But some twelve thousand
armed French soldiers, bearing the body of General Kléber and with their
wives and children, began their march for Rosetta, accompanied by British
troops. Menou, with some seven thousand troops, remained locked into
Alexandria, saying 'I know how to die, but not how to capitulate.' He
remained hopeful that with another attempt Ganteaume might yet succeed
in bringing in supplies and troops. And, indeed, had the French strategy
been different; had Linois remained in the Mediterranean; had Admiral
Dumanoir got his five French-manned Spanish ships through the Straits
from Cadiz; and had those forces then joined with Ganteaume, who could
say what such a force might not have achieved in delivering to Egypt
the thousands of soldiers Napoleon had stationed at Neapolitan ports to
embark from there for Alexandria? Realistically there was probably little
actual possibility of that. Everything, the Army of Egypt included, had
combined against every strategy that Napoleon had sought to retain his
hold on Egypt.

Menou finally capitulated on 2 September. The soldiers in Alexandria
followed those of Cairo in departing with full honours of war and all their
weapons and equipment. One should again recall that this was what Sidney
Smith and Kléber had agreed to at El Arish in January 1800. The British
government's rejection of the treaty and its sudden change of mind was a
fuddle for which thousands of French, Turkish and British soldiers paid
with their lives.

A special order issued by Napoleon on 9 October awaited the Army of
Egypt as it returned to France. General Kléber's body was not to land: it
would remain in a prison fortress on an island near Marseilles. Napoleon
was never likely to forget that letter dated 8 October 1799 that Kléber had
sent to the Directory after the First Consul's flight from Egypt, least of all
its heavy emphasis that possession of Egypt required a powerful lever: '. . .
and that lever is a navy. Ours has ceased to exist.' A truth now painfully
relived just two years on especially since Napoleon at this time nursed a
great bitterness against Kléber for his desire at the El Arish negotiation to
withdraw the French Army from Egypt. It was as though all had proceeded
badly from that. If Kléber had evacuated Egypt, he said, he would have
brought him to trial on his return to France. But at St Helena, as with so
much else, it was all revalued. If Kléber had lived, the British would never
have taken Egypt, he told his aide, Comte de Las Cases. And to his surgeon
O'Meara, 'Kléber was an irreparable loss to France and to me. He was a
man of the brightest talents and the greatest bravery.'

XXXI

AMIENS

NELSON returned from the Baltic on 1 July 1801 to a nation gripped by fear of invasion, and arising from that came an immediate, persuasive demand that he return to active service instead of the repose he ardently wished for.

He at once began to work out his strategy for the defence of the island's vulnerable coasts on the Narrow Seas. On 25 July he presented to Admiralty his hastily composed memorandum on the matter. And on 27 July, just over three weeks after landing at Yarmouth, he hoisted his flag aboard the frigate *Unite* at Yarmouth to start his watch on home waters.[1] He was required to maintain watch against invasion with several cruiser squadrons to cover the Narrow Seas from Dieppe to Flushing, himself lying at the Downs.

What had caused the stir in London and across southern England was the immense preparation that had been observed in the French Channel ports, Boulogne especially, for an apparent invasion. A great flotilla of gunboats, flatboats for carrying troops and other small craft was being assembled. At Boulogne in the middle of July a camp was established for the thousands of troops that were being gathered there, all of this even as peace negotiations between Britain and France were advancing. Conclusion to the negotiations seemed likely at any time. There was broad suspicion, therefore, that the invasion threat was merely being mounted by Napoleon to hasten the peace negotiations thereby to win as much as possible of his full demands from Britain.

Napoleon already feared the possibility of retreat from Egypt and wanted peace before Alexandria would have to be surrendered. Without news of success in Egypt and at the Straits of Gibraltar Britain had to take menace at the Channel with full seriousness. St Vincent and Prime Minister Addington therefore wanted Nelson's name to the fore in defensive preparations against invasion as one quick means of calming public fears but also as a warning to France. As St Vincent told Nelson, with peace negotiations advancing, 'I need not add, how very important it is that the enemy should know that *you* are constantly opposed to him.'

Nelson's own hasty, handwritten assessment of the Boulogne threat discounted the idea of a full invasion of the sort that had always been dreaded. He saw instead the possibility of a powerful thrust such as a raid on London that might throw the whole country into fear and turmoil, and thus hasten the peace that Napoleon wanted.

The swift assembly of his ideas laid down the immediate form of the island's defences against what might come across the sea. The blockades of the Texel, Brest, Boulogne and the Biscay ports were increased. All cruisers lying at the Downs were ordered to sea. Twenty additional watch frigates were stationed along the French coast, from Le Havre to Dunkirk. The captains and officers of ships of necessity in port or lying off were ordered to sleep on board instead of going ashore. Guard ships manned by pike men were stationed at Harwich and other ports. Nelson and St Vincent nevertheless believed that the cardinal point of their defence should be that the enemy had to be kept as far from the British coasts as possible, with the navy 'able to attack them the moment they come out of their ports'.

In a striking demonstration of British desire to remind the French coast of the readiness of their watch ships and what they were capable of, a daring attack was launched across the Channel. In a war of outstanding boat operations this one would perhaps remain one of the most remarkable.

Four British frigates, *Beaulieu*, *Uranie*, *Robust* and *Doris* were part of the watch on Brest. They lay close in, with the combined French and Spanish fleets in whole view before them. Brest was protected by an encrustation of heavy batteries as well as flotillas of gun ships. A French corvette, *Chevrette*, lay under the batteries of the bay of Cameret in the roadstead of Brest. She had every reason to feel as secure there as any of the ships of the line within Brest itself. But a desire to seize her had suddenly possessed the British officers daily observing her. On the night of 20 July 1801 they decided to cut her out and bring her away.[2]

Boats from *Beaulieu* and *Doris*, manned entirely by volunteers, set off but in the dark they became separated. One lot of boats lay on their oars at the entrance of the bay until dawn, waiting to be joined by the others. When those failed to appear they returned to the frigates, but before they got back to their ships the French spotted them.

Chevrette understood at once that an attack had been intended. That morning, the 21st, her officers moved her a mile and a half up the bay and moored her immediately below batteries. Troops were brought on board from the shore. Arms and ammunition were brought on deck. Her main guns were loaded with grape shot. The batteries, too, were in a state of preparation, with further temporary redoubts thrown up about them. A gun vessel with two 32-pounders was brought up and moored in advance of *Chevrette* as a guard boat.

All of those preparations were observed from the British frigates. In the afternoon, with the defences apparently completed, *Chevrette* hoisted a large French ensign above a British one, its signal of defiance. For the British sailors it was incitement.

Far from intimidating the onlookers the extensive preparations they had witnessed became part of the challenge, to the sailors of *Beaulieu* in particular. As the French prepared, so did they, putting their arms in order, grinding their cutlasses, which had to be sharp to cut boarding nettings, the rope nets suspended from a ship's yards down to the water as a barrier to boarding.

At nine thirty that night six boats from *Beaulieu* joined boats from *Doris*, *Uranie* and *Robust*. *Beaulieu*'s boats were manned by between eighty and ninety officers and men, all volunteers, under Lieutenant Maxwell. The operation was under the command of Lieutenant Losack from one of the other frigates. With a moon above, Losack told them to lie on their oars or pull easy as it was too early for the attack. But Losack then went off, accompanied by other boats, in pursuit of a boat that was assumed to be the enemy lookout. When, by half-past midnight, Losack had failed to return argument arose between the boats on whether to proceed or call it off. The moon was sinking below the horizon. The wind had fallen. It was flat calm. Maxwell, who was now the senior officer, decided to continue and sent a midshipman after the boats that, with Losack's absence, had begun pulling back towards their ships.

Maxwell then gave his orders, that immediately on boarding, while others were fighting on deck, the smartest of *Beaulieu*'s topmen, who had accompanied him, should fight their way aloft and cut the sails loose with their cutlasses. Other sailors he singled out to cut the cables and to take the helm.

The moon had set but the sky was clear and they were spotted and hailed as soon as they came in sight of *Chevrette*. A drenching fire of musketry and grape shot descended upon them as the boats drove forward, with many dropping dead or wounded before they got alongside. In this hail of metal one of *Beaulieu*'s lieutenants, Martin Neville, stood up in his boat, cheering the oarsmen forward until alongside. They were then into the thick of hand-to-hand fighting as savage as could be imagined, battling to get aboard even as French soldiers dropped down into the boats to fight there. The French were fighting with firearms, sabres, tomahawks and pikes. It was so fiercely close that the British soon lost all their firearms and were left with only their cutlasses. Terrible wounds were suffered. Many British sailors had their arms cut off by tomahawks as they tried to board.

The sailors Maxwell had delegated to get themselves aloft had to fight desperately to get there. Several were killed, others hopelessly wounded. The others, bleeding from their wounds, got aloft but found that the foot ropes were still strapped. They therefore had to scramble out on the yards upon their hands and knees, somehow still managing their cutlasses. But, minutes after the boats had come alongside, with half the British sailors killed or wounded, they cut the three topsails and courses. Simultaneously the cable was cut and *Chevrette* began casting away.

Lieutenant Neville had run on to the quarterdeck, where he found the French captain. In the fight that followed the captain was run through with Neville's cutlass and fell lifeless at the wheel. Henry Wallis, quartermaster of *Beaulieu*, fought his way to the wheel and, although severely wounded and bleeding, began steering *Chevrette* as she slowly came underway.

When the sails fell the French sailors were briefly paralyzed in their astonishment. Some jumped overboard, others threw down their arms and rushed down the hatchways. Within five minutes of boarding the British sailors were in possession of the quarterdeck and forecastle, which were covered with dead bodies. The French sailors who had retreated on to the main deck were laying trails of powder and threatening to blow up the quarterdeck. The British split into two parties, one to return the fire from below, using firearms picked up from the deck, while the other party made sail and threw overboard the bodies around them, including some of the fallen British.

A breeze was gently carrying *Chevrette* out, but shot and shells were flying about, through the ship's sides, masts, sails and rigging. The state of the boats alongside prevented them from towing. Instead they sought to tow away boats with dead and wounded from under the fire of the batteries. By this time the action had lasted two hours. The British sailors managed to set every sail, even while being fired on by the French sailors and soldiers on the main deck. Once clear of the batteries the British threatened to show no quarter unless the firing stopped, which it then did. By then *Chevrette* was well away, making towards the British frigate squadron, carrying to them sight of the frightful carnage on her decks.

It was truly an episode without parallel. Lieutenant Maxwell and his sailors had rowed into the most powerfully defended waters on the French coast and brought out a French ship from under the batteries, in sight of the Grand Fleets of France and Spain. Unlike most boat operations this one had been pressed forward without the advantage of its originally intended surprise. The sailors went in face of the fullest preparation against their assault. Their courage as they rowed towards what they knew was prepared for them is intimidating to reflect upon, as is their unflinching zeal as they fought their way up from their boats to the decks of a corvette, to be cut by that chilling assortment of weapons, and able withal to get the sails loose and the ship underway.

Quartermaster Wallis, savagely cut and bleeding at the helm, on being told by an officer that he should be relieved because of the severity of his wounds, answered that it was only a prick and a graze from a cutlass, that it would not prevent him from going again on another such expedition, and indeed wished it were the following night.

Chevrette was taken to Plymouth, where she arrived on 26 July, the day before Nelson raised his flag aboard *Unite* at Yarmouth.

Chevrette was a fitting example for Nelson himself when, a few weeks later, he prepared his own boat operation, against Boulogne. By now his scepticism of the whole invasion threat was deep. To St Vincent on 7 August he wrote, 'I pronounce that no embarkation can take place at Boulogne; whenever it comes forth, it will be from Flanders, and what a forlorn undertaking! Consider cross-tides, etc. etc. As for rowing, that is impossible! It is perfectly right to be prepared against a mad government; but with the active force your Lordship has given me, I may pronounce it almost impracticable.' The time for an invasion was gone, he declared.

Nelson nevertheless wanted to hit hard while he had the opportunity to do so. He, too, wanted a 'cutting-out' operation, to capture and bring away vessels of the French flotilla. British alarm was principally focused upon the so-called 'flats', stoutly built rafts that carried thirty seamen, 150 soldiers and mounted one mortar and a 24-pounder. More than a hundred of these lay at Boulogne, guarded by a line of gun ships, including brigs of 200–250 tons with between four and eight heavy guns, 24-, 18- and even 36-pounders. The flotilla was under the direct supervision of Admiral Latouche-Tréville, who demanded that his gun ships lie before the port, prepared as if for battle and constantly on high alert. And it was to raid and destroy as much of that line as possible that Nelson sent in a large force of boats on the night of 15 August.

Nelson, aboard the frigate *Medusa* off Boulogne, saw his own force of fifty-seven boats, mostly the British form of flatboats armed with howitzers and carronades, move off from alongside at eleven thirty. They were in four divisions, each with its specified attack point in the French line of gunboats. But strong currents separated the boats and spoiled the intention of a concerted attack. The French were waiting in force for the British assault. And, although the British, armed with pikes, cutlasses and tomahawks, managed to fight their way through the heavy netting that shielded the ships to board several of them, they were driven off by grape shot from the guns and the heavy musket fire of the soldiers on board.

The British were forced to return without even having been able to burn any of the boats they boarded. Nelson had supposed that the human loss would not be much. Instead he had forty-five dead and some 130 wounded. Not since Tenerife had Nelson experienced such a setback, and for much the same reason, namely the dispersion of his attacking craft. It at least provided the consolation that the currents that had spoiled his operation promised the same misfortune to any invasion attempt from Boulogne: 'The craft which I have seen, I do not think it possible to row to England; and sail they cannot.'³

After Boulogne he wished only to be with Emma, whom he had charged to buy a house for them. He wanted to go up to London to see her but St Vincent refused it. 'The public mind is so much tranquillised by your being at your post, it is extremely desirable that you should continue there,' St Vincent replied. Nelson complained also that he could not stand the autumn cold. Apart from the cold he was miserably seasick aboard his frigate as it rocked and plunged at anchor in the gale-driven seas that rolled in below the Downs, crying to Emma in his letters how damned sick he was of the sea. Relief came in September when the Hamiltons came down to Deal and stayed a fortnight. But their departure simply intensified the pain. Returning to the empty ship he cried, 'I came on board, but no Emma. No, no, my heart will break . . . Good God, what a change! I am so low that I cannot hold up my head.' But the end was in sight.

Just ten days later, on 1 October 1801, the Preliminaries of Peace were signed, with the formal end to hostilities set for 22 October. Nelson was told that on that date he could come ashore, and ashore he went that very day, and on to London, and from there to the house that Emma Hamilton had bought for them near the village of Merton in Surrey.

For Napoleon peace was a banquet, far more than he should have hoped to have, given that British sea power had entirely constricted his dreams of global reach.

To France, the Batavian Republic (Holland) and Spain, Britain restored practically all her conquests. It was a giveaway to ensure a peace that it was hoped might endure. 'I am the friend of peace,' Nelson was to write, once he had settled in at his new home, of which he had been ecstatic, 'for my politics are to let France know that we will give no insult to her government . . . if Buonaparte understands our sentiments, he will not wish to plunge France in a new war with us.' But for Napoleon, as was promptly made evident, peace was an interlude.

Of all her conquests, Britain kept only Ceylon and Trinidad. In the Mediterranean she returned Malta, Minorca and gave up her garrison on Elba. In the West Indies Tobago, Martinique, Santa Lucia and the Dutch colonies in Guiana went back. The Dutch got back the Cape of Good Hope. They and the French also got back their Indian stations. Egypt was to be restored to the Ottomans (when the Preliminaries were signed the capitulation of Alexandria was still not known). Portugal was to regain the territory she had lost in the attack on her that Napoleon had compelled Spain to make. France withdrew her troops from Naples, the Papal States and the Ionian Islands.

What mattered for most in Britain was simply the return of peace, which coincided with a fine harvest. Pitt described the peace terms as not all that might have been wished, nevertheless 'highly creditable and on the whole advantageous'. The former Secretary of State, Grenville, thought otherwise and attacked the treaty in parliament. He and others from Pitt's departed government predicted that war would soon be resumed and that what had been surrendered would have to be fought for all over again. But the illuminations and rejoicing across the land expressed the popular satisfaction and lack of misgiving. Peace it was, and that was all that mattered.

France, too, was ebullient. Peace was what all had wanted, and this was a peace that only recently had seemed unimaginable. France's considerable natural resources were restoring a prosperity that built on gains from its victorious campaigns. Napoleon was supreme. The nation, in gratitude for what he had won and restored, was soon to agree by plebiscite that he should be named Consul for Life.

In Britain there was intense curiosity to see this extraordinary individual who had so unpredictably changed the fortunes of all of Europe. He was thirty-three. The British artist Joseph Farington was among those who went over to France to satisfy their curiosity. His observation point was on a landing of the great staircase in the Tuileries. A large crowd awaited Napoleon and accompanied him as, with frequent halts, the First Consul passed up the steps. Farington's diary entry of the occasion was that of the painter taking in his subject:

As all circumstances are remarkable about an extraordinary man, I noticed that he picked his nose very much – sometimes took snuff, and would take off his hat and wipe his forehead in a careless manner – I also remarked that some of the officers occasionally spoke to him, *without his having addressed them*, and seemed only to be making such remarks as persons who are on an easy footing do to each other . . . He stood about three yards from me about ten minutes reading a paper which had been delivered to him by an officer to whom he put several questions – having dismissed this application . . . another officer presented a paper which he looked at and gave an answer. He took off his hat and wiped his forehead and I noticed that all his actions were *unstudied* and quite easy and natural and calm . . . He proceeded to the next flight of steps and passed me so close that I could have touched him. His eye having glanced on strangers, when he came opposite to me he looked me full in the face which gave me an opportunity to observe the colour of his eyes, which

are lighter, more of blue grey, than I should have expected from his complexion
... I thought there was something rather feverish than piercing in the expression
of his eyes, but his general aspect was milder than I had before thought it ... His
person is below the middle size. I do not think more than 5 feet 6, I judge him
to be rather less than that measure ... He is not what can be called thin. He is
sufficiently full in the shoulders and body and thighs for his age and height.[4]

The treaty of peace was finally and formally concluded at Amiens on
27 March 1802. But between signing the preliminary peace on 1 October
and before the formal signing at Amiens nearly five months later, Napoleon
sought to reassert his colonial and oceanic ambitions.

France's intended purchase of Louisiana from Spain was now known
to the world. That France sought to re-establish itself in North America
and its waters was a shock to both Britain and the United States. France
also wanted enlargement of the stations in India that were destined to be
returned under the treaty. That too was refused. But Napoleon subsequently
sent out a squadron under Admiral Linois, with six thousand troops. It
appeared off Pondicherry when that station had not yet been restored to
the French.

Meanwhile, on the Continent itself Amiens appeared to have guaranteed
nothing. On the contrary, that balance of power that Britain had always
sought to ensure there was gone. Britain entered the treaty believing that
the independence of the new republics, Switzerland, Holland, Cisalpine
and Liguria, was recognized. Napoleon had agreed to it in the earlier treaty
with Austria. Before the end of 1802, however, that as well as much else
that had been agreed in principle at Amiens had already been remodelled
by Napoleon.

Whatever its critics thought of it, this peace represented a line sharply
drawn across the age. Nine years of war had changed the face of everything.
The age of revolution in which it had begun had subsided, but the impact
of that upheaval was inscribed upon the world. Deep change sat upon the
Western mind and outlook. The ordinary individual's whole sense of his
world and his time was altered. There was an enveloping expectation that
touched everything. There was conviction of rights, of what was beholden
to the humblest. However indistinct it remained among some, it nevertheless
was there, ever broadening and expanding: the true legacy of American independence and the French Revolution. And accompanying this free-ranging
ascent of the individual had come a fuller grasp of the boundless range of
the secular, of what inventive knowledge might yield that was entirely new,
the limitless possibilities for the questions that might now be asked of the
entrenched and hitherto infallible. The surging mechanical inventiveness
of the industrial revolution in Britain and elsewhere offered the practical

side of the epoch's restless mind. The soaring music, poetry and art of the time was the other side to it.

Britain and the monarchical states of Europe had been drawn into war against Revolutionary France with the avowed purpose of restoring the French monarchy. But the preliminaries of peace in 1801 forgot the Bourbons entirely. France was obviously the most changed society in Europe, but it had advanced beyond the revolutionary. Jacobinism was history. Napoleon and Talleyrand had together laid that to rest. But Napoleon embodied the new in many other striking ways, for he was teaching more than generalship. His creative sensibility was changing the face and layout of Paris, to serve as the permanently glowing example for other cities. His practical military vision of connection expressed through the roads and canals he was laying down was permanently changing communication on the Continent as much as in France itself. A lessened sense of distance, easier assumptions of accessibility and contact, were thus alive. Great public works in France required a new institutional system to maintain and govern them and from that sprang the bureaucracy of the select, *auditeurs*, those brought in as exceptionally talented young men who rose to manage the higher levels of the civil service. It was a system whose independence prevented any suggestion of it ever existing as mere adjunct to military dictatorship, therefore a brilliant model for others. And it was fed by talent from a wholly new, secular educational structure.

What Amiens nevertheless underscored was the military impact, and through it the shifting balances of power that had become the inescapable influence upon everything awakened or springing alive at that time. It was a military character that had been entirely moulded by the period of belligerence that the peace treaty now closed. As such it had come to represent the ultimate evolution of the contest between the power of Land and that of Sea. Each had its own particular balance to show.

Ships told the story of the balance upon the sea. Britain had captured fifty French ships of the line and lost only five to France. Britain had started the war with 135 line ships and 133 frigates. She finished with 202 line ships and 277 frigates. France had started with 80 line ships and 66 frigates, finishing with 39 and 35 respectively. But the land balance, on the Continent of Europe, was quite different. French power and influence lay solidly upon central and southern Europe, and for reasons apart from military dominance, for the revolutionary principle of secular republicanism had become entrenched across much of Europe. At many points it allied itself to the French.

French control of the Batavian Republic was strengthened. There was no withdrawal of French troops. The hold upon the Italian republics and the Swiss Republic (Helvetia) similarly tightened. The Cisalpine Republic, centred upon its capital Milan, was renamed the Italian Republic, and called to Napoleon to become its president. The Ligurian Republic, Genoa, was under French military control. Piedmont was annexed and the Kingdom of Sardinia was now confined to the island of that name. With Austria subdued and the Spanish and German rulers entirely under his influence, Napoleon could survey a continent that he could satisfactorily regard as prone before his demand. He was shortly to impel the Swiss canton of Valais to give him the Simplon route through the Alps for his armies should he require it. And beside all of that he could with even greater satisfaction regard the fact that in necessity he had implicit mastery of the coasts from the North Sea to the boot of Italy. The terrified Ferdinand of Naples was prostrate before him. If Naples and Sicily were needed the French armies would run down swiftly to take possession. For France there was therefore no immediate sense of lack of any military or political advantage where it mattered in Europe, though Russia and its young tsar required steady and persuasive diplomatic effort for a relationship that could bear upon French intentions in the Levant. With his Continental land position so secure, Napoleon was at once able to turn his attention fully upon the sea where it had gone wrong for him, where he had lost his vision of global power centred upon the Orient and its wealth. Egypt remained for him the strategic centre of that pursuit. More immediately pressing, however, was the need to restore the flow of colonial wealth from the West Indies.

French possession of St Domingue (it would become Haiti) was merely nominal, though still on the colonial books as hers. Britain, after her disastrous military campaign there, had abandoned the island to the former slave Toussaint L'Ouverture, who had brought order to the former colony after the slave revolt that followed the revolution in France. Toussaint had come to believe that his independence was established. In May 1801 he had declared himself governor for life. He had also seized the Spanish half of the island, Santo Domingo. Before the French Revolution and its slave revolt sequel in St Domingue the plantations there had accounted for more than half of France's oceanic commerce, and restoration of that was one of Napoleon's immediate demands after the end of hostilities on 1 October 1801. At the end of that month Talleyrand appealed to the British government for help in supplying provisions from Jamaica for a proposed expedition to 'destroy the new Algiers being organized in American waters'.

The British did not exactly welcome this just three weeks into a still raw peace. They liked it even less as France began assembling the largest force it had ever sent to sea: thirty-three ships of the line together with a similar number of frigates as well as other lesser naval vessels and transports. They were to carry more than twenty thousand troops to St Domingue to seize back the island from Toussaint. On 14 December 1801 the first squadron sailed from Brest under Admiral Villaret-Joyeuse: fifteen ships of the line escorted by frigates and carrying some seven thousand troops. Five of the line ships were Spanish, under Admiral Gravina.

It was peace and Britain was in no position to protest French desire to seize back a rebellious colony. Britain nevertheless promptly decided to send a force of matching strength under Rear Admiral George Campbell to re-enforce the weak squadron at Jamaica. That hasty response, as Mahan said, 'partook more of panic than of reasonable fear', for it overlooked the enormous inferiority of French naval power upon which tenure of the West Indian colonies had to depend, and also ignored the disastrous experience of Britain in attempting to wrest St Domingue from Toussaint. That memory and fear of what Toussaint's example still set for the slaves on the British colonial plantations nevertheless allowed the *Naval Chronicle* to say that the French intention to wrest St Domingue from 'the destructive domination of Toussaint and his ferocious followers' was in the interest of Britain 'to forward rather than obstruct'. That undoubtedly reflected the view of those in Britain influenced by the West Indian lobby and interests.

There was to be poignant cost to Britain for this St Domingue venture, for the mustering of Campbell's fleet produced one of the saddest episodes within the Royal Navy itself during that war.

For sailors who had been locked into their ships for years, some for as long as the war itself had lasted, and who expectantly saw peace as imminent release to homes and families so long unseen, the sudden command to weigh and sail for the West Indies was too much to bear. The war was over. It was their time for love and laughter, for shore life and England again. They heard their own officers declaring that *they* would rather retire on half-pay than go because nothing would be gained by sailing to the West Indies. And then, releasing their own voice over a dramatic ten-day period, from December 1 to 11 1801, one group of sailors forcefully expressed themselves aboard Admiral Campbell's flagship, the 98-gun *Temeraire* lying at Bantry Bay.

XXXII

TEMERAIRE

WITH the long-awaited peace fallen upon the land so enticingly around them, the bitterness of sailors aboard *Temeraire* turned savage with confirmation that there would be no stepping on shore for them and that instead they would be off to sea at once on an indefinite mission.

The mutiny that began on 1 December 1801 built up through the next ten days until, inevitably, as with anything so ultimately hopeless, it expired on 11 December. On 6 January 1802 fourteen of those regarded as ringleaders were put on trial at Portsmouth. For anyone passing through the record of that court martial it all comes alive in a manner that is unique, offering a living fragment of the navy of the day, for within it one goes below deck, into corners rarely glimpsed so directly, and in the testimony of ordinary sailors hears their voice.

The snatches of the testimony from individual sailors offered below allow the reader a small sense of that.

On trial were John Mayfield, captain of the forecastle, James Ward, belonging to forecastle, James Chesterman, also forecastle, John Fitzgerald, captain of the foretop, Thomas Cross, also foretop, James Lockyer, maintop, John Cumings, maintop, Christopher White, maintop, William Hillier, foretop, John Collins, ship's butcher, John Daley, Joseph Rowland, a carpenter, Thomas Jones and William Cooke, seamen of HMS *Temeraire*.

Evidence from two of the witnesses:

John Anfrey, seaman, sworn: 'On the 1st December, in the larboard bay, in the morning, I saw nineteen or twenty people; they were drinking either grog or wine; they swore to be true to each other. When they were going to begin they said, "Drink to us like British heroes, there is no fear, we will go through the business; shake hands like brothers, stick to each other, there is no fear if there are no informers." Fitzgerald was present, Mayfield, Ward, Lockyer, Rowland, Cooke and Chesterman. On Saturday morning the 5th at nine o'clock, Fitzgerald, Collins, Chesterman and Cooke asked the ship's company if they were willing to come aft, to tell their officers, now the war was over, that they did not wish to go out of the land. They went aft, halfway the gangway, and made a stop – "Come and speak to your officers like men, now is the time." and they went aft directly, it was then about eleven o'clock. They spoke to lieutenants Douglas and Gore. Mr D. asked them what they wanted. They said they were informed they were going out of the land and did not wish to go. The admiral came on deck and asked the same question; they answered that they wanted to know where they were going, and that they would not heave the anchor to go out of the land. The admiral desired them to go down and be quiet; that the *Temeraire* had an excellent character, and he should be very sorry to report mutiny in the ship. They all then went down to the lower deck. Fitzgerald, Cooke and Ward said, nobody should drink more than their allowance, and in case any should drink more than their allowance and get drunk they would cob them. The word was passed fore and aft the same evening that the first man who was caught lying on the yard to bend sails would be punished by themselves. I heard Fitzgerald for one saying this . . .

'On the 6th of December about one o'clock, as the men were at dinner, I saw Mr Lawrence, the master's mate, going round the deck. After he came, Fitzgerald, Chesterman, Allen, Lockyer and Taylor said, "Now is your time, lower the ports down; douse the ports," and they were all down but one, which Allen lowered himself. Lieutenant Douglas came and asked what noise that was, when they began to cheer. He desired them to come aft on the quarterdeck, and let the admiral know what they wanted, and if he could grant it he would. They all began to cry, No, No, and cheered. They then went up to the quarterdeck, when the admiral asked the ship's company what they wanted, and why they made so much noise and confusion? Jones said they wanted to know where they were going. The admiral asked if they had ever been made to know where they were going? Jones said, no. The admiral then said they had better be quiet, not to be obstreperous, as they would gain nothing by it; he said he did not know himself where he was going; he was ordered to sea on a cruise, and must obey his orders; that it was enough when he called all hands, and then he hoped they would go with goodwill. Many cried, "No, no; we will not go from the land, we will go to England." On Sunday morning at ten I espied a few cannon cartridges of powder in the locker nippers, and a match lighted on the larboard side, in a small washing tub covered with two shirts. Daley, when I was looking over the locker, asked me what I wanted in the manger. I asked why he wanted to know; I told him I wanted to see the manger, in case it should be wanted to heave up. Daley desired me to be gone; and if I did not he would make me. On Monday 7th James Ward ordered me not to bring my hammock up until piped up, and that every man should drink his allowance among themselves, until it was all settled; that the war was over, and they would not go out of the land; that the first man who was found drunk should be punished among themselves. Ward passed these orders round to every man's berth. There was a great quantity of people consulting together, and when the officers used to come round every man used to go to his berth, and come out again when they were gone.

Lockyer said he would be damned if he would ship the capstern bar to go out of the land, and he hoped everybody was of his mind. Mayfield said he had been eight or nine years in the service, and he would like to go and see his friends now the war was over. Everyone was told by Chesterman, if they fetched the hammocks up before they were piped, they would be knocked down the hatchways with their hammocks. On the same night Taylor wrote a letter under the bowsprit. Lieutenant Forfar came down close by the bowsprit, and Taylor ran over to the starboard side between two hammocks until the officer was gone, and when gone he came back. They had different password while the letter was writing. First they said, "Catch the rat, take hold of the rat". It was a notice of an officer's coming. Another watchword was "Give me a chew of tobacco". I saw many tell Taylor what to put in the letter. On the next morning nineteen or twenty were looking at the paper in Chesterman's berth. I could not tell what was in the paper. Chesterman asked me if I was willing to go out of the land. I told him I should not like to go, but if I was forced or asked, I must go . . . The boatswain's mate having been drunk he was cobbed, he received a dozen and a half from Chesterman, with a pea squeezer; Lieutenant Bogden came down and asked what noise it was, they told him it was only a man going to be cobbed. Lieutenant Bogden told them they should punish nobody with their own hands, but send them aft to be punished. Collins said it was only a cobbing match; immediately Lieutenant Bogden was shoved in the crowd, I saw a man strike him, I cannot tell who it was. An alarm came directly afterwards, and . . . the people went up and made a rush to go aft to take possession of the arms and disarm the sentries, and go upon the forecastle, and kill all the officers; they said they would soon clear those gentlemen quality off the forecastle, and send them away, and began cheering all the way as they went. They stopped and did not go aft when they found the marines were under arms . . . On Thursday, in the forenoon, the admiral called all hands on the quarterdeck, concerning the letter that was sent to him respecting the ship's company, that they were willing to fight for their king and country, but not to go out of the land; that the most part of them had been five, seven or eight years in the service, and now the war was over they wished to go home. Admiral Campbell desired to know if the marines were in the same mind with the sailors. Admiral Campbell came to the marines to try to make them quiet. A few sung out, stand your ground, you buggers. On that day all the prisoners were picked out, except Daley and Hillier. I heard Dixon and Comayne say, and many more with them, near one hundred and fifty, they would take knives and stab the marines when they were asleep in their hammocks. I was present, Miles, the captain of the waist, Shackleday, Harris, Whitaker, and Williams, all belonging to the same mess. George Comayne was close by the fore bits. George Dixon said to me, he did not think I was fit to be among true Britons; he thought I would report them, and begged me to go; I would not, and he knocked me down twice. On the 11th day, about ten o'clock, he told me I should not go home; he would make me sick before the week was out; I told him I did not mind it. He and George Comayne sung out loud as they could, that in case they could not destroy the marines, they would kill the officers out of revenge;

that their comrades were gone out of the ship, and if that would not do, they would blow the ship up. Thomas Simmonds, a fore-top man, was there at the same time, and said to me, he was sorry he had not killed the officers on Sunday; he had it in his power at that time, as he had a crow bar in his hand. George Dixon gave me a kick, and I went away, and never went there again.'

James Richardson, sworn: 'I went down to the lower deck for a sheet of writing paper. On the starboard side I found Edward Taylor, and asked him to write a letter. He said, you had better wait till this business is settled. I then asked him what it was. I dared say it was nothing concerning us. He answered, yes; it was concerning the whole ship's company. He then told me, the ship was going to the West Indies, and that all hands were going on the quarterdeck, to tell the admiral they would not go. I then looked round, and saw Chesterman and John Snowden discoursing together, and a number listening to them. I heard Chesterman ask Snowden, if he was agreeable to go to speak to the admiral. Snowden said he had no objection, if he could get another or two to speak with him; which was agreed to. Chesterman said, all we have to do is, to tell the people in the middle deck who do not know it. Taylor answered, here is one who belongs to the middle deck will do. Chesterman then touched me on the shoulder, and asked me if I would go and let the people of the middle deck know it. I then went up, and told my messmates, John Clements and Joseph Wynn. They began to laugh at me, and said there was nobody there wanted to hear of it. I then went on the poop, and stayed until my watch was out. When I went to dinner my messmates told me the word had been passed when hands were turned up to bend sails, to go down to the lower deck. Chesterman in the afternoon desired me to see that every person and messmate in the middle deck drank their grog, and that any man who was drunk would be turned down on the lower deck, and cobbed. On Sunday morning the word was passed as before, when hands turned up to bend the sails to go down on the lower deck as before. The hands were turned up about eleven to bend sails, which was done as usual. After sails were bent, I went down to dinner. After I got dinner I went to the lower deck, where I saw Chesterman in his own berth. I asked him what they were going to do, whether to unmoor the ship or not? He answered, he did not know. Taylor came down and asked what we were to do. Chesterman said we must soon know, there was no time to be lost, as the hands would be turned up to unmoor as soon as they had got their dinner. I then went to the middle deck to my berth, where I stayed until my grog was served out. As soon as I got my grog, a man came and passed word for us to go down below. I went down to the lower deck and stood alongside Ward. Hillier was in the manger, and, putting his hand to his mouth, singing out with a loud voice, what do you say, lads, one and all, fore and aft, lower away ports? The ports were lowered accordingly and the people all began cheering, and asked where the ship was going. Some of the ladders were unshipped, but the officers got down below, and sent all the people on the quarterdeck. The admiral asked what all that noise was below; a great deal passed but I could not hear it. I went away. On Monday morning I met Taylor on the middle deck, and asked him again about my letter; he said I had better wait another day or two. Cumings came up and said, there is Franey on the foregratings as drunk as hell, and quarrelling with everybody that comes past. After dinner, as I was carrying my dirty water to the head, I saw a parcel of people standing at the foremost gun of the main deck; I saw Franey over the breech of the gun, and Chesterman with a pair of pea-squeezers in his hand, to cob him with. Before he began he pulled off his hat and said he was going to cob him for breaking the rules and laws of the ship's company, he then gave him a dozen. Five o'clock in the evening of Monday I was going down the starboard side of the lower deck when I met Cooke, who said they were going to do some business. I went into Chesterman's berth, where Fitzgerald and Chesterman were talking. Chesterman called William Lockwood and asked him if he would look out; he then went out of the berth and was taking a man out of every berth all the way aft to the main hatchway; as he came back he gave the watchword. If any officer came forward the watchword was, give me a chew of tobacco; then he went into the midship berth under the bowsprit, along with Taylor, who began to write a letter. There was no other man near, except the people looking out; an officer came forward, and they sang out, who will give me a chew of tobacco; the candle was put out till the officer was gone, when they began again. An officer came down, and the light was put out again, the watchword was 'I want to water'. After the letter was finished and directed some conversation passed between Chesterman and Taylor to know which way it was to be conveyed to the admiral. Fitzgerald came up and asked if the letter was gone, Taylor answered, no; he said if you give it to me I will give it to James Shaw, the marine, who will have the middle watch tonight, and he will put it in the admiral's steward's berth. I heard no more of the letter till I heard it read on the quarterdeck.'

Testimony on the characters of the accused:

Lieutenant Walsh: Mayfield has been in the ship two years, always behaved pretty well, and had a good character. Ward has a very good character in the ship. But Chesterman was always looked upon as a very dangerous character. Fitzgerald sometimes very troublesome. Hillier's character has been very fair, a very good active man till the mutiny. Cumings a very good decent man till the mutiny. Daley, a very good character, a man very much respected; no officer ever thought it necessary to look after him.

Lieutenant Brown: Ward has behaved himself particularly well; has never been found fault with. Hillier I have never heard a complaint against; he was particularly attentive to his duty; I never saw him drunk. Daley, a very good character; has been noticed by every officer in the ship for his good character.

Douglas, boatswain: Ward's character was very good before this business, Hillier the same, Collins the same.

Hillier called *Admiral Pole*, who said, I believe Hillier a very good man, he was active, I sent him on dangerous services and he performed them well.

Lieutenant Forfar: I don't recollect any complaint of Fitzgerald, he always did his duty.

Lieutenant Gore: I never heard any complaint of Cumings. And as to Daley, he is one of the best men in the *Temeraire*, for his general good conduct. As to Ward, he always did his duty with the greatest activity. I always considered him a very good man.

Daley called *Mr Jones*, the master, who said he is a particularly good man; very attentive, not only in his mess but his watch; a trusty man, and a good moral character. Hillier has always done his duty remarkably well. Ward the same.

The Court found the charges proved against all and sentenced them to be hanged at Spithead or in Portsmouth harbor.

The naval historian Edward Brenton in his comment on the affair offers one of those many small portraits that particularly distinguish his work, and compensate for the unevenness of some of it. These pictures always come from his own naval service in the Great War. In this case, he spoke with the authority of an officer in that very West Indies squadron of Admiral Campbell. He offered these images in his *Life of St Vincent*.

Brenton believed that 'the language of the officers at the wardroom table was, in all probability, the chief exciting cause, and, because *they* were not punished, *the seamen were*, with a degree of severity which, although it *might* be justified under the peculiar situation of the empire, yet I shall never cease to deplore as one of the most fatal blots on our naval annals. It was an unkind and ungrateful return to the brave fellows who, during a war of unexampled success and glory, had faithfully served their country.'

Brenton was present at the court martial in Portsmouth and described the prisoners as he saw them there.

They were the noblest fellows, with the most undaunted and prepossessing mien I ever beheld – the beau ideal of British sailors; tall and athletic, well-dressed, in blue jackets, red waistcoat, and 'trowsers white as driven snow'. Their hair, like the tail of the lion, hung in cue down their back. At that time, this last article was considered, as indeed it really was, the most distinguishing mark of a thorough bred seaman. Unfortunately, these gallant fellows were ignorant as they were impatient, and the custom of the time was to hang every one who should dare to dispute the orders of his superior officers . . . The execution of Chesterman and the other mutineers of Temeraire cost us more than I am willing to believe or to own; but it certainly lost us for a time the goodwill and affection of our sailors. Of this truth I was made fully sensible, not only in our passage to the West Indies, with Admiral Campbell, but in all the subsequent years of the war up to 1814. We could perceive among the seamen a sullen and lifeless obedience, a scrupulous attention to all orders, but no voluntary service; they did their duty from fear, not love.

XXXIII

RESUMPTION

THE peace that now lay upon Europe was an interlude trusted by few, though most prayed for it to last.

'I think our peace is strong if we act, as we ought, with firmness, and allow France to put no false constructions on the words, or on omissions in the Treaty,' Nelson wrote on 1 May 1802. And then asked dismissively, 'But for what am I getting into politics?' He was embraced by all the pleasures that were new to him: the uninterrupted company of Emma Hamilton, enjoyment of the country place she had bought and prepared for them, travels beyond it that brought adulation wherever he appeared, the visits of friends and family and the distinction of his maiden speech in the House of Lords. But the far-reaching intentions of Napoleon clarified steadily through 1802, by the end of which everyone knew that Britain and France were heading back into war.

The French grip upon Italy had strengthened. Thirty thousand French troops marched into Switzerland in September. Communications with Italy were being improved with roads over the Simplon and other Alpine passes, leading Napoleon to say in August 1802 that the Simplon road alone 'has changed the system of war to be adopted in Italy'. The French reach down Italy was always read as preliminary to the reach for Egypt and India.

Only in the Caribbean were things going wrong for Buonaparte. His force under General Leclerc, his brother-in-law, had arrived in February. Toussaint was seized. Leclerc continued his attempt to subdue the island but his troops, as expected, were brought down by fever as the British earlier had been. Toussaint was sent to France, where he later died in prison. Leclerc, some twenty of his generals and the greater part of the thirty thousand troops succumbed to the fever. What remained of the French garrison clung on but, in face of continuing ferocious reprisals from the freed blacks, any hope of restoring St Domingue to its former colonial productivity and tranquillity was gone by the end of 1802. Admiral

Campbell's fleet returned as early as June 1802: it had, as Brenton said, been an unnecessary rush across the Atlantic.

Crisis remained over the intended cession of Louisiana by Spain to the French. Thomas Jefferson had become President of the United States in March 1801. In November his minister in London sent evidence that Spain had secretly agreed to give Louisiana back to France the year before. Events accelerated thereafter. Jefferson in alarm in April 1802 wrote a letter to the American minister in Paris, Robert Livingston, declaring that from the moment France took possession of Louisiana 'we must marry ourselves to the British fleet and nation'. Jefferson showed the letter to his close friend Pierre Dupont de Nemours, who carried it to Paris, from where Dupont advised making an offer to buy Louisiana from France. On 1 May Secretary of State James Madison instructed Livingston to ascertain the price for which France might sell New Orleans and the Floridas.[1]

On 15 October 1802 Spain formally transferred Louisiana to France. That same month Spain ordered New Orleans and the lower Mississippi closed to American ships. By then the commerce in the port was increasingly with the Americans, particularly westerners who used New Orleans as a transhipment point for products from the interior to the eastern states or abroad. That trade had stimulated western population growth, which in 1800 already registered nearly half a million.

News of the transfer reached Washington in November. American outrage flared in the eastern states. The talk once more was of war against France, or of outright seizure of New Orleans and Florida. But Dupont soon after wrote from Paris to say that the United States could probably buy Louisiana for six million dollars.

France's disaster in St Domingue had changed the Louisiana purchase dramatically. Talleyrand's and Napoleon's concept of a new colonial empire in the west had seen that as centred jointly upon St Domingue and Louisiana. Though far apart, the two, if paired, had substance and viability. Louisiana would help sustain the island with timber, cattle and non-tropical foodstuffs, to cut the cost of maintaining St Domingue and thereby raise the profitability of the island's sugar and coffee exports. But Louisiana was vulnerable and difficult to defend without an intermediate naval station between Europe and America. That intended station was St Domingue. Without it tenure of Louisiana looked impracticable. Henry Adams was to write, 'The colonial system of France centered in St Domingo. Without that island the system had hands, feet, and even a head, but no body. Of what use was Louisiana when France had clearly lost the main colony which Louisiana was meant to feed and fortify?'[2]

The first week of January 1803 Napoleon got the news of Leclerc's death and the necessary abandonment of the expedition, and thus ultimately the island. His guests at a small dinner were discussing wine and coffee when Napoleon startled them by suddenly crying out, 'Damn sugar, damn coffee, damn colonies!' It was his write-off of any ambitious western world empire, but the prospect of an eastern one appeared large three weeks later through the report of a special envoy he had sent to the Levant, François Sebastiani.[3]

The First Consul had sent Sebastiani off in September to assess the situation in Egypt. The British chargé d'affaires in Paris had written to London on 25 September 1802 saying that Sebastiani had gone to Egypt with 'regular powers and instructions, prepared by M. Talleyrand, to treat with Ibrahim-Bey for the purpose of creating a fresh and successful revolt in Egypt against the power of the Porte, and of placing that country again under the direct or indirect dependence of France . . .' That had been absorbed without undue alarm.

Sebastiani returned to Paris on 25 January 1803. On 27 January Talleyrand told the British ambassador, Lord Whitworth, that Napoleon demanded to know when the British intended to evacuate Malta, as agreed under Amiens. Three days later, on 30 January, Sebastiani's full report on his mission appeared in the official newspaper *Moniteur*. In it Sebastiani declared that the defences and fortifications of Egypt were ruinous, the state of its Turkish defenders hopeless, the British troops there closeted in their camps, and that 'six thousand French troops would at present be enough to conquer Egypt'.[4]

The British were powerfully affected, particularly since Napoleon's demand on evacuation of Malta followed directly on publication of Sebastiani's report. The two events immediately changed the British attitude on Malta, retention of which then became fixed, providing the point upon which peace was finally to be shattered.

Many explanations were proffered on the reason for such an amazing provocation right then. Some saw the dramatic focus upon Egypt as a means of distracting attention from the scale of failure in St Domingue and the subsequent intention to dispose of Louisiana to America, the sale of which was unpopular with those who saw a new Canada, including some of Napoleon's brothers.

President Jefferson had nominated James Monroe as minister extraordinary to France to negotiate a sale. But even before Monroe arrived at Paris Napoleon had informed his ministers that he intended to sell Louisiana. On 11 April 1803 Talleyrand saw the resident US minister Livingston and proposed the sale. Monroe fortuitously arrived the next day. The sale price of fifteen million US dollars was agreed and the treaty was signed on 2 May.

The dramatic run of events in those early months of 1803, between news of St Domingue reaching Paris and the signing away of Louisiana, suggested that Napoleon was stubbornly reforming his grand strategy, at the heart of which was eventual reconquest of Egypt. Publishing Sebastiani's report was a flaring symptom of his anger and impatience over British slowness to evacuate its soldiers from both Malta and Egypt. After Sebastiani, however, the chances of quick British departure from Malta were slim. Everything on both sides now accelerated into final crisis. Lord Whitworth increasingly became the victim of Napoleon's irascibility, with the First Consul continuing ever more forcefully to press for British departure from Malta.

On 8 March the king sent a message to the House of Commons declaring that Britain should adopt precautionary measures against the French preparations in the Dutch and Channel ports. Two days later he suggested calling out the militia, and the day after, on 11 March, the Commons voted ten thousand additional seamen, atop fifty thousand sailors and marines already voted in December 1802.

Napoleon summoned the British ambassador to the Tuileries on 13 March. 'And so you are determined to go to war,' the First Consul demanded.

'No,' Whitworth replied. 'We are too sensible of the advantages of peace.'

'We have just finished a war of fifteen years.'

'That is already too much.'

'But you want another fifteen years, and you are forcing me.' And he added, 'Why, then, these armaments? Against whom these measures of precaution? I have not a single ship of the line in the French ports but if you wish to arm I will arm also; if you wish to fight, I will fight also.' The French ships of the line were, of course, all in the West Indies.

'We wish neither the one nor the other.'

'You must respect treaties then, woe to those who do not respect treaties. They shall answer for it to all Europe.'

Whitworth had considered Napoleon too agitated to prolong the conversation.[5]

In that harangue Napoleon appeared to ignore the fact that France that very month was in rush to rebuild its own navy. Ten ships were put on stocks at Flushing, and at Nantes, Bordeaux and Marseilles. Twenty-two others were to be built at Brest, Lorient, Rochefort, Toulon, Genoa and St Malo. By 1805 a powerful new fleet would be in existence.

It was not Britain's own preparation that sat so hard upon Napoleon. It was Malta. Britain and France had moved into irreversible positions. Napoleon had now effectively made British departure from Malta an absolute. Sebastiani's report had brought British determination to hold on to it. Addington was yet prepared to withdraw its garrison if a favourable compromise could be reached. Britain proposed that she should hold Malta for ten years, but any agreement should include the evacuation of French troops from Holland and Switzerland. Intense discussion failed to bring resolution. On 23 April the British government told Whitworth that he was to leave Paris within seven days if the proposal was not accepted. When the period expired Whitworth asked for his passports. There was further futile talk, with Talleyrand and Joseph Buonaparte urging conciliation, until on 12 May Whitworth left Paris. On the 16th George III told parliament that negotiation with France was over. On the 18th a Declaration of War in the name of the king was delivered.

Malta and its significance for Egypt had inflamed Napoleon as nothing else could at that time, but if he had held on to peace he would have had the time and the possibility perhaps of gaining what he most sought. Britain at that moment was removing two great obstacles to French naval deployment. British soldiers left Alexandria on 17 March. They had withdrawn from the Cape of Good Hope the month before. Both would have been inestimable gifts to the future of a Napoleon who allowed himself time. So, too, the new ships he was building. It would be another two years before they were afloat and in service. He would then have a navy that was a closer match in numbers and quality against the British, with the old navy also refurbished and retrained. 'Peace,' he had said, 'is necessary to restore a navy, peace to fill our arsenals empty of material, and peace because then only the one drill-ground for fleets, the sea, is open.' But, by publishing Sebastiani's report in the manner in which it was done Napoleon had brought on war, and with it disadvantage where he least could afford it: at sea.

This was another war in another dawning. The industrial revolution was advancing pell-mell. Technological inventiveness was at this time in a new burgeoning phase. Steam, though yet in its infancy, was nevertheless the fast-rising symbol of the conviction of great things to come, the greatest interest in it naturally focused upon its propulsive capability on water. Henry Bell tried a steamer on the Clyde in 1800. The American Robert Fulton tried two boats on the Seine in this very year of 1803. He was to go on to contract for a steamboat on the Hudson.

Available to both sides for development in this new war was the most astonishing experiment of all, Fulton's Diving Boat or, as the French called it, *bateau plongeur*. Fulton, in his early thirties, had come to Europe to study painting and went to live in Paris where his fascination with new technology overcame painting. He offered his first boat to the Directory, the second to the First Consul, declaring it to be a boat that 'would deliver France and the world from British oppression'. Buonaparte instructed his officials to report on an experiment with the *bateau plongeur* at Brest in July 1801 and another at Le Havre. Along with the boat itself, Fulton demonstrated the weapon it carried, its torpedo.

When in Paris Joseph Farington obtained from a friend a direct description of the boat and its first use of the torpedo. On the surface the boat had masts and two sails. These were struck for a dive. At Brest an old vessel was anchored about a mile and a half from the shore. When the diving boat approached within a quarter of a mile of it, Fulton, who was in it with eight men, put his boat into a dive. He then sank the vessel with his torpedo. 'In about a quarter of an hour,' Farington related,

the vessel was blown up so entirely that nothing was left of her, and sometime after Fulton's boat appeared again upon the surface of the water in an opposite direction from where she sunk. The manner in which he blows up a ship is by enclosing a certain quantity of gunpowder in a small machine which appears externally like the back of a porcupine having small pipes or quills standing out in every direction, anyone of which being touched occasions something like the lock of a gun to go off, and the powder blows up . . . he lets one of these machines go in a direction to touch the bottom of the hull of a vessel; off goes the piece and the vessel is sent in to the air. The boat can be kept under water eight hours at a time, and when raised to procure fresh air, it is only necessary to allow her to rise so high as that the valves which are to receive the air may be above water; the vessel may then again be sunk to any depth, forty fathoms or more; he has also a means of obtaining light. He can go under water at a rate of three miles an hour. This most dangerous and dreadful contrivance is said to be fully understood only by Fulton. He will show the machine but there are certain mysteries about it which he has not yet communicated and says *he will not but in America.*[6]

Further and more insightful observation came from a member of the Tribunate, St Aubin, who witnessed the demonstrations at Brest and Le Havre.

In making his experiments at Havre, Mr Fulton . . . held his boat parallel to the horizon at any given depth. He proved the compass points as correctly under water as on the surface . . . It is not twenty years since all Europe was astonished at the first ascension of men in balloons; perhaps in a few years they will not be less surprised to see a flotilla of diving boats which, on a given signal, shall, to avoid the pursuit of an enemy, plunge under water, and rise again several leagues from the place where they descended . . . with these qualities it is fit for carrying secret orders to succour a blockaded port, and to examine the force and position of an enemy in their own harbours . . . Mr Fulton has already added to his boat a machine by means of which he blew up a large boat in the port of Brest; and if by future experiments the same effect could be produced on frigates or ships of the line, what will become of maritime wars, and where will sailors be found to man ships of war, when it is a physical certainty that they may every moment be blown into the air by means of a diving boat, against which no human foresight can guard them?

That remarkable appraisal and foresight, published in Paris, was reprinted in the *Naval Chronicle*, and there presumably read by all, including Nelson. Napoleon had turned down making use of Fulton's boat. Fulton then offered his invention to the Admiralty who had a demonstration in sight of Pitt's home, Walmer Castle, with Pitt watching. But, for all its wonder, this 'mischievous and horrid mode of destroying vessels of any size while floating in the water', as the *Chronicle* put it, had as little appeal for the British as for the French.[7]

It can seem astonishing that such an achievement should have been ignored by both sides at the start of a war that was quite clearly marked by each for destruction of the power of the other. But in a new war that had come on too fast, where both sides suffered insufficiency of one sort or the other whether of ships or men, immediate dependence was on bringing the tried and true up to scratch. There was no time, patience or willingness for experiment.

XXXIV

BOULOGNE

HAVING erred in bringing war upon himself sooner than he really wanted, indeed was prepared for, Napoleon at once applied himself to the one course that he had always supposed to be the basic solution for conquest of Britain and suppression of her rivalry.

Ruled by his immediate impatience, angered by British obduracy, doubt-less suffering chagrin at being wrong-footed on it all and then finally caught out by Britain's peremptory ultimatum, Napoleon reverted to that which alone offered any hope of finishing it all off sooner than anything else: invasion.

Without the navy he had hoped to have, there immediately appeared to be no alternative for achieving the ultimate victory of Land War over Sea War. The impact of the collapse of Amiens upon Napoleon was severe. His hatred of England now matched Nelson's of France.

What began was, finally, direct engagement between Napoleon and Nelson themselves. The issue fell plainly upon them as it never had before, even at the Nile, when Nelson was not yet the specific adversary he subse-quently became.

As this battle had become for Napoleon the necessary triumph upon which his global ambitions rested, he took full command of the strategy and planning. And, as this confrontation could only be decided by supremacy on the water, the one who countered him had to be Nelson. That Napoleon knew, and for the next two years the manner of his direction was to draw out upon the seas the diversions and distractions that might fool and baffle his opponent, to create the proper opportunity for his grand assault. It was personal, and both knew it. So did the navies behind each of them, as well as the Grand Army that patiently waited for this resolution.

It was the start of the principal contest in history between the mind of Land War and the mind of Sea War, between history's greatest sailor and its greatest general, and in the two-year progress of it there would be witnessed as well the longest military wait for an action that never came and the greatest naval race ever thrown upon the seas.

Britain was alone. This was the essential fight for her survival. Napoleon had no immediate distractions on the Continent to shift his focus away from what he was set on accomplishing. The lack of distractions did not suppose, however, that he would not create them. From the outset the critical question for Admiralty, therefore, was the immediate validity of the threat across the Channel, or whether it covered, as all suspected, some other design such as Egypt, or Ireland. Nelson, therefore, had been marked even before the start of the war as Commander in Chief for the Mediterranean. The wisdom of that appeared justified when, before the end of May, Napoleon sent an army through the Papal States and Naples and reoccupied Brindisi and Taranto, making concrete the fears for the Levant.

Nelson's unique intimacy and knowledge of that sea alone made his command there necessary for not since 1798, before the Nile, had French command of the Mediterranean been so sweeping. Spain was neutral but Napoleon's dominance over her meant that Spanish ports, while open to the French, were hostile to British ships. With Italy similarly under his sway, British operations in the western basin were severely hampered, all of which was sufficient need for Nelson's familiarity and experience there.   .

The British navy moved swiftly to station after the declaration of war on 18 May. Nelson raised his flag aboard the 100-gun *Victory* at Portsmouth on the 20th and he sailed for the Mediterranean. Admiral Cornwallis sailed from Plymouth to maintain the blockade of Brest. Keith had the Downs and the North Sea.

On 8 July Nelson arrived off Toulon, where the hitherto Mediterranean commander Admiral Sir Richard Bickerton was waiting aboard his 80-gun flagship *Gibraltar* supported by the rest of the Mediterranean squadron, four 74s, two 64s and two frigates. Then began the longest sea-time watch of his career, for it would be near two years before he stepped off *Victory* again.

The tremendous preparations that continued for invasion nevertheless left no doubt that, if this were truly the intent, it was for an assault that in its meticulous detail was unlike any other ever planned. And indeed it was.

Napoleon was beholden to no one. His power was supreme. He commanded what he wanted. And he went to it as he would in planning any major military campaign on the Continent; if anything, more seriously, for upon this, he plainly believed, rested everything.

The plans he had had for 1801 were modified and enlarged. An army of 160,000 would be landed on the Channel shores in two waves with the intention, in the words of Jurien de la Gravière, to repeat the Battle of Hastings on the shores of Kent or Sussex. An initial assault would land 120,000 to 130,000 men, with another thirty thousand to follow. The main assault was to set out from Boulogne and three small adjacent harbours, Vimereux,

Ambleteuse and Etaples. The reserve embarkation was to be from Calais, Dunkirk and Ostend. Extensive enlargement was undertaken at Boulogne, with special quays where the flotilla craft lay, with up to nine of the craft at a single quay.

This vast army was to cross in flotillas of small flat-bottomed boats which had originally been designed for the projected invasion of 1797. A typical craft was sixty feet long, sixteen broad, designed to draw around two feet, and with sides three feet above the water. It carried an 18- or 24-pounder in the head and an 8-pounder in the stern. Each boat was to carry a hundred men. Each had a mast but was moved by oar, twenty-five on each side. In these the army was to cross the forty-mile-wide Channel. Apart from delivering the army to the opposite shore, they also had to bear the horses, artillery and supplies. Some six thousand horses were to be transported across.

The huge cost of all of this was sufficient affirmation of Napoleon's serious intent. It was also reflective of the arm-wringing power he possessed on the Continent. While some of the expense was met by the funds brought in by the sale of Louisiana, Napoleon demanded subsidies from Spain, Italy and the Dutch.

As always, the question was, even with all that he was putting together, could he pull it off?

From the way Napoleon was going about this invasion it was, for many, an extraordinary proposition. In 1801 Nelson had already dismissed its feasibility. Other doubters followed. The Dutch, upon whom descended responsibility for delivering some of these craft, regarded them as unseaworthy, with a Dutch admiral advising Napoleon that 'nothing but disgrace could be expected' from dependence upon them. A British admiral who examined one of the captured flotilla craft reported on 23 November 1803, 'It is impossible to suppress for an instant that anything effective can be produced by such miserable tools, equally ill-calculated for the grand essentials in a maritime formation, battle and speed.' The guns were fixtures 'so that, literally, if one of our small boats was to lay alongside there would be nothing but musketry to resist, and those in the hands of poor wretches weakened by the effect of sea-sickness, exemplified when this gun-boat was captured – the soldiers having retreated, incapable of any energy or manly exertion . . . In short, sir, these vessels in my mind are completely contemptible and ridiculous, and I therefore conclude that the numbers collected at Boulogne are to keep our attention on the *qui vive* and to gloss over the real attack meditated from other points.'[1]

For a successful attack the assault would require an extended calm. This danger could never be ignored by the British. A calm, or even light, shifting winds, could mean that frigates and ships of the line might be incapable of sustained attack upon an invading flotilla if they lacked sufficient wind. Furthermore, as Nelson recognized, fast tides and currents, and choppy or rough seas, could make those shallow, flat-bottomed craft unmanageable, and scatter any attempt at steady formation.

The French had already discovered perhaps the greatest disadvantage of all: a seemingly insurmountable problem was simply getting away. It would require several tides to clear that huge flotilla from Boulogne and the other ports. While gradually assembling off the ports such a mass would be vulnerable to sustained attack from the British. Nelson and St Vincent had laid down in 1801 that, were such a large invasion to be launched against the British coasts, the main defence against it would be to attack it before it got halfway across. Nelson's failure at Boulogne that year had demonstrated the danger of going in for direct close assault upon such a tightly assembled armada.

Neither side could take anything for granted, or make any safe assumptions. Napoleon in 1803 was determined upon his invasion. He believed first of all that the hugeness of the effort carried its own momentum, an enormity that would roll forward and overwhelm. The difficulty about that for him was that he was thinking land. Currents and tides did not flow on the maps in his mind. Besides Napoleon, like Nelson, saw chance and luck as abiding elements of the belief in risk that was fundamental to his outlook. He therefore saw no reason to suppose that the conditions and circumstances propitious to invasion could wholly evade him: 'Let us be masters of the Channel for six hours, and we are masters of the world.' In one form or another this conviction was to be repeated.

Whatever scepticism was expressed by some over the practicalities and general feasibility of this invasion, the threat nevertheless lay heavily upon Britain. Lying in huge encampments above Boulogne was this force of more than 100,000 soldiers, the finest of Napoleon's veterans, who formed the most experienced and best drilled army in the world. If landed, Britain had nothing to match it in experience. In 1797 Home Riggs Popham had established a volunteer coastal defence force known as the Sea Fencibles. That was now revived, and by the end of the summer of 1803 more than 300,000 had been enrolled. But these were simply men of all classes and ages, without experience and little of drill, driven by patriotic desire to be on hand should the call come. St Vincent believed it was a system 'of no further use than to calm the fears of old ladies'. Dependence would rest with the regulars.

Nelson in 1801 had recognized the deficiencies of British coastal defences, and with that the serious possibility that, in spite of British naval mastery, an invasion might be successful.

Ironically, it was St Vincent who was now damned in much of public apprehension, for it was upon him that a great deal of blame for lack of preparation fell. Nelson himself was to be a critic. In his sea service St Vincent had, like many in the navy, railed against the corruption, waste and laggardliness in the naval dockyards. As head of Admiralty he had set about trying to eradicate what he could. He had sought economy and efficiency and accordingly had laid harsh new regulation upon the navy, cutting supplies and stores, reducing naval staff and workmen in the dockyards. Where the French were rushing to build a new navy the British navy found itself in a situation where, in its heavily restricted dockyards, new ships could not be built, old ones unable to be repaired. Many ships in commission were in poor state to be at sea on hard duty. This would be particularly felt by Nelson in the Mediterranean when he began operating there with a squadron that had hastily been pushed to sea when hostilities began.

Upon St Vincent's masterful command of strategy nevertheless rested the immediate defence of Britain in 1803. He tenaciously held to the belief that the right naval defence should lie away from Britain's own coasts, for 'to guard our ports, inlets and beaches would, in my judgment tend to our destruction'. He accordingly from the start laid tight blockade upon Brest and the French coast.

Brest had always been the principal focus of blockade. It had to be since it was the main French naval base opposite England and the place where the Grand Fleet sheltered. That made it the natural point for directing operations against Britain, apart from its value for sending off squadrons to other seas or receiving the fleets of Toulon and Spain. Brest lay on a bay deep inside a system of channels and headlands. It was beautifully secure, unlike its approaches where blockading vessels were exposed to powerful winds and dangerous shoals.

Strong argument had long existed on the tactical nature of blockade, but particularly so in the Great War. The issue was between two forms of blockade: close blockade and open blockade. Close meant a strong force lying just beyond the range of the coast batteries, as a challenge for the other force to come out and fight or, if it were unwilling, to hold it locked in to prevent it from slipping out and causing mischief elsewhere. Open blockade was to lie far out, over the horizon, as a stronger lure for the other to take his chances, but positioned so that contact was assured if the other came out. This was what Nelson preferred.

St Vincent saw differently. No ship was allowed to retire from the watch on Brest unless it had special orders from him or from Admiralty. He brought the watch stations closer in. He himself set stern example. In violent storm he sat in an armchair lashed to the quarterdeck, and from there gave his orders. When St Vincent moved to Admiralty and Cornwallis took over the Channel fleet he maintained St Vincent's policy as firmly as St Vincent himself had done. By then the threat of invasion left no alternative.[2]

Thus, simultaneously with Cornwallis off Brest, Nelson off Toulon, Pellew off Ferrol and a patrol line maintained from the Straits of Gibraltar to Cape Clear at southern Ireland and through into the North Sea, the extended vigilance of 1803–5 began: an endeavour to ensure the survival of Britain to be matched eventually only by its equivalent in 1940. Mahan summarized the collective effort: '. . . that tremendous and sustained vigilance which reached its utmost tension in the years preceding Trafalgar . . . They were dull, weary, eventless months, those months of watching and waiting of the big ships before the French arsenals. Purposeless they surely seemed to many, but they saved England. The world has never seen a more impressive demonstration of the influence of sea power upon its history. Those far distant, storm-beaten ships, upon which the Grand Army never looked, stood between it and the dominion of the world.'[3]

By the end of 1803, however, Napoleon had begun to assimilate what his admirals, including Decres, Minister of Marine, and Bruix, commander of the flotilla, sought to impress upon him, namely that trying to get his gigantic flotilla across from Boulogne to Dover was an invitation to terrible disaster without cover and support from a strong fleet.

Napoleon had continued to believe that his flotilla could beat off attack, its sheer size sufficient to get the greater part of his army ashore. But that supposed his crowded, unwieldy, oar-driven flatboats could easily avoid Keith's squadron of line ships off the Downs and the 150 or so British frigates, sloops and brigs that patrolled the British coastal waters and which would immediately converge on their target. All this apart from the fact that he also required the proper weather conditions merely to assemble his flatboats. Invasion nevertheless remained his unshakable commitment.

To create that necessary protective fleet for his flotilla in face of the blockade of all his naval forces at their different bases set an intricately difficult strategic puzzle before the First Consul, who nevertheless applied himself to it with the same confidence of success that would accompany solution of a land deployment problem. To put together the sort of naval strength he required meant composing it from the ships of the line that were distributed between his bases. He had twenty-one in Brest, nine or ten at Toulon, and five at Rochefort, all of which were under British blockade. The rigid blockade maintained by Cornwallis on Brest meant that dependence upon the fleet lying there was immediately questionable. To release it, he needed a diversion, and to create that he had to call on the fleets that lay elsewhere. Upon them he would principally have to depend to get his flotilla across the Channel.

Napoleon therefore began to lay out the strategy through which he sought to attain his objective. It focused upon Toulon. That was inevitable. And in December 1803 he wrote to Ganteaume at Toulon instructing that the Toulon squadron, commanded by Admiral Latouche-Tréville, had to sail for Cadiz on 10 January 1804, subsequently to be joined by the Rochefort ships. Together they would be off Boulogne the middle of February to escort the flotilla across.

Nelson's blockade of Toulon therefore was the obvious first concern in all of this. But Napoleon saw no problem with that. Raise the spectre of French thrust towards Egypt and the Levant, and Nelson would be off to Alexandria. Then, with the right circumstances and good judgement, the Toulon fleet could lay a false trail. In preparation for such a ruse naval personnel at Toulon were told that the intended destination of the fleet was Taranto and the Morea (Peloponnesus), that forty thousand French troops would be embarked at Taranto. Troop movements were made in Italy as if to confirm that. As for the Toulon fleet itself, when it finally sailed it would steer a course that suggested eastwards. Then, when its pursuers were lost sight of, it would make for the Straits of Gibraltar. The principle of it, Napoleon told Ganteaume, had to be managed 'so that Nelson will first sail for Alexandria'.

Upon Toulon and Nelson the issue therefore decisively rested, which was no more than what Nelson expected when he arrived to start the watch that would run through an ensuing twenty months to its resolution off Trafalgar.

XXXV

TRIPOLI

As Nelson waited impatiently for his action off Toulon, the Americans were already heavily involved with theirs on the other side of the Mediterranean, against Tripoli.

The Bashaw of Tripoli had watched with interest and envy the arrival at Algiers in the autumn of 1800 of the American frigate *George Washington* with tribute for the Dey of Algiers and the subsequent compulsory diplomatic mission to Constantinople imposed upon the frigate's captain, William Bainbridge. Having absorbed that, the Bashaw told the American consul at Tripoli that he would wait six months for similar tribute, failing which he would declare war on the United States. On 14 May 1801, the time of his ultimatum having expired, the Bashaw ordered the flagstaff of the American consulate to be cut down as a declaration of war.

Bainbridge's rough experience had not sat well with an American government proud of the successful demonstration of the prowess of its young navy against France. A show of force to the Barbary powers had already been decided. A squadron of three frigates and a sloop was assembled and then sailed from Hampton Roads for the Mediterranean.

Command of the squadron was given to Commodore Richard Dale, who raised his pennant on the 44-gun *President*. Bainbridge was back, as captain of the 32-gun *Essex*, with Captain S. Barron commanding the 38-gun *Philadelphia*. Lieutenant Andrew Sterret had the 12-gun schooner *Enterprise*. American merchantmen were convoyed out and the flag shown, at Tripoli, Algiers and Tunis. Only at Tripoli was there belligerence and the first action in America's second naval war fell to the smallest member of the squadron, *Enterprise*.

On 1 August 1801 *Enterprise* encountered a 14-gun Tripolitan polacre. During a three-hour action the Tripolitan struck twice but immediately rehoisted colours when it thought that, with the pause, advantage had been gained over the American. *Enterprise* then decided to sink her without allowing further opportunity for trickery. But under heavy fire the polacre's captain appeared on deck, threw his ensign overboard and stood bowing low, until the American's fire stopped. *Enterprise* showed little damage. None of her crew was hurt.

The polacre, doubtless to its own considerable surprise, evaded being taken as prize. Dale's squadron had sailed with the curious stipulation that a ship that struck could not be taken as prize. Lieutenant Sterret accordingly threw all her armament overboard and stripped her of everything but a single sail and one spar to get her home. Such a peculiarity in a war where neutral Americans had too frequently found themselves held as prizes was hard for this young navy to swallow. Such a startling form of apparent innocence in that whole world at violent war could only have been regarded by all the other combatants as perversely inexplicable. President Jefferson explained it to Congress on 8 December 1801 in referring to the *Enterprise* incident after the squadron returned home: 'Unauthorised by the Constitution without the sanction of Congress, to go beyond the line of defence, the vessel being disabled from further hostilities, was liberated with its crew. The legislature will doubtless consider, whether, by authorizing measures of offence also, it will place our force on an equal footing with that of its adversaries.' And early in 1802 Congress authorized the capture and condemnation of any Tripolitan ships encountered by the American navy.[1]

By 1803 the Americans had established blockade of Tripoli as well as their own efficient protective watch on trade through the Straits of Gibraltar and across the Mediterranean. But in October 1803 they suffered severe setback.

The Americans were entirely on their own. The fact that the British had their own troubles with Barbary did not necessarily create any warmth between them and the Americans. Dangerously tense occasions could arise between them. Commodore Edward Preble of the 44-gun *Constitution* found himself alongside a large ship in the darkness of the Straits of Gibraltar. Through his trumpet Preble hailed the other and yelled the name of his ship, country and his rank. When he got no answer he threatened to fire a shot. 'I am about to hail you for the last time; if not answered, I shall fire into you.'

'If you fire a shot, I'll return a broadside. This is His Britannic Majesty's ship Donnegal, sixty guns.'

Preble told the stranger he doubted the truth of that and that he would lie alongside until morning until he could verify the identity. At daybreak *Donnegal* sent over a boat and the thing was amicably settled. But challenge from an American did not sit well with the British, who increasingly saw the build-up of the American navy as a threat they might yet have to confront on a larger scale.[2]

The command ships of the American Mediterranean squadron at this time were Preble's *Constitution* and 38-gun *Philadelphia*. On 31 October 1803 *Philadelphia*, commanded by William Bainbridge, was on station off Tripoli to intercept the Bashaw's privateers. He gave chase on sight of a ship close inshore. With Tripoli in plain view some three miles off Bainbridge decided to abandon the chase. They had come too far inshore and he wanted to get back to deep water. The wind was nearly a-beam and *Philadelphia* was doing a good eight knots. But even as Bainbridge ordered the helm a-port the lead gave new shallows and, before the ship lost any of her way she struck a reef, so hard that the whole vessel lifted up between five and six feet.

A desperate effort began to lighten *Philadelphia* and attempt to get her off. Guns were run aft in hopes of making her slide off astern. Then all guns were flung overboard, except for a few kept for defence. Anchors, too, were cut from the bows. The Tripolitan gunboats had begun to assemble. Bainbridge next ordered the water casks emptied, all heavy articles thrown overboard and the foremast cut. But the ship remained immovable. To save lives Bainbridge finally decided to lower his colours. Before the Turks and Arabs boarded the magazine was flooded, the pumps made useless and holes bored in the hull to make *Philadelphia* a complete loss.[3]

The Corsairs came on board, stripped the Americans of all their possessions and clothes, leaving them half-naked, and then took their prisoners ashore. They were delivered into the main hall of the Bashaw's palace before the Bashaw himself. It could hardly be otherwise. He had before him what was tantamount to treasure, for the 315 officers and men represented a golden ransom. The American officers were seated. After some interrogation they were all taken to another hall, where a meal was laid out. And then, fittingly, conducted to the house that had been the American consulate.

Apart from considerable ransom that now was inevitable, the Tripolitans also had one of the finest frigates on the high seas sitting before them. They immediately began to try to get her afloat and, in the course of a gale in November, she lifted off the reef. She was kept afloat by pumping and filling the holes that had been bored. Then, with the guns and anchors recovered from the seabed, Tripoli had the best ship that had ever been in Barbary possession. It was not to be for long.

In February 1804 one of the young officers with the Mediterranean squadron, Lieutenant Commodore Stephen Decatur, took his ketch *Intrepid* into Tripoli on a moonlit night intent on retrieving *Philadelphia*. He had an Arab-speaking Maltese pilot, who took *Intrepid* in slowly, with her officers and sailors all lying low on deck, concealed by the bulwarks. Decatur alone stood by the pilot. When *Philadelphia* hailed *Intrepid* the pilot answered that the ketch was Maltese on a trading voyage, that she had lost her anchors in a recent gale and wished to lie beside *Philadelphia* for the night. The North Africans then helpfully lowered a boat with fasts, cables for bringing the other ship alongside. *Intrepid* sent out her own boat and took the fasts, which were delivered to the men lying low and who, from where they lay, began drawing the ships close. But as they closed the Corsairs saw that *Intrepid* had anchors and began cutting the fasts, shouting 'Americanos'.

The Americans with strong pull then got *Intrepid* alongside. Decatur was the first aboard *Philadelphia*, followed by the others. After brief resistance the Corsairs leaped overboard. The frigate had not a sail on a yard and lacked her foremast. Getting her immediately underway was impossible. *Philadelphia* was then swiftly set alight. The fire spread so rapidly that *Intrepid* itself was endangered. The sweeps (long oars carried for when wind failed) were manned and the ketch got away.

The recapture and destruction of *Philadelphia* were canonized to become one of early heroic legends of the United States Navy.[4]

The American blockade of Tripoli and assault on its gunboats and armed xebecs continued, with *Constitution* and a small fleet of gunboats lying off the North African fortress. Decatur was to win more fame for himself when, in August 1804, on a mission to bombard Tripoli, he led an American force of gunboats and bomb vessels against the city's defending force of Tripolitan gunboats and galleys. The presence of the galleys provided the proper touch to what followed, for this was to be fighting that was the whole history of Barbary: galley fighting. Decatur learned that swiftly on jumping aboard the first of the enemy gunboats.

The Turkish captain was a man as large and powerful as the American. Decatur rushed him with a pike, which was seized by the Turk, wrenched away, and then turned on Decatur, who parried the blow. He slashed at the pike with his sword, to cut off its head. The sword broke on the iron. The Turk made another thrust. Decatur was weaponless. He had only his arm, which deflected the pike sufficiently that it merely tore at the flesh of his breast. Pushing the pike from his wound, he leaped along it to grab his opponent. The pike fell between the two. But the Turk's physical hold was greater than the American's. They fell down, and Decatur broke free from the Turk's grasp as they lay side by side. The Turk was reaching for his dagger but Decatur had hold of his hand. Decatur drew a small pistol from the pocket of his vest and passed his free arm round the body of the Turk and fired. The ball passed through the Turk and lodged in Decatur's own clothes. He jumped up. The Turk was dead, but another had his sabre raised above Decatur. As he brought it down a young American sailor sought to intercept the blow, and suffered his arm cut off. So it went among the others. Decatur's brother was among the fallen. The Turks eventually fell back, but they left behind memory of one of the fiercest close-combat encounters of the Great War; more distinctively, the first such of the United States Navy.[5]

This four-year war finally concluded by treaty on 4 June 1805. The United States had increased its force in the Mediterranean. No one was served by extending the struggle. Tripoli had been ready for peace before *Philadelphia* was wrecked. With so many prisoners in hand, continued confrontation had its value. The price of peace was $200,000 for the prisoners. This was lowered to $60,000, no further tribute to be paid. As many British sailors did, some Americans from *Philadelphia* were said to have been converted to Islam and had been taken into service aboard Tripolitan fighting ships and privateers.

It was hardly a grand victory, but America had won benefit from the war in that it had forcefully asserted warning to Barbary that it would no longer tolerate piracy on its commerce. The lesson had registered elsewhere. The British disliked every new manifestation before them of American naval power. This was a subject ever more frequently discussed in the pages of the *Naval Chronicle*. The easy cost of potential American naval enlargement was marvelled at by one *Chronicle* correspondent who, speaking of the 'formidable' navy of the United States, listed the total appropriations of the United States Navy for 1805 as merely $1,235,000. That sum covered everything, from pay for officers and men, to provisions, medical stores, repairs of vessels, marines and navy yards. All of that, he pointed out, was 'not much more than the yearly charge of two line-of-battle ships in the English navy, manned and with a year's provision'.[6]

XXXVI

WATCH

This longest watch, already six months underway off Toulon in January 1804, would remain as one of the finest examples of unrelieved duty and fully sustained seamanship that the naval world has known.

No one but Nelson could have maintained it in the sustained form that he gave to it. As Mahan put it: 'Nelson before Toulon was wearing away the last two years of his glorious but suffering life, fighting the fierce northwesters of the Gulf of Lyon, and questioning, questioning continually with feverish anxiety, whether Napoleon's object was Egypt again or Great Britain really.'

Cornwallis's ships were close to home waters. When necessary they could go off singly or in pairs to Plymouth or Portsmouth for repair, supplies or watering. For Nelson no such option existed. Minorca had gone back to Spain with peace. But the Spanish ports were under instruction to give him no assistance. Gibraltar and Malta were neither well provided nor well equipped. All the once-familiar ports on the Ligurian Sea were under French control or dominance. And with French troops already in Taranto and Brindisi his old friends the Neapolitan king and queen were in a perpetual panic to avoid provoking the French into seizing what remained of their kingdom. And nothing in the way of spares was sent out to him. His squadron therefore had to fend for itself in a Mediterranean as hostile or intimidated by France as he ever had known it.

Steady vigil upon Toulon had to be maintained but Nelson was responsible for the whole of the Mediterranean, not merely the watching ground of the western basin around the Golfe du Lyon. His watch ran as well across to the Levant, into the Adriatic, North Africa and through the Straits into the Atlantic even as far as Cape St Vincent.

Through all of this Nelson's fleet was on constant passage, when not watering and collecting provisions. The only ones who got ashore were those of the watering parties or similar excursions. Nelson himself never considered going ashore anywhere. 'I have made up my mind never to go into port till after the battle, if they make me wait a year,' he had said at the outset. And that commitment was resolutely kept. 'We cruise, cruise, and one day so like another that they are hardly distinguishable,' he could say when those days were calm and sunny. 'But hopes, blessed hopes, keeps us up, that some happy day the French may come out, then I shall consider my duty to my country fulfilled.'

Expectation was naturally high when he first arrived on station. That some great purpose was alive in Napoleon's mind and afoot everyone knew. But what? The mystery of it was the great excitement that drove and initially lifted Nelson. Battle was what he hoped for at once so that the victory he was sure of would simultaneously frustrate any thrust towards the Levant and eliminate the Toulon fleet from all further strategic calculations. But month after month the Toulon fleet gave no indication of stirring. For Nelson it was a bafflement that became an increasing strain upon spirit and steadily depleting resources. In one report to Prime Minister Addington he said Toulon was hard at work equipping two new 80-gun ships, therefore 'perhaps they wait for their being ready before they give us a meeting'. The effort to predict Latouche-Tréville's ultimate purpose grew ever more uncertain. To add to the strain there was concern about the intentions of the considerable French army gathering in southern Italy. Nelson believed Napoleon meant to go into Morea as a preliminary to Egypt. More immediately worrying was whether it intended invasion of Sicily. The calculations and predictions continued. On 16 January 1804 Egypt or Ireland were regarded as possibilities. On 10 February, 'Egypt is Bonaparte's object.'

That whole patrolling watch of the Mediterranean was organized through a pattern of numbered rendezvous, some of which served as the operating base for a cruiser or a small ship, with whom messages or instructions could be left. On any extensive operation ships could be instructed to rejoin or find instructions at a particular rendezvous, such as Number 97 at Cape St Sebastian, where a ship was always kept, and it always knew where at a particular time Nelson might be found. Message points were also established on shore at certain places.

What this widespread system finally rested upon, however, was Nelson's mode of blockade. The watch upon Toulon was central to everything. What he longed for, and with increasing anxiety waited for, was a movement of the fleet there, the fundamental reason for his own presence. But with the demand for so much movement and deployment constantly imposed upon his limited force extreme caution was necessary for maintaining the watch and yet coping with all the other demands. The French should always be kept guessing, never to know where they were with Nelson.

When Nelson arrived off Toulon the commander whom he succeeded there, Admiral Bickerton, was following St Vincent's principle of close inshore watch. Nelson changed that immediately and moved the fleet thirty to forty miles offshore. The object of that was twofold, principally for the empty sea before Toulon to lure the French out to battle but also for the watchers on the heights above the harbour never to know the real strength of the British force out there. 'Every opportunity has been offered the enemy to put to sea, for it is there we hope to realize the hopes and expectations of our country,' Nelson said, in despair for the lack of the required response.

How to meet the oncoming first winter was nevertheless his main preoccupation. 'My crazy fleet,' Nelson wrote. 'If I am to watch the French, I must be at sea, and if at sea must have bad weather; and if ships are not fit to stand bad weather they are useless.' The Golfe du Lyon was notorious for the ferocity of its weather. In their first winter there it was particularly bad. By September the weather was already intimidating, 'three days gale of severe blowing weather out of the seven, which frequently comes on suddenly, and thereby exposes the topmasts, topsail yards and sails, to great hazard, under every care and attention, and there are no topsail yards in store, either at Gibraltar or Malta'.

Nelson's knowledge of the Mediterranean enabled him to seek shelter points off the Spanish coast where the force of the gales was less. '. . . such a place as all the Gulf of Lyons, for gales from the N.W. to N.E. I never saw,' he wrote to the Duke of Clarence, 'but by always going away large, we generally lose much of their force and the heavy sea. By the great care and attention of every captain, we have suffered much less than could have been expected . . . I have always made it a rule never to contend with the gales; and either run to the southward to escape its violence, or furl all sails and make the ships as easy as possible . . . with nursing our ships, we have roughed it out better than could have been expected.'[1]

Seamanship could carry them far but eventually scarcely further as strain and lack of spares made ships unserviceable. Nelson was bitter as he watched the new French construction rising at Toulon. His affection and admiration for St Vincent could not suppress the anger he himself felt over the lack of foresight that had so reduced the navy. 'The French navy is daily increasing, both at Toulon and Brest, whilst ours is clearly going down hill,' he wrote in July. 'We made use of the peace, not to recruit our navy, but to be the cause of its ruin . . . if Admiralty do not very largely reinforce this fleet, so as to enable me to send some ships home, and others into port to refit, it cannot be kept at sea another winter.' He was resentful, too, of the greater flexibility in period on station that Cornwallis's ships got at Brest. 'If I was to do as they do in the Channel, I have not, by that mode of judging, four sail fit to keep the sea. I absolutely keep them out by management; but the time must come when we shall break up . . .'

Nelson's dominant suspicion that the preparations at Toulon and the heavy troop movements to the south of Italy were intended for a French invasion of Morea and eventually on to Egypt meant watch on Taranto and Brindisi. Companion to those fears was fear of seizure of Sicily. The Straits of Messina therefore had to be watched. There was constant fear for the safety of his old Neapolitan friends, King Ferdinand and Queen Maria Carolina. To ensure their escape should the French seize Naples itself Nelson sacrificed a ship of the line from his overstretched resources to lie in readiness at Naples. Genoa was blockaded because, as Nelson said, it served as 'the granary of the south of France and the north of Italy', meaning it brought in supplies from North Africa. With Nelson something close to a state of war in any event existed with Algiers. He took as deliberate insult the Dey of Algiers's expulsion of the British Consul-General, compounded by Algerine seizures of Maltese ships with enslavement of their crews. The Dey was threatened with a deadline for response after which British ships would be under orders to sink every Algerine ship they met. 'I will try and take or destroy his whole fleet, for I can stretch over to the coast of Barbary, between Tunis and Algiers.' Above all, the British trade convoys to and from the Levant had to be safely conducted.

Protection of convoys had become a particularly painful responsibility laid upon the central brief of Toulon. Apart from the Barbary predators, French privateers swarmed out of the Italian ports, as well as Spanish and North African ports. The situation had become such that no merchant vessel could sail without protection. 'I am pulled to pieces by the demands of merchants for convoys,' Nelson was to say. The Straits of Gibraltar had become a particular problem, with privateers operating from Algeciras, Ceuta and Tangier. That situation compelled convoys to be escorted at least as far as Cape St Vincent, where others took over. For Nelson the main problem was the same he had suffered in 1798, a lack of frigates, 'the eyes of the fleet', as he called them. He complained that from Cape St Vincent to the Adriatic he had only eight. There were nine other stations that should have been filled. 'I want ten more than I have in order to watch that the French should not escape me, and ten sloops besides, to do all duties.' To his old friend William Ball at Malta he bitterly declared, 'I wrote to the Admiralty for more cruisers until I was tired, and they left off answering those parts of my letters.'

When he had to, Nelson went into Spanish ports to demand provisions. But he established his main support at Sardinia's Madalena Islands, which lay off the north-east coast. There he found an anchorage where he could get water and wood, meat and fruit. He would declare that if Sardinia were lost, 'I do not think that the fleet can then be kept at sea'. Sardinia was worth fifty Maltas.[2] But as important as that was to him, greater still was the need for more ships: '. . . at this moment, when from the bad condition of many of the ships under my command, I can barely keep a sufficient force at sea to attend to the French fleet, I have not ships to send to Madalena: not less, my Lord, than ten frigates, and as many good sloops, would enable me to do what I wish, and what, of course, I think absolutely necessary.'

After just short of a year in the Mediterranean, Nelson could report 'not a ship refitted in any way, except what was done at sea'. Apart from *Victory* and *Amphion*, the other ships had been in the Mediterranean for years and were showing the wear and tear of it. They had been in constant expectation during the peace of going home, for repair and to give the men a rest. St Vincent's watch on the pennies was blamed for keeping them in the Mediterranean. Apart from lack of cordage, rigging and sails, there was a shortage of men, each ship in the squadron lacking around one hundred. But the severity of the manning problem in Britain itself meant he got nothing. 'We can send you neither ships nor men,' St Vincent was to write in response to the appeals that Nelson was to make for winter.

By keeping his crews constantly busy to steady routines Nelson kept their minds occupied and controlled any restlessness. As important as that, he always believed, was the health and wellbeing of his crews. It became even more so with such a seemingly endless unrelieved shipboard confinement. 'The health of this fleet cannot be exceeded,' he was frequently to say. Scurvy was rare, and instantly taken care of. In the Channel, by contrast, there were occasional severe outbreaks. Even after twenty months on that watch a new surgeon boarding *Victory* found that only one of her crew of 840 was confined to bed. It was the same with the rest of the fleet.

Nelson outlined his principles on health in a letter to an old medical friend, Dr Moseley at the Chelsea Hospital: 'The great thing in all military service is health; and you will agree with me, that it is easier for an officer to keep men healthy, than for a physician to cure them.' He recognized the necessity of mental change as well as the dietary, adding, 'Situated as this fleet has been, without a friendly port, where we could get all the things so necessary for us, yet I have, by changing the cruising ground, not allowed the sameness of prospect to satiate the mind – sometimes by looking at Toulon, Ville Franche, Barcelona, and Rosas; then running round Minorca, Majorca, Sardinia and Corsica; and two or three times anchoring for a few days . . . but shut very nearly out from Spain and only getting refreshments by stealth from other places, my command has been an arduous one.'[3]

He did better with the Catalans than elsewhere. When he sent one of his ships with sick on board into Rosas for provisions he instructed her captain to remain seven days, 'and during that time you are to cause your people to be supplied with fresh beef every day, with as many onions as you and the surgeon may deem necessary to remove any taint of scurvy which may have introduced itself among them. You are . . . to purchase fifty head of good sheep for use of the sick aboard the different ships, with sufficient corn and fodder to last them for a month . . . procure thirty thousand good oranges for the fleet, with twenty tons of onions, or any other vegetables that will keep eight or ten days . . . as many live bullocks for the ships' companies as you can conveniently stow, with fodder . . .'[4] To such captains who were sent in to get supplies for themselves and the fleet, he ordered 'strictest attention to ascertain the real quality of the provisions'. They were to cut pieces from the salted pork and meat they bought and then boil them, to see that they were good and did not shrink. Pease had to be similarly tested. All this 'for preventing complaints or discontent amongst the seamen, from the issue of bad provisions'.

His own health by comparison with that of his crews was, by his own constant account, poor and deteriorating. His failing eyesight was a main concern: 'I am nearly blind; however I hope to fight one more battle.' He always wore a green shade over his forehead to protect his eyes from strong light. He had no use of his injured eye. The strain upon the good eye was ceaseless, from hours of daily writing and reading official reports in the uncertain light of the Great Cabin as well as constant use of the telescope when on deck. His concern became more acute. To his agent Davison he confessed, 'My eyesight fails me most dreadfully. I firmly believe that, in a very few years, I shall be stone blind. It is this only, of all my maladies, that makes me unhappy.' He had reason for his fear, for the intensive post-mortem on him after Trafalgar was to confirm that if he had lived a few years longer and continued at sea he would have lost his sight totally. He suffered spasms, which his surgeon attributed to indigestion, and a persistent cough. And, as always in rough seas, from seasickness.

In those two years all was not, however, always the tedium of weariness and anxiety. When the weather was good and the pressures consequently eased there could be a comforting rhythm to his days. From the record of a typical such day in the summer of 1804 left by two of his doctors, Nelson's regimen as described by them strikes a distinctly modern note in its respect for moderation under exacting circumstances. He ate lightly and took a lot of exercise, walking the deck six or seven hours in the day.

Nelson rose at daybreak and breakfasted at six in summer, seven in winter. As one of the physicians recorded, 'At six o'clock my servant brings a light, and informs me of the hour, wind, weather and course of the ship, when I immediately dress and generally repair to the deck. Breakfast is announced in the admiral's cabin, where Lord Nelson, Rear Admiral Murray (the captain of the fleet), Captain Hardy, commander of the Victory, the chaplain, secretary, one or two officers of the ship, and your humble servant assemble and breakfast on tea, hot rolls, toast, cold tongue, etc., which when finished we repair on deck to enjoy the majestic sight of the rising sun.' The meals were prepared by Nelson's Italian chef, Gaetano.

Between seven and two p.m. Nelson was busy reading or writing letters and despatches, or examining reports from the rest of the fleet. In between he would walk a lot. At two the ship's band played, until three, when dinner was announced. There were seldom fewer than eight or nine at the table. If the weather was good admirals and captains from other ships were invited over. The meal usually consisted of three courses and a dessert of the best fruit, together with three or four of the best wines, as well as champagne and claret. 'At dinner he was alike affable and attentive to every one: he ate very sparingly himself; the liver and wing of a fowl, and a small plate of macaroni, in general composing his meal, during which he occasionally took a glass of champagne. He never exceeded four glasses of wine after dinner, and seldom drank three; and even those were diluted with either Bristol or common water.'

Coffee and liqueurs closed dinner about half-past four or five, after which the party walked the deck, with the band again playing. At six tea was announced and all returned to the Great Cabin where tea was served before seven, 'and, as we are inclined, the party continue to converse with his Lordship, who at this time generally unbends himself, though he is at all times free from stiffness and pomp as a regard to proper duty will admit, and is very communicative. At eight o'clock a rummer of punch with cake or biscuit is served up, soon after which we wish the admiral a good night.'

Whether Nelson would then retire was doubtful. One of the surgeons, Sir William Beatty, wrote that Nelson

possessed such a wonderful activity of mind, as even prevented him from taking ordinary repose, seldom enjoying two hours of uninterrupted sleep; and on several occasions he did not quit the deck during the whole night. At these times he took no pains to protect himself from the effects of wet, or the night air; wearing only a thin great coat: and he has frequently, after having his clothes wet through with rain, refused to have them changed, saying that the leather waistcoat which he wore over his flannel one would secure him from complaint. He seldom wore boots, and was consequently very liable to have his feet wet. When this occurred he has often been known to go down to his cabin, throw off his shoes, and walk on the carpet in his stockings for the purpose of drying the feet of them. He chose rather to adopt this uncomfortable expedient, than to give his servants the trouble of assisting him to put on fresh stockings; which, from his having only one hand, he could not himself conveniently effect.[5]

Those hours that he spent away from the quarterdeck with his papers were some of the heaviest, if only because of the strain upon his eyes, though the brain work was scarcely less. The multitude of issues he was called on to deal with meant, as it always did in the Mediterranean, endless diplomatic correspondence, and frequently direct diplomatic negotiation. The main part of this correspondence was with the British ministers or consuls at all the key points of the Mediterranean, drawing intelligence, offering his own judgement on issues. A key communication was with the British Embassy at Madrid, to ensure being always informed on Spanish intentions, and to communicate his own formal objections when facing problems on the Spanish coast.

The paperwork was enormous. Aboard *Victory* Nelson had two secretaries, one of whom, the Rev. Alexander Scott, was also chaplain. Scott was an accomplished linguist, an invaluable asset in the Mediterranean, where correspondence and documents at any point they touched invariably embraced use of several languages. Letters and documents found aboard prizes or taken from neutral ships were all carefully examined for intelligence. *Victory* at this time was probably better informed on events in Europe than Cornwallis at Brest. While news and correspondence from England could take at least two months and even three to get to *Victory* by sea, Spain's neutrality meant that it served as a medium for quicker communication. And through Spain Nelson got the French newspapers ten days to a fortnight after publication. He was fortunate that even in his isolation the French, Spanish and Italian papers allowed him a full grasp of the developments beyond his scene during one of the strangest and most politically eventful years of the Great War.

Britain, alone in a war whose real direction none could yet fathom, lay in unprecedented crisis at the start of the year. George III at mid-February fell ill and appeared to be losing his senses. What constitutional formula was there for such a crisis at such a time? The country, Pitt said, was in a state of difficulty and danger 'dissimilar to any former one'. With the king's illness and invasion threatening, the political scene became one of turmoil. In parliament Pitt on 15 March delivered a heavy censure on St Vincent for the poor state he had brought on a navy upon which the nation's survival depended. It provoked furious party exchange but touched painfully raw nerves as the flatboat fleet at Boulogne continued visibly to increase, and new ships rose to completion on the stocks from Flushing to Toulon.

On 7 May Addington's government collapsed and Pitt formed a new administration. Nelson knew of it in under two weeks. Henry Dundas, now Lord Melville, replaced St Vincent at Admiralty. On 18 May Pitt took his seat in parliament on his re-election. On the same day in Paris Napoleon was declared Emperor of France. Creation of a Napoleonic dynasty was seen as a counter to royalist insurrection and Bourbon revival. By associating Buonaparte with nobility reconciliation was sought with the Old France.

It proved surprisingly successful. Off Toulon on 3 June Nelson observed a heavy *feu-de-joie* salute for the declaration of emperor. 'There ends, for a century, all Republics!' he wrote to Emma.[6] He saw prospect of peace in that. But then hopefully added, 'I rather believe my antagonist at Toulon begins to be angry with me; at least, I am trying to make him so; and then he may come out, and beat me, as he says he did, off Boulogne. I owe him something for that.' But the watch was wearing him down ever more rapidly, especially since Latouche-Tréville had been making occasional brief sorties, none with any suggestion of challenge. These fleeting enticements totally unsettled Nelson. The tension and frustrated expectancy they raised over close to two years had worn him down. It was becoming unendurable. He applied for leave to return to England. If there were to be another winter on that command, he said, 'I shall be done up. The mind and body both wear out.' But then, with his usual resilience, 'I must not be sick until after the French fleet is taken.' And that in essence was what it was about. He wanted out, but knew he had to stay in.

What he in reality was suffering from was not a chronically weak physique but the huge weight of that frustration combined with the multiple allied responsibilities that lay upon him, for he was in remarkably good shape. In spite of his frequent complaint in his letters that he was unwell, one of the physicians aboard *Victory* was to say that 'though Lord Nelson's constitution was not of that kind which is generally denominated strong, yet it was not very susceptible of complaint from the common occasional causes of disease necessarily attending a naval life'. The post-mortem after Trafalgar would provide even stronger testimony of how fundamentally fit he was, declaring that 'all the vital parts were so perfectly healthy in their appearance, and so small, that they resembled more those of a youth, than of a man who had attained his forty-seventh year'. He, and his country, were therefore fortunate that the man upon whom all depended had a constitution that could continue to carry him through those two years of narrow confinement aboard his ship and the strain of coping on every day of it with an immovable burden of necessary deductions, any of which might be fatally wrong. By the end of 1804, however, it began to seem that he really could hold out no longer.

Then, as it seemed to be with everything that memorable year, there was sudden change. At the start of the war the British minister at Madrid had been instructed to warn Spain that peace with England absolutely depended upon 'the cessation of every naval armament'. But in September 1804 Napoleon had sent more sailors to the French ships at Ferrol there and the French, Spanish and Dutch ships in the harbour all showed signs of preparation for some operation together. The ambassador at Madrid was told to demand that all these activities cease. Simultaneously instructions were sent to Nelson to intercept four frigate treasure ships inbound to Cadiz from South America. The ships were to be held until Spain complied with the British demands. Four frigates were sent on this mission. The Spanish resisted and one of their frigates was blown up in the action. War with Spain was inevitable, a war that Nelson had not wanted, laying more burden upon him. Yet, it was that war and the movement it would bring that, as Mahan suggested, was probably the determining reason why Nelson at the last moment decided to remain in the Mediterranean instead of going home.

A surprising change had, meanwhile, occurred at Toulon. Admiral Latouche-Tréville had died unexpectedly on 20 August 1804 aboard his ship at Toulon. Command of the Toulon fleet passed to Admiral Villeneuve.

To Hugh Elliot, British Minister at Naples, Nelson wrote on 19 December, 'My cough, if not removed, will stay by me for ever. On the 12th the French fleet were safe in Toulon; but I am firmly of opinion before this day fortnight they will be at sea. What would I give to know their destination!' His firm surmise was based on the fact that seven thousand troops were reported to have been embarked.

Nelson's diary, 19 January 1805: Hard gales N.W. At three p.m. the *Active* and *Seahorse* arrived at Madalena, with information that the French fleet put to sea from Toulon yesterday. These frigates were close to them at ten o'clock last night, and saw one of them until two o'clock this morning. Unmoored and weighed. At twenty-eight minutes past four, made the general signal for each ship to carry a light, and repeat signals during the night, made by the admiral . . . From their position when last seen, and the course they were steering, S.or S.b.W., they could only be bound round the southern end of Sardinia.'

XXXVII

CHASE

THE long-deferred chase appeared to be over soon after it had begun, with Nelson repeating the error of the earlier chase of 1798 by making for Alexandria.

He had even less reason to blame himself than before. The winds and gales of the Mediterranean winter that he knew so well seemed to allow assured calculation. 'The French sailed with a strong gale at N.W. and N.N.W., steering South or S.W. on the 19th,' he wrote, when he already knew they were back in Toulon. He nevertheless still believed that he had been right. 'I have not a shade of doubt, but that Egypt was the original destination of the Toulon fleet when they sailed on January 17 1805.' For him at that moment such presumably it would be when they set out again.

With his scouting frigates fanning out before him, Nelson took the squadron to point after point on his way to the Levant, Cagliari, Palermo, Messina, Koroni, and arrived at Alexandria on 7 February. He was at Malta on the morning of 19 February, to learn there that the French fleet was back at Toulon in a badly crippled state.

The brief drama that played out in the western Mediterranean in January and February 1805 was the sad one of a fleet without sea time and experience and setting out at the worst possible season in defiance of that. But Villeneuve, who now commanded the Toulon fleet, had had no option. He had been ordered to set forth. With seven thousand troops embarked he had taken his fleet out into Toulon Roads on 17 January and sailed on the 18th with a strong gale that became tempestuous in the night. They were being driven so hard that *Seahorse*, the frigate that reported their departure to Nelson, had to work up to thirteen knots to get out of their way. By that time things would already have been going seriously wrong for Villeneuve. 'The Toulon squadron looked very well at anchor, with the crews well dressed and going through their exercise well; but when the storm came things were very different; they were not exercised for storms,' Villeneuve reported to Minister of Marine Decres. 'The few sailors mixed up with the soldiers were no longer to be found, while the latter could not stand on the decks, and only encumbered them. It was impossible to work the ship, and hence the yards carried away and the sails split, for in all the damages incurred there was as much clumsiness and inexperience as defectiveness in the articles supplied by the dockyards.' What had occurred had not surprised him. 'I had a presentiment of this before I sailed; I have now too painfully experienced it.'¹

Nelson offered a more dryly concise summation when he heard they were back in Toulon: 'Those gentlemen are not accustomed to a Gulf of Lyons gale, which we have buffeted for twenty-one months, and not carried away a spar.'

Napoleon naturally was displeased, and scornfully so: 'What is to be done with admirals who allow their spirits to sink, and determine to hasten home at the first damage that they receive? It would be requisite to give up sailing, and to remain wholly inactive, even in the finest weather, if an expedition is to be prevented by the separation of a few vessels. But the great evil of our Navy is, that the men who command it are unused to all the risks of command.'

Villeneuve could hardly be blamed for a situation forced upon him. He was indeed a man seemingly wary of risk, as at the Nile, where he had made practically no attempt to engage. Napoleon's choice of him to command the Toulon fleet after Latouche-Tréville's unexpected death accordingly had met with some surprise. His background was brave enough, and certainly experienced, but, as Jurien de la Gravière said, his 'mild and melancholy disposition, his retiring and ascetic temper, were ill suited to the ambitious part which the emperor intended for him'. Collingwood, who had Villeneuve as his prisoner for several days after Trafalgar, was to say, 'Admiral Villeneuve is a well-bred man, and I believe a very good officer; he has nothing in his manners of the offensive, vapouring and boasting which we, perhaps, too often attribute to Frenchmen.'

Villeneuve was forty-two, just five years younger than Nelson; between them now, to be played out over the next eight months, lay this final round in Napoleon's strategy of conquering Britain by invasion: what might be called the great chase to Trafalgar.

Napoleon was now on his third grand scheme within a year for bringing his whole fleet to support the Boulogne armada to enable it to cross the Channel. One way or another circumstances had meant that the first two schemes had fallen away. The schemes all supposed release of the ships blockaded at Brest, Rochefort and Toulon to form a single force. Central to the present plan and its predecessor was a divergence to the West Indies to draw Nelson there, the false trail, followed by a combined move upon the Channel. This third plan, like the others, was wildly ambitious in its supposition that all three forces could, when required, evade their blockades and, like armed detachments marching to a fixed rendezvous, easily form a union on fixed dates at fixed places. With this last scheme, however, there was an important new element. Spain had declared war on Britain on 12 December 1804. It had promised to have between twenty-five and twenty-nine ships of the line ready to serve with the French before the end of March.

With Villeneuve back in Toulon, on 2 March 1805 Napoleon gave new instructions to Villeneuve and Ganteaume. The Rochefort squadron of five line ships and four frigates under Admiral Missiessy had already got away and was in the West Indies. Ganteaume was to escape from Brest and go to Ferrol and release the fifteen French and Spanish ships in the port. He was then to make for Martinique where he would meet Villeneuve and Missiessy. He was to allow thirty days for Villeneuve to arrive if he was not yet at the rendezvous when Ganteaume got there. The combined force would then make for the Channel, where Napoleon hoped they would arrive between 10 June and 10 July. Ganteaume at that point would be commander in chief.

Villeneuve's orders were to clear Toulon as soon as possible, go to Cadiz, wait outside for the Spanish and one French ship in Cadiz to come out, and then head for Martinique, where he would wait forty days for Ganteaume.

The French fleet sailed again during the night of 29–30 March. Nelson's two watch frigates followed. One went off to inform Nelson, the other continued but then lost sight of the French. Nelson got the news on 4 April. Once again the nightmare conundrum of deciding where Villeneuve was heading. 'I am, in truth, half dead; but what man can do to find them out, shall be done,' he wrote to Ball at Malta. 'But I must not make more haste than good speed and leave Sardinia, Sicily or Naples for them to take, should I either go to the eastward or westward, without knowing something more about them.'[2] Scouting frigates were sent in every direction, but it was two weeks before he got positive information, from Gibraltar, that the French had passed through the Straits.

Villeneuve had passed Cartagena, where six Spanish ships lay. He had asked them to join him but the Spanish admiral needed time to load powder. Villeneuve did not want to wait and pressed on down to the Straits, through which he passed on 9 April. That same evening he anchored off Cadiz, after Sir John Orde had hastily retreated from that station with his five ships at sight of the superior force.

The Spanish commander at Cadiz was Admiral Gravina, who had played such a prominent role as British ally at Toulon in 1793. Cadiz sheltered the appearance of a mighty fleet, sixteen ships of the line, but they were in sorry state and short of crew. The fever that had recently ravaged Cadiz had carried away many of its sailors. Only six ships were serviceable, but only two of those managed to join Villeneuve in the few hours there. The others were left orders to steer for Martinique when they were ready. Gravina embarked sixteen hundred soldiers and at two in the morning Villeneuve was under weigh again.

The situation in which Nelson meanwhile found himself provided another classic example of the barrier that the Straits of Gibraltar represented if the wind was wrong for passing through, whether at the Mediterranean end or the Atlantic. Villeneuve had the good fortune to arrive on an east wind and to be borne swiftly through. After that a westerly set in. Strong west wind combined with the fast inflowing current from the Atlantic made passage through the narrow Strait a self-defeating effort.

On 26 April Nelson could say, 'From March 26, we have had nothing like a Levanter, except for the French fleet. I believe easterly winds have left the Mediterranean . . . It has half killed me; but fretting is of no use.'[3]

Nelson was off Tetuan on 4 May. This was the Moroccan bay close to Gibraltar, behind the headland on which Ceuta lay, and which the British navy used for watering and obtaining beef. While there a frigate from Gibraltar brought report that the French after clearing the Straits were rumoured to be bound for the West Indies. Nelson immediately made for Gibraltar. In the short time at Tetuan he had managed to water the whole fleet. He had called in all the transports that provisioned his fleet and was now clearing them of all they carried in preparation for a long, fast pursuit into the Atlantic.

Rounding Ceuta, still against a westerly, on 6 May *Victory* anchored in Gibraltar Bay, where the transfer of supplies from the transports continued. Officers from the ships, expecting to lie there until a levanter set in, sent their washing ashore. But, as can happen at the Straits, there was suddenly hint of change. As Nelson's secretary and chaplain Alexander Scott recorded, 'Off went a gun from Victory, and up went the Blue Peter, whilst the Admiral paced the deck in a hurry, with anxious steps, and impatient of a moment's delay. The officers said, "Here is one of Nelson's mad pranks." But he was right.' An east wind had begun to set in. They had arrived at two p.m. Four hours later they were on their way again. As Nelson said, 'The fleet was unmoored, the transports taken in tow, and at six o'clock the whole fleet was under sail, steering through the Gut.' In a few hours they were out in the Atlantic. Upon such caprice of wind, and such swift determined response, naval fortunes and naval history could turn.

Through ineptitude or hostility against Nelson, Orde had failed to send a frigate to the mouth of the Straits to await Nelson and give him some information on the last observed position of the French and the direction in which they were sailing. For Nelson such dereliction, such a total lack of conscience over necessary intelligence for an operation upon which the fate of Britain might depend, was incomprehensible. 'God only knows, my dear friend,' he wrote to Alexander Davison on 7 May, 'what I have suffered by not getting at the enemy's fleet, and when I naturally consoled myself that, at least, time would be given for Sir John Orde's frigates, who were naturally sent after them, to return to Gibraltar with information for me, I had the mortification yesterday to find that none had been sent there. Nor was it generally believed that Sir John Orde had sent after them; but this I cannot believe, and I must suppose that they have all been unfortunately captured.' The generosity of that supposition was a measure of his incredulity over such a fault.[4]

By now the mystery of the French fleet's destination and objective was stirring great alarm in Britain. The nation stood prepared for the massive assault it now fully expected. To match the camp of the Grand Army around Boulogne the British Channel coast had itself become a vast military camp. Various forms of soldiery, the regulars and others formed for the emergency, were camped around the towns or at the big army camps at Warley Common in Essex and Coxheath near Maidstone. New military roads connected the camps and new defensive positions. Along the South Coast dozens of Martello towers had been raised, with heavy guns able to fire in any direction. Across Romney Marsh a zigzag canal was being dug between Hythe and Rye, lined by earthworks, bastions and redoubts against which the Grand Army would have to fling itself. The Thames with its access to London was heavily defended, with a line of Indiamen moored across the river below Gravesend. These had been converted into floating batteries with 24-pounders providing heavy broadside. Heavy batteries flanked both banks of the river. In every town within twenty miles of the sea farm carts had been assembled for the quick evacuation of women, children under nine, the aged and the infirm. With any alarm, all horses, cattle and sheep were to be driven inland, or have their throats cut. Enormous beacons were set up on headlands and high ground reaching far inland, these to be set alight day or night in case of a landing by the French. A complete blackout was laid along the southern coast, with heavy punishment for anyone striking a light that might be interpreted as a signal to the enemy.

At Boulogne, too, all was at a pitch of readiness. The invasion flotilla had been stowed with all the ammunition, weaponry, saddles and rations that the Grand Army would need as it got ashore. Embarkation of the troops aboard the two thousand flotilla craft had been meticulously rehearsed to avoid wasting any minute of a tide. Already the advance guard of twenty-five thousand men could be embarked in less than ten and a half minutes, and could disembark in attack formation in less than thirteen minutes.

Forty signal stations between Le Havre and the Texel would flash news
of the arrival of the Combined Fleet and the launch of the invasion. And,
maintaining his personal watch on all of this, Napoleon riding his white
charger, Marengo, daily passed among his soldiers or along the cliffs, from
where he gazed down at the narrow band of water upon which he believed
his greater destiny would be borne.

With such a fevered state of apprehension laid upon it, Britain sought
news of the French fleet with increasing anxiety. The westerlies that had
so delayed and buffeted Nelson between Malta and Gibraltar had meant an
equally long gap in providing insight on the situation to Admiralty, where
another change had occurred. Lord Melville, the former Henry Dundas,
had been replaced as First Lord by Lord Barham, the former Charles
Middleton. Coming into office in the middle of this crisis, Barham was
angered by the lack of news from Nelson.

Nelson had been here before. The criticism and questioning were repetition of what had fallen upon him during the 1798 chase after Napoleon's
armada. He was again, as in 1798, on a long haul through obscurity and
speculation to determine the enemy's purpose and destination, he and he
alone in a position to do so, the one upon whom all depended, and for
that therefore poised to be as capriciously vilified as glorified. Over and
over again one is reminded of the rare and indomitable qualities of this
remarkable man, for one is continually confronted by the extremity of the
demand upon him: the double burden that irremovably lay upon him, of
diligent pursuit of the enemy in blinded circumstances that simultaneously
had to provide comforting reassurance of meaningful achievement to an
ever-volatile public mood.

At this moment, in an effort to end Britain's isolation, Pitt with his new
administration was trying to build a Third Coalition against France with
Russia and Austria. With Russia the effort had been stalled by the tsar's
request that, as a sop to Napoleon and to help restore European peace,
Malta should be garrisoned by Russians. Pitt's reply in refusing such a thing
forcibly brought it all back to Nelson and his squadron: 'It will not save
Europe. The Mediterranean, the Levant and Egypt, will be in the power
of France the moment a British squadron ceases to have for base a good
port protected by formidable fortifications . . . So, whatever pain it causes
us (and it is indeed great) we must give up the hope of seeing the alliance
ratified, since its express condition is our renunciation of Malta. We will
continue the war alone. It will be maritime.'

Nothing could have delivered with greater clarity the concerns that then
rested upon Nelson. Nor indeed that this was Sea against Land in a final
determination.

While agitation about Nelson's and the French fleet's whereabouts was

building in London, Nelson had arrived at Cape St Vincent, where he lay
to complete five months of provisioning. He now had more concrete intelligence. An American brig that had lain in Cadiz reported that the West
Indies had been regarded as the greatest probability. Nelson got the same
information from a British admiral who had just been dismissed from the
Portuguese service and who came aboard *Victory* at Cape St Vincent.

Apart from pursuit of Villeneuve, another chore had suddenly been laid
upon Nelson. Pitt, stirred by his new worries over Malta, had decided to
send five thousand soldiers to the Mediterranean. They were to be based at
Malta for the defence of Sicily if needed, with some for Gibraltar. Nelson
had been informed at Gibraltar that he was required to protect the inbound
convoy. He was therefore compelled to wait at Cape St Vincent until it
arrived, which was imminent. On 10 May he sent a sloop to Barbados, to
announce that he was coming, and wrote to Admiral George Campbell,
recently with him in the Mediterranean: '. . . tomorrow I start for the West
Indies. Disappointment has worn me to a skeleton, and I am, in good truth,
very, very far from well.'

The convoy arrived the following day, 11 May. Two ships of the line
formed the convoy's main protection. Nelson gave another from his fleet
for greater protection against the gunboats and privateers that lurked in the
Straits. Then he was on his way. *Victory*'s log recorded: 'At 6.50, bore up
and made sail. Cape St Vincent N.W. by N, distance 7 leagues.'

En route to Barbados Nelson prepared his plan of attack for when he
met Villeneuve. This appears to have been the first of the various outlines
that preceded that of Trafalgar. Its fundamental principle was the one that
remained with all of them, melee: 'The business of an English Commander-
in-Chief being first to bring an Enemy's Fleet to Battle, on the most
advantageous terms to himself, (I mean that of laying his ships close on
board the Enemy, as expeditiously as possible) and secondly, to continue
them there, without separating, until the business is decided.' How to arrive
at melee became, however, the main tactical problem. Nelson saw two
principal possibilities, or modes. One was to pass in traditional line, out of
gunshot, until the van ship of the British line was opposite the centre ship
of the enemy line. Then, at the signal, the British line would fall upon the
five or six lead ships of the enemy line, passing through the French line if
necessary. The other mode was simply Breaking the Line, cutting through
about the sixth ship from the van, with all the enemy's lead ships becoming
heavily engaged. With all of it an important principle was that in such close,
heavy battle every commander should have a clear sense of his individual
commitment. 'Signals from these moments are useless, when every man is
disposed to do his duty. The great object is for us to support each other,
and to keep close to the enemy, and to leeward of him.'[5]

On 3 June Nelson's scout frigate, *Amphion*, spoke to two British merchantmen, who confirmed that the French fleet was in the West Indies. The following day, at noon, the squadron arrived at Carlisle Bay, Barbados. Waiting for him was a report that had just arrived from Brigadier General Brereton, commanding the troops at Santa Lucia, that the enemy's fleet of twenty-eight sail had passed there during the night of 28–29 May. The local admirals and generals believed that Villeneuve's objective had to be Tobago and Trinidad. Nelson was urged to embark two thousand soldiers. He sailed the following morning for Trinidad, expecting that something like the battle at Aboukir Bay would follow when he entered the Gulf de Paria. But when he sailed into Paria on 7 June, cleared for action, they found only wide, hot and empty water. The information had been completely false.

Emerging from the Gulf on the 8th he got a report that the French were still at Martinique and had planned to sail from there on 4 June to attack Grenada and Dominica. Nelson made for Grenada and arrived noon on 9 June. All was safe. But there he received direct eyewitness that the French were seen on the 6th near the Saints, running northward, perhaps towards St Kitts and Grenada. On 12 June, off Antigua, he was told that Villeneuve at Guadaloupe had relanded all troops and stores that he had previously embarked there, and that last seen the French had passed Antigua and were standing to the northward, clearly on the way back across the Atlantic. Nelson then himself made for Antigua. On the morning of the 13th he landed the troops he had embarked, and scribbled a hasty note to his friend Alexander Davison: 'I have only one moment to say I am going towards the Mediterranean after Gravina and Villeneuve, and hope to catch them.'

For just two weeks they had had this chase among the islands. It was bad enough to finish on this inconclusive note, but far more shattering was the realization that they had been painfully close to a resolution of the chase. But for false information at the start, he told the Duke of Clarence, 'I should have been off Port Royal, as they were putting to sea; and our battle, most probably, would have been fought on the spot where the brave Rodney beat De Grasse.'[6] When he arrived at Barbados on 4 June Villeneuve was at Martinique, just a hundred miles away. One place or the other, their meeting would have been inevitable. All of it made the false run south from Barbados to Trinidad so much more galling. The name Brereton was to remain like an unremoveable irritant in Nelson's mind.

Villeneuve had been twenty-six days in the West Indies. He had been ordered to stay at least thirty-five, waiting to see whether Ganteaume would show up. But on 8 June he had captured fourteen British sugar ships. From them he learned that Nelson had arrived with his squadron. Villeneuve decided to cut, heading northwards for the prevailing westerlies that would carry him to Europe. On 28 June, before he could know the outcome of any of this, Napoleon remarked, 'I think that the arrival of Nelson may lead Villeneuve to return to Europe.' He knew his man.[7]

Napoleon at this time was in Italy. He had left Boulogne to have himself crowned as King of Italy at Milan Cathedral on 26 May. But his attention remained fixed on the grand strategy at Boulogne, trusting that Villeneuve and Ganteaume might yet accomplish their union, though the latter remained, as ever, tightly locked in at Brest by Cornwallis.

On course back to the Straits of Gibraltar Nelson in his letters justified his own decision in sailing back to Europe. 'I may be mistaken that the enemy's fleet is gone to Europe; but I cannot bring myself to think otherwise . . . My opinion is as firm as a rock, that some cause, orders, or inability to perform any service in these seas, has made them resolve to proceed direct for Europe.' One marvels again at the courage that such a decision required, the astuteness of it, followed by the resolution to stick with it, with the man being always aware that court martial and ignominy might fall as easily upon him as a shower of praise and decorations. As Mahan said of this, 'If Nelson had been an average commander he would have remained in the West Indies until he had tangible evidence that the French fleet had left them. This is no surmise. Many strongly urged him so to remain; the weight of opinion was against him; but he possessed that indefinable sagacity which reaches just conclusions through a balancing of reasoning without demonstrable proof.'

That sagacity had further remarkable demonstration on the way across. One of his frigates encountered an American merchant ship that reported having fallen in westward of the Azores with an abandoned ship that had evidently been set on fire. The American ship had taken away the logbook and some seamen's jackets, all of which the frigate's officers took and brought aboard *Victory*. The last entry in the logbook was 'Two large ships in the W.N.W'. That, said Nelson, indicated that the derelict had been a Liverpool privateer operating west of the Azores. The logbook contained a small scrap of paper. Nelson identified the characters as French. 'I can unravel the whole,' he said. 'This privateer had been chased and taken by the two ships that were seen W.N.W. The prize master who had been put on board in a hurry omitted to take with him his reckoning, and this dirty scrap of paper contains his work in his endeavour to find out his situation by back-reckonings. The jackets I find to be the manufacture of France, which proves the enemy was in possession of the privateer. I am satisfied those two ships were the advanced ones of the French squadron, and fancying we were close at their heels, they set fire to the vessel and abandoned her in a hurry. I infer from it they are gone more to the northward, and more to the northward I will look for them.'[8]

They were for a while surprisingly close. On 18 June Nelson wrote several letters marked with his position as two hundred leagues north of Antigua. The next day, 19 June, the brig *Curieux*, which he had sent off with his despatches to Admiralty on the night of 12 June, sighted the French fleet three hundred leagues north-north-east of Antigua. But thereafter, with Villeneuve on course for Ferrol and Nelson steering for the Straits, their courses diverged.

On 30 June Nelson sent *Amphion* to race ahead and to find out from the British consul at Tangier whether the French fleet had been seen passing through the Straits into the Mediterranean, instructing *Amphion* to rendez-vous with *Victory* off Cape Spartel.

'Private Diary. 18th July 1805. Cape Spartel in sight, but no French fleet, nor any information about them; how sorrowful this makes me, but I cannot help myself!'

Victory continued through the Straits to Gibraltar, where Nelson anchored on the 19th.

'Private Diary. 20th July 1805. I went on shore for the first time since the 16th of June 1803; and from having my foot out of Victory, two years, wanting ten days.'

It was, for the British navy, and history, a time of enormously critical decisions. Captain Bettesworth of *Curieux* made one of the most important of them.

It was already a week since he had parted with Nelson at Antigua when he saw the Combined Fleet. Fearing that he might miss Nelson if he sought to return to him, Bettesworth continued for Britain under a press of sail. He reached Plymouth on 7 July and raced to London, arriving there late the following night. At daybreak on the 9th the eighty-year-old First Lord, Barham, was given the news that Villeneuve was on his way back to Europe. Barham, angry that he had not had the news the night before, began giving his orders without bothering even to dress.

With astonishing rapidity Barham laid the net to catch Villeneuve and Gravina and their combined fleet. Orders were immediately sent to the blockade commanders at Brest and Rochefort to leave their stations and to be ready to meet Villeneuve at sea and bring him to battle. Cornwallis had his orders on the 11th to temporarily lift the Brest blockade, send some of his ships to Sir Robert Calder, then blockading Ferrol with ten ships. Cornwallis himself was to patrol in the Bay of Biscay. The Rochefort ships joined Calder on 15 July. They moved out into the Atlantic. Barham thus laid his net effectively across the course for Ferrol upon which the inbound Combined Fleet presumably would be set.

At eleven on the morning of 22 July, 112 miles off Cape Finisterre, Calder's force of fifteen ships of the line and two frigates sighted the

Combined squadrons with their twenty ships of the line, five frigates and three brigs.

Here at last was the action that all of Britain had been waiting for, the battle after which Nelson for two years had so earnestly sought and relentlessly pursued, for which he had lingered off Toulon season after season, weathered those countless gales, chased across the Mediterranean to Alexandria and back, and then across the Atlantic to the Caribbean and back. But battle it was not even to be.

The weather was foggy during the four-hour action and at times was so thick that ships could barely see those either ahead or astern of them. When the action had faded, Calder had two prizes, both Spanish, 74-gun *Firme* and 80-gun *San Rafael*, and considered that he had a victory, though he made no immediate claim of it. 'The victory was decidedly ours,' he was to say much later. Villeneuve, for his part, believed that he himself had had the better of it. 'As far as I could see, all the advantage of the combat was with us,' he said in his own report of the action. Two of Gravina's ships had struck, but Villeneuve himself had made no attempt to shy away from the action.

On the morning of the 23rd the two fleets were in sight of one another soon after light. But Calder made no further attempt to engage the Combined Fleet. Villeneuve believed that Calder was avoiding renewed action: 'At peep of dawn, I made signal to bear down upon the Enemy, who had taken their position at a great distance and endeavoured by every possible press of sail to avoid renewing the action.' Calder's own senior admiral, Charles Stirling, who had commanded the Rochefort blockade, and whose own ship *Hero* had been van ship in Calder's line, affirmed that the Combined Fleet had several times during the day formed line and descended towards the British. 'We never attempted to renew the action, or to lay our heads towards the enemy,' he told the court martial that eventually followed. 'It appeared to me that the Admiral's object was to cover the crippled ships.'

The same held true for the 24th, with the two fleets still in sight of one another. Did Calder take any step to direct the British fleet to bear up after the enemy on the 24th, Stirling was asked. 'I do not know any objection to the British fleet following the enemy, if the Admiral thought proper to do so,' he answered. 'We continued steering from the enemy.'

Calder's justification for not renewing the action was fear that, with blockade removed from Ferrol and Rochefort, the French and Spanish ships lying there were likely to come out to the assistance of the Combined Fleet, 'or they might be pushing to England, the invasion of which was an event daily expected'. He therefore 'thought it best to keep my squadron together, and not to force the enemy to a second engagement, till a more favourable opportunity'. His defensive pleas were echoed by his opponent.

Villeneuve, miserable with this operation from the start, wrote bitterly to Minister of Marine Decres: 'If, as I had reason to hope, I had made a quick passage from Martinique to Ferrol, had found Admiral Calder with six ships, or at most nine, and beat him, and . . . had I effected a junction at Brest, and cleared the road for the grand expedition, I should be the first man in France. Well! All that should have happened . . . Two gales have done us some damage, because we had bad masts, bad sails, bad rigging, bad officers and bad sailors. Our crew fell sick, the enemy had received information of us . . . The weather favoured him; unaccustomed to battles and fleet manoeuvres, each captain during the fog had no other idea than that of following his second ahead, and here we are the laughing stock of Europe.' And that, then, with those two dispirited reviews, was all there was to it.

In Britain the *Naval Chronicle* reflected the dark tone of public reaction: 'The French fleet did not run away; but on the contrary, owing to the particular manoeuvres of the Action, they may be said even to have pursued us . . . The account which the French have published in the *Moniteur*, allowing for their natural boasting and vanity, contains a greater portion of truth than usual.' For that to have appeared in the *Chronicle* so soon meant that naval officers must have been talking.[9]

Calder and Villeneuve lost sight of one another on 26 July. Villeneuve made for Vigo, and then Corunna/Ferrol, where twenty-nine French and Spanish ships were brought together. Calder joined Cornwallis off Brest on 14 August.

At the Straits of Gibraltar on 25 July Nelson received a newspaper account of the news of Villeneuve that *Curieux* had delivered to Barham. He immediately took his squadron north, believing that Villeneuve was bound for Biscayan ports, and hoping that opportunity had not yet entirely evaded him. On the afternoon of 15 August he joined Cornwallis off Ushant, just a day after Calder had joined. Here he was mortified to get the first news of the action with Villeneuve.

For Nelson, of course, smarting that he had missed by a notch what he had suffered so much to obtain, there could not have been a more favourable opportunity than the one that Calder had had. He was immediately regretting that Captain Bettesworth with *Curieux* 'did not stand back, and try and find us out. I feel very unlucky.' Calder, who after the battle of Cape St Vincent had sought reprimand from Jervis against Nelson for breaking the line, had always been among those jealous of Nelson, or who resented his public fame. But, as one who only recently on his pursuit of Villeneuve had himself been feeling again the sting of public fickleness, Nelson's sympathy for Calder was spontaneously generous. When he received a packet of newspapers from his old colleague,

Captain Thomas Fremantle, to whom he immediately wrote, he said, 'I was in truth bewildered by the account of Sir Robert Calder's Victory, and the joy of the event; together with the hearing that *John Bull* was not content, which I am sorry for. Who can, my dear Fremantle, command all the success which our Country may wish? We have fought together, and therefore well know what it is. I have had the best disposed Fleet of friends, but who can say what will be the event of a battle? And it most sincerely grieves me, that in any of the papers it should be insinuated that Lord Nelson could have done better. I should have fought the enemy, so did my friend Calder; but who can say that he will be more successful than another? . . . You will forgive this dissertation, but I feel upon the occasion.' How could he not? He was expressing that incalculable balance of win and lose upon which every risk in military fortune rested, upon which every reputation precariously swung, and where he himself had so often come close.[10]

Cornwallis, sympathetic to all that Nelson had endured, dispensed with the customary formal visit that Nelson would normally make to his commander in chief and told him instead to proceed at once to Portsmouth to take his long-deferred leave. On 18 August Nelson anchored at Spithead. A post-chaise hired in Portsmouth the next day took him home, where he arrived at six in the morning on the 20th. No one summed up his achievement of the past two years better than Hugh Elliot, British minister at Naples: '. . . you have extended the powers of human action. After an unremitting cruise of two long years in the stormy Gulf of Lyons, to have proceeded without going into port, to Alexandria, and from Alexandria to the West Indies, from the West Indies back again to Gibraltar; to have kept your ships afloat, your rigging standing and your crews in health and spirits, is an effort such as was never realised in former times nor, I doubt, will ever again be repeated by any other admiral.'[11]

XXXVIII

PRELUDE

THERE was now a fast quickening of events that suggested that some form of climax must soon be reached, though whether on land or sea or both still remained unpredictable.

On 26 May 1805 Napoleon had crowned himself King of Italy in Milan. Nine days later, on 4 June, he annexed the Ligurian Republic, which to the world meant Genoa with its rich commerce, banking and great strategic significance in the Mediterranean. That ended the tsar's cavilling with Pitt over Malta. On 9 August Russia pledged itself to the new coalition with Britain and Austria. War on the Continent now appeared inevitable.

The seizure of Genoa and the Milan coronation had harshly signified Napoleon's increased domination of Italy, which at once became as alarming to the tsar as it was to Pitt. Both feared the loss of Naples and Sicily, Russia because of threat to its possession of Corfu and its new position in the Levant, Pitt of course fearing for Egypt and India.

Between them they wanted evacuation of Italy, restoration of the king of Sardinia, restored independence for Holland and Switzerland, and withdrawal from Hanover and northern Germany. There was small chance of winning any of that from Napoleon. The emperor nevertheless was in haste to launch his assault across the Channel before he was landed with a new war on the Continent. The Austrians were already moving troops westwards. On 31 July Napoleon wrote to Talleyrand, 'All my news from Italy is warlike, and indeed Austria no longer observes any concealment.'

Napoleon returned to Boulogne on 8 August and he there got news of Villeneuve's action with Calder off Finisterre. Villeneuve's failure to cope with the British fleet and to make it to Brest, together with the new urgency beyond the Rhine, made volatile Napoleon's impatience to launch his move across the Channel. On 7 August Villeneuve had outlined his intentions to Minister of Marine Decres. He would increase his fleet, he said, with the five French ships that had been blockaded in Ferrol and would send a frigate to find the Rochefort squadron of five. With his enlarged force he would then make for Brest. Villeneuve added the proviso, however, that should he consider that circumstances were against him, he would then make for Cadiz to await a better opportunity. Napoleon had allowed him that discretion in a letter on 26 July, but only as something of dire emergency.

Villeneuve's continuing distress with what lay upon him and his own disbelief in its feasibility was expressed to Decres on the 11th. After the encounter with Calder he had even less faith than before in the ability of his worn twenty-nine ships of the line and their inexperienced crews to stand up to a British force, even an inferior one. He knew that he was under close watch and that the main British fleet would be directed upon him as soon as he sailed. 'I am about to set out, but I know not what I shall do,' he said. And that had to be perhaps the most despairing cry ever uttered by any commander, land or sea, upon whom the main tactical thrust of a mighty campaign rested. He added, 'I am far from being in a position, I deeply regret to say, in leaving this place with twenty-nine ships, to be able to engage a similar number of the enemy. I do not fear to tell you, indeed, that I should be hard put to it if I met with twenty.' But the assumption nevertheless was that he would be heading for Brest when he sailed on 13 August.[1]

Although he set out for Brest, Villeneuve began by seeking the Rochefort squadron of five. A frigate had been sent out in advance to find them and deliver them to rendezvous. On 15 August, off Finisterre, Villeneuve sighted three warships on the horizon: two were British, the third the frigate he had sent in search of the Rochefort ships and which had been captured. He then encountered a merchantman who told him that a force of twenty-five British ships was in the offing. The information was entirely false, fed to the Danish skipper by the captain of one of the British watch frigates previously in sight. Still believing himself inadequate to meet any large British fleet Villeneuve that evening ordered course for Cadiz.[2]

That same day Napoleon, in full expectation of Villeneuve's imminent arrival, held a grand parade of his army on the sands by Boulogne. He was at the height of his expectation. So complete was it that a letter was sent by special courier to Villeneuve at Brest: 'Vice-admiral, I trust you have arrived at Brest. Make a start. Lose not a moment and come into the Channel, bringing our united squadrons, and England is ours. We are all ready; everything is embarked ...' But, as his aide-de-camp, de Ségur, was to express it, 'At the very moment when the advent of this unhappy Villeneuve was more than ever hoped for and expected before Brest and in the Channel, the admiral was turning his back on us.'[3]

The first man to feel the impact of that was Pierre Daru, the historian who at that time was Chief Clerk in the War Department. On arriving for a consultation with the emperor Napoleon walked up to him and cried,

'Do you know, do you know where Villeneuve is now? He is at Cadiz! – at Cadiz!' And that very morning he dictated to Daru his first instructions for the silent withdrawal from Boulogne of several divisions of troops, to be moved by rapid marches to the Rhine.

When Cornwallis heard that Villeneuve had sailed from Ferrol he sent Calder and most of the Brest blockade south. Only sixteen ships were left on station. With the force off Brest so reduced it was argued that Villeneuve had missed his one great opportunity. But that and the severe censure of Villeneuve overlooked his true state of mind. After the action with Calder off Finisterre he was quite incapable of any strategic compulsion such as was required of him. Once out of Ferrol he wanted away, and he went. His overwhelming emotion appears to have been dread of further humiliation. On his way to Cadiz he wrote a despatch explaining his action: 'The reunion of the forces of the enemy and their knowledge of all my proceedings since my arrival on the coast of Spain has left me with no hope of being able to carry out the great object for which the fleet was destined.'

Napoleon unleashed upon the unfortunate Villeneuve a flood of invective and insult that embraced the entire navy. 'What a navy! What an admiral! What sacrifices for nothing! My hopes are frustrated.'[4] Villeneuve was accused of 'excessive pusillanimity'. But the worst outburst followed when Decres sought to restore a sense of proportion.

In a letter to Napoleon Decres declared what he himself and Ganteaume as well as Gravina had always believed, that the idea of using the Combined Fleet to release the Brest fleet had been impracticable, that Villeneuve never would have succeeded against the full concentration of British naval power and that Napoleon was fortunate that 'an act of Destiny preserves your Majesty's fleet for other operations'. Napoleon's response on 4 September, unsurprisingly, was apocalyptic. Decres and everyone connected with the navy were incapable. The English would be reduced when France had two or three admirals who were willing to die. Ganteaume was a clod, Gravina was an ass, Villeneuve was a coward and a traitor who had no plan, no courage, no insight, and who would sacrifice everything to save his own skin. As for Decres himself, he had better not write a letter like that again.

On those histrionics history turned. By 25 August Napoleon had begun moving his soldiers out of the vast camps above Boulogne. The invasion was over. By 28 August the army was in full movement. On 29 August the Army of England became the Grand Army. Some regiments were left to guard the flotilla, obstinate belief that the chance might yet be there for its use, but the main force of soldiery was marching towards the Rhine. Napoleon himself remained at Boulogne until 3 September. By 7 October he stood at the head of an army of 200,000 before the Danube, where the Austrians were holding the bridges between Ingolstadt and Ulm.

Villeneuve had entered Cadiz on 22 August. Collingwood's blockade of three ships of the line and a frigate was immediately augmented by Calder's eighteen line ships and another four from Gibraltar. Once again, Villeneuve and his fleet were tightly locked in. He sat down to further justify his diversion to Cadiz in a series of letters to Decres, pleading the fleet two thousand short of its strength, suffering frequent desertions and with seventeen hundred men in hospital. He was, he said, plunged into 'an abyss of misfortune', overcome by his inability to do his part in 'the grand design'. His immediate situation in Cadiz only added to that despair.

The French found themselves intensely unpopular in Cadiz. The loss of the two Spanish ships in the action with Calder had caused great distress in the city because they were based in Cadiz and manned from there. The news was fresh when Villeneuve arrived. The belief was that the Spanish ships had been deserted and sacrificed by Villeneuve. The Spanish navy held a historic command in Cadiz more consciously felt than in the other naval centres of Spain. Such a sense of injury to naval pride was therefore intense there. The city, besides, was in mourning from a yellow fever epidemic that had raged for a year. Supplies were short and the sudden demands of the Combined Fleet added to the resentment. Everything was scarce, food as well as material for refitting the ships. The authorities refused to give anything without hard money, refusing French paper money. They only complied when ordered to do so from Madrid. The hostility of the Cadiz populace caused leave ashore to be stopped aboard the French ships because of insults and attacks upon seamen. It was said that hardly a night passed without the dead bodies of assassinated French seamen being found on the streets. Admiral Gravina, who shared the prevailing feelings over the Calder action and the lost Spanish ships, had wanted to resign but was prevailed upon to stay by Godoy, the Spanish Prime Minister. Apart from all of that, Villeneuve was also conscious of criticism of his leadership among his own officers, of not pursuing Calder, of not continuing to Brest. Against that background Villeneuve began to receive from Decres the violent criticisms from Napoleon, though much softened in transition by the sympathy and affection Decres felt for Villeneuve, whom in many ways he sought to protect.

On 16 September, a week before leaving Paris for the Danube, Napoleon sent Villeneuve new instructions. The Combined Fleet should at once pass into the Mediterranean, pick up the Spanish fleet at Cartagena, land the four thousand soldiers he carried at Tarentum and then take the fleet to Toulon. Suddenly the presence of the fleet at Cadiz fitted perfectly Napoleon's new campaign on land and its thrust into the Mediterranean. That would seem to have justified Decres's statement that destiny had preserved the fleet for other operations. Whether Napoleon then recognized that or not, no such admission escaped the emperor. He had, in any event, ordered Villeneuve to be superseded by Admiral Rosily, who was to leave Paris on 24 September and was told to hand the recall personally to Villeneuve. That pending demission Decres hesitated to pass on immediately to Villeneuve. His compassionate feelings for Villeneuve put him in such an emotional state that he was barely able to draft the order of recall to give to Rosily. As Jurien de la Gravière tells it, 'He wrote the draft of the order of recall with a trembling hand. He, whose pen was so ready, whose style was so clear and flowing, now blotted and altered twenty times the five or six lines by which he informed that unhappy officer of his recall, and the emperor's intentions.'[5]

Nelson's respite was to be three weeks and a day. It was in the domestic sense without doubt the most tranquil and happy period of his life, if not entirely blissful because of the hovering call back to duty that was ever present.

He had been happy before, even with his wife, Fanny, particularly during the period when she had tended his wounded arm after Tenerife. But Fanny had never been a passion. She existed behind the screen of gentility, the demure and the polite, that had offered nothing to match or meet his own spirit, offering instead a motherly protective concern for his safety and wellbeing that could be an irritant, someone to retreat to for a recuperative interlude, then to escape. Emma Hamilton's own concern derived from the emotional power of her passion. Her whole life offered a blaze of spirit, tumult equal to his own. In her exuberance, even in her coarseness, Nelson found the necessary union that satisfied him. They both understood the wild and the rough. But now in their new home at Merton there was something new. It was experience of the settled, the taste of a calm that each of them had finally come to and now wanted more than that which had driven them.

Merton to its visitors at this time offered a warm family atmosphere, as the Earl of Minto found when he paid a visit. At dinner he was surrounded by Nelson's surviving brothers and sisters and their families, with Emma at the head of the table and Emma's mother at the other end, and Horatia among the many children. 'I had a hearty welcome,' Minto said. 'He looks remarkably well and full of spirits. His conversation is a cordial in these low times. Lady Hamilton has improved and added to the house and the place extremely well, without his knowing she was about it. He found it already done. She is a clever being, after all: the passion is as hot as ever.'[6]

Promptly gone, it seemed, were the hot flushes from tension, the dejected weariness, headaches and low-spirited outlook that had accompanied him as far as Spithead. A nephew who called at this time wrote, 'Lord Nelson in private life was remarkable for a demeanour quiet, sedate, and unobtrusive, anxious to give pleasure to every one about him, distinguishing each in turn by some act of kindness and chiefly those who seemed to require it most ... in a little knot of relations and friends, he delighted in quiet conversation, through which occasionally ran an undercurrent of pleasantry, not unmixed with caustic wit. At his table he was the least heard among the company, and so far from being the hero of his own tale, I never heard him voluntarily refer to any of the great actions of his life.'

The only interruptions to this descent upon him of the quietly loving and sedate were necessary visits to London. For the first two weeks of his stay in England nothing was known of the whereabouts of Villeneuve, whether he was on his way to Brest or Ireland or the Mediterranean. It was hoped that Calder with his eighteen ships might meet him. 'Mr Pitt,' he wrote on 29 August, 'is pleased to think that my services may be wanted. I hope Calder's victory (which I am most anxiously expecting) will render my going forth unnecessary.' That easy deferring of the main action to another would have been quite unimaginable at any other time.[7]

Nelson was mobbed wherever he went in London. 'It is really quite affecting to see the wonder and admiration, and love and respect of the whole world,' Minto wrote, after experiencing that public enthusiasm alongside Nelson, 'and the genuine expression of all these sentiments at once, from gentle and simple, the moment he is seen. It is beyond anything represented in a play or in a poem of fame.' It does indeed seem remarkable for a time when there was nothing remotely resembling the saturation that all public faces get from the twenty-first century's news media.

On one of his visits to London Nelson found himself in an anteroom with a military figure. Neither knew who the other was. The other man was Sir Arthur Wellesley, the future Duke of Wellington who, in recall of their initial exchange, said, 'He could not know who I was, but he entered at once into conversation with me, if I can call it conversation, for it was almost all on his side and all about himself and, in reality, a style so vain and so silly as to surprise and almost disgust me.' Nelson, guessing some stature in the man, went outside to ask who he was. When he returned Wellesley found someone quite different. 'All that I had thought a char-latan style had vanished and he talked of the state of the country and of the aspect and probabilities of affairs on the Continent with a good sense and a knowledge of subjects both at home and abroad that surprised me equally and more agreeably than the first part of our interview had done; in fact, he talked like an officer and a statesman.'

Thus the two figures that for Britain symbolized the Great War briefly met.

The summons that Nelson knew was inevitable arrived at five in the morning on 2 September. Henry Blackwood, whom Collingwood had imme-

diately despatched in *Euryalus* to take to London the news of Villeneuve's
arrival at Cadiz, had demonstrated his affection for Nelson by going straight
to Merton. Nelson was already up and dressed when Blackwood arrived.
'I am sure you bring me news of the French and Spanish fleets,' Nelson
said even before Blackwood delivered his news, adding, 'and I think I shall
yet have to beat them.' The following day he wrote, 'I hold myself ready
to go forth whenever I am desired, although God knows I want a rest; but
self is entirely out of the question.' Two days later his luggage went to
Portsmouth.

Nelson was particularly touched by Pitt's courtesy when they took leave:
'Mr Pitt paid me a compliment which, I believe, he would not have paid
to a Prince of the Blood. When I rose to go, he left the room with me and
attended me to the carriage.'

On 12 September Minto went to Merton and to say farewell. 'I stayed
till ten at night and I took a final leave of him. He goes to Portsmouth
tonight. Lady Hamilton was in tears all day yesterday, could not eat, and
hardly drink, and near swooning, and all at table.'[8] The following night, 13
September, Nelson left Merton, after going to Horatia's bed and praying
over the sleeping child. His diary said, 'At half past ten drove from dear
dear Merton, where I left all which I hold dear in this world, to go serve
my king and country.' He arrived at Portsmouth at six a.m. and at two
p.m. embarked from the beach where the 'bathing machines' were kept,
to avoid crowds at the usual place. But they came all the same, many in
tears, some kneeling down before him to bless him as he passed. 'I had
their huzzas before,' he said to Hardy in the boat. 'Now I have their hearts.'
From *Victory* he wrote to Emma: 'I intreat, my dear Emma, that you will
cheer up; and we will look forward to many, many happy years, and be
surrounded by our children's children . . . My heart and soul is with you
and Horatia . . . For ever, ever I am yours most devotedly.'

On 26 September *Victory* joined the fleet off Cadiz. 'The reception
I met with on joining the fleet caused the sweetest sensation of my life.
The officers who came on board to welcome my return, forgot my rank as
commander-in-chief in the enthusiasm with which they greeted me.' He laid
before them his intended plan of attack 'and it was not only my pleasure to
find it generally approved, but clearly perceived and understood'.

The question now was how to extricate the Combined Fleet from Cadiz
and to bring it to battle. The fear of Villeneuve taking the fleet into the
Mediterranean was always present. Both Nelson and Collingwood, ignorant
of Villeneuve's new instructions, believed that to be the intention. Daily,
with increasing impatience and exasperation, they watched and waited.

On 1 October, in preparation for leaving port, Villeneuve began
embarking the four thousand soldiers who had been put ashore. A persistent

westerly prevented an immediate attempt to sail. When the wind changed
to the east on the 7th Villeneuve immediately signalled to weigh but, as was
common at that season, the wind swung back to the west. The following
day Villeneuve called a Council of War aboard the flagship, with seven
French and six Spanish officers. These included Villeneuve's flag officers,
his second Rear Admiral Dumanoir le Pelley and Rear Admiral Charles
Magon, and the Spanish admirals Gravina, Alava, Cisneros and Escano.

It is notable that the three principal French commanders had all come
up from the old navy. Villeneuve, Jurien de la Gravière said, was 'undoubtedly the most accomplished officer, the most able tactician, whatever people
may say, though not the most resolute man, that the French navy then
possessed',[9] which can seem a remarkable compliment to a man who had
sat out the Battle of the Nile. Dumanoir le Pelley, thirty-five, had been
second-in-command under Linois at Algeciras. Magon had been with
de Guichen in the three battles with Rodney during the American War.
Relations between Villeneuve and the other two were said to have been poor.
Dumanoir had resented being superseded by Villeneuve at Toulon after the
death of Latouche-Tréville; Magon had been incensed that they had not
renewed action with Calder at Finisterre. Of the three Spanish chiefs, two,
Gravina and Alava, had both seen service in the American War. Gravina,
forty-nine, was of course especially well known to the British having been
second to Hood at Toulon. Cisneros, thirty-five years in the Spanish navy,
had been a commander at the Battle of Cape St Vincent.

The council was a charged, bitter gathering, fraught with implications
from the French of a lack of will and even courage on the part of the Spanish
and from the latter sharp reminder that they took the brunt at Finisterre.
What both sides agreed, however, was that the Combined Fleet was not in
fit state for battle, that the ships were ill-equipped, short of men and that
many of those they had lacked training. The fleet nevertheless began to
move from the inner harbour to the roadstead.

As the prospect of unavoidable action loomed, Villeneuve reviewed his
own tactical possibilities, with frank acknowledgement that his difficulty
was abandonment by Nelson of the established and conventional. Villeneuve
therefore broadly anticipated Nelson's battle plan. 'He will not confine
himself to forming a line of battle parallel to ours,' he told his officers. 'He
will endeavour to surround our rear, cut through our line, and to bring
groups of his ships upon those he has cut off, to enclose and overwhelm
them.' To counter that he proposed the very thing that Nelson himself
sought, melee. Villeneuve would form line, but he, too, was giving licence
to abandon the former strict rule of keeping station. 'All the efforts of our
ships should be directed to the support of those attacked, and to closing
round the Admiral, who will set the example . . . It is much more by his

own courage and love of glory that each captain should be directed, than by the Admiral's signals; who, being himself engaged, and enveloped in smoke, may not, perhaps, have the power of making any.'[10] Nelson was to issue practically the same instruction.

Villeneuve, meanwhile, had learned unofficially that Rosily was to succeed him. Rosily was already in Madrid. He should have left there on 14 October but his carriage had broken down and, once repaired, the journey from Madrid to Cadiz would require at least ten days.

On the 18th the wind appeared to be shifting eastward. Several of Nelson's ships had been seen entering the Straits. This was a frequent occurrence as ships were detached to go and fetch water and fresh provisions. This was Villeneuve's opportunity. He sought to restore himself and had no intention of leaving the action to Rosily. He ordered the fleet to start moving out, a slow process that only ended on the morning of the 20th. No sooner out than the wind appeared to be changing to a south-west. Nothing could have been more convenient for passing along the coast, past Cape Trafalgar, and into the Straits.

Within two hours of the Combined Fleet starting to work out of Cadiz the news reached Nelson, lying fifty miles off. The watch system had been beautifully laid out, with signals passing from Blackwood's *Euryalus* posted close off Cadiz to the 'repeating' frigates, which were spaced for swift visual passage of messages masthead to masthead. A midshipman aboard *Euryalus* wrote, 'The morning of 19th October saw us so close to Cadiz as to see the ripple of the beach and catch the morning fragrance which came out of the land, and then as the sun rose over the Trocadero with what joy we saw the fleet inside let fall and hoist their topsails and one after another slowly emerged from the harbour mouth.' Blackwood himself sat down to write to his wife, 'What think you, my own dearest love? At this moment the enemy are coming out and as if determined to have a fair fight . . . At this moment (happy sight!) we are within four miles of the enemy, and talking to Lord Nelson by means of Sir H. Popham's signals . . . You see, dearest, I have time to write to you and to assure you that to the last moment of my breath, I shall be as much attached to you as man can be . . . The day is fine and the sight magnificently beautiful.'

In Cadiz itself it seemed that the whole of the city's people had crowded to the harbour walls to watch the departure. Every church had been packed through the day with wives and mothers and other family members. At some churches the people had to be admitted in relays. So recently struck by yellow fever, this seemed another holocaust upon them, for the men they were sending off had little faith in the action to come.

On the 20th, with the whole Combined Fleet outside, the wind was from the south-west and strong. But it gradually went down. Through that day

Blackwood in *Euryalus* and with the rest of his frigates maintained watch on the Combined Fleet while Nelson sought to place himself between Capes Spartel and Trafalgar to prevent Villeneuve passing into the Straits. Nelson, entertaining a number of midshipmen at dinner, said, 'Tomorrow I will do that which will give you younger gentlemen something to talk and think about for the rest of your lives, but I shall not live to know about it myself.' This assumption of his death was a familiar refrain from him before battle. Given his exposure on the quarterdeck it was always a natural one. But this time it was something that was not as lightly taken as before. Everything that he had expressed at Merton and in his correspondence suggested that he earnestly wished to survive and return to Emma, Horatia, his new home and the rewards that would be his. In his last letter to Emma he said, 'May the God of battles crown my endeavours with success; at all events, I will take care that my name shall ever be most dear to you and Horatia, both of whom I love as much as my own life. And as my last writing before battle will be to you, so I hope in God that I shall live to finish the letter after the battle.' The same wish for 'a speedy return to dear Merton' was expressed in the letter he wrote to Horatia, and signed 'your Father'.

It was the moment for all to sit down to express, possibly for the last time, feelings of affection and devotion to those they loved. Captain George Duff of *Mars*, who had just embarked his thirteen-year-old son, Norwich, as a midshipman, wrote to his wife, 'My dearest Sophia, I have just time to tell you we are going into action with the combined fleet. I hope and trust in God that we shall all behave as becomes us, and that I may yet have the happiness of taking my beloved wife and children in my arms. Norwich is quite well, and happy. I have however ordered him off the quarterdeck.' Mail was collected from all the ships. The boat with the mail had already left *Victory* when Nelson was told that a petty officer who had been preoccupied on a job had been unable to put a letter to his wife in the ship's mailbag. 'Hoist a signal to bring her back' was Nelson's immediate order. 'Who knows that he may not fall in action tomorrow. His letter goes with the rest.'

There followed a strange night that all in both fleets knew preceded a battle that could no longer be avoided. The two fleets were some ten miles apart and had not yet had sight of one another. But the night, moonless and heavily dark, was full of light from the signals that ceaselessly passed within the two fleets. The Combined Fleet appeared to be 'like a well lit up street six miles long'. The British used blue lights that were particularly bright and penetrating in the dark. During the night Villeneuve was signalling to form line of battle and to clear for action.

While in Cadiz Villeneuve had drawn up his 'Line of Battle'. He had composed a line whose van was led by the Spanish second-in-command,

Vice Admiral Alava, fifty-two, with thirty-nine years in the Spanish navy, sailing aboard his 112-gun flagship *Santa Ana*. In the van Villeneuve had three of the sharpest of his captains, Julien Cosmao-Kerjulien on *Pluton*, Louis Baudoin on *Fougueux* and Louis Infernet aboard *Intrépide*, all three 74s. At the centre he had himself aboard *Bucentaure*, the Spanish third-in-command, Rear Admiral Baltazar Cisneros aboard the splendid 130-gun *Santissima Trinidad*, and among the outstanding captains there were Jean Lucas on *Redoutable* and Felipe Cagigal, on *San Augustin*, both 74s. In his rear he placed his own second-in-command, Rear Admiral Dumanoir le Pelley aboard the 80-gun *Formidable*, supported by three French and three Spanish ships. A strong force of twelve ships under the Spanish commander in chief, Admiral Frederico Gravina, who was also second-in-command of the Combined Fleet, formed a Squadron of Observation, whose station was to be windward of the fleet, available to reinforce any part of the line that was hard pressed. Gravina sailed aboard the 112-gun *Principe de Asturias* and among the commanders of the twelve ships he had under him were other notable French and Spanish officers, Cosmé de Churruca, aboard the *San Juan Nepomuceno*, 74, Gabriel Denieport, *Achille*, 74, Rear Admiral Charles Magon, *Algesiras*, 74, and Pierre Gourrege, *Aigle*, 74. Several of these ships and their commanders would offer some of the most heroic episodes of the day to come.

Through the night of 20–21 October Villeneuve sought vainly to bring together the line he had planned for his thirty-three ships, eighteen French and fifteen Spanish. The fleet had been completely dispersed after nightfall. At daybreak on the 21st Villeneuve restored his line, though imperfectly. Then, by a change of course that put their heads towards Cadiz, the order of the line was completely inverted from what he had drawn up on shore. The rear under Dumanoir became the van, the van became the rear and furthermore was all mixed up with the Squadron of Observation.

It was a change that was to be of enormous, critical significance to the battle that day, and for Villeneuve his ultimate source of despair.

For the moment, however, only honour and glory were before them. The confrontation which had been so dreaded and that now finally and unavoidably presented itself, became a sudden brightness to them quite as much as it was to the British. In that dawn on the 21st all the despair, pessimism, doubts and misgivings that had afflicted the Combined Fleet as it lay in Cadiz fell away, a weight cast off as if in relief. As drums and fifes beat stations, an exultant surge of spirit seized the ships, from which came cheers and roars of '*Vive l'Empereur!*', '*Vive le commandant!*', even as similar joy and cheers and cries of 'Rule Britannia' floated over the British ships.

XXXIX

TRAFALGAR

THE greatest and grandest battle fought under sail was to have as its setting an Atlantic headland that was deeply familiar to all involved and therefore especially fitting, but one that nevertheless lent its own grandeur to the event.

The fleets were off the shoals below Cape Trafalgar on the south-western coast of Spain where the circumstances had delivered them. At dawn on 21 October 1805 both fleets lay within the space of sea between Cape Spartel on the North African coast and Cape Trafalgar on the Spanish. It is a gulf that narrows towards the entrance of the Straits, which are guarded by Cape Malabata on the Moroccan side and Tarifa directly opposite.

The Spanish coast between Tarifa and Cape Trafalgar today is another character from the more familiar Costa del Sol on the other side of the Straits. Although touristic development has come, it has not yet obliterated the striking beauty of the Atlantic shore, which until even twenty years ago remained seemingly untouched. Instead of the ash-grey volcanic sands of the Costa del Sol the Atlantic coast shines whitely from its long, broad beaches and coves, dunes and the broad, high-ascending blankets of wind-blown sand that decorate the sides of the mountains. Here the sea is bluer, more effervescent. And it is the same on the African side, with the great beach of Tangier, and the endless south-running sands beyond Cape Spartel. On both sides of this wide Atlantic space that encloses the entrance to the Straits the mountains rise massively rough, precipitately tumbled but green.

It can be an area dominated, as we have repeatedly seen in this account, by the easterly levanter and the alternating westerlies. Especially memorable, therefore, in that small corner of hard-blowing winds are the days that can lie between these winds. A fierce levanter might die suddenly and then, before a westerly sets in, the whole world is still, or almost still, only the lightest breath of air to stir the tranquillity or disturb the purity of a light that has joyously lost the brittle refraction of wind. And so it was on 21 October 1805.

It was a day whose dawning clarity and quietness might have seemed created for the sort of reflection inevitable to the occasion. It would have held an emotive power quite unlike other scenes of naval engagement where familiarly there would be some inevitable sense of rush, elements of discordance, tension and apprehension. None were here. A calm lay upon all, as only a sense of the measured, fateful advance of what was specially awaited and mindfully prepared for could bring. Such a dawn revealing such a scene could only enlarge that. And in that air before that scene, with all its freshness and vivacity, there had to be an enhanced joy of mere existence, which could only have been felt more vividly among those regarding it through reminder of the possibility of imminent death. Whole in youthful body and mind, fully sensible of every taste of the living air through which they moved, they had this final gift as they moved towards sudden irruption of fire and iron.

What the sea itself offered was a spectacle equal to the surrounding land and its matchless air. Seventy-three vessels lay upon the sea in two groups. Nelson had twenty-seven ships of the line, four frigates, a schooner and a cutter. Villeneuve commanded thirty-three of the line, fifteen of them Spanish, with five frigates and two brigs. In the clear sunshine on a blue sea they all glittered gloriously as only such vessels could do, with their white sails, bright, freshly painted sides and their elegantly windowed and ornamented stern quarters, while idling on the air above them were the colourful ensigns and the banners of their commanders. Something so magnificent, yet in portent so awful.

The British scouting frigates had the Combined Fleet in sight soon after five that morning. *Victory* logged the enemy sighted at six a.m. ten or eleven miles distant. At six forty *Victory* made the signal 'Prepare for Battle'. At eight thirty Villeneuve made the signal for his ships to wear together and form line in close order on the starboard tack. That stood them headed towards Cadiz and made Nelson fear of an attempt to escape. But the compact discipline of the line indicated to those watching from *Victory*'s quarterdeck that their opponents were committed to a determined effort to show themselves in this battle when they came to it. An officer of *Victory* was to say, 'They appeared to seek the action with as much confidence as ourselves.' The French believed they had good reason for their confidence, as a lieutenant aboard *Intrépide* related, 'The British ships reaching us one by one and at a very slow speed seemed bound to be overpowered in detail by our superior forces.'

The lightness of the breeze meant that manoeuvres within the fleets as well as their approach to one another was very slow, the British fleet moving at only three miles an hour. But that was better than the Combined Fleet, for the British fleet had the wind. It was also aided by a heavy swell that indicated approach of a gale later that day. Even at the better advance of the British, however, with the two fleets some twelve to thirteen miles apart, action was still at least six hours off when they first stood in clear sight of one another. That could have meant a long, painfully slow morning of protracted anticipation. But for everyone there was occupation for every minute of it.

There was besides the sustained activity of preparation aboard the ships of both fleets. Aloft the most extensive preparation of all, to provide support of masts and rigging for when they might be severely damaged. On every deck on every ship in every fleet, gunners, carpenters, topmen, surgeons, marines and soldiers were preparing for the emergencies that might arise, the wounded that would come, the weapons that would be required. Preparation of the magazines and movement of shot and powder to the guns. The laying-out of medical instruments. Decks sanded to prevent slide by the bare feet of the gunners. One of the seamen aboard *Santissima Trinidad*, obviously a conscript and new to the ship, was to describe his reaction to the preparation for battle that morning. Watching sailors distributing sacks of sand on deck and throughout the lower decks he asked a boy what it was for. "'For the blood," he said, very coolly. "For the blood!" I exclaimed, unable to repress a shudder. I looked at the sand – I looked at the men who were busily employed on this task – and for a moment I felt I was a coward."'

Nelson toured *Victory* to view all of his own ship's activity, addressing the crew at their stations. There was concern for Nelson's safety among his officers. The surgeon and his two secretaries, the two Scotts, intended to plead with Nelson to remove or at least cover the brilliant decorations he wore, to make him less of a target for French marksmen shooting from high in the rigging. They found no opportunity easily to do so, fearing his irritation. But the senior captain of his frigates, Henry Blackwood, when called to *Victory* for a final conference, went even further and suggested that Nelson move his flag to Blackwood's frigate, *Euryalus*, to allow better view of the battle and because of the high value of his life to the country. Nelson considered that a poor example to set. Blackwood then sought yet another alternative for protecting Nelson. As *Victory* was then the van, he pleaded that since the flagship would be singled out for concentrated attack one or two other ships should lead her into action. To that Nelson agreed, but the feeble wind prevented *Temeraire* from coming up and *Victory* remained the lead ship, with *Temeraire*, *Neptune* and *Leviathan* close behind.

At eleven thirty Nelson told his flag lieutenant, John Pasco, to prepare a signal to the fleet. Nelson said, 'You must be quick, for I have one more to make, which is for "Close Action". I wish to say "England confides that every man will do his duty".'

Pasco had the new and far more efficient system of signals. This code had a vocabulary offering many words that could be transmitted with a single flag bearing a number in the vocabulary book. Other words had to be spelled out letter by letter. Nelson's demand for haste led Pasco to say, 'If your lordship will permit me to substitute *expects* for *confides* the signal will soon be completed, because the word *expects* is in the vocabulary, and *confides* must be spelt.' Nelson was happy with that. 'That will do, Pasco, make it directly.' And Pasco hoisted, 'England expects that every man will do his duty', greeted by three cheers from every ship.

The action began near simultaneously with that signal. The Combined Fleet lay in a long line with van and rear extended over approximately four to five miles. The British fleet approached the centre of that line in two distinct columns, some two miles apart.

There was nothing upon that broad stretch of ocean to suggest how naval battle until recently had been fought. With the old system the two fleets would have sought to pass parallel to one another. Only the Combined Fleet offered semblance of that here. But its lengthy line was curved and disorderly, with many of its ships close or doubled upon one another. Against this line the British approached like two arrows aimed at the heart of Combined Fleet's body. The lead column, led by *Victory*, headed for the Combined Fleet centre, specifically for Villeneuve's flagship *Bucentaure* and the 130-gun *Santissima Trinidad*, ninth and tenth in the line.

The second column, led by Cuthbert Collingwood in the 100-gun *Royal Sovereign*, made for the Combined Fleet's rear. *Royal Sovereign* was sailing well, having recently had her hull coppered. She was therefore closer to the Combined Fleet's rear than *Victory* yet was to the van. It was evident that the first action might fall to Collingwood.

At eleven thirty, with the wind light, the sunshine bright, the sea surface smooth over the backs of a heavy swell rolling in, the French 74 *Fougueux* opened fire on *Royal Sovereign*, which delayed her own fire until up to the Combined Fleet line. The French centre then began firing on *Victory* as it came up.

Aboard *Victory*, Nelson took leave of Blackwood as shot began flying overhead. 'God bless you, Blackwood,' Nelson said, 'I shall never speak to you again.'

The possibility of that was dramatically evident even as Blackwood clambered down into his boat alongside, to carry Nelson's last instructions to the other ships. For the next forty minutes *Victory* took the concentrated fire of the 80-gun French flagship *Bucentaure* and other ships in the Combined van. The shots began to fall rapidly upon the flagship. One tore through the main topgallant sail. Eight marines were mown down by a shot, another tore apart Nelson's secretary, John Scott, who was talking to Captain Hardy close by. His body was immediately thrown overboard along with those of the marines. 'Is that poor Scott who is gone?' Nelson asked, to be told that it was. The clerk who took Scott's place was himself killed soon after. Then *Victory*'s wheel was smashed, which meant that the ship had to be steered by forty sailors manning the massive tiller on the lower gun deck, with orders sent down by messenger. With many of her sails already gone *Victory* became slower in the water.

During its refit at Portsmouth, Nelson had removed the skylight over his cabin and had the space decked over to enable him to walk amidships during action, clear of the quarterdeck guns and ropes. Here Nelson and Hardy positioned themselves during the action, walking to and fro together. A shot passed between them and struck a block of timber nearby. Some of the splinters caught Hardy's foot, bruising it without serious injury. They stopped, each to see if the other was all right, then, smiling, Nelson said, 'This is too warm work, Hardy, to last long.' At this time *Victory* had still not fired a shot.

As *Royal Sovereign* bore down upon the two ships that led the rear line of the Combined Fleet, the Spanish *Santa Ana* and *Fougueux*, Collingwood told his sailors to lie down at their quarters, to reduce casualties on the approach. *Fougueux* fired the first shot from the French line, hoisting her colours as she did so. She closed up with the intention of preventing *Royal Sovereign* from going through the line but at ten minutes past noon *Royal Sovereign* broke through the enemy line. She came up to *Santa Ana* and fired into her, a broadside with the guns double-shotted. It was done with such precision that the slaughter was terrible. That single broadside killed or wounded nearly four hundred of the Spanish ship's crew. *Royal Sovereign* then ranged alongside *Santa Ana*, so close that the guns were nearly muzzle to muzzle. As *Fougueux* came up, yardarm to yardarm, she, too, took a broadside. 'I thought the Fougueux was shattered to pieces – pulverized,' her master-at-arms later said. 'The storm of projectiles that hurled themselves against and through the hull on the port side made the ship heel to starboard. Most of the sails and rigging were cut to pieces, while the upper deck was swept clear of the greater number of seamen working there.'

Differences on the times of engagement were registered between the many logs of the British ships, obviously due to the pressures under the heat of the action. Blackwood's watch frigate *Euryalus* recorded all times, and these were to be regarded by some after the battle as perhaps the most reliable. According to *Euryalus* at twelve sixteen p.m. the British admirals raised their respective flags and the White Ensign. One minute later Collingwood opened fire. *Victory* had been under heavy fire since before noon, though she herself had not yet fired a shot. Her log recorded that she opened fire at four minutes past twelve. But *Euryalus* recorded

Victory's first shot at twelve twenty-three. Whatever the differences, battle nevertheless had begun, some ten miles below Cape Trafalgar.

Two other ships, *San Leandro* and *Indomptable*, bore up upon *Royal Sovereign* and for fifteen minutes *Royal Sovereign* was the only British ship in close action, taking such incessant, heavy fire from her four opponents that her crew frequently saw shots striking each other.

What was now underway became melee with a ferocity that could never have been imagined in any earlier generation. It was what both sides sought. The light wind allowed them slowly to draw close, but once close they too often remained thus, with limited allowance of manoeuvrability. The swell also helped roll the ships into entanglement.

Nelson all along had wished to make for the French flagship. The wind had died to a 'mere breath'. But the British did at least have such wind as there was in their favour. *Victory* was driven onward by riding the swell. She continued to take heavy fire from three ships, *Bucentaure*, *Santissima Trinidad* and *Redoutable*. As she drew near to *Bucentaure* Nelson's wish and intention were to break through the line astern of the flagship and then to 'run on board', meaning to pass through the line and come up alongside the flagship on the other side. But Hardy declared that to be impracticable because of a tight cluster of ships beyond. They could pass close under *Bucentaure*'s stern, Hardy said, but they could not pass through the line without running on board one of the other ships lying close to *Bucentaure*. Nelson replied, 'It does not signify which we run on board of. Go on board which you please: take your choice.' So *Victory*, her sails riddled or shredded, passed within thirty feet astern of *Bucentaure*. And as *Victory* did so a carronade on her forecastle fired one round shot and a keg filled with five hundred musket balls right into the stern cabin windows of *Bucentaure*. Then, as she drew ahead, the full fifty guns of her broadside, double- and even treble-slotted with balls, blasted upon the French flagship.

The barely two minutes of that entire action left *Bucentaure* in a practically defenceless state. The destruction within the ship was severe, judging by the dense smoke that poured from her, filling *Victory*'s own interior, threatening to suffocate her crew, and covering those on the quarterdeck with dust from the shattered woodwork of *Bucentaure*'s stern. Aboard *Bucentaure* nearly four hundred lay dead or wounded. This was at one p.m.

From beyond *Bucentaure*, *Victory* was already engaged by two French ships, *Neptune* and *Redoutable*, both of which poured fire upon her. *Victory* ran foul of *Redoutable* and at one ten p.m. the two ships lay alongside one another, moving slowly before the wind. Firing was now merciless one upon the other. *Redoutable* was firing her main deck guns into *Victory* but her musketry from the portholes and from the rigging was creating particular havoc on *Victory*'s decks. Of the 110 men on *Victory*'s gangways and quarterdeck at the start of the action barely twenty were left unwounded.

What now followed was, heroically, the defining moment of the battle for both sides, harrowing for the British and exemplary for the French. *Redoutable* was to take Nelson's life. But by engaging the 100-gun *Victory* in the manner it did this French 74 wrote its own special chapter in French naval history for its courage and defiance.

At one fifteen Nelson fell, victim to one of the musketeers stationed aloft aboard *Redoutable* and no more than fifteen metres from where Nelson and Hardy were walking. The ball struck the epaulette on his left shoulder and passed into his chest. He fell face down at the place where his secretary, John Scott, had fallen. Nelson's clothes were soiled by Scott's blood. A marine and two seamen rushed to his side and began lifting him.

'They have done for me at last, Hardy,' Nelson said, when Hardy turned and rushed to him. 'I hope not.' 'Yes, my backbone is shot through.'

The three men carried Nelson down to the cockpit, where the wounded and dying lay crowded upon one another. The heavy firing that *Victory* had taken had already filled the place with wounded of all ranks. One officer, Lieutenant Ram, had just been brought down severely wounded. He only saw how bad his wound was when the surgeon began applying ligatures. Ram then tore them off with his own hand and bled to death. To the surgeon Nelson said, 'Ah, Mr Beatty! You can do nothing for me. I have but a short time to live. My back is shot through.' Nelson was stripped of his clothes, put on a bed and covered with a sheet. When the chaplain, Dr Scott, who was administering lemonade to the wounded, hurried to his side, Nelson said, 'Doctor, I told you so. Doctor, I am gone.' Then, in a low voice, 'I have to leave Lady Hamilton and my adopted daughter Horatia as a legacy to my country.' It was a refrain that he was to repeat several more times during the long, painful hours ahead, most eloquently to Hardy.

The surgeon examined the wound and asked Nelson what he felt. Nelson replied that he felt a gush of blood every minute within his breast, that breathing was difficult, he had no feeling in the lower part of his body but had severe pain at the spine where the ball had struck. 'I felt it break my back.' From that and from Nelson's pulse Beatty recognized that Nelson's state was hopeless. But the news was to be kept from all except Hardy, who was compelled to return to the deck at once. Nelson nevertheless kept calling for him. Messages were sent to Hardy. Nelson often impatiently exclaimed, 'Will no one bring Hardy to me? He must be killed. He is surely destroyed.' But Hardy's aide-de-camp, a midshipman, came down to say that 'circumstances respecting the fleet' required Hardy's presence on deck.

Hardy and *Victory* at that moment had as their opponent *Redoutable*'s captain, Jean Lucas, perhaps the outstanding seaman of the French fleet that day. He had been training his men for months with an uncommon zeal of the sort that Nelson and St Vincent believed in exercising. In particular, he said, 'My thoughts ever turned on boarding my enemy in any action I fought, and I so counted on finding my opportunity that I made that form of attack part of our daily exercises, so as to ensure success when the hour arrived.' With his attack on *Victory* the hour appeared to have arrived.

Redoutable had been the third ship astern of Villeneuve's flagship *Bucentaure*. The two intermediate ships, lacking wind, had fallen out of station when *Victory* and *Temeraire* bore down upon *Bucentaure*, which was thus left unsupported. 'We had all unanimously determined to lose our own ship than witness the capture of our admiral,' Lucas and his officers wrote in the statement they compiled after the battle. It was a vow of remarkable commitment for *Redoutable* for, apart from the 100 guns of *Victory*, the French 74 was simultaneously pitted against the 98 of *Temeraire*, which was coming up fast behind *Victory*.

Heavy cannonade from *Victory* sought to force *Redoutable* from its station defensive of *Bucentaure*. 'They were, however, unable to move us. We determined to range ourselves alongside the enemy's admiral, and in that situation we gave and received a number of broadsides,' Lucas's report said. 'The enemy, however, could not prevent us from lashing ourselves fast to Victory. Our captain then gave orders to board, whereupon our brave crew, with their officers at their head, instantly made ready for the onset.'

These were the circumstances that took Hardy hurriedly back on deck from Nelson's side. When Nelson was carried below the quarterdeck was practically deserted. *Redoutable*'s musketry had created such fast destruction on *Victory*'s decks that the way looked open for *Victory* being boarded by French sailors. The few British sailors left were carrying their wounded comrades below. When Hardy returned from below he had only the marine captain, Charles Adair, and one or two other officers beside him.

For Lucas the attempt to board *Victory* proved unexpectedly difficult because her upper deck stood so much higher than that of *Redoutable*. But by climbing up by an anchor from *Redoutable* a midshipman and four sailors reached *Victory*'s deck and others prepared to follow them, led by a lieutenant. Jean Lucas ordered the main yard of *Redoutable* to be lowered to serve as a bridge for the rest. A party of *Victory*'s officers and men rushed up from the lower decks to repulse boarders. In the close fight that followed Adair and several seamen and marines were killed. 'A few minutes more and Victory was ours,' Jurien de la Gravière was to say. It could well have been so had *Temeraire* not been so close. When *Victory*'s guns fell briefly silent *Temeraire* drew up and sent a volley of shot and musketry across *Redoutable*'s decks, killing and wounding some two hundred. 'In less than half an hour our ship had been so fearfully mauled that she looked little more than a heap of debris,' Lucas said. Out of a crew of 634 *Redoutable* already had lost 300 killed and 222 wounded. Nevertheless, when *Temeraire* demanded surrender Lucas ordered soldiers to fire at her decks. In their mutual exchange *Redoutable*'s mainmast fell across *Temeraire* and *Temeraire*'s topmasts came down aboard *Redoutable*, which then lay enclosed by *Victory* and *Temeraire*. The three ships were held together by their fallen masts. Thus they drifted, with *Temeraire* and *Redoutable* still fighting, the latter with soldiers and sailors aloft throwing hand grenades down at *Temeraire*'s decks or clearing them with musketry. This became so fierce that *Temeraire*'s captain, Eliab Harvey, sent all his crew below.

Then *Fougueux* came up, having drifted down a wide space of sea from her engagement with *Royal Sovereign*. Since her starboard broadside was clear, *Temeraire*'s first lieutenant, Thomas Kennedy, directed its fire upon *Fougueux*. The havoc was severe. Although already crippled, *Fougueux* was now an unmanageable hulk as she drifted on to and became entangled with *Temeraire*. Her sailors having been sent below, the empty decks of *Temeraire* suggested to *Fougueux*'s sailors that the British ship had suffered such a devastating loss of men that she could easily be taken. Crying '*à l'abordage*' *Fougueux*'s sailors rushed with cutlasses and tomahawks to board. Again the superior height of a three-decked British ship served as advantage over a 74. The French were driven back by musketry fired down upon them, and then the British themselves boarded in a rush. The French captain, Louis Baudoin, and his second were both killed on the quarterdeck. Savage fighting between the four ships locked together continued until shortly after two p.m. when *Victory* drifted away, leaving the other three to fight it out, between them forming 'one mass which drifted at the mercy of the wind'. British sailors got on to the deck and then into the main rigging of *Fougueux* and hauled down the French colours. By then *Redoutable* was too shattered to continue and Lucas surrendered. In summary of that ferocious contest *Redoutable*'s Jean Lucas paid tribute to all involved: 'Never could the intrepid Nelson have fallen in action with foes more worthy of his courage and his grand reputation.'

During that close, grappling encounter the sniper who had shot Nelson was himself marked out and shot. He was one of two who were seen firing from the mizzen top of *Redoutable*. He was seen by one of *Victory*'s quartermasters. One of the midshipmen kept firing at the mizzen top and when one of the Frenchmen there fell on *Victory*'s poop the quartermaster cried out, 'That's he – that's he.'

With Nelson dying in the cockpit below, the fight for possession of *Victory* becomes perhaps the most curious episode of that whole battle. Had it succeeded it could only have been temporary. It could not have survived the immediate onslaught of *Temeraire*, whose own sailors anyway would have immediately rushed to join *Victory*'s resistance. But without *Temeraire*'s fortuitous arrival it might, as Jurien de la Gravière thought, have been different. The ultimate outcome of the battle by then was already evident as a British success. But what would have been the impact if Jean Lucas had been able to have presented his personal admiration and respect to Nelson in *Victory*'s cockpit? Or the demoralizing effect upon the rest of the British fleet to have seen *Victory*'s colours descend, if only temporarily? They are uncomfortably intrusive questions of the sort that history so often leaves upon large events.

At this time, five minutes after two, the French flagship *Bucentaure* also surrendered. Perhaps no commander of naval battle was ever more unfortunate than Villeneuve was that day. As the action unfolded everything seemed set against him personally. The glory of the day fell upon others in his fleet, but very little upon him, for reasons mainly beyond his control. He was simply the unluckiest of men.

The most distressing aspect of the day for this long-suffering man was the absence from the main battle of practically his entire van. It was an extraordinary development that simply seemed to gather its own momentum, initiated by the rearrangement of line at dawn. As *Victory* broke the French line and became engaged with the principal ships there, *Bucentaure* and *Santissima Trinidad*, the ten ships that composed the rest of the French van under the division's commander, Rear Admiral Dumanoir le Pelley aboard the 80-gun *Formidable*, drew away, and continued to do so, leaving their commander in chief practically on his own, the centre left to fend for itself. At the start of his engagement with *Victory* Villeneuve had ordered that every ship not engaged should get into action. Dumanoir made no movement in response. Villeneuve, totally preoccupied, did not repeat his signal until it was too late to save him from his embattled situation. *Bucentaure*, already wrecked by *Victory*'s broadside, had subsequently been closely engaged by three British ships, the 98-gun *Neptune* (each fleet had a *Neptune*) and two 74s, *Leviathan* and *Conqueror*; and, after suffering further destruction, had hauled down her colours at five minutes past two and been taken possession of by *Conqueror*. Villeneuve was not prepared, however, to concede the battle lost. Before offering to surrender at one fifty p.m. he had again signalled that ships not engaged should rapidly move into action. Dumanoir, on receipt of that, finally sought to take his ships back to the centre, where the full heat of the battle had already passed.

Bucentaure was useless. Her main- and mizzen masts had come down. The greater part of her guns were dismounted by broadside with others made useless by the fall of the masts. Villeneuve nevertheless had still expected to continue command of the battle after lowering his colours to save lives. He had kept his barge prepared to take him aboard another ship in the event of *Bucentaure* being dismasted. But when he ordered it to be launched it, like everything else around it, was found to be crushed by shot and the fall of the masts. He then hailed *Santissima Trinidad*, just ahead, and asked her either to send a boat or to take the flagship in tow. But there was no answer to the hail. The Spanish three-decker was too hotly engaged. That moment of resignation was expressed in Villeneuve's official report: '. . . the main deck having had to be abandoned, heaped up with dead and wounded, with the ship isolated in the midst of the enemy and unable to move, I had to yield to my destiny. It remained only to stop further bloodshed. That, already immense, could only have been in vain.' Such was the final burden upon that cruelly luckless man. His bitter complaint expressed to another officer at that moment was that fate had spared his life, that amid all the slaughter there seemed to be not one bullet for him.

Captain Israel Pellew of *Conqueror* was unable to spare his first lieutenant to board *Bucentaure* to accept Villeneuve's sword. Instead he sent Captain James Atcherley of the marines to take possession of the French flagship. As Atcherley arrived on *Bucentaure*'s upper deck four French officers stepped forward, bowing, to present their swords. One was Villeneuve. 'To whom,' asked Villeneuve in good English, 'have I the honour of surrendering?'

'To Captain Pellew of the Conqueror.'

'I am glad to have struck to the fortunate Sir Edward Pellew.'

'It is his brother, sir.'

'His brother! What are there two of them? Hélas!'

Atcherley, with a fine sense of form, suggested that the swords be handed to an officer of superior rank to himself, Captain Pellew. Villeneuve and his officers then kept their swords. Atcherley went below to secure the magazines, passing among the dead 'thrown back as they fell, lying along the middle decks in heaps'. He locked the magazines, pocketed the keys and posted sentries at the doors of the admiral's and flag captain's cabins, before conducting the officers down to the boat alongside.

Dumanoir, in his belated response to Villeneuve's appeals, had appeared to windward of *Victory*, arousing fear that his ships would likely advance on her. That had provided further reason to keep Hardy on the quarterdeck and prevent his descent to the cockpit in answer to Nelson's cries for him.

Meanwhile, the three British ships that had attacked *Bucentaure* passed on to the *Santissima Trinidad*. An officer aboard the 100-gun *Britannia* gave a sad description of the beginning of the end of this, the then largest and grandest ship in the world. 'We passed under the stern of this magnificent ship, and gave her a broadside which shattered the rich display of sculpture, figures, ornaments and inscriptions with which she was adorned. I never saw so beautiful a ship. Luffing up alongside her four-decked side, of a rich lake colour, she had an imposing effect.'

The initial broadsides between *Santissima Trinidad* and *Victory* and the damage done to the British flagship fired the enthusiasm of the Spanish. 'It seemed as though the Victory must fall into our hands, for the Trinidad's fire had cut her tackle to pieces, and we saw with pride that her mizzenmast had gone by the board.' But *Santissima Trinidad* became surrounded by the ships in line behind *Victory*. They pounded *Santissima Trinidad* and, after two and a half hours, as one Spanish seaman described it,

The scene aboard Santissima Trinidad was simply infernal. All attempts at working the ship had to be abandoned. She could not move . . . The English had torn our sails to tatters. It was as if huge invisible talons had been dragging at them. Fragments of spars, splinters of wood, thick hempen cables cut up as corn is cut by the sickle, fallen blocks, shreds of canvas, bits of iron, and hundreds of other things that had been wrenched away by the enemy's fire, were piled along the deck, where it was scarcely possible to move about . . . Blood ran in streams about the deck, and in spite of the sand, the rolling of the ship carried it hither and thither until it made strange patterns on the planks. The enemy's shot, fired as they were from very short range, caused horrible mutilations . . . The ship creaked and groaned as she rolled, and through a thousand holes and crevices in her hull the sea spurted in and began to flood the hold . . . The Bucentaure surrendered before our very eyes. When once the leader of the fleet was gone, what hope was there for other ships?

By two thirty this celebrated Spanish 130-gun lay an unmanageable wreck on the water. But she continued firing and in an interval of this arose one of the strangest incidents of the battle. Politeness and courtesy, of which there was a remarkable amount on display between the two sides in this battle, saw perhaps its most delicately framed occasion on the decks of *Santissima Trinidad*. Seeing that her colours had been shot away Captain Henry Digby of the 64-gun *Africa*, one of the attacking ships, sent an officer, Lieutenant John Smith, to the Spanish ship to ask for the sword of her commander and to take possession. When Smith reached the quarterdeck and declared his mission he was politely told that it was through oversight that the colours had not been rehoisted. They were getting up fresh ammunition from below, that was why they had stopped firing. Instead of detaining Smith he was escorted off the quarterdeck, bowed off the ship and allowed to return to his vessel before firing resumed. But half an hour after *Bucentaure* had surrendered *Santissima Trinidad* did as well.

At two thirty Hardy felt able to go down to the cockpit again. Nelson asked, 'Well, Hardy, how goes the battle? How goes the day with us?'

Hardy gave Nelson what he knew he would prefer to hear. 'Very well, my lord. We have got twelve or fourteen of the enemy's ships in our possession. But five of the van have tacked, and show an intention of bearing down upon Victory. I have therefore called two or three of our fresh ships round us, and have no doubt of giving them a drubbing.'

'I hope none of *our* ships have struck, Hardy?'

'No, my lord. There is no fear of that.'

'I am a dead man, Hardy. I am going fast. It will all be over with me soon. Come nearer to me. Pray let my dear Lady Hamilton have my hair, and all other things belonging to me.'

'I hope Mr Beatty can yet hold out some prospect of life.'

'Oh no, it is impossible. My back is shot through. Beatty will tell you so.'

Hardy then returned to the deck. Nelson compelled the assistant surgeons attending him to go to the other wounded for, he said, 'you can do nothing for me'. But a few minutes later he asked to see the surgeon, Beatty. 'Ah, Mr Beatty! I have sent for you to say, what I forgot to tell you before, that all power or motion of feeling below my breast are gone, and *you* very well *know* I can live but a short time.'

Beatty replied, 'My lord, unhappily for our Country, nothing can be done for you.' Beatty was so affected that he turned about, to hide his emotions.

Nelson said, 'I know it. I feel something rising in my breast,' putting his hand on his left side, 'which tells me I am gone.'

Asked whether his pain was great he said it was so severe that he wished he were dead, then added, 'Yet one would like to live a little longer, too.' And, after a pause, 'What will become of poor Lady Hamilton if she knew my situation?'

Hardy, back on the quarterdeck and with Nelson's immediate responsibility of overall command on him until he could transfer it to Collingwood, was surveying the intensity of the battle scene around him. For the past two and a half hours, since the serious action had begun around noon, the fiercest battle that had ever lain upon the sea had resounded against the cliffs of that coast below Trafalgar, and been listened to in wonder in Tangier, Cadiz, Tarifa and all around. Whatever had been said before of the lack of experience and training or lagging activity of the French and Spanish sailors now had to be forgotten. They had fought with a determination and bravery as unrelenting as that of their opponents. And at that time, between two and three o'clock on that sunlit afternoon of 21 October, a great deal more was yet to be required of all.

British ships of the line had never taken as much punishment as they got at Trafalgar. The close action that Nelson had demanded was not only close but hours long as ships lay locked together pumping shot into one another, even as others came up to thicken the fire and increase the burden of mutual destruction. Never had open decks seen such slaughter as each side raked the top decks of the other. Quarterdecks took heavy loss. Nelson early on lost two captains, George Duff of *Mars* and John Cooke of *Bellerophon*. The close-fighting ships accumulated smoke that was often so thick below that gunners could not see one another at the same gun, working as though blindfolded.

Collingwood's *Royal Sovereign*, which fired the first British shot, was thereafter immediately into her own melee. At two fifteen, after two hours of uninterrupted engagement between *Royal Sovereign* and *Santa Ana* the Spanish 112-gun struck to *Royal Sovereign*. The British ship by then was practically as wrecked as the Spanish. Her mizzen, main- and foremasts were down.

Belleisle, immediately behind *Royal Sovereign* in line, had already suffered between fifty and sixty dead and wounded from the rear ships of the Combined line before she herself exchanged broadsides with three ships. She had already lost her main topmast when *Fougueux* engaged her and in ten minutes shot away her mizzen mast. When *Fougueux* fell away towards her engagement with *Victory* three other ships surrounded *Belleisle* and continued cannonading her. Her sails and rigging were cut to pieces. By two ten p.m. *Belleisle* had lost her mainmast, lying across the poop. The French *Neptune* joined the assault and at two forty-five p.m. *Belleisle*'s bowsprit and foremast were gone. At three fifteen three British ships came up and drew away *Belleisle*'s stubborn attackers. Shattered and dismasted, with even her boats and anchors gone, *Belleisle* had nevertheless withheld submission. A Union Jack was suspended at the end of a pike that was mounted on the stump of the mizzen mast.

Astern of *Belleisle*, *Mars* was quickly drawn into that same close-grouped melee in which *Royal Sovereign* and *Belleisle* were fighting. Like *Belleisle*, she took such a pounding from the rear ships of the Combined Fleet before coming into action herself that she was already badly damaged by the time she cut the enemy line and became engaged with five different ships. Her principal opponent became the French *Pluton*. At practically the same time that Nelson fell a shot took off George Duff's head. He was standing by the gangway looking over the side to judge the firing of his guns when it hit him. Two seamen standing behind him were also killed. By that time *Mars* was practically unmanageable with masts either shot away or shattered.

The 80-gun *Tonnant*, captured by Nelson at the Nile, had come to the aid of *Mars* and became heavily engaged with the ships that had surrounded her, particularly with the Spanish 74, *Monarca*, and the French 74, *Algesiras*, flying the flag of Admiral Charles Magon. *Tonnant* hauled up alongside *Monarca*, which dropped astern, struck her colours, but then later rehoisted them as *Tonnant* became fully engaged with *Algesiras*, which had closed in alongside her. *Tonnant* had already lost her fore topmast and main yard. *Algesiras* made an attempt to board at *Tonnant*'s bowsprit, which was entangled with the French ship's rigging. But the boarders were mown down by heavy fire. Admiral Magon, with a tomahawk in hand, was leading the boarding party when hit in the leg and the shoulder. He refused to go below and a shot cut him nearly in half. The masts came down one by one. One of *Tonnant*'s lieutenants said, 'Only one man made good his footing on our quarter-deck, when he was pinned through the calf of his right leg by one of the crew with his half-pike, whilst another was going to cut him down, which I prevented and desired him to be taken to the cockpit.' *Algesiras* struck her colours at two fifteen p.m. after a gallant and intensive effort to master *Tonnant*.

Cosmé de Churruca's *San Juan Nepomuceno* had also been in that melee, before which he had been engaged by six different ships. His final opponent was *Dreadnought*. A cannonball hit his right leg and almost severed it. 'It is nothing, go on firing,' he said, but he died, after which the crew lowered colours. 'A sudden paralysis seemed to seize the crew; their grief at losing their beloved leader apparently overpowered the disgrace of surrender,' one account said. By then, however, half the *San Juan*'s crew were already dead or wounded. Most of the guns were disabled. All masts except the mainmast were gone. The rudder was useless.

Another ship in Collingwood's lead, *Bellerophon*, whose name became recorded in popular legend as 'Billy Rff'n', had drawn up into the melee around *Tonnant*, but found herself lying within her own contest with six different ships, suffering cannonade from all sides. At one p.m. her main- and mizzen topmasts had gone. Minutes later her commander, John Cooke, was killed. The hardest fight was with the French 74 *Aigle*, lying alongside with rigging entangled with *Bellerophon*'s. Musketry and grenades from *Aigle*'s tops caused great loss on *Bellerophon*'s decks. *Aigle*'s captain, Pierre Gourrege, made several attempts to board but these were repulsed. *Bellerophon* by this time was unmanageable but continued to lay equal damage upon her assailants. Breaking away from *Bellerophon*, *Aigle* first engaged *Revenge*, from whom she receive two broadsides that so crippled her that she was prevented from making sail. But, falling in with *Defiance*, *Aigle* continued action. At three p.m. *Defiance* ran alongside *Aigle*, boarded her, lashed themselves to her and rushed to haul down the colours. But an intense fire of musketry was opened on the boarders from the forecastle, waist and tops, and the British sailors were forced to withdraw. *Defiance* cut loose the lashings, stood off, and cannonaded *Aigle*, which finally submitted. Gourrege was among those killed.

That touching empathy that always had a place in these battles was demonstrated again in this action. It was recorded by Sir John Franklin, the Arctic explorer who was a signal midshipman aboard *Bellerophon*. He was on the poop of his ship. Most of those around him had been brought down by the musketry of those in the tops and on the poop of *Aigle*. When *Bellerophon*'s colours had been shot away for a third time a sailor named Christopher Beaty, yeoman of signals, climbed the mizzen rigging with the largest Union Jack he could find. He spread it as wide as possible across the shrouds but came down unhurt. The French riflemen, who previously had picked off every man who appeared before *Bellerophon*'s mizzen mast suspended their fire while Beaty was busy, in apparent admiration for his courage. They resumed as soon as he was down.

These actions between Collingwood's column and the Combined Fleet's rear, together with the simultaneous actions between Nelson's column and the Combined Fleet's van, were packed into the first three hours of the engagement. By three p.m., however, the heaviest was over. By then eleven of the thirty-three ships of the Combined Fleet had surrendered, one-third of the Combined force.

Dumanoir did eventually approach the centre of the battle, where *Bucentaure* and *Santissima Trinidad* lay surrounded by a strong British force. The five van ships that remained with Dumanoir in passing fired on the cluster of *Victory*, *Temeraire*, *Redoutable* and *Fougueux*, killing British and French alike, for which Dumanoir was to be excoriated as much as for having held off. In his fleeting engagements with other British ships a shot aboard *Conqueror* left the sort of strangely distressing incident that always stood out amidst all the hundreds of other deaths. Third Lieutenant William St George while passing the first lieutenant, Robert Lloyd, good-humouredly tapped him on the shoulder to congratulate him on his approaching appointment as a commander. As St George turned to smile at Lloyd a cannonball took off Lloyd's head and knocked St George dead on to the deck. It would seem to have been the fleeting warmth of friendship, the reference to future and the swift severance of that possibility which to those who were present made this moment so memorably touching amidst so much other dying.

After taking some damage themselves, Dumanoir's *Formidable* and the other ships with him began drawing off again from the battle scene. Dumanoir had the wind. He did not wish to lose it. He made off. 'To bear down at this moment on the enemy would have been an act of desperation, which could only have tended to increase our losses,' he was to say in exculpation of his actions.

Through the period after Hardy had returned to the quarterdeck all in the cockpit had listened attentively to the noise beyond. *Victory*'s crew cheered whenever they saw an enemy ship surrender. Nelson, roused by it, would ask what the noise was about. His signal officer, Lieutenant Pasco, who by then had also been wounded, lay nearby, and told him another ship had struck. Nelson's satisfaction was immediately apparent. He kept on calling to be fanned with paper, and for drink. Around three o'clock when Dumanoir had fired on *Victory* and *Victory* had returned the fire, 'Oh Victory, Victory, how you distract my poor brain,' Nelson cried. Then, reflectively, 'How dear life is to all men!'

At about three forty-five p.m. Hardy once more felt able to go down to the cockpit. He and Nelson shook hands again. Hardy held on to Nelson's hand and congratulated him on his brilliant victory. He did not know then exactly how many ships had surrendered and repeated fourteen or fifteen. 'That is well,' Nelson said, 'but I bargained for twenty.' Then, '*Anchor*, Hardy, *anchor!*'

'I suppose, my lord, Admiral Collingwood will now take upon himself the direction of affairs?'

'Not while I live, I hope, Hardy.' Nelson then tried to raise himself from the bed. 'No.' And added, 'Do you anchor, Hardy?'

'Shall we make the signal, sir?'

'Yes, for if I live, I'll anchor.' It was a strange and moving suggestion of him trying to cling to the sense of life that the idea of command retained. It was also something more, the last evidence of his cognitive powers, for the swell that signalled a powerful gale to come had made him concerned about eventually being able to anchor in the shelter of Cape Trafalgar if necessary. He followed that by saying that in a few minutes he would be no more. 'Don't throw me overboard, Hardy!'

'Oh! No, certainly not.'

'You know what to do. Take care of my dear Lady Hamilton, Hardy. Take care of poor Lady Hamilton. Kiss me, Hardy.'

Hardy knelt down and kissed his cheek. Nelson said, 'Now I am satisfied. Thank God I have done my duty.' Hardy stood gazing down at him for a minute or two and then knelt down again and kissed Nelson's forehead. Nelson said, 'Who is that?'

'It is Hardy.'

'God bless you, Hardy.'

Hardy returned to the quarterdeck. Fifteen minutes later Nelson appeared to fall unconscious. His steward called the surgeon to his side. Beatty took up Nelson's hand, which was cold, and felt the pulse. It was gone. The surgeon went off to the others. Doctor Scott was rubbing Nelson's breast. Nelson opened his eyes, looked up, then shut them again. The surgeon was called over. He pronounced Nelson dead. It was four thirty. The battle was practically over. The final actions were diminishing. Nelson had died knowing it was a triumph.

At three p.m. Admiral Gravina in his flagship *Principe de Asturias* had been involved in his own final action. His flagship was severely damaged. This, the last, was a series of engagements with the 98-gun *Prince* and three 74s, *Revenge*, *Defiance* and *Thunderer*. *Principe de Asturias* managed to get away when others came to her assistance. Gravina had been seriously wounded. The *Principe* was taken under tow by a frigate. As second-in-command Gravina signalled to ships that had not struck to rally round him. Seven ships joined him, and they made for Cadiz together, this at four forty-five p.m. As *Principe de Asturias* bore away other ships broke off and accompanied her. Eleven ships of the line moved off with her towards Cadiz.

When Dumanoir made off two of his van ships broke from him and made a serious attempt to go to the assistance of *Bucentaure* and *Santissima Trinidad*. Captain Felipe Cagigal of the *San Augustin*, 74, made for the *Santissima Trinidad* and at about three p.m. was intercepted by *Leviathan*, also 74. *San Augustin* sought to rake *Leviathan*, which put her helm hard a-port and, having more wind, was able to bring her guns to bear before the Spanish vessel, whose mizzen mast and colours came down. *Leviathan* laid herself alongside. Seamen and marines then managed to overcome *San Augustin*. The action produced an occasion of British stoicism that was hallowed as part of the enduring Trafalgar example. Thomas Main, a gunner on *Leviathan*'s forecastle, had his arm taken off by shot. When his companions sought to help him down to the cockpit he said, 'I thank you to stay where you are; you will do more good there.' He went down by himself to the cockpit. The surgeon, who knew him well, wanted to attend to him immediately but Main said, 'Avast, not until it comes to my turn, if you please.' When the surgeon came to amputate his arm near the shoulder Main sang the whole of 'Rule, Britannia'. He was to die in Gibraltar hospital after being landed.

The other van ship was the *Intrépide*, 74, whose commander, Louis-Antoine-Cyprien Infernet, belonged to that special gallery of sailors for whom it would always be all or nothing. Infernet, at five feet ten tall for a French sailor of the day, had begun his sea life as a cabin boy and powder monkey. Born near Toulon, he was rough and uneducated but popular. He had been deeply unsettled from the outset by Dumanoir drawing away from the scene of the action. A sub-lieutenant of his ship, Marquis Giequel des Touches, wrote a powerful account of their dismay.

Our captain, Infernet, with his eyes fixed on Formidable, expected Admiral Dumanoir every moment to make the signal to go about and take part in the battle. But no signal went up. Time passed, and the van division slowly drew off from where the fighting was going on: it became soon but too plain that its chief was keeping out of the battle. Admiral Villeneuve, meanwhile, while he had a mast standing on which to hoist a signal, was ordering our ships to put about and come to action. Undoubtedly, owing to the lightness of the wind and the swell, the

evolution was a slow and difficult one; but it might at least have been attempted . . .
Happily Captain Infernet took another view of his duty, and his honour. Although
we were immediately under the orders of M. Dumanoir, we had already made
several unsuccessful attempts to put about; but the wind had been entirely stilled
by the cannonading and the very heavy ground swell, presage of an approaching
storm, made it difficult for the ship to answer the helm . . . When at length we
drew near where the Bucentaure and Redoubtable lay, their masts had fallen, their
fire was almost silenced; yet the heroism of those on board kept up an unequal
and hopeless struggle . . . against ships from the ports of which broadside after
broadside flashed incessantly. It was into the thick of this fray that our Captain
Infernet led us to rescue Admiral Villeneuve and take him on board. It was a reckless and forlorn hope, a mad enterprise, and he himself could not doubt it. It was
the pretext Infernet gave for continuing the fight . . . We soon had the honour of
drawing on us a number of the enemy – Leviathan, Africa, Agamemnon, Orion,
the Britannia of 100 guns. They all set on us fiercely and when, after five in the
evening, we had to lower our colours, the only flag on our side that still flew, the
Intrepide had not a lower mast left standing. She had lost two-thirds of her men
and was lying riddled with shot holes; the port lids torn away, and with water
pouring in below everywhere.

Intrépide was the last ship that struck her colours at Trafalgar. Infernet
got off all the wounded and then, with his ten-year-old son, crossed to one
of his attackers, *Orion*, commanded by Edward Codrington. Infernet by
then had earned great admiration from his opponents. A lieutenant aboard
Conqueror, Humphrey Senhouse, said of *Intrépide*: 'Her captain surrendered
after one of the most gallant defences I ever witnessed. The Frenchman's
name was Infernet, and it deserves to be recorded in the memory of those
who admire true heroism.' Codrington advanced Infernet £100 on leaving
Orion and wrote to his wife and asked her to do all she could for him
while he was a prisoner of war in England. 'He is much like us in his open
manner,' he told her, '. . . and endeavours to make himself agreeable to all
in the ship. He fought most stoutly, and had I not had the advantage over
him of position and a ready fire whilst he was engaged with others, we
should not have escaped as well as we did.'

The last event in the drama of Trafalgar followed half an hour after
Intrépide's surrender. The French 74 *Achille*, Captain Gabriel Denieport,
had been in action since the earliest. At one thirty p.m. *Achille* had joined
the attack on *Bellerophon* and fought there until three forty-five p.m. when
Swiftsure engaged her. By that time *Achille* had lost her main- and mizzen
topmasts. Her captain and all senior officers were dead. More than four
hundred of her crew were dead or wounded. She was then commanded by
a sub-lieutenant, Ensign Cauchard, who extricated her from the melee but

then encountered the 98-gun *Prince*, whose broadside, fired high, caused an explosion in the arms chest in *Achille*'s foretop. That caused a fire. Cauchard and his men decided to cut the mast to let it drop overboard. Then *Prince* fired again, cutting the mast with its shot. The burning wreckage of the top fell on to the deck below. The ship was soon ablaze. Those on board began jumping overboard, after stripping off all their clothes to enable them to swim easily. *Prince* lowered boats to rescue as many as possible.

At five fifty p.m. *Achille* blew up. With that, the Battle of Trafalgar ended.

XL

AFTERMATH

AFTER the human storm, nature delivered hers, and it began to fall almost instantly upon the appalling scene that lay upon the ocean just a few miles off Cape Trafalgar.

The gale could be said to have contained the sea's own final tribute to Nelson, for it affirmed the final order he gave as he lay dying. 'Do you anchor, Hardy?' he had pressed upon his captain. 'Shall we make the signal, sir?' 'Yes, for if I live, I'll anchor.'

Nelson had read from the great, rising swell that heavy weather was moving in from the south-west. Aware that the action was drawing to a close, the damage that *Victory* had already suffered had obviously raised his concern for the wellbeing of his own ship and the others once it was all over.

That he had been right in his final perturbed command was soon to be made clear. The ships of the fleet and their prizes were in no state to contend with a rising gale. *Victory*'s mizzen mast toppled overboard about the same time that action ceased. Collingwood gave the order to anchor at nine p.m. But, as he himself then said, 'The whole fleet were now in a very perilous situation; many dismasted, all shattered, in thirteen fathom water, off the shoals of Trafalgar; and when I made the signal to prepare to anchor, few of the ships had an anchor to let go, their cables being shot.'

Collingwood's own flagship *Royal Sovereign* had lost her masts except for a tottering foremast. At five fifty-five, the firing having ceased, Collingwood boarded Blackwood's *Euryalus* and raised his flag there. At six fifteen *Euryalus* took *Royal Sovereign* in tow for the second time, a first towing cable at the height of the battle having been shot away. Blackwood now went to *Victory* on his behalf to know the fate of Nelson. Collingwood had been informed at the height of the battle that Nelson was wounded but as the battle closed he still did not know that Nelson was dead and that he himself was now commander in chief. Hardy returned with Blackwood and on board *Euryalus* gave this news to Collingwood, along with Nelson's final instruction to anchor as soon as practicable.

The scene at the sunset then upon the sea was in proportion as truly awful as that of dawn had been magnificent. The glorious forest of masts of twelve hours since lay to various extent stumped upon all the ships in view. The ships were like battered hulks, British and prizes alike, seeking some form of management under remnants of sail. Aboard all of them frantic effort was underway with the gathering storm to clear fallen masts and yards and rigging, to erect jury masts, to manage pumps against inflow from wounded hulls, to effect what immediate order was possible from shambles, and to care for the wounded and pile the dead, all of whose blood lay thick on all the decks.

The final count for the Combined Fleet was nearly seven thousand killed and wounded; the British loss nearly seventeen hundred killed and wounded. For the French and Spanish it had been a massacre. The French engineer Forfait, quoted by Jurien de la Gravière, explained why. The cannon alone gave law at sea, Forfait said, '. . . to hear people enter into long arguments about the causes of British superiority . . . four words explain it . . . they have ships well fitted, guns well served, and they manoeuvre well . . . with you it is all the contrary . . .'[1] The French had once been masters of shipboard artillery, but the Revolution had abolished the privileged stature of naval gunners and their mastery had never been recovered. It now firmly belonged to the British. Collingwood made a habit of telling his gunners that if they could fire three well-directed broadsides in five minutes, no vessel could resist them. Practice had enabled them to do that in three and a half minutes.

It was the devastation of the opening British broadsides that fundamentally decided the issue at the start. Broadside was in the plural. That is, ship-length lines of guns on two or three decks firing simultaneously on to and into an opponent, with each gun double- or even three-shot-slotted. *Victory*'s first broadside had immediately put *Bucentaure* virtually out of action. *Royal Sovereign* similarly disabled *Santa Ana*. The terrible effect of such a broadside was described by Jurien de la Gravière:

If any one will picture to himself the destructive effects to be expected from a mass of iron, whose total weight sometimes exceeds 3000 lbs., driven through space with a velocity double that of sound, travelling 1600 feet in a second, and suddenly arrested in its course by a penetrable substance which tears and flies into splinters more fatal than the shot itself, he will understand the formidable power of a line-of-battle ship's first broadside. Instead of frittering away this irresistible force as we used to do then, in the hope of cutting some ropes . . . or for the mere chance of destroying some important rigging or wounding a mast, the English better taught, concentrated it upon a more certain object, the enemy's batteries. They heaped our decks with slain while our shot passed over their ships.

In those last words lay the answer to the British victory at Trafalgar, and to the frightful carnage that the British officers confronted when they went to take possession of surrendered ships.

Of the thirty-three French and Spanish ships that had lain in solemn acceptance of challenge before Nelson that morning eleven were now following Gravina towards Cadiz, four were following Dumanoir northwards, seventeen floated as prizes, and the fragments of one, *Achille*, floated upon the water where she had exploded. Eight of the prizes had not a mast standing. Others were partially dismasted. Some, like *Redoutable*, were slowly sinking. The Royal Navy had suffered no loss of ship. Nor did any British ship lower its colour. But of the British ships eight were either unable to move or barely so. The others had all suffered various losses of masts and yards. It was an example of how the Rodney/Clerk principle of melee and disregard of the former strictures of line had passed beyond the British navy. Villeneuve was the only French admiral of that epoch and of the wars before to issue melee as a battle instruction. And it was obedience of that fierce assault, solitary or in group, that left the British themselves so severely punished.

The outcome was effectively settled in the melees that dominated the battle: those of Collingwood with *Santa Ana*, *Fougueux* and *Indomptable*; *Belleisle* with *Fougueux*; *Victory* and *Temeraire* with *Bucentaure*, *Santissima Trinidad* and *Indomptable*; *Tonnant* with *Algesiras*, *Monarca*, *San Juan*; *Bellerophon*, *Aigle*, *Bahamo*, *San Juan*. All took terrible punishment from one another. But this concentration of the action had worked to the British advantage. It is what they had prepared for and sought. Trafalgar had been, finally, the first fully planned and meticulously plotted 'breaking the line' battle on the open sea: long deliberated upon, earnestly longed for, and here achieved. It was the first such, but it was also to be the last. Nothing resembling such tactical melee was ever to follow.

The last action of Trafalgar was fought by Dumanoir's four fugitive ships when they were intercepted by Commodore Sir Richard Strachan, who had been sent in search of them. Strachan aboard his 80-gun flagship, *Caesar*, was accompanied by four 74-gun ships and two frigates. All four of Dumanoir's ships were taken after a fierce two-hour battle off Cape Finisterre.

There could be no real joy for anyone as the sun went down, even for the British in victory, for the loss of Nelson descended like a cloud upon all. His death was suspected even before it was communicated to all. They feared the truth when they saw no lights on board *Victory* and then saw that the commander in chief's lights had shifted and now shone from *Euryalus*, where Collingwood had hoisted his flag.

Aboard *Victory*, as there was no lead to make a coffin, a cask called a leaguer, the largest type on board, was brought up. Nelson's hair was cut off and his clothes removed except for the shirt. The body was then put in the cask, which was filled with brandy. It was secured in his Great Cabin.

The last hour of fading light was occupied with the final task of the battle itself, rescuing survivors from the exploded 80-gun *Achille*. Boats picked up the French sailors and distributed them among the British ships. Some were badly wounded. All were naked, having stripped off their clothes to swim better to floating debris. This was where the rage of battle fell away. Humanity asserted itself. Many of the rescued were taken to *Revenge*, where the purser was told to issue each man a complete set of clothes. The only one among them in jacket and trousers was found to be a woman. One of *Revenge*'s lieutenants gave her his cabin. She too had thrown off her clothes but British sailors in the boat that picked her up had hastily dressed her with their own clothes. Aboard *Revenge* clothing materials and other gifts were pressed upon her. The woman's name was Jeannette and she was eventually reunited with her sailor husband.

The night that now descended, and the two days that followed, matched the horrors of battle with those of its aftermath. As the storm rose and raged its ferocity seemed to be something previously unimaginable to those aboard all the ships, especially the drifting prizes and the British that had lost their anchors and were unable to make it to the shelter of Cape Trafalgar. Aboard the prizes the hundreds of wounded were screaming in agony as they were flung about. Little could be done for ships or men until the storm spent itself. Aboard every prize there were images of hell that remained ineradicable with those who had survived battle and with the British seamen who had been placed on board. For one British officer the night after battle was worse than the battle itself.

The officer, from *Bellerophon*, was in the party that took possession of the Spanish *Monarca*. He, another officer and eight men were left with 150 Spanish on board. Writing home afterwards, the British officer recounted:

I can assure you I felt not the least fear of death during the action, which I attribute to the general confidence of victory which I saw all around me; but in the prize, when I was in danger of, and had time to reflect upon the approach of death, either from the rising of the Spaniards upon so small a number as we were composed of, or from the violence of the storm, I was most certainly afraid, and at one time the ship made three feet of water in ten minutes, when our people were almost all lying drunk upon deck, when the Spaniards, completely worn out with fatigue, would no longer work at the only chain pump left serviceable, when I saw the fear of death so strongly depicted on the countenances all around me, I wrapped myself up in a Union Jack, and lay down upon the deck a short time, quietly awaiting the approach of death; but the love of life soon after roused me . . .

British and Spanish then resumed their effort to save the ship. It was a common experience that the British sailors who were put aboard the prizes lost no time in getting to the wine stocks on board.

Fougueux was the first ship to be lost. She broke from her tow and drifted ashore on the morning after the battle. She was without masts. The boats were smashed. Only desperate pumping kept her afloat as water poured in through holes from stem to stern. 'The water had risen almost to the orlop deck,' her master-at-arms, Pierre Servaux, recalled. 'Everywhere one heard the cries of the wounded and dying, as well as the noise and shouts of insubordinate men who refused to man the pumps and only thought of themselves. The scenes of horror on board the ship that night were really the most awful and fearful that imagination can call up.' *Fougueux* was driven ashore and most on board were lost, including thirty British seamen from *Temeraire*.

The same scenes were being enacted aboard *Redoutable*. British and French seamen worked together all night pumping, stopping leaks and blocking portholes on a ship strewn with dead and wounded. But when the water continued to gain on the pumps the British ship towing her, *Swiftsure*, sent boats across in towering seas to take off as many as possible. Wounded were brought up and laid out on the poop. One of *Swiftsure*'s lieutenants, Thomas Sykes, took his boat as close alongside as possible. 'In consequence of the tremendous rolling of the Redoutable in the heavy seas which had set in, he found it impossible to get close to her, and all he could do was to watch the lee-roll of the ship, and drag into his boat as many as could be laid hold of.' But *Redoutable* went down before all could be rescued. *Swiftsure*'s boats continued in the high seas to try and find and pick up as many as possible. When brought aboard, British seamen clothed the French sailors from their own small stock.

Storm enabled prisoners to retake one of the prizes. *Algesiras* was without masts and anchor and drifting when Lieutenant Charles Bennett of *Tonnant*, with fifty British seamen, was put in charge after she had lowered her colours. The ship's 270 officers and crew were under the hatches. But in the rising weather the British were unable both to guard the prisoners and rig jury masts to get the ship under control. When she began drifting towards the shoals the prisoners were released. One of *Algesiras*'s officers, Lieutenant de la Bretonniere, then told Bennett that they were retaking the ship and that British and French should work together to save the ship and themselves, if not the British would be thrown overboard. The British had no choice. Together with the French they raised three topgallant masts as jury masts, and the ship was brought into Cadiz.

Matching that was a bold attempt from Cadiz to repossess some of the prizes. Captain Cosmao-Kerjulien of *Pluton* persuaded four other ships, the 80-gun *Indomptable*, 80-gun *Neptune*, 100-gun *Rayo* and 74-gun *San Francisco de Asis* to follow him out into a lull of the storm. They encountered *Santa Ana* with the wounded Alava on board under tow by *Thunderer*. The British ship took off the prize crew and cast off *Santa Ana*, which was picked up and taken into Cadiz. Another prize, *Neptuno*, had broken adrift from the British ship towing her and was also taken into Cadiz. But more was lost than gained from the sortie. *Indomptable* and *San Francisco de Asis* were wrecked as they tried to regain Cadiz. *Rayo* lost her masts and was taken prize by the British *Leviathan*, only to be totally lost shortly after.

Villeneuve's *Bucentaure* was under tow by *Conqueror* when Cosmao-Kerjulien's force came out. *Conqueror* cast off the tow and *Bucentaure* ran ashore near Cadiz. Those still on board and the British prize crew got ashore, with the British subsequently sent back to Collingwood under a flag of truce.

Collingwood finally decided that the effort to save his shattered prizes in such weather was pointless and ordered their destruction. With that came the end of the finest warship created under sail, *Santissima Trinidad*. The British had hoped desperately to get this magnificent trophy first to Gibraltar for repair, eventually to England. Instead, the *Santissima Trinidad* became the last tragedy of Trafalgar.

The Spanish naval historian Perez Galdos gave a moving survivor's account of the situation aboard *Santissima Trinidad* after the battle:

Night fell, increasing the misery and horror of our situation . . . the elements lashed us with their fury as though heaven thought our cup of misfortune was not yet full . . . the winds and waves tossed and buffeted our ship in their fury, while, as she could not be worked, she was utterly at their mercy. The rolling was so terrible that it was very difficult even to work the pumps; and this, combined with the exhausted condition of the men, made our condition grow worse every minute . . . Those who had escaped unhurt were doing what they could to aid the wounded, and these, disturbed by the motion of the vessel which prevented their getting any rest, were so pitiable a sight that it was impossible to resign oneself to sleep. On one side, covered with the Spanish flag, lay the bodies of the officers who had been killed; and in the midst of all this misery, surrounded by so much suffering, these poor corpses seemed really to be envied.

Worse followed when Collingwood signalled destruction of the prizes. British sailors went aboard *Santissima Trinidad* and, by opening the gun ports on the lower deck, ensured that on every roll the ship took in tons of water. She was rolling so violently that the inrush of water meant that there was little time before she went down. As Lieutenant John Edwards of *Prince* related,

After driving about four days without any prospect of saving the ship or the gale abating, the signal was made to destroy the prizes. We had no time before to remove the prisoners, and it now became a most dangerous task; no boats could lie alongside, we got under her stern, and men dropped in by ropes; but what a sight when we came to remove the wounded, which there were between three and four hundred. We had to tie the poor mangled wretches round their waists, or where we could, and lower them down into a tumbling boat, some without arms, others no legs, and lacerated all over in a most dreadful manner . . . we had got all out, to about thirty-three or four, which I believe it was impossible to remove without instant death. The water was now at the pilot deck, and taking in tons with every roll, when we quitted her, and supposed this superb ship could not remain afloat longer than ten minutes. Perhaps she sunk in less time, with the above unfortunate victims . . .

The haste produced hard decision. A seaman from *Revenge* recounted one painful scene:

A father and his son came down the ship's side to get on board one of our boats. The father had seated himself, but the men in the boat, thinking from the load and the boisterous weather that all their lives would be in peril, could not think of taking the boy. As the boat put off the lad sprang from the ship into the sea and caught hold of the gunwale of the boat, but his attempt was resisted, as it risked all their lives; and some of the men resorted to their cutlasses to cut his fingers off in order to disentangle the boat from his grasp. At the same time the feelings of the father were so worked upon that he was about to leap overboard and perish with his son. Britons could face an enemy but could not witness such a scene of self-devotion: as it were a simultaneous thought burst forth from the crew, which said, 'Let us save both father and son or die in the attempt.'

The pair were eventually landed at Gibraltar and exchanged with other prisoners. Another British rescue was the ship's cat, which ran out on the muzzle of one of the lower-deck guns and was plucked off by a British seaman.

The battle had been watched from the shore in Spain and was clearly visible from the hills above Tangier. In the days that followed the battle wreckage and bodies were continually coming on shore on both coasts. Burying parties were stationed along the beaches around Cape Trafalgar. A remarkable feature of the days immediately after the battle was the relationship that developed between the British and the Spanish at Cadiz.

Collingwood had touched the Spanish deeply by offering to deliver all the Spanish wounded to Cadiz. The city's governor, Marquis Solana, responded in kind. 'Judge of the footing we are on,' Collingwood wrote, 'when I tell you he offered me his hospitals, and pledged the Spanish honour for the care and cure of our wounded men. Our officers and men who were wrecked in some prize ships were kindly treated: all the country was on the beach to receive them, the priests and women distributing wine, and bread and fruit, amongst them.' The Spanish seamen who came ashore with their captors from the wrecked prizes were particularly noteworthy in their responses. After having rushed to see their families they returned and, as one British seaman reported, '. . . they bought us some bread, and some figs, and some wine, for we had scarcely tasted anything the last twenty-four hours, and the Spaniards behaved very kind to us'.

Admiral Gravina died of his wounds on 9 March 1806. His remains were embalmed and transferred to the Panteon de Marinos Illustres at San Fernando near Cadiz.

In one of history's great balances of fortune France, meanwhile, was able to celebrate a great victory before it got news of Trafalgar. The day before Trafalgar, on 20 October, Napoleon resoundingly defeated the Austrian military commander, General Mack, at Ulm. Twenty thousand troops and three thousand horse surrendered their arms before him. It was the beginning of the swift end of the Third Coalition. Napoleon then marched on Vienna, which he was to enter on 14 November.

Rumour of a battle at Cadiz in which Nelson had destroyed the Combined Fleet was already alive in London on 2 November. So were rumours of Ulm. It was a strange fog of the good and the bad. Belief in a possible Nelson victory was easy. Such early disaster in the Continental campaign against Napoleon was, however, difficult to accommodate, especially since Pitt was in the midst of an effort to bring Prussia into the coalition. Lord Malmesbury dined with Pitt that night and mentioned the reports of Ulm. 'Don't believe a word of it; it is all a fiction,' Pitt replied. But the next day Malmesbury brought a Dutch newspaper whose detailed account of the battle allowed no further doubt.

The gloom that instantly settled on Pitt soon lay upon all. If Buonaparte carried the Continent, would he be back at Boulogne soon enough to renew that threat?

Collingwood sent off his Trafalgar despatch on 27 October with Lieutenant John Lapenotiere, who commanded the 8-gun schooner *Pickle*. It was a rough nine-day voyage. Off Land's End *Pickle* met *Superb* and Lapenotiere went on board to give the news to Nelson's close friend, Richard Keats. He left behind a ship stricken with grief over Nelson's death and arrived off the Lizard at two in the morning of 4 November. He was ashore at ten by Pendennis Castle and on his way to London in a post-chaise that, changing horses nineteen times, arrived at the gates of Admiralty at one in the morning on 6 November. William Marsden, First Secretary of the Board of Admiralty, was about to go to bed when he was told that a naval officer had just arrived with important despatches. 'In accosting me,' Marsden was to write, 'the officer used these impressive words: 'Sir, we have gained a great victory, but we have lost Lord Nelson!' The effect thus produced it is not to my purpose to describe: nor had I time to indulge in reflections, who was at that moment the only person informed of one of the greatest events recorded in history, and which it was my duty to make known with the utmost promptitude.' Candle in hand he went to Lord Barham's chamber. 'Drawing aside his curtains with a candle in my hand, I woke the old peer from a sound slumber . . . he showed no symptoms of alarm or surprise, but calmly asked, "What news, Mr Marsden?" We then discussed, in a few words, what was to be done, and I sat up the remainder of the night with such of the clerks as I could collect, in order to make the necessary communications . . .'[2]

Pitt had the news at three a.m. A colleague later described the Prime Minister's reaction. 'He observed that he had been called up at various hours in his eventful life by the arrival of news of various hues; but whether good or bad, he could always lay his head on his pillow and sink into sound sleep again. On this occasion, however, the great event announced brought with it so much to weep over as well as to rejoice at, that he could not calm his thoughts; but at length got up, though it was three in the morning.'

Three days later Pitt attended the Lord Mayor's Day at Guildhall, where the Lord Mayor proposed his health as 'the Saviour of Europe'. Pitt rose and said, 'I return you many thanks for the honour you have done me; but Europe is not to be saved by any single man. England has saved herself by her exertions, and will, as I trust, save Europe by her example.' He sat down.[3]

'That was all; he was scarcely up two minutes; yet nothing could be more perfect,' said Arthur Wellesley, who was present. It was the shortest speech of Pitt's entire career. And it was, perhaps, in its own way, symptom of a deep-felt reflection in the wake of Nelson's death, expression of a different situation: the start of the post-Nelson era, and a different dependence. Perhaps also an instinctive recognition that, with his failing health he, too, like Nelson, would soon be out of the picture.

The nation took the news of Trafalgar uniquely as an expression of grief and joy. Typical was the alternate tolling of bells, exultant tolling alternating with solemn for Nelson. Lord Malmesbury, describing the illumination of London, said: 'I never saw so little public joy. The illumination seemed dim and as it were half-clouded by the desire of expressing the mixture of contending feelings; every common person in the streets speaking first of their sorrow for him, and then of the victory.'

Admiralty sent a messenger, Captain Whitby, immediately to break the news to Emma Hamilton before it reached the newspapers and the public. Her own account of it was, 'He came in, and with a pale countenance and faint voice, and said, "We have gained a great victory." "Never mind your victory," I said, "my letters – give me my letters" – Captain Whitby was unable to speak – tears in his eyes and deathly paleness over his face made me comprehend him. I believe I gave a scream and fell back, and for ten hours I could neither speak nor shed a tear.'[4]

Never before nor since was there in Britain, or perhaps in any other nation, such undiluted grief for the loss of one man. In London *The Times* reflected what was felt across Britain: 'The victory created none of those enthusiastic emotions in the public mind which the successes of our naval arms have in every former instance produced. There was not a man who did not think that the life of the Hero of the Nile was too great a price for the capture and destruction of twenty sail of French and Spanish men of war. No ebullitions of popular transport, no demonstrations of public joy, marked this great and important event. The honest and manly feeling of the people appeared as it should have done: they felt an inward satisfaction at the triumph of their favourite arms; they mourned with all the sincerity and poignancy of domestic grief their Hero slain.'

It had to be, after the high, tense expectation of assault across the Channel. 'At Trafalgar,' said Mahan, 'it was not Villeneuve that failed, but Napoleon that was vanquished; not Nelson that won, but England that was saved.' Explaining that Mahan said, 'The English people, from long immunity, were particularly sensitive to fears of invasion, and their great confidence in their fleets, if rudely shaken, would have left them proportionately disheartened.'

With Britain something of her distinctive insular security and its special brand of confidence could have been lost if the Army of England had managed to get ashore, irrespective of the greatness of resistance. It was, as Mahan rightfully points out, what was fundamentally understood and feared. In Nelson they had recognized the only man they believed could preserve them from that risk. Faced by Boulogne, the island had stood in greater widespread alarm than ever before. Upon the sea had rested all its trust. Nelson had embodied that trust as no one else could have done. They had wanted that reassurance in their home waters, of which Trafalgar was viable extension. Much of the greatness of the man lay in his own suffering understanding of that, and the disproportionate weight it laid upon him compared to that which fell upon the very best of the others around him. But the appeal of him became, of course, far more. It was luminous in a

manner that was his alone. In his waywardness, in his openness, in his lack
of formal severity, he closed a distance that was unbridgeable between the
public and others. Jurien de la Gravière summed that up as well as anyone
could: 'Far from entrenching himself from a mistaken idea of dignity in inaccessible forms, Nelson, on the contrary, mixed himself up with the daily life
of all on board, becoming its very centre, and, winning all hearts and wills
to himself, directed them to one object – the annihilation of our fleets.'

Villeneuve was landed at Gosport on 29 November. He and the other
French officers were accommodated in country homes. The French heroes
of Trafalgar, Captains Lucas and Infernet, who were lionized in England,
received the same in France when they returned on exchange. They were
promoted to rear admiral and received by the emperor. Villeneuve was
released in April 1806 on an exchange of prisoners. He landed at Morlaix
and went on to Rennes, from where he reported to Decres that he was
in France. He got no reply from Decres and on the morning of 22 April
Villeneuve was found in bed in his hotel room, a table knife in his chest.
There was never to be satisfaction that it was suicide rather than murder.

Napoleon received the news of Trafalgar on 18 November, on his march
to the next encounter with the Austro-Russian armies at Austerlitz. He was
at table when handed a despatch detailing Trafalgar. He pocketed it and
said nothing. His only public reference to it was in his Imperial Address on
2 March 1806, one sentence: 'The tempest caused us loss of some ships
after a battle imprudently sought.'

PART THREE

THE CONCLUSIVE STRUGGLE,
1805–1816

XLI

APPRAISAL

It became at once a new and different war and, in hastening prospect, another world.

From his victory at Ulm, Napoleon marched on Vienna, which he entered on 14 November 1805. After Ulm Emperor Francis II and Tsar Alexander rallied their armies around the town of Austerlitz, just north of Vienna in Moravia. There on 2 December Napoleon's Grand Army routed the Austro-Russian combination in what was to stand as perhaps his greatest and most decisive victory. It broke the Third Coalition.

With the Treaty of Pressburg signed on 27 December Austria lost her place in Italy and Germany. She surrendered Venetia, Istria, Dalmatia and the Tyrol and Vorarlberg and was compelled to recognize the independence of Bavaria, Württemberg and Baden. Loss of the first three virtually handed the Adriatic to Napoleon, a prize of prizes for a man still intent on Egypt.

Things might have been different had Prussia been drawn into the Third Coalition. Pitt and Napoleon had been engaged in a strenuous diplomatic tug of war over Prussia, Pitt to persuade her from neutrality into the coalition, Napoleon to prevent it. The weak, indecisive Prussian emperor, Frederick Wilhelm, vacillated before deciding against involvement on strength of a promise from Napoleon that there would be no objection to Prussia marching into Hanover.

At the time of Trafalgar, Pitt, in alliance with the Swedes and Russians, had launched upon a mad effort to recover Holland involving a total of twenty-five thousand British troops, one of the largest British forces yet assigned to Continental war. It scarcely got beyond occupation of Bremen for, after Austerlitz, its position looked untenable and on 15 February 1806 it returned to Britain.

A sickly Pitt, at full cost to his health, had put all his diplomatic effort and personal hopes into success for the Third Coalition. Ulm had been bad enough. Then news of a further great defeat had reached him in fragmented reports. When the disaster of Austerlitz was confirmed to him he asked for a map to see where it was. He said, 'Roll up that map; it will not be wanted these ten years.' He then asked to be left alone.

His own effort to gain a military foothold on the Continent and to wrest Holland back from the French stood large as the pathetic effort it had been. Once more had millions been paid out in subsidies to Austria and Russia and nothing gained from it other than defeat. This total disaster – headlong flight of the two emperors from Austerlitz and the shock of a third, Frederick Wilhelm of Prussia, toying with his neutrality to win French agreement to his possession of Hanover – was blamed for Pitt's swift decline and death. The Third Coalition, Pitt's laborious construct to achieve a safer balance of power in Europe, had crumbled before Napoleon's military genius and the greater form of power that was emerging from it. Pitt had been in a poor state for some time, suffering badly from gout. The overload of disappointment crushed him. He died on 23 January. His last words were 'Oh, my country. How I love my country!'

Trafalgar and Austerlitz: never could it have been imagined that two such victories in such close conjunction would be able so decisively to declare the confrontational issue of Sea and Land in such ultimate terms of the power of each.

'The sea must be subdued by the land,' Napoleon now declared, and for him upon the exercise of that premise the future would move instead of upon any further unrealistic dependence upon sea to cope with sea. That spelled out the fundamental difference of what lay ahead.

A profound change in any event existed through the death of the two principal influences upon the British conduct of the Great War. That Nelson and Pitt should have gone almost simultaneously might at any other point have seemed fatal, but the two, together and individually, had delivered Britain to a position that ensured the nation's ability to withstand and surmount the great forces that would now be pitted against it. They had laid the foundation upon which all would rest. Britain and Europe had both been quite unprepared for what settled upon them with the Great War. Pitt and Nelson selected themselves to acquire the necessary education to ensure survival of an island nation. The burden finally proved too much. But they had ensured continuity.

Nelson had the easier death, conscious of absolute achievement. Pitt's was an agony of fear, reflective of the immediate imponderables that hastened his end. But he left behind a nation that he had raised to a pinnacle of commercial success despite thirteen years of war. His military sensibilities were faulted, but never his commitment to the navy. There was never likely to be sacrifice of the 'maritime code' to satisfy the demands of an ally such as Russia.

The legacy of each was unique. Pitt had left a new concept of economic structure, Nelson an entirely new one of naval warfare. Pitt founded the British nineteenth century, Trafalgar guaranteed it.

Given that the war would continue another ten years, did Nelson really save Britain at Trafalgar? The common assertion is that Trafalgar saved Britain from invasion which, if successful, it could not have withstood. It was Villeneuve who actually saved Britain from invasion from Boulogne when he turned south to Cadiz instead of continuing to the Channel as he was meant to do, thus terminating Napoleon's Boulogne preparations. Napoleon took his army from Boulogne as soon as he got news of Villeneuve's retreat. He was already two months gone from the beach when Trafalgar was fought. Boulogne nevertheless realistically represented the biggest fright that Britain had suffered in centuries. For the British, Trafalgar in every sense therefore symbolized immediate release from that.

Napoleon never gave up the idea of invasion. He went back to Boulogne to ponder on its sands. He continued to build his navy. He saw Antwerp and the Scheldt as the launching point for another, grander, effort. What Nelson effectively demolished at Trafalgar, however, was any such future grand purpose and intent for the French navy and any combination that it might form through the rest of the war. Napoleon recognized that. With his prompt retaliatory commitment to Land, Napoleon's own commitment to navy was distinctly killed at Trafalgar. His navy was left demoralized by defeat. And, locked into Brest, Rochefort and Toulon, it lost efficiency and will.

One can then ask whether, truthfully, Britain could have come to that insular security at that time without a Nelson. What if Villeneuve had continued to Boulogne instead of turning south, perhaps the most interesting question of all. But Villeneuve's extraordinary lack of will and impulse, as first seen at Aboukir Bay, never suggests that as a serious possibility. One must, nevertheless, pursue the question of whether Britain's finally achieved naval security was really so fully owed to Nelson. There were many other fine officers, so who else could have carried it all forward as he did?

The gifts and drive of Nelson are so unique that only one man seems to come close through the entire period before Trafalgar: Cuthbert Collingwood. But blockade was where Collingwood saw most of his time and he was never given real opportunity until Nelson's death brought him his first significant operational command.

An evaluation of Nelson has to start with the fact that at the beginning the Royal Navy found itself heir to a new concept of naval battle that allowed individual daring and found in Nelson the natural practitioner of it. With Nelson, John Clerk's tactical enlightenment became much more than the licence of breaking the line and creating melee. What Nelson gave to it was entirely original to him, defining the value in attack even of the weak against the strong: the principle of a smaller but more efficient force hurling itself against superior numbers and, though defeated, creating sufficient havoc with the opponent to affect an entire campaign and its strategic objectives. That is, a battle 'wisely lost' for wider gain. This motivation of risk and daring to strike a punishing blow against the odds was always with him. What he had meant to a nation watching the rise of the astonishing individual and military genius across the Channel was that Britain had its own heroic genius to oppose the intimidation of the other.

Given the benefit derived from Rodney and Clerk, could no other naval officer similarly have determined the nation's fate? A simple answer is that for most the risk involved was too intimidating. Few, indeed, if any, were willing to set themselves unnecessarily against disciplined structures of the Royal Navy, thereby calling down upon themselves all the wrath and jealousy that any show of independence and the unconventional would provoke. Perhaps the most mystifying aspect of Nelson's career is how he survived at all to deliver what he eventually did.

For the general run of officers there was little of inspirational example at the top. They found it among themselves in the lesser rated ships, the frigates especially. Apart from Howe at 'the First of June' and Duncan at Camperdown there were no others in the critical pre-Trafalgar period who stood as decisive example for the younger generation in ship-of-the-line battle. Hood, in the unusual circumstances in which he perplexedly found himself at Toulon and Corsica, needed a resourceful officer. He found such a man in Nelson, for whom it was an unusual opportunity quickly seized upon. But Nelson soon enough found how wayward Hood's allegiance could be. It was the laxity and indolence of the commanders, Hotham and Hyde Parker, who succeeded Hood, that helped Britain to lose the Mediterranean at the critical point of Napoleon's career there. At the battle from which he took his title, St Vincent stood steadfastly in traditional line until Nelson had the courage and daring to provoke the melee that defeated the Spanish. Though others instantly followed his example, none of them had possessed the effrontery to initiate such an action. Fury arose over Nelson getting the assignment to search for Napoleon's expedition to Egypt, and he was lucky to hold on to the command after arriving at Alexandria and finding the port empty, then retreating to Sicily before returning to Alexandria and passing on to Aboukir Bay. Nelson knew all that time that he was pursued by jealousy from many directions. As Mahan said of that voyage, if he had missed the French a few weeks longer 'he might have lost his command, so great was the popular clamour over his first failure; and there was scarcely another British admiral at that time fitted to deal decisively with an equal enemy'. The same was true later with the mission to Copenhagen, under Hyde Parker, who ultimately but only after extended resistance gave Nelson his way to direct that hazardous action to the victory that ensured the Baltic. The odds seemed always to be against Nelson being able to deliver what was necessary at the right moment.

Whichever way one moves the picture, and search as one might, there simply was not anyone else, as Mahan said, fitted to deal as Nelson did at those pivotal actions upon which so much turned. Courage others had, but little or none of Nelson's unique intuitive tactical insight and irrepressible zeal, and even less of his appetite for risk, upon which his entire career ultimately depended. One only has to think of Howe's captain of the fleet, Roger Curtis, crying out his cautions against risk in the midst of 'the First of June'. Or of Robert Calder in the same position with Jervis at St Vincent, questioning Nelson's unauthorized departure from line. That made Calder's poor showing later against Villeneuve off Cape Finisterre more understandable.

How Nelson survived his personal follies is another question altogether. His commitment to risk guaranteed his exposure, in a physical sense as well as throughout his career. He lost an eye and an arm as a result of the former. His career could have been broken at Corsica when he sought a landing against a force whose superior strength he concealed from Hood. He sought, and fortunately did not get permission for, a foolish landing at Leghorn. He involved himself in the disastrous attempt by the Neapolitan king and queen to chase the French from Rome. His biggest folly was Tenerife. But all that mattered was that in the end he finally delivered what he sought and what Britain needed. It could be said that, had he survived Trafalgar, nothing more would have been required of him. It is doubtful that he would have gone to sea again. His deteriorating eyesight would have discouraged it. He himself at the end was, besides, ardently praying not merely to be away from the sea, but simply to be left at his ease at Merton with Emma and Horatia.

Challenge of the scale of Trafalgar had anyway left the seas. That is, the war of grand battle was gone, already pictures on the wall of the past. It would nevertheless continue as a war of intense naval activity on all the seas and oceans, a war of operational squadrons largely dependent on 74s and frigates.

A striking aspect of Pitt and Nelson falling away at practically the same time was thus that the war was simultaneously set on its entirely new course, away from what it had been, from the struggle as they had known it. It was, in a way, the legacy they bequeathed to the weak government that succeeded, known as 'All the Talents', with Lord Grenville as Prime

Minister, Edward Fox as Secretary of State for Foreign Affairs and William Windham as Secretary of War.

Napoleon's formula for Land's ability to subdue Sea, which meant to conquer Britain without recourse to tactical deployment of great fleets, was to proclaim a total blockade on all British commerce with Europe, where much of her prosperity lay. As he saw it, that for Britain would mean a battle for survival quite as determining as if he had managed to get across from Boulogne with his forces.

As great and demanding as that was, for Napoleon it nevertheless remained ancillary to the greater vision: the oriental empire he never lost sight of. And for that he required absolute mastery of the Mediterranean, '*the principal and constant aim of my policy*'. That ensured that the burden upon Collingwood steadily became heavier and more complex for the Mediterranean was to be inseparable from Napoleon's march across Europe during 1806 and 1807. Villeneuve's departure from Cadiz was intended by Napoleon to be in support of all of that. Had he got through the Straits before Nelson managed to confront him, the war would have been set on another, quite different, course.

There were to be three principal aspects to the character of the Great War after Trafalgar. War on commerce was, of course, the principal, for upon that Napoleon would direct all his intent and resources. But in a war propositioned as Land against Sea there had to be a military element of sea power. There was nothing new about that. Throughout the Great War so far landings of some sort or the other had been frequent. But this time the military element would be crucially different, with great campaigns fed from the sea. Just as the first phase of the Great War saw the rise to supremacy of the British navy, so the final one of the war would see a dramatic ascent of the British Army, through circumstances nevertheless entirely dependent upon the Royal Navy. That, then, was the second aspect.

The third significant aspect to the Great War after Trafalgar was to be American involvement. That was inevitable with the all-out war on commerce and quarrel over the rights of neutral flags. For the Americans this rapidly became another 'quasi-war' which, unlike the previous one, finally became full-scale war with Britain. During the five years preceding actual war between Britain and America the situation between them would become a bitter and acrimonious one through impressment of Americans, desertion of British sailors to America, and incidents of naval and commercial confrontation.

It was against the rapidly evolving background provided by those three forms of pressure and activity that the Great War now continued, making its final phase so distinct from what went before that it becomes a conflict that practically stands on its own.

XLII

RAMPAGE

Napoleon returned to Paris from the Ulm and Austerlitz battlefields on 24 January 1806 as a man without reason to doubt that he could already consider all Europe prostrate before him, even though Prussia was yet to bend the knee.

Given the bludgeoning performance so far witnessed, it would have been difficult to doubt that in their turn the Prussians surely would do so. A new, unstoppable human machine had been released upon the world, driven by the fury of frustration experienced on the western edge of the Continent and by the maritime defeat that had further compounded that.

Napoleon Buonaparte was on a rampage, the ultimate satisfaction and destination of which was yet too difficult to define except in terms of the universal and the sweeping, for, in alleviation of Trafalgar, Ulm and Austerlitz had unstoppered a release of himself and the boiling genius within that looked unrestrainable. He had been launched upon what would prove to be an astonishing twenty-four-month odyssey of conquest and diplomatic manipulation the swiftness and extent of which neither he nor anyone else could properly have foreseen, even though all of it was within the embrace of his broad ambitions. That he would push and the structure would fall as easily as it had done had nevertheless been quite unpredictable, especially by those who had so easily tumbled.

The fact that they had tumbled before him with such facility made Napoleon's determination to shut Britain out of Continental commerce seem so much more realizable. For anything so all-embracing to be effective, however, required direct command of, or influence over, all maritime trade from the Levant to the Baltic, and that he now sought to establish. At the start of 1806 that could yet seem an unrealistic demand, even after Ulm and Austerlitz. By the end of 1807, however, it appeared to be reality. By then this new Charlemagne had shackled or shrunk the ancient dynasties of Europe and created his own. Atop his rule as King of Italy he soon established his brothers as kings of Naples, Holland and Rome.

Between November 1805 and November 1807, every calculation on outcome that had seemed ponderable at the time of Trafalgar was to be swept away, with Britain at the end of it once more isolated, an isolation starker and more cold-walled than any previous.

Two days after Napoleon's return to Paris he, as if in token example of his new sway for any who might doubt it, declared the reign of the Bourbons Ferdinand and Maria Carolina and their Neapolitan kingdom to be at an end. Naples had agreed to a treaty of neutrality but Maria Carolina had invited an Anglo-Russian force of twenty thousand into Sicily, with later intent in Italy. Enraged, Napoleon sent an army down to seize Naples. The Neapolitan throne was decreed to his elder brother Joseph.

On 13 January 1806 Ferdinand and Carolina, their family and Court once more fled to Palermo and in March Napoleon installed Joseph as King of Naples. The Treaty of Pressburg had given Napoleon strong position on the Adriatic, which took him closer to the Ottomans and the Levant. On 9 June he sent on special mission to the Ottomans the celebrated Sebastiani, whose earlier mission to the Levant in 1802 had helped to end the Peace of Amiens. Sebastiani now sought to close the Bosporus to Russian and British ships.

The battered and virtually defunct Third Coalition had so far delivered only military disaster. For Britain it brought a particular diplomatic one as well. Her relationship with the Ottomans had been warm. Their treaty of alliance with the Turks had followed Napoleon's invasion of Egypt. But alliance with Russia put Britain in a different light with the Turks. Under Sebastiani's influence the Turks refused to renew their treaty with the British. Fears for the safety of Egypt were now badly compromised. The only relief from that was, for the moment, Napoleon's preoccupation with Prussia.

For his control of British commerce to be effective Napoleon needed control of the Baltic. He therefore needed to win, conquer or intimidate Prussia, which had the strongest army after his own. His tactic was to proffer Hanover to Prussia, in return for closing the Baltic to British commerce. A treaty to that effect was confirmed by Frederick Wilhelm on 26 February. Prussian troops occupied Hanover. Prussian ports were closed to British trade and on 21 April Britain responded by declaring similar hostility against all Prussian sea trade.

Between the capitals of Europe at this time weirdly changeable diplomatic currents were ceaselessly in flow from the crisscross of Napoleon's many designs. Then, clouding the picture, Britain and France once more entered negotiation towards peace, initiated by Edward Fox as Foreign Secretary. Fox longed to see the end of the war. For that he had an ally in Talleyrand, who increasingly recognized Napoleon as running out of control. Napoleon

himself was not averse to peace with Britain, for with it he saw opportunity
to negotiate for Sicily, the one piece of the picture he now required to
make concrete French predominance over the eastern Mediterranean. And,
having just assented to Prussian possession of Hanover, Napoleon was just
as easily disposed to reverse that and concede Hanover to Britain instead,
in return for Sicily.

Talleyrand had designated a British *bon vivant*, Lord Yarmouth, as the
British negotiator he preferred. Yarmouth was among the Britons who
had been detained prisoner in France at the renewal of war. More alive to
the loose-tongued society he was accustomed to than that of diplomacy,
Yarmouth soon made his own contribution to the prevailing diplomatic
confusion.

Russia was still at war with France, though her troops had retreated home
from the European battle zone. But on 20 July Russia's envoy, M. Doubril,
and Talleyrand signed a peace treaty. The treaty recognized cession of Sicily
to Joseph Buonaparte as King of Naples. Napoleon showed this to Yarmouth
and with that made his offer of Hanover to Britain as well as recognition
of British right to Malta *if* Britain, too, would allow cession of Sicily to
Joseph, with Ferdinand and Maria Carolina sent into exile. Edward Fox,
surprisingly, was finally prepared to give way on Sicily, if it brought the
peace he wanted. On 26 July Yarmouth therefore gave his agreement, but
he then let slip to the Prussian ambassador that Napoleon had guaranteed
Hanover to Britain. That inevitably inflamed Frederick Wilhelm who, on
Napoleon's earlier promise, already saw Hanover as his own.

All of it, however, fell apart. Yarmouth's agreement was overruled by
his successor, Lord Lauderdale, who insisted that Sicily would remain with
the Bourbons. The tsar rejected the treaty of his envoy Doubril. Frederick
Wilhelm, outraged by Napoleon's apparent double-dealing on Hanover,
began to mobilize his army and to demand the withdrawal of French troops
from points they had been occupying along the Rhine in north Germany.
Frederick Wilhelm promptly reopened the North German ports to British
commerce.

Fox died on 13 September. Talleyrand sought to continue the peace
negotiations, which for Napoleon still centred on possession of Sicily, but on
6 October the talks were finally broken off. By the time the talks ended
Napoleon had already left to muster his troops, refusing to evacuate them
from Germany until Frederick Wilhelm demobilized his own army. On 14
October 1806 in the twin battles of Jena and Auerstadt the Prussian army
was shattered. Thirteen days later Napoleon made his triumphant entry
into Berlin. Frederick Wilhelm had retreated eastwards with the remnants
of his army.

Occupation of Prussia allowed Napoleon preparation for the continuing war with Russia. Preceding that, however, came enunciation of the next stage of the maritime war. On 21 November 1806, from Berlin, Napoleon proclaimed the decree that placed absolute embargo on British trade and commerce upon the seas, along the coasts and within the nations and territories he controlled. All trade with Britain or in British goods, or British colonial produce, was forbidden. Mere possession of British goods was criminal. Any ship of whatever nationality that touched at British ports or carried British goods would become a prize of war. This was now more practicable than it had ever been, for the humiliation and subjection of Prussia gave Napoleon the rivers and ports upon which Britain was particularly dependent for shipping goods into Europe. With London as depot, commerce had flowed in and out of Europe principally through the north German ports on the Weser and Elbe rivers: Bremen, Cuxhaven, Hamburg.

Russia's fate was next. The tsar was now in two wars. In December 1806 his army attacked the Turks in Wallachia, modern Romania, and entered Bucharest But the tsar remained determined to support his ally Frederick Wilhelm. In a terrible winter campaign in 1807 the Russians and Prussians were narrowly defeated at Eylau on 7 February.

Britain, meanwhile, had decided on a show of flag and force at Constantinople in support of the Russians in their war with the Turks. There never was a clear definition of the naval mission, except as a counter to Sebastiani's influence at Constantinople, 'to detach the Turks from the French'.[1] Admiral Duckworth led a squadron of eight ships of the line through the Dardanelles to moor off Constantinople. The Turkish fleet was told to surrender, failing which Constantinople was to be bombarded. Duckworth lay ten days off Constantinople without any satisfaction, while behind him, along his way of retreat, the Turks directed by Sebastiani were preparing armament. Duckworth decided to get out, losing one ship on the way, from fire on board.

The Dardanelles show was a miserable failure. So was the near-simultaneous landing of six thousand soldiers in Egypt. Alexandria was taken but lack of supplies meant it could not be held. It was too much of a drain on British forces and resources in the Mediterranean. Five months later they were evacuated. Nothing had been achieved, except to warn Sebastiani that the British were ever on the watch against Napoleon's eastern intentions. Or, as the military historian J.W. Fortescue put it, 'The Cabinet sent six thousand men to Alexandria for a vague object which it could not define.'[2]

Meanwhile, the eastward retreat of the Prussian and Russian allies continued until, on 14 June 1807, near the Prussian town of Friedland, the Russians and Prussians were again defeated. Tsar Alexander and Frederick

Wilhelm retreated eastwards again to reassemble their forces at Tilsit on the River Niemen, in what is modern Lithuania. Alexander was persuaded by his generals to arrange an armistice with Napoleon. The three emperors met on a raft in the middle of the river. There, afloat, the future of the entire European continent appeared to be decided. On a lavishly decorated floating platform Napoleon completed the triumph of mustering the Continent for the encircling destruction of British commerce that was his goal.

Julian Corbett described the wholly new aspect that Napoleon had now brought to land warfare, a difference as profound as Nelson's at sea: 'War on land seemed to have changed from a calculated affair of thrust and parry between standing armies to a headlong rush of one nation in arms upon another, each thirsting for the other's life, and resolved to have it or perish in the attempt. Men felt themselves faced with a manifestation of human energy which had no counterpart, at least in civilized times.'[3] But of course the soldier who drove this rampage was one like no other before.

In the Treaty of Tilsit signed on 9 July 1807, the map of Germany and north Europe was rearranged. Prussia lost half its territory, reduced to half its previous population. In that dismemberment Napoleon's brother Jerome was given a new kingdom, Westphalia. To Louis of Holland went an enlargement that gave him Frisia and the port of Hamburg. Dantzig was declared a free city but garrisoned by the French. Prussia's Polish territories went to Russia. Tsar Alexander, in secret articles, agreed that Cattaro in the Adriatic and the Ionian Islands should go to France, that Joseph Buonaparte be recognized as King of Sicily as well as Naples. The Bourbons Ferdinand and Maria Carolina would be exiled to the Balearics or Crete, or wherever. Tsar Alexander agreed to stop fighting the Turks.

Throughout this campaign Alexander had looked to Britain to deliver some assistance to the last vestige of the Third Coalition that the Russian resistance specifically represented. There was no funding, no military help, not even significant naval assistance at points along the Baltic coast where it might have helped, such as Dantzig and Königsberg. An embittered tsar, impressed by Napoleon's persona, was therefore far more easily drawn under Napoleon's influence at Tilsit than otherwise might have been.

At Tilsit Alexander offered to mediate peace with Britain. Napoleon accepted, on condition that if agreement had not been reached by 1 December Russia would join France in war against Britain. Ultimatums would be sent to Denmark, Sweden and Portugal to close their ports to Britain and make war on her.

Travelling back to Paris from Tilsit Napoleon was in such a buoyant state that he even decided to revive the flotilla at Boulogne. Prospective possession of the Danish and Portuguese navies would undoubtedly have helped stimulate such thought, reviving the whole concept of invasion. He was in for a quicker surprise than he could have imagined. A British agent at Tilsit had hastened home with full details on the treaty and the menace it represented through its intent on Portugal and Denmark. Britain was left no option other than instant action with both Portugal and Denmark to secure their fleets.

The Baltic had priority. Denmark had a fleet of sixteen ships of the line manned by sailors whose seamanship and resourcefulness were as fine as Britain's. Napoleon's acquisition of such a force had at all costs to be prevented. When it was considered that Russia had a fleet of nineteen or twenty line ships to add to Denmark's fleet the balance of naval power on the Baltic was clearly Napoleon's. There was sufficient force to completely freeze Britain out of the Baltic, upon which access to naval stores and much of her export commerce were dependent. This was the heart of a crisis that Fortescue considered 'the most serious for England since the outbreak of the war in 1793'.[4]

Never was a major naval decision more swiftly taken by Britain. News of Tilsit had reached London about 16 July. Ten days later a fleet of seventeen ships of the line, twenty-one frigates and assorted flotilla vessels sailed from Yarmouth for the Sound, to compel surrender of the Danish fleet. The force was under Admiral James Gambier aboard his 98-gun flag-ship *Prince of Wales*. Twenty thousand troops embarked. Their second in command was Sir Arthur Wellesley. The orders were simultaneously sent to the force still at Stralsund to embark and proceed to the Sound, where on 12 August the two expeditions joined.

The Danish Prince Regent was assured that the British had come not for war but solely with demand that the Danish fleet and its stores be surrendered to them on full promise that all would be restored when Europe returned to peace. That was peremptorily rejected. The campaign was short and different from Nelson's in that this time the main job was left to the army. Gambier, like Hyde Parker before him, was a cautious man. The shores were more heavily defended than before and he held the fleet well above Copenhagen but ships were distributed to cut off the island of Zealand from Denmark. The troops were landed on the 16th and advanced on Copenhagen, which was encircled and besieged. The British proceeded to erect batteries. When the Danes, on 2 September, again refused to surrender their fleet the batteries began a merci-less bombardment of the city, much of it with the new weapon, Congreve's rockets. It continued for three days, after which the Danes submitted and surrendered their fleet and its stores.

Copenhagen was devastated, at least one-quarter of the city flattened to the ground, the first evidence of the destructive power of the rockets. There was much unease in Britain over this, but the satisfaction of stripping Napoleon of further recourse to any form of naval advantage over Britain outweighed the sense of brotherhood that the British always had with the Danes. Moral repugnance over the action was more easily borne, moreover, at sight of the Danish fleet being ushered into Yarmouth. For Napoleon it was a surprise that drove him berserk, as Joseph Fouché recalled in his memoirs, describing '. . . violent transports of fury'.[5]

Napoleon's ultimatum to Portugal had gone off as soon as he was back. At a diplomatic levee on 2 August he reminded the Portuguese ambassador: 'Your Court knows that she must break with England before the 1st of September. You must break either with England or France before the 1st of September.'[6]

On 20 October the Prince Regent of Portugal decided to comply with the demand to close his ports to the British. By that time, an army of twenty thousand under General Junot was marching down through Spain to ensure that closure and to seize the Portuguese fleet.

Foreign Secretary George Canning responded swiftly by seeking to persuade the Regent, the rest of the Braganza family and their Court to flee to Brazil, escorted there by the Portuguese fleet and a British squadron. The Regent vacillated week after week as Junot, under strong pressure from Napoleon, advanced upon the capital. Sidney Smith was finally sent out with a squadron of six ships of the line to advise the Regent and his Court to embark for Brazil or suffer the rigours of the blockade that Britain would impose. The Regent finally assented and on 29 November he and his entourage sailed out escorted by the Portuguese fleet of twelve line ships accompanied by Sidney Smith's five. Junot was simultaneously marching into Lisbon, just in time to be able to see the Combined Fleet yet visible, standing towards the horizon and the Brazils.

Sea had again denied Land a prize it had rushed to possess, but with Junot's army in Lisbon there could be no great celebration. Portugal, Britain's oldest ally, had provided a steady base on the Tagus to cover the Mediterranean approaches. Obtaining both the Danish and Portuguese fleets did not lessen the unpleasant fact that Napoleon had greatly enlarged his means for enforcing his war on commerce in the Baltic and along the Atlantic.

By the swift progression of conquest from Ulm and Friedland to Lisbon, Napoleon had laid his command upon the Continent. He now even had the Turks on side. He could say, 'England sees her merchandise repelled by all Europe, and her ships, loaded with useless wealth, seek in vain, from the Sound to the Hellespont, a port open to receive them.'

It was yet too early to be so emphatic upon success, but no ruler had ever possessed such complete enforced obedience on the Continent. Look where you would, every significant port or base that sat on Europe's entire shoreline was there to serve the French and their emperor's commitment to the destruction of British commerce, thereby elimination of British power.

XLIII

SANDY HOOK

EARLY afternoon on 25 April 1806 a familiar sight greeted the pilot craft, revenue cutters and assorted merchantmen that were either lying off the New Jersey shore or standing in to pass Sandy Hook lighthouse and on in to New York.

Three British warships had appeared, the 50-gun *Leander* and *Cambrian* and a brig. All were from the Canadian naval base at Halifax and were on regular station along that coast, off New York, there to board homeward-bound American ships they suspected of contravening British definitions of contraband, or of carrying British deserters. Their closeness to the American shore reflected the aggressive British determination to enforce all of that.

Several American ships, including the coasting sloop *Richard*, were coming up from the south. *Leander* and *Cambrian* began firing at the ships, as signal to stop and await boarding party. The firing appears to have been carelessly wide. Jesse Pierce, master of the *Richard*, was busy with the main sheet, his brother John Pierce at the helm, when a shot from *Leander* struck the quarterdeck, passing through the binnacle and killing John Pierce. The American ships all hove to, but no boarding parties were launched. The British ships then made off.

The British squadron was familiar to the pilots and revenue cutter men that lay off Sandy Hook lighthouse, as well as in the port of New York where the three ships sometimes went for provisioning. On this occasion they had been sent down from Halifax specifically to make a show off Sandy Hook for, as a British court martial subsequently revealed, on a previous cruise off Sandy Hook American ships had 'obstinately persisted in not attending to the first shot fired by Leander'.

The Americans had set their maritime jurisdiction as three miles out. The British ships were all judged to have begun their action at about a mile and a half from the shore.

Richard sailed into New York and landed John Pierce's body, which the next day was put on public view. Elections were then underway in New

York, to be immediately inflamed by the assault. The British flag was burned in front of the British consul's house. The British were sent a demand to surrender *Leander*'s captain, Henry Whitby, for violation of American neutrality and for the wilful murder of Pierce. President Jefferson, meanwhile, issued a proclamation prohibiting any further dealings with *Leander*, *Cambrian* and *Driver* at New York or elsewhere along the east coast.

Relations between Britain and the United States were already in a fast deteriorating state on neutrality issues and actions of the British navy. That represented a sudden and unexpected change in what during recent years had become a remarkable mutually satisfying commercial accord. The first crisis over the neutrality of the American flag at the start of the Great War had fallen away as Britain gave virtual free play to neutral shipping to help carry her trade. The United States had been the principal beneficiary of that. The tonnage of American shipping in foreign trade rose from 363,100 in 1791 to 848,300 in 1807. The Americans had benefited from a device known as 'continuous voyage'. A ship would load, say, a cargo of sugar in French Martinique, carry it to an American port where it would be registered as import. Then, without any of it being discharged, the ship might sail for a French port carrying the sugar as export on its manifests. There were countless variations of this. But in 1805 the High Court of Admiralty had ruled against the practice in the case of a ship, *Essex*, that broke a voyage between Barcelona and Havana by calling at Salem, Massachusetts. *Essex* was intercepted by a British cruiser on the way from Salem to Havana. Ship and cargo were subsequently declared prize by the Admiralty prize court.

The *Essex* decision, one of the most critical in the history of Anglo-American relations, changed everything on the sea for American merchantmen for it brought the first serious indication of a changed attitude in Britain from gratitude to something harder over the role of the Americans and other neutrals in maintaining the flow of British commerce, upon which funding of the war depended. An Admiralty lawyer, James Stephen, had published a book, *Frauds of the Neutral Flags*, that declared that the neutrals were keeping alive the commerce and prosperity of Britain's enemies and that, far from benefiting Britain, they were waging 'a war in disguise' against her. Stephen was reflecting a viewpoint that had already become established among British ship-owners and merchants. It readily attached itself to the established fear of future American rivalry in global trade.[1]

The *Essex* was the dominant international issue in Washington when the *Leander* squadron appeared off Sandy Hook. The week before, on 18 April, Congress had retaliated against the *Essex* seizure with an act prohibiting the importation of certain British manufactures. The act was postponed, however, to await the outcome of new diplomatic negotiations with the

British that Jefferson had decided were urgently required. A Washington lawyer, William Pinkney, was to go to London at once to support James Monroe, the American minister there, in negotiating a new agreement with the British. *Leander* obviously brought further urgency to that.

Impressment was now an even greater emotional issue than it had been twelve years before when the Jay Treaty had been negotiated. The instructions that Pinkney took from Jefferson were to win a British commitment to abandon 'the licentiousness' with which impressment was pursued. Apart from indignation over the impressment of Americans, equal indignation was felt over the seizure from American ships of British deserters or Britons with American papers. On trade, Pinkney and Monroe were to seek clearer definition of contraband and of continuous voyage.

In this already tense situation *Leander* had gone too far too soon after *Essex*. Britain therefore sought to make an especially expressive gesture of conciliation for the *Leander* squadron's action. Captain Whitby was ordered for court martial and the principal American witnesses were brought over to England for it. Apart from anything else, their evidence aboard HMS *Gladiator* in Portsmouth harbour just a year after the incident offered a telling picture of the brash manner of British inshore intrusion and peremptory halting of American merchantmen at the very entrance to New York harbour. Caleb Brunster, captain of the American revenue cutter *Vigilant*, speaking of the morning of the action, said,

I got under weigh in Ratigan Bay, and went out past the lights at the Hook. As soon as I got out I discovered three men of war. I discovered a number of sail of vessels to the southward of me, along the Jersey shore, standing in for Sandy Hook. I saw these three ships stand in for the land, the Cambrian, the Leander and Driver. I knew the ships, I have been all around them fifty times. The Cambrian was the headmost ship; she stood in for the land, and began to fire at the headmost vessels that were coming from the southward, and brought them to. I suppose the Cambrian to be about a mile and a half from the shore. The Leander came up right astern of her, went past her, and began to fire at the brig Sally, that was in shore of him, and the sloop Richard, Jesse Pierce, master. She fired a number of shot before she went about, and as she went about she fired a number of shot at those two vessels. I saw a number of them strike in the water near those two vessels, one of them struck in the surf, the next struck on the beach, and made the sand fly ten feet high.

There was no indication of from where the merchantmen were inbound. Coming from the south the likeliest possibilities could have been either coastal or from the Caribbean. It was the latter possibility that made them targets, on suspicion of carrying French colonial produce.

Whitby was acquitted but refused further service in the Royal Navy. A year later, however, he was quietly reinstated.[2]

The Pinkney–Monroe mission came to naught. On 31 December 1806 they actually signed a treaty in London in which some further definition of contraband was made but the British withheld any commitment on impressment. Without the latter Jefferson refused to submit the treaty to Congress.

Essex and *Leander* were the sparks that set off the serious descent of British and American relations in the last phase of the Great War. A greater, more explosive, issue followed just six months later. At all events, an active transatlantic reach of the war had been firmly established.

Simultaneously with *Leander*, a great foolishness was underway in the other Americas where one of the Royal Navy's boldest captains, Sir Home Riggs Popham, had decided on an impromptu grab at Buenos Aires and the River Plate.

Here, irrepressibly alive again, was the British lost dream of the Americas.

While Nelson was still in London and Villeneuve's ultimate destination still imponderable, Pitt and Barham, weighed by all those uncertainties, had decided that it was urgently necessary to repossess the Cape of Good Hope, so generously returned to the Dutch with Amiens. On 1 September 1805 a force of six thousand soldiers in a convoy of sixty-one transports escorted by nine men of war sailed from Cork on mission to recapture the Cape of Good Hope. The Dutch colony had not endeared itself to the British during the ten years of their occupation. Their final assessment of its value saw it as a 'burden rather than an advantage'. St Helena and Madagascar were considered better staging posts to India. That had also been the Portuguese view of the Cape after they first discovered it. The place itself was seen as worthless, the indigenous inhabitants troublesome. But Napoleon's persistent Indian preoccupations prompted new British concern about it in mid-1805. And, besides, in 1796 an American Indiaman, *Hercules*, had been wrecked on the southern African coast. Her master, Captain Benjamin Stout, of Boston, had been so impressed by the country that he recommended establishment of an American colony there, suggesting to President Adams that South Africa was 'open to American adventure'. That was more than enough to set a different value on the place with the British. An American had already occupied the island of Tristan da Cunha, south of St Helena, and raised the American flag there.[3]

American adventure, but of different aspect, was what Captain Popham shared with Captain Stout. Britain had become increasingly drawn to the idea of South America as an area for its own exploitation. On 4 January 1806 Popham brought his fleet to anchor off Cape Town. After a brief resistance the Cape capitulated on 18 January. Major General Baird's firm instructions had been to send half his troops on to India after garrisoning the Cape. Popham's brief was to stand by until the Cape was captured, then to return home. Instead, with the naval force at his disposal, he decided on seizing Buenos Aires and Montevideo. He persuaded Baird to provide him with sixteen hundred soldiers under Colonel W.C. Beresford.

Popham sailed from the Cape on 14 April and arrived off the Plate on 8 June, after a stop at St Helena, where he had wrung more troops from the governor. At the Plate the soldiers were put ashore in small craft and on 27 June the governor of Buenos Aires surrendered that city of seventy thousand with its powerful river fort of eighty-six guns. It all happened so quickly that the colonists found the British flag flying over them before they could get themselves together. But resentment was swift.

Unhappily for Popham and Beresford it was all short-lived. A French colonel in the Spanish service, Chevalier de Linieres, aided by the Bishop of Buenos Aires, organized the colonists on both sides of the River Plate. The city was infiltrated as the British stood at church parade. Beresford was compelled to surrender after a fierce battle in the centre of Buenos Aires. After an extended futile struggle around the River Plate, the British gave up completely on July 7 1807.

All of it was a sorry disaster blown up from the arrogant self-esteem, contempt for authority and determination on quick enrichment of a British naval captain who had a small squadron at his disposal and decided to make it serve his own ends. The whole had been based on casual assumptions of a supine colony that would easily be walked over by a band of British soldiers and sailors, and whose inhabitants would then obediently swear allegiance to the British flag. Taking the Cape had been easy, but that had been expected. The Dutch had never mounted a heavy defence there. What had not been counted upon was the fact that the Spanish colonists, far from bowing in servile submission, would find in foreign occupation the unifying cause towards the independence they sought. 'The inveteracy of every class of inhabitants was beyond belief,' Rear Admiral George Murray reported from Buenos Aires. These were tough people who knew the worth of their fruitful, prospering land and were ready to defend it. Once roused, Rio Plata failed to settle down again. Six years later Argentina was independent.

This had been yet another miserably ill-prepared and incompetently directed military excursion to add to the sad list of those many others like it since the start of the Great War.

Popham went to trial and got away with it. Expectations had been raised in Britain of possessing new American empire and markets just as Buonaparte began to demonstrate a real possibility of Land choking Sea after all, by bringing commerce to a halt. Tilsit had changed the face of Europe, and with it the course of the war, and of history. The humiliating subjection of Prussia had given Napoleon the north German and Baltic ports that were essential for successful imposition of his ban on British commerce. Against that, the South American delusion was at least understandable.

XLIV

CHESAPEAKE

DUSK was thickening on the evening of 7 March 1807 when Midshipman Robert Turner of the British sloop of war *Halifax*, lying in Hampton Roads, was ordered to take five seamen into the jolly boat to weigh the kedge anchor, which had been laid out for swinging the ship. The kedge was a small anchor used in harbour or at anchor to assist movement of the ship, particularly with the approach of bad weather. Rain was closing in as Turner shoved off. The weather was thick when they got to the kedge hawser and prepared to haul up the anchor. In that rapidly diminishing visibility four of the seamen took over the boat. They began rowing for shore. Turner hailed the ship for help. His seamen told him to keep quiet or have his brains knocked out and himself then thrown overboard.

Aboard *Halifax* First Lieutenant Thomas Carter saw the sailors making off and immediately concluded mischief. He ordered a fire of musketry, and then some of the big guns to be pointed and fired. But the boat disappeared into the dusk. When it got to the beach the sailors shoved it back into deep water, with Turner, who jumped out and waded ashore.

The next day when *Halifax*'s commander, Captain Lord James Townshend, and other officers went ashore at Norfolk, Virginia, to report the incident the first sight that greeted them was that of the deserters parading the streets with the American flag. They had just signed for service aboard the 38-gun frigate *Chesapeake*, which was recruiting for her next spell of duty with the American squadron in the Mediterranean. Townshend made an ineffectual attempt through the recruiting officer and local officials to have his men returned to him. Townshend was probably a disliked captain for, on encountering some of his seamen in the streets, he was vigorously insulted by them. The abuse was said to be personal, particularly from one seaman, Jenkin Rutford. Advising Rutford and the others to return to the ship, Townshend was told to mind his own business. They would do as they liked, Rutford said, since they were now in the land of liberty.

The episode appears to have caused apoplexy for the British commander of naval forces on the North American station, Vice Admiral George Berkeley, who, in spite of the tensions already building with the United States over *Leander*, trade and impressment, ordered all ships on his command to seek out *Chesapeake* and get back the deserters.[1]

A complaint against *Chesapeake* for recruiting British seamen had been lodged even before the *Halifax* desertions. Three sailors had deserted from the British warship *Melampus* and had enlisted aboard *Chesapeake*. But the British complaint had been indignantly received and rejected at Washington for at least two of the *Melampus* deserters were proven to be Americans, one of them a coloured man.

Chesapeake's preparation for her departure to the Mediterranean had been leisurely. By the time of sailing her new crew of 375 had only three times been at quarters, the drill that summoned them to their action stations. On none of those occasions had the guns been exercised.

At eight a.m. on 22 June 1807, *Chesapeake*, under the broad pennant of Commodore James Barron, with Captain Charles Gordon as captain, sailed from Hampton Roads for the Mediterranean. Lying off the roads was a British squadron, the *Bellona*, 74 *Melampus*, 38, and *Leopard*, 50. When *Chesapeake* was seen to have weighed *Leopard* lifted her own anchor and set a course that kept her several miles ahead of *Chesapeake*.

At about three p.m. *Leopard*, then about a mile to windward, wore round and descended upon *Chesapeake*, which she hailed, saying that she had a despatch for her. This had become a habit. An American ship outbound for the other side might be asked by a British warship to take letters or despatches. That sort of informality was still alive. Commodore Barron said he would heave to and receive a boat. Some of *Chesapeake*'s officers then noticed that *Leopard*'s lower gun ports were up and that the tompions (wooden stoppers for the gun muzzles) were out of her guns.

The British officer who boarded was received by Barron, who was handed a letter from *Leopard*'s captain that included the general order that Admiral Berkeley had issued against *Chesapeake*, stipulating that the British officer who boarded was required to search for deserters. As a sop to likely indignation Berkeley's order provided assurance that the British were willing to allow the Americans the same right on the British ships. Barron replied that, to his knowledge, he had no British deserters and that he would not allow his men to be mustered by any officers but his own. He wrote a note to that effect to *Leopard*'s captain, Humphreys.[2]

So high-handed a demand from a fighting ship of one nation upon one of another flag was a belligerence unknown outside of war. The possibility of resistant action was what Barron and Captain Gordon now had to contemplate.

As the *Leopard*'s boat returned, the British ship's own readiness for immediate action was more plainly evident. She lay within pistol shot but clearly it was not musketry she intended. Her guns were trained and matches were burning, with the men at quarters. Barron told Gordon to clear the gun deck and to bring *Chesapeake* to quarters with as little noise and visible action as possible. He stopped the tapping of the drum that began to beat to quarters.

Action was the last thing that *Chesapeake* had prepared for as she weighed out of Hampton Roads. Apart from the fact that her crew now at quarters had not yet been exercised at guns, the ship itself was in disarray. Her officers were fortunately experienced men and had the guns loaded and shotted only to find at every station that they lacked one thing or another, whether rammers, wads, matches, gunlocks or powder horns. Besides, *Chesapeake*'s cables had not yet been coiled away; baggage, stores and cabin furniture still stood on the decks, awaiting transfer below.

Barron was at the gangway watching the return of *Leopard*'s boat. *Chesapeake* was hailed immediately after. Humphreys signalled that Admiral Berkeley's order had to be obeyed. Barron answered that he did not understand the hail. *Leopard* then fired a shot ahead of *Chesapeake*. When two more shots were ignored Humphreys fired a broadside. An attempt was made by *Chesapeake* to fire her own broadside, but there was no priming powder or matches. Meanwhile, two more broadsides from *Leopard* drove into *Chesapeake*. Barron ordered the colours to be hauled down. Before they were completely down *Chesapeake* finally managed to fire one gun, ignited by a live coal brought up from the galley and which the officer at the post had applied with his bare fingers. It was the only shot fired by *Chesapeake*.

A boat was sent to *Leopard* to say that *Chesapeake* was at the disposal of Captain Humphreys, being now his prize. Humphreys declared that he had no wish to hold *Chesapeake*. Two of *Leopard*'s lieutenants and several midshipmen boarded *Chesapeake*, mustered the American seamen and sought out those they knew as deserters or suspected to be. The man they particularly wanted was Jenkin Rutford, who had abused Captain Townshend of the *Halifax* in the streets of Norfolk. They found him in the coal hole.

Once the seized Britons were on board, *Leopard* made off, bearing them to Halifax, Nova Scotia. *Chesapeake* was left in sorry state. Six seamen had been killed, twenty-three wounded. Twenty-one shot had struck the hull. All three masts had been damaged, rigging cut and the sails riddled. Barron had himself been wounded in the leg by a splinter. *Chesapeake* was back in Hampton Roads that same evening.

Norfolk that night was in a state of anti-British riot. British sailors ashore were lucky to escape with their lives. A watering party from the frigate *Melampus* escaped as their two hundred water barrels were destroyed. The British navy would never again water there.

Outraged national pride, a deeply felt sense of impotence and humiliation of the flag, sent a storm of rage whirling through the United States. Following so hard on the *Essex* and *Leander* events, the political and public uproar looked unappeasable. A declaration of war appeared to hover. The episode rankled as nothing had done since the War of Independence. Its impact was to be lasting, with effects on both nations that became disastrously far-reaching for both. The *Chesapeake* affair fast brought a new and critical course in British and Americans relations. America was spurred to a dramatic, ill-considered response that was to rebound upon her while Britain, soon to be fighting for her commercial survival, found that *Chesapeake* had deprived her of her most dependable source of support, the American trade. The price of Captain Lord Townshend's patrician pride injured in the streets of Norfolk proved to be high.

The British navy immediately lost all privileges on the American coast. On 2 July President Jefferson issued a proclamation ordering the departure of all British armed vessels from American harbours and waters. All future intercourse with the officers and crews of British warships was forbidden, and they were to be denied all supplies, aid and any form of pilotage. Parties that landed for water were chased back to the sea.

Under the new Portland government with George Canning as Foreign Secretary, Britain made some demonstration of regret. Admiral Berkeley was recalled from his command at Halifax and Captain Humphreys removed from *Leopard*. He was not given another ship on grounds that he had exceeded his instructions. *Chesapeake*'s Commodore Barron paid heavily. The shortcomings aboard *Chesapeake* made it inevitable with such an emotional issue. Lack of experience could no longer excuse this young navy which by 1807 had three naval wars behind it. *Chesapeake*, after all, was sailing to a scene of possible naval action. Brought to trial on several charges, Barron was found guilty of failing to clear his ship for action after it became plain that *Leopard* intended action. He was suspended for five years without pay. *Chesapeake*'s gunner was cashiered for failing to fill the priming horns.

At Halifax the deserters seized from *Chesapeake* were promptly court-martialled. Jenkin Rutford received a surprising commendation from the captain he had publicly abused. Townshend said that before the desertion he had behaved himself as a 'quiet, steady man'. But he was, as expected, sentenced to death and hanged from the yardarm. The others were to receive five hundred lashes each, but were afterwards pardoned.

The British increased their watch off the American coasts but British warships were no longer seen close inshore off the American harbours, where they so had often detained ships and impressed men. The United States Navy no longer sent its ships to the Mediterranean.

On the wider stage of the Great War a dramatic aspect of *Chesapeake* was that it appeared as a prospective transatlantic backup for Napoleon's plans to kill British commerce, even if not complicitly with American support.

The American dilemma was painful. In the changing Western world that was emerging so rapidly after Tilsit, the United States stood as the only independent nation outside the all-enveloping struggle, into which she was now ever more tightly drawn. The irony was that the most active source of America's resentment in this titanic struggle was against the only other truly independent nation that now existed, and whose ideals she shared. Neutrality was a state that, if it retained any significance at all, now had real existence only with the American flag on the western seas and oceans. But the constrictions laid down by both Britain and Napoleon during 1806 and 1807 had made the concept of neutrality more farcical than it had ever been. With both countries edict continued to follow edict in violation of neutrality.

The situation that finally arrived was, at its simplest, that if an American ship touched at a British port on the way to the Continent his ship and cargo were liable to confiscation by the French or their agents. The same, in reverse, applied with the British. Neutral ships were liable to seizure if they traded with France or her allies, or wherever the British flag was excluded. The British offered one loophole: American ships could trade with enemy ports provided they first put in at British ports and paid duty on their merchandise. Apart from thereby exposing themselves to the fullest censure of the French, heavy duties were imposed on foreign goods passing through British customs houses, particularly on cotton and tobacco, America's two main domestic exports. Such a system, if submitted to, John Quincy Adams said, 'would have degraded us to the condition of colonists'.[3]

In face of all these restrictions, together with the lack of reparation for the *Chesapeake* action and the British refusal to make any commitment on impressment, President Jefferson and Congress on 22 December 1807 resorted to their own extraordinary and completely unprecedented embargo. American ports were closed to foreign shipping. American merchantmen were forbidden oceanic trade. Coastwise trade between American ports alone was to be allowed. This, James Madison told Congress, was 'an armor and an attitude demanded by the crisis', which he particularly blamed on Britain 'whose practices have the character as well as the effect of war on our lawful commerce'. The embargo was consequently seen as the alternative to open war.

Britain badly needed the American market for its manufactures.

Punishment of Britain the act therefore certainly delivered, but it was, far more, an incomprehensibly savage self-inflicted blow to a large and active American merchant marine, pride of the New England seaboard, employing some sixty thousand seamen and annually handling sixty million dollars' worth of foreign produce.

For navy man Mahan, looking back scathingly upon the whole, it was an indescribable folly, attributable to President Jefferson's aversion to all things oceanic and his moralizing elevation of the rural simplicities of colonial America. 'The American nation was to take as its model the farmer who lives on his own produce, sternly independent of his neighbor; whose sons delved, and wife span, all that the family needed. This programme, half sentiment, half philosophy, and not at all practical, or practicable, was the groundwork of Jefferson's thought.' Or, as Jefferson himself expressed it, 'I trust that the good sense of our country will see that its greatest prosperity depends on a due balance between agriculture, manufactures, and commerce, and not on this protuberant navigation, which has kept us in hot water from the commencement of our government.'

Whether for merchant ships or navies, Mahan said, the sea was odious to Jefferson's conception of things, 'for that ample use of it which had made the greatness of Holland and England, he had only aversion . . . Opposition to England was to him a kind of mission. His best wish for her had been that she might be republicanized by a successful French invasion.'[4]

This was a bitter Mahan who, at the end of the nineteenth century, was striving to restore the naval vision of the early years, so much of which had fallen away after the Great War. But his bitterness was more than justified by the distress, loss, ruin and disorder that Jefferson's absurd embargo laid upon the land, New England especially. It was naturally evaded wherever possible. Smuggling became rife through Canada. American harbours were like forests of tall, dry trees as ships were tied up. Perhaps the most bitter aspect, certainly the most ironic, was that American seamen began to look to British ships for employment, exposing themselves to more impressment.

The blindness of the embargo was extraordinary in that American ships could have continued trade with Britain since the possibility of French intervention was negligible, unless the ships went on to the Continent. The American merchantmen could have continued as well with the West Indies and South America and, as war came to Iberia, those coasts lay open to them, quite apart from the China and oriental trade in which they had been building their competition with Britain. But, except for New England, elsewhere in the United States that rage against Britain justified the weird self-denial of America's hitherto ambitious mercantile reach for the wide world.

That admirable sailor Vice Admiral Collingwood, commanding in the

Mediterranean, commenting on the episode, gave an insight on how the British were operating with impressment merely in the Mediterranean. A return he had from only a part of the ships in his squadron revealed that those alone had 217 Americans. In returns from one ship a 'supernumerary' was reported received from an American ship. 'I hope he was given up in an amicable way,' Collingwood wrote. 'The affair in America I consider as exceedingly improvident and unfortunate, as in the issue it may involve us in a contest which it would be wisdom to avoid. When English seamen can be recovered in a quiet way, it is well; but when demanded as a national right, which must be enforced, we should be prepared to do reciprocal justice.' The journal of another ship told him that they had pressed a man out of an American merchantman bound from Leghorn to Salem. 'What should we say if the Russians were to man themselves out of English ships?'[5]

XLV

ABOMINABLE

For the 100,000 or more sailors indefinitely incarcerated aboard the warships of the Great War sexual longing was a denial that had to be lived with, conscious that release from it belonged to a day beyond any prediction, or to rare special circumstances.

Many women were afloat, wives or those who passed as such, ones who got on board and stayed. They gave sterling service in battle, tending to the wounded or even carrying powder to the guns. Since sailors were only allowed ashore in exceptional circumstances it was common, especially lying off home ports, for women to come out. There followed the riotous, bawdy scenes so denounced by the evangelicals. But after years at sea it was well-deserved relief, something which for most rarely, if ever, came.

It was hardly surprising, therefore, that homosexual relations between sailors occasionally surfaced. The instances of them coming to notice were rare, which was understandable since sodomy was a capital crime. Culprits were hanged. It is therefore difficult to make any judgement on the extent of its existence. One historian of the eighteenth-century British navy declared, 'Everything suggests that it was an insignificant issue.' But that seems merely wishful, difficult to accept against the intense intimacy of shipboard existence, and the inevitable irruption of homosexual bonding that such extended circumstances had always produced.

Some insight is provided from publicly reported courts martial held when the charges of homosexual relations were brought ashore from a voyage. Otherwise, with rigid disciplinarians like St Vincent, who hanged two men off Cadiz for it, there could be little more than the bare logged fact of culprits found guilty under the 29th Article, which dealt with sodomy. Two particular courts martial, in 1807 and 1810, provided unusual images of what could occur aboard ship. One case, that of 1807, becomes especially affecting.

The first lieutenant of HMS *Hazard*, William Berry, was charged by his captain under the 29th Article, 'the horrid and abominable crime which delicacy forbids us to name'. His exposure came from a woman, Elizabeth

Bowden, who had been on board the ship for eight months. 'Curiosity had prompted her to look through the key-hole of the cabin door, and it was thus she became possessed of the evidence which she gave.' She was a woman who clearly had regular access to the officers' quarters, probably used as a cleaner there. Her suspicions had obviously been raised by the visits of a boy of the ship, Thomas Gibbs, to Berry's cabin. Malice certainly, perhaps even envy, took her to the keyhole, for Berry was an unusually attractive young man: 'The unfortunate prisoner was a native of Lancaster, and only in his 22nd year, about six feet high, remarkably well made, and as fine and handsome a man as in the British navy. He was to have been married on his return to port.'

Berry asked time for his defence and was granted until the next day. But 'having maturely and deliberately weighed and considered the same' the court found the charges proved and sentenced him to hang. There is no indication of what his defence was, but the boy had 'proved the offence'. He had been questioned and, doubtless in terror, had sought to save himself.

Berry was hanged aboard his own ship.

At nine o'clock he appeared and mounted the scaffold with the greatest fortitude. He then requested to speak with the Rev. Mr Birdwood on the scaffold; he said a few words to him, but in so low a tone of voice they could not be distinctly heard. The blue cap being put over his face, the fatal bow gun was fired, and he was run up to the fore-yard-arm, with a thirty-two pound shot tied to his feet. Unfortunately the knot had got round under his chin, which caused great convulsions for a quarter of an hour. After being suspended the usual time, he was lowered into his coffin, which was ready to receive in a boat immediately under, and conveyed to the Royal Hospital, where his friends meant to apply for his internment.

A strange attempt was made to save him. A woman brought a letter saying that she could save him, since she was there to marry him. She was brought on board and put under guard. Questioned by the captain and clergyman after the execution she said she had dreamed a dream the previous night, that if she went on board *Hazard* and Lieutenant Berry would marry her, he would not suffer death. She had told her dream to some women who also lived on the dockside. They had told her to go to the ship to save him. 'She was admonished, and sent on shore.'

The trial in 1810 was of quite a different order. James Nemehiah Taylor, surgeon of HMS *Jamaica*, was found guilty of an 'abominable offence' with Thomas Ashton, a boy of the Royal Marines, his servant, when the ship came in on a voyage from Halifax. He was thirty-eight and had been surgeon at sea for nineteen years.

Taylor was clearly a product of the Age of Reason, alive to his times: 'He was a man of good education, strong natural abilities, and very extensive reading; but his principal reading, as he said, was in Voltaire, Bolingbroke, and other infidel authors. His manners were easy and courteous, and his quick flow of observations, upon almost every subject, shewed a well-stored mind.'

What was particularly insightful from him was his declamation on the widespread character of homosexuality in the world of his day. As was common with those going to execution, he did so as a repentant confessional to the ship's chaplain, Rev. Howell:

He said, 'Now sir, I am willing to make a full disclosure of all my sins, for I feel I must unburden my heart and mind of them. I will tell you with whom I have been concerned in this hateful crime, which I have practised so long and so often, and who are the persons that have tended to bring me into this baneful practice. Sir, this crime is more general than you are aware of – *there is a society formed for the practice of it*! And, belonging to it, are some men whom the public look up to' – He was proceeding to make this painful and disgusting disclosure, when Mr Howell desired he would not mention any names as, in his present situation, it could be of no service, and only tend to ruffle his mind, and break off his communications with the Deity, which above all things he should endeavour to preserve. He proceeded: In London, in France, and in the Mediterranean, he had seen the act committed, and it was not considered a crime; that having taken up the vile and baneful opinion, *that he had a right to do it himself as he pleased*, and was not accountable to God, he had frequently committed it; and so powerful was the control of the vice over him, that when objects did not present themselves to him, he sought them.

Given the apparent intensity of his former passion, in his nineteen years at sea Surgeon Taylor must have encountered or successfully sought many 'objects'. The many boys on a ship clearly were among such. Boys were the partners of both Berry and Taylor. That would not be unusual in navies of a later age when such dire punishment no longer existed. Boy Seaman Samuel Leech in his record of the moral licence aboard a man of war spoke of 'licentiousness in its most shameful and beastly garb; vice, in the worst of its Proteus-like shapes, abound there'. The message therefore is clear, especially since Leech drew clear distinction between all of that and what went on when the ship was in port.

Through the whole history of men in prolonged isolation from their mainstream world such relationships have always existed, especially afloat. At that very time, in the penal colonies of Australia, the transported men turned to one another for permanent relationships. In a later Royal Navy of easier tolerance it was commonplace. So how could it not also have been within the tight, prolonged intimacy on board during the Great War, in spite of the terrible penalties? The difficulties and dangers were great. Only officers and others such as surgeons had privacy with their own cabins. But even for the others, an eighteenth-century warship had its dark, hidden corners. There were many spaces and opportunities for the resourceful.

Whether it came to actual sexual expression or not, there was nevertheless a natural bonding with intense attachment that evolved within that prolonged confinement and the harsh endurance it demanded. Deep loving relationships were naturally formed. A later comparable situation was to be that of the relationships of the 1914 war. For that one has the moving testimony of the poets, Wilfred Owen and Siegfried Sassoon notably. Martin Taylor's *Lads: An Anthology of Comradeship*, an anthology of love poetry of the trenches, provides special insight into the intensity of the emotional bond that built between men surviving close together under extreme duress without discernible hope for release. As in the trenches of 1914–18, so in that navy of the Great War.

Terrible grief was expressed after every action by men who had lost their closest comrades. They were prepared to die for one another, as frequently occurred, in one instance recounted in a letter by an officer from HMS *Barfleur*:

A sailor of our's on watch, by some accident, fell overboard; the sea running very high at the time, prevented the poor fellow from catching any of the ropes which were thrown to him, and upset two boats which put off to his assistance: everybody was now on deck, the man sinking, and nobody able to afford him the least relief; when a comrade of his, struck by the supplicating countenance of the miserable man cried suddenly – 'By heavens, Tom, I can't bear that look; I'll save you or go with you!' All eyes were directed to the man who spoke; but what was our astonishment, when we beheld him plunge into the merciless waves, gain his comrade, and seize him with his left arm, while, with his right, he supported both himself and the man through the high running sea, and thus gave time for another and more fortunate boat to rescue them both from an untimely death.

XLVI

PENINSULA

As Napoleon stood supreme over Europe and its broken sovereignties and Britain simultaneously confronted transatlantic hostility, the British government in viewing its stark isolation was compelled to take stock of its overall means of defence.

The first thing to discard was the illusion that Trafalgar had left Britain in unchallengeable naval command. On 8 January 1808 the Earl of Westmorland, Lord Privy Seal in the Portland administration, presented the cabinet with a memorandum on the naval forces that disturbed the confident sense of command that Trafalgar had allowed.

The command that Napoleon had laid upon Europe or exercised through alliance meant that, just a little over two years since Trafalgar, he now had at his disposal 121 sail of the line, 88 of which were ready for sea, with 23 in 'ordinary' (laid up) and 40 building. Britain had 206 sail of the line, only 107 of them in commission or manned. The danger of what stood against her was in the distribution of the enemy. In the Baltic and North Sea Napoleon had 49 line ships against Britain's 5. In the Channel and on the Atlantic coast he had 33, against 32 British. In the Mediterranean it was 42 against 27 British. It is against those figures that the importance of securing the Danish and Portuguese navies has to be appreciated, for with those thirty ships Napoleon would have had more fully manned and equipped warships in commission than Britain.[1]

Tilsit had made vividly clear that, in spite of Napoleon's retreat from Boulogne, the ambition remained solidly with him, enforced by the realistic possibility of uniting all the naval forces of the Continent against Britain, in alliance with his own new navy-to-be.

For Britain this was no longer a pre-Trafalgar situation, a matter compelling a line ship action that could settle the balance of forces. Napoleon's naval acquisitions allowed strong enforcement of his war on commerce. It provided as well the means for harassment and deployments in all theatres, something that could stretch British naval resources beyond their capability.

And, most particularly, augmentation of his naval power made another invasion attempt far more likely of success.

In Britain's favour was the fact that the French navy remained inert in its havens, losing skill and efficiency, demoralized after Trafalgar. Spain was out of it. Nevertheless, a special British concern was the Scheldt, there where her fears of Continental menace had ever been, the arrow at the heart of Britain, as Napoleon himself described it. Traditionally Britain's fear was for hostile possession of the Scheldt, which in effect meant fear of that great maritime passage directly opposite the Thames being held by the French. Well, there they were now, as formidably established as only imagination at its worst could have visualized. Napoleon had constructed magnificent · new fortified docks at Antwerp, capable of holding forty sail of the line. It was now his chief naval establishment, with thirty-five sail of the line finished or under construction. He was in the process of reviving Boulogne, with a new army established there, but Antwerp would be the centre of any future invasion plan, able to send across to the Thames a fifty-ship armada defended on either side by flotillas of the allied navies.

Pitt, in his recurrent speculations on how militarily to retrieve the Netherlands, had in 1797 put forth the idea of seizing what was then the island of Walcheren (now attached to the mainland by reclamation) and its harbour of Vlissingen, or Flushing as the British called it. By thus holding the entrance to the Scheldt, Antwerp would be locked in. It was a concept that now took new life with Secretary of War Castlereagh. But any such venture seen in light of the heavy imbalance of military forces that confronted Britain first required a new look at the British Army.

Sea's war with Land and the prowess of the military genius on the Continent declared to all with foresight that a greater call for offensive action was likely to be laid upon the British Army in this definitive struggle ahead than anything seen so far in this war. Castlereagh was the visionary. His revival of the idea of Walcheren made that plain. It was clear to him that British survival would require a different army for the rest of the war, as much as it had required a different navy at the start. It would also need a fuller, more efficient operational involvement between army and navy. Their joint success at Copenhagen provided example for that.

A focused military grasp that had so far appeared elusive, at least with the governing body, at last seemed to present itself. From the disastrous West Indies campaign at the start of the war through to the paltry recent efforts at Buenos Aires and in Egypt, the British Army had suffered valiantly but failed to leave any mark upon the main struggle. Only a Royal Navy captain, Sidney Smith at Acre, had so far delivered a decisive and smarting, highly personal British military blow at Napoleon.

The British had clung resolutely to their established distrust of a 'standing army'. While Frederick II and then Napoleon had created new concepts of military organization and control, the British Army had remained tied to its ill-defined status of a service hovering between the professional and one never quite regarded as indispensable to national security, as the navy was.

The first firm attempt to reorganize the army in this war had been passed in 1802. Castlereagh as War Secretary brought new urgency to the matter. In 1808 he created an entirely new military system for Britain. The regular standing army would be at least 220,000 strong, liable to be sent anywhere and to be kept up by ordinary recruiting and volunteers from the militias. Cabinet gave swift approval and put it into effect. And on 1 February 1808 Britain already had what the Duke of York described as the largest military force the country had ever possessed, with a regular strength of 93,000 on foreign service and 217,000 on home service.[2]

It was almost as if Castlereagh had acted with uncanny foresight, some strange instinct that had called out the moment, for at that moment some ninety thousand of Napoleon's troops were already south of the Pyrenees and descending into Spain. There was no suggestion that Castlereagh or anyone else foresaw the great Iberian Peninsula military struggle that would be underway before the year was out. On the contrary, a wild urge to let loose foreign expeditions for imperial aggrandizement had flared in the wake of the fatal Buenos Aires venture. As former War Minister Windham's mad idea of a march across the Andes from Chile to the River Plate had suggested, the failure at Buenos Aires had not brought total disillusionment. When, with the new government, Castlereagh succeeded Windham as Secretary of War and Colonies, he seized upon a memorandum that Sir Arthur Wellesley had prepared on stripping Spain of its South American colonies. Venezuela and Guiana were the first marked for seizure, but Wellesley advised against that since the slave trade was about to be abolished and the rich agriculture of the territories would be unmanageable without slaves. Naval-military operations against Mexico and the River Plate were therefore decided upon. This folly was intended by Castlereagh for the spring of 1808. As these assaults were to be undertaken with the troops who had so successfully attacked Copenhagen, Castlereagh had marked Wellesley for command of the expedition to wrest Mexico.

The war on commerce gave urgency to the search for new markets and, after Popham's attempted seizure of the River Plate, South America stood large in all such calculations.

With similar ventures in mind, there was no immediate consideration of military response from Britain to the French intrusion upon Iberia. There were still too many other preoccupations. Napoleon was making a new thrust to seize Sicily and to occupy Corfu. Eight thousand British troops were sent to Messina, and the French thrust was stayed. In the Baltic, Napoleon's ally, Russia, was at war with Sweden. In May ten thousand soldiers under Sir John Moore went to Gothenburg to assist Gustavus of Sweden. Events in Iberia were nevertheless rapidly accelerating.

With the Braganzas in flight from Portugal, Napoleon saw the Bourbon dynasty of Spain as ready to follow them into oblivion, with a member of his own family on the throne. The Bourbons themselves simplified the task for him. They first of all allowed fifteen thousand Spanish soldiers to be sent at Napoleon's demand to the Baltic to assist in the war on commerce. Spanish troops had also assisted Junot in his march upon Portugal, which supposedly was to have been divided between France and Spain. While all of that facilitated the French entry into Spain, bitter quarrel between King Charles IV and his heir, Ferdinand, the Prince of Asturias, hastened the dynasty's fall. Ferdinand secretly sought collusion with Napoleon on marriage with a Buonaparte princess and was arrested by his father for 'high treason', until compelled to beg the king's pardon. But Charles IV decided to abdicate after all and on 19 March 1808 Ferdinand was declared king. Charles then repented his abdication. As the factions of this divided house vented their wrath upon each other the French troops under Murat had entered Madrid. Murat, seeing advantage in the Bourbon quarrel, called on Napoleon to intervene. Napoleon had arrived at Bayonne. A swiftly engineered set of invitations got the whole Spanish royal family to Bayonne where, closeted with Napoleon, they found themselves manipulated into obeisance. On 5 May, Charles IV conceded the crown of Spain and its empire to Napoleon, who declared that his brother Joseph, king at Naples, would now rule at Madrid instead, Murat becoming King of Naples. Charles IV and Ferdinand both received pensions and castles in France. It was perhaps the most ruthless betrayal within Napoleon's conquest of the Continent. 'I embarked very badly on the Spanish affair, I confess,' he was to say on St Helena; 'the immorality of it was too patent, the injustice too cynical, and the whole thing wears an ugly look since I have fallen; for the attempt is only seen in its hideous nakedness deprived of all majesty and of the many benefits which completed my intention.'

Possibly in the long run Spain would have been the beneficiary if Napoleon's stamp had remained upon it, as his biographer Holland Rose suggests: 'Political and social reforms had hitherto consolidated the work of conquest; and those which he soon offered to the Spaniards might possibly have renovated that nation, had they not been handed in at the sword's point; but the motive was too obvious, the intervention too insulting, to render success possible with the most sensitive people in Europe.'[3]

The Spanish people certainly were not taking it. They rose spontaneously, 'in unanimous, energetic revolt'. It was an astonishing phenomenon that exploded in Madrid on 2 May. Murat's executions of the patriots remains eternally alive in the canvas of Goya. Word of the uprising flew to all corners of the land. Patriotic mobs took over wherever there was any sign of deference to the French. On 25 May the general assembly of Asturias declared war on France. The other regionally governing Juntas followed suit. The war effort thereafter lay in the hands of the Juntas, acting virtually as sovereign states.

The Junta of Asturias sent delegates to London to ask for British help. Like the Juntas of Seville, Murcia, Valencia, Aragon, Galicia and Catalonia, they wished to keep control of their own troops and command. From the start, therefore, any assistance from outside confronted difficulties with all. After years of regarding Britain as enemy, it was difficult at first for many Spanish to lose their suspicions of the British, even with hatred of the French being expressed with a ferocity that the latter had not encountered elsewhere.

By the time the great insurrection of May 1808 began the French were well established. They held the fortresses of San Sebastian and Pamplona and controlled the central line of communication from the Pyrenees down through Vitoria, Burgos and Madrid to Toledo. But they had lost all control beyond the actual positions they held. The main forces of the insurgent Spanish armies were concentrated in Galicia and Andalusia. Galicia had seized the arsenals of Corunna and Ferrol. For Napoleon the other naval establishments, the great ones of Cartagena and Cadiz, were therefore his most urgent objectives. For his war on British commerce and for his control of the Mediterranean the Iberian coastlines had served as a prime motive for his seizure of the Peninsula. From every point of view they were indispensable to the world he sought to make.

Through Gibraltar the insurgents got their first help from Britain. The Rock's governor, General Sir Hew Dalrymple, maintained confidential relations with the Spanish military commander in Andalusia, General Castanos, even while Spain was still at war with Britain. After the Madrid revolt Dalrymple began supplying Castanos with what arms and ammunition he had available. But it was upon Vice Admiral Lord Cuthbert Collingwood, the Mediterranean commander in chief, that the burden of forging a new alliance between Britain and the Spanish initially descended. His responsibility for the Mediterranean coasts of Spain, in effect from Cadiz to Rosas, now had an entirely different weight. For it was along those coasts that a particular form of naval war henceforth was to be fought, closely allied to partisan fighting ashore.

XLVII

COLLINGWOOD

IT was British good fortune that Collingwood was still on station to take on his new responsibility, not yet recalled as he so fervently wished.

His was now a delicate, difficult task that by another might easily have been mishandled, for the situation was fraught with possibility of deep and dangerous offence, of further provoking a people already at an extremity of rage against a brutal foreign presence. Whatever the strength of hostility against the French – and it was powerfully there even before they came marching in across the Pyrenees – the Spanish had been at war with the British for too long now easily to lay aside suspicions of British intent, upon their bases and their empire. Collingwood had to placate a confused, jealously explosive people, to ensure that at the outset a necessary working relationship should be established. In the most difficult of circumstances he achieved far more, a trust, urgently necessary in Andalusia, the most vital point at the start of the war.

With Collingwood the Mediterranean after Trafalgar had shifted into a broader, more complex responsibility as Napoleon marched across Europe. Napoleon's command of the entire northern Mediterranean shoreline, from the Straits of Gibraltar to the Strait of Messina, down the Adriatic to Corfu and, given his influence with the Turks, on to the Dardanelles, meant that the Mediterranean had become Britain's biggest naval operational area. It was a harsh, solitary task for the man who had to deal with it, year after year without relief, unique in its diverse demands, upon which depended sound response to the continuously unfolding scenarios that Buonaparte set in motion.

Collingwood had to be at once deductive strategist for the ever-changing political map around the whole sea upon which he moved, ever watchful of enemy deployments for Egypt or against Sicily, constantly deploying his own frigates and line ships to scout the French, ever a battle-ready admiral. In addition he was required to be military commander moving troops to whatever point they might be required, and persuasive diplomat besides, whether seeking to win back the Turks, draw on side an Albanian warlord, soothe the Egyptians or to placate Barbary. All of that and a great deal more formed Collingwood's daily preoccupations. He had, of course, to maintain the watch on Toulon and the steadily enlarging French fleet that lay there. The harassing possibilities that Toulon represented were always present. Especially onerous was the obligation to defend Sicily while Napoleon remained determined to acquire it. With that task came the irritation of coping with the schemes and plots of the Sicilian Bourbons. He nevertheless saw less of them than Nelson had done because, sensibly, with the Adriatic, Corfu and the Dardanelles as centres of ceaseless activity, he stationed himself at Syracuse instead of Palermo.

Collingwood said goodbye to his wife and daughters in March 1805. He was never to see them again. His only devoted daily companion thereafter was his terrier, Bounce. During the years that followed Trafalgar he rarely stepped off his ship, first the *Ocean*, later the *Ville de Paris*. Through that time he moved ceaselessly between the Atlantic and the Levant, between Cadiz, Toulon and off the Dardanelles. By lamplight or the sunlight streaming through the high ornamental windows of his stern quarters he quilled the endless stream of correspondence that detailed his thoughts and actions, Bounce ever at his side. From those letters there stands forth a remarkable portrait of a naval man indispensably directing over an extended period one of the principal theatres of action in the Great War. Those letters simultaneously offer an affecting and touching image of the human quality at its resolute best, of a man filled with longing for home and family, contemplating small possibility of it, and persisting without pause or self-pity in his commitment to his unassailable concept of duty.

As remarkable as anything about this constant passage from one point of demand to another is how Collingwood maintained the endurance of his fleet and his seamen as well as his own mental and physical strength, though by 1808 his had begun to suffer. The fitness of his sailors was an example to all. With him, so it had always been. 'I have been long at sea, have little to eat, and scarcely a clean shirt; and often do I say, Happy lowly clown. Yet, with all this sea work, never getting fresh beef nor a vegetable, I have not one sick man in my ship.'[1]

Ocean usually had eight hundred men. On one occasion during this service she was more than a year and a half without going into port. During that time she never had more than six and generally only four on her sick list. Collingwood was loved by his sailors, for their wellbeing that he maintained and because his was a ship where punishment did not exist without good reason. For Collingwood loss of any man, particularly the skilled, had become grave concern. Being so long in the Mediterranean meant that manning had become even more of a problem than it already was elsewhere with this protracted war. In the Mediterranean there were now few merchantmen from which the navy could impress sailors.

From his outpost Collingwood saw a post-Trafalgar navy sliding into torpor. He saw it on his quarterdeck. 'It is not the fashion for young men to be seamen now,' he commented. 'They are more attentive to the outward furniture of the head, than to anything within it; and they all dress a la Bonaparte, as if a great hat and tassels constituted a hero. I could laugh at their nonsense, if the public interest were not too much affected by it.' Speaking of a midshipman who had just joined him he said, 'I have little hope of his being a sailor. He does not take notice of any thing, nor any active part in his business; and yet I suppose when he has dawdled in a ship six years he will think himself very ill-used if he not be made a lieutenant. Offices in the navy are now made provision for all sorts of idle people.' And of another: 'He will not be qualified for a lieutenant in sixteen years, and I should be very sorry to put the safety of a ship and the lives of men into such hands. He is of no more use here as an officer than Bounce is, and not near so entertaining.' Addressing the First Lord of the Admiralty, Lord Mulgrave, on having 'very inexperienced' youths as lieutenants, Collingwood said, 'The difficulty of getting officers is such, that the subject has been much upon my mind. Few line-of-battle ships have more than two or three officers who are seamen. The rest are boys, fine children in their mothers' eyes, and the facility with which they get promoted makes them indifferent as to their qualification.'[2]

For Collingwood since Trafalgar the navy had clearly lowered its standards. Like Nelson at the end, Collingwood's own disillusion and loss of enchantment with the sea began to express itself under the enormity of the pressures upon him, and to which he nevertheless gave himself with absolute commitment. 'You will suppose that this is a very anxious time for me, but I study day and night what is best to be done, and I trust in God that the event will be happy for our country,' he wrote to a friend in April 1808. 'My health is pretty good – as well as I ought to expect, considering the cares upon my mind; but they have worn me very very much ... I shall go home as soon as I can, and never after have anything to do with ships.'

Collingwood's fierce longing for home and family equalled Nelson's for Merton, Emma and Horatia in his last days at sea. 'My dear wife,' Collingwood wrote in a particularly moving letter, 'I think of you as being where alone true comfort can be found, enjoying in your own warm house a happiness which in the great world is not known. My heart yearns for home, but when that blessed day will come in which I shall see it, God knows. I am afraid it is not so near as I expected. I had before mentioned my declining health to Lord Mulgrave, and he tells me in reply that he hopes I will stay, for he knows not how to supply my place. The impression his letter made on me was one of grief and sorrow, that with such a list as we have, there should be thought to be any difficulty in finding a successor of superior ability to me.'[3]

Mulgrave was undoubtedly right in seeing no one of sufficient stature to replace Collingwood. In any event, by the time Collingwood wrote that letter to his wife all Iberia was already covered by war, which alone meant small chance of Collingwood being relieved. And, cruel to say, certainly better for Britain that right then he was not.

XLVIII

CADIZ

In the middle of May 1808, having at Bayonne won from Charles IV of Spain and his heir Ferdinand their agreement to cede to him their throne and empire, Napoleon apparently felt that he could regard his acquisition of Spain safely concluded, for he immediately once more applied himself to Eastern venture.

On 17 May he wrote to Decres, the Minister of Marine: 'There is not much news from India. England is in great penury there, and the arrival of an expedition would ruin that colony from top to bottom. The more I reflect on this step, the less inconvenience I see in taking it.' Two days later he wrote to Murat at Madrid: 'I must have ships, for I intend striking a heavy blow towards the end of the season.'¹ But he soon got news that Madrid had exploded, followed by the rest of Spain, and at the end of June in another letter to Decres he said that they would have to postpone the idea of sending a fleet far from European waters.

Napoleon was anyway again too late, for Collingwood once more hastened to foil him in the acquisition of ships.

Collingwood, aboard *Ocean*, was off Toulon on 29 May 1808 when he received news from the governor of Gibraltar of the turmoil in Spain and that General Castanos had raised the matter of the squadron of French ships of the line still at Cadiz. For Collingwood uncertainty at Cadiz posed the question of the fate of the Spanish ships there besides the French ships that had remained after Trafalgar.

Collingwood had been off Toulon because of another futile chase. Admiral Ganteaume's Rochefort squadron had escaped British vigilance off that port. Its arrival in the Mediterranean had again raised fears for Sicily. Ganteaume had eluded Collingwood by following the North African coast until he made it into Toulon, where strict watch was immediately laid upon him. But the alarm they raised passed. Even before receiving the Gibraltar governor's communication Collingwood had already suspected something afoot, for he had intelligence at Toulon that the French troops in Italy had been much reduced. Ganteaume's ships had then been prepared in a way that indicated no intention to leave the port soon, and they subsequently had moved to the inner harbour.

Those observations, together with the news from Gibraltar, led Collingwood to conclude that the threat against Sicily had been lifted. After passing the Toulon command to another admiral, on 1 June Collingwood sailed for Cadiz. 'I left a station which had almost worn me out with care,' he wrote to his wife, 'to be upon the spot where a great revolution was taking place in Spain, and to give my aid to it. I am a poor lack-linen swain, with nothing but a few soldier's shirts, which I got at Gibraltar. All my own were left at Malta and Palermo, and when I shall get them I know not; but such wants give me little disquietude.'[2]

Collingwood arrived at Cadiz on the 11th. By that time the Spanish were besieging the five French line ships and one frigate that lay at Cadiz. Admiral Rosily had moved his ships away from the town and out of reach of its cannon. Under constant attack from the Spanish, however, Rosily surrendered his ships on 14 June. The British who landed were surrounded by Spanish crying '¡Vivan los Ingleses!' but there was strong resistance at first to any soldiers coming ashore. The proposal for British troops to land at or in the neighbourhod of Cadiz was also rejected. There was, Collingwood recorded, 'a visible suspicion that we had views particular to ourselves, and which had nothing to do with preserving their independence as a nation; and that their jealousy was less disguised as the number of troops in ships off Cadiz increased'. To that Collingwood immediately applied himself. 'That there might be no appearance of assuming control over their measures,' he reported, 'I desired them to point out how the British force on the coast could be most useful to them.'[3]

Collingwood in any event had already launched the naval strategy that was to be one of the British navy's greatest contributions to the Peninsular War. It was from Cadiz, through the Straits and on along the eastern coast of Spain that the navy had to maintain its most extended active harassment of the French, to disrupt their movements along the coast, and to support the unique new form of fighting that emerged fully in Spain – guerrilla warfare. At Cadiz the Spanish gave Collingwood his own preliminary intimation of the latter: 'They say that Buonaparte has hitherto had only armies to contend with, but that now he has a nation, where every man is a soldier.'[4] No single fact of that war was to be truer. While the main course of the war that Britain was subsequently to fight would lie from Andalusia through Estremadura, Castile and Leon to the northern provinces, drawing on naval support from Portugal to Corunna, the eastern side of Spain with its great ports of Valencia, Cartagena and Barcelona formed practically its own war. Catalonia was to become the most distinctive part of that. It was to that coast that Collingwood despatched Captain Lord Thomas Cochrane on 21 June 1808.

No man was more fitted for that task. Cochrane, as we already have seen, had made his reputation by harassing that very coast while Spain was in the war. He therefore knew his scene. He had been busy there when things changed and he had hastened to join Collingwood at Cadiz to ascertain his own role in this new situation. His assignment in hand, Cochrane sailed up the coast in his frigate *Imperieuse* with both British and Spanish colours flying at the main.

Collingwood then had further demonstration of Spanish suspicions. On suggesting to the governor of Cadiz, General Morla, that the Cadiz fleet be prepared for sea to join the British navy if French movement made it necessary, the Spanish ships, like the French, were immediately moved to the upper harbour and work began to dismantle them. Morla then got approval from the Supreme Council of Seville for what he had done. But Collingwood persisted and gave Morla two reasons for them immediately to stop unrigging their ships: that if the French marched against Cadiz neither the batteries nor the town would be able to give them sufficient protection, and that the ships were needed as well to defend the Spanish colonies against a French attempt to seize them. Collingwood urged that one of the ships be sent at once to the Caribbean to carry the news of the changed situation in Spain. The Junta agreed to stop dismantling the ships.

Collingwood emerged from this standing high in the estimation of the Supreme Council of Seville which, in a letter to Morla, declared, 'No Spaniard could have pleaded the interests of Spain with a warmer zeal than Lord Collingwood has done.' It had consented 'with much grief' to Morla's proposal to disarm the Cadiz squadron, the Council said, adding, 'The misfortunes suffered by our navy demand a contrary measure: the whole monarchy and its colonies require an armada . . . the assistance which they should mutually lend, and the preservation of the Americas, render the maintenance of one indispensable . . . We breathed therefore when we observed the same ideas in the letter of Lord Collingwood.'[5]

In his letters to the head of Admiralty, Mulgrave, Collingwood frequently drew distinction between those seeking to lead the insurgency and the spirit of the populace: 'The people, irritated to the greatest degree against the French are raised to enthusiasm and would do anything. Their Councils, maintaining the gravity of their national character, would let this ardour cool and do nothing . . . it is the populace that is the spirit which gives vigour to their measures; and if their Councils can keep this spirit alive, and direct it judiciously, all may be well.' And, more succinctly in another letter, 'Every peasant is a soldier, every hill a fortress.' That, in effect, was what the guerrilla war was to be all about.[6]

For all his admiration of the patriot spirit, Collingwood nevertheless saw the jealousies between the Juntas as likely to prove fatal: '. . . there never was a nation more disjointed, and I consider its safety as very doubtful. If they do not constitute one sole Government, which will combine the powers of the country, it will be lost'.[7] And with that followed his note of fatalism for himself, for it was a contest that was wearing him down still more: 'These subjects, and my cares for them, are wearing me to death; but much that I see in the world reconciles me to its approach, whenever it shall please God.'

Napoleon, directing operations from Bayonne, made two major moves. In June General Moncey left Madrid to descend upon the Juntas of Valencia and Murcia. General Duhesme seconded him. General Dupont went south to take Andalusia. Moncey was beaten off in his attempt to take Valencia and was compelled to retreat to Madrid, where he arrived on 15 July. Dupont had passed down from Toledo through the Sierra Morena to Baylen in Jaen. There on 23 July his eighteen thousand soldiers were defeated by Castanos with thirty-four thousand men, many of them raw peasants. The terms of truce were that the French soldiers were to be shipped to Nantes but the Junta of Seville refused to allow it and the French were instead shipped to the island of Cabrera off Majorca where more than half of them were to die of starvation by the end of the war. Spain's new monarch, Joseph, had entered Madrid on 20 July, only to retire from it on 1 August.

Baylen was a shock that rang out across an astounded Europe. Invincible Napoleon no longer was. It was a turn of the Napoleonic tide, merely suggestive at this point, nevertheless one that gradually gathered its strength. Through the four years ahead the Iberian Peninsula was to become the implacable harassment, the confounding frustration, of Napoleon's greater dreams, for here he raised two different forces against himself. Across Spain an entirely new military phenomenon had arisen, a patriotic insurgency which, though raw, impetuous, unruly, invented guerrilla warfare in the sense that we fully understand it today. Napoleon quickly realized its essential character: 'In civil wars it is the important posts that must be held: one ought not to go everywhere.'[8] But in that wild, rough terrain, whose peasants were as hard and rough as the landscape itself, this style of warfare became uniquely different from anything so far. The Duke of York was to be succinct about it in a memorandum on 1 August: 'The Spaniards are the first people that have risen in one mass, and that have enthusiastically united in support of their own cause against the common enemy; they are the first nation upon the Continent that appear to have made their country's cause individually their own.'[9]

The other new force was to be the British. Through these early stages a British force of some four thousand had been sailing up and down the coast around Seville, waiting to be called upon but constantly refused permission to land at Cadiz, in spite of Collingwood's efforts. It eventually made for the Tagus. Castlereagh anyhow had in mind something far larger than another of the sort of petty, ultimately ineffectual, expeditions that Pitt had liked to send off. The changes that Castlereagh had in the past months brought to the army allowed him for the first time since Marlborough to consider a major military effort on the Continent, having now available to him a British force which, at sixty thousand, would be double that of Marlborough's. For Iberia Castlereagh immediately contemplated forty thousand. In that, he had the active support of Sir Arthur Wellesley.

When Spain exploded into insurgency the five thousand British soldiers who had been intended for the seizure of Mexico still waited to embark at Cork. They were now conveniently available when, in May 1808, Wellesley in a memorandum to the cabinet formally suggested that a force be sent to Portugal, where Junot had concentrated his army around Lisbon. The Portuguese, like the Spaniards, had also risen in insurrection. At Castlereagh's urging the cabinet agreed and the force, now nine thousand strong, sailed from Cork on 13 July. After calling at Corunna on the 20th for consultation with the Junta of Galicia, Wellesley landed his men at Mondego Bay, near the coastal fortress of Figueira between Oporto and Lisbon. While there a reinforcement of fifteen thousand arrived.

Wellesley took the coast road down towards the Tagus and, on 17 August, in his first action with the French at the village of Rolica, he captured one of Junot's subordinates, General Delaborde, and his force of four thousand. And on 21 August, at the village of Vimeiro on the Maceira River, Junot himself was defeated. On 31 August Junot agreed to the entire evacuation of Portugal, provided he could take his troops away with him. This was agreed to by the British generals. Junot and his soldiers were transferred to France in British ships.

The convention that allowed Junot to extricate himself and his soldiers without becoming prisoners of war was fiercely criticized in Britain and Wellesley was summoned home to attend a court of inquiry, where he defended the action. He argued that the French had been in a position to retire towards Lisbon, able then to resume and prolong the fight. But the real gain was that the end of the war in Portugal left the British forces free for operations in Spain. Britain, besides, retrieved operational use of the Tagus, with all of Lisbon's forts, arsenals and dockyards and, to top it all, acquired the twelve Russian ships of the line that lay there.

So began the Peninsular War, as it came to be known. There was to be a long, difficult and painful way to go for all concerned – the French, the British, the Spanish – but Napoleon had been struck a severe blow, in prestige as well as strategically. He had lost Portugal, which he had earnestly desired for his empire, and needed for his economic warfare. His newly confident naval outlook, upon which his irrepressible Eastern vision depended, was shaken as he saw the maritime advantage of the entire Iberian run of coastline slipping from his grasp. And, of course he had lost the Spanish ships and the remnant at Cadiz of his own Trafalgar fleet.

XLIX

CATALONIA

WHAT became the greatest campaign yet undertaken by the British Army on the continent of Europe would from 1808 work steadily towards successful advance from Iberia into France, able to do so for one outstanding reason: it was fought on land surrounded by sea, enabling the British navy to sit in close support on all sides.

It was a unique collaboration, delivered to this unmatched union of the two services through the careless impatience and reckless delusion of invincibility of Napoleon Buonaparte at what appeared to be the fullest moment of his career.

Major Continental military expeditions of the past were in line with what was known as 'War limited by contingent'. That had meant Britain providing an ally or allies with an auxiliary force of a stipulated strength in certain contingencies, the common form of token military assistance to a subsidized ally such as Austria. But for Iberia Julian Corbett gave contingent war a new definition, seeing it as an objective 'to wrest or secure from the enemy a definite piece of territory that to a greater or less extent can be isolated by naval action'. Such was the Iberian Peninsula.[1]

Mahan defined more closely the difference the Peninsula would make to this whole war: 'The theatre of war, surrounded on the three sides by water, was for the French, a salient thrust far out into the enemy's domain on the sea . . . To the British the Peninsula offered the advantage that the whole coast line was a base of operations, while every friendly port was a bridge-head by which to penetrate, or upon which, in case of reverse, to retire, with a sure retreat in the sea beyond.'[2]

That encirclement of Land by Sea created a struggle, Mahan said, 'eminently alien to the emperor's genius'. Or, as Wellington would justify, '. . . it is our maritime superiority [that] gives me the power of maintaining my army while the enemy are unable to do so'.

As the determining factor in this decisive confrontation between Sea and Land, the Royal Navy assumed a role as critical as that which finally had necessitated Trafalgar, one that progressively had to be played out now alongside the conclusive struggle with the 'Continental System', the war on commerce. And it was along the Catalan coast in particular that a new form of Land–Sea naval warfare that became integral to the Peninsular War was initiated. It was there that the necessary model was provided of close involvement between partisans and British sailors, and where the navy's adventuristic zest and unstinted bravado was especially demonstrated. The man who would stand as the exponent of it all was Captain Lord Thomas Cochrane, together with his closely knit ship's company aboard the frigate *Imperieuse*.

Sailing up the coast from Gibraltar Cochrane made forceful expression of the new alliance when he hove to off Barcelona, fired a twenty-one-gun salute, and then displayed British colours over French followed by Spanish colours over French.

As he progressed close in along the Catalan coast, with intimate closeness becoming the fundamental tactic of this form of engagement, boats filled with people from the towns came out, men and women, bringing presents and, more important for Cochrane, intelligence. One place after another brought bitter tales of French plundering and the burning of towns, accompanied by merciless killing of the inhabitants. With *Imperieuse* becalmed off one village, the inhabitants came out to say that their church had been plundered and forty-five houses burned to the ground. They brought word that the French had entered the town of Mataro, just above Barcelona, and requested Cochrane's assistance, for General Duhesme was advancing along the coast road with reinforcement for Barcelona. Cochrane's response set the example for all that followed in this unique, new partnership of sea and shore.

The road in question ran along the face of precipitous rocks just above the sea. Landing with a party of seamen, Cochrane took the local insurgents into his team for them to learn from what he did, so as to continue the same elsewhere. He blew down overhanging rocks to block the road and destroyed bridges to prevent cavalry and artillery from passing. But when he returned there shortly afterwards the French had used the enforced labour of the peasants to clear the roads. The gaps blown in the road had been filled with everything moveable from the village, even agricultural implements, furniture and clothing. To stop the Spanish from again interfering with the roads the French had sacked and burned all the houses in the neighbourhood.

Taking marines ashore Cochrane once more blew up the road and created fresh obstacles. The French had created a battery on the cliff above: seamen and marines destroyed this and threw its brass 24-pounders over the cliff, where they were recovered and taken aboard *Imperieuse*. Ingenuity swiftly rose before such tasks. At another new battery created on the top of a high cliff the brass guns taken were got on board *Imperieuse* by means of hawsers carried from the frigate to the cliff, with one end made fast to the masthead and then, using capstan and tackles, 'the guns were thus hopped on board'. Cochrane took another party of sailors and marines ashore and, for two days, continued destroying roads in every direction, blowing them up or blowing down rocks upon them, with the peasants 'aiding heart and soul, anxiously listening to every suggestion for retarding the enemy's movements'.

With General Duhesme continuing his attempt to relieve the French garrison at Barcelona, Cochrane passed on to Mongat, ten miles from the city, to attempt to destroy the fort there. As they did everywhere, on sight of *Imperieuse* standing in under the combined colours of Britain and Spain, the inhabitants came out to beg for help. The fortress at Mongat guarded a pass on the road. Cochrane went ashore and climbed the heights over-hanging the fortress. Encouraged by the presence of *Imperieuse* the Spanish insurgents charged up a hill where the French had established an outpost close by the fortress. The Spanish seized the outpost as the fortress sought to dislodge them by heavy fire. But Cochrane had returned to *Imperieuse* and brought her closer into shore. After several well-directed broadsides against the fortress, flags of truce were hung out. Landing with a party of marines to accept the surrender, Cochrane had difficulty bringing his prisoners away, the Spanish peasantry wanting to murder them in revenge for their suffering. The French were marched down to the boats 'and glad enough they were to get there, for the Spaniards accompanied them with volleys of abuse'. Cochrane then blew up the fortress, with Spanish colours planted on the ruins, 'hoisted amidst the hearty cheers of thousands with arms in their hands'.

All of this was on 31 July 1808, the day Wellesley landed at Mondego Bay. To Thomas Cochrane therefore can be credited the first serious British tactical engagement and triumph against the French in Iberia, three weeks before Wellesley's victory at Vimeiro. Through his actions Cochrane had forced Duhesme to take an interior road to reach Barcelona. He had done so by swiftly establishing the manner of this unique form of warfare required for that coast: to 'out boats' with landing parties of sailors and marines for surprise harassment, to remove vital but isolated posts, or to cut communications and supplies, all supported if necessary by bombardment with broadsides from close inshore, with *Imperieuse* serving as a formidable floating battery. But central to this form of guerrilla warfare had to be the cooperative bond between the ship and the patriots on shore. And with that went instruction of the peasants in how to be effective, to be methodical rather than rashly impetuous.

As J.W. Fortescue points out, the rough and often impassable nature of the Spanish terrain meant that the French were compelled to defer to it because their troops could not pass easily from one district to another. This was particularly true of Catalonia which 'remained from beginning to end of the struggle practically a distinct seat of war'. And, as Cochrane found, Catalonia nurtured a spirit that helped to give it that distinction. 'The Catalans made capital guerilla troops, possessing considerable skill in the use of their weapons, though previously untrained,' Cochrane said. 'A character for turbulence was often attributed to them; but, in a country groaning under priestcraft and bad government, the sturdy spirit of independence, which prompted them to set the example of heroic defence of their country, might be . . . set down for discontent and sedition . . . One quality they eminently possess, viz. patience and endurance under privation; and this, added to their hardy habits and adventurous disposition, contributed to form an enemy not be despised – the less so that they were in every way disposed to repay the barbarities of the French with interest.'[3] All of which might just as easily have been written in 1936, in the circumstances of that later time.

As he had for the moment successfully frustrated the French along that coast, Cochrane passed to the French coast beyond, making for Marseilles, to create sufficient alarm between Perpignan and Marseilles to divert the French from despatching more troops to Catalonia from there. What developed from that was yet another advantage offered by this close inshore strategy. On anchoring off the mouth of the Rhône, abreast of a signalling station that was sending out word of their presence to the other stations along the coast, Cochrane saw a new mission. Sending in ninety men aboard gunboats, the station was destroyed. From that he proceeded to destroy station after station. His favourite time for attack was at night, believing that the French at the signal stations would not venture far out in the dark. Typically of such an operation, '. . . we marched along the beach in line towards a battery, observed on the previous evening, skirmishing as we proceeded, our boats meanwhile covering us with their nine-pounders; the French also keeping up a constant fire with their guns, but in a wrong direction'. Before destroying the signal semaphores Cochrane made sure to find the signal books. All other papers were burned, to allow the French to suppose that the signal books too had been burned when the station was destroyed. For daylight operations masthead watch was maintained and, if any danger was feared, recall guns were fired. 'It is wonderful what an amount of terrorism a small frigate is able to inspire on an enemy's coast,'[4] Cochrane found himself bemusedly declaring in assessment of the strategical values he was discovering in this new form of naval operation. 'Actions between line-of-battle ships are, no doubt, very imposing; but for real effect, I would prefer a score or two of small vessels, well handled, to any fleet of line-of-battle ships.' With that he defined post-Trafalgar.

Ingenuity remained constantly to the fore. At the entrance to the Rhône, *Imperieuse* ran low on water and the men were put on short allowance. Passing into the river, *Imperieuse*'s fore topmast studding sails were sewn up and converted into huge bags. These were sent high upstream in the boats, filled with fresh water, and then towed alongside the ship, the water being pumped into the hold by means of the fire engine.

Cochrane's original and energetic operations had been keeping *Imperieuse* and its zestful crew fully occupied for five hectic months when, in November, the situation in Catalonia and throughout Spain changed drastically.

When Wellesley had been recalled to Britain to help in the inquiry on why Junot and his army had been allowed to return to France, taking all their booty with them, command of the British forces had passed from Sir Hew Dalrymple to Sir John Moore, recently returned from the futile excursion to Sweden to help King Gustavus against Russia. An indecisive period had followed, with the Spanish generals holding their own and gaining successes, and General Castanos in Madrid. But the Spanish forces were still unable to reach agreement on a commander in chief. As the Spanish argued about that and about a national government, the British were dallying over their method of cooperation and whether or not they should take their army from Portugal to Spain. The principal French forces at this time had been driven beyond the line of the Ebro into a pocket embracing the western Biscayan provinces. Moore, who had always had his doubts about success in Spain, finally started from Lisbon on 28 October with twenty-five thousand troops to enter Spain.

The subjugated Continent had come alive after the Spanish and British victories, stirring Prussia and Austria to reconsider their supine position before Napoleon. The Austrians had begun rearming. That compromised Napoleon's intention of a new offensive to reaffirm his power and hold on Spain, but before launching that he needed to subdue Austria and to quieten Prussia. He therefore met Tsar Alexander at Erfurt, to gain assurance of Russian support against Austria. To stop Austrian rearmament Napoleon sought Alexander's cooperation in sending an ultimatum to the Hapsburgs to halt their military revival. Alexander refused to go along. In a new treaty signed on 12 October, however, he agreed to support France in a war with Austria.

The Erfurt meeting was perhaps more conspicuously marked by the searing betrayal of Napoleon by Talleyrand, who had sought to distance himself since the ruthless deposition of the Spanish Bourbons, to which he had strongly objected. Talleyrand saw the old Europe that he valued and respected fast disappearing. As Duff Cooper outlined in his profile, Talleyrand saw the conservative influence of Austria as being as essential to the maintenance of the structure of Europe as the liberalizing, anti-autocratic spirit of England. 'If the English constitution is destroyed,' he had said on one occasion, 'the civilization of the world will be shaken to its foundations.'[5] At Erfurt both those values had appeared in peril and he had said to the tsar, 'Sire, it is in your power to save Europe, and you will only do so by refusing to give way to Napoleon. The French people are civilized, their sovereign is not. The sovereign of Russia is civilized, and his people are not. The sovereign of Russia should therefore be the ally of the French people.' Unless the tsar stood up to Napoleon, he argued, they would all be dragged to their destruction. Talleyrand's influence played upon Alexander throughout the Erfurt meeting, but the tsar had his own reasons for denying Napoleon all he wanted, principally because he had little reason to believe that he would get from Napoleon the support he himself ultimately desired for acquiring Constantinople and the Dardanelles.

Napoleon turned away from Erfurt to give his full attention to Spain. He returned to Bayonne and French troops began pouring into Spain. On 4 November Napoleon left Bayonne to take over command in Spain and on the 6th established himself at Vitoria. He now had 150,000 troops in Spain, thirty thousand in Catalonia and the rest for the descent from the Ebro. Defeat fell successively upon the various Spanish commands. On 4 December Napoleon occupied Madrid. He then turned his focus on the British. Moore had reached Salamanca by 23 November but, as reports of the new French force and Spanish collapse began to reach him, he decided to evacuate Spain: '. . . we have failed,' Moore wrote to Castlereagh, 'for, situated as we are, success cannot be commanded by any efforts we can make if the enemy are prepared to oppose us'.[6] It was that defeatism which he was said to have expressed even before leaving London, namely that the Iberian expeditionary force could never succeed.

As Moore began a steady retreat north towards Corunna, Cochrane set himself to confront the strengthened French thrust down the main road from Perpignan to Rosas. The French had been turned out of Rosas but had established themselves at various points around the town, awaiting a powerful force of the new French inrush advancing upon it.

The defence of Rosas depended upon two structures: a citadel in the town and Fort Trinidad, a strong fortress on the cliff above the town. Two 74s from the main fleet off Toulon, *Excellent*, Captain West, and *Fame*, Captain Bennet, had preceded Cochrane to Rosas when Spanish reinforcement expected from Gerona failed to arrive. 'The Spanish army would do nothing,' Collingwood reported. 'No argument could move them from Gerona, to raise the siege. Every day brought an excuse: they were ill-armed, they had not provisions, they were without clothes – in short, they would not come. To the captain–general I represented what must inevitably be the consequence of this delay. I shewed him Catalonia lost, if he did not raise the siege.'[7]

First West of *Excellent* then Bennet of *Fame*, sent to replace West, sought to prop up the siege but decided it was hopeless and the latter withdrew the men he himself first placed in the fort. When Cochrane, who had been off Barcelona, heard of the imminent fall of the Rosas forts he returned there at once, arriving on 20 November. He found the Spanish defenders who had been left behind in the citadel and fort ready to abandon both. Cochrane decided to defend and hold the strongholds until the promised reinforcements arrived from Gerona. He took a hundred men ashore to augment the Spanish still there, the landing covered by covering fire from *Imperieuse*. The defences in both fortresses were strengthened, ingeniously with encircling wire armed with fishhooks to deter assault. The French took the citadel, however, and continued their attempts to rush upon the fortress. In the largest and most near-successful of the French attacks on Trinidad, Cochrane found himself aiming at the last man to leave the breach from which the French were retreating. 'Finding escape impossible, he stood like a hero to receive the bullet, without condescending to lower his sword in token of surrender. I never saw a braver or a prouder man. Lowering my musket, I paid him the compliment of remarking that so fine a fellow was not born to be shot down like a dog, and . . . he was at liberty to make his way down the ladder, upon which intimation he bowed as politely as though on parade, and retired just as leisurely.'[8]

The Gerona reinforcement finally arrived but it was too late. The odds against Fort Trinidad were daily greater and on 5 December Cochrane took away his own men and the Spanish garrison. He refused to sacrifice more of his men 'to the preservation of a place which could not be long tenable'. Typical of his care for his men was that, while the French lost hundreds in their assaults, at Fort Trinidad Cochrane lost only three.

From Rosas Cochrane continued his harassment along the coast. And as he maintained those activities the largest army that Britain had ever sent from home shores was in disastrous retreat to Corunna, where it arrived on 17 January. Nothing so calamitous had ever been experienced by the army. Order was hard to maintain as the soldiers gave themselves to drink all along the way. As the rearguard fought the enemy it simultaneously collected the drunken strays who had fallen behind. Cold and hunger meant that men were daily dropping in numbers. The customary burden of women and children made the suffering and anguish even greater. In a last strong stand against the French at Corunna Moore was killed. By then his force had lost close to six thousand men. On 18 January 1809 the last soldiers of that unhappy army had embarked.

It was a day of humiliation and defeat, and considered such. But Mahan was to see it otherwise. Moore's march from Lisbon, he believed, helped change the war and Napoleon's future: 'The threat to the French communications arrested Napoleon's advance, postponed the imminent reduction of Spain, gave time for Austria to ripen her preparations, and entailed upon the emperor, in place of a rapid conquest, the protracted wasting Peninsular War, with its decisive ultimate effects upon his fortunes.'[9]

Cochrane, meanwhile, was still energetically waging what then amounted to the only British campaign against Napoleon's forces in Iberia. Yet Cochrane was to get no public praise or reward from Admiralty or government, though Collingwood in his reports described Cochrane's 'zeal and energy' as exciting 'the highest admiration. His resources for every exigency have no end.'

That, unfortunately, was to be the sum of Cochrane's Catalan accomplishments. He had with a single frigate seriously affected the war in Catalonia. His effort was akin to that usually expected of an entire expeditionary force aided by a squadron of line ships. He had slowed the advance of the French, destroyed their batteries wherever they sought to plant them on that coast, attacked and blown up fortresses, blown up roads, destroyed their semaphoric communications all the way along the Golfe du Lyon to Marseilles, had instructed and supervised the peasants in a more effective guerrilla warfare and, on occasion, taken his sailors and marines far inland on specific military sorties. As he himself rightly said of his effort, '. . . if with a single frigate I could paralyse the movements of their armies in the Mediterranean – with three or four ships it would not be difficult so to spread terror on their Atlantic shores, as to render it impossible for them to send an army into Western Spain'. His hope of persuading the British government to give him a small squadron to attempt precisely such an enterprise was one reason that led him then to apply for permission to return to Britain, where he arrived on 19 March, to find himself immediately involved in something fatally different from what he had had in mind.

L

BASQUE ROADS

Oh Nelson! Nelson, Nelson where were you? Never could the absence of the man from a scene of action clearly designed for his drive and decision have been more painfully alive than at Basque Roads on the night of 11 April 1809.

A Nelsonian figure was certainly present, in the person of Captain Lord Cochrane, of the frigate *Imperieuse*, arrived from Catalonia in time to deliver here the hazardous assignment of the night. Where Nelson and his spirit were missing was in the command.

What transpired at Basque Roads that night forms one of the strangest episodes in the history of the Royal Navy in which every aspect of its diverse character stands revealed: all the aspects of a service of which one might so easily balance the stressful worst against the glorious best were there apparent, all the elements of the good and the bad, the best and the worst, all flailingly set against one or the other. Here one saw the old navy, never lacking valour, but deep set in its cautions, its imbued hesitation before the price and penalties of risk which might chance a national setback and a ruined reputation. This was the old navy of which Collingwood was the contrary example. Here, too, was the entrenched permanence of acrimonious rivalry, the jealousies of opportunity and advancement, the ever-simmering hatred by one of being passed over by another, and on top of it all even a showing of the rising antipathy between the evangelical and the secular. But fortunately here, too, was Cochrane's example of Nelsonian daring and initiative. In reality, the Basque Roads story was entirely to do with the latter, the need for it, the urgent enlistment of it, then jealousy of it and, finally, the quick riddance of the new embodiment of it.

Far from sharing the national despair over the ignominious return of the British Army from Corunna, War Minister Castlereagh had a positive view of the future, on two grounds.

His immediate resolve was to go back to Iberia, the other to move into Europe at another point on the Continent. In the case of Iberia, Castlereagh began immediate discussions with Sir Arthur Wellesley on conducting a new campaign there. This time Wellesley firmly intended to become commander of the expeditionary force. His memorandum on the matter was presented to cabinet in March 1809, was approved, and preparations began at once to assemble thirty thousand troops to join the ten thousand still in Portugal. As regards the other strike into Europe, Castlereagh was intent on reviving Pitt's scheme of going for Antwerp. In Pitt's plan the island of Walcheren at the mouth of the Scheldt was the focal point for such a landing. Castlereagh adopted that for his own proposed expedition. There was urgency to both schemes for Austria and France were at war again on 9 April, which meant that Napoleon was moving troops to the Danube from all points, an opportune moment to strike him where and when he least expected it, and to assist Austria by laying on another front. Unfortunately Castlereagh and Admiralty had a more immediately pressing matter to deal with, on the Channel.

After the attack on Copenhagen Admiral Gambier was appointed to block the fleet at Brest. But the eight line ships and two frigates lying there got out when a storm at the end of February drove Gambier off his post. Admiralty and the home fleet were back in a familiar situation. Where had the Brest ships gone? To strengthen Toulon? Intelligence was sought at Cadiz and at Madeira. Then it was found that they had simply gone to Lorient, collected the ships lying there, and proceeded to Rochefort to reinforce what remained of that force. The assembled squadron was destined to pass on to the West Indies to defend France's richest colonies there, Martinique and Guadeloupe.

Gambier had immediately started to block Rochefort. Admiralty decided that the fleet had to be destroyed, but where they lay presented great difficulties in getting at them. The fort and town of Rochefort were on the Charente River at the end of a deep inland penetration of the Atlantic. The French ships lay in front of the fort, anchored in two curved lines in a narrow channel that formed the direct approach. Their anchorage was between an island, Aix, and a mud shoal called Les Palles. The approach was from the Atlantic across the Basque Roads and past an extended shoal called the Boyart, which was so submerged that it was scarcely seen even at low tide. Batteries on Aix and the opposite shore covered this approach. Assault on the French ships therefore had to pass between these batteries while easing along the uncertain line of the Boyart shoal.

Timidity reigned as the matter came up for discussion. Direct attack was regarded as impracticable. Fire ships were seen as the only alternative, even though that, too, was regarded as impracticable by some. Gambier had himself said of fire ships that 'it is a horrible mode of warfare, and the attempt hazardous, if not desperate'.

First Lord Mulgrave and the Admiralty remained in this quandary until Cochrane brought *Imperieuse* into Plymouth Sound on 19 March. When by custom Cochrane presented himself at Admiralty two days later Mulgrave was ready with a surprising proposition, that Cochrane direct the fire-ship attack on the Rochefort fleet. Cochrane's zeal and exploits on the Spanish coast made him the obvious choice, and, besides, he had served on the Rochefort station and knew it well. He had once actually presented a plan for destruction of its defences. Handing Cochrane the letter in which Gambier had expressed his reservations, Mulgrave said, 'You see that Lord Gambier will not take upon himself the responsibility of attack, and the Admiralty is not disposed to bear the onus of failure by means of an attack by fire-ships, however desirous they may be that such an attack should be made.'

Cochrane balked at once. As he saw it: 'They wanted a victory and the admiral commanding plainly told them he would not willingly risk a defeat. Other officers had been consulted, who had disapproved of the use of fire-ships, and, as a last resource, I had been sent for, in the hope that I would undertake the enterprise. If it failed the consequence would be the loss of my individual reputation, as both ministry and commander-in-chief would lay the blame on me.' He refused the assignment, declaring that as a junior officer he would incite too much jealousy, and that Gambier himself might regard it as presumptuous of him to accept it.

Mulgrave protested that since all the officers who had been consulted had deemed the fire-ship attack as impracticable it was unlikely that they would be offended by the action being given to an officer who believed otherwise. Cochrane still refused. He was called back the next day. Mulgrave told him, 'My lord, you must go. The Board cannot listen to further refusal or delay. Rejoin your frigate at once. I will make you all right with Lord Gambier. Make yourself easy about the jealous feelings of senior officers. I will so manage it with Lord Gambier that the *amour propre* of the fleet shall be satisfied.'

Cochrane still tried to get out of it, but Mulgrave would not accept and ordered him back to his ship, advising that a secret letter would be written to Gambier 'directing him to employ your lordship on the service which we have settled against the Rochefort fleet'. There was no way out of that.

Upon Cochrane now rested the preparations. Fire ships had a history that went back to the Armada. They were small craft packed with explosives that were conducted as close as possible to the target vessels, a form of slow fuse was lit, and the crew then jumped into a boat they were towing and made off as fast as possible. Twenty-one fire ships were prepared. These were made especially flammable as well as explosive. They were lined with tarred canvas and loaded with turpentine, resin and other combustible materials. In addition Cochrane prepared his own design of explosive vessels. Three of them were built. They were composed of casks into which fifteen hundred barrels of powder had been emptied. These were tightly bound into a compact mass with several hundred shells and three thousand hand grenades. But all these craft carried something new as well. They offered another prophecy of twentieth-century warfare: rockets.

In the Great War, as it would be with the Second World War, new invention eagerly propositioned itself. Around 1804 William Congreve had begun to experiment with rockets as a serious military weapon. By 1806 a metal-encased 32-pound rocket had reached a range of three thousand yards. They were tested against Boulogne and used by the military at Copenhagen. Cochrane had used them off the Catalan coast and would now do so again. They were loaded aboard the fire ships and his own explosive vessels.

Cochrane then sailed out to Basque Roads, leaving the explosive flotilla to follow, together with a ship carrying Congreve himself and a detachment of marine artillery.

When Cochrane arrived off Aix on 3 April 1809, Gambier received him with perfect amiability. He had accepted that Cochrane would conduct the actual attack, but had again guardedly expressed his reservations to Admiralty: '. . . *if* their Lordships are of opinion that an attack on the enemy's ships by those of the fleet under my command is practicable, I am ready to obey any orders they may be pleased to honour me with, however great the risk may be of loss of men and ships'. And with that he explicitly dissociated himself from blame if things went wrong. Along with that emphatic message to Cochrane, that all risk was now laid entirely upon him, Cochrane saw that, as he had feared, he had earned the resentment of all the other captains. 'Every captain was my senior,' he later wrote, 'and the moment my plans were known, all regarded me as an interloper, sent to take credit from those to whom it was now considered legitimately to belong.' For the moment, however, that anger exploded in quite different fashion.

The resentment of Cochrane by the other captains was as nothing to that directed against Gambier by the second-in-command at Rochefort, Rear Admiral Eliab Harvey, who only knew of the intended operation after Cochrane's arrival.

When details of the mission reached him Harvey stormed across to the flagship, *Caledonia*, and into Gambier's Great Cabin to vent his rage that the assignment had not fallen to him or any of his officers. But what exploded there had as much to do with the dislike of Gambier that many in the navy bore as it did Cochrane's mission. Cochrane was seated in the apartment next to the Great Cabin with Sir Harry Neale, captain of the fleet. Through the open doors he and Neale listened to a rage of insult without precedent between two of the most senior officers in the Royal Navy.

Cochrane and Neale heard Harvey demanding of Gambier that Harvey and his officers aboard his ship, *Tonnant*, be given Cochrane's assignment. Unless the direction of it came to him he would strike his flag and resign his commission. Gambier replied that, regrettable though that might be, Admiralty had fixed on Cochrane and he could not deviate from that. Harvey then let loose a torrent of clearly long-suppressed loathing of Gambier: that he never saw a man so unfit for command of the fleet as Gambier, who so far had made no soundings in preparation for an attack, nor checked whether any mortars had been placed in front of the French ships. That instead of such vital preparations he merely mustered the ships' companies for 'catechetical examinations of the men'. Had Nelson been there, Harvey concluded, he would not have anchored in Basque Roads at all but would have dashed at the enemy at once.

Harvey then went into Neale's cabin, shook hands with Cochrane saying there was nothing personal in what he had heard but that bringing Cochrane in from outside could only be regarded as an insult to the fleet. That the Admiralty had sent him was none of his own seeking, Cochrane replied. 'Well,' said Harvey, 'this is not the first time that my services have not been attended to in the way they deserved, because I am no canting Methodist, no hypocrite, no psalm-singer, and do not cheat old women out of their estates by hypocrisy and canting.' The latter reference was to some scandal involving Gambier.

They all went on the quarterdeck where, before all who were within sight and hearing, some thirty seamen and officers, Harvey continued his ranting, repeating that Gambier's treatment of him was proof of his 'Methodistical, Jesuitical conduct' and of his vindictive disposition. Cochrane and Neale, walking the quarterdeck, were unable to restrain their laughter, saying 'Hear him, hear him.' But Cochrane's irrepressible laughter hid a now bitter and sobering regret that he had not stuck to his refusal with Mulgrave and thereby avoided 'the hornet's nest' into which he had delivered himself. 'The fact was that the fleet was divided into two factions, as bitter against each other as were the Cavaliers and Roundheads in the days of Charles I,' he was to write. He himself duly received from Gambier packets of evangelical tracts for distribution to his crew, but he found them 'silly and injudicious' and refused to distribute them.

Cochrane had his first setback when the fleet of fire ships arrived on 10 April. He wanted an immediate attack that night, rightly believing that on recognizing the fire ships the French would make changes to their defences. Gambier's reputation for caution was at once to the fore. He refused, declaring that the fire ships might be boarded and their crews murdered.

Cochrane pointed out how illogical that was; given that the ships were destined to be used the risk of casualties was likely to be greater afterwards since the French would be then expecting them. Anyhow, as the explosion ships bearing the Congreve rockets and crewed by himself and his volunteers would precede the fire ships, all risk would fall upon them.

Gambier replied that if Cochrane chose to rush on self-destruction that was his own affair but it was his, Gambier's, duty to take care of the lives of others, and he would not place the crews of the fire ships 'in palpable danger'. To that Cochrane stubbornly answered that the use of the explosion vessels that he himself had devised being new to naval warfare, it was unlikely that, after seeing the effect of the first explosion, the enemy's officers and men would board a single fire ship.

Gambier's objections probably had less to do with logic than his repugnance of fire ships now to be complemented by Congreve's rockets. Evangelical protest against Congreve's rockets had already appeared in the *Naval Chronicle* in an essay decrying 'the inhumanity of introducing them into naval warfare'. That protest against the rockets in 1809 offered yet another note from the Great War that could re-echo in the twentieth century: 'In all other battles there is hope – in all other warfare may be heard the songs of triumph but in this diabolical contention hope itself must expire, triumph can be but in idea, for the vanquishers only can be distinguished from the vanquished by the last terrible explosion.'

On that unlikely note the Basque Roads operation began. As Cochrane predicted, the French lost no time in preparing for the fire assault, striking their topmasts and getting as much inflammable material as possible down from aloft. Instead of lying in two lines overlapping each other the French ships were rearranged at their anchorage to offer a less easy target to the attack. They were additionally protected by an enormous boom, of which nothing was known until the attack since Gambier had failed to take soundings.

The following day, 11 April, with a strong wind from the sea, a dark night and a full tide flowing towards the French fleet, Gambier agreed to launch the attack, but he held the British fleet some six miles off Aix. The officers and seamen who had volunteered to command the fire ships were aboard the flagship *Caledonia*, where they got their last instructions from Cochrane, who then sailed in aboard his own explosion vessel towards the boom. Off the boom he lit the fuse. He and the others then jumped into the dinghy they were towing and began rowing against the sea to get away. The fuse burned faster than they had planned and the explosion vessel blew up dangerously close to them, a massive force of powder, shells, grenades and rockets that raised a wave that nearly swamped their boat. It had blasted open the boom. This was the achievement that would allow success to the entire operation, for the tremendous explosion created a fear among the French that wrecked their fleet. One of the grandest artificial spectacles imaginable, Cochrane described it: 'the sky was red with the lurid glare . . . the sea was convulsed as by an earthquake, rising in a huge wave on whose crest our boat was lifted like a cork'. By contrast, the fire ships achieved nothing. Of the twenty-one fire ships only four reached the French position and not one did any damage. 'The way in which they were managed was grievous,' Cochrane was to record. 'I could scarcely credit my own vision when I saw the way in which they were handled; most of them being fired and abandoned before they were abreast of the vessels anchored as guides.' The fire ships nevertheless had great effect for they caused the French to fear them as threatening the same force as Cochrane's explosion vessel. As one witness recorded, 'They appeared to form a chain of ignited pyramids, stretching from Ile d'Aix to the Boyart shoal; while Congreve's rockets flying through the air in various directions and, like comets, dragging a fiery train behind, formed a scene at once the most grand and terrific that can be imagined.' Confusion reigned in the French fleet.

As the French ships hastily sought to remove themselves deeper into the basin beyond Aix some simply cut their cables and were seen drifting broadside to the wind and tide that carried them in. Others made sail to get away. But at daylight, except for two, every other vessel of the Rochefort fleet was seen to be ashore, stranded on Les Palles. Admiral Alemand's 120-gun flagship *L'Ocean* and four others lay in a position vulnerable to attack, which they would be unable to return.

At just before six a.m. on the 12th Cochrane signalled to Gambier, 'Half the fleet can destroy the enemy. Seven on shore.' The signal was acknowledged but no answer sent. He signalled again at six forty, 'Eleven on shore.' Then at seven forty, 'Only two afloat.' To neither signal was there any response other than the answering pennant confirming Message Received. At nine thirty a.m. he finally signalled 'Enemy preparing to heave off.' The tide had started to run and the French were preparing to lift off. For Cochrane the lack of decisive response to his signals was incomprehensible. He had waited for the fleet to move in and bombard the stranded vessels. At eleven the British fleet began to move but soon after it went to anchor again. Gambier's eventual defence of this lack of urgency to destroy the French fleet was that 'as the enemy was on shore, he did not think it necessary to run an unnecessary risk of the fleet, when the object of their destruction seemed to be already obtained'.

At one p.m. on the 12th Cochrane took it upon himself to do what Gambier appeared unwilling to do. He let his frigate *Imperieuse* drift with the wind and tide past the island of Aix whose guns Gambier had feared. They fired at *Imperieuse* but all fell short. In an attempt to compel action

from Gambier and the fleet at one forty p.m. he signalled 'Enemy superior to chasing ship but inferior to fleet'. That drew no attention so five
minutes later he signalled 'In want of assistance'. As he engaged three of
the French ships he at last saw motion from the fleet as seven ships began
to move towards *Imperieuse*, to join the attack. By sunset that evening two
of the French had struck, one had blown up and two, abandoned by their
crews, had burned and also blown up. All but one of the British support
ships withdrew during the night. Cochrane remained, intending to attack
the flagship *L'Ocean*, but at daylight on the 13th *Caledonia* sent a recall
signal followed by a letter from Gambier delivered by boat. Cochrane still
sought to remain to attack but a final peremptory message from Gambier
left him no alternative but to withdraw.

Aboard *Caledonia* Cochrane pleaded with Gambier for the work of
destruction to be completed, declaring that if no more were done 'a noise
would be made in England'. To which Gambier angrily replied, 'If you
throw the blame upon what has been done, it will appear like arrogantly
claiming all the merit to yourself.' Cochrane was then told to sail for England
with despatches. He replied that he preferred to finish the job entrusted to
him by Admiralty, namely destruction of the Rochefort fleet. Gambier cut
him short by handing him written orders to leave for England. *Imperieuse*
sailed for home the next day, 15 April.

Against Cochrane's youthful zeal, daring and insight had stood the flabby
cautions, the absence of drive and weak assessments of Gambier. The whole
dismal performance, Gambier's 'mollesse', lack of backbone, as Jurien de la
Gravière described it, had through Cochrane's distinctive effort seriously
incapacitated what survived of the Rochefort fleet. Three ships of the line
had been destroyed and the rest of the squadron so damaged that they were
subsequently dismantled. What made it a notable victory was that it entirely
spoiled the French intention to send the Rochefort squadron to the West
Indies to defend Guadeloupe and Martinique, which in due course were
captured by the British.

What now followed in London, however, brought further distortion
of it all, precipitated by Cochrane, thereby finally converting the Basque
Roads operation into one of the ugliest episodes in the internal history of
the Royal Navy.

The Gambier despatch that Cochrane carried home gave credit to God
and Cochrane in equal measure for a great success. God had strongly
favoured His Majesty, the Nation and the fleet under Gambier in that
success. Gambier wrote, 'I cannot speak in sufficient terms of admiration
and applause of the valorous and gallant attack made by Lord Cochrane
upon the French-line-of-battle ships which were on shore, as well as of the
judicious manner of approaching them, and placing his ship in a position

most advantageous to annoy the enemy and preserve his own ship, which could not be exceeded by any feat of valour hitherto achieved by the British navy.' More Cochrane could not have asked for. It was certainly a lot more than Nelson got for some of his most audacious early exploits. And, as the first great naval success since Trafalgar, Basque Roads was publicly seen as a major victory, enough to light bonfires and raise Cochrane's name as a new hero. But when Cochrane heard that a vote of thanks was proposed in the House of Commons for Gambier's 'glorious' and 'brilliant' success, he told Mulgrave that, being a member of parliament, he would oppose the motion on the grounds that Gambier had done nothing to merit a vote of thanks but had neglected to destroy the fleet at Aix when he was able to do so. Mulgrave immediately begged him to avoid that. He already had full credit with the public for what he had done at Basque Roads, so why deny some recognition for Gambier? And he could only bring high government displeasure upon himself!

In face of Cochrane's determination to expose Gambier, Mulgrave made a remarkable offer. 'Now, my lord, I will make you a proposal. I will put under your orders three frigates, with *carte blanche* to do whatever you please on the enemy's coasts in the Mediterranean. I will further get you permission to go to Sicily, and embark on board your squadron my own regiment, which is stationed there. You know how to make use of them.' It was an offer the like of which such a young officer had never before received. The inherent opportunities for success, glory and riches were easily comparable to Nelson receiving the Mediterranean squadron that took him to the Nile, but for Cochrane the principle he was defending was greater than any of that. His contempt for the corruption so deeply entrenched in the war effort and public life, the weakness of the government and its uninspired conduct of the war was too great. 'I told his lordship that, were I to accept his offer, the country would regard my acceptance as a bribe to hold my peace, whilst I should regard my acquiescence in the same light . . . The anxiety of the Government was, no doubt, to convert the little that had been effected in Aix Roads into political capital, as a victory which merited the thanks of parliament; my tacit acquiescence in the object of Government would have subjected me, and rightly, to a total loss of political confidence in the estimation of those with whom I acted.'

The official retaliation was immediate and merciless. Gambier demanded a court martial before the matter was raised in parliament. He was told to make a new despatch on the action at Basque Roads. In it he deleted the praise given to Cochrane in the earlier report. That set the nature of the court martial that followed. Every possible means of thwarting any serious assault by Cochrane on Gambier's reputation or conduct of the Basque Roads operations was exercised. Gambier was honourably acquitted of any failures at Basque Roads. The vote of national gratitude and praise of him was duly passed in parliament.

After Basque Roads it is easier to understand the disenchantment that Collingwood had expressed from the Mediterranean on the quality of the new generation as well as the officers in general. In praise of Cochrane, while foreseeing a great future for him and lamenting over what was veiled over by the courts martial of Gambier and Harvey, the *Naval Chronicle* saw reason to compare Napoleon's handling of the different generations in his army with that prevalent in the British navy:

The very name of Cochrane will be as dreadful to him as was that of Nelson; if our ministers will only muster up courage enough to look our old admirals in the face, and permit our young hero to obtain volunteers among the young officers, to burn and destroy everything that may be within the reach of youthful courage and youthful vigour. It is the active spirit, and not helpless seniority, to which our vigilant enemy entrusts the execution of his operations . . . It is to youthful talents that Buonaparte is indebted for the enormous and successful strides which he has made towards universal power. The decrepitude of ancient experience may adapt itself to our councils of war; but the rapid ardour of youth ought to be employed to execute those daring schemes, by which alone the most daring enemy we ever had to encounter can be defeated.

Such hopes were quickly shown to be forlorn.

The proof of that was to be the treatment of Cochrane after Gambier's court martial. Admiralty set about trying to edge Cochrane out of immediate service in the navy, duly accomplished just a year later. It was a tragic loss to a navy that had urgent need of his talents. Before that, however, Admiral Harvey had to be dealt with. He was court-martialled for 'imputing disrespect to his superior officer', found guilty and dismissed the service. The *Naval Chronicle* provided a moving final image to the whole sad business. Its observer at Harvey's trial wrote, '. . . we felt sincerely at seeing this brave man, after receiving sentence, walking up alone from the Sally Port to his house. He left Portsmouth immediately.'

L I

EXPEDITIONARY FORCES

From the start of his time in office as Secretary of War, Castlereagh had taken it upon himself to counteract any belief that after Trafalgar a sense of urgency no longer attached to the navy and its role. He had immediately sought to formulate a clear post-Trafalgar naval policy tied to his military urgency. Of the struggle with France he said, in a letter to Chancellor Spencer Perceval on 1 October 1807: 'The more I have had time to reflect on our future prospects in this war, the more impressed I am with a conviction that neither peace nor independence can be the lot of this nation till we . . . counteract at sea what [France] lawlessly inflicts and enforces on shore.'

This was the most decisive retort yet to Napoleon's 'Sea must be subdued by Land', for with Castlereagh it meant that Britain's response had to combine land and sea: seaborne military. For that he and the Duke of York had remodelled the army. His strategy for the combination of the two services became broadly to take advantage of Napoleon's increasing entanglements on the Continent to move substantial military force by sea to points where a new front could add to the emperor's problems. Iberia, of course already established that. But Napoleon's renewed war with Austria gave it further and immediate urgency.

In the spring of 1809 the island of Walcheren had appeared already to be the natural target from both a naval and military point of view. The naval aspect had the greatest priority. As the Westmorland memorandum had made clear, Napoleon's dominance of the Continent had given him a naval strength that could hardly have been foreseen in the immediate aftermath of Trafalgar. With it an invasion of Britain appeared more assured of success. But through Castlereagh's swiftness of decision after Tilsit, first at Copenhagen then at Lisbon and Cadiz, much of that possibility had been demolished, though by no means entirely. Napoleon had been neatly deprived of the Danish, Portuguese and Spanish fleets. All of this had been the achievement of sea-military. What remained, however, was the powerful centre of Napoleon's naval confederacy, Antwerp and the Scheldt: that menace permanently feared by Britain.

Walcheren was the largest island between the main channels that divided the mouth of the Scheldt. The channel of the western Scheldt flowed in past Vlissinge at its entrance and continued beyond through a tortuous forty-mile course to Antwerp.

Castlereagh had demanded haste when the project was first seriously proposed in March 1809, but it was not to be until 21 June that he finally got cabinet approval. The circumstances for a strike at the Scheldt had never looked better. Apart from Napoleon's preoccupations in Austria, Antwerp was poorly defended. But the situation had changed when the expedition finally sailed on 28 July. Napoleon had defeated Austria at Wagram and the French had begun to prepare to confront the greatest combined navy and military armament that had ever set sail from Britain: 120 warships and transports carrying forty thousand troops.

The French forces on the Scheldt were by no means sufficient to cope with that oncoming strength. But during the desultory preparation of the expedition the British had been warned that the midsummer period for any operation at Walcheren was fast disappearing for the approach of autumn brought a sickly season conducive to fevers. The British began landing troops fourteen hours after their departure from the Downs. Just three weeks later they began their withdrawal. Of that mighty force, only 106 had been killed in action, but four thousand had died of fever, with 11,500 still in hospital. These were undoubtedly the most astonishing casualty figures of any campaign in this war.

The search for blame exploded in Britain, and it continued long after the war. Julian Corbett offered the most insightful view. He saw it as that necessary fusion of the military and the naval required to meet Napoleon's declaration that Land would defeat Sea. For Britain it was the tactical union of the two services that was about to prove itself in the Iberian Peninsula, there to establish one of the distinct differences between the war before and the one after Trafalgar.

Walcheren had left a bitter sense of futility. As the tremendous cost was considered Britain sought consolation elsewhere, together with replenishment of a rapidly depleting Treasury.

A natural instinct in those circumstances was to look eastwards. On this occasion it was to the Indian Ocean, for immediate material gain, but equally for firmer assurance of the security of Britain's flow of wealth from India and the Orient. Accordingly there were two immediate objectives. These were seizure of France's principal Indian Ocean base, the two islands that composed Mauritius, Ile de France and Ile de Bourbon, and of the Dutch Spice Islands, as Sumatra and Java were known.

Mauritius had always been a source of huge concern to Britain, a fear enhanced by Napoleon's irrepressible eastern aspirations. The two islands were rich enough on their own in sugar, coffee, indigo, ebony and spices to be of immediate value. Far more important, however, was their value to France as a base at the centre of the Indian Ocean, commanding all strategic passage across it. As such, they formed one of the few points on the world's seas where the French navy remained highly and successfully active.

Mauritius provided the base and rendezvous for a fleet of frigates and other vessels that had the trade of the Indian Ocean as their natural target: Indiamen out of India, and merchantmen out of China or wherever else they came from in the East. The taking of Indiamen was constant, a significant drain on the cargoes that passed from India to Britain. The captured vessels were brought to the islands, which became the depot for their cargoes, much of which the British angrily accused the Americans of delivering to Europe on behalf of the French.

After one successful assault on the Ile de Bourbon from the Cape in September 1809, another attempt was made in March 1810. Ile de Bourbon was taken in July after protracted effort but in the attempt against the adjacent Ile de France the British lost three frigates. A more determined effort from India brought capitulation of the Ile de France in December 1810.

As a sideshow to this came the last naval engagement of the war on the Indian Ocean. A French squadron of three frigates, *Renommée*, Captain Roquebert, commodore of the squadron, *Néréide*, Captain Le Maresquier, and *Clorinde*, Captain St Cricq, got out of Brest on 2 February 1811, intended for reinforcement of Mauritius but with instructions to proceed to Java if they encountered problem at Mauritius. They arrived off the Ile de France on 6 May and quickly discovered that the British were in possession. The British, holding the signal books, tried to lure them in, but the French commanders at once surmised the situation and made off for Tamatave, Madagascar, with the British in pursuit. At noon, 20 May, off Tamatave, the British came in sight of the French squadron, but in a perfect calm.

What followed was one of the most resolutely fought frigate actions of the Great War, effectively one of the last true naval engagements between the British and French navies in that war, for little of comparable distinction or consequence was to follow elsewhere in what remained of the conflict. As such, the two squadrons proved entirely deserving of that particular honour, their showing highly creditable to each.

The ships were absolutely matched. It was a strange action with scarcely any wind most of the time, mainly a light breeze alternately benefiting one side or the other. Thus, off and on, it extended through a dark night during which the opponents sought to identify their own by occasional brief light signals. Both sides suffered severely. Two of the French frigates were lost to the British, but the latter suffered heavily in damage and killed and wounded. *Clorinde* had also lowered its colours but then escaped from its heavily disabled opponent. *Clorinde* was pursued by two of the British ships, so close at one point that their bowsprits nearly touched *Clorinde*'s stern. But at quarter past four in the morning Captain St Cricq had his last sight of his pursuers. He had long since lost touch with all his own ships. *Clorinde* then began her long voyage home to Brest.

It was a voyage of survival. Taking stock at dawn Cricq had a badly damaged ship, with smallpox, scurvy and fever among the crew, and reduced water and provisions. He made for the Seychelles, where he took on board turtles, coconuts and water. Thereafter they survived on what they took from passing ships, including a British packet captured after doubling the Cape of Good Hope. From her they took biscuits and salt meat sufficient to get them home. On 24 September, approaching the entrance to Brest in a fresh wind, a British man-of-war in full sail came down hard upon them, to cut them off. The British ship maintained too much sail in a strengthening gale. She was within pistol shot, cannonading *Clorinde* severely, when Cricq had the good fortune to see the Briton's maintop and mizzen top go. His pursuer was obliged to haul off. At five that afternoon Cricq anchored in Brest Roads, eight months after his departure from there. His arrival closed the expulsion of France from the Indian Ocean.

Meanwhile, at Ile de France the Royal Navy was dealing with an unpleasant surprise that accompanied its seizure of the island.

Some fifty seamen, sailors and marines who had arrived there as prisoners from different ships taken by the French, including ships involved in the recent operations against the island, had gone over to the French. Worse, they had gone into the French army and worn the uniform of French soldiers, prepared to fight for France. Yet another galling aspect of the defections was that several had taken advantage of the terms of surrender by which French soldiers and their families were conveyed to France and had been allowed to get away with those.

Twelve of the deserters were carried back to Britain to be dealt with in special circumstances that would serve as intimidating example. On 10 February 1811, at Horsemonger Lane in Southwork, they appeared before a Special Commission, headed by the Lord Chief Justice Baron MacDonald, on charges of high treason. The crowd seeking to enter the court was so large that only a fraction could get admittance.

The prisoners were defended by Henry Brougham. The witnesses against them were mainly other sailors who had also entered the French army but whose testimony would earn them their liberty.

The case against all was broadly identical. They had joined the French army and worn its uniform. They had helped to guard their former ship-mates, often jeering at them through the bars. They had publicly insulted their own officers when they encountered them on the streets of Port Louis. Although the seamen and marines were imprisoned when their ships were captured, it was the custom in that war for officers to move about freely on parole.

In a war where desertion from the Royal Navy was continuous and enlistment in another navy common, the character of this hearing was extraordinary. Sailors could be, and were, hanged for desertion to another navy, even in the case of desertion to the American navy when America was not a belligerent. But those were tried by court martial, usually at Portsmouth aboard the vessel reserved there for Marine Law hearings. But why would High Treason not have been the solemn charge in such cases? The charge of High Treason was, of course, the essential difference in this case. It was a rare event, and the first and only one in this war involving the navy.

The unusual nature of the process and the charge itself therefore raises curious questions. How was the extreme offence of High Treason arrived at? A possible answer is that the sailors had put on French army uniform, a gravity attached to this case of a different order from anything preceding it, as Lord Justice MacDonald's summary and horrendous sentence made clear:

The scene passing here is one which I least expected Great Britain would ever see. Scarcely a session of parliament passes, that we do not find the conduct of the British navy spoken of in terms of high eulogium, and thanks voted to them for their unparal-leled bravery. How unexpected then do I this day see so many seamen of Great Britain convicted of high treason, and of having deserted their king and country, and of having entered the service of the enemy. Next to lifting your hand against your Sovereign, your crimes could not have assumed a blacker dye. Under these circumstances it now only remains for me to pass that sentence upon you which the law dictates; a duty which, as I am growing old, I did hope to escape; but which, painful as it is, I am bound to perform. It is that each of you be taken on a hurdle to the place of execu-tion, where you shall be hanged by the neck, but not till you are dead; that you be severally taken down, while yet alive, and your bowels taken out, and burnt before your faces. That your heads then be cut off, and your bodies cut in four quarters, to be at the king's disposal.

The prisoners 'heard the awful sentence with becoming fortitude and, after crying for mercy, re-conducted to their cells'.

LII

TIMOR

AFTER the conquest of Mauritius the British moved on to remove the French presence entirely from the Indian Ocean, by seizing Java and the rest of the Spice Islands.

That unique archipelago, long held by the Dutch, was, with its spices and tropical produce such as coffee and rice, a source of mercantile wealth then comparable only to India. But it also commanded the principal sea passages from across the Indian Ocean to China, either through the Malaccan Straits or the Strait of Sunda.

For those reasons Napoleon saw obvious value in Java. He had attached further significance to it, however, as complementing the strategic importance of Mauritius through which French presence on the Indian Ocean was maintained and, in the far view, as a base for any assault on India. In 1808 he had, therefore, through two trusted Dutch generals, Daendels and Janssens, set about fortifying Java. French soldiers were sent out to back up the Dutch forces in defence of the islands.

For the British, Java and the islands represented another naval-military venture to a strange and unpredictable scene of the sort that had become so distinctive to this war. But for the senior naval and military officers, always conscious of prize money, whatever the difficulties, it was an expedition to be pressed forward. The submission of Java was accomplished remarkably swiftly.

As in the case of Mauritius, Lord Minto, the governor-general of India, assembled the forces at Madras in the spring of 1811. The naval force consisted of three 74s, one 64, fourteen frigates and seven sloops of war, under the command of Rear Admiral Stopford. Their sailors and marines were to bolster a military force of twelve hundred. The expedition arrived off Batavia on 4 August and a landing made the same day. Batavia was abandoned almost immediately by the Dutch and French, who retreated to an inland, heavily fortified position. Once more, as so often since Nelson at Corsica, sailors dragged guns up to form batteries. On 24 August the naval batteries opened intense fire. The next day the military assault was launched and the place taken. Meanwhile, all around Java and the islands the other fortified French bases were also taken. On 19 September Janssens, who had been pursued halfway down Java, signed a capitulation of Java and all its related islands.

As always in large operations such as that of Java there were often those who found themselves launched upon their own separate and special adventures. Such was the experience of Captain C. J. Thurston of the sloop of war *Hesper*.

Thurston's was another of those naval episodes of the Great War in which a man might find himself alone, baffled by weather and unfamiliar scene, fearing the worst, but then emerging into his own singular contribution to the whole. It is a small, superb story of seamanship and mastery of the unexpected.

In December 1811, with all of Java and its dependencies seemingly in British possession, report was received of the escape from Brest of Roquebert's squadron. Although Mauritius was already in British hands, news of the fate of those frigates, *Néréide*, *Clorinde* and *Renommée*, had still not reached Java. The commander in chief, Rear Admiral Stopford, therefore accurately assumed that they had been intended for the relief of Java and might show up there. Stopford ordered Thurston to sail from Surabaya for the Straits of Bali to watch the southern entrance for the French.

Of his original crew of 120, Thurston had only between eighty and ninety left, fifty of whom were stricken, as the entire British operation had been, by tropical fevers. He sailed to a familiar anchorage in the Straits to take on water and while *Hesper* was doing so the westerly monsoon suddenly set in violently, as it could do, accompanied by blinding downpour. Thurston stood pondering the wisdom of putting to sea.

In the long account that he subsequently wrote, Thurston said, 'I determined to run all risk and stood to sea early one morning with the intention of returning to the anchorage in the evening if the severity of the weather or strength of currents outside should render it necessary.' But within half an hour after clearing the Straits a particularly heavy squall came on and entirely hid the land.

I stood on for a few hours and then tacked, in the expectation of reaching my anchorage in the Straits before dark. The weather during the whole day had been so extremely thick, that we were never once enabled to see more than half a mile distant. About four o'clock p.m. I calculated that I was at the mouth of the Straits which I had left in the morning. The weather as we approached in shore became more moderate, the land at no great distance. I stood in with full confidence, when to our astonishment, the face and form of the Straits had entirely changed their character, and I soon discovered that it was in vain to search for our old friendly anchorage *here*. I now comprehended that the easterly current, for which it was impossible to calculate, had driven me in spite of all my endeavours to keep to windward, into the Straits of Lombok, between Bali and the island of Lombok. I endeavoured to gain the offing, as the only rough manuscript chart in my possession, represented these Straits as extremely dangerous, from the extraordinary currents there prevailing. But it was too late to recede, the wind had almost at once fallen to a dead calm, and I found myself irresistibly drawn into this gulf, with a rapidity most alarming.

Hesper became completely ungovernable from the lack of wind, thrown about by the capricious effects of the currents. 'At one moment all was calm and smooth as a mirror, not a ripple to be seen or heard, and in an instant a mountainous wave rose at a short distance, and directed its course to the vessel, boiling and roaring with a noise and velocity most appalling. It then broke over the ship on both sides, carrying on its course with the same wild appearance for a hundred fathoms more, and then, all at once, the surge ceased, and all was still again. This phenomenon ceased only to appear again instantaneously, and during the whole of this awful scene the Hesper was turned round and round in the most alarming manner, a plaything in the hands of the genii of this whirlpool.'

Thurston was then confronted by another peril. *Hesper* was being driven towards the breakers along the shore with a rapidity that declared the situation hopeless. 'Then, at the very moment when we had lost the hope of deliverance, a counter current caught us with the same violence, and hurried us over to the opposite shore. I now found that independently of the counter currents, the direction of the whole movement was to the northward, through the Straits, with such velocity that at the expiration of two hours we had the northern entrance, and I gained the same night the entrance of the Java Sea without any accident, and in the course of the following morning again entered the Bali Straits, but by a northern passage.'

Hesper had gone round Bali from south to north, from the Indian Ocean into the Flores Sea and back to their former anchorage. Exhausted, battered, they sought respite. 'The weather was now for a day or two tolerably settled, so that notwithstanding the experience I had gained in my first attempt to remain at sea, I was induced to make a second experiment. Accordingly I started again by the same route. The morning was fine, and the easterly current outside did not appear too rapid to prevent my holding my ground, but towards the afternoon it grew black to the S.W. and in a short time a gale of wind came on with great fury; it blew a perfect hurricane all night, and in the morning when I stood in for the land I discovered by my observations

of chronometer that I was now opposite the coast of the island of Sumbawa.'
Return to Java was for the moment impossible, 'unless I had chosen to cross
the equinoctial line, and thus profiting by the contrary monsoon which blew
to the northward of the equator.'

Hesper was short of provisions, the crew exhausted and the sick
sinking.

I cast my eyes over the chart and saw no place where I could find refreshment nearer
than Timor, and although I had no local knowledge of the state of the settlement
and hoped that possibly before this time the British government might have sent a
garrison to take possession of it, I decided, therefore, to make the best of my way
to that place, and ran down before the wind, running a great risk from the coral
reefs, which were not marked down in the chart.

I found myself the next day in the open sea between Sandal Wood Island and
Timor island. The weather was now occasionally clear, though still blowing with
undiminished violence. I was fortunately able to determine with tolerable precision the
latitude by double latitudes, which was of the utmost consequence, as my intention was
to enter the straits which are formed by the two small islands lying to the westward
of Timor. At eight o'clock in the evening I was exactly in the latitude of the straits,
at the supposed distance of about fifty miles. I therefore ordered the ship to be hove
to for the night, and not to attempt a nearer approach until next morning.

I remained on deck all night, during which the weather was excessively bad,
and the ship drifting fast to eastward. The day had not yet broken when the alarm
was given – 'breakers on the lee bow'; the vessel was instantly wore round, and
scarcely had she gone on the other tack, when again – 'land ahead'; and the surf
was seen breaking over the rocks with tremendous fury. I could now only hope that
we were in the Straits, but our preservation depended on various circumstances –
upon the correctness of the latitude of the Straits, as marked down in the chart on
the precision of my observations the preceding day, and on the exactitude of our
cruise during the night. It was a fearful moment, if we were in the Straits I knew
we were safe, but if a quarter of a mile to the northward or southward, nothing
could possibly save us from destruction. The day was not yet clear, we wore round
frequently to avoid the tremendous breakers on either side; the Straits were not
half a mile in breadth, a perfect silence prevailed on board, every individual seemed
absorbed in the contemplation of the imminent danger which surrounded them, and
the rapid execution of every order, shewed the superiority of British seamen over
every other in the hour of danger. I had sent men aloft to report if any opening
could be observed between the land to leeward; when at once on the dispersion of
a dark and heavy squall, which kept back the day, several voices exclaimed, 'we
are in the Straits, sir', and the opening appeared every moment more manifest. *We
had stood the cast of life or death and the throw was successful.*

I now steered confidently into the Straits, and we were soon in that part of them formed by the northernmost of the two islands and Timor. Here we were perfectly sheltered from the fury of the monsoon, but our difficulties were not all over. Our chart, owing to the illiberal conduct of the Dutch government, whose invariable practice was to preclude strangers from all knowledge whatever of their seas, contained no details, and I knew not in what part to look for an anchorage. Our sounding lead could never reach the bottom with forty fathoms, and the day was employed in a vain search in the Straits. I continued in the Straits all night, and in the morning sailed out to explore the northern coast of Timor. I found a deep bay to the northward. I stood in for a considerable time, but no signs of habitation appearing. As I put my eye to the glass for the last time, I imagined, I perceived a red habitation peeping from among the trees. The picturesque town of Cepang [Kupang] presented itself, protected by the battery of Vittoria, which stood high on a cliff to the westward.

Our colours were now hoisted, and a signal gun was fired, and I expected the British flag hoisted on the fort, but you may judge my embarrassment when I observed the Dutch flag wave. I immediately despatched an officer with a flag of truce ashore, bearing a letter to the governor, in which I informed him of the reduction of the Dutch settlements at Batavia by the English, and demanding the surrender of the colony, and his immediate attendance on board. The officer returned with the answer of the governor, that he could not comprehend the affair, that he had no communication with Java for nearly two years, and begged me to come on shore to explain.

I was received on the beach with military honours, the battery was manned, and the troops and militia drawn up. I proceeded to the government house, and commenced the conversation with a recapitulation with the late events at Java. He required to see my authority, and the written orders usually given on such occasions. I was obliged to be frank with him, and represented to him the truth, that accidental circumstances had brought me to Timor, where I expected to have found a British garrison, but that not being the case, it became my duty as a British officer, to haul down an enemy's flag wherever I might find it. I now summoned him in my own name to surrender to me, as an enemy of superior force, stating that I had on board 300 men, who waited only for my return to come ashore and commence an immediate attack. I warned him also that the blood that might be shed in this contest must rest on his head.

He was immensely agitated and undecided what part to take. To compel him to decision I drew out my watch, 'Sir, I give you ten minutes for deliberation; if, at the expiration of that time, you are not decided, I *am*, and shall return on board, and you abide the consequences of a bombardment.' His inquietude increased. I whispered to my Dutch interpreter whom I had on the ship to proceed to the fort and endeavour, by feigning himself to be the bearer of orders to that effect, to haul down the flag. He executed his commission so well that before ten minutes were expired and the governor was still hesitating, the flag of Holland was lowered and the British ensign waved in its stead. It was too late for him to retract.

It was a neat gamble for, as Thurston declared, against the substantial forces that the Dutch governor commanded, *Hesper* now had fewer than forty able men, insufficient to garrison the fort let alone rule the rest of the station. But, after the Dutch and 'Malay' troops and local inhabitants had taken an oath of allegiance to the British flag, harmony was sealed with a ball on the portico of Government House.

LIII

CHINA–JAPAN

HYDROGRAPHY, they called it, the word that encompassed the accelerating expansion of the modern world through nautical survey and charting that the late-eighteenth-century mastery of longitude had empowered, and to which the Great War had brought its own drive.

The Western world was beset by an intense urgency to have the globe fully realized before it, to accurately map the seas and oceans and their coasts, the gulfs, channels, straits of passage, the islands that offered shelter and succour. What was wanted by all was an ability to sail the seas and oceans with greater safety and confidence, to approach even familiar coasts with less fear, to have fewer of the terrible human and financial losses of shipwreck because of old, undependable charts.

Hydrography became the titular instrument for that large goal to comprehend the globe and everywhere safely navigate it. In practical terms that was represented by the collation by Admiralty, Trinity House, the East India Company and the various scientific societies of everything possible on navigation and exploration. Naval and merchant navy officers were expected to send in observations and experiences, especially the new and unfamiliar, from their missions and voyages. This they did with admirable zeal.

The Great War had naturally provided huge expansion of those ambitions in all the seagoing protagonists. The search for navigational insight developed its particular urgency with each. Apart from advantage to be gained within the war itself, for all of them the projection was upon the future. Prospective rivalry in commerce was of course a dominant aspect of hydrography. And, along with the mercantile, strategic demands and incipient colonialism had also become vital aspects of this new and more diligent opening up of the world.

The French, through the first four years of the new century, were exploring and surveying the coast of Western Australia for colonial establishment, provoking a British observation, 'The facilities that will be afforded them of communicating with India are superior to those we enjoy from our colony at Port Jackson in New South Wales.' The Russians were turning to the Pacific and to the Arctic passage that might bring them closer to north-west America. The Americans, already on the Pacific, were building trade there, as well as practically everywhere else, from the Baltic to Canton. The Dutch were building new factories in West Africa and, while already holding so much of South-East Asia, were the only ones who had established themselves with Japan. Next to the British in India, theirs was the most enviable mercantile grip on Asia. Like all the others, the British themselves were seeking entry into Japan.

Typical of the efforts in the first years of the new century to fulfil the obsessive demand to have as close an observation of the accessible world as possible was that provided by John Turnbull, who went round the world from 1800 to 1804, passing from Madeira to the Brazils, the Cape of Good Hope, Botany Bay and Norfolk Island, and on to the principal islands of the Pacific. His published account detailed every aspect of life and nature as he encountered it. But Turnbull was only one of many. The great preparation for the imperial and colonial nineteenth century was feverishly underway.

Wherever else they were going, whatever else the seagoing Western powers had in mind, all concern and impulse were still dominated by what had always been fundamental to their ventures eastwards beyond the Cape of Good Hope: the China trade.

In spite of an established familiarity, the long run to the Orient never-theless remained a dangerous passage, fraught with risk in the great variety of its passages through different climates and seas and oceans with all their varying winds, currents and tides, and frequently erroneous charts.

The finest contribution to overall knowledge of the passage came in 1805 when the geographer James Horsburgh published his *Directions for sailing to and from the East Indies, China, New Holland, Cape of Good Hope, and interadjacent ports made during twenty-one years' experience in navigating those seas*. It was a compilation that offered the sum of all existing experience. Apart from Horsburgh's own experience he drew from the journals of 234 ships, his preface declaring, 'This work commenced at the solicitation of some navigators, who frequent the Oriental Seas . . . my chief aim has been to trace out error, and approximate truth . . . having once suffered shipwreck by the inaccuracy of the charts in general use, I considered it my duty to point out to other navigators such errors as were perceived to prevent them, if possible, from similar misfortune.'

In the first years of the Great War Horsburgh had produced three revi-sions of his own chart of the China voyage. As well as the surveying he conducted he had continued scientific experiments for navigation during the first five years of the century, among them exhaustive experiments in the efficiency of chronometers and the rise and fall of mercury in marine barometers, all of it in different seas. Typical of so many of that time, he was a self-taught man.

The China voyage was a passage of many months. That involved its own problems of survival among the crew, who might be decimated by fevers, scurvy and other health problems on the way out as well as the way back. A safe return never existed in any form of certainty for any sailor embarking for China or the East.

In 1811 Captain Byng of the 64-gun frigate *Belligueux*, with a crew of 491, decided to make his return voyage from China to Britain an experiment in shipboard health. *Belligueux* sailed from Macao Roads on 14 February with six bullocks for slaughter at sea and twelve dozen capons for the sick. Larger quantities than usual were loaded of potatoes, pumpkins, onions and carrots. Two thousand pounds of onions and nopal (cactus) leaves were pickled on board with vinegar, nutmeg, mace, cinnamon, ginger and pepper. The voyage took six months and every man on board was landed alive and well. During the voyage 133 men were put on the sick list. The sick had been given 'a light and proper diet of fresh food'. Every man who came down with scurvy was given one pound of potatoes on the four days in the week when not served fresh mutton or beef. When the beef was consumed, the bones were boiled with a variety of vegetables for soup. When salt meat was served it was accompanied by an unlimited allowance of pickles. Soup was made with the capons, onions and pumpkin. Mock apple pies were baked from the pumpkins, lime juice, orange peel and spices.[1]

All the resourcefulness that was going into making the oriental voyage navigably safer and healthier could not alter the fact that arrival there presented its own problems, for which the new age of scientific and philosophical pondering, or the international diplomatic suavity that was now at its apogee in Europe, had no immediate solution. At the end of the voyage lay the barrier of oriental suspicion, with its resistance to western appeal for inroads beyond the stipulated approaches and contemptuous indifference to occidental culture, all of it done with exquisite courtesy. Britain had got its first embassy to China into the capital in 1793 but, after lavish exchange of gifts, it was given twenty-four hours to quit Pekin. The British puzzled whether 'it was an enlarged view of national interest, which it was supposed the propositions of Great Britain would not tend to advance', or something else. They got nowhere. It was early October and the Chinese simply said that the approach of winter meant that the journey from Pekin to Canton could become difficult. An attempt in 1806 by the Tsar of Russia to send a similar embassy bearing lavish gifts to the Chinese emperor was refused admission into Pekin.

The sole emporium of the China trade was at Canton, modern Guangzhou, inland on the Canton River. In Britain's case this remained a trade managed and supervised by the East India Company, though with the British navy always on hand. Merchant ships picked up their Chinese pilot in the Macao Roads and were then conducted in stages of rigid inspection and customs evaluation up to Canton itself, where cargo was discharged and paid for in Mexican dollars. Here there was attitude more familiar to the westerners. The diplomatic reserve of the mandarins was replaced by the hard commercial dealing of the merchants. Foreign trade was hardly the necessity for China that it had become for Britain. There was nothing from the West they wanted. Instead western traders had to bring the Chinese those materials and luxuries their demand for which centuries of Indian Ocean commerce had developed: tin, cotton, sandalwood, pepper, rattans, birds' nests, shark fins, ivory, rhinoceros horns, pearls and precious stones.

In that first decade of the century the Great War also saw the first serious confrontation between Britain and the Manchu dynasty, a brief affair that demonstrated the vulnerability of the trade, the acute sensitivity of the mandarins while also suggesting western strong-arm to come.

Fears of assault on their China trade by marauding French frigates prompted the British to land troops at Macao in October 1808. China immediately stopped all trade and intercourse with Britain until the troops were removed. When the Chinese rejected all attempts to negotiate on the matter the British sent two frigates and a 74 up the river as far as the second bar. The squadron commander, Admiral Drury, then sent all the boats from his ships, packed with armed men, to lie off Canton for two days. Drury was courteously received by the principal mandarins but refused access to the Viceroy. When Drury withdrew his boats, in face of continued Chinese refusal to discuss the issue, the Chinese assembled troops around Canton and moored war sampans filled with troops across the river three miles below Canton. On 28 November 1808 Drury took a force of boats against that barricade but was fired on. He then made a lone attempt in his barge, standing on the stern sheets and with a Portuguese padre as interpreter. The Chinese threatened to fire whenever the Portuguese tried to speak. Drury then took his squadron away altogether. This was the deepest that the Great War reached into the Orient.[2]

On 16 December the British withdrew their troops from Macao. On the 22nd the Chinese allowed commercial relations to resume. An audacious demonstration of British naval power had failed. It failed to break or jar Mandarin resolution. The future nevertheless had spoken. Thirty years ahead lay the so-called Opium War that for Britain would bring 'Extraterritoriality', the term that would eventually attach to all western lodgment on Chinese territory, in Britain's case to mean colonial possession of Hong Kong opposite Macao.

*   *   *

While it could be expected that any of the seagoing flags of the Western world might be found lying at Canton in season, no contact with the Occident existed at any Japanese port, except Nagasaki, where the Dutch had long been allowed a trading post.

Japan was so tightly locked by its shoguns against intrusion from the oceans that, accepting the impossibility of success, none except the Russians seriously sought to gain entry. The Dutch, holding such an exclusive possession, zealously worked on the Japanese against all likely competitors who sought the same privilege. As further protection of that, they offered the rest of the world little intelligence or observation on Japan or the Japanese, who remained an unknown people, a tantalizing and frustrating mystery to the explorative minds of the new age in the West.

The Russians, with their defensive interest and ambitions in the Sea of Okhotsk, the Kurile Islands and the northern Pacific, persistently sought access to the Japanese hierarchy to establish relations, and to obtain use of Nagasaki. Catherine the Great had made an attempt in 1793. In 1803 Tsar Alexander sent his chamberlain, Resanoff, who was told that no Russian ship would be permitted to approach the coasts of Japan. In the event that a Russian ship was driven upon the coasts of Japan by storm the Russian crew would be repatriated in Dutch not Russian ships. Correspondence found by the British aboard a captured Dutch ship described how the Dutch interpreters used during the Resanoff visit had been principally responsible for turning the Japanese wholly against the Russians.

As with so much else, hydrography produced one of the most striking portraits of the Japanese of that time. It came from the Russian navigator Captain Golovnin, who was captured on shore by the Japanese in 1811 after he had landed from his sloop of war, *Diana*, which had the special imperial assignment of surveying and charting the Sea of Okhotsk and the Kurile Islands.[3] He remained a Japanese prisoner until 1813. He had excused his presence on the coast of one of the Japanese Kurile Islands by pleading that he was in search of wood and water. 'The real motive of our visit could, however, on no account be disclosed. It would have been impossible to have made such a people as the Japanese comprehend how a state completely foreign to them, could be induced, by mere curiosity, and without having some secret design in view, to fit out ships to explore distant countries.' What was nevertheless remarkable about the continuous interrogation to which he was submitted was the curiosity of his captors themselves. Golovnin was exasperated by the apparent fatuousness of the questions.

Time after time he and his officers and sailors were brought before the Bunyo, viceroy, of the island of Matsumai, in his reception hall, whose screens were 'all gilded and adorned with Japanese paintings of landscapes, quadrupeds and birds'. Seated cross-legged on finely worked tapestry, the Bunyo wished to know how the Russians buried their dead, what sort of monuments they erected over their graves, whether any difference was made between rich and poor.

In this manner it continued during the first months of their captivity, every day or every other day, usually the greater part of the day.

If he put one interrogatory concerning any circumstance, he asked fifty, which were unimportant, and many which were ludicrous . . . We once stated plainly that we had rather they would put an end to our existence at once, than torture us in the way they did. When I was taken, I had ten or twelve keys of my bureau and drawers. The Bunyo wished to be informed of the contents of every drawer and every box. When I pointed to my shirt, and told him that my drawers contained such things as these, he asked how many I had? I told him, with some degree of ill-humour, that I did not know, and that it was my servant's business to keep that reckoning. Upon this he immediately inquired how many servants I had, and what were their names and ages? I lost all patience and asked the Japanese why they teazed us with such questions and what use such information could be to them, since neither my servants nor property were near me? The governor then, with great mildness, observed that he hoped we were not offended by his curiosity; that he did not intend to force any answers from us, but merely questioned us like a friend.

The examinations continued exhaustively. What kind of dress did the Emperor of Russia wear? What did he wear on his head? What kind of birds were found in the neighbourhood of St Petersburg? What would be the price in Russia of the clothes they were wearing? How many cannon were placed round the imperial palace? What wool was made use of in Europe for cloth? What quadrupeds, birds and fish were eaten in Russia? In what manner did the Russians eat their food? What dress did ladies wear? What kind of horse did the emperor ride? Who accompanied him when he went abroad? Were the Russians partial to the Dutch? How many windows did the imperial palace contain? How many times did the Russians go to church in one day? Did the Russians wear silk clothes? Where did the sailors live in St Petersburg? Told that they lived in barracks, the Bunyo asked the length, breadth and height of the barracks, the number of gates, windows and doors they contained, in what part of the building the sailors lived. Where did they themselves live? How large were their houses, how many servants did they keep? Everything was taken down.

Expressing his exasperation, Golovnin said, 'I frequently thought that the Japanese took pleasure thus to torment us; for to reply to all their questions which their insatiable curiosity induced them to put to us, was a real martyrdom. We sometimes absolutely refused to answer them, and told them that they might if they pleased put us to death. The Bunyo would then endeavour to reconcile us by expressions of regard, but he would soon resume his childishness.'

When a party of officers was formed to take the news of their presence and all the information extracted from them to the Emperor of Japan they were all measured for 'the inhabitants of the capital to be enabled to form a notion of the tall stature of the Russians'. Their portraits were then sketched. All their books were to go to the emperor, leading to the question, how was it that foreign books in Golovnin's chest were handsomely bound and printed on fine paper, whereas the Russian ones were printed on coarse paper? 'I replied that the Russians, as well as other nations, occasionally printed their books either on fine or coarse paper.' Every other article that had been taken from them was labelled with details of purpose, manufacture and cost.

Curiosity there obviously was, but not yet enough to set the doors ajar for the rest of the world. It would be another half century before the pressure for that began to tell.

LIV

CRISIS

AFTER Walcheren and its companion setback, Wagram, a future of deepening uncertainty and apprehension lay upon Britain and the Continent through the two years that followed. Success on the Indian Ocean was insufficient solace.

The concerns on all sides were over a darkening economic future and the dynamically persistent Napoleonic ambitions inseparable from that. Those together formed a depressive outlook that intensified after 1809, on through 1810 and 1811.

Europe was now in tighter subjection. Austria had seen Napoleon's preoccupation with the Iberian Peninsula as opportunity for renewed war to attempt its own and Continental release from Napoleonic grip. Instead war had produced Wagram and cost the Hapsburgs loss of more of their empire as well as demand from Napoleon for heavy indemnity.

Britain was back, trying again, on the Iberian Peninsula before the Walcheren expedition sailed. Sir Arthur Wellesley had landed at Lisbon on 22 April 1809 with forty thousand men to reinforce the ten thousand left behind by Sir John Moore to defend it. On 12 May Wellesley defeated General Soult at Oporto, which Soult had seized after Moore's departure. Wellesley then advanced into Spain, hoping to take Madrid. He engaged the French on 28 July at Talavera, a two-day affair that was close, allowing Wellesley the nominal claim of a victory, which helped cover the immediate and necessary retreat back into Portugal. Wellesley was raised to the peerage as Viscount Wellington. The scepticism that some attached to that was reflected in the *Naval Chronicle*: 'Lord Wellington, in addition to his *double* peerage, and the thanks of Parliament, is to have an annuity of £2000 for himself and his two next heirs, for the *victory* of Talavera!!'

Peace with Austria allowed Napoleon huge reinforcement in the Peninsula. Soult overran Andalusia and laid siege to Cadiz. Suchet moved into Valencia and Catalonia. But the main struggle for the Iberian Peninsula began in the summer of 1810 when Masséna, with a force of 130,000, advanced into Portugal to recapture Lisbon. Wellington, however, put a check on Masséna at Busaco and then withdrew towards Lisbon, to make his stand at Torres Vedras, twenty-five miles north of the capital.

At Torres Vedras Wellington retired behind two powerful lines packed with six hundred cannon. A fleet and transports lay at Lisbon ready to carry away his army if necessary. But he did not fear that. For, as he expected, when they arrived before Torres Vedras, Masséna's troops were already sick and starving. Wellington's soldiers, on the other hand, were fully nourished, principally on American corn, which could move to Spain and Portugal after Jefferson eased the restriction of American merchantmen trading overseas. In 1811, 802 American vessels entered the Tagus to 860 British, and only seventy-five others. As a result, flour at this time was cheaper in Lisbon than at Liverpool. In Britain, and France as well, failure of the harvest had raised bread prices and provoked riots. Torres Vedras at this point provided perhaps the supreme lesson on the power of command at sea: the supply it ensured for the one who had it, the weakness of the one who lacked it. Nothing made that point more illuminatingly.

In spite of any satisfaction that could come from that, the Great War had nevertheless reached what was arguably its most critical point. There was strong conviction among many in Britain that the sooner Wellington and his army were aboard the fleet and transports lying at Lisbon and on their way home the better, for the British were being compelled to ask whether they could afford this war in Iberia. And, as the campaign for long periods assumed a static quality, the question became more pressing.

Britain was in dire, and rising, economic crisis. It was the price on the one hand of her wilful actions with American shipping, merchant and naval, that in retaliation had brought Jefferson's Non-Intercourse Act. Further to that, Napoleon's Continental System, the destruction of her commerce, had begun to work: by 1811 British exports to Europe and the United States had dropped drastically. It was the American drop that had the greatest impact. Annual British exports to the United States had stood at fifteen million pounds, worth more than all Britain's other markets together. In 1811 that had dropped 25 per cent below the level of 1810. What went to America had to go in through Canada or offshore smuggling.

Total British exports, which had stood at sixty one million pounds in 1810, fell to thirty-nine and a half million in 1811. The pound depreciated in value to even lower than the French franc on the Continent, even though France itself was in severe economic straits.

The year 1811 was the one that threatened to break Britain. The situation had become a scarcely credible reversion of the extraordinary prosperity that had been steadily accumulative through the war. Both bread and meat reached prices the poor could not afford. As exports fell and factories closed, disorder had to be suppressed by the military, and by the scaffold. Bankruptcies multiplied. Together with a weak, unsteady government and George III's mental instability that had brought in the Regency of a dissolute Prince of Wales, Britain appeared to be on a slope into the unpredictable. With the country in apparently such a dire state, how could she continue to pay for an apparently static campaign on the Iberian Peninsula? The Iberian War had now reached the cost of just over five million a year. The French on the Peninsula paid for nothing. They simply took it all from the land they were on. Britain had to pay for everything, in gold.

France and the rest of the Continent were, however, in extremity as well, their own trade and economy severely shaken by the economic dislocation that Napoleon's Continental System had also laid upon them. Rampant smuggling helped break the system. They were all going down together. Some relief nevertheless began to emerge as Napoleon became absorbed in another grand strategy, a drive into Russia. By the end of 1811 something of the old activity and contact between Britain and the Continent began to revive, though the American crisis remained.

With the war in Portugal there was still not any real sense of comparable relief. Wellington had failed to attack Masséna's weakened army as it lay through the winter at Santarem, some twenty-five miles from Torres Vedras. When Masséna's lack of supplies forced him to leave Santarem in March, Wellington advanced behind him across Portugal to the Spanish frontier. Many in the British government still saw this as a seemingly limitless campaign, unproductive of decisive outcome, waged far inland in a difficult country at an insupportable cost. Wellington nevertheless retained their support as, through 1811, the war on the Peninsula became focused on the three great fortresses that controlled the main routes between Spain and Lisbon – Ciudad Rodrigo in Leon, Almeida, on the Portuguese side close by, and Badajoz in Estremadura.

When the French moved out of Portugal at the end of 1811 Wellington was himself still unable to enter Spain, held up by the two fortresses on the Spanish side of the frontier, Ciudad Rodrigo and Badajoz. Upon those points the future of his own campaign rested as the Atlantic world entered the fateful year of 1812.

LV

BREAKDOWN

ON the western seas, meanwhile, the human wear and tear of this protracted war increasingly manifested itself shipboard through episodes that offer their own disturbing insight into the price of that endurance.

The breakdown could occur on any of the carefully structured levels of shipboard society, with all regard for the consequences gone, suddenly flung away. Whether it occurred on the quarterdeck or on the messdecks it was release of a fury interminably suppressed. It could be like repossession of a lost self, a pride of defiance. It could be the explosion of a temper too long restrained from flinging out its damnation of the world it viewed. It could be from something seemingly inconsequential that abruptly was more than enough on top of that which was brooding within the person. Whatever the spark that released it, the consequences of any such impulse were bound to be tragic.

A few instances, therefore, of some of those who broke, with, first of all, the case that involved both the upper deck and the lower.

The general tenor of Richard Stewart Gamage's conduct as first lieutenant of the sloop *Griffon* was, it was said, so mild, so forbearing to those under his command, that he secured the affection of the meanest individual. And 'as a messmate, and as a gentleman, he was gentle, friendly and sincere, abounding in social virtues'.

When he joined *Griffon* in June 1812 Gamage was twenty-seven. In 1804 he had got public mention for jumping from his ship at night to save a marine who had fallen overboard.

On the morning of 20 October 1812 *Griffon* was lying in the Downs. When the midday dinner was piped and the officers met in the gun room Gamage took his seat 'with his accustomed smile of good humour and complacency'. He left the table for the change of watch at one o'clock. At one thirty the officers below heard sudden tumult and a cry from above.

One of the officers came rapidly down the companion ladder and said, 'Gamage has stabbed Sergeant Lake!'

Rushing up they found the marine sergeant lying near the mainmast surrounded by a crowd of sailors. He died as they watched. Gamage stood by, stunned speechless by his action. 'When he recovered himself sufficiently to speak, he called the ship's company together, expressed his deep contrition at the rash act he had committed, and surrendered himself to justice, by giving command to the second lieutenant.'

When he had come on watch Gamage had received a complaint from the ship's carpenter, who said that the marine sergeant, Lake, had threatened 'in the most riotous and disorderly manner' to beat him up. Gamage then sent for the sergeant and ordered him to walk the quarterdeck with shouldered musket, a mild summary punishment. As Gamage himself put it, 'I, with a lenity natural to me, ordered him a slight punishment, too trifling in its nature, merely to walk the quarterdeck with a musket in his hand, and to which I was induced, by a prepossession in his favour, and a wish to preserve him from condign punishment, which must have been the consequence, if the regular steps had been taken.'

For many, and certainly for anyone from the old navy, such a view of the matter must have seemed bewilderingly inexplicable. Since the carpenter was senior to the sergeant the latter by naval regulation could have been sentenced to a flogging and certainly lost his rank for his actions. Men suffered dire severity for much less.

Instead of gratitude, what followed between Sergeant Lake and Gamage was even more astonishing. As Gamage himself explained it, 'with insufferable contempt, expressed by the carriage and countenance and eye, than by language, he refused to submit. I again and again commanded further compliance, the same provocation was renewed.' Gamage then ran below and brought up his sword. When he returned to the deck with it he found that Lake was at least holding the musket in his hand. Gamage then struck the musket several times with sword, ordering Lake to start walking the quarterdeck as previously ordered.

Lake shouldered his musket and Gamage returned the sword to its scabbard. The stand appeared to be over. But only for a minute. Gamage was turning away when the sergeant 'threw the musket down, and, with a loud oath, asserted his determination to persist in his disobedience'.

All of this, it should be remembered, was passing before the whole of the ship's company then on deck. They were watching something the like of which had never before occurred in that navy, could not even have been imagined. The consequences for Lake, unless Gamage somehow allowed him to get away with it, would have been a hanging for mutiny. No one could have had any doubt of that. Instead, as Gamage explained, 'in the very same moment, my soul still glowing with indignation at his outrageous audacity of air and aspect, he again refused compliance, and dared me to the fatal act. The imposing attitude of the man, the fierce arrangement of his features, his high ingratitude and disdain working on my imagination, already infuriated by irritated exasperation, that like a flash of lightning across my brain, reason forsook its seat, raging madness usurped the sway, and my sword was passed into his body.'

The court martial was assembled on 27 October still on board *Griffon*. Gamage made a long and eloquent self-defence. 'No pencil can portray the anguish which preys upon my mind at this moment, yet I feel some consolation in thinking that this man was formerly the object of my lenity – when, from motives of compassion, and the just sense I entertained of his professional abilities, I had shielded him from punishment, though implicated in the serious charge of mutiny. I know myself incapable of committing an ill action, and am horror struck at the magnitude of this.'

The verdict was announced that same evening. 'Amidst a profound silence, and in a low and tremulous tone of voice, the judge-advocate pronounced the awful sentence of – Death. Lieutenant G. heard no more; he fell into the arms of a friend, and was carried from the court in a state of insensibility, whilst the ejaculations of "God bless him", resounded from every mouth.' Gamage's execution was set for 23 November.

The night before it Gamage sent for several of the ship's company 'and in pathetic terms expressed his gratitude for the affection they had shewn towards him, and bade them a final adieu. The poor fellows, melted by his appearance and manner, shed abundance of tears, and spreading the affecting tale amongst their messmates, the whole ship presented but one scene of commiseration and distress.'

Naval executions were performed with a dreadful, measured solemnity, never more so than this. All ships at the Downs were ordered to send two boats with witnesses to lie alongside *Griffon*. An order from the commander in chief at the Downs further declared that those who remained on board the ships had to be on deck to watch from there, and 'that the attention of the officers and ships companies may not be diverted from the melancholy scene, nor the salutary reflections to which it may give occasion be interrupted, no work is to be begun till after body has been lowered down'.

Gamage rose at six and dressed in black instead of in uniform.

At a quarter after nine, he was joined in fervent prayer by the officers of the ship, who assembled for that purpose in the gun room; he then partook of some warm wine, and again retired to his cabin; at a quarter before ten, he heard the dreadful annunciation of 'Readiness', without the alteration of a single feature, he replied, 'I am prepared, my Saviour is with me'. He then ascended the companion ladder, and proceeded along the deck with a slow but steady step, to the foot of the platform; he there leaned, for a short time, on the shoulder of a friend, he requested permission to look around him and take his farewell of the sun, which now shone with much brilliancy; his face was covered, he gave his last adieu; the appointed signal was given, and the ill-fated Gamage was hurried into eternity amidst the sorrowful tears of every man on board the Griffon, and the surrounding spectators.

Gamage had asked to be buried alongside the man he killed, Sergeant Lake. This was done in the burial ground of the Navy Hospital at Portsmouth. Captain Trollope and the officers as well as some of the crew of the *Griffon* attended the funeral.

It was altogether a strange, moving tragedy, and might seem puzzling in its implications. That Gamage was different from most in the mildness and softness of his nature was repeatedly referred to. The ship's company had benefited from that since Gamage was so clearly averse to punishment. They demonstrated their concern and pity for him throughout his subsequent ordeal. There appeared to be real affection for him. Sergeant Lake was obviously a powerfully assertive, reckless character. He regarded Gamage's softness differently, and was explicit about it. He somehow understood that he could go as far as he did when he did. He appeared to believe that he could get away with it. Perhaps all along he had read something in Gamage that allowed him that assumption. That might have been a detectable personal interest in him conveyed from Gamage, even if innocently. To such a man as Lake evidently was, such a thing could never be hidden. There was too much to be gained from it. But contempt for what he read as weakness could enrage if, instead of submission, it stood up to him. Gamage's own words on his feelings towards Lake, 'a prepossession in his favour, a wish to preserve him from condign punishment', were certainly unusual. So was his wish to be buried alongside the man. But the way he felt towards Lake was probably the way he would have felt towards anyone else on that ship. There is nothing that allows one to make anything of it other than as another of the desperately sad stories of the Great War, and that from everything available on the case Gamage simply appears to have been victim of his own gentle innocence.

A strikingly similar situation had occurred just a few months before the *Griffon* episode. This was how it was reported in the *Naval Chronicle*:

On the 3rd of June, Andrew Abchurch, ordinary seaman on board H.M.S. Union, then on her passage from Plymouth to the Mediterranean, sent word to Captain Linzee, through the first lieutenant, that he wished to speak to him. Captain L. went up on the quarterdeck with Lieutenant James, to hear what he had to say, when Abchurch, in a low tone of voice, said 'there was a mutiny in the ship'. On Captain L., asking Lieutenant James what the man said, Abchurch replied, 'There is a mutiny in the ship – take that – I am the man!', and at the same instant plunged a knife into Captain Linzee's breast. The blow was evidently aimed at the heart; but either from Captain L's suddenly turning, or from the confusion of the assassin, the knife penetrated obliquely between the sixth and seventh ribs three inches deep, struck the breast bone, and then turned to the right side instead of the left. The man was instantly secured; and on the arrival of the ship at Lisbon (into which port, for the preservation of Captain Linzee's life, it was necessary to go), was tried by a court martial, and executed. He was repeatedly urged, in the most solemn manner, by the chaplain of the Union, to declare what his motives were for attempting so atrocious a deed, and he unequivocally declared that he never had received any sort of treatment from Captain Linzee which could justify it; but that a sudden thought came into his mind that he must commit murder, and he then determined to do so on the captain, to which he thought he must have been instigated by the devil. He exculpated his shipmates, not one of whom, he said, had the slightest knowledge of his intention; that he alone contrived and perpetrated the act; he entreated Captain Linzee would forgive him, then he should die in peace.

Also in an edition of the *Naval Chronicle*, headlined 'Blasphemy and Disloyalty':

A court-martial, of which Rear-admiral Sr Isaac Coffin was president, was held at Portsmouth, for the trial of the surgeon of H.M.S. Jamaica, for disorderly behaviour, by provoking and insulting speeches and gestures, to the officers, etc., in breach of the articles of war. Among the witnesses called for the defendant, was the purser of the ship – but his evidence was objected to, on the ground, that he had been heard to blaspheme our Saviour Jesus Christ; to vilify the character of the Virgin Mary, to ridicule the Bible and say it ought to be burnt by the common hangman, with other grossly aesthetical expressions, which decorum forbids us to repeat: it will not be wondered at, that the same person should – the king, call him an old fool, etc. – the court resolved, that after proof adduced of the infidelity and disloyalty of the purser, his evidence could not be received; and that the president be requested to represent his behaviour to the Lords Commissioners of the Admiralty. The president accordingly wrote to their lordships; and the purser was dismissed H.M.'s service.

The Tale of Seaman Jefferey, as recounted through a sequence of issues of the *Naval Chronicle*:

Robert Jefferey, a twenty-one year old blacksmith from Polpero, Cornwall, had shipped himself aboard a privateer schooner in the summer of 1807, only to find himself impressed when his ship stopped at Falmouth. He was put aboard the 18-gun brig *Recruit*, commanded by Captain Warwick Lake, and was appointed to serve as armourer's mate. Jefferey was described as about five feet four inches in height, 'with a light complexion and rather slender made.'

Recruit cruised in the West Indies for three months until she ran low on water. Allowances were cut. Jefferey, already regarded as a *skulker* by Lake, went to the beer cask and drew off two quarts into a bucket. He drank most of it and left the remainder in the bucket. One of the crew saw him and reported him to Lake, who put Jefferey on the black list. He said that he would not keep such a man in the ship. Three days later, December 13, Recruit came in sight of a desert island, Sombrero. Lake ordered his second lieutenant, Richard Mould, to put Jefferey ashore on the island. Mould remonstrated, pleading for another mode of punishment. Lake told him to carry out the order.

Captain Lake told Jefferey to go ashore as he was and refused to allow him to take his clothes or anything else. In the boat rowing to shore Jefferey begged the crew to drown him. They refused, saying they had to obey the captain's orders. When the boat got to shore Jefferey clung to it but the men forced him onto a rock. The only food they had to give him was a few biscuits and a piece of beef.

Jefferey was barefoot and cut his feet as he struggled on the rock. One of the men in the boat gave him a pair of shoes and a knife. Mould gave him some money, which Jefferey refused, saying it was of no use there. He lieutenant then gave him the boat hook and three handkerchiefs, to hoist as signals. They then left him.

Sombrero was an absolute wasteland, without water, covered in rough grass weed. There was no house or inhabitant on it. No water.

News of Jefferey's abandonment reached the commander of the station, Admiral Cochrane, he ordered Lake to return to Sombrero to take off the man. They found no one.

When *Recruit* returned to England Lake said to Lieutenant Mould, 'I hope when I have another ship, we shall sail together.'

Mould replied, 'No, never. Recollect Jefferey.'

Lake was never to have another ship. He was court-martialled and dismissed from the navy.

Some time afterwards American newspapers reported that Jefferey had been taken off the island by an American ship and landed in America. The episode had now won public attention. Jefferey's family, backed by a group of philanthrophists, as evangelicals were commonly described, set out to trace him. Jefferey was found to be working as a blacksmith at Marblehead, Massachusetts, earning twenty-three dollars a month. He had seen many vessels pass and attempted to hail them without success. Then, nine days after being abandoned, the schooner *Betsey* of Marblehead had spotted his signals and taken him off. Jefferey had survived by eating limpets scratched off the rocks and drinking either salt water or fresh found in the crevices of the rocks after a rainfall.

Jefferey was brought back to England, given a free discharge from the navy, paid his arrears and from Lake's family received a 'liberal compensation'. 'He left London immediately, in high spirits, with his money to see his mother. Some people were after him, to make him exhibit himself for money; but he got his discharge from the service upon an understanding, as is supposed, that he should quit the metropolis . . . By the time that they reached the village all the inhabitants were prepared to receive him, and it is hardly possible to express the cordial greeting and exulting transport that attended his arrival. The meeting between Jefferey and his mother was particularly affecting. Jefferey repeatedly declared that the kind attention and generosity of the Lake family would never be effaced from his memory – that he entirely forgave Captain Lake himself, and could take him by the hand with sincere goodwill if he were on the spot.'

MELANCHOLY ANECDOTE ON BOARD THE BUFFALO MAN OF WAR ON PASSAGE FROM NEW SOUTH WALES TO ENGLAND.

It was Christmas Eve, and we were sitting round a good fire, anticipating the pleasure of the ensuing day, for which great preparations had been making for several days, when we heard a great noise on the main-deck, which we soon learnt was occasioned by Mr L. one of the midshipmen, who was excessively intoxicated. Stripped to his trowsers, his face flushed with liquor, his countenance dark and malignant, and his mouth foaming with passion, he was uttering the most horrible oaths, and threatening to strike or destroy every person near him. He refused obedience to the orders that were given to confine him to his cabin, which was under the half-deck, till menaced to be punished at the gangway. He then went in, and the door shut upon him, but not fastened. In less than five minutes afterwards he appeared, stark naked, just under the main-chains on the gangway, having got out at the port in his cabin. He was discovered standing on the gangway, by his calling out, 'Make haste, messmates, bear a hand, I am going to drown myself; bear a hand, messmates, tell them I am going to drown myself'. All hands thronged to that side of the ship: he looked up and said, 'Call my messmates, tell them that I am going to drown myself: I wish well to all the Buffalo ship's company', and instantly plunged into the deep, before any means could be used to prevent him. The ship was going at a rate of seven knots, directly before the wind, a considerable sea was on, and night had just set in, it being between nine and ten o'clock, so that he must have been out of reach before a boat could be lowered. To describe the horror and dismay it occasioned throughout the ship is impossible.

Whatever one might seek to make of it all, these anyway were for all insufferably harder times by now in a navy for which there was no rest, from which there was no escape, and where the ceaseless activity of watch and blockade had mainly become unrelieved monotony. Most sailors had now been at sea for years without going ashore, some for ten years or more.

One might well ask how they managed to sustain it, without becoming unsettled, and for how much longer? It is a question that could have applied to both the men who carried the name Lake. There were other frequent examples of breakdown in various forms of those who had got as far as they could go in that harsh and long enduring confinement, but all of a sudden no further.

All of it simply laid heavier emphasis upon the fact that this was a war too long lasted and heavy, and not getting easier.

LVI

SWALLOW

AWAY from the Peninsula and from the intensifying activity on the American coast, and with the inaction of the grand fleets, it could often seem that serious naval engagement had broadly fallen away, or become negligible.

Action there nevertheless was on all the European and Mediterranean stations where high vigilance had to be maintained, minor but brave, often heroically so, encounters that soon faded into obscurity.

Frigates produced the most notable engagements. Once in a while there might be an action between one or two line ships. In the Adriatic in March 1812 a British 74, *Victorious*, took the 84-gun French *Rivoli* in a furious action of four and a half hours within half-pistol shot, with severe loss of life on both sides. The actions more easily passed over were those involving the lowest classifications in the navies, such as the brigs, sloops and schooners. These were frequent because those ships were intensely engaged, in the widest scope of activities: close inshore work of every sort, escort of convoys, pursuit of privateers, support of frigate squadrons – the task list was endlessly varied. Those engagements were often the most violent of the war. Such was the case with the 18-gun brig *Swallow*, on watch off Fréjus on 16 June 1812, when she ran in with a French brig and schooner.

Three accounts of the battle survive. The first was from the *Swallow*'s purser, Ryan, who recorded his experience immediately it was over:

This afternoon we have had a very severe engagement with two enemy's vessels, nearly double our own force; it was preconcerted by them for several days, and they stood pledged to the inhabitants to take us into Frejus that evening, or both go down alongside of us. We engaged, guns nearly touching, and after an action most sangui-nary (in which they four times attempted to board, being full of troops), they made all sail, and took refuge under the batteries of the town. We have been desperately cut up, and I am sorry to add, lost several brave fellows. It is now ten o'clock – the bell tolling, after burying the dead, and I have just left the deck, after performing the last and melancholy rites due to Christians. This task was the more painful, as in reading the funeral service over the dead, it also fell to my lot to perform that office for the clerk, who was killed in act of speaking to me; a person whom I was exceedingly partial to, and one of the finest young men I ever knew. The captain did me the honour to place the marines and boarders under my direction: my hat was twice knocked off by a doubled-headed shot; I was twice knocked down – but, thank God, have all my legs and arms hanging about me; nor did I suffer any injury, but a contusion of little consequence in my side. These are circumstances I would not acquaint you with, but as all my messmates are writing to their friends, I do not see why I should not do the same, particularly as you will see the business in the papers.

Letter from a young seaman named Dennis Graydon, of Cork, dated 20 June.

We have just come from fighting one of the most bloody actions that ever was fought in these seas; but, thanks to the Lord, I have escaped, and I shall always be grateful to him for it. We had a great many killed and wounded, and followed the French, who ran away into the harbour. Mr Ryan, who is the purser, had his hat shot off, and one time fell all covered with blood; when his servant, an old marine, took him in his arms, and was carrying him below, he got to himself on the ladder, and said, 'Where are you taking me?' The servant said, with tears in his eyes, 'Down below'. 'Well then', says he, 'take me back again, for I am only stunned, and this here blood is not mine'. I was near to him when he was knocked down, as he was cheering the men at the after guns, and going to fire one. The French fought very well for some time – they had five times as many men as we, and the slaughter must be dreadful. We have not a mast, nor rope, nor sail in the ship but what is cut to pieces; and we expected we shall have to go to England, where all our officers will be promoted. They wanted to board us four times, but we beat them off every time: one time, when we were engaged with the largest on one side, the other came round our bow – the captain saw her – she was full of men with large blue caps, who were in the rigging, and everywhere to board. The captain desired Mr Waller, one of the officers, to get five guns ready at that side, but while he was doing it, his leg was shot off; then Mr Ryan came to us (myself was at those guns), and, says he, 'My boys, load with double canister, and don't fire a gun until I tell you'. We had then 64lbs of small shot in every gun; they thought we did not see them in the smoke – the men were mad to fire at them, but the purser said, he 'would not fire a gun until he rubbed the muzzles of the guns against her sides'. With that, as they were close alongside, he ordered us to put a bag of musket balls at the mouth of every gun – these bags had 32lbs each, and we had then 96lbs of shot in every gun. After we fired there was not a man to be seen, but we heard the most dreadful cries, and a great many of them fell overboard, and they never came near us after that.'

Letter dated Port Mahon, 1 July.

The Swallow has just anchored here, after a most obstinate and sanguinary engagement: her masts, sails, rigging, are desperately cut up. The action, on the part of the enemy, had been in agitation for several days. The largest of the French vessels was called the Reynard, and the commander of her was formerly commandant of the Prosperine frigate, at Toulon, with 80 chosen men; and he stood pledged to the minister of marine to bring the Swallow into Frejus, or to forfeit his existence: nor did he, at the time, bargain for the auxiliary assistance of a sixteen gun schooner, which he also brought into action with him. The America arrived last night: she boarded a fishing boat, who informed her the brig had every gun dismounted but one, by the shot from the Swallow; her starboard side almost completely stove in, and 150 men killed and wounded in her and the schooner, the greater part of whom fell in the several attempts they made to board the Swallow. The little town of Frejus was a scene of mourning, from the number of people belonging to that place who served as volunteers in the enemy's brig and schooner. There were several troops embarked in the morning preceding the action who all received a promise of being enrolled in the Legion of Honour, after the capture of the Swallow: they were ranged along the gangways, bowsprit and rigging, coming out. The Swallow passed between the brig and the schooner, within 30 yards of the former, and ten of the latter, opening a fire of 64 pounds of canister and 32 pounds of musket balls, from every gun on both sides. The enemy's brig had a long 9 pounder in her bridle-port, one on each side of her forecastle, and nine 32lb carronades on each side; and the schooner eight long 9-pounders on each side. Thus they were more than double the force of the Swallow; had every advantage, as the water was smooth; and were beaten and followed in under their batteries by fair artillery, the Swallow's superiority in tactics being lost, as there was neither wind nor sea. The Swallow's loss has been severe: but from the nature of the action it could not be expected to be otherwise.

MELANCHOLY AND INTERESTING NARRATIVE FROM ONE OF THE OFFICERS OF THE SWALLOW.

There was a seaman named Phelan, who had his wife on board: she was stationed (as is usual when women are on board in time of battle) to assist the surgeon in the care of the wounded. From the close manner in which the Swallow engaged the enemy, yard-arm and yard-arm, the wounded, as may be expected, were brought below very fast: amongst the rest, a messmate of her husband's (consequently her own), who had received a musket ball through the side. Her exertions were used to console the poor fellow, who was in great agonies, and nearly breathing his last: when, by some chance, she heard her husband was wounded on deck: her anxiety and already overpowered feelings could not one moment be restrained; she rushed instantly on deck, and received the wounded tar in her arms; he faintly raised his head to kiss her – she burst into a flood of tears, and told him to take courage, 'all would be well', but scarcely pronounced the last syllable, when an ill-directed shot took her head off. The poor tar, who was closely wrapt in her arms, opened his eyes once more – then shut them forever. What renders the circumstance the more affecting was, the poor creature had only three weeks been delivered of a fine boy, who was thus in a moment deprived of a father and a mother. As soon as the action subsided, 'and nature began to take its course', the feelings of the tars, who wanted no unnecessary incitement to stimulate them, were all interested for poor Tommy (for so he was called); many said, and all feared, he must die; they all agreed he should have a hundred fathers, but what could be the substitute for a nurse and a mother? However, the mind of humanity soon discovered there was a Maltese goat on board, belonging to the officers, which gave an abundance of milk; and as there was no better expedient, she was resorted to, for the purpose of suckling the child, who, singular to say, is thriving and getting one of the finest little fellows in the world; and so tractable is his nurse, that even now she lies down when poor little Tommy is brought to be suckled by her. Phelan and his wife were sewed up in one hammock, and, it is needless to say, buried in one grave.

Lines intended for a stone to be placed over two seamen, late belonging to *Swallow*, interred in the Naval Burying Ground at Port Mahon:

> Courses up and topsails handed,
> Life's main-stay-sail carry'd awa';
> Weather sheet and bowlines stranded,
> Here death piped they last belay.

LVII

TARRAGONA

ALTHOUGH Thomas Cochrane had vanished from the naval stage, the example he had established on the Mediterranean coasts of Spain was being vigorously maintained by a worthy successor, Captain Edward Codrington, aboard his 74, *Blake*.

If the critical importance of naval support and sustenance in a difficult war offered one dramatic aspect of its value at Lisbon and Torres Vedras, it continued to demonstrate another and particular character on the other side of the Peninsula. As Cochrane so brilliantly initiated in 1809, even before Arthur Wellesley had stepped ashore for the first time in Portugal, the British navy had become a mainstay of guerrilla warfare, the new form of combat that had spontaneously arisen among the Spanish peasants.

As the regular Spanish armies collapsed or were broken by the French in the south and in the interior, the Spanish regulars and the guerrillas together maintained intense resistance in Valencia and, most notably, Catalonia. Their main opponent was General Suchet, probably the best of Napoleon's Peninsula commanders. It was practically a separate war from that being fought by Masséna, his successor Marmont, Soult and the other generals. The very landscape and the character of the people in north-eastern Spain were different. For Napoleon it was a vital war, for its obvious Mediterranean importance as well as for the easy connection from Perpignan. For Suchet the promised reward for conquest there was elevation to marshal.

Except for the British navy, the Spanish in these provinces were on · their own. The British armies had never approached Valencia, Catalonia, or even Malaga. The British involvement therefore remained with the navy. Collingwood died aboard his ship in March 1810, worn out by the complex burdens of the Mediterranean command. He was finally on his way home in *Ville de Paris* but his weak state denied him getting there. He was carried home and buried beside Nelson in St Paul's. His command passed to Admiral Sir Charles Cotton, and under him the vital assignment of patrolling the Spanish Mediterranean coast went to Captain Edward Codrington, who was given a squadron for the task. Codrington went out from participation in the Walcheren expedition and for more than two years, from 1810 to 1812, applied himself with a commitment to the Valencian and Catalan guerrillas as zealous as Cochrane's had been, and with that he came to an admiration for the Catalans especially that equalled Cochrane's. For, through that entire period, right to the very end of the war, the Catalans were to make probably the most distinctive stand of any one group or people within the resistance in Spain. And, as Codrington was to witness, they suffered heavily for it.

Along the eastern coast of Spain, off Catalonia especially, the value of command of the sea was demonstrated as cogently as anywhere in the Great War, particularly because it was so vividly continuous. It meant that Napoleon's armies along that coast were tied to inland routes as they sought to gain coastal command. Codrington's ships, his sailors and his marines, continued the harassment by gunfire, blockade, military excursions ashore, ferrying or rescuing forces of the Valencian and Catalan armies and giving broad assistance to the guerrillas (*migueletes*), all of it in the form that Cochrane initiated.

In their original descent the French had taken Barcelona but the city was then tightly blockaded by the British fleet. It was a city dependent upon import of its food, mainly by water. Starvation descended upon it, and it became incapable of sustaining a garrison. What the French urgently required for their Catalan campaign was free movement down the main road from Perpignan through Figueras, Gerona, Barcelona, Tarragona, Tortosa and on to Valencia beyond. Barcelona sat in the middle of it all. The British navy made the coastal road from Rosas impossible for the French, but they were not much better off on the inland road. The French held Figueras, twenty miles from their frontier, 'the bulwark of northern Catalonia', but the Spanish armies still had Gerona, Tarragona, Tortosa and Valencia, the siege of which the French had abandoned.

To have clear possession of that line of communication had become Napoleon's urgent objective for 1810. Gerona surrendered on the last day of 1809. In March 1810 Suchet laid siege to Valencia but withdrew because of the city's powerful defences. Tortosa, the inland Catalan citadel on the Ebro that commanded the road between Catalonia and Valencia, was the next objective, to cut off communication between the two. But it was another year before Tortosa surrendered, on 2 January 1811. Tarragona, Catalonia's greatest fortress, was the next objective in this drawn-out struggle for domination of the province.

Suchet appeared before Tarragona on 3 May 1811 with a force of fifteen thousand. Tarragona was a formidable obstacle. It lay on a sharp slope with the main city at the top and the harbour with the old city below. Both were walled and heavily fortified. It was defended by the Marquis Campo Verde with some ten thousand soldiers. Codrington aboard *Blake* and accompanied by another 74 and two frigates was lying in the harbour. They turned their fire on the large fort for heavy guns that Suchet began building at the mouth of the Francoli River that wound past Tarragona. The British ships maintained heavy fire on it but the work continued to rise until, on 13 May, it received its heavy guns.

Codrington's squadron then began a rush to help save Tarragona, to bring reinforcement, arms and other military supplies from Valencia, Peniscola and Alicante. But the siege had advanced steadily. The lower city and harbour fell on 21 June. 'The exertion and ability of the French in besieging this place has never, I believe, been exceeded,' Codrington wrote to Admiral Cotton on 23 June.

The task now was to hold the upper city. The squadron was set busy making more than three thousand sandbags to help fill the breaches cut into the upper city's walls by French cannonade. Codrington was also sending away those who had fled the lower city. 'The poor wounded, the women and children, who crawl down to such little crevices of the rocks as they think will best admit of their embarkation, and there wait patiently some-times through a whole night for the possibility of our boats taking them off, become the constant object of the enemy's fire.'[1] Having been driven from the harbour, the ships were lying in the roadstead.

The British Army then made a belated effort to send some assistance. General Graham at Cadiz detached a force of 1,147 infantry composed of two crack regiments used against the French at the siege of Cadiz. They arrived on 26 June under Colonel Skerret. Graham had stipulated that communication with the British squadron should always be maintained, with Skerret free to withdraw the troops if surrender looked imminent. And to Codrington he said, 'Do not put them in a situation to be taken or to capitulate.'[2]

On arrival the surf was too high for a landing. A sailor swam ashore with a letter for the Tarragona governor, General Contreras, detailing the conditions under which the troops might land, but from their immediate observation Codrington and Skerret believed that it was already too late. They agreed that they might have saved the garrison had the British arrived before the harbour and lower city were taken. As they now saw it, all that they might achieve if they landed the force would be to prolong the fate of Tarragona, but at the certain sacrifice of the British force. In the evening they decided, however, that they themselves should go ashore to verify the situation.

Contreras believed that Tarragona was untenable. Once the walls were

The American frigate *Chesapeake* under attack from HMS *Shannon*, 1 June 1813.
Before (*above*) and after (*below*) impact.

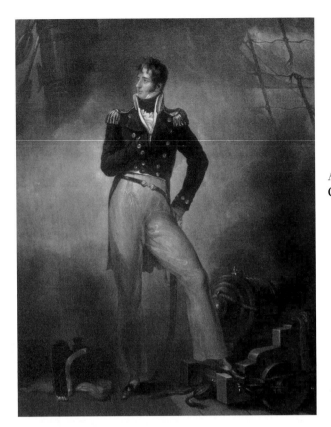

Admiral Sir Alexander
Cochrane, 1807

Admiral Lord Viscount Exmouth

Commodore Stephen Decatur, U.S.N.

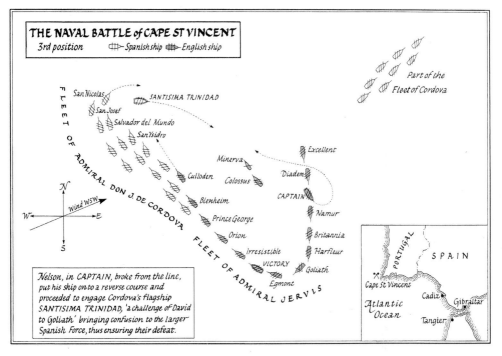

The Naval Battle of Cape St Vincent, 14 February 1797

Admiral Lord Nelson

(*Below left*) Admiral Villeneuve, commander of the French fleet at Toulon, captain of the *Bucentaure*, the French flagship at Trafalgar. (*Below right*) Admiral Gravina, Captain of the Spanish flagship *Principe de Asturias*

British sailors boarding the Spanish man-of-war *Hermione*, 25 October 1799

The capture of four French gun vessels by a boat party commanded by Lieutenant Blyth,
2 August 1811

Sackett's Harbour on Lake Ontario

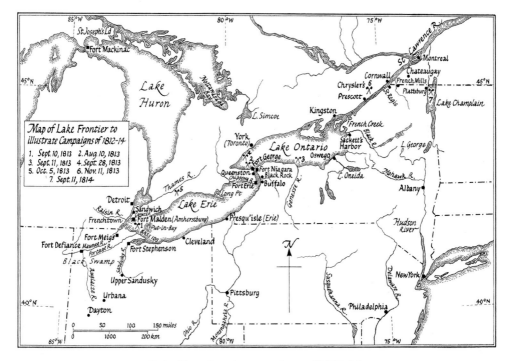

Lake Frontier, the campaigns of 1812–14

The Sailor's Return

Manning the Navy: the Press-Gang on Tower Hill

breached by Suchet's cannon he intended to abandon the place to pass to the forces of the Marquis Campo Verde outside and hoped the British would join him. Codrington and Skerret narrowly escaped with their lives on their return. The French, suspecting that the troops might land in the dark, poured gunfire on their boat, with one shell landing under it. For Codrington that alone affirmed the dangers of a landing. But Skerret went ashore again the next day to confer with Campo Verde at his inland post. Skerret returned on the 28th unimpressed by what he saw there. By then Tarragona's upper city was in flames. The French breaching batteries had opened their assault on the town at dawn that day. A breach in the walls was made at five thirty in the afternoon and three columns rushed in through it. Skerret and Codrington affirmed the decision they had already made: Graham's troops would not land.

This one effort of the British Army to make a contribution to the war in Catalonia thus came to nought. In his exhaustive seven-volume study of the Peninsular War published in 1902, Charles Oman declared that the departure of the British after thirty-six hours in the roadstead without landing a man was an active cause of the demoralization of the Spanish defenders, for it 'appeared to prove to the garrison of Tarragona that their own condition was hopeless'. It would have been far better, Oman believed, had the expedition never appeared.[3]

The fall of Tarragona became another of the horror stories of the Great War. More than half the four thousand slain in the town by the inrush of the French were civilians, including hundreds of women and children. Hundreds of soldiers and civilians tried to make it to the British fleet. All the boats of the squadron and the transports were sent to assist those who had stripped and were swimming to the ships or hiding under rocks to escape the French musketry that swept across all.

In the days that followed, as more and more fugitives were picked up from the shore, Codrington found his decks crowded with women and children, accommodated under an awning spread for them. 'What I am to do with them Heaven knows!' They were allowed the freedom of the ship.

I never refuse the people the gratification of seeing my cabin as well as the rest of the ship; and at this minute I am sitting, with a large crowd standing betwixt me and the stern windows, staring and making their observations upon me and my bald pate, as well as the rest of the furniture. The band is playing a Spanish country dance at the same time . . . At present my people have scarcely a shilling amongst them, and are moreover almost naked themselves from having handsomely clothed those who were not quite so. As most of those whom we picked up when swimming on the night of the fall of Tarragona were without a rag to cover them, my ship's company came aft to ask my leave to give them some of their clothes; to which I consented, although it is contrary to order for any man to dispose of the clothes which he has been allowed to take up from the ship upon charge against their pay. And I also ordered the squadron to clothe the naked generally, as well as feed the hungry, for which the Navy Board may perhaps stop my pay.

The Admiralty did in fact give him an indemnity for the gesture.[4]

The price of Tarragona was high to the French and Spanish both. Casualties among the soldiers on both sides during the siege were severe. The French lost some six thousand, but the Army of Catalonia lost between fourteen and fifteen thousand, nearly two-thirds of the regular troops of that force. Tarragona had been the base of Spanish resistance in Catalonia. The one fortified harbour was gone. As Codrington concluded, 'A partisan warfare is all which can now be supported.'[5] But, as Suchet turned away from Catalonia to launch his deferred blow against Valencia, the Catalan army had a new captain-general, General Luis Lacy, who began to rebuild the force of regulars and with it gradually began a new, semi-guerrilla offensive against the French garrisons and lines of communication.

Upon Codrington and his squadron now fell the task of assisting Lacy, and of harassing the French at every point along that coast. They continued for close to another year and a half. It was wearisome work, passing from point to point reports of French movement or occupation, moving reinforcements and supplies, landing guns and sorties, bombarding Tarragona and Barcelona to disturb and preoccupy the forces there. All the while, they were also assisting the build-up in Valencia. The latter never meant the same to Codrington as his work on the Catalan coast. The intimacy he had created with the Catalans led him to observe as he sailed back from activity off Valencia, 'I am now on my way from Valencia to Peniscola, and thence to what we now familiarly term *our own coast* again.'

Codrington, like Cochrane, had developed great respect and affection for the Catalans. 'The spirit of the Catalans rises with the increase of their difficulties; and the French will yet bury many men in this principality.' His depiction of them, again, as with Cochrane, often reads as many such would read in 1936: 'In Cataluna the people have ever a notion of rights unknown in the other provinces, although, poor souls, they are very backward in the knowledge of real freedom; but it is this temper and disposition, which has made them the objects of jealousy to the kings and courtiers of Spain, that has made them so exemplary in their present resistance.'[6]

Through all of it he was to meet the numerous principal soldiers and characters involved. 'There appear to me to be, speaking generally, but two classes of people in the Peninsula: the high being the worst, and the low the best I have ever met with.'[7] Among the many portraits he offered was a memorable one of someone who was of the higher class but certainly of the best. Writing from Arens, just north of Barcelona:

I had an interview during my stay on shore this morning, with the heroine of Tortosa, Dona Candia, whose history, if well given, would show England of what some Spanish women are capable. When her masculine voice, which still rings in my ears, uttered the fervent ejaculation that 'she wished she were a man leading a body of troops against the enemy', the ardour of her expression made me accuse nature of having committed a most unaccountable error. Her mind, her movements, her language, and her stature, are all masculine . . . and she seemed to me a woman only in her goodness of heart, in the benevolence of her disposition . . . To Lacy she says, 'Well, general, so we must become French after all, eh?' 'No, no, never.' 'Oh, but I see they are gaining ground every day, and you have not the power to interrupt them!' Lacy must have discernment enough to understand this sarcasm . . . To Milaus, who is brave enough though boasting, and, though debauched and profligate, endowed with the genuine Catalan hatred of the French, she says, 'You complain of the weakness of your division, when it is your own neglect which makes your soldiers desert you. Instead of seeing that your troops are properly clothed and properly fed, you are following your own selfish propensities'. But she likes Milaus because he fights and hates the French; and this is the general feeling of the people. She lost her whole property at Tortosa, her native place . . . Suchet took great pains to gain her over to him, and placed an officer and four men to guard her in her own house. Whenever this officer tried to persuade her that Suchet would befriend her, and that he was a very great man, she replied in terms of the most decided contempt. At length she made the officer and his four men drunk, and effected her escape . . . The poor soul receives seventeen and a half dollars a month for her services as a commandanta; and out of this she gives the principal part towards the clothing and feeding of the soldiers who happen to be ill provided, unasked for. To one she says, 'You have no alpargatas; here take this and buy yourself a pair directly'. To another, 'You are filthy, take this money and get your clothes washed'. And when she sees a whole corps thus ill provided she goes to the Justicias of the town and claims assistance as their right . . . This poor creature is of a noble family, which one could not find out by her language or appearance; for she certainly swears as loudly as the best of us without the smallest ceremony. She is, as you may well suppose, beloved by all the soldiery, who universally call her 'mother'.[8]

Codrington followed in the example of Nelson and Collingwood. After nearly three years on that station he was able to view his ship, *Blake*, and still find it a harmonious and contented community. At Christmas 1812 he could write to his wife, 'I was amused upon going round the ship to see a whole sheep roasting in the galley, stuffed with potatoes and onions.

It seems the mess to which this belonged had bought it, like many others, for a Christmas dinner ... It is very satisfactory, both to myself and the officers, that the ship's company at this Christmas time should have shown so much mirth and good-humour without drunkenness and quarreling. You would have been much amused to see their dinners and suppers on Christmas day ... There was not a table that had less than double what the mess could eat on it ... and at supper some of the tables were lighted up with ten or a dozen wax candles.'[9]

His next Christmas, in the cypress swamps of New Orleans, would be very different.

LVIII

AMERICA

PRESIDENT Jefferson's effort to lock American ships into their home ports through his embargo upon oceanic trade at the end of 1807 had instead locked his young nation into the crisis that steadily evolved towards a war that became widely predicted, and with some openly sought.

The embargo had been seen as the means of avoiding war. What it released was quite the contrary, a new set of provocations that fast raised the temperature of ill feeling.

The idea that closing and sealing all doors to the outside world might somehow obtain distance from its intrusion had simply enlarged the crisis and, as always with the ill-considered, had added new problems. Jefferson himself appeared closed to the consequences, to all the likely implications, of a merchant marine that was second only to that of Great Britain being told to furl its sails and go permanently to moorings.

American outrage over British actions against its ships and citizens on the high seas had built steadily after the seizure of the merchantman *Essex* in 1805 and the incident of the *Leander* off Sandy Hook. The *Chesapeake* episode had inflamed those beyond measure, to become the running sore, the unhealed wound, that continued to poison relations, especially since any reparation appeared to be permanently deferred. But far from quelling any of that bitterness, Jefferson's embargo became a savage inversion of it all.

What followed with this Jeffersonian destruction of the American global commerce that had been the pride of the eastern seaboard was the flight of American seamen into the services of the British in preference to beggary at home. It also enriched Halifax, Quebec and Montreal, which became the entrepôts of the commerce lost to Boston and New York. Nothing was therefore achieved by the embargo other than misery and deprivation across the most prosperous and developed regions of the United States, accompanied by lawless flouting of the embargo act along the land and coastal frontiers with Canada. Imports and exports flowed across them, raising costs and prices.

The years 1808–9 would always stand as the harshest in the history of American mercantile seagoing. Ignoring shock and outrage along the eastern seaboard, the administration made strenuous efforts to maintain the prohibitions of the embargo. Coasting ships were compelled to load only under the supervision of Revenue officers. Ships had to get a bond six times the value of their cargo and had to return with a certificate from the point of discharge. Gunboats and revenue cutters maintained watch on the ports and coasts for smuggling. But coasters never intended for venture on the deep sea nevertheless used the coasting licence to make it to the West Indies. Great Lakes schooners in the fur trade found a new function across those waters. Winter saw hundreds of sleighs moving between Montreal and Vermont. Smuggling became a phenomenon rampant across the entire line of the Canadian frontier, to remain unequalled until it found its equivalent with alcohol in Prohibition America.[1]

Town meetings and street protests conveyed the violent feelings of New Englanders. Civil officers who sought to maintain the embargo at ports were threatened with having their houses burned. For the American merchants and sailors their bitterness was enlarged as the Peninsular War opened Spanish and Portuguese ports for trade, themselves left out of it. Jefferson's naivety over it all was revealed in a letter to Secretary of the Treasury Albert Gallatin on 11 August 1808: 'This embargo law is certainly the most embarrassing we ever had to execute. I did not expect a crop of so sudden and rank growth of fraud, and open opposition by force, could have grown up within the United States.'[2] But America had to wait a while yet before he gave that insight practical effect. On 1 March 1809, three days before James Madison became President, Jefferson agreed to a milder measure, the Non-Intercourse Act. Through it American ships were allowed back on to the ocean but banned from trading with Britain or France. That was suddenly a lesser irritant since the Portuguese and Spanish ports were now open to them. Supplying the British forces in the Peninsula merely with flour for their bread began to restore New England fortunes. The China trade too was open again. But the Non-Intercourse Act solved nothing in settling the issues that were the source of all the trouble: impressment and British commercial harassment.

The American quarrel was with France as well. But the French did not impress Americans and, though they had seized American ships in French ports, they had no power on the oceans and were unable to exercise vigilante interference at sea as the British did. The neutral maritime states that once sided with America no longer could, all being now controlled by Napoleon. It was therefore essentially for the British and the Americans to sort themselves out, not without Napoleon playing a duplicitous game on the side, pretending to lift his own decrees on merchant shipping in an effort to hold the Americans on side in his war on British commerce.

For the next three years London and Washington became rancorously entwined in ineffectual diplomatic wrangling on their fundamental disagreement, the same issues over and over again, with delegates passing from one capital to the other to seek resolution. The Americans wanted guarantees on impressment and free movement of their merchantmen. The British insisted that the United States lift its ban on British imports. More simply, what it amounted to was Britain scrapping its Orders-in-Council that ruled its interference with trade, and America laying aside its Non-Intercourse Act. Each remained inflexible until the other gave way, which neither did, in spite of some false starts. In America exasperation hastened talk of war.

With such a national mood gathering strength it might have been supposed that some attention would have been given to the navy, the one force capable of defensive action and retaliation against British maritime harassment off the American coasts. The fierce passions aroused by the *Chesapeake* incident alone should have prompted enlargement and development of a navy that had so finely demonstrated its quick acquisition of spirit and experience with Barbary. Nothing, meanwhile, had been done to add to or proficiently maintain the existing navy. When Jefferson came to the presidency in 1801 the United States Navy had been provided with seasoned timber for six 74-gun ships. None was built. Instead of investing in those 74s Jefferson, with his obdurate sense of closing off the Atlantic at the shoreline instead of defensively reaching outward upon it, had built two hundred gunships. These were merely gun platforms, unable to venture any distance offshore and impractical even for the coastal defence for which they were intended, being unable to function except with the backing of the coastal batteries. The existing navy had only contempt for them.

As the navy wasted away in the eleven years that followed, as the wrangling over trade and impressment continued, more than nine hundred American merchantmen were taken by Britain, more than six thousand Americans impressed. Small squadrons of British frigates operated freely off the American coasts, though after *Chesapeake* they stayed further out than before. Anxious to avoid incurring more American wrath, the squadrons were told to be particularly careful not to give 'just cause of offence to the government or subjects of the United States of America', and to stay out of American ports.

The American coast had as much reason to fear French privateers at this time as the British. Privateering piracy was so uncontrolled in those waters that when two French privateers tied up at Savannah their heterogeneous crews of French, Italians, Venetians, Sicilians and Portuguese rampaged through the town, killing seamen and others who first sought to resist them. But when drums beat the whole town to arms the privateers were boarded and set alight.[3]

The morale of a neglected navy had fallen so far that William Bainbridge, who had gained so much esteem on the Barbary patrol, asked leave to make a commercial voyage to China because of poor finances, saying, 'I have hitherto refused such offers, on the presumption that my country would require my services. That presumption is removed, and even doubts entertained of the permanency of our naval establishment.'[4]

A token effort to restore American naval pride came in 1810 when Commodore John Rodgers was allowed a squadron of frigates and sloops to patrol the coasts northward from off the Capes of the Chesapeake, '. . . to vindicate the injured honor of our navy, and revive the drooping spirit of the nation'. Rodgers issued a personal vow to his captains that plainly bore the angry hurt of *Chesapeake*'s dishonour. A shot by a British ship at an American while the latter's colours were flying would be 'a menace of the grossest order . . . an act of hostility meriting chastisement to the utmost extent of all your force'.[5]

A published profile of Rodgers at the time described a rough character who had started his sea career in the slave trade, in which he rose to being a master, with nicknames such as Bully Rodgers and Black Jack. He had joined the American navy in 1798 but he was later dismissed from the service for striking one of his midshipmen. He was brought back into the navy during the wars with Barbary. 'He has been often known to strip himself to his shirt, and fight with one of his foremast hands; if conquered, he confessed it, and was always the friend of his conqueror; but where the reverse was the case, he always shewed his superiority of strength by tyranny. He is about five ten inches in height, very muscular, has a dark but not unpleasant countenance . . . he is very illiterate, but allowed by every person who knows him to have great judgment in the working of a ship. He is a native of Maryland, born at Havre de Grace, where he has a very handsome seat, highly romantic.'[6]

On 14 May Rodgers, commanding the frigate *President*, 44, was at Annapolis, Maryland, when he got word that a British man of war had seized two Americans from an American coaster passing between two coastal ports. Rodgers sailed at once, with everything prepared for an action. On the 16th, fifty miles east of Cape Charles, the 18-gun British sloop of war *Little Belt* was sighted and given chase. The next morning, when they were within pistol shot, Rodgers gave orders for the men to stand by their guns but not to fire until orders were given. He first wished the ship to identify herself. There was to be strenuous argument over what followed.

As so often happened with these episodes, mutual acknowledgement of flag and name of ship was slow on demand. An American inquiry found that *Little Belt* had fired the first shot, the British inquiry at Halifax, to which *Little Belt* returned, accused the Americans of opening hostilities. Two

British seamen who were serving aboard *President* at the time of the action told the Halifax inquiry that the first shot had been fired from *President* but it had been an accident, for, as one of them testified, '. . . no orders were given from the quarter deck to fire; the guns had locks, and all were cocked. After the action he was informed by the men in the waist that a man was entangled with the lanyard of the lock, that occasioned the gun to go off.' *Little Belt* returned the fire and got half an hour of broadsides in return. The British sloop's colours were shot down but when Rodgers asked if she had struck he was told that she had not. Seeing her crippled state he nevertheless held off. Only then did each ship learn the name of the other. Rodgers, expressing his regret for what had happened, offered her captain New York to refit his ship. But *Little Belt*'s Captain Bingham took her back to Halifax and in his report said, 'I asked his motive for having fired at all; his reply was that we fired the first gun at him, which was positively not the case. Nor is it probable that a sloop of war within pistol shot of a large forty-four gun frigate should commence hostilities.'[7]

The two British seamen from *President* who gave evidence at Halifax presented a curious insight into the conflict of emotion that could work in a British sailor of the day. They were typical of those whom British squadrons sought to demand from American ships. They had joined and happily served the American navy but the heavy broadsides laid upon the weaker *Little Belt* by *President* brought an upsurge of loyalty to their former flag. Both deserted and went to Canada when *President* went into New York.

Ironically, at that moment a British minister was in Washington finally to make reparation for the *Chesapeake*. This was done, with the British apparently ready to let the new incident die quietly. Some sort of balance, perhaps, had been achieved against the *Chesapeake* affair. But the existing tensions between the two navies were alive when American naval ships called at British ports, which they constantly did in carrying diplomats and communications to and fro. A distressing incident occurred when the 32-gun *Essex* lay at Portsmouth on one such visit. A British naval officer came on board saying that they had learned that one of the crew was British and a deserter. *Essex*'s commander, Captain Smith, thought it impossible to protect the man, who admitted his identity and the desertion, but said he had been impressed into the Royal Navy and after desertion had become an American. He saw an axe where the carpenter had been working, seized it, and with one blow cut off his own left hand. In his bleeding state he presented himself to the British officer and thrust the severed hand at him.[8]

Around the same time, late 1811, a more dangerous incident at Portsmouth was more firmly handled by Captain Hull of the 44-gun *Constitution* when a deserter from a British ship nearby was seen keeping himself afloat with blocks of wood alongside the American ship. Brought aboard he declared himself an American, though speaking with a strong Irish accent. The next day the deserter was inquired after. No formal demand was made after it was intimated that he would not be given up. But it was known that *Constitution* was to sail that night and in the course of the day two British frigates came and anchored near her. When *Constitution* changed her anchorage preparatory to departure the frigates followed her, so close that the pilot expressed fear of getting foul of one of them. As *Constitution* prepared to sail Captain Hull ordered the ship cleared for action. The lanterns were lit fore and aft and the men went to their quarters by beat of drum, 'every officer and man on board believing that the affair of the Chesapeake was about to be repeated'. But when the ship lifted her anchor she moved out without being followed. A more concrete menace followed, however, at her next point of diplomatic mission, Cherbourg. On sailing from there, mission accomplished, *Constitution* omitted to make on time the agreed signal that distinguished her from the British ships blockading the port. The French batteries opened up on her, with two shots striking *Constitution* before the necessary signal was made, at which the batteries stopped firing. The diplomatic passages by American warships increased during the early months of 1812. The naval vessels involved thus gained valuable experience of those belligerent waters, and with it practice of alert readiness for action.[9]

In a message to Congress at the end of 1811, President Madison gave further notice of the possibility of war. He laid blame for the encounter between *President* and *Little Belt* firmly on the latter. Then, accusing the British cabinet of withholding remedy of wrongs 'so long and loudly calling for it', he believed that 'Congress will feel the duty of putting the United States into an armour'. The demand for a breach with Britain began to grow steadily, but armament was now for more than the maritime question. On the northwestern frontier forces of regulars and militia had been assembled, as Madison put it, to deal with 'murders and depredations committed by Indians, but more especially by the menacing preparations and aspect of a combination of them on the Wabash'.

By mid-1811 Michigan, Indiana, Illinois and Missouri were in continual tension with the Indian tribes as the whites sought to push their agricultural settlements forward. The rise of the Shawnee chieftain Tecumseh had brought an entirely new element to that. A striking note to this was that it was just on fifty years since the first powerful Indian uprising against white settlement, that of the great Ottawa chieftain Pontiac, who had led his resistance across the very same territory pivoted upon Detroit. Tecumseh was attempting to form a united front of all the tribes against the frontiersmen, as Pontiac had done. He was drawing into his confederacy tribes of the south as well, as Pontiac also had sought. By seeking to influence southern tribes he aligned the southern states in Congress with the northwest when the latter began to speak of war with Canada.

The northwest believed that Tecumseh and his twin brother, known as Prophet, were in league with the British commanders along that frontier. While the British military commanders may not have been in active conspiracy with Tecumseh against the American frontiersmen, they nevertheless made every effort to win over the Indians as allies in the event of war. From those tensions had developed a desire in the northwest territories for a move into Canada.

The northwesterners saw early acquisition of Canada as a given. The broadly accepted view of the feasibility of that was expressed by Jefferson in a letter to James Monroe as war approached in 1812: 'The acquisition of Canada this year as far as the neighbourhood of Quebec will be a mere matter of marching.'[10]

How could they be wrong, seeing as the British had merely 4,500 regular troops in Canada, three thousand of which were garrisoned in Montreal and Quebec? The rest of the British regulars were distributed along a line of forts sparsely positioned on the St Lawrence above Montreal, along the shores of Lakes Ontario and Erie, and with a lonely outpost at the head of Lake Huron. The military governors of Canada had already been informed that, with British involvement in the Iberian Peninsula, they could expect no reinforcement, nor indeed specie to pay for an expensive campaign. In effect, they should stand fast as best they could, where they could, in face of the overwhelming manpower that the Americans seemingly had to draw upon as required, in one form or another.

The reality was that never had a nation been less prepared for war than the United States right then, whether on land or ocean. A standing army of ten thousand had been authorized some time back by Congress. Some five thousand only were in the ranks in 1811. Congress subsequently voted to add twenty-five thousand more regulars and to allow for fifty thousand volunteers, but the difficulties in raising those was considerable with a people who disliked being tied down to any form of restriction of their lives and independence. During the eleven years of Jefferson's and this early stage of Madison's presidency the army in any event had, like the navy, fallen into a state of inefficiency and neglect. The states and territories had their militias but militiamen had the option of refusing to serve beyond their home territories.

Whether or not the United States was ready for war, the fever for it was expressed by Andrew Jackson, commander of the militia in western Tennessee: 'We are going to fight for the re-establishment of our national character, misunderstood and vilified at home and abroad; for the protection of our maritime citizens, impressed on board British ships of war and compelled to fight the battles of our enemies against ourselves . . . in fine, to seek some indemnity for past injuries, some security against future aggressions, by the conquest of all of the British dominions upon the continent of North America.'

There it all was. But, finally, it was a war that should not have happened at all, for now came perhaps the bitterest irony of Anglo-American history.

On 1 June 1812 President Madison delivered a long message to Congress on the wrongs America had suffered from Britain and requesting decision on peace or war. On 4 June the House of Representatives voted seventy-nine for war and forty-nine against. The Senate followed on 17 June with nineteen for, thirteen against. The following day, 18 June, the United States was at war with Britain. Five days later, the British government annulled the Orders-in-Council that, together with impressment, had been the source of the trouble. Castlereagh had returned to government in March 1812 as Foreign Secretary determined to change things. In parliament the restrictions upon American trade and shipping embodied in the Orders-in-Council had consistently been attacked by the Scottish radical Henry Brougham who had entered parliament in 1810 as a Whig. Castlereagh left the argument for repeal of the orders to Brougham.

'It is not a figure of speech,' Brougham said,

but the simple truth, to affirm that . . . there is not an axe falls in the woods of America which does not put in motion some shuttle, or wheel, or hammer, in England. Is it the miserable, shuffling, doubtful traffic in the north of Europe and the Mediterranean, which we prefer to the sure, regular and increasing North American trade – a trade placed beyond the reach of the enemy's power, and which supports at once all that remains of the liberty of the seas, and gives life and vigour to the main pillar within the realm – the commerce and manufactures of England? . . . the inevitable consequence will be that the Americans will be driven to the necessity of supplying themselves with manufactures . . . The nation is already deeply embarked in the Spanish war; let us not then run the risk of adding another to the league of our enemies . . .'[11]

The repeal of the Orders-in-Council that followed was unconditional, except that the American government was expected to follow suit by cancelling its Non-Intercourse Act against Britain. It would, of course, be weeks before each knew of the other's actions. Too late then by far. The Atlantic had never been wider.

LIX

WAR

THE great distinction that this North American war would carry was clear from the start: a war upon two waters, salt and fresh.

That is, upon the ocean along its coastlines the United States would have to maintain its pre-eminent line of defence against whatever naval force Britain decided to send against it, while naval activity upon the expansive inland seas and river routes of northwestern America was the required support for an offensive land campaign that sought conquest of Canada.

In neither case had there been serious preparation for war, by the militant frontiersmen least of all. That is, afloat on their inland waters where it mattered they were unprepared. Nevertheless, when they began marching, imbued by the aggressive optimism of their widely unfolding new frontiers, they saw easy acquisition of Upper Canada, the colonial territory that fronted Lakes Ontario and Erie from the St Lawrence to Detroit and along the Lake Huron shore beyond. Their optimism rested confidently upon the meagre 4,500 British regulars that represented the main force with which Britain held Canada, that being thinly stretched from Quebec to the head of Lake Huron.

The first thrust into Canada had been assigned to the Michigan Territory's governor, Brigadier William Hull, who had declared, 'The British cannot hold Upper Canada without the assistance of the Indians, and that they cannot obtain if we have an adequate force at Detroit.'[1] But Tecumseh and his Indian forces were already firmly allied to the British when, on 12 July, Hull took sixteen hundred of his force of 2,500 regulars and militia and crossed from Detroit to the Canadian village of Sandwich opposite. He should have passed on swiftly to the British military and naval post of Amherstberg just beyond but delayed, thereby allowing reinforcement as well as an armed brig with eighteen 24-pounders to arrive at Amherstberg. On 8 August Hull found himself compelled to return to Detroit. On the same day the British military commander in Upper Canada, General Isaac Brock, embarked 300 Canadian militia on Lake Erie and, with 700 British regulars and 600 Indians under Tecumseh, laid seige to Detroit on 16 August. Hull first deployed his men before the fort but withdrew inside as Brock approached. To the British general's astonishment a white flag was then suspended from the walls and Hull surrendered at once. Together with this critical fort came all its stores, an armed brig lying alongside, the whole of the northwest's arms and, in effect, the rest of Michigan's posts and garrisons. The first American invasion of Canada had been a pathetic failure. Hull's plea was fear of Indian vengeance should he and his forces fall to them.

Could the navy do better? Whether the United States Navy had any serious active role to exercise was still being questioned even after war was declared. James Monroe, in correspondence with Jefferson, wondered whether 'the best disposition which could be made of our little navy would be to keep it in a body in a safe port, from which it might sally, only on some important occasion, to render essential service'.[2] There was broad support within the administration that the navy should be kept in port. But when William Bainbridge and another captain saw orders for the Rodgers squadron then lying in New York to be confined there instead of putting to sea they demanded and got an audience with the President to plead against it. Against opposition within the cabinet Madison agreed to change the instructions.[3]

For such options of inaction to be so seriously considered was hardly surprising, however, coming as it did from men who had stood by the neglect of the navy during the past decade. Of the thirteen large frigates that had been built in response to the crisis with Barbary only nine remained serviceable at the outbreak of war. Together with lesser classifications the United States Navy had altogether only seventeen ships for oceanic service. The British navy by comparison had some eight hundred cruising ships in a fleet of more than one thousand vessels. It is perhaps understandable, therefore, that there should have been reluctance among some to risk such a small force against the overwhelming weight of the other. So it could look on paper. But the British navy was so fully engaged on the other side of the Atlantic that there was little extra to spare or divert for the war with America.

The American frigates were formidable ships, moreover, far in advance of anything classified as frigate in the British navy. What they had besides was a spirit that had remained defiant in face of naval neglect. Their seamanship was second to none. The small size of the United States Navy nevertheless provoked strong argument even among its own officers on how the fleet should best be employed, whether in combined operation or allowed individual movement. All agreed, however, that whether singly or together the ships of the United States Navy had to move out on to the ocean, to protect American shipping and to deploy itself against British commerce, even in British waters.

A force of five ships commanded by Commodore Rodgers was lying in New York harbour when war was declared. Rodgers, aboard the 44-gun *President*, had with him two other frigates, *United States*, 44 and *Congress*, 38, as well as the 18-gun sloop *Hornet* and a 16-gun brig, *Argus*. The force was divided into two squadrons, however, with Commodore Stephen Decatur, captain of *United States*, having under him *Congress* and *Argus*. When news of the declaration of war reached them on 21 June the five ships were heading for sea within an hour.

The United States Navy proved itself with a rapidity that became an unpleasant surprise for the British, who by now took their supreme command on the seas completely for granted. It offered a jolt as well to a Congress that had so easily dismissed any prospective oceanic function for the navy even as it declared war.[4]

On 23 June, just two days into the war, the first naval encounter came when a 36-gun British frigate from Rodgers's squadron was sighted and given chase. It became a brief, inconclusive action between *President* and the British ship, *Belvidera*. Sailing straight ahead, with her stern to her immediate pursuer, *President*, the British ship had the advantage that the chasing ship could not fire ahead, except with a forecastle chase gun, which Rodgers himself fired when *Belvidera* came within gunshot. The shot penetrated the British ship's stern and passed into the gun room. To hit *Belvidera* more effectively, *President* had to turn sideways to bring its main guns to bear. *Belvidera*, on the other hand, had four guns on her stern. She brought these into play directly upon her pursuer, simultaneously seeking to escape the squadron by dumping boats, spare spars, anchors and 14 tons of drinking water to lighten her, get away and make it back to Halifax. As *President* yawed, allowing a gun immediately below the forecastle to be pointed, the gun burst as it was fired, blowing up the forecastle deck, killing and wounding sixteen men. Rodgers was thrown into the air, breaking a leg as he fell. The *President* finally hauled up and fired three broadsides before *Belvidera* got away. Thus to the United States Navy fell the first shots of the war, and to *Belvidera* the task of communicating to the British navy at Halifax that war had been declared.

The British commander at Halifax, Admiral Sawyer, immediately formed a squadron under Captain Broke of the 38-gun *Shannon*, accompanied by four other frigates, to go in pursuit of the Americans. *Belvidera*, repaired, was part of the force. Off Sandy Hook the squadron made the first British capture of an American ship of war, the 14-gun brig *Nautilus*, which was immediately manned by the British and included in the squadron.

Meanwhile, the 44-gun *Constitution*, Captain Isaac Hull, had been lying at Annapolis taking on board a new crew. She sailed on 12 July and five days later, off the New Jersey shore, encountered the 38-gun *Guerriere*, belonging to Broke's squadron. The rest of the squadron then appeared and closed in towards gunshot range. Hull found that he had seven ships in different positions around him. From this hopeless situation he was saved by a calm that produced undoubtedly the most unusual chase of the Great War. Lacking wind, the attacking ships had to be towed within range, to be able to fight. Or, in the case of *Constitution*, hauled beyond it.

For two and a half days, from dawn of 18 July to close to noon on the 20th, pursued and pursuers moved their ships by sheer muscle power, either by towing their vessels or by hauling them forward by anchor. Ships' boats were launched, packed with oarsmen and, hauling one behind the other in a long line, pulled their vessels forward. Or kedge anchors, normally used to warp ships from one berth to another in harbour, were carried forward half a mile ahead by cutter, dropped, and the crew on signal 'walked away with the ship' on deck, drawing her slowly forward. Hull aboard *Constitution* was the first to use this method to move ahead and gain distance on his pursuers but the British soon followed suit. *Shannon*, by adding the boats of other ships to her own, closed towards gunshot range. But *Shannon* had to exercise caution because it would have been easy for her own towing boats to be targeted by the stern guns of *Constitution*.

Two sailing fleets manoeuvring on a battle scene under tow by oarsmen: in this painful manner, through one day and night, and then again another day and night, lacking wind, *Constitution* and the British ships sought movement on the small patch of ocean that contained them. The nearest ships of the British squadron, *Shannon* and *Guerriere*, tried steadily to close with their powerful adversary to cripple her. At times the British sought with probing fire to reach *Constitution*, especially when sudden upsurge of light wind in their sails gave them advantage. *Constitution* itself would then seek range. The Americans' greatest fear was that in those baffling winds the British would suddenly be favourably placed to windward, then to descend swiftly upon them.

The men slept by their guns as the others hauled on kedge anchors from deck. Those who hauled occasionally fell down to sleep briefly where they were. Then midday on the 20th there was wind enough for *Constitution* to abandon towing and kedging. The boats were brought in rapidly. The canvas filled and, on a flat sea, the lost sound of a bow wave and of the wash alongside were heard again. *Constitution* gained ground rapidly, flew away at a rate of eleven knots, lost her pursuers and Hull took her to Boston.[5]

This romantically heroic episode brought mutual admiration of skill, persistence and ingenuity. It would stand as unique example of the resourcefulness and physical endurance that had to be drawn upon when the motoring idiosyncrasies of wind left sail inert. For the British it was their first real encounter with the quality of seamanship and determination of the young American navy. Not since the Dutch wars of the mid-seventeenth century had they faced the prospect of naval war with sailors fully equal and as consciously alive as they themselves were to a convinced sense of mastery at sea.

Constitution and *Guerriere* had yet another encounter ahead of them. Hull sailed on 2 August, headed towards the mouth of the St Lawrence to intercept British trade, and then turned south and on 19 August sighted a British frigate, which indicated it was ready to engage 'in a fair yard-arm-and-yard-arm fight'. The opponent was *Guerriere*. The preparatory sequence for action between two such well-matched ships always offers, as much as anything can, a fine image of the grandeur and tactical alacrity of sail that accompanied imminence of battle, as a report from *Constitution* detailed:

. . . at four, coming up with the chase very fast; at quarter before five, the chase laid her main-top-sail to the mast; took in our top-gallant sails, stay sails, and flying gib; took a second reef in the top-sails, hauled the courses up, sent the royal yards down, and got all clear for action; beat to quarters, on which the crew gave three cheers; at five, the chase hoisted three English ensigns; at five minutes past five, the enemy commenced firing; at twenty minutes past five, set our colours, one at each mast head, and one at the mizen peak, and began firing on the enemy, and continued to fire occasionally, he wearing very often, and we manoeuvering to close with him, and avoid being raked; at six set the main-top-gallant sail, the enemy having bore up; at five minutes past six brought the enemy to close action, standing before the wind . . .[6]

At six thirty it was all over. *Guerierre* submitted. She was so badly damaged that she sank the following day. In his report to Admiral Sawyer at Halifax, written from Boston, *Guerriere*'s captain, James Dacres, ascribed loss of his ship to the early fall of the mizzen mast, which fell over the weather side and hampered the helmsman's efforts to bring the ship's head up to the wind. The fore- and mainmasts then fell over the side. She suffered seventy-eight killed and wounded against seven killed and seven wounded aboard *Constitution*. Dacres himself was wounded. He emerged from this action with two fine gestures to his credit. When the action began Dacres allowed the ten impressed Americans he had on board to go below when they refused to fight their countrymen. In his report to Admiralty he said, 'I feel it my duty to state that the conduct of Captain Hull and his officers to our men has been that of a brave enemy, the greatest care being taken to prevent our men losing the smallest trifle, and the greatest attention being paid to the wounded.'

So here was the first serious action between the British and American navies. The impact of it in both Britain and the United States was tremendous. The surprise and dismay on the one hand and joy and celebration on the other were swiftly enlarged as other American victories followed in the same month. For the British the sudden requirement was a complete reassessment of the quality and ability of the American naval forces, small though they were. The same could be said for the Congress that had failed to strengthen the navy. But, naturally, all the navy's former congressional opponents unashamedly shared the elation and festivity, particularly since things had not gone well on the front that they themselves had promoted, for which the war had so aggressively been launched.

The War of 1812 was by now merely one aspect of a radically altered situation in the Great War, the other being Napoleon's invasion of Russia.

Relations between Napoleon and Tsar Alexander had been deteriorating since 1810. Alexander's refusal to commit himself to the Continental System had convinced Napoleon that Russia was returning to belligerence on Britain's side. Alexander strengthened his position when the Ottomans finally decided to sign a peace treaty with him. On 25 June 1812, two days after the American Congress went to war with Britain, Napoleon with a force of 450,000 crossed the Niemen on his swift way, he believed, to Moscow. 'I have come to finish once and for all with the colossus of the barbarian north,' he told his secretary Caulaincourt. All too soon it looked the other way round.

What he saw of Moscow when he got there on 14 September was a deserted city. On 19 October his force, already severely reduced, sick and demoralized, began the long march back, the most calamitous retreat in history. On 3 December a bulletin was issued declaring that 'an atrocious calamity' had befallen the Grande Armée. Two days later Napoleon abandoned his army and raced for Paris, which he reached at midnight on 18 December. Behind him 330,000 surviving soldiers were dragging their way back across the icy Russian plains.

LX

MACEDONIAN

SUNDAY at sea aboard British ships of war would customarily be a day of rest. After breakfast the crew, dressed in their best, would be mustered on deck for church service read by the captain. So it was aboard the British frigate *Macedonian*, on course from Madeira to Halifax, on the morning of 25 October 1812.[1]

This day, however, there was to be no church service. Breakfast was barely over before the masthead lookout cried a sail in sight. Captain John Carden for days had appeared in a nervous state, constantly demanding lookout to be alert. The cry that morning had therefore agitated him, with constant demands to the masthead for description of the approaching vessel, eventually determined to be a large frigate.

For the crew gathered on deck and commanded to be silent as the captain listened for word from aloft the speculation had been that the oncoming ship was American and that they would have to fight her. Although reports of war with America had been circulating on board as *Macedonian* approached American waters there had been no certainty of it. But that came at eight thirty as the other ship, now some three miles distant, turned to stand on a different tack and showed her colours. *Macedonian* was immediately cleared for action.

Macedonian inevitably had on board its own group of impressed Americans. One of them immediately presented himself to Carden and said the Americans objected to fighting their countrymen. Carden lacked the humanity of Dacres of *Guerriere*. He had a reputation for cruelty. He ordered the Americans to their action quarters saying that anyone who again made that demand would be shot. The sailor who had done so was to be one of those killed in the action.

The ship before them was the *United States*, Stephen Decatur.

The boy seaman Samuel Leech, who had started his naval career aboard *Macedonian*, gave in his memoirs one of the most vivid descriptions of an action in that war. It has particular impact for conveying the first experience of action for a boy such as he then was.

My station was at the fifth gun on the main deck. It was my duty to supply my gun with powder, a boy being appointed to each gun in the ship on the side we engaged. A woollen screen was placed before the entrance to the magazine, with a hole in it, through which the cartridges were passed to the boys, and covering them with our jackets hurried to our respective guns. Thus we all stood, awaiting orders, in motionless suspense. A strange noise, such as I had never heard before, next arrested my attention; it sounded like the tearing of sails, just over our heads. This I soon ascertained to be the wind of the enemy's shot. The roaring of cannon could now be heard from all parts of our trembling ship, and made a most hideous noise. I heard the shot strike the sides of our ship; the whole scene grew indescribably confused and horrible, like some awfully tremendous thunder-storm, attended by incessant streaks of lightning, rendered more horrible by the torrents of blood which dyed our decks. I saw blood suddenly fly from the arm of a man stationed at our gun. I saw nothing strike him. In an instant the third lieutenant tied his handkerchief round the wounded arm, and sent the groaning wretch below to the surgeon.

The cries of the wounded now rang through all parts of the ship. These were carried to the cockpit as fast as they fell, while those more fortunate men who were killed outright were immediately thrown overboard. As I was stationed but a short distance from the main hatchway, I could catch a glance at all who were carried below. A glance was all I could indulge in, for the boys belonging to the gun next to mine were wounded in the early part of the action, and I had to spring with all my might to keep three or four guns supplied with cartridges. I saw two of these lads fall nearly together. One of them was struck in the leg by a large shot; he had to suffer amputation above the wound. A stout Yorkshireman lifted him in his arms, and hurried him to the cockpit. Two of the boys stationed on the quarterdeck were killed. A man who saw one of them killed, told me that his powder caught fire and burnt the flesh almost off his face. In this pitiable situation, the agonized boy lifted up both hands, as if imploring relief, when a passing shot instantly cut him in two. I was eye-witness to a sight equally revolting. A man named Aldrich had one of his hands cut off by shot, and almost at the same moment he received another shot, which tore open his bowels in a terrible manner. As he fell two or three men caught him in their arms and, as he could not live, threw him overboard.

The battle went on. Our men kept cheering with all their might. I cheered with them, though I confess I scarcely knew for what. Certainly there was nothing very inspiriting in the aspect of things where I was stationed. So terrible had been the work of destruction round us, it was termed the slaughterhouse.

Our men fought like tigers. Some of them pulled off their jackets, others their jackets and vests; while some had taken off their shirts and with nothing but a hand-kerchief tied round the waistbands of their trousers fought like heroes. I observed a boy named Cooper, stationed at a gun some distance from the magazine. He came to and fro on the full run, and appeared to be 'as cheery as a cricket'. The third lieutenant cheered him along, saying, 'Well done, my boy, you are worth your weight in gold'.

I have often been asked what were my feelings during this fight. I felt pretty much as I suppose every one does at such a time. That men are without thought when they stand amid the dying and the dead, is too absurd an idea to be entertained a moment. We all appeared cheerful, but I know that many a serious thought ran through my mind: still, what could we do but keep up a semblance, at least, of animation? I satisfied myself by repeating again and again the Lord's prayer.

Grape and canister shot were pouring through our portholes like leaden rain, carrying death in their trail. The large shot came against the ship's side like an iron hail, shaking her to the very keel, or passing through her timbers, and scattering terrific splinters, which did a more appalling work than even their own death-giving blows. Suddenly the rattling of the iron hail ceased. We were ordered to cease firing. A profound silence ensued, broken only by the stifled groans of the brave sufferers below.

Macedonian had surrendered to the *United States*. She had suffered thirty-six killed, seventy-two wounded. *United States* had seven killed, five wounded.

Leech then went to help with the wounded and to throw the dead overboard. He offers striking comment on the bonds between seamen and those they lost.

There was one poor boy there crying as if his heart would break. He had been servant to the boatswain, whose head was dashed to pieces. I met one of my mess-mates, who showed the utmost joy at seeing me alive, for, he said, he had heard that I was killed. There were also two boatswain's mates, named Adams and Brown, who had been messmates for several years in the same ship. Brown was killed, or so wounded that he died soon after the battle. It was really a touching spectacle to see the rough, hardy features of the brave old sailor streaming with tears as he picked out the dead body of his friend from among the wounded, and gently carried it to the ship's side, saying 'O Bill, we have sailed together in a number of ships, we have been in many gales and some battles. Now we must part!' Here he dropped the body into the deep, a fresh torrent of tears streaming over his weather-beaten face.

Decatur struck an unusual note for the British when he came over to inspect *Macedonian*, for 'he wore an old straw hat and a plain suit of clothes, which made him look more like a farmer than a naval commander'.

Both ships then sailed for the American coast. Some of the British sailors remained aboard *Macedonian*, others were transferred to their captor, Leech among the latter. In both cases the sailors found common ground. 'I soon found myself perfectly at home with the American seamen; so much so that I chose to mess with them,' Leech said. 'My shipmates also participated in similar feelings in both ships. We ate together, drank together, joked, sung, laughed, told yarns; in short, a perfect union of ideas, feelings and purposes seemed to exist among all hands.' That was aided by the fact that a large proportion of the *United States*'s crew was British. Over two of the gun ports aboard the American ship were the words Victory and Nelson. The men quartered at those guns had served many years with Nelson and had even been his own bargemen. *Macedonian*'s men recognized many old shipmates. One of them even found his own brother among the crew. At New York Leech and great numbers of the *Macedonian* sailors now took every opportunity to, as Leech put it, escape 'the obnoxious discipline of the British navy'. So that at the end it was 'the fragment that remained of them' that was eventually shipped home. Leech returned aboard *Macedonian* to get his clothes. While on board he was invited to join the victory parade through New York. That triumphant parade was led by *Macedonian*'s band, which when taken aboard *United States* had immediately decided to go over to Decatur and ship with him.

Already that same month the 18-gun brig *Wasp*, on a cruise out of Delaware, had taken the 18-gun British sloop-of-war *Frolic*, only to find itself taken together with its prize by a British 74. For the Royal Navy, however, further serious shock followed two months later when the *Constitution*, Commodore Bainbridge, captured the 49-gun British frigate *Java*, carrying the new governor of Bombay and his staff out to their post. *Constitution* intercepted *Java* off the coast of Brazil. The American navy at this time was ranging far out across the North and South Atlantic in search of British prize, naval or merchant. *Java*'s commander, Captain Lambert, was killed by rifle fire from the *Constitution*'s main top. *Java* lost all her masts and was a wreck after nearly two hours of action. She was in such poor state that she was blown up instead of being taken to the United States. Her British officers and men were landed at San Salvador.[2]

The Royal Navy was, however, soon to have some compensating uplift. Still serving the British blockade on the American coast was Captain P. B. V. Broke of the 38-gun British frigate *Shannon*. *Guerriere*, taken by *Constitution* in the first dramatic American success, had been part of Broke's squadron. Broke and *Shannon*, it might be recalled, had been leaders of the masterful towing race in pursuit of *Constitution* after the taking of *Guerriere*. Broke at all events was a man thirsting for satisfaction.

Broke had descended on Boston in the belief that his old adversary *Constitution* and another ship were lying there. They had left before he arrived. Instead, the frigate *Chesapeake* had come in. *Chesapeake* was already part of British and American naval history, from the episode in 1807 when

HMS *Leopard* had forcefully boarded her to remove British seamen. Broke lay off, waiting for her to come out and, to speed the process, sent a letter of challenge ashore: 'Sir: As the Chesapeake appears now ready for sea, I request that you will do me the favour to meet the Shannon with her, ship to ship, to try the fortune of our respective flags.'

The letter was sent off too late to reach *Chesapeake*, Captain James Lawrence, before she was observed moving out past Boston Light on 1 June 1813. *Chesapeake* had been intended to sail out on a cruise but, with *Shannon* so defiantly lying close in, it would have been difficult for *Chesapeake* to avoid the clearly visible challenge. She came out at five thirty p.m. flying three ensigns, including a flag bearing the slogan 'FREE TRADE AND SAILORS RIGHTS'. About twenty miles off Boston Light the two ships came up slowly to one another on a gentle breeze, watched by hundreds on shore, and by others from yachts and small craft that ventured out. When *Chesapeake*'s foremast was in line with *Shannon*'s mizzen mast *Shannon* began firing.

It was one of the fastest actions of the Great War, over in fifteen minutes. Its swiftness was bloody, as it inevitably would be with the ships eventually entangled. The raking fire of *Shannon* played havoc on *Chesapeake*'s decks. Lawrence, a tall, powerful figure, fell almost immediately, shot by an officer of the marines. Broke cried out, 'Follow me who can,' and leaped on to *Chesapeake*'s quarterdeck where, in close combat with three American seamen, he was severely wounded on the head. A distinctive fight took place aloft when the yardarms of the two ships locked together. Two *Shannon* midshipmen fought their American opponents in the main top and the fore top. One of them, finding himself screened by the foot of the topsail, lay down on the main yardarm to fire and shot three of the Americans. Then suddenly it was over, the British colours flying. *Chesapeake* had forty-eight killed and ninety-eight wounded, *Shannon* twenty-three killed and fifty-six wounded.

In spite of the blood running on their decks, in his report Broke could say, 'Both ships came out of action in the most beautiful order, their rigging appearing as perfect as if they had only been exchanging a salute.'

Three hours later *Shannon* and her prize sailed for Halifax, where they arrived five days later. As could be expected, *Chesapeake* had many British on board. Thirty-four were identified, one of them subsequently hanged at Spithead. The Royal Navy always wanted that example. The British were surprised by the contrast they drew between their own sailors and the American. As William James noted, 'The Chesapeake's crew were remarkably stout, healthy young men; especially when contrasted with Shannon's; most of whom were rather below middle stature, and a great proportion old or elderly men.'

LXI

REFLECTION

In Britain the American navy's successes against the Royal Navy brought surprise joined to deep shock.

The Royal Navy found self-examination thrust upon it, in a manner to which it was entirely unaccustomed, particularly after Trafalgar, which had allowed the navy to fall back comfortably upon what it always preferred to take for granted: conviction of superiority, the indisputable mastery of its seamanship. But here, suddenly, was an unwelcome exposure to shortcoming. For a British navy that seldom assumed that it had anything much to learn from any other, the experience that now began with the Americans forced harsh, even bitter, reflection on many aspects of what they were encountering.

The sudden requirement was a complete reassessment of the quality and ability of the American naval forces, small though they were. William James was to say, 'While ... a feeling towards America, bordering on contempt, had unhappily possessed the mind of the British naval officer, rendering him more than usually careless and opinionative, the American naval officer, having been taught to regard his new foe with a portion of dread, sailed forth to meet him, with the whole of his energies roused. A moment's reflection assured him; that his country's honour was now in his hands; and what, in the breast of man, could be a stronger incitement to extraordinary exertions?' That was quite a tribute from James who, though regarded as reliably accurate throughout the whole of his subsequent work, nevertheless often appears savagely dismissive whenever dealing with anything concerning the American navy.[1]

Though they knew that ultimately the Royal Navy, through sheer numbers and weight of ships, had to overpower the United States Navy, the experience of *Guerriere* and others that immediately followed was regarded by the British not only as humiliating but, perhaps more importantly, as unsettling prediction of a dangerous future power to contend with.

An intense naval debate was launched, not to be equalled until the end of the nineteenth century with the rise of German and Japanese naval power. That naturally found its home in the *Naval Chronicle*, where navy men by now were accustomed anonymously to express themselves in a manner whose forthrightness might not have served them too well elsewhere.

British sailors had always conceded that the French built better ships; here nevertheless was seen an impressive advancement on all. In the 44-gun American frigates the British now saw something different and, given that these ships had already been visible to them in the Mediterranean and as visitors to British ports, chagrin was expressed that the difference had not been fully recognized and exploited before.

The American frigates were widely regarded as virtually the equivalent of a British ship of the line, the dependable 74 now obviously considered as the viable opponent to the Americans. 'Fortune has invariably favoured the Americans, in having their largest class frigates opposed to ours . . . each of them mounting 56 guns, and 480 men, were all built on the scantlings of 74-gun ships, and were intended to be such, when their keels were laid down. They were built equal in strength to any of our line-of-battle ships; their sides are thicker, their masts tauter, yards squarer, and breadth of beam greater, than our 74-gun ships,' a *Chronicle* correspondent, 'Naval Patriot', commented, adding that nearly a quarter of the crews of the American ships were British deserters. Then,

Having said so much concerning the heavy American frigates, I will explain the reason of their working their guns, and handling their ships, superior to any other nation, and not inferior to our seamen. In general most of the men who have deserted from our service to theirs are *prime seamen*, with whom, and almost all *real seamen*, are the American ships manned . . . Look at our ships, how they are manned at the breaking out of a war, and compare them with the generality of ships now commissioned, and the difference will be most striking. The vast number of ships at this time in commission are now manned by a very small proportion of able seamen, and the remainder filled up with good, bad and indifferent, viz. Ordinary seamen, landsmen, foreigners, the sweepings of Newgate, from the hulks, and almost all the prisons in the country; with such a motley crew . . . it must take some considerable time before such a ship's company can be well regulated and brought to good discipline, and much longer to make them good sailors or trusty men. [The largest ships that served in the United States fleet through the early years of the war were the 44-gun *Constitution, President, United States, and Guerriere*, which entered service in 1814. That same year the 74-gun *Independence* was launched at Boston, to be followed by the 74 *Franklin* in 1815, and the 74 *Washington* in 1816.]

The spleen on this filled many pages in successive issues of the *Naval Chronicle*. 'I do not know what information the government may have possessed respecting the largest class of American ships of war, called by them frigates,' said one contributor. 'But I remember being told, twenty years ago, by one who had been in their service, that if ever we should have war with that country, our frigates could be no match for them, as they were laid down for ships of the line. Recent events have proved the correctness of the observation.'

Another writer demanded, 'If we wish to preserve our naval character on its former footing, why resort to large ships? Build frigates of the same dimensions as the Americans, and let them have the same weight of metal, then I trust our national glory will soon put it to the proof.'

The published reports of the American engagements were keenly studied. Bafflement was common: 'It may be asked, how the French, who always fire high in order to destroy the masts and rigging, have never succeeded in capturing our ships as the Americans have done? The answer is plain – the French, by directing only one gun to a particular mast, had but small chance of striking it, or if the ball did strike, it most frequently only wounded the mast . . . But as the Americans do not apply their whole broadside to the destruction of the masts . . . I think it is but fair to conclude, that extraordinary means have been used against us.' Or, as 'Half-Pay Officer' pondered, 'I should like to ask them – Is the exercise of their guns, and arrangement at quarters, like ours? Have they fixed ammunition? Are their rammers, sponges, worms, wads, shot, crows, handspikes, cartridges, tubes, powder horns, or tackles different? In short, what have they better, or what can we learn from them?'

The common conclusion was that the American model of frigate was perhaps the best thing in naval warfare and should be adapted, as advocated by 'Albion': 'The ample experience we have already had since the commencement of the present American war of the inadequate force of our frigates and sloops, to cope with American ships of the same designation, must have taught our present Board of Admiralty the propriety, nay, the necessity of preparing and keeping effective a force, and that not a small one, of a similar description to that possessed by our active, enterprising and successful enemy . . . the frigates henceforth ordered to be built should be the largest construction fit to cope with any ship termed frigate either by the Americans or the French . . .'

Commenting on the higher death toll aboard the British ships compared to that of the Americans, another contributor said, 'You must allow for their sides being so very thick, and their men better sheltered; also their being so much larger than our ships, and with such great breadth of beam, they have less motion in a sea, or swell, and of course can with more accuracy point their guns.' Another factor was the American riflemen picking off officers and men from the tops. These marksmen were marines. As James pointed out in his *Naval Occurrences*: 'Very distinct from the American seamen are the American marines. They are chiefly made up of natives of the country . . . In the United States every man may hunt or shoot among the wild animals of the forest. The young peasant or backwoodsman carries a rifled-barrel gun . . . To collect these expert marksmen, when of proper age, officers are sent into the western parts of the Union; and to embody and finish drilling them, a marine-barrack is established near the city of Washington, from which depot the ships are regularly supplied.'[2]

In his *Chronicle* letter 'Naval Patriot' angrily asked: 'Did not the memorable battle of Trafalgar point out to our rulers, by the fall of Nelson, the necessary propriety of having riflemen in *our* tops, to oppose the French in theirs? . . . by which means we should then be able to pick off a few of the opposing officers and the best men, as the Americans did ours in the late battles.'

A striking aspect of this *Naval Chronicle* correspondence was the critical examination it prompted of much of the fixed outlook of the Royal Navy, as provoked by the example that the Americans now set. The American sailor suddenly appeared as one quite distinctly apart on the seas. The comparisons were all unhappy ones, the spirited bond of 'picked' men with everything in common between them, their high seamanship, the limited period of their service instead of the indefinite bondage that was the lot of the British sailor, who suffered as well the cruel punishments inflicted upon him. That so many British deserters should be found serving aboard the Americans and thereby delivering their own experience to them was especially galling. And that raised the uncomfortable issue of desertion, as expressed by 'Albion', in a different letter: 'There are comparatively few so blind, as not to perceive . . . in the serious injustice so long practised on the seamen, which the absurdity of our antiquated naval institutions and "customs" permits . . . and which together with the impress, have been tolerated with incredible indifference and ignorance by successive administrations . . . Hence obviously that dread of the service of their country among sailors . . . Until the legislature shall cause a revision of the naval articles of war . . . there can exist neither satisfaction nor good will in that service.'

'Albion' was to express another view that, however, was probably of far more concern to many than injustice in the navy. 'The Americans have fought us bravely at sea, they have, almost in every instance, been successful; and there cannot be a doubt, they will speedily become . . . a truly formidable naval power. We have, I fear, been lulled asleep by our former glorious victories over the fleets of France, Spain and Holland; and have, until too late, despised this new, but rapidly rising rival of our maritime greatness . . . Let us then profit by *dear-bought experience*; let us build ships of adequate force; let our line of battle ships, frigates and sloops, be no longer incapable of meeting and contending with this rising enemy.'

LXII

NORTHWEST

In spite of early success, American command on the ocean could never be supposed in this war, even off the coasts, but on the inland waters it had to be assured if the conquest sought of Canada were to be realized.

However impressive individual naval actions on the ocean might be, lakeland was where advance and gain had to be won by those who had sought and then propelled the United States into war by invading Upper Canada. The start of what they had so hotly demanded had been spectacularly unpromising.

Hull understandably became the war's first scapegoat. When the British released him he was, on his return to the United States, immediately court-martialled and sentenced to be shot, which was commuted by Madison. Whatever his deficiencies, Hull had to pay for the lack of thought and preparation behind the fevered drive to war. The most conspicuous fault was the lack of any serious effort to ensure naval strength on the lakes, where the British had naval superiority.[1] Not greatly so, but enough to allow early command, strengthened for them at the start by the armed brig they collected at Detroit.

For any military man surveying the vast spread of water linking the potential field of conflict laid across middle America, free movement was clearly the first requirement. Wellington recognized that from afar in the Peninsula. 'Without naval control of those lakes,' he wrote, 'successful land operations are impossible on that frontier.' There was no real difference between such an expanse of water and the ocean so far as naval operation was concerned. Water was the connection, providing the lines of supply and communication between the bases: the surface upon which control needed to be contested and resolved. Those lines were long and complex, as with the ocean, alternating safe anchorage with intricate shallows that demanded hours of soundings, assaulted by storms that could pound and throw a vessel as violently as the Atlantic, or lay down calms and variable winds that could frustrate movement and manoeuvre as much as any capricious part of the Mediterranean.

Those inland seas are truly one of the great unsung natural wonders of this planet, for even with many who live in the great cities on their shores and who have never ventured out on them they are something casually taken for granted: an open expanse of water disappearing into the humid mists of summer, a featureless white stretch of ice reaching out from the shore and breaking open far off in winter. So it might seem at Toronto, Chicago, Cleveland, Milwaukee. But to sail upon them, to pass from one to the other, is something else. One is strongly tempted to call them oceans, seas at any rate, Superior especially. And, if the writer may digress, he can say that at different times in the past he has sailed on them from one end to the other, in many sorts of vessel, in all their seasons, and from his very first sight of Lake Superior from a Canadian Pacific train in 1950 they have remained for him, through countless memories of their natural beauty and the variety in character of sailing and seamanship, a permanent wonder and source of attraction.

The line of hostile vigilance for both sides in 1812 was a 1,500-mile front from Quebec to the head of Lake Huron, following the St Lawrence past Montreal into Lake Ontario, along the Niagara Strait into Lake Erie, thence along the Detroit River, past Detroit, and on up Lake Huron to Mackinac and the Sault at the approach into Lakes Michigan and Superior.

The northwest lakeland was a vast wilderness with thick forest mostly right down to the water's edge on all the lakes. Such small scattering of posts and villages as existed lay along both shores of Lakes Ontario and Erie, but particularly at or near to the points of transit between the lakes, such as at Detroit and the Niagara Strait. Settlements and cultivated land were all close to the shore. Roads, where they existed, were bad, seldom more than tracks and usually impassable. Water thus necessarily linked every post and inhabited place on the lakes. So it had always been, whether for trade, military or communication. As one British commander was to report, an army could achieve in two days by water what otherwise would involve two to three weeks of marching. Every movement of any significance therefore depended upon the water for speed, surprise and conservation of strength. All of which made it difficult to understand why neither side made any serious naval preparation for a war that both were expecting.

Schooners were the vessels habitually used on the lakes, varying in size from 30 to 100 tons. Many of these were soon to be armed and pressed into service. In naval armament the British had a slight edge on the lakes. On Lake Ontario they had one ship of 300 tons and three smaller vessels. The Americans had one armed brig. On Lake Erie the Americans had one armed brig and four or five schooners. The British had nothing there. An important distinction between the British and the Americans was that while the American ships were manned by sailors of the United States Navy the British had not yet brought in their own navy for their lake ships, which were usually manned by Canadian militia.

As with any war of invasion and aggressive intent, this war had to arrange itself according to the American reach for and possession of primary objects.

On the face of it, the primary objects of all had to be Montreal, the heart of Canadian commerce, and Quebec, the seat of the colonial government. This reach of the St Lawrence west of Lake Ontario was called Lower Canada. American seizure of Montreal and Quebec meant the fall of all of Canada. Montreal and Quebec together were garrisoned by three thousand of the 4,500 regulars Britain had in Canada. But with the Americans holding an easy line for supply and reinforcement up the Hudson and through Lake Champlain there was no strong conviction of holding out in face of strong assault. The governor-general of Canada in 1807 had declared, 'Quebec is the only post that can be considered tenable for the moment. If the Americans should turn their attention to Lower Canada, which is most probable, I have no hopes that the forces here can accomplish more than to check them for a short time. They will eventually be compelled to take refuge in Quebec, and operations must terminate in a siege.' Nothing had changed since then.[2]

For Upper Canada in the event of war the primary points were Mackinac and Detroit. Together those controlled access to and movement within the great northwest.

Mackinac was the vital transit point between Michigan and Superior and the other lakes. It was the established passage for Indians and white fur traders. The Americans had a fort, Mackinac, on the island of Michilimackinac at the passage into Michigan. The British had a fort on St Joseph's Island fifty miles from Mackinac, the guardian of the passage into Superior. Between them these two posts controlled movement between the three biggest lakes. Equal in significance, as the northwest's transit point between Michigan and Upper Canada and for communication between the upper and lower lakes, was the Detroit River. There the Americans had Fort Detroit and the British-maintained Amherstberg across the way. Well before the war, as the British military governors in face of rising war fever in the United States made their strategic assessments, Detroit and Mackinac appeared to be the necessary points to possess, for control and assurance of Indian alliance. 'If we could destroy the American posts at Detroit and Michilimackinac,' wrote the lieutenant-governor of Upper Canada in 1808, 'many Indians would declare for us; if not, they will surely be against us.'[3]

Upper Canada's governor in 1812, General Isaac Brock, also had that in mind the moment he got word that war had been declared. He too believed that 'unless both Detroit and Mackinac be in our possession at the commencement of hostilities, not only Amherstberg but most probably the whole country must be evacuated as far as Kingston'.

The moment Brock got news of the war on 28 June he sent orders to his commander at St Joseph's to seize the American fort at Mackinac. When Brock's instruction reached him on 17 July that officer immediately took his force of forty-five British regulars, 180 Canadian militia and four hundred Indians in boats across to Mackinac, whose garrison of fifty-seven surrendered at once.

Thus, by having their defensive strategies well considered before the outbreak of war, and with quick decision after Brigadier Hull's retreat back to Detroit, the British in under two months held both that fort and its transit passage and Mackinac with its control of the upper waters. The war in lakeland would now essentially be fought on Lakes Erie and Ontario, on their shores and at the connecting points between them.

Lake Erie is 231 miles long, sixty-four wide. Amherstberg was the only naval and military base the British had on it. The American shore had several posts and settlements, the principal of which was Presqu'île, later named Erie, with a sizable town and a dockyard where new ships were to be built. At the entrance to the fast-flowing Niagara River the British had Fort Erie, which was without a cannon at the start of the war. Opposite it were the American villages of Buffalo and Black Rock, two miles apart. Where the Niagara flowed into Lake Ontario the British had the village of Queenstown with the American village of Lewistown opposite. At the outflow into Lake Erie the British had Fort George, matched opposite by the American Fort Niagara. Fort George was no more than earthen ramparts and palisades of dry cedar. Fort Niagara was a strongly built stone structure. On the north shore of Lake Ontario, about ninety miles from Niagara, was York, the capital of Upper Canada, with no more than three hundred houses. At the far end of the lake, at the entrance into the St Lawrence River, was Kingston, the largest British military and naval base on the lakes and also the most substantial Canadian lakeland town. Some thirty miles across on the other side of the wide St Lawrence mouth the Americans had their own principal military and naval post, Sackett's Harbour.

With the British holding Detroit that meant that the next thrust by the Americans on the lake frontier would be at Niagara, where they had mustered six thousand men. General Brock with twelve hundred awaited the attack, and on the night of 13 October some sixteen hundred Americans under General Stephen van Rensselaer, head of the New York militia, crossed the Niagara from Lewistown to take Queenstown, whose heights commanded the river. The Americans took the ridge, the British regulars and Canadian militia retook it. Brock was killed in the action. The Americans returned to their boats and crossed back to the other side. The Americans failed in another landing at another point on the Niagara. An American attempt to retake Detroit was disastrous. American failure at Niagara was blamed on New York militiamen refusing to embark with the others, saying they had turned out to defend their homes not invade Canada. Thus petered out the much-vaunted northwest land campaign for 1812. The talk of an easy march across Canada faded away as the Americans went into winter quarters.

A majority in Congress had demanded a war which appeared too much of a walkover for there to be any serious strategic planning, let alone zealous preparation. A dangerous assumption had been that the Canadian settlers would be brought on side against British governorship to embrace independence with their American cousins. Instead Upper Canada militiamen had mainly carried the fight for Queenstown heights. For a conquest that to many had appeared a guaranteed success the conspicuous defect was the lack of the obvious: an immediate full thrust at Montreal and another at Halifax. Before the War of Independence American colonials under Colonel Pepperell of Maine in 1745 had captured the strongly defended French base of Louisbourg, just north of where Halifax was then soon to be. If in 1745, why not in 1812, with a strong American naval force moving in from the Atlantic? One factor, of course, was that the former American Loyalists who had moved into Canada's maritime provinces from New England with the American War of Independence would have offered stiff resistance. Whatever doubts may have existed of that coastal proposition, the overwhelming logic of an attack upon Canada should have been with Montreal then Quebec as the main objectives, which of course was what the British themselves had expected and feared.[4] Logistically everything favoured it, with that easy communication line up the Hudson and over Lake Champlain. 'The conquest of Lower Canada,' a recent governor-general of Canada had declared, 'must still be effected by way of Lake Champlain.'

Seven thousand men had been assembled at Plattsburgh on Lake Champlain. A patrol sent by them against a watch post manned by Canadian militia at a bridge was repulsed. Nothing else was attempted and that whole force, too, went into winter quarters. In this desultory manner did it all fade away as the leaves began to fall and the ice to form.

Every operation so far, American or British, had involved movement on water, but there had not yet been any regular form of naval engagement between the two sides.

The seizure of Mackinac had been the first waterborne operation. Whether moving armies close by or far, much of it was by oar. Nowhere during the Great War was there more dependence upon the oar than upon the North American inland waters, pulling with muffled oars at night across Niagara, hard against the rapids of the St Lawrence, or hundreds of miles across a lake. When General Brock set off from York to take command at Amherstberg after Hull had retreated back to Fort Detroit, he put his force of seven hundred regulars and militiamen into open boats and passed down to Burlington, near Niagara, before marching them across to Long Point on the north shore of Erie. From there he had embarked them in another fleet of open boats for the two-hundred-mile, week-long voyage to Amherstberg, through storm and heavy rain, off a coast often so rugged that it allowed no creek for rest or shelter. Such were the demanding necessities of lakeland operation.

The largest American ship on the lakes was the brig *Oneida*, carrying eighteen 24-pound carronades and commanded by Lieutenant Melancthon Woolsey of the United States Navy. *Oneida* was lying at Sackett's Harbour on 19 July when a five-strong British squadron appeared off the fort.

The British ships included the *Royal George*, 22, the *Prince Regent*, 16, and the *Earl of Moira*, 14. It was a combined force of metal able to make quick work of *Oneida*. The British sent in a boat with a demand that *Oneida* surrender to them. Woolsey decided to try his chances. He got underway and ran down to windward of the enemy squadron, to escape if possible. It proved impracticable so he beat back into the harbour and anchored his brig from where he could rake the entrance. He unloaded his guns on the shore and mounted these, forming a full battery of sixteen 24-pound carronades.

The British, turning with the wind, came within gunshot and opened fire, which they maintained for two hours, until they made off for Kingston, having done little damage. That had been the actual start of naval war on the Great Lakes. Preparation on both sides for something fuller than that had a way to go yet. The British had a larger force than the Americans, but hardly adequate for the immense expanse of water upon which they had to move. Nor did they have trained naval personnel. A member of the Canadian governor's staff reported that there was not a man fit to command a ship of war since they had not yet brought in officers and sailors from the Royal Navy to serve on the lakes, as the Americans had done.

American command on the lakes was given to the head of the New York navy yard, Captain Isaac Chauncey, who brought his own touch of the new age to this war by setting off from New York by steam on the Hudson. Sackett's Harbour, at the outflow of the St Lawrence at the eastern end of Lake Ontario, had already been selected as the centre for naval operations. Chauncey arrived there on 6 October and immediately set about building the naval force that long since should have been provided.

Chauncey selected another naval officer, Lieutenant Jesse Elliott, to build a fleet on Lake Erie, where the Americans were without any naval vessel. Erie was strategically the most vital of the northwest waters. It was the connection to the upper lakes and commanded the western reach of Upper Canada. But British possession of Detroit had deprived the United States of much of Erie's strategic advantages, and had as well sealed the bond with Tecumseh and his warriors.

Elliott established himself at Buffalo, opposite the British Fort Erie at the inflow of the Niagara River, to fit out schooners and to build two large ships of 200 tons each. On 8 October two of the largest ships that the British had on the lakes, the brigs *Caledonia* and *Detroit* (captured from the Americans at Detroit) arrived at Fort Erie. Both were manned by Canadians. Observing across the river from Buffalo, Elliott saw opportunity. At one o'clock the following morning he put one hundred sailors and soldiers into boats and, pulling hard against the fast outflow from Lake Erie into the Niagara Strait, they came alongside the ships, boarded and took them. *Caledonia* was carried off but *Detroit* ran aground and was lost. At a stroke Elliott had provided the Americans with one of the best ships the British had on the lakes. And by the close of the navigation season at the end of November Chauncey and Elliott had two ships of 24 guns under construction at Sackett's Harbour and two 20-gun brigs on Lake Erie. Chauncey had already launched the largest ship on the lakes, the 24-gun *Madison*, 590 tons. She had been built in forty-five days. That provided a notable difference between naval warfare on the lakes and on the oceans beyond, as Chauncey pointed out: 'Nine weeks ago the timber she is composed of was growing in the forest.'[5]

LXIII

LAKELAND

As the thaw of the winter of 1812–13 approached, the American War Administration remained focused upon the northwest in viewing the imminent renewal of campaign on the Canadian frontier, once more disregarding the tactical logic of an early, powerful thrust at Montreal.

Instead of the close by and more directly accessible, the strategic simplicity presented by the Hudson and Lake Champlain which, arrow-like, pointed straight at the obvious target, American intent remained, as Mahan put it, 'upon the extremity of the enemy's power, instead of upon its heart'.[1]

The failure of the confident optimism that had launched the war appeared to bring little serious subsequent reflection on the value of this time moving into Lower Canada instead of Upper Canada, thereby cutting at Montreal and Quebec the direct oceanic connection with Britain, without which the war on the St Lawrence and beyond could not be maintained by the British. With the Americans, the northwest was where the war was launched, and that was where the assault was required to remain. But for them the moment to move against Lower Canada was propitious in a manner it never would be again. Britain was still unable to send serious reinforcement for any ambitious counter against the Americans. Napoleon had returned to Paris just before Christmas, to explain to a shocked nation, equally well a stunned Europe, the calamitous loss of an army of 400,000, the remnants of which were still struggling back through the snows from Moscow. Wellington, who had retreated from Madrid soon after taking it, was pondering the season ahead from his winter headquarters at Ciudad Rodrigo. Everything in Europe was on a balance, liable to tip which way no one could yet predict. British preoccupation with all those uncertainties had become fatally taken for granted by the American government, which appeared unable to give up on the original vision of the seeming ease of conquest through the northwest. Supportive of that, however, was the strenuous effort on both sides through the winter to build naval strength on the lakes.

The war through 1813 was to be a war for naval power on the Great
Lakes, specifically on Lakes Ontario and Erie. Nothing meaningful could be
accomplished there, offensively or defensively, without that naval command.
That had not been nearly so evident at the outset since the motivating
American assumption had been an easy land conquest of colonial Upper
Canada from Detroit and Niagara. Failure where success had seemed
foregone had made the forthcoming campaign entirely dependent on the
inland waters. Only afloat could any meaningful new strategy be borne.
Free movement on and across the lakes alone could now ensure tactical
movement, communication, supply and reinforcement.

The British, now holding Detroit, needed naval power on Lake Erie to
maintain that valuable position, for its connection to the upper lakes as well
as the transit passage across the Detroit River, which was highly valued by
the Indians. Without both those the British knew that they could quickly
lose Indian support.

The seat of naval power for both the Americans and the British was,
however, on Lake Ontario, at the eastern end of which, at the outflow into
the St Lawrence, both powers had their principal naval bases, virtually
opposite one another. The British had theirs at Kingston, the Americans at
Sackett's Harbour. With only thirty miles between them it was inevitable
that sooner or later one side would attack the other. Such was Chauncey's
plan for the opening of navigation. To have seized and held Kingston would
effectively have eliminated British naval position on the lakes. Chauncey
was overruled. Instead the early objectives in the new campaign became
York, followed by repossession of Detroit. An attempt by General William
Henry Harrison to retake Detroit in the early winter had failed. Harrison
had then built a new fort at the rapids of the Maumee River, some thirty
miles below Detroit.

Around the lakes there could be no movement until the ice was sufficiently gone, which could only be from around early April. Even then
large floes could still make passage on the lakes hazardous. The coastal
roads, such as existed, would be impassable until hot sun had hardened
the sodden ground. Roads, anyway, were often no more than rough tracks
whose course could only be followed by marks cut on the trees. For the
impending campaign, therefore, it all came back to the waters. And to the
naval operations there that would have their own unique place in the history
of maritime conflict: naval warfare to be fought remote from the ocean yet
conducted by all the forms and standards of oceanic navy for, in Mahan's
succinct phrase, 'although on a small scale, the lakes were oceans, and the
forces that met on them were fleets'.[2]

New naval officers had been appointed to the lakes. Chauncey received
as his second lieutenant Oliver Perry, who was given the command on Erie

while Chauncey remained at Sackett's Harbour on Ontario. The Royal Navy had sent Captain Sir James Yeo, who arrived with a small body of tars to take command at Kingston. Yeo was joined by Captain Robert Barclay, who was given command at Erie, to be Perry's opponent there.

The ice began to break at Sackett's Harbour in mid-April. On the 25th Chauncey and Perry sailed out with eighteen hundred men under General Zebulon Pike for the assault on York. The two-day voyage brought them off York on the 27th. The landing was successful. The Americans remained long enough only to destroy the public buildings and much of the rest of the town. General Pike was killed by a magazine explosion. A 16-gun ship was taken and a 30-gun on the stocks destroyed. The force then moved on to Niagara, where the British Fort George was taken on 27 May. With their principal fort gone, the British evacuated the whole of the Niagara Peninsula, withdrawing to Burlington, halfway along the road between Niagara and York. For the British Burlington was a necessary point for, with Niagara lost, it now provided the essential communication with Amherstberg and Detroit. From Burlington a road ran to the harbour on Lake Erie, Long Point, from where troops and supplies needed to embark for the passage to Amherstberg. It was the route Barclay had to take in June when he went to assume naval command at Amherstberg.

What followed through the succeeding months of that summer was a shifting campaign of gain and loss, of attempt and tentative gain, of assault and retreat, veering from one side to the other as each sought naval ascendancy and control of Ontario and Erie. In absence of land campaign it was, in military terms, a fight for the bases from which the squadrons operated and from where the soldiers skirmished. The British retaliated for York and Fort George by trying to seize Sackett's Harbour, and nearly succeeded, bringing damnation upon the head of the British governor-general, Sir George Prevost, for failing to do so. General Harrison at Fort Meigs sought to regain control of Detroit while the commander at Amherstberg, General Proctor, retaliated by laying siege to Fort Meigs. These northwestern lakeland skirmishes were hard and brutal. Much of it was forest fighting, which the Indians preferred. But a substantial part of Harrison's army consisted of Kentuckians, just as adept in the forests. For Indians and Kentuckians alike, there was no quarter. They scalped their victims, alive or dead. Proctor was being pushed into these assaults by Tecumseh, whose people saw their own survival tied to a return to their unrestricted movement across the northwest. Proctor needed to hold the Indians in alliance but they had become a heavy burden. Fifteen thousand Indians, men, women and children, had accumulated inland of the north shore of Erie and had to be provisioned. All supplies had to move by ship the two hundred miles from Long Point to Amherstberg.

The Long Point supply route was the natural target for Perry's fleet once he had it fully assembled. The British evacuation of Fort Erie had allowed Perry to remove five ships that had lain at Black Rock. They had previously been unable to pass into Lake Erie under the batteries of Fort Erie. Even so, getting them into the lake still meant them doing so against the hard current of the inflow from Erie into the Niagara River. This Perry accomplished by hauling the ships to the lake with teams of oxen, yet another operation unique to naval warfare that this Great War delivered. At his base of Presqu'île, he was completing two 500-ton brig-rigged warships, as well as armed schooners.

Perry's prospective opponent, Captain Barclay, who had lost an arm at Trafalgar, arrived at Amherstberg in June to take command of the small British squadron. He brought a few British sailors with him. Apart from those, his five ships were manned by British regulars or Canadians, none of whom had seamanship experience, which somehow they now had to get before facing the challenge that would settle the fate of the northwest and continuance of the Indian support.

Meanwhile, the same resolution towards obtaining naval power was being sought on Lake Ontario between Chauncey and the new British commander there, Captain Yeo. Upon the outcome of that depended the maintenance of British hold on Upper Canada. It was consequently a more critical contest since defeat on Lake Ontario had to mean loss of Erie as well, as the British at Detroit and Amherstberg could not possibly hold out on their own, being dependent upon supplies coming across Lake Ontario from Long Point.

Yeo had six ships of different sizes, all built for war. Chauncey had three brigs and ten schooners built for war. In July Chauncey added to his fleet the biggest ship on the lakes, *General Pike*, armed with twenty-six 24-pounders. Until the *Pike* was completed on 20 July Yeo moved freely on Lake Ontario, capturing supply ships, attacking stations. With *Pike* afloat, it was a different situation, and a strange one. They were about equal in force but, while moving constantly in unavoidable challenge to one another, they did so without bringing that to full action. On three occasions they came close enough to it, compelled into all the tactical manoeuvring of battle, with exchange of shots, but without taking the engagement into decisive action. It was naval engagement as determined as on the ocean but, as in the old days on the ocean, what each side sought to avoid was the very thing that latterly determined oceanic action, melee. Chauncey and Yeo were each of them painfully aware that neither could afford a serious loss to their small fleets that could decide the outcome on that frontier. For, as Chauncey admonished Perry, 'The first object will be to destroy or cripple the enemy's fleet; but in all attempts upon the fleet you ought to use great

caution, for the loss of a single vessel may decide the fate of the campaign.'
It was what Chauncey himself assiduously practised on Lake Ontario.

For the rest of the year, until the end of the navigating season on the lake,
Yeo and Chauncey moved through this inconclusive confrontation. Each had
to maintain watch on his opponent's position and intentions. Close encounter
was therefore unavoidable, which meant that close action often appeared
imminent. It was a duel that began properly on 7 August off Niagara. For three
days, until 10 August, the two squadrons manoeuvred through constantly
changing winds, sailing in parallel line when circumstances allowed, firing
between ships that were within range, bearing away when advantage appeared
questionable. Each side would blame the other for evasion.

A determining issue was the difference in the firepower of the two. The
ships on both sides carried two forms of gun, long-range cannon and short-
range carronades. In long guns the Americans were four times as strong as
the British; in carronades the British were twice as strong as the Americans.
In the summation of William James: 'The immense disparity in long guns
accounts for Sir James Yeo's endeavoring to get the weather-gage; without
which, his wary opponent would have hammered the British squadron to
pieces; and remained himself comparatively uninjured.'[3] As the winds on
the lake were extremely variable, perpetually seeking to be to windward of
the Americans was therefore a difficult game to play, but play it they both
zealously did. For the British that essentially meant avoiding the broadsides
of the *Pike*, which had brought to the lakes the equivalent power of a 74.

That first extended engagement ended, something of an anticlimax, at
midnight on 10 August. Yeo, in pursuit of two schooners that had lagged
behind Chauncey's force, found himself within gunshot of the two biggest
American ships, including *Pike*. Instead of the action that everyone expected,
aboard *Pike* especially, *Pike* bore away. As one officer aboard *Pike* related:

On the 10th, at midnight, we came within gun-shot, everyone in high spirits. The
schooners commenced the action with their long guns, which did great execution. At
half past 12, the commodore fired his broadside, and gave three cheers, which was
returned from the other ships – *the enemy closing fast*. We lay by for our opponent,
the orders having been given, not to fire until she came within pistol shot, though
the enemy kept up a constant fire. Every gun was pointed, every match ready in
hand, and the red British ensign plainly to be described by the light of the moon;
when, to our utter astonishment, *the commodore wore, and stood* S.E. leaving Sir
James Lucas Yeo to exult in the capture of two schooners, and in our retreat; which
was certainly a very fortunate one for him.[4]

Chauncey's response to that was, 'At twelve midnight, finding that I must
separate from the rest of the squadron, or relinquish hope of saving the two

which had separated, I reluctantly gave up the pursuit.'⁵ The nature of that first engagement remained the character of the two subsequent encounters between Chauncey and Yeo. It enabled them to preserve their squadrons intact to the end of the season.

On Lake Erie it was to be quite different. There, on 10 September, the main naval battle on the lakes was fought. By early August Perry had completed his squadron. He then moved his ships to Put-in-Bay opposite Amherstberg. This anchorage guarded the two forts below Detroit that the Americans under General Harrison now occupied. Tecumseh was still pushing General Proctor at Amherstberg to attack those forts but, as with the earlier attempts, it was ineffectual. Perry's presence killed all further possibility, for this in effect was now close blockade of the whole British position on and around the Detroit River. Unless Barclay came out to meet him, any supplies or reinforcement for the British passing on the water from Long Point would be intercepted. Fear of Perry's squadron had already seriously impeded the flow. At Amherstberg it had become a matter of go out and fight, or die. Barclay and General Proctor both recognized that. Governor-General Prevost himself urged the confrontation in a letter to Proctor, declaring, 'Barclay has only to dare and he will be successful!'⁶

When Barclay arrived off Put-in-Bay on 10 September Amherstberg had 'not a day's flour in store' for its garrison and the thousands of Indians who had to be fed. Barclay's ill-assorted crews were on half-rations. On that they had to dare and be successful.

Barclay was aboard his flagship *Detroit* and Perry on his flagship *Lawrence*. On the water Barclay was at a disadvantage from the start. He lost the early benefit of having the weather-gauge, which meant that Perry, being to windward, could choose his distance to give full effect to his long guns 'while the British carronades dropped their high-priced shot uselessly in the water',⁷ as James described it. Barclay affirmed in his official report, 'The weather-gauge gave the enemy prodigious advantage, as it enabled them not only to choose their position, but their distance also.' But the battle, as outlined by Mahan and the American novelist and early naval historian James Fenimore Cooper, was a great deal more complex and close than simply that. The battle, Cooper said, 'for near half its duration, appears to have been fought, so far as efficiency was concerned, by the long guns of the two squadrons. This was particularly favoring the Detroit and the American gun-vessels.' Barclay's official report declared that soon after the start of the action, just before midday, *Detroit* and *Lawrence* 'came to close action'. It 'continued with great fury until half past two'. By that time both flagships were completely shattered. More than half of *Lawrence*'s ship's company lay dead or wounded on her decks. She had only one gun left but her colours were still up. *Lawrence* then dropped astern of *Detroit* and Perry was seen to pass in a boat from *Lawrence* to his second ship, *Niagara*. As he boarded *Niagara* the colours on *Lawrence* came down. As Barclay put it in his report, Perry moved to the other ship 'seeing that as yet the day was against him'. The *Niagara*, Barclay said, 'was at this time perfectly fresh'. Under the continued fire that fell upon *Detroit* and its companion vessels surrender followed soon after. *Detroit* by then lay 'completely unmanageable, every brace cut away, the mizen top-mast and gaff down, all the other masts badly wounded, not a stay left forward, hull shattered'.[8]

Barclay, who was severely wounded soon after and taken below, nevertheless believed when he left the deck that the squadron had won, though he accepted that *Detroit* would have to strike as well. Or so it would appear from an account offered by Cooper: 'When the Detroit was taken possession of, the boarding officer went into the cabin, where he found Captain Barclay suffering under his wound, but still flushed and excited. "You are sent for my sword, sir?" he cried. "No, sir, I have come to take possession of the ship." "Well, sir," continued Captain Barclay, "I would not have given sixpence for your squadron when I left the deck!"' It was the only surrender of a complete squadron in British naval history.[9]

Barclay and Perry had fought with conspicuous bravery. Their mutual respect in that was registered by Barclay's comment, 'Captain Perry has behaved in a most humane and attentive manner, not only to myself and officers, but to all the wounded.' Particularly reflective of the ferocity of the action was the loss of Barclay's officers, most of whom fell, which was seen by Barclay as a factor in his defeat: 'Manned as the squadron was, with not more than fifty British seamen, the rest a mixed crew of Canadians and soldiers, and who were totally unacquainted with such service, rendered the loss of the officers more sensibly felt, and never in any action was the loss more severe; every officer commanding vessels, and their seconds, was either killed or wounded so severely as to be unable to keep the deck.'

The Americans were now masters of Lake Erie. General Proctor abandoned Detroit and Amherstberg and retreated across western Upper Canada. General Harrison moved from Fort Meigs and followed the British to an inland point halfway across the north shore of Erie. What remained of the mixed force of British regulars and Indians attempted a stand. Proctor galloped away on the first exchange of fire, for which he was subsequently court-martialled. Resistance was maintained by the Indians, until Tecumseh fell. It was the end of the Indian alliance. Tecumseh was said to have been scalped by the Kentuckians in Harrison's force. Harrison returned to the Detroit River to take possession of the fort there and of the British stations opposite. Michigan and the American northwest frontier were thus regained.

Finally and belatedly the American government decided to go for Montreal. The end of October was hardly the best time, with the leaves in their vivid-turned colours already falling. The task was given to a new military commander in chief, General James Wilkinson, who took eight thousand men down the St Lawrence while another force under General Wade Hampton marched from Plattsburgh. One of the American columns was stopped by a force of Canadians entirely on their own without British regulars, in what was to become an episode of intense patriotic pride in the new concept of a distinctive Canadian identity that this war brought. The other column retreated to winter quarters at Plattsburgh. And so ended the second attempt on Montreal.

At Niagara the British sprang a surprise with the final campaign of the season. Aware that the Americans had withdrawn troops from Fort George for the Montreal operation, they marched on the fort and retrieved it. In their retreat from Fort George the Americans destroyed the town of Newark, driving the inhabitants out into the snow. It was an act of brutality that left a deep mark upon the Canadians. The British continued their advance and on 19 December took Fort Niagara. They passed on to Black Rock, Buffalo and other villages and settlements on the American frontier line. These were destroyed as retaliation for Newark. With this savagery on both sides the second year of the war ended, fairly evenly balanced in triumph and disaster between the two. For the British triumph at that moment was particularly acute, for apart from repulsing the move against Montreal they greeted the New Year with full possession of the Niagara Peninsula.

LXIV

TORPEDOES

OF the new weapons devised for the Great War, two now came into more active use, Congreve's rockets with the British and Fulton's torpedoes with the Americans.

Both these startling inventions caused revulsion and fear, the Congreve rockets even with those who used them. In the American side of the war the torpedoes finally became a thing of dread for the British navy in their coastal operations, and eventually of vengeful rage with Nelson's former captain, Thomas Hardy.

At the start of the war Fulton had tried to sell his submarine and torpedoes to both the French and the British. Neither was interested so he took his machines home to America. What was called torpedo was in principle more like what was to become known a century later as a 'mine'. The torpedo was a case of powerful explosives that was submerged, supported by a small buoy, and then directed by currents or tide alongside a ship. Once contact was made a line attached to the machine was pulled and the explosion took place. Or, as Fulton had demonstrated at Brest and before Pitt at Walmer Castle, the torpedo could be carried aboard his submarine alongside an enemy ship and the explosive then attached to the hull.

Hardy, in his ship *Ramillies*, was off New London on 25 June 1813, in command of a squadron of ships of the line, when his boats captured an American schooner that was found to have been abandoned. The schooner was laden with provisions. The initial idea was to lay her alongside *Ramillies* to unload the provisions, but Hardy ordered her kept at a distance. One of his officers and thirteen men went on board. They were no sooner on board when the schooner exploded. All but three of the men survived. Trains had been laid to several barrels of gunpowder, the trails set to explode at a given time by sparks provided by clockwork. The automatic system was that of the torpedo. The ruse signalled an attempt by the Americans to launch their own particular warfare against the British coastal assaults, led by submarine warfare, something the British already seriously feared, accounting for Hardy's wariness.[1]

The loss of his men had enraged Hardy, who applied himself, through informers, to obtain what intelligence he could on all such American operations in Long Island Sound. What he heard was that further torpedo assaults were intended. Submersible attempts had already been made against a British 74, *Victorious*, and at Chesapeake against a brig. The first crude attempt at submarine warfare was thus seriously underway.

Re-enter now into this narrative Joshua Penny, not so long since returned to his home after his impressment and African adventures previously recorded in these pages. Penny had acquired his own small coasting ship, which he sold as soon as war was declared, 'resolved to put myself in an attitude to annoy the enemy of my country, and the scourge of the terrestrial globe'. Penny's home was at Three Mile Harbour, close to East Hampton. Men from *Ramillies* were frequently landing on Gardiner's Island, in Gardiner's Bay at the end of Long Island. Gardiner's Island was at that time occupied by the same Captain Gardiner who had given the place its name. When Hardy once more appeared there Penny crossed to New London, where Commodore Stephen Decatur aboard *United States* was blockaded by Hardy's squadron. Decatur put four boats under one of his lieutenants, Lieutenant Gallagher, with Penny to direct them.

Landing on Gardiner's Island they watched 160 marines and sailors fitting out nine boats, two launches, four cutters, two barges and a gig from *Ramillies* and its attendant frigate, *Orpheus*, for an apparent assault. The British became aware of them and tried to cut off their escape. They were pursued by shot from the ships. 'Our enemy returned to Gardiner's Island to abuse Mr Gardiner for suffering us to come there, as if he could help it,' Penny said. 'He is very critically situated – in the power of the British, and consequently censured by both parties.'

A short while after the Gallagher sortie, Penny was asked to assist in a torpedo operation against the ship. Penny's house was open to the bay and in sight of the British ships, but the ships kept shifting their anchorage and the project was abandoned. But in July 1813, while again lying off New London, the deck sentinel cried out, 'Boat ahoy!' A form like a porpoise had risen to the surface a few feet astern of *Ramillies*. The alarm gun was fired and all hands called to quarters. But the submarine, which it was suspected to be, had submerged and vanished. *Ramillies* hastily cut her cables and got underway. The submarine, observing all through its telescope, rose again and then, as if having positioned itself, dived. Moving at three miles an hour it went alongside the keel of the British ship but the man aboard the submarine was unable to attach its explosive device. The craft got away. Hardy remained on the station but when anchored encircled *Ramillies* with boats.

Penny wanted a commission in the naval service from Decatur and, having obtained various local recommendations, was about to return to New London, expecting to receive command of a row-galley. But, on the morning of 20 August 1813, a boat was seen taking soundings in the creek near his house. Penny called to a neighbour to get his arms and they made for the boat, which pushed out and went alongside *Ramillies*. 'I suspected their design, for I saw them viewing with a glass, and pointing to my house.'

Penny decided to move his wife and three sons to a safer place the next day. He was awakened early that evening by a knock on the door. In answer to his demand as to who was there the reply came, 'Decatur's people. Mr Penny, we want you to get up immediately.' He, however, was satisfied that they were 'the Prince Regent's people' and ran for his gun in the kitchen. He had one hand on his gun when they burst in the door and surrounded him. The first lieutenant of *Ramillies* fired at him but missed.

Penny said, 'Officer, you are determined, I see, to murder me. I hope you will be gentleman enough to take me out of sight of my wife and children first.'

The lieutenant, Lawrence, replied, 'It is Sir Thomas Hardy's orders to blow your brains out if you should make the smallest resistance.'

Penny was marched to the shore in his nightshirt. On the way to *Ramillies* Lawrence offered gin, and asked, 'Where are your documents which you obtained yesterday at Sag Harbour, to carry to Decatur?'

'They are in my pocket, and if you had been gentleman enough to have let me got my clothes, you could have had my papers.' Penny knew that because of fears of the East Hampton militia Lawrence would not return.

Lawrence said, 'Damn the clothes, we've got him, that's enough.' And to Penny, 'Well, your papers will never do *you* any good. You'll be disappointed obtaining a commission in a row-galley. Your character has been given me by a fellow in that boat which you saw taking soundings, and a damned good description of your house he gave us. You have some damned good friends who live close by you, or you would not have met with this misfortune. I have been informed by one of your countrymen, that you deserted from a British ship of war; and are the most inveterate enemy of the British within five hundred miles of here. You have been assisting in Decatur's expeditions, and also concerned in conducting those damned torpedoes!' Lawrence added that Penny would undoubtedly suffer death, because torpedoes were 'contrary to the law of nations'. *Ramillies*, when they got there, was surrounded by its boats as a shield. Penny was put in irons.

Meanwhile, at Sag Harbour and New York, Penny's abduction had caused outrage. The commander of the American troops at Sag Harbour, Major Benjamin Case, had immediately sent to Thomas Hardy aboard *Ramillies*, under flag of truce, a demand that Penny be released. The letter was carried by one of Case's officers, Lieutenant Hedges, who was instructed to return with Penny. Penny, Case declared, being a non-combatant and 'attached to no vessel as a mariner or corps of artillery whatever, but was taken by force by your men from his own house unarmed'. Hardy replied from *Ramillies*, still at Gardiner's Bay, on 23 August: '. . . this man conducted a detachment of boats sent from the United States squadron under the command of Commodore Decatur, now lying in New London, from that port to Gardiner's Island, on the 26th of July last, for the express purpose of surprising and capturing the captain of His Britannic Majesty's frigate Orpheus and myself . . . The next account I had of him was his being employed in a boat under the command of Thomas Welling, prepared with a torpedo, to destroy this ship . . . I therefore cannot think of permitting such an avowed enemy to be out of my power . . . Thomas M. Hardy.'

Hardy sent another letter back with Hedges, addressed to Justice of the Peace Terry at Southold. In it Hardy was blunt. Any further attempt with torpedoes would see every house along the Long Island shore destroyed.

On 8 September the *Long Island Star* reported, '. . . it appears that com. Hardy's persecution of Joshua Penny is principally on account of his having piloted a torpedo boat, commanded by Thomas Welden; which boat was discovered by guard-boats, and made its escape only by frequent *diving*. The commodore threatens to lay waste the towns and show no mercy to the inhabitants that harbour torpedoes, which, as he informed Lieutenant Hedges, had given him so much inquietude that it had taken almost all the hair from his head!'

At Halifax Penny was taken under escort of one sergeant, a corporal and nine men to the prison. During his first weeks there Penny was constantly interrogated by Lawrence on Hardy's instructions, to extract all they could on torpedoes and the plans for them. He was told that he would be set free and get three thousand dollars if he told all. 'I felt too much insulted to answer him.' Lawrence said that Hardy had paid two hundred dollars to the informer who betrayed Penny.

Penny came down with a severe fever. He was released after he recovered, under further pressure from the Americans. He arrived home nine months and nine days after being kidnapped. Penny concluded his memoir: 'I had not been long at home before I was invited to engage in another torpedo enterprize; but this failed in consequence of bad weather. It was never my good fortune to command a torpedo; and perhaps I might then have been unsuccessful; but I should be pleased to have the privilege of terrifying John Bull and avenging myself while I was engaged in the service of my beloved country.'

LXV

ELBA

As winter locked in activity on the North American lakes, a totally altered prospect on the war was emerging on the other side of the Atlantic.

For an American administration that had taken too much for granted in supposing Atlantic distance from the war in Europe to be an advantage for its assault on Canada, concern over changing circumstances had built steadily through 1813 as Napoleon's assumed invincibility appeared to crack and tumble. As 1814 dawned, the Western world optimistically saw a real prospect of peace more surely than at any other time during the past twenty-one years.

The shock that the Russian campaign had dealt to the Napoleonic myth was limited. Napoleon had lost a vast army but a major portion of it had consisted of men drawn from different parts of his empire – Germans, Dutch, Italians and others. Many of the best French troops and his ablest generals had survived. And the two sovereigns best able to revive any stand against him, Frederick Wilhelm of Prussia and Emperor Francis of Austria, remained intimidated. But Tsar Alexander began strong effort to draw the two into renewed war with France. A Russo-Prussian accord against France was arrived at in March 1813 after the Russians, in renewal of their pursuit of Napoleon, reached Berlin, and then Hamburg.

Austria was effectively ruled by its chancellor, Metternich, who steadily held out from this coalition. But, although he was disturbed by where Europe was going under Napoleon, he preferred that Austria should await its own properly judged moment before joining the armed effort against Napoleon. His caution appeared justified when Napoleon in quick succession defeated the new alliance at Lützen on 2 May and Bautzen on 20 May. It nevertheless was quickly noted, by Metternich especially, that the two victories had by no means been overwhelming. Napoleon's new army, bolstered by raw young recruits, lacked the discipline and tenacity of the former Grande Armée. His casualties had been heavier than those of the allies, who had not been routed but retired in good order.

Metternich saw opportunity in offering to mediate an armistice. In that function, he hoped to isolate Britain from any peace negotiation, from which he sought a new map of Europe advantageous to Austria. To serve Austria's interests he wanted peace talks confined to France, Russia and Prussia, himself orchestrating it all. But British strength of position was suddenly on a different basis altogether, apart from the subsidies that she was paying out as usual.

During the past four years of the Peninsular War Wellington had never had more than thirty thousand troops, and never any direct control over the Spanish and Portuguese forces. But at the start of the Peninsula campaign in the spring of 1813 Wellington was not only given full control of the Iberian troops of both nations but Castlereagh in London had worked strenuously to get him a stronger force of British regulars. As a result the start of the 1813 campaign saw him with an army of 100,000 under his full command. In May 1813, as he started from his winter quarters at Ciudad Rodrigo, he was opposed by Napoleon's Spanish king, Joseph, and General Jourdan. Both retreated steadily before him. In six weeks Wellington advanced five hundred miles and crossed six rivers until Joseph and Jourdan made a stand at Vitoria in Alava. There, on 22, June 1813, Wellington inflected severe defeat. The road into France opened before him as Joseph fled.

On 26 June Metternich met Napoleon at Dresden. For nine hours they discussed how to have a peace in Europe that would be allied to the sweeping changes that Metternich demanded of the imperial map, including restoration to Austria of much of its lost territory. The latter was the price of Austrian neutrality in another war. Napoleon furiously declared, 'If I accept your policy, I am required to evacuate Europe, half of which I still hold, and lead back my legions across the Rhine, the Alps and the Pyrenees and, signing a treaty which amounts to a vast capitulation, deliver myself like an idiot to my enemies, and rely for a doubtful future on the generosity of those whom today I am conquering.'

Metternich recalled Lützen and Bautzen. 'I have seen your soldiers,' he said. 'They are no more than children. And when these infants have been wiped out, what will you have left?'

Flinging his hat away in his rage, Napoleon yelled: 'You are not a soldier. You know nothing of what goes on in a soldier's mind. I grew up on the field of battle, and a man such as I am cares little for the life of a million men.'

'If only the words you have just uttered could be heard from one end of France to the other!'

At the end, as things grew calmer, Napoleon demanded of Metternich, 'Well now, do you know what will happen? You will not make war on me?'

To which Metternich replied, 'You are lost, sire; I had the presentiment of it when I came: now, in going, I have the certainty.' And, asked by those crowding the anteroom whether he was satisfied with what had passed with Napoleon, he said, 'Yes, he has explained everything to me; it is all over with the man.'[1]

That night, as if in a strange affirmation of that verdict, news of Wellington's victory at Vitoria reached Dresden. With that, Europe believed that it finally saw clear end for Buonaparte. Tsar Alexander called for a special *Te Deum* mass. Vitoria was believed to have greatly influenced Metternich. Austria joined the Russo-Prussian coalition and on 12 August declared war against France. In October Napoleon was defeated at Leipzig. On 2 November he retreated across the Rhine. By then Wellington was already across the Pyrenees and on French soil. The great rampage had drawn in upon itself within France.

Through the winter and spring of 1814 the participants found themselves locked into a strange imbalance of diplomatic negotiations and continuing military effort. Fighting in one corner, bargaining in another. As regards the latter, Britain was finely equipped. On 28 December 1813 Castlereagh left London for Basle, the allied headquarters, to present the British demands. Europe was suffering the coldest winter ever known, during which the Thames was to freeze solid. Landing at The Hague, Castlereagh travelled on from there with his assistants in four carriages without stopping, unable to see through the ice-encrusted windows of his carriage, in which he slept at night. He arrived at Basle on 10 January 1814 and immediately established a satisfactory relationship with the suspicious Metternich. What he learned from Metternich was that peace was by no means as imminent as London believed.[2]

A peace conference had already been decided for Châtillon, where Napoleon's new Foreign Minister, Armand de Caulaincourt, the Duc de Vicenza, had arrived on 21 January.

On 1 February the Prussian General Blücher and the Austrian commander in chief, Prince Schwarzenberg, defeated Napoleon at La Rothière. With the allies on the road to Paris, the belief was that this finally was the end. The Châtillon conference opened on 5 February, to attempt agreement on the Europe that should emerge with peace. But yet another twist of fortune followed. After two French victories, Montmirail, 11 February, and Montereau, 18 February, the conference was suspended and, on 22 February, the allies began a retreat, the earlier confidence shattered. The tsar, it was said, had gone to pieces, while Frederick Wilhelm 'talks like Cassandra'.

Schwarzenberg advised Alexander and Frederick Wilhelm to request an armistice. Castlereagh then persuaded Metternich to make a stand against that. To give way so easily was without dignity and would simply reinforce Napoleon's conviction of power. Castlereagh was imposing the British intrusion that the others resented. What was holding the coalition together, he believed, was simply 'the consciousness that without Great Britain the peace cannot be made'.

Castlereagh's determination was quickly justified. On 9 March Napoleon was defeated by Blücher at Laon. On 12 March Wellington entered Bordeaux. Paris capitulated on 31 March, when the Czar, accompanied by the King of Prussia and Austria's Prince Schwarzenburg, rode into the city. Napoleon abdicated on 11 April. The following day Caulaincourt took to Napoleon at Fontainebleau the terms of abdication agreed by the coalition, known as the Treaty of Fontainebleau. By it, Napoleon renounced all rights of sovereignty for himself and his successors, but he and Empress Marie Louise would retain their rank and title in their lifetime. He would retire to the island of Elba, over which he would have sovereign authority. He would receive an annual pension of two million francs from the French Treasury. On reading it, Napoleon said, 'Life has become unbearable for me. I have lived too long.' That night he made an unsuccessful attempt to commit suicide.

On 16 April he began his journey to Fréjus in a convoy of fourteen carriages. HMS *Undaunted*, Captain Usher, awaited him at Fréjus, where he arrived by moonlight on 28 April. Fréjus was where Napoleon had landed on his return from Egypt. The Austrian cavalry which had escorted him formed a square at the embarkation point, where one of *Undaunted*'s boats awaited him, three British marines on each side of it.

Captain Usher was present and introduced himself. Napoleon responded to him with full affability. To complete the courtesy Napoleon asked for the boat's officer to be presented to him. The boat was commanded by Lieutenant George Sidney Smith. On hearing the name so bitterly associated with his defeat at Acre and the end of his Oriental vision Napoleon repeated it and remained silent the whole way off to the ship.

LXVI

SNOW MARCH

As so often was to happen in this war, British sailors in Canada found themselves involved in an operation remote from the decks they trod, of a character previously unimaginable within the tight confines of shipboard existence.

So it was for Lieutenant Henry Kent, two other officers and two hundred sailors sent to augment Captain Yeo's forces at Kingston in Upper Canada. This was the naval reinforcement that Yeo had been pleading for. But they arrived at Saint John, New Brunswick, at the end of January 1814, in the depth of the northern winter when the St Lawrence was closed to navigation.

To reach Kingston on Lake Ontario for the opening of the navigation season on the lakes the sailors therefore confronted a forced march of some nine hundred miles across the frozen landscape of some of the roughest country in eastern Canada. It was the longest march that sailors were called upon to make in that war, perhaps any war. Lieutenant Kent left a fine account of it in a letter to his father written from Kingston.[1]

As they disembarked on 29 January the rigging of theirs and all the other ships in Saint John was manned with crews cheering them, in apparent clear understanding of the resolution required for the ordeal that lay ahead. They first set off on sleighs that took them to the capital, Fredericton, which they reached the next day. The seamen were then divided into two divisions, one under the senior officer, Captain Collier, and the other under Kent. 'The country after leaving Fredericton, is but thinly inhabited; a settlement you may see occasionally, but never more than three houses together.' On the third day one of the sailors died of the intense cold. On the 7th they reached a barrack at Presqu'île, where they left the sleighs and

began making preparations for our march, each of us being furnished with a pair of snowshoes, two pairs of moccasins, a toboggan between every four men, a camp kettle to every twelve, with axes and tinder-box. As you may not know the use of those articles by their Indian names, I will endeavour to describe them: Snow shoes are of a singular shape, something like a pear, formed by a hoop, and the bottom of them netted across with the hide of some animal; they are fixed on a strap around the heel, and tied across the instep, as you do a pair of skates; they are about two feet in length, and one in breadth. Moccasins are made of buffalo hide, sole and tops in one, roughly sewed up with twine, a stripe of hide run through notches, cut round the quarters, to haul it tight on your foot. Toboggans are hand sleighs, about four feet in length, and one in breadth, made of such light wood that they do not weigh above four pounds. On these you lash your provisions and clothes, and with the bight of a rope over your shoulder, drag it with great ease on the snow.

Thus equipped for the totally unfamiliar they set off, marching fifteen to twenty-two miles daily, 'with snow up to our knees as much as any man could do'. It was apparently a fixed route, with small huts between occasional French settlements. They slept in the huts when they found them. Otherwise they slept in the open, in the woods. The march from the French settlement of Grande Rivière to another, Madawaska, 'was beyond anything you can conceive; it blew a gale of wind from the northward, and the drift of snow was so great, it was almost impossible to discern a man a hundred yards distant; before I got halfway, the men lay down, saying they could not possibly go further; I endeavoured by every persuasion to cheer them, and succeeded in getting about one half to accompany me. We reached it about nine o'clock at night, almost fainting . . . The following morning, having sent all the midshipmen in search of the men, got them all collected, but out of 110, only 10 able to proceed on our march, leaving a midshipman and 12 men behind sick, chiefly frost bitten.' And so it progressed, across part of American territory, hauling their sick, 'continually marching up and down hill, and the snow upwards of five feet deep', past Quebec, constantly stopping to collect those who fell behind. Marching through Montreal on 12 March, six weeks into their journey, 'passing the monument erected to the memory of the immortal Lord Nelson, halted, and gave three cheers, which much pleased the inhabitants'. From there the going was easier, less of the trackless wilderness, here few settlements but many scattered houses and then, skirting the many rapids of the St Lawrence, they arrived at Kingston on 22 March, with all the officers and seamen there brought out to cheer them in.

The lakeland navigation season had not yet begun, nor any of the naval hostilities that had brought them there, but as they snow-shoe marched across New Brunswick and upper Maine peace had arrived in Europe. Thus, for the sailors who had just arrived at Kingston, and for those who cheered them in, there was already a strong sense of approaching climax to this war, for the very arrival of these sailors as well as increased Royal

Navy presence on the American coast declared that the British attention to
the war in North America would shortly be a different thing.

The naval reinforcement arrived to find heavy preparation underway for
the next round of the naval contest for command of Lake Ontario. The
British and the Americans alike had indulged in more shipbuilding. Yeo
had two ships ready for launching, the 58-gun *Prince Regent* and the 40-gun
Princess Charlotte. Kent was immediately assigned as first lieutenant of the
Princess Charlotte. Under construction was a mammoth 102-gun vessel,
more formidable than most ships of the oceanic navy. Yeo had laid her
down without authority from home. Across the water at Sackett's Harbour
Chauncey had launched his own prize vessel, the 62-gun *Superior*. He had
another smaller ship under construction.

Both sides were building big for the battle that was expected to settle
decisively the naval command of lakeland. Yeo's two new 58-gun and 40-gun
ships were launched on 14 April and afloat ready for action eleven days later.
With those ships Yeo had immediate ascendancy over Chauncey, who was
anxiously awaiting the long guns for *Superior*. Chauncey had his two big ships
of the previous season as well as two armed brigs. He was therefore perfectly
capable of meeting a challenge from Yeo. The guns he was waiting for could
only reach Sackett's Harbour by water from Oswego. Chauncey, conscious of
Oswego's vulnerability, took the precaution of assembling most of his guns at a
point twelve miles inland. It was wise, for on 5 May Yeo raided Oswego. The
British took possession of the only nine guns that Chauncey had there. The
guns were then brought to the shore from their depot in the woods. Nineteen
bateaux were loaded with twenty-one long guns and thirteen lighter pieces
and with one hundred and fifty army riflemen on board skirted the coast and,
despite a British attempt to intercept them, got safely to Sackett's Harbour.
Had Yeo succeeded in preventing their entry into Sackett's, which he had
been blockading, his command of Lake Ontario would have been virtually
unchallengeable. Yeo had retained free movement throughout the lake until
Chauncey had armed *Superior*. But even with a stronger force Yeo, as in the
previous season, was still unprepared to risk engagement with Chauncey. 'The
enemy,' he wrote, 'are not in sufficient force to undertake any expedition in the
face of our present squadron, but any disaster on our side might give them a
serious ascendancy.' Chauncey for his part declared, 'I shall sail the first week
in July to offer the enemy battle.' But it was not until 1 August that he sailed
out of Sackett's Harbour. He then in his turn blockaded Kingston, where Yeo
awaited completion of his 102-gun ship, *St Lawrence*.[2]

For all this potential power afloat, it was to be another season of their
strange continuing inertia on the water. Yet never had dependence on the
water passage been greater. The winter on the lakes had been unusually
mild. That had prevented transport during the winter of military supplies

across the ice or on the usual hard snow surface of the roads, which instead were deeply soggy, with movement over them impossible.

The 1814 campaign in lakeland nevertheless was to be essentially land, with nothing decisive on water other than supply and communication, and that too often lagging on both sides. Once more the American government saw the northwest as its primary objective, principally to be recovery of Niagara, assigned to General Jacob Jennings Brown, whose opponent in Upper Canada was the military governor there, General Sir Gordon Drummond. Brown crossed the Niagara Strait on 2 July with a force of some three thousand. In that month on that unique peninsula the two most distinctive battles of the American War (of 1812) were fought, before the final one at New Orleans at the end of the year. The first of these was above and the other below the Niagara Falls.

On 5 July the Americans confronted a British force of eleven hundred regulars and three hundred Canadian militia and Indians, under Lieutenant General Riall, on open ground by the Chippawa River that flowed into the Niagara. The Americans moved with a regularity and discipline different from anything experienced so far. As Fortescue described, 'both sides now advanced, halting from time to time to pour volleys into each other'. The American fire was superior, with the British suffering so severely that they were compelled to retreat. The British casualties at just over five hundred killed and wounded were nearly double those of the Americans. On 25 July on the heights close to Queenstown, at a point called Lundy's Lane, Brown and Drummond went into action late in the afternoon and for three hours their forces fought savagely at close quarters, all order lost in the darkness with opposing companies becoming intermixed, 'and the fight was carried on with the bayonet, with the butt, with any weapon that came to hand'. This time the Americans withdrew. Brown and Drummond were both severely wounded. It was, Fortescue declared, 'the best contested fight of the whole war . . . honourable alike to Americans and British'.[3] Casualties of each numbered over eight hundred.

For Mahan, Brown's retirement on 26 July marked 'the definitive abandonment by the United States of the offensive on the Canadian frontier'. Practically the same could be said of the naval contest on Lake Ontario. Brown had counted on Chauncey for support but Chauncey had remained at Sackett's Harbour pleading that to quit it was to leave it exposed to attack by Yeo from Kingston opposite. Yeo similarly confined his efforts until his big new ship was launched. That was to be on 10 September but not for another month would she be said to be completely equipped. But for both that was already the end. Neither again set out against the other. Having obsessively built for naval warfare on the lakes by oceanic standards, they then let naval warfare on the upper lakes effectively die with the closing of the season, for there would not be another season of it.

LXVII

PATUXENT

A burningly acrimonious view of the Americans had come alive with the British political and military hierarchy, though not necessarily with the lower orders, who continued to desert in numbers, the soldiers now that they had opportunity on American soil as much as the sailors when anywhere given the chance.

The venom directed against the Americans by those disposed to it could express itself brutally when opportunity offered. This was something broadly distinct from the way things usually were in war with the French, where outright hatred of them (such as Nelson's) or a general contempt were rare. The burning of Newark and other Canadian villages had helped to unleash this despising of the Americans. But it went far deeper.

There was to this fierce view of the Americans naturally something of the unforgiving quality of a bitter, vengeful and never healing family quarrel. Naval and military leaders on both sides were, after all, too often men who had opposed one another in the War of Independence. The Americans in making their second challenge to Britain were doing so as the nation that the British had not yet fully recognized. For those who still regarded them as colonial rebels it reopened the wound, doubling the resentment that lingered.

A companion distinctive fact of the War of 1812 was its gift also to Canadians of their own clarified sense of a patriotic identity they probably had not consciously carried before. When the Americans went in at the northwest they had fully expected the Canadians of Upper Canada to fall in with the idea of being incorporated within the United States. The contrary soon became apparent. On the Niagara Peninsula and south of Montreal the Canadians, conspicuously on their own, several times drove back American assault. A notable fact, according to General James Carmichael-Smyth in his *Précis of the Wars in Canada* was that, though British regulars among them frequently deserted to the Americans, not a single Canadian militiaman did.[1]

The American navy's startling early successes had provoked a spreading alarm of the United States as a potential power in the Western world. It was with the Royal Navy especially that resentment lurked deep. And never more succinctly expressed than by the new naval commander of the Atlantic and American Gulf coast station, Vice Admiral Sir Alexander Cochrane, who thus described his intentions towards the Americans: 'I have it much at heart to give them a complete drubbing before peace is made, when I trust their northern limits will be circumscribed and the command of the Mississippi wrested from them.'[2]

Cochrane's words expressed the underlying sense emanating from the British political and military establishment of this being a war both to undermine the United States as a power and redefine its frontiers where possible. Wresting New Orleans from it for use as a future naval base, as Cochrane indicated, was one objective with many. Another was for the Great Lakes to be drawn within the Canadian frontier, with the Americans retaining only right of commerce on them. A great slice of northern Maine was also considered, to keep Americans at a greater distance from the St Lawrence. The British were determined on the punitive, as was soon made clear to the American diplomatic mission sent to Ghent in June 1814 to negotiate peace with Britain. Secretary of the Treasury Albert Gallatin found that the British 'mean to inflict on America a chastisement which will teach her that war is not to be declared against Great Britain with impunity'.[3] That came indirectly from Castlereagh himself. The *Naval Chronicle* at this time, however, in the spirit of the peace just come to Europe and of peace talks with America being underway, gave clear warning on making too much of that: 'The great mass of the American population are deeply imbued with an anti-Britannic spirit. If we aim at the conquest of the United States, we may create an inextinguishable spirit of hatred and revenge. We may capture her cities, and lay waste her coasts; but in doing so, we shall waste and consume our armies, and too probably – wither the laurels gathered in Europe. Let us rather secure the respect of America, by our justice and moderation – and accept of her proffered amity, whenever we can do it on terms compatible with our honour and safety.'

Admiral Cochrane was to have none of that, however, as he made plain in his instructions to his naval commanders, who were urged to use measures of retaliation 'against the cities of the United States, from the Saint Croix River to the southern boundary near the St Mary's River . . . to destroy and lay waste such towns and cities upon the coast as may be found assailable . . . and you will spare merely the lives of the unarmed inhabitants of the United States'. As Mahan points out, on 26 July he quickly had the last phrase expunged, since it might be understood as something more drastic than he meant.

Cochrane knew that he had the full backing of the home government. The lemon was to be squeezed to the full. The new Secretary of War, Earl Bathurst, instructed the officer who would command troops sent to the American east coast from the Peninsula campaign: '. . . if in any descent you shall be enabled to take such position as to threaten the inhabitants with the destruction of their property, you are hereby authorized to levy upon them contributions in return for your forbearance'.[4]

Cochrane's policy of wanton destruction was nevertheless now applied with immediate spectacular impact. As a prime lesson, the destruction of Washington had been decided upon in London, partly in retaliation for the destruction of the Upper Canada capital, York, and Newark.

The great inflow of Chesapeake Bay beyond Capes Henry and Charles, with all its naval and commercial points from Norfolk on up to Baltimore and Washington on the Potomac had always been a natural target for Atlantic squadrons, particularly in 1813. The British had established a base on Tangier Island, the first of a cluster of islands lying across the mouth of the Potomac.

The American defence of that critical juncture had fallen to Commodore Barney, a renowned seaman who came in from successful privateering to take command of the only naval force on the bay that could offer some resistance. He established his flotilla of thirteen galleys and gunboats on the Patuxent River, a stream just above the Potomac. The Patuxent was navigable for forty miles to a point just fifteen miles below Washington. Large ships could not progress far into it, which made it a natural refuge for Barney since the British were now moving freely on the bay, with 74s lying off the Potomac.

On 15 August 3,400 troops who had embarked at Bordeaux straight from the campaign in the Peninsula arrived at Tangier Island, where four 74s and other ships of war under Cochrane had already assembled. The force was there brought up to over four thousand. Two days later, on August 20, the expedition, commanded by Major General Ross, began moving up the west bank of the Patuxent. Barney, trapped on that river, removed his crews and destroyed his ships as the British advanced.

A small British squadron, two frigates and five smaller ships, simultaneously passed up the Potomac against the main defence on the river, Fort Washington, which was abandoned. The squadron passed on to Alexandria, where it anchored.

Washington was practically defenceless. When the new gravity of the American situation precipitated by peace in Europe was realized, the American administration had hastily put out a summons for just over ninety-three thousand militiamen. Fifteen thousand were allocated to Brigadier General Winder who was assigned the defence of the capital. But when on 24 August Winder had to make a stand at Bladensburg, five miles from Washington, he had no more than five to six thousand. From Bladensburg a broad, straight road crossed a bridge and ran into Washington. Here the Americans put up a strong barricade. The British ran straight for the bridge. The head of their column was cut down by American riflemen. But the British then used the weapon that, since Walcheren, they had been employing whenever confronted by a difficulty, the rocket. The psychological impact was always effective, as it now again was at Bladensburg. Winder's line broke and the men began to run.

It remained to Commodore Barney to bring up his sailors and the guns they had carried away with them. They held up the British until, as Barney reported, 'not a vestige of the American army remained, except a body of five or six hundred, posted on a height on my right, from whom I expected much support from their fine situation'. But they, too, retired. Barney's ammunition was finished. The drivers of his ammunition wagons had joined the panic. Barney was severely wounded, his other officers either killed or wounded. His sailors stayed with him until he told them to go, he being unable to move. He was taken prisoner and when Ross and Admiral Cochrane appeared he was, he said, 'treated like a brother'. It was invariably like that on the battlefields or in the naval actions of the Great War: courage and intrepidity in the opponent were accorded due respect and ungrudging admiration, whatever the hostility beforehand.[5]

The British entered Washington at eight o'clock that night and lost no time in destroying every one of its principal structures. The Capitol, the White House and other public buildings, including the library, printing offices and national archives were put to the torch. So were all naval and military establishments. One of the outstanding British military figures of the nineteenth century, Harry Smith, a captain at Washington and who had come straight from the Peninsular War, was one of many who, in his words, entered Washington 'for the barbarous purposes of destroying the city'. He added that Admiral Cochrane would have burned the whole, but Ross would only consent to the burning of the public buildings. For himself Smith said, 'I had no objection to burn arsenals, dockyards, frigates building, stores, barracks, etc., but fresh from the Duke's [Wellington's] humane warfare in the south of France, we were horrified at the order to burn the elegant Houses of Parliament and the President's house.'[6]

Perhaps the most bizarre image of all was the banquet that Madison had laid on at the White House, presumably for the victors of a successful defence of the capital. Smith and other British officers who entered the White House found 'a dinner table spread, and covers laid for forty guests.

Several kinds of wine, in handsome cut-glass decanters, were cooling on the side-board; plate-holders stood by the fireplace, filled with dishes and plates; knives, forks, and spoons were arranged for immediate use . . . in the kitchen spits loaded with various joints turned before the fire.' The food was ready, and still warm. As Smith and the others sat down to dine at Madison's table the British sailors who had accompanied them set about burning the place. 'I shall never forget,' Smith said, 'the destructive majesty of the flames as the torches were applied to beds, curtains, etc. Our sailors were artists at the work.'

Ross withdrew his troops from Washington on the 25th and on the 29th they were back at the lower Patuxent, just nine days since they had begun their march towards Washington. The British then moved against Baltimore. Here the Maryland Militia put up a different show from that of the Virginia men. The British were beaten back. General Ross was one of the first to fall, having ridden to the front as soon as the firing began. Captain Peter Parker of the 38-gun *Menelaus* led a party of sailors and marines in the assault on the night of 30 August. Parker was killed. A touching episode involving one of his sailors was recorded. Twenty-four-year-old James Perring was severely wounded. He insisted that his companions go on and leave him. He crawled to a tree against which, in great agony, he propped himself, cutlass in one hand and pistol in the other. At daylight, after the British had retreated, the Americans returned to the field to collect the wounded. When they found him they called to Perring to surrender. He answered that no American would take him alive. They assured him that they only wanted to carry him to hospital. He still refused to allow them near him. He was told that if he continued to refuse to give up his arms they would have to fire on him. Perring shouted back, 'Fire away, and be damned! No Yankee shall ever take me alive; you will only shorten an hour's misery.' Admiring his bravery, the Americans left him to die quietly against his tree.[7]

The British wound up their landing parties on the Chesapeake after Baltimore, but to ensure that this punitive lesson from an affronted Britain be as broadly understood as possible the British navy continued landings and seizure or destruction of all the shipping encountered. The governor of Nova Scotia took possession of the fort at Machias and Penobscot Bay.

The territory from Penobscot to New Brunswick was declared British, and likely to remain so. To the peace talks at Ghent, however, Foreign Secretary Castlereagh declared, 'The views of the government are strictly defensive. Territory as such is by no means their object; but, as the weaker power in North America, Great Britain considers itself entitled to claim the use of the lakes as a military barrier.'[8]

The wisdom of that was about to be challenged. Britain had suffered one severe defeat on the inland waters. It was now about to experience another.

Lake Champlain had been regarded by the Americans as their military highway direct to Montreal, though they had spectacularly failed to use it as such. Obversely it offered itself as a natural descent into the United States. For those reasons naval control of the lake was sought by both. Champlain runs narrowly, eighteen miles at its broadest, for some eighty miles from just above the head of the Hudson to the entrance of the Richelieu River, which carries the waters of Champlain along its fifty-mile length into the St Lawrence. Since the lake fell wholly inside American territory the British had their base at Isle-aux-Noix on the Richelieu.

Strong British reinforcements had been arriving steadily at Montreal through July and August. Some sixteen thousand British soldiers were already assembled in Lower Canada. As stalemate settled upon Lake Ontario and the northwest, the governor-general of Canada, General Sir George Prevost, set his attention upon Lake Champlain and the wide opening it represented for any descent into the United States. He began preparations for taking Plattsburgh on the north-western shore of the lake before the season ended. To achieve that required elimination of American naval command on the lake. There appeared no sound reason to doubt a satisfactory outcome. The British had made successful harassing sorties upon the lake in 1813.

The Americans had naval superiority on the lake, under Captain Thomas Macdonough, but the British force, commanded by Captain Downie, had on 25 August launched a powerful new 27-gun ship, *Confiance*, to oppose Macdonough's 26-gun flagship *Saratoga*. Both sides had as well brigs, schooners, sloops and gunboats. The Americans also had galleys, making Champlain probably the last occasion in history when anything answering that description was used in naval combat.

On 3 September Prevost marched at the head of some eleven thousand men against the spare force of fifteen hundred regulars and seven hundred militia under Brigadier General Macomb that awaited them. Prevost continued down to Plattsburgh, which he entered on 6 September. Macomb retired across the Saranac River that divided the town. Macdonough's squadron lay off Plattsburgh, beyond range of the batteries that Prevost established. For Prevost, destruction of the squadron was essential. He had more than enough strength to overwhelm Macomb but the American general, in his retreat down to Plattsburgh, had demonstrated skill in using the forest through which his troops moved to create every manner of obstacle. The roads were poor, with soggy ground. Supply therefore would depend on the water. Provisions were already running short. Macomb had retired behind the established forts and works adjacent to Plattsburgh town and, with American militia flooding in to assist him, was strengthening his position. Prevost therefore urged Downie to move to action, but Downie, who had taken command only on 2 September, had found the new ship *Confiance*, upon which all depended, still needing much work.

Prevost intended to storm Macomb's position jointly, as Downie took on the American squadron. Under Prevost's intense pressure Downie felt compelled to sail from where he lay at the head of the lake. He did so at midnight on 10 September. Arriving off Plattsburgh at dawn on the 11th, he found, as a midshipman with Downie described it, 'the Yankee fleet lying off Plattsburgh, with springs on their cables, and all in line of battle, ready to receive us'. Given the variable winds on that confined water Macdonough intended to fight from anchor. Here, then, was a smaller version of the Battle of the Nile, so to speak. Macdonough put his strongest ships to northward, windward, allowing the best manoeuvrability on the cables. Downie formed his own plan as his ships approached in column, assigning the strongest to their equals, with Macdonough's flagship *Saratoga* as *Confiance*'s own opponent.

The fight started with an intensity that was maintained for the full three hours of the action. *Confiance*'s first broadside struck down forty of *Saratoga*'s crew. Downie was himself killed fifteen minutes after the action began. The whole of it was neatly condensed in a letter to his brother written from hospital by the aforementioned young midshipman:

At nine a.m. (just after breakfast) we beat to quarters; at half after nine made signals to our fleet to form the line of battle; at forty minutes after nine ran down alongside the Yankee commodore's ship, and came to anchor, when the action commenced by a vigorous cannonade of all the Yankee fleet on our ship, which we immediately returned: a little before ten o'clock the action was general, and kept up with the greatest spirit until twenty-five minutes after noon, when our spring and rudder were shot away, and all our masts, yards and sails were so shattered, that one looked like so many bunches of matches, and the other like a bundle of old rags . . . her hull like a riddle, for she was foundering very fast, we were necessitated, though with the greatest reluctance, to strike to the enemy. I received a wound from a grapeshot, which after striking my foot, passed through the palm of my left hand, my fingers are very much shattered. The havoc on both sides is dreadful, I don't think there are more than five of our men, out of three hundred, but what are killed or wounded. Never was a shower of hail so thick as the shot whistling about our ears; were you to see my jacket, waistcoat and trowsers, and hat, you would be astonished how I escaped as I did, for they are literally torn all to rags with shot, and splinters; the upper part of my hat was also shot away. There is one of our marines who was in the Trafalgar action with Lord Nelson, who says it was a mere flea-bite in comparison with this.[9]

Prevost retreated at once back to Canada. 'The battle of Lake Champlain,' said Mahan, 'more nearly than any other incident of the War of 1812 merits the epithet "decisive."' It effectively closed the war in Canada.

In the Pacific, off Valparaiso, another naval encounter was resolved, this time favouring Britain. It was, on the face of it, further example of the adventurism of American naval power in the war but it also came about as an action arising from the increased British anxiety over future American mercantile rivalry.

The 32-gun American frigate *Essex*, belonging to Commodore Bainbridge's squadron, had been successfully cruising and taking prizes off South America through 1812. In January 1813 her commander, Captain David Porter, decided to take her into the Pacific. The British, meanwhile, had assigned the 42-gun *Phoebe* to proceed to the north-west Pacific to destroy an American fur establishment on the Columbia River that had established a rich trade in furs to China.

Phoebe, accompanied by two sloops of war, *Cherub* and *Racoon*, sailed from Britain in March 1813 and arrived in the South Atlantic in June, when *Phoebe*'s commander, Captain James Hillyar, heard of *Essex*'s prize-taking. He set off in pursuit. *Essex*, meanwhile, had rounded Cape Horn, the first United States ship-of-war to show the Stars and Stripes on the Pacific. Porter, running short of provisions, sought British whalers, which he knew to be well stocked for their extensive voyages. After stopping at Valparaiso he continued to the Galapagos Islands, where he took twelve British whalers, one of which was converted into a companion raider named *Essex Junior*. At Galapagos Porter heard that a British squadron, *Phoebe* and her consorts, was on its way to the Pacific. Porter took *Essex* to the Marquesas, where she was refitted and provisioned. He then sailed for Valparaiso, which he reached on 3 February 1812. Just five days later, on the 8th, *Phoebe* and *Cherub* came in, *Racoon* having been delegated to continue north to destroy the American fur depot at the Columbia River.

After a refit and provisioning, the British ships took up position off Valparaiso Roads. Porter, believing himself outmatched in armament, remained at anchor awaiting opportunity to escape when circumstances allowed. On 28 March action was forced on him when a fierce squall parted *Essex* from one of her cables. The other cable had to be cut. Then another squall took away the main topmast. *Essex* sought to stay within the three-mile neutral waters but the two British ships had moved against her. In difficult wind conditions at four p.m. the British made a ten-minute attack before drawing off again.

The action was renewed shortly after five thirty. *Phoebe*, with long guns of greater range, inflicted heavy damage on *Essex*. The action was so fierce that one gun aboard *Essex* successively lost three of its crews, fifteen men altogether. *Phoebe*'s tactic was to edge away when fire from *Essex* got too warm. Then, out of range, her long guns played destructively on the American. In face of this, Porter decided to run ship ashore, allowing his men to escape. She was within musket shot of the beach when a shift of wind drew her back into the action, closing with *Phoebe*. Porter therefore sought to board. Unable to do so, the fight intensified and continued at its hottest for nearly another hour. When *Essex* caught fire Porter gave permission for anyone to swim ashore to escape the ship blowing up. Some of those who attempted it were picked up by *Phoebe*. The majority remained and the fires were controlled, but the losses were too severe to continue. At six twenty *Essex* lowered her colours.

Essex suffered fifty-eight killed, sixty-five wounded. *Essex Junior* was disarmed and the American sailors of both ships returned to the United States as paroled prisoners of war. *Phoebe*'s Captain Hillyar paid high tribute to *Essex* in his official report: 'The defence of the Essex, taking into consideration our superiority of force; the very discouraging circumstance of her having lost her main-top-mast, and being twice on fire, did honour to her brave defenders, and most fully evinced the courage of Captain Porter, and those under his command. Her colours were not struck until the loss in killed and wounded was so awfully great, her shattered condition so seriously bad, as to render further resistance unavailing.'[10]

An outstanding action closed a remarkable cruise during which *Essex*, apart from showing American colours in the Pacific, had captured 4,000 tons of shipping (some of which was recaptured) and played havoc on the British whale fishing in the southern seas. She had provisioned herself from her captures, and paid her crew from prize money.

LXVIII

NEW ORLEANS

BRITAIN's defeat on Lake Champlain, which ended the war in Canada, should have meant the end of the war altogether, but Britain's punitive intentions remained active and Admiral Cochrane's ambitions large.

Castlereagh wanted more leverage at the peace talks at Ghent. Before General Ross was killed at the Chesapeake, he and Cochrane had proposed a programme of intensive punitive assault against the United States that had full support of the cabinet. That ranged from occupation of Rhode Island and coastal points of Georgia and the Carolinas, ending with attack on New Orleans and Mobile. Canadian governor-general Prevost's retreat from Champlain had no affect upon Cochrane's determination to persist with the Mississippi operation. For that he retained the support of the government, although with the government there was already fear of renewed war in Europe, and Britain urgently wanted relief from the escalating costs of war. For both reasons reinforcement was therefore limited. For these remaining operations a new commander in chief, Sir Edward Pakenham, had been appointed, to replace Ross.

After Washington all discretion on how to proceed against New Orleans had been left to Cochrane and Ross and, encouraged by the success of Washington and Cochrane's other coastal operations, two thousand extra troops were marked for the Mississippi operations. Ross's death meant that decision and planning rested entirely with Cochrane, now commander in chief until Pakenham arrived. He had wanted to command in America before operations began, especially since he distrusted Cochrane, who controlled Ross but knew he would not have the same with Pakenham, who was late in arriving. Cochrane saw opportunity for the navy to retain immediate command and, believing that he knew the field of operations better than a new arrival could, went quickly ahead.

In preparation for the Mississippi venture Cochrane went to Jamaica, where he awaited the new arrivals allocated to him from the Peninsular War and collected two West Indian regiments composed of black West

Indians. His total force amounted to six thousand. The British government had defined its own objectives for the expedition: 'First, to obtain command of the embouchure of the Mississippi, so as to deprive the back settlements of America of their communication with the sea; and, secondly, to occupy some important and valuable possession, by the restoration of which the conditions of peace might be improved, or which we might be entitled to exact the cession of, as the price of peace.' New Orleans and Mobile fulfilled all of that.

A century later, the British military historian J.W. Fortescue was cynical about the motives of Alexander Cochrane and his fellow admirals in pressing for New Orleans. It was, he said, due chiefly to their desire for prize money. They saw the prospect of finding at New Orleans stores of cotton, sugar and tobacco worth millions, of which they would get handsome cut, apart from it replenishing the Treasury's ceaselessly draining coffers.[1]

Cochrane and his fleet and transports arrived off one of the islands in the Mississippi Sound, near the mouth of Lake Borgne, on 8 December 1814. As he still had not yet been joined by Pakenham, the operations that then unfolded were entirely devised and set in motion by Cochrane, with his new second, General Keane.

New Orleans did not present an easy and readily accessible target. Approaching New Orleans direct from the sea – up the delta of the lower Mississippi – was impracticable because of the forts on the river but above all because of the strong current that prevented adequate manoeuvre among the shallows, and because ships would have to be tied to trees if the wind failed them. There was also the risk of logs coming downstream and in that fast current striking the ships with sufficient impact to damage them dangerously.

The alternative was scarcely simpler. With Isle au Chat, Cat Island, as their base and anchorage, the British were to land at the entrance to one of the bayous, the marshy creeks that wove through the cypress swamps that composed the isthmus between Lake Borgne and Lake Pontchartrain. They were to go through that swampland to descend to the west bank of the Mississippi along which a road ran direct into New Orleans. There they would launch their assault.

Cochrane had been busy sending officers to the Mississippi Sound and had some knowledge of that coast. None of them now with Cochrane, however, had the least knowledge of the swampland that they were about to penetrate. The Spanish fishermen they had acquired as guides assured them that the disaffected French and Spanish inhabitants of New Orleans would rise up to welcome and aid them. Victory would be theirs.

The guides chose their own village at the entrance to Bayou des Pêcheurs as the landing point for the troops from Cat Island. That established the first grave underlying fault of the whole operation. From Cat Island, where the fleet lay, to Bayou des Pêcheurs was some sixty miles. From there to the west bank of the Mississippi was some ten miles more through the swamps. All of it was to be done in open boat by oar. Upon the British sailors therefore would descend the longest and hardest boating task ever to be endured. This expedition was to be entirely dependent upon sailors pulling at oars days on end, often with scarcely a break. Merely to get the soldiers from ship to landing point was a twelve-hour pull.

The dangers, and lack of foresight, with this expedition were further illustrated by the fact that the whole fleet had boats to move only one-third of the army at a time, each movement involving more than thirty hours.

The expedition had arrived with one month's provisions and military supplies for its force of 2,400 soldiers and the sailors of the fleet. The business of maintaining supply and reinforcement to wherever the force arrived on the Mississippi was clearly to be desperately slow and arduous. Transport between the fleet and the shore, and then through the swampland, was undertaken totally without apparent semblance to logistical reasoning. A swift conquest was taken for granted. So far in all previous coastal sorties the assailants had always been bountifully provided with all the luxuries so long denied them in other theatres. The same easy acquisition of hogs, poultry and other produce experienced at the Chesapeake was assumed for the wholly different landscape and climate of New Orleans.

The first experience of the madness of the distances the British imposed upon themselves came with having to deal with the five American gun ships that mounted guard on Lake Borgne. On 12 December a fleet of fifty ship's boats rowed by sailors and carrying marine riflemen began pulling against strong winds and currents towards the American ships, which were commanded by Lieutenant Jones. It took thirty-six hours for the British boats to approach within range of Jones's guns. After that ordeal they had to pull wildly to try to come alongside for boarding, with Jones's shot taking off heads in the boats while others collapsed upon their oars as grape shot rained down. Once they managed to get alongside a gun ship they had to cut away the defensive netting as American rifle fire and grenades fell upon them. Some boats, with most of those on board, sank beside the gun ships. For those who managed to clamber aboard, the sailors with swords and the marines with small arms, it was ferocious hand-to-hand combat. The first gunboat that was won by the British turned its guns on the others. The Americans fought staunchly but were finally forced to surrender.

The fight for Lake Borgne was another of those close naval combats that would fall from sight against the larger naval events of the Great War. For anyone returning to them, however, they evoke a more terrible intimacy than practically anything else: the unhesitant rush into close combat against severe odds, the unflinching endurance once locked into it, the terrible wounding suffered. Those were the qualities required for all hand-to-hand fighting approached through a curtain of fire. But the Royal Navy's constant demand for open-boat operations and the gruelling boarding involved meant that sailors saw a greater frequency of it than most. In this instance they had set off on the 12th but only at noon on the 14th did they come to action, throwing themselves into it after a day and a half without sleep in the open boats, where they had rested on the oars only long enough to eat their hard rations.

With Jones's force disposed of, the way was now clear for Cochrane and General Keane to bring their force ashore. Two naval officers with the guides had first reconnoitred by canoe the passage through the bayous to a point where they had to leave the canoe and pass on foot to the road running along the west bank of the Mississippi. They found themselves six miles below New Orleans. They saw no sign of preparation by the Americans. Cochrane had believed the Americans quite unaware of their arrival. This appeared to confirm it.

The Americans had in fact received intelligence of the British expedition from a trading vessel that came in from Jamaica, where the destination of the expedition was common knowledge. General Andrew Jackson accordingly had been sent to New Orleans, where he arrived on 2 December. He had brought down a large force of troops, who had been fighting the Creek Indians.

On 22 December General Keane took an advance force of sixteen hundred troops with two pieces of cannon into the cypress swamps for the advance to the Mississippi. Many sailors had been four to five days continually at oar to get the force ashore. The passage through the bayous had been more difficult than suggested by the two men who had done it by canoe. As one naval officer with the force later wrote, 'The place we landed in, the Americans say, was never before explored but by alligators and wild ducks; it was up a creek narrow and completely hid by canes . . . the upper part became so narrow that we were unable to pull our oars, but tracked the boats by the shore.' From the Bayou des Pêcheurs they passed to the Bayou Bienvenue and down through tributary creeks until those were too narrow for the boats. They were compelled to leave the boats some miles from the road they were making for.

By this time the sailors had been in the boats for eight days and nights, the soldiers for six. The weary sailors then turned the boats about and went back to fetch the rest of the force as Keane led his men marching in column of twos towards the Mississippi, through swamp, often halted by streams either too wide to be leaped or too deep to be forded. The reeds became woods and they finally emerged into orange groves and among farmhouses, whose inhabitants they took prisoner. The escape of one of these civilian prisoners meant the end of any secrecy the British thought they possessed. They reached the road leading into New Orleans, continuing for about a mile until they arrived at a small green plain about a mile wide. It was bounded on one side by the Mississippi and on the other by cypress swamp. On a rise stood a large house surrounded by twenty wooden huts, the slave quarters. Behind these stood a smaller house, which Keane appropriated as his headquarters. This, they were told, was the estate of one M. Villere. The abandonment of it suggested that word of their imminent arrival had preceded them.

Upon this small plain hemmed in by the river and cypress swamps, with a slow, tortuous course behind them in the event of a retreat, the British Army arrived at midday on 23 December, 'with their knapsacks on, their arms in their hands'. New Orleans lay before them, five and a half miles off. Rear Admiral Edward Codrington, now with this force, summed up their confident expectation. They were ready, he said, 'to impress on the New Orleans people the folly of resistance'.[2] Unfortunately, this small square of green plain was as far as they were to get in that effort.

Having been on the move for ten days, in two stages from ship to island, island to shore, then through the fevered isthmus, the soldiers surveyed their situation with weary relief. Between the road and the river a high, strong embankment had been thrown up to prevent inundation of the plain they occupied. The only object in sight on the river was a sloop, far downstream, assumed to be a merchantman.

Advance picquets were posted. A generous air of relaxation then prevailed. From the Villere house hams, fowls and wine were brought and divided up. Fires were lit and blazed up as the men began to cook. Happy, they stretched out by the fires or went to the river to bathe. As darkness settled, the fires blazed higher. At eight o'clock a loud splash was heard. Dimly recognized in the dark, the sloop seen downriver had come up and anchored. Her sails were being furled. She lay with her head to the current, broadside to the British bivouac. A loud voice was then distinctly heard, 'Now, damn their eyes, and give them this for the honour of America!' And broadside upon broadside from the ship's eighteen guns, together with grape shot, poured upon the encampment.

The soldiers scattered, seeking protection behind the house, among the trees, but mostly under the raised embankment of the river. There they lay for an hour until musket fire was heard from one of the advance picquets. Then the British found themselves surrounded.

Jackson had received report early that afternoon from his own posted militiamen that the British had arrived at the plantation outside New Orleans, Villere. He had immediately mustered fifteen hundred men. With

these he had advanced after dark upon the unsuspecting British encampment. What followed was another close combat with the distinctive feature
unique to the American War (of 1812), as at Lundy's Lane on the Niagara
Peninsula. The fighting was of a ferocity that held its own distinction. The
disorder that language brought, with opponents crying out in the same
language, meant that too often each side was attacking its own. In the tumult
of shouts and cries it was too difficult for each easily to recognize the accents
of the other. Sometimes in the dark two combatants had to pause to correctly
identify one another before getting back to the task of killing. Some British
and Americans were to be found lying tightly pinioned together in death,
their knives and bayonets in one another. The British fought with bayonets, the Americans with their long hunting knives. Cutting and slashing
with those, or striking with rifle butt, they laid upon one another with a
savagery that was particularly memorable. As one soldier recounted, 'No
man could tell what was going forward in any quarter, except where he
himself chanced immediately to stand; no one part of the line could bring
assistance to another, because, in truth, no line existed.'[3]

The fight had started at eight. It died away at three in the morning,
when the Americans withdrew. Seven hours of fighting of that intensity
had drained them all. Each side had lost close to one-third of its force in
killed and wounded. But for the British it was not yet over for, at daylight,
the sloop *Carolina*, her decks crowded with riflemen, opened up again.
The British again sought shelter under the Mississippi bank, where they
lay all day.

The description of the night's battlefield, given by an officer who went
in search of a friend, is one of the most terrible in the Great War, because
of the disfiguring wounds that came from the close combat and through
which 'the dead exhibited the most savage and ghastly expressions', instead
of the relative tranquillity that could lie upon men cleanly shot.[4]

General Keane was to come under strong criticism for having halted where
he did instead of pressing on to attack New Orleans directly. Whether the
British would have done any better had they immediately moved against New
Orleans is hard to say. But these were hard men straight from the Peninsular
War. And, as one of the officers was to write, 'The rapid movements of
Napoleon Bonaparte in these modern days were fresh upon the recollection
of every one – did *he* halt when the enemy were in view, or when winning
a victory did he cease to follow it up? But here the rapidity of a Bonaparte
or the decisive lines of a Caesar were both alike disregarded.' They had
arrived at midday and as yet Jackson had not thrown up any defences on
the riverside road. As that same officer observed, the houses there had not
been barricaded or loop-holed, 'nor were trees felled or abbatis formed by
the British in case of a reverse . . . it behoved the general more particularly

to form a stronghold either to give a greater disposable force for attack, to cover any hostile landing that might be made from the right bank of the Mississippi, or in like manner to cover a retreat if necessary'. He savagely concluded, 'This square mile was therefore ultimately digged into holes, and became the soldiers' burial place, without prayers, coffins or tombstones . . . the deplorable consequences of indecision at this remarkable spot of ground will figure in history . . .' To Andrew Jackson, however, he ultimately gave full marks, to which was attached further bitter reflection on the Peninsular War: 'General Jackson had shown himself a general of the first class both in attack and defence, since his first surprise. And although so far the Americans possessed the most consummate and able tactician, still the British general commanded the best troops . . . from discipline and brilliant deeds in the field their conduct could not be surpassed, the very elite of His Majesty's dominions.' As indeed they had to be, he declared, coming from years fighting across the rough Iberian landscape and successfully scaling the great walls of cities such as Ciudad Rodrigo and Badajoz.[5]

Keane could at the very least, it was felt, have attacked a vulnerable two-gun American battery halfway between the British position and New Orleans and then used those guns against *Carolina*, and eventually turned them on Jackson's militiamen. Instead the British lay inert all day through the 24th while Jackson began building his line a mile and a half away, and doing so with the very people whom the British had been told might regard them as liberators. As one officer commented, 'Instead of an easy conquest, we had already met with vigorous opposition; instead of finding the inhabitants ready and eager to join us, we found the houses deserted, the cattle and horses driven away, and every appearance of hostility.' And they were compelled to listen as 'the very fiddlers and the French horn-players from New Orleans struck up their notes within hearing of the British sentinels'. Understandably, by now the British had discarded their Spanish guides, in mistrust of everything they had been told by them.

Jackson added two more guns to the battery that, it was believed, had been within British ability to capture. His barricade, of sugar casks and bales of cotton, mounted solidly from the banks of the river, across the road, to the cypress swamps. Another ship, *Louisiana*, had joined *Carolina*, to anchor a mile upstream. All was in place to greet the balance of the British force when they arrived. Those were on their way through the swamps the night before, when they heard the noise of the battle. The sailors had redoubled their efforts, pulling the overloaded boats to get the soldiers to where the water passage ended and from where the men had to begin their march to the road. The soldiers began arriving at the owner Villere's plantation after dark on the 24th. That night Keane got all his men into the huts of the slaves, allowing more distance from *Carolina*'s guns. The next day, Christmas, Pakenham himself arrived accompanied by his second-in-command, General Gibbs.

Pakenham, who so far had been quite unable to exercise any decision within his command, having had no say in the deployment he now witnessed, was aghast by the situation into which Cochrane and Keane had landed his army. Though commander in chief, his entire role with this expedition so far had been nominal. It was created as a naval operation, and such it essentially remained, wholly dependent upon the navy and its sailors, with the distant fleet as its base and only supply point. The ones who had planned it were all there before him, his headquarters staff so to speak, Admirals Cochrane, Malcolm, Codrington, Hardy, Troubridge and Gordon. Navy and army had faced off at Corsica, but never with the vehemence that was to be recorded here, with poor Keane somewhere in the middle of it all.

Pakenham gave full vent to his rage before all, with the soldiers as his approving audience. The force of it was memorable for its very public nature, and for language of a sort never before heard from someone of his rank before the men. He had, said one of the memorialists of the occasion, 'arrived to see his troops brought into a situation from which all his abilities could scarcely expect to extricate them'. It was what the troops themselves had come to believe. They had been 'murmuring' their dissatisfaction. They greeted his outburst 'with a hearty cheer'.[6]

Pakenham's dismay was justifiable from every viewpoint. The British in their small redoubt were in an impossible situation. Before them was Jackson's steadily fortifying barricade. The Americans were bringing forward guns from the gunboat flotilla lying at New Orleans. Their artillery power had increased prodigiously. They now had cannon on the opposite bank as well. On the river the Americans had their two naval vessels. Encircling the redoubt were the cypress swamps. The source of the British supplies, whether provisions or ammunition or whatever, was some eighty or more miles away with the fleet off Cat Island. Whatever was now needed had to cover that distance by open rowboat. The track from the landing place where the water route through the swamps ended was four miles from the camp. It was so bad after the frequent rains that anything landed from the boats had to be carried to the camp on the backs of sailors. There was no source of local supply. They had cleaned out all that the Villere plantation had had to offer.

Pakenham's first move was to take the guns he had brought by boat down to the banks of the Mississippi as soon as it was dark. Working parties created a battery. At dawn a heavy cannonade was directed at *Carolina*. The sloop caught fire. The crew abandoned her and she blew up. It was a small recompense for what had been endured during the past forty-eight hours. The other ship was immediately moved further upstream.

Destruction of *Carolina* meant that the British could at last move about more freely and form up within their redoubt. Pakenham next tried an advance against the American line. Jackson's fire combined with fire from *Louisiana* fell upon the British, who were called back. As one British officer angrily commented, 'This reconnaissance, as the phrase went, cost the British well nigh fifty men, principally by grape and cannon shot, without accomplishing any good, and causing a bad *morale* to creep into the ranks.' Pakenham made another effort on New Year's Day 1815, and the British were again forced back, even compelled to abandon the artillery they had taken forward against the American line.

The situation was getting rapidly worse. Jackson had increased his artillery prodigiously. He had also established two batteries on the opposite bank of the Mississippi, their fire directed upon the British batteries. Jackson's harassment of the British was maintained without let-up. His artillery fire was ceaseless, day and night. Sharpshooters harassed the British picquets, producing a cry of unfairness in war, since it had become accepted on the Peninsula that opposing sides gave one another their rest once battle was called off, with no creeping up on picquets. So at least one of these Peninsula officers claimed.

What the British now had to face was that if they directly stormed the American line they exposed themselves to sweeping destruction from shot and grape. It was the only course open to them, however, for the circumstances of river and cypress swamp allowed them no flanking movement. They had no ostensible means of getting across the river to tackle the American batteries on the west bank. But it then fell to the instigator of the whole enterprise to come up with the next effort to retrieve something from the seemingly hopeless situation in which they found themselves. Cochrane proposed a way of getting them across to the west bank of the Mississippi.

A narrow irrigation canal ran across the Villere plantation from the bayou where troops and supplies had been landing. Cochrane suggested widening and deepening the canal and taking it up to the Mississippi embankment, which would be pierced sufficiently to allow the boats to be brought up and launched on to the river. That would enable a force to cross to seize the American batteries on the west bank and turn the guns there on the American line opposite, which would simultaneously be attacked by the full force of the British.

Lacking alternatives, the idea was accepted. The British force now totalled some eight thousand soldiers, sailors and marines. It was divided into work parties to work day and night without interruption, supervised by naval officers. Pakenham's distrust of Cochrane transferred to this project. He predicted misfortune. Nevertheless, he planned the operation that would accompany its completion. The need for action had become imperative for desertions were mounting steadily, depleting the force and bearing away intelligence.

Pakenham set 8 January for mounting a full assault on the American positions. That became the day that the fate of New Orleans, or of the British siege, would be decided.

The work on the canal was completed on the 6th. The same day a reinforcement of sixteen hundred under Major General Lambert reached the camp. Fourteen hundred men under Colonel Thornton were to embark in armed naval boats before midnight on the 7th to cross to the west bank. But, as Pakenham had feared, there was trouble with the canal so hastily broadened and deepened. The boats got stuck and the sailors had to drag them to the camp, where they only appeared after one in the morning, but then only enough of them to carry four hundred men across. Thornton nevertheless embarked that number of soldiers, sailors and marines and crossed the Mississippi, eight hours late and with only a third of the intended force. Pakenham's plan was for a rocket signal to be fired before dawn, to launch Thornton's attack and his own simultaneous assault by three columns on Jackson's line, with one detachment carrying sixteen ladders made from sugar cane to enable the British to scale Jackson's barricade. But with the delay to Colonel Thornton's crossing, the diminution of his force and dawn near to breaking, Pakenham had doubts about firing his rocket signal and launching the whole operation. He called in his assistant adjutant-general, Harry Smith, and said, 'Thornton's people will be of no use whatever to the general attack.'

Smith replied, 'There is still time before daylight to retire the columns now.'

'It will cost more men but the assault must be made.' Smith again urged a pull back.

While they were talking the first streaks of daylight began to appear. Smith repeated his plea to hold off. Pakenham replied, 'It is now too late; the columns would be visible to the enemy before they could move out of the fire, and would lose more men than they will in the attack. Fire the rocket!'

As the light increased and they became visible, the British were brought down in hundreds while they stood waiting for orders. Upon all the sides that they advanced after the rocket went up the British were mown down. The havoc brought such confusion that, at one point, some soldiers had to throw themselves to the ground to avoid being shot in the back by their own side. The chaos was appalling. Three companies managed to overcome the advance redoubt of the Americans but two out of every three had fallen before they captured it. They had taken four guns and waited for the intended support to come up but those had been driven back with heavy loss and the men in the redoubt were themselves then compelled to retreat. The assault on the American barricade was heavily paid for. Some soldiers nevertheless reached the barricade. The ladders were lost in the mix of rout on the one hand and determination on the other to push forward. To scale the parapet without ladders was impossible. Some tried by mounting on the shoulders of one another and even got to the top, but most of those were killed or taken prisoner. Pakenham, riding to and fro to control disorder, was wounded at the same time that he lost his horse. Mounting another, he was scarcely in the saddle when he was shot dead. His second, General Gibbs, was then struck down, fatally wounded. Keane was also seriously wounded. A demoralized army gradually retreated back to its camp. But for five hours thereafter, from that fatal dawn to the middle of the day, the Americans plied the British lines with round shot and grape. 'During the tedious hours we remained in front,' one officer recorded, 'it was necessary to lie on the ground, to cover ourselves from the projectiles.'

In face of such defeat, there was, however, surprising success, where it had been least expected. Colonel Thornton, with only one-third of his intended force, had captured Jackson's two west bank batteries, one of them taken by sailors. The Americans had fled from both when attacked. With those guns Thornton was in a position to severely harass Jackson's main defence line where the main battle was raging. Thornton's men were racing forward already two miles beyond the captured batteries when word reached them of the failure on the other side, and with an order to return.

The deaths of Pakenham and Gibbs and the wounding of Keane had left the new arrival, General Lambert, in command. At midday he asked for and obtained a twenty-four-hour truce. But for the British it was the end, and the Americans knew it. The British had lost nearly two thousand killed, wounded or missing, one-third of their entire force. Three generals, seven colonels and seventy-five officers were among the fallen. The Americans were said to have lost no more than fourteen killed and wounded.

In his brittle description of the end Harry Smith said, 'The Admirals came to the outlying picquet-house with faces as long as a flying jib: a sort of council of war was held.' Smith had passed among the troops to see how they stood. He found that 'Those who had received such an awful beating and so destroyed were far from desirous to storm again.' When Codrington said, 'The troops must attack, or the whole will be starved', Smith replied, 'Kill plenty more, Admiral; fewer rations will be required.' To General Lambert he said, 'General, the army are in no state to renew the attack.' Even if such a 'desperate event' had success, which was unlikely as things stood, they would not even have the troops to occupy New Orleans, he declared. Lambert agreed.[7]

Cochrane had brought the fleet to Mississippi Sound with supplies for only a month, so convinced had he been of a swift conquest. Those were diminishing steadily but in their camp at the Villere plantation outside New Orleans they were all still entirely dependent on what had to be brought from the fleet. Communication between fleet and the camp at New Orleans, already one of the outstanding acts of endurance by British sailors in the Great War, became even heavier after the final battle. One of the military officers paid tribute to that in his record of the expedition: '. . . for owing to adverse winds and the necessity of carrying the wounded down to the shipping by Lake Borgne, a distance of sixty miles, and bringing up in return provisions, the sailors were quite exhausted. They had been exposed for more than a month in the depth of winter to all kinds of weather, sweating on the oars by day, or perishing with cold in the open boats by night. The consequence was that consumption was beyond the produce; on some days we did not taste food, and when we did, it was served out in such small quantities as only to tantalize our voracious appetites . . .'

All of that meant that for the British a major new problem had presented itself, that of the manner of retreat. Extricating themselves from what Cochrane had got them into was suddenly a far greater problem than the original penetration of the cypress swamps had been. Even once all the wounded had been got away, they had not enough boats to take more than half the army at a time. If separated in that manner, both parties could be destroyed. If the Americans became aware of the exodus, and it was hard to suppose that they would not be for negro slaves had begun to wander back to their old quarters, the half that embarked could be intercepted or waylaid in the swamps. Or those left behind might be obliged to cope with the entire American force. The possibility was of at least one division, and perhaps even both, being lost. The solution was that the soldiers had to move out together. The only way it could be accomplished was for the army, in a body, to walk through the alligator-infested swampland all the way back to Lake Borgne. This was something that even those few locals who sometimes canoed through the swamps could not have imagined.

As no road existed, or could exist, an attempt began to make one. As there was no firm footing for miles all that could be done was to bind together large quantities of reeds, which were laid across the quagmire. Large branches were taken into the swamps from the woods and used to form bridges across creeks. This rudimentary passage was completed in nine days. During that time the Americans maintained continual fire on the small level, exposed camp of the British. 'We never closed our eyes in peace, for we were sure to be awakened before many minutes elapsed, by the splash of round-shot or shell in the mud beside us,' one of the officers was to write. At the outposts there was constant skirmishing. The Americans were endlessly increasing their strength on both banks of the river and fired from both sides. Simultaneously, they renewed their attempts to win deserters, and were daily successful.

Finally, on the night of the 18th, the retreat began. 'Trimming the fires, and arranging all things in the same order as if no change were to take place, regiment after regiment stole away, as soon as darkness concealed their motions, leaving the picquets to follow as rear guard, but with strict instructions not to retire till day-light began to appear.'

Like so many things on this fateful operation, the journey through the swamps on the path of reeds was a march like no other:

. . . resting upon a foundation so infirm, the treading of the first corps unavoidably beat it to pieces; those which followed were therefore compelled to flounder on in the best way they could . . . not only were the reeds torn asunder and sunk by the pressure of those who had gone before . . . the consequence was that every step sunk us to the knees, and frequently higher . . . as the night was dark, there being no moon, it was difficult to select our steps, or even to follow those who called to us that they were safe on the opposite side. At one of these places I myself beheld an unfortunate wretch gradually sink until he totally disappeared. I saw him floundering, heard his cry for help, and ran forward with the intention of saving him, but I myself sunk at once as high as the breast . . . I was forced to beg assistance for myself; when a leathern canteen strap being thrown to me, I laid hold of it, and was dragged out just as my fellow sufferer became invisible.

At dawn they reached the shore of Lake Borgne. Some of them were to lie there for a month, without shelter, 'the only provision some crumbs of biscuit and an allowance of rum', awaiting their turn in the boats, until eventually the ceaselessly labouring sailors got them all back aboard the ships. 'We, who only seven weeks ago had set out in the surest confidence of glory, and of emolument, were brought back dispirited and dejected. Our ranks were woefully thinned, our chiefs slain, our clothing tattered and filthy . . . A gloomy silence reigned throughout the armament, except when it was broken by the voice of lamentation over fallen friends; and the interior of each ship presented a scene well calculated to prove the short-sightedness of human hope, and human prudence.'

Once the whole force had been embarked the fleet sailed for what had been designated its other objective, Mobile. A leisurely siege was laid upon the fort at Mobile and on 12 February 1815 the American garrison marched out and laid down its arms. Two days later, on the 14th, news of the peace arrived from England.

The fleet anchored off while the troops laid out camp on a small sandy island alive with snakes and alligators. Snakes would be found in their beds, alligators entered the tents. In this desolate place and this altered state of alarm and agitation they had to remain until advised of promulgation of the peace by the American President. That finally arrived on 15 March and they sailed for home, a savagely embittered and disillusioned body of men. As one of their officers put it, in summary of the whole American War (of 1812), most of which he had experienced, there had been little in any of it 'to flatter our vanity, or increase our self-importance . . . Except a few successes in Canada, at its very commencement . . . it will be found that our arms have been constantly baffled or repulsed on shore.'[8]

J.W. Fortescue was more savage in his summary, with high praise for the sailors and damnation for their chief admiral: 'So ended this ill-fated expedition, of which it may be said that it provides perhaps the most striking warning . . . against conducting operations ashore upon the sole advice of naval officers. The whole project was based on the expectation of prize-money only . . . The man who should have been tried by court-martial and shot was Sir Alexander Cochrane. The callous manner in which he deliberately placed the troops in a dangerous situation, and then worked his faithful blue-jackets to death to keep them there – all with the principal object of filling his own pockets – cannot be too strongly condemned . . .'

A different side to military bitterness at New Orleans was expressed by one of the other military officers there: 'New Orleans was a military prize of the first class; had it been taken possession of at the onset, the world would have only talked or written of it as a dashing marine enterprise, and the British general would have obtained little credit for its capture . . .' The implication was that the British Army instead had to bear the ignominy of the defeat, one of the most crushing in its history. Fortescue, still at it, provided the final verdict: 'There is no nobler service than the Royal Navy; but there are two sentences which should be writ large on the inner walls of the Admiralty and of the Cabinet's meeting-place: Never employ the fleet alone for operations which require the combined forces of Army and Navy. Never use those combined forces upon the sole advice either of a naval or of a military officer.'[9]

Fortescue, in his bile, omitted to lay any blame against War Minister Liverpool, Castlereagh and the rest of the cabinet who had given their eager support to the New Orleans operation in the belief that at the peace talks possession of it would strengthen their territorial demands in the Gulf and at the Great Lakes. But Prevost's defeat at Lake Champlain had already undermined much of the British bargaining strength. Wellington finished it off when, refusing the offer of command in America, he said the existing military situation gave England no ground for demanding territory. Only naval superiority on the lakes could give force to such demands and that had been lost. If he went to America it would only be to sign a peace treaty, 'which might as well be signed now'.

There were to be many arguments over what the army itself might have done to ensure a victory, or at least something better than the way it turned out, what Keane or Pakenham could have done or should have done. And, as one of the officers indicated, the army no less than the navy expected rewarding prize at the end had New Orleans been taken. But what point to all of that with such an ending? For there it was, the war anyway already over by the time they all stumbled out of the cypress swamps! Peace had been concluded at Ghent on Christmas Eve, the day before Pakenham's arrival before New Orleans. The battle had been without value, the terrible loss of life and suffering in vain. Victory for the British at New Orleans would have brought nothing except prompt evacuation, since Ghent stipulated restoration of all occupied territory. New Orleans, like the invasion of Canada, had been for nought.

The Ghent Treaty had arrived at New York on 11 February. It was ratified by Madison on the 17th. What was gained by it all? Of the negative there was plenty. Britain gave nothing on impressment or neutral rights. It would be another forty years before the world saw any international agreement on that. But the United States had a new stature, within and without. Albert Gallatin expressed the within: 'The war has renewed and reinstated the national feelings and character which the Revolution had given, and which were daily lessening. The people have now more general objects of attachment, with which their pride and political opinions are connected. They are more Americans; they feel and act more as a nation; and I hope that the permanency of the Union is thereby better secured.'[10] What Gallatin said for the Americans could be said for the Canadians as well. For Americans they had seemed as amorphous neighbours whose land had appeared up for easy grabs. The Canadians had fought resolutely in their resistance to that assumption, and in doing so had declared their own distinct character, thereby gaining a patriotic sense of self upon which their own immediate future was now to be built.

As with the land, there was yet to be more action on the ocean before news of the peace was widely known.

For the Americans, resounding victory at New Orleans was clouded by loss of one of their finest frigates, *President*, Commodore Stephen Decatur. *President* had been blockaded in New York, waiting opportunity to get out to sea. Decatur saw opportunity with a powerful gale on the night of 14 January 1815. The pilots had marked the channel out from Staten Island but through some error in that operation *President* grounded on the bar, where she was stuck for an hour and a half, beating on the bottom. She was extensively damaged and Decatur wanted to return to port but the raging northwester was against him.

Decatur shaped his course for fifty miles along Long Island and then headed into the Atlantic. At five a.m. he was sighted by the British blockading squadron of three frigates, the 40-gun *Endymion* and two 38-guns, *Pomone* and *Tenedos*. *President* from her grounding had lost speed and manoeuvrability, but she held her lead in the chase until five p.m. on the 15th, when *Endymion* caught up with her. They exchanged broadsides for two and a half hours, until eight thirty p.m., when *Endymion* fell back. At eleven p.m. *Pomone* and *Tenedos* caught up with *President*. *Pomone* fired two broadsides. *President* then struck her colours.

On both sides it became a controversial battle. All subsequent accounts gave the victory to *Endymion* although she was not in sight when *President* struck. 'It appears that some differences have taken place between the British frigates engaged, as to the honour of having captured the President,' the *Naval Chronicle* commented. Later the publication declared, 'Much has been said relative to this engagement, but a perusal of Endymion's logbook must convince most men that the victory decided belonged to that ship.' This ostensibly was on the basis that the *President* suffered crippling damage in the two-and-a-half-hour fight with *Endymion*. One British report from Bermuda said that when *Pomone*'s boats boarded *President*, Decatur had insisted that his sword be sent to the captain of *Endymion*. This was subsequently denied.''

President's precipitate submission bothered Mahan. He believed that, 'Had Decatur appreciated at the moment that his speedy surrender to Pomone would be attributed to the subjection to which the Endymion was supposed to have reduced his ship, he very probably would have made a second fight of it.' Decatur's report said, 'with about one fifth of my crew killed or wounded, my ship crippled, and a more than fourfold force opposed to me, without a chance of escape left, I deemed it my duty to surrender'. Decatur had lost most of his officers, he himself was wounded and, according to one British report, his ship had six feet of water in her holds from her grounding. Mahan's conclusion: 'Physical and mental fatigue, the moral discomfiture of a hopeless situation, are all fairly to be taken into account; nor should resistance be protracted where it means merely loss of life. Yet it may be questioned whether the moral tone of a military service, which is its breath of life, does not suffer when the attempt is made to invest with a halo of extraordinary heroism such a resistance as Decatur made, by his own showing. Unless the President was really thrashed out by the Endymion, which was the British assertion, she might have put one of His Majesty's frigates, the Pomone, out of commission for a long time.' The fact was that she did not, and upon that the matter finally had to rest.

The Americans nevertheless got the last word after all. On 20 February *Constitution* encountered a British frigate, *Cyane*, and a sloop, *Levant*, off Madeira. She took them both in a short running action.

An interesting sidelight on the *President* was that when she sailed she was fully laden for a long cruise down the South Atlantic where she was to rendezvous with other members of her squadron at the island of Tristan da Cunha, west of the Cape of Good Hope. As we have already seen, the island had been uninhabited and an American had laid claim to it by establishing himself there. The two ships intended to sail with *President*, the sloop *Hornet* and brig *Peacock*, left New York five days after *President* got out. Hornet was first to arrive at Tristan da Cunha from where, on 23 March, she saw a passing sail and pursued it. Her quarry proved to be the British sloop-of-war *Penguin*.

There, in that great remoteness, on the fringe of the Southern Ocean, those two small vessels closed upon one another for the last naval engagement of the American War (of 1812), indeed the last action altogether of that war. It was brief, a mere twenty-two minutes. *Penguin* had attempted to board but the American crew opened such intense musket fire on the British assembling on their forecastle that *Penguin* surrendered immediately. And so, as it had begun, on a note of American naval success ended the American War of 1812.

LXIX

ADRIATIC

AFTER Trafalgar there was one officer in the Royal Navy who more than most can be said to have steadily maintained Nelson's example in intrepidity, zeal, commitment and flair: William Hoste.

There was a great deal of outstanding heroism in many, with remarkable examples of enterprise and daring. What stood out with Hoste, however, was the extended consistency of his performance in a career which involved more naval action than most others saw after Trafalgar. But his modesty and lack of the official recognition he deserved eventually helped to take him quietly away out of historical view.

William Hoste, Thomas Cochrane and Edward Codrington were fortunate that after Trafalgar they found themselves under Admiral Collingwood, who admired them and gratefully gave them their due in his reports. Hoste and Collingwood might rightly be regarded as the principal of those who became the forgotten heroes of the Great War. But, fortunately, their correspondence and journals were compiled and published soon after the end of the Great War, so that their experiences and reflections survive. Although legend never attached to their names, they nevertheless remain with us in those volumes, as poignantly as Nelson's letters serve him.

Captain William Hoste had a particular distinction in that he was one of those who saw the war through from its first days to its last. He was one of Nelson's first midshipmen, also at Tenerife, at the Nile, and flamboyantly paraded through Palermo by Emma Hamilton. Just before Trafalgar, Nelson gave him a 36-gun frigate, *Amphion*. To his everlasting regret, Hoste missed Trafalgar because Nelson sent him on a mission to Algiers. After Trafalgar, Collingwood moved him from one point after another in the Mediterranean, which, by the end of the first decade of the new century, Hoste probably knew better than anyone in the fleet. French activity in Calabria and the menace it represented to Sicily took Hoste into the Adriatic in 1808. Collingwood wanted him there and asked for his return from a brief visit home 'for he is active, vigilant, and knows the coast, and more depends upon the man than the ship'. In that last phrase Collingwood concisely summarized the character and value of William Hoste.

Like Cochrane and Codrington in their individual though similar ways, Hoste symbolized the form of naval warfare that prevailed after Trafalgar. The main character of naval warfare became coastal and close inshore, from the Adriatic to the Baltic, the tightest offshore watch yet, distinct from mere blockade of specific ports for watch on the grand fleets. Several factors compelled that closer-drawn, extended vigilance, among them Napoleon's complete control of the Continent, his war on British commerce, the threat from Antwerp and the Scheldt, the Peninsular War.

The Adriatic was never still. Its demands were constant. Apart from French ambitions to take Sicily, French control of Dalmatia and the Italian ports demanded vigilance, particularly upon French supply and reinforcement movement between the Adriatic and Corfu. In the last six months of 1808 alone Hoste, aboard *Amphion*, took and destroyed 218 merchantmen. The prizes should have made him rich but he had no place other than Malta to take them, a long way off his station, so they were destroyed.

The Adriatic became Hoste's special operational area, his name thereafter to be principally and permanently associated with it. His squadron was enlarged by two more frigates, *Active*, 38, and *Cerberus*, 32. Together they began practising some of the most daring landings and boat operations of the war. In 1809 *Amphion*'s boats rowed into the anchorage at Venice and destroyed six Venetian gunboats. In 1810, cruising in the Gulf of Trieste, the boats of *Amphion* chased a convoy of several ships laden with naval stores into the harbour of Grao. Sailors and marines landed to take the town. The French soldiers defending the town confronted the British in close combat with bayonets. The French were compelled to surrender. Grao was taken and the twenty-five ships there destroyed before the British retreated back to their ships. These operations were typical.

Hoste's opponent in the Adriatic was a French squadron under Commodore Dubourdieu, who kept his force at Ancona. Hoste used as rendezvous point the island of Lissa (Vis) off the Croatian coast, usually a base for British privateers. Dubourdieu raided Lissa late in 1810 and took three merchant ships that lay there. Hoste had long sought a confrontation with him. After the Lissa raid he was resolutely set upon it. Having refitted and provisioned his ships at Malta in the spring of 1811, he arrived off Lissa on 12 March. His timing was providential since Doubourdieu had sailed from Ancona the day before with the most powerful force yet assembled on the Adriatic, carrying between four and five hundred Italian soldiers to seize and garrison Lissa. Dubourdieu had four 44-gun French and Venetian frigates, two French 40-gun frigates, a 16-gun brig-corvette, one 10-gun schooner, a 6-gun xebec and two gunboats.

Dubourdieu was off Lissa before dawn on the 13th. He was immediately detected by one of Hoste's ships. At dawn Hoste, with his three frigates and a 22-gun corvette, sailed forward to confront a force more than double the strength of his own. As the four ships closed with the enemy Hoste telegraphed, 'Remember Nelson!', which was greeted by loud cheers from all the ships.

Dubourdieu, intending to board *Amphion*, stood with the French crew on the forecastle. But as his ship approached to within a few yards a brass howitzer on *Amphion*'s quarterdeck discharged upon the French forecastle seven hundred and fifty musket balls. Dubourdieu, was among those who fell. 'I must say that he set a noble example of intrepidity to those under him,' Hoste was to say afterwards. Dubourdieu's ship soon after hit rocks and remained hard aground until the end of the action, when her crew blew her up.

The action that began at nine a.m. continued until almost two p.m. It was close and ferocious, but at the end it was an outstanding British victory. *Amphion* itself took two of the French frigates. Her companion frigates took another. The gunboat was sunk and what remained of the force was taken into Lissa harbour.

During the action an explosion threw Hoste violently into the air. He suffered burns, and then a musket shot in the arm. When requested to go below for treatment he said, 'Never, but with death.' All the ships had suffered severely. *Amphion* had her masts and rigging so shot through that her return to Britain for repair was inevitable.[1]

In a war where formal line ship battle had passed away, naval engagement in its fullest and formal sense now belonged to frigates and lesser rates. The French still had powerful fleets. They continued to build and launch large ships at Toulon. But there, and elsewhere, they remained. Saumarez lay with a fleet in the Baltic but none of the hostile fleets there challenged him. Basque Roads and Walcheren offered example of the sort of operations that supplanted formal battle. In such operations and in small cruising squadrons, line ships were, of course, heavily employed, the ubiquitous 74s especially. But frigates, always the hound dogs of the navy, were the ones upon which had descended combat in its fiercest form, of the character that the public glorified. And so it was with Hoste's decisive achievement in the Adriatic. Such actions had become rare, their impact therefore greater.

Hoste returned to the Adriatic in a new ship, *Bacchante*, 38, to find that command there now belonged to Admiral Fremantle, who had far stronger force, of three line ships and six frigates. The tumultuous new movement within the Continent in 1812 had brought new focus upon the Adriatic. Hoste's relationship with Fremantle was to be something opposite from that with Collingwood.

During the next two years Hoste wore himself down with the increasing weight of activity in the Adriatic and off Corfu. The journal of one of the officers aboard *Bacchante* offered a memorable observation on the sort of rough close-combat operations in which they could find themselves, in this instance the boarding of a gunboat: 'You may cut sailors to pieces, but you cannot conquer their spirit. One of them had his right arm shattered whilst in the act of boarding a gun-boat; instead of retreating, he took his cutlass with his left hand, and continued to press forward as long as he could stand, holding up the bleeding remnant as a signal for his comrades to avenge him.'

Hoste maintained a happy ship, in the manner of Nelson and Collingwood. The same journal recorded:

His conduct, both to officers and men, is most steady and impartial; strict when strictness is necessary, and indulgent whenever it is admissible. The ship is in the best state of discipline; for the men are well aware that their duties must be done, and that there is an eye over them that cannot easily be deceived. But there is no severity, nothing of the Tartar; punishment, of course, happens now and then; but never except when absolutely necessary. Hoste cannot bear to punish men, and so great is his dislike of it, that when we meet at breakfast, I can almost always tell by his looks when there is to be any punishment in the course of the morning. He is easy and familiar with his officers, and accessible to his men, and most scrupulously attentive to their comforts.

The re-entry of Austria into the war in 1813 intensified Hoste's involvement as the Austrians descended to free Dalmatia and the coast from Trieste to Ragusa (Dubrovnik) and Cattaro (Kotor). The years of practically uninterrupted activity had begun to tell on Hoste. As his surgeon later said, 'During the summer of 1813 his health was manifestly declining . . . yet never was he more actively employed than through the whole of that summer along the Illyrian coast, most of the strong places in which we either reduced alone or assisted others in doing so.' Then, at the end of the year, Admiral Fremantle ordered Hoste with *Bacchante* to capture the fortresses of Cattaro and Ragusa.

It was an unprecedented demand, to all appearances unrealistic. Cattaro mounted ninety guns, Ragusa 194. They were mountain strongholds on that high coastline, Cattaro deep inside a difficult inlet. A single 38-gun frigate with its sailors and marines was now required to lay siege to and take both citadels. No such task had ever been laid upon a single ship.

Fremantle refused any support, or was unwilling to give it. There is a suggestion in the journal kept by one of *Bacchante*'s officers that the enormity of the task was deliberate, perhaps vindictive in its expectation of failure: 'Sensible of the inadequacy of his own frigate to carry on a siege against two fortresses of the strength of which they possessed, and aware that his commanding officer was alive to that in a greater degree than himself, Captain Hoste requested a body of marines, and some guns and mortars, to carry on the siege, but the admiral refused every assistance. No way daunted by an apparent determination on the part of another to prevent the success of an enterprise which himself was projecting, Captain Hoste quitted his presence with the noble determination to perform to his utmost the duty entrusted to him.'

Malice and envy were steadfastly present in that navy, as Nelson ever experienced. Hoste was always conscious that he had no 'interest' to back him when necessary, in promotion especially. 'Lord Collingwood is my friend, and that is all my chance,' he had written to his father while Collingwood was alive. With Collingwood gone, he was alone.

The broad understanding of the task was that Hoste should give the Austrians any assistance they needed in taking the fortresses. But the Austrians offered no assistance for Cattaro and Ragusa and showed no move or effort of their own in that direction. It was, therefore, not a matter of assisting them. It was doing the job for them. Here, then, was something like a repetition of the circumstances affecting Nelson in his relations with the Austrians on the Ligurian coast and Genoa in 1796, begging Hotham and Hyde Parker for more frigates, instead seeing some of his force actually withdrawn from him by Hyde Parker. As with Nelson, Hoste found himself entirely alone on his mission. Cattaro was in Montenegro, and upon the Montenegrins, Serbs, he would have to depend for any extra help he needed.

Cattaro became the first objective. Passing Ragusa on his way to Cattaro Hoste encountered a small British scouting force, the armed brig *Saracen* and two gunboats, which he took under his own orders. Cattaro sat at the head of the great roadstead Bocca di Cattaro, whose fortresses commanded the main approach and had to be subdued. They were garrisoned by Croats and Italians under French officers. *Bacchante* arrived there on 13 December 1813.

Hoste first sent *Bacchante*'s boats to an island where four French gunboats lay. The gunboats and the island were already in possession of Serbs who, on appearance of the British ship, threatened to kill the French officer unless he surrendered. *Bacchante*'s boats therefore brought back the island's armament of twelve brass guns and a mortar. Hoste, meanwhile, had sent a demand to the Bocca fortress to surrender, which followed quicker than he expected. 'We have been very fortunate in obtaining possession of it so soon,' he wrote, 'for the fort is much stronger than we fancied.' But the assault on Cattaro was delayed for two months when Hoste was compelled to assist the Austrians at two other coastal operations.

At the end of November he was back at Bocca di Cattaro, to be again refused all assistance by the Adriatic commander in chief, Admiral Fremantle. And 'on the side of the Austrians none came forward to share in the dangers and difficulties of regaining that territory, of which they intended finally to become possessed'.

On 12 December Hoste was trying to get *Bacchante* up the difficult course from the roadstead to Cattaro, through the narrow channels and against the strong currents that passed among the islands of the inlet. The ascent was achieved laboriously by alternatively warping and sailing. Once anchored closer to Cattaro, Hoste sailed up the rest of the river in his gig and then ascended to the hills adjacent to Cattaro to reconnoitre its batteries. He decided to form a battery on a mountain, Mount Theodore, that completely commanded Cattaro and its fort. The battery was to consist of two 18-pounders, long guns and two eleven-inch mortars.

The artillery was landed the following morning, 14 December, together with fifty-four officers and men. By dusk the first gun had reached the base of the mountain. More height was gained on the 15th. On the 16th a kedge anchor was buried in rock to help get the gun further. So it continued in cold and heavy rain day after day. A tent was raised under a projecting rock for shelter and stores carried up to it. 'They have sent me here to take a very strong place without the means of doing it,' Hoste wrote to his mother on 18 December. 'However I can but do what lies in my power.'

As the struggle with the gun continued so did the effort to get *Bacchante* further upstream. Most of the crew being on shore 'the hands were so few on board that it was to the surprise of all that she could even be got under weigh'. Cattaro had now begun to fire on her continually.

The ascent on Mount Theodore had become a desperate struggle: 'The weather increased in fury; torrents of rain and gusts of wind, so stormy as at times to disable the men from standing up at their work. Yet the indefatigable little party, with their heavy gun, ceased not their labours through all the hardships of severe seasons; the want of shoes, which were destroyed by the rocky soil; the insufficiency of their machinery to perform so heavy a work – still encouraged by their leader, they increased their exertions, and on the 20th their efforts were rewarded by placing their gun on the summit of the mountain.' The next day it was mounted in the battery. Through this time Hoste frequently slept on the open mountain in all that weather, so that his health grew steadily worse. Hoste's first lieutenant, Lilas Hood, in a letter in 1830, recalled that 'frequently for nights would his clothes remain on him, wet as they were, in a climate either at freezing point, or drenching us all in torrents of rain. How the people stood it, God only knows! And from my heart, I believe, with no other man could they have done what they did.'

Another battery, meanwhile, was built on a less precipitous hill over-looking Cattaro. Altogether four batteries of different strength were created, as well as a point for firing rockets. On 25 December all opened fire together on Cattaro, which had already itself opened constant and heavy fire on the British positions. The assault continued until 2 January 1814, when a party of Montenegrins, who had been assisting Hoste, stood ready to make an assault. Terms of surrender had been sent under flag of truce to the French commander, General Gauthier, who first refused but then decided to discuss them.

A military passenger aboard *Bacchante*, Captain Angelo, went to Cattaro with the flag of truce. Gauthier complained to him of the use of rockets, and described it as unmilitary. Angelo answered, 'Do you know with whom you are contending? You are not engaged with soldiers, who do all these things in a regular technical manner: you are opposed to sailors; people who do nothing like other men, and they will astonish you before they have done with you.'

Gauthier surrendered on 5 January. Seamen and marines took possession of Cattaro. Gauthier and his garrison of three hundred were embarked. For the next ten days all the armament and stores were brought on board. The seamen and marines were withdrawn from Cattaro and the town left in the hands of its magistrates. The whole operation had taken Hoste five weeks.

Meanwhile, the Austrians had finally arrived at Bocca di Cattaro. Their general, Metutenovitch, asked Hoste to convey his troops to Cattaro, as he was fearful of being attacked by the Montenegrins. For Hoste, who had himself got no help whatsoever from the Austrians, it was too much. He replied that he had accomplished what he had been asked to do, capture Cattaro, and as soon as he had all his material on board he would sail for Ragusa, his other instructed assignment. Metutenovitch himself then decided to withdraw, being too intimidated by the Montenegrins. For that response Hoste was immediately censured by the British ambassador at Vienna, the Earl of Aberdeen, but particularly for having used the Montenegrins who, instead of the Austrians, were now in possession of the area. To that Hoste also forcefully replied: 'I wrote repeatedly both to the British admiral and the Austrian general, requesting a force might be sent to support their interests; and to the latter particularly, that he would hasten his march . . . Notwithstanding this, though General Metutenovitch did advance, it was not till the place had surrendered . . . I do say that it is entirely their own fault that the Austrians are not at this moment quiet possessors of the province of Cattaro. I could not have acted otherwise than I did; I had no force to garrison the place, and the Bacchante was wanted for other service.' This forthrightness in defence of actions on a lone, unsupported mission was certainly something that Nelson would have understood.

Bacchante arrived off Ragusa on 19 January. Hoste landed and recon-noitred those points from which a successful attack could be made on this town with its one hundred and fifty guns. He decided to establish three mountain batteries, and the same laborious struggle began to get the guns to their positions, six miles from the landing, passing round the back of the mountain and then up it. On the 27th the guns were placed and ready to open fire on the city when the French asked for truce and then surrendered. At Cattaro Hoste had lost only one seaman, and at Ragusa also only one. Only Nelson at Bastia and Calvi could show anything equal to this achieve-ment of the conquest of the two Dalmatian mountain fortresses.

Admiral Fremantle had only just heard of the fall of Cattaro and the intended assault on Ragusa. And, as the memoir of Hoste's achievement recounted, the admiral 'struck with astonishment at the performance of what he had considered wholly impracticable with so small a force, he immediately despatched the Elizabeth frigate, Captain Gower, to assist and to supersede the command of Captain Hoste. Fortunately she only hove in sight while the capitulation was going on; and on Captain Hoste coming down from the town to give up the command, Captain Gower very properly declined to pluck away those glories which he could have no claim to, and the terms were signed by those who had conquered.' Austria did at least express its gratitude. The emperor sent Hoste the Order of Maria Theresa.

Bacchante returned to a previous station off Corfu. Hoste's health had deteriorated so badly from exposure at Cattaro and Ragusa that he suffered a rheumatic attack and lost use of both his legs to the point that he could barely stand.

Hoste's last operation was on 26 March 1814, as the war was drawing to an end in Europe. Bearing up to Corfu harbour to reconnoitre the forces there *Bacchante* ran on to a mud bank in sight of the harbour. Hoste's extraordinary career appeared about to end in capture. A French frigate lay off the harbour, likely to come out and get the better of the immov-able *Bacchante*. But Hoste said, 'Let there be no confusion; if the ship will not back off, take in all sail altogether, that the enemy may not suppose us aground, but to have only anchored for the night, for coolness must be the order of the day.' The ship was then made to all appearances snug at anchor as every effort was made to get her off.

As Duncan had done at Camperdown, signal flags were intermittently hoisted as if in communication with ships out of sight. Anchors were carried out to try and move the ship, provisions were put aboard Turkish shore boats that were in the vicinity, the pumps worked ceaselessly, and Hoste was seated on a chair from where he supervised operations. Even in the chair, his surgeon said, he seemed scarcely able to overcome his own faint-ness and weakness. Main deck guns were thrown overboard and everything else done to lighten the ship.

At daylight, with high water, *Bacchante* floated. Then, a strangely appropriate footnote. A gunboat came out bearing a flag of truce. It was loaded with fruit and vegetables, a present from the governor of Corfu. On board the gunboat was a French army captain and his wife. The captain had come out expressly to thank Hoste for his handsome conduct to his wife when she had found herself a prisoner on *Amphion* in 1808. *Bacchante* was, of course, familiar in those waters, along that coast, so her commander was known.

Hoste was too ill to continue. *Bacchante* took him to Malta to await a ship home. Lilas Hood described the parting at Malta. 'When it was known to the ship's company that he was no longer to command them, they appeared to me no longer the same men. The people being about to cheer him, were stopped by me, in consequence of my perceiving his state of agitation on quitting us, until we had, for the last time, lowered him to his boat, when the ship was instantly manned, and I believe no man ever received three more hearty cheers. In a moment, as from sudden impulse, he rose on his legs for the first time in three months, and returned the compliment; then dropping into the arms of the surgeon as if in a fit, was rowed on shore regretted by all.'

This moving mutual salute and tribute to their harmony and long endurance together aboard such a hard-working frigate provides a conclusive note to the Royal Navy's heroic Great War upon the seas and oceans, as fine an example as anything else that one might think to choose.[2]

For a twenty-first century witness emerging from close insight into the naval battles and actions of the Great War, one question constantly arises. Were those who fought these battles truly a different sort of man? Their courage in so many striking circumstances compels one to ask also, what was the nature of fear with those men at that time?

Courage has never been an easy quality to define. The prospect of battle demands, through anticipation, its own distinctive form of courage, through solemnly tolling reminder to the individual that there is no retreat. Whatever fear there might be is bounded by commitment to the inescapable. What was passing in the minds of those standing by their guns at noon on 21 October 1805, off Trafalgar, could hardly have been any different from what was in the minds of those on their way to the Normandy beaches at dawn on 6 June 1944. Nevertheless, what stands out are the particular qualities of fighting in the Great War that seem to remain awesomely distinctive. That especially has to be the zeal and frenzy of close combat which, in its many forms, was the constant demand, the most frequent and likely form of encounter.

One thinks of the very eagerness for close combat, most notably with Nelson, but more widely on smaller actions, as with the assualt on the frigate *Chevrette* lying at Brest. It was zeal for the most terrible intimacy of all. The emphasis falls on the navy, because naval images naturally predominate in a struggle where a fully concerted military involvement mainly belonged to the last six years of a twenty-two-year struggle. But there could hardly be any line of difference or balance of merit between the two, army and navy. What demand could be more horrendously foredoomed than mounting the ladders laid against the walls of Badajoz and Ciudad Rodrigo, what grappling struggle more intensely close than the fighting at Lundy's Lane and New Orleans? But could such eager zest, which is almost a hunger for such combat, still exist? And so broadly based? Does the apparently mindless fearlessness of it retain any such broad existence in modern society? It is one of the measuring questions of then and now that arises when one emerges from the pages of that time. For it is the element of an ingrained and committed sense of self-sacrifice that so strongly implies a difference that can seem difficult to grasp.

Some answer to that was sought by Lord Moran in his *Anatomy of Courage* and its theme of the soldier's struggle against fear. Published in 1945, after his second experience of close observation of war, Moran's thesis was, however, almost entirely focused upon the First World War, drawn from his active service as a medical officer from 1914 to 1917. What he sought were the qualities of fearlessness.

Moran saw in the trenches yet some connection with an unspoiled England of the past, where the 'courage of insensibility' was still not extinct. The sort of soldiers he was referring to were those he called yokel soldiers: 'There were whole battalions, where the men did not seem to think at all. They came from a part of England that had not been touched, or at any rate had been but slightly affected by the industrial age, which elsewhere was slowly eating away at this happy remnant of another and simpler time. The strength of the yokel soldier lay in his obstinate refusal to recognize danger when it was all around him.' As for the rest, they suffered more in the war, Moran said, 'not because it was more terrible but because they were more sensitive . . . We were moving away from that primitive valour, fumbling for a type of soldier whose courage was a thought-out thing . . . It was not that the horror of battle had been raised to a pitch no longer tolerable, but that their resistance to fear had been lowered. Some subtle change in men's nature which was not the effect of the war, but of the conditions of life before the war, had taken place, that left them unprotected, the sport of battles.'[3]

LXX

ADIEU

WITH Napoleon on Elba and a Bourbon once more on the French throne, what now had to be faced and conclusively decided was the new face of Europe.

What that really was about was the new face of power, the critical positioning of the future, who had what and where, the essential balances between the Quadruple Powers, Britain, Russia, Austria and Prussia.

After such a war, it might have been supposed that division of the spoils entered large. Naturally, there was something of that. But a war that had dealt so much shock to all exercised its own unique cautions. These were expressed by Metternich in what amounted to the most prescient glimpse of an ultimate future. It was the first concept of the need for a fundamental unity among nations, a 'Concert of Europe'. As Metternich saw it, the isolated state no longer existed: '. . . we must always view the *Society* of states as the essential condition of the modern world'. Memorably, in line with that, as if with strange intuition, Metternich was to write, 'I should have been born in 1900 and have had the twentieth century before me.'[1]

Metternich's view of what mattered was the essential postscript to twenty-five years that had witnessed and endured the greatest social, political and military convulsion in history. The map of Europe had changed ceaselessly as old frontiers were removed, new ones established, and eventually those, too, altered. Dynastic history was overturned. Monarchies were removed, new ones installed. Enemies became allies, before changing again repeatedly. Through all of that the very nature of society had changed for ever. The Enlightenment and the Revolution had already changed men's minds. But Napoleon with his civil codes, his original concepts of civil service and his reorganization of education set examples that offered an illumination to all everywhere. And the concept of the secular had become irremovable from thought and much of governance. So what might emerge now as the practical fusion of it all? It was a new world, within as well as without Europe, and all therefore had to come to terms with that, in whatever form. They sought their answers at the Congress of Vienna, called for 1 October 1814.

Castlereagh's guiding hope was that, once they had satisfied themselves that their individual security was assured, the big Continental powers would settle into peaceful coexistence. Much had already been settled through earlier conferences such as Châtillon and then the Treaty of Paris. Holland and Switzerland were to have their independence, Prussia was enlarged, the German states would have their independence with a future union envisaged, the Italian states would be restored, France would return to her frontiers of 1792. To ensure a lack of resentment that might help revive Bonapartism, there was to be no demand upon France for reparations. In the world beyond, France had her overseas possessions returned to her, except Tobago, St Lucia and Mauritius. The Dutch got back their Spice Islands but not the Cape of Good Hope and Guiana. Britain kept Malta.

While France, in the interests of a permanent peace, had got a settlement more generous than many could have imagined, on the eve of the Congress she did not yet rank in the minds of the others as a power equivalent to themselves. Talleyrand had arrived at Vienna on 23 September to find himself excluded from all the counsels of the four great powers that preceded the Congress. He circulated the reminder that a France thus antagonized might itself very well become antagonist again. As a result, on 30 September he found himself included with the big four's illustrious negotiators, Austria's Metternich, Britain's Castlereagh, Russia's Count Nesselrode and Prussia's Prince Hardenberg in their last meeting before the formal opening of the Congress. Castlereagh said, 'The object of today's conference is to acquaint you with what the four Powers have done since we have been here', and handed Talleyrand the protocol. Talleyrand glanced swiftly at it and was seized by the word 'allies'. And he demanded, had not peace been made? If they were still at war, whom was it against? Not Napoleon: he was at Elba. Surely not against the king of France! He was the guarantee of the duration of the peace. 'Let us speak frankly, gentlemen,' Talleyrand then said. 'If there are still "allied powers" this is no place for me.' The document was withdrawn. In that manner Talleyrand established France's own place there, and the Big Four became Five.[2] The episode was a memorable anticipation of de Gaulle's pained cry in 1942: 'Fighting France has only one reason and only one justification for finding herself in the camp of freedom; that of being France herself, and treated as such by her co-belligerents.'

As the Congress got underway, Castlereagh, powerfully fending for Britain, stood adamant on three issues tied to its maritime concerns. These were abolition of slavery and the naval enforcement of it on the high seas, off Africa especially; Britain's 'Maritime Rights'; and absolute exclusion

of France from any naval establishment on the Scheldt, especially at
Antwerp.

The Scheldt had already been solved by recognition of the independence of the Netherlands, embracing Belgium and therefore Antwerp. By
'Maritime Rights' Britain meant retaining the right in war to board and
search neutral vessels. She remained insistent on maintaining the action that
had helped to bring on the war with the United States only just concluded.
And, as they had been doing vigorously since the middle of the eighteenth
century, the other states objected to that as violation of 'The Freedom of
the Seas'. They got no further on it than they had before, or America had
done. The argument therefore slunk away before the obvious fact of British
command of the seas. There was never likely to be any British give on that.
They all knew it. For Britain anyway the right to board suspect vessels at sea
had transferred from wartime seizure of prohibited commerce to the rescue
of slaves from slave traders. It thus had its new moral justification.

The slavery abolition question itself was, however, unavoidably
different from all the other matters affecting Britain during the Congress.
For Castlereagh it was the one issue where emphasis had to be on hard,
unrelenting demand. That was imperative for, driven by the Evangelical
Movement, total universal abolition had become a passionate commitment across Britain. The justifiable conviction for action at Vienna was
that a peace concluding a war that Britain had largely paid for, at a cost
of seven hundred million pounds in gold and specie, had surely earned
her the right to that demand. A 'Conference' was appointed within the
Congress to consider abolition, and on 8 February 1815 it unanimously
declared that slavery was inhuman and should be condemned. But it was
clear that progress to total abolition would not be immediate among all
the signatories, least of all with Spain and Portugal. Furthermore, abolition of trade did not yet mean emancipation, certainly not yet even for
Britain itself with all its West Indies slave plantations.

The Congress of Vienna continued forward, month after month, into the
New Year, the biggest party of the nineteenth century. There would never
be anything like it again. Apart from minor royalties, there were four kings,
one queen, two heirs to thrones, two grand duchesses and three princes. As
Duff Cooper so nicely related, 'The courtiers followed in the train of their
sovereigns. The flower of European nobility, the richest, the most distinguished, the most beautiful, all who played any part either in the political
or in the social sphere flocked to Vienna. The majority were not there for
work. They never had worked and never meant to. The eighteenth-century
tradition of pleasure still lingered.'

Away from that, where the work was actually being done, the concentration was on the controversial issues determining the immediate future:

the partitioning or independence of Poland; the constitutional unity of Germany; Tsar Alexander's manoeuvrings westwards and eastwards atop his acquisition of Finland; the enlargement of Prussia through acquisition of Saxony which made her the leading power in northern Germany, prompting Talleyrand to write that Prussia 'would in a few years form a militarist monarchy that would be very dangerous for her neighbours'. Fears of Russia and Prussia developed so swiftly that on 3 January 1815 Talleyrand got Britain and Austria to join France in a secret treaty to act together and defend whichever one of them might be attacked. Against that background Wellington arrived at Vienna a month later, on 3 February, to succeed Castlereagh as Britain's plenipotentiary. He was therefore on site when, four weeks later, news of Napoleon's escape from Elba reached Vienna.

All dissension was put aside and the Grand Alliance swiftly recomposed. The proclamation of it made clear that it was against Napoleon and not against France that war was declared. In the 'hundred days' that preceded Waterloo the dispersing armies were recalled and mustered. Waterloo was fought on 18 June. Napoleon abdicated for a second time on 22 June.

The day after his abdication Napoleon asked Minister of Marine Decres to prepare two fast frigates, to carry him out of Rochefort to the United States. He reached Rochefort on 2 July. The British were already conscious of his intentions. Captain Frederick Maitland, aboard *Bellerophon* at Basque Roads, had got news of Napoleon's imminent arrival on 1 July.[3] On receiving that news on the 5th, Vice Admiral Sir Henry Hotham, commander on that coast, immediately sent a squadron of frigates to blockade Rochefort.

For the next week the frigates stopped every ship coming out of Rochefort to search for Napoleon, for whom the focus upon Rochefort meant that any chance of getting away in one of the frigates was passing. But arrangements were made for him to escape in two smaller Channel craft, *chasse-marées*, two of which were prepared. The plan was to sail by night and lower the sails during the day. Napoleon's brother Joseph offered to stay behind to impersonate him. It might have worked, but Napoleon hesitated too long. Rochefort had remained Buonapartist but a Bourbon *préfet* was on his way to take over. Finally, on 10 July, Napoleon sent his former Minister of Police, Savary, and his secretary, Las Cases, to negotiate with Captain Maitland of *Bellerophon*, which was then joined in the roads by Hotham aboard *Superb*.

On 14 July Napoleon advised Maitland that he would board *Bellerophon* between four and five the following morning. He sent a letter written on the 13th for delivery to the Prince Regent, asking asylum and British protection. A French brig, *Epervier*, delivered Napoleon to *Bellerophon*. As he boarded the British ship cries of '*Vive l'Empereur!*' rang from the brig. It was the last time Napoleon would hear that salute.

Napoleon had pronounced the final contest of the Great War to be Land against Sea. Within that definition it could seem appropriate that to sea fell the formal act of his own submission. It was, in any event, his preference at the very end. He was to say to the admiral who became his captor, 'I have given myself up to the English; but I would not have done so to any other of the allied powers. In surrendering to any of them, I should be subject to the caprice and will of an individual – in submitting to the English, I place myself at the mercy of a nation – Adieu.'

That deliverance on the deck of a British ship of the line was perhaps the rarest of all tributes to the Royal Navy as the embodiment of the nation it had defended, succoured and saved.

Hotham had crossed to *Bellerophon* to meet Napoleon. Hotham's nephew, Captain William Hotham, accompanied him and left a full description of the emperor's first day in British captivity aboard *Bellerophon*:

On arrival we were introduced in the front cabin to Madame Bertrand, the Duke of Rovigo, the Count de Montholon and his wife, and the Count Las Casas. After waiting there a few minutes we were ushered into the after-cabin and introduced to Napoleon. We were received by the ex-emperor with all his former dignity.

His figure is bad, he is short with a large head, his hands and legs small, and his body so corpulent as to project very considerably, his coat made very plain, and from being very short in the back it gives his figure a more ridiculous appearance than it has naturally. His profile is good and is exactly what his busts and portraits represent him, but his full face is bad. His eyes are a light blue, heavy, his teeth are bad, but the expression of his countenance is versatile, and expressive beyond measure of the quick and varying passions of the mind. His face at one moment bears the stamp of good humour and again immediately changes to a dark, penetrating, thoughtful scowl denoting the character of the thought that excites it. He speaks quick, and runs from one subject to another with great rapidity. His knowledge is extensive and very various, and he surprised me much by his remembrance of men of every character in England. He spoke much of America and asked many questions concerning Spanish and British America, and also of the United States.

After an interview of nearly an hour, during which time the ladies and attendants were all kept in the front cabin, dinner was announced to Napoleon by his Maitre d'Hotel.

He plays the Emperor in everything, and has taken possession of Maitland's after cabin. As a specimen, he sent this morning to Captain Maitland to request the pleasure of his company to breakfast at Maitland's own table. In consequence of this assumption Napoleon walked into the dinner cabin as into his own palace, and Marshal Betrand was left to usher in the strangers and staff. Dinner was served entirely in the French style by Napoleon's domestics. Without any ceremony, he commenced eating, no notice was taken of any individual, and we had all only to eat and drink as fast as the servants plied our plates and glasses with food and wine.

Directly after dinner we had coffee and then adjourned to the after-cabin; very little conversation took place: afterwards we were principally amused by seeing a very compact camp bed of Napoleon's set up and his bed made by 3 or 4 of his valets. It was rather singular that from want of height in the cabin there was no room for the ornament for the top of the bed – a golden ball. A small portable library was brought in with his other luggage, in which I saw a Bible.

Soon after this we went to the Quarter Deck, by Napoleon's desire, with the ladies, and remained until half past seven. At dinner Napoleon said little but ate very heartily; as little was said afterwards, and on going on deck he amused himself much in talking with the subordinate officers and midshipmen by turns, and walking the deck with Bertrand. At an early hour he retired to bed, apparently much fatigued.[4]

Napoleon created an impressive bond with the officers and men of *Bellerophon* on the ten-day voyage to Torbay. For the *Bellerophon* sailors this was one of the Royal Navy's truly unique experiences of the Great War, as it undoubtedly was for Napoleon himself. This was, after all, his first experience of a British man-of-war, of Nelson's world. The British navy had, naturally, always fascinated him. This was his opportunity. 'Nothing escapes his notice; his eyes are in every place, and on every object, from the greatest to the most minute. He immediately asked an explanation of the ropes, blocks, masts, and yards, and all the machinery of the ship. He sent for the boatswain, to question him; that officer always fitting out the French ships. He requested the marines to pass in review before him, examining the arms, evolutions, dress, etc., etc. and expressed himself highly pleased. He inquired into the situation of the seamen, their pay, prize-money, clothes, food, tobacco, etc. and when told of their being supplied by a purser or commissary, asked if he was not a rogue.'

Napoleon knew why Nelson had won. He saw French superiority in better ships and better guns. Beyond that, in battle, they failed. In his memoirs he detailed his reasons for that, and revealed his own appreciation of breaking the line and melee:

Although often superior in force to the English, we never knew how to attack them, and we allowed their squadrons to escape whilst we were wasting time in useless manoeuvres. The first law of maritime tactics ought to be, that as soon as the admiral has made the signal that he means to attack, every captain should make the necessary movements for attacking one of the enemy's ships, taking part in the action, and supporting his neighbours.

This latterly [was] the principle of English tactics. Had it been adopted in France, Admiral Villeneuve would not have thought himself blameless at Aboukir, for remaining inactive with five or six ships, that is to say, with half the squadron, for twenty-four hours, whilst the enemy was overpowering the other wing.

All of this was, for him, belated insight, if we accepted Mahan's view that Napoleon, to the end of his career, was never able rightly to appreciate the conditions of naval warfare: 'His perfect military insight was not mistaken in affirming that the principles of war upon the sea must be the same as upon land; it was by the failure to comprehend the circumstances to which the principles must be applied – the failure to realize the possibilities and the limitations of the naval warfare of his day – that the general and the emperor were alike led into fatal miscalculations. The Nile and Trafalgar, each the grave of a great conception, proclaimed the same cause and effect; underlying each was the inability of Napoleon to understand what ships could do and what they could not, according to the conditions of the sea and the capacity of the seamen.'[5]

At St Helena Napoleon defined somewhat strangely the essential differences he saw between the marine and the land commander: 'The marine general needs but one science, that of navigation. The commander by land requires many, or a talent equivalent to all, that of profiting by experience and knowledge of every kind. A marine general has nothing to guess; he knows where his enemy is, and knows his strength. A land general never knows anything with certainty, never sees his enemy plainly, nor knows positively where he is . . . It is by the eyes of the mind, by the combination of all reasoning, by a sort of inspiration, that the land general sees, commands and judges.'

Napoleon certainly never underrated Nelson's gifts and achievement. Whatever passion he felt against the man during the war appeared to have vanished, for, according to Surgeon O'Meara on St Helena, he spoke in very high terms of Nelson. One is thereby brought to reach a final balancing view of the two protagonists, Nelson and Napoleon.

On the face of it they could seem too different to reveal much in common. They are a strangely contrasted pair. Yet much seems to bind them, in addition to their propulsive qualities. They naturally were equally driven by the sense of predestined self, far more so with Buonaparte, the junior of the two, child of the Revolution, and thereby invested with the missionary zeal of change in that epoch. The two were similarly distinctive, however, in the particular and unusual qualities each brought to authoritarian station at that time. They were vain, of course, driven by vanity, its glory-seeking and the conviction of being select. They were alike human, alive to conscience, approachable instead of aloof, and unswervingly generous. They gave opportunity and encouragement to the deserving, regardless of social background. They were equally ruthless in whatever might stall their immediate objectives. Each had his particularly infamous black mark. For Napoleon it was the execution at Jaffa of the thousands of prisoners of war. For Nelson it was the execution of Caracciolo and the toleration of the savage vengeance of the Neapolitan rulers upon those who had supported the French occupation of Naples.

Like Nelson, Napoleon built his popularity within his army upon the unstinting loyalties of those who served under him, particularly the lower ranks. He would pass across a battlefield searching out the wounded and dying. With Napoleon this direct approach to his men had, of course, a different basis than that of Nelson. The impact of the French Revolution's libertarian levelling principles were ever with Napoleon. Nelson's relationship with his men had the particular distinction that he established a sense of devoted camaraderie that reached beyond the Royal Navy's customary formalities of mute obedience. He nevertheless remained bound to the disciplinary code of the British navy, respected and exercised it though with considerably more lenience than most.

Napoleon had always been horrified by any account of the British navy's system of flogging. But, with reservation, he admired the disciplinary system. In his memoirs he indicated that he had indeed sought to learn from the British. He wrote, 'The English are superior in discipline. The Toulon and Scheldt squadrons had adopted the same practice and customs as the English, and were attempting as severe a discipline, with the difference belonging to the character of the two nations. The English discipline is perfectly slavish; it is patron and serf. It is only kept up by the influence of the most dreadful terror. Such a state of things would degrade and abase the French character, which requires a paternal kind of discipline, more founded on honour and sentiment.' While that stood largely true, he was nevertheless ruthless in summarily punishing those who went against him or let him down.

Their fundamental view of society was wholly opposed. There was little place for a potential meeting ground between them. For Nelson the concept of revolution was anathema. Napoleon saw and desired a changed universe, Nelson sought only to preserve and defend the world he knew. The hatred he so often expressed against Napoleon and the French arose from the Revolution's challenge to his English world of rural gentility, and to its king and its God: to his world as it existed. And challenge it certainly was.

The 'regeneration' of Europe was what Napoleon sought, as he explained to his aide Comte Las Cases on St Helena. He was First Consul at the time of the projected Boulogne invasion. Had he succeeded he would have created a Great Britain republic, as he had done with others on the Continent, for 'the people of England groaned under the yoke of an oligarchy'. He would have arrived in London, he said, not as a conqueror but as a liberator, 'as brothers, who came to restore to them their rights and liberties'. Though he subsequently established his own monarchical forms he saw nothing contrary or perverse in supplanting republicanism with his own forms of kingship, the justification being that the latter were different from the old oligarchies precisely because they rested on what he had brought forward from his Revolutionary ideals. On St Helena he saw both his systems, republican and monarchical, as equally good, 'since both would have been attended by the same result'.

Against Nelson's fervent affirmation in God, Napoleon was secular. He sometimes disavowed being an atheist. But at the end he said, 'I am glad I have no religion. It is a great consolation. I have no imaginary fears. I do not fear the future.' His secular vision, however, was part of his greatness, through the legal, administrative, educational and other social institutions that he laid upon France and elsewhere within his reach.

Finally, there really is no effective measure of the greatness of one against the other. For they palpably belong inseparably together within the mystifying circumstances that simultaneously raised at the changing of the world the emergence of the greatest sailor and the greatest soldier in history, the designated commanders in what can seem, the further we go from it, as their near mythical contest of Sea against Land.

Captain Maitland of *Bellerophon* was to say, 'From the time of his coming on board ship, his conduct was invariably that of a gentleman.' Unlike William Hotham, Lieutenant Bowerbank thought that he was a good-looking man, his manners 'very engaging'. When Maitland asked a member of his crew what the ship's company thought of Napoleon, the verdict was, 'Well, they may abuse that man as much as they like, but if the people of England knew him as well as we do, they would not hurt a hair of his head.' And when they got to Torbay on 24 July the ship was surrounded by boats filled with sightseers who, when Napoleon bowed to them, took off their hats. Not a disrespectful or abusive word escaped from anyone, Bowerbank said.

Telegraphic orders forbade any communication between ship and shore and the following day *Bellerophon* was ordered to Plymouth, where hundreds of boats packed with the curious and an estimated ten thousand people on shore gathered for sight of Napoleon. He was frequently on deck and, again, the crowd not only took off their hats to him but cheered, 'apparently with the view of soothing his fallen fortunes, and treating him with respect and consideration'. Soothing it must have been but Napoleon's concept of himself as being a guest of England was now to be brutally shattered.

The government did not like the enthusiastic reception he had already got from the public. An initial idea had been to intern him in Scotland, but at a Cabinet Council held at the Foreign Office on 28 July it was decided to send him to St Helena. He was no longer to be treated as an emperor but as a general on retired pay, General Buonaparte. The decision for St Helena was hastened when a British sympathizer and admirer of Napoleon obtained a writ of habeas corpus to obtain delivery of the prisoner. *Bellerophon* was ordered to sea to await the arrival of the ship that would take him to St Helena, *Northumberland*, commanded by Admiral George Cockburn.

The shock registering on Napoleon as he received the news was severe. He could not conceive that any possible objection could be made to his living quietly in England the rest of his life. His assumption on the propriety of surrendering to an English man-of-war was turned upside down. His surprise was more painful at being addressed as general instead of emperor. 'You have sent ambassadors to me as a Sovereign Potentate, you have acknowledged me as First Consul.' He was taking snuff as he protested. The British officers listened silently. They had no answers, themselves not entitled even to try.

At noon on 7 August Napoleon boarded *Northumberland*. The marines were lined up to receive him. He took off his hat as they presented arms. To an officer he said, 'In what corps do you serve?' The officer replied, 'In the artillery.'

'I myself came out of that service.'

LXXI

ALGIERS

THE last major naval actions of the fleets and sailors that fought the Great War were in the Mediterranean against the last enemy, Barbary.

The Dey of Algeria, aware of America's war with Britain, had taken advantage of it by seizing American merchantmen. He had ordered the American consul and all American citizens to leave Algiers and, on pain of immediate imprisonment, had demanded a substantial ransom from the consul before he left. Americans from the captured merchant ships were held in captivity. On 23 February 1815 President Madison recommended to Congress that war against Algiers was necessary since the peace with Britain meant that American commerce would be moving freely through the Mediterranean again. Congress accordingly declared war on 2 March, less than a month after news of the Treaty of Ghent arrived at New York.

In May Commodore Stephen Decatur aboard the new *Constellation*, accompanied by a powerful squadron, sailed from New York. Outside the Straits of Gibraltar they encountered and captured a 44-gun Algerian frigate. Appearing in full strength off Algiers the Americans found most of the other Algerine cruisers to be at sea. The head of the Algerine navy, Hamida, made some resistance and was killed. On 13 June the Dey submitted completely to every one of twenty-two American demands in a treaty peremptorily thrust at him. These included no more tribute to be paid on any pretext whatever; delivery to the squadron of all American citizens, with a full compensation paid to them; any American taken into captivity through any circumstance was to be liberated immediately. The treaty was taken back to America and signed by President Madison at Washington on 26 December. The fleet was to remain in the Mediterranean, henceforth to winter there.

This virile demonstration, following within six months after the end of the war with Britain, naturally caused some shock to the British that the Americans should reappear so actively so soon in European waters, and even provoked resentment that the Americans acted for themselves and not on behalf of all. As one report submitted to Admiral Sidney Smith declared: 'This treaty removes the United States from the number of tributary powers. The Americans had merely their own interest in view, and were more intent on that than renown; a most favorable opportunity for crippling the maritime power of Algiers, already prostrate, was ingloriously lost. The captured vessels and prisoners are to be returned without stipulating at the call of humanity, anything in behalf of some of the objects there, which the occasion so much favoured.'

The British were already under demand to confront Barbary, more specifically to end 'white slavery' there. That historic humiliation of captured westerners enslaved in the Barbary states had been raised at the peace talks as something that finally had to be dealt with, an intolerable subjection too long taken for granted. The issue sprang naturally from the debate at the Congress of Vienna on the abolition of negro slavery. That by association had instantly brought up the much closer and more emotional 'white slavery' of North Africa: '. . . by what spell is Algier, and the inferior though no less active States of Tunis and Tripoli, permitted to pursue unrestrained their wonted course of piracy and enslavement'. Here, clearly, action *could* be immediate.

Once aroused, the impetus to the punitive had never before been so collective among the European powers. Barbary, in this instance more specifically meaning Algiers, Tunis and Tripoli, had brought retribution with unusual haste because their depredations had mounted violently during the last stages of the Great War. In 1815 even as the question of white slavery took hold in Europe the seizure of white slaves appeared to reach new extent. Algerines took several hundred men from a fishing fleet in the Adriatic. Three hundred others were taken off Bone. Seven hundred men and women were taken off the Sardinian coast at Alghieri. The raids were so frequent that coastal settlements were being abandoned. The entire Italian coast was suffering. Ships of all nations were stopped at random all over the Mediterranean and Christians, men, women and children, taken for ransom or slavery.

New horror stories of the treatment of the Christian slaves were recorded at Vienna by Sidney Smith, who had taken upon himself to lead the campaign against 'white slavery'. He had been through the Barbary ordeal when captured by Tunisians in 1798.

A month after the American appearance off Algiers a British naval commander, Walter Croker, was sent to Algiers by Lord Exmouth, the former Edward Pellew, who was now British commander in the Mediterranean.

Croker took his ship, HMS *Wizard*, to Algiers on 25 July, for a reconnaissance of its defences. A strong Dutch squadron of five frigates, one 20-gun ship and a brig had preceded him off Algiers. The Dutch were there to seek renewal of the treaty between Holland and Algiers that had existed before Holland's submersion into the Napoleonic Empire. Croker found himself witness to humiliation of the Dutch. An Algerine frigate and corvette came in from the sea and, by passing among the Dutch ships, provoked an action. The Algerines got into port. The Dutch then raised a flag of truce, seeking to complete their mission. In reply the Dey told them to haul it down as he was coming out to fight them, moreover that he wanted Holland to pay the arrears in tribute for the whole period when Holland was annexed to France. Croker, who intended visiting the Dutch, was advised against it by the British consul, lest he himself further enrage the Algerines. The Dutch, anyway, then sailed off.

Croker went ashore and, with his report on the fortifications of Algiers, surreptitiously gathered as he moved about, he delivered horrifying account of the sufferings of the Christian slaves. While there more than three hundred newly acquired slaves arrived after capture at sea. 'They were landed at Bona [Bone], whence they were driven to Algier like a herd of cattle. Those who were no longer able to walk were tied on mules, and if they became still more enfeebled, they were murdered . . . at the public quarries saw the Christian slaves and the mules driven to the same labor by their infidel masters . . . in going into the country, I met the slaves returning from their labor. The clang of the chains of those who were heavily ironed called my attention to their extreme fatigue and dejection; they were attended by infidels with large whips . . . I tasted of their bread, and, I must own, I tasted of sorrow.' Whatever amelioration might have existed in other times obviously now no longer did. Croker was allowed this freedom of movement because the influence of the British consul was much greater than that of the consul of any other nation, though limited, for it 'extends to being able to avoid insult to his person and house, and barely that'. It could, however, be a vicarious tolerance. Croker himself saw a Spanish vice consul in heavy chains working with the other slaves.

In 1816 Exmouth obtained treaties with Tripoli and Tunis prohibiting the enslavement of Christians. But at Algiers the Dey said the treaty he had made with America was already at an end and that the enslavement of Christians was a system too established to do away with. For Exmouth, force was now the only alternative. The Dutch allied themselves to the proposed British expedition.

On 27 August 1816 ships from the two navies and a single French frigate stood before Algiers in challenge to the Dey and his powerful naval and military forces. It was not, finally, a naval engagement so much as a battle between the attacking ships and the powerful array of batteries of the land, though the Dey's ships were strongly equipped and manned for boarding.

The British force was formidable. Exmouth's flagship was the 110–gun

Queen Charlotte, 96-gun *Impregnable*, three 74s, one 50 gun, two 40s, two 36s, three 18s, and a variety of others. The Dutch force, commanded by Admiral van de Cappellen, had four 44s, one 30 gun and one 18.

The demand sent ashore under a flag of truce was immediate delivery of all Christian slaves without ransom and solemn promise to cease enslavement of Christians. The Dey sent back that within a short while the British would be whitewashing the walls of his city. At two thirty p.m. Exmouth made the signal, 'Are you ready?', and was immediately answered by all, 'Ready'. The ships then passed from the outer bay to their allotted anchorage positions. 'Anxiety to combat was depicted on every countenance, and every bosom throbbed high to cover themselves with honour, and rescue their fellow Christians from ignominious slavery.'

This last action was as fierce as any in the war, fought through long, terrible hours with conspicuous courage on both sides. The bravado of the British was especially outstanding for Exmouth took his flagship sixty yards off the Mole Head, close to the ships beyond and under three batteries. As a midshipman on another ship observed, 'To give Lord E. his due, he certainly took Q.C. into a place where I expected her to be blown out of the water; she lay within half pistol shot of three immense batteries, and had about two hundred guns bearing on her alone.'

The other ships followed *Queen Charlotte*, anchoring in succession all close under the batteries. Their exposure was to be fearful. The British entered into action with their starboard broadsides, the Dutch engaged on the larboard (port) side. In typical situation, the *Superb*, 74, and *Granicus*, 36, lay under sixty 18- and 32-pounders.

The action began as *Queen Charlotte* anchored at two fifty p.m. The Dey had assembled a force of fifty thousand on shore and aboard his ships. A midshipman aboard *Queen Charlotte* described the start of the action: 'I cannot describe to you the immense crowd of men that covered the Mole and all parts of the marine; they were as thick as hops; thicker I suppose than the hops are this year, unless the weather mended – Well, just as the old lady was going to let fly her broadside, the Admiral, I suppose, had pity on the poor devils, for he stood on the poop and motioned with his hand for them to get out of the way – but there was such a crowd that was impossible, even if they had wished; but I don't suppose they understood what the admiral meant – at last, Fire! Fire, fire – I think I saw 500 or 1000 of them bang down in an instant.'

The logbook of *Leander*, 50, a ship with an especially long and active history in that war, recently back from the war in America, recorded the commencement of the action: 'Observed the effect of our fire had totally destroyed the enemy's gunboats and row galleys and defeated their intention of boarding. The battle now raged with great fury, officers and men

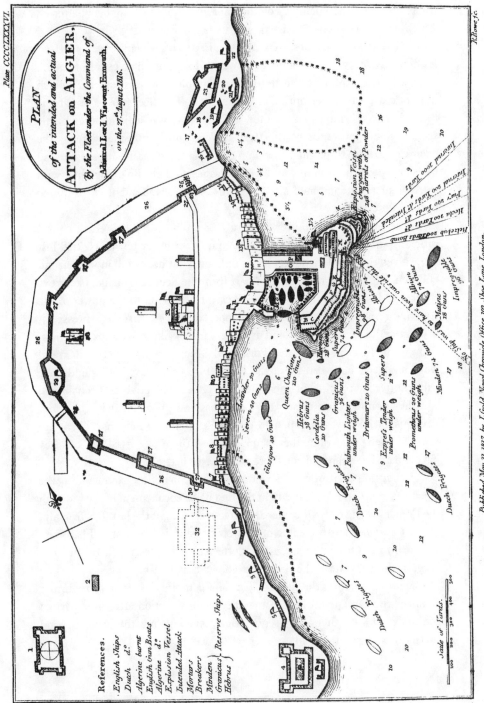

falling very fast, and masts, yards, and rigging cutting in all directions. At three, observed the enemy's colours shot away in some of their batteries, which were very soon re-hoisted, and their fire obstinate.'

With that near-ceaseless ferocity the Battle of Algiers began, and, as Exmouth wrote, 'a fire as animated and well supported as ever witnessed, from a quarter before three until nine, without intermission, and which did not cease altogether until half past eleven'. The fleet moved out at one thirty in the morning to the outer anchorage. It was a fittingly climactic scene. 'The appearance of the fleet standing out, with the glare of the enemy's burning ships and arsenal on their shattered masts and sails, added to heavy peals of thunder and vivid flashes of lightning, together with torrents of rain, combined altogether to form a scene awful and sublime beyond description.'

In the morning Exmouth sent in a flag of truce. The Swedish consul brought out word that the Dey would comply with any terms. He had lost some seven thousand men, besides an unknown but heavy toll in women and children. Algiers was devastated. Apart from the fleet cannonade, Congreve rockets had rained upon the city. Full credit was given to the power of the Algerine resistance. The midshipman aboard *Queen Charlotte* expressed it in a letter home: 'Turbans and trowsers are so like caps and petticoats, that you in England think the Turks and Moors are little better than old women. If you had seen them the day before yesterday, you would have had a different opinion of them ... They were as active as Frenchmen, and they pointed their guns with a coolness and precision that would not have disgraced any gentlemen in cocked hats and pantaloons. There are few Christians who value their skins less than these pagans. They say they have a paradise prepared for those who die in battle.'

It was curious that Admiral Exmouth, as Captain Pellew, commanding the frigate *Nymphe*, in 1793 had fought the first naval engagement of the war with the French frigate *Cléopâtre*. Here he effectively fought the last. His flagship, *Queen Charlotte*, was the name of Howe's flagship in the first full battle on 1 June 1794. The first Queen Charlotte had been destroyed by fire but here, in the last battle, the name served again as flagship.

There was, finally, the positive fact of a combined operation by former enemies, the Dutch and British together again in action after more than a century, and with that one French frigate symbolizing the peace beyond that now enclosed them all.

LXXII

POSTSCRIPT

AT some distant moment, one might have felt, a time so different as to be almost difficult to recall, the world had entered the tunnel from which it now emerged, blinking in the glare of the transformation of all about it.

So it must have seemed. The Great War had seen more than transition from one century to another. In mind and expectation the Western world had crossed a bridge to a new shore, from a past age to a wholly new, where all was evolutionary, visibly and dominantly so.

All that had been inventively emergent in the decade before Revolution and the start of war was now functionally established: the machines and factories, iron, steam, and the social turbulence that accompanied it all, into which peace delivered its own discordance as the war machine wound down and unloaded its own dissatisfactions and disaffections. On British streets, where the press gangs just a while ago had ruled, impoverished seamen now begged. But the Great War had left Britain predominant. She had at that moment no rivals in sea power and its commerce, none in industry and finance, or in colonial possession.

None of her wartime rivals was immediately, or soon likely to be, in a position in that new century to challenge her. The war had weakened and reduced them too much. But, as they all recovered, there was anyway steadily less reason for the old rivalry since the mercantilism that had generated so much of the heat and jealousy in the past began rapidly falling away. And, as Britain proclaimed herself defender of the seas and free trade, the others were content to leave it to her to maintain and pay for.

Britain's fierce defence of 'Maritime Rights' at the Congress of Vienna and in the peace talks at Paris had hardly suggested her as defender of the 'freedom of the seas' for in 1814 that still meant freedom on her sufferance, since she retained the right to stop and search any vessel on the oceans if it served her interests. But on 8 May 1820 the House of Commons was presented a petition from British merchants for abandonment of the 'protective or restrictive' in trade, pleading that 'a policy founded on

these principles would render the commerce of the world an interchange
of mutual advantages, and diffuse an increase of wealth and enjoyment
among the inhabitants of each state'. And in 1821 and 1822 parliamentary
acts threw out the system of Navigation Laws which for a century and a
half had sought to protect British shipping against foreign competition.
Upon the mercantile freedom that thereafter swiftly built upon those, the
nineteenth century's genuine freedom of the seas became well established
by mid-century.

In the immediate aftermath of the war, however, as Britain surveyed
the maritime supremacy and commercial dominance that she had acquired,
she was alarmed by the one threat she saw to all that she had attained: the
United States.

The American War of 1812 was in many respects the real war of independence of the United States. The British recognized something like that. So
did Europe, for the War of 1812 had conclusively put the United States
before the world as a new power in the balances of the future.

The United States itself shared that surprise. It had emerged from
the war with a new nationalism, an alert grasp of its defensive abilities,
and, above all, a totally transformed comprehension of its own continental
immensity and the potential strength and vision it represented.

Naval strength and world stature had been the very least associations
that Britain was likely to attach to the United States before the war. The
general despising of the thirteen colonies was too deep. Independence had
been resentfully conceded when there was no alternative. The idea merely
of nationhood remained hard to concede. Not surprisingly, the interior
boundaries of the United States had remained ill-defined or uncertain.

The British had wanted an Indian barrier state and until 1796 kept their
posts at Michilimackinac, Detroit, Niagara and Oswego. The intended
Indian Barrier State would have embraced the southern shores of Lakes
Superior, Michigan, Huron and Erie and run down to the juncture of the
Ohio and the Mississippi. Britain never wished to relinquish the Great
Lakes and did so reluctantly. After the war, however, aided by acquisition
of Louisiana and incorporation of the Floridas, and through the Boundary
Treaty of 1818, the northern boundary of the United States already ran
from just beyond the western head of Lake Superior, from Lake of the
Woods along the forty-ninth parallel to a yet uncertain termination in what
was being called Oregon. In descent below that the boundary wandered
uncertainly along the Continental Divide of the Rockies towards the Gulf
of Mexico. Much remained to be argued and negotiated, especially in the
far northwest where Russia, Spain and Britain all had claims. Nevertheless,
already there for all to see and speculate upon was the shadowy emer-

gence of a vast new and potentially powerful state. Pittsburgh was already an industrial centre served by the astonishing steamship traffic on the Mississippi and its connecting rivers. Its industries had aided Commodore Chauncey's shipbuilding activities during the war on the Great Lakes. For Britain, however, the most disturbing aspect was that this new America had so powerfully demonstrated itself as a naval power. That fact, tied to America's established oceanic commerce, declared that although competition with her old Continental rivals had faded, a new and formidable competitor that had not been in sight before the war now confronted her on the other side of the Atlantic.

It was notably in the pages of the *Naval Chronicle* that those who saw themselves most affected, the sailors and the merchants, expressed their fears and resentment, as well as wonder and some admiration, for what had been revealed to them.

During the sixteen years since its first appearance this outstanding publication with its detailed survey and view of the naval war had become the very voice of the British navy. It was perhaps the closest existing bond between Nelson and Napoleon. Both read it keenly. Now, with the war over, the *Chronicle* was about to cease publication, which it did with its fortieth issue in 1818. In its final issues the main subject in its correspondence and discussion was America and what America now meant to the world, and to Britain specifically.[1]

The swift return of the American fleet to the Mediterranean at the end of the war and its immediate subjection of Barbary had given urgency to their alarm. It was noted that the squadron sent to the Mediterranean under Commodore Chauncey was the strongest ever sent to sea by the United States, 'so it has commenced its cruise by demands, affecting in no small degree the interests of England in regard to trade, as well as *naval supremacy* in those seas . . . already we see the American squadron acting as if masters in the Mediterranean'.[1]

That last was reference to a fracas between British and Americans at Messina. Tensions between the British and the Americans in the Mediterranean were obviously high, when they came together in the same port. The fracas in question occurred when the American squadron under Commodore Stephen Decatur put into the Sicilian port.

An American sailor from the frigate *Java* was found aboard a British merchantman and suspected of theft. He was flogged by the British sailors. The American consul laid the matter before the Sicilian authorities. When the captain of the British merchantman went ashore he was confronted by three American officers. He was severely beaten in turn. Soon after two of *Java*'s boats, packed with sailors armed with pistols and cutlasses, sought to attack the British ship. They were held back when the merchant-

man's officers threatened to blow them out of the water with the ship's
own guns. Other disturbances broke out between American officers and
British captains at Messina. When the British ship eventually sailed, the
new American 74, *Washington*, Commodore Stephen Decatur, sent two
boats to board her. The British crew was mustered and one of them, said
to be an American, was taken off. The episode was thus closed with the
Americans defiantly replicating the arbitrary boarding that they themselves
had suffered from the British during the recent war.[2]

As if to make it all sink in, in January 1818 the United States sent over on
a formal visit its latest 74, *Franklin*. The impact of *Franklin* was profound.
The ship provoked surprise and consternation. The largest cause of alarm
was that her armament and construction were seen as superior to anything
in the British navy. One correspondent described in detail her superiority
to any British 74, or even 100-gun ship. 'The *Franklin*'s broadside . . .
amounts to . . . more than two to one against our 74s; this is a formidable
odds.' British 100-gun ships were said to discharge one-quarter less shot
than *Franklin*. *Franklin* would therefore enter contest with either a British 74
or 100 'with every prospect of success'. The Americans, the correspondent
said, had through genius, skill and foresight designed their line of battle
ships 'into their present state of perfection, which has rendered them nearly
irresistible in single conflicts, for which they appear peculiarly adapted; and
in the event of hostilities taking place, this will certainly be their mode of
fighting, in preference to that of fleets.' In face of that the Royal Navy
should look to total revision of its armament: '. . . whatever is intended to
be done, let it be done quickly; for it is evident, that the Americans are
now looking forward to the time, when they shall be fully supplied with
the means of successfully disputing with us, the sovereignty of the ocean;
and when this period shall arrive, we may expect their cruisers to be the
first carriers of this unwelcome news, by sweeping our coasts.'[3]

Many of the letters published in the *Chronicle* were addressed to Lord
Melville, back in government as First Lord of the Admiralty, on the justifiable assumption that Melville, as head of the navy, had to be a diligent
reader of the *Chronicle*. One of those letters declared: 'As the war of the
French Revolution introduced new tactics into the military science, so
the late short war between Britain and America bids fair to bring upon
the ocean, in naval warfare, a new description of ships, as to capacity for
carrying heavy artillery . . . which, for war, are more effective than any
ships in the British navy.' The letter concluded with an exhortation that
the British government rebuild its fleet on similar design to meet a predictable threat: 'Your lordship must be aware, that the American government
is not only stalking with gigantic strides, in imagination, from the Atlantic
to the Pacific; from the Lakes of Canada to Iceland and the frozen sea;

from Georgia to the isthmus of Darien; but is also sweeping the seas with her victorious fleets; and even pursuing the British, vanquished, on their own shores ... Let this country then ... triumph over this new enemy, as she has done over all others ... the republican spirit is restless, proud and overbearing. While it talks aloud of liberty and freedom, it desires to domineer and extend its power.'

Another letter addressed to Melville said, 'We have just seen the Franklin depart from our ports ... we have no ship in the navy at present capable, as now armed, to contend on anything like equal terms with her. When war again agitates the world, it is with the navy of America that Britain will have to contend in *earnest*; and sooner or later, my Lord, the gauntlet will be thrown down ... Shall we see these fine and doubly armed American ships within our ports, their squadrons sweeping the Mediterranean Sea, and the South American shores, and making settlements in the Pacific Ocean, and *be still?*'4

A more reflective view offered in the *Naval Chronicle* turned to the ultimate future America: 'The prodigious extent of territory yet unoccupied but fertile, gives to the United States immense resources of future growth in population and wealth; for all the prosperity of pacific enterprise; for all the comprehensive energy and perseverance of protracted warfare. So that there can be no comparison between the capabilities and resources of any other country and those of the United States, provided the federal union lasts, and increases in strength as it advances in age.'5

Those British fears of American global naval and commercial belligerence soon dimmed and receded, of course, as Britain and the United States settled down amicably to dispose of the final issues left to the arbitration commissions of the Treaty of Ghent. Neither had cause for the hard reflections on recovery that lay on all the other participants of the war. The two were the great beneficiaries of the Great War. Britain had her imperial nineteenth century before her. The United States turned inward and gave its attention to the infinite promise of its westward reaching vastness, to wait until the end of the century for one of her naval captains of that later time, A. T. Mahan, to return to it a renewed concept of navy.

It was Mahan who at the end of the nineteenth century delineated the remarkably persistent influence of the Great War.

For a Western world in transition the Great War marked the beginning of the end of the great age of sail. The final glory of sail with the clipper ship lay just ahead. But the end of the motoring value of sail was already recognized. By the last quarter of the nineteenth century it had been fully superseded by steam. Nevertheless, the Great War continued to dominate naval outlook. The most strenuously sustained contest in the maritime

history of the world failed to lose its significance as naval example, even
with the passing of sail. It extended its influence and impact from the turn
of one century to the eventual turn of the other, simply because after 1816
there were no further sea wars of global consequence until the 1904–5 naval
confrontation between Russia and Japan in the Far East. By then, of course,
it was a confrontation between ironclad battleships.

What could be more different from the square-rigged past? Everything
was technologically new. The new navies nevertheless represented a curious
anomaly for, as Mahan was to point out, 'the great preponderance of
historical experience continues to rest upon sailing fleets'.

For the existing and putative masters of the seas and their navies of
iron ships and steam propulsion the Great War remained the only source
of instruction in naval strategy and tactic. Although steam had changed
everything by removing the propulsive uncertainties of wind and current,
the steam navies had not yet any history of their own to provide the new
operational lessons. 'Hence theories about the naval warfare of the future
are almost wholly presumptive,' wrote Mahan in 1890 in *The Influence of
Sea Power upon History*, the classic volume that would establish him as the
pre-eminently original naval historian and strategist of his time, soon to be
joined by his British contemporary, Julian Corbett.

Mahan, then an American naval captain and university lecturer, wrote
with the serious purpose of re-creating the United States Navy, which
had never been allowed to develop further after the Great War. He was
compelled by the imminence of the Panama Canal to deliver his work, foreseeing 'the growth of the United States to be a great Pacific power, and in
her probable dependence in the near future upon an Isthmian canal for the
freest and most copious intercourse between her two ocean seaboards'. The
other factor that worked on him was 'that the greater rapidity of communication afforded by steam has wrought, in the influence of sea power over
the face of the globe, an extension that is multiplying the points of contact
and emphasizing the importance of navies'.

The impact of Mahan's work reached far beyond the United States. Four
new navies were created in the last decade of the nineteenth century, the
American, German, Russian and Japanese. The German was the brainstorm
of Kaiser Wilhelm II who, influenced by reading Mahan, saw naval power
as an instrument of his own ascendancy. The Americans were stirred to
naval strength by Mahan and the adventurist Spanish–American War of
1898. In their reach for naval power the Japanese for their part saw the
threat of Russian dominance around them, especially by Russia's intrusion
upon Manchuria to finish the Siberian Railway.

The Russian and Japanese navies met in the Straits of Tsushima on
27 May to fight the first major naval battle between iron-built, steam-

driven battleships. All the naval powers sought to draw from the Battle of Tsushima, and from Mahan's close study of it in a new volume, *Naval Strategy*, the urgent lessons they needed for this new oceanic reality so fast upon them. For all of them, however, the Great War yet provided the principal tactical and strategical reference. Such was the fog of the new. And, as the shadows of a likely naval confrontation between Britain and Germany began to hover over the Atlantic world in 1911, it was still the war of 1793–1815 whose instructional symbols and command lay upon the new navies. Britain, convinced that its mastery of the seas remained unchallengeable, went to war in 1914 confidently dependent upon the heroic example of Trafalgar to which its navy tightly clung. At Jutland Britain and Germany staged the last of great battles of line, disastrous to both.

With Britain, the lingering mind and structure of Nelson's navy only vanished finally and for ever when Japanese bombers sank the *Prince of Wales* and the *Repulse* off the Malayan coast on 10 December 1941, taking with them the last of battleship mentality in the Royal Navy with its fixed concept of line and broadsides. Then, on 7 April 1945, the Japanese battleship *Yamato*, largest in the world, shared the fate of *Prince of Wales* and *Repulse* when sent to the bottom by American carrier aircraft at Guadalcanal. It was the final end of big guns afloat.

As the Cold War and the last big-power confrontation upon the seas vanishes into history, it is now difficult seriously to profile the look of a naval future, outside of the submarine. For someone such as me who, as a correspondent, spent much time with different navies on different oceans during the Cold War, all of it now seems weirdly remote. How strange to have been aboard a cruiser on the Indian Ocean pondering the strategies of maintaining oil supply lines from the Middle East in a possible war! Or wondering whether the Russians were really intent on establishing a base on the island of Socotra as answer to Diego Garcia. But the Russian navy collapsed at the end of the Cold War, European powers lost interest in navy, which in any event few of them could afford, and Britain's Royal Navy even found itself intimidated by the Iranian navy in the Persian Gulf, once a pivotal point of its global assertion. Only the US Navy today stands supreme, with a power beyond anything imnaginable in the past. Can that hold deeper into the twenty-first century? If not, what then of the future?

Professor Paul Kennedy of Yale in his magisterial work *The Rise and Fall of British Naval Mastery* (2004), offers perhaps the most succinct survey presently available of naval power as it was, as it now exists embodied by the US Navy, and of how the future of it all may proceed. China's economic surge would appear to make it the obvious challenger to the United States with confrontation across the Pacific. But Kennedy is doubtful of that in the near future, given the enormous economic investment of each in the other. Instead: 'What might need to be taken much more seriously by the U.S. Navy in the next few years, however, is the prospect that rising Asian nations, India as well as China, will develop sophisticated sea-skimming or even ballistic missiles to force American carrier groups to stay further and further away from the continent's shores; in other words, it might not require an equally-large Chinese high seas fleet to blunt or deny the application of American naval mastery in the western Pacific.'

Against all of that, it should be of particular interest to readers of this book that, for Professor Kennedy, Mahan and Corbett retain their impact upon naval history. Mahan has tended to be a controversial figure among British naval historians. That an American naval captain should have written the initial, internationally accepted masterwork on naval power and strategy never sat well with some of them. Kennedy, himself a British historian, acknowledges that Mahan's work cannot today be uncritically accepted. Nevertheless, Kennedy declares, '. . . any survey of British naval history should commence with him, for his contribution to the subject was unique and his influence has been unparalleled; and the very fact that this present study will take issue with his conclusions at many points should be regarded less as a denigration than as a reflection of his importance. Mahan is, and will always remain, the point of reference and departure for any work on "sea power".' And, '. . . if Mahan, Corbett and other navalist writers of a century ago were brought back to life and given a look at the *USS Kitty Hawk*, and the dozen others like it, and informed of the role they play in today's international scene, they would see proof of their contention that maritime power would always be of significance in our volatile, anarchic world.'

Ultimately, whatever is to be the new on the seas, it is the deeper past that rightfully will continue to grip us, and so it should, especially the twenty-three years of the greatest war under sail, for it will always stand as the grandest of Western man's sea stories.

The island of St Helena sits like an unbreachable fortress mysteriously rising sheer from the ocean. Approaching it, the impression of unassailable impregnability is strengthened rather than diminished. For the heavy South Atlantic swell, slow rolling in from the great Southern Ocean beyond, smashes heavily against those cliffs, declaring no safe place to land.

The soaring height and sheer of the island's wall-like sides suggest the unscalable. Then suddenly that solid front is parted, narrowly, no more than a reluctant crack, viewed from the sea. That tight fissure holds the island's tiny capital, Jamestown. There is no harbour, just a strong jetty, the only landing point for the island whose roughly tumbled heights allow no approach from the air. St Helena remains as sealed to easy access as it ever was through the centuries.

Up through Jamestown the narrow road climbs to the summit, winding along the precipitous sides of the hills, through the thick woods, steadily upwards, to arrive finally before a long, sprawling Georgian country house, Longwood.

I have twice travelled that road to Longwood, walked through the spacious rooms, past the long table where Napoleon, the Bertrands, Las Cases and the rest of that mournful suite gathered for those pellmell meals that Napoleon peremptorily finished by rising and moving away to the card table. But it is in his bathroom where you stand the longest, before the small metal bath in which he lay for hours nursing his discomfort before he died. Nowhere else can one today get a more powerful sense of the man, certainly not at the grandiose tomb at the Invalides. In the silence of the empty house – for visitors are rare – in the weighted recollection of those bright rooms, there is an unspoiled sense of the heavy memories recounted there and bitterly reflected upon. There, you feel, if you listen keenly into the quietness of the house, that all of that history yet remains within hearing, lurking, biding, for nothing has yet come to that remote place to overwhelm the complete yet living sense of its presence. You never quite lose the strong memory of that. You feel that you came away with some touch of what was there.

NOTES ON SOURCES

1. Ocean (pp. 3–13)

Extensive reading across the wide array of work available on such a large subject has meant being drawn back to the works of particular historians and writers. High among them have been J.H. Parry, for *The Establishment of European Hegemony, 1415–1715* and his *Spanish Seaborne Empire*; C. R. Boxer for *The Portuguese Seaborne Empire, 1415–1825, The Tragic History of the Sea, 1589–1622* and *The Dutch Seaborne Empire, 1600–1800*; Fernand Braudel's three-volume masterwork *Civilization and Capitalism* and his *The Mediterranean in the Age of Philip II*; Henri Pirenne's *A History of Europe*, for the medieval age.

More particularly, I have turned to Julian Corbett's *Drake and the Tudor Navy, The Successors of Drake*, his two-volume *England in the Mediterranean*, and *Some Principles of Maritime Strategy*, a work that will retain its presence throughout this book. For the Indian Ocean I have drawn upon Professor K.N. Chaudhuri's landmark *Trade and Civilization in the Indian Ocean from the Rise of Islam to 1750*. Among other works useful to this chapter have been L. Carrington Goodrich's *A Short History of the Chinese People*; R. C. Andersen's *Oared Fighting Ships*; Jacques Mordal's *Twenty-Five Centuries of Sea Warfare*; Alan Villiers' *Sons of Sinbad*.

1. Chaudhuri, *Trade and Civilization*, pp. 6, 14.
2. *ibid.*, p. 14.
3. Villiers, *Sons of Sinbad*, p. 24.
4. Corbett, *Drake and the Tudor Navy*, p. 5.
5. Corbett, *Strategy*, pp. 54–5.

2. Navy (pp. 14–22)

As this chapter essentially concerns the rise of Western navies and the inception of the first great tactical manoeuvres under sail, I have particularly drawn upon Admiral Mahan's initial classic *The Influence of the Sea upon History* (Mahan, *SPH*) and his later *Naval Strategy* (*NS*), as well as Corbett's *England in the Mediterranean*, vol. 1. The finest succinct summary on the origin of 'breaking the line' forms the appendix of *England in the Mediterranean*, vol. 2. On the naval ship, one of the most accessible references is the summary of its development and that of its armament provided in the first part, 'The Sailing Ship', of F. L. Robertson's *The Evolution of Naval Armament*.

1. Corbett, *Mediterranean*, vol. 1, p. 227.
2. Mahan, *SPH*, p. 107.
3. *ibid.*, p. 125.

3. Century (pp. 23–43)

The dramatic release of the British navy from tactical paralysis by Rodney's action at the Saints and the insight of Clerk of Eldin, together with the Royal Navy's controversial reaction to it, are covered by the *Naval Chronicle* (*NC*) in the following volumes and pages: *NC* 1, pp. 32–41, 378; *NC* 20, pp. 120–27; *NC* 36, pp. 357–9, 464–7; *NC* 37, pp. 50–54; and in Clerk's *An Inquiry into Naval Tactics*.

The *Naval Chronicle* is heavily drawn upon in this book. Through its forty volumes, from 1799 to 1819, the *Chronicle* presented a profile of the fighting Royal Navy and its adversaries that is like no other. Apart from offering the Admiralty reports, it sought so far as possible to offer its own reports and comment on the naval actions that occurred, as well as portraits of the main actors. Sailors were invited to offer their stories, as they did, something from which this book has so richly benefited.

As well as the *Chronicle*, one of the most impressive gifts of that period for anyone preparing a book such as this has to be the range and variety of publications available. The last quarter of the eighteenth century saw a riotous eruption of publishing in all its forms, to feed an avidly demanding, better-educated public. Atop it all, however, was the triumphantly free active press. The demand to be informed, to share experience and to comment was alive as never before. When it began, the Great War was to be a war more closely scrutinized and reported upon than could have been imagined before. The government itself kept the people up to date. Through the *London Gazette* the government weekly released its Admiralty or War Ministry accounts of naval and military action.

A particularly valuable reference was the *Gentleman's Magazine*, a marvellous cornucopia of observation on every aspect of life and affairs of the time. Equally useful are the volumes of *The Farington Diary*, offering observations of the artist Joseph Farington at the turn of the century.

1. Rediker, *Between the Devil and the Deep Blue Sea*, p. 10.
2. Robinson, *The British Tar in Fact and Fiction*, p. 137.

3. Campbell, *Lives of the British Admirals*, vol. 7, p. 385.
4. *ibid.*, p. 326.
5. Mitchell, *The Maritime History of Russia*, p. 317.
6. Mahan, *SPH*, p. 377.
7. Clerk of Eldin, *Inquiry*, pp. 138–9.
8. *NC* 25, p. 401.
9. William Laird Clowes, *The Royal Navy: A History*, vol. 8, p. 464.
10. *ibid.*, p. 467.
11. Mahan, *SPH*, p. 391.
12. Mahan, *SPH*, p. 491.

4. Decade (pp. 44–59)

For William Pitt I principally draw upon Earl Stanhope's *Life of Pitt*, J. Holland Rose's *William Pitt and the Great War* and John Ehrman's *The Younger Pitt*, as well as the compiled volumes of official Pitt correspondence.

1. Tocqueville, *Ancient Regime*, p. 190.
2. Stanhope, *Life*, vol. 1, p. 122.
3. *Gentleman's Magazine*, 1783, vol. 2, p. 559.
4. *ibid.*, p. 207.
5. *ibid.*, p. 772.
6. Stanhope, *Life*, vol. 1, pp. 240–41.
7. *ibid.*, p. 237.
8. *Gentleman's Magazine*, 1784, vol. 1, pp. 91, 171–3.
9. *ibid.*, 1783, vol. 1, pp. 144, 433.
10. *NC* 2, p. 409 ; *NC* 3, p. 169; *NC* 4, p. 12; *NC* 6, p. 95.

5. Wood (pp. 63–76)

1. Albion, *Forests and Sea Power*, p. 4.
2. Corbett, *England in the Seven Years War*, vol. 2, pp. 366–7.
3. *NC* 3, p. 464.
4. Chapelle, *The Search for Speed Under Sail*, p. 31.
5. *NC* 38, pp. 237–42, 403–12.

6. Shipboard (pp. 77–95)

Professor Michael Lewis's *A Social History of the Navy* offers the most accessible portrait of the shipboard society of the sailing navy. Matching it is Brian Lavery's *Nelson's Navy: The Ships, Men and Organization*. Extremely valuable is the portrait of ship management in Augustus Phillimore's *The Life of Sir William Parker*, pp. 66–70 and, more broadly, pp. 196–205. Of similar value is N.A.M. Rodger's *The Wooden World: An Anatomy of the Georgian Navy*. On a smaller scale we have Christopher Lloyd's equally helpful social survey of the British navy, *The British Seaman*. For an especially direct picture I have drawn on Samuel Leech's *A Voice from the Main Deck; A Selection from the Public and Private Correspondence of Vice-Admiral Lord Collingwood* (Collingwood) and

Edward Brenton's *The Life and Correspondence of John, Earl of St Vincent* (*St Vincent*). Much of shipboard life has been drawn throughout the book from Nelson's Dispatches.

1. *NC* 34, p. 136.
2. *NC* 40, p. 26.
3. *NC* 30, p. 223.
4. *ibid.*, p. 337.
5. *NC* 7, p. 164.
6. *NC* 30, p. 339.
7. Leech, *A Voice from the Main Deck*, p. 25.
8. Lloyd, *British Seaman*, pp. 259, 263.
9. *London Medical Journal*, vol. VIII, part II, 1787. Quoted in the *Gentleman's Magazine*, 1788, vol. 2, p. 709.
10. *NC* 17, p. 467.
11. *NC* 6, p. 72.
12. *NC* 16, p. 243.

7.   Toulon (pp. 96–108)

This chapter initiated reference to Sir Harris Nicolas's *The Dispatches and Letters of Vice-Admiral Lord Viscount Nelson*. Other principal reference works from this chapter onwards were Mahan's *The Influence of Sea Power Upon the French Revolution and Empire, 1793–1812* (Mahan, *R/E*) and his *The Life of Nelson* (Mahan, *Nelson*); and Jean-Pierre Baptiste Edmond, Jurien de la Gravière, *Sketches of the Last Naval War* (Gravière), two volumes. The *Naval Chronicle* offers probably the finest summary available of the capture and loss of Toulon, the highly controversial first major naval event of the Great War. Much of it is summarized in what all called 'The Toulon Papers'. The *Chronicle* sources are *NC* 2, pp, 25–37, 106–17, 288–302, 378–84; *NC* 37, pp. 249–55, 425–33.

1. Nicolas, *Nelson Dispatches*, vol. 1, p. 299.
2. Gravière, vol. 1, p. 54.
3. Nicolas, *Nelson Dispatches*, vol. 2, p. 316.
4. Private letter Lt. Cooke, *NC* 2, pp. 378–84.

8.   Buonaparte (pp. 109–118)

For broad historical narrative and perspective on Napoleon I have largely consulted J. Holland Rose's two-volume *The Life of Napoleon* and found useful for quick reference a smaller life, John Markham's *Napoleon*. As a guide to the whole study of Napoleon, I have found Pieter Geyl's inestimable *Napoleon: For and Against* indispensable. My own preference has been Adolphe Thiers' *Histoire du Consulat et de l'Empire* and the work of Pierre Lanfrey. The first chapter of the English translation of vol. 1 of the *Mémoires* provides Napoleon's own account of the 'Siege of Toulon'. Holland Rose provides a fine summary of Toulon in vol. 1 of his *Life of Napoleon*, pp. 48–57.

1. Napoleon, *Mémoires*, vol. 1, p. 201.
2. *NC* 8, p. 230.

9. Corsica (pp. 119–130)

The intense bitterness that arose between the Royal Navy and the British Army on Corsica is recounted from the army's point of view in Chapter 8, Book 2 of volume 4 in J. W. Fortescue's *A History of the British Army*. Nelson's involvement is drawn from *Nelson's Dispatches*, vols 1 and 2. As *Nelson's Dispatches* forms the most common source in all the volumes on Nelson, I have restricted myself throughout this book only to those I have judged to be either indispensable or not commonly used. Mahan's *The Life of Nelson*, vol. 1, pp. 118–33, covers Bastia.

1. *Nelson's Dispatches*, vol. 1, p. 361.
2. *ibid.*, p. 358.
3. *ibid.*, p. 372.
4. Napoleon, *Mémoires*, vol. 1, p 195.
5. *Nelson's Dispatches*, vol. 2, p. 6.

10. Battle (pp. 131–153)

I have drawn upon all the following: The *Naval Chronicle* reported comprehensively on 'the First of June' in *NC* 1, pp. 19–23, 25–8, 277; *NC* 2, p. 365; *NC* 3, pp. 31–3, 252–8; *NC* 4, pp. 144–5; *NC* 5, p. 405; *NC* 7, pp. 178–9; *NC* 8, pp. 194–5; *NC* 12, pp. 106–8; *NC* 19 pp. 222–6, 230–31; *NC* 22, p. 103. Mahan's extensive examination of the battle is on pp. 122–161 in vol. 1 of Mahan, *R/E*. Two fine personal accounts are provided by Edward Codrington, *The Memoir of Sir Edward Codrington* (Codrington), pp. 1–33, and, particularly moving, that of young William Parker in *The Life of Sir William Parker*, at pp. 49–57. Other account is provided by Collingwood, pp. 16–20; Sir John Barrow, *The Life of Earl Howe*, pp. 221–95. The battle is, of course, extensively covered in the two considerable histories of the time, William James's six-volume *The Naval History of Great Britain* (James) and Edward Pelham Brenton's two-volume work with the same title, *The Naval History of Britain* (Brenton). Corbett, in *Some Principles of Maritime Strategy*, has comment on pp. 196, 209.

11. Uncertainty (pp. 154–171)

1. Fortescue, *History*, vol. 4, p. 197.
2. *Nelson's Dispatches*, vol. 2, p. 8.
3. *ibid.*, pp. 10–17; James, vol. 1, p. 257.
4. *Nelson's Dispatches*, vol. 2, pp. 50–52.
5. *ibid.*, pp. 80–84.
6. *ibid.*, p. 92.
7. *ibid.*, p. 98.

8. *ibid.*, p. 102.
9. *ibid.*, p. 119.
10. *ibid.* p. 116.

12.   Change (pp. 172–192)

Brenton's *The Life and Correspondence of John, Earl of St Vincent* is an important source for the critical period in the Mediterranean covered by this chapter, supplementing *Nelson's Dispatches* and Mahan's *The Life of Nelson* (Chapter vii) and Mahan, *R/E*, vol. 1, pp. 195–220; Brenton, *St Vincent*, pp. 154–5, 187, 210-13, 219–20, 264–7, 275.

1. Mahan, *Nelson*, vol. 1, p. 182.
2. This episode, accompanied by a profile of Sidney Smith and his escape from the Temple, is covered in M.W. Stirling, *The Life of Sir William Hotham, Pages and Portraits from the Past*, pp. 298–305.
3. *Nelson's Dispatches*, vol. 2, p. 136.
4. *ibid.*, p. 142.
5. *ibid.*, p. 156.
6. *ibid.*, p. 171.
7. *ibid.*, p. 248.
8. *ibid.*, pp. 257–8; Mahan, *R/E*, vol. 1, pp. 214–15.
9. *Nelson's Dispatches*, vol. 2, p. 257.
10. *ibid.*, pp. 331–2.

13.   Triumph (pp. 193–201)

The Battle of St Vincent is covered by Collingwood in his *Public and Private Correspondence of Collingwood*, pp. 16–20; *Nelson's Dispatches*, pp. 331–51; Mahan, *Nelson*, pp. 267–89; Mahan, *R/E*, pp. 221–32; and *NC* 2, pp. 500–503; *NC* 3, pp. 174–7; *NC* 6, p. 100; *NC* 37, pp. 212–15, 361–5.

1. Gravière, vol. 1, p. 156.
2. Mahan, *R/E*, vol. 1, p 228.

14.   Mutiny (pp. 202–216)

A standing reference work for this shattering occurrence remains the work of G.E. Mainwaring and Bonamy Dobree, *Mutiny: The Floating Republic*. For other sources, the mutiny forms a major part of Barrow's *The Life of Howe*, pp. 321–55. Stanhope's *Life of Pitt* also covers it extensively, vol. 3, pp. 23–48; Brenton's *St Vincent*, pp. 264–5; *NC* 4, pp. 98–104; *NC* 20, pp. 90–91; and, of course, it receives extensive coverage in the histories of James and Brenton.

1. Mainwaring and Dobree, *Mutiny*, p. 9.
2. *ibid.*, p. 11.
3. *Life of Admiral Gambier*, vol. 2, p. 145.
4. *NC* 4, p. 103.
5. *NC* 20, pp. 90–91; *Nelson's Dispatches*, vol. 2, pp. 408–9.
6. *NC* 7, pp. 263, 347 ; *NC* 16, p. 343.

15. Tenerife (pp. 217–224)

NC 23, pp. 10–16, 374–5; *NC* 24, pp. 56–61. Also, *Memoirs and Letters of Captain William Hoste* (Hoste), p. 72 (vol 1); Brenton's *St Vincent*, vol. 1, p. 362; Collingwood's *Public and Private Correspondence of Collingwood*, p. 52 etc.

1. *Nelson's Dispatches*, vol. 2, pp. 425–33.
2. *ibid.*, p. 420.
3. *ibid.*, p. 422.
4. *ibid.*, p. 434.

16. Camperdown (pp. 225–236)

For this difficult period of Pitt's premiership I have substantially relied on Stanhope, *Life of Pitt*, vol. 3, J. Holland Rose's *William Pitt and the Great War* and vol. 1 of Holland Rose's *The Life of Napoleon*. In their naval histories James (vol. 2, p. 96) and Brenton (vol. 1, p. 347) give accounts of the Battle of Camperdown, but in Stirling, *The Life of Sir William Hotham*, Hotham, who was present at Camperdown with the rank of post-captain commanding the 50-gun *Adamant*, severely questions their account of the action. In *Hotham*, see pp. 102–7, 122–9, 132–45. A brief biography of Hotham is in John Marshall's *Royal Naval Biography*, pp. 580–82. A biography of Admiral Duncan is provided in *NC* 4, pp. 94–113, with a detailed report of the battle contained within that same volume, *NC* 4, pp. 108–12. *Hotham* includes a portrait of Duncan, pp. 236–9.

1. Holland Rose, *Pitt and the Great War*, p. 325.
2. Stanhope, *Life*, vol. 3, p. 68.
3. *ibid.*, p. 71.

17. Duel (pp. 237–245)

The entire account of this strange event is found in *NC* 22, pp. 303–24, 423–83, 481–92. Farington comment, *The Farington Diary*, 7 March 1804, p. 199.

18. Offensive (pp. 246–260)

For Napoleon's armada and his campaign in Egypt I have drawn on J. Holland Rose's *Life of Napoleon*, Napoleon's *Mémoires*, vol. 2, pp. 95–380 and J. Christopher Herold, *Bonaparte in Egypt*, J. Ross, *Memoirs and Correspondence of Admiral Lord de Saumarez*, W. H. Fitchett, *Nelson and His Captains*.

1. Holland Rose, *Pitt and the Great War*, p. 366.
2. *ibid.* p. 367.
3. *Nelson's Dispatches*, vol. 3, p. 24.
4. Napoleon, *Correspondance*, VIII, p. 644, quoted Mahan, *R/E*, vol. 1, p. 252.
5. *Nelson's Dispatches*, vol. 3, pp. 18–19.
6. *ibid.*, pp. 26–7.

7. *ibid.* p. 31.

8. Mahan, *Nelson*, p. 333.

9. *ibid.*, p. 336.

10. *ibid.*, p. 337.

11. *ibid.*, p. 334.

12. Herold, *Bonaparte in Egypt*, p. 56.

13. *ibid.*, p. 1.

19.　Nile (pp. 261–278)

The coverage of this monumental battle is considerable. The *Naval Chronicle*: *NC* 1, Narrative by an Officer, pp. 43–65; French account, *NC* 1, pp. 149–53; Nelson's Report, *NC* 1, p. 532; *NC* 2, p. 440; *NC* 3, p. 181; *NC* 4, pp. 144, 199–202; *NC* 6, pp. 103–4; *NC* 8, pp. 228–38; *NC* 37, pp. 140–44; *NC* 38, pp. 474–6. *Nelson's Dispatches*, vol. 3, pp. 48–71; Narrative of Captain Miller, vol. 7, Addenda, pp. cliv–clxi; Mahan, *Nelson*, pp. 344–61; Mahan, *R/E*, vol. 1, pp. 263–73; Mahan, *NS*, pp. 183, 260; Gravière, *Sketches of the Last Naval War*, vols 1 and 2; Herold, *Bonaparte*, pp. 102–11. Among miscellaneous comments, Barrow, *Life of Howe*, p. 247; Hoste, pp. 96–103; Corbett, *Some Principles of Naval Strategy*, p. 240; John Marshall, *Post-Captains*, p. 375; and *Royal Naval Biography*, p. 180.

20.　Barbary (pp. 279–289)

The involvement of the American navy commences with this chapter. For this and the ongoing chapters featuring the American navy I have relied substantially on, among others, J. Fenimore Cooper, *History of the Navy of the United States of America* (Cooper), vols 1 and 2; and Mahan, *Sea Power in its Relation to the War of 1812*, also John Henry Sherburne, *The Life of Paul Jones*.

1. *NC* 22, p. 295.

2. *NC* 36, p. 148.

21.　Neutrality (pp. 290–298)

An invaluable and frequently consulted reference on American foreign policy has been Julius W. Pratt, *A History of United States Foreign Policy*; also Steven Watson, *The Oxford History of England. The Reign of George III, 1760–1850: Amiens to Trafalgar*.

1. Pratt, *United States Foreign Policy*, chapter 6, pp. 68–85.

2. Mahan, *R/E*, vol. 2, p. 229.

3. *ibid.*, p. 232.

4. *ibid.*, p. 251.

5. *ibid.*, p. 219.

6. Cooper, vol. 1, p. 318.

22.　'Quasi-war' (pp. 299–305)

1. Cooper, vol. 1, p. 324.

2. *NC* 1, p. 338.

3. *NC* 1, p. 539.

4. Cooper, vol. 1, p. 356; *NC* 4, pp. 144, 514.

5. Cooper, vol. 1, pp. 377–89.

23. Impressed (pp. 306–314)

This chapter is compressed from *The Life and Adventures of Joshua Penny*, published by Joshua Penny himself in Brooklyn, New York, in 1815. I have, however, drawn my selection from a reprint of the original published by the South African Library, Cape Town, 1982.

24. Naples (pp. 315–328)

The principal source is *Nelson's Dispatches*, vol. 3.

1. Fortescue, *A History of the British Army*, vol. 4, book 12, chapter 20, p. 565.

2. Dispatches, vol. 3, p. 214.

3. *ibid.*, p. 216.

25. Acre (pp. 329–344)

This, one of the outstanding episodes of the Great War, is superbly covered by the *Naval Chronicle*: *NC* 2, pp. 437–9, 610–25; *NC* 3, pp. 400–401; *NC* 8, p. 390; *NC* 34, pp. 265–88, 353–76. Also Isaac Schomberg's *Naval Chronology*, vol. 3, pp. 309–26; Herold, *Bonaparte in Egypt*, pp. 272–303.

26. Return (pp. 345–359)

1. *NC* 1, p. 533.

2. Mahan, *R/E*, vol. 1, p. 305; Mahan, *Nelson*, p. 422.

3. Earl of Dundonald, *Autobiography of a Seaman*, vol. 1, p. 81.

4. *ibid.*, pp. 84–6; Mahan, *Nelson*, p. 452; Mahan, *R/E*, vol. 1, pp. 315–21.

5. *Nelson's Dispatches*, vol. 3, p. 391.

6. Mahan, *Nelson*, p. 429.

7. *Nelson's Dispatches*, vol. 3, pp. 391–2 ; Mahan, *Nelson*, pp. 432–5. Captain Foote retained great bitterness over this episode. See *NC* 23, p. 312.

8. Quoted Tom Pocock, *Horatio Nelson*, p. 204.

9. *Nelson's Dispatches*, vol. 3, p. 498.

10. *ibid.*, p. 409.

27. Consul (pp. 360–369)

1. *Nelson's Dispatches*, vol. 4, p. 24.

2. Stanhope, *Life*, vol. 3, p. 498.

3. Corbett, *Strategy*, p. 198.

4. Mahan, *R/E*, vol. 1, p. 331.

5. Mahan, *Nelson*, vol. 2, pp. 24–31; *Nelson's Dispatches*, vol. 4, p. 218; *NC* 4, pp. 233–6.

28. Home (pp. 370–381)

1. *NC* 30, pp. 19–23.

2. Stanhope, *Life*, vol. 3, pp. 234–5; *Nelson's Dispatches*, vol. 4, pp. 216–17.

3. *NC* 30, pp. 16–23.

4. Stanhope, *Life*, vol. 3, p. 238.

5. *Gentleman's Magazine*, 1800, p. 1092.

6. Holland Rose, *Pitt and the Great War*, p. 387.

7. *NC* 4, pp. 157–9, 240–41, 302–5, 512–13; *NC* 5, pp. 81–2, 89, 174–5, 177.

8. Stanhope, *Life*, vol. 3, pp. 262–3.

29.   Baltic (pp. 382–402)

The *Naval Chronicle* and *Nelson's Dispatches*, vol. 4, are mainly drawn upon; *NC* 5, pp. 334–55, 451–3; *NC* 6, pp. 117–223; *NC* 13, pp. 463–9; *NC* 14, pp. 391–9; *NC* 21, p. 458; *NC* 26, pp. 16–19; *NC* 37, pp. 444–52. *Nelson's Dispatches*, vol. 4, pp. 292–4; Colonel Stewart's Narrative is pp. 299–304, 307–13.

30.   Straits (pp. 403–412)

Among the principal sources for the Battle of Algeciras are *NC* 6, pp. 85, 94–5, 146–50, 194–8 (Spanish account); *NC* 2, pp. 44–6; *NC* 2, p. 41; and Brenton, vol. 1, pp. 546–53. Other sources for this chapter are *NC* 8, pp. 167, 231; *NC* 22, p. 5; Marshall, *Royal Naval Biography*. *Royal Naval Biography*, p. 174, on Admiral Saumarez, p. 43 for Admiral Keith; Dundonald, *Autobiography of a Seaman*, vol. 1, pp. 129–40. I have also referred to Thomas. Walsh, *Journal of the Late Campaign in Egypt*.

31.   Amiens (pp. 413–423)

1. Nelson's memorandum on the island's defences, *Nelson's Dispatches*, vol. 5, p. 425.

2. *NC* 7, full narrative of *Chevrette*, pp. 319–25; 216. Also *NC* 6, pp. 61, 73–4; *NC* 39, pp. 268–72.

3. *NC* 13, pp. 53–5; *NC* 14, pp. 400–405; Gravière, vol. 2, pp. 136–42.

4. Farington, *Diary*, 1802, p. 54.

32.   *Temeraire* (pp. 424–429)

The court martial is contained in *NC* 7, pp. 46–7. Brenton's comments are in his *St Vincent*, p. 101. Other sources for this chapter are *NC* 3, pp. 310; *NC* 4, p. 156; *NC* 5, pp. 6–7; *NC* 7, pp. 268, 347; *NC* 16, p. 343.

33.   Resumption (pp. 430–436)

1. Holland Rose, *Life of Napoleon*, vol. 1, p. 369; Pratt, *United States Foreign Policy*, p. 92.

2. Pratt, *United States Foreign Policy*, p. 96.

3. *ibid.*

4. Holland Rose, *Life of Napoleon*, vol. 1, p. 411.

5. Farington, *Diary*, 1803, p. 136; O'Meara, *Napoleon in Exile*, vol. 1, p. 500.

6. Farington, *Diary*, 1803, p. 103.

7. *NC* 7, p. 270.

34. Boulogne (pp. 437–443)

1. Holland Rose, *Life of Napoleon*, vol. 1, p. 485.
2. Brenton, *Life and Correspondence of St Vincent*, vol. 2, p. 35.
3. Mahan, *R/E*, vol. 2, p. 118.

35. Tripoli (pp. 444–448)

1. Cooper, vol. 1, p. 411.
2. *ibid.*, vol. 2, p. 8.
3. *ibid.*, p. 14.
4. *ibid*, p. 30; *NC* 12, p. 149.
5. Cooper, vol. 2, p. 54.
6. *NC* 18, p. 279.

36. Watch (pp. 449–458)

1. *Nelson's Dispatches*, vol. 6, p. 156.
2. *ibid.*, vol. 5, p. 406.
3. *ibid.*, p. 438.
4. *ibid.* p. 437.
5. Mahan, *Nelson*, vol. 2, pp. 224, 227.
6. *Nelson's Dispatches*, vol. 6, p. 50.

37. Chase (pp. 459–471)

1. Gravière, vol. 2, p. 173.
2. *Nelson's Dispatches*, vol. 6, p. 399.
3. *ibid.*, p. 415.
4. *ibid.*, p. 427.
5. *ibid.*, p. 443.
6. *ibid.*, p. 455.
7. Mahan, *R/E*, vol. 2, p. 162.
8. *Nelson's Dispatches*, vol. 7, p. 2.
9. *NC* 14, pp. 163, 168–72; *NC* 15, pp. 79–85, 162–75; *NC* 17, p. 90 ; *NC* 27, pp. 441–52.
10. *Nelson's Dispatches*, vol. 7, p. 5.
11. Mahan, *R/E*, vol. 2, p. 310.

38. Prelude (pp. 472–482)

Nelson's Dispatches, vol. 7; Gravière, vol. 2; Mahan, *Nelson*, vol. 2, Mahan, *R/E*, vol. 2 and Fraser's *The Enemy at Trafalgar* all help provide background to this chapter.

1. Gravière, vol. 2, p. 202.
2. *ibid.*, p. 208.
3. Fraser, *Enemy at Trafalgar*, p. 20.
4. Holland Rose, *Life of Napoleon*, vol. 1, p. 503.
5. Gravière, vol. 2, p. 236.
6. Mahan, *Nelson*, vol. 2, p. 326.
7. *ibid.*, p. 327.
8. *ibid.*, p. 334.

9. Gravière, vol. 2, p. 231.
10. *ibid.*, p. 231.

39.   Trafalgar (pp. 483–502)

A vast library exists on Trafalgar. My own selection of sources is as listed below. The human story has seldom, if ever, been better told than in Fraser's *The Enemy at Trafalgar*, on which I have drawn for much of the French and Spanish account. As one would expect, Mahan in his *Nelson* and volume 3 of *R/E* is expressive and concise on the tactical manoeuvres. He is admirably complemented by Gravière. Mahan wrote at the end of the nineteenth century, influenced by the maritime and political pressures of that time. But he grew up at the end of the fighting age of sail, though. He was inducted into it and trained by it. That is sealed into his work and it is what gives it its enduring distinction above all else, for he understands the age as few could truly do after. For all those reasons I regard his *Life of Nelson* as the finest of all the biographies, with his understanding of the tactical gift of mastery of wind and sail providing the central impulse of the work, as well as his comprehension of the man himself. It is a work of great study and powerful intellect.

The most compactly accessible account of Trafalgar is that offered by volume 7 of *Nelson's Dispatches*, continuous from page 142. It was principally written by the historian William James in painstaking detail, including the narrative of Dr Beatty on the death of Nelson, the logs of all the British ships, the flag signals, the dispatches of Vice Admiral Collingwood, as well as other private letters. James's own history and that of Edward Brenton are, of course, also established sources on Trafalgar.

Gravière, vol. 2; *Nelson's Dispatches*, vol. 7; Mahan, *Nelson*, vol. 2; Mahan, *R/E*; Fraser, *Enemy at Trafalgar*; and the *Naval Chronicle*, *NC* 14, pp. 411–15, 422–3, 503–4; *NC* 15, pp. 14–15, 203–8, 272, 370–75; *NC* 17, pp. 360–61, 361–2.

40.   Aftermath (pp. 503–513)

For this chapter see *NC* 15, pp. 15, 27, 45–52, 207–8; *NC* 18, pp. 199–201, 466–7. Also Mahan, and I have again borrowed from Fraser's *Enemy at Trafalgar*.

1. Gravière, vol. 2, p. 242.
2. Hibbert, *Nelson: A Personal History*, p. 381.
3. Stanhope, *Life*, vol. 4, p. 347.
4. Hibbert, *Nelson*, p. 379.

41.   Appraisal (pp. 516–521)

No notes for this chapter.

42. Rampage (pp. 522–528)

Among the varied sources of this central chapter I consulted J. Holland Rose, *Life of Napoleon*, vol. 2, chapters 24, 25, 26; Fortescue, *A History of the British Army*, vol. 6; Augustus Stapleton, *George Canning and His Times*; Robert Bell, *Life of the Rt. Hon. George Canning*.

1. Collingwood, p. 248.
2. Fortescue, *History*, vol. 6, p. 24.
3. Corbett, *Strategy*, p. 17.
4. Fortescue, *History*, vol. 6, p. 59.
5. Stapleton, *Canning*, p. 137.
6. Holland Rose, *Life of Napoleon*, vol. 2, p. 147.

43. Sandy Hook (pp. 529–534)

1. Pratt, *United States Foreign Policy*, pp. 116–17.
2. *NC* 18, pp. 72–81.
3. *NC* 26, pp. 225–6.

44. Chesapeake (pp. 535–541)

1. *NC* 18, pp. 116–28, 335–42; Crichton, *Admiral Broke*, pp. 156–257; Phillimore, *Life of Sir William Parker*, pp. 344–5.
2. Cooper, vol. 2, pp. 114–33; Pratt, *United States Foreign Policy*, p. 115.
3. Mahan, *Sea Power in its Relation to the War of 1812*, vol. 1, p. 178.
4. *ibid.*, p. 187.
5. Collingwood, p. 276.

45. Abominable (pp. 542–545)

NC 18, p. 342; *NC* 23, p. 172 ; *NC* 25, p 454.

46. Peninsula (pp. 546–550)

1. Alison, *The Lives of Lord Castlereagh and Sir Charles Stewart*, vol. 1, p. 235.
2. *ibid.*, p. 236.
3. Holland Rose, *Life of Napoleon*, vol. 2, p. 167.

47. Collingwood (pp. 551–554)

1. Collingwood, p. 310.
2. *ibid.*, p. 361.
3. *ibid.*, p. 411.

48. Cadiz (pp. 555–560)

1. Holland Rose, *Life of Napoleon*, vol. 2, p. 176.
2. Collingwood, p. 326.
3. *ibid.*, p. 329.
4. *ibid.*, p.327.
5. *ibid.*, p. 365.
6. *ibid.*, p. 361.

7. *ibid.*, p. 379.
8. Holland Rose, *Life of Napoleon*, vol. 2, p. 169.
9. Alison, *Castlereagh and Stewart*, vol. 1, p. 247.

49. Catalonia (pp. 561–568)

1. Corbett, *Strategy*, p. 59.
2. Mahan, *R/E*, vol. 2, pp. 352–57. Here Mahan delivers a summary of the Great War post-Trafalgar. In principle, Mahan's Great War ends at Trafalgar. His preoccupation beyond Trafalgar is concentrated on in his *Sea Power and its Relation to the War of 1812.*
3. Dundonald, *Autobiography of a Seaman*, vol. 1, p. 268.
4. *ibid.*, pp. 270, 334.
5. Cooper, *Talleyrand*, Chapter 7.
6. Alison, *Castlereagh and Stewart*, vol. 1, p. 257.
7. Collingwood, p. 419.
8. Dundonald, *Autobiography of a Seaman*, vol. 1, p. 311.
9. Mahan, *NS*, p. 241.

50. Basque Roads (pp. 569–578)

NC 21, pp. 316, 344–6 (Official Report), 368–74, 395–7 (Account of an Officer), 412–14 (Account of a Midshipman); *NC* 22, pp. 102–3, 107–30 (Court Martial), 215–42 (Court Martial); *NC* 25, pp. 211–13 (Cochrane and Fire Ships).

51. Expeditionary Forces (pp. 579–583)

Walcheren: *The Letters and Despatches of Viscount Castlereagh*; Corbett, *Strategy*, pp. 64–5; Marshall, *Post-Captains*, pp. 71–2.
Mauritius: *NC* 25, pp. 72–3, 157–9, 162–3, 234–7; *NC* 27, p. 152 (High Treason); *NC* 29, pp. 414–17.
Clorinde action: *NC* 26, pp. 388–94; 431–5; *NC* 28, pp. 151–7.

52. Timor (pp. 584–589)

Java: *NC* 26, p. 435 ; *NC* 27, pp. 73–83, 137–41; Marshall, *Post-Captains*, p. 198, *NC* 40, p. 371.

53. China–Japan (pp. 590–596)

1. *NC* 28, p. 58.
2. *NC* 24, pp. 27–8.
3. Golovnin, *Memoirs of a Captivity in Japan.*

54. Crisis (pp. 597–599)

Mahan, *R/E*, vol. 2, from p. 328, and Watson, *The Oxford History of England*, Chapter xviii, 'Economic Warfare', helped provide background to this chapter.

55. Breakdown (pp. 600–607)

Gamage: *NC* 28, pp. 501–6; *NC* 29, pp. 25–31.

Seaman Jefferey: NC 23, pp. 261, 386–7; NC 24, pp. 303–8, 389.
Melancholy Incident: NC 20, p. 201.

56. *Swallow* (pp. 608–611)

NC 28, pp. 194–6.

57. Tarragona (pp. 612–618)

1. Codrington, p. 224.
2. *ibid.*, p. 225.
3. Oman, *A History of the War in the Peninsula*, vol. 4, p. 521.
4. Codrington, p. 233.
5. *ibid.*, p. 231.
6. *ibid.*, p. 287.
7. *ibid.*, p. 261.
8. *ibid.*, pp. 276–8.
9. *ibid.*, p. 299.

58. America (pp. 619–626)

1. Pratt, *United States Foreign Policy*, and Mahan, *1812*, vol. 1 (p. 199 etc.), give vivid descriptions of the drastic impact of Jefferson's embargo.
2. Mahan, *1812*, vol. 1, p. 194.
3. *NC* 27, pp. 10–11.
4. Mahan, *1812*, vol. 1, p. 257.
5. *ibid.*
6. *NC* 26, p. 282.
7. *NC* 26, pp. 32–41, 81–4, 424–5; *NC* 27, pp. 58–65; Mahan, *1812*, vol. 1, p. 258; Cooper, vol. 2, p. 241.
8. Cooper, vol. 2, p. 159.
9. *ibid.*
10. Mahan, *1812*, vol. 1, p. 291; Pratt, *United States Foreign Policy*, p, 127.
11. Alison, *Castlereagh and Stewart*, vol. 1, p. 523.

59. War (pp. 627–632)

1. Mahan, *1812*, vol. 1, p. 338.
2. *ibid.*, p. 280.
3. Cooper, vol. 2, p. 169.
4. Mahan, *1812*, vol. 1, p. 323; Cooper, vol. 2, p. 177.
5. *ibid.*, p. 328; *ibid.*, p. 180.
6. *ibid.*, p. 330; *ibid.*, p. 194; *NC* 28, pp. 346–7, 370–71.

60. *Macedonian* (pp. 633–637)

Leech, *Voice*; Cooper, vol. 2, p. 206; James, *Naval Occurrences of the Late War between Great Britain and the United States of America*, p. 154; *NC* 29, p. 77; *Java*, *NC* 29, pp. 346–7, 404–8, 414–17, 452; *Wasp*, Cooper, vol. 2, pp. 200–216; Mahan, *1812*, vol. 2, p. 4; *NC* 30, pp. 69, 83–4, 160–62; Cooper, vol. 2, pp. 220–25; Crichton, *Admiral Broke*, pp. 156–257; Mahan, *1812*, vol. 2, p. 132; James, *Naval Occurrences*, 239.

61.   Reflection (pp. 638–641)

British naval reaction to the American War (of 1812) may, among others, be found in *NC* 29, pp. 113–19, 206–8, 291–2, 466–8; *NC* 30, pp. 225, 310; *NC* 32, pp. 142, 207, 330–33, 408, 409, 486.

1. James, *Naval Occurrences*, p. 97.
2. *ibid.*, p. 96.

62.   Northwest (pp. 642–648)

1. Mahan, *NS*, p. 99.
2. Mahan, *1812*, vol. 1, pp. 304–5.
3. *ibid.*, p. 306.
4. *ibid.*, p. 309.
5. *ibid.*, p. 366.
See also *NC* 33, pp. 158–9; *NC* 31, pp. 250–53, 496

63.   Lakeland (pp. 649–656)

1. Mahan, *1812*, vol. 2, p. 29.
2. *ibid.*, p. 101.
3. James, *Naval Occurrences*, p. 303.
4. *ibid.*, p. 299.
5. Mahan, *1812*, vol. 2, p. 59.
6. *ibid.*, p. 75.
7. James, *Naval Occurrences*, p. 287.
8. Mahan, *1812*, vol. 2, p. 80, etc.; Cooper, vol. 2, p. 463, etc.; *NC* 32, p. 242.
9. Cooper, vol. 2, p. 467.

64.   Torpedoes (pp. 657–660)

Further excerpt from *The Life and Adventures of Joshua Penny*.

1. Broadley, *Nelson's Hardy, His Life, Letters and Friends*, p. 163; *NC* 30, pp. 348–9.

65.   Elba (pp. 661–664)

1. Nicolson, *The Congress of Vienna*, pp. 41–3; Holland Rose, *Life of Napoleon*, vol. 2, p. 318.
2. Nicolson, *Congress*, p. 64.
See also *NC* 35, p. 480.

66.   Snow March (pp. 665–668)

1. *NC* 33, pp. 123–7.
2. Mahan, *1812*, vol. 2, pp. 290–91.
3. Fortescue, *History*, vol. 5, p. 109.

67.   Patuxent (pp. 669–677)

1. Smyth, *Précis of the Wars in Canada*, p. 175.
2. Mahan, *1812*, vol. 2, pp. 330, 332.
3. *ibid.*, pp. 347–8; *NC* 30, p. 162; *NC* 32, p. 247, etc., 341–7, 503–7.
4. Smith, *The Autobiography of Lt.-Gen. Sir Harry Smith*, vol. 1, p. 200.
5. *NC* 35, pp. 344–6.

6. Mahan, *1812*, vol. 2, p. 355.
7. *NC* 32, pp. 155, 245–6, 474–5.
8. Mahan, *1812*, vol. 2, p. 334; Mahan, *1812*, vol. 2, p. 331.
9. *NC* 13, pp. 168–9.
10. Cooper, vol. 2, p. 260, etc.

68. New Orleans (pp. 678–694)

1. Mahan, *1812*, vol. 2, p. 385; Fortescue, *History*, vol. 10, chapter 20, p. 120.
2. Codrington, p. 331.
3. Gleig, *The Campaigns of The British Army at Washington and New Orleans 1814–1815*, p. 292.
4. *ibid.*, p. 294.
5. Cooke, *The Attack on New Orleans*, pp. 204, 205, 212, 214.
6. Gleig, *Campaigns*, p. 301.
7. Smith, *Autobiography*, vol. 1, pp. 236, 238.
8. Gleig, *Campaigns*, pp. 340, 342, 347, 374.
9. Fortescue, *History*, vol. 10, chapter 20, pp. 177, 180.
10. Mahan, *1812*, vol. 2, p. 436.
11. *ibid.*, p. 397; *NC* 33, pp. 156, 215, 260, 283, 370; *NC* 37, p. 384.
See also *NC* 33, pp. 337–43, 484–8; *NC* 35, 464–71.

69. Adriatic (pp. 695–704)

1. Hoste, vol. 2, pp. 54, 169; *NC* 25, pp. 423, 429–31; *NC* 37, p. 384.
2. The greater part of this sequence is drawn from Hoste, pp. 159–259.
3. Moran, *The Anatomy of Courage*, pp. 9, 11.

70. Adieu (pp. 705–714)

1. Nicolson, *Congress*, p. 38.
2. *ibid.*, p. 141; Cooper, *Talleyrand*, p. 205.
3. Maitland, *Narrative of the Surrender of Napoleon*, p. 72; *NC* 34, pp. 118, 127; *NC* 34, p. 209.
4. Stirling, *Hotham*, pp. 3–7; Maitland, *Surrender of Napoleon*, p. 75, etc.
5. Napoleon, *Mémoires*, vol. 1, pp. 198–9.

71. Algiers (pp. 715–720)

Pratt, *United States Foreign Policy*, pp. 111–12; *NC* 35, p. 481; *NC* 35 pp. 82, 482; *NC* 36, p. 50; *NC* 36, p. 148; *NC* 36, p. 81; *NC* 36, pp. 287–95, 309–13, 397–404; Marshall, *Post-Captains*, pp. 151, 235; *NC* 36, p. 289.

72. Postscript (pp. 721–729)

1. *NC* 36, pp. 470–72.
2. *NC* 37, pp. 27.
3. *NC* 39, p. 56.
4. *NC* 39, p. 207.
5. *NC* 40, p. 152.

SELECT BIBLIOGRAPHY

(Works are published in London unless otherwise stated.)

Albion, Robert, *Forests and Sea Power* (Cambridge, MA, 1926)

Alison, Sir Archibald, *The Lives of Lord Castlereagh and Sir Charles Stewart* (Londonderry, 1861, vol. 1)

Andersen, B.C., *Oared Fighting Ships* (1962)

Annual Register

Barrow, John, *The Life of Richard, Earl Howe* (1838)

Baynham, Henry, *From the Lower Deck: the old Navy 1780–1840* (1969)

Bell, Robert, *Life of the Rt. Hon. George Canning* (1846)

Bovill, E.W. *The Golden Trade of the Moors* (Oxford, 1968)

Braudel, Fernand. *Civilization and Capitalism, 15th–18th Century* (1983, 3 vols)

Brenton, Edward Pelham, *The Naval History of Great Britain from the year 1783 to 1836,* (1837, 2 vols)

———————— *The Life and Correspondence of John, Earl of St Vincent* (1838)

Briggs, Asa. *The Age of Improvement, 1783–1867* (1979)

Broadley, Alexander M., *Nelsons Hardy: his life, letters, and friends* (1909)

Campbell, John, *Lives of the British Admirals* (1814, 7 vols)

Carel, Auguste, *Pré´cis historique de la guerre d'Espagne et de Portugal, de 1808 à` 1814* (Paris, 1815)

Chapelle, Howard I., *The Search for Speed Under Sail* (New York, 1967)

Charnock, John, *Biographia Navalis* (1794, 6 vols)

Chaudhuri, K.N., *Trade and Civilization in the Indian Ocean from the rise of Islam to 1750* (Cambridge, 1985)

Chatterton, Lady, *Memorial of Admiral Lord Gambier* (1861)

Cipolla, C.M. *Guns and Sail in the Early Phase of European Expansion* (1965)

Clark, James and McArthur, John, eds, *Naval Chronicle* (1799–1819, 40 vols)

Clerk, John of Eldin, the Elder, *An Inquiry into Naval Tactics* (Edinburgh, 1782)

Clowes, William Laird, *The Royal Navy: A History* (1897–1930, 7 vols)

Codrington, Edward, *A Memoir of the Life of Sir Edward Codrington* (1873, 2 vols)

Collingwood, Lord Cuthbert, *The Correspondence of Vice-Admiral Lord Collingwood, Interspersed with Memoirs of his Life* (1828)

Cooke, Capt. J.H., *A Narrative of Events in the South of France, and of the Attack on New Orleans, in 1814 and 1815* (1835)

Cooper, Duff, *Talleyrand* (1958)

Cooper, J. Fenimore, *History of the Navy of the United States of America* (1839, 2 vols)

Corbett, Julian S., *Drake and the Tudor Navy* (1898)

———————— *The Successors of Drake* (1900)

———————— *England in the Mediterranean* (1904, 2 vols)

———————— *England in the Seven Years War* (1907, 2 vols)

———————— *The Campaign of Trafalgar* (1910)

———————— *Some Principles of Maritime Strategy* (1911)

Creswell, J. *British Admirals of the Eighteenth Century, Tactics in Battle* (1972)

Drinkwater, John, *A Narrative of the Battle of Cape St Vincent with Anecdotes of Nelson, Before and After the Battle* (1840)

Dundonald, Thomas, Earl of, *Autobiography of a Seaman* (1860, 2 vols)

Ehrman, John, *The Younger Pitt* (1983)

Farington, Joseph, *The Farington Diary* (1922, 8 vols)

Fitchett, W. H., *Nelson and his Captains* (Murray, 1910)

Fortescue, John W., *A History of the British Army* (1899–1933, 13 vols)

Foy, Count Maximilien Se´bastien, *History of the war in the Peninsula under Napoleon* (1827, 2 vols)

Fraser, Edward, *The Enemy at Trafalgar. An account of the battle from eye-witnesses' narratives and letters and despatches from the French and Spanish fleets* (1906)

———————— *The Sailors whom Nelson Led* (1913)

Geyl, Pieter, *Napoleon: For and Against* (1949)

Gentleman's Magazine

Gleig, G.R., *The campaigns of the British Army at Washington and New Orleans 1814–1815* (1879)

Golovnin, Vasily Mikhailovich, *Memoirs of a Captivity in Japan 1811–1813* (1973)

Goodrich, L. Carrington, *A Short History of the Chinese People* (1948)

Gravière, Jurien de la, Jean-Pierre Baptiste Edmond, *Sketches of the Last Naval War* (1848, 2 vols)

Halévy, Elie, *England in 1815* (1987)

Harland, John, *Seamanship in the Age of the Sail: An Account of the Shiphandling of the Sailing Man-of-war 1600–1860* (1984)

Henderson, W.O. *The Industrialization of Europe, 1780–1914* (1969)

Herold, J. Christopher, *Bonaparte in Egypt* (1962)

Hibbert, Christopher, *Nelson: A Personal History* (1994)

Hobbs, J. S., *Sailing Directions for the Mediterranean Sea* (1864)

Hoste, Harriet, *Memoirs and Letters of Sir William Hoste* (1833, 2 vols)

James, William, *A Full and Correct Account of the Chief Naval Occurrences of the Late War between Great Britain and the United States of America* (1817)

———————————— *A Full and Correct Account of the Military Occurrences of the late War between Great Britain and the United States of America* (1818)

———————————— *The Naval History of Great Britain from 1793 to the accession of George IV,* (1837, 6 vols)

Jones, J.R., *Britain and the World 1649–1815* (1980)

Jones, Paul, *Memoirs* (1830)

Kemp, Peter, ed., *The Oxford Companion to Ships and the Sea* (Oxford, 1976)

Kennedy, Paul M. *The Rise and Fall of British Naval Mastery* (2004)

———————————— *The Rise and Fall of the Great Powers* (1988)

Lanfrey, Pierre, *Histoire de Napoléon* (Paris, 1867)

Las Cases, Emmanuel Auguste Dieudonné', *Journal of the Private life and conversations of the Emperor Napoleon at Saint Helena* (1823, 2 vols)

Lavery, Brian, *Nelson's Navy: The Ships, Men and Organisation* (1989)

Leech, Samuel, *A Voice from the Main Deck* (1999)

Lewis, Michael, *A Social History of the Royal Navy, 1793–1815* (1960)

Lloyd, Christopher, *The British Seaman, 1200–1860* (1908)

Mahan, A.T., *The Influence of Sea Power Upon History* (1890)

———————————— *The Influence of Sea Power Upon the French Revolution and Empire 1793–1812,* (1892, 2 vols)

———————————— *The Life of Nelson* (1898)

———————————— *Sea Power in its Relation to the War of 1812,* (1905, 2 vols)

———————————— *Naval Strategy* (1911)

Mainwaring, G.E., and Bonamy Dobree, *Mutiny: The Floating Republic* (1935)

Maitland, Capt. F.L., *Narrative of the Surrender of Napoleon* (Dresden, 1826)

Markham, John, *Napoleon* (1966)

Marshall, John, *Royal Naval Biography* (1823)

———————————— *Post-Captains* (1823)

Minto, Countess of, ed., *The Life and Letters of Sir Gilbert Elliot* (Bastia, 1874, 3 vols)

Mitchell, Maírín, *The Maritime History of Russia* (1949)

Moran, Lord, *The Anatomy of Courage* (1945)

Mordal, Jacques, *Twenty-Five Centuries of Sea Warfare* (1965)

Mundy, G.F., *The Life and Correspondence of Admiral Lord Rodney* (1830)

Napier, W.F.P., *History of War in the Peninsula*

Napoleon I, *Mé'moires pour servir à`l'histoire de France sous Napoléon, écrits à Sainte Hélè`ne, par les géné'raux qui ont partagé' sa captivité'* (Paris, 1823)

———————————— *Correspondance de Napoleon 1er* (Paris, 1868)

Naval Chronicle (1799–1819, 40 vols)

Nicolas, Sir Harris, *Dispatches and Letters of Vice-Admiral Lord Viscount Nelson* (1844, 7 vols)

Nicolson, Harold, *The Congress of Vienna* (1946)

Oman, Charles, *A History of the War in the Peninsula* (1903)

O'Meara, Barry, *Napoleon in Exile* (1822, 2 vols)

Panikkar, K.M., *Asia and Western Dominance: a Survey of the Vasco da Gama Epoch of Asian History, 1498–1945* (Kuala Lumpur, 1959)

Parker, Geoffrey. *The Dutch Revolt* (1988)

Parkinson, C.N. *War in the Eastern Seas, 1793–1815* (1954)

Parry, J.H., *The Establishment of the European Hegemony, 1415–1715* (1966)

Penny, J., *The Life and Adventures of Joshua Penny* (Cape Town, 1982)

Perkins, B. *Prologue to War; England and the United States, 1805–1812* (Berkeley, 1961)

Phillimore, Augustus, *The Life of Sir William Parker* (1876)

Pirenne, Henri, *A History of Europe* (New York, 1958, 2 vols)

Plumb, J.H. *England in the Eighteenth Century* (1963)

Pocock, Tom, *Horatio Nelson* (1987)

Pratt, Julius W., *A History of United States Foreign Policy* (Englewood Cliffs, NJ, 1955)

Rediker, Marcus, *Between the Devil and the Deep Blue Sea* (Cambridge, 1987)

Rodger, N.A.M., *The Wooden World: An Anatomy of the Georgian Navy* (1986)

Robertson, F.L., *The Evolution of Naval Armament* (1921)

Robinson, Charles Napier, *The British Tar in Fact and Fiction* (1909)

Rose, John Holland, *The Life of Napoleon* (1902, 2 vols)

———————————— *William Pitt and the Great War* (1911)

Ross, J., *Memoirs and Correspondence of Admiral Lord de Saumarez* (1838, 2 vols)

Seward, Desmond. *The Hundred Years War* (New York, 1978)

Sherburne, John Henry, *Life and Character of the Chevalier J. Paul Jones, a Captain in the Navy of the United States, during their Revolutionary War* (Washington, 1825)

Schomberg, Isaac, *Naval Chronology* (1815, 3 vols)

Scoffern, J., *Projectile Weapons of War* (1858)

Smith, Sir Harry George Wakelyn, *The Autobiography of Lt.-Gen. Sir Harry Smith, 1787–1819* (1910, 2 vols)

Smyth, James Carmichael, *Précis of the Wars in Canada* (1826)

Stanhope, Philip Henry, *The Life of the Right Honourable William Pitt* (1861, 5 vols)

Stapleton, Augustus, *George Canning and his Times* (1859)

Stirling, M.W., *The Life of Sir William Hotham, Pages and Portraits from the Past* (1919)

Thiers, Adolphe, *Histoire du Consulat et de l'Empire*

Thompson, E.P., *The Making of the English Working Class* (1968)

Tocqueville, Alexis de, *The Ancient Regime and the French Revolution* (1966)

Villiers, Alan, *Sons of Sinbad* (1940)

Walsh, Thomas, *Journal of the Late Campaign in Egypt* (1803)

Warner, Oliver, *A Portrait of Lord Nelson* (1958)

Watson, Steven, *The Oxford History of England. The Reign of George III, 1760–1850: Amiens to Trafalgar* (1960)

Willyams, Rev. Cooper, *A Voyage in the Mediterranean* (1802)

———————————— *An Account of the Campaign in the West Indies* (1794)

Yongue, C.D., *The Naval History of Great Britain* (1886)

INDEX

The page numbers in *italics* refer to illustrations.

28 DAYS

DATE DUE

JUN 2 1 2009		
	WITHDRAWN	

GAYLORD | | | PRINTED IN U.S.A.